D0212854

Uncritical acceptance
of US claim WMD in Iraq
in sense that little discussed
re how points to publish of
I dent WMD

P178
CB 2010 Report

Suitcase not addressed

# AVOIDING THE ABYSS

## Praeger Security International Advisory Board

*Board Cochairs*

Loch K. Johnson, Regents Professor of Public and International Affairs, School of Public and International Affairs, University of Georgia (U.S.A.)

Paul Wilkinson, Professor of International Relations and Chairman of the Advisory Board, Centre for the Study of Terrorism and Political Violence, University of St. Andrews (U.K.)

*Members*

Vice Admiral Arthur K. Cebrowski, USN (Ret.), former Director of Force Transformation, Office of the Secretary of Defense (U.S.A.)

Eliot A. Cohen, Robert E. Osgood Professor of Strategic Studies and Director, Philip Merrill Center for Strategic Studies, Paul H. Nitze School of Advanced International Studies, The Johns Hopkins University (U.S.A.)

Anthony H. Cordesman, Arleigh A. Burke Chair in Strategy, Center for Strategic and International Studies (U.S.A.)

Thérèse Delpech, Senior Research Fellow, CERI (Atomic Energy Commission), Paris (France)

Sir Michael Howard, former Professor of History of War, Oxford University, and Professor of Military and Naval History, Yale University (U.K.)

Lieutenant General Claudia J. Kennedy, USA (Ret.), former Deputy Chief of Staff for Intelligence, Headquarters, Department of the Army (U.S.A.)

Paul M. Kennedy, J. Richardson Dilworth Professor of History and Director, International Security Studies, Yale University (U.S.A.)

Robert J. O'Neill, former Chichele Professor of the History of War, All Souls College, Oxford University (Australia)

Shibley Telhami, Anwar Sadat Chair for Peace and Development, Department of Government and Politics, University of Maryland (U.S.A.)

Jusuf Wanandi, co-founder and member, Board of Trustees, Centre for Strategic and International Studies (Indonesia)

Fareed Zakaria, Editor, Newsweek International (U.S.A.)

# Avoiding the Abyss

## Progress, Shortfalls, and the Way Ahead in Combating the WMD Threat

*Edited by Barry R. Schneider
and Jim A. Davis*

PRAEGER SECURITY INTERNATIONAL
Westport, Connecticut · London

## Library of Congress Cataloging-in-Publication Data

Avoiding the abyss : progress, shortfalls, and the way ahead in combating the WMD threat
/ edited by Barry R. Schneider and Jim A. Davis.
     p. cm.
Includes bibliographical references and index.
ISBN 0-275-99033-8 (alk. paper)
   1. Weapons of mass destruction. 2. Arms control. 3. Nuclear nonproliferation. 4.
National security—United States. I. Davis, Jim A. II. Schneider, Barry R.
   U793.A86 2006
   327.1′745—dc22          2006006637

British Library Cataloguing in Publication Data is available.

Copyright © 2006 by Barry R. Schneider and Jim A. Davis

All rights reserved. No portion of this book may be
reproduced, by any process or technique, without the
express written consent of the publisher.

Library of Congress Catalog Card Number: 2006006637
ISBN:   0–275–99033–8

First published in 2006

Praeger Security International, 88 Post Road West, Westport, CT 06881
An imprint of Greenwood Publishing Group, Inc.
www.praeger.com

Printed in the United States of America

The paper used in this book complies with the
Permanent Paper Standard issued by the National
Information Standards Organization (Z39.48–1984).

10 9 8 7 6 5 4 3 2 1

The views expressed in this publication are those of the authors and do not necessarily reflect the official policy or position of the U.S. Government, Department of Defense, or the USAF Counterproliferation Center.

# Contents

# Acknowledgments

Publishing a book covering the progress, the shortfalls, and the way ahead of the Department of Defense (DoD) Counterproliferation effort from the early 1990s to today, and the successes and failures of the Homeland Security Program since September 11, 2001, until the present, has been no small task. Identifying and bringing together 22 world-class authors and subject-matter experts to share their insights and conclusions with us on the subject was a lengthy process, but the end product is one that should benefit the DoD in combating the threat posed by those adversaries pursuing or in possession of chemical, biological, radiological, and/or nuclear weapons. We wish to thank the contributors of each of the chapters for their quality work and for bearing with the editors through this long and sometimes arduous process.

This is the only book of its kind attempting to cover this subject, and it would not have been possible without the funding and encouragement from two important defense organizations and their leadership. A special thanks goes to the office of the Deputy Assistant to the Secretary of Defense for Chemical and Biological Defense, Dr. Klaus Schafer, and his predecessors in that office, Brigadier General Patricia Nilo and Dr. Anna Johnson-Winegar, who ordered this study, and to the Chemical and Biological Directorate of the Defense Threat Reduction Agency under Dr. Charles Gallaway, who funded the study.

Likewise, there were many other individuals and organizations that have supported this project by furnishing information and perspectives. Particularly, we are grateful for the continuous expertise and funding support from the Air Staff's Nuclear and Counterproliferation Directorate, XOS-FC now directed by Colonel Tom Billick and overseen by Brigadier General (Select) Robert Holmes and Major General Roger Burg. Thanks are due also to their very supportive predecessors in those positions, Colonel Franklin Wolf and Major General Robert Smolen.

Of course the tedious work of bringing the project to fruition was the result of hundreds of hours of behind-the-scene efforts from our USAF Counterproliferation Center (CPC) staff in drafting, typing, editing, and coordinating the chapters of this volume. Most notable in their contributions to this project are our Assistant Director, Mrs. Jo Ann Eddy, and our Associate Editor for CPC Publications, Mrs. Abbey Plant. In addition, Mrs. Brenda Alexander was also a very diligent worker behind the scenes in this project. If it had not been for these staffers and their attention to detail and hard repetitive work, this project would not have succeeded. Thanks also are due to our outside reviewers, Dr. James Miller, a subject-matter expert who reviewed each of the chapters in great detail and whose substantive comments made this a much-improved product, and Mr. Armin Reitz, who ranks at the top of the world of copy editors. Mr. Randy Honnet also made significant contributions to the book by supplying valuable information to the authors from a previous study on Scud hunting detailing the United States' progress and shortfalls in capabilities to locate, target, and neutralize enemy mobile missile launchers in a time of crisis or war. Captain Tammie Fell, through many hours of research, also provided important data on DoD's Counterproliferation funding and the status of WMD programs of various states. We also express our gratitude to Master Sergeant Henry Mayfield for his support of the editors in checking on the status of programs for biological and chemical sensors, and individual and collective protection equipment.

Last but not least, both editors owe their greatest gratitude to their wives, Brenda Davis and Judy Keegan (Schneider). Their unwavering support to us during the countless hours we spent on this book instead of with them and our families shows their kindness toward us and their similar passionate desire that the United States be better able to protect its forces, citizens, and allies against enemies who might use weapons of mass destruction.

Jim A. Davis
Barry R. Schneider

CHAPTER 1

# Over a Decade of Counterproliferation

*Jim A. Davis*

This book marks the end of more than a decade of counterproliferation since Secretary of Defense Les Aspin's announcement of the Counterproliferation Initiative on December 7, 1993.[1] His initiative was a response to several important developments and served to actively address a newly recognized and emerging threat—proliferation of weapons of mass destruction (WMD) in the hands of rogue states as well as other adversaries.

Although in the 1980s Iran and Iraq fought a war using chemical weapons at a level of intensity unseen since World War I (WWI), the international community did not react to the extent the event deserved. Tens of thousands of Iranians and Iraqis died from the use of chemical weapons. In August 1990, when Iraq invaded Kuwait, the United States and others decided to respond. This presented a new danger since this coalition of states found themselves at risk in facing an adversary that had recent operational experience employing chemical weapons on a massive scale.

In the same year as the 1990–1991 Gulf War, the Soviet Union was unraveling, ultimately splitting into 15 independent states in December 1991. Most of the 15 republics possessed tactical nuclear weapons; 4 had longer-range nuclear weapons.[2] Moreover, there was the fear of "brain drain" of Soviet bioweaponeers, chemical weapons specialists, and nuclear scientists leaving the USSR bound for employment in rogue states. There was also the dread of the possibility of nuclear technology and resources drifting to other states, dampening an excitement over what seemed to be the emergence of world peace.

It was well-known that the USSR had possessed a vast chemical weapons arsenal, but, when revealed, the size of the biological arms program was a surprise. Soviet defectors during this period exposed, for the first time, a gargantuan covert biological weapons program. Over 60,000 people working at dozens of facilities had created enough biological agents to kill every human on the planet several times over.[3] The United States and other Western nations realized that much of this biological expertise, equipment, and stockpile of biological warfare (BW) agents could also be for sale and might eventually be scattered to many nations or groups around the world.

The findings about Iraq's significant nuclear and chemical weapons programs by the United Nations Special Commission on Iraq and International Atomic Energy Agency inspections after the 1990–1991 Gulf War, combined with the proliferation problems caused by the rupture of the USSR, caused Secretary Les Aspin to launch a new Department of Defense (DoD) Counterproliferation Initiative (CPI) on December 7, 1993. In the unveiling of the CPI, Aspin stated that he saw several chief threats to the United States, including the following:

- the danger posed by the increased threat of proliferation of WMD caused by the breakup of the Soviet Union,
- regional dangers posed by rogue nations pursuing WMD, such as Saddam Hussein's Iraq,
- the danger that democratic and market reforms would fail in the former Soviet Union (FSU), and
- dangers to the economy of the nation.

Aspin's chief concerns appeared to be the rapid spread of technology, the dissolution of the Soviet Union, and the lack of nonproliferation and counterproliferation (CP) programs to adequately address concerns posed by the spread of weapons of mass destruction to dangerous rivals and the need to counter and dilute such threats. In an effort to add emphasis to his December 1993 speech, he quoted President Clinton, "One of our most urgent priorities must be attacking the proliferation of weapons of mass destruction, whether they are nuclear, chemical, or biological; and the ballistic missiles that can rain them down on populations hundreds of miles away … . If we do not stem the proliferation of the world's deadliest weapons, no democracy can feel secure."[4]

Aspin stated that the Department of Defense's Counterproliferation Initiative would not diminish the U.S. effort to prevent proliferation, but would now also include a new military mission he called protection, later labeled counterproliferation.[5] Figure 1.1 is the chart he presented in his December 1993 speech in which he laid out a multifaceted approach, including protection, and stated, "What's new is the emphasis on the right side of the chart where the Defense Department has a special responsibility."

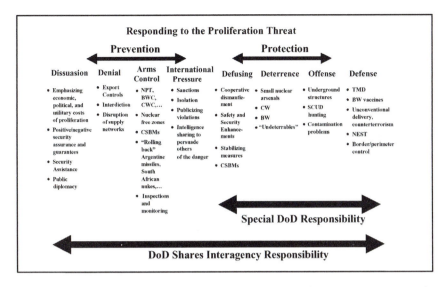

**Figure 1.1** Chart Presented by Les Aspin on December 7, 1993, to Launch the Department of Defense Counterproliferation Initiative (CPI)

This book seeks to document what happened throughout the 1990s and early 2000s as the United States reacted to this new threat, efforts which were spurred forward by the 1993 Counterproliferation Initiative. Specifically, it provides an overview of U.S. counterproliferation efforts during this period. Each of the chapters provides an analysis of how far we have come in specific areas since 1993 and what still needs to happen to provide an adequate or optimal U.S. capability in each dimension of our counterproliferation capabilities.

## What Has and Has Not Changed

Since 1993, many positive changes have occurred in the field of counterproliferation. Regime changes in Iraq and South Africa have removed some WMD proliferation threats. Saddam Hussein, who wielded chemical weapons against Iraq and his own Kurds and who pursued nuclear and biological arms, has been overthrown, and a new Iraq is beginning to emerge. South Africa's clandestine WMD program has apparently ended, and many, but not all, of the secrets of its biological and chemical programs have been revealed.[6] Libya announced it has given up its previous efforts to have active WMD programs. The Taliban and al-Qaeda have been routed in Afghanistan, probably delaying al-Qaeda's efforts to develop or buy WMD, although perhaps only temporarily.

In 1992, it appears that all tactical nuclear weapons formerly possessed by the USSR armed forces were relocated back on Russian soil, after the initial consolidation to four key republics of the FSU. In 1994, the Ukraine, Kazakhstan, and Byelorussia all decided they would prefer not to remain states with strategic nuclear arms so they shipped their weapons to Russia, thereby preventing the creation of multiple new nuclear states.[7]

The U.S. Cooperative Threat Reduction program has forged new levels of economic and scientific cooperation with former Soviet Union states. In 2002, 11 nations joined together in an interdiction program called the Proliferation Security Initiative (PSI) aimed at preventing the flow of WMD technology or weapons to dangerous states.

On the domestic front, the U.S. Department of Homeland Security was established after the al-Qaeda attacks of September 11, 2001, and Secretary Tom Ridge began the arduous task of bringing together over 40 agencies and thousands of federal employees to perform that mission. The U.S. military has created a new combatant command, U.S. Northern Command (NORTHCOM), focused solely on protection of the homeland. The U.S. Air Force has developed a new concept of operations that allows it to fight in the midst of chemical attacks on its air bases. Also, the Global Positioning System and laser guidance systems have allowed the creation of a family of precision-guided munitions (PGMs) for very accurate targeting of fixed installations and other known targets.

Counterterrorism laws such as the U.S. Patriot Act have been enacted. Information sharing between nations united in the Global War on Terrorism has improved.[8] Increased funding has allowed the United States to acquire more stocks of smallpox, anthrax, and other vaccines to protect U.S. forces and civilians against biological warfare attacks. We now have a Strategic National Stockpile of vaccines and medicine deployed at a dozen locations across the United States to help provide immediate medical assistance to guard against chemical, biological, radiological, nuclear, and high-yield explosive terrorism or warfare. Commercially produced polymerase chain reaction (PCR) research and testing have catapulted our biodetection capability forward. Biodefense efforts within the Department of Health and Human Services and the Department of Homeland Security (DHS) had grown to $5.2 billion by 2004, resulting in huge gains in public health emergency preparedness.[9] The Internet has created an environment for first responders, the military, statesmen, and citizens around the world to become well-informed about WMD issues with the click of a button. The list of positive steps in countering weapons of mass destruction goes on and on, but it is still hard to say the world is a safer place today than it was in the early 1990s.

States continue to develop and export WMD and/or their delivery systems. India and Pakistan have now joined the club of nations that have tested nuclear weapons and have acknowledged programs. Abdul

Qadeer Khan, the scientist who directed the Pakistani A-bomb program, has now admitted selling nuclear weapons designs and nuclear enrichment equipment to Libya, Iran, and North Korea. His colleagues also have held discussions with al-Qaeda representatives. Ayman al-Zawahiri, number two in the al-Qaeda chain of command, claims that the terrorist organization has several suitcase A-bombs from the former Soviet Union. It appears clear to many that Iran has a desire to develop nuclear weapons in spite of its recent partial and temporary cooperation with the United Nations' International Atomic Energy Agency. Syria still has a chemical weapons program. North Korea's WMD profile has escalated with its show of the Taepo Dong missile test launch with a flight path over Japan.[10] U.S. intelligence now credits North Korea with enough fissile material to have weaponized as many as seven nuclear weapons. Likewise, multiple allegations have been made by individuals claiming to be eyewitnesses charging that North Korea experimented with chemical and biological agents on humans.[11]

Many other countries, perhaps as many as 30 states, are still believed to have either a nuclear, biological, or chemical weapons program. Some have all three. In fact, the total number of nation-states thought to have active nuclear, biological, or chemical programs has not changed radically since the introduction of the Counterproliferation Initiative, even with Libya's recent decision to disarm and comply with nonproliferation treaties, Saddam Hussein's demise in Iraq, and the dismantlement of South Africa's nuclear, biological, and chemical programs. (See Table 1.1.)

And, of course, the 1990s and the turn of the millennium brought with it attacks on the World Trade Center in 1993, the Oklahoma City bombing in 1995, the Tokyo subway sarin nerve gas attack in 1995, the Khobar Towers attack in 1996, and the September 11, 2001, attacks on the United States. These were just a few of many terrorist events worldwide. Most concerning for counterproliferation experts was the fact that more and more terrorist groups appeared to be interested in WMD.[13]

In 1983, the United States experienced its first major biological attack launched by a group in Dalles, Oregon, known as the Bhagwan Shree Rajneesh cult.[14] In 1995, 12 persons were killed and 5,500 fled to hospitals in the wake of a sarin attack in Tokyo initiated by the Aum Shinryko cult that had accumulated a net worth of over $1 billion.[15]

In Afghanistan, al-Qaeda experimented with chemical agents on animals as validated in live video footage captured and later shown on CNN.[16] A white supremacist terrorist recently captured in Tyler, Texas, was discovered to possess a bomb containing cyanide.[17] During arrest and police raids, Islamic extremists have been found to have ricin or ricin-making equipment in "Britain, France, Spain, Russia, Georgia, and Kurdish-controlled northern Iraq."[18] Israel uncovered cyanide bombs in Gaza.[19]

**Table 1.1**    WMD Status of States in Early 1990s and Early 2000s in Unclassified Reports[12]

| Country | WMD 1990–1993 | | | WMD 2000–2004 | | |
|---|---|---|---|---|---|---|
| | **Nuclear** | **Chemical** | **Biological** | **Nuclear** | **Chemical** | **Biological** |
| Algeria | Discon. | | | R&D | Interest | R&D |
| Argentina | Discon. | | | Discon. | | |
| Belarus | Discon. | | | Discon. | | |
| Belgium | | | | | Discon. | |
| Brazil | Discon. | | | Discon. | | |
| Canada | Discon. | Discon. | Discon. | | Discon. | Discon. |
| China | Confirm | Confirm | Suspect | Confirm | Confirm | Suspect |
| Cuba | | | | | | R&D |
| Egypt | R&D | Suspect | Suspect | R&D | Suspect | Suspect |
| Ethiopia | | Suspect | | | Suspect | |
| France | Confirm | Confirm | Discon. | Confirm | Discon. | Discon. |
| Germany | | Discon. | Discon. | | Discon. | Discon. |
| India | Confirm | Confirm | | Confirm | Suspect | R&D |
| Iran | R&D | Confirm | Suspect | R&D | Confirm | Suspect |
| Iraq | R&D | Confirm | Suspect | R&D | Suspect | Suspect |
| Israel | Confirm | Suspect | Suspect | Confirm | Suspect | Suspect |
| Italy | | Discon. | | | Discon. | |
| Japan | | Discon. | Discon. | | Discon. | Discon. |
| Kazakhstan | Discon. | | Discon. | | | |
| Libya | R&D | Suspect | R&D | R&D | Suspect | R&D |
| Myanmar | | Suspect | Interest | | Interest | |
| North Korea | R&D | Suspect | Suspect | R&D | Suspect | Suspect |
| Pakistan | Confirm | | | Confirm | R&D | R&D |
| Panama | | | | | Discon. | |
| Russia | Confirm | Confirm | Suspect | Confirm | Confirm | Suspect |
| Saudi Arabia | | | | | Interest | |
| South Africa | Discon. | Suspect | Suspect | Discon. | Discon. | Discon. |
| South Korea | Discon. | Confirm | | Discon. | Discon. | |
| Sudan | | Interest | | | R&D | R&D |
| Syria | | Confirm | | | Suspect | R&D |
| Taiwan | | Suspect | | Discon. | Interest | Interest |

| | | | | | | |
|---|---|---|---|---|---|---|
| *Ukraine* | Discon. | Discon. | | Discon. | Discon. | Discon. |
| *United Kingdom* | Confirm | Confirm | Discon. | Confirm | Discon. | Discon. |
| *United States* | Confirm | Discon. | Discon. | Confirm | Discon. | Discon. |
| *Vietnam* | | Interest | | | Interest | |
| *Yugoslavia (Serbia & Montenegro)* | | | | | Discon. | |

*Key:* Confirm = possession confirmed (production or stockpile); Suspect = probable or suspected possession; R&D = suspected research/development; Interest = possible interest but inconclusive evidence; Discon. = discontinued program; Blanks indicate none or no information.

The list goes on and on, and as technology and information sharing continue to improve, so will the ability of terrorists to gain information on how to obtain, weaponize, and effectively deploy WMD. Terrorists may also be realizing they do not have to make WMD to create a contaminated toxic danger. Hazardous materials are all around us and all terrorists may have to do is blow them up. For instance, on March 14, 2002, two suicide bombers blew themselves up in Ashdod, Israel, where many suspected their objectives were strategic and their targets were tanks storing bromide, ammonia, and fuel. If they had been successful, thousands downwind of the industrial site could have been killed or injured.[20]

A newspaper official in Florida and the television network headquarters of ABC, CBS, and NBC, along with the U.S. capital area, have been attacked by those using biological weapons.[21] Anthrax-filled letters were delivered by mail in October through December 2001 to members of the U.S. Senate in their offices. An extremely small amount of anthrax was used, less than a teaspoon in all the letters combined, and the delivery mode was unsophisticated. Nevertheless, 22 people became ill and 5 died from the fall of 2001 anthrax letter attacks. If the same quality of anthrax in larger quantity had been actively sprayed over an area in Washington, D.C., with certain weather conditions, the results could have been much more devastating. The attacker has still not been identified, demonstrating that a terrorist might be able to attack, cause massive devastation and panic, and never be identified. In March 2004, the U.S. capital area was again put at risk when a Senate office received a letter thought to contain ricin. Fortunately no one became ill from this event.[22]

During the 1980s, the Internet was but a dream, but today it has become a tool for terrorist organizations to communicate and disseminate information. Books on how to produce chemical and biological agents have been freely purchased off the Internet.[23] Terrorists also use the Internet to recruit and give operational commands to their members.

While most of the world community has signed the three major nonproliferation treaties covering nuclear, biological, and chemical weapons possession and use, it is clear those barriers will not prevent the WMD programs of determined proliferator states. The Chemical Weapons Convention (CWC)[24] went into force in 1997 and is being actively administered through an international UN inspectorate, the Organization for the Prohibition of Chemical Weapons at The Hague. The Biological Weapons Convention (BWC)[25] of 1972 has never had a verification and compliance inspection regime and is therefore often seen as having significant weaknesses. The Nuclear Non-Proliferation Treaty (NPT)[26], on the other hand, has been somewhat successful in keeping most of the world free of nuclear weapons, with the United States, Russia, China, France, United Kingdom, Israel, India, Pakistan, and, possibly, North Korea being the most notable exceptions. Although the United States has supported these three major nonproliferation treaties, the George W. Bush administration abrogated the Anti-Ballistic Missile Treaty because the United States concluded that it needed missile defenses against certain potential adversary nations, and the treaty hampered U.S. ability to develop adequate protection against such threats.

Much has been accomplished since the Counterproliferation Initiative was launched in 1993, but much work to slow proliferation and defend against those who would use WMD still lies ahead.

How much funding has the U.S. Department of Defense applied toward counterproliferation? It is difficult to ascertain exact dollar amounts because during the 1990s various counterproliferation programs were categorized differently. But it appears that while the DoD budget increased 144 percent ($252.6 billion to $363.9 billion) from 1995 to 2003, the funding for counterproliferation activities increased 275 percent ($4.1 billion to $11.3 billion). (See Table 1.2.) These figures are not adjusted for inflation, but represent the actual dollar amounts. Nevertheless, counterproliferation funding has increased at almost twice the rate as has the DoD budget.

Also most interesting is how the DoD has decided to spend its counterproliferation dollars. While $2.7 billion was spent on missile defense (or 66 percent of the entire counterproliferation budget) in 1995, by 2003 the amount budgeted for missile defense was $8.7 billion (or 77 percent of the entire counterproliferation budget). (See Figure 1.2.)

When confronting a world of over 190 sovereign states and scores of terrorist organizations, how can the United States and its allies work to reduce the number of states that possess or could acquire chemical, biological, radiological, and nuclear weapons? There is no single answer to

**Table 1.2** Estimated Counterproliferation Funding in Relation to the DoD Budget, 1995 and 2003[27]

|  | DoD Budget | CP Funding | CP as a Percent of Total DoD Budget |
|---|---|---|---|
| **Fiscal Year 1995** | $252.6 billion | $4.1 billion | 1.6 percent |
| **Fiscal Year 2003** | $363.9 billion | $11.3 billion | 3.1 percent |
| **Percent Increase** | 144 percent | 275 percent |  |

that question. Rather, there are multiple remedies to the problem that, taken together, help reduce the number of WMD parties to a more manageable number. The basic counterproliferation remedies are focused primarily at states, but are also thought to have a significant effect on terrorist organizations. These remedies have yet to prove themselves against the twenty-first century terrorist threat.

## The Counterproliferation Elements

No single element of a counterproliferation program can succeed in reducing the WMD proliferation problem significantly on an individual

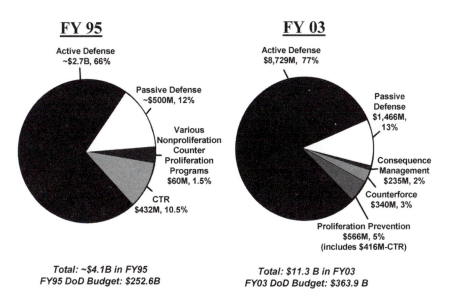

**Figure 1.2** DoD's Counterproliferation Pillar Funding Breakout[28]

basis. Figure 1.3 shows how each element, working in tandem with all the others, reduces the WMD threat.

Were it not for the many states' decisions not to pursue WMD, it is likely that the problem of WMD proliferation would be so serious that the U.S. military never would be able to counter the threat. Even with all elements of counterproliferation in operation, the WMD threat might become so great as to be unmanageable unless sustained and substantial support continued to be available over many years to construct far more robust U.S. and allied deterrents, active defenses, passive defenses, counterforce, and consequence management capabilities.

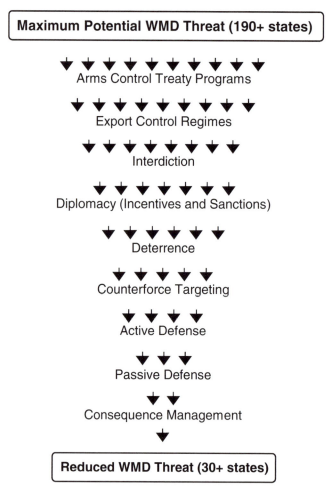

**Figure 1.3**   Counterproliferation Elements

The definition of "counterproliferation" has evolved over time and indeed has meant different things to different audiences at any given time. The current National Strategy to Combat Weapons of Mass Destruction includes three elements: interdiction, deterrence, and defense and mitigation, and it considers nonproliferation and consequence management as separate. Because counterproliferation was initially defined very broadly to include all of these activities and because this book is intended to track progress over the past nearly 13 years, we use a broader definition that includes the following areas: arms control treaty programs, export control regimes, interdiction, diplomatic/economic/political persuasion and sanctions, deterrence, counterforce, active defense, passive defense, and consequence management.

Each of the elements of the U.S. counterproliferation effort is covered below briefly and in more detail in subsequent chapters in this book.

## International Arms Control Treaty Programs

It is easiest to explain the importance of each component of the U.S. counterproliferation effort by understanding how they build on each other's previous success or failure. In 2002, the United Nations had 191 member states, up from 184 in 1993.[29] Each of those 191 states represents a potential proliferator of WMD. Yet, the majority of these states have willingly signed and appear to have abided by international arms control treaties. While some are violators of these treaties, such as Iraq in the early 1990s, North Korea, and potentially Iran, most states have adhered to their arms control treaty commitments. For instance, the NPT of 1970 has grown from 140 member states in 1990 to 188 member states in August 2004, with only three nations abstaining membership, that is, India, Israel, and Pakistan. Since 1993, only two countries, India and Pakistan, are known to have acquired nuclear weapons, and only one other country (North Korea) is suspected to have them.

Although international arms control treaties help *keep honest nations honest,* deceitful nations would probably sign these treaties and cheat to acquire these systems regardless of any treaty. The Biological Weapons Convention, an outgrowth of the U.S. unilateral repudiation of biological warfare in 1969, came into being in 1972 and entered into force in 1975. Initially, agreement was reached by 103 cosigning states and as of August 2004, 167 states had signed the agreement.[30]

In spite of being one of the initial cosigners, the USSR saw the Biological Weapons Convention as an opportunity to steal a unilateral advantage with its clandestine offensive biological warfare program, covertly developing the largest biological warfare program ever known to have been developed. Likewise Iraq, a signatory of the Biological Weapons

Convention, was exposed in the 1990s as developing a BW program in direct violation of its commitments under the Biological Weapons Convention. The lack of adequate verification and compliance measures has plagued the Biological Weapons Convention since its inception; hence several signatories to the Convention have been some of the greatest violators and have had the most extensive biological warfare programs.

The Chemical Weapons Convention opened for signatures in 1993 and went into force in 1997. Learning from the shortcomings of the BWC, it was designed with greater compliance-verification measures providing significantly more international clout. In 1997, 87 countries ratified the CWC to become the original states parties. As of February 2005, the number of member states had grown to 161 states.[31]

## Export Control Regimes

Since international arms control treaties cannot stop all nations from acquiring WMD, the next step is to make it difficult for nations to obtain the equipment or precursors required to develop WMD. Nations that have proven themselves untrustworthy or as particularly threatening have been identified by U.S. and allied intelligence. For instance, the U.S. State Department publishes a biannual list of "states of concern."[32] These states share a cluster of negative traits. They are declared adversaries of the United States or its allies. They seek to acquire WMD. They are state sponsors of terrorism. They are security threats to their neighbors and to the United States.

Besides the unilateral restrictions that states like the United States place on their own materials and technology exports, there are international organizations that also help set some standards. The Australia Group, based in Paris, had grown from its original 15 members in 1985 to 38 members plus the European Union by 2005. These countries form a standing diplomatic conference, share information, and take action to keep materials and equipment used to produce chemical and biological weapons out of the hands of states desiring to acquire them.

Likewise, the Missile Technology Control Regime (MTCR) was formed in 1987 by seven states (including the United States) as a voluntary, informal group with shared goals of stopping proliferation of unmanned delivery systems (usually considered missiles) that could deliver weapons of mass destruction. By 2004, the membership of the MTCR had increased to 34 states.

While the United States and other states have their own mechanisms and policies to limit exportation of certain sensitive materials, the Australia Group and the Missile Technology Control Regime have served to slow the spread and elevate the awareness of transfers of ballistic and cruise missile components and associated equipment transfers and their delivery systems among member states.

## Interdiction

Interdiction is another means of keeping WMD-related materials and technology out of the hands of rogue states. When international arms control treaties and export control regimes have failed to prevent the flow of materials and technologies to the wrong people, another means of denial and prevention is intercepting, seizing, destroying, or otherwise neutralizing them while in transit, whether on the high seas, in international airspace, or on land. (See Denial in Figure 1.1.)

Interdiction was not considered a major component of the U.S. counterproliferation program seeking to deter the spread of WMD until the United States led an international effort called the Proliferation Security Initiative. It was felt that another tool was needed to stop the flow of WMD-related materials and technologies to dangerous rival states and terrorist groups. Therefore, on May 31, 2003, President George W. Bush announced the PSI would be a means to coordinate more effective mechanisms "to impede or stop shipments of WMD, delivery systems, and related materials."[33]

## Diplomacy (Incentives and Sanctions)

Diplomatic persuasion is one of the standard tools available in efforts to influence regime leaders to cease their WMD programs or roll them back. For example, a combination of rewards and punishments appear to have persuaded Muammar Qaddafi to reverse Libya's policies and give up its nuclear and chemical weapons programs. Two decades of diplomatic isolation, travel restrictions, economic trade sanctions, and possible military conflict seem to have influenced Libya's ruler to seek the economic and political benefits of a cooperative policy.

Sanctions work best when all or most other states also cooperate in concert with the United States to pressure the proliferant regime to reverse its path and renounce the pursuit or possession of WMD. Embassies may be closed and travel bans to the noncompliant state may be imposed. Companies and states that continue to deal with the proliferant state might also be penalized to bring them into conformity with the pressure policy.

Carrots as well as sticks are part of nonproliferation diplomacy. Diplomatic recognition, renewed trade and increased international financial aid, lifting of embargoes, removal of threats of military intervention, and reopening of travel to and from the state of concern are all carrots that can be offered in exchange for giving up a WMD program and cooperating with on-site inspectors to verify compliance with nonprolifer-ation goals. Thus a policy of diplomatic rewards and punishments can, in certain situations, help move noncompliant states toward cooperation.

## Deterrence

What can be done when nonproliferation mechanisms have failed to prevent a nation from acquiring WMD? Deterrence, a major tool of the Cold War, can be the counterbalance that holds in check the rogue state WMD threat. To effectively deter an adversary requires a capability, or perceived capability, to inflict unacceptable retaliatory damage on an adversary. It also requires a clear communication of the willingness to use this capability, and it is effective mostly when confronting a rational opponent.

The rise of terrorist groups that seem to be motivated more by religious or ideological motives rather than by a logical cost-gain calculus has com-plicated our ability to deter attacks or escalation of conflict. Those that kill in the name of God are operating on a different wavelength than most state or terrorist leaders. Moreover, terrorists often are difficult to pin-point. Sometimes it is difficult to determine the source of the attack and their location. Deterrence operates best when the potential attacker has a return address you can visit with your retaliatory strikes. Nevertheless, if a terrorist group's motivations can be accurately analyzed and determi-nations can be made about what the group holds of value, deterrence should not be ruled out as a possible tool; yet, further study is needed to answer the many unknowns about deterring nonstate actors.

## Counterforce

If deterrence fails, and warfare ensues, then the United States, when faced with a WMD-armed adversary, must have the ability to destroy those enemy WMD assets before they can be launched against U.S. and allied targets. This requires very effective counterforce weapons and intel-ligence, surveillance, and reconnaissance (ISR) capabilities to detect WMD locations. Optimally, in wartime, U.S. and allied forces must destroy the WMD on the adversary's territory before they are used. Hav-ing an effective counterforce program may help deter an adversary from acquiring WMD, but if not, it also can degrade an adversary's potential threat to friendly forces so as to decrease the burden on active defense, passive defense, and consequence management. The counterforce compo-nent of the U.S. counterproliferation program requires effective and timely intelligence, sophisticated command and control, and a suite of appropriate weapons.

To offset time-sensitive targets like WMD assets that must be neutralized before their terrible effects can be visited upon U.S. and allied personnel, the United States needs a combination of lethal, PGMs with ISR sensors that give 24/7 target identification, tracking, and battle damage assessment. Moreover, the command and control of such counterforce assets, be they air to ground, ground to ground, or sea to ground, must be so rapid and accurate that sensor-to-shooter times are reduced to a few minutes and target coordinates are accurate to within the circular error probable[34] of weapons employed.

Counterforce targeting must also defeat three particularly difficult types of WMD-asset-related target sets if it is to be successful. First, deeply buried hardened shelters may shield some adversary WMD assets. This compels U.S. forces to develop better penetrating weapons or to attack otherwise invulnerable sites with the idea of inflicting a functional defeat rather than physical destruction by destroying power, water, or air supplies. Second, the U.S. forces must develop an ability to locate, attack, and destroy mobile missile launchers by a combination of better intelligence, surveillance, and reconnaissance; command and control; precision-guided munitions; coordination of attack aircraft; unmanned aerial vehicles; forward deployed special forces; cruise missiles; and ground-launched ballistic weapons, all directed by accurate intelligence against moving targets. The proper intelligence preparation of the battle space will enable planners to identify probable launch zones, assign kill box coordinates, monitor the latter continuously, and identify time-sensitive target locations in real time. The outcome of future "Scud hunts" with potential WMD-armed missiles could determine whether U.S. and allied forces face casualties numbering in the dozens versus in the tens of thousands.

Finally, successful counterforce strikes require suppression of WMD assets with a minimum of collateral damage to civilian populations and adjacent friendly troops in the region. This requires a new family of agent defeat weapons that are now starting to reach the field after years of research and development efforts.

## Active Defense

If one fails to prevent an adversary from acquiring WMD, fails to deter their use, and cannot destroy the WMD on adversary territory, then the U.S. and allied defenses against land, sea, or air attacks with such weapons must be effective to blunt the attacks and protect against them. For example, if the attack takes the form of a missile or aircraft strike, an effective active defense interceptor program must be in place. Israel has now deployed its high altitude terminal phase antiballistic missile, the Arrow, alongside the U.S.-supplied Patriot-3 to provide its national missile defense. The United States has been developing multiple theater ballistic missile defense programs for nearly 13 years. As noted, one, the Patriot-3 terminal defense system, has been deployed. Five others are in various stages of research, development, and testing. In 2004, the United States deployed interceptor missiles designed to protect U.S. territory, the Ground-based Midcourse Missile Defense.

## Passive Defense

Since no active defense system can be 100 percent effective and because there are other ways to deploy WMD than missiles or planes, a passive defense system must be effective, as it is literally the last line of defense. Personal protective equipment (masks and suits), detectors, vaccines, antidotes, decontamination procedures, collective protection shelters, and more are relied upon by U.S. military forces to provide the means to survive a chemical, biological, radiological, or nuclear attack and continue to carry out their missions. Likewise, passive defenses are needed to provide protection for the civilian community so it can survive an attack and get back to life as usual. Today, many of the U.S. forces have received new masks and suits, but these improve protection only against certain chemical agents and hinder military personnel in fighting in conventional combat. Although millions of dollars have been put into research and some promising vaccines are being advanced, no new vaccines have been made available to U.S. forces during the last 13 years. Improvements in environmental biological agent detection have occurred through the use of new technologies such as PCR, but there are still huge deficiencies in the number of agents that can be detected even if they are at levels that are hazardous to humans. For identification of biological agents, it still takes time to produce lab results, and false positives and false negatives continue to plague biodetection technology.

## Consequence Management or Survive to Operate

An adversary may still succeed in producing, deploying, and employing WMD despite our best nonproliferation and counterproliferation efforts. For this reason, an effective consequence management program is also required to allow the military to survive, recover, and then continue operations and to help the civilian community recover and restore order. If the adversary perceives the United States has a good consequence management program, it might help deter the use of WMD altogether.

The U.S. military has conducted several Advanced Concept Technology Demonstration (ACTD) programs to help learn how to survive and operate in a WMD environment. The most notable of these are the Restoration of Operations (RestOps) ACTD and the Contamination Avoidance at Seaports of Debarkation ACTD. These have allowed the testing of a myriad of technologies and concepts of operations, as well as tactics, techniques, and procedures for operating in a chemical or biological environment. For example, the U.S. Air Force has developed a new counterchemical warfare concept of operations for keeping U.S. Air Force sortie rates high even during a chemical warfare barrage of a forward air base, based largely on lessons learned from the RestOps ACTD.

## The Renewed Emphasis on Homeland Security

Although the Homeland Security program is separate from the U.S. counterproliferation effort, it overlaps in multiple areas. In fact, each counterproliferation component contributes to the vital protection of the homeland. And although the concept of homeland security was not explicitly articulated when the 1993 Counterproliferation Initiative was announced, the mission of homeland protection is as old as the republic, and there has been renewed emphasis placed on this old mission that greatly accelerated after September 11, 2001.

The Department of Defense has reorganized to create NORTHCOM dedicated to protecting U.S. military forces, facilities, and installations in the United States homeland. In the same regard, the National Guard finds itself increasingly called upon to protect the homeland from terrorists and especially those that might have WMD. Homeland defense pertains to the defense of U.S. military installations in the continental United States. Homeland security pertains to the defense of the entire nation. NORTHCOM may be drafted by the DHS to help do both in a crisis, but DHS has the lead.

President Bush has said repeatedly in speeches that he sees weapons of mass destruction in the hands of terrorists as one of the gravest dangers our nation faces. A series of presidential directives and executive orders even before September 11, 2001, helped the numerous agencies involved with homeland security begin to at least think about it. President Bush's first *National Strategy for Homeland Security*[35] was published on July 15, 2002. The new Department of Homeland Security came into being on March 11, 2003, consisting of 22 agencies. Clearly, one of the major overlaps between the counterproliferation mission and that of homeland security is to protect U.S. personnel and vital interests against the WMD threat posed by adversaries.

## Challenge

The era following Les Aspin's Counterproliferation Initiative, announced on December 7, 1993, has seen the United States take many positive steps in preparing to slow, stop, deter, or defend against enemy WMD. Yet, the world is not demonstrably safer today than then. Rogue states such as North Korea and Iran move toward more potent WMD capabilities, and the fear of terrorist use of WMD grows. There is an intense race to prevent and prepare against the contingency of a megaterrorist or a WMD war event.

# CHAPTER 2

# The WMD Proliferation Threat

## *Jonathan B. Wolfsthal*

The proliferation of weapons of mass destruction (WMD) by states,[1] including nuclear, chemical, and biological weapons and ballistic missiles, emerged as the top security threat to the United States in the wake of the Cold War. Several factors put concerns about weapons of mass destruction at the top of the list of concerns, including the breakup of the Soviet Union and the proliferation consequences stemming from that major event. One Soviet state became 15 independent republics, 4 with strategic nuclear weapons deployed on their soil. There have also been serious problems with the security of the former Soviet nuclear, biological, and chemical arsenals as well with protecting hundreds of tons of fissile material and over 40,000 tons of chemical weapons. Further, there has been a concern that thousands of nuclear, biological, and chemical weapons scientists and technicians could share their knowledge with would-be WMD proliferators. The breakup of the Soviet Union threatened to dramatically worsen the already formidable challenge of containing the WMD proliferation threat that previously existed.

A second reason for concern in the early 1990s was the confrontation with Iraq in the 1990–1991 Gulf War and its aftermath. Iraq under Saddam Hussein was known to have employed chemical weapons in the 1980–1988 Iran-Iraq War, as well as against their own Iraqi Kurds. After Operation Desert Storm, UN inspectors discovered a multipronged and very ambitious Iraqi nuclear program. Then, later in 1995, a defection by Saddam Hussein's sons-in-law led to an admission by Iraq that it also had possessed a substantial biological weapons research and development program prior to Desert Storm.

These events triggered alarm bells and caused the United States to initiate the counterproliferation program. It was decided that the previous nonproliferation regime consisting of nonproliferation treaties [Nuclear

Non-Proliferation Treaty (NPT), Chemical Weapons Convention (CWC), and Biological and Toxins Weapons Convention (BTWC)], export control regimes, UN sanctions, and state-to-state diplomatic efforts were not sufficient in and of themselves to prevent determined proliferators from acquiring weapons of mass destruction and that other tools would be needed.

The Counterproliferation Initiative of 1993 was designed to augment traditional nonproliferation activities with new activities to strengthen U.S. counterforce, active defense, passive defense, and consequence management initiatives. Fearing that WMD proliferation might not be contained, counterproliferation measures were accelerated to prepare the U.S. military to survive, fight, and win in conflicts where the enemy might use chemical, biological, radiological, or nuclear weapons in addition to conventional arms. It was further hoped that possessing these capabilities would help deter states from getting involved with WMD in the first place.

Proliferation concerns grew in the 1990s and early years of the twenty-first century as both transnational groups and states sought, and some acquired, a basic WMD capability. In 1995, the Aum Shinrikyo cult led by Shoko Asahara drew the world's attention with a sarin gas attack on passengers on five trains in the Tokyo, Japan, subway system, killing a dozen persons and sending 5,500 to the hospital.[2] Subsequent investigations of the group indicated that it had attempted nine biological weapons attacks and seven chemical weapons attacks on targets in Japan. One of those targets was a U.S. naval base. The Aum Shinrikyo had experimented with anthrax, sarin nerve agent, VX nerve agent, botulinum toxin, and cyanide. The cult also sought nuclear weapons and owned land with uranium deposits, although no real progress toward a nuclear capability was achieved by the cult.

Al-Qaeda has also shown an interest in acquiring weapons of mass destruction. Osama Bin Laden has called acquiring nuclear weapons a religious duty and al-Qaeda leadership is reported to have had meetings with Pakistani nuclear weapons scientists to ascertain the shortest path to such arms. In the aftermath of Operation Enduring Freedom, U.S. forces in Afghanistan found evidence of al-Qaeda interest in and experiments on animals with chemical weapons.

If all this were not serious enough, both North Korea and Iran have accelerated their nuclear weapons programs and the A. Q. Khan black market network has helped both programs by sharing centrifuge technology and designs as well as other nuclear weapons manufacturing expertise. There is growing concern that these programs, if unchecked, would trigger other nuclear programs by their neighbors to offset and deter their use. Japan, the Republic of Korea, and Taiwan and Iran's neighbors including Egypt, Saudi Arabia, and even Turkey may be tempted to acquire nuclear weapons in response to regional proliferation. Trade in missile and WMD technology and expertise promises to increase the potential for future WMD use either by states or terrorist organizations.

Moreover, the security situation is darkened by other proliferation developments. Both ballistic and cruise missile technology have spread widely. For example, it is now estimated that over 75 countries have some form of short- or even longer-range cruise missiles in their inventories. North Korean missiles and related technologies are being spread to other states such as Iran. If these lead to Intermediate Range Ballistic Missiles (IRBMs) and Intercontinental Ballistic Missiles in the hands of rogue states, the United States and its allies will be in increased danger, although these capabilities have spread more slowly than some believed just a few years ago.

Another great uncertainty is how far biological weapons programs have or have not spread. Biological warfare programs can be effectively hidden and leave few signatures that can be detected by national technical means. The lack of a legally binding verification regime for the Biological Weapons Convention further hinders biological warfare (BW) nonprolif-eration efforts. Further, states with even basic biomedical or health-care industries can sustain a basic biological weapons program. Such weapons are easily hidden and are well within the budgets and expertise of many countries. Indeed, even small groups or individuals are deemed capable of manufacture and using basic types of biological agents, although effective weaponization and dissemination remain major impediments to mass casualties, if not mass panic. Note the anthrax through the mail attacks in the United States in late 2001 that created such major disruptions.

While the weapons of mass destruction proliferation situation since 1993 has not been a happy story, the story is far from one dimensional. There have been some notable and surprising nonproliferation success stories in the 1993–2004 period, but the future is far from certain.

## WMD Proliferation Becomes a Top Policy Priority

While the three post-Cold War U.S. presidents have used different language to characterize this threat, presidents George H. W. Bush, William J. Clinton, and George W. Bush have all cited the threat of weapons of mass destruction as a top security concern for the United States. Statements by current Bush administration officials indicate that concern over proliferation will continue to seize U.S. policy makers for the foreseeable future. As laid out by President George W. Bush,

> The gravest danger our nation faces lies at the crossroads of radicalism and technology. Our enemies have openly declared that they are seeking weapons

of mass destruction, and evidence indicates that they are doing so with determination. The United States will not allow these efforts to succeed.[3]

Even before September 11, 2001, America's global presence and interests, as well as its overwhelming conventional superiority, necessitated a direct focus on weapons of mass destruction proliferation.[4] The potential connection to terrorism has elevated the risk posed by proliferation into a top tier security concern for the public and policy maker alike.

Despite the intense focus given to this issue, and the considerable investment in U.S. time, energy, and resources, a number of countries have continued to pursue weapons of mass destruction capabilities. As the then CIA Director George Tenet testified in 2003, "we have entered a new world of proliferation." He continued, "the 'domino theory' of the 21st century may well be nuclear."[5]

While this may eventually prove to be true, it is not a certainty and echoes doom-filled predictions from the 1960s and 1970s that never came to pass, in large part because of U.S. efforts to reduce the supply and demand for weapons of mass destruction. Not only are a relatively small number of states seeking nuclear weapons, but a number of countries have abandoned nuclear weapons programs or actual weapons.[6] People tend to forget the success stories inherent in the decisions by Belarus, Kazakhstan, and Ukraine to give up nuclear weapons they inherited from the Soviet Union, as well as South Africa's voluntary rollback of its nuclear weapons arsenal. Libya's recent rejection of weapons of mass destruction is another case in point, as is Iraq's apparent decision to destroy all of its weapons of mass destruction in the 1990s.

Despite the new dire predictions, the number of states seeking or possessing nuclear weapons has remained largely static and has even declined over the past decade. Not all nations that had nuclear weapons programs continued them, and not all that pursued programs have yet succeeded in acquiring such weapons, but the desire remains among a few very important states and this desire could spread. Indeed, if Iran and North Korea continue with their nuclear weapons programs, and if states such as Pakistan and China continue to share nuclear technology, the world might see a surge in the numbers of nuclear states. Indeed, the spread of nuclear arms to even a couple of new states such as Iran and North Korea is almost sure to whet the appetite for such weapons by their neighbors who feel threatened. It would not be surprising to see renewed interest in atomic weapons, for example, in South Korea and Japan, just to name a few candidates.

If the nuclear weapons proliferation story is mixed, the proliferation of potential weapons of mass destruction delivery vehicles is largely negative. Each of the nuclear weapons countries of concern to the

United States has constantly improved its missile capabilities. The North Koreans have tested No Dongs and Taepo Dongs. The latter, tested only once, has the potential to reach the West Coast of the United States if further testing takes place and is successful. Moreover, North Korea has been collaborating with states such as Iran, Syria, and Pakistan by selling missiles and missile technology to improve their strategic reach. China also slowly continues to modernize its Intercontinental Ballistic Missile force.

The degree of chemical and biological weapons proliferation since 1993 is shrouded in uncertainty. Numerous chemical and biological programs are suspected, but proof remains elusive. The recent experience in Iraq where no substantial evidence was found of active weapons of mass destruction programs should make us wary of speculations by the Intelligence Community, unless rock-solid evidence is provided to substantiate such judgments in the future.

Locating hidden chemical or biological programs is like finding a needle in a haystack. One of the problems is that we do not know what we do not know. Biological weapons programs, in particular, can be very hidden and use accessible equipment that has other commercial civilian uses. Moreover, these programs are far cheaper than nuclear or even chemical or missile programs. Chemical weapons manufacturing can also be hidden easily within chemical or pharmaceutical plants, and neither chemical nor biological programs have very large or easily detectable signatures. This creates a very large uncertainty for U.S. intelligence as to how many states have chemical and biological weapons programs or even what the trend has been since 1993. Judging the military utility of such weapons is even harder.

However, the threat from nonstate actors seeking weapons of mass destruction clearly appears to have grown in the last decade. The past few years, dating back before September 11, 2001, has given rise to concerns over the ability of subnational groups to acquire weapons of mass destruction capabilities, either through their connections to states or on their own. The Aum Shinrikyo case noted above is an active case in point.[7]

In the period from 1990 to 1995, the Aum Shinrikyo cult in Japan launched seven terrorist attacks using chemical weapons (sarin, VX, and hydrogen cyanide) in Tokyo, Matsumoto, and Osaka. Over that same period, the cult also launched nine attacks using aerosolized biological agents (anthrax and botulinum toxin) with murderous intent, but with no visible result because of delivery system problems or use of ineffective strains of the biological warfare agents. One of these biological warfare targets was Yokosuka Naval Base, the main port of the U.S. Seventh Fleet in the eastern Pacific.

There are other examples of nonstate actors seeking WMD. Evidence was discovered after the war in Afghanistan that al-Qaeda was pursuing chemical weapon capabilities. Some terrorist(s) of unknown origin used anthrax to attack, via the mail, members of the U.S. Congress and U.S. mass media headquarters in late 2001. Bush administration officials raised the concern that Saddam might pass weapons of mass destruction to terrorist groups before the recent Iraq War.

Traditional approaches to prevent nonstate acquisition of such weapons have had questionable utility against nonstate actors. The threat of weapons of mass destruction finding their way into the hands of terrorists raises major challenges to the diplomatic and military establishments to develop new ways to protect American interests. These efforts will be successful mainly insofar as they recognize that even subnational groups must exist and operate within the borders of existing states, failed or otherwise. This reality creates potential solutions to those that are tasked with countering weapons of mass destruction terrorism.

In addressing proliferation before or after it occurs, it is vital to understand the motives that underlie weapons of mass destruction proliferation and the decisions to abandon such programs. The motives often cited for pursuing such weapons are to acquire their deterrent or war fighting capabilities, to overcome a real or perceived insecurity (military or otherwise), to pursue regional or global influence or prestige, or to secure domestic political gains. Nonstate actors, such as terror groups, have additional motivations, including a desire for power, influence, wealth, revenge, or simply to create mass casualties and chaos among those perceived as adversaries.

In the group of countries that have continued to seek weapons of mass destruction, all of the state-related motives for proliferation are present, often several at the same time. These motives are powerful and often have prevailed in spite of significant strengthening of U.S. nonproliferation policies over the past 13 years, including the formalization of a counterproliferation strategy. In addition, several of the states pursuing weapons of mass destruction also have ties to terror groups or are active sponsors of state terrorism. These states quickly rise to the top of states that concern the United States, given the new focus on the links between terrorism and weapons of mass destruction.

The fact that some states have continued their programs in the face of U.S. pressure and growing U.S. counterproliferation efforts does not mean that they have not altered their approaches to pursuing or their potential strategies for employing such weapons. These facets of each state's national policy are highly secret, and open sources on such information are scarce and notoriously unreliable. Nevertheless, there is growing evidence that states are increasingly seeking to hide their programs from U.S. intelligence and are increasingly going underground, literally, to avoid detection or destruction.

## Recent Developments

Since 2001, the U.S. military has removed regimes from two countries that were state sponsors of terrorist organizations and, in the case of Iraq, one was thought to be engaged in the pursuit of weapons of mass destruction. This is unlikely to be the norm for dealing with proliferation threats, but it demonstrates the ability and willingness of the United States to take direct action to address perceived or actual weapons of mass destruction threats. Both cases are special.

The war in Afghanistan was directly tied by the Bush administration to the aftermath of the September 11, 2001, terror attacks in New York and Washington, D.C., and was not fought principally with the threat of weapons of mass destruction in mind. In addition, Operation Iraqi Freedom (OIF) came on the heels of the 1990–1991 Gulf War, 12 years of efforts to enforce the UN resolutions banning Iraqi pursuit or possession of weapons of mass destruction, and the increased threats perceived by U.S. political leaders as a result of the events of September 11, 2001.

The decision by Libyan leader Colonel Muammar Qaddafi is another recent development that will influence the future course of nonproliferation and counterproliferation activities. Those analysts who believe primarily in the role military power is playing in dissuading states from challenging the United States might cite the willingness of President Bush to go to war in Iraq over the weapons of mass destruction issue as a primary influence in Libya's decision.

Others note, with some authority, that Libya's offers to disarm date back to the 1990s and are likely as influenced by a desire to eliminate sanctions as to avoid destruction. The truth is likely somewhere in the middle, since both motives seem sensible. The nature of the regime and the recent nature of events make a complete analysis difficult, and additional work to understand the true nature of the Libyan decision would be beneficial to the future development of nonproliferation policies.

## Sources and Methods

Tracking weapons of mass destruction programs is an inexact science. Over time, information about a country's programs emerges as a mosaic of statements, intelligence assessments and reports, press accounts, and leaked information. Many of these sources are uncertain and may be driven by unseen political or military motivations. Even without the controversy over U.S. intelligence about Iraq's weapons of mass destruction programs that emerged after Operation Iraqi Freedom, one should understand that such national intelligence estimates are usually based on limited evidence and contain a greater or lesser degree of uncertainty. Generally, reliance on government reports, public statements, and reliable media reporting can provide an outline of basic weapon programs. They often fail, however, to provide operational details or specifics regarding the exact amounts of material acquired or the logistics associated with weapon programs. To gain an accurate assessment of the direct effects the U.S. counterproliferation program has had on proliferants, a much greater level of detail, including how weapon programs are hidden or protected, would be needed. Much of this information is simply unavailable in assessments of weapons of mass destruction trends, especially at the unclassified level.

In the wake of the failure to find weapons of mass destruction in Iraq, however, there should be an increased amount of scrutiny applied to publicly available government reports about WMD proliferation. Inaccurate statements, broad conclusions, and politically motivated leaks of information can all prevent people outside the government system from obtaining an accurate sense of which countries are developing what types of weapons, how soon these programs might reach maturity, and what type of threat they may actually pose to the public and military of differing countries.

## Seven Cases of State Trends in WMD Proliferation

This analysis now focuses on seven key states where weapons of mass destruction programs have been pursued and maintained in the first 13 years of the Counterproliferation Initiative, starting with an unclassified look at the program in Iran.

### Iran

In the wake of Operation Iraqi Freedom, Iran quickly jumped to the top of the U.S. concerns about proliferation. Iran has signed and ratified the NPT as well as the Chemical and Biological Weapons Conventions. Despite these legal commitments, Iran is reported to be pursuing the full suite of nuclear, chemical, and biological weapons and ballistic missiles (see Table 2.1) and is widely believed to be much closer to being able to

**Table 2.1** Iran's WMD Status (1993–2005)

|  | Nuclear | Chemical | Biological | Missiles |
|---|---|---|---|---|
| **1993** | No | Yes | Yes? | Yes |
| **1997** | No | Yes | Yes? | Yes |
| **2005** | No | Yes | Yes? | Yes |
| Overall Trend: Rapidly developing nuclear, missile capabilities | | | | |

produce nuclear weapons than previously thought. Moreover, the International Atomic Energy Agency Board of Governors has concluded that Iran failed to meet all of its obligations by not reporting nuclear activities to the Agency, as required under its safeguards agreement.

Iran's nuclear acquisition programs have been under way for several decades and are motivated by a variety of factors, including the extended conflict between Iran and Iraq, a desire by Iran to counter Israel's weapons of mass destruction capabilities, to deter possible U.S. attempts at regime change, and as a possible source of power and influence in the region. According to the U.S. Department of Defense,

> Iran's national security efforts are designed to increase its influence and prestige in the Middle East and throughout the Islamic world, to deter Iraq and any other regional threats as well as to limit U.S. influence and presence in the region, especially in the Persian Gulf. Iran recognizes that it cannot match U.S. military power and therefore seeks asymmetric means to challenge and/or deter the United States. Iran's efforts include the acquisition of nuclear, biological and chemical weapons and missiles and use of terrorism.[8]

Iran is thought by U.S. intelligence to have begun chemical weapons production in the mid-1980s after Iraq used chemical weapons on Iranian troops and cities. Iranian forces initially used captured Iraqi chemical weapons in that conflict and then stockpiled and used indigenously manufactured cyanogen chloride, phosgene, and mustard gas. After the conflict was terminated in 1989, Iran was reported to have begun new agent production. Iran signed and ratified the BTWC in late 1997, but is believed still to possess a clandestine chemical warfare (CW) program.

The case of Iran poses a particularly difficult nonproliferation challenge for the United States. The historical problems between the two states, dating back even before the Islamic Revolution, compound the problem of trying to change the behavior of the ruling regime in Tehran without alienating the Iranian reform movement the United States hopes to encourage. A key issue is whether the United States can effectively restrain Iran's nuclear program without alienating the reform movement or making the nuclear effort a point of nationalistic pride for that same movement.[9] U.S. skepticism about Iran's motives have also restricted U.S. support for efforts beginning in 2003 by major European powers to engage Tehran to end their nuclear activities.

Iran's nuclear weapons program is the most prominent of its weapons of mass destruction activities. In 2003, it was revealed that Iran had hidden an active program to develop the means to produce weapons-usable nuclear material from the International Atomic Energy Agency (IAEA) and the international community. For the bulk of the 1990s, the U.S. effort to prevent Iran from pursuing nuclear capabilities was focused on the relationship between Tehran and Moscow. Russia is nearing completion of a modified VVER-1000 power reactor at Bushehr, Iran, and the United States has objected to the construction of the reactor on the basis that Iran was using the commercial program as a cover for its nuclear weapon ambitions. It is now known that Iran has acquired considerable uranium-enrichment capabilities through the black market network run by Pakistan's A. Q. Khan.

Some question why Iran, which is the possessor of nearly 10 percent of the world's proven oil reserves, should make such a major investment in nuclear power and enrichment if it did not have nuclear weapons ambitions. Whether Iran has or does not have a nuclear weapons program is still debatable, but it is certain that Iran's ability to pursue nuclear weapons is increasing. Iran has successfully pursued the acquisition of weapons-related technology, including an ability to produce centrifuges for the enrichment of uranium. It was disclosed in late 2002 that Iran's nuclear program had, without detection by the international community or presumably U.S. intelligence, progressed much further than U.S. officials and the international community thought possible. IAEA inspectors were surprised and even shocked at the extent and sophistication of Iran's uranium-enrichment program after having been allowed to tour the Natanz facility in February 2003.

The Natanz facility is located in central Iran, approximately 200 miles south of Tehran. The complex itself is extensive and covers nearly 100,000 square meters. Many of the largest structures within the complex are buried underground. The two largest of these structures enclose about 60,000 square meters collectively. The full facility is still under construction and is not scheduled for completion until 2005. According to U.S. officials and IAEA specialists, there are currently 160 centrifuge machines at the facility that are considered operational, and parts are in place for another 1,000 machines. Iran denies that it has violated its safeguards agreement or that it had tested centrifuges with uranium outside of safeguards. When completed, the Natanz facility is expected to house 5,000 gas centrifuges and could produce enough fissile material for two nuclear weapons a year.

In early 2004, it was revealed that Dr. Abdul Qadeer Khan, father of Pakistan's nuclear bomb program, admitted to running a black market operation that sold nuclear expertise and technology to Iran, Libya, and North Korea. It was disclosed that Pakistani centrifuges were shipped to Iran through a company located in Dubai in the United Arab Emirates, called the SMB Group. Khan's group also supplied Iran with used centrifuge components and designs.[10] Pakistan's government claims this was an unauthorized transfer of technology and expertise carried out by Khan and his associates, although it has declined to prosecute the popular Dr. Khan after he issued an apology.[11]

There has been much speculation about Iran's decision to place the most sensitive sites underground. In a press briefing in December 2002, U.S. State Department spokesman Richard Boucher said,

> It appears from the imagery that a service road, several small structures, and perhaps three large structures are being built below grade, and some of these are already being covered with earth. Iran clearly intended to harden and bury that facility. That facility was probably never intended by Iran to be a declared component of the peaceful program. Instead, Iran has been caught constructing a secret underground site where it could produce fissile material.[12]

In addition to its nuclear activities, Iran has been working to expand its chemical and biological weapons capabilities throughout the past decade. In 1993 testimony before Congress, CIA Director James Woolsey confirmed that Iran "can … manufacture hundreds of tons of chemical agent each year. Although it produces primarily choking and blister agents, Iran may also have a stockpile of nerve agents. Biological weapons, if not already in production, are probably not far behind." Another CIA nonproliferation specialist, Dr. Gordon Oehler, stated in the same Congressional hearing that Iran's biological warfare program "could be operational."[13] Iran's chemical weapons capabilities were vividly demonstrated by that country's use of chemical weapons during the Iran-Iraq War. Russian intelligence reports concur with Woolsey's 1993 assessment, reporting, "Iran possesses at least two types of chemical weapons."[14]

By the early 2000s, Iran was continuing its pursuit of chemical and biological warfare capabilities, but remained dependent on outside sources of material and technology. Meanwhile, Iran has made significant progress in its missile capabilities. Iran benefited from its collaboration with North Korea, having obtained both missiles and missile production capabilities from Pyongyang. Whereas it was limited to Scud missiles in the early 1990s, by 2003 it had tested and begun serial production of a domestically produced 1,300-kilometer version of the North Korean No Dong missile, the Shahab-3. This missile puts all of Israel and some of the southeastern flank of NATO within Iran's reach. Such longer-range missile development, with its expensive investment price tag, makes little strategic sense if it were to be mated only with a conventional warhead. The expense and rapid pace of research, development, and testing of the Shabab-3 naturally raises the question as to whether Iran has a parallel nuclear, biological, or chemical warhead development program to mate with such a delivery system once it is deployed operationally. If so, most of Southwest Asia and Southeast Europe would be within reach of Iran's weapons of mass destruction.

In addition to Scud-Bs and Cs, indigenous Mushak missiles, and the Shahab-3 and Shahab-4 missiles, Iran is also credited with a growing inventory of Silkworm, Harpoon, Sunburn, Kyle, and Kitter cruise missiles as well as seven types of fighter-bomber aircraft.

At the broadest level, there is no outward sign that U.S. planning in the region has directly affected Iranian procurement. In fact, as stated by U.S. Government sources, Iran is thought to be pursuing weapons of mass destruction capabilities specifically because of the divergence between U.S. and Iranian conventional capabilities. There are some outward signs that Iran has sought to protect its weapons of mass destruction assets by using dual-use facilities and, in the case of the nuclear program, by building covert and buried facilities, which may be attempts to prevent the United States from using preemptive military strikes against Iran's weapons of mass destruction capabilities.

Iran's continued links to terror groups, in combination with its weapons of mass destruction programs, place that country squarely in the center of U.S. regional security concerns. The 2002 edition of the State Department's *Patterns of Global Terrorism* stated the following:

> Iran remained the most active state sponsor of terrorism in 2002 ... Iran's record against Al Qaeda appears to be mixed. While it has detained and turned over to foreign governments a number of Al Qaeda members, reportedly other Al Qaeda members have found safehaven there and may be receiving protection from elements of the Iranian Government.[15]

## North Korea

The Democratic People's Republic of Korea (DPRK), commonly called North Korea, represents the most challenging case for U.S. proliferation policy. The isolated and secretive regime has successfully pursued the development of the full suite of weapons of mass destruction capabilities (see Table 2.2) and may already possess nuclear weapons. Moreover, North Korea is poised to rapidly expand its nuclear weapon production capabilities over the next few years and could undermine the entire international security system if it chooses to export nuclear materials or fully

**Table 2.2**  North Korea's WMD Status (1993–2005)

|      | Nuclear | Chemical | Biological | Missiles |
|------|---------|----------|------------|----------|
| 1993 | Yes?    | Yes      | Yes?       | Yes      |
| 1997 | Yes?    | Yes      | Yes?       | Yes      |
| 2005 | Yes?    | Yes      | Yes?       | Yes      |
| Overall Trend: Rapid pursuit of nuclear capabilities, development and testing of IRBM systems | | | | |

constructed nuclear weapons. North Korea has withdrawn from the NPT (the first ever to do so) and is a member of the BTWC, but not the CWC.

The motives for North Korea's weapons programs appear to be focused on regime survival. The export of ballistic missiles to states including Pakistan, Iran, Syria, and Yemen is a major source of hard currency for the North Koreans, and their nuclear and missile programs are also designed to deter any U.S. or allied military attack against Pyongyang. There is a serious debate over the willingness of North Korea to give up its unconventional weapons in exchange for incentives from the United States.

North Korea's nuclear and missile capabilities are the focus of U.S. security concerns in Northeast Asia. By 1994, when the United States and North Korea negotiated the Agreed Framework, which froze North Korea's known nuclear infrastructure until late 2002, North Korea had built the capability to produce and refine plutonium for use in nuclear weapons. It is not known with any certainty how much plutonium North Korea may have produced before the freeze took effect in 1994, although unclassified reports of the U.S. Intelligence Community concluded that it is likely that North Korea produced enough plutonium prior to the agreement for perhaps one to two nuclear weapons.[16]

In addition, North Korea had produced an additional 25–30 kilograms of plutonium, enough for five to six nuclear weapons, that was contained in 8,000 irradiated fuel elements in storage at Yongbyon until North Korea evicted IAEA inspectors from the country in December 2002. According to April 2004 press reports, several U.S. intelligence agencies now believe that North Korea may possess at least eight nuclear weapons.[17] Pakistan black marketeer A. Q. Khan reported seeing three devices that North Korean officials showed him, claiming they were nuclear weapons.

In addition to nuclear weapons in North Korea's possession, the isolated DPRK regime is also working to build a robust nuclear material production capability that includes large-scale plutonium production, as well as a significant uranium-enrichment capability. This uranium program reportedly was only discovered in mid-2002 by U.S. intelligence, and unsubstantiated reports that North Korea was building a uranium centrifuge facility by North Korea led to the collapse of the Agreed Framework and the restart of that country's nuclear program. In October 2002, Assistant Secretary of State James Kelly confronted North Korean officials with facts that suggested North Korea was pursuing, in violation of its agreements, a secret uranium-enrichment facility. Surprisingly, the North Korean officials admitted such an activity was indeed taking place and that North Korea had decided to pursue the acquisition of a nuclear weapons stockpile. This program reportedly was detected by tracing North Korea imports of specialized materials and equipment, as well as other means.[18] It is believed that the bulk of the technology, if not the actual material for this program, was transferred to North Korea from Pakistan.[19] North Korea admitted to Kelly that it was pursuing this alternate nuclear program, which led to the unraveling of the Agreed Framework and the escalation of tensions in the region.

The exact location of any uranium-enrichment plant is unknown outside of North Korea, which hampers any discussion of military action by the United States to end North Korea's pursuit of nuclear weapons. In addition, the location of any extracted plutonium or actual nuclear weapons is also unknown, meaning that any military action by the United States and its allies would be unlikely to eliminate North Korea's nuclear arsenal. North Korea does have three nuclear reactors (one is operating, two are under construction) and an above-ground plutonium processing plant, which in a conflict would be vulnerable to targeting. Its loss would reduce near-term ability to produce large amounts of additional plutonium. Left unchecked, North Korea could produce up to 250 nuclear weapons by 2010.[20]

Another significant development regarding North Korea's nuclear program took place in 1998 when U.S. intelligence raised concerns that North Korea was constructing an underground nuclear facility at Mount Kumchangri. It was suspected that complex could house a nuclear facility that might begin operation in 2003, but the exact function of the facility was unknown. Intelligence reports indicated that the site could "be intended as a nuclear production and/or storage site."[21] The United States successfully pressured North Korea to accept bilateral inspections at the site, which revealed it to be an empty underground facility, but the event reinforced concerns that North Korea could use hidden facilities to advance its nuclear program. It is suspected that the uranium-enrichment plant thought to have been built by North Korea is underground. Indeed, the DPRK regime reportedly has the world's most extensive complex of deeply buried hardened facilities and protected tunnels drilled into the sides of hills and mountains to protect its missile and artillery forces dug in north of the demilitarized zone.

North Korea also possesses a robust ballistic missile capability and remains the foremost exporter of short-range ballistic missiles in the developing world. North Korea has successfully produced and exported Scud and extended-range Scud missiles with ranges from 300–1,000 kilometers and has tested a longer-range missile with a suspected top range of 2,000 kilometers.[22] North Korea possesses over 500 Scud and extended-range Scud missiles. The most significant missile-related event during the 1990s was the August 1998 test of the North Korean Taepo Dong 1 missile that overflew Japan and landed in the Pacific Ocean. Although the three-stage missile failed to place a small satellite in orbit, the launch demonstrated the ability of North Korea to build and test multiple stage missiles and signaled its intention to acquire missiles with ranges beyond East Asian targets. North Korea, however, remains under a self-imposed missile flight test moratorium which has hindered, although not crippled, its ability to advance its missile capabilities.

According to the U.S. Department of Defense,

> North Korea also moved forward with the development of other longer-range missiles, which has become a matter of growing international concern. North Korea is developing the Taepo Dong 2 (ICBM), which could potentially deliver a several-hundred kilogram payload to Alaska or Hawaii, and a lighter payload to the western half of the United States … but Pyongyang in September 1999, announced it would refrain from testing long-range missiles while high-level talks to improve bilateral relations with the U.S. are ongoing. The DPRK subsequently reaffirmed the moratorium in June 2000, and again, in writing, in the October 2000 Joint Communiqué issue[d] at the conclusion of Vice Marshal Jo Myong Rok's visit to Washington.[22]

North Korea retains the ability to build and test longer-range ballistic missiles.

North Korea's biological weapons program probably dates back to the 1960s. U.S. officials believe that North Korea could produce biological warfare agents including anthrax, cholera, and plague and possesses a basic ability to weaponize such agents. North Korea is not known to actually possess weaponized biological warfare agents, and the BW program is the least advanced of all of North Korea's weapons of mass destruction programs. It is believed that "North Korea likely has the capability to produce sufficient quantities of biological agents for military purposes within weeks of a decision to do so."[24]

North Korea possesses chemical weapons and a large amount of chemical precursors for the production of such weapons. It is believed by U.S. intelligence to have the ability to produce bulk quantities of nerve, blister, choking, and blood agents. North Korea maintains facilities involved in producing and storing chemical weapons, agents, and precursors. It has at least eight industrial facilities that can produce chemical agents, although the rate of production at the facilities is uncertain. Many of these facilities are believed to be underground. North Korea is believed to possess a stockpile of some 180–250 metric tons of chemical weapons and agents, with some estimates running as high as 5,000 metric tons.[25]

## Pakistan

Pakistan has conducted nuclear tests and possesses a number of nuclear weapons, perhaps 24 to 48.[26] In addition, it possesses the Ghauri Intermediate-Range ballistic missile system capable of reaching Madras, India. At present, their main delivery systems for nuclear weapons would likely be F-16 strike aircraft. (See Table 2.3.)

**Table 2.3** Pakistan's WMD Status (1993–2005)

|        | Nuclear | Chemical | Biological | Missiles |
|--------|---------|----------|------------|----------|
| 1993   | Yes     | ?        | ?          | Yes      |
| 1997   | Yes     | ?        | ?          | Yes      |
| 2005   | Yes     | ?        | ?          | Yes      |

Overall Trend: Possession of nuclear weapons since 1984; development and testing of IRBMs

Pakistan is one of the frontline states in the Global War on Terror and may have significant numbers of al-Qaeda and Taliban hidden inside its borders. There remains considerable animosity toward the United States within Pakistan and significant numbers of the Pakistani intelligence service are still sympathetic to al-Qaeda and Taliban purposes, despite the fact that Pakistan's President Musharraf has thrown his support to the United States.

The black market operations of Dr. A. Q. Khan, "the father of the Pakistani Atomic Bomb," led to the transfer of Pakistani centrifuges, centrifuge parts, warhead designs, and other nuclear expertise to North Korea, Iran, Libya, and perhaps to other potential nuclear weapons proliferators. The Pakistani government and army claim not to have approved such transactions, which made Khan and his associates rich men; how Khan could have transferred such items without at least tacit approval of some parts of the Pakistani government and/or army strains belief.

This country with a large Islamic population, a large part of it radicalized, is politically unstable and appears to have been the accelerator of other rogue state nuclear programs in the past 13 years. It appears that Pakistan traded nuclear secrets to Kim Jong Il's North Korea in return for missile technology help from Pyongyang. Pakistan also has received nuclear weapons and missile assistance from China.

## Syria

Syria reemerged as a focal point for U.S. nonproliferation concern in 2004. Allegations that Iraq may have shipped its weapons of mass destruction assets to Syria in order to evade capture and detection by U.S. forces after Operation Iraqi Freedom compounded statements by U.S. officials before the war regarding Syria's chemical, biological, and ballistic missile capabilities and its nuclear intentions (see Table 2.4). Despite these charges and U.S. Government official statements or inferences to the contrary, there is no compelling evidence that Iraq possessed

**Table 2.4**  Syria's WMD Status (1993–2005)

|  | Nuclear | Chemical | Biological | Missiles |
|---|---|---|---|---|
| **1993** | No | Yes | Limited | Yes |
| **1997** | No | Yes | Limited | Yes |
| **2005** | No | Yes | Limited | Yes |

Overall Trend: Slow development of CW capabilities, advancing missile acquisition, and possible BW advances

chemical or biological weapons at the start of the Iraq War or that any such weapons, if they did exist, were shipped to Syria or any other countries in the region.

Syria's own weapons of mass destruction programs have existed for several decades with sporadic progress reported in their chemical warfare capabilities and missile programs. Syria is a signatory to the NPT and the BTWC, but has refused to join the CWC, citing the threat from Israel's nuclear arsenal. Not being legally bound by prohibitions on its chemical capabilities, Syria reportedly has developed a moderately robust chemical warfare program, and despite its obligations under the BTWC is believed to continue to pursue a biological warfare capability. Syria has acquired an arsenal of short-range ballistic missiles from sources outside of the Middle East.

Syria's weapons capabilities appear to be designed for strategic defense. "Since the loss of its Soviet sponsor a decade ago and its inability to achieve conventional parity with Israel," the U.S. Department of Defense assessed, "Syria has increasingly relied on a strategic deterrent, based on ballistic missiles and chemical warfare capabilities as the ultimate guarantor of regime survival against potential regional adversaries."[27] But the assessment of the U.S. Government also considers Syria to be a rational actor in considering the use of its weapons of mass destruction assets. "Syria would likely refrain from using chemical or biological weapons against Israel … unless the regime's survival is at stake."[28]

Syria's President Bashar al-Asad has not demonstrated a strong interest in acquiring nuclear weapons, but there are concerns that Syria may also have purchased items and technology from the A. Q. Khan network. The Department of Defense reported in 2001 that Syria "is not pursuing the development of nuclear weapons," although subsequent reports have expressed concern over Syrian interest in acquiring nuclear technology from various sources.[29]

Syria possesses chemical weapons and is pursuing more advanced chemical warfare capabilities. The Department of Defense reported that

Syria possesses stockpiles of the nerve agent sarin and is trying to develop more toxic and persistent nerve agents, such as VX. However, these reports note that Syria remains dependent on foreign supplies of precursor chemicals and production equipment for such weapons.[30]

Syria remains interested in a biological warfare capability, but does not appear to have aggressively pursued this capability. According to unclassified U.S. estimates, "Syria's biotechnology infrastructure is capable of supporting limited agent development. However, the Syrians are not believed to have begun any major effort to put biological agents into weapons. Without significant foreign assistance, it is unlikely that Syria could manufacture significant amounts of biological weapons for several years."[31]

Syria also continues to be of concern to the United States because of its links to terrorist organizations. Syria has been cited in U.S. terrorism reports for providing support to a number of Palestinian groups that are directly linked to terror activities, including Hizballah, the Islamic Jihad, and Hamas.[32] Syria maintains that offices of these organizations in Damascus are related only to political and information activities, but the links between such terrorist groups and a country with a known weapons of mass destruction capability pose a disturbing challenge to U.S. and allied security.

## Iraq

Official U.S. intelligence assessments now conclude that Iraq did not maintain WMD or substantial missile programs after the early 1990s. U.S. and British intelligence estimates, as well as long-standing UN concerns about unaccounted for weapons of mass destruction capabilities in Iraq, have not been confirmed or validated two years after the end of Operation Iraqi Freedom. It now appears likely that Iraq eliminated all of its weapons of mass destruction in the early 1990s. (See Table 2.5.)

Iraq did continue a modest program of ballistic missile development and deployment beyond the limits permitted in the cease-fire agreements that ended the 1990–1991 Gulf War. Interviews with key former high

**Table 2.5**  Iraq's WMD Status (1993–2005)

|      | Nuclear | Chemical | Biological | Missiles |
|------|---------|----------|------------|----------|
| 1993 | No      | Yes?     | Yes?       | Yes      |
| 1997 | No      | No?      | No?        | Yes      |
| 2005 | No      | No?      | No?        | No?      |

Overall Trend: Regime change eliminates WMD in near term; no WMD found; future uncertain officials of Saddam Hussein's government indicate that he was very likely to have reconstituted his weapons of mass destruction programs had he succeeded in getting UN sanctions lifted and if OIF had not terminated his regime and quest for such weapons.

The history of Iraq's weapons of mass destruction programs in the 1990s is closely linked to the broader political and security dynamics of the decade. After the eviction of Iraqi forces from Kuwait, Iraq was required under the terms of the Gulf War cease-fire UN Resolution 687 to accept complete inspections, to eliminate its weapons of mass destruction programs, and was banned from possessing missiles with ranges over 150 kilometers.[33]

Throughout the decade, Iraq sought to evade inspections, retain prohibited items and programs, resist efforts to uncover past and ongoing activities, and in general weaken the political support for inspections within the UN Security Council and more broadly. This effort was intimately tied with Iraq's efforts to evade, weaken, and eventually eliminate the UN sanctions imposed as a result of the invasion of Kuwait and after the 1990–1991 Gulf War. Initial inspections uncovered massive weapons of mass destruction programs in all four areas (i.e., nuclear, biological, chemical, or missile programs) and made progress in eliminating prohibited items.

The loss of sustained political support for sanctions and inspections within the UN Security Council allowed Iraq to erode the effectiveness of these efforts. This led to the suspension of all inspections in 1998, precipitating Operation Desert Fox. Inspections resumed for a few months in 2002 and 2003 under the terms of UN Resolution 1441, but were ended with the start of Operation Iraqi Freedom on March 19, 2003.

In the wake of Operation Iraqi Freedom, Iraq does not have any significant nuclear facilities or nuclear weapons production capability. Before the 1990–1991 Gulf War, Iraq had been engaged in a wide-scale effort to produce a nuclear weapon. Post-Desert Storm UN inspections discovered that Iraq's nuclear program was more diverse and extensive than had been known even to U.S. intelligence before the war. Over the next several years, the IAEA, which had jurisdiction over nuclear inspections and disarmament in Iraq under the UN Security Council's mandate, is believed by many experts to have completely neutralized Iraq's nuclear program.

In the months prior to Operation Iraqi Freedom, there were serious and growing concerns about Iraq's weapons of mass destruction capabilities. Throughout the 1990s, Iraq was engaged in a cat-and-mouse game with UN inspectors over its weapons of mass destruction capabilities. From 1991 until inspections stopped in 1998, the UN Special Commission on Iraq (UNSCOM) was able to confirm that Iraq had possessed large stocks of chemical weapons, and they oversaw the destruction of large amounts of Iraqi chemical weapons and chemical weapon precursors. UNSCOM confirmed that before the start of the Gulf War, Iraq had produced enough precursor chemicals for the production of 500 metric tons of VX nerve gas. Hundreds of tons of tabun, sarin, and mustard gas were also produced by Iraq before the war.[34] UN inspectors destroyed more than 480,000 liters of chemical agents and 1.8 million liters of chemical precursors in Iraq.[35]

UN inspectors believed at the time that even after these efforts, Iraq may have retained enough chemical precursors to produce an additional 600 metric tons of chemical weapons although they lacked any direct evidence that such weapons or precursor chemical still existed after 12 years of inspections. U.S. intelligence reports were dire, stating in October 2002 that Iraq had "begun renewed production of chemical warfare agents."[36]

Iraq's biological weapons program was smaller in numbers of people involved, facilities, and investment than its chemical program, but was uncovered in 1995 as a result of UN inspections and Iraqi defections. After repeated denials that Iraq had possessed an offensive biological warfare program, Iraq admitted in 1995 that it had been developing biological warfare agents.

> Iraq declared … that it had produced approximately 30,000 liters of bulk biological agents and/or filled munitions. Iraq admitted that it produced anthrax, botulinum toxins, and aflotoxins and that it prepared biological agent filled munitions, including missile warheads and aerial bombs.[37]

These, however, according to Iraqi officials were destroyed shortly after the 1990–1991 Gulf War. The fact that the Saddam Hussein government in Iraq had continually engaged in years of repeated "cheat and retreat" tactics against the UN inspectors led to conclusions that this Iraqi leadership was dishonest and lying about its elimination of weapons of mass destruction programs. The constant lack of cooperation with UN inspectors, and ultimately Saddam Hussein's refusal to allow any further inspections, led to a continuation of UN oil embargo sanctions that cost Iraq in excess of $100 billion in oil revenue in the dozen years following the 1991 Gulf War.

The high price Saddam Hussein appeared willing to pay to avoid coming completely clean about his weapons of mass destruction programs led to the natural conclusion that he had something to hide.

Before inspections ended in 1998, Iraq refused to provide a full accounting of its activities related to biological warfare, and UN inspectors remained concerned that Iraq may have retained a stock of biological weapons and related manufacturing capability. The U.S. Intelligence Community report on Iraq released in October 2002 stated, "All key aspects—R&D, production and weaponization—of Iraq's offensive biological warfare program are active and most elements are larger and more advanced than they were before the Gulf War."[38]

The status of Iraq's missile programs also generated debate and concern during the 1990s. Iraq fired 88 extended-range Scud missiles at allied forces in Saudi Arabia and at Israel. Previously, Iraq had extensively used missiles in its war against Iran during the 1980s. After the Gulf War, Iraq declared to UN inspectors that it possessed 48 ballistic missiles with ranges in excess of the 150-kilometer limit laid down in UN Resolution 687. In March 1992, however, Iraq admitted that it had withheld 85 banned missiles from inspectors and had destroyed them without the observation or verification of UN inspectors. This, along with other evidence, gave rise to allegations that Iraq continued to maintain a small force of Scud missiles as late as 2002. "Gaps in Iraqi accounting to the UN Special Commission on Iraq suggest that Saddam retained a covert force of up to a few dozen Scud-variant short-range ballistic missiles with ranges of 650 to 900 km."[39]

Prior to the start of the war, it was feared that Operation Iraqi Freedom could witness the use of Iraqi chemical and biological weapons against U.S. and allied troops. No such weapons or evidence of active programs to produce those weapons has been discovered in Iraq. Iraq appears to have destroyed all of its operational chemical and biological weapons well before the start of the war for a combination of reasons, the exact nature of which remain unclear.

According to former Iraqi officials under Saddam Hussein, one reason the dictator wished to leave the impression he still retained weapons of mass destruction, even after his regime had disposed of them, was to deter attacks by Iran, Israel, and the United States. He felt weakness would encourage his opponents, both domestic and foreign, to use force against his regime. Saddam Hussein was also deemed likely to have restarted the Iraqi programs once sanctions had been lifted.[40]

It appears that the combination of sanctions, inspections, and the threat of military action were effective in containing the potential and stated interest by Iraq to develop and field such weapons. This may justify an additional investment of resources by the United States into exploring more effective and focused diplomatic activity to pressure would-be proliferators.

In addition, it may illustrate the real and powerful deterrent effect of the U.S. military in the minds of at least some national leaders of adversary states. The threat that any conclusive evidence that Iraq possessed and was prepared to use such weapons would trigger U.S. military action—and the hope that the lack of such evidence would forestall such action—may have been a more powerful motivation in the mind of Saddam Hussein than anyone knew. It may be difficult, if not impossible, to directly apply the experience to other countries, but it suggests that much less is known about the calculations that take place in the minds of a country's leadership than may have been previously thought.

## Libya

Libya is a member of the NPT, the BTWC, and the CWC, having joined the last in the first few months of 2004. Libya decided in December 2003 after several years of negotiations with the United States and Great Britain to abandon all of its weapons of mass destruction and ballistic missile programs. This stark decision is a major positive development in international efforts to reduce the threat of weapons of mass destruction and is being implemented with the active support of the United States and the international community. While no explicit promise of rewards was made to Libya for the decision, the United States and other countries are moving quickly to lift economic and trade sanctions against Tripoli. Libya possessed chemical weapons and ballistic missiles and is one of the few countries to have used chemical weapons in warfare since the First World War when it used mustard gas against Chad in 1987. Libya was also a customer of the A. Q. Khan nuclear black market centered in Pakistan and acquired many of the raw materials and equipment needed to produce enriched uranium for nuclear weapons. Libya lacks the advanced industrial infrastructure to support the wide-scale development of weapons of mass destruction on its own and had to rely on outside sources for much of its program. (See Table 2.6.)

Colonel Muammar Qaddafi's motives for abandoning his weapons of mass destruction capabilities appear to center on his desire to rejoin the international community and to expand oil exports and production capabilities through access to Western technology. The sudden move reinforces the unpredictable nature of the Libyan regime, and the commitment to abandon weapons of mass destruction programs will have to be carefully verified.

Can a leopard change its spots? That is the kind of question analysts are now asking about Muammar Qaddafi of Libya. For many years Qaddafi was the poster boy of international terrorism and weapons of mass destruction proliferation. He extended sanctuary, financial aid, training, weapons, and encouragement to numerous international terrorist

**Table 2.6** Libya's WMD Status (1993–2005)

|  | Nuclear | Chemical | Biological | Missiles |
|---|---|---|---|---|
| 1993 | No | Yes | No | Yes |
| 1997 | No | Yes | No | Yes |
| 2005 | No | Yes, but | No | Yes, but |

Overall Trend: Has begun program to give up its WMD and adhere to CWC and NPT with transparency organizations from the Irish Republican Army to the Abu Nidal Organization. In addition, Qaddafi's regime attempted to buy a nuclear weapon from China in 1970 and later on the black market, gave financial support and yellowcake uranium to aid the Pakistani atomic bomb project, and produced many tons of chemical weapons, some of which it used against a neighboring state, Chad. At one time or another under his radical leadership, Libya has been at war with each of its neighbors, and Qaddafi has been implicated in numerous assassination plots against domestic and foreign adversaries.

The greatest revelations from Libya centered on its nuclear program. Libya's decision to purchase centrifuges and other enrichment technology from A. Q. Khan's network appears to date back into the 1990s. Yet, there appear to be major questions about Libya's potential to pursue the production of nuclear weapons even with the technology and equipment it acquired. Nevertheless, even with the significant help from Khan, Libya was years away from producing enough enriched uranium to produce a nuclear weapon when the decision to abandon the program was made.

Given all this negative history, it is little short of amazing that Qaddafi's Libya now appears to be coming out against terrorism and has renounced its own weapons of mass destruction programs. As part of a December 2003 agreement worked out between Libya and the governments of the United States and the United Kingdom, Tripoli agreed to terminate any support to terrorist organizations. In addition, Libya has agreed to cooperate in the dismantlement of its nuclear, chemical, and most of its missile programs.

On March 5, 2004, Libya declared that it possessed 23 metric tons of mustard gas, 1,300 metric tons of precursor chemicals, and two chemical weapons storage sites at Rabta and Tarhuna, facts later verified by inspectors of the Organisation for Prohibition of Chemical Weapons (OPCW).[41]

Further, the OPCW "verified the complete destruction of more than 3,500 unfilled bombs" designed to carry such chemical warfare agents.[42] This UN organization has also reached agreement to verify the destruction of Libya's remaining chemical warfare stockpile.[43] Unaccounted for, as yet, is any declaration by Libya of holdings of nerve agents like sarin or VX which they are suspected to have produced.

As of this writing, "the United States has removed all of Libya's longest-range missiles and most elements of its nuclear weapons program."[44] Libya has also promised to accede to the CWC and has agreed to an additional protocol to its IAEA safeguards agreement giving that UN agency additional inspection authority to verify its compliance with the NPT.[45]

As a result of its agreements, Libya has allowed 13 kilograms of 80 percent highly enriched uranium (HEU) fuel to be returned to Russia to be blended down for commercial use. Such HEU might otherwise have been further enriched to make nuclear weapons had it not been removed.[46] Moreover, in January 2004, Libya cooperated in letting the United States remove its "centrifuge components, uranium hexafluoride, ballistic missile guidance systems, and other nuclear designs … ."[47]

In addition to its chemical capabilities, Libya also possesses a small arsenal of short-range ballistic missiles. In fact, Libya is one of the few countries to have used such systems in combat, having launched Scud missiles at a military base on the Italian island of Lampedusa "in response to the U.S. air attack against terrorist and military infrastructure."[48] Libya is believed to possess just over 200 aging Soviet era Scud-B missiles, but until recently it continued to express interest in acquiring longer-range systems from North Korea, including the 1,000-kilometer range No Dong missile from North Korea.

According to the agreements with Libya, the United States has already, in 2004, removed all of Libya's longest-range missiles. The United States and the United Kingdom have also agreed "in principle" to permit Qaddafi's regime to keep a number of medium-range Scud-B missiles if it conforms to the agreed range and payload limitations. The United States and the United Kingdom have insisted that any remaining missiles conform to the guidelines set by the Missile Technology Control Regime limiting them to no more than a 500-kilogram payload with no more than a 300-kilometer range.[49]

In recent years Libya has also agreed to pay reparations to the families of victims of two airliners downed by Libyan directed terrorist actions. These negotiations over payments are largely completed, but not completely resolved. During the Clinton administration, Libya began sounding out whether a deal could be arrived at with the United States to end its economic and political sanctions in return for dismantling its chemical stockpile. The United States rejected any such deal so long as Libya refused to admit its complicity in those terrorist events and pay appropriate damages. The George W. Bush administration began these nonproliferation negotiations with Libya in early 2003 once it was clear that a settlement was near over the two airliner downings.

It is likely that a mixture of carrots and sticks brought Libya to its current counterterrorism and counterproliferation position. Libya has been diplomatically isolated for two decades and economic sanctions have greatly hindered its trade and economic growth. Air travel to Libya was cut off by many countries and Qaddafi has been unsuccessful in achieving much traction as a leader of the Arab world, one of his lifelong goals.

His support of terrorist activities almost got Qaddafi killed when President Ronald Reagan ordered Operation Eldorado Canyon in 1986 in retaliation. Indeed, it is reported that the retaliatory raid narrowly missed the

Colonel and killed his daughter. After this traumatic event, Qaddafi's visible support for terrorists was seen to decline markedly.

According to Qaddafi's son, Saif Al-Islam Qaddafi, the motivations for Libya's new decisions were made for "political, economic, cultural, and military gains" and because it was "on a dangerous path … with the Western countries."[50] He also suggested that such weapons were no longer needed for Israel since the Israeli-Palestinian peace process had made such preparations unnecessary.[51]

It is likely that Qaddafi was spurred by the U.S. actions in Afghanistan (2002) and Iraq (2003) and the willingness of the United States to forcibly remove such radical regimes that sponsored terrorism and that embraced weapons of mass destruction programs. Furthermore, the U.S. discovery that Libya, along with North Korea and Iran, had been secretly paying Abdul Qadeer Khan's network to supply nuclear weapons equipment and designs may have convinced Qaddafi that Libya might become the next target of a U.S. intervention if it did not take further cooperative steps to roll back its weapons of mass destruction programs and open itself to inspections.

In return, Libya is asking for a removal of sanctions and normalization of relations, a step-by-step process that has begun but will not be complete until Libya lives up to its promises in a verifiable manner.

## Egypt

Egypt is a close ally of the United States in the Middle East and is one of two neighboring states that have signed a peace agreement with Israel. Egypt is a member of the NPT, but has not signed the CWC or ratified the BTWC citing Israel's refusal to sign the NPT. Despite its relationship with the United States, Egypt continues to pursue both chemical and biological weapon capabilities and possesses a small but significant arsenal of short-range ballistic missiles. Moreover, Cairo's long-term interest in nuclear weapons is a growing question, especially in light of Iran's ongoing program (see Table 2.7). Its motives for possessing such weapons

**Table 2.7**  Egypt's WMD Status (1993–2005)

|        | Nuclear | Chemical | Biological | Missiles |
|--------|---------|----------|------------|----------|
| **1993** | No | Yes | Yes | Yes |
| **1997** | No | Yes | Yes | Yes |
| **2005** | No | Yes | Yes | Yes |
| Overall Trend: Static, little major development of WMD capabilities | | | | |

have changed somewhat over the life of its programs, but were begun and continue to be primarily directed to counterbalance Israel's nuclear weapons capabilities. Although the likelihood of hostilities between the two states is low, political and institutional pressures in Egypt have worked to maintain the capability to build and employ WMD in the event there is a regional conflict.

By the time the DoD Counterproliferation Initiative was launched, Egypt was known to possess weapons of mass destruction programs, including a capability to produce chemical weapons and biological agents. In fact, Egypt is one of the few countries since the First World War to use chemical weapons in combat, having used both mustard and phosgene gas in Yemen during the civil war in the 1960s.[52] There were also substantial allegations that Egypt used G-series nerve agents during the war. Egypt is widely believed by analysts to have also developed VX nerve gas in the following several decades.[53] Although Egypt has used and is thought to possess chemical agents, the most detailed intelligence reports suggest that Egypt's "stockpiles of chemical agents available at this time are insufficient for broad-based operations, but the industrial potential would make it possible to produce additional quantities in a relatively short time."[54] Some sources indicate that Egypt supplied Syria with chemical weapons in the early 1970s and supplied Iraq with chemical warfare agents and technology during the Iran-Iraq War in the 1980s.[55]

Cairo also continues to develop its biological weapons capabilities. In 1993 testimony before the Senate Governmental Affairs Committee, CIA Director James Woolsey confirmed Egypt possessed a biological weapons program.[56] There is very little open source reporting, however, that provides details into the character and location of Egypt's BW related research or the extent of its capabilities. Foreign intelligence sources maintain that Egypt possesses a military biological warfare research program but stated, "no data has been obtained to indicate the creation of biological agents in support of military offensive programs."[57] Egypt signed the BTWC in 1972, but has not yet ratified the treaty.

Egypt's missile capabilities are well documented, with the country having received a regiment of Scud missiles from the Soviet Union during their Cold War military alliance. It is widely reported that some of these missiles were transferred to North Korea and that those systems provided Pyongyang with the capability to reverse engineer and become the largest exporter of such systems in the developing world. Altogether, Egypt is credited with possessing over 100 Scud-Bs with a 300-kilometer range and 985-kilogram payload. They possess approximately 90 project T missiles with a 450-kilometer range and 1000-kilogram payload, and an unknown number of Scud-C missiles, with a range of 500 kilometers and a payload capacity of 600 kilograms. Egypt also has deployed a number of cruise missiles including the AS-5 Kelt, the Harpoon, the AS-1 Kennel, HY-2 Silkworm, the Otomat Mk1, the FL-1, the Exocet, and SS-N-2a Styx. It also possesses nine different variants of fighter aircraft capable of WMD delivery.[58]

## Conclusions

The past decade has witnessed the continuation of weapons of mass destruction programs in a well-defined set of countries, mainly in the Middle East, but not the widespread proliferation of weapons of mass destruction capabilities predicted by some. The proliferation schedule of at least three states, Libya, North Korea, and Iran, were advanced by the sales of nuclear technology, designs, and expertise by the A. Q. Khan clandestine network of suppliers. Of these, only Libya has reversed field after several decades of pursuing weapons of mass destruction capability. Existing programs, for the most part, are motivated by issues unrelated to the United States or its security interests, and therefore they have not been overwhelmingly impacted by U.S. policies related to slowing the spread of weapons of mass destruction. The major exception to this is Iraq, where U.S. military action was taken repeatedly since 1991 in actions such as Operation Desert Storm, Operation Northern Watch, Operation Southern Watch, Operation Desert Fox, and Operation Iraqi Freedom to reduce Saddam Hussein's pursuit of weapons of mass destruction, and Libya, although the exact reasons for Tripoli's decisions remain shrouded. In addition, U.S. forces were responsible for removing the Taliban protection of al-Qaeda and heading off efforts by al-Qaeda in Afghanistan to develop and acquire chemical and biological weapons and radiological dispersal devices, but terrorists continue to pursue WMD capabilities.

U.S. counterforce targeting improvements have had an effect in some of the ways in which countries have chosen to proliferate, for example, by persuading adversaries to hide their facilities underground. Reportedly,

> more than 70 countries now use underground facilities (UGFs) for military purposes. In June 1998, the Defense Science Board Task Force on Underground Facilities reported that there are over 10,000 UGFs worldwide. Approximately 1,100 UGFs were known or suspected strategic (weapons of mass destruction, ballistic missile basing, leadership or top echelon command and control) sites. Updated estimates [from the Defense Intelligence Agency (DIA)] reveal this number has now grown to over 1,400. A majority of the strategic facilities are deep underground facilities.[59]

As a result, the United States has initiated research on new conventional and nuclear counterforce weapons to hold these targets at risk. States that are pursuing weapons of mass destruction have observed the lessons of the first Gulf War and the Israeli strike against the Osirak reactor in Iraq in 1981, and they are seeking ways to hide and protect their WMD-related facilities from detection and attack.

U.S. interest in targeting such facilities in foreign countries has not dissuaded all of them from going after weapons of mass destruction. In fact, it appears that U.S. declaratory policies designed to deter the acquisition of weapons of mass destruction by determined adversaries has not had an appreciable effect. At most, U.S. counterforce preemptive threats, whether verbal or just inferred by U.S. improvements in accuracy, may have delayed the North Korean nuclear weapons program by temporarily closing down its nuclear complex and delaying its acquisition of a larger nuclear arsenal. If anything, it appears that U.S. statements reserving the right to take action—including the use of nuclear weapons if necessary —to deter, prevent, and respond to the acquisition and use of weapons of mass destruction may, in some cases, be helping to drive proliferation. This is most likely the case in North Korea and Iran. Surprisingly, U.S. threats may have had the exact opposite effect in Iraq, where that leadership may have eliminated its deployable weapons of mass destruction assets to avoid detection or attack from the United States, while retaining an ability to resume production once UN sanctions were lifted.

Where U.S. and international efforts have been successful in preventing proliferation is in the cooperative arena. The removal of nuclear weapons from Belarus, Kazakhstan, and Ukraine in the 1990s and the elimination of South Africa's arsenal of six nuclear weapons were the result of cooperative policies and the ability of the international nuclear nonproliferation regime to positively affect the security of states that were for a time straddling the nuclear fence. The motives for nuclear possession in these four states were met in other ways, directly tied to security assurances, financial assistance, and the lure of readmission to the international community. If Libyan declarations regarding dismantling of its weapons of mass destruction program are carried to completion, it will be another case of successful rollback.

The United States needs all the tools in its tool kit to thin out the proliferation threats that could and do exist. Nonproliferation treaties, treaty verification mechanisms, export controls, the Proliferation Security Initiative, and strong carrot and stick incentives in U.S. diplomacy are all potent nonproliferation tools that are needed to reduce the number of states that attempt to acquire weapons of mass destruction. Without such active nonproliferation measures, the job of the U.S. military will be much more difficult, perhaps impossible, as the number of rivals armed with weapons of mass destruction expands.

On the other hand, a strong nonproliferation regime, coupled with an equally staunch counterproliferation capability, may make the problem manageable, and still within the power of the United States and its allies to contain. In the end, a broad array of tools will be needed to reduce the risk posed to U.S. interests and military personnel from the spread of nuclear, chemical, and biological weapons and the delivery vehicles that could carry them. Integration of effective nonproliferation and counterproliferation programs and policies will not only be beneficial to this process, it is essential.

In summary, these 13 years have provided a number of mixed messages and lessons for those interested in preventing and responding to proliferation. This review suggests the need to apply greater resources into understanding why countries seek weapons of mass destruction and a broader, more integrated effort to bring all possible nonproliferation tools to bear on a problem before the counterproliferation tools of the U.S. military become the only practicable solution.

# CHAPTER 3

# Weapons of Mass Destruction Terrorism[1]

*Jerrold M. Post, Laurita M. Denny,*
*and Polina Kozak*

There is a heightened concern in the United States over the specter of cata-strophic chemical, biological, radiological, and nuclear (CBRN) terrorist attacks. Billions are being invested in training first responders for what is acknowledged to be a high-consequence/low-probability event. But while substantial investment is being devoted to protecting our vulner-able society from such a devastating act, there is very little attention being devoted to who might do it and why and, as important, who might not do it and why not. After a historical review, this chapter analyzes the spec-trum of terrorism and the spectrum of CBRN terrorist acts, identifying those groups motivated to use this class of weapons and the types of acts which they would be likely to carry out.

## Historical Context

Terrorism is not a modern phenomenon. It has been with humanity for centuries. Accounts of political assassination can be found in ancient documents including the Bible. The history of the Roman Empire, Byzan-tium, and Europe is rich in plots to murder rulers with poisons, daggers, and pistols. The first organized terrorist groups devoted to systematic ter-rorism and acting across borders were fueled by religious convictions. The Jewish terrorist group the Zealots, also known as the Sicarii after the sacred daggers they employed, was committed to the expulsion of Romans from the Holy Land in the first century. Armed with daggers, the Zealots started out by murdering individual victims, eventually stirring an unsuccessful uprising, which led to the Jewish exile from Palestine.[2] In the eleventh century, a Shiite religious extremist group called the Order of the Assassins committed to the purification of Islam appeared in the Middle East. For two centuries, the Assassins planned and executed attacks on prominent political and religious figures who did not share their religious conviction. Although their actions did not have a significant impact on the religious thought of the Muslims, the Assassins are credited with originating the suicide mission concept: the guaranteed passage to heaven as a reward for the assailant's death on the mission.[3] In India, the worshipers of the goddess Kali, called Thugs, terrorized travelers for 600 years. The motive for the Thugs' murders—apart from robbery—was to bring a sacred offering to their deity.

Just as terrorism is as old as organized society, exotic weaponry is by no means a modern phenomenon. Exotic weaponry has been utilized for centuries not only to exterminate the enemy but also to win wars by evoking fear. According to Jessica Stern, "The Peloponnesians left Attica not because they feared the Athenians, who were shut up in their cities, but because they feared the Plague of Athens, described by Thucydides in the second book of the *Peloponnesian Wars*."[4] In the fourteenth century, the Tatars besieged the Genoese fortress on the coast of Crimea and catapulted plague-infested cadavers over its walls. The disease, which was attributed to divine vengeance, was brought to Europe on board Genoese ships. In the eighteenth century, the British used biological weapons against the Indians in Pennsylvania. They distributed blankets from the smallpox hospitals to the Native American population as a way of dealing with the disaffected tribes.

Given the relative ease with which crude biological and chemical weapons can be produced, it is striking how infrequent the use of such weapons by terrorists has been in modern times. In 1995, the world witnessed a chemical terrorist attack in the Tokyo subway system carried out by the Aum Shinrikyo religious cult. Prior to the use of anthrax in 2001, there had been only one moderately large-scale successful act of biological terrorism. The followers of the Rajneeshee cult used Salmonella bacteria in 1984 against the local population of The Dalles, Oregon, in an attempt to win a local election. By contaminating salad bars, the Rajneeshees hoped to render ill enough voters so as to win the election and eliminate the threat to their *Bagwhan*—bioterrorism as a political "dirty trick."

Past biological and chemical weapons attacks have, for the most part, been on a small, tactical scale, not the catastrophic "superterrorism" of which experts have dolefully warned. While much has been said about the vulnerability of society to catastrophic terrorism, little regard has been given to assessing the motivations, incentives, and constraints for terrorist groups to commit such attacks. In fact, there is a major disconnect between the weapons technology community and the community of academic terrorism experts, with the former being focused on vulnerabilities of our society and what might happen in terms of technological possibilities, and the latter, who study terrorist motivation and decision making, being underwhelmed by the probability of such an event *for most, but not all*, terrorist groups.

It is useful to consider the term "weapons of mass destruction" terrorism. Usually referring to chemical, biological, radiological, or nuclear weapons, it is a semantically confusing term. Conventional weapons, such as the fertilizer bomb that Timothy McVeigh used at the Alfred P. Murrah Federal Building in Oklahoma City at a morning hour in order "to obtain maximal body count," the bombs that destroyed the U.S. embassies in Nairobi, Kenya, and Dar es Salaam, Tanzania, in 1998, and the hijacked planes that flew into the World Trade Center and the Pentagon, can produce mass destruction. Moreover, the so-called weapons of mass destruction, especially biological and chemical weapons, can be employed with exquisite discrimination to produce low-level casualties, to the point of being employed for the assassination of lone individuals. In this chapter, we use the term weapons of mass destruction (WMD) terrorism to mean terrorist attacks with CBRN weapons.

## Changed Threat Since the Collapse of the Soviet Union

Perceptions of the source and risks of WMD terrorism have changed greatly over the past decade. Prior to the 1990s, the major concern for the source of CBRN terrorism was with state actors supporting terrorism, but that began to change in the early 1990s. The growth of religious extremists, especially radical Islamist fundamentalist groups and violent millennial cults, led to mounting concerns that terrorist organizations would independently pursue CBRN weaponry.

The threat was not altogether new. During the Cold War, both superpowers fielded chemical, biological, and nuclear weapons in arsenals of awesome size. Earlier, the use of chemical weapons in the First World War and the use of nuclear weapons in the Second World War revealed their full and devastating potential. Despite the seriousness of state-supported political terrorism during the Cold War, the superpower rivalry, which provided a certain degree of stability and constraint, helped control the proliferation of weapons of mass destruction. The superpowers developed chemical, biological, and nuclear capabilities to target and/or deter each other, while restricting the development of similar programs in satellite states because of concern as to the dangerous consequences if these weapons were to proliferate. Technological advances and the buildup of weapons of mass destruction on both sides of the Iron Curtain served as a deterrent against conflict between the United States and the Soviet Union, both of which shared a concern that these weapons not proliferate. Despite tough nonproliferation practices by the superpowers, however, some states did manage to acquire or develop WMD during the Cold War. But WMD remained under the control of states, not terrorists.

The collapse of the Soviet Union in the late 1980s, marked by the fall of the Berlin Wall in 1989, did not bring the expected sense of security. With the end of the relatively stable superpower rivalry, multiple regional powers and nonstate actors replaced the Cold War concept of a single ideological enemy. States that had depended heavily on U.S. financial support witnessed deteriorating economies and a plunge in living standards as the United States began cutting foreign aid. The United States' political and economic role as the global leader became the basis for animosity from friends and emerging nonstate actors. Anti-American sentiments became a rallying point for disenfranchised populations throughout the world.

The disintegration of the Soviet Union created new security concerns beyond the global balance of power. When the Russian state suddenly cut funds traditionally allocated to military, industrial, and research facilities, thousands of scientists, technicians, and military personnel formerly employed in this sector lost their livelihoods, creating a dangerous situation. Some unemployed scientists were ready to sell their knowledge of weapons of mass destruction to the highest bidder. Some demoralized military personnel as well as underpaid workers with access to strategic storage facilities engaged in theft of nuclear material with intent to sell it abroad. Organized crime and corruption within the Russian government created an environment in which weapons of mass destruction could be exported to rogue states. Poor maintenance and general apathy within the army added to the concern over "loose nukes." To highlight this problem, Jessica Stern in her book *The Ultimate Terrorists* quoted General Lebed's claim that out of 132 "suitcase bombs," he was able to locate only 48.[5]

In addition to many of the other factors above, the final move from conventional to unconventional terrorism is determined by the character of the group itself. A group's ideology is central in determining the presence or lack of constraints on the use of CBRN weapons. Osama Bin Laden issued a fatwa in 1998, "Jihad against Jews and Crusaders," that called on Muslims to fulfill their duty to God, asserting that "to kill the Americans and their allies—civilians and military—is an individual duty for every Muslim who can do it in any country in which it is possible to do it."

This ruling removed constraints on the number of casualties and made it legitimate to kill civilians. It invoked religious doctrine not only as a justification for killing American civilians, but also made it an imperative to act. The motive behind the Aum Shinrikyo sarin gas attack was an apocalyptic vision of an imminent end of the world, the survival of the chosen few, and the desire to force the end by use of chemical and biological weapons.

Although the United States had been the target of international terrorism prior to the 1990s, all involved attacks on U.S. property and individuals abroad. The United States' perceived immunity to international terrorism on its own territory created a sense of invulnerability and complacency about counterterrorism policy at home. America, operating behind its two ocean barriers, had enjoyed a zone of peace unknown to much of the rest of the world. The uneventful history of little domestic terrorism was mistakenly interpreted as an indicator that counterterrorism measures in place were effective in deterring terrorists and did not require revision.

Several important events of the 1990s have contributed considerably to the changed perception of the CBRN terrorist threat to the United States. This decade showed a shift in the terrorist motivations, the types of groups and their composition, and the evolutionary progression of violence.

In the beginning of the modern era of terrorism, usually dated to the late 1960s, early 1970s, dramatically exemplified by the Palestinian terrorist takeover of the Israeli Olympic Village at the 1972 Munich Olympics, two types of terrorist groups predominated: social revolutionary terrorist groups, such as the Red Brigades of Italy and the Red Army Faction of Germany, steeped in Marxist-Leninist ideology, and the nationalist-separatist terrorists, who sought a separate nation for their minority group, exemplified by radical Palestinian secular terrorists, including Fatah, the Popular Front for the Liberation of Palestine (PFLP), and the Abu Nidal Organization; the Provisional Irish Republican Army of Northern Ireland (PIRA); and the Basque insurgent terrorist group ETA (Basque Fatherland and Liberty). Both types of terrorist organizations sought to influence the West and regularly claimed responsibility for their acts, often with multiple claims of responsibility for the same act. They were seeking to call attention to the West to their group's cause. In his examination of the link between terrorist motives and methods, Brian Jenkins observed that the goal of the terrorists was not the number of bodies but the size of the audience. He observed further that the *capacity* of terrorist groups to kill has always been greater than the *actual number* of deaths they have caused, a discrepancy reflecting self-imposed restraint, for too much violence would be counterproductive for the cause.

And then, from the late 1980s to the early 1990s, a new trend developed, so that in upward of 40 percent of terrorist acts committed, no one claimed responsibility for them. These were the acts of radical Islamist fundamentalist terrorists who did not seek to influence the West, but instead sought to expel completely the corrupt, secular, modernizing West. They did not require a *New York Times* headline or CNN story to call attention to their authorship of the act. They were "killing in the name of God," and God already knew.

The bomb that exploded in the underground parking garage of the World Trade Center in 1993 killed six and injured over 1,000 people— tragically signaling the first instance of international terrorism in the United States. Had the bomb been bigger and placed slightly differently, it might have brought down both towers and resulted in tens of thousands of deaths. The goal was assuredly mass destruction. Law enforcement also intercepted plans by the same organization to simultaneously bomb the UN complex, the Lincoln and Holland tunnels, and a bridge linking New Jersey to Manhattan. They reportedly also planned to attack the Federal Bureau of Investigation's New York headquarters and various U.S. military installations, political and judicial offices, and foreign heads of state.[6]

The World Trade Center, a public symbol of the economic might of the United States, was clearly a civilian target and was chosen to terrorize the American public. The radical Islamist perpetrators, enraged by U.S. foreign policy in the Middle East, namely, the support for Israel and moderate Arab regimes, sought to inflict massive casualties. This attack awakened the United States to the domestic danger of international terrorism. It also brought home the willingness, indeed motivation, of terrorists to inflict mass casualties.[7] The serious implications of the 1993 attack were not fully realized at the time. Domestic counterterrorism measures were almost entirely limited to investigating the incident as an act of conventional terrorism, prosecuting its perpetrators, and putting in place tighter security measures in New York.

## New CBRN Terrorism

The awakening to the dangers of mass casualty nonconventional (CBRN) terrorism occurred in 1995 when Aum Shinrikyo staged a sarin gas attack in the Tokyo subway. Eleven packages with sarin were placed on five trains, and the contents were haphazardly released by Aum members during rush hour. The toxic gas that formed killed 12 and sent 5,500 people to the hospital.[8] As was the case with the 1993 World Trade Center bombing, the attack was less lethal than intended. Had it not been for a mistake in the preparation of the sarin nerve agent and the inferior dissemination system, chemical weapons experts estimate that tens of thousands could have been killed.[9]

The Aum Shinrikyo attack shattered the belief that a nonstate actor could not acquire the sophisticated technological base for production of CBRN weapons. According to then-Director of Central Intelligence, John

Deutch, Aum had attempted to mine uranium in Australia and to purchase a full nuclear warhead from Russia.[10] The investigation of Aum's activities unveiled chemical and biological research, development, and production on an unprecedented scale for a nonstate actor. Even more alarming was the fact that Aum pursued the development of CBRN weapons without attracting the attention of the Japanese government or foreign intelligence agencies. Aum managed to acquire the necessary technology and specialists through recruitment of scientific professionals in various fields from Japan and Russia—nuclear physicists and engineers, organic and inorganic chemists, and microbiologists and virologists. They were simultaneously pursuing the development of all three types of weapons of mass destruction. The crude method of delivery of the poisonous gas in Tokyo's metro system demonstrated that terrorists do not need sophisticated technology to disperse toxic agents. Today, "WMD devices can be transported on small trucks, in cargo containers, or even in a lunch box,"[11] although effective dissemination of toxic agents remains a significant challenge.

The 1995 Tokyo sarin attack provoked a debate among security professionals over the degree of threat from biological or chemical weapons attacks by terrorists and how best to prepare for such attacks. The investigation into Aum's activities, and its previous attempts to disperse toxic agents, also highlighted the technological difficulties associated with weaponization of a chemical or biological agent that terrorists would most likely encounter. It was clear that with the necessary financial and technical resources, a determined group could overcome the obstacles and stage a chemical or biological attack.

That same year, Chechen leader Shamil Basayev demonstrated that the *threat* of terrorists obtaining nuclear materials was real. Chechen separatists planted a case with radioactive material in a Moscow park to substantiate the claim that they had the necessary materials to stage a nuclear attack within Russia if the government did not withdraw troops from Chechnya. A television station crew, informed by the Chechen leader, discovered 32 kilograms of cesium-137 in the park.[12] This was the first instance where radiological material actually was found in the possession of a terrorist group. Notably, it was *not* intended to inflict casualties, but rather to create fear among the population and demonstrate the group's credibility. In addition to the concern over terrorist groups obtaining nuclear materials, the incident also highlighted concern over the lack of security at Russian nuclear facilities.

In 1995, the largest incident of domestic terrorism, as of that date, took place in the United States. A truck bomb exploded in Oklahoma at the Alfred P. Murrah Federal Building, killing 168 people and injuring over 500. Perpetrated by Timothy McVeigh and his accomplice, Terry Nichols, the attack demonstrated the threat of just an individual or two, a prime example of the threat posed by the right-wing community of extremist belief in the United States. The assumption that mass casualty terrorism requires an extensive knowledge and organizational base was clearly not valid. Indeed, McVeigh indicated that the timing of the attack was in order "to obtain maximal body count." Inspired by Christian white supremacist ideology (in particular, "the bible" of the right wing, *The Turner Diaries*, in which a neo-Nazi group uses a fertilizer bomb to destroy the FBI headquarters in Washington), and having limited resources, Timothy McVeigh easily obtained the necessary instructions and materials to create a fertilizer bomb. The case shed light on the vulnerability of modern society to terrorist acts by individuals who find moral support through the Internet. The case also provides an insight into the psychology of unstable individuals like McVeigh, who may find particular comfort in a group identity that provides justification for and inspires extreme actions, including potentially the use of CBRN. "Christian Patriots are especially troubling because they are often organized to evade detection by authorities," wrote Jessica Stern, referring to the concept of the "leaderless resistance," in which individuals act alone or in very small cells to avoid being infiltrated. "They are interested in WMD, and they have demonstrated an ability to acquire chemical and biological agents."[13]

## Al-Qaeda and the September 11, 2001, Attacks

September 11, 2001, marked the most lethal terrorist attack in history, resulting in the loss of over 3,000 lives when al-Qaeda members hijacked four airliners and flew two of them into the World Trade Center, the iconic symbol of U.S. economic might, and another into the Pentagon, the symbol of U.S. military might, while the fourth airliner, believed to have been targeted at either the White House or the U.S. Capitol Building, symbols of U.S. political authority, crashed en route into a field in Pennsylvania. While this reflected an unprecedented scope and level of coordination, these were conventional attacks that caused mass destruction.

Al-Qaeda, the terrorist network responsible for the attacks, had cast aside any constraint regarding mass casualties and raised the level of deadliness of terrorism to an unprecedented level. But it did not involve CBRN weapons. With a religious justification of terrorism as "any Muslim's duty" and the desire to inflict mass casualties "in the name of Allah," there is little doubt that they would be willing to use the most potent CBRN weapons. There have been reports of al-Qaeda members seeking to purchase nuclear materials and having meetings with at least two retired Pakistani nuclear scientists. Moreover, in several of his interviews, Bin Laden has spoken of the need to use whatever weapons are at their disposal to counter the superior military strength of the West.

The demographic portrait of the September 11, 2001, suicidal hijackers significantly differed from the typical profile of the religiously motivated suicide bombers in Israel. There, Palestinian suicide bombers were younger (17 to 22 years in age), uneducated, unmarried, and unemployed. Unformed youth, they were persuaded by the suicide bomb commanders that their prospects in life were bleak, that by carrying out a martyrdom operation they could do something significant with their lives, that they would be enrolled in the hall of martyrs, and that their families would be proud of them and would gain prestige and financial awards. They were recruited at the last moment and kept under supervision until the attack to prevent them from backtracking.

The attackers of September 11, 2001, in contrast, were older (28 to 33 years in age). Several had higher education—the alleged ringleader Mohamed Atta and two of his colleagues were in graduate training in the technological university in Hamburg—and they came primarily from affluent Saudi and Egyptian families. They traveled extensively around the world and lived in Western society for extended periods of time, upward of seven years. While blending in with Western society, they carried within them their mission to take thousands of casualties while giving their own lives. They were fully formed adults: "true believers" who had subordinated their individuality to the destructive charismatic leadership of Osama Bin Laden, his group, and its cause.[14]

These men harbored deeply radical religious beliefs with intense resentment of the West; their ideas had been shaped and reinforced by Bin Laden's al-Qaeda ideology. With financial assistance and coordination by al-Qaeda leadership, yet without being under direct control of al-Qaeda leaders, they had planned and carried out the attacks. These new types of terrorists, technically knowledgeable and motivated to sacrifice their lives in an attack, increase the risk of a CBRN attack.

## 2001 Anthrax Attacks

The anthrax-contaminated letters mailed to the offices of U.S. media outlets and prominent U.S. politicians following the September 11, 2001, attacks have added to the fear in the United States of biological terrorism. Public panic over the anthrax attacks far exceeded the ultimate number of casualties. The majority of people were treated with antibiotics and never showed symptoms. Although five people did die from anthrax exposure, the attacks triggered a disproportionate level of panic across the country.[15] The source of the anthrax letters has not been identified, and this reinforces a sense of vulnerability in an already sensitized population. In the milieu of fear that ensued, people stocked up on antibiotics and gas masks, displaying distrust in government officials' ability to deal with the situation. A flood of hoaxes that intensified the atmosphere of fear after the devastating terrorist attacks of September 11, 2001, further complicated the matter.

Individuals who chose to capitalize on the fear produced by real anthrax contamination have exploited the momentum of public anxiety over chemical and biological weapons. Of all the terrorist attacks, we have been the least prepared for hoaxes, and yet these can be highly effective in terrorizing a population. The traditional psychological and technological factors constraining terrorists are not applicable in a hoax situation since the intent is not to physically kill or injure. Previous acts that give terrorists credibility in their claims, such as burying nuclear materials in a Moscow park by the Chechen leader Shamil Basayev, gives potential terrorists more leverage in creating a believable hoax. A terrorist group with technical capabilities could use a credible hoax, prior to or shortly after an actual attack, to amplify the terror effect of their actions.

## Combating an Ever-Widening Range of Terrorism

Much has been done to circumvent terrorist activity, to undermine their infrastructure, to improve state-to-state cooperation, to increase transparency of arms control programs and banking systems, and to prepare for the possible consequences of an attack. However, huge gaps still remain in counterterrorism policy. The events of the last decade demonstrate how unprepared we are for an escalation of terrorism on U.S. soil. Our policy has been reactive with improvements in security measures following, not preceding, the terrorist incidents. One of the greatest challenges today is to move from this reactive state of counterterrorism to proactivity by creating safeguards that precede attacks and reduce existing vulnerabilities. Two serious weaknesses in the state of preparedness in countering terrorism are in the areas of public communication and information technology.

The novelty of CBRN agents, secrecy of the government, and sensational media reports could greatly contribute to anxiety in the community. The media often unwittingly assists terrorists in spreading fear through the population. In his discussion on terrorism, media, and public opinion, Bruce Hoffman writes that disproportionate coverage of terrorism by the American mass media leads to the perception that CBRN terrorism presents a greater danger than other life-threatening acts. The media's unbalanced attention on terrorism not only shapes public opinion but also can affect the priorities of policy makers.[16] Jessica Stern suggests that a single unconventional terrorist attack might upset the democratic balance between civil liberties and public safety, a debate that has raged since September 11, 2001.[17] Unless public fears are addressed in a calm and balanced manner, a CBRN terrorist act or a credible threat of such an attack, could lead to very negative social consequences.

Another emerging and not fully addressed problem has to do with the role of information technology in the future of WMD terrorism. The precedent has already been set. In 1998, a group of hackers broke into the computer system of the U.S. Department of Defense and claimed to have downloaded sensitive satellite control software.[18] On another occasion, a group of hackers penetrated the computer system of Indian nuclear research facilities and created concerns about the security of India's nuclear program.[19]

Information, or cyber, terrorism has not been commonly associated with the massive loss of human life. Indeed, it has been characterized as more disruptive than destructive. But information systems terrorism (IST), if coupled with conventional terrorism, could seriously impair emergency response by, for example, a denial-of-service attack on the 911 telephone system. Moreover, such IST attacks could potentially move into the field of conventional or WMD terrorism if cyberterrorists were to take control of command and control apparatuses. Many serious scenarios could occur from hackers breaking into air-traffic control systems, to knocking out the power grid, or to disrupting the work of a nuclear reactor.

In industrialized nations with high levels of computerization, societies are becoming increasingly reliant on information systems and computer networks. Those who control the information environment, both offensively and defensively, will dominate the twenty-first century battlefield. So far, the gap between what could happen in terms of technological feasibility and what has actually happened is very large. However, bridging that gap, a gap that is narrowing as terrorists become increasingly sophisticated in the tools of the information age, is only a matter of time.[20]

## Differentiating the Threat of WMD Terrorism by Terrorist Group Type

Terrorism is not a homogeneous phenomenon. It is useful to examine the spectrum of terrorist groups to differentiate those that are significantly constrained from committing acts of mass destruction and those that might be less inhibited and, indeed, might find incentives to commit such acts. There is a broad spectrum of terrorist groups and organizations, as described in Figure 3.1. (This graphic is a modification of one introduced by Alex Schmid, 1983.[21]) Each terrorist type has a different psychology, motivation, and decision-making structure. Indeed, one should not speak of terrorist psychology in the singular, but rather of terrorist psychologies.

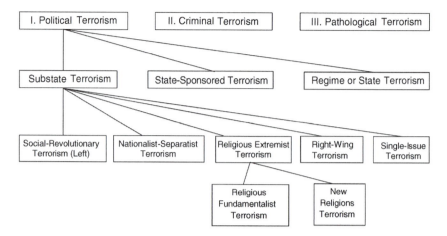

**Figure 3.1** Typology of Terrorism

In the top tier of Figure 3.1, political terrorism is differentiated from criminal and pathological terrorism. While criminal and pathological terrorists have the potential for using WMD, the likelihood is much less than for political terrorists. Studies of political terrorist psychology do not reveal severe psychiatric pathology. Indeed, political terrorist groups do not permit obviously emotionally disturbed individuals to join their groups, for they represent a security risk. Seriously disturbed individuals tend to act alone.

In the middle tier, there is state-sponsored terrorism and regime or state terrorism. State-sponsored terrorism refers to a state lending its resources to an international terrorist group in order to carry out attacks against mutual enemies. Such ties are usually kept secret and give the sponsoring states a measure of deniability for the acts they help sponsor, helping protect them against retaliation. State-supported terrorism is of major concern to the United States. As of 2002, the Department of State had designated seven countries as state sponsors of terrorism: Iran, Iraq, Libya, Sudan, Syria, North Korea, and Cuba.[22]

State terrorism is where a government directly engages in attacks on citizens or officials of another state using their own personnel to plan and execute such attacks. The North Korean assassination of 18 South Korean officials in Rangoon in 1983 is such an example. The Democratic People's Republic of Korea operation that blew up a South Korean Airliner in 1987, killing 115 passengers, is another. A third example was the attempt by Saddam Hussein's Iraqi Intelligence Service to assassinate George H. W. Bush during his visit to Kuwait in 1993. A case of biological weapons assassination occurred in London in 1978 when the Bulgarian secret service killed Bulgarian dissident Georgi Markov by stabbing him with an umbrella tip laced with ricin.

Another type of terrorism, as cited above, is regime or state terrorism which refers to states that use their police, military, secret security services, judiciary, and other resources against their own citizens to stamp out dissent, as exemplified by Argentina's "dirty war" against its own citizens to stamp out dissent between 1976 and 1983. Saddam Hussein's use of chemical weapons against his own Kurdish citizens in 1988 was state chemical and biological warfare (CBW) terrorism.

In the lower tier of Figure 3.1, a diverse typing of substate terrorist groups is specified: social-revolutionary terrorism, nationalist-separatist terrorism, religious extremist terrorism, subsuming both religious fundamentalist terrorism and terrorism perpetrated by nontraditional religious groups, right-wing terrorism, and single-issue terrorism. Their motivations are examined below.

## Social-Revolutionary Terrorism

Social-revolutionary terrorism, also known as terrorism of the left, includes those acts perpetrated by groups seeking to overthrow the capitalist economic and social order. Social-revolutionary groups are typified by the European "fighting communist organizations" active throughout the 1970s and 1980s (e.g., the Red Army Faction in Germany and the Red Brigades in Italy). While social-revolutionary terrorist groups have experienced a significant decline over the last two decades, paralleling the collapse of Communism in Europe and the end of the Cold War, social-revolutionary terrorism and insurgency are still under way, as exemplified by the Japanese Red Army, Sendero Luminosa (the Shining Path) and the Tupac Amaru Revolutionary Movement in Peru, several Colombian terrorist groups, such as the Revolutionary Armed Forces of Colombia which are also associated with narcoterrorism, and the Zapatista Army for National Liberation of Chiapas, Mexico.

These are complex organizations, however, not groups per se. The decision-making locus is outside of the action cells. In these secret organizations, there is a tension between security and communication. This leads to more decision-making latitude for the action cells than might be present in a more open organization. Thus, policy guidelines may be laid down, but specific planning concerning the target and the tactics has been delegated to the group. Nevertheless, for a matter as grave as the strategic decision to deploy weapons of mass destruction, the decision making would assuredly be conducted at the highest organization levels.

## Nationalist-Separatist Terrorism

Nationalist-separatist terrorism, also known as ethnonationalist terrorism, includes those groups fighting to establish a new political order or a state based on ethnic dominance or homogeneity. The Irish Republican Army (IRA), the Liberation Tigers of Tamil Eelam of Sri Lanka, the ETA in Spain, and radical Palestinian groups, such as Fatah, the Abu Nidal Organization, and the PFLP are prominent examples. Nationalist-separatist terrorists are usually attempting to garner international sympathy for their cause and to coerce the dominant group. Thus, ETA is attempting to pressure Spain to yield to its demands for an independent Basque state. These causes of the nationalist-separatist terrorist groups and organizations are particularly intractable, for the bitterness and resentment against the dominant ethnic group has been conveyed from generation to generation.[23] Nationalist-separatist groups operating within their nation are particularly sensitive to the responses of their internal constituency, as well as their international audience. This provides a constraint against acts as violent or extranormal as to offend their constituents, as exemplified by the attack by the Real IRA (RIRA) [a splinter group of the Provisional IRA (PIRA)] in Omagh (Northern Ireland) in 1998 in which 29, mostly women and children, were killed. The resulting uproar from their Irish constituents was so extreme, that the RIRA apologized and forswore future violence.

## Religious Extremist Terrorism

Religious extremist terrorism is characterized by groups seeking to maintain or create a religious social and political order. These include two types of groups and organizations. First, there are those adhering to a radical fundamentalist interpretation of mainstream religious doctrines. Second, there are nontraditional religious groups representing "new religions," such as the Aum Shinrikyo, responsible for the 1995 sarin nerve gas attack on the subway system in Tokyo and an earlier sarin attack on a residential neighborhood in Matsumoto, Japan.

### *Religious Fundamentalist Terrorism*

In the 1970s and 1980s, most of the acts of terrorism were perpetrated by nationalist-separatist terrorists and social-revolutionary terrorists. They wished to call attention to their cause and, accordingly, would regularly claim responsibility for their acts. They were seeking to influence the West and the establishment. As noted above, in the past 15 years, no responsibility is claimed for upward of 40 percent of terrorist acts. That terrorist attacks have become increasingly anonymous in recent decades corresponds with an increasing frequency of terrorist acts by radical religious extremist terrorists, which are not seeking to influence the West but to expel the West and seek revenge against the West.

Traditional groups include Islamic, Jewish, Christian, and Sikh radical fundamentalist extremists. In contrast to social-revolutionary and nationalist-separatist terrorists, for religious fundamentalist extremist groups, the decision-making role of the preeminent leader is of central importance. For these true believers, the radical cleric is seen as the authentic interpreter of God's word, not only eliminating any ambivalence about killing, but endowing the destruction of the defined enemy with sacred significance.

The radical cleric, whether ayatollah, rabbi, or priest, has used sacred text to justify killing in the name of God. Ayatollah Khomeini employed a radical interpretation of the Koran to provide the ideological foundation for his Islamic revolution and selected verses to justify terrorist extremity, such as "And slay them where ye catch them, and turn them out from where they have turned you out. ... Such is the reward of those who suppress the faith."[24] In a radio broadcast of June 5, 1983, Khomeini exhorted his followers: "With humility toward God and relying on the power of Islam, they should cut the cruel hands of the oppressors and world-devouring plunderers, especially the United States, from the region." To those who died fighting in this holy cause, Khomeini assured a higher place in paradise. In inciting his followers during the Iran-Iraq War, he rhetorically asked: "Why don't you recite the *sura* of killing? Why should you always recite the *sura* of mercy? Don't forget that killing is also a form of mercy." He and his clerical followers regularly found justification for their acts of violence in the Koranic *suras* calling for bloodshed.[25]

### New Religions Terrorism

New religions have also been associated, and cults based upon them can sometimes also lead to terrorist activities. An example of one such group was the Aum Shinrikyo group led by Shoko Asahara in the 1990s. Originally based in Japan, the membership of the group grew to about 40,000 members by the mid-1990s with roughly 10,000 adherents in Japan, 30,000 in Russia, and several hundreds spread in small cells located in the United States, Western Europe, Sri Lanka, and Australia. Before the group was discredited following its deadly sarin gas attacks in Matsumoto and Tokyo in 1995, it controlled over $1 billion in resources and pursued a wide diversity of weapons for its use including several types of chemical and biological arms. Asahara's vision was apocalyptic, expecting another world nuclear war where his cult had to arm itself to survive and seize power in Japan. Consequently, the Aum Shinrikyo cult was organized as a shadow government.[26]

Another such cult is the Rajneeshees, a cult that began in the 1960s in India and spread to Europe and the United States in the 1970s. This cult relocated to the United States after encountering considerable opposition from the government of India and eventually grew to a membership of 10,000, most of whom settled in a rural area of Oregon in Jefferson and Wasco counties.[27] Their ranch was close to The Dalles, Oregon, and the relations between the local townspeople and the very different cultists led to numerous tensions. The Rajneeshees resorted to poisoning town water supplies and salad bars with *Salmonella enterica* bacterium in September 1984 to attempt to influence a local election by keeping the voter turnout low by causing severe gastroenteritis in the public, aiming to elect a friendlier group of county officials, an effort that failed.[28] The community did not learn that the biological attack that sent 751 sick people to hospitals and physicians had been a deliberate act until a year later when one disgruntled cult member informed the authorities, which led to a number of criminal convictions and a crackdown on their organization, dispersing it.

## Right-Wing Terrorism

Right-wing terrorism includes those groups seeking to preserve the dominance of a threatened ethnic majority or to return society to an idealized "golden age" in which ethnic relations more clearly favored the dominant majority. These groups generally espouse fascist ideologies, including racist, anti-Semitic, and antigovernment "survivalist" beliefs. These groups in the United States fear the federal government, which they see as contributing to the decline of the majority's dominance. Commonly, such groups believe that a certain group dominates government decision making—often the Jews, referred to as ZOG, the Zionist Occupied Government—and accordingly, that government is illegitimate.

## Single-Issue Terrorist Organizations

Some terrorist groups, such as antiabortion, animal rights, or ecoterrorist groups, are organized around a single issue. It is interesting and contradictory that some in these groups, such as antiabortionists, are willing to take the lives of abortion doctors and nurses in their right-to-life cause. Similarly, some animal rights activists are willing to commit violence against their own species to attempt to achieve less violence against other species.

An example of such a single-issue terror organization is the Animal Liberation Front whose Internet site "proudly lists hundreds of attacks on the property of meat-packers, grocery chains, and the like."[29] Another type of such single-issue group is Earth First, an ecoterror group that would save the forests from loggers by sabotaging logging machinery.[30]

## WMD Terrorism

In considering which groups in the spectrum of terrorist groups might be inclined to carry out acts of chemical, biological, radiological, or nuclear terrorism, it is important to differentiate the spectrum of such acts as well. It is useful to group WMD terrorist acts into six types:

- large-scale casualties with conventional weapons;
- CBRN hoaxes;
- a conventional attack on a nuclear facility;
- a limited-scale chemical or biological attack, or radiological dispersal;
- a large-scale chemical or biological attack, or radiological dispersal; and
- CBRN strikes (superterrorism), in which thousands of casualties may result.

The crucial psychological barrier is not the choice of weapon, but rather the willingness to cause mass casualties, and this threshold has already been crossed for some groups. Groups motivated to cause mass casualties are characterized by a realization that they do not have a position of strength from which bargaining can be successful, the public will no longer respond to lesser attacks, and popular support has been lost because of the social paralysis caused by previous attacks.[31] In addition, groups carrying out such mass casualty attacks can be seeking revenge and playing to their own internal constituencies.

Besides the motivation or the willingness to inflict mass casualties by any means, terrorists must possess the technical and financial capabilities to obtain the necessary materials and skills to weaponize those materials and carry out an attack. For CBRN terrorism, all three elements have to be present. Chemical and biological weapons may pose a risk to the terrorists themselves, and caution might deter them from using such weapons. Some incarcerated Middle East terrorists interviewed about their interest in CBRN weapons indicated their concern about the danger of using such weapons.[32] The technical hurdles and lack of "know-how" can prevent even a willing terrorist from staging a mass casualty terrorist act. Given the skills and hazards in working with radiological and nuclear materials in particular, some groups might question the necessity to move into this technologically difficult and dangerous area, when they could inflict mass casualties and mass terror by using conventional weapons as was vividly demonstrated in the attacks of September 11, 2001. Sham attacks or hoaxes lack the psychological constraints of radiological and nuclear attacks but, at the same time, such threats can cause devastating psychological effects, even if there is no release of ionizing radiation or large-scale firestorms or explosive yields.

Considering the likely inability of terrorists to build or acquire nuclear weapons, chemical and biological agents pose the greatest danger. These are the simplest kinds of weapons of mass destruction in that they could be produced with relative ease from available components. Chemical agents have been defined as man-made poisonous substances that can kill or incapacitate.[33,34] Biological agents, unlike chemical, are comprised of naturally occurring viruses, bacteria, rickettsia, or toxins that can be used against other living things.

The advantages and incentives for terrorist groups to use biological weapons are, first, related to the fact that they are difficult to detect with traditional antiterrorist sensor systems. They can be relatively easily disguised, transported, and introduced into a target area compared to nuclear or radiological weapons. Biological weapons utilizing contagious disease agents, in particular, have a potential to quickly disseminate on their own, so only a very small amount of an agent might be necessary for a widespread effect. Both chemical and biological weapons affect only human beings and other living organisms, thereby leaving infrastructure and buildings intact. Biological weapons also offer terrorists the advantage of having a delayed effect. A time lag between the time of the release of an agent and its perceived effects on humans associated with biological weapons aids a perpetrator in escaping capture. Both chemical and biological weapons are cheaper, easier to manufacture, more mobile, and easier to disguise than nuclear weapons. Biological weapons provide the greatest lethality for the investment, and minute quantities can achieve the same or greater impact as chemical weapons.

The disadvantages of biological weapons use in a terrorist attack are related to their "silent" nature. They do not necessarily produce a sharp dramatic effect that would allow terrorists to exploit the event's immediate shock value.[35] In using biological agents, the lagged release of an agent may make the event difficult to determine and for terrorists to take credit. Sometimes the target population does not even know when it has been attacked. Disease outbreaks can be blamed on natural causes and, if the strike fails, there may be no recognizable evidence of an attack. According to Ron Purver, terrorists tend to prefer "things that shed blood and go bang and explode in a fairly well-circumscribed place and time."[36] Biological agents are also significantly more dangerous and unpredictable than chemicals. Precautionary measures have to be taken to minimize the risk of self-infection. Pathogens might also lose virulence over time, change under various environmental conditions, and weaponizing biological weapons is hazardous and technically difficult.

Some terrorists also have shown interest in acquiring radiological weapons. There is a large amount of radiological material available worldwide from numerous sources such as spent fuel from nuclear reactors and medical x-ray and other imaging machines, so terrorists have opportunities to secure radioactive materials. Further, radiological weapons might be chosen because of their long-term area denial capability, the difficulty of cleaning up the contaminated area, and the public fear of radioactivity. However, there are also serious drawbacks to radiological weapons use. Radiological weapons, depending on the radioactive substance used, can pose a health risk to those handling or manufacturing them. Gamma rays, protons, and neutrons are dangerous to those in the vicinity and alpha particles are dangerous when ingested or inhaled. Intense radiation can incapacitate persons exposed in a matter of hours or days. However, lesser dosages of radiation act more slowly and symptoms of sickness or cancer may take months or years to develop. Additionally, there are serious logistic problems associated with acquisition, safe transportation, and storage of radioactive materials.[37] On the other hand, radiological weapons are easier to produce than nuclear weapons, require little technological knowledge, and material necessary for their production could be obtained with relative ease from nuclear, industrial, or research facilities. Gavin Cameron characterized radiological weapons as "the least catastrophic" nuclear device, possessing the least lethal potential, but a weapon of mass destruction that could inflict strong psychological damage on the population.[38]

The most dangerous WMD that terrorists could possess are either contagious lethal biological weapons, such as smallpox, or a nuclear bomb. Today, the prevailing thought is that without state technical and financial support a terrorist group is unlikely to be able to obtain and employ nuclear explosive weapons. State support of terrorism has generally been a prerequisite for a successful international terrorist group. However, the cases of the Aum Shinrikyo and al-Qaeda demonstrate that nonstate actors are becoming particularly dangerous, not in the least due to their mobility and facade of legitimacy. The know-how of WMD is increasingly available in open literature and on the Internet. Dual-use technology and commercially available materials for chemical, biological, and radiological weapons production make it difficult to control their proliferation. Black marketeers selling deadly agents or toxic materials, particularly nuclear materials, and cadres of trained, underpaid specialists in biological, chemical, and nuclear fields in Russia and other states of the former Soviet Union could enable terrorist groups to pursue the development of WMD, granted they have strong financial support.

Besides the choice of weapon for the attack, the symbolism of a physical target is very important for terrorist groups. Civilians may be chosen as targets of violence to extend the effect beyond the immediate victims. Four targets of terrorism can be identified:

1. target of violence—the immediate physical target and victim of an attack;
2. target of terror—the population that shares the same characteristics with the victim of a terrorist act and consequently can become a potential target;

3. target of compliance—the national governments that the terrorists seek to force to accept their demands; and

4. target of influence—the larger community, usually encompassing the world, to which the terrorist is trying to bring attention to the cause.

In evaluating the risk that terrorist groups will use CBRN weapons, it is useful to include the distinction between random and discriminate violent acts. Writing in *Disorders and Terrorism,* The Report of the Task Force on Disorders and Terrorism, more than 20 years ago, R. W. Mengel distinguished four different means by which terrorists attempt to achieve their goals.[39] He observed there is a distinct difference between discriminate and random target selection. Whereas discriminate target selection can be used in support of bargaining or to make a political statement, random targeting is associated with the motivation to cause social paralysis or to inflict mass casualties. In evaluating the risk that terrorist groups may use chemical or biological weapons, it is useful to employ this distinction in differentiating among terrorist groups. Considering the degree to which they view the impact of the act upon internal and external constituents, some groups might well contemplate CBW attacks only in a bounded area, limiting casualties, which would significantly militate against negative reactions from their constituents, both local and international. These groups would be significantly constrained against acts in a region in which their constituents might well be adversely affected as a result of physical proximity to the area of attack. These bounded acts are specified as discriminate. Indiscriminate attacks, in contrast, are attacks in which no consideration is given to the selection of specific victims, or the impact of the act upon internal or external constituents.

For each of the terrorist group types described, there are varying constraints against the use of CBRN weapons and mass casualty terrorism.

## Social-Revolutionary Terrorists

Insofar as these groups are seeking to influence their society, they would be significantly constrained from indiscriminate acts that cause significant casualties among their own countrymen or cause negative reactions in their domestic and international audiences. But discriminate acts against government or symbolic capitalist targets could be rationalized by these groups.

## Nationalist-Separatist Terrorists

These groups are significantly constrained from acts that indiscriminately involve mass casualties and negatively affect the group's reputation with their constituents and their international audience. But discriminate acts against their adversary, in areas where their constituents are not present, can be rationalized. Just as the rash of suicide bombings in Tel Aviv and other predominantly Jewish cities in Israel was implemented by absolutist Palestinian groups, some of which were radical Islamists, the prospect of tactical chemical and/or biological weapons in such areas is quite conceivable. Such discriminate attacks could also be implemented in revenge against U.S. targets. But a chemical or biological weapons attack in Jerusalem, by secular Palestinian terrorists that might affect their own constituents, is considered highly unlikely.

## Radical Religious Fundamentalist Terrorists

These organizations are hierarchical in structure. The radical cleric provides interpretation of the religious text justifying violence, which is uncritically accepted by his "true believer" followers, so there is no ambivalence concerning use of violence that is religiously commanded. These groups are particularly dangerous, for they are not constrained by Western reaction, indeed are driven to expel secular modernizing influences and achieve revenge against the West, focused especially upon the United States. They have shown a willingness to perpetrate acts of mass casualty terrorism, as exemplified by the bombings of Khobar Towers in Saudi Arabia, the 1993 attack on the World Trade Center in the United States, the 1998 U.S. embassy bombings in Kenya and Tanzania, the 2000 attack on the USS *Cole,* and the 2001 attacks on the World Trade Center and the Pentagon. Osama Bin Laden, responsible for these events, has actively discussed the use of weapons of mass destruction in public interviews. Thus, in contrast to the social revolutionaries and the nationalist-separatist groups, the constraints against CBRN mass terrorism are not present, and such terrorists are considered especially dangerous.

### *New Religion Terrorism*

The Aum Shinrikyo "attempted to use aerosolized biological agents against nine targets, two with anthrax and seven with botulinum toxin."[40] Although all these biological warfare attacks failed because they made mistakes in production or dissemination of the biological agents, they were more "successful" in their use of chemical weapons. Their chemical attacks killed 12 and injured over 1,000 in April 1995[41] when they used sarin on the Tokyo subway and their earlier sarin attack in Matsumoto killed 7 and injured another 500 persons. This group was also experimenting with Q fever and was shopping for Ebola virus in East Africa and had bought nuclear weapons components from individuals in the former Soviet Union. They also owned a uranium mine in Australia and obviously had future nuclear weapons aspirations.

The pursuit of the full spectrum of nuclear, chemical, and biological weapons by the Aum Shinrikyo cult, and the resulting casualties in Tokyo and Matsumoto, Japan, was a wake-up call to the United States, signaling that the era of superterrorism featuring unconventional or CBRN weapons was upon us. This eventually led to U.S. Congressional Hearings and legislation such as the Nunn-Lugar-Domenici Act that increased defensive counterterror preparations against potential WMD events in the United States.

## Right-Wing Terrorism

Because right-wing terrorists generally dehumanize their enemies, attacks on target groups, such as blacks or, in Europe, on enclaves of foreign workers, are justified by their ideology. Because of their delegitimization and dehumanization of the government, government facilities are targeted by such groups, including attacks on the seat of the federal government as represented in *The Turner Diaries*.

Many of the case studies of chemical-biological terrorism developed by the Center for Nonproliferation Studies at the Monterey Institute for International Studies, the first group of which was published as *Toxic Terror,* [42] were acts committed by individuals with a right-wing ideology, but not belonging to a formal group or organization per se. The case study by Jessica Stern of Larry Wayne Harris, a former neo-Nazi, is a case in point. Timothy McVeigh is an exemplar of such individuals seeking to cause mass casualty terrorism, using conventional weapons. McVeigh was enthralled by *The Turner Diaries*, which he sold below cost at gun shows. At the time of his capture, glassined,[43] highlighted pages from this bible of the radical right were found in his car. Individuals in this category are a significant threat for low-level chemical and biological attacks but, because of resource limitations, probably do not represent a threat of mass casualty chemical or biological terrorism.

The role of the Internet in propagating the ideology of right-wing extremist hatred is of concern, for an isolated individual consumed by hatred can find common cause in the right-wing Web sites, feel he is not alone, and be moved along the pathway from thought to action, responding to the extremist ideology of his virtual community.

## Single-Issue Terrorists

To date, the single-issue terrorists, such as antiabortion terrorists, ecoterrorists, and animal rights radicals, have not used mass casualty weapons to make their point, probably because these are indiscriminate weapons that target too wide a spectrum of victims, not just those whom they object to most strenuously. It is possible that they would not want to inflict such levels of damage because it would adversely affect public acceptance of their agendas. Finally, some might be deterred by the amount of government pursuit that such actions might catalyze.

## A Spectrum of Groups, A Range of Incentives and Constraints

This differentiated motivational spectrum is represented in Figure 3.2. It should be emphasized that a check mark does not indicate that these groups are strongly motivated to carry out CBRN terrorism attacks, but that they are less constrained. The asterisk designates those groups that might make discriminate attacks but which would be inhibited from indiscriminate attacks affecting their constituents. A few points should be kept in mind. The horrors of September 11, 2001, demonstrate that conventional attacks may be sufficient to cause mass destruction. In addition, incarcerated radical Islamist terrorists interviewed under the auspices of the Smith Richardson Foundation, while open to considering weapons of mass destruction, for the most part said, "Just give me a good Kalishnikov," and several indicated that the Koran prohibited the use of poisons.[44] Yet, as the graphic reveals, it is radical religious fundamentalist terrorists that are least constrained and pose the greatest danger.

| Group Type | Large-scale Conventional | CBRN Hoax | Limited Scale CBR | Large-scale CBR | Superterrorism/ Catastrophic CBRN |
|---|---|---|---|---|---|
| Social-Revolutionary | ✓* | ✓ | ✓* | X | X |
| Nationalist-Separatist | ✓* | ✓ | ✓* | X | X |
| Religious Fundamentalist | ✓ | ✓ | ✓* | ✓* | ✓* |
| New Religious Extremists (closed cults) | ✓ | ✓ | ✓ | ✓ | ✓ |
| Right-Wing | ✓ | ✓ | ✓ | X | X |
| Single-Issue Extremists | ✓ | X | X | X | X |

| | |
|---|---|
| * | Designates reduced constraints against *discriminate* but not indiscriminate WMD terrorism. |
| X | Designates major constraints against WMD terrorism. |
| ✓ | Designates reduced constraints against WMD terrorism. |

**Figure 3.2**  Differentiating Motivations and Constraints for WMD Terrorism by Group Type

## Conclusions and Outlook

There are many lessons to be drawn from the terrorist attacks of the past decade, both home and abroad. State-supported terrorism and CBRN proliferation have been addressed at the highest levels. New organizations have been established at the federal, state, and local levels to plan, coordinate, and deal with the consequences of the future terrorist attacks. Academic seminars have discussed the spectrum of CBRN agents that could be used by terrorists and the measures that need to be undertaken in each case. Yet, we need to focus more on the psychology of terrorists to be able to not only prevent attacks from already known groups, but also to identify the groups at risk of resorting to WMD terrorism. Just as important as knowing who might resort to weapons of mass destruction terrorism and why is determining who would not want to do it and why not. Evaluating the motivations, constraints, and resources of different groups is crucial in the future of counterterrorism.

Terrorism has evolved over the last decade into deadlier forms. The U.S. Government has shifted its concerns from the Soviet Union as the principal perceived sponsoring threat to other states such as Iran, Iraq, Syria, Libya, Sudan, Cuba, and North Korea. Three of these states—Iran, Iraq (prior to Saddam Hussein's ouster), and North Korea—comprise the so-called "axis of evil." These states either possess, possessed, or were seen to be on the verge of possessing major CBRN capabilities. Indeed, a major espoused motivation for the 2003 conflict with Iraq was the threat that Iraq would provide WMD to the terrorist groups it supported. Iran has been identified as the major state sponsor of terrorism. However, the leadership of these nations likely would judge it to be hazardous to pass these weapons to a terrorist group not under full control, realizing if the group employed such weapons and the link back to the state were to be traced, the consequences could be catastrophic as the United States retaliated.

After the Aum Shinrikyo sarin gas attack in Tokyo in April 1995 and the al-Qaeda attacks in New York and Washington, D.C. on September 11, 2001, followed by the anthrax mail attacks of late 2001, the focus of concern has increasingly shifted to nonstate actors, with the recognition that autonomous terrorist groups and organizations or even lone individuals are now willing and able to conduct mass casualty terrorist acts. Motivation to commit violent acts is growing stronger, reinforced by pseudoreligious backing. In the past decade, mass casualty constraints and taboos have been broken, and there is little doubt that some terrorists will use CBRN weapons in the future.

The supply of resources available to terror networks continued to expand in the 1990s with chemical, biological, and nuclear materials increasingly available from the Russian black market or commercial and industrial sources. This danger is compounded as many terrorist organizations have developed vast financial resources, permitting them access to these black-market commodities. Information on how to build a CBRN weapon is widely available from public sources on the Internet and in print and may be assisted by unemployed Russian scientists willing to trade their expertise for good pay. Constraints against mass casualty terrorist attacks are eroding. For the majority of terrorist groups and organizations, however, there still remain major disincentives to CBRN mass casualty terrorism.

Most terrorists will not be attracted to the use of chemical, biological, radiological, or nuclear weapons because they would see such WMD use as counterproductive to their cause. The constraints are particularly severe for groups that are concerned with the reactions of their constituents, for example, social-revolutionary and nationalist-separatist terrorists, although they might consider discriminate low-level CBW attacks. Right-wing extremists, because of their tendency to dehumanize their victims and delegitimize the federal government, pose a distinct danger of initiating low-level conventional discriminate attacks against their demonized targets: Jews, blacks, and ethnic minorities, as well as federal buildings.

If other nontraditional religious extremist groups resembling Aum Shinrikyo were to emerge, they could be attracted to WMD use and might be a great threat, but most millennial cults are not led by religious belligerents, but instead passively await the final days.

Religious fundamentalist terrorist groups, who follow the dictates of destructive charismatic religious leaders, are not constrained by their audience on earth. God is the audience in their minds. They are more of a threat to execute mass casualty attacks, although to the degree they have a constituency, as does Hamas, they are also constrained. Having demonstrated an unconstrained goal of committing mass casualty destruction and of maintaining America in a continuing state of insecurity, the al-Qaeda group of Osama Bin Laden is not constrained and is particularly dangerous. Because of the series of successful attacks, with increasing levels of violence, and the expanding mission of its grandiose leader, this organization is considered as the highest risk to move into chemical and biological terrorism. Bin Laden is innovative and continually seeks to create an escalating terror. Because of resource and technological constraints, however, small local attacks are the most likely, rather than chemical or biological superterrorism. This limitation would be removed were the group supported by a state with the necessary technological resources.

Given the severe constraints against catastrophic WMD terrorism for most groups, this argues for continuing to protect against the greatest likely event—conventional terrorism—and to devote significantly increased intelligence resources to monitoring much more closely the groups posing the greatest risk of chemical and biological weapons use. These are right-wing extremist groups and religious extremist groups, both nontraditional cults similar to Aum Shinrikyo and especially religious fundamentalist terrorist organizations. These are the emerging WMD terrorist threats, groups that came on the scene in force only in the past decade. The improvements made in the U.S. counterproliferation and homeland security programs are not likely to dissuade such terrorists from using WMD, but will make it more difficult and will lend protection and consequence management capabilities that can help reduce such terrorist WMD effects.

CHAPTER 4

# Nonproliferation—
# Challenges Old and New

*Brad Roberts*

Since the advent of the nuclear era in 1945, Americans and others have been debating whether or how it might be possible to prevent the proliferation of nuclear and other weapons of mass destruction (WMD). As each new proliferation challenge has emerged, debate about the shortcomings of the various policy tools for coping with proliferation has intensified. These debates have grown only more intense in the last 10 to 15 years. Despite such debates, American presidents have steered a fairly consistent course—promoting nonproliferation, innovating along the way, while also coping with its periodic failures.

The end of the Cold War seemed to make new things possible for nonproliferation, with the promise of even more cooperation between East and West on specific proliferation challenges. And the Persian Gulf War of 1990–1991 seemed to make new things necessary, as the United States faced the first regional war under the shadow of weapons of mass destruction. First President George H. W. Bush and then President William Clinton committed the federal government to significant political efforts to strengthen the tools of nonproliferation policy.

At this juncture, a decade or so hence, it is useful to take stock. What was the "strengthening agenda" that they launched? How has thinking changed over three administrations—and in the wake of 9/11—about the means and ends of policy? More specifically, how has thinking about the balance between nonproliferation and counterproliferation evolved? How much progress has been made? Is there a future for nonproliferation? Where might national efforts most effectively be focused?[1]

## The "Strengthening" Agenda

The first Bush administration committed itself in the early 1990s to seek a strengthening of nonproliferation in various ways.[2] Early priority was given to conclusion and rapid entry into force of a global ban on chemical weapons. This was a Bush priority since his time as vice president when he proposed a draft treaty in 1984 which resulted in conclusion of the Chemical Weapons Convention (CWC) in the very last days of the Reagan administration.

Anticipating the 1995 review conference of states parties to the Nuclear Non-Proliferation Treaty (NPT), the first Bush administration began to work for a decision to extend the treaty indefinitely. It also sought a strengthening of the safeguards system policed by the International Atomic Energy Agency (IAEA).[3] The Bush administration sought to lead an effort to strengthen the Biological and Toxin Weapons Convention (BTWC), with special focus on dealing with compliance challenges. Strengthening cooperation on export controls was also an administration priority, with focus on improved coordination in the ad hoc supplier groups such as the Australia Group and the Missile Technology Control Regime (MTCR).

The first Bush administration also focused on a string of specific problem cases. It took steps to promote North Korea's compliance with its IAEA and NPT obligations. To deal with rising concerns about Russian BWC compliance, it promoted a trilateral inspection effort involving the United States, the United Kingdom, and Russia. In regions of proliferation concern, it promoted various steps. In Latin America it promoted the strengthening of the nonproliferation regime, including the Mendoza Declaration outlawing chemical weapons there. In the Middle East it promoted the Arms Control and Regional Security process. It continued pressures on India and especially Pakistan. The administration also exploited the end of the Cold War to recast the military environment in Europe by using the agreement on Conventional Forces in Europe, the Vienna Confidence and Security Building Measures, and the Open Skies Treaty as tools for providing predictability and transparency.

At a more strategic level, the administration took the lead in mobilizing consensus among the permanent members of the UN Security Council to issue an unprecedented statement at the head-of-state level on weapons of mass destruction proliferation. In their January 1992 summit statement, they declared the proliferation of unconventional weapons to be a threat to international peace and security (code words for justifying the use of force under the UN Charter) and committed themselves to concerted follow-up actions to strengthen nonproliferation—with special though not sole focus on Iraq.[4]

The Clinton administration inherited this agenda and proposed no significant departures from it. An early priority was to secure ratification of the CWC and its rapid entry into force, though on this effort it stumbled badly, not least in the failure to anticipate deep-seated opposition to the treaty from within the Republican Party. Finally the treaty did enter into force with U.S. participation, but only after the administration acceded to a plan of the Senate Republican Committee for an overhaul and contraction of the federal arms control process (i.e., elimination of the Arms Control and Disarmament Agency).

The Clinton administration successfully brokered the 1995 decision of states parties to the NPT to extend the treaty indefinitely. This was a significant achievement in the face of the desire of many states to extend the treaty only for a fixed period of time and with certain explicit conditions. It was won in part on the promise to conclude and bring into force the Comprehensive Test Ban Treaty (CTBT). But this ultimately foundered in the U.S. Senate, in part because of limited senior level engagement and poor bureaucratic follow-up of the kind that bedeviled CWC ratification. The Senate CTBT debate also revealed a wide chasm of thinking among American experts on the role of nuclear weapons in the post-Cold War environment. The efforts to strengthen the BTWC continued under the Clinton administration. The technical exploration of means to strengthen verification launched by the Bush administration was redirected with formation of an ad hoc international group of experts to consider broader questions associated with strengthening compliance.[5]

The special processes on problem cases were carried forward and adapted by the Clinton administration. Achieving the denuclearization of the non-Russian republics of the former Soviet Union was an especially important early nonproliferation success for the Clinton administration—especially in the case of Ukraine, where denuclearization was hard won. Working with Congressional leaders Sam Nunn and Richard Lugar, the administration also launched the Cooperative Threat Reduction (CTR) effort to address concerns about the so-called "loose nukes" and "brain drain" problems in the former Soviet Union (the threat that weapons, sensitive technologies or materials, and expertise might migrate from the former Soviet weapons complex to proliferators in the Middle East and elsewhere). Along the way, concern about the Russian biological warfare (BW) problem seemed to slip from the list of top priorities, in part because the trilateral inspection process had been stymied by the Russians.

The regional agenda also continued to receive high-level attention in the Clinton administration. The mounting crisis over North Korea led to near war and then adoption of the 1994 Agreed Framework, brokered by former President Jimmy Carter, which seemed to promise an avoidance of war on the bet that the Democratic People's Republic of Korea (DPRK) would not survive long enough in the post-Cold War environment to realize its nuclear weapons ambitions. Efforts to promote regional approaches to nuclear nonproliferation were frustrated by developments in both South Asia and the Middle East and by international division about how to deal with threats that had not taken clear shape.

On export control, the Clinton administration continued the effort to adapt Cold War mechanisms to post-Cold War realities. It promoted an expansion of membership in some of the ad hoc mechanisms (e.g., Australia Group). It led the effort to replace the Cold War vintage Coordinating Committee for Multilateral Export Controls (CoCom) with the Wassenaar Arrangement on Export Controls for Conventional Arms and Dual-Use Goods and Technologies, a much looser mechanism, though also one seemingly better attuned to the requirements of an era of globalization. This, too, was much criticized by Senate Republicans, as an abandonment of the types of coercive measures that had served American interests well in the past.

With regard to the other major powers, the Clinton administration made some progress with Moscow in addressing the loose nukes problem, though less progress in preventing Russian nuclear and missile aid to others, especially Iran. The administration made more progress with Beijing in drawing China into the global nonproliferation effort—including Chinese membership in the NPT and CWC and support for the objectives of the Australia Group and MTCR—though China did not bring its export behaviors fully into alignment with Washington's preferences. And vis-à-vis the European allies, the Clinton administration suffered continued frustration in building common approaches to Iran, North Korea, and others. And on the Clinton watch, the United Nations Special Commission on Iraq enjoyed both its greatest successes and suffered its ultimate collapse as consensus on the Security Council about how to deal with Iraq finally dissolved.

The Clinton administration also addressed as an urgent priority the need to come to terms with the military planning requirements of proliferation. In doing so, they were directly following a line of thinking advanced earlier in the Pentagon under Secretary Richard Cheney. Throughout the Cold War, the challenges posed by the chemical, biological, and nuclear weapons of the Soviet Union were so daunting that any other challenge was simply a lesser-included problem. But with the collapse of the Soviet Union and following a decade (the 1980s) of rapid proliferation of chemical and, possibly also, biological weapons, U.S. military planners had to begin to think more seriously about the operational requirements of projecting power and prevailing against regional powers armed with weapons of mass destruction. The near brush with Iraqi weapons of mass destruction in 1990–1991 only confirmed this view.

Thus in the Cheney Pentagon the term "counterproliferation" was coined to encompass such efforts, and a plan was developed to reorganize the Pentagon in a second Bush administration. Cheney's successor, Les Aspin, arrived from his former post as chairman of the House Armed Services Committee with a keen interest in this particular problem. Embracing the term counterproliferation and the intended reorganization, Aspin launched his Defense Counterproliferation Initiative on December 7, 1993, and with it a top-level effort to motivate the Services, Joint Staff, and regional commands to take seriously the challenges, especially of chemical and biological weapons. The term counterproliferation was used and misused in many different ways—to suggest an emphasis on counterforce attack operations or a rejection of nonproliferation or new nuclear missions—with the result that the Clinton National Security Council brokered an agreement across the U.S. Government about the means and ends of nonproliferation and counterproliferation. A key theme was that the two objectives are mutually supportive.[6] Nonproliferation requires that the weapons proliferators might acquire not be useful, whether militarily or politically, for blackmailing the United States and others who are confronted with WMD-armed aggression. Counterproliferation is easier to achieve if the number of WMD-armed states is few and their capabilities are restrained by the lack of access to global markets, foreign expertise, and extensive testing.

Against this backdrop there were three further important developments in the decade after the Persian Gulf War. One was the rising concern about the proliferation of ballistic missiles. In the late 1980s, the MTCR enjoyed its original success in stifling development of the Condor missile (a joint development program pursued by Egypt, Argentina, and others). As a result of cooperation by technology suppliers facilitated by the MTCR, cooperation among Third World missile developers was sharply curtailed, and this fueled optimistic predictions about the future of missile nonproliferation. By the late 1990s, an entirely different view of missile proliferation had taken hold in Washington, in part through the prodding of the Commission on Ballistic Missile Proliferation chaired by Donald Rumsfeld and in part through the emerging threat from North Korea and the unfolding nuclear and missile competition in South Asia. Washington policy makers became increasingly concerned about the convergence of nuclear and missile proliferation trends and the possibility that the United States might, sooner rather than later, come within range of emerging rogue ballistic missiles.

The second important development was the emergence of intensified domestic political debate about the tools of nonproliferation. In a certain sense, this reflected a return to normalcy in American politics. The notion that "politics stops at the water's edge" held true through much of the Cold War but not in the decades since. In the 1990s, as the risks of nuclear Armageddon receded, it thus seemed natural to some national leaders to try to exploit divisions on foreign and defense policy issues for partisan gain. But to cast the history of this era as one marked by a return to partisanship in the debate about nonproliferation would be misleading, as the most intense debates about how to deal with proliferation challenges seemed to unfold within the Republican Party rather than between the two major parties. This debate touched on many issues central to nonproliferation. On the utility of arms control, for example, former Congressman Newt Gingrich took aim at part of his own party in describing a "difference between those who rely on lawyers to defend America and those who rely on engineers and scientists" as he made his case for missile defense.[7] On the virtues of multilateralism as opposed to unilateralism there was an equally intense debate among Republicans. The Clinton administration seemed increasingly unable to set its own agenda on nonproliferation and national policy and its strategy in the face of Republican opposition in the Congress. At the same time, the deeply divided Republicans were unable to agree on an alternative agenda.

The third important development was rising concern about the linkage between proliferation and terrorism. The 1993 truck bomb attack on the World Trade Center, the 1995 Oklahoma City bombing, the 1995 attack on the Tokyo subway with sarin nerve gas, and a dramatic spike in the number of anthrax hoaxes all contributed to newfound concern about whether and when terrorists might resort to weapons of mass destruction. This concern affected nonproliferation in a number of ways. It fueled the broader political attack on arms control and nonproliferation from the right wing of the Republican Party, on the argument that nonproliferation regimes have little relevance to the emerging terrorism threat.

The increasing focus of the United States on domestic preparedness also magnified concerns among friends, allies, and others that the United States was beginning to turn inward and thus away from the leadership role it had played in dealing with international problems. The rising concern about weapons of mass destruction terrorism also affected the counterproliferation effort in the sense that it became a serious distraction, by diverting fiscal, operational, and intellectual resources. Military counter-WMD assets, already stretched to the limit to deal with the planning and operational implications of regional adversaries armed with weapons of mass destruction, were shifted increasingly to deal with the domestic counterterrorism mission.

Thus, through the 1990s there was both continued progress in the effort to strengthen nonproliferation and a mounting crisis of confidence in the overall regime. The continuity from Bush I to Clinton was striking. The architecture of the regime was developing further. Specific challenges were being addressed. But at the same time, the efficacy of nonproliferation in delivering security came increasingly into question. The failures of nonproliferation in South Asia and the Middle East were sharp and compelling and of far more political and military interest than the successes in many other parts of the world.[8] That crisis of confidence was felt acutely by small and medium powers around the world that had forsworn WMD in the global treaties, and they wondered increasingly about whether the bet they had made was a sound one. But it was also felt acutely by those Republicans that for a decade and more had fought the Bush/Clinton strengthening agendas.

## The George W. Bush Administration

Given the diversity of opinion that emerged in preceding years, it is hardly surprising that the new Bush administration seemed in its first year or so to pursue an inconsistent nonproliferation policy.

At first there was a certain reactive quality to the Bush administration's policy—an effort to correct the many perceived deficiencies of the Clinton administration. In the words of William Schneider, a senior advisor to Secretary Rumsfeld in his capacity as chairman of the Defense Science Board, "the Clinton administration is fighting the proliferation of missiles and weapons of mass destruction with the tools of a bygone strategic era."[9] He argued further,

> [T]he political constituency for ... multilateral agreements is losing strength. Americans are less and less interested in arms control measures that have not in fact stopped the proliferation of these weapons and actually impede our own ability to provide security for ourselves and our allies in the face of that proliferation ... the Clinton administration has enacted policies which have actually accelerated proliferation rather than retarding it.[10]

This view led to early efforts to move away from the Agreed Framework with North Korea, to resurrect something like CoCom in the export control domain, to talk tougher to Russia and China about their continued trade with proliferators—and to deploy ballistic missile defenses as rapidly as possible.[11]

Also, during this period, the administration gave serious consideration to the possibility of significantly curtailing the CTR program with Moscow, on the arguments that its time had passed and that the Clinton administration had not figured out that the CTR program was being exploited by the Russians to divert resources to purposes not intended by the United States. The reaction to eight years of Clinton policy also contributed to the decision to reject the package of measures designed to strengthen the BTWC that had been the focus of international effort since the first Bush administration had helped set the process in motion a decade earlier.[12]

At the same time, others in the administration seemed to be making contrary claims. Under Secretary of State for Arms Control and International Security, John Bolton, asserted that "our commitment to multilateral regimes to promote nonproliferation and international security never has been as strong as it is today."[13] He voiced strong administration commitment to the NPT and pushed for increased funding for the IAEA.[14] He also expressed support for the CWC and spearheaded an effort to eject the director of the Organisation for the Prohibition of Chemical Weapons on the charge that he was ineffectual. But Bolton also resisted use of the challenge inspections provisions of the CWC to pursue allegations of noncompliance by Iran and others.

This ambiguity was partially caused by the institutional perspectives of persons from different departments. But it also reflected uncertainty in the administration about the value of both arms control and multilateralism more generally. Its opposition to bilateral arms control with Russia was evident from the start, with the desire to move away from the restraints embodied in the Anti-Ballistic Missile Treaty but also the reluctance to negotiate any kind of successor to the Strategic Arms Reduction Treaty. The opposition to bilateral arms control was often couched in language dismissive of arms control more generally, though some in the administration were careful to argue that the desire to move away from the Cold War strategic framework with Moscow did not also connote a desire to move away from multilateral arms control mechanisms for dealing with weapons of mass destruction proliferation.

Others seemed perfectly content to dismiss all arms control, both bilateral and multilateral, as a dangerous placebo that should be struck down and dismantled so that Americans are no longer fooled by the illusion of security these critics associate with negotiated measures. Moreover, for many in the administration, multilateralism was seen as something being promoted by those resentful of American power and wishing to compel American restraint.

Behind closed doors in the policy studies community in this period, it was not uncommon to hear some heretical ideas about nonproliferation offered by appointees or affiliates of the new administration. Some were willing to argue that the nonproliferation battle had been lost completely —that the nuclear jungle is here or just right around the corner, given the emergence of second-tier suppliers, such as North Korea as well as the continued proliferation behaviors of Moscow and Beijing, and that it is time to get over nonproliferation and to see it as a lost dream of the Cold War. Others were willing to argue that more proliferation may be perfectly acceptable to the United States—as it promises new friends and allies in the next major international competition.[15] It was not uncommon to hear talk about the possibility of collapsing the global treaty regime, on the argument that we would then be free of the delusion that it protects us.

And then came 9/11, and with it the need to sort out the various opinions, impulses, and perspectives represented in the administration. For the president at least, the lessons of 9/11 as they bear on the proliferation question were clear enough. More proliferation is not tolerable. The threat posed by the crossroads of weapons of mass destruction technology and tyranny is clear and present and cannot be allowed to go further. Rather than acquiesce, the United States must pursue rollback. The axis of evil —his term of reference for "rogue states"—must be confronted and pacified now, with preventive wars of preemption if necessary, before they can pose imminent threats to America. Wars for regime removal are necessary because arms control has proven itself incapable of compelling their compliance with international norms. The national strategy to combat weapons of mass destruction was to be revitalized, and along with it the commitment to nonproliferation renewed and updated.

Such thinking was evident first and foremost in the *National Security Strategy* of 2002, and then in more detail in the *National Strategy to Combat Weapons of Mass Destruction* of late 2002.[16] In spring 2003, the Bush administration supplemented these strategies and the associated initiatives with an effort to promote enforcement of existing agreements with stronger international cooperation for interdiction of illegal shipments—the so-called Proliferation Security Initiative.[17] In February of 2004, the president also gave a wide-ranging address at National Defense University in which he gave strong endorsement to the principles and mechanisms of nonproliferation and proposed seven new steps to strengthen them.[18] Readers of these documents who are also conversant with the proliferation-related developments over the last decade in the global landscape and in American politics cannot help but be struck by the essential continuity in national policy envisioned by the White House. The embrace of a broad strategy encompassing political and military and unilateral and multilateral measures echoes the thinking of the preceding Clinton and Bush administrations.

Indeed, the aspects of the strategy deemed most unprecedented by some opinion makers, i.e., the emphasis on preemption and interdiction, can readily be found in the strategic logic of the 1993 Defense Counterproliferation Initiative. There is at least one striking disconnect between the two Bush administration documents: the logic of preemption elaborated so forcefully in the *National Security Strategy* can barely be found in the *National Strategy to Combat WMD*, even though the latter appeared months after the former. Moreover, there is also a striking silence about the risks of proliferation to friends and allies of the United States in contrast to the constant refrain about the risks of proliferation to enemies.

In addition, as part of his commitment to eliminate "gathering threats," the president took the nation to war in Iraq to expel Saddam Hussein from power. More than two years after the end of major combat operations, the legacy of this effort for nonproliferation remains uncertain and deeply debated. The Bush administration argued that regime removal was necessary to remove the imminent threat of Iraqi weapons of mass destruction, though as U.S. weapons of mass destruction inspector David Kay subsequently famously argued, "[W]e were almost all wrong," regarding the existence of such arms.[19] The administration also apparently believed that only by beginning with an effort to democratize Iraq could the larger political transformation of the Middle East occur, with the apparent hope that this would contribute both to an easing of the terrorist threat and of weapons of mass destruction proliferation pressures. On the other hand, the exercise of unilateralism has proven deeply injurious to the will of others to cooperate with the United States in postwar Iraq. For some observers, it has raised questions also about whether a more interventionist United States might generate additional proliferation pressures of its own.

Thus, in its fourth year, the Bush administration had undertaken some bold initiatives of its own while also drawing closely to key continuities in U.S. strategy vis-à-vis proliferation as it has been pursued for the last 15 years, and longer. The flirtation with heresies during its first year has given way to a concerted national strategy built around clearly defined presidential priorities and encompassing both nonproliferation and military measures.

## Taking Stock 1990–2004

What has this strategy accomplished over 15 years? How much progress has been made in strengthening nonproliferation in the period since the end of the Cold War and the Persian Gulf War?

The effort to strengthen the global treaty regimes has fallen far short of the expectations of over a decade ago. Membership of the NPT has grown (especially with the addition of China, France, and Ukraine, among others) and the treaty has been extended indefinitely, but the effort to strengthen the safeguards system has moved only a few steps and the challenges of noncompliance by a handful of states remain acute. Both India and Pakistan have demonstrated their weapons and apparently continue to acquire additional capabilities.

The CWC was concluded and entered into force and is moving through the phase of its work focused on the destruction of declared stockpiles of chemical weapons and their production facilities, but it has yet to tackle the problems posed by suspicions of undeclared capabilities and to initiate the use of challenge inspections.

The effort to strengthen the BTWC produced a package of verification and other measures, but these were rejected by the United States and were not warmly received by others concerned with their impact on the interests of biodefense and biotechnology.

The efforts to strengthen the supporting export control ad hoc coordinating mechanisms have produced some incremental measures; but with the growing importance of dual-use technologies in all of these areas (i.e., those with both civilian and military applications), such mechanisms seem to offer decreasing utility in the years ahead.

The effort to address specific proliferation problems has generated various processes but few actual results. The long and tortuous process to address the North Korean nuclear problem has yet to result in restoration of North Korea's compliance with its NPT obligations (withdrawal from the treaty has not legitimized or legalized the activities that it pursued in violation of the treaty).

North Korea's program has been helped by the transfer of uranium-enrichment technology and advice from the A. Q. Khan black-market operation out of Pakistan. North Korean representatives have admitted to a significant uranium-enrichment effort and claim to already possess atomic weapons. The DPRK has now withdrawn from the NPT and may now possess as many as seven nuclear weapons according to claims.

The process to turn back the Iranian nuclear weapons program has garnered some grudging support from Moscow and Beijing and elsewhere, but has not so far resulted in cessation of the effort to build reprocessing capabilities. Indeed, Iran and North Korea are continuing to press toward nuclear weapons capabilities. They loom as the two most significant nuclear proliferation challenges and both promise to pose serious challenges in the immediate years ahead. Iranian and North Korean nuclear programs might well provoke similar programs in countries such as Japan, the Republic of Korea, and interest in nuclear weapons in Saudi Arabia.

The process to pressure India and Pakistan to roll back their nuclear capabilities or, at least, to agree to some form of mutual, formal restraint has yet to result in such agreement. The CTR program continues its work in the former Soviet Union, but the Russian biological warfare problem remains unaddressed, as do concerns about China's noncompliance with the BTWC. As argued above, the Iraqi weapons of mass destruction problem has been resolved with the war to expel Saddam and the Ba'ath Party, though at the same time the failure (at this writing) to find evidence of any such weapons seems likely to poison future U.S. efforts to build international coalitions against states and regimes with weapons of mass destruction ambitions. Fortunately, as of this writing, no state-developed weapons of mass destruction appear to have been acquired by terrorist groups by purchase or theft, or at least such acquisition has not yet resulted in weapons of mass destruction use.[20]

The effort to strengthen the commitment of the major powers in their role as international security guarantors to deal with weapons of mass destruction proliferation has reached a crucial crossroads. On the one hand, the second Bush administration is clearly loath to pursue the agenda of the first Bush administration to utilize the UN Security Council as a venue for fashioning and demonstrating such commitment (on the general argument that deference to the Council is an infringement of U.S. sovereignty). Its willingness to proceed to war against Saddam without a clear Security Council mandate is testament to its antipathy to this mechanism and its unwillingness to defer to the concerns of the other major powers in the effort to reach agreement.

On the other hand, the Bush administration has worked diligently in bilateral as opposed to multilateral modes to elicit the support of Moscow and Beijing in dealing with the specific proliferation challenges of Iran and North Korea. The administration's rejection of the UN Security Council for these roles reinforces a general lack of U.S. leadership of the multilateral treaty regimes. The United States remains engaged, but is not leading. Absent U.S. leadership, the effort to strengthen nonproliferation has faltered, not least because no other nation or group of nations can play that leadership role. This raises basic and profound questions about the future of efforts both in the United States and internationally to strengthen nonproliferation.

This stocktaking summary should look beyond the effort to strengthen nonproliferation to the broader question of the status of nonproliferation. Over the last decade, and despite all of the rising concern about proliferation, the number of nuclear-armed states or states deeply committed to achieving a nuclear capability has not grown. Indeed, over the last decade, the states that have abandoned nuclear weapons (Ukraine, Belarus, Kazakhstan, and South Africa) or nuclear weapons capabilities (Argentina, Brazil, and Libya) outnumber the states that have moved forward (North Korea and Iran). Over the last decade India and Pakistan became overt nuclear weapon states (though the tests they conducted in 1997 were clearly demonstration shots rather than developmental ones, aimed at revealing capabilities developed in preceding decades). The number of chemically armed states has not increased and may well have decreased as the CWC has been implemented. The number of states understood to be seeking or possessing biological weapons jumped dramatically in the early 1990s but seems to have held steady since then. These rough statistics suggest that whatever the various shortcomings of the tools of nonproliferation—and the rising debate about the efficacy of those tools—nonproliferation has enjoyed some important successes.

## Looking to the Future

Over the early decades of the nuclear era, a certain way of thinking about the weapons proliferation problem emerged and, despite various and sometimes intense debates, a significant measure of consensus emerged internationally and in the United States about the nature of the problem and what to do about it. In the period since the end of the Cold War, this consensus has given way to greater uncertainty and increasing division over the premises and principles of policy. Continuity of presidential commitment promises a measure of continuity in U.S. nonproliferation strategy. But it seems reasonable to anticipate an increasingly broad and deep debate about the fundamentals of proliferation and nonproliferation in the period ahead. In this author's view, that debate will revolve around the following core questions:

*What is the problem?* Writing more than four decades ago, Albert Wohlstetter provided a classic definition: "n plus one."[21] By this definition, the proliferation problem equates with the next state in line desiring to acquire nuclear weapons. In the wake of 9/11 another view of the problem has taken hold in some quarters, to the effect that "the problem" is no longer proliferation to states but has become proliferation to nonstate actors, even individual terrorists and criminal extortionists.

But these are both oversimplifications. Even in an era of rising concern about terrorist use of weapons of mass destruction, concern remains strong about the proliferation of nuclear weapons to additional states— hence President Bush's commitment to rollback of the so-called axis of evil. And n plus one touches on only one facet of the state proliferation problem. It is useful to think of different types of state problems. The vast majority of states would greatly prefer not to have nuclear weapons and not to live in a world in which they are a customary tool of security and war. A tiny number of states appear deeply committed to acquiring nuclear weapons—and even among these high-risk proliferators it would seem that some are more committed to being seen to be moving toward having a future capability than to actually possessing such weapons. Some larger number of states have forsworn nuclear weapons on a contingent basis—they have the technical sophistication to acquire such weapons but abstain because of feared negative consequences of nuclearization (and because some viable alternatives exist, such as alliance with the United States).[22] These states tend to develop latent capabilities as a hedge against a future breakdown in their security environment and the need to pursue an autonomous nuclear stance. In fact, many of them are "repentant nuclear powers" that have previously had nuclear ambitions but stopped short.[23]

In this world, many types of proliferation are possible: by the n plus one country, by the hedging latent states, in subregions such as East Asia where these factors coalesce, and more globally if proliferation patterns in different subregions interact with one another. Between n plus one and a complete breakdown of the prevailing nuclear order are many conceivable interim states. For example, a wave of nuclearization by states in East Asia is conceivable as is a separate wave in the Middle East; if both were to occur, the results would likely be felt elsewhere—e.g., Central Asia and Europe. The larger forms of breakdown spanning multiple regions and involving large, developed countries would seem to require a catalytic event of some kind. For the hedging latent states, the single most important factor would seem to be the United States. If the United States somehow discredits itself as a security guarantor, then such states are likely to question whether the United States can be an effective steward of their interests. Ironically, it might be years after such a breakdown before it was recognized as having happened—as the latent states covertly turn their weapons potential into breakout capabilities.

*What is winning (and is it possible)?* One version of "winning" the nonproliferation battle is defined as preventing n plus one, i.e., stopping the next states desirous of nuclear weapons from achieving that ambition. This is an important, indeed central, definition of winning, and it has sometimes proven possible to achieve. But as suggested above, there are other definitions of winning. One is ensuring that the latent hedgers do not choose to turn latent capabilities into overt ones, even in time of crisis. A variant of this is ensuring that the repentant powers do not turn recidivist.[24] Winning by this definition has obviously been possible, though the conditions of future success are unclear. Another definition of winning is ensuring that the large ranks of leaders of states opposed to nuclear weapons and hopeful of the future possibility of eliminating them from the affairs of states do not lose that hope and do not begin to think that they should invest in their own hedges against a future breakdown of the prevailing nuclear order. Winning here also looks promising but cannot be assumed. President Bush has reminded us of an important additional definition of winning: rollback, i.e., restoration of the status quo ante (i.e., the prenuclear status).

Secretary Rumsfeld has argued that the number of nuclear-armed states could double over the next decade (without any indication of what categories and calculations led him to this number).[25] One version of winning is limiting the damage to just a doubling. Another version is ending up a decade from now with even fewer nuclear-armed states—clearly the president's objective.

Consider for a moment the reverse question: What is losing? Losing means more than an incremental addition to the number of nuclear-armed states. It means rising fears of nuclear competition and war, as, for example, seen in South Asia since 1998. It means fears of the spillover effects from one subregion to another. More parochially, from a U.S. perspective, losing could mean also the partial eclipse of U.S. power. After all, if some of the "repentant" powers such as Japan or South Korea or Taiwan opt for nuclear weapons in reaction to some event(s) that has discredited the United States as a security guarantor, their decision to acquire nuclear weapons will reflect a loss of confidence in the United States and will signal an increased autonomy in their international relations. The United States may find them occasional willing partners in some U.S. initiative, but it seems less likely to be able to count on them as full allies in some new American project.

Moreover, the fact that they might have moved to nuclear status while under the cover of the U.S. nuclear umbrella would be interpreted by many international observers as a U.S. violation of the commitment under the NPT not to assist others to acquire nuclear weapons. If winning is possible, so too is "losing" as defined here, at a cost to U.S. political and security interests that is difficult to calculate.

Winning remains possible and should not be abandoned even in the face of setbacks on the n plus one" challenge.[26] In concluding its *National Strategy to Combat WMD,* the Bush White House has argued as follows: "The requirements to prevent, deter, defend against, and respond to today's WMD threats are complex and challenging. But they are not daunting. We can and will succeed in the tasks laid out in this strategy; we have no other choices."[27]

*What policy tools work best for nonproliferation?* Especially in recent years there has been a strong debate about whether political or military tools are better suited to deal with the proliferation problem. This question is a red herring. Different tools are suited to different challenges. Dissuading and deterring potential proliferators is best done with military capabilities that promise them defeat in war and successful rollback of one or two of the high-risk proliferators; such military prowess ought to have some positive impact on the thinking of other potential proliferators. Dissuasion and deterrence can be reinforced by political measures that promise exposure and punishment of illicit activities especially in the case of those states that pursue weapons not for purposes of national survival but for purposes of aggression and coercion.

On the other hand, assuring the repentant powers and other allies and friends of the United States that they remain secure without nuclear weapons is best done with political instruments—alliances, security guarantees, legal regimes, and other mechanisms for international security cooperation. "Best for what?" is the right answer to the question posed above. The glaring present shortcomings of treaty regimes in ensuring compliance by especially willful malefactors do not make them irrelevant to the other facets of the proliferation challenge—to reassuring the latent states and to facilitating international cooperation to deal with those other than the aggressive cheaters.

*Are multilateral approaches a help or a hindrance?* The traditional nonproliferation community has seen such approaches as the sine qua non of nonproliferation.[28] Some in the Bush administration have given a strong endorsement to multilateralism, while others have attacked it as a form of restraint on the exercise of American power.[29]

Multilateral approaches to proliferation encompass the specific treaty regimes, the ad hoc supporting mechanisms, and the international institutions such as the United Nations. The drawbacks to such approaches are numerous and well-known. Multilateral approaches are often reduced to the lowest common denominator, and what is possible often substitutes for what is necessary. Over the last decade multilateral approaches have been conspicuously ineffective at securing compliance by states such as Iraq and North Korea with self-accepted treaty obligations. And as the case of the UN Security Council debate on military action against Iraq suggests, multilateral approaches sometimes constrain American power. For all of the debate about the proper balance between unilateral and multilateral approaches, few in America would argue that unilateral action is never justifiable. The question for Americans then must be: What can multilateralism add beyond unilateralism?

Excessive unilateralism comes with its own costs: it suggests to many foreign observers that the global problem today is posed not by rogue regional challengers but by an unpredictable America that has put itself above the law in its pursuit of hegemony.[30] This may induce a new wave of proliferation, as others react to the increasing unpredictability of American power or arm themselves in fear of U.S. intervention.[31] Especially as the United States pursues an ambitious war against terror of global reach and as it confronts Iraq, North Korea, and potentially other WMD-armed regional powers, it has a strong interest in dampening fears that it will widen the war beyond the scope necessary to these ends and in refuting the argument that a rogue America is the new international security problem. Anchoring its actions in the legitimizing frameworks of multilateralism can help secure this interest. Secretary Rumsfeld has argued that proliferation

> is not a problem that individual nations can handle by themselves. ... We face three intersecting dangers today: the growing arsenal of rogue, failed or failing states; the exponential growth in trade among these states in WMD-related materials, technologies, and delivery capabilities; and the relationship between these state and terrorist networks that are seeking to obtain chemical and biological and nuclear material. If we are to deal with these new dangers, we need new tools of international cooperation, including new authorities to prevent—and, if necessary, interdict—the import, the export, and the transshipment of weapons of mass destruction, ballistic missiles, and WMD-related materials from and between and to terrorist states.[32]

He goes on to identify strengthening and reforming the institutions of multilateral action as a top priority.

*Do norms matter?* Underlying the debate about political measures and multilateral institutions is a debate about nonproliferation norms. Are they relevant to success in meeting the proliferation challenge?

Nonproliferation norms lack the coercive power of other tools of policy. The fact that they are not universally adhered to is what causes them to exist—behaviors exist that people find intolerable. But the importance of such norms is growing, not declining, in an era in which high-leverage technology is diffusing from states to nonstate organizations and even individuals. Views of right and wrong help to shape the behavior of individuals and organizations whose behaviors cannot be policed effectively all or any of the time.

U.S. policy makers tend to talk about the virtues of creating nonproliferation norms. But with rare exception, norms are not promulgated. They exist, as derived from human experience of things people consider wrong. The word itself derives from the Latin for a carpenter's set square. The set square tells the carpenter what a right angle is "expected and required" to be. … An international norm defines "expected and required" behavior in the society of states. The existence of a norm, at any level, does not imply permanence, still less divine edict.[33] Norms are an unreliable basis for persuading the malefactor to improve his behavior, because he sees his behavior as required and warranted by his circumstance. But without norms, no behavior is right or wrong, and thus no behavior can be punished. Norms are more reliable for promoting cooperation to deal with the malefactor than in affecting his behavior directly. In the current international climate of unipolarity, whenever the United States fails to explain its uses of powers in terms of accepted norms of international behavior, it undercuts these norms and fuels the perception that nothing more than a competition of power and interest is at stake.

*What role can and should the United States play?* In combating proliferation, the United States has no choice but to lead. If it abandons its leadership position, others can be expected to fill the gap with projects of their own, projects that cannot always be expected to show the same respect for U.S. interests as those conceived in Washington. But the ability of any other state or coalition of states to fill the gap is very doubtful. Sustained retreat by the United States from its historic leadership of the nonproliferation project could well help precipitate a breakdown of the prevailing nuclear order. Even if that breakdown would have many explanations, it seems highly likely that the blame for its breakdown would fall on Washington. After all, nuclear nonproliferation has been a special American project from the advent of the nuclear era, and American defection from this effort would lead others to predict the imminent collapse of existing approaches.[34] Moreover, as the most powerful actor in the international system, blame naturally attaches to the United States for any and all developments that others would have wished avoided.

What mode of leadership best suits U.S. interests in nonproliferation? The two White House strategy documents, the *National Security Strategy of the United States* (2002) and the *National Strategy for Combating Weapons of Mass Destruction* (2003), provide many useful answers. But leadership also requires an effort to build a shared vision of how to achieve desired objectives and a willingness to work at keeping people focused when distractions arise. Coming to a unified position on an approach to solving the weapons of mass destruction threat is difficult for we are not all of one mind on how best to pursue our nonproliferation goals. Indeed, there are entrenched and powerful opponents who provide a direct challenge to a president who seeks to lead a national strategy that is integrated, synergistic, and has the backing of the public.

The questions and answers provided in this chapter are constructed with a focus on nuclear weapons. Do they fit the other problems we face, especially the proliferation of biological weapons? The biological weapons proliferation problem is analogous to the nuclear problem in the sense that the number of proliferators remains few. There are perhaps a dozen or so states with biological weapons or actively seeking to acquire them. But the number could increase in different ways and over different thresholds in response to some catalytic event. Winning here means some rollback of the BW capabilities of specific actors (especially Russia, but also North Korea, Iran, and perhaps China). It also means accepting a high degree of latent capability among all states, given the diffusion of dual-use biotechnologies. In the biological weapons domain, both military and political tools are applicable, as in the nuclear domain. But the military tools remain badly underdeveloped, especially relative to the focus on nuclear security, and the political tools seem largely abandoned by an administration that sees the BTWC as unverifiable. Unilateral approaches cannot "solve" the biological weapons problem just as they cannot solve the nuclear one—but they have a role to play. Norms matter, even more in the biological weapons realm than in the nuclear, given the relative ease with which states and substate groups can produce and employ these weapons. Here as in the nuclear area, there is no substitute for U.S. leadership, as no other actor has a global view of the problem or a comprehensive view of the tool kit to work it.

The biological weapons problem seems, however, to hold out the possibility of future engagement with two new constituencies not relevant to the effort to prevent nuclear proliferation. One is the international scientific community seeking to develop biotechnologies for peaceful purposes. The other is the U.S. industrial community in the pharmaceutical, agricultural, and other domains that has a stake in promoting society's acceptance of its new products. Both of these constituencies resist engaging in the effort to police compliance with international norms against the misuse of their expertise, but both are increasingly essential as partners in that effort. The biotechnology revolution is making bioweapons more accessible to small states as well as terrorist groups. Thus, it is all the more important to bring scientists and biotech firms into new regimes.

To do so will require new thinking and new cooperation between the U.S. Government in partnership with key firms working together within a framework of guidelines and regulations designed to keep the BW genie in the bottle.

## The Next Strengthening Agenda

A decade or so ago the United States committed itself to leadership of an international effort to strengthen nonproliferation. Despite a widening and a deepening of debate about the fundamentals of strategy and policy, national leadership appears committed to sustained pursuit of nonproliferation objectives. Looking ahead another decade or so, how might the United States best focus its efforts to strengthen nonproliferation?

Part of the answer is found in the context of the treaty regimes. Despite some Bush administration misgivings about the shortcomings of multilateral arms control, the United States remains a party to the three core treaties and remains central to the effort to strengthen them. In 2005, states parties to the NPT will again convene in a review conference to evaluate progress in implementing the terms of the treaty, and a successful review conference will oblige Washington to have a strategy that takes account of the various developments since the 1995 review and extension conference, including U.S. rejection of the CTBT, the emergence of India and Pakistan as de facto nuclear weapon states, the Bush administration's Nuclear Posture Review and New Strategic Framework, and the challenges of rollback, as so far pursued against Iraq, Libya, Iran, and North Korea. Over the coming decade, most of the stockpiles of chemical weapons declared by states parties to the CWC will have been destroyed and the emphasis of states parties will shift increasingly to dealing with noncompliance and thus with challenge inspections. The effort to strengthen the BTWC will also continue, though it is unlikely that the Bush administration or its successors will easily be persuaded that the treaty can be made verifiable at a cost that the United States (and others) are willing to pay—a fact that could help keep states parties focused on myriad other projects of utility to the regime.

But, of course, treaty regimes are only part of the "answer." Expect continued efforts to tighten export controls and the associated ad hoc coordinating mechanisms—as well as continued frustration with the utility of such measures in an era of globalization and a broadening array of dual-use (civil-military) technologies.

Expect also continued efforts to promote international partnerships to deal with particular problems—partnership, for example, with Russia and China and with other conduits of weapons of mass destruction technology and expertise to proliferators. Expect continued efforts to interdict shipments of sensitive materials, technologies, and weapons when other measures have failed.

An important new question has emerged about how to reap the benefits for nonproliferation of the Bush administration's efforts to confront "gathering threats at the crossroads of technology and tyranny." Some in the administration have spoken privately about their hope that these efforts will "reset" international norms by demonstrating that the United States in partnerships with coalitions of the willing will see to it that flagrant violations will not go unpunished. In other words, having eliminated the Taliban, suppressed al-Qaeda, driven Saddam from power in Iraq, and tightened political and economic pressures on North Korea and Iran, are there opportunities now to roll back others without recourse to war and to reinforce nonproliferation more broadly?

Richard Perle, among others, has offered up one logical implication: that other proliferators, watching military action against these actors, ought to conclude that the possible costs of weapons of mass destruction far outweigh the benefits and, thus, the next round of proliferators ought to be dissuaded by the action of the Bush administration.[35] Libya's decision to give up its nuclear program would seem to buttress this claim. Of course, some (such as North Korea) may conclude that they had better rush to complete nuclearization before they face serious prospect of a U.S. effort to remove their regime.

Another possibility is that other states will come to appreciate the seriousness of the United States in its desire to confront weapons of mass destruction proliferators and will no longer object to U.S.–led efforts to pressure those suspected of noncompliance. This message may be especially powerful for Moscow and Beijing, who also desire greater partnership with Washington on various other concerns. Of course, success in this regard would seem to require some vindication of the intelligence that led to Bush administration claims that Iraq possessed weapons of mass destruction. Failing to uncover such vindication, the United States may find it considerably more difficult to build such coalitions in the future.

These possibilities suggest that the future focus of U.S. policy makers will remain on the challenges of compliance and not on the challenges of constructing new pieces of the nonproliferation architecture. But to a significant extent, this would seem to depend on the political winds.

## Conclusions

After a decade or so of intensifying debate about the means and ends of nonproliferation, remarkable continuity prevails in the main scope and thrust of policy. Despite debate about whether winning is possible, judging by its actions the United States remains strongly committed to winning. Despite debate about whether nonproliferation is an anachronistic concept with roots in an era now past, the United States remains committed to the effort to strengthen nonproliferation mechanisms. Despite debate about the proper balance between military and political tools of policy, there is broad consensus that both sets of tools are necessary to deal with the various facets of the nonproliferation problem.

Events may trigger new nonproliferation possibilities in the future. For example, if there were a major use of nuclear, biological, or chemical weapons, whether by a state or terrorist group, this could create new dynamics, including perhaps new demands and opportunities for increased international cooperation and perhaps also increased regulation of sensitive industries (e.g., biotechnology, pharmaceutical plants, chemical factories, and the nuclear power industry). It could also create a new potential for armed conflict, especially if a state made the attack or is believed to have assisted.

A consistent long-term U.S. goal of this importance deserves consistent, strong policy support, especially in the face of what seems to be a growing proliferation challenge. But looking to the future, continued debate about both the means and ends of policy seems likely—with a harmful effect on the ability of the United States to achieve its objectives and to lead others toward that end. Indeed, fundamental questions deserve broader and deeper exploration as the Cold War recedes further into the past and the new challenges of technology diffusion, mass casualty terrorism, and weak and collapsing states come into sharper focus. But for the coming decade at least it seems that no American president will want to be tarnished with a rapid and broad proliferation of nuclear weapons. As the *National Strategy to Combat WMD* concludes, there is too much at stake for the United States to allow this to come to pass.

CHAPTER **5**

# Progress in Counterforce 1993–2004

*Barry R. Schneider*

Counterforce targeting is one of the important means of removing potential weapons of mass destruction (WMD) threats to the United States and its allies and is one of the multiple means available to thin out the weapons of mass destruction threat.

To fully understand what progress the United States has made in counterforce capability, as well as the continuing shortfalls and the way ahead, one has to search for answers to a few key questions, namely,

- What would the ideal counterforce capability entail?
- How has weapons accuracy changed warfare?
- What are the implications of stealth technology for counterforce?
- How can the U.S. military neutralize deeply buried hardened facilities, and what challenges do these present to U.S. forces?
- How can the U.S. military defeat the threat of adversary missiles fired from transporter erector launchers (TELs)? How capable are we at present? What needs to be done to neutralize such future "Scud hunt" threats?
- How can the U.S. military eliminate enemy WMD assets without major collateral damage? How far have we come in creating thermobaric and agent defeat weapons for this purpose?
- What strides has the United States taken in science and technology to improve U.S. counterforce weapons capability?
- What advantages do new U.S. counterforce targeting planning tools such as the Counterproliferation Analysis and Planning System (CAPS) provide to commanders?
- When should and should not the U.S. leadership elect to employ counterforce attacks in a preemptive or preventive war mode?

- Finally, what future steps in organizing, training, and equipping U.S. forces need to be taken to make U.S. counterforce capabilities adequate to the challenges of finding, fixing, tracking, targeting, assessing, and engaging adversary WMD and other military assets in a time of war?

## The Ideal Counterforce Capability

If one wanted to construct the ideal U.S. counterforce capability against potential adversary WMD assets, what might be its attributes? Clearly, one thing that would be essential to have is accurate target information. U.S. targeteers would need answers to such questions as follow:

Where, precisely, are all the weapons, production facilities, storage facilities, and launchers?

What are the vulnerabilities of these assets?

How could these assets be destroyed?

Is a direct kill possible? If so, how? Or, must we be satisfied with inflicting a functional defeat? If so, how?

In the case of attacking mobile or relocatable targets, how long do we have before they are likely to move again?

If the target is a TEL about to launch a missile, how long is that launch cycle?

If the target is a production or storage facility for WMD assets, what kinds of U.S. agent defeat weapons would be effective in either destroying it, disabling it, or denying access to it in such a way as to prevent collateral damage to adjacent civilians or friendly forces in the region?

Further,

How do we assess the results of strikes on known or suspected WMD targets, especially strikes with standoff weapon systems?

Have these strikes released WMD agents into the atmosphere? What agent? How much? Where is it going?

These questions are very hard to answer with current capabilities. Clearly, you cannot target enemy weapons of mass destruction if you do not know where they are. Nor can you efficiently negate them if you are uncertain about target characteristics or the results of your own strikes against such targets.

In addition to ascertaining precise target coordinates and characteristics, the ideal counterforce fighting force should be able to deliver its blows with great accuracy. Counterforce units will need precision-guided munitions (PGMs) to hit the bull's-eye when the balloon goes up.

Also required, when striking at such important targets, is a force that can apply discriminate lethality for tailored effects and minimal collateral damage. To get to targets before they are launched or moved, the ideal counterforce strike should minimize the time to target. Counterforce weapons should be able to penetrate unharmed to target, maintain all-weather precision, operate from extended range if necessary, or to be present continuously over likely target sets to reduce the sensor-to-shooter-to-target times. The counterforce weapon system used should match the appropriate weapon to each target to achieve the effects sought. Further, the ideal counterforce attack plan will minimize the dangers to aircrews and ground units utilized in the attacks.[1]

Finally, for counterforce operations to be optimally employed, the United States needs a strategy and military doctrine that guides when, where, and how such counterforce actions should be triggered by top U.S. decision makers. Further, reasoned decisions will be improved if policy makers address some key questions before deciding on a particular course of action.

In the years since Operation Desert Storm, the U.S. military has dramatically improved its counterforce capabilities. Several areas deserve particular emphasis, such as the revolutions in accuracy, stealth, penetrating warheads, other hard target defeat tools, various programs to track and destroy mobile missile launchers, agent defeat weapons, and analytic tools to assist the targeteer. Perhaps the single most significant improvement to the U.S. capability to attack and destroy enemy weapons of mass destruction targets in wartime is in the realm of accuracy.

## The Revolution in Accuracy

There was a quantum leap in improvements in bombing accuracy from World War II to Desert Storm. A similar improvement in bombing accuracy and lethality occurred between Operation Desert Storm (1991) and Operation Iraqi Freedom (2003), as U.S. forces employed far more PGMs than were used in the first Gulf War.

During World War II very few aerial bombs dropped by aircraft ever hit their target. As many as a thousand sorties might be needed to destroy a single target in the era of the "dumb" bomb. Indeed, according to the United States Strategic Bombing Survey, issued at the end of the conflict, only about one in five bombs ever landed within 1,000 feet of their intended targets.[2]

In World War II targeteers talked in terms of numbers of sorties per target destroyed. Today, with the advent of smart weapons with great accuracy and lethality, targeting specialists speak of targets destroyed per sortie since a single aircraft may destroy multiple targets in a single flight.

As Lieutenant General David A. Deptula, USAF, has noted, "even when control of the air was wrested from the Luftwaffe in the spring of 1944 and allied aircraft were free to roam the Axis skies, the level of 'precision' bombing still required a thousand aircraft to succeed against one target."[3]

During the last years of World War II, even with air superiority, Allied bomber attacks against various German industrial sectors took months of bombing to achieve even modest success against fixed targets. Massed air attacks and tons of bombs were required to eliminate targets such as a bridge or a factory.[4]

The progressive introduction of precision-guided munitions into the inventory has allowed the U.S. military to substitute precision for sheer tonnage and has reduced dramatically the numbers of sorties required. Precision weapons have given a new meaning to the concept of *mass*. As Lieutenant General (USAF–Ret) Buster Glosson noted, "what we historically achieved with volume we now can accomplish with precision."[5] General Deptula estimates that whereas 1,000 B-17 sorties dropping 2,000-pound bombs were required to destroy one target in World War II, only 20 F-4 sorties, dropping 176 of the first laser-guided bombs, were needed in Vietnam to accomplish the same task.[6] By 1991, only one F-117 dropping two PGMs could destroy two targets. By 1998, in the air war against Serbia, a B-2 bomber was capable of destroying 16 individual targets with bombs launched in a single sortie.[7]

The circular error of probability of such weapons had shrunk from 3,200 feet in 1943 to 20 feet by 1998. This increased accuracy made PGMs the weapons of choice as they became available. By the time of Desert Storm in 1991, as one commander noted, "of the 85,000 tons of bombs used in the Gulf War, only 8,000 tons ... were PGMs, yet they accounted for nearly 75 percent of the damage."[8] Note the evolution of PGMs' use from Desert Storm to the Kosovo air war in Table 5.1 below. By the time of Operation Iraqi Freedom in 2003, PGMs were used most of the time.

**Table 5.1** U.S. Airpower in Recent Regional Conflicts[9]

|  | Desert Storm | Serbia/ Kosovo | Afghanistan |
|---|---|---|---|
| **Precision-Guided Bombs Delivered** | 20,450 | 8,050 | 12,500 |
| **Percentage of Total Munitions That Are Precision Guided** | 7 to 8 percent | 35 percent | 56 percent |
| **Percentage of Precision-Guided Weapons Delivered by the United States (versus others in coalition)** | 89 percent | 80 percent | 99 percent |

Precision-guided munitions make up the majority of the overall U.S. munitions budget. As one report states, "dozens of smart-munitions programs are in development or production today by the Army, Navy, and Air Force. About 60 percent of the munitions budget is spent on precision-guided weapons, and that 60-40[10] breakdown is expected to continue in the foreseeable future."[11]

Precision-guided munitions can provide a number of battlefield advantages over less accurate arms. First, PGMs can reduce collateral damage, allowing commanders to strike enemy targets that are near the civilian population or near sensitive cultural assets such as churches, mosques, cultural symbols, hospitals, schools, and businesses, while minimizing noncombatant casualties and avoiding destruction of valued nonmilitary facilities.

Second, PGMs can more rapidly quiet enemy firepower by employing more effective targeting and less ordnance. PGMs allow more standoff target kills, responsive kills, and one-shot kills. They also allow commanders to send missiles and guided bombs rather than men and women aviators against targets, thus reducing allied casualties while accelerating the engagement and defeat of enemy forces. As General Glosson has written, "each (WWII) Schweinfurt raid placed 3,000 airmen in harm's way. Today, we can do the same job with just two airmen."[12]

Third, the widespread use of PGMs reduces the logistics tail of friendly forces. Accurate "smart" weapons can inflict damage equivalent to that of much larger numbers of dumb munitions.

Smart bombs also reduce the inventory of bombs needed to destroy a given set of targets. General Glosson noted that, "according to the Gulf War Air Power Survey data base, we used approximately 180 tons of precision munitions a day in Desert Storm. Our airlift capacity from the continental United States (CONUS) to Southwest Asia was 6,500 tons a day. Nine C-141s (of the 234 available) a day could supply the daily precision-guided munitions expenditures of Desert Storm."[13] PGMs provide orders of magnitude increases in per-weapon lethality and far fewer weapons are needed to accomplish the same objectives. In summary, PGMs reduce collateral damage, improve lethality, enhance survivability, reduce logistical demands, and accelerate enemy defeat.

One such precision-guided munition, the Joint Direct Attack Munition (JDAM), has had a particularly dramatic impact on targeting effectiveness. As General Glosson summarizes, the JDAM "will allow a single B-2 to precisely destroy 16 separate targets on a single pass."[14] The JDAM guidance kit converts existing unguided bombs (dumb bombs) in the inventory into precision-guided smart munitions. The tail section of JDAMs contains a global positioning system (GPS) and an inertial navigational system that can guide either the 2,000-pound MK 84 or the 1,000-pound MK 83 warheads to target when air launched against ground targets by an F/A-18 aircraft. Testing of JDAMs indicates they have a 95 percent system reliability and are accurate to within nine meters in all kinds of weather.[15]

Between 1997 and 2003, the United States had acquired 87,000 JDAMs in its inventory and it became a weapon of choice against many targets in Operation Iraqi Freedom in 2003, dropped by B-52s, B1-Bs, B-2s, F-15s, F-16s, and F/A-18s.

However, the JDAM is just one of a large family of new U.S. smart weapons or PGMs employed in the U.S. inventory and improved in the past decade to provide greater accuracy and lethality with far fewer weapons employed.[16] General Glosson noted that "the Joint Standoff Weapon (JSOW), coupled with the Sensor-Fuzed Weapon (SFW), would leave destroyed the armor of the Iraqi Hammurabi and Medinah divisions, if they had been available in Desert Storm. This would have prevented their use in quelling the Shiite rebellion after the 1991 Gulf War."[17] These Iraqi Republican Guard Armor Divisions were destroyed by such PGMs in Operation Iraqi Freedom 12 years later.

Further, in the past decade, the United States also has developed and acquired over 60,000 PGMs.[18]

This PGM revolution, in sum, means that the U.S. and allied militaries will be able to achieve targeting objectives utilizing far fewer flights while achieving more targets killed per delivery.

## Implications of Stealth for Counterforce Targeting

This revolution in accuracy and accompanying lethality has also been coupled with a significant improvement in the ability of air forces to penetrate unscathed to a target through the introduction of new stealth technology. As General Deptula has stated, stealthy aircraft like the F-117 flew only 2 percent of the combat sorties in Desert Storm, yet accounted for 43 percent of the targets stuck, since they were all but invisible to Iraqi air defense radars.[19] Stealth allows full penetration to optimal launch points and helps ensure survivability of the aircraft and crew during the mission. Thus, the combination of weapons lethality gained by accuracy, and bomber survivability gained by stealthiness, maximizes the counterforce capabilities of U.S. air forces, a revolution augmented by robust acquisition programs in the 15 years since Desert Storm (in 1991).

## Solving the Challenge of Hardened, Deeply Buried Targets

As the United States improves its counterforce weapons by drastic improvements in stealth and accuracy, adversaries are countering U.S.

capabilities by placing their own weapons, production facilities, storage facilities, and command and control assets inside hardened and, at times, deeply buried facilities. U.S. precision-guided munitions and air superiority have sparked a "mole" response as adversaries have taken to tunnels, caverns, deep underground bunkers, and cut-and-cover facilities.

These underground facilities are likely to be shielding high-value time-sensitive enemy assets such as their

- leaders and top staff;
- command, control, and communications centers;
- weapons of mass destruction;
- nuclear enrichment assets;
- WMD munitions storage;
- TELs; and
- chemical, biological, radiological, and nuclear (CBRN) production facilities.

As one Department of Defense (DoD) report states,

the limitations of weapons capabilities during the (1991) Gulf War, as well as the increasing availability of advanced tunneling technologies, have brought about a clear worldwide trend in tunneling to protect facilities. Hardened cut-and-cover facilities may be vulnerable to current air-to-surface conventional penetrations but remain a substantial challenge when standoff attack is desired. Some facilities housed in tunnels or deep underground shelters, however, are nearly invulnerable to direct attack by conventional means.[20]

Potential military adversaries such as North Korea have turned to tunnels and hard and deeply buried facilities to shield their military forces from the ever-more lethal PGMs of the United States.

Reportedly,

more than 70 countries now use underground facilities (UGFs) for military purposes. In June 1998, the Defense Science Board Task Force on Underground Facilities states that there are now over 10,000 underground facilities worldwide. Approximately 1,100 underground facilities were known or suspected strategic (WMD, ballistic missile basing, leadership or top echelon command and control) sites. Updated estimates [from the] Defense Intelligence Agency reveal this number has now grown to over 1,400. A majority of the strategic facilities are deep underground facilities.[21]

During World War II, the German high command shielded itself from Allied bombing by building a series of leadership bunkers. Indeed, Adolf Hitler died in his bunker as Allied forces closed in around him in the spring of 1945. During the Vietnam War, the Viet Minh and Viet Cong made frequent use of tunnels to hide forces, weapons caches, and to provide secure transportation routes. During the Cold War, Soviet leaders and forces attempted to protect themselves from possible attack by building thousands of hardened bunkers and underground facilities to try to place themselves in safe positions. Similarly, the U.S. leadership, beginning with the Eisenhower administration in the 1950s, built a network of leadership and critical asset shelters in a Federal Relocation Arc, around Washington, D.C., 50 or more miles outside the city, scattered throughout the countryside in an area including North Carolina, West Virginia, Virginia, Maryland, Pennsylvania, and the District of Columbia, to protect against a possible Soviet attack.[22]

Intercontinental ballistic missile forces on both sides were placed in hardened silos in an attempt to protect them against possible attacks, ranging all the way from those that could withstand a few hundred pounds per square inch (psi) of overpressure to some that would remain intact and withstand up to 100,000 psi of overpressure.

When the U.S. Peacekeeper (MX) missile was in development, over 30 different basing modes were explored, most of which looked at some form of protected basing such as in hardened silos, tunnels drilled into hillsides, or deeply buried facilities inside a butte or mountain. Survivability, in many of the basing modes explored, used a combination of hardening, mobility, and location deception.

Muammar Qaddafi in Libya has built a huge underground facility at Tarjunah and has since admitted that this was one of two chemical weapons manufacturing and storage sites. (Qaddafi showed a willingness in 2004 to roll back his weapons of mass destruction programs, cooperating in their dismantlement.) North Korea has built many thousands of hardened tunnels and hardened underground shelters for its artillery, missiles, and leadership. Saddam Hussein's regime also went underground into bunkers beneath buildings to escape the potential wrath of a U.S. adversary, and such facilities became important targets of General Tommy R. Franks and his targeteers from U.S. Central Command in Operation Iraqi Freedom.

In the past decade, the U.S. Department of Defense has initiated the Hard and Deeply Buried Target Capability (HDBTC) program "to develop conventional (non-nuclear) weapons systems capable of denying access to, disrupting operations of, or destroying defended, hard and deeply buried facilities."[23]

One of the counterforce achievements of the past 13 years, since the inception of the DoD Counterproliferation Initiative in late 1993, has been the initiation of the DoD Tunnel Defeat Demonstration Program that "seeks to develop, assess, and demonstrate end-to-end targeting capabilities (from detecting, identifying, and characterizing facilities to targeting, attacking, and performing damage assessment) across all warfighting options."[24]

Detection of deeply buried hardened facilities can be done by access to human intelligence, by remote sensors that record construction or operations, or by close-in inspections that uncover the presence of power lines, sewage systems, water pipes, camouflaged antennas, air vents, entrances, exits, and telltale heat, and acoustical, electromagnetic, or other emissions. Details of underground layouts might be acquired by getting blueprints from the foreign contractors originally involved in constructing the facility or by educated guesses based on the standard layout done by the relevant contractor in previous projects.

Hiding the existence of tunnels, cut-and-cover[25] facilities, and deeply buried bunkers can become a cat-and-mouse game as rival "hiders" are pitted against the intelligence, surveillance, and reconnaissance (ISR) "seekers" of the United States. Adversaries, for example, become aware of the times when U.S. reconnaissance and surveillance satellites pass overhead and may do their construction work or operations only when they believe they will be unobserved.

In this contest of hiders and seekers, U.S. intelligence, surveillance, and reconnaissance technologies have improved significantly over the past 13 years since Secretary of Defense Aspin announced the DoD Counterproliferation Initiative in December 1993. First, satellite sensors have been improved as multispectral sensors have been developed and deployed since 1993. The view from high altitudes has come into increasingly sharp relief.

The U.S. Department of Defense, over the past decade, has made improvements in the ability to measure hot spots, gravitational fields, electrical fields, magnetic fields, seismic tremors, radioactive emissions, sonar pings, ground shock movements, biological and chemical agent presence, and other indicators. Moreover, ground-penetrating radars can give indications of underground structures and voids, and multispectral sensors can detect an array of smells, emissions, noises, and vibrations that help to locate and characterize subsurface operations and structures.

Further, the United States has now developed an improved and very capable group of unmanned aerial vehicles (UAVs) such as Predator and Global Hawk to loiter over suspect sites and provide more constant coverage of activities on the surface and near entrances to underground facilities. This increased overhead presence makes it increasingly difficult for an adversary to build and operate from tunnels and underground facilities without detection.

Characterizing the nature of the hidden site is still problematic for the seeker, although a mixture of technologies can help solve the puzzle, including improved seismometers, gravimeters, instruments that map the electromagnetic field of a site, and other remote types of sensors. In the past 13 years, progress has been made in the technologies employed to characterize underground facilities from either the surface or the atmosphere, although this is far from an exact science and hiders have great advantages over seekers in this arena. Hiders can make the opponent's (e.g., the United States seeker) job even more difficult by masking, camouflage, decoys, deception, insulating hot areas, covering sharp edges, and painting surface equipment in earth hues.

Even if a hardened tunnel or underground facility has been identified, located, and accurately characterized, it may still be difficult to defeat. Any deeply buried facility with 2,000 feet or more of overburden may be invulnerable to a direct attack even if nuclear weapons were employed.

The U.S. counterforce attack may attempt either a direct attack aimed at destroying the facility altogether or a functional defeat attack aimed at causing "a militarily significant reduction in its capacity to perform its function for a militarily significant period of time."[26]

A functional defeat may be achieved by various means: closing ingress/egress portals, destroying external umbilicals such as electrical power lines, phone lines, and radio antennas, or by denying life-support systems relating to air and water supplies. Internal equipment might be caused to malfunction due to blast vibrations that were too weak to destroy the structure but which, nevertheless, might disable the technology within it. Also, entombment can inflict a functional defeat as effectively as crushing the facility through blast overpressure.

A good deal of original thought has gone into the analysis of ways to defeat buried hardened facilities in wartime. In addition to use of earth penetrators or other explosive means to penetrate the overburden and crack or shatter the structure, counterforce analysts have examined ways of sealing vents and exits, cutting off the power, water, air, and sewage flows, and of entombing the complex. Thought has been given to the use of insulation foam to seal openings and tunnels. Fuel air explosives might be used to suck up the oxygen within a complex, and mobile robotic probes and sensors could allow invaders to preexplore tunnels and openings. Were it not prohibited by the Chemical Weapons Convention or the Biological Weapons Convention, incapacitating agents, choking gas, narcotics, sleep agents, and other toxins might be forced deep into the underground voids via air vents. Other vent weapons might include use of acoustical arms, tear gas, smoke, molds, allergens, mildews, or fungi. Further, the underground or tunnel facilities might be shorn of electrical power by use of electromagnetic pulses, cutting power lines, destroying electrical nodes, or by microwave attacks. Computer systems within the protected shelters could be neutralized by either destroying their antennas, cutting power, or introducing computer viruses.

Unfortunately, once a hardened tunnel or underground complex has been struck, our battle damage assessment (BDA) is still relatively primitive and inadequate for discerning what the effect was inside the targeted tunnel or underground shelter. Yet, BDAs need to be accurate if the United States and its allies are to continue to disable the enemy site through timely restrikes and stay ahead of the enemy by blocking his efforts to dig out after the facility's portals have been closed.

The longer the United States has had to identify, characterize, and plan either a functional or destructive strike on a given hardened buried target, in most cases the greater its probability of wartime success against it. The past decade has seen an arms race of sorts between the moles in states of concern and the growth of U.S. PGM and ISR capacity. At this juncture it is not clear whether, in a net assessment, the defense or the offense has made a significant gain. Identifying, characterizing, and killing a hard target set, especially one drilled into the side of mountains or constructed deep underground, are still very difficult problems just as in 1993, and much counterforce research and development work still need to be done to change that fact.

In short, while the United States has come a considerable distance since 1993 in its ability to identify, locate, characterize, attack, and assess damage, it still has far to go since adversaries continue to respond asymmetrically to great U.S. advantages in airpower, intelligence, surveillance, and reconnaissance, and to U.S. precision-guided munitions by going underground and hardening their facilities to protect their weapons, leadership, and industry.

## Solving the Challenge of Targeting Mobile Missile Launchers

During Desert Storm the United States' military capability to counter the Iraqi missile threat was very limited. Iraq launched 88 Scud-type ballistic missiles, 42 of which were aimed at Israel. According to the Gulf War Air Power Survey (GWAPS), coalition forces directed 1,500 air sorties against Iraqi missile launchers. Despite these numerous air strikes, GWAPS concluded that not a single Scud launcher kill could be confirmed.[27] This finding was disputed by General Wayne Downing, (USA–Ret), commander of U.S. Special Operations Forces (SOF) in Desert Storm, who asserts that SOF "took out six to eight Scuds, including a couple destroyed by anti-tank missiles launched by the teams."[28]

Nevertheless, the Gulf War Air Power Survey indicated that

[t]he actual destruction of any Iraqi mobile launchers by fixed-wing coalition aircraft remains impossible to confirm. Coalition aircrews reported destroying about eighty mobile launchers. Special operations forces claimed another score or so. Most of these reports undoubtedly stemmed from attacks that did destroy objects in the Scud launcher area. But most, if not all, of the objects involved now appear to have been decoys, vehicles such as tanker trucks that had infrared and radar signatures impossible to distinguish from those of

mobile launchers and their associated support vehicles, and other objects unfortunate enough to provide "Scud-like" signatures.[29]

The best that could be said about the intensive allied Scud hunt of Desert Storm, even if it resulted in few or zero kills, is that the operation at least kept the Iraqi Scud-launch teams continually moving, hiding, and taking evasive actions. It almost surely reduced Iraq fire rates and the number of salvos.

During the 1991 war with Iraq, allied forces allocated about 5 percent of all aircraft sorties in the counter-Scud offensive. However, several factors accounted for the meager results. Iraqi mobile TEL survival strategies included the following:

- shoot and scoot tactics;
- use of decoys and other camouflage, concealment, and deception techniques;
- hide sites (under bridges, inside buildings, and in tunnels);
- use of fixed sites as target magnets to draw off enemy resources otherwise devoted to destroying mobile missile launchers; and
- rapid launch sequences to limit "dwell time."

Further, the allied forces in Desert Storm hindered their own efforts by not taking the Scud threat seriously at the inception of the planning process, by not deploying maximum Special Operations Forces into the Iraqi desert at the beginning to ferret out Scud transporter-erector-launcher locations, and by a sensor-to-shooter time lag of 60 minutes. The present goal is to try to reduce this sensor-to-shooter time to 15 minutes or less in order to get within the enemy firing cycle and to destroy the mobile missile launchers, once pinpointed, before they can move and relocate.

In addition, the Scud hunt against mobile missile launchers in 1991 ignored the use of some of the available sensor/platform technology that had proven effective in tests, but which had not yet been deployed. The officer in charge of the 1991 Scud hunt air campaign had never previously commanded or participated in plans or exercises designed to destroy mobile missile launchers.

During Desert Storm the primary mission for both the United States' Delta Forces and the United Kingdom's Special Air Service was to locate and then designate targets for coalition aircraft such as U.S. Air Force A-10s, F-15s, F-16s, Air Force Special Operations Command C-130 gunships, and MH-53J Pave Lows. Delta Forces on the ground were also equipped with 50-caliber sniper rifles to target Iraqi missiles, launchers, and their teams. Unfortunately, Allied Special Forces could rarely get within rifle range and the aircraft response times averaged an hour, permitting the Iraqi mobile launch teams to fire and move away before coalition land and air forces could close in and destroy them.

## U.S. Scud Hunt Needs and Shortfalls

Considerable technical progress can be reported in developing new U.S. technologies and concepts of operation to be successful in future engagements against an enemy operating with ballistic missiles launched by a mobile transporter erector launcher.

To succeed against the mobile "Scud-type" threat the United States needs to be able to do the following:

- improve its persistent and mission-dedicated intelligence, surveillance, and reconnaissance capabilities to locate enemy mobile missile launchers in a timely, targetable way;
- preemptively destroy suspected enemy hide sites or potential hide sites in the expected launch zone;
- shorten the sensor-to-shooter handoff time to 15 minutes or less;
- prioritize Scud hunt missions in the Air Tasking Order (ATO); and
- organize, train, and equip joint air assets, intelligence, surveillance, and reconnaissance assets, and SOF ground assets for this role.

There are certain deficiencies in the Scud hunt capabilities that need to be corrected to provide nuclear, biological, chemical, and missile (NBC/M) counterforce against such time-sensitive, time-critical targets. As Lieutenant Colonel Tim Lindemann has summarized in a study of U.S. counterforce capabilities,

> Warfighting commands and service planners have done a thorough job of identifying and analyzing capability gaps—or unfulfilled needs—of NBC/M mobile targeting. With regard to intelligence, reconnaissance, and surveillance these needs consistently include:
>
> - intelligence preparation that supports pre-launch operations;
> - wide area surveillance;
> - rapid sensor retasking;
> - precise target location;
> - tracking, classification, and identification;
> - data exchange and cross-cueing between sensors; and
> - foliage penetration.[30]

With regard to battle management and command, control, and communications, Lieutenant Colonel Lindemann indicates that the needs include the following:

- rapid data exchange between platforms;
- automated battle management tools for data fusion;
- target tracking; and
- tasking (dynamic battle management);
- a common view of the battlespace (i.e., a common operational/tactical picture); and
- integrated fire control of service platforms.[31]

Still, a challenge is the job of finding and fixing the Scud transporter-erector-launcher targets or the infrastructure that supports such systems (e.g., garages, roads, hide sites, command and control, maintenance, logistics, etc.). The current buzzword to improve battle management and targeting is "horizontal fusion" or integration of all sources of data and from all sensor suites to facilitate the intelligence preparation of the battle space, intelligence, surveillance, and reconnaissance collection planning, dynamic cueing, target data fusion, target data identification, and target data validation. These data must be synthesized and translated into usable targeting information to be used by the shooters.

To provide more persistent overhead intelligence, surveillance, and reconnaissance capabilities it is suggested that more airborne platforms, including attack aircraft and tankers, carry sensors. Likewise, some additional assets designed for ISR purposes might be equipped as shooters as well (e.g., such has been done with the Predator). All airborne platforms would become multipurpose to facilitate the Scud hunts of the future.

The intelligence challenge will be to provide the war fighter with a global situation awareness and persistent surveillance of the battle space. Finally, as Lindemann has suggested regarding weapon systems, the needs consistently include the following:

- Having sufficient [and] numerous theater air assets assigned to the Scud Hunt mission;
- ability to acquire, identify, and engage targets in an adverse weather environment;
- having enough attack aircraft to cover all the "kill boxes" on the map;
- having enough intelligence, surveillance, and reconnaissance assets to discover the presence of Scud transporter-erector-launchers in "kill boxes" on a continuous basis;
- having highly responsive shooters with available weapons accepting in-flight target updates;
- employment of automatic target recognition capabilities;
- having shooters in close proximity to targets when needed; and

- weapons must be capable of neutralizing nuclear, biological, and chemical agents without excessive collateral damage.[32]

Prior to the launch of Operation Iraqi Freedom, U.S. forces practiced against mobile transporter-erector-launcher targets at a CONUS air-base location to perfect teamwork and attack operations against possible Iraqi transporter erector launchers. This practice and certain other practices led U.S. commanders to believe they would do significantly better in Scud hunting in Operation Iraqi Freedom than was the case in Operation Desert Storm. The possible outcome will never be known because no Iraqi Scuds surfaced to fight in Operation Iraqi Freedom.

Nevertheless, unlike Operation Desert Storm, in Operation Iraqi Freedom numerous Special Operations Forces teams were deployed forward at the outset of hostilities, U.S. attack aircraft were better trained to engage mobile missile launchers, U.S. ISR assets were improved and more persistently in place over the target zones, and the intelligence team assembled before and during the operation better prepared the battle space, fused the various collections of intelligence data, and better prepared the target characteristics for the ATOs that followed.

During the Operation Iraqi Freedom Scud hunt operation, the Time-Sensitive Targeting cell of the Combined Air Operations Center did, indeed, become such a potential force multiplier that it could be considered a weapons system in its own right. A tactical ballistic missile intelligence federation made up of 15 different intelligence agencies and operational commands combined to do the intelligence preparation of the battle space for Operation Iraqi Freedom. Potential launch areas or "Scud baskets" were identified. Geospatial data and analysis were generated to identify roads and paths Scud transporter erector launchers might traverse or potential hide sites. Intelligence on the potential Iraqi missile order of battle was combined with named areas of interest, coordinates were assigned, and "kill boxes" were identified and plotted. Then, had an engagement with Iraqi Scud transporter erector launchers taken place in Operation Iraqi Freedom (OIF), the triad of ISR, Special Operations Forces, and attack platforms would have combined to attempt to destroy the Scud threat.

Despite some significant advances over the first Gulf War Scud hunt operations, OIF success still would have been limited by such problems as follow:

- limited nighttime surveillance,
- limited sensor capabilities,
- inability of ISR assets to monitor launch areas, persistently, and
- too few attack aircraft were available to cover the entire potential launch areas.[33]

At present, the United States is making a number of upgrades to its Scud hunting/mobile targeting capabilities. One such very recent program upgrade is the Predator unmanned aerial vehicle equipped with two Hellfire Thermobaric Blast/Frag warheads upgrade to target and defeat highly mobile or relocatable targets.[34] Another such program is the USAF Low Cost Autonomous Attack System (LOCASS), an affordable precision-attack guided munition capable of broad area search for transporter erector launchers and a system that can execute both the location and destruction missions.

As currently envisioned, LOCASS is a turbojet powered, GPS navigated, and Laser Detection and Ranging guided munition. It has a 90–100+ nautical mile range and has 30 minutes of powered flight. It can be used as a standoff weapon, can be launched from an aircraft or missile, and can use its Automatic Target Recognition feature to engage in a target search and close to destroy the targets located and identified.[35]

To improve the nation's Scud hunting capabilities, the United States needs to improve in four operational areas of the so-called "kill chain": target sensing, attack decisions, target engagement, and poststrike assessment. Note these elements (see Figure 5.1) that go into the attack operations (AO) kill-chain steps to be taken when targeting an enemy asset such as a mobile ballistic missile transporter erector launcher. Strengthening all is the path to real effectiveness.

As Dr. George W. Ullrich, Director, Weapons Systems Office in the Office of the Secretary Defense has stated, mobile targets demand a wide-to-spot area search capability; rapid target cueing and fingerprinting; the presence of overhead weapons platforms, unmanned, mobile

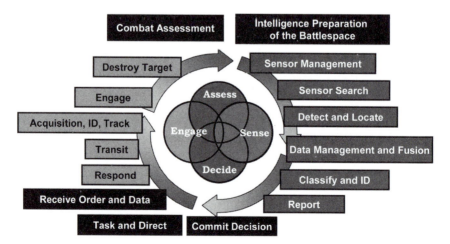

**Figure 5.1** Attack Operations: Joint Operational Elements

sensor platforms, and prompt sensor-to-shooter linkages, likely integrating both sensors and weapons delivery on the same platforms. Persistence is one way to address the engagement portion of the kill chain. Another would be through development of high-speed weapons to reduce the time-of-flight portion of the kill chain, especially in antiaccess scenarios where "persistence" solutions would be vulnerable to integrated air defenses.

Some of the more important new technologies being developed to improve U.S. attack operations versus enemy mobile transporter erector launchers are the following:[36]

- *Automatic Target Recognition Technology* in U.S. synthetic aperture radars combined with a wide-area search capability on U.S. overhead sensors, as may be placed on platforms like the U-2 aircraft, the Joint Surveillance and Target Attack Radar System (JSTARS) aircraft, or the Global Hawk unmanned aerial vehicle;
- *Semi-Automated Imagery Intelligence Processing System* to more rapidly assist image analysts in locating and identifying targets and help in transmitting targeting data to the tactical commander faster and more accurately;
- *Affordable Moving Surface Target Engagement System* to integrate sensors with precision standoff weapons to attack moving targets in all weather scenarios without visual confirmation; and
- *Targets-Under-Trees Program* uses synthetic aperture radars to find, identify, and destroy enemy hide sites for ballistic missile launchers despite his use of camouflage foliage, or other deception and denial practices.

This list is suggestive, not exhaustive. Other interesting research and development projects that could improve future U.S. Scud hunting capabilities are the following:

- Mobile Killer Units;
- Improved Synthetic Aperture Radars;
- Improved Technology for Measurement and Signature Intelligence (MASINT);
- Multispectral scene generation for critical mobile missiles;
- Advanced Remote Unattended Ground Sensors;
- National imagery and mapping agency support to targeting;
- Overhead Specific Emitter Identification;
- Countercamouflage, concealment, and deception projects;
- Polarimetric Measurement and Signature Intelligence (MASINT) Collection Capability;
- Advanced Remote Ground Unattended Sensor;
- Real Time Synthetic Aperture Radar Battle Damage Assessment;
- Fusion of Electro-Optical and Radar Sensor Data;

- Intelligence Preparation of the battle space support vis-à-vis Critical Mobile Missile Targets; and

- Space-Based Radars, perhaps positioned in geosynchronous orbit over the battle space to give 24/7 persistence in ISR support.

In order to take advantage of these developing new counterforce weapons, ISR, and targeting decision technologies, the United States is going to have to increase its acquisition of low-density/high-demand assets like the U-2 and JSTARS aircraft and unmanned aerial vehicles such as Global Hawk. The technologies to improve elements of the kill chain must be incorporated into one or all of these overhead platforms.

Even with such improvements in place, the burden of proof will still be upon the U.S. military to prove it has solved the challenge of tracking, targeting, and destroying mobile missile launchers in combat. During 1991's Operation Desert Storm, the official tally was 0 for 88 in our confirmed ability to destroy Scuds and Scud variants before launch. In the 2003 Operation Iraqi Freedom no missiles appear to have been fired from mobile transporter erector launchers. It appears that Iraqi forces relied on fixed launchers only, which should have been far easier to identify, locate, and destroy. However, 22 ballistic and cruise missiles were fired at U.S. and allied forces, without any being detected before launch.

Thus, no country, not even the United States, has yet demonstrated the capability to conduct successful attack operations against rival ballistic missile mobile launchers, and the jury is still out on our ability to find and target all fixed missile launchers prior to launch. The United States is gaining on the solution to this counterforce problem, but will have to lean most heavily on its active and passive defenses until attack operations reach a much higher level of capability.

Within the U.S. Government for some years there was no single office or agency exclusively dedicated and empowered to develop technology and concepts of operation to conduct a "Scud hunt." The effort now falls in numerous domains, including the individual U.S. armed services, the Joint Theater Air and Missile Defense Organization (JTAMDO), and the combatant commanders (e.g., such as the Special Operations Command).

Prior to 1997, theater air and missile defense (TAMD) systems were developed by the individual services to satisfy the unique requirements of each, and this was not a joint coordinated program. Rather, each service went its own way.

Finally, because TAMD was deemed increasingly important due to the proliferation of weapons of mass destruction in the hands of potential adversaries and the wastefulness and inefficiency of parallel go-it-alone theater air and missile defense service programs, JTAMDO was created to "define system interoperabilities and operational architectures and to validate the developing joint theater air and missile defense capabilities."[37]

There are three areas within theater air and missile defense that JTAM-DO is responsible for developing requirements, including the following:

- active defense,
- passive defense, and
- attack operations.

Thus, if an enemy aircraft or missile threatens a U.S. or allied force or asset in wartime, it can either be destroyed on the ground prior to launch (attack ops), intercepted while in flight toward the target (active defense), or those in the targeted area can be protected from harm via passive defensive measures such as dispersion, using shelters, wearing protective gear, and making advance medical preparations. JTAMDO was directed to (1) develop joint U.S. theater and missile defense capabilities requirement for the armed services, (2) design the joint mission architecture, and (3) plan a joint theater air and missile defense capabilities road map. The organization was to become the U.S. Defense Department's operational proponent for TAMD (including attack operations) with oversight over Defense Department planning coordination and oversight over TAMD operational requirements. In short, oversight over U.S. Scud hunt enabling programs is JTAMDO's responsibility, a job that it has failed to accomplish due to limited resources and a primary focus on other elements of its tasks.

## Solving the Challenge of Targeting WMD Assets: Thermobaric and Agent Defeat Weapons

The threat posed in Operation Desert Storm by Iraqi chemical and biological weapons brought home to U.S. defense officials the need to develop weapons that could destroy, disable, or deny such production facilities and stockpiles to remove that chemical and biological menace.

At present, the U.S. military is mostly limited to conventional warheads as the tools to eliminate adversary chemical and biological weapons capabilities. Unfortunately, conventional explosives directed against an enemy bunker, storage facility, or production plant may cause the scattering of lethal agents over substantial adjacent areas that may be inhabited by civilians and friendly forces. This could also contaminate the local environment. If infectious diseases were released, such targeting could result in widespread infections.

The U.S. Thermobaric (TB) and Agent Defeat Weapons (ADWs) programs were accelerated and upgraded to meet special war fighting needs after the September 11, 2001, attacks on the World Trade Center and the Pentagon sparked the U.S. declaration of a global war on terrorism, including the state sponsors of terrorist groups. Two counterforce TB programs were put on the fast track. One was the Bomb Live Unit (BLU)-118B Thermobaric Penetrator which was rushed into the hands of the war fighter after a 90-day transition period of tunnel and open-air tests of weapon effectiveness that preceded delivery of this ADW complete with warheads, guidance kit, and fuzes to theater. The BLU-118B Thermobaric Penetrator can be used for defeating hard and deeply buried targets housing chemical and biological weapons.[38]

The second post-9/11 thermobaric weapons delivery to the theater, Predator unmanned aerial vehicles equipped with Hellfire Thermobaric Blast and Fragmentary warheads (AGM-114M), took 11 months to get into the possession of relevant commands.[39] Thermobaric weapons are optimized, or tailored, blast weapons. Generally speaking, less blast is better when detonating in the vicinity of weapons of mass destruction. The Defense Threat Reduction Agency (DTRA) sponsored two quick-reaction programs: the AGM-86D Conventional Air Launched Cruise Missile (CALCM) Penetrator and the BLU-119 Crash Prompt Agent Defeat (CrashPAD) gravity bomb. The CALCM-P was developed, demonstrated, and fielded as part of the DTRA-led Counterproliferation II Advanced Concept Technology Demonstration (ACTD). CrashPAD was sponsored by the DTRA, in collaboration with the Air Force Research Laboratory (AFRL) and was fielded in 9 months as the first weapon designed specifically to defeat biological agents.

In addition to these quick-reaction TB and ADWs programs, the U.S. Defense Department has in the last decade also begun work on a number of other new classes of ADWs that could be air delivered to deny an adversary the use of its chemical and biological stockpiles and facilities with minimal collateral damage.

Put another way, as Thomas A. Ricks reported in the *Wall Street Journal,* the agent defeat weapons program is unique. "Its mission is to produce the first truly new weapon of the post-Cold War era, a bomb whose effectiveness is to be measured by how many people it doesn't kill—while it destroys stockpiles of horror weapons."[40]

While the details of such agent defeat weapons are classified, suffice it to say that at least eight agent defeat weapons programs are in progress and are designed to neutralize enemy chemical and biological assets by the following:

- high incendiary temperature weapons attack utilizing so-called "thermobarics" to burn the enemy chemical or biological munitions and materials in place;[41]

- fragmentary weapons attacks designed to puncture chemical or biological containers within facilities without major explosions because major explosions might blow the agents outside the walls of those bunkers or laboratories;

- keep-out weapons attacks that so contaminate the chemical or biological assets that enemy personnel could not retrieve them in a timely manner;
- blast weapons coupled with hard target smart fuzes and penetrating warheads that are designed to collapse or implode bunkers rather than explode them so that the structures struck collapse onto and cover the chemical or biological munitions and agents, denying easy access to enemy personnel;
- other means of sealing off or rendering hardened tunnels or deeply buried facilities nonfunctional, denying opponents entry or exit from such chemical or biological locations, and destroying facility umbilicals.

The agent defeat weapons coming into the U.S. arsenal have been tested in three ACTD programs:

- The Counterproliferation II Advanced Concept Technology Demonstration program administered by the Technology Division of the Defense Threat Reduction Agency;
- The Agent Defeat Weapons Advanced Concept Technology Demonstration program begun in 2002 administered by the U.S. Navy; and
- The Thermobaric Advanced Concept Technology Demonstration program begun in 2002; the thermobaric operational sponsor is the U.S. forces, Korea command, with the DTRA as the technical manager.[42]

In addition, the AFRL at Tyndall AFB, Florida, began work on air-delivered agent defeat weapons in 1999. The overall agent defeat weapons program is designed to be compatible with U.S. arms control commitments and the agent defeat weapons Advanced Concept Technology Demonstration program is developing analysis tools to predict agent release plumes, internal dispersion and venting outcomes, and agent defeat weapons lethality against weapons of mass destruction targets.

The ADWs that are being designed are to be compatible with insertion into or to replace the 2000-pound BLU-109 warhead and will be compatible with USAF guidance kits for a number of other U.S. bombs and warheads, including the GBU-31, Joint Direct Attack Munition or JDAM.[43]

During Operation Enduring Freedom in Afghanistan, the BLU-118B thermobaric warhead was employed against al-Qaeda and Taliban forces entrenched in caves and tunnels at Gardez.[44]

According to a report by the Jane's Information Group, although the official goal of the Agent Defeat Weapons ACTD project was "to fabricate eight weapons by fiscal year 2004 for flight tests and validation and to have another 20 to leave for operational use," … nevertheless there was a push to get the weapons ready in time for a U.S. war with Iraq.[45] Luckily, such agent defeat weapons were not needed in Operation Iraqi Freedom.

Of the 58 original ideas considered for research and development by the U.S. Government, only eight agent defeat weapons programs have been seriously pursued, but it is still uncertain which ones might be worth full-scale acquisition and deployment. The problem is that some enemy chemical and biological weapons storage facilities may be so deeply buried and hardened as to require a nuclear weapon on an earth penetrating warhead to have any reasonable chance of destroying that kind of target. Thus, the agent defeat weapons research and development (R&D) process goes on, still in search of a more effective agent defeat weapon that remains a conventional weapon. This is a problem still awaiting a solution.

## Counterforce Science and Technology Support

Much of the progress in U.S. counterforce programs in the past 13 years is the product of work done at the Defense Threat Reduction Agency which conducts and supports R&D programs in such areas as the following:

- The Counterproliferation I and II ACTDs;
- WMD Combat Assessment Systems;
- Agent Defeat, Deny, and Disrupt Technologies;
- Hard Target Defeat;
- WMD Database Maintenance;
- Target Planning and Assessment tools [e.g., Hazard Prediction and Assessment Capability (HPAC), Munitions Effects Assessment (MEA), and Integrated Munitions Effects Assessment (IMEA)];
- Weather Modeling;
- Survivability Assessments;
- Hazard Prediction;
- Force Protection Assessments;
- Structural Response Technology;
- Weapons Effects Phenomenology;
- Nevada Test Site Operations;
- Counterproliferation Analysis Planning System (CAPS);
- Test and Simulator Operations; and
- Nuclear Stockpile Stewardship.

DTRA is an amalgam of diverse parts. Its directorates focus on such programs as counterforce development, chemical and biological warfare defense, nuclear technology, combat support, weapons elimination, counterterrorism science and technology, on-site inspections to verify arms control compliance, as well as management of the U.S. Defense Department's participation in the Cooperative Threat Reduction program in partnership with the states of the former Soviet Union. The Defense

Threat Reduction Agency's predecessor was the Defense Nuclear Agency, which temporarily was named the Defense Special Weapons Agency, before it morphed into its present DTRA form in 1998.

DTRA's counterforce philosophy is to first develop enabling technologies and then demonstrate those through testing, advanced demonstrations, and ACTDs. DTRA then provides such capabilities to the war fighter, procures limited numbers of unique counterforce systems, and offers the combatant commanders support in the operational use of such counterforce systems.[46]

The Counterproliferation I and Counterproliferation II Advanced Concept Technology Demonstrations have provided the combatant commanders with some new bunker buster weapons (as well as AFWs) designed to destroy hardened targets and to limit downwind fallout of biological, chemical, or nuclear contamination. The Advanced Concept Technology Demonstration program has been utilized to do as follows:[47]

- ensure mature advanced technology is integrated into enhanced/new counterforce capability that meets the war fighter's needs, providing early and affordable evaluations;

- perform a military utility assessment of the new technology and associated concepts of operations and tactics, techniques, and procedures, usually evaluating this in a combatant commander's military exercise;

- leave behind new counterforce technology at the bases or other sites when the Advanced Concept Technology Demonstration is completed; and

- provide a counterforce program transition from research, development, test, and evaluation status to acquisition of new counterforce technologies, weapons, and tools for use by U.S. forces.

The DTRA-managed Counterproliferation Advanced Concept Technology Demonstrations have been aimed at providing the U.S. war fighter with improved counterforce or direct strike options against possible enemy WMD-related targets. Some of the products tested and provided to field commands via the Counterproliferation I Advanced Concept Technology Demonstration are the hard target smart fuze, the advanced unitary penetrator, a targeting concept of operations, the low altitude navigation and targeting infrared for night.

## Counterforce Targeting Planning Tools

Other Defense Threat Reduction Agency products have aided the war-fighting community in its ability to plan counterforce operations and predict outcomes. One such tool is the IMEA, which helps targeteers do prestrike planning and poststrike assessments by using weapons and target characteristics as inputs to predict collateral effects.[48] "The IMEA provides an end-to-end capability to analyze results and collateral effects."[49]

Other valuable counterforce targeting planning tools recently developed are the MEA, a WMD planning tool that estimates damage and the amount of agents released, and the HPAC tool that predicts downwind hazards, collateral effects, and nuclear weapons effects.

Another very significant improvement in counterforce targeting capabilities over the past 13 years has been the CAPS, a U.S. Strategic Command and Defense Threat Reduction Agency classified computer-based program based at the Lawrence Livermore National Laboratory where intelligence is collected, analyzed, and displayed on the chemical, biological, radiological, and nuclear weapons programs of states of concern.

CAPS allows targeting analysts to identify key nodes in the infrastructure of chemical, biological, radiological, nuclear, and missile programs of such states and supplies a comprehensive fused intelligence picture of their weapons of mass destruction assets.

Thus, the key function of CAPS is "to provide comprehensive and timely counterproliferation target planning information to the combatant commander."[50] CAPS allows U.S. defense specialists to analyze another state's specific approach to weapons production, identifying critical processing steps or production facilities which, if denied, would prevent that country from acquiring weapons of mass destruction.[51]

CAPS can also be useful to guide arms control verification efforts to assist in discerning compliance or noncompliance of other states with various nonproliferation regimes they have agreed to, such as the nuclear Non-Proliferation Treaty, the Chemical Weapons Convention, or the Biological and Toxin Weapons Convention.

## Counterforce Employment and Preemption Decisions

As the *U.S. National Strategy to Combat Weapons of Mass Destruction* states,

> Because deterrence may not succeed, and because of the potentially devastating consequences of weapons of mass destruction use against our forces and civilian population, U.S. military forces and appropriate civilian agencies must have the capability to defend against WMD–armed adversaries, including in appropriate cases through preemptive measures. This requires capabilities to detect and destroy an adversary's weapons of mass destruction assets before these weapons are used.[52]

The United States, therefore, in this national strategy, has stated that "[w]e will not permit the world's most dangerous regimes and terrorists to threaten us with the world's most destructive weapons." Put another way, "we cannot afford to be the unready confronting the unthinkable."[53] To this end, better counter-CBRNE (chemical, biological, radiological, nuclear, and high-yield explosive) preparedness, the U.S. Counterproliferation Initiative was dedicated 13 years ago in December 1993 when Secretary of Defense Les Aspin announced the beginning of the Counterproliferation Program. An important component of this counterproliferation readiness effort is the capability to launch effective counterforce operations to eliminate the weapons of mass destruction threat posed if that action was deemed necessary.

Since Operation Iraqi Freedom there has been a debate about the wisdom of the United States' decision to preempt against what was perceived as a growing weapons of mass destruction threat from Iraq. The overthrow of Saddam Hussein's regime was partially motivated by a sense of growing peril and a desire to extinguish that weapons of mass destruction threat before it was turned full force on the United States or its allies.

The failure to find concrete evidence of the Iraqi weapons of mass destruction arsenal after Operation Iraqi Freedom points out one of the hardest problems of a policy of preemption, namely, the need for very accurate actionable intelligence to pinpoint the weapons of mass destruction assets that the U.S. forces would have to destroy, disrupt, disable, deny, interdict, neutralize, or seize in a counterforce operation. It is hard to design an air tasking order or special operations plan without precise target location information.

The hardest case is where a relatively peaceful situation exists, but where the U.S. authorities have evidence that leads them to believe that a malevolent regime is about to acquire a dangerous new weapons of mass destruction capability that U.S. officials believe will be used against the United States or an ally in the not-too-distant future. If the regime leadership has a history of aggression, is a state sponsor of international terrorist groups, and has an evident and active hatred of the United States, such a new weapons of mass destruction capability is generally seen as especially dangerous. In such scenarios, U.S. authorities may contemplate preemption as a means of removing that threat, if it appears all peaceful approaches have been explored and are unsuccessful and if the threat is viewed as imminent.[54]

Of course, if the United States is already at war with such a heavily armed adversary, the decision to forcibly disarm its weapons of mass destruction assets is relatively noncontroversial. Here, a good offense (i.e., a good series of counterforce targeting operations) is perhaps the best defense. Better to eliminate these chemical, biological, radiological, nuclear, or high-yield explosives rather than have the enemy strike with them. However, even in wartime, such counterforce strikes can backfire if the adversary sees himself forced into a "use or lose" mode. Such wartime or peacetime counterforce strikes need to be decisive in eliminating the threat early in a developing crisis or the United States may face the wrath to come from those enemy WMD-equipped forces missed in the first attacks.

Unfortunately, real-world decisions often have to be made when time is short and information is incomplete. Crises are generally marked by high stakes, surprise, and a short time for decision making. Unfortunately, at the very time when rational decisions are most necessary, the pressure and stress of such situations add an extra difficulty for those in command. However, seeking answers to the questions raised above may be a step toward making a well-considered decision on whether or not to initiate action against enemy weapons of mass destruction. Clearly, such decisions will never be made lightly and preemption is rightly an option of the very last resort, if it is to be exercised at all.

Such analysts and legal authorities argue that preemption is illegal in international law since it is an act of war against a hitherto peaceful state. The argument is made that all aggressors give some defensive rationale before they invade their neighbors and that a doctrine of preventive war would lead us back to the law of the jungle in international relations where the strong nations can make the rules to fit their own situation.

Others argue that the spread of weapons of mass destruction presents a new imperative in international relations. These argue that no state can tolerate an enemy weapons of mass destruction strike, due to the enormous damage and mass casualties such weapons can cause, if it has the means to uncover an impending attack and to neutralize it before it happens.

These argue that the United States has an inherent right of anticipatory self-defense. They argue that in some very few, very special cases the best and perhaps only means of effective defense is a good offense, that it is better to disarm by military action an adversary poised to inflict massive harm on U.S. forces or population rather than to suffer catastrophic losses due to, say, an enemy biological or nuclear attack.[55]

As Elihu Root wrote in 1914, "International Law does not require the threatened state to wait in using force until it is too late to protect itself."[56] Just-war theory, if applied to the concept of preemption and anticipatory self-defense, would limit such actions only to occasions where preemptive actions were taken only in situations of evident self-defense, after peaceful remedies were exhausted, where there was a reasonable chance of success, taken in actions either proportional to or less than the injury or anticipated injury about to be suffered, and executed on the decision of a competent authority.[57]

Another just-war theorist, Michael Walzer, concludes that, given compliance with these conditions, "states can rightfully defend themselves against violence that is imminent, but not actual."[58]

Thus, the United States might legally, in certain situations, have the right to preemptively disarm a WMD-armed opponent, if an attack was seen to be very likely.

Perceptions of impending catastrophic attacks by an adversary might, therefore, dictate U.S. preemptive action in an extreme case. Indeed, no U.S. president could likely survive a later impeachment trial if it were proven after such a horrific weapons of mass destruction attack that he had substantial knowledge of an impending weapons of mass destruction strike and failed to take preventive action that was in his power to order.

Thus, the United States will continue to include the preemption option in its repertoire of possible policy responses to those that threaten the United States and its allies with weapons of mass destruction. Counterforce capabilities, if mated with accurate and comprehensive intelligence, could be effective in blunting a weapons of mass destruction attack. Coupled with improved active and passive defenses, a respected deterrent capability, and aggressive nonproliferation diplomacy, perhaps the threat posed by such unconventionally armed rivals can be minimized or neutralized. In both crises and wartime such counterforce operations may be all too necessary.

## Counterforce: The Way Ahead

While weapons of mass destruction targets are, without a doubt, high priority for combatant commanders, the weapons and assessment systems best suited to address these targets (e.g., agent defeat/disrupt/deny weapons, standoff missiles with penetrating, low-yield conventional explosive payloads, UAV-based combat assessment systems, etc.) have not fared well in terms of dedicated service investment in them. This is likely for two reasons. First, the weapons of mass destruction target set, although important, is not large in comparison to the non-WMD target set. Second, the services' investment decision-making process tends to favor higher visibility, higher probability of employment systems than "niche" systems. Additionally, development and fielding of small numbers of specialized weapons/systems, i.e., niche capability, brings with it the requirement to maintain proficiency with the systems and to sustain them in the field. Providing the combatant commander with the tools needed to accomplish the WMD counterforce mission is likely to remain challenging under the current Defense Department investment construct.

Despite funding limitations, the U.S. armed forces have acquired a significant improvement in their ability to execute successful counterforce strikes against future enemy weapons of mass destruction assets. The revolution in precision-guided munitions has dramatically improved the lethality of U.S. forces against such time-critical targets.

Stealth aircraft can also penetrate unscathed to target in a manner not seen prior to Operation Desert Storm. Unmanned aerial vehicles, like Predators equipped with Hellfire Missiles, can provide a continuous overhead and lethal counterforce presence not available when Secretary of Defense Aspin announced the Counterproliferation Initiative in 1993.

U.S. agent defeat weapons, now in research and development, show promise, one day, of successfully destroying, disabling, or denying access to enemy weapons of mass destruction sites without spreading their lethal contamination downwind. Analytical tools for characterizing targets and weapons effects also make life easier for planners given the task of mating the right weapon to a given enemy weapons of mass destruction target, and predicting effects. Thus, in all of these ways, there have been major technological improvements in accuracy, penetration to target, target area coverage, agent defeat weapons, and analytical tools.

However, the adversaries have not been asleep while all this U.S. technological progress has been achieved. The North Koreas, Irans, and other actual and potential rivals have hidden their weapons of mass destruction assets, using camouflage, concealment, and deception techniques. Unfortunately, as the United States is finding out in Iraq, an adversary may be very successful in concealing weapons of mass destruction programs and finding them may be like finding a needle in the proverbial haystack.

It is close to impossible to execute successful counterforce attacks when the target locations are unknown. Thus, target identification and location is the key to counterforce success or failure. Position location uncertainty also robs the United States of its ability to successfully implement a preemptive strategy, so good intelligence on enemy weapons of mass destruction is an absolute requirement.

Nor have adversaries been asleep in other ways. Adversaries like North Korea, for example, have burrowed into hills and mountains and moved their assets into tunnels, cut-and-cover structures, and deeply buried facilities. The mole strategy has been adopted to frustrate improved U.S. counterforce strike capabilities and, at present, there is only a partial U.S. capability against adversaries who have taken their weapons of mass destruction maintenance, storage, and production assets underground.

Finally, adversaries have increasingly turned to deploying mobile missile launchers whose shoot and scoot tactics, coupled with numerous decoys, make counterforce targeting extremely perplexing and difficult. After a dismal failure in Desert Storm "Scud hunting," the U.S. military still lacks an adequate counterforce capability to find and destroy missiles on transporter erector launchers. The mobile or relocatable missile launcher problem is still a good way from being solved despite numerous improvements since 1991.

Thus, in the foreseeable future, despite significant technological and procedural improvements, U.S. counterforce applications can promise only a partial means of diluting and reducing the threat posed by enemy weapons of mass destruction. Much of the burden remains on nonproliferation means, deterrence, active and passive defense, and the ability to manage consequences after an attack.

# CHAPTER 6

# Emerging Missile Challenges and Improving Active Defenses

*Jeffrey A. Larsen and Kerry M. Kartchner*

## The Rationale for Missile Defense

The 1993 Counterproliferation Initiative (CPI) was an implicit recognition by the U.S. Government that despite the best efforts of the international community in nonproliferation and arms control, some weapons of mass destruction and the means for their delivery were going to fall into the hands of the world's bad actors. Since that was likely to happen, it was only prudent to prepare.

The CPI specifically called upon the U.S. military to include planning for active and passive defenses in its spectrum of defense responsibilities. Its focus was primarily on tactical concerns, as defenses in the theater would "neutralize or mitigate the effects of WMD [weapons of mass destruction] and enable U.S. forces to fight effectively even on a contaminated battlefield."[1] In this context, it was envisioned that tactical and strategic ballistic missile defenses would play an integral role in protection of our deployed forces, our allies, and the American homeland.

In the realm of strategic ballistic missile defense of North America, however, the need is not so clear-cut, nor is there a consensus regarding deployment. The need for a new defensive concept was articulated by President Ronald Reagan and caught the public's attention in 1983 and in the years immediately thereafter. In the early 1990s a somewhat fragile consensus was formed, including both Republicans and Democrats, that a limited national missile defense (NMD) system was needed, particularly after North Korea began testing its No Dong and Taepo Dong missiles and it became evident that Kim Jong Il's government was selling this technology to other states such as Iran and Pakistan.

This missile defense system was simultaneously praised by proponents as deliverance from assured destruction and reviled by opponents as too expensive, too destabilizing, and too technologically challenging. This debate was finally settled by the George W. Bush administration that withdrew the United States from the Anti-Ballistic Missile (ABM) Treaty in 2002 and deployed the first operational system in late 2004.

Some missile defense proponents rejected the idea that a world of mutual assured destruction (MAD) is somehow safer, that we should simply accept that the bomb is the ultimate weapon for which there is no defense. Rather, they believe that this reflects an immoral abrogation of a government's fundamental purpose: the protection of its citizens. The shift to a defense-dominant relationship between major powers is possible and must be pursued, according to this perspective.

Opponents have developed a standard set of criticisms that they roll out each time a new missile defense system is proposed: it will not work; it will cost too much; it will upset strategic stability by changing the accepted rules of international behavior; it could easily be overcome by offensive weapons and countermeasures, hence leading to an arms race; and (prior to 2002), it would violate the spirit of the ABM Treaty, thereby undercutting the cornerstone of arms control. Such beliefs, in fact, led the United States and the USSR to sign the ABM Treaty in 1972. This treaty and its restrictions on strategic defenses legitimized a world without defenses, one in which societal vulnerability was seen as the best way to ensure that logic prevailed between the two superpowers. If neither side could win a nuclear exchange, it was argued, no rational actor would ever start a war.

Tactical or theater missile defenses have been regularly highlighted in the annual Counterproliferation Program Review Committee reports, in which the regional Combatant Commanders prioritized their requirements in a list of Areas for Capability Enhancements (ACE). In every ACE list made public during the late 1990s, an active missile defense capability was ranked in the top five priorities. It was called different things each year: "active defense" (ranked 2nd) in 1995, "interception of cruise missiles" (2nd) in 1996, "theater ballistic missile active defense" (4th) in 1997, and "theater missile defense with minimum collateral effects" (5th) in another part of the 1997 report.[2]

The world has changed in the last few years, enough, in fact, to allow the deployment of a limited missile defense that is not strategically significant and therefore nonprovocative to Russia. This provides some modest defense against rogue states in a world where ballistic missile technology is proliferating to multiple countries, some of which may be undeterrable in the classic sense, and many of whom do not like America. The Bush administration is following in the footsteps of its predecessor, William Clinton's administration, by proposing a modest, limited missile defense system that includes both national and theater missile defense elements. The ABM Treaty is no longer an issue or impediment, and there was little international reaction to U.S. withdrawal from the treaty or its plans to deploy a limited system, given the reduced international level of tension between the United States and Russia. In addition, the world recognizes an acknowledged threat from rogue states, such as North Korea, and the likelihood of further multinational expeditionary military actions in far-flung corners of the world. Given this, and with defensive technology getting better, even some former opponents now say that missile defenses have finally reached the point where they make sense.[3]

## Background: Early Efforts at Missile Defense[4]

After World War II and before the invention of the intercontinental ballistic missile (ICBM), the United States initially focused its air defense efforts against manned bombers. It investigated some early concepts for antimissile and antisatellite defensive systems, but these did not really catch the public eye until 1957, when the Soviet Union tested an ICBM and launched Sputnik. Suddenly, the country felt vulnerable to an adversary who could threaten America's heartland from above. Furthermore, the Soviets began to deploy their own Galosh ABM system around Moscow in the early 1960s. Clearly, something had to be done. Over the past five decades, the United States has been developing missile defense programs (see Table 6.1) to meet this evolving threat.

## Missile Defense Programs, 1957–1993

### Nike Zeus

The first effort at developing an ABM missile used a spin-off of the Nike Hercules intermediate-range ballistic missile system. Nike Zeus proved itself capable of downing a satellite with a nuclear warhead. It was successfully tested in the late 1950s, but had many technical difficulties.

### Nike X

The successor to Nike Zeus, Nike X, was an Army program in the early 1960s. This research and development effort witnessed many advances and proposed a two-tier layered defense system to defend the country. Nike X became the Spartan missile, and the program was rolled into the first true NMD effort, the Sentinel program.

**Table 6.1**   Major U.S. Missile Defense Programs Since World War II

| Decade | Program Name | Goal | Threat | Key Elements |
|---|---|---|---|---|
| 1960s | Sentinel | "Thin" national protection | China | Spartan, Sprint missiles |
| 1970s | Safeguard | Point protection of offensive forces | USSR | Spartan, Sprint missiles |
| 1980s | Strategic Defense Initiative (SDI) | National or global protection | USSR | Exotic defenses, including space-based, plus missiles |
| 1990s | Global Protection Against Limited Strikes (GPALS) | Global and theater protection | Russia (limited strikes), rogue states | Ground- and space-based missiles |
| 1990s | Theater Missile Defense (TMD) and National Missile Defense | Theater first; national secondary | Rogue states | Ground- and sea-based missiles |
| 2000s | Missile Defense | National and theater | Adversary state, accidental launch | Ground- and sea-based missiles, airborne laser |

## *Sentinel*

President Lyndon Johnson made a decision in 1967 to deploy a thin national defensive system against a Chinese threat. Originally, proponents of Sentinel called for a robust missile defense network that could thwart the Soviet offensive missile threat. But recognition that it would be nearly impossible to create a perfect defense against a large Soviet threat, and the Soviet unwillingness to negotiate away their strategic defenses at the June 1967 Glassboro (New Jersey) Summit, convinced Johnson to pressure Congress into approving deployment of Sentinel.

The Sentinel plan called for placing several hundred Spartan and Sprint missiles at 14 locations across the United States, including 10 major cities. This, in turn, led to public concern about nuclear warheads exploding overhead, or the possibility that merely deploying defenses could provoke a Soviet first strike attack to take out the system (making these sites "megaton magnets"). Sentinel was thus a compromise program between demands in some quarters for a system that would provide limited protection and those who argued it was a mistake to deploy any defensive system, using the standard arguments described above. Its public rationale was, in part, to provide a defense against the emerging Chinese long-range ballistic missile threat, while avoiding an action-reaction phenomenon in U.S.–Soviet relations that could lead to an arms race.[5]

## Safeguard

President Richard Nixon changed the name for his smaller version of Sentinel. This was a system that no longer attempted to be nationwide and moved the ABM sites away from cities in order to protect U.S. second-strike forces at bomber bases and ICBM missile fields. Safeguard was originally envisioned to be based at 6 to 12 sites. Two of those actually began constructing their silos for the interceptor missiles: Grand Forks AFB, North Dakota, and Malmstrom AFB, Montana. Safeguard would employ only a few hundred Spartan and Sprint missiles, using the same two-layered approach as was planned for Sentinel. The 1972 ABM Treaty limited each side to two sites (the United States chose to defend the ICBM fields at Grand Forks and the national capital of Washington). The 1974 Protocol to the ABM Treaty further limited each side to one site. Grand Forks was the only location to become operational. On October 1, 1975, the Safeguard site began operations, the only such capability the United States had fielded until 2004. The next day, Congress cut its funding, questioning the value of a single site in the north central Midwest. It closed in February 1976.

## The Strategic Defense Initiative

In March 1983, President Ronald Reagan called upon American scientists to undertake what has since become the nation's largest and most expensive weapons system program. In a visionary speech, Reagan asked the United States to build a defensive system that would make nuclear weapons "impotent and obsolete." As he put it,

> What if free people could live secure in the knowledge that their security did not rest upon the threat of instant U.S. retaliation to deter a Soviet attack, that we could intercept and destroy strategic ballistic missiles before they reached our own soil or that of our allies?[6]

Reagan created the Strategic Defense Initiative Organization (SDIO) in 1984 to lead the effort. Initially, SDIO focused most of its research on exotic weapons, including directed energy weapons and space-based systems. The arguments for and against SDI were virtual repeats of those heard during the Sentinel and Safeguard debates of the previous two decades. Nonetheless, the magnitude of the effort scared the Soviet Union, which tried desperately to eliminate this latest U.S. threat to MAD stability. The Soviet concern was evidenced by its willingness to trade away its strategic offensive forces at the arms control negotiating table in return for constraints on SDI. (This was most obvious in Soviet Secretary General Mikhail Gorbachev's proposal at the Reykjavik Summit in October 1986.)[7] The program became less grandiose after a couple of years of research showed that space-based systems had a long way to go before they would be mature, deployable weapons. In 1985, Paul Nitze, a senior State Department arms control adviser, had provided a formula for deployment that included three criteria. These were similar to the four-part approach that the Clinton administration would take 10 years later. In order to be considered, according to Nitze, ballistic missile defenses had to be effective, survivable, and cost effective at the margins (in order to prevent the other side from simply deploying more offensive forces).[8]

### Theater Missile Defense

President George H. W. Bush sponsored a review of the SDI program from 1989 to 1990 led by Ambassador Henry Cooper. While Cooper remained an advocate of a national missile defense program that included a space-based system involving thousands of small satellites called Brilliant Pebbles, the findings of his study called on the United States to shift its defense research emphasis from strategic defenses over North America to the protection of deployed forces and allies against limited attacks.[9] The coalition's experience with Iraqi Scuds in Operation Desert Storm in 1991 certainly influenced this recommendation. These suggestions to focus on theater defenses became policy.

### Global Protection Against Limited Strikes

President Bush changed the strategic defense program dramatically in 1991. Given the supposed success of Patriot ABM batteries in the first Gulf War, Bush reinvigorated the ballistic missile defense program. The new program, while robust, was smaller than SDI. GPALS was composed of three main parts: a ground-based NMD comprised of 750 missile interceptors at six sites, a ground-based theater missile defense, and a space-based global defense (using Brilliant Pebbles). The Missile Defense Act of 1991 (discussed below) lent badly needed Congressional support to the revised program.

### Accidental Launch Protection System (ALPS)

Senator Sam Nunn (D-GA) suggested a compromise approach that would provide an alternative to GPALS with a smaller and more affordable system, one that would be able to defend against an accidental launch of a few missiles or a small attack by a rogue commander. ALPS would require improved theater missile defenses and modest adjustments to the ABM Treaty that would allow the deployment of limited national missile defenses to counter accidental launches and limited strikes. While this was a system offered as a compromise and was never officially blessed, it is of interest today because it reflects much of the current system deployed in 2004.

## Programs Since 1993

The Defense Counterproliferation Initiative was released in 1993. That same year, the Bottom-Up Review of U.S. security policy and the Defense Department was published. This study laid out a three-part missile defense program, which gave top priority to TMD efforts. Its key elements included the Patriot antiaircraft missile and its upgrades, the army's Terminal High-Altitude Air Defense (THAAD) missile, and the navy's Aegis Area Defense program.

When the Clinton administration arrived in Washington, Secretary of Defense Les Aspin renamed SDIO the Ballistic Missile Defense Organization (BMDO) to reflect this new emphasis on TMD. To many, this signaled the end of the SDI decade—though even Aspin gave SDI credit for helping win the Cold War. As discussed later in this chapter, in its second term the Clinton administration agreed to pursue a national missile defense system, and George W. Bush came into office in 2001 convinced of the need to push such a system forward to actual deployment.

Before reviewing the events and systems of the past 13 years, however, we need to examine the post-Cold War threat to the United States that has driven concern over the need for theater and ballistic missile defenses.

## The Current Threat

In addition to the obvious desire to protect one's homeland from the ravages of missile attack, many analysts today believe that theater missile defenses are a necessary component of any expeditionary military operation. The growing number of countries that possess short- or intermediate-range missiles makes it crucial to have TMD to protect one's forces and allies. Some 20 states have ballistic missiles today, and one count places the number of nations with cruise missiles at 77.[10] Given the precedents set in recent wars, states are not hesitant to use cruise or ballistic missiles when it serves some military purpose. Witness the Iran-Iraq War (1980–1988), the first Gulf War in 1990–1991, and the increasingly common U.S. reliance on land-attack missiles as shown in Operations Desert Fox (Iraq, 1998), Allied Freedom (Kosovo, 1999), Enduring Freedom (Afghanistan, 2001), and Iraqi Freedom (2003).

The technology necessary to develop ballistic or cruise missiles is no longer exotic or difficult. Many states in all regions of the globe have at least a rudimentary force of missiles, and some rogue nations are pursuing longer-range systems that can threaten the United States or its allies in Europe and East Asia.

The current U.S. push for deploying an initial missile defense capability is driven by a perception of a growing and increasingly unpredictable ballistic missile threat. While some have argued that the proliferation of ballistic missiles is actually declining and that the number of long-range missiles is actually decreasing from the levels of the Cold War, the ballistic missile threat to the United States, its friends, allies, and forces deployed abroad can best be understood in view of the following key assertions frequently attested to by Intelligence Community officials.

First, the U.S. Intelligence Community has repeatedly asserted that missile capabilities are growing. Those countries with ballistic missile programs continue to improve their capabilities in terms of range, payload capacity, and reliability.

Second, the number of missiles of all ranges is increasing. Medium- and short-range ballistic missile systems already pose a significant threat to U.S. interests, forces, and allies overseas.

Third, there has been increased trade and cooperation among countries that have been recipients of missile technologies. According to an unclassified summary of a recent National Intelligence Estimate (NIE), "Proliferation of ballistic missile-related technologies, materials, and expertise—especially by Russian, Chinese, and North Korean entities—has enabled emerging missile states to accelerate missile development, acquire new capabilities, and potentially develop even more capable and longer-range future systems."[11] Ballistic missile technology based on early Russian Scud missiles, in particular, has been widely distributed and proliferated. In some cases, such as Pakistan and North Korea, countries that were at one time the recipients of ballistic missile technology (Pakistan from both the United States, in terms of space launch technology, and North Korea from the Soviet Union, in terms of military hardware) have now become exporters of expertise, components, systems, and production capabilities.

Fourth, a small number of countries continue to work toward longer-range systems, including ICBMs, often under the guise of developing a peaceful space launch capability. Once a nation has achieved the ability to place an object in space, it has in effect acquired the ability to also deliver a comparably sized weapons payload anywhere on the face of the earth.

Fifth, while only a relative handful of countries have significant ballistic missile capabilities, some of those countries are among the least responsible in the world, have expressed the most hostility toward the United States, and have demonstrated a disregard for international agreements and norms of behavior. Moreover, these regimes are seeking to acquire both long-range ballistic missile capability and weapons of mass destruction, including biological, chemical, and nuclear weapons. It is this confluence of WMD proliferation and ballistic missile technology that is particularly worrisome. This is partly why the U.S. Intelligence Community has assessed that "the probability that a missile with a weapon of mass destruction will be used against U.S. forces is higher today than during most of the Cold War, and will continue to grow."[12]

Ballistic missiles are not the only emerging threats of concern. Over the next 10 years, the U.S. Intelligence Community believes that at least nine countries will be involved in producing cruise missiles, and of these, several will make their missiles available for export.[13] Cruise missiles are easy to build or acquire, they are relatively cheap, they are easily transportable, and they require less maintenance, training, and logistical support than either manned aircraft or more sophisticated ballistic missiles. They have long flight ranges and potentially high accuracy. Because they can fly at low altitudes, they are difficult to detect by traditional radar. This difficulty (or advantage) is compounded by a low radar cross section, which can be reduced even further by using signature reduction technologies. Moreover, the effective employment of U.S. Navy and Air Force cruise missiles for precision strikes against land-based targets in both the 1991 and 2003 Gulf Wars has reinforced the perception that cruise missiles are an attractive counterforce option. The United States also has, on several occasions, employed them in a retaliatory or coercive role.[14] Currently, it is estimated that there are over 80,000 cruise missiles in the arsenals of over 70 nations. Consequently, virtually all U.S. theater missile defense systems have been designed and tested with some capability against cruise missiles.

U.S. intelligence has also addressed the question of the political motivation behind the growth in ballistic missile technology. In Senate testimony, intelligence officials have stated the following:

> [A]cquiring long-range ballistic missiles armed with a weapon of mass destruction probably will enable weaker countries to do three things that they otherwise might not be able to do: deter, constrain, and harm the United States. To achieve these objectives, the missiles need not be deployed in large numbers; with even a few such weapons, these countries would judge that they had the capability to threaten at least politically significant damage to the United States or its allies. They need not be highly accurate; the ability to target a large urban area is sufficient. They need not be highly reliable, because their strategic value is derived primarily from the implicit or explicit threat of their use, not the near certain outcome of such use. Some of these systems may be intended for their political impact as potential terror weapons, while others may be built to perform more specific military missions, facing the United States with a broad spectrum of motivations, development

timelines, and resulting hostile capabilities. In many ways, such weapons are not envisioned at the outset as operational weapons of war, but primarily as strategic weapons of deterrence and coercive diplomacy.[15]

## The Rumsfeld Commission Report

Current ballistic missile threat perceptions, as they pertain to political support for the U.S. missile defense program, are largely a product of two key events: the publication in July 1998 of the Rumsfeld Commission Report and the August 1998 launch of the North Korean Taepo Dong, a prototype long-range ballistic missile, which was widely interpreted as confirming the assessments contained in the Rumsfeld Commission Report. This section provides some background on perceptions of the emerging ballistic missile threat that precipitated the current missile defense program and how those threat perceptions evolved up to the present.

In November 1995, the National Intelligence Council, which is made up of 13 intelligence agencies, released its 1995 NIE.[16] According to reports that began appearing in newspapers, this NIE concluded "no country, other than the major declared nuclear powers, will develop or otherwise acquire a ballistic missile in the next 15 years that could threaten the contiguous 48 states or Canada." This conclusion was controversial, especially in Congress. Many Republicans, who had assumed majority control a year earlier in the 1994 elections, charged that the NIE's conclusions had been leaked to the press in order to help defeat support for increased funding for missile defenses.

Critics charged that this report contained a number of flaws, contradictions, and ambiguities. They also charged that the authors of the report had downplayed the potential impact of foreign assistance to countries developing ballistic missiles, had underestimated the impact of space launch vehicle development on missile proliferation, and assumed that countries that currently have missiles will not sell them. It was further asserted that the report discounted the threat posed by long-range missiles in China and Russia. To congressional representatives of Alaska and Hawaii it was especially troublesome that the report had excluded their respective states from the territory to be defended against missile attack.

Consequently, Republican leaders in Congress ordered the Intelligence Community to reexamine the evidence, to assess whether the intelligence conclusions were justified, and to determine whether the Clinton administration had exerted undue influence in "politicizing" the process, thus impairing the integrity of this Intelligence Community product.

Robert Gates, former deputy national security adviser and director of the Central Intelligence Agency during the first Bush administration, was chosen to chair the panel, which reviewed the available intelligence and the process used to compile the NIE's conclusions. It issued its own report in December 1996. The Gates Panel concluded that "the Intelligence Community has a strong case that for sound technical reasons, the United States is unlikely to face an indigenously developed and tested intercontinental ballistic missile threat from the Third World before 2010."[17] Further, the Gates Panel determined that there was "no breach of the integrity of the intelligence process." In nearly every respect, the Gates Panel endorsed the findings of the earlier 1995 estimate and dismissed the idea that the United States would soon be threatened by long-range ballistic missiles launched from rogue states. Thus, it provided additional ammunition to those claiming that there was little pressing need for increasing funding for missile defenses.

This did not satisfy the supporters of missile defense in the U.S. Congress. Unhappy with the Gates Panel conclusions, Congress chartered another group of outside experts to take a second look at the 1995 estimate. This time, Donald Rumsfeld, former Secretary of Defense in the Ford administration, was chosen to chair the panel, formally known as "The Commission to Assess the Ballistic Missile Threat to the United States," but more commonly known as the Rumsfeld Commission. This panel not only reviewed the intelligence used to produce the 1995 estimate, but interviewed scores of outside experts on missile technology and proliferation. It issued its report on July 15, 1998, and, unlike the endorsement of the Gates Panel, this report challenged many findings of the reported 1995 estimate.

The Rumsfeld Commission's principal conclusion was that a country such as North Korea could deploy an ICBM "within about five years of a decision to develop" one.[18] Among its other key findings, the Rumsfeld Commission concluded that the ballistic missile threat to the United States was real and growing; this threat was greater than previously assessed, and the United States may have little or no warning of new threats. The report's conclusions were spelled out in an executive summary:

- Concerted efforts by a number of overtly or potentially hostile nations to acquire ballistic missiles with biological or nuclear payloads pose a growing threat to the United States, its deployed forces and its friends and allies. These newer, developing threats in North Korea, Iran and Iraq are in addition to those still posed by the existing ballistic missile arsenals of Russia and China, nations with which we are not now in conflict but which remain in uncertain transitions. The newer ballistic missile-equipped nations' capabilities will not match those of U.S. systems for accuracy or reliability. However, they would be able to inflict major destruction on the U.S. within about five years of a decision to acquire such a capability (10 years in the case of Iraq). During several of those years, the U.S. might not be aware that such a decision had been made.

- The threat to the U.S. posed by these emerging capabilities is broader, more mature and evolving more rapidly than has been reported in estimates and reports by the Intelligence Community.
- The Intelligence Community's ability to provide timely and accurate estimates of ballistic missile threats to the U.S. is eroding. This erosion has roots both within and beyond the intelligence process itself. The Community's capabilities in this area need to be strengthened in terms of both resources and methodology.
- The warning times the U.S. can expect of new, threatening ballistic missile deployments are being reduced. Under some plausible scenarios—including re-basing or transfer of operational missiles, sea- and air-launch options, shortened development programs that might include testing in a third country, or some combination of these—the United States might well have little or no warning before operational deployment.[19]

In certain key respects, this report directly contradicted earlier reports. For example, both the 1995 intelligence estimate and the Gates Panel assumed that the United States would have ample warning of the development of a strategic ballistic missile threat in time to allow an adequate missile defense to be developed to counter that threat. In contrast, the members of the Rumsfeld Commission concluded unanimously that the United States needed to assume that there might be *no strategic warning* of a rogue state's acquiring the capability to strike the United States with a long-range ballistic missile.

The Rumsfeld Commission Report explained that three crucial factors were shaping the emerging ballistic missile threat.

1. *Different Standards:* Missile developing countries don't use the same accuracy, safety or environmental standards as would the United States. Therefore, their programs can move ahead much faster than assumed.
2. *Foreign Assistance:* Sale of components or even complete missile systems, together with substantial technical assistance from foreign powers, can help accelerate the development of a rogue state missile threat much faster than assumed.
3. *Concealment and Deception:* Rogue states determined to pursue developing ballistic missiles take great care to conceal their ballistic missile and WMD programs from Western intelligence services—which makes it much harder for the Intelligence Community to accurately predict these threats.[20]

## The North Korean Missile Test

The Rumsfeld Commission Report was released in late July 1998. Had it not been for an event that transpired within weeks of its release, this report may have simply been additional fodder in the partisan battles over missile defense funding and the fate of the ABM Treaty. However, on August 31, 1998, North Korea launched a ballistic missile named the Taepo Dong, thus confirming that North Korea did, in fact, have a program for developing long-range ballistic missiles. Even though the missile ultimately failed to place its payload into orbit, this launch was widely interpreted as validating the Rumsfeld Commission's conclusions. While the U.S. Intelligence Community had anticipated this launch, the missile itself demonstrated several key characteristics that caught Western intelligence services by surprise.[21]

In particular, the Taepo Dong missile launched by North Korea contained a third stage, considered an important feature of an intercontinental-range ballistic missile. It demonstrated the technology for third-stage separation. It demonstrated advanced fuel technology. It showed that North Korea had critical command and control capabilities for launching and guiding such a missile. It had previously been assumed that these technical barriers to acquiring long-range ballistic missile capability would be hard for a rogue state to surmount.

In addition, the missile's flight demonstrated one other often overlooked feature with tremendous political ramifications that would reverberate for years to come. It overflew the territory of Japan. This violated an unwritten taboo in international space launch practice that dictated that flight tests of missiles should not overfly the populated territory of another nation, for the sake of avoiding the appearance of initiating a surprise attack. The fact that North Korea ignored this taboo had the effect of precipitating growing interest in and support for missile defense in Japan, Taiwan, and Australia.

But its most important consequence was to confirm the conclusions of the Rumsfeld Commission Report, to energize and consolidate support for missile defense in the U.S. Congress, and to force the Intelligence Community to revise its threat assessment.

In response to both the Rumsfeld Commission's criticisms of its assumptions and methodology and to the political furor in the wake of the North Korean Taepo Dong launch, the Intelligence Community set about producing a new, revised report. This was released to Congress in 1999. According to Senate testimony by senior Intelligence Community official Robert D. Walpole, this report differed from previous reports in three important ways. First, it extended the period of assessment from 2010 to 2015. Second, the Intelligence Community, drawing on expertise both inside and outside the Intelligence Community, focused more on when a country *could* acquire an ICBM, in addition to assessing when they would be *likely* to do so. Third, the report recognized that a threat to the United States from a rogue state ballistic missile program would materialize before such a state had deployed an arsenal of missiles in the traditional sense; therefore, the Intelligence Community adopted the approach of using the first successful flight test to indicate an "initial threat availability."[22]

The 1999 NIE was entitled "Foreign Missile Developments and the Ballistic Missile Threat Through 2015." Preempting the possibility of a leak to the press, and in response to criticism that secrecy promoted the possibility of politicization, the CIA took the unusual step of preparing an unclassified summary of this report.[23] According to this public version,

> [m]ost Intelligence Community agencies project that before 2015 the United States most likely will face ICBM threats from North Korea and Iran, and possibly from Iraq—barring significant changes in their political orientations—in addition to the longstanding missile forces of Russia and China.

In addition, the Intelligence Community confirmed that short- and medium-range ballistic missiles "already pose a significant threat overseas to U.S. interests, military forces, and allies."[24]

Finally, the 1999 NIE addressed the debate over whether rogue states would use technologically complex long-range ballistic missiles to deliver weapons of mass destruction to U.S. territory or whether they would resort to other, less expensive, and less complex means of delivering weapons, such as by truck, ship, or airplane. The report asserted that, for the immediate future, attack by these other means was actually much more likely than attack by long-range ballistic missile, "primarily because nonmissile delivery means are less costly, easier to acquire, and more reliable and accurate." However, the report also stated "[m]issiles provide a level of prestige, coercive diplomacy, and deterrence that nonmissile means do not."[25] Subsequent NIEs have not varied substantially from the 1999 edition.

## U.S. Efforts Since 1993

To understand the priorities of U.S. missile defense efforts over the course of the years that began in 1993, it is necessary to review the lessons learned from U.S. experiences with missile attack and missile defense in the 1991 Gulf War. This experience led to the formation of an unprecedented political consensus for developing and deploying TMD systems, reflected in the 1991 Missile Defense Act. However, this consensus did not extend to developing national missile defense systems or defense against ICBMs, primarily due to a disagreement whether a long-range threat existed. There was also skepticism about the technology for such a defense as well as continued support for the ABM Treaty, which limited defenses against long-range ballistic missiles, but did not restrict the development of defenses against short- and medium-range ballistic missiles, or against cruise missiles.

## Theater Missile Defense Programs[26]

Prior to the 1990–1991 Gulf War, it was assumed by many defense planners that opponents armed with ballistic missiles would either be deterred from firing them against U.S. targets for fear of devastating retaliation or U.S. forces would be able to relatively easily and quickly identify ballistic missile launchers with existing surveillance capabilities. Once such launchers had been identified, they would be targeted and destroyed before they could pose a substantial threat to U.S. or allied assets. It was further assumed that even if deterring such attacks failed, and even if the U.S. Air Force or Army Special Forces were unable to effectively preempt such threats, attacks by missiles would have relatively little strategic or political impact.

The reality of the U.S. experience in the first Gulf War, however, challenged and refuted these assumptions. The Iraqis were not deterred from using their ballistic missile assets, even against noncombatants such as Israel. Mobile Scud launchers proved much more elusive than expected, and even more difficult to destroy with confidence. Even those that were damaged were often quickly reconstituted or replaced by reserve units. On February 25, 1991, a single Iraqi Scud missile slammed into a warehouse being used as billeting quarters for U.S. military personnel in Dhahran, Saudi Arabia, killing 27 Army reservists and injuring nearly 100 others. This was the single largest loss of life by any ally in the war. It marked a turning point in the debate over missile defense, and it led directly to renewed calls for developing and deploying theater missile defenses. It became clear in the aftermath of this attack that some kind of active theater missile defense would have to play an important role in protecting forward deployed forces in any future conflict.

The Dhahran attack also helped forge a new consensus in Congress on the need for theater missile defenses and resulted in passage of the Missile Defense Act of 1991. Among many other provisions, this legislation urged the president to pursue immediate discussions with the Soviet Union on amending the ABM Treaty to permit deploying additional missile defense interceptors, to increase utilization of space-based sensors, and to clarify the distinctions between TMD and ABM systems. This, in turn, led to a sustained programmatic emphasis on TMD acquisition that is now bearing fruit. The United States has begun deploying a family of highly capable TMD systems that are serving as the technological and operational precursors to more capable strategic missile defenses.

A consensus was building that TMD was necessary for America to carry out its foreign policy. As one analyst put it,

> a compelling case can be made for theater missile defense deployments in strategically sensitive areas where U.S. allies and friends face growing threats … well-designed, forward-deployed theater missile defenses could

alleviate allied concerns, signal U.S. resolve for friends in need, and possibly intercept missiles carrying lethal weapons. The downside risks of having forward-deployed theater missile defenses near or in troubled regions are far lower than the risks of abstention.[27]

By 1993, two years after the conclusion of the Gulf War, the army, the navy, and the air force had all initiated new TMD development programs or had accelerated existing ones. These programs can be divided into two categories: lower-tier interceptors, those that cover an area of 20 to 30 miles in diameter and seek to intercept missiles in range at altitudes of 10 to 20 kilometers, well within the atmosphere; and upper-tier interceptors, those that can protect a much broader area and seek to intercept intermediate-range missiles at the edges of the atmosphere or even in outer space. The U.S. Army's Patriot missile and the U.S. Navy's Aegis air defense system are the most prominent examples of lower-tier systems, and the U.S. Army's Terminal High-Altitude Area Defense program is the most promising and mature of the terminal phase systems.

Multiple systems are under consideration for the TMD mission. These have been undergoing continuous refinement and change for years as testing validates some and eliminates others.[28] Three systems were originally identified in 1993 as key elements of TMD; in addition, a fourth system was under consideration and would be decided in a "runoff" that would select either the Navy Upper Tier, the Air Force Airborne Laser, or the Army Corps Surface-to-Air-Missile (which later was removed from this competition when it became the multinational medium-range extended air defense system, or MEADS).

Other TMD programs that have been under development since 1993 include THAAD (under revision, no tests since 1999), Patriot Advanced Capability (PAC-3) (tested most successfully in Iraq, March 2003), Navy Aegis Ballistic Missile Defense (first deployments scheduled in 2005), and the Airborne Laser (which has had test flights for the aircraft platform). In addition, the United States has three international programs that are fairly well advanced: Arrow, a joint production venture with Israel; a new program under way jointly with Japan; and MEADS, using the PAC-3 missile, with Germany and Italy.

## Patriot

The army first introduced the Patriot air defense system in its antitheater missile defense role during the first Gulf War, where its performance was the subject of a fierce postconflict debate.[29] The Patriot missile system was initially designed in the mid-1980s to be effective against both aircraft and short-range ballistic missile threats. However, due to concerns over possibly violating the ABM Treaty, its antimissile capabilities were greatly constrained. Only when it appeared that a conflict with the Scud-armed forces of Iraq appeared imminent did the U.S. Army move rapidly to upgrade the Patriot missile systems' antimissile defense capabilities on the eve of the war.

In the aftermath of the first Gulf War, it became clear that a more reliable and effective theater missile defense system was needed, and the army contracted for the development of a follow-on to the Patriot system. The new system, dubbed the Patriot Advanced Capability 2, or PAC-2, incorporated hit-to-kill technology, rather than proximity blast fragmentation kill mechanisms. The PAC-2 came on line around 1995. This was immediately followed up by an even newer, more capable version of the Patriot system, based on an entirely new, much smaller, but faster missile, called the Patriot Advanced Capability-3. This system could defend a larger footprint than the older Patriots and PAC-2s. Even though it was faster and had greater range, it was a significantly smaller missile than the older Patriot, so that four missiles could be carried in the same container that before could carry only one. With four containers per mobile launcher, this increased the firepower of a Patriot unit from 4 missiles to 16 missiles each. Each missile contained its own radar for homing in on targets, rather than relying on a common, ground-based radar.

The first PAC-3 units were ready for deployment just prior to the second Gulf War, in 2003, where they were held largely in reserve for use against Scud missiles, which ultimately were never fired against allied forces. The older, less capable PAC-2s scored most of the successes against those shorter-range Iraqi missiles that were engaged. By 2005, some 350 Patriots had been modified to provide additional terminal protection against long-range missile threats. PAC-3 has been designed to defend against cruise missiles, as well, and has been shown to be effective in this role in tests against cruise missile-type targets.

## Aegis

The U.S. Navy has a long history of developing capabilities for defense of its ships against threats from the air, including cruise missiles, antiship missiles, and, more recently, short- and medium-range ballistic missiles. With the post-Gulf War emphasis on theater missile defense, the navy moved to upgrade its existing Aegis Combat System to give it antiballistic missile defense capabilities. The Aegis air defense system was first deployed in the 1970s, based on the standard family of guided surface-to-air missiles. In 1997, the navy established a requirement for an upgraded missile that would have improved capabilities for intercepting ballistic missiles. This new missile entered development soon thereafter and was dubbed Standard Missile (SM)-3.

Aegis-equipped cruisers are deployed by other nations as well, which makes their conversion to TMD capabilities much easier. Japan operates four modified Arleigh Burke-class Aegis destroyers and plans to purchase two more. Spain is currently operating or building four F-100 class Aegis frigates, and Norway is procuring five of this same type. South Korea is building Aegis-equipped variants of its KDX destroyers, and Australia is also considering acquiring Aegis-equipped "Air Warfare Destroyers" that could, at a later date, be adapted for a theater missile defense role.

By early 2005, another two Aegis destroyers were equipped with the new Standard Missile-3 interceptor, while 15 such ships are to be fitted with the surveillance and radar tracking systems that support the SM-3. By the end of 2005, the navy had three Aegis destroyers equipped with a total of 22 SM-3 interceptors. SM-3 missiles will also be designed with an inherent capability to defend against the cruise missile threat, just as is the case with PAC-3.

## THAAD

In September 1992, the army initiated the Theater High-Altitude Area Defense program, or THAAD.[30] Currently, this is the most mature of the upper-tier terminal phase TMD systems in development. With a range of over 200 kilometers and a maximum intercept altitude of 150 kilometers, THAAD is designed to intercept both short- and medium-range ballistic missiles either within or above the atmosphere. THAAD will have a significantly more capable radar than the PAC-3, with the ability to acquire missile threats at ranges up to 1,000 kilometers. In combination with the PAC-3, it will provide layered missile defense protection (that is, a shoot-look-shoot capability) for deployed forces as well as population centers. Low-rate initial production of up to 40 missiles per year is currently planned to begin in 2006. The U.S. Army is expected to acquire 80–99 THAAD launchers, 18 ground-based radars, and a total of 1,422 THAAD missiles. Like each of the other TMD systems discussed above, THAAD will also have a built-in counter-cruise missile capability.

## Airborne Laser (ABL)

The air force's contribution to tactical missile defense is a modified Boeing 747 aircraft carrying a large chemical oxygen-iodine laser. The laser will shoot down missiles during their first phase of flight, the boost phase. As originally planned, it will be able to hit short-range ballistic missiles but eventually ICBMs, as well. The aircraft is currently undergoing test flights, but for technical reasons it has not yet been mated with its laser. Plans call for two or three operational ABL platforms to be available between 2006 and 2008.

## Long-Range Missile Defense Programs

Spending on TMD systems substantially increased following the first Gulf War and the passage of the 1991 Missile Defense Act, but funding for national missile defense programs actually decreased throughout much of the 1990s. The issue continued to be tied up in a rancorous debate over the fate of the ABM Treaty. (See Figure 6.1.)

The contentious status of this debate began to change in the summer of 1998, with the release of the Rumsfeld Commission Report and the North Korean launch of an intercontinental-range Taepo Dong. These consecutive events forced the Clinton administration to realign its priorities on missile defense, and it subsequently devised the so-called "3 + 3" plan. Under this plan national missile defenses would be developed and evaluated over a three-year period, following which, if a decision were made to deploy them, a three-year deployment plan would be adopted. The assumption was that given three years' warning, the United States could deploy up to 100 interceptors (the ABM Treaty limit) at the old Safeguard site in North Dakota.[31]

The Clinton administration determined that it would evaluate any proposal to deploy missile defenses on the basis of four criteria: (1) whether the emerging ballistic missile threat justified proceeding with deploying missile defenses, (2) whether existing or prospective missile defense

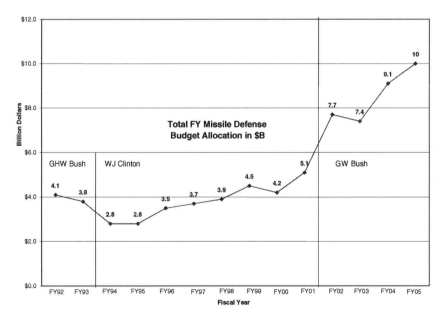

**Figure 6.1**  U.S. Missile Defense Budget Allocations by Fiscal Year (FY), 1992–2005

technologies were sufficiently effective and mature, (3) whether they were affordable, and (4) an assessment of the ramifications of such a deployment on international strategic stability and U.S. arms control commitments. The administration also proposed a basic system architecture that would have consisted of 100 interceptors, a new ABM radar, and upgrades to five existing early warning radars. The primary purpose of announcing this architecture was not to provide a blueprint for the Defense Department but rather to provide overall negotiating guidance to those diplomats working to convince Russia to amend the ABM Treaty to allow such a deployment.

However, on September 1, 2000, President Clinton announced his decision to defer deployment of a NMD system, saying "the system as a whole is not yet proven," instead urging further research, development, and testing.[32]

## Missile Defense and the Bush Administration

Upon taking office in January 2001, the George W. Bush administration immediately began setting a radically different course for missile defense, making it the centerpiece of his new strategic framework for national security. President Bush and his senior foreign and defense advisers did not dispute the validity of the four criteria considered by the Clinton administration, but believed that each of these criteria had been or could be met: The threat was imminent, the technology was available (or could be developed given freedom from ABM Treaty constraints), it was affordable, and the diplomatic and arms control ramifications could be managed. The Bush administration took a much more hostile stance toward the ABM Treaty. Rather than thinking of the Treaty as the "cornerstone of strategic stability," it was viewed more as an outdated "millstone" around the neck of American national security.

The administration soon dropped the "N" from "NMD" and began referring to "missile defense" more generically. This recognized that the distinction between TMD and NMD was becoming technologically blurred, especially for some U.S. allies. This move was also intended to signal that the distinction was an artificial construct of the ABM Treaty and that all missile defense systems should be considered as making a contribution to defeating the threat of ballistic missile attack. The administration announced that it would seek the necessary amendments to the ABM Treaty to allow more robust testing of missile defense systems and their possible deployment in ways then prohibited by the ABM Treaty. But it also made clear that should Russia refuse to grant such amendments, the United States was prepared to exercise its right under Article

XV to withdraw from the Treaty upon the expiration of a six-month advance notification.

President Bush began laying the conceptual basis for missile defense by stating in a speech on May 1, 2001, that the United States needed "new approaches to deterrence," approaches that relied on both offensive and defensive means.[33] This was also part of a broad push for a "new strategic framework" for U.S.–Russian relations, one that would reduce the centrality of nuclear weapons and formal arms control agreements in the relationship. Finally, the administration restructured the BMDO, elevating its status by renaming it the Missile Defense Agency (MDA) and seeking substantial funding increases for a range of missile defense programs.

There was an increased recognition by all Americans of the real meaning of vulnerability following the September 11, 2001, attacks on New York City and Washington, D.C. If hijacked airplanes could wreak such devastation, wondered analysts, what damage could ballistic missiles with nuclear, chemical, or biological warheads do to the country? This led to a nonpartisan call for larger defense budgets, including funding for ballistic, cruise, and theater missile defense.

At about the same time, consultations began in earnest at all levels of diplomatic contact with Russia over amending the ABM Treaty. However, Russia resisted this and warned that U.S. deployment of missile defenses would provoke a renewed arms race, obligate Russia to withdraw from the START (Strategic Arms Reduction Treaty), destroy further chances for new arms control agreements, lead to the utter collapse of the whole international arms control regime, undermine international efforts to combat the proliferation of weapons of mass destruction, and lead to a new Cold War between Russia and the United States. Consequently, these consultations did little to narrow the gap between the Bush administration and Russia over amending the ABM Treaty, or alternatively, fashioning a cooperative exit from the Treaty.

However, several converging factors forced a resolution of the impasse between the United States and Russia over amending the ABM Treaty in the fall of 2001. The administration believed that a long-range ballistic missile threat to the United States could emerge at any time and was determined not to wait until such a threat had actually materialized to begin preparing for it. The longest lead-time item in the administration's missile defense program involved the construction of a new ABM radar on the island of Shemya, Alaska, where the short construction season mandated pressing ahead with an early decision to start. However, it was not clear at what point such construction plans would cross the line of noncompliance with the ABM Treaty. If the United States wanted to avoid outright violation of the Treaty, it would have to provide the requisite notice of withdrawal six months prior to the beginning of the 2002 construction season in Alaska—early in the fall of 2001. Furthermore, the administration wanted urgently to begin exploring other technological approaches to missile defense then banned by the ABM Treaty, and it wanted to test certain theater missile defense assets, such as the radars on Aegis cruisers, against strategic ballistic missile threats—a step that was also banned by the Treaty.[34]

## The Decision to Withdraw from the ABM Treaty

On December 13, 2001, President Bush announced that the United States had given Russia formal notice of its decision to withdraw from the ABM Treaty, stating that "the ABM Treaty hinders our government's ability to develop ways to protect our people from future terrorist or rogue state missile attacks."[35] Within just a few hours of this announcement, the Russian government released a statement by President Vladimir Putin characterizing the U.S. decision as "a mistake," but stating that it was not a security threat to Russia (thus, there would be no arms race response), that Russia was determined to sustain improvements in U.S.–Russian relations (thus, there would be no return to the Cold War), and urging the United States to enter into a legally binding agreement on further reductions in strategic offensive arms (thus, there would be prospects for further arms control arrangements between the United States and Russia).

It appears from later statements by key administration players that negotiations over amending the ABM Treaty finally broke down over apparent Russian insistence on granting the United States relief from ABM Treaty testing constraints only on a "case-by-case" basis, which President Bush was entirely unwilling to do. In any event, this announcement set in play several things. First, in what amounted to a de facto quid pro quo, President Bush reversed his earlier opposition to a legally binding strategic offensive arms reduction agreement along the lines of the U.S. and Russian unilateral pledges issued at the November 2001 Crawford Summit. The Strategic Offensive Reduction Treaty—a follow-on to the START Agreement—was quickly negotiated and signed in Moscow on May 24, 2002. Second, U.S. withdrawal from the ABM Treaty became effective on June 14, 2002. But even prior to that date, the Defense Department began putting into place plans for several activities:

- testing TMD systems against long-range ballistic missile targets,
- planning an outreach effort to allies,
- calling on allies to participate with the United States in the development of a missile defense system, and
- developing ideas for deploying missile defenses outside the limits previously allowed by the ABM Treaty that would be presented to the president later in the summer of 2002.

Finally, and most importantly, these proposals to the president led to a second announcement from the White House, almost exactly a year later, that the United States would proceed to deploy an "initial defense capability" by the end of 2004.


## Initial Defense Capability

Having secured virtual acquiescence from the Russian Federation in its break from the ABM Treaty, the MDA to conduct a series of tests that incorporated heretofore prohibited activities, including notably the participation of ship-based radar in two successive missile interceptor tests. Meanwhile, the Department of Defense began drafting plans for rapidly moving toward deploying some form of defense against long-range missiles by the end of the president's first term in office. Such plans were presented to the president in August 2002.

It is not clear from the public record exactly what options the Defense Department recommended to the president in August, but a few months later, on December 17, 2002, President Bush announced that he had directed the Secretary of Defense to proceed with fielding "an initial set of missile defense capabilities" by 2004.[36] He noted that these capabilities would serve as a starting point for fielding improved and expanded missile defense capabilities later. His announcement also explicitly eschewed defining an "architecture" for the system or a broad outline of how all the pieces would fit together. In an accompanying Department of Defense news release, the administration simply said that there would be "no final or fixed missile defense architecture. Rather, the composition of missile defenses, including the number, type, and location of systems deployed, will change over time to meet the changing threat and take advantage of technological developments."[37]

The announcement contained midterm as well as longer-term objectives. Future capabilities would be a product of the "spiral development" approach to evolving the system architecture, whereby new components would be evaluated for incorporation into the operational force at intervals, or "blocks," every two years. The capabilities planned for operational readiness in 2004 and 2005, or the first block, according to this announcement, would include the following:

- 20 ground-based interceptors, of which 16 would be located at Fort Greely, Alaska, and 4 at Vandenberg AFB, California;

- up to 20 sea-based interceptors (using the Standard Missile-3) on three existing Aegis ships, whose radar and data processing systems would be upgraded to accommodate these missiles;

- additional Patriot Advanced Capability-3 units;

- upgraded sensors based on land, at sea, and in space, including upgraded radars at Shemya, Alaska, and Fylingdales, United Kingdom, and upon approval from the Danish government, at Thule, Greenland; and

- an expanded Pacific Test Bed to provide greater flexibility in testing geometry (allowing, for example, launches of interceptors on a more realistic west to east trajectory, instead of the existing restriction of launching from Vandenberg in an east to west trajectory).

This first set of initial capabilities falls far short of what the acquisition community would normally refer to as "Initial Operational Capability," or IOC, and has therefore been given a different moniker: "Initial Defensive Operations" (IDO) to denote that these capabilities will represent little more than test assets but will have some operational capability as well. For example, no actual test launches of missiles will be conducted from the silos at Fort Greely, since this would require flying over populated territory, something the United States has avoided throughout the nuclear era. All such tests will be from Kodiak Island, off the coast of Alaska, from the Vandenberg Air Force Base facility, or from the island of Kwajalein in the Pacific. However, the silos at Fort Greely will contain actual operational missiles that could be launched in the event of a crisis.

Under the approach announced by the president, and subsequently elaborated by Office of the Secretary of Defense (OSD) officials, this IDO capability may be improved in the future through additional deployments at subsequent two-year intervals or blocks, such as deployment of additional ground- and sea-based interceptors, including the following:

- Patriot (PAC-3) units;
- initial deployment of THAAD;
- deployment of the Airborne Laser system;
- development of a family of boost-phase and midcourse hit-to-kill interceptors based on sea-, air-, and ground-based platforms; and
- development of enhanced sensor capabilities; and development and testing of space-based defenses.

## Surveillance Systems

The radar and surveillance component of this initial capability could ultimately be its most important and lasting legacy. Several key programs are under way to upgrade U.S. and allied early warning and tracking capabilities as a contribution to the missile defense mission. They include the following:

### X-Band Radar

In order to discriminate between reentry vehicles and decoys or other countermeasures, the system requires an improved radar system in the

X frequency band. Cold War radars, such as the Ballistic Missile Early Warning System (BMEWS) at Thule, Greenland, Fylingdales Moor, England, and Clear, Alaska, operate in the L band and lack the fidelity to differentiate between similar objects in space—a capability that has been shown during missile intercept tests by the prototype X-band radar on the Kwajalein Atoll. Accordingly, the plan calls for upgrades to the BMEWS sites and the development of a floating mobile X-band radar built on an offshore oil platform that, by 2005, could be moved to the region of greatest threat. In the interim, the Cobra Dane radar (an L-band system) on Shemya Island, Alaska, will be upgraded to provide some discrimination capability along the route of the most likely attack corridor from Northeast Asia.

### Space-Based Infrared System (SBIRS)

Formerly called the SBIRS-High system, this will consist of six satellites: four in geosynchronous orbit and two in an elliptical orbit. These will replace the existing Defense Support Program satellites and provide early warning of missile launches, nuclear detonation, or other thermal activity around the globe. In particular, they will track and discriminate among missiles during their flight and provide sensor data to the battle management system. The first new satellite is scheduled for launch in 2006.

### Space Surveillance and Tracking System (SSTS)

Formerly called SBIRS-Low, this system envisions a constellation of satellites in low-earth orbit that would track and discriminate between incoming warheads and decoys. While SBIRS-Low originally projected a requirement for some 30 satellites to maintain global coverage, SSTS will initially deploy only two satellites, to be launched in 2007. At least 18 satellites will eventually be necessary to cover key areas of concern around the world.

## The Bush Plan for Missile Defense

In January 2002, Secretary of Defense Rumsfeld described the administration's missile defense objectives this way:

> First, to defend the U.S., deployed forces, allies, and friends. Second, to employ a Ballistic Missile Defense System (BMDS) that layers defenses to intercept missiles in all phases of the flight (i.e., boost, midcourse, and terminal) against all ranges of threats. Third, to enable the Services to field elements of the overall BMDS as soon as practicable.[38]

The specifics of the system were outlined in the 2001 Nuclear Posture Review, highlights of which were publicly released in January 2002, and at a Defense Department press conference in December 2002. Leading government officials identified the parts of the missile defense plan that they envisioned putting in place by the year 2008. These include an airborne laser to shoot down missiles during their boost phase, a ground-based interceptor force to hit reentry vehicles during the midcourse phase of their trajectory, sea-based missiles for defense against incoming warheads in the mid and terminal phases, terminal defenses against any long-range missiles that reach the United States, and a satellite system that can track missiles from launch to terminal phase and distinguish between warheads and decoys. All of this would be tied together by a far-flung command and control system. The program's goal was no longer to deploy a complete, working system to defend against specific threats; rather, it was to field missile defense capabilities as they became available and then link them to the existing infrastructure.

The current plan for a layered missile defense of the United States and its deployed forces and allies therefore contains a number of different systems. The first part, tactical Patriot PAC-3 missiles, has already been deployed with U.S. forces in Iraq and proven themselves in combat testing there. The second phase is the Ground-Based Midcourse Missile Defense (GMD), which saw its first interceptor missiles placed on operational status in 2004.[39] Other elements of the complex system are under development, as well. The aircraft for the Airborne Laser has had its first test flight; major strategic warning radar systems from the Cold War are being upgraded to handle the more stringent requirements of missile defense and warhead discrimination; sea-based point defense weapons and ships are being readied for deployment a year after GMD; the two space-based infrared satellite systems are under development, and testing continues on additional tactical missiles, as well as a battle management system to tie everything together.

## The Way Ahead

This will not be the first time the United States has attempted to deploy an operational antiballistic missile defense system, leading some individuals to ask whether "the third time will be the charm."[40] The chances that the current efforts will lead to a lasting missile defense capability will be enhanced by the fact that U.S.–Russian relations have successfully survived U.S. withdrawal from the ABM Treaty. Moreover, the United States faces a greater number of missile-armed and potentially hostile states than during the Cold War, even if it faces fewer numbers of long-range ballistic missiles overall. In addition, current missile defense systems benefit from advances in key technologies over the past 35 years and have a more modest objective than did earlier U.S. ABM systems, whose effectiveness was judged by how well they could defend against thousands of highly sophisticated Soviet ICBMs and submarine-launched ballistic missiles.

Over a decade after the Defense Counterproliferation Initiative was announced, the U.S. missile defense program has made solid technological and political strides. Yet its future is far from certain. Many elements of the American political spectrum oppose the effort that is being invested in missile defenses and highlight the treasure that a robust, working defensive shield will cost in the future. On the other hand, advocates of strategic and tactical missile defenses point out that the cost is less than the bill for strategic offensive weaponry in the Cold War and that this is a propitious time to move from a defense based on assured destruction to one based on defenses.

Given the concerns over stability during the Cold War, such a major shift in our strategic thinking then would have been unthinkable. But today a number of factors make such a change possible: Russia's change from adversary to partner; the rise of small, potentially undeterrable threats with WMD and the means to deliver them; and the increasing use of U.S. military power in an expeditionary mode, where it becomes vulnerable to localized missile attack. All of this makes a logical case for the development of missile defenses. To the degree it is possible, few would disagree that we need to shield our fighting forces and allies from missile strikes to the extent our technology and funding permit.

The Bush administration came into office in 2001 with a Republican majority in both houses of Congress and a mandate to deploy a missile defense system "as soon as technologically feasible."[41] They have begun to do just that, and their reelection in 2004 means that the deployments will continue. While the strategic defensive system they will initially field looks a lot like the National Missile Defense system of the Clinton years, there have been some notable improvements and changes.

For one thing, the initial 2004 deployment will not be an end point; rather, it will mark simply the first step in a long, evolutionary process of continuous improvements in what will become a layered defense of North America. Second, the concept of layering means that systems previously considered tactical (both for operational reasons and because of the classification restrictions of the ABM Treaty) will now be included in any U.S. missile defense system.

Third, the system will be deployed in stages or blocks, as noted above, using what the Pentagon is calling a spiral development model. In this concept, every move up the spiral requires additional testing and change. The system is not simply developed, fielded, and forgotten. Proponents point out that this way the United States can field something, which is "better than nothing." (More formally, it will "serve as a starting point for improved and expanded capabilities later.") Regular block improvements over the next 10 years will continue to enhance the system's capabilities.[42]

Opponents argue that this is a recipe for continuing cost increases and unproven technology. Rather than procuring a system the way it has been done for the past 50 years, the spiral approach can lead to changed priorities, a shortened and relaxed testing schedule, premature deployment, and potentially an ineffective defense. According to this argument, "the Pentagon is ready to place the system on operational status even without the parts needed for it to be effective."[43]

## Conclusion

The ideological nature of the debate over past deployment attempts in the George W. Bush administration was muted by the fact that missile defense proponents were running the White House and both houses of Congress. The end of the ABM Treaty and the advocacy of proponents in all the key offices had, as one writer put it, "allowed the Missile Defense Agency to focus on developing a missile defense system without being whipsawed by high-stakes political fights." Furthermore, the September 2001 terrorist attacks "empowered the president on national security issues, reduced the public's focus on missile defense issues, and made opposing the president on defense programs tough."[44]

There have been both significant progress and important shortfalls in U.S. attempts to achieve viable theater and national ballistic missile defenses in the period from 1993 to 2004. Some of the major changes in this era include the following:

- There has been steady and significant progress in development and testing of theater missile systems, with relevant systems demonstrating improved capability. For example, the Patriot-3 TMD system is an improvement over the PAC-2 systems deployed in Operation Desert Storm. Five other TMD systems are in various stages of research, development, testing, and evaluation: THAAD, MEADS, ABL, and the two Navy Aegis-based systems.

- There has been a watershed change in U.S. attitudes on national missile defense issues. The election of President George W. Bush and his NMD supporters, the termination of the ABM Treaty, and the aftermath of the September 11, 2001, attacks on the U.S. homeland, along with the first deployment of NMD interceptors in 2004, probably means national missile defense is a nonreversible program.

- There has been a blurring of the distinction between NMD and TMD, partly due to technological changes, partly because of the mixing of the same technologies in both, and partly because TMD and NMD can now use technologies and architectures previously limited by the ABM Treaty.

- Spending on both TMD and NMD has increased dramatically under President Bush, to an estimated combined total of $10 billion in FY 2004, by far the largest portion of the U.S. counterproliferation budget.

- Despite the progress in ballistic missile defense, the United States is still years away from effective defenses against a robust threat in either national or theater defense.

- There has been little apparent progress in developing effective cruise missile defenses, a serious deficiency since these weapons are widely available to potential enemies and provide a less expensive and probably more effective means of delivering biological munitions than are ballistic missiles. Indeed, far poorer states such as Iran, North Korea, China, and others can present an emerging threat to U.S. personnel by combining this delivery system with the poor nation's most available and effective weapons of mass destruction.[45]

It is clear that more needs to be done to solve the ballistic and cruise missile threats that are emerging in the twenty-first century.

In addition to strategic missile defenses that defend the American homeland from small-scale attacks or accidental launch, the United States needs theater ballistic and cruise missile defense systems that are deployable, readily available to regional commanders, effective, proven, sustainable, survivable, and flexible.[46] The goal of theater missile defense should be more than simple protection for forward-deployed forces. It can also serve to strengthen the resolve of friends and allies, deter or dissuade an adversary from going to war, or from escalating a conflict already under way. In this regard, robust defenses can complement other efforts at peacekeeping that make the use of force less likely, including arms control and diplomacy, as well as offensive counterproliferation operations.

The future of missile defense systems for the United States in this, its latest attempt to deploy defenses, is now becoming clear. In coming years we can expect to see the creation of a layered defensive shield that begins with short-range, tactical defenses over our troops and allies in distant theaters. Additional layers will include sea-based interceptors and airborne lasers to attack missiles in their boost phase, and ground-based midcourse defenses that will track, target, and engage missile payloads during their flight. All these systems will be linked via a sophisticated battle management system that relies on terrestrial and space-based sensors. Given the political will, public support for deployment, and the threats facing this country today, missile defenses are likely to play a central role in U.S. deterrence and counterproliferation policies over the coming decades.

CHAPTER 7

# Passive Defense against the WMD Threat: Progress and Shortfalls

*Walter L. Busbee, Albert J. Mauroni, and John V. Wade*

One means of countering the threat posed by adversaries armed with chemical, biological, radiological, and nuclear (CBRN) weapons is to employ effective passive defenses,[1] namely, actions taken to protect U.S., allied, and coalition forces against CBRN weapons effects, including measures to provide the following:

- detection and warning using sensors and alarm systems to detect and characterize CBRN attacks and tell U.S. forces to protect themselves;

- individual protection equipment (IPE), including ground and aircrew protective masks and suits and ancillary equipment;

- collective protection (COLPRO) shelters to provide a "clean" environment for personnel operating in aircraft, armored vehicles, ships, command and control centers, and other shelters;

- decontamination agents to provide protection and restoration capabilities for both personnel and equipment after an adversary uses chemical, biological, or radiological weapons; and

- medical systems to provide preexposure protection, CBRN casualty management, and postexposure treatment and therapies.

These passive defense areas collectively support the joint chemical, biological, radiological, and nuclear defense concept, whose elements are sense contamination, shape the battle, shield the force, and sustain operations.

Between 1993 and 2004, the concept of chemical, biological, radiological, and nuclear defense has morphed multiple times, in ways that have not yet been fully recognized by the general military community. It has changed from a largely stand-alone aspect of military operations during the Cold War to an integral pillar of the counterproliferation strategy in the early 1990s, a part of homeland security in the late 1990s, and an aspect of the military's antiterrorism efforts today.

This metamorphosis is the result of changes in the perceptions of what level of threat chemical, biological, radiological, and nuclear weapons presented over the years, how the threat should be addressed, and who would be responsible for executing this plan. Over the last decade, the Department of Defense (DoD) Chemical and Biological Defense Program was created, has evolved, and was adapted to these changes, but it has not followed an easy road.[2] The range of reactions to the need for CBRN defense has gone from apathy during peacetime to extreme concern during wartime.

Throughout the decade some progress has been made, in doctrine, in materiel developments, and in understanding what the threat is and is not. However, significant shortfalls still exist in the passive defense capability to counter the use of CBRN weapons. The next few years will be increasingly critical as a transition point for how the military addresses the future threat of what we now call chemical, biological, radiological, and nuclear hazards.

A number of important questions need to be addressed if we are to understand how U.S. passive defense programs have evolved during the period since Operation Desert Storm in 1991 to the present, namely, the following:

1. How prepared were U.S. forces for a chemical or biological weapons attack at the time of Operation Desert Shield/Desert Storm in 1990/1991?

2. What progress had the U.S. military made in chemical and biological passive defenses at the inception of Operation Iraqi Freedom (OIF) in 2003?

3. How far from the ideal passive defensive program is the present U.S. military and what areas need the most attention to improve U.S. security against CBRN attacks on our forces in wartime?

4. How has the CBRN defense process been changed to improve the Department of Defense's acquisition and management of defensive equipment since the inception of the U.S. counterproliferation program?

## U.S. Passive Defense Capabilities in Operation Desert Storm

The post mortems from Operation Desert Storm resulted in a comprehensive series of assessments in the defense and intelligence communities, all of them leading to the conclusion that we were unprepared to defend against any sustained use of chemical or biological weapons by the Iraqi forces. That realization, coupled with the continued proliferation of CBRN capabilities to additional states at a time when the United States had only limited counterforce and active defense capabilities, underscored the notion that robust, passive chemical, biological, radiological, and nuclear defenses really had to be the *first line of defense* of U.S. fighting forces.

The partial failure of various international nonproliferation regimes ultimately resulted in the conclusion by U.S. leaders that we should consider adversary use of weapons of mass destruction (WMD) as "a likely condition of future war." Thought had previously been given at various levels of the defense establishment about the need to enhance U.S. CBRN defenses and to prepare against future weapons of mass destruction use on the battlefield, but a coherent, comprehensive strategy with credible passive defense funding was not yet in place to capitalize on this new reality.

Many lessons were learned from the 1990–1991 Gulf War with Iraq in the area of passive defense against the chemical and biological (CB) threat posed by the Iraqi military forces. Our defensive posture was focused on certain knowledge of the Iraqi chemical offensive capability. U.S. authorities knew far too little about the latent Iraqi biological weapons programs, the magnitude of which was not known until 1995.[3]

## Desert Storm: Detection and Warning

The U.S. joint operational concept of contamination avoidance was simply not executable, given the limited number of chemical weapons detectors available across the force structure, as well as their inherent operational and reliability problems.

In 1991, there were too few robust and reliable point chemical agent detectors with a functional alarming or warning capability. The M8A1 chemical agent alarms were capable of being connected in an array around a fixed site; but due to high maintenance and false alarm rates, the perception was that their reliability was very suspect for the nominal three agents they could detect, and that in a static, and relatively benign, environment.

These detectors had little utility for troops on the move. The "dust buster" configured Chemical Agent Monitor (CAM) provided forces on the move some limited capability for large liquid contamination detection, but it was prone to false readings from ubiquitous battlefield interferents such as diesel fumes and burning explosives.

The provision of a number of German engineered Spurpanzer Fuchs (also known as the Fox vehicle) nuclear, biological, and chemical (NBC) reconnaissance vehicles, which could detect chemical agent vapor and liquid puddles on the move with an external sampler and an on-board mass spectrometer, demonstrated the future course for real-time chemical detection and identification.

Although these vehicles could maintain pace with mechanized fighting forces, there were few of them available when offensive operations commenced in the first Gulf War. Further, they were not integrated into the existing command and control and early warning structure, effectively limiting their integrated use and contributions.

In after-action reviews with units equipped with Fox vehicles,[4] it was reported that many were pressed into service during Desert Storm as alternate command and control vehicles, or used in non-CBRN related scout missions, because of their mobility and air-conditioned comfort, an engineering design feature that is essential for the vehicle's sophisticated detection systems to work properly. The standoff chemical agent detection systems, based on infrared technology, were not effective in the intense heat, blowing sands, and atmospheric turbidity of the desert.

Fundamentally, at the time of Operation Desert Storm, there were no mature biological agent detection capabilities. The United States and the United Kingdom fielded several biological agent detection teams that traveled through the theater with air samplers, manually testing samples with antibody assays for two suspect threat agents. The sensitivity and specificity of these crude biological warfare (BW) detection suites limited their utility since false positive rates were unacceptably high.

Of course, the medical community in theater was capable of conducting limited epidemiology surveys of sick troops after their exposure and when symptoms manifested themselves. Unfortunately, most advanced diagnoses and treatment would have had to be performed out of theater (e.g., Europe or the United States) with a time delay too great to be of any real utility for the troops who may have been exposed in the war zone.

## Desert Storm: Individual and Collective Protection

The state of individual protection in 1990–1991 was approximately as it had existed during the Cold War, with an ensemble of heavy-duty boots, gloves, and overgarments designed more for the cool plains of central Europe than for the normal conditions in the desert or tropics. The heat load and loss of visual acuity and manual dexterity while wearing this ensemble were severe. The majority of our troops had been issued the M-40 series protective "gas" mask that offered a number of improved performance features over the older M-17 masks first fielded widely in the 1970s.

In spite of the burden imposed by wearing this mission-oriented protective posture (MOPP) gear, a number of units that had trained with this gear in a disciplined manner before hostilities began clearly demonstrated the ability to maintain their operational tempo in the face of a significant chemical and biological threat.[5] However, for those who have not trained extensively in protective gear, there was a sharp drop off in combat effectiveness.[6]

The proficiency of the coalition ground combat divisions in Operation Desert Storm to sustain operations in a chemical, biological, radiological, or nuclear contaminated environment varied widely. Collective protection shelters played a limited role, partly because their quantities in theater were so low and, as a result, could provide protection only for a few key fixed sites, such as command and control centers and medical facilities.

## Desert Storm: Decontamination Capabilities

The U.S. forces in Iraq in 1991 had to rely primarily on corrosive solutions such as bleach to provide a rudimentary chemical or biological decontamination capability. The water-hungry characteristics of the mechanical decontamination systems, and the logistical burden of supporting them, were major problems in providing any kind of robust agent decontamination capabilities for either people or critical equipment.

The hot weather in Kuwait and dusty conditions that would help to isolate and evaporate some liquid agents probably provided more real decontamination capability or protection from exposure than all the designed systems brought into the theater combined. Nature's decontaminants and agent aging also exacted less of a toll on sensitive equipment, such as electronics, which would have been essentially destroyed by corrosive decontamination fluids that were administered.

An Operation Desert Storm contingency plan had to be formulated in the event we had to conduct mass burials of U.S. and allied chemical, biological, or radiological fatalities in the theater of operations because we lacked the doctrine, concepts and technologies, or systems to decontaminate human remains for shipment home to be buried. A less gruesome, but nevertheless troubling, fate would have awaited any large equipment, such as commercial aircraft pressed into cargo service and exposed to chemical, biological, or radiological contamination, because there was neither decontamination equipment nor any standards for deciding what was acceptably clean. The capabilities to bring such aircraft home clean simply did not exist and remains a huge problem still to be solved today.

Fortunately, coalition forces never had to cope with Iraqi chemical, biological, and radiological weapons attacks in the 1990–1991 Gulf War. Had such attacks occurred, the results would likely have been very serious.

The general mediocre state of U.S. and allied chemical and biological passive defenses and readiness to sustain even the minimum scale attacks, such as those that Saddam Hussein's forces had launched against Iranian forces in the Al-Faw Peninsula campaigns in the mid-1980s or the Kurdish populations in northern Iraq, was simply appalling. A prioritized and well-conceived "get well" plan with adequate funding was urgently needed to enhance the chemical and biological force protection and survival chances for U.S. and allied forces in future conflicts.

## Desert Storm: Medical CB Defense Capabilities

With the 1990 Iraqi invasion of Kuwait, the United States was faced for the first time since World War I with the imminent hostile use of chemical and biological weapons against its deployed forces. At that time, the number of readily available and fielded, U.S. Food and Drug Administration (FDA)-approved medical chemical and biological countermeasures was very limited.

Medical chemical defense products included the Mark I Nerve Agent Antidote Kit, the Convulsant Antidote Nerve Agent (CANA) diazepam auto injector for treatment of the chemical warfare (CW) nerve agents sarin (GB) and cyclosarin (GF). Pyridostigmine bromide (PB) tablets, intended for use as a nerve agent pretreatment, were an Investigational New Drug (IND) not yet fully approved by the FDA for use.

Medical biological defense products were limited to Anthrax Vaccine Adsorbed (AVA), Pentavalent Botulinum Toxoid (PBT) (as an IND), and Botulinum antiserum (as an IND) for immuno-prophylaxis against the respective BW agents.

While the medical chemical defense products were available in sufficient quantities to support Operation Desert Storm, the relatively recent fielding of CANA and the necessity of using PB tablets under an emergency waiver of traditional investigational new drug documentation requirements caused considerable confusion regarding doctrinal use of these products.

In contrast, the two biodefense vaccines were available in only limited quantities of anthrax vaccine and PBT. Only AVA was fully licensed and its use was problematic due to the lengthy required six-shot regimen. Those service members deployed to the Gulf received only one or two doses, and there was insufficient vaccine to complete the entire series for those who received the two shots.

## Pre-OIF (Late 1990s) CB Defense Improvements

Following Operation Desert Storm, Congress directed the creation of a single Office of the Secretary of Defense (OSD) program to manage and execute the DoD CB Defense Program. This program was executed between 1994 and 2003 through a number of joint service committees, chaired by the army with the four services' requirements and acquisition action officers as voting members. In the years after the conclusion of Operation Desert Storm and prior to Operation Iraqi Freedom the following passive defense improvements were made:[7]

- The M22 Automatic Chemical Agent Detector/Alarm replaced the M8A1 alarm, and the M21 Remote Sensing Chemical Agent Alarm and the Improved Chemical Agent Monitor were fielded to the force.
- The navy developed and fielded an interim biological agent detector.
- The army fielded biological integrated detection systems for a reserve and an active duty company.
- Central Command and Pacific Command received Joint Portal Shields for fixed site biodetection.
- The services procured Dry Filter Units as inexpensive biological air samplers for their installations.
- The army and marines received a common M40 and M42 protective mask and a protective assessment test system.
- All services benefited from the new protective suits, the Joint Service Lightweight Integrated Suit Technology (JSLIST).
- The army and marines procured the AN/VDR-2 radiacs through the program, replacing the outdated AN/PDR-27 radiacs.
- The army also had procured new AN/UDR-13 pocket radiacs to replace their old IM-93 dosimeters.
- The medical community was getting new COLPRO systems, the chemical and biological protective shelter and the Collective Protection Deployable Medical Shelter.
- There was a sorbent decontamination system to replace the individual and crew equipment decontamination solutions.

## Operation Iraqi Freedom: Passive Defense Capabilities

One of several reasons the administration of President George W. Bush had decided to forcibly remove Saddam Hussein's regime from power was to locate and eliminate Iraq's weapons of mass destruction program and to prevent the possible transfer of such weapons to terrorist organizations.[8]

Intelligence briefs on Iraq's capabilities focused on the possibility that Iraq had reconstituted its WMD program between 1998 and 2002. It was suspected that Iraq had developed chemical and biological weapons and was pursuing a nuclear weapons program, but probably did not have any nuclear weapons. The CIA's (unclassified) National Intelligence Estimate in October 2002[9] assessed Iraq as stocking between 100 and 500 metric tons of CW agents, including mustard, sarin, cyclosarin, and VX. The CIA noted that the UN inspectors had not accounted for 6,000 aerial bombs developed during the 1980s as well as 15,000 chemical rockets and 550 artillery shells filled with mustard agent. The CIA also estimated that Iraq stocked anthrax, botulinium toxin, ricin toxin, and possibly smallpox.

President George W. Bush's administration stressed that it believed that Saddam was continuing to seek the ability to develop nuclear weapons. As far as delivery systems, the CIA noted Iraq's past experience in weaponizing chemical and BW agents in artillery shells, rockets, and bombs. The CIA report suspected Iraq's new short-range ballistic missiles, the al-Samoud and al-Ababil-100, as exceeding the 150-kilometer range mandated by the UN security resolution. Of special concern was Iraq's Unmanned Aerial Vehicle (UAV) program that could be delivery platforms for chemical and biological warfare agents. The CIA report noted these UAVs could "threaten Iraq's neighbors, U.S. forces in the Persian Gulf, and if brought close to, or into, the United States, the U.S. Homeland."[10]

Although it now appears that the intelligence estimates of Iraq's WMD program were inaccurate, the U.S. military had to deploy forces into a theater that at the time most leaders believed would include the adversarial use of chemical and biological warfare agents.

There had been some significant improvements in U.S. chemical and biological defense capabilities from Desert Storm to OIF. As Deputy Secretary of Defense Paul D. Wolfowitz stated,

> U.S. forces that deployed for Iraq Operations (OIF) enjoyed the high level of protection offered by anthrax and smallpox vaccinations. They also brought important capabilities that were not available to our forces during the earlier Persian Gulf conflict, including new and improved biodetectors, a new chemical detector that will trigger fewer false alarms than the ones we used 12 years ago in Desert Storm, lighter and more durable protective suits and masks, and the latest generation of short-range missile defense systems in the form of the PAC-3, which represented—and I know this from personal experience—an enormous improvement over the PAC-2s we deployed in Desert Storm.[11]

Planners in U.S. Central Command worked with the Office of the Secretary of Defense and the Joint Staff between May 2002 and January 2003 to outline their most critical requirements to provide CBRN defense capabilities, to include a large-area decontamination system, an interim decontaminant to replace the Chemical Decontaminant DS-2 (use of which had been halted subject to being eliminated from the U.S. inventory), additional biological point detectors, JSLIST protective suits, and medical chemical and biological defense countermeasures. The OSD directed that U.S. forces deployed in Korea stop receiving anthrax vaccine in order to prioritize the treatments for forces deploying to the Middle East.

The OSD counterproliferation policy office led a working group at the National Defense University in July and August 2002 to develop a concept for weapons of mass destruction exploitation and elimination. Plans were prepared for a small group of specialists to move in behind the main military force to quickly capture, document, and ensure the destruction of Iraq's weapons of mass destruction storage, production, and research facilities.

While there was no military force organized or equipped at that time to conduct this mission, the army was tasked to develop a structure and to support such a group. The army chose the 75th Field Artillery Brigade headquarters to be the nucleus of what would be known as the 75th Exploitation Task Force, a unit that would oversee actions of a group of military specialists including those from the Technical Escort Unit, the Defense Threat Reduction Agency, Aberdeen Proving Ground, and the navy. In addition, U.S. Special Operations Command had Task Force-20 searching for WMD sites in western Iraq, and the CIA had its CB Intelligence Support Teams moving behind the coalition forces as they advanced.[12] There was no question as to the intent to seize any WMD assets found and ensure that Iraq's WMD program was eliminated once and for all. The challenge was finding the Iraqi weapons and support infrastructure.

## OIF: Detection and Warning Capabilities

Military leaders all expected Iraq to use or threaten to use its chemical and/or biological weapons to ensure regime survival. To guard against this contingency, U.S. Central Command developed a Joint Task Force for Consequence Management, manned by several coalition CBRN elements, to support Kuwait's government in the event that Iraq attacked Kuwait with these weapons.

Lieutenant General James Conway, commanding the 1st Marine Expeditionary Force, thought that there were at least four "triggers" for employment of weapons of mass destruction.[13] He did not go into details, but one might postulate that those triggers might have been when the

1. U.S. and allied forces were readying themselves in Kuwait,
2. Coalition ground forces attacked and overran Najaf,
3. U.S. Army 3rd Infantry Division crossed through the Karbala gap, and/or
4. Coalition ground forces crossed the "red line" circling Baghdad on their way to bringing down the Saddam Hussein Ba'athist regime.

During Operation Iraqi Freedom there was no evidence of Iraqi chemical or biological weapons employment. Nor was there any definitive evidence that Iraq had reinitiated its program after Operation Desert Storm to produce and stock chemical, biological, radiological, or nuclear weapons. All that has been found were some older chemical munitions produced prior to 1991 mixed in stockpiles of their conventional weapons.

The lessons learned from this conflict are still being accumulated and analyzed. Preliminary reports indicate that the U.S. military has probably solved the CW agent false alarm problem with the fielding of the M22 automatic chemical agent disarmament alarm, as the replacement for the error-prone M8A1 alarm. Nonetheless, some U.S. units deployed to Kuwait and Iraq with chickens and pigeons that they used as their sentinels because they did not have confidence that these systems would be available or configured in an integrated network that would provide real-time warning of a CW agent attack.

Partly because U.S. military forces could not be sure of getting adequate immediate warning of a chemical, biological, or radiological weapon contaminating their area after release, U.S. units in OIF treated each Iraqi missile launch as a CBRN threat that required a reciprocal protective action. Therefore, the rule was to don one's protective mask anytime an air raid or incoming missile was reported.

Sadly, in case after case, well-trained chemical warfare specialists, a dozen years after Operation Desert Storm, still had to use obsolete chemical agent detection paper or the handheld CAM to screen suspect drums at remote Iraqi laboratories in a search for possible chemical weapons stockpiles.

## OIF: Decontamination Capabilities

In preparations for Operation Iraqi Freedom combat, the U.S. Army deployed elements from both of its biological detection companies, the 310th and 7th Chemical Companies, as well as the 2nd Chemical Battalion, 83rd Chemical Battalion, the 468th Chemical Battalion headquarters, and many other chemical companies from both the active and reserve components.

In early 2003, just prior to the OIF attacks, the U.S. Army faced a shortage of lightweight and heavy decontamination applicators and chose to procure commercial decontamination applicators in their place, which caused some training and logistics challenges. The OSD approved the limited release of an interim decontaminant known as DF-200, which was available in small quantities. U.S. Central Command would get the last of its Portal Shield detectors in January 2003 and a limited number of Joint Biological Point Detection Systems rushed off the production line, but would not receive the large-area decontamination system it desired.

## OIF: Individual and Collective Protection Capabilities

It was a widely shared view in the U.S. military that there was a need for the new Joint Service Lightweight Integrated Suit Technology. The JSLIST protective overgarments are lighter, cooler to wear, and can be washed and used more often than the older battle dress overgarments. The problem, in the short-term, was that the services had too few of either the new or old protective suits.[14]

There were barely enough quantities to ensure everyone would receive two new suits each, meaning service members would have to rely on the older battle dress overgarment suits as backups should the two newer suits be contaminated.

By the time Operation Iraqi Freedom kicked off in April 2003, the U.S. military had provided some new collective protection shelters against toxic weapons that had not been in the inventory in the dozen years prior when Operation Desert Storm took place.

Added to the U.S. passive defense capabilities were the Chemical Biological Protective Shelter, the Chemically Protected Deployable Medical System, the Simplified Collective Protection Equipment, the Transportable Collective Protection Shelter, and the Collective Protection System Amphibious Backfit.[15] Had the Iraqi military used chemical weapons in OIF, the U.S. forces would have been much better equipped in both individual protective equipment and collective protection equipment than they were in Operation Desert Storm.

Nevertheless, this is not to say that all allied forces would also have been adequately protected. This was far from the case, except for the U.K. forces. Nor were all U.S. forces fully equipped against all types of chemical or biological attacks. Fortunately, none occurred.

## OIF: Medical CB Defense Capabilities

At the inception of OIF and in early 2005, there were three main biodefense medical countermeasures in the U.S. tool kit. First, there is AVA/BioThrax,™ currently the only FDA-licensed biodefense vaccine. Full immunization consists of six injections administered. After the first vaccination, subsequent doses are to be administered at the end of the second and fourth weeks and sixth, twelfth, and eighteenth months thereafter. These six injections are then followed by an annual booster shot.

A second biodefense tool available at the time of Operation Iraqi Freedom is PBT, a product effective against five types of Botulinum Toxin (A, B, C, D, and E). Unfortunately, there is no current manufacturer of Pentavalent Botulinum Toxoid, and all U.S. Defense Department stocks available at the onset of Desert Storm have expired as of 2004.

Finally, at the time of OIF, there was the biodefense provided by Dry-Vax™ Vaccinia (smallpox) Vaccine, the original smallpox vaccine given to eradicate the naturally occurring disease. The existing stockpile is held and maintained by the U.S. Centers for Disease Prevention and Control. Contracts for new production of a similar product have been awarded by both the Department of Defense and the National Institute of Health, but neither is fully FDA licensed at the time of this publication.[16]

## The Way Ahead: Future Capabilities Needed

There are several startling similarities in Operation Iraqi Freedom to the first Gulf War, notably the lack of any substantial advancement in the areas of decontamination, collective protection shelters, and medical countermeasures. While U.S. Central Command enjoyed increased capabilities in chemical-biological-radiological-nuclear detection and protective ensembles that would have helped more military personnel to survive a CBRN weapons attack, it remains unclear still if U.S. and allied forces could have sustained effective combat operations in an all-out chemical and/or biological warfare environment, lacking critical decontaminants, shelters, and vaccines in particular.

The U.S. Department of Defense and its Combatant Commands still lack an effective policy outlining how to handle contaminated human remains and formerly contaminated equipment, ships, and planes more than a dozen years after this challenge had been identified. During Operation Desert Storm, U.S. Central Command had the Technical Escort Unit operating under the direction of a Joint Captured Material Exploitation Center to conduct chemical and biological agent sampling and to escort the samples back to U.S. and U.K. laboratories for verification. Yet, the U.S. Army 75th Exploitation Task Force suffered the same challenges and learning curves, including a lack of organic communications and transportation support that the soldiers in 1991 also had to overcome.

### Future CBRN Sensor and Warning Issues

Although the U.S. military still does not have the detect-to-warn capability against aerosolized clouds containing biological agents, there have been significant upgrades in both U.S. biological and chemical sensors since Operation Desert Storm. Ten new chemical sensors and seven new types of biological sensors are now fielded. (See Chapter 12, "Seeking a Port in the WMD Storm," in this book.)

Unfortunately, in the face of possible biological weapons attacks by future military opponents, the United States was at the time of OIF, and is still, in a "detect-to-treat" mode of operations rather than a "detect-to-warn" status; yet it is far simpler to avoid casualties by donning masks before contamination rather than treating casualties after they have been infected. Our BW sensors and warning procedures were and are still inadequate.

There will be a much reduced risk of mass casualties from chemical and biological attacks once U.S. and allied military forces have transitioned from a detect-to-treat situation to a detect-to-warn capability. Once sensors can reach out and interrogate clouds of airborne CB agents, forces can be warned in time to go to shelter and don protective overgarments and masks, thus preventing exposure to lethal BW and CW agents.

## Future Individual and Collective Protection Issues

The future U.S. military forces will need more numerous individual and collective protection equipment than is now in the inventory. The present system provides two suits for each combatant deployed to a conflict area, but what happens when these suits are contaminated and no replacements are at hand? Furthermore, if forward based U.S. forces are fighting side by side with allied forces that do not have sufficient suits and masks and toxic-free shelters, the combined forces might be overrun by adversaries deploying CBRN weapons, thereby killing or wounding large numbers of allied fighters.

While toxic-free shelters are in place in far more bases than was the case a decade ago, the United States still needs to provide more state-of-the-art collective protection equipment to its forces both abroad and in the continental United States.

Further, the protective suits, masks, and shelters need to be made secure not only against the more traditional kinds of biological and chemical weapons, but must be able to cope with so-called fourth generation chemical agents. This means the United States needs to do some substantial research and development (R&D) on new suits, masks, and shelters, as well as on sensors and decontamination agents to meet this new emerging threat.

## Future Medical CB Defense Issues

Passive defense against CB agents has traditionally been divided into "medical" and "nonmedical" countermeasures. Nonmedical countermeasures, as previously discussed, focused on providing a physical barrier between an individual and exposure to the threat agent. This included IPE such as protective masks, suits, gloves, and collective protection systems where people could work inside in a toxic-free "shirt sleeve" environment protected from contamination.

This is a sound enough philosophy, because the best way to *not* become a chemical or biological casualty is *not* to be exposed. Unfortunately, IPE cannot be worn indefinitely, and it would be impractical to remain in collective protection shelters, even if an entire force could be so protected. In spite of the best individual or collective protection systems, if chemical or biological agents are used, casualties *will* occur.

Thus, medical countermeasures are needed. Required will be skin decontaminants, pretreatment or therapeutic drugs for chemical defense, and vaccines, antibiotics, therapeutic antibodies, and antiviral drugs for biological defense. Skin decontaminants must be extensively tested for both safety and efficacy and their use regulated by the FDA. Rapid decontamination can be looked upon as "early treatment."

The first specific medical countermeasures, beginning with the introduction of atropine sulfate as an antidote to nerve agent exposure, were viewed as the emergency response to a failure of the nonmedical systems. Military personnel might be exposed to nerve agents if they do not get a good seal when donning their masks or protective overgarments. They might also get contaminated while removing their MOPP gear if it has been exposed. The immediate remedy is to get treatment from others or administer it to oneself.

In keeping with the precept that it is easier to prevent disease than it is to treat it, medical pretreatment or prophylactic countermeasures have been developed that augment the effectiveness of protective suits and shelters, the efficacy of postexposure therapeutics, or all combined. Complementing these traditional medical countermeasures are the necessary *diagnostic* capabilities, essential to the proper treatment of chemical and biological casualties, preferably as soon as possible postexposure, before the onset of symptoms, and while there is a higher likelihood of success.

Currently, the only specific, fielded U.S. chemical defense countermeasures are directed against the nerve agents [GA (tabun), GB (sarin), GD (soman), GF, and VX]. Although these nerve agents differ in their properties and relative toxicities, as a class they are some of the most potent and rapidly acting toxic chemicals known. They are all hazardous in either their liquid or vapor states and can cause death within minutes of exposure by paralyzing the nervous system.

One medical countermeasure available for certain chemical agents is PB tablets that should be administered as one 30 milligram tablet every eight hours to be taken before nerve agent exposure. PB improves the efficacy of the Mark I Nerve Agent Antidote Kit in neutralizing the effects of the nerve agents soman (GD) and cyclosarin (GF).

A second medical countermeasure is Skin Exposure Reduction Paste against Chemical Warfare Agents (SERPACWA), the most recently FDA-approved chemical defense countermeasure. Topically applied SERPACWA forms an effective barrier that prevents absorption of nerve and blister agents, thus preventing or delaying intoxication. This protective paste is currently the only fielded countermeasure effective against the blister agents.

A third medical defense against chemical weapons attacks is the Mark I Nerve Agent Antidote Kit. This is a true nerve agent "antidote." As many as three Mark I injections can be administered as self-aid.

A fourth medicine to use against nerve agents is the CANA. In some cases where Mark I injections are not sufficient to arrest convulsive seizures, CANA should be administered as buddy aid.

Fielding of the only new chemical defense medical product, SERPAC-WA represents an advance in topical protection against chemical warfare agents, but is neither well understood nor doctrinally integrated into the services' chemical warfare protective posture.

Two major problems have contributed to the lack of progress in the medical chemical defense program. The first, and foremost, has been the difficulty in moving products through the FDA regulatory process. This has become more difficult due to the problems generated by the use of PB as a nerve agent pretreatment during Desert Shield/Desert Storm and the later unsubstantiated attribution of it to Gulf War Syndrome. The second major issue is the minimal funding of the advanced development of medical chemical defense related products.

Progress has also been slow in providing an adequate medical defense against chemical agents. Concerns that PBT tablets might have in some way contributed to "Gulf War Syndrome" all but eliminated this potentially effective product from the Defense Department inventory until such time that it achieved full FDA licensure. Fielding of SERPACWA, while representing an advance in topical protection against chemical warfare agents, was, in the authors' opinion, neither well understood nor adequately integrated into the services' protective posture.

The lack of U.S. preparedness against adversaries capable of engaging in biological warfare was the reason for the establishment of the Joint Program Office for Biological Defense in 1993. Its charter identified two major functions: (1) the establishment and fielding of a biodetection capability and (2) the identification, production, manufacture, and licensure of effective biodefense countermeasures against those biological warfare agents identified on the Chairman of the Joint Chiefs of Staff validated threat list.

By 2004, over a decade later, the U.S. medical preparedness to face a BW-capable adversary is somewhat better, but still faces challenges. Production and regulatory difficulties experienced by the sole manufacturer of AVA in the late 1990s have been corrected and there are more than enough doses of this vaccine available to protect any deploying force. Studies sponsored by the Centers for Disease Control and Prevention to reduce the required number of doses from six to three are progressing on schedule and should allow for FDA approval, making this a far more "deployment friendly" product. On the other hand, there is no current manufacturer of PBT, and all remaining stocks have been placed on hold by the FDA due to a loss of potency. Finally, it is a disappointment and potential danger that there have been no additional biodefense vaccines licensed since Operation Desert Storm.

The Department of Defense has funded research in medical biological defense as a joint program since fiscal year 1996, in accordance with legislative direction provided in Public Law 103-160, which also identified the army as executive agent for the program. Research is driven by the appropriate joint future operational capabilities documents which translate into operational requirements documents generated primarily by the Army Medical Department Center and School (with input from the other services and coordination by the Medical Program Sub-Panel of the Joint Requirements Office through the U.S. Army Training and Doctrine Command requirements process).

As one defense analyst has noted regarding the status of the vaccine programs,

> A quick look at the current status of the U.S. program gives some idea of the ground that needs to be made up in biological defenses. Of the fourteen diseases that experts deem most lethal, effective and weaponizable, the United States currently has FDA-approved vaccines for only four disease agents (anthrax, smallpox, cholera, and plague), and the plague vaccine is not approved for use against pneumonic plague. Five are in the Investigational New Drug (IND) category (Q fever, tularemia, Venezuela equine encephalitis, viral hemorrhagic fever, and botulinum toxin) and may be years from final approval.
>
> In the case of five other diseases (glanders, brucellosis, staph enterotoxin B, ricin, and T-2 mycotoxins) no human vaccines currently exist.[17]

This is not the end of the problem. Even though vaccines exist for cholera and plague, not enough of these vaccines has been produced and stockpiled to inoculate more than a small percentage of the U.S. armed forces, and U.S. pharmaceutical firms have not yet been provided sufficient financial incentives to manufacture more. Hopefully, this will change now that the U.S. Congress has passed the Bioshield legislation in late 2004.

## Future Needs: Areas for Capability Enhancement

Significant progress has been made in the U.S. passive defense program since Operation Desert Storm in 1991. Yet, much work in this area still needs to be done before it can be declared adequate to counter the threat. Major problems remain.

There are several areas that U.S. combatant commanders feel must be strengthened to achieve success in the U.S. chemical and biological defense program. Each year these commanders list their top 16 counter-proliferation capability requirements, the so-called "areas for capability enhancement" (ACEs).

In 2003, in the realm of CB defense, these combatant commanders listed areas they believe need the most improvement in passive defenses against CBRN weapons:

- the "detection, identification, characterization, location, prediction and warning of CW and BW agents,"

- the capability to "enable sustained operations in a WMD environment through decontamination, and individual and collective protection,"

- the "medical protection, training, diagnosis, treatment, surveillance and countermeasures against NBC agents, to include surge manufacturing capability and stockpile availability of vaccines, pretreatments, therapeutics and other medical products," and

- the "defense against, and detection, characterization and defeat of paramilitary, covert delivery, and terrorist WMD capabilities (including protection of critical installations in the United States and abroad)."[18]

In conclusion, while some substantial progress has been made in U.S. passive defenses against chemical, biological, radiological, and nuclear threats, there are still significant shortfalls in the CBRN-defense program.

Despite some improvements in its ability to fight and survive in a chemical or biological war, it still appears that the U.S. Department of Defense has done far too little research, development, and acquisition of vaccines, individual protection equipment, collective protection equipment, and improved chemical and biological sensors.

The U.S. military still is not fully equipped with adequate numbers of JSLIST suits, protective masks, and collective protective shelters. U.S. protective equipment needs improvement against so-called fourth generation chemical agents. Individual and Collective Protection equipment is also in much scarcer supply among U.S. allied forces, and this is particularly troubling in areas where the potential for CBRN weapons use is especially high, on the Korean Peninsula and the Persian Gulf area, for example.

Progress has also been made in developing decontamination capabilities against both chemical and biological attacks, but the most promising progress remains in R&D and not, as yet, in the field.

U.S. sensors to detect CB agents have improved significantly since Operation Desert Storm in 1991 to 2006. Nevertheless, particularly in the biological warning area, U.S. and allied forces are still in the detect-to-treat mode rather than the far better detect-to-warn mode because sensors have not yet been created to reliably scan the horizon to detect clouds of BW agents floating their way. Until that capability is created, U.S. forces may know they have been biologically attacked only after the disease symptoms appear among their ranks. A detect-to-warn capability would permit forces to respond to threats by donning masks and taking protective shelter to avoid becoming infected by such attacks.

Vaccine programs currently provide anthrax and smallpox protection to inoculated personnel, and significant quantities of vaccines and medicines have been purchased to cope with a biological warfare or terror attack with either of these two lethal agents. Unfortunately, this cannot be said about protection against the many other types of likely biological agents an adversary might employ, and much work needs to be done to provide workable new vaccines in adequate amounts to protect the force against these diverse biological warfare threats.

While progress continues to be made in various elements of the passive defense program, in individual protective equipment, in collective protective equipment, in decontaminants, sensors, vaccines, medicines, and in the way the Department of Defense has organized itself for CBRN defense, it is well to remember that progress is not success. There are numerous ACEs that must be addressed before we can say the U.S. military is adequately prepared to survive, fight, and win against enemies using CBRN weapons.

Despite some improvements in its ability to fight and survive in a chemical or biological war, it still appears that the U.S. Department of Defense has not fully supported the research, development, and acquisition of vaccines, individual protection equipment, collective protection equipment, and improved chemical and biological sensors.

There continues to be concerns that the U.S. chemical and biological defense programs are relatively underresourced, if all of the medical products are being developed in parallel with the same priority. While medical biological defense programs have grown substantially over the past six years, funding still falls short of the accepted and oft-quoted estimates of $100 million to $300 million per vaccine for full FDA licensure.[19]

The soldiers, sailors, marines, and airmen of the United States still need better passive defense protection, and if it is not available when our forces next take the field against an enemy force armed with chemical, biological, radiological, or nuclear weapons, the outcome could be extraordinarily costly in American and allied lives.

# CHAPTER 8

# Consequence Management

## *Bruce W. Bennett and Richard A. Love*

In the past decade, as the threat from rogue states and terrorist groups has increased, the United States and its allies have devoted far greater attention to how to manage the consequences of prospective uses of weapons of mass destruction (WMD). Consequence management[1] is a process *to mitigate the effects* of the use of weapons of mass destruction, including

- detecting and characterizing weapons of mass destruction attacks;
- measures that protect public health, ensure safety, and protect the environment;
- measures to medically counter the effects of weapons of mass destruction attacks;
- measures that restore essential services to government, businesses, and individuals; and
- planning, training, and equipping to coordinate/synchronize the civil-military response.[2]

A thorough review and discussion of U.S. plans for consequence management will include the following:

- The *history* of consequence management of the effects of weapons of mass destruction, with particular focus on the period since 1993.
- The *mandate* for consequence management in the recent *U.S. National Security Strategy* and *National Strategy to Combat Weapons of Mass Destruction.*[3] These strategies direct U.S. efforts both in the homeland and in support of U.S. forces and allies overseas, though these efforts are organized differently.
- The *potential effects* of weapons of mass destruction, including the types of weapons of mass destruction threats and the kinds of damage such weapons could cause to military forces and civilian society.

- *Current concepts* of consequence management, how it would be organized, and how the capabilities for consequence management have changed since 1993.

- The *potential ability to improve* consequence management in the future, especially in response to developing threats.

## History of WMD Consequence Management

When the late Secretary of Defense Les Aspin announced the Defense Counterproliferation Initiative on December 7, 1993, a formal concept of a coordinated response to deal with the consequences of a weapons of mass destruction event did not exist. While the Federal Emergency Management Agency (FEMA) would likely have taken the federal lead due to its disaster relief mandate, it was not until 1995 that consequence management as a concept developed within the U.S. Government counterterrorism community. Consequence management in many ways originated from the dispute over the drafting of Presidential Decision Directive 39 (PDD 39), signed on June 21, 1995. It established the Clinton administration's counterterrorism policy. In particular, it addressed the potential for mass casualty terrorism resulting from weapons of mass destruction. A dispute developed regarding the responsibilities of various federal agencies, specifically between the Federal Bureau of Investigation (FBI), which had the lead for domestic counterterrorism, and the Federal Emergency Management Agency, which had the lead for managing federal agency responses to disasters. To clarify the situation, PDD 39 distinguished between crisis management, where the FBI had the lead to prevent an incident or to conduct law enforcement investigations, and consequence management, where FEMA was the lead federal agency.[4]

PDD 39 also focused attention on the need to respond to the threat of chemical, biological, and nuclear terrorism, stating that "[t]he United States shall give the highest priority to developing effective capabilities to detect, prevent, defeat and manage the consequences of nuclear, biological or chemical materials or weapons used by terrorists."[5]

Although PDD 39 was a significant step, efforts to implement the new policy highlighted certain key problems. First, responsibilities were diffused throughout the government. There was no senior government official who had clear authority over the many agencies with a legitimate role in consequence management. As a result, the Clinton administration discovered that it was difficult to resolve interagency disputes or to ensure that agencies were taking the steps needed to fulfill their responsibilities in this arena.

Second, efforts to develop responses in the area of chemical, biological, and nuclear terrorism revealed that the division of authority between the FBI and FEMA failed to resolve many of the bureaucratic difficulties entailed in managing responses to terrorism incidents. Specifically, the distinction between crisis and consequence management proved less clear in practice than it seemed in theory. There was no obvious time line to define when crisis management would transition to consequence management. Indeed, it became apparent that both sets of activities might be under way at the same time. Thus, PDD 39 failed to provide clarity over the issue of who, within the federal government, would have the overall lead.

Additionally, it became obvious that there was a need to coordinate crisis activities taken by law enforcement agencies with consequence management efforts under the supervision of FEMA. Thus, it was extremely plausible to believe the site of a terrorism incident would be a crime scene that the FBI would need to manage to protect evidence, investigate leads, and prosecute perpetrators. Yet, at the same time, other agencies might need access to the site to assist victims of an attack.

Widespread concerns about the inadequacy of PDD 39 generated considerable support within the administration for another presidential decision that would resolve some of these bureaucratic obstacles. Unfortunately, it proved extremely difficult to negotiate a solution satisfactory to all the parties.

In 1996, Congress passed the "Defense Against Weapons of Mass Destruction Act" also known as the Nunn-Lugar-Domenici Act. The purpose of this congressional initiative was to prepare local first responders for a biological, chemical, or nuclear attack in the interval before federal resources become available. The Nunn-Lugar-Domenici Act called on the Department of Defense (DoD) to develop and provide training and equipment for first responders in 120 U.S. cities.

In 1998, President Clinton signed Presidential Decision Directive 62, in part to rectify the shortcomings of PDD 39. The new Presidential Decision Directive, PDD 62, made substantial changes in the federal government's bureaucratic structure for counterterrorism. The new directive clarified organizational responsibilities and strengthened the authority of the National Security Council over those agencies. Second, the president asked Congress to provide $294 million in additional funding—above funding levels requested when the budget was submitted earlier in the year—for programs enhancing responses to biological and chemical terrorism.

PDD 62 was adopted to resolve widely recognized bureaucratic problems. It detailed a new and more systematic approach to fighting terrorism by bringing a program management approach to U.S. counterterrorism efforts. The directive created a National Coordinator for Security, Infrastructure Protection and Counter-Terrorism, who had the responsibility to oversee a broad variety of relevant policies and programs, including areas such as counterterrorism, protection of critical infrastructure, and consequence management for weapons of mass destruction. In addition, the National Coordinator could provide advice on the counterterrorism budget and was to coordinate guideline development for crisis management. The National Coordinator position was added to the National Security Council staff.[6]

The National Coordinator position was a compromise solution. One group of advocates argued that the administration needed to establish a czar who would control the federal budget for counterterrorism and could thus exert considerable control over the activities of the many agencies involved in counterterrorism. In contrast, other agencies opposed the creation of a position with such broad authority, and at least some are believed to have not concurred with the final proposal that was approved giving the National Coordinator more limited powers.

Responding to biological terrorism was the primary focus of the president's $294 million supplemental funding request. These funds were directed into three areas:

- $94 million for Department of Health and Human Services to create a pharmaceutical stockpile of antidotes and antibiotics to treat the victims of biological attack and to enhance public health surveillance and detection systems for disease outbreaks resulting from these weapons.[7]

- $10 million for the National Institutes of Health to conduct research on biological agents and possible treatments.

- $190 million to the Department of Health and Human Services, the Department of Justice, and the Federal Emergency Management Agency for efforts to enhance chemical and biological terrorism response capabilities. The bulk of these funds were to go to state and local governments, and the rest was directed to the Federal Bureau of Investigation to enhance its capabilities.[8]

The *1997 Quadrennial Defense Review* (QDR) expressed the official views of the Secretary of Defense and carried considerable weight within the Defense Department. The QDR[9] discussed the need to counter asymmetric threats, reflecting concerns that hostile states, bent on countering the overwhelming conventional power of the United States, might focus on responses that exploited U.S. vulnerabilities using weapons that differed from those relied upon by the U.S. military or against which the U.S. military was not well prepared to respond.

The strategic implications of chemical, biological, radiological, and nuclear (CBRN) weapons, including in terroristlike operations, were drawn out in a November 1997 study commissioned by the Office of the Secretary of Defense, *Assessment of the Impact of Chemical and Biological Weapons on Joint Operations in 2010* (also known as the *CB 2010 Study*).[10] This report focused on the impact that chemical and biological weapon use could have on the ability of the United States to project military power. The sponsors of the report were specifically interested in the impact of chemical and biological (CB) weapon use on the ability of the United States to prosecute major theater wars. They wanted to draw attention to the U.S. military's reliance on force projection from the continental United States, which could be targeted by CBRN. The study examined a baseline scenario, which involved Iran and Iraq conducting a coordinated campaign against U.S. interests in the Persian Gulf arena in the 2010 time frame.

The study team concluded that the United States could frustrate the campaign if the adversaries used only conventional war-fighting capabilities. When the attackers also employed chemical and biological weapons against key power projection nodes, the results changed dramatically.[11] The most significant conclusion reached by the study group was that "our military must be able to counter and cope with limited, localized CB attacks," but "massive battlefield use of chemical and biological weapons … is no longer the most likely threat."[12]

Comparing the baseline and the excursion involving chemical and biological weapons use, the study participants concluded, "The chemical-biological scenario resulted in delays, mispositioning of forces, and severe degradation of operational tempo."[13] Based on this result, the study team concluded, "Our nation's ability to project power is vulnerable to limited chemical/biological intervention in the force projection phase, including employment in the continental United States."[14] The study also emphasized the vulnerability of civilian, contractor, and host nation support personnel. Finally, the study worried about the potential impact of attacks on civilian populations.

Finally, it should be noted that President Clinton's direct interest in WMD threats and the need for an adequate consequence management response had a large impact on the progress made in the 1993–2000 period. His reading of *The Cobra Event* and subsequent discussion with a small panel of experts motivated not only staff on the National Security Council, but also those in the Department of Defense and other agencies.

It was during this time that for a period, the Defense Department created a new post, the Assistant to the Secretary of Defense for Civil Support, who led DoD efforts in the interagency process and who integrated internal DoD consequence management efforts. This position later morphed into what today is the Assistant Secretary of Defense for Homeland Defense. The Department of Defense also began to help in the planning that led to the setting up of what became the crisis responder unit now named the WMD civil support teams. Despite the lines of demarcation now laid out about who is responsible for what in responding to a WMD crisis in the United States, there is still some disagreement about the role that the Department of Defense personnel will be called upon to play should the United States suffer from an attack in the homeland with very large or widespread consequences. In such cases other departments or agencies with the formal consequence management responsibility might be overwhelmed, leaving the DoD as the only department with enough resources to do the job.

## Mandate for Consequence Management in the National Security Strategy

Until recently, the role of WMD consequence management in U.S. national security strategy has been somewhat vague, but several recent documents clarify this role. The 2002 United States' *National Security Strategy* identifies one major element of U.S. strategy as "[p]revent our enemies from threatening us, our allies, and our friends with weapons of mass destruction."[15] In turn, one of the three components of this strategy element is defined as "[e]ffective consequence management to respond to the effects of WMD use, whether by terrorists or hostile states."[16] The National Security Strategy states that

> [m]inimizing the effects of WMD use against our people will help deter those who possess such weapons and dissuade those who seek to acquire them by persuading enemies that they cannot achieve their desired ends. The United States must also be prepared to respond to the effects of WMD use against our forces abroad and to help friends and allies if they are attacked.[17]

Three major roles for consequence management against WMD effects are stated in the *National Strategy to Combat Weapons of Mass Destruction*. First, "[d]efending the American homeland is the most basic responsibility of our government. As part of our defense, the United States must be fully prepared to respond to the consequences on our soil, whether by hostile states or by terrorists."[18] The United States "... will develop and maintain the capability to reduce to the extent possible the potentially horrific consequences of WMD attacks at home."[19] Second, "[w]e must be prepared to respond to the effects of WMD use against our forces deployed abroad, and to assist friends and allies."[20] Third, these capabilities will help deter adversary WMD use and dissuade some adversaries from even acquiring weapons of mass destruction.

Part of the responsibility for the first two of these three roles is defined in the same document.

> The White House Office of Homeland Security will coordinate all federal efforts to prepare for and mitigate the consequences of terrorist attacks within the United States, including those involving the continental United States. ... These issues, including the roles of the Department of Homeland Security, are addressed in detail in the *National Strategy for Homeland Security.*[21]

Presumably, the White House Office of Homeland Security will also coordinate consequence management in the United States in response to attacks by hostile states. Meanwhile,

> [t]he National Security Council's Office of Combating Terrorism coordinates and helps improve U.S. efforts to respond to and manage the recovery from terrorist attacks outside the United States. In cooperation with the Office of Combating Terrorism, the Department of State coordinates interagency efforts to work with our friends and allies to develop their own emergency preparedness and consequence management capabilities.[22]

However, this document does not specify who coordinates consequence management outside the United States against a hostile state attack, though it likely would not be the Office of Combating Terrorism, especially in the context of a war. In wartime, it would be the responsibility of the U.S. State Department together with the host nation that would take the lead in consequence management after any weapons of mass destruction attack, though the State Department would likely rely heavily on assistance from the Department of Defense.

The *National Strategy for Homeland Security* argues that the consequences of a weapons of mass destruction attack on the United States "could be far more devastating than those we suffered on September 11, 2001—a chemical, biological, radiological, or nuclear terrorist attack in the United States could cause large numbers of casualties, mass psychological disruption, contamination and significant economic damage, and could overwhelm local medical capabilities." It indicates that existing responses to terrorism

> … are based on an artificial and unnecessary distinction between "crisis management" and "consequence management."
>
> Under the President's proposal, the Department of Homeland Security will consolidate federal response plans and build a national system for incident management in cooperation with state and local government.[23]

It later indicates that a national incident management system will be created as one of the major homeland security initiatives.

## WMD Threats and Their Potential Effects

Weapons of mass destruction are not a single category of weapons. The term weapons of mass destruction includes chemical, biological, radiological, and nuclear weapons, and there are major differences in the effects among them. There are also some major differences even within these categories. The variety of weapons of mass destruction threats we face are described in Table 8.1,[25] which indicates how rapidly these weapons usually affect people, the relative potential for mass casualty events, and examples of the specific agents or weapons that fit into each class. These are the threats against which consequence management was designed in 2004; relatively little effort has yet gone into consequence management of advanced chemical or biological weapons.

**Table 8.1** Different Kinds of WMD Threats[24]

| Class of WMD | Speed of Effect | Potential for Mass Casualties[a] | Example of Specific Agent/Element |
|---|---|---|---|
| *Chemical weapons* | | | |
| Choking | Secs-Hours | Low | Chlorine, Phosgene |
| Blood | Secs-Minutes | Modest | Hydrogen cyanide |
| Blister | Hours-Days | Modest | Mustard, Lewisite |
| Nerve[b] | Secs-Minutes | High | Sarin, VX, Soman, Tabun |
| Riot control | Secs-Minutes | Very low | Tear gas |
| Toxic industrial chemicals | Secs-Days | Low-High | Ammonia, Malathion, Parathion |
| *Biological weapon[c]* | | | |
| Bacteria | Days-Weeks | Very High | Anthrax, Plague, Tularemia |
| Toxins | Hours-Days | High+ | SEB, Botulinum |
| Viruses | Days-Weeks | Very High | Smallpox, Hemorrhagic fevers |
| *Radiological* | Hours-Weeks | Low-Modest | Cesium, Strontium, Cobalt 60 |
| *Nuclear effects* | | | |
| Blast | ≤Seconds | Very High | Fission (Plutonium, Uranium), and Fusion (Tritium, Deuterium) |
| Crater | ≤Seconds | High | |
| Prompt radiation | Immediate | Very High | |
| Thermal radiation | Immediate | Very High | |
| Fallout | Hours-Weeks | High | |
| EMP/TREE[d] | Seconds | Low | |

[a]Describes the relative potential for mass casualties per quantity of WMD used. Thus, compared to nerve agents, the effects of chlorine are low, while the effects of biological weapons can be very high. [b]Some nerve agents are persistent (e.g., VX), others are not (e.g., sarin). [c]Some viral and bacterial biological agents are contagious (e.g., plague and smallpox). There are some other forms of biological agents, but these are the most commonly considered for biodefense. [d]EMP means electromagnetic pulse and TREE means Transient Radiation Effects on Electronics. Both are radiation effects created by a nuclear explosion.

With most nuclear effects (blast, heat, and prompt radiation) and most chemical weapons, the effects occur very rapidly, before mitigating intervention can occur. In these cases, consequence management is largely limited to acting in the aftermath of the onset of effects unless personnel have strategic and/or tactical warning and are prepared before the attack. Biological weapons give time after exposure to begin prophylaxis that can prevent the disease effects, at least with bacterial diseases and others for which treatments have been developed. With radiological weapons and fallout, the key is detecting the threat and then staying away from it. Radiation and some chemical weapons tend to be very persistent, remaining in an area long after initially being spread. On the other hand, many other nuclear effects are transient and most biological weapons decay fairly quickly in the air, especially in sunlight.

Dr. Ken Alibek, a former deputy director of the 30,000 technicians and scientists of Biopreparat, making up half of the Soviet biological weapons program, has stated that biological weapons can be employed in three ways:

- contaminating water or food (water purification systems tend to protect water, but contaminated food can affect a modest number of people);

- releasing infected vectors like mosquitoes or fleas (inefficient and can affect the attackers); and

- creating an aerosol cloud (can affect masses of people, depending upon how the cloud is produced, what agent is used, and the wind and weather).

Of these three, the aerosol cloud is the most effective in causing mass casualties.[26] Chemical weapons and toxic industrial chemicals can also be spread as an aerosol cloud, and fallout and radiological weapons can be dispersed similarly. But most nuclear effects are generated by a nuclear explosion and radiate in a circular pattern from that explosion.

## Characterizing the Damage That WMD Could Cause

To illustrate weapons of mass destruction effects, Table 8.2 compares prompt nuclear, biological, and chemical effects from quantities of WMD that might be available, suggesting the areas that would be covered and the fatalities that might result if people are not medically treated. The chemical and/or biological weapons effects here assume delivery as an aerosol, presumably coming as a line source produced by an aircraft or vehicle with a sprayer. The areas affected would therefore differ by atmospheric conditions. In contrast, the prompt nuclear effects are roughly constant across these conditions. A biological agent such as anthrax covers a larger area than a greater quantity of a chemical agent such as sarin because the biological agents tend to be far more toxic, by several orders of magnitude.[28] A biological weapon such as anthrax might even affect a

**Table 8.2** Comparing the Potential Lethality of (Untreated) WMD Attacks[27]

| Weapons | Area Affected, Fatalities[a] | | |
| --- | --- | --- | --- |
| | Clear, Sunny Day | Overcast Day | Clear, Calm Night |
| Nuclear: 12.5 Kt, blast effects | | 7.8 km$^2$, 23,000–80,000 | |
| Biological: 10 kg of anthrax | 4.6 km$^2$, 13,000–46,000 | 14 km$^2$, 42,000–140,000 | 30 km$^2$, 100,000–300,000 |
| Chemical: 1,000 kg of sarin | 0.74 km$^2$, 3,000–7,000 | 0.8 km$^2$, 4,000–8,000 | 7.8 km$^2$, 30,000–80,000 |

[a]Assuming an aerosol release of sarin and anthrax, with 3,000 to 10,000 unprotected people per km$^2$.

larger area than a nuclear weapon of the size that a terrorist or new nuclear power might possess. But nuclear casualties would occur promptly whereas the biological casualties would develop over time and could, for some agents, including anthrax, be more easily prevented by proper treatment after the attack is recognized.

In practice, weapons of mass destruction use does not just cause casualties and fatalities. Such use can cause various disruptions to military operations and society, and it would be expected to cause particularly large-scale psychological disruptions. These impacts combined could lead to serious operational and strategic effects. For example, an examination of the casualties in the Tokyo sarin subway event showed that about 4,000 "worried well"[29] and only about 1,000 actual casualties sought hospital care. In turn, this behavior led to overwhelming the medical care system; a really large-scale weapons of mass destruction attack as depicted in Table 8.2 could cause so many casualties that the health-care system would fail, and people might take action against the government because of this failure.

Indeed, if hundreds of thousands of people are just seeking antibiotic treatment, local supplies could be exhausted for some period of time. The impact of weapons of mass destruction persistence was illustrated by the efforts to decontaminate the Senate Office Building and their high cost, as well as the duration of work disruption associated with the attack. Secondary effects on the economy as occurred after the September 11, 2001, attacks would almost certainly cause crippling effects from events of the magnitude suggested here.

## Delivering Weapons of Mass Destruction

The potential delivery means for weapons of mass destruction are described in Table 8.3. As indicated earlier, chemical and biological

**Table 8.3**  Delivery Means for WMD[30]

| Kind of WMD | Expected Delivery Means | Likely Covert? | Other Delivery Means |
|---|---|---|---|
| Chemical weapons | Artillery, ballistic/ cruise missiles, aircraft | No | SOF[a] |
| Toxic industrial chemicals | SOF attack storage tanks | Yes? | SOF attack tankers |
| Biological weapons | SOF with sprayers, cruise missiles, UAVs[b] | Yes | Ballistic missiles, aircraft, ships, SOF in food/water |
| Radiological | SOF with bombs | Maybe | SOF deposit |
| Nuclear | Ballistic missiles | No | Cruise missiles, aircraft, ships, SOF |

[a]SOFs are Special Operations Forces; terrorists could also fill this role. [b]UAVs are unmanned aerial vehicles.

weapons would typically be sprayed as an aerosol and carried by the wind.[31] A large quantity (hundreds of kilograms or more) of chemical weapons would be required to cause a mass casualty event, making an aircraft or large missile the likely source for creating the spray, though artillery could also be used if enough rounds are fired. Most nuclear weapons are also large and would normally be delivered by a missile or aircraft. Because individuals such as Special Operations Forces (SOF) can deliver only a small quantity, they are not a primary delivery means of chemical weapons unless the objective is to cause very selective and limited damage. A release from toxic industrial storage tanks is another way to cause mass casualties, as happened in Bhopal, India.[32]

Because much smaller quantities of biological weapons are required to cause mass casualties, Special Operations Forces or terrorists could deliver these weapons. Radiological weapons would usually be carried by the wind after an explosion disperses the radiation, and these would tend to pose persistent threats in the areas where the radiation settles. Radiological materials could also be used without being dispersed, though they would affect a much smaller area and number of people.

In terms of consequence management, the delivery means for weapons of mass destruction affects the ability to detect such weapons attacks and to attribute them. The delivery means also help determine the area and number of people affected.

## Methods for Managing the Consequences of WMD Use

This section addresses the requirements of WMD consequence management and how far consequence management has progressed since 1993. Because there was little capability for consequence management of weapons of mass destruction incidents in 1993, most of the current capabilities represent advances, especially outside of the nuclear area.

### Detection, Warning, and Confirmation

The steps in detection, warning, and confirmation are first, recognizing that a weapons of mass destruction attack has occurred, second, determining what type of WMD was used, third, warning potential victims of the attack, and fourth, confirming the detection and identifying the type(s) of weapons of mass destruction involved.

Considering detection, there are three basic ways in which an adversary weapons of mass destruction attack could be observed: (1) detection of the delivery vehicle, (2) detection of the weapon of mass destruction and/or its immediate effects, and (3) detection of the effects of weapon of mass destruction on people. Detection of a delivery vehicle, at most, provides a cue to one of the other forms of detection, because the vehicle might not carry weapons of mass destruction; detection is most likely when a delivery vehicle has only military applications (e.g., a ballistic missile). The ability to do this has advanced only a little in the last 13 years.

Detection of the effects of a nuclear explosion is the easiest to achieve because of how dramatic those effects are. Detection of the effects of chemical, biological, and radiological attacks requires the appropriate kind of detector. Radiation detectors are and have been the most commonly available; detectors of the presence of chemical weapons have become far more available and capable, and detectors for biological weapons have emerged that did not even exist in 1993. Still, biological agent detectors are not yet widely available, perform only point detections, and are relatively slow to achieve a detection. The roughly 30 minutes required generally does not allow action to be taken soon enough for people in the vicinity of the detector to protect themselves after being warned. Thus biological weapon detectors are usually referred to as "detect-to-treat" rather than "detect-to-protect" systems.

The relative unavailability of biological weapons detectors makes it fairly likely that victims of a biological warfare (BW) attack will seek medical care before a detector gives warning of the attack. This was the situation with the anthrax letters in late 2001. At that time, the medical personnel dealing with the first cases failed initially to recognize the symptoms of anthrax. It is now more likely (though far from certain) that small numbers of biological weapon cases would be recognized because of enhanced education and improved diagnostic procedures for detecting these symptoms, especially for anthrax.

Once sensors or observers signal that a WMD attack has been launched and/or its effects have been detected, the community must be warned immediately about the threat. This warning should encourage people to seek shelter or other protection when possible to avoid exposure to weapons of mass destruction effects. The warning should also alert medical personnel to be looking for certain effects and encourage those who were likely exposed to seek appropriate medical care. Warning should be supported by appropriate information of the weapons of mass destruction effects, seeking to reduce panic and other psychological effects. It should also reach out to the affected community, but not far beyond, to limit the number of worried well who would otherwise become psychosomatic casualties. Most U.S. cities were ill-prepared to provide such warning in 1993 and are not much better prepared today.

Once chemical, biological, or radiological weapons effects are detected, it is essential to confirm the detection and identify what type(s) of weapons of mass destruction are involved. Some detectors (especially for biological weapons) are prone to false positives that could lead to unnecessary and potentially harmful treatment, and there is not a universal procedure for treating all WMD victims. Confirmation and identification is generally a laboratory process. Laboratory confirmation and identification of biological weapons was very limited in 1993, with only two reference laboratories available in the United States for most forms of biological weapons, one at the Centers for Disease Control and another at the U.S. Army Medical Research Institute for Infectious Diseases. In the aftermath of the 2001 attacks involving the anthrax letters, laboratory capabilities have been more widely disseminated and improved (quicker options are now available), allowing for more rapid confirmation and identification.

## Assessment

After a weapons of mass destruction attack has been confirmed, the assessment process determines who has been affected and what resources will be required for managing the consequences of the attack. It also seeks to attribute the attack to the responsible parties. With any weapons of mass destruction use, one of the first actions is to determine the area affected. This is relatively easy to do for most nuclear effects because of the physical evidence of damage, but more difficult for chemical weapons, biological weapons, and various forms of radiation, including fallout, because of the lack of a visual damage pattern. For prompt nuclear effects and chemical nerve agents, this area determines both where most of the casualties will be located and where residual contamination may also be.

With weapons of mass destruction that cause delayed effects (more than a few minutes, especially with biological weapons and radiation weapons), it will also be essential, albeit potentially very difficult, to determine when the attack occurred and to provide this as a reference to determine who was likely in the affected area at the time. While it is usually assumed that the casualties will promptly seek health care, some may be incapacitated, and medical care may need to enter the affected and surrounding areas to seek out these people.

The ability to estimate the time of the attack and the area affected was relatively poor in 1993. There were some simple models of WMD effects that required information on the quantity and characteristics of the weapons of mass destruction, how and where it was disseminated, and the wind and other atmospheric conditions at that and subsequent times during the dissemination process. Unfortunately, little of this information would be known in the aftermath of a WMD attack.

The United States has sponsored at least one effort to develop a system that would estimate the attack timing and area affected based upon post-attack observables, but that effort has not yet led to a completed system. Thus, even today this aspect of assessment would be difficult to accomplish. At best, a rough approximation of the affected area would be developed over time.

The next step is to determine who was in the area affected and how seriously they were each affected by weapons of mass destruction. This is more difficult to do with weapons that have a delayed effect like biological weapons, because it may be days before the attack is detected and many people who were in the area attacked will have moved to other locations. At the very least, the assessment needs to estimate the number of people potentially affected, though the limited databases on population location (largely census based and thus not showing population fluctuations by time of day) made this a difficult process in 1993, and this is only marginally easier today.

Even today, there is no basic system available to determine who was in an affected area at the time of an attack; improvisation and broad questioning could provide at least some of this information. Whether people will be affected is in part a function of where they were located and what they were doing at the time. For example, some people might have been relatively protected, having been indoors or in an underground location. Moreover, some people may have greater resistance to weapons of mass destruction. There is relatively little information of this type available to help adjust raw estimates of the people affected.

The third step is to determine the requirements for treating those who have been affected. If one knew the degree to which each person was exposed to weapons of mass destruction effects, one could roughly estimate medical requirements. Naturally some people have more resistance to WMD effects, and some have less.[33] Some computer models that did not exist in 1993 exist today to help make such estimates,[34] but even these produce only very rough estimates.

The final step is attribution of the attack. The victim will normally want to identify who was responsible for the attack. If the attacker has used a delivery system like a ballistic missile, the origin of the attack can be easily determined, though the country of origin could claim that a renegade group was responsible. Otherwise, unless the attacker is apprehended or other intelligence information is available on the culprit, it is very difficult to attribute the attack. Some laboratory analysis may be able to determine a unique country or area of the world from which a particular chemical or biological weapon originated, though this is still not definitive in providing attribution. While some advances have been made in attribution since 1993 (e.g., the entire genome effort relative to different kinds of biological weapon agents), capabilities in this area are still very poor.

## Medical Resolution

In addition to public health efforts, medical resolutions of weapons of mass destruction threats can be divided into five categories: (1) prevention, (2) pretreatment, (3) postattack prophylaxis, (4) immediate treatment, and (5) long-term treatment. To begin any of these interventions, the nature of the medical challenge must first be determined. For example, people's symptoms may be quite similar from various biological agents, yet the medical intervention would be quite different depending upon the disease. There are also significant differences in medical interventions required, depending upon the type of WMD effect to which the person was exposed.

In addition, it is normally assumed that affected people will seek medical care on their own. However, many people may be incapacitated or unaware that they are being affected; a more proactive effort to find casualties may be required, especially in a mass casualty event. Yet many of the personnel who might perform such a search would be involved with the treatment of casualties. In addition, the affected area may not be well-known. It is therefore unclear when and how such a search would be initiated.

Before most people exposed to weapons of mass destruction can receive medical treatment, they must be decontaminated. Personnel decontamination relative to chemical and radiological agents is relatively easy because detectors can promptly define areas on the body requiring decontamination. It is more difficult to decontaminate people exposed to biological weapons because of the lack of a prompt detector for them.

## Prevention

Most prevention actions are actually not a part of consequence management, but are, rather, a part of passive defenses. Nevertheless, because all medical interventions are often included in consequence management, we discuss these actions briefly. Usually, there are not preventive medical actions against chemical or nuclear weapons, though good health condition is a preventive means with some effectiveness against all forms of weapons of mass destruction.

With biological weapons, vaccines are the key preventive means. In 1993, while there were various vaccines in use to protect researchers in the biological defense program, no vaccines against biological weapons were applied to broader populations. In the last few years, the vaccines for anthrax and smallpox have been applied more broadly as preventive means. However, for a number of biological agents that could be weaponized, there still does not exist a means of disease prevention for the broader military and civilian populations. Many in the community are also concerned that the evolution of threats, new or modified diseases, is outpacing the development of new vaccines.

## Pretreatment

Pretreatments are used to prepare personnel for treatment, making treatment eventually effective. For example, the nerve agent soman requires pretreatment with pyridostigmine bromide tablets within eight hours prior to nerve agent exposure for the nerve agent antidote kit [(NAAK)—discussed under immediate treatments below] to work properly. Pyridostigmine bromide tablets were used for pretreatment during Operation Desert Storm, but some suspected that it became a potential cause of Gulf War Syndrome, and, thus, the military plans use of these tablets only in very specific situations. Only if a clear soman threat or some other threat requiring pyridostigmine bromide treatment is part of the established chemical weapons threat is it likely that these tablets would be issued today. This may leave some U.S. and allied forces unprepared if soman use is not appropriately anticipated.

## Postattack Prophylaxis

Postattack prophylaxis is treatment of people who might be exposed to a disease or medical hazard but who have not yet shown symptoms. For example, in response to the anthrax letters in late 2001, antibiotics were given to thousands of people who might have been exposed to the anthrax. Because antibiotics can defeat bacterial diseases such as anthrax, the use of antibiotics before the development of symptoms was intended to prevent people from getting sick at all, a clear preference with a disease as serious as anthrax. Prophylaxis is most appropriate for diseases that have incubation periods of at least a few days, and which can be cured by the use of one or more medicines. Thus, prophylaxis applies primarily to biological agents.

In 1993, it was understood that antibiotics could defeat bacterial diseases, but the procedures for prophylaxis were not well developed. Indeed, the U.S. Food and Drug Administration (FDA) did not approve the use of antibiotics before the development of disease symptoms. Nevertheless, many experts felt that personnel exposed to anthrax, for example, would die if not provided antibiotics prior to the development of symptoms.[35]

Interestingly, some experts still feel this way despite the survival of anthrax letter victims who did not receive antibiotics until days after the development of symptoms.[36] Since 1993, procedures for prophylaxis have been identified,[37] and the FDA has approved some drug uses for postexposure prophylaxis. From a military perspective, military commanders can now order the use of antibiotics for prophylaxis in the aftermath of a presumed biological weapons exposure. Nevertheless, the lack of medicines to cure many kinds of biological weapons, especially the toxins and viruses, and the potential antibiotic resistance of even bacterial agents leaves postexposure prophylaxis an incomplete response.

Nuclear explosions create a radioactive iodine threat. This iodine can be absorbed in the human body. Potassium iodide pills can be used to block the absorption of the radioactive iodine if given as a prophylaxis. Since 1993, the U.S. Government has developed supplies of potassium iodide for just such a use.

## Immediate Treatment

With some chemical weapons, especially nerve agents, treatment must begin extremely promptly after exposure. As indicated in Table 8.1, effects occur in seconds to minutes. Therefore, the initial treatment must usually be self-administered with on-hand supplies. Because of the focus of the chemical defense community on the nerve agents, this early treatment has been packaged for military purposes in a NAAK, which has self-injectors carrying atropine, 2-Pralidoxime chloride, and diazepam.[38] These treatments are effective only against nerve agents, and against the nerve agent soman, they are effective only after the pyridostigmine bromide pretreatment discussed above. In 1993, only some of the U.S. military personnel serving in the forward area had nerve agent antidote kits; today, these kits are generally available for forward deployed personnel, though normally they are kept in central storage until a specific threat is perceived to reduce what troops must carry and prevent use of the nerve agent antidote kits in inappropriate circumstances.

With biological agents, immediate treatment usually begins after the disease is recognized, which could be as long as days after the development of symptoms. As noted above, bacterial diseases are normally susceptible to treatment with antibiotics, though in the case of anthrax it is now recommended that multiple antibiotics be given simultaneously.[39] Some toxins can be treated with antitoxins, and some viruses may be treated with antivirals, though often only supportive treatment is available for these diseases. In 1993, the antivirals were not available, and the national antibiotic stocks had not been acquired. These are significant advances today. But there is still much to do in treatment, as the difficulty in treating the viral illness Severe Acute Respiratory Syndrome (SARS) has shown.

With nuclear weapons, there is a combination of effects that require medical treatment. Medical injuries associated with blast effects usually require typical trauma treatment familiar to hospitals. But with small nuclear weapons the size that terrorists or new nuclear states may possess, prompt radiation will tend to be the primary source of injury and fatalities. This prompt radiation is released in the first minute after an explosion; while it consists of many components, the principal ones in terms of radiation effects are gamma rays and neutrons. The weapon also will release fission products that decay over time, causing the radiation that can contaminate downwind areas in the form of nuclear fallout. Immediate medical treatment against such injuries is critical, and U.S. capabilities are relatively advanced, as shown in the 1986 Chernobyl case. Advances in U.S. radiation treatment and trauma care since 1993 make the United States better prepared to deal with such threats, though the number of expected casualties from even small nuclear weapons used in a city would likely overwhelm locally available hospital care, even today.

## Long-Term Treatment

We refer to long-term treatment as care required after the initial medical crisis-causing injury has been addressed. Much of long-term care is supportive. For nerve agents, this care should begin within hours of exposure; for many biological agents, this care will begin within several days after symptoms develop. With nuclear weapons, this care would also likely begin within days.

An example of this kind of care was the hospital treatment given to the anthrax letter victims. Five of the six survivors who developed anthrax symptoms remained hospitalized for 18 to 25 days after symptoms initially developed, and even when released from the hospital they required follow-up care.

U.S. capabilities for long-term care have advanced since 1993, providing better abilities to return WMD victims to health. Nevertheless, many victims will have protracted care requirements, which very likely would challenge the U.S. medical system in a mass casualty environment. With regard to military populations, it is likely that many weapons of mass destruction victims will need to be evacuated even for parts of the immediate treatment and certainly for most long-term treatment, making an early return to duty unlikely.

## Protecting Public Health and Preventing Panic

Medical treatment is only a part of the medical requirements for consequence management. Additional action is required to contain whatever contamination exists, including the potential requirement for quarantine or other movement restrictions. Also, human remains must be properly handled. Finally, both because many casualties will be self-diagnosed and because the psychological effects of weapons of mass destruction use can be severe, efforts are required to provide appropriate information to the public and use this information to establish calm and control.

### Quarantine and Isolation[40]

Quarantine involves separating people or products that might have been exposed to a disease or other form of WMD contamination from people and products that are not exposed. Quarantine continues until (1) decontamination can be accomplished, (2) the incubation period of a disease has passed and it can be confirmed that the people will not develop symptoms, or (3) the people develop symptoms and are moved to isolation. Quarantine seeks to prevent the spread of disease or other weapons of mass destruction contamination. Isolation involves separating people who have disease symptoms to prevent the spread of that disease. Quarantine and isolation are usually applied in the case of contagious human disease, but could be applied more generally to reduce fear or other psychological reactions.

U.S. procedures for quarantine and isolation exist and are practiced with various endemic diseases. The World Health Organization has defined diseases that it monitors and could take action to control.[41] In addition, President Bush has recently issued an executive order that updates the list of diseases where quarantine should be applied in the United States.[42] However, the Defense Department regulation on quarantine is dated and mainly focused on preventing the spread of agricultural diseases.[43] The military medical system normally assumes that military casualties will be stabilized in forward conflict areas and then moved for most treatment to major medical centers in the United States. But it does not establish rules for when biological casualties or those who may have been exposed to BW can be moved or procedures for moving them.

The United States Transportation Command developed (March 25, 2003) an interim policy on how to handle such movements, but it applies to only seven diseases with bioterrorism potential and focuses mainly on isolation during movement of those already showing symptoms. But there is a developing sense that it would be best not to move contagious casualties, and there is some concern about properly applying quarantine and prophylaxis in moving those who may have been exposed to contagious disease.

Thus, while some progress is being made, there remain many issues for resolution, such as how to move patients back into the United States or through foreign countries en route to the United States, or how to apply mass quarantine/isolation to the tens of thousands of noncombatants who may be evacuated to the United States in some future contingency which involves biological weapons use.

## Travel Restrictions

Even in cases where quarantine or isolation is not called for, weapons of mass destruction contamination may require some forms of travel restrictions. Some travel restrictions are applied on a normal basis with endemic diseases and could be extended to other kinds of contamination, including biological agents. For example, when the SARS virus developed in China and other countries, travel warnings were issued to limit the people going to those areas and potentially exposing themselves to a contagious disease. Similarly, travel restrictions could be established around an area contaminated with residual radiation by a radiological or nuclear weapon.

With biological agents, some further procedures may be required to limit psychological reactions. For example, if an anthrax attack were detected in area A, it may be appropriate to "quarantine" the entire area A to prevent people who may have been exposed from traveling to area B where they could become sick with anthrax and create anxiety that an attack had also occurred in area B. Neither the requirements nor the procedures for these travel restrictions are well developed.

## Dealing with Human Remains

Human remains contaminated with chemical, biological, or radioactive agents pose a hazard that must be dealt with. Unless these remains are promptly interred, they could lead to other outbreaks of disease. Proper interment requires decontamination of the remains (especially for those chemically and radiologically contaminated), cremation, or sealing the remains in pouches that will leak neither liquids nor gases. Otherwise, ground water and soil could also become contaminated.

Without individual protection for those performing these functions, it may be difficult to handle these remains. These efforts may be very difficult to complete after a mass fatality attack. Consider, for example, the difficulties of burying tens of thousands of fatalities in crowded urban areas or on a battlefield. Mass graves may be required at least as an interim solution, but finding a location for such graves may require moving the fatalities out of an urban area. An alternative health measure may be to cremate the remains, especially to destroy the disease-infested dead.

Recent work in the RESTOPS ACTD (Restoration of Operations Advanced Concept Technology Development) program has helped to develop procedures for handling remains and examined appropriate remains pouches, though it did not find a fully acceptable candidate. Before Operation Iraqi Freedom, the Defense Department examined alternatives to returning U.S. military weapons of mass destruction fatalities to the United States, but an acceptable solution was not found.[44] Thus, considerable work is still required in this area.

## Public Information

The effects of some weapons of mass destruction attacks will be obvious (e.g., a nuclear crater or thermal and blast effects). In other cases, people will not understand that they have been exposed. And in either case, people may not know what to do about casualties or when/how to apply prophylaxis or medical treatment. Thus, one function of public information is to help people self-diagnose their exposure or potential exposure to weapons of mass destruction effects and take appropriate action in response. The reverse of this is information that would help people conclude that they have not been exposed and do not need prophylaxis or treatment—essential to limiting chaos and panic and the consumption of scarce medical services and supplies, thereby reducing the size of the worried well population. Even as late as the anthrax letters in 2001, it was clear that the United States did not have standard public information packages to fulfill these functions, though the U.S. Centers for Disease Control and Prevention and other Web sites have now posted some information to help in these areas. The Department of Homeland Security is working more on these functions.

In the aftermath of a weapons of mass destruction attack, public information also needs to provide a more general, calming function and seek to sustain governmental control in the affected area. This information should be synchronized with efforts to provide adequate medical assistance, resolve contamination, and restore services. Experience with the anthrax letters suggests that the inconsistent instructions provided by multiple sources undermined the credibility of those sources and caused employees to question whether they could trust their bosses. A coherent and consistent response plan was needed; the U.S. Government published the National Response Plan in December 2004 that helps define roles of government officials and bridge this gap.

## Resolving Contamination and Restoring the Environment

Each form of weapons of mass destruction leaves a different kind of contamination residual. Some chemical agents, such as hydrogen cyanide, chlorine, and phosgene, rapidly become gases in most weather conditions and disperse fairly quickly, leaving negligible residual contamination. Even the nerve agent sarin is like water, evaporating and dispersing within minutes in many weather conditions, depending upon the particle size. Many biological agents decay rapidly when aerosolized, within an hour or so, including plague, tularemia, and botulinum toxin. And most nuclear effects, such as cratering, blast, thermal radiation, and prompt radiation, are over very quickly. But other forms of weapons of mass destruction persist for a long time, including chemical agents like VX nerve agent, which has an oily consistency, biological agents like anthrax, which forms spores resistant to decay, and some forms of nuclear fallout/ radiation. These longer-term threats generally require some form of decontamination effort to restore the ability of people to live and work in contaminated areas.[45] Indeed, it is reported that there are places in France that still show signs of chemical contamination from World War I.

Before decontamination can begin, it must be determined what areas have been contaminated. Decontamination of chemical and biological weapons effects can then be done with various liquids and foams. Most of these decontaminants can damage sensitive electronics, and some are toxic and/or can cause damage to metals and other surfaces. A wider range of decontaminants are available today compared to 1993, but the damage that they can cause still limits their potential use. Moreover, the waste products from decontamination require special handling so as not to damage the environment, including soil and water tables. While there has been some progress on addressing these issues, much yet needs to be done.[46]

## Restoring Services and Confidence

If the weapons of mass destruction attack were to happen on the territory of the United States, some unique challenges would need to be faced. Certainly, one of the most difficult challenges to state and federal authorities following a weapons of mass destruction event is the timely restoration of government services and the need to retain confidence in the government's ability to manage the event effectively. Affected populations must see government elements quickly moving to contain damage, provide real and immediate services to ease suffering, and make assurances that plans and procedures are being implemented for prompt restoration of critical services.

According to the Federal Emergency Management Agency, recovery includes all types of emergency actions dedicated to the continued protection of the public or to promoting the resumption of normal activities in the affected area.[47] The FEMA definition encompasses a broad array of activities, crossing many functional areas and intergovernmental jurisdictions. Emergency actions range from attributional forensics and intelligence, to law enforcement and police activities to ensure the functioning of services, to logistics actions to enhance survivability of affected populations to medical countermeasures. However, it is important to note that the jurisdictional component does not stop at the public sector. Large private sector ownership of critical infrastructures also requires that plans and policies for recovery take their interests as stakeholders into account. Indeed, involving the private sector in response plans can enhance the reach of essential services and buttress the likely strained resources of state and local actors as they respond to a weapons of mass destruction incident. Essential to restoring services and thus promoting government confidence is developing robust intergovernmental plans across federal, state, and local authorities that are flexible, adaptable, and tested and retested through training exercises.

## Planning and Coordination

Under the previous Federal Response Plan (FRP), the lead federal agency for crisis management was the FBI and for consequence management operations was FEMA. To implement new presidential guidance, the National Response Plan (NRP) was published in December 2004 and combined the requirements for both of these.[48]

> The plan incorporates best practices and procedures from incident management disciplines—homeland security, emergency management, law enforcement, firefighting, public works, public health, responder and recovery worker health and safety, emergency medical services, and the private sector—and integrates them into a unified structure. It forms the basis of how the federal government coordinates with state, local, and tribal governments and the private sector during incidents.[49]

The function of crisis management operations is still primarily a law enforcement function and consequence management is still an emergency management function, including measures to protect public health and safety, restore essential government services, and provide emergency relief to governments, businesses, and individuals affected by the consequences of a WMD event. Yet, the NRP now provides established protocols to be followed with a new multiagency coordination structure that addresses many of the shortfalls of the FRP and blurred lines of responsibility between crisis and consequence management.

Under the National Response Plan, multiple new coordinating features have been created to respond to crisis in an all-hazards approach. Those new coordinating features include Homeland Security Operations Center, National Response Coordination Center, Regional Response Coordination Center, Interagency Incident Management Group, Joint Field Office, and the Principal Federal Official.

## Domestic vs. Overseas Consequence Management

Overseas consequence management operations have significant political-military implications for the Department of Defense, even though the State Department is the lead agency for the conduct of overseas consequence management operations in support of foreign governments or to assist U.S. civilians. The reason is simple: the State Department has virtually no response capabilities of its own and relies on other agencies to provide assets needed for consequence management operations.

Thus, the Department of Health and Human Services would provide expert medical advice to State in the event of a chemical or biological incident, while the Environmental Protection Agency would assume a similar role when addressing chemical incidents. The Office of Foreign Disaster Assistance in the Agency for International Development would provide critical support in coordinating international responses to an incident, as well as providing access to certain resources needed on a time-sensitive basis.

Despite the significant role that non-DoD agencies may play in U.S. Government responses to a consequence management operation in support of a foreign government, the U.S. military will probably be the most important single source of resources. Thus, the Department of Defense airlift capabilities will probably be responsible for transporting response assets to the scene of the incident. Depending on the nature of the incident, DoD personnel, supplies, or units could provide a significant portion of the deployed response capabilities.

### *Limited DoD Ability to Assist Overseas Civilian Populations*

This capability is always constrained and is likely to become even more limited in the context of contingency operations in a chemical or biological environment. DoD has relatively few consequence management capable units, the time required to deploy such units to distant incident scenes is excessive, and there is likely to be a high demand for such units in prosecuting a war fight and protecting the homeland.

## *DoD Depends Heavily on Host Nation Consequence Management Capabilities*

The Department of Defense has limited consequence management resources to support its military forces deployed overseas. Only during periods of crisis is the U.S. military likely to expand its overseas force deployments with significantly enhanced consequence management capabilities. As a result, under many circumstances, U.S. military forces operating overseas must rely on host nation capabilities. For example, in many countries the United States has limited medical facilities and must rely on host nation hospitals for treating mass casualties. Most U.S. installations have only limited ability for chemical defense or dealing with hazardous materials. In addition, reliance on host nation resources may be a preferred option to enhance the timeliness of response and minimize the impact of the same constraints that limit Department of Defense support for overseas civilian populations. Nevertheless, host nation populations (both military and civilian) will usually be affected in large numbers by a weapons of mass destruction attack that also targeted U.S. forces overseas. In such cases, the host nation will tend to focus on taking care of its own people, leaving little resources available for taking care of U.S. personnel.

## *Support to Coalition Partners Often Seen as Secondary to War Fighting*

Many people in the Department of Defense tend to believe that consequence management activities in support of coalition partners should be a lower priority than domestic responses or support of combat operations. From many perspectives, this attitude is perfectly understandable. The Department of Defense faces many constraints in its consequence management activities, partially due to the extent to which its capabilities depend on assets that are in short supply or that are needed to support war-fighting capabilities. The cost of diverting such assets could be a significant threat to the ability of the United States to prosecute wars against adversaries armed with weapons of mass destruction.

Consequence management capabilities would become even more limited in the context of contingency operations in a chemical or biological environment. As has been noted, the Department of Defense has relatively few units available to perform consequence management. It takes a great deal of time and expertise to create such units, and there is a high demand for their services in other missions, such as protecting the United States and carrying out U.S. war-fighting contingencies.

At the same time, some officials with responsibility for managing alliance relationships point out that circumstances may not permit the United States to ignore requests for consequence management support.

Access rights and coalition solidarity would likely depend upon the United States responding to requests for protection against weapons of mass destruction and providing consequence management assistance. There are numerous recent examples of the United States diverting scarce, high-value, high-demand military assets for such reasons. In 1991, the United States supplied Patriot missile batteries to Israel as part of a campaign to convince the Israeli government that it should stay out of the war against Iraq even if attacked with Scud missiles. Similarly, in February 1998, the Department of Defense reportedly provided Israel with chemical and biological defense supplies at a time when the United States was preparing to initiate hostilities against Iraq. More recently, this kind of support was provided during the conflict in Iraq by a NATO deployment of Patriot air defense missile systems to Diyarbakir and Batman in South Eastern Turkey.

## Toward a Capabilities-Based Approach

Much has been done to improve consequence management capabilities since 1993. Nevertheless, even against existing threats, current capabilities are clearly inadequate, and against some threats (like aerosolized hemorrhagic fevers), current capabilities are seriously inadequate. Investments by the United States and its allies to create defenses for these areas will gradually enhance U.S. and allied capabilities. However, to complicate matters even more, the threat is also evolving. Key concerns include the following:

- New kinds of chemical weapons are being developed. One example is the Russian fourth generation agents, about which the Pentagon has said,

… since 1992, Russian scientists familiar with Moscow's chemical warfare development program have been publicizing information on a new generation of agents, sometimes referred to as "Novichoks." These scientists report that these compounds, some of which are binaries, were designed to circumvent the Chemical Weapons Convention and to defeat Western detection and protection measures. Furthermore, it is claimed that their production can be hidden within commercial chemical plants. There is concern that the technology to produce these compounds might be acquired by other countries.[50]

- The genetic revolution raises many new possibilities for the evolution of biological weapon threats. Even before the recent advances in genetics, before the demise of the Soviet Union, its biological weapons program was pursuing a variety of antibiotic resistant strains of biological agents and also strains that would suppress the immune system. They also worked on variants of serious diseases that would potentially thwart existing vaccines or treatments.[51] Further advances in these and other areas can be expected.

While some ongoing defensive efforts may help to counter these evolving threats, it appears to be the case that the offensive weapons of mass destruction capabilities are both well ahead of the defensive/consequence management capabilities and, in some areas, moving even further ahead.

Part of the challenge in this area is the requirement that defenses focus on established threat lists. For example, Defense Department counters to biological weapons are focused on an established threat list of biological agents that intelligence sources have sufficient information to confirm. This approach focuses new defensive efforts on the offensive threats that emerged usually two or more decades ago. Moreover, this approach is inconsistent with the strategy laid out in the Defense Department's 2001 Quadrennial Defense Review, which called for capabilities-based, as opposed to threat-based, planning.

In a capabilities-based planning framework, one focuses more on the most serious threats that could plausibly exist, for example, smallpox or some hemorrhagic fevers, and fields defenses prioritized against those threats.[52] Indeed, the Quadrennial Defense Review includes a strategy component referred to as "Dissuasion," which seeks to develop capabilities against the most serious threats before adversaries can even develop those threats in an effort to dissuade adversaries from pursuing the threats in the first place.[53] In terms of military competition, dissuasion seeks to put the United States in the lead of the "challenge and response cycle,"[54] giving it a leading rather than a trailing role. But such an approach is generally not allowed or followed today.

To pursue a capabilities-based approach, sufficient funding must be applied to enhance the capabilities needed for consequence management of weapons of mass destruction attacks. While this funding has been increasing significantly in recent years, especially in terms of homeland security, the funding is still well short of being adequate. As Secretary of Defense Rumsfeld has said,

> It would be reckless to press our luck with false economies or gamble with our children's future. This nation can afford to spend what is needed to deter the adversaries of tomorrow and to underpin our prosperity. Those costs do not begin to compare with the cost in human lives and resources if we fail to do so.[55]

# CHAPTER 9

# Counter-WMD Concepts of Operations at U.S. and Allied Air Bases

*Charles R. Heflebower, Laura J. LeGallo, John P. Lawrence, and Bert A. Cline*

In the face of U.S. military superiority, potential adversaries have begun to turn to asymmetrical means as a way to counter that capability. Our adversaries understand that U.S.–led coalitions will dominate the battle space, if given the opportunity to flow their forces. Likewise, adversaries may try to inflict casualties on U.S. and allied forces early in the conflict in an attempt to make the coalition lose its "will" to fight. Such attacks are likely to include one or more elements of chemical, biological, radiological, nuclear, and high-yield explosives (CBRNE) warfare.

Recent events, such as the terrorist attacks of September 11, 2001, the subsequent dispersal of anthrax-contaminated letter threats, North Korea's October 2002 declaration of the reactivation of its nuclear facilities and missile testing programs, and the threat, fortunately unrealized, of Iraqi use of chemical and biological weapons against coalition forces in Operation Iraqi Freedom, highlighted the specter of weapons of mass destruction (WMD) use and brought it to the forefront of our national security challenge as well as our national interest. Of equal concern is the availability of an extensive range of advanced weapons and technologies, dual-use production and storage facilities, and scientific/technical know-how that has accelerated the proliferation of WMD capabilities.

The number of likely adversaries pursuing these weapons is growing, and the potential for increased production and sales of weapons of mass destruction between both state and nonstate actors, such as terrorist groups, is of serious concern. Secretary of Defense Rumsfeld addressed this increasing capability of our adversaries in June 2001.

> We do know that countries that do not wish us well have an enormous appetite for weapons of mass destruction and the ability to deliver them. We know North Korea does, and we know they've launched a two-stage [missile] with a kick motor for the third. With an ounce of luck, it could have been in orbit and would have inter-continental ballistic missile range. Everyone said they couldn't do it; how could those people who were starving, how could they possibly develop the kinds of system integration capabilities that would enable them to do that? They did it.[1]

Since the end of the Cold War, the threats and challenges faced by U.S. and allied forces changed dramatically. Many of the assumptions that had long dominated U.S. defense strategy, policy, doctrine, and force requirements no longer apply in today's new security environment, characterized by the rise of well-armed regional aggressors as well as smaller, nonstate actors with the demonstrated desire and intent to acquire or develop WMD along with suitable delivery means. While a new focus has emerged regarding the homeland threat, the United States still faces serious threats to its military forces overseas. Potential regional adversaries are very likely to turn to WMD, particularly chemical weapons, as a way to blunt superior U.S. military strength during the course of hostilities. This chapter explores, in depth, the improvements that have been made to operate in the chemical threat and, just as importantly but in less detail, the biological and radiological weapons threat.

## USAF's New Understanding of the Chemical Threat

Since U.S. Air Force (USAF) units traditionally deploy to strategic forward operating locations early in a conflict, they are extremely vulnerable targets to chemical warfare (CW) attacks. This is particularly significant given the USAF need to freely operate and sustain high sortie generation operational tempo from these fixed sites, and it is crucial to deterring and defeating the adversary. However, until recently, the ability to resume flying operations in the wake of a chemical attack has been hampered by assumptions of a "worst-case" scenario in all cases, which required personnel to don their protective equipment and remain in mission-oriented protective posture level four (MOPP 4)[2] for extended periods of time.[3]

A central feature of the prevailing worst-case approach was the familiar "slimed base" environment. The underlying assumption was that enemy missile, air, and Special Operations Forces (SOF) attacks could strike with enough frequency and intensity to create chemical hazards that were highly lethal, pervasive, and persistent. Consequently, the base populace was forced to spend extended periods in MOPP 4 until chemical reconnaissance efforts either (a) determined that a chemical agent had not been used or, more typically, (b) remediated the hazard, generally through a lengthy and resource-intensive decontamination process.[4] Regardless, it was anticipated that personnel would likely spend hours to days operating and living in MOPP 4. This worst-case approach had driven air force planners to accept substantially degraded operations as an unavoidable consequence of a CW attack. Considering this an unacceptable result, air force senior leaders directed a reexamination of these threats and the associated concepts of operation to mitigate the effects of a CW attack.[5]

Subsequently, tests, studies, and analyses sponsored by the USAF, Defense Threat Reduction Agency (DTRA), Joint Service Materiel Group, West Desert Test Center, and the Naval Surface Warfare Center (NSWC) at Dahlgren, Virginia, provided a greater understanding of chemical effects on air-base operating surfaces. These results, coupled with a more detailed understanding of the threat and the delivery environment, including the real-world limitations of the delivery systems, overlaid on the operations at a fixed site, revealed that by improving tactics, techniques, and procedures and adding several new technologies, aircraft sortie rates could be maintained even after CW strikes. As highlighted in the Air Force Senior Leaders Guide Update 2002, a revised understanding of the CW threat was evident. Many of the previous passive defense measures underpinning the USAF Nuclear, Biological, and Chemical Defense concepts of operations (CONOPS) and procedures were disproportionate to the actual threats, risks, and hazards, even in worst-case scenarios.

Perhaps the most significant conclusion to emerge from the past several years of testing and analysis is the realization that an air force counter-chemical warfare concept of operations (C-CW CONOPS) must be tailored to address a range of potential contamination environments. The extensive analyses suggested that developing CONOPS designed to exploit less severe environments, while retaining the ability to survive and operate in worst-case environments, provided the potential for significant operational payoff. This approach was consistent with the common operational philosophy of protecting against the worst case, but planning for the "expected case." See Figure 9.1 for a graphic representation of this shift in thinking from the traditional (worst-case) assessment to the current (expected-case) assessment. This adaptable and responsive philosophy (current assessment) underlies the approach the USAF recently has taken in developing a revised CONOPS for air-base operations in a chemically contaminated environment.

The C-CW CONOPS includes procedures and risk-based decision aids that are designed to improve leadership's ability to determine the specific nature of contamination following a CW attack. While it requires new guidance and training, the CONOPS is expressly designed to be institutionalized throughout the existing doctrine, organization, training,

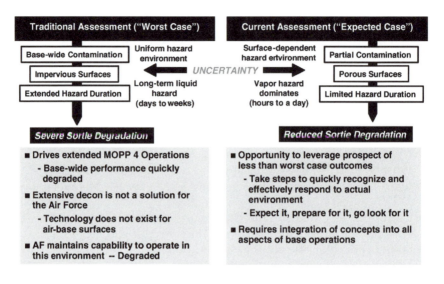

NOTE: *The uncertainty in the ability of an air base to complete its mission in the event of a CW attack is driven by the level to which that air base is able to implement and leverage the C-CW CONOPS*

**Figure 9.1** Range of Potential Contamination Environments from Worst Case to the Expected Case

material, leadership, personnel, and facilities (DOTMLPF) readiness domains of the air force.[6]

With a properly trained force, this knowledge allows appropriate post-attack actions to be taken that increase operational capability. The ultimate effectiveness of the C-CW CONOPS is driven by an installation's ability to implement and manage a decentralized split-MOPP[7] environment, the availability and employment of chemical contamination avoidance mechanisms, and tailored, site-specific procedures that balance force (personnel and equipment) survivability and mission production.[8]

Although the primary focus over the last few years has been directed at understanding and quantifying the chemical threat, the air force is beginning to apply that same rigor to understanding the biological, nuclear, radiological, and high-yield explosive threats that exist in today's battle space. While the C-CW CONOPS is approved and is being implemented throughout the USAF, the development of counterbiological, radiological, nuclear, and (high-yield) explosives CONOPS elements should ultimately lead to a singular, unified C-CBRNE CONOPS. This is the goal of the USAF C-CBRNE Master Plan and its road maps.

## Background: History of the Air Force Counterchemical-Warfare Readiness Initiative

In the mid-to-late 1990s, a series of high-level war games and exercises[9] raised concerns about the air force's ability to fly strategic airlift into an air base contaminated with chemical warfare agents.[10] In 1998, DTRA and USAF Headquarters, Nuclear and Counterproliferation Directorate (HQ USAF/XON) cosponsored a study to address this issue.

This analysis, commonly referred to as the "Aerial Port of Debarkation (APOD) study,"[11] found little basis for the generalized assumptions regarding the impact of chemical weapons on airlift operations. The relatively limited agent payload and inaccuracy of theater ballistic missile-delivered chemical weapons made it unlikely that the threat could contaminate an entire air base on a repeated basis. Moreover, the existing hazard duration estimates which came from existing manuals did not address concrete, asphalt, and painted metal equipment used at air bases. Existing test data suggested significantly shorter liquid contact and vapor hazard duration than traditional estimates. The APOD study quantified the operational opportunities that the expected shorter hazard duration period created in terms of risk to aircraft contamination and impact on deployment flow. This, in turn, raised the operational importance of developing a better understanding of the fate of chemical agent on different surfaces.

The results of subsequent live agent testing[12] at Dugway, the Czech Republic, and the Naval Surface Warfare Center confirmed that the liquid contact and vapor hazard duration is likely to be significantly shorter than previously assumed.[13]

Based on this new understanding and the comprehensive reexamination of historical test results, the Commander of the Pacific Air Forces (COMPACAF), General Pat Gamble, in June 1999, directed Headquarters Pacific Air Forces (HQ PACAF) to develop revised procedures for air-base operations in a chemically contaminated environment.

The Pacific Air Forces C-CW CONOPS[14] was built on the premise that it was possible to achieve dramatic improvements to mission-critical measures of success (i.e., sorties flown) while simultaneously strengthening the overall force protection posture of the air base. This called for a "holistic" approach that took an end-to-end look at current and emerging threats, conducted thorough hazard analyses, and applied the best available science to determine the safest, most effective passive defense measures consistent with the operational imperative of continuing the mission.[15]

In December 2000, COMPACAF sent out a memorandum that directed his forces to implement the revised C-CW CONOPS and recommended its implementation throughout the air force. In January 2002, the Chief of Staff, United States Air Force (CSAF) directed its implementation air force–wide.[16]

## The USAF C-CW CONOPS

The USAF C-CW CONOPS has four major tenets based on a risk-management approach that recognizes there are gaps in the underlying empirical knowledge base. (See Figure 9.2.) The CONOPS articulates this better understanding of the hazard environment in an operationally meaningful way. It provides procedures and tools that enable commanders to determine the specific nature of the contamination after an attack and take appropriate preattack (contamination avoidance procedures) and postattack (command and control decision making) actions to leverage opportunities to increase operational capability.

## USAF C-CW CONOPS Execution

When warning of an attack is received, it will be disseminated across the base, and personnel will don their protective equipment (MOPP 4), seek cover, and the basic flow of C-CW CONOPS (Figure 9.3) will be followed. Personnel will remain under cover in MOPP 4 until directed to resume operations. In all but the most time-sensitive, critical mission operations, it is prudent to limit operations outside until the droplet

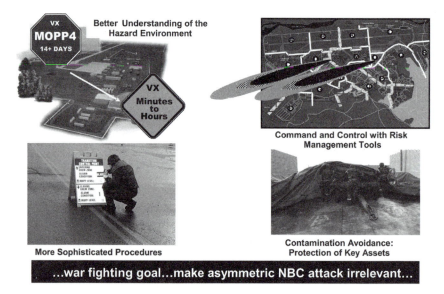

**Figure 9.2** Four Major Tenets of the USAF C-CW CONOPS

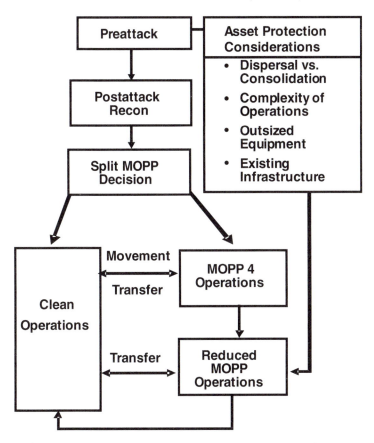

**Figure 9.3**   Basic Flow of Operations on an Air Base under the USAF C-CW CONOPS

deposition period is complete to minimize the risk of direct liquid contamination. Once the attack is over, postattack reconnaissance activities will be conducted to determine the extent of contamination across the base. The results of this reconnaissance will allow the commander to direct portions of the base that were not contaminated during the attack to reduce MOPP levels while operations in contaminated areas will continue in MOPP 4.[17]

Due to the lack of automated liquid agent detectors or vapor detectors sufficiently sensitive to detect liquid deposition of low volatility agents, like VX, prepositioned M8 paper[18] must be used to determine where the contamination occurred. Follow-on monitoring of surfaces known to have been contaminated enables the base to determine for itself whether or not the agent has sorbed[19] into the operating surfaces. Again, using M8 paper, base personnel can determine the contamination status of vehicles, equipment, and aerospace ground equipment/materials handling equipment (AGE/MHE).

Operations in contaminated areas will continue in MOPP 4 until the hazard from the concrete and asphalt operating surfaces no longer requires this level of protection. This time frame, when personnel will be required to wear MOPP 4, will be driven by the vapor hazard generated by the off-gassing of agent sorbed into the operating surfaces. This determination will initially be based on detector readings.[20] In most cases, existing detectors will not be sufficiently sensitive to detect low levels of off-gassing agent, requiring the commander to assess his/her mission requirements against the risks associated with reducing MOPP levels in these areas. The range of hazard times depends on height of burst of the missile, wind speed, air temperature, and air stability. This range of hazard times illustrates the uncertainty that commanders must be aware of when reducing MOPP levels since it represents a time of rapidly decreasing risk, where the agent is below acute lethal or incapacitating effects and designed to protect personnel from the lowest-level eye effects.[21]

Even after MOPP levels in contaminated areas have been reduced, MOPP 4 operations will continue when operating in or directly around vehicles, equipment, AGE/MHE, and munitions that were contaminated during the attack. These items represent both painted and bare metal surfaces that are expected to support a longer-term hazard than the surrounding concrete and asphalt operating surfaces. The C-CW CONOPS provides procedures for limited operational decontamination to remove any liquid that may be remaining on these surfaces. These expedient decontamination actions will not be sufficient to reduce MOPP levels solely because of their completion. Rather, expedient decontamination of these specific surfaces can minimize the risks and probabilities of inadvertent personal contact and cross-contamination. The inability of any fielded decontamination technique to neutralize all chemical hazards is primarily due to the porous quality of most surfaces found on an air base, to include the paint used on most USAF assets.[22] Much like the operating surfaces, these paints sorb the agent within minutes. While the liquid contact and transfer hazard dissipates quickly, a vapor hazard will remain for some period. The ability of an air base to have vehicles, equipment, AGE/MHE, and munitions covered at the time of attack is an important element of contamination avoidance, because of the inability to completely neutralize chemical agents once they have sorbed into most surfaces. The benefits of covering critical assets preattack are increased personnel safety, the absence of cross-contamination through inadvertent agent transfer, and reduced MOPP 4 time lines.

Procedures for managing operations in MOPP 4 must be maintained. These include capabilities for shelter management, contamination control areas, and chemical exposure control activities. These procedures remain in place to ensure the air base can continue to safely operate in MOPP 4 for as long as the hazard warrants. If the hazard is of relatively short duration, the air base is positioned to determine this and take advantage of the opportunities afforded. If, on the other hand, the hazard is of a longer duration, then all the procedures to sustain MOPP 4 operations are provided.[23]

## Understanding and "Operationalizing" the Science

As mentioned previously, the APOD family of studies[24] offered an alternative view to the air force's long-held assumptions and practices. The study concluded that chemical attacks are likely to affect a much smaller portion of fixed sites than originally believed. Likewise, pickup and transfer hazards to equipment are likely to be of much shorter duration than previously assumed. While the chemical effects data on which these findings rest remain limited, all the available data point strongly to the conclusion that chemical agents will sorb quickly into porous concrete and asphalt surfaces of fixed facilities. While this will not eliminate the hazard posed by agents deposited on nonporous surfaces, it does suggest that with the appropriate command level understanding, command and control, CONOPS, and training, the operations tempo should be sustainable and war plans executable.

Building on the APOD family of studies, recent analysis of air-base operations in a chemically contaminated environment as well as exercise results from Osan Air Base (AB) in the Republic of Korea show that the negative impact on sortie generation under the C-CW CONOPS could be less than 10 percent after a CW attack rather than the expected degrade of 40 percent or more when using traditional approaches.[25] (See Figure 9.4.) The 51st Fighter Wing (FW) at Osan AB achieved this through a process that took the risk management guidance, tools, and procedures provided in the PACAF Counter-Chemical Warfare Commanders Guide and Technical Report, and with the assistance of a team of technical experts provided by the HQ USAF, tailored them to the Osan AB infrastructure and functional operations. The analytic results were most recently validated through operational exercise results during the air force–led, DTRA-executed Restoration of Operations Advanced Concept Technology Demonstration at Osan in February of 2001.[27] Key to the 51 FW success in reducing the negative impact of a CW attack on sortie generation was their ability to assess operations across all wing functionals within the context of the new understanding of the air-base CW environment as well as the ability to identify which operations, if contaminated, posed the greatest risk to full operational recovery, and develop strategies for mitigating those risks.

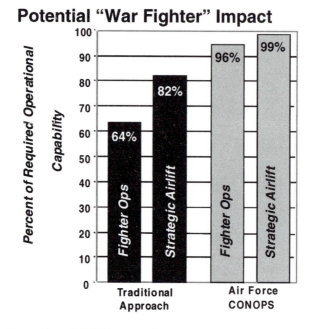

## Potential "War Fighter" Impact

—Based on USAF operations at multiple installations
—Degradation due to CW effects only

**Figure 9.4** Potential Operational Buyback Gained from Understanding and Implementing the C-CW CONOPS[26]

It is important to note that the air force C-CW CONOPS is a passive defense approach against chemical weapons. The air force must take an  integrated and comprehensive approach across the counterproliferation spectrum, including proliferation prevention, counterforce/attack operations, active defense, and passive defense in order to achieve the maximum potential effectiveness in countering chemical weapons. This is critical to mitigating the threat.

## The Chemical Threat and Current Air Force C-CW CONOPS Implementation Initiatives

### Comparison of Efforts from 1993 to the Present

The air force has made dramatic improvements in CW defense over the past decade. As a result, air force personnel have demonstrated the ability to significantly improve mission accomplishment while using tactics, techniques, and procedures (TTPs) that are much safer than those utilized circa 1993. Additionally, the air force has upgraded protective equipment and initiated and sustained a Mask Fit Validation Program. The following are some of the major differences between CW defense operations in 1993 versus those of today.

## Evaluation of Probable Threat Environment at Air Base (Rear Area Fixed Sites)

While in 1993 the air force understood that tactical ballistic missiles were the primary threat, versus manned fighters/bombers, the knowledge essentially stopped there. Over the past few years beginning in 1999, the air force conducted a scientific and analytical review to quantify the types and extent of probable chemical threats to the typical air base. Specifics of the review included missile payloads, missile accuracy, SOF delivery methods, and CW agent droplet sizes at time of release, deposition patterns, and more.

## Use of Split-MOPP Operations

In 1993, while not a new concept, no air force–level guidance existed for split-MOPP operations, and the practice was not widespread. Consequently, a chemical attack would have resulted in an ineffective one-MOPP level attack response methodology. A split-MOPP response allows personnel in uncontaminated areas to rapidly reduce their protective posture and return to full operational capability with a minimum of risk.

## Demasking Techniques

In 1993, the standard demasking technique was to use available chemical detectors to check for the presence of contamination and then direct demasking once chemical contamination ceased to register on the instruments. Upon further study, the air force determined this practice was unsafe. Although the liquid contact and transfer hazard dissipates quickly (most detection instruments only read liquid hazard), a potential vapor hazard will still remain thereafter for a certain amount of time depending on such factors as surface and weather conditions, during which masks will still be required until directed by the commander. The commander can use guidance in the USAF C-CW CONOPS to assist in this decision process.

## Hazard Duration Projections

In 1993, the only document used throughout the air force that contained chemical hazard duration projections was the Allied Tactical Publication (ATP) 45, *Reporting Nuclear Detonations, Chemical and Biological Attacks, and Predicting and Warning of Associated Hazards and Hazard Areas*. The hazard duration table in ATP 45 is very general in nature, giving estimations such as three to ten days in the hazard area and four to six days downwind of the hazard area. Upon further study, the USAF determined these projections were extremely conservative and did not provide operationally useful information. Consequently, the air force departed from the ATP 45 table and began to follow Persist 2, a chemical persistency program used by USAF Civil Engineer Readiness (CEX) personnel. As more information was provided and additional test results became available, the USAF then transitioned from Persist 2 to today's hazard duration charts.

## Automated Hazard Prediction Plotting

In 1993, the air force did not possess an automated chemical hazard prediction plotting capability. Since that time, the air force has distributed an automated CW hazard prediction plotting capability to each CEX flight. This automated plotting capability is contained within the Vapor Liquid Solid Tracking (VLSTRACK) software package included as part of the Joint Warning and Reporting Network (JWARN) program. The air force provided training at each major command (MAJCOM) regarding automated CW hazard prediction plotting during C-CW CONOPS training sessions.[28]

## Deemphasis of the M17 Decontamination Apparatus and Specialized Contamination Control (Decontamination) Teams

In 1993, the air force had not finished reviewing the studies and test results that facilitated the removal of the M17 decontamination apparatus from wartime chemical-biological equipment sets.[29] The air force also still maintained a requirement for area (civil engineer), munitions, vehicle (transportation), and aircraft (maintenance) decontamination teams. Over the past 13 years, the futility of using the M17 decontamination apparatus for chemical decontamination hours after an attack has been clearly established,[30] and studies have shown that large-scale decontamination efforts do not significantly reduce contamination in the expected threat environment. The subsequent air force elimination of the decontamination requirements has led to increased productivity and lessened the manpower requirement for wartime operations.

## Matching Equipment and Resources to the Threat

In 1993, the individual protective equipment (IPE) authorizations existed only for high chemical and biological warfare (CBW) threat areas. The concept of a medium threat area did not exist. Consequently, people were in an "all or nothing" condition in regard to IPE authorizations.

The introduction of authorizations designed for areas that required some, but not all, IPE rectified this shortfall.

Further, in 1993, the air force's collective protection, or shelter program, was essentially nonexistent. The collective protection facilities in Korea were unserviceable and those in Europe were in the process of being removed or placed into long-term storage. Today, the collective protection facilities have been repaired and transportable collective protection systems have been introduced.

## Incorporation of Nuclear, Biological, Chemical, and Conventional (NBCC) Defense Training into Basic Military Training (BMT)

The air force recognized that all airmen required basic NBCC Defense Training, regardless of whether or not they were going to be assigned to a mobility position at their first installation. Consequently, NBCC Defense Training is now part of the Warrior Week segment of enlisted Basic Military Training.

## Incorporation of Automated Chemical Detectors into a Base-Wide Network

In 1993, all chemical detectors were stand-alone units—there was no system available that integrated the detectors into a single network that could be monitored and controlled from the Wing Operations Center. Today, those air force installations equipped with the Portal Shield biological detection system also have the M22 Automatic Chemical Agent Detection Alarm[31] included as part of a single, integrated chemical-biological detection network.

## Operational Effectiveness Assistance

In addition to revisions to air force publications [AFI 10-2501, AFH 10-2502, Air Force Manual (AFMAN) 10-2602, AFMAN 32-4005, and AFMAN 32-4006] and the Full Spectrum Threat Response Plan 10-2, an important piece of the C-CW CONOPS implementation process, particularly for units forward deployed or responsible for contingency operating locations, is Operational Effectiveness Assistance (OEA).

Optimum C-CW CONOPS implementation benefits are realized when installations are able to manage a split-MOPP environment and identify and resolve vulnerabilities to chemical attack. Generally, such vulnerabilities may include a lack of infrastructure or barrier materials (or plans and procedures to use such contamination avoidance measures) to protect key assets prior to and during an attack. Examples of potential key assets may include munitions build and delivery equipment and vehicles as well as flight line maintenance equipment, etc. Additionally, inadequate command and control attack response procedures and time lines or lack of proper plans and procedures for establishing base sectors for split-MOPP operations can be other examples of vulnerabilities that are likely to require operations to be conducted in MOPP 4 unnecessarily. Resolving such issues can greatly improve both the timeliness and the accuracy in understanding and resolving the actual contamination environment. The specific operational vulnerabilities are unique to each installation and are addressed accordingly through the OEA process. An OEA visit is performed by a team of subject-matter experts. The OEA provides a detailed analysis of CW vulnerabilities at an installation and quantifies the impact of mitigation techniques to minimize the effects of a CW attack. This is accomplished by developing a quantitative "operations baseline" of the installation's capability, key infrastructure, threats, and mission critical assets and then running models such as EXPEDITER, to identify high leverage, site-specific actions and mitigation strategies to improve mission capability in a contaminated environment. This offers the installation a tailored strategy for the C-CW CONOPS TTPs.

It is wise to tailor such TTPs to specific installations to achieve maximum operational payoff in sortie generation and airlift operations. An example of this tailored approach can be seen in Figure 9.5, where

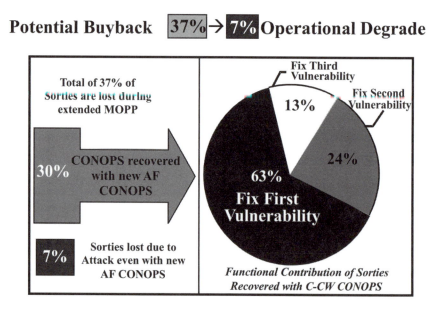

**Figure 9.5** Example of the Impact of Base-Specific Tailoring of the C-CW CONOPS on Sortie Generation Capabilities

30 percent of the operational capability at a notional air base was regained by implementing the C-CW CONOPS and resolving specific operational vulnerabilities.

In this example, the base lost its ability to generate 37 percent of its sorties using the traditional CONOPS, but by introducing the USAF C-CW CONOPS, 30 percent of the sorties were recovered, leaving a total degradation of only 7 percent of the sorties. What was required to gain back the 30 percent? In this example, three vulnerabilities were identified and each had a different level of improvement when the vulnerability was mitigated.

## Education and Training

Successful implementation of the C-CW CONOPS in the air force requires a comprehensive program of education and training. This education and training regime must focus on the individual, his/her unit, and the larger wing organization. (See Figure 9.6.)

At the individual level, airmen need to have a basic understanding of the C-CW CONOPS, the significance of various surfaces to potential contamination, and the basic concepts behind split-base and split-MOPP operations. The airman must be able to use and care for his/her chemical protection equipment.[32] Finally, the airman must receive C-CW CONOPS

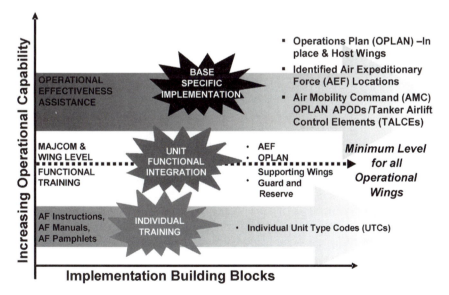

**Figure 9.6** Levels of Training Necessary for the Full Benefits of the C-CW CONOPS To Be Realized

training relevant to his/her technical skill. This is best done during technical training. For example, a munitions specialist must understand the CONOPS in the context of munitions storage area operations.

At the unit level (flight/squadron) training must be provided in postattack contamination assessment and reporting procedures.

At the wing level, within the command post, training needs to focus on assimilating reports and on assessing contamination and the associated impact on operations. Finally, the decision process to determine split base/split MOPP must be exercised using the various tables available. During exercises, the wing commander must assess the responsiveness of all subordinate units to the direction provided.

In a host of professional military education courses, the C-CW CONOPS must be taught and understood. Efforts are under way to infuse this course of instruction into Air War College, Air Command and Staff College, the Squadron Officer's Course, Basic Military Training, and a variety of commander's courses.

Finally, the air force needs to accommodate C-CW CONOPS training within the context of the Air Expeditionary Force (AEF). "Just-in-time" training at fixed locations and the use of mobile training teams will facilitate meeting this need. Additionally, training at the Air Mobility Warfare Center at Fort Dix, New Jersey, provides a basis of knowledge to future AEF support teams.

## Command and Control (C2)

Successful implementation of the Air Force C-CW CONOPS requires a robust command and control structure from the Joint Force Air Component Commander level through the wing level. (See Figure 9.7.)

First, early detection of a theater missile launch is essential in order to start the theater warning process. Timely launch warning is fundamental to passive defense. Rapid dissemination of the launch warning throughout the theater command and control structure (and civil defense) requires a robust, redundant, C2 system.

Once warning is received at the wing level, the alert must be disseminated quickly and efficiently throughout the base. In established forward bases, this may involve Giant Voice (a base-wide loud speaker system), closed circuit TV, Theater Battle Management Computer Simulation, and telephone alerting. At expeditionary bare bases, the alerting requirement is no less real, but the means available to the wing commander may be limited. Base deployment kits need to accommodate this requirement. Base personnel must be able to receive the warning, don protective equipment, and take shelter within the remaining time of flight of the theater missile.

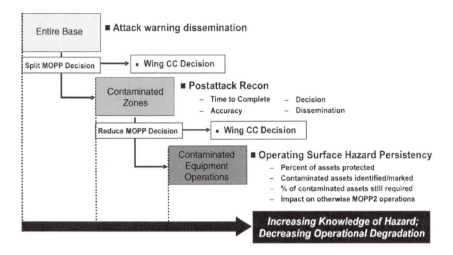

**Figure 9.7**   Critical Areas of a Robust Command and Control with Regard to Postattack C-CW CONOPS Operations

At the wing level, the wing commander must have the command and control tools to facilitate upward postattack reporting in order to efficiently make the necessary operational decisions needed to restore combat capability. The C2 architecture must then support the dissemination of those decisions.

## Areas Still Being Addressed in the C-CW CONOPS[33]

Despite great strides in reducing degradation of operational capability through C-CW CONOPS implementation, there is significant room for improvement. The following items represent some examples of additional work to be done:

- Additional demasking guidance is needed.
  - Tools specifically designed to assist in determining when it is safe to demask inside facilities that had chemical and/or biological contamination drawn in through the heating, ventilation, and air conditioning systems should be created.
  - An automated tool that factors in diurnal weather patterns into chemical hazard duration projections should be developed.
  - Criteria for determining when it is safe to demask when an overt release of CW agents has been detected, factoring in agent, weather, terrain, etc., should be established.
  - Tools specifically designed to assist in determining when it is safe to reuse tents and other temporary living/working quarters after they have

been directly exposed to chemical or biological contamination should be considered.

- Contamination Control Area (CCA) activities require additional attention. A CCA is an area in which chemically contaminated individual protective equipment is removed; people, equipment, and supplies are decontaminated to allow processing between a toxic environment and a toxic-free area (TFA); and people exiting a TFA may safely don IPE.[34]

  - Streamlined CCA procedures for ground crew, medical, and aircrew processing should be cultivated.

  - Clear guidance on "who" must process through chemical CCAs does not exist (e.g., should everyone in a known contaminated area process through a CCA or only those with physical contamination on their ensembles?).

  - Definitive guidance does not exist in regard to the specific steps required for processing people (in IPE and/or civilian clothes) that have been exposed to a CW environment through a CCA.

  - Chemical mask refurbishment activities may not be cost-effective, especially when the availability of "required resources" is considered.

- All aspects of aircrew operations in a chemical and biological (CB) environment require additional attention.

  - Given aircraft environmental and life support systems, what protection is actually required to be furnished by CB IPE?

  - What individual protective equipment should aircrew have available during each phase of mission operations (i.e., preparing to fly in MOPP 2, preparing to fly in MOPP 4, postengine start, landing, etc.?)

  - Are current NBCC Defense and flying (in CB IPE) requirements sufficient?

- Standardized performance criteria should be developed for use at all levels of the air force in the Research, Development and Acquisition program to ensure adequate specifications are included as key performance parameters in Joint Operational Requirements Documents. An example would be that all chemical vapor detectors have the ability to detect and measure agents (to include known foreign variants) down to a level where miosis would not be reached after two hours of continuous exposure.

- All aspects of reconstitution operations require attention.

  - What specific special handling procedures are required for resources that were contaminated during hostilities?

  - What specific decontamination procedures will be used (resource by resource) to achieve the lowest possible level of contamination?

  - What will be done if detectors do not possess the sensitivity required to verify that contamination has been reduced to peacetime exposure standards?

- Specific guidance is required for contaminated waste disposal.

- Development and utilization of standardized Inspector General criteria for core CBRNE items should be implemented air force–wide, regardless of where the unit is located.

## The Biological Threat and Current Initiatives

Biological weapons also pose a serious concern to national security. Recognizing this threat, the air force has made several great strides in the challenging area of biological defense since 1993.

### Vaccination Programs

In 1993, the air force population as a whole was not vaccinated against biological warfare (BW) agents. As seen in Operation Desert Storm, the response technique when entering a threat environment was to vaccinate personnel at the time of contingency plan execution. In most cases, air force personnel were vaccinated during deployment at the forward location rather than in the predeployment phase.

For the past several years, until late 2004, target populations received BW vaccinations based on their job and assignment/deployment status. However, in late 2004 and early 2005, anthrax vaccinations were halted due to a restraining order by a federal judge who mandated further safety tests. As of December 2005, the FDA passed an order deeming the Anthrax Vaccine Adsorbed as "safe and effective against all routes of exposure to anthrax spores, including inhalation.[35] As of this writing the DoD continues voluntary vaccinations, but only to eligible personnel. Up to the time when the vaccination program was stopped, it had become routine for personnel stationed in or deployable to BW high-threat areas to receive anthrax vaccinations, regardless of the current defense condition level. Further, many medical care providers across the air force have been vaccinated for smallpox, regardless of whether or not they were stationed in or deployable to a BW high-threat area. Given the shortcomings of BW agent detectors, these vaccination programs, if permitted, will provide the backbone of the personnel protection program, although many U.S. vaccines are either ineffective or are in very short supply against biological agents other than anthrax and smallpox, which are considered the top two BW threats.

### Recognition That Response to BW Agents Is not the Same as Response to Chemical Warfare (CW) Agents

In 1993, there was little guidance available for how to respond to a BW attack. As a result, the conventional wisdom among leadership was to respond to BW attacks in the same manner as CW attacks. Over the last 13 years, the air force has come to realize that chemical and biological agents are very different from one another. For example, biological agents are very difficult to detect, and delayed symptoms may complicate medical detection. Further, the contagious nature of some BW agents and the toxicity of BW agents in comparison to CW agents lead to different considerations for BW vs. CW. Due to these factors and others, the air force recognized that BW response should differ from CW attack response protocols in several key areas. For example:

- Recognition of BW attacks will likely occur as a result of trigger events that do not involve the actual detection of a BW agent through the use of a machine. These trigger events include intelligence warning, weapons event, and/or sentinel casualties. This use of trigger events differs from CW attack scenarios in that the use of detectors such as M8 paper will provide confirmation in most cases that CW agents were used in an attack.

- The use of split-MOPP procedures is generally not recommended for BW attack situations. Conversely, the effective use of split-MOPP procedures is one of the cornerstones of CW attack response.

- Use of personal equipment (M291/M295 kits[36]) to accomplish operational decontamination of resources and work areas is not a useful technique in the majority of BW attack situations because of the delay expected between attack and detection. This differs from CW attack scenarios where operational decontamination can be very useful if the personnel were unable to adequately protect their assets in the preattack phase.

- Biologically contaminated remains must be separated from chemically contaminated and uncontaminated remains. Further, biologically contaminated remains are separated into three distinct categories while they are temporarily stored: noncontagious pathogen (anthrax for example), contagious pathogen (smallpox for instance), and toxin (ricin would be an example).[37]

- The ongoing concern regarding the transportation of biological warfare casualties or contaminated remains across national or international boundaries complicates base response to biological events due to the contagion factor in many biological agents.

- Crisis management is a more important component of response to a biological event due to the latency of biological agents. Further, the requirement to identify and track those possibly exposed to a biological agent and the potential need to restrict or quarantine these individuals reiterates the importance of maintaining an accurate and continuous flow of information to the targeted populace. This is not necessarily the case when dealing with a CW attack.

- The likelihood of individuals in the surrounding base community to be exposed to a biological agent as the result of an attack against the base increases the need for a regularly exercised, integrated C2 structure for civilian-military interagency cooperation and resource sharing.

- Inhalation of BW is generally the greatest hazard concern and simple/ inexpensive individual and collective protection measures may go a long way toward reducing risk. The air force has begun some analysis and experimentation on expedient BW protection.

## Biological Detection

In the 1993 time frame, the air force had not developed or fielded a biological detector that could be used in a field environment to sample and provide early warning of airborne or surface contamination. It was a virtual certainty that BW detection would occur at a medical treatment facility through the exhibition of symptoms and/or slow (several hours to days) laboratory tests. Today, while not every installation possesses a full suite of BW agent detectors, and there are still significant issues in the area of BW agent detection, most air bases have some biological detection capability outside of the laboratory. Table 9.1 provides a summary of the types of BW detectors commonly found at many air force installations.

**Table 9.1**    BW Detectors Currently in Use at USAF Installations

| Type BW Detector | Purpose | Location |
|---|---|---|
| DoD Sampling Kits (aka Handheld Assays) | Sampling of surface areas | Most CEX and BEE offices in the air force[a] |
| Portal Shield Network | Sampling of air at multiple places around installation | Several selected locations in high CB threat areas (Korea and SWA[b]); some CONUS[c] units scheduled to receive system |
| Portable Collector Concentrators (Spincon, Dry Filter Units, Portable Biological Aerosol Sampler, etc.) | Sampling of air at location where portable collector concentrator is positioned (normally 1–3 per installation) | Selected locations in medium and high CB threat areas; some CONUS sites |
| Ruggedized Advanced Pathogen Identification Device | Identification of BW agent contained in environmental or fluid samples | Several medical facilities (normally maintained by BEE or laboratory personnel) throughout air force |

[a]CEX = Civil Engineer; BEE = Bioenvironmental Engineer. [b]SWA = Southwest Asia. [c]CONUS = Continental United States.

## Automated Hazard Prediction Plotting

In 1993, the air force did not possess an approved biological hazard prediction plotting capability. In essence, since no guidance materials existed, the ad hoc response of most CEX personnel was to plot BW agents in the same manner as the farthest-reaching CW agents. Since that time, the air force has published manual BW hazard prediction plotting procedures.[38] More importantly, the air force distributed an automated BW hazard prediction plotting capability to each CE Readiness Flight. This automated plotting capability is contained within the VLSTRACK software package included as part of the JWARN program. The air force provided training regarding automated BW hazard prediction plotting at each MAJCOM C-CW CONOPS training session to include provisions for a detailed step-by-step checklist.

## Initiation of Joint Service Installation Pilot Program and Weapons of Mass Destruction First Responders Program

In 1993, the air force did not have a program that was specifically designed to provide installations with the equipment and training required to effectively respond to terrorist use of WMD. Although in its early stages, the air force has actively participated in Joint Service and air force–wide programs that are ultimately designed to significantly increase force protection at air bases. In the case of the *Joint Service Installation Pilot Project (JSIPP),* networked BW sensors (Portal Shield) are scheduled to be placed at three CONUS bases initially, with follow-on installations identified if the program is proven to be cost-effective. First Responders and other Disaster Response Force members are scheduled to receive specialized terrorist attack response equipment as part of both the JSIPP and WMD First Responder's programs. The specific equipment items are contained on the Baseline Equipment Data Assessment List. Further, both programs possess a training component that highlights BW response actions and includes field and tabletop exercise events.

## Availability of Information

As stated earlier, in 1993 there was very little guidance available regarding response to BW attack situations. Since then, the air force, DoD, and other U.S. Government agencies have developed and published a wide range of reference and procedural guidance documents. While much work remains to be done, the following list provides some insight into how much more information is readily available today as compared to 1993.

- Interim Biological Defense Plan. Prepared by an air force level Biological Defense Task Force, distributed to the major commands, and posted on the

AF/XOS-FC Web site.[39] The execution tasks within this document are being combined into the standardized Full Spectrum Threat Response (FSTR) 10-2 template. NOTE: This document did not exist in 1993.

- FSTR 10-2 template. This template is used by all air force installations as the starting point for developing the installation FSTR 10-2 plan. Installation responses to BW attack and terrorist use of BW agents are required portions of this plan, with the information being located in Annex C (enemy attack) and Annex D (terrorist use of WMD), respectively. NOTE: This standardized template did not exist in 1993. In fact, in 1993, it was not a requirement for the installation Disaster Preparedness Operations Plan to have an Annex outlining response procedures for a terrorist attack involving WMD.

- AFMAN 10-2602 and AFMAN 32-4017 both contain informational segments regarding BW agents and delivery systems. NOTE: These documents did not exist in 1993.

- AF Handbook 10-2502, USAF WMD Threat Planning and Response Handbook, contains information outlining how to tell if a BW attack has occurred, what response actions are appropriate, and agent-specific material. NOTE: This document did not exist in 1993.

- The current NBCC Defense Course contains far more BW-related information than the corresponding course in 1993. In 1993, the course material was constrained to limited protective actions individuals should take before, during, and after a BW attack. The current course discusses agent characteristics, delivery methods, recognition of trigger events, and decontamination methods in addition to containing information that addresses protective actions.

- In 1993, few had access to the Internet, and the Web was just coming into existence. Since then, it has become a valuable conduit for distributing information about biological defense-related activities. A few examples of information available on the Web are as follows:

  - USAF Counterproliferation Center: http://www.au.af.mil/au/awc/awcgate/awc-cps.htm.

  - DoD Anthrax Vaccine Immunization Program: http://www.anthrax.osd.mil.

  - The AF/XOS-FC Commanders' ChemBio Website is a repository for all current Air Force guidance on CBW response: https://www.xo.hq.af.mil/af/xo/xos/xosf/xosfc/ccbrne_resource/index.ays.

  - BW agent technical information and fact sheets from the Center for Disease Control (CDC): http://www.bt.cdc.gov/Agent/Agentlist.asp.

  - The Medical Management of Biological Casualties handbook from the U.S. Army Medical Research Institute of Infectious Diseases can be downloaded from http://www.usamriid.army.mil/education/instruct.htm.

## Development and Initiation of Specific Handling and Packaging Criteria for BW Samples

In 1993, the air force did not have published procedures or criteria for the handling and packaging of BW samples, to include chain-of-custody requirements. This information is now contained in documents such as AFMAN 10-2602 and the Interim Biological Defense Plan, with air force personnel (mostly CEX and BEE) taking courses and receiving certification for handling/packaging activities through the International Air Transport Association.

# Nuclear and Radiological Threat and Current Initiatives

The biggest differences between the 1993 time period and the present in regard to nuclear attack response techniques involve the following items.

## Detection Equipment

The air force has replaced up to four separate radiation instruments with the ADM 300, a detector with far superior capabilities. The largest improvements are the ADM 300's ability to detect all types of radiation of interest, the digital readings versus scale depictions—which provides increased accuracy and the ability to set audio warning alarms. (See Table 9.2.) In addition to directly translating to operational advantages, this has lessened the maintenance times required, reduced the numbers and types of consumable supplies (such as batteries on hand), simplified the training requirements, etc.

**Table 9.2**   Various Radiation Instruments and Their Individual Operational Capabilities

| Type of Instrument | Type of Radiation Detected/Measured | Specificity of Reading |
|---|---|---|
| AN/PDR 56F | Alpha, x-ray | Needle on scale |
| PAC 1S | Alpha | Needle on scale |
| AN/PDR 27 | Beta, gamma (low range) | Needle on scale |
| AN/PDR 43 | Beta, gamma (high range) | Needle on scale |
| ADM 300 | Alpha, beta, gamma, neutron, x-ray | Specific digital reading |

## Awareness of Hazards Associated with Depleted Uranium (DU)

As a result of exposures that personnel received during and after Operation Desert Storm, the air force instituted a DU awareness training program. This training was made a mandatory part of the NBCC Defense courses that everyone "in or deployable to a medium or high CB threat area" is required to receive. This training segment consists of information that defines addressing what DU is, the specific sources that personnel may come into contact with, the hazards associated with the material, and protective actions that can be taken.

## Awareness and Ability To Respond to Attacks Involving Radiation Dispersal Devices (RDD)

Radiation weapons were not considered a mainstream threat within the air force in 1993. Consequently, there was no specific training on the subject for air force personnel unless they were assigned to a highly specialized, national-level team such as the Nuclear Emergency Search Team. At the present time, more information is available to the air force population regarding the characteristics of radiation weapons and additional information has been incorporated into hazardous material training courses and in air force policy and guidance.[40]

- Deployable units have an automated RDD plotting capability available in every CEX Flight. The Hazard Prediction and Assessment Capability software can predict areas and intensities of radiation contamination that was distributed as part of the JWARN program.
- The Full-Spectrum Threat Response plan contains requirements for all air force installations to develop procedures for response to situations where the air base is in the downwind hazard plume of a radiation weapon.[41]

## Modification of Installation Response Mechanisms Regarding Enemy Attacks Involving Nuclear Weapons

The air force NBCC defense programs remain focused on the dominant threat(s) at the time. Consequently, there has been a deemphasis on nuclear warfare response activities from 1993 to the present, with a corresponding increase focusing on other threats. For example, the historically nuclear-oriented shelter management training requirements in Table 9.3 of Air Force Instruction (AFI) 10-2501 state that "installations assessed as low threat areas will train only upon increase in threat posture or as directed by Air Staff, with the exception of covering natural disaster sheltering." This shift in philosophy is also contained in such AFMAN 32-4005 items as follows:

- In addition to response to nuclear attack, installation protective shelters can be used for major accidents, natural disasters, and other civil emergency relief operations. This includes specifying that Air Force units are allowed to use War Reserve Materiel (WRM) supplies to support shelter operations for major accidents, natural disasters, and other civil emergency relief operations.[42]

- Differing numbers of required shelter management team members for nuclear attack, CB attack, and natural disaster/major accident response situations need to be specified.[43]

- Radiological exposure control procedures need only be developed for each shelter if the threat warrants.[44]

## Summary and Way Ahead

The air force has made dramatic improvements in countering WMD over the past 13 years. In the area of chemical warfare, results from testing and analyses showed quite convincingly that many previously accepted operational concepts were based on inaccurate assumptions and were largely ineffective. Whereas previously a worst-case operating environment had been assumed, new information about the physical characteristics of chemical agents, agent sorption, and the expected delivery methods led to the conclusion that the worst-case scenario was unlikely. While the effects of a CW attack are still not trivial, commanders implementing the C-CW CONOPS can now make risk assessments and informed decisions in order to continue the war fight. At the operational level, through active defense, counterforce operations, and passive defense, much of the current CW threat can be negated.

The air force needs to continue to capitalize on this momentum, especially in the area of testing. Additional testing in agent fate is still needed in order to validate and extend the results of the existing testing and analyses. Due to uncertainties inherent in the data, operational commanders must understand the risks inherent in the hazard duration ranges and take a conservative approach to ordering measures (e.g., reductions in MOPP levels) to restore operational capability and reduce the physical stress placed on personnel. Sustainment requirements, such as institutionalized training, are also still necessary at all levels of the air force. Further research and analysis is also needed to determine the proper attack response procedures when considering fourth generation chemical agents and other possible future improvements in chemical warfare.

In the area of biological warfare defense, the air force has begun to make great strides in recognizing that, although the same or greater rigor applied to the chemical warfare threat is necessary, responding to biological threats is very different and more challenging. As a result, the air force has implemented a vaccination program, biospecific hazard prediction plotting, and has also published a wide range of reference and procedural guidance documents for understanding and responding to a biological warfare event.

The air force has also continued to hone response procedures to counter nuclear and radiological threats. As a result of the reemergence of nuclear and radiological warfare as realistic threats, the air force has dramatically improved its capability to detect these types of weapons and has significantly increased its training and education in the area of hazardous exposure to nuclear and radiological material.

In the future, the weapons of mass destruction capabilities of adversaries will continue to grow and become more sophisticated. To counter them, the air force must continue its significant material and operational investment in command and control, passive defense, active defense, and attack operations, as well as training, education, and CONOPS development to fight and help win the nation's wars.

CHAPTER **10**

# U.S. Counterproliferation Cooperation with Allies

*Peter R. Lavoy and Gayle D. Meyers*

With the enactment of the Defense Counterproliferation Initiative (CPI) by the late U.S. Secretary of Defense Les Aspin in December 1993, the U.S. Department of Defense accelerated its efforts to prepare U.S. military forces to fight and win a full spectrum of military conflicts, even when its adversaries threaten to use or actually use weapons of mass destruction (WMD). For over the next decade, as improvements were made in the organization, training, and equipping of U.S. armed forces to conduct operations under chemical and biological conditions, U.S. defense planners recognized that even an extremely well-prepared U.S. military could not overcome the vulnerabilities that an adversary's use of chemical and biological weapons would pose for the troops and populations of American allies and coalition partners. Thus, counterproliferation had to go international.

As Pentagon planners were beginning to integrate significant counterproliferation improvements into the wide-ranging activities of the four military services, the regional combatant commands, and other combat support entities, the Office of the Secretary of Defense (OSD) undertook a series of new policy initiatives to help Washington's closest allies and coalition partners gain a better understanding of their own vulnerabilities to WMD use and to take effective steps—with or without U.S. assistance—to address these vulnerabilities. After several years of international counterproliferation cooperation, many U.S. allies in Europe, Southwest Asia, and Northeast Asia have a better understanding of current weapons of mass destruction threats and possible weapons of mass destruction countermeasures for both their military forces and their domestic populations. Some countries have taken significant steps to enhance their own ability to combat weapons of mass destruction use, while others thus far have not been able to overcome the vexing political, bureaucratic, or resource challenges that impede real improvement of their counterproliferation and homeland security capabilities. This chapter describes U.S. efforts to internationalize counterproliferation and assesses the successes, failures, and remaining challenges of this crucial endeavor.

## The Logic of International Counterproliferation Cooperation

After the sudden collapse of the Soviet Union in 1991, American defense planners soon came to recognize that the greatest threat to U.S. security was posed not by potential peer military competitors, such as the new Russian Federation or China, but by state and nonstate adversaries that might have access to weapons of mass destruction and might be willing to use them as part of asymmetric military strategies. Saddam Hussein's invasion of Kuwait in August 1990 had highlighted the threat regional military powers could pose to the national security interests of the United States and its allies. Even more daunting was the discovery after the 1991 Gulf War that Baghdad secretly had assembled large-scale chemical and biological warfare (CBW) production programs, had a dynamic nuclear weapons research and development effort that was possibly 18 months short of producing Iraq's first nuclear bomb, and also had acquired short- and medium-range SCUD missiles to deliver weapons of mass destruction to targets throughout the region.

During the Cold War the United States and the Soviet Union both had extensive chemical weapons arsenals, and leaders in both alliances expected that a major war in Europe would involve chemical weapons use. U.S. and other NATO intelligence services suspected, but could not prove, that they would someday face Soviet and Warsaw Pact biological attacks as well. Despite these threat perceptions, U.S. and allied military forces had not made preparations for fighting a CBW-armed adversary much of a priority during the Cold War because the massive superpower stockpiles of nuclear weapons deterred a hot war from arising between the United States and the Soviet Union. Even if deterrence had failed during the Cold War, the resultant military conflict would have been dominated by the use of nuclear weapons, against which there was no practical defense at the time. In the wake of Saddam's invasion of Kuwait, however, Pentagon officials correctly realized that U.S. armed forces were extremely vulnerable to the use of CBW by new adversaries. Prior to, during, and after Operation Desert Storm, U.S. defense planners conducted a series of tabletop exercises and assessments of the possible impact of

Iraq's projected use of CBW-filled SCUD missiles against coalition forces and the regional nations that hosted U.S. forces. Because of additional revelations about the weapons of mass destruction proliferation potential of other hostile states,[1] concern quickly spread throughout the U.S. defense establishment that the timely and effective employment of CBW and missiles, and possibly even nuclear weapons, by a small military adversary could lead to heavy allied casualties and possibly even present an otherwise dominant U.S.–led military coalition with defeat.

It was this alarming scenario that prompted Secretary Aspin to launch the Defense Counterproliferation Initiative. According to the Secretary of Defense, weapons of mass destruction proliferation had become one of the most urgent dangers confronting U.S. security and international stability. Aspin contrasted the old threat of a massive Soviet nuclear first strike with that of "perhaps a handful of nuclear devices in the hands of rogue states or even terrorist groups." As he described it, "the engine of this new danger is proliferation." He also declared,

> With this initiative, we are making the essential change demanded by this increased threat. We are adding the task of protection to the task of prevention. … At the heart of the Defense Counterproliferation Initiative, therefore, is a drive to develop new military capabilities to deal with this new threat.[2]

## International Reactions to the Counterproliferation Initiative

Defense Secretary Aspin's initiative produced confusion and unrest in many governmental and nongovernmental circles, especially outside the United States. Particularly troubled was the international arms control community, which viewed the Defense Counterproliferation Initiative as a declaration of war on the various weapons of mass destruction nonproliferation regimes that had taken decades to establish. By signaling a shift in the priority of the U.S. Government—or at least in the mission of the U.S. Defense Department—away from the long-practiced diplomatic instruments of nonproliferation treaties, supplier cartels, export controls, sanctions, and arms control, and toward more assertive military efforts to deter and combat the use of weapons of mass destruction, Secretary Aspin seemed to many nonproliferation advocates at home and abroad to convey the impression that traditional nonproliferation efforts were doomed to fail.[3] Often overlooked at the time, however, was the Secretary's carefully considered declaration that "prevention remains our preeminent goal. … The [Counterproliferation Initiative] in no way means we will lessen our nonproliferation efforts."[4]

The international nonproliferation community reacted particularly negatively to statements made by the Assistant Secretary of Defense for

International Security Policy, Ashton Carter, that the Pentagon's use of preemptive military strikes might be a desirable and effective means to eliminate weapons of mass destruction proliferation threats before they could be developed sufficiently to hold American civilian and military populations at risk.[5] In fact, it was the nonproliferation community's apprehension over this potentially unilateral and aggressive element of counterproliferation that initially set it against the Counterproliferation Initiative. Despite these early anxieties, 10 full years elapsed after the introduction of the Defense Counterproliferation Initiative before a U.S. administration actually engaged in a preventive military attack to destroy an adversary's weapons of mass destruction capability and remove its regime. Ironically, the target was Saddam Hussein's Iraq, the same adversary that triggered the CPI in the first place.

The United Kingdom was the first of Washington's international allies to welcome the Counterproliferation Initiative. Six weeks after Aspin announced it, the British defense minister expressed his approval: "the American administration has made countering proliferation a major policy priority. We warmly welcome this, and we are looking forward to discussions with our North Atlantic Treaty Organization (NATO) allies on this important subject over the coming months."[6] The British Ministry of Defence has to this day been the most consistent supporter of U.S. counterproliferation policies, plans, and operations. It also has contributed a great deal to American thinking about how best to mitigate CBW and missile threats on the battlefield. The Washington-London counterproliferation connection is a mutually valuable two-way partnership.

France also supported the new policy, but in a more guarded manner. A French defense white paper issued in March 1994 devoted six pages to the need to improve deterrence against weapons of mass destruction and called for a new military strategy to protect French military forces from the effects of an adversary's use of weapons of mass destruction.[7] When the United States proposed the creation of a new policy group within NATO to improve the Atlantic Alliance's preparedness against weapons of mass destruction risks, France initially hesitated but ultimately supported the formation of the NATO Defence Group on Proliferation (DGP), with the conditions that France would be the body's first European cochair and that a Political Group on Proliferation also be established to coordinate the Alliance's nonproliferation policies and activities. As it turned out, the early support provided by London and Paris helped to legitimize Washington's counterproliferation concept not only within NATO but also throughout the broader international community.[8]

Other NATO allies were more circumspect about the American defense initiative and tried to limit the DGP's work on counterproliferation to intelligence sharing and defensive military preparations—in other words, *not* to include preventive military strikes. However, the biggest strain was not among the allies' defense ministries, but actually between this group and its foreign ministry colleagues.[9] The tensions among NATO allies and between counterproliferation and nonproliferation were highlighted in the Ten Point Nonproliferation Initiative German Foreign Minister Klaus Kinkel issued on December 15, 1993—just eight days after Secretary Aspin announced the Counterproliferation Initiative. Based on the timing of Kinkel's speech as well as its content, his initiative appeared to be intended as a diplomatic—and perhaps European—alternative to the Counterproliferation Initiative. In particular, the final point of the German initiative tried to preempt Washington's declared interest in enhancing its ability to execute counterforce strikes and improve its active and passive defenses against enemy weapons of mass destruction by insisting that military enforcement actions—except in the case of self-defense against armed attack—always must require UN Security Council approval.[10]

Most of Washington's other non-NATO allies responded to the new U.S. counterproliferation policy with caution, refusing to embrace an ambiguous initiative that might end up provoking their neighbors into overreaction and/or causing them to devote scarce resources to expensive, American-built missile defense systems and other costly counterproliferation equipment. At the same time, while these allies either did not recognize the immediacy of the new weapons of mass destruction threats or were unable to devote significant resources to counter these threats, they did not oppose the plan because of its potential to mitigate the growing international threats of weapons of mass destruction proliferation and use. For several years, Japan and South Korea, for example, said very little about Washington's Counterproliferation Initiative probably because they did not want to agitate North Korea, which was then understood to have initiated a small nuclear weapons program, and because of the economic crisis that had befallen them in the mid-1990s.[11]

Australia, another key American ally, also adopted a noncommittal stance on counterproliferation. Possibly, it did not perceive an immediate WMD threat to its security because of the distance separating its territory from the Middle East and Northeast Asia. The other reason for Australia's lukewarm reaction to Washington's Counterproliferation Initiative is that the Canberra government still preferred to emphasize traditional diplomatic approaches to combat the global spread of nuclear, biological, and chemical (NBC) weapons and associated delivery means.

In sharp contrast, Israel embraced its own counterproliferation programs from the outset and in the last 13 years has viewed the threat of weapons of mass destruction use in more urgent terms than it generally had been treated in the United States or anywhere else. This is not surprising considering the number of hostile, regional military powers in Israel's neighborhood that are believed to possess weapons of mass destruction. In addition, the Defense Counterproliferation Initiative seemed to validate an approach Israel already had taken. After all, Israel conducted a successful preventive military attack against a major weapons of mass destruction facility when it attacked Iraq's Osirak nuclear reactor in 1981.[12]

Other foreign governments remained generally quiet when Washington spoke about counterproliferation, waiting to see how the programs and policies that the Defense Counterproliferation Initiative would produce would affect their security and their political and economic interests. When the United States initiated counterproliferation consultations with the Gulf Cooperation Council (GCC) countries in the late 1990s, for example, the participants showed great interest since the new counterproliferation policies were aimed largely at their neighbors, Iran and Iraq, but the GCC states initially declined to cooperate in any formal sense.[13] This attitude gradually changed over time. By the 10-year mark of counterproliferation, at least seven Middle Eastern countries—the GCC nations Bahrain, Kuwait, Oman, Qatar, and the UAE, along with Jordan and Egypt—have come to participate in some capacity in important cooperative counterproliferation programs with the United States.

Washington's erstwhile adversaries Russia, Ukraine, and a few other countries voiced serious apprehension about Washington's new military approach to WMD proliferation. Having just emerged from decades of Cold War military competition with the West, Moscow and Kiev understandably viewed the Defense Counterproliferation Initiative with intense suspicion. Recognizing this concern, the Pentagon conducted early counterproliferation dialogues with these countries. In the words of former Deputy Assistant Secretary of Defense Mitchell Wallerstein, these consultations were intended "both to demonstrate that these efforts are *not* directed at them and to explore common ground for possible exchange of information and exploration of complementary approaches."[14]

## Counterproliferation Cooperation in Europe

After launching the CPI, the United States turned first to its European allies to internationalize counterproliferation. Because the threat of weapons of mass destruction was viewed primarily as a menace to battlefield operations (as opposed to civilian populations), it was logical to cooperate with the countries most likely to join a military alliance with the United States. High-level cooperative programs and dialogues were established within NATO and then bilaterally with the United Kingdom and then France. These cooperative efforts have continued at varying levels of intensity. They have changed over time as the perceived threat to civilians increased—first from long-range missiles, and then after the September 11, 2001, terrorist attacks against New York and Washington, D.C., from terrorist groups, such as al-Qaeda.

## NATO

As noted above, NATO established the Defence Group on Proliferation in 1994. At the same time, it established a companion group, the Political-Military Group on Proliferation, reflecting a desire on the part of military as well as diplomatic agencies to formulate Alliance policy on nuclear, biological, and chemical weapons proliferation.

The long-term Defence Group on Proliferation program to counter emerging weapons of mass destruction threats comprised defense planning and policy, intelligence, and the acquisition of new counterproliferation capabilities by member nations. NATO intensified its attention to weapons of mass destruction proliferation matters in 1999 with the adoption of a new strategic concept, the Weapons of Mass Destruction Initiative (WMDI), and the Defence Capabilities Initiative, all of which were launched at the summit marking the 50th anniversary of the Atlantic Alliance. NATO also established a staff element—the Weapons of Mass Destruction Center at NATO Headquarters in Brussels—to facilitate dialogue and coordination relating to threat assessment and to develop effective defense and diplomatic responses to such threats. At the Prague Summit in November 2002 the allies made firmer commitments to develop effective capabilities to respond to weapons of mass destruction threats. The new measures include the Prague Capabilities Commitment (PCC) and the NATO Response Force.[15]

Progress in improving real NATO counterproliferation capabilities has been slow. Although NATO's Defence Capabilities Initiative sought to improve the military capabilities required to counter weapons of mass destruction threats, "only 50 percent of [Defense Capabilities Initiative] commitments" had been met by May 2001, according to Ambassador Alexander Vershbow, then the U.S. Permanent Representative to the North Atlantic Council.[16] At the 2002 Prague Summit, NATO allies committed to an even more ambitious program of capability improvements, including national improvements and five Alliance initiatives: a Prototype Deployable NBC Analytical Laboratory, a Prototype NBC Event Response team, a virtual Center of Excellence for NBC Weapons Defense, a NATO Biological and Chemical Defense Stockpile, and a disease surveillance system.[17] According to one analyst, this PCC "may have better prospects for success than the [Defense Capabilities Initiative] due to the firm commitments of individual allies. In contrast, the [Defense Capabilities Initiative] lacked specific deadlines and comparable national commitments."[18]

At the Prague Summit, the allies also endorsed a new military concept for defense against terrorism. The concept is part of a package of measures to strengthen NATO's capabilities in this area, which also includes improved intelligence sharing and crisis response arrangements, as well

as a commitment to implement plans for the improvement of civil preparedness against possible attacks against the civilian population with chemical, biological, or radiological agents. This change was a direct result of
the September 11, 2001, terrorist attacks on the United States, after which
the threat of terrorist use of chemical or biological weapons and the
need to protect populations took a more prominent role at NATO. Politically, the Atlantic Alliance's new counterterrorism initiatives brought
committees whose primary focus is civil emergency planning into the
fight against the proliferation and possible use of weapons of mass
destruction.

## U.S.–U.K. Counterproliferation Cooperation

In line with its support of the WMDI, the United Kingdom has undertaken broad and deep collaboration with the U.S. Government on counterproliferation. A U.S.–U.K. Joint Venture Oversight Group (JVOG) on
the defense response to the threat posed by chemical and biological weapons was established in December 1998. Led in the United States by the
Office of the Secretary of the Defense, the JVOG has managed a robust
program of policy coordination, operational assessment, and technical
cooperation. Shortly after the JVOG's founding, U.K. Secretary of State
for Defence George Robertson testified to Parliament that "[w]e will build
on this exchange as a means of developing further the already strong
defence capabilities of both countries."[19]

Since its inception in 1998, the JVOG has met regularly and frequently.
Various working committees have been formed to further assist in the
coordination of U.S. and U.K. approaches to counterproliferation. The
senior leaders of JVOG met in July 2003 at Edgewood Chemical Biological
Center in the United States. Approximately 40 people with specializations
in policy, research and development, medical issues, and operations were
involved in the meeting.[20]

This cooperation paid off during the 2003 Iraq War, when military planners on the U.S. Central Command staff and their British counterparts
benefited by being intimately familiar with each other's doctrine for
chemical and biological warfare defense operations. Although Iraq did
not use chemical or biological agents against coalition forces, these forces
certainly were far better prepared to operate effectively on a CBW battlefield than they were in 1991—an achievement that owes a great deal to
U.S. and U.K. cooperative counterproliferation efforts. The contribution
the JVOG has had on combined U.S. and U.K. counterproliferation capabilities is likely to grow further as this body considers the lessons from
the Iraq War and uses them to guide future activities.

## Counterproliferation Cooperation in Southwest Asia

Because Southwest Asia is considered the global region with the greatest weapons of mass destruction proliferation problem, and it is of central strategic concern to the United States, cooperative counterproliferation efforts take on a very important role in this part of the world. The six states of the Gulf Cooperation Council were a natural choice for cooperation based on Washington's counterproliferation logic. Located within missile range of Iraq and Iran and home to a large U.S. troop presence, these countries were viewed as likely coalition partners in one of the two major theater wars for which the Pentagon was preparing in the 1990s.

Internal military assessments, such as the OSD-sponsored DESERT BREEZE seminar series conducted at U.S. Central Command (CENTCOM), highlighted the importance of Gulf airfields and seaports to any potential U.S. military operation in the region and how they could be put in jeopardy by the threat or use of chemical or biological weapons. For example, civilian dock workers who were not trained or equipped to operate in an environment contaminated by chemical agents would not be able to unload military cargo from incoming ships, or governments concerned about biological threats to their populations might be pressured to ask U.S. troops to withdraw.

The main focus of counterproliferation cooperation with these countries, therefore, was to help their civilian and military authorities identify ways to improve their preparedness to defend against and manage the potential consequences of chemical and biological weapons use. In addition, increased regional weapons of mass destruction proliferation sparked a concern that regional allies might begin to shift their focus from a reliance on active and passive defenses against weapons of mass destruction to the acquisition of their own offensive, long-range strike assets to offset the growing capabilities of their neighbors. These concerns led to the creation of the Cooperative Defense Initiative and a bilateral U.S.–Israel Counterproliferation Working Group (CWG).

### Cooperative Defense Initiative

The Office of the Secretary of Defense launched the Initiative on Cooperative Defense against weapons of mass destruction in Southwest Asia—eventually shortened to "Cooperative Defense Initiative," or CDI—in 1998. The CDI is an effort led jointly by the Office of the Secretary of Defense and U.S. Central Command to enhance the ability of the GCC states along with Jordan and Egypt to prepare their forces to operate effectively in chemical and biological environments, to improve the interoperability of these forces with U.S. troops, and to increase the capability of these countries' domestic agencies to deal with a weapons of mass destruction event on their territory.[21]

The OSD Counterproliferation Policy Office began developing the project in 1997 by surveying the weapons of mass destruction preparedness of the six Gulf countries. Next, in January 1998, the Office of the Secretary of Defense approached U.S. Central Command to partner in a major policy initiative to counter WMD proliferation in Southwest Asia. The U.S. CENTCOM Combatant Commander at the time, General Anthony Zinni, agreed that his Directorate of Policy and Plans (J-5) would take the lead in promoting the Cooperative Defense Initiative. Finally, the OSD Counterproliferation Policy Office began close cooperation with the Office of the Deputy Assistant Secretary of Defense for Near Eastern and South Asian Affairs in December 1999 to coordinate the policy guidance required for this initiative. This close collaboration within the Office of the Secretary of Defense ultimately was instrumental to the success of the Cooperative Defense Initiative because it put counterproliferation on the agenda of bilateral military cooperation between the United States and the states in the region.

The Office of the Secretary of Defense led two trips to the Gulf region in March and June 1999, in which the GCC states, Jordan, and Egypt were formally approached and asked to participate in the Cooperative Defense Initiative. Each government was requested to form a subcommittee devoted to CDI, which would meet under the auspices of existing annual defense cooperation talks (Military Consultative Committees and Joint Military Committees). These, in turn, would oversee a set of cooperative activities in five areas: theater air and missile defense; command, control, communication, computers, and intelligence; NBC defense; medical countermeasures; and consequence management (CM).

The goal of the Cooperative Defense Initiative has been for partner countries to undertake their own efforts to "institutionalize" counterproliferation by acquiring effective CBW defense capabilities, revising their military plans, training their personnel to practice the latest counterproliferation procedures, and preparing their homeland security organizations to effectively mitigate the consequences of a weapons of mass destruction event on their own territory. This goal has been met to differing degrees in each country. For example, Bahrain participated in a combined tabletop exercise with U.S. defense officials and augmented its small chemical corps. As recently as November 2003, the Bahrainis exercised relevant civil defense capabilities in *Exercise Desert Sailor*.[22] Jordan put particular focus on improving its medical countermeasures in the event of a chemical and biological warfare attack. Saudi Arabia focused on enhancing its missile defense.

At a November 2003 conference hosted by the National Defense University, the Army War College's Center for Strategic Leadership facilitated a discussion and an assessment of the weapons of mass destruction CM portion of the Cooperative Defense Initiative. Based on insights offered by a forum of representatives from Bahrain, Jordan, Kuwait, Oman, Qatar, Saudi Arabia, and the United Arab Emirates,[23] the assessment found that overall, the CM program was successful in serving the region's counter-proliferation needs. There were, however, specific areas of concern raised, including interagency myopia among many senior ministries that remain unaware or unconvinced of the severity of the threat, constrained re-sources, and reticence of civil first responders to work in contaminated areas. In spite of these concerns, however, "the prevailing atmosphere of the forum showed a clear inclination toward expanding cooperative efforts in the region."[24] It is hard to say how far the actual counterprolifer-ation and consequence management capabilities have come, however, because they have yet to be tested and all concerned parties treat these issues with a great deal of sensitivity.

There is also a multilateral component to the Cooperative Defense Ini-tiative, known as *Eagle Resolve*. This recurring coordination exercise, attended by senior defense officials and staff from all of the partner nations, validates the education and training functions of the Cooperative Defense Initiative and ensures that the political-military requirements associated with managing coalition cohesion in the face of threatened or actual chemical and biological warfare use are met. Additionally, this exercise improves the ability of regional partners to protect their own forces, facilities, and population from chemical and biological warfare use.[25] *Eagle Resolve* has been held regularly for several years.

During *Eagle Resolve 2001*, held in Manama, Bahrain, participants used a hypothetical crisis scenario to structure their discussion, and they pro-duced a conceptual architecture, an operational concept, and a draft of procedures for establishing a Gulf Cooperation Council Regional Coordi-nation Cell (RCC). They envisioned that the RCC would serve as a clear-inghouse for information and a communications center for intranational and multinational cooperation to permit quick response to both military and civilian crises in the event of a weapons of mass destruction event in the Persian Gulf region.[26]

Within the U.S. Government, responsibility for implementing the Coop-erative Defense Initiative has fallen primarily to Central Command subject-matter experts, with policy oversight and assistance from the Office of the Secretary of Defense Office of Counterproliferation Policy. It has been fully institutionalized at Central Command and is supported today by a staff of contractors. More recently, the Cooperative Defense Initiative was expanded to include the Central Asian nations in Central Command's area of responsibility.

The results of the Cooperative Defense Initiative to date are mixed. On the one hand, the initiative has helped keep chemical and biological warfare defense on the agenda of military-to-military relations between the United States and its Gulf Cooperation Council partners and Jordan. It has helped ensure that Central Command includes chemical and biological warfare scenarios in combined exercises. It also has been remarkably flexible. It has provided a venue for engaging Central Asian states, and it has been adapted to include a broad spectrum of topics under the consequence management and homeland security umbrella.

The Cooperative Defense Initiative is not set up to track partner states' acquisition of chemical and biological warfare defense equipment, but it appears that they have made a few relevant purchases. The U.S. State Department has issued licenses for the export of gas masks, protective equipment, and chemical agent detectors to Bahrain, Egypt, Jordan, Kuwait, Qatar, Saudi Arabia, and the United Arab Emirates in recent years. Perhaps even more significantly, several of the desert countries have started storing their protective masks and suits in air-conditioned environments instead of leaving them in unprotected warehouses where they tended to melt. This change in practice is a direct result of assessments and recommendations made by a U.S. Army team under Cooperative Defense Initiative auspices.

On the other hand, the partner states do not appear to have integrated these new capabilities throughout their forces or significantly improved their ability to work interoperably with each other or with U.S. forces. As Colonel Mustafa Juma, Deputy Director of Kuwait's Civil Defense Force, described during an October 2002 Cooperative Defense Initiative exercise, it is a 70 percent success. "It was good as a start, I hope we're ready to deal with any possible chemical and biological warfare use … .[27] Luckily, that threat never materialized. Table 10.1 provides a summary of the Cooperative Defense Initiative activities and direct commercial sales licenses issued.

Still to be seen will be the impact of the 2003 Gulf War on the interest of the Cooperative Defense Initiative partner countries to make some progress in fielding the capabilities required to counter weapons of mass destruction use in the region. Kuwait distributed 200,000 gas masks to civil defense workers in advance of the war, and a Czech chemical defense unit deployed to Kuwait and exercised with both U.S. and Kuwaiti forces, marking an important milestone for both NATO and the Cooperative Defense Initiative.[29]

The fact that Iraqi troops did not seem to possess and certainly did not employ WMD as U.S.–led coalition forces marched on Baghdad is a double-edged sword with regard to Cooperative Defense Initiative progress. Perhaps the U.S. and U.K. defensive preparations for chemical and biological warfare deterred Iraqi CB weapons use, if indeed they had such weapons, which now appears to have been unlikely. It is doubtful that CDI preparations would have deterred Iraq if they had had such

**Table 10.1**    CDI Activities and Direct Commercial Sales Licenses Issued[28]

| Country | Activity | Value of Direct Commercial Sales Licenses Issued |
| --- | --- | --- |
| Bahrain | **1999, 2000, 2001:** *Eagle Resolve* seminar: All GCC states, Jordan, Egypt, and the United States conduct senior-level tabletop exercise and briefings on CBW defense and coordination.<br>**2000:** Exercise *Neon Falcon:* 7,000-person exercise for Bahrain, U.S., French, and British units—included a field training exercise to refine CBRN defense operational tactics, techniques, and procedures.<br>**2003:** Exercise *Desert Sailor:* Bahraini and U.S. troops exercised emergency response procedures. | **2002:** Breathing equipment (gas masks, etc.): $34,397<br>**2003:** Chemical agent detection equipment: $274,949 |
| Egypt | **1999, 2001:** Exercise *Bright Star:* Major joint and combined exercise added NBC defense component.<br>**1999, 2000, 2001:** *Eagle Resolve* seminar: All GCC states, Jordan, Egypt, and the United States conduct senior-level tabletop exercise and briefings on CBW defense and coordination. | **1999:** Protective equipment (suits, gloves, etc.): $755<br>**2000:** Protective equipment (suits, gloves, etc.): $76,064 |
| Jordan | **1999, 2000, 2001:** *Eagle Resolve* seminar: All GCC states, Jordan, Egypt, and the United States conduct senior-level tabletop exercise and briefings on CBW defense and coordination. | **1999:** Protective equipment (suits, gloves, etc.): $814,000<br>**2001:** Breathing equipment (gas masks, etc.): $121<br>**2003:** Chemical agent detection equipment: $62,480 |

CDI Activities and Direct Commercial Sales Licenses Issued (cont.)

| | | |
|---|---|---|
| **Kuwait** | **1999, 2000, 2001:** *Eagle Resolve* seminar: All GCC states, Jordan, Egypt, and the United States conduct senior-level tabletop exercise and briefings on CBW defense and coordination. **2002:** CBW defense drill for Kuwait, U.S., and German forces. | **1999:** Breathing equipment (gas masks, etc.): $1,650  **2001:** Protective equipment (suits, gloves, etc.): $532,500 **2002:** Chemical agent detection equipment: $152,000; Protective equipment (suits, gloves, etc.): $539 **2003:** Breathing equipment (gas masks, etc.): $69,000; Protective equipment (suits, gloves, etc.): $182,322 |
| **Oman** | **1999, 2000, 2001:** *Eagle Resolve* seminar: All GCC states, Jordan, Egypt, and the United States conduct senior-level tabletop exercise and briefings on CBW defense and coordination. | |
| **Qatar** | **1999, 2000, 2001:** *Eagle Resolve* seminar: All GCC states, Jordan, Egypt, and the United States conduct senior-level tabletop exercise and briefings on CBW defense and coordination. | **2003:** Breathing equipment (gas masks, etc.): $30,706 |
| **Saudi Arabia** | **1999, 2000, 2001:** *Eagle Resolve* seminar: All GCC states, Jordan, Egypt, and the United States conduct senior-level tabletop exercise and briefings on CBW defense and coordination. | **1999:** Breathing equipment (gas masks, etc.): $410 **2001:** Breathing equipment (gas masks, etc.): $82,860 **2002:** Breathing equipment (gas masks, etc.): $1,657 **2003:** Breathing equipment (gas masks, etc.): $3,530 |
| **UAE** | **1999, 2000, 2001:** *Eagle Resolve* seminar: All GCC states, Jordan, Egypt, and the United States conduct senior-level tabletop exercise and briefings on CBW defense and coordination. | **1999:** Protective equipment (suits, gloves, etc.): $1,539 **2001:** Protective equipment (suits, gloves, etc.): $3,606 **2002:** Chemical agent detection equipment: $2,152,260 **2003:** Protective equipment (suits, gloves, etc.): $30,650 |

weapons, given the limited CDI improvements at the time and considerable shortfalls in GCC state counterproliferation efforts to date. Clearly, the absence of Saddam Hussein's weapons of mass destruction threat, and indeed widespread questioning as to whether Iraq actually posed a serious weapons of mass destruction threat to its neighbors in 2003, might reduce future interest in pursuing the Cooperative Defense Initiative throughout the Persian Gulf region.

## Counterproliferation Cooperation with Israel

In the late 1990s, the United States and Israel formed a CWG to focus on the strategy, policy, and technology of chemical and biological defense. This body meets twice annually in conjunction with the Joint Political Military Group, which coordinates bilateral defense cooperation between the United States and Israel. As noted above, because the Israeli government treats weapons of mass destruction use as an urgent military menace, and because it has developed significant scientific, military, and political expertise in countering regional weapons of mass destruction threats, Tel Aviv has emerged as one of the most important partners of the United States in countering the international threats posed by the proliferation and possible use of weapons of mass destruction. The bilateral counterproliferation relationship between Washington and Tel Aviv is also quite sensitive; most cooperative activities remain classified by both parties.

## Counterproliferation Cooperation in the Asia-Pacific Region

Because of their proximity to one of Washington's most vexing WMD-armed adversaries, the Democratic People's Republic of Korea (DPRK, or North Korea), Japan and the Republic of Korea (ROK) quickly became the focus of U.S. counterproliferation efforts in the Asia-Pacific region. Bilateral cooperative efforts have been aimed at establishing an ongoing dialogue with each of these allies to discuss the military risks posed by North Korea's growing weapons of mass destruction capabilities, improving allied military capabilities in the face of these weapons of mass destruction threats, and identifying areas for cooperation in counterproliferation programs and activities.

### Japan

Like most countries, Japan's approach to international weapons of mass destruction proliferation problems during the Cold War emphasized diplomatic activities to strengthen the nuclear, chemical, and biological nonproliferation regimes. Very little attention was given to improving Japan's own defense capabilities to defend against or manage the consequences of chemical and biological warfare attacks. For example, the 1996 white paper, *Defense of Japan,* did not refer to the military challenges posed by weapons of mass destruction in Asia, but instead observed, "Transfers and proliferation of such weapons constitute an immediate matter for the international community, and efforts to prevent transfers and proliferation of mass destruction weapons through strengthening non-proliferation regime are being made."[30] The document made no reference to counterproliferation. Because of the different perspectives held by American and Japanese defense officials of the problems posed by weapons of mass destruction proliferation in the Asia-Pacific region, counterproliferation cooperation in the mid-1990s was restricted mainly to general consultations.

However, in the aftermath of the deadly Tokyo subway sarin attack in March 1995 and North Korea's August 31, 1998, Taepo Dong I multistage missile launch over Japanese territory, the government of Japan dramatically altered its view of the military threat posed by regional WMD proliferation and use. Compared to the 1996 document, Japan's 2002 white paper on defense treated the DPRK threat in a more ominous tone:

> Taken together with its suspected nuclear weapons program, the ballistic missile development and deployment by North Korea constitutes a destabilizing factor not only for the Asia-Pacific region, but for the entire international community, and there are strong concerns regarding the development.[31]

The key turning point for Japan was the weapons of mass destruction terrorism committed by Aum Shinrikyo, or "Supreme Truth." In fact, the March 20, 1995, sarin attack on the Tokyo subway had nearly the same cathartic impact as did the September 11, 2001, attacks on the United States. What was especially alarming to the Japanese, however, was the fact that the Aum cult actually had committed attacks, using chemical weapons (sarin and cyanide) several times and biological weapons (anthrax and botulinum toxin) nine times previously in an ongoing campaign of terror against the Japanese government and population.

Aum Shinrikyo began its weapons of mass destruction terror campaign on June 27, 1994, when cult members drove a converted refrigerator truck loaded with sarin nerve agent into a residential neighborhood in Matsumoto, a city of 300,000 located 200 miles northwest of Tokyo. After the truck was parked in a secluded parking lot behind a stand of trees, a computer-controlled device was activated to float a small cloud of sarin toward a group of private homes, apartments, and a small dormitory, which housed all three judges sitting on a panel hearing a lawsuit over a real-estate dispute in which Aum Shinrikyo was the defendant. The

Aum's lawyers had advised the sect's charismatic leader, Shoko Asahara (whose real name was Chizuo Matsumoto), that the decision was likely to go against him. Unwilling to lose the case, Asahara sent a team to Matsumoto to kill or injure the judges so they could not hand down an adverse judgment. As calculated, a light breeze gently pushed the deadly aerosol cloud of sarin into the neighborhood's open windows and doorways. Although the wind suddenly shifted away from the judges' residence, one judge was injured, and the trial ended up being postponed indefinitely. More significantly, this incident killed seven people, severely injured more than 150–200 people, and caused an additional few hundred other individuals to be transported to local hospitals.[32]

Aum Shinrikyo's next major sarin attack took place 10 months later. On the morning of March 20, 1995, specially trained cult members placed plastic bags filled with a toxic sarin compound and wrapped inside newspapers on five different trains in the Tokyo subway system. At a designated time, the operatives punctured each bag with a sharpened umbrella tip, allowing the chemical liquid to spill onto the floor of the subway car and then evaporate, causing the vaporous sarin to spread throughout the car. Because the attacks occurred on subway cars many miles apart, the resulting deaths and injuries occurred over a vast portion of central Tokyo. The first pleas for help came from the inner suburbs and then, very quickly, workers at one subway station after another reported widespread illnesses. The attacks formed a tight ring around the Kasumagaseki station, which serves the buildings that house most of the key agencies of the Japanese government—including most of the major ministries and the national police agency. By the end of the day, 15 subway stations in the world's busiest subway system had been affected. According to a Centers for Disease Control and Prevention source, the attacks injured about 3,800 people, out of which nearly 1,000 required hospitalization. Twelve people were killed.[33]

Japan also has developed a new appreciation of the very real threat posed by biological warfare because of Aum Shinrikyo's WMD terrorist activities. In early 1990, the cult's researchers launched a program to produce botulinum toxin as a biological agent. Three years later, Aum completed a new biological research facility designed to produce *Bacillus anthracis*, the bacteria responsible for producing the anthrax infection. In addition, the cult is believed to have experimented with Q fever and the spores from a poisonous mushroom, and it also sent agents to Zaire to acquire Ebola.[34] Media reports suggest that the Aum attempted to use aerosolized biological agents against nine targets, two with anthrax and seven with botulinum toxin. The target set included the Diet (Japan's parliament); the town of Yokohama and the Yokosuka Naval Base (the U.S. Navy's most important facility in the east Pacific); Narita International Airport, one of the world's most important airports; downtown Tokyo (to disrupt the planned wedding of Prince Naruhito, Japan's Crown Prince); the Imperial Palace in Tokyo; and the Tokyo subway. The failure of this last operation on March 15, 1995, led the cult to use sarin on the subway five days later.[35]

The Aum scientists evidently made mistakes either in the way they produced or disseminated the agents, and all the attacks failed. Nonetheless, subsequent reports of these intended acts of bioterrorism created a chilling stir inside Japan's national security apparatus. Based on the lessons Japan learned from the outbreak of the Tokyo subway sarin incident in 1995 and the *Bacillus anthracis* attack in the United States in 2001, the Japan Defense Agency has adopted an entirely new appreciation of the importance of counterproliferation against BW threats.

Japan's 2002 defense white paper indicates that a comprehensive biodefense strategy was essential because biological weapons can be produced easily and with low cost, ordinarily have several days of incubation period from exposure to becoming ill, cannot be detected easily when used, can have a strong psychological effect even if not actually used, can possibly cause a large number of casualties, and also because "there have been mounted risks of acquisition, development, production or use of biological weapons by some countries or terrorists, which may be used for attack to military targets or attack or terrorism to ordinary citizens."[36]

In January 2002, Tokyo also released a new document outlining its "Basic Concept for Dealing with Biological Weapons." According to the new policy,

> the Agency must secure the capability to properly take action at such time as the defense operations by acquiring [the] ability to protect [its] own unit[s] and that [a] biological weapons response capability and necessary base in areas of detection, protection, decontamination, disease control, rescue and medical treatment must be maintained comprehensively and steadily under the restricted financial circumstance.[37]

Japan also has identified new organizational responsibilities and procedures for dealing with a biological terrorist attack on Japanese soil. The Japanese government understands that its police or fire fighting agencies, or the Ministry of Health, Labor and Welfare, will be the primary responders to a biological attack. The Self-Defense Force

> will perform rescue activity for victims mainly by the chemical unit of the Ground Self-Defense Force and the medical unit of each Self-Defense Force. … [I]n addition to performing emergency transportation requested by concerned ministries and agencies, the Self-Defense Force engage in such activities as transfer of patients, provision of treatment facilities and medical treatment, transportation or dissemination of preventive or treatment drug, or detection, prevention of expansion and decontamination by the disaster dispatch based on the request of prefectural governors, etc. And, according

to the situation, the Self-Defense Force will respond by police operation or defense operation.[38]

Similar policies would be followed in the event of a chemical terrorist attack against the Japanese population. To assist first responders, such as police or fire fighting agencies,

> the Self-Defense Force will be able to respond to and protect from chemical weapons by such equipment as chemical protection suit or chemical protection vehicles allocated to the chemical protection unit, etc. of the Ground Self-Defense Force. In detail, in addition to performing emergency transportation requested by concerned ministries and agencies, the Self-Defense Force engage in such activities as specification of chemical agent used by using chemical detection equipment, transfer of wounded or injured persons, decontamination or medical treatment by the medical protection unit of the Ground Self-Defense Force and the medical units of ground, maritime and air Self-Defense Force in the contaminated area by the disaster relief dispatch based on the request of prefectural governors, etc. Even in a case in which the action of the Self-Defense Force is not required, the Self-Defense Force are capable of providing equipments such as chemical protection suit or dispatching experts of chemical protection to concerned organizations.[39]

Although the Japanese government has not publicized any specific cooperation with the United States in countering the proliferation and use of chemical and biological warfare, the United States and Japan have explored new opportunities for cooperation to improve both nations' consequence management and weapons of mass destruction defense capabilities, under the auspices of the long-standing U.S.–Japan Security Consultation Committee. Much hard work lies ahead to field effective counterproliferation and homeland security capabilities, but Japan now ranks among the few countries that actually have undertaken widespread changes in the way it plans, organizes, trains, and equips to counter weapons of mass destruction threats.

## Korea

The U.S. Government places a very high priority on counterproliferation cooperation with the Republic of Korea because that country is confronted with perhaps the world's greatest military threat of nuclear, biological, and chemical weapons use. North Korea's long-standing inventory of biological and chemical weapons and associated means of delivery is now believed to be complemented by a small number of nuclear weapons. In April 2004, U.S. President George W. Bush stated,

> In the Pacific, North Korea has defied the world, has tested long-range ballistic missiles, admitted its possession of nuclear weapons, and now threatens

to build more. Together with our partners in Asia, America is insisting that North Korea completely, verifiably, and irreversibly dismantle its nuclear programs.[40]

Efforts to negotiate a peaceful termination of North Korea's weapons of mass destruction programs have not enjoyed any success. It also is not clear if any negotiated agreement would be honored by the Pyongyang regime. As former Central Intelligence Agency Director James Woolsey stated with regard to compliance, "any agreement with North Korea is worse than worthless."[41] Because of the unavoidable prospect that North Korea will pose a serious and growing WMD threat to its neighbors for many years, the United States and the Republic of Korea will have a powerful incentive to improve their mutual counterproliferation preparedness.

At the tail end of the Clinton administration, the United States and South Korea formed a Combined Counterproliferation Working Group to serve as a forum for discussion of policy issues and a source of guidance for an affiliated Counterproliferation Operations Group, cochaired by U.S. forces, Korea, and ROK Joint Chiefs of Staff military experts. Several operationally focused subgroups have been established and now meet regularly to improve U.S. and ROK WMD-related defense capabilities. The working groups address operational NBC defense issues associated with ground force equipment and operations, air-base and seaport operations, medical defenses, modeling and simulation, and weapons of mass destruction consequence management. Their focus is on practical measures to improve combined operations in a chemical and biological warfare environment. Much of the impetus for this progress came from the CORAL BREEZE series, a set of tabletop chemical and biological warfare defense exercises cosponsored by the Office of the Secretary of Defense and the Commander of U.S. Forces, Korea. While these exercises initially involved only U.S. forces, they gradually evolved to encompass Korean as well as American participants.

The Seoul government has demonstrated its commitment to counter weapons of mass destruction threats by increased spending on WMD defense capabilities for its military forces. The Commander of U.S. Forces, Korea, also launched a Family and Force Protection Initiative to extend chemical and biological warfare protection to dependents of U.S. military service members, civilian Department of Defense employees, and their families through the distribution of protective masks and hoods. Although South Korea has a long way to go before it will possess an effective military and homeland security capability against weapons of mass destruction threats, it has made significant progress in working closely with the United States.

## Assessment and Future Challenges

The U.S. Government has been concerned about the proliferation and possible use of weapons of mass destruction since chemical warfare agents were used against American troops in the First World War and U.S. adversaries started to develop biological warfare agents, chemical weapons, and nuclear weapons during and after the Second World War. While weapons of mass destruction were viewed during and immediately after the Cold War as weapons of last resort, the Bush administration's main national strategy document for weapons of mass destruction aptly observes that rogue states see their increasingly sophisticated and extensive nuclear, chemical, biological, and missile arsenals as

> militarily useful weapons of choice intended to overcome our nation's advantages in conventional forces and to deter us from responding to aggression against our friends and allies in regions of vital interest.[42]

While these words could have been written by the late Secretary of Defense Les Aspin, or by former Secretary of Defense William S. Cohen, who said that "our unrivaled supremacy in the conventional military arena is prompting adversaries to seek unconventional, asymmetric means to strike what they perceive as our Achilles heel," and that among our adversaries, we especially must be prepared to counter "fanatical terrorists" armed with weapons of mass destruction,[43] there is a clear sense of urgency in the Bush administration's statements about weapons of mass destruction, which did not exist before September 11, 2001. Just as the American people viewed the Japanese military threat in a new light after the attack on Pearl Harbor, so too does the public and its elected officials see a palpable change in the threat posed by state and nonstate owners of weapons of mass destruction after the September 11, 2001, terrorist attacks against Washington, D.C., and New York City.

Because of Washington's heightened concern about weapons of mass destruction proliferation and its growing awareness of the vulnerability of U.S. coalition partners and allies to weapons of mass destruction use, after a three-year delay the Bush administration has continued much of its predecessor's policies with regard to international counterproliferation cooperation.[44] The current U.S. deterrence posture against weapons of mass destruction use still rests on a strong declaratory policy and effective military forces, but there has been a not-so-subtle shift in the balance of deterrence from long-standing promises to *punish* any adversary that contemplated weapons of mass destruction use against U.S. interests, to increasingly credible threats to *deny* adversaries any meaningful political or military advantage from using weapons of mass destruction. The Bush administration remains adamant about the U.S. Government's "right to respond with overwhelming force—including through resort to all of our options—to the use of weapons of mass destruction against the United States, its forces abroad, and friends and allies." In addition, the new strategy calls for improved military and civilian capabilities to defeat and defend against weapons of mass destruction use—including missile defenses and force enhancements such as intelligence, surveillance, interdiction, and even domestic law enforcement—which combine to strengthen deterrence by "devaluing an adversary's weapons of mass destruction and missiles."[45] Predictably, U.S. international counterproliferation cooperation reflects these changes in defense priorities.

Recognizing that deterrence may not succeed and that weapons of mass destruction employment against the U.S. population or military forces could be devastating, the new strategy requires U.S. military forces and appropriate civilian agencies to be prepared to "detect and destroy an adversary's weapons of mass destruction assets before these weapons are used" and to have in place "robust active and passive defenses and mitigation measures" to enable U.S. authorities to accomplish their missions and to assist friends and allies when weapons of mass destruction are used. Once again, this approach has much in common with previous U.S. policies, but the stress placed on missile defenses, and the unprecedented resources devoted to them, is a hallmark of the Bush administration's defense strategy. Also receiving new and appropriate emphasis is the development of specifically tailored policies to counter biological weapons which, because of their unique effects and detection and response requirements, cannot be lumped together with chemical weapons.

The most dramatic innovation in counterproliferation policy is the new stress on interdiction, and this aspect has had the greatest impact on international counterproliferation cooperation. President Bush announced the Proliferation Security Initiative (PSI) on May 31, 2003, in Krakow, Poland. He stated,

> When weapons of mass destruction or their components are in transit, we must have the means and authority to seize them. … The United States and a number of our close allies, including Poland, have begun working on new agreements to search planes and ships carrying suspect cargo and to seize illegal weapons or missile technologies. Over time, we will extend this partnership as broadly as possible to keep the world's most destructive weapons away from our shores and out of the hands of our common enemies.[46]

The 2003 seizure of a North Korean ship carrying SCUD missiles bound for Yemen is evidence of this new approach. Because the missiles were going to a close ally in the war on terrorism, the shipment was allowed to sail on to Yemen, but the outcome would have been different had the ultimate recipient been a U.S. adversary, such as Iraq, or a stateless terrorist group, such as al-Qaeda. This new interdiction strategy has led to the implementation of the PSI, an international venture to improve the preparedness of Washington's overseas friends and allies to interdict transfers of weapons of mass destruction and weapons of mass destruction-related technology and materials.

Because of the daunting legal, intelligence, and operational challenges presented when more than a dozen countries partner together to share intelligence and interdict illicit weapons of mass destruction shipments, the Proliferation Security Initiative will demand a tremendous amount of attention from the participating nations—a development that has the potential, if not managed effectively, to undermine the significant progress made to date in realizing Secretary Les Aspin's vision in the more "traditional" areas of counterproliferation. A key challenge facing U.S. defense planners and their international partners in the next decade is to integrate new counterforce and interdiction plans and capabilities into a more coherent and robust international counterproliferation strategy. If they manage to do so, the effect could be to make WMD proliferation even more difficult and costly, thus ultimately minimizing the threat of WMD use.

Another potentially troubling issue for international counterproliferation efforts is the fallout from the 2003 Gulf War. According to the Comprehensive Report of the Special Advisor to the Director of Central Intelligence on Iraq's Weapons of Mass Destruction, it now seems certain that there was no large-scale Iraqi weapons of mass destruction capability to deter in Operation Iraqi Freedom (OIF).[47] As a result of this finding—and the mistaken judgments the U.S. policy and intelligence communities had made about Saddam Hussein's WMD capabilities—U.S. friends and allies might not believe they need to devote so much government expenditure and energy to preparing their military forces and their homeland authorities to fight through and survive a weapons of mass destruction attack as they did before the OIF false alarm. This would be a grave mistake.

In the next war with a rogue state, the result could be very much different. Because weapons of mass destruction remain in the possession of several radical regimes, 13 years after the launching of the Defense Counterproliferation Initiative, the United States ought to redouble the efforts it initiated in December 1993 to forge, or reforge, a strong international consensus that weapons of mass destruction proliferation and use constitute the most dangerous threats to international peace and stability and that close international diplomatic and military cooperation is required to deter and defeat this growing threat.

# CHAPTER 11

# Securing the Homeland

## The First Decade

### *Randall J. Larsen and Patrick D. Ellis*

*Defending our Nation against its enemies is the first and fundamental commitment of the Federal government. Today, that task has changed dramatically. Enemies in the past needed great armies and great industrial capabilities to endanger America. Now, shadowy networks of individuals can bring great chaos and suffering to our shores for less than it costs to purchase a tank. Terrorists are organized to penetrate open societies and to turn the power of modern technologies against us.*

President George W. Bush
The National Security Strategy of the United States
September 20, 2002

On September 20, 2001, the developers of the DARK WINTER exercise met with Vice President Richard Cheney and his staff to discuss the lessons learned from this simulated smallpox attack on America.[1] The vice president asked, "What does a biological weapon look like?" One of the briefers reached into his pocket and pulled out a small test tube filled with a white powder. "Sir," he said as he eyed the two Secret Service agents standing by the door, "It looks like this ... and by the way ... I did just carry this into your office." "Three decades ago," the briefer continued, "only large industrial nations had the technical capability to produce such a weapon. However, due to the revolution in biotechnology, this sample was produced with equipment bought on the Internet for less than $250,000."[2]

The powder was weaponized *Bacillus globigii*. Genetically, it is nearly identical to *Bacillus anthracis*—the bacteria that causes anthrax. However,

*Bacillus globigii* is frequently used as a simulant. Most nations that have weaponized anthrax, including the United States, and the Soviet Union, first weaponized *Bacillus globigii* to test their production and delivery processes. Weaponization refers to the production of a biological agent at the three- to five-micron size (a human hair is about 100 microns wide), which is perfect for release in the air and is the optimal size to enter and remain lodged in the lung of the target.

Three weeks following this conversation, Robert Stevens, a photojournalist for American Media, Inc., in Boca Raton, Florida, died from inhalational anthrax. Four other Americans would also soon die from anthrax-laced mail. During the next several weeks, citizens across the nation began to question their security. Major newspapers stopped accepting letters to the editor, farmers in Iowa wondered if it was safe to open their mail, and most Americans began to appreciate how technology had changed the international security equation.

In 1828, a young Abraham Lincoln said, "No European or Asian power, even with a Bonaparte in command, could march across this continent and take a drink of water from the Ohio or make a track on the Appalachian trail."[3] This is still true, but today it is irrelevant. America's enemies no longer need to put an army on our soil or missiles in our skies to threaten our homeland. Small adversary groups can penetrate American society covertly and, undetected, could release invisible, odorless biological agents.

Homeland security is the most complex endeavor this nation has ever faced. Some see this new mission as just the next evolutionary step in the national security process. This is not the case—it is a change in kind, not degree. Since the late 1800s, national security took place in Washington, D.C., and overseas. The key players were all in the federal government, most notably, the Departments of Defense, State, and the Intelligence Community.

Today there are 57 federal agencies, 50 states, 8 territories, and 3,066 counties involved in U.S. homeland security. In fact, there are 87,000 different governmental jurisdictions that play roles in homeland security.[4] Furthermore, the private sector plays a major role in homeland security, and this role is not limited to logistical support. Corporate America is required to play a major operational role in homeland security.

In any analysis of homeland security issues facing the United States after the al-Qaeda attacks of September 11, 2001, a number of important questions must be addressed:

1. What changes does the leadership and citizenship need to make about national security in the post 9/11 world?

2. What new style of terrorist are we confronting that could lead to mass casualty events?

3. What sequence of terrorist events since 1993 has led us to the conclusion that we are confronting a new breed of terrorist?

4. What policy changes has the U.S. Government initiated to cope with this new terrorist security threat?

5. What commissions were organized to provide ideas on how to respond, and what did they recommend?

6. What analytic framework informs the new U.S. Homeland Security program? How, and when, should the United States deter and prevent attacks on the homeland? When, if ever, should it preempt to nip attacks in the bud? How should it manage incidents? Attribute blame? Respond to limit damage?

7. How should the Homeland Security program deal with the threat of weapons of mass destruction (WMD) use?

8. What is the character of the 2001 attacks on the U.S. homeland that caused the United States to form the Department of Homeland Security (DHS)?

9. What were the first steps taken by DHS once formed? And what is the crux of the *National Strategy for Homeland Security*?

10. What are the U.S. agencies and departments consolidated under DHS?

11. What key issues remain to be resolved before the United States has a coherent and effective Homeland Security Program? For example, how do we integrate intelligence and law enforcement? What is the role of U.S. Northern Command? How do we reconcile *Posse Comitatus* issues? How do we integrate all levels of government in a united effort?

12. How do we prioritize threats and spending to offset them in the Homeland Security Program in such a way as to strike a balance between security and freedom?

The changes that have and will continue to occur make it difficult to even decide which questions to ask, much less, how to answer them. Perhaps the first step will be to change how we think about security in the twenty-first century.

A young reporter once asked Albert Einstein what his theory of relativity had changed. He thought about it for a moment and then said, "The unleashed power of the atom has changed everything save our modes of thinking, and we thus drift toward unparalleled catastrophes."[5] If we are to secure the American homeland from twenty-first century threats, we must learn to do something that is very difficult … we must change the way we think. Therefore, the purpose of this chapter is to help readers change the way they think about homeland security, no easy task.

First, it is important to realize that U.S. territory is no longer in a zone of peace largely free of threats. We can and will be attacked on our own soil. Some of those attacks will be by terrorist organizations such as al-Qaeda.

Some might be by homegrown terrorists such as Timothy McVeigh or, perhaps, the person(s) who used the U.S. mail system to launch anthrax poisonings in late 2001.

Second, Americans everywhere in the world are now considered targets, whether they reside in barracks such as Khobar Towers, Saudi Arabia, the USS *Cole* anchored off Yemen, or Iraq.

Third, we can no longer go about business as usual but must be ever conscious of security as we check into airports, visit public buildings, handle cargo coming into our ports, or handle the daily mail.

Fourth, we must also become more prudent in how we admit foreign persons into the United States and in monitoring their activities while here.

Fifth, we must be vigilant in protecting the critical infrastructure of America and intelligent in defending it so that our own resources such as airliners and the postal system can be used less easily against key nodes in our society. Overall, a keen awareness of the threat and a prioritized defense of American lives and assets is required in the new security environment. Further, this awareness needs to be the job of every citizen, not just that of the Federal Bureau of Investigation (FBI), the police, and a few concerned officials. Vigilance is the price of liberty and safety.

At the same time, we must respect the rights of Americans and non-Americans alike, at home and overseas both because it is a core value to do so and because America's prestige and long-term power depends on it. Respect for human rights and democracy, both of which will be subject to tensions as we pursue the war on terrorism, are central to the foreign policy goals of the United States.

## Homeland Security in the 1990s

The current concepts of homeland security—protecting the homeland from large-scale attacks where small nation-states or well-financed terrorist organizations would use WMD—began in late 1990 as America prepared for war with Iraq. This was the first war in almost 40 years where Washington seriously considered the possibility of enemy attack on the homeland. Airports introduced new security procedures. At border crossing points there was increased surveillance, and the FBI monitored the activities of Iraqis in the United States. Reportedly, several special operations-type units were dispatched from Iraq. However, cooperation among allied intelligence and law enforcement organizations deterred and prevented Iraqi attacks on the American homeland.

For most Americans, homeland security entered the common lexicon on September 11, 2001. However, the modern era of homeland security began in earnest in 1993. Throughout the later half of the twentieth century, terrorists had conducted small-scale attacks to bring attention to their causes. Some have described this as "blowing up something to get a seat at the table." In the 1990s, a new age of terrorism emerged. The attackers chose to remain anonymous, they had no specific demands, and their primary goal appeared to be the killing of large numbers of people. Some terrorists no longer wanted a seat at the table; they just wanted to "blow up the table." This new style of terrorism came to the American homeland on February 26, 1993.[6]

## World Trade Center Bombing 1993

On February 26, 1993, a large explosion ripped through the B-2 level of the basement under the World Trade Center, creating an L-shaped crater measuring 130 by 150 feet across and approximately seven stories deep. Almost unbelievably, the blast and subsequent debris killed only six, but injured more than 1,000 people. The bomb, 1,200 pounds of nitro urea supplemented by hydrogen cylinders, created over 6,000 tons of rubble and produced acrid smoke, which rose up to the 46th floor. Total property damaged reached $300 million.[7] Four men, led by Ramzi Yousef, planned this operation to topple both of the Twin Towers.

## Tokyo Subway 1995

For the next two years, the world was quiet in respect to major terrorist events. Then, on June 27, 1994, several terrorists released sarin nerve gas in an apartment complex in Matsumoto, Japan, killing seven and sending 150–200 residents to the hospital.[8] This was an indication of things to come. Nine months later, during the morning rush hour on March 20, 1995, this same Japanese domestic terrorist organization, Aum Shinrikyo (Aum Supreme Truth), released a crude form of sarin gas (GB) in the Tokyo subway.

The sarin attack on the Tokyo subway system killed 12, injured 3,800, and traumatized thousands. The residents of Tokyo were fortunate the numbers were not higher. Aum's chemical team had been testing several chemical agents at a large ranch they owned in Australia. The quality of the sarin used in this attack was very poor because it came from a batch that had been hastily prepared the weekend before, after senior leaders in the Aum received a tip that the Tokyo police would soon raid their headquarters. The delivery system also was primitive. Plastic bags filled with the poor quality sarin were placed on subway cars and punctured with umbrella tips. Had this been a high quality sarin delivered in a more sophisticated manner, deaths would have been in the hundreds or even thousands.

This attack initially appeared to be the first terrorist use of a weapon of mass destruction. However, documents presented during the criminal trials of senior Aum leaders painted a completely different picture. Between 1990 and 1995, the cult conducted at least 19 attacks, 10 using chemical agents and 9 with biological agents.[9] The cult had experimented with chemical nerve agents such as sarin, tabun, soman, VX, and other agents such as hydrogen cyanide, phosgene, and mustard blister agents. Aum's interest in biological agents extended to anthrax, Q fever, and hemorrhagic fevers such as Ebola. In the end, none of the Aum Shinrikyo biological attacks were effective, but it did have limited success with its chemical program. The cult also had shopped for nuclear weapons components in the former Soviet Union, although little progress was made toward acquiring nuclear weapons.

Aum's subway attack released a floodgate of information on the group's extensive chemical and biological weapons development programs—all of which went undetected by the intelligence and law enforcement communities. It sent shock waves through the domestic and international law enforcement, intelligence, and first-responder communities, which first were amazed to realize the types of weapons that were being prepared and, second, were surprised to discover the stated purpose of such attacks—the creation of mass casualty events for the purpose of toppling the government.

Despite the obvious differences between Aum Shinrikyo and al-Qaeda in terms of culture, religion, and organization, their goals are nevertheless similar: to completely upset political and social order through the use of massively destructive weapons.

## Murrah Federal Office Building 1995

It has been said that whatever was left of America's innocence, in reference to terrorism, was lost on April 19, 1995. For the senior leadership in the Clinton administration and Congress, the first-responder community, and virtually all Americans who stared at television screens that day, the nightmare of catastrophic terrorism had become reality in the American heartland.

Initially, many assumed the attack came from Islamic fundamentalists, but in less than 48 hours an even more disturbing story emerged. Just like the Japanese had difficulty believing that some of their "own" could launch such a murderous attack on the Japanese homeland, Americans now had to deal with a homegrown catastrophic terrorist—a Gulf War veteran who intentionally parked a large truck bomb in front of a child-care center. Shock, horror, grief, and anger were the emotions of the day.

Timothy McVeigh and his accomplice Terry Nichols had built a 4,000-pound ammonium nitrate fuel oil bomb and placed it into a Ryder rental truck, which McVeigh then drove to the Alfred Murrah Federal Office Building. The front of the building was destroyed, leaving 167 people dead and more than 500 injured. The eventual crime scene stretched over some 200-city blocks, and the sheer magnitude of response agencies overwhelmed existing communications systems. Besides high physical and personal costs, mental health costs were $4.1 million during the following year and continues yet today.

While there are few similarities between the al-Qaeda terrorist atrocities and Timothy McVeigh's Oklahoma City bombing, one commonality is apparent. None of the instigators had any hesitation or regret at killing innocents.

Nothing is more disturbing than to hear pundits and apologists for terrorists say, "One man's terrorist is another man's freedom fighter." There is a major difference between attacks on child-care centers, pizza parlors, or high-rise office buildings and legitimate military targets. When the marine barracks in Beirut was attacked with a truck bomb—some called it terrorism. It was not. A U.S. Navy battleship was sitting off the coast firing 1,600-pound shells at military targets in Beirut. In response, an attack was launched on a U.S. military unit. Call it asymmetric warfare or guerilla warfare, but do not confuse it with those who intentionally bomb office buildings in New York City, subways in Tokyo, and child-care centers in Oklahoma.

Some looked at the 1993 attack on the World Trade Center, the 1995 attacks on the Tokyo subway, and the Federal Office Building in Oklahoma City as random events. Others realized that a new international security environment was emerging. One of those individuals representative of this new environment was arrested in Pakistan and returned to the United States for trial. His name was Ramzi Yousef.

The head of the FBI in New York, Bill Gavin, was escorting Yousef to New York City for arraignment. As the FBI helicopter flew up the Hudson River, Gavin eased the blindfold from Yousef's eyes, "'Look down there,' ... gesturing toward the twin towers. 'They're still standing.' Yousef squinted and looked out of the window. 'They wouldn't be, if I had had enough money and explosives,' he replied defiantly."[10]

## The Role of the Early Commissions

The terrorist attacks in New York City, Tokyo, and Oklahoma City led to the appointment of several high-level commissions that would examine both the threat and America's state of readiness for this new type of catastrophic terrorism. In retrospect, the reports from these commissions were for the most part right on target with both their descriptions of the threat and the actions required to deter, prevent, and respond to such threats. Unfortunately, few listened.

The first mention of the term *homeland security*, in a post-Cold War government report, appeared in *Report of the National Defense Panel* (NDP) in

December 1997, chaired by Phil Odeen. Section 924 of the Military Force Structure Act of 1996 had directed the report. The term *homeland defense* was used interchangeably with homeland security for several years. The NDP Report contained one paragraph on homeland defense:

> Protecting the territory of the United States and its citizens from "all enemies both foreign and domestic" is the principal task of government. The primary reason for the increased emphasis on homeland defense is the change, both in type and degree, in the threats to the United States. Besides the enduring need to deter a strategic nuclear attack, the United States must defend against terrorism, information warfare, weapons of mass destruction, ballistic and cruise missiles, and other transnational threats to the sovereign territory of the nation. In many of these mission areas, the military will necessarily play the leading role; however, many other threats exist which will require Defense to support local law enforcement agencies, as well as a host of other federal, state, and local entities.[11]

However, homeland security today is used to mean defense of all U.S. territory and citizens who reside there, whereas homeland defense is now normally used to refer to the defense of U.S. military installations and personnel in the continental United States (CONUS).

President Clinton signed Executive Order 13010 establishing the *President's Commission on Critical Infrastructure Protection.* The report was released in October 1997. This was the first of several key commissions that laid the groundwork for how we understand homeland security today.

The initial charter of the commission was to look at all aspects of critical infrastructure protection, but the final report almost exclusively focused on the cyber threat to infrastructure. According to Phil Lacombe, the Executive Director of The President's Commission on Critical Infrastructure Protection (PCCIP), the commission narrowed its focus because considerable work had already been accomplished on the physical vulnerabilities of critical infrastructure, but little had been done on the cyber threats. Four key infrastructures were initially identified: information and communications, banking and finance, energy (including electrical power, oil, and gas) physical distribution, and vital human services. The one element these infrastructures had in common was that they were each highly vulnerable to cyber attacks. In demonstration after demonstration, the commissioners were shocked to learn how easy it was to hack into systems. The report noted, "A personal computer and a simple telephone connection to an Internet Service Provider anywhere in the world are enough to cause a great deal of harm."[12] Highlights of the report included the following:

- Deregulation in the energy industry had driven corporations to look for ways to trim costs. This meant less redundancy. Energy systems were operating at near maximum capacity, so that even a minor event could cause a cascading effect. The report noted, "Because of the complexity, some of these dependencies may be unrecognized until a major failure occurs."

- The threats examined ranged from natural events and accidents to disgruntled employees, recreational hackers, criminal activity, and terrorism. The commission noted that most things entering the United States must go through some sort of screening: the Immigration and Naturalization Service (INS) screened people, the Postal Service examined the mail, airplanes pass through an air defense identification zone, trucks and containers are checked by border patrol and customs, food stuffs are inspected by Food and Drug Administration and United States Department of Agriculture, but electrons, coming on the Internet enter this country every moment of every day, and nobody was checking.

- The commission also highlighted how outdated America's concepts of defense and prevention had become. They asked, "Who would be responsible for investigating a cyber attack?" According to the commission report, "With the existing rules, you may have to solve the crime before you can decide who has the authority to investigate."

The commission's number one recommendation, a recommendation that should be a top priority for all homeland security issues, was to develop a program of awareness and education. Additionally, it recommended a partnership with industry including the creation of the Infrastructure Sharing and Analysis Centers (ISACs) to allow industry and government to share critical security information in an environment that would protect the proprietary interests of industry and the government from the Federal Advisory Committee Act (FACA) restrictions.[13]

The **National Commission on Terrorism** was created by Congress and led by Ambassador L. Paul Bremer III.[14] The commission report, released in June 2000, concluded that international terrorists would impose an increasingly dangerous and difficult threat to the American homeland. The commission said that today's terrorists seek to inflict mass casualties, are less dependent on state sponsorship, and are forming loose transnational affiliations, making terrorist attacks more difficult to detect and prevent. This new type of threat would require significantly enhanced efforts by the U.S. Government.

The commission provided several recommendations; three of these would receive considerable attention after September 11, 2001: (1) increased integration of law enforcement and intelligence communities, (2) creation of a cadre of FBI officers who would distill and disseminate terrorist information once it is collected, and (3) an increase in intelligence collection on all states that support terrorists.

The commission also noted that terrorist attacks involving a biological agent or nuclear material, even if only partially successful, can profoundly affect the entire nation. Many in the press misinterpreted one recommendation. The report stated, "the Department of Defense must have detailed plans for its role in the event of a catastrophic terrorist attack, including criteria for decisions on transfer command authority to DoD in extraordinary circumstances." Several major newspapers interpreted this to mean that the Department of Defense (DoD) should have the lead role in consequence management. That was neither the intention of the commission, nor what the report said. Had the reporters read more than the executive summary they would have understood that this statement referred to a situation in which state and local authorities were completely overwhelmed and unable to respond to an incident, which was considered to be the extreme exception, not the rule.

**The Advisory Panel to Assess Domestic Response Capabilities for Terrorism Involving Weapons of Mass Destruction,** also known as the Gilmore Commission because its chairman was Governor James Gilmore III of Virginia, released its first report in December 1999, and issued its fifth and final report on December 15, 2003.[15]

The legislation creating this commission directed them to assess federal efforts to enhance domestic preparedness and highlight deficiencies in federal programs for response to terrorist incidents using weapons of mass destruction. The Gilmore Commission's first report introduced the debate: whether to focus on preventing and dealing with *high-probability/ low-consequence* versus *low-probability/high-consequence* scenarios. The initial report acknowledged that the low probability/high consequence could happen, but chose to focus on high probability/low consequence. The report stated,

> Conventional explosives, traditionally a favorite tool of the terrorists, will likely remain the weapon of choice in near term as well ... increasing attention must now also be paid to the historically more frequent, more probable, lesser consequence attack, especially in terms of policy implications for budget priorities or allocation of other resources, to optimize local response capabilities.[16]

The report went to great length describing the current difficulties in acquiring and developing mass casualty weapons, drawing on the example of Aum Shinrikyo, a terrorist organization with several hundred million dollars in assets and "highly-educated scientists," who failed after numerous attempts to produce a successful biological weapons program.[17] Information that was not available to the commission at that time later explained why the Aum's biowarfare program failed. Court testimony revealed that the graduate student, who was directed to acquire the sample of *Bacillus anthracis* (anthrax) from a laboratory, got cold feet and instead provided a sample of anthrax vaccine.[18] Fortunately, it was the nonlethal vaccine strain that was mass-produced and released in 10 different attacks in Japan rather than lethal strains. The Gilmore report also stated many well-trained scientists worked on this program, when in fact, it was mainly chemists and physicians working on the bioweapons program. Not a single Ph.D. level microbiologist participated in the program.

Nevertheless, the Gilmore Commission did provide several useful recommendations, primarily emphasizing the need for better cooperation and coordination of federal, state, and local governments and a reorganization of Congress to ensure proper policies and funding were coordinated for homeland security. The commission also stated that more cooperation was needed to obtain and share information on terrorist threats at all levels of government.

Later Gilmore Commission reports, released after the September 11, 2001, attacks, had a significantly changed attitude about weapons of mass destruction and became more in line with the recommendations of the initial Hart-Rudman report of September 1999.

**The U.S. Commission on National Security/21st Century,** also known as the Hart-Rudman Commission after its cochairmen, Senators Gary Hart and Warren Rudman, concluded that America will become increasingly vulnerable to hostile attacks and that Americans will die in their homeland, perhaps in large numbers.[19] The two new threats this commission was most concerned about were the result of rapid advances in information and biotechnology: terrorist organizations might attack not only humans, but also the economic infrastructure of nations. This commission expressed concern about the porous nature of borders and also addressed numerous other challenges America will face in the twenty-first century not directly associated with homeland security, such as education and problems with the civil service system.

One of the most notable features of the third Hart-Rudman Report, released in February 2001, was the recommendation to create a Department of Homeland Security. The vast majority of organizations consolidated into the new Department of Homeland Security in March 2003 were the same ones recommended two years earlier in the release of this report. In the summer of 2001, Representative Mac Thornberry (R-TX) used the commission report as the basis for the bill he introduced in the House of Representatives. This bill served as the blueprint for the legislation that eventually created the new department.

All high-level commissions that studied the issue of homeland security came to similar recommendations, some more prescient than others. These commission reports, combined with the open testimony of the director of the CIA, George Tenet, forewarned America of what was to come on September 11, 2001.[20] These reports were produced in a bipartisan manner by some of the most experienced national security leaders in the nation. Sadly, very few Americans listened.

# 9/11 Commission and Beyond

The attacks of September 11, 2001, and December 7, 1941, have many things in common: the heavy loss of life, the inability to understand all the warning signals before the attacks, and the changes to the American way of life after the attacks. Just as those studying the Pearl Harbor attack would comment on the obvious signs presented before the attack, we too can see "similar" noticeable signs post-September 11, 2001. The National Commission on Terrorist Attacks upon the United States (commonly referred to as the 9/11 Commission) states, "we write with the benefit and handicap of hindsight."[21] Hindsight is indeed "20-20." Thus, the task of the 9/11 Commission was to understand the why's and how's of this attack. President Bush's charter for the Commission was for the final report to "contain important recommendations for steps that can be taken to improve our preparedness for and response to terrorist attacks in the future."[22]

## About the Commission

On November 27, 2002, the 107th Congress passed Public Law 107-306, *Intelligence Authorization Act for Fiscal Year 2003*, establishing the 9/11 Commission. This independent bipartisan Commission was composed of 10 members equally divided between the Republican and Democratic parties of Congress. The president appointed the chairman of the Commission and the Senate's Democratic Party leader selected the vice-chairman.[23] One Democratic and one Republican representative were selected from both the Senate and House of Representatives. The staff was made up of roughly "80 full-time employees, contractors, and detailees"[24] working in teams. They researched eight topics ranging from al-Qaeda and the organization of the 9/11 attacks, border security, terrorist financing, commercial aviation and transportation security, to national, state, and local level response. The Commission's original budget was programmed for $3 million; however, the final budget would total $15 million.[25] The Commission had, by law, 18 months to submit a final report (containing findings, conclusions, and recommendations agreed on by the majority) to the President and Congress of the United States.[26] In the end the Commission's deadline was extended by two months.[27]

## The Commission's Purpose

The Commission was given two overall tasks to complete. The first came in the form of a charter. It was "to prepare a full and complete account of the circumstances surrounding the September 11, 2001, terrorist attacks, including the preparedness for and the immediate response to the attacks."[28] The second task was a mandate, "to provide recommendations designed to guard against future attacks."[29] After thorough investigations, interviews with over 1,000 people in 10 countries, and 13 public hearings with testimony from 110 federal, state, and local officials, and experts from the private sector, the tasks were completed and a final report compiled and released to the public on July 22, 2004.[30] The Commission officially closed a month later on August 21, 2004.[31]

## The Commission's Report

"We have come together with a unity of purpose because our nation demands it. September 11, 2001, was a day of unprecedented shock and suffering in the history of the United States. *The nation was unprepared*" (emphasis added).[32] With this statement the 567-page narrative, *9/11 Commission Report*, became available for the free world to review. This exposé on America's unpreparedness would cover, in 13 chapters, the attack on 9/11, to al-Qaeda and the new terrorism, how the nation responded, the heroism and nightmare of a people under attack, an understanding of Islam, how our world has changed and how we as a nation are to prepare and organize for this new world, and the war on terrorism. The report provides a critical observation of America's general ignorance of the world around it and of the need to have taken Osama Bin Laden's threats more seriously. It asserts, "The history, culture, and body of beliefs from which Bin Laden shapes and spreads his message are largely unknown to many Americans."[33] His fatwa, telling every Muslim to kill all Americans was taken as all his other proclamations were, with a dull ear. This behavior is reminiscent of 1930s Europe when Adolf Hitler pronounced to the world his intentions in his book, *Mein Kampf,* which was ridiculed by many non-Germans. Only after the fact was the world to see its shortsightedness. The 9/11 Commission's report also reveals our nation's shortsightedness for not taking previous commissions' suggestions, to deal with terrorism, more seriously. The Commission would "say with confidence … that none of the measures adopted by the U.S. Government from 1998–2001 disturbed or even delayed the progress of the Al Qaeda plot."[34]

## General Findings of the Commission

The Commission highlighted four broad areas where we failed: imagination, policy, capabilities, and management. The Commission stated that of the four findings, imagination was the "most important failure."[35] Interestingly, none of the previous commissions ever identified this as a major issue. Why imagination?

1. *Imagination.* In general, U.S. Government leadership did not see the seriousness of the al-Qaeda threat. Nor did they understand the "new brand of terrorism" emerging on the horizon. Our governmental system was designed in such a way that it could not perceive the change from Islamic terrorist, of previous decades, to the terrorist organization of September 11, 2001. This lack of imagination led to errors in policy.[36]

2. *Policy.* The Commission concluded, "Terrorism was not the overriding national security concern for the U.S. Government under either the Clinton or the pre-9/11 Bush administration." Both administrations were presented with a dilemma of not having a hard and fast "just cause" to invade the Taliban-controlled Afghanistan.[37] Interestingly, President Roosevelt faced a similar dilemma prior to Pearl Harbor. War changes everything.

3. *Capabilities.* The Commission concluded the 9/11 attacks revealed serious shortfalls in our capability to deal with this new transnational terrorist threat. How could this be? Was not the United States the remaining superpower with the number one military in the world? What was revealed to us? First, that we tried to fight this new war with the capabilities of the last one (Cold War) and it failed. Second, our intelligence apparatus, mainly the CIA, had limited abilities to conduct paramilitary operations and limited human intelligence collecting capability. Third, our homeland defense did not look inside the nation, only outward. Fourth, and considered by the Commission as the "most serious," was the Federal Bureau of Investigation's incapability "to link the collective knowledge of agents in the field to national priorities."[38] These and many other shortfalls in our capabilities directly attributed to us not being able to stop the September 11, 2001, attacks, which leads to the final general finding, the issue of Management.

4. *Management.* The Commission postulates the U.S. Government's shortfall, pre-9/11, as a failure of management to adapt. "The missed opportunities to thwart the 9/11 plot were also symptoms of a broader inability to adapt the way government manages problems to the new challenges of the twenty-first century."[39] This "inability to adapt" was no less apparent than in the Intelligence Community. With their critic's familiar "a failure in Intelligence" mantra ringing in their ears, senior government management, collectively, did not understand the big threat picture. This was especially true when it came to al-Qaeda and how to coordinate government efforts for sharing intelligence and other resources. Consequently, there were differing thoughts and ideas on how to set priorities and allocate resources.[40]

## Specific Findings of the Commission

The Commission also highlighted more specific areas to guide America's efforts toward a better-prepared nation. These findings point out specific areas where we failed before and on September 11, 2001.

- *Unsuccessful Diplomacy.* The U.S. Government, unsuccessfully, tried to use diplomatic pressure, warnings, and sanctions to persuade the Taliban to expel Bin Laden and al-Qaeda from Afghanistan. Efforts with Pakistan to pursue the Taliban failed. Finally, Saudi Arabia provided limited and inconsistent help pre-9/11.[41]

- *Lack of Military Options.* Policy makers were often frustrated with the range of options provided by the military to attack Bin Laden. Getting Bin Laden was key; however, inability to decide over the various strike options (pros and cons) and associated risk versus the possibility of making a mistake resulting in significant collateral damage and missing Bin Laden was the source of this frustration. Another source of frustration was actionable intelligence. "On three specific occasions in 1998–1999, intelligence was deemed credible enough to warrant planning for possible strikes to kill Bin Laden. But in each case the strikes did not go forward, because senior policymakers did not regard the intelligence as sufficiently actionable to offset their assessment of risks."[42]

- *Problems within the Intelligence Community.* "The Intelligence Community struggled throughout the 1990s and up to September 11, 2001, to collect intelligence on and analyze the phenomenon of transnational terrorism."[43] The reason for this was a combination of too many priorities, a constrained budget, bureaucratic rivalries, and an antiquated system. Just as with management, the Intelligence Community failed to rise to the new threat.

- *Problems in the FBI.* Since the first World Trade Center bombing in 1993, the FBI began to take an interest in Islamic extremism. However, the problems facing the FBI up to 9/11 were institutional. Throughout its existence, the FBI's main effort was to pursue criminals and prosecute them. The same undertaking was done after terrorist attacks. "The FBI's approach to investigations was case-specific, decentralized, and geared toward prosecution. Significant FBI resources were devoted to after-the-fact investigations of major terrorist attacks."[44] Attempts at changing the FBI's ability to prevent attacks instead of responding to them were made to no avail. Problems of collecting intelligence, analysis, and sharing information within and out of the Bureau blindsided the FBI on September 11, 2001.

- *Permeable Borders and Immigration Controls.* The 9/11 terrorist plot exposed the porous nature of our borders and the shortcomings of our immigration system. Only in hindsight were we able to see the details. Confronted with false passports, violated immigration laws, and unlawful entrances, the Commission could say "protecting the borders was not a national issue before 9/11."[45] The big picture was that the State Department and Immigration were never connected to the national counterterrorism effort.

- *Permeable Aviation Security.* Aviation security also had gaping holes. The hijackers made a great effort to study all publicly available security material to defeat existing security systems and procedures. Several of the terrorists were on a national watch list; however, the Federal Aviation Administration (FAA) did not use these data.[46]

- *Financing.* It cost between $400,000 and $500,000 to execute the 9/11 attacks. The attackers predominantly used banks in the United States.

- *An Improved Homeland Defense.* The Commission found civilian and military airspace defenders unprepared for an attack from within. Terrorist hijackers with box cutters turning airliners into flying missiles never entered the nation's collective mind. However, in the midst of this surprise attack, the FAA and military effectively controlled aircraft during the nation's first total ground stoppage. Highlighted, once again, were the inefficient or nonexisting relationships at the senior government management level. "Senior military and FAA leaders had no effective communication with each other. The chain of command did not function well."[47]

- *Emergency Response.* Who can argue the heroic deeds performed by emergency responders on September 11, 2001? However, in hindsight, flaws in key functional areas impaired effective decision making. The Commission identified two key problem areas: a lack of unified command and control and poor communications. Command and control over the multitude of agencies responding were hampered by different operating procedures. Communication problems stemmed from agencies not having compatible radio frequencies or sets.

- *Congress.* "The Congress, like the executive branch, responded slowly to the rise of transnational terrorism as a threat to national security. The legislative branch adjusted little and did not restructure itself to address changing threat."[48]

- *Are We Safer?* Are we safe from future terror attacks? In reply, the Commission says,

Even as we have thwarted attacks, nearly everyone expects they will come. How can this be? The problem is that Al Qaeda represents an ideological movement, not a finite group of people. It initiates and inspires, even if it no longer directs. In this way it has transformed itself into a decentralized force. … His (Bin Laden) message of inspiration to a new generation of terrorists would continue."[49]

## An Analytic Framework for Homeland Security

Homeland security in the twenty-first century presents America with an incredibly complex challenge. Despite the fact that a few high-level commissions, think tanks, and military schools have examined the concept of homeland security since 1997, the vast majority of Americans first heard the term only after the attacks of September 11, 2001.

Following these attacks, journals, congressional hearings, and press reports began to examine this new security challenge. Traditional national security scholars and pundits soon learned that the analytical frameworks of the Cold War were inadequate for examining homeland security.

While some elements of the Cold War model remain relevant, such as deterrence, prevention, and retaliation, new elements such as crisis management, consequence management, attribution, and prosecution emerged. Furthermore, the national security framework of the Cold War was exclusively focused on activities of the federal government, primarily the Departments of State and Defense and the Intelligence Community. However, a complete analytic model of homeland security must be suitable for use by federal, state, and local government organizations (ranging from defense and law enforcement, to public health, food security, immigration, and border control), plus the private sector.

The Strategic Cycle of Homeland Security consists of six elements: deterrence, prevention, preemption, incident management, attribution, and response.

**Deterrence** must be a central element of any homeland security framework. The consequences of attacks on the homeland made possible with twenty-first century technology can be devastating. In some cases, modern technology could enable a small nation, or perhaps even a well-financed terrorist organization, to bring a superpower to its knees. Therefore, the United States must have policies and postures to deter enemies from attacking the homeland.

Classical deterrence is based on two elements: punishment and denial. The threat from both nation-state and nonstate actors, which might employ nuclear and bioweapons, demands a shift in how deterrence is practiced. Throughout the Cold War, deterrence was based on mutual assured destruction—the ability to deliver incalculable punishment under any circumstance. Given the nature of modern homeland security threats, the United States must increase its ability to deter enemies by denying them the effects they seek. In some cases, this will be accomplished through methods, institutions, and programs that have not been considered elements of deterrence. For example, a robust public health system that would significantly mitigate the effects of a biological attack may act as a deterrent to biological terrorism. Would a nation-state or terrorist organization risk massive retaliation if it knew that America was able to identify the perpetrator and significantly mitigate the affects of a biological attack? In the Cold War, civil defense was not a significant factor in deterrence. This is not the case in the twenty-first century. Resource allocation should reflect this new reality. There will be times when deterrence efforts fail, perhaps if only because some enemies may be undeterrable. In those cases, the United States will have to rely on prevention capabilities.

**Prevention** incorporates a wide group of active and passive measures that can stop an attack. U.S. prevention activities are defensive in nature and range from arms control treaties to aerospace, maritime, and land defenses to border control and other law enforcement measures. A former speaker of the U.S. House of Representatives stated that foreign aid such as "a Marshall plan for the Arab world" could help prevent terrorism.[50] Others say that searches for "root causes" are exactly the wrong strategy when responding to terrorist acts because it serves to legitimize the acts.[51] Because some modern attacks could take the United States beyond the point of recovery, our nation must also possess the capabilities and associated policies that allow us to preempt attacks on our homeland.

**Preemption** is the policy that is fraught with political and military risks. In the Cold War, preemption would have meant first use of nuclear weapons, possibly resulting in a global nuclear war. Further, aggressors have frequently cloaked their initiation of war with claims that they were only preempting an attack on their homeland. Preemption in the homeland security context does not have to call for the initiation of nuclear war or occupation of another nation's territory. It requires the selective use of all elements of national power, to include military force and law enforcement to preempt terrorists before they launch their attacks. Preemption options can span the range from a precision-guided 2,000-pound bomb delivered by a B-2 bomber to an arrest by a U.S. law enforcement official working with allies in overseas nations.

**Incident management** has changed in two important ways over the past decade. The first major change occurred in 1995 when President Bill Clinton signed Presidential Decision Directive 39 (PDD 39), *U.S. Policy on Counterterrorism.*[52] This directive codified the United States' emerging national policy on counterterrorism and how we would respond. The PDD 39 coined two important terms, *crisis management* and *consequence management*, each having an assigned lead federal agency. Crisis management begins when intelligence information suggested an attack might occur until the actual attack. The FBI was assigned as the lead agency for crisis management. Consequence management was defined as the effort to provide emergency services to government, business, and individuals to restore public health, safety, and the economy after an attack, with the Federal Emergency Management Agency (FEMA) assigned as the lead federal agency for consequence management. Consequence management could persist for an indeterminate amount of time. For example, the direct economic impact of the September 11, 2001, attacks on New York City was still clearly visible in the spring of 2003. According to the *New York Times*, more than 12,000 restaurant workers had been laid off due to a major downturn in tourism. Economic analysts have linked this to public concern over future terrorist attacks.

In February 2003, President George W. Bush signed the Homeland Security Presidential Directive/(HSPD-5), *Management of Domestic Incidents,* ushering in the second major change in Incident Management.[53] This new directive's main emphasis was in the creation of a single comprehensive national approach for handling domestic incidents. Its major objective was to have all levels of government across the United States effectively work together during any response. To this end, HSPD-5 combined *crisis management* and *consequence management* into a single, integrated function, rather than two separate functions. There are several reasons the Bush administration chose to combine these two elements into the concept of *incident management.* This aligns the terminology used by the president with the terminology that has been used many years by state and local first responders. These two elements also were combined because in some attacks, such as biological and cyber, there is significant overlap between the crisis and consequence management phases.

By far the most important piece of HSPD-5 was the creation of the National Incident Management System (NIMS). Approved by DHS Secretary Tom Ridge on March 1, 2004, NIMS effectively "establishes standardized incident management processes, protocols, and procedures that all responders—federal, state, tribal, and local—will use to coordinate and conduct response actions … when a homeland security incident occurs—whether terrorism or natural disaster."[54] Response organizations at all levels would use NIMS in their planning.

The directive also tasked the federal government to develop a single *National Response Plan (NRP),* which would integrate all "Federal Government domestic prevention, preparedness, response, and recovery plans into one all-discipline, all-hazards plan."[55] Effective response was being impeded by not having a single entity to coordinate and manage these independent plans. To get from this multitude of plans to a single NRP, the Department of Homeland Security created an interim plan called the *Initial National Response Plan,* dated September 30, 2003. This 11-page document, designed to "harmonize" all existing response plans with the "strategic direction" provided by HSPD-5, was to act as a "bridging document" until the NRP was completed.[56] As for the NRP, it "shall, with regard to response to domestic incidents, provide the structure and mechanisms for national level policy and operational direction for Federal support to State and local incident managers."[57]

**Attribution** occupies a critical place in the homeland security strategic cycle. U.S. enemies are likely to disguise their identity to avoid retaliation. The 1990s witnessed a new trend in attacks wherein the attacker chose to remain anonymous (e.g., the Pan Am 103 bombing, World Trade Center bombing in 1993, bombing of the Khobar Towers in 1996, the USS *Cole* in 2000, and the anthrax letters of 2001). Improving U.S. attribution capabilities will demand more creative scientific methods and technologies as well as greater integration of the relevant law enforcement and intelligence efforts. The responsibility for attribution clearly resides with the Department of Justice; however, it has neither the scientific capability nor the budget to successfully complete this mission. The Department of Health and Human Services and the Department of Defense laboratories, as well as the private sector, will be required to play significant roles in attribution. Without attribution, there can be no response.

**Response** has two roles in homeland security. The first is to eliminate the capability of the attacker to cause further harm. This might be achieved through arrest and prosecution, the use of military force, or covert actions. Certainly, the nature of response would depend on a range of factors, not the least being whether the attacker is a domestic or international actor. The Bush administration's actions after 9/11 illustrate the potential range of response options. Second, the ultimate goal of any response must be the reestablishment of deterrence. For America, the purpose of war is to establish a "better peace." In the homeland security strategic cycle, the purpose of response is to eliminate the attacker's offensive capability and to reestablish deterrence by sending a very clear message to all who wish America harm. Both elements of response were transmitted loud and clear in Afghanistan following the 9/11 attacks. The regime that supported al-Qaeda was removed from power, and al-Qaeda's command and control, logistical, financial, and training functions were severely disrupted. Additionally, terrorists and tyrants across the globe took notice of America's decisive action and global reach. As the president said, "Whether we bring our enemies to justice, or bring justice to our enemies, justice will be done."[58]

There are cases in which there is overlap within this framework, and at times, certain actions could fit in more than one category. Following the attacks on American embassies in Kenya and Tanzania, the cruise missile attacks on al-Qaeda were called preemptive by the Clinton administration, but one could also argue they were a response.

All models have limitations. In fact, there is an old saying in the defense community that *all models are wrong, but some are useful*. Many within the homeland security community find this model useful. In fact, many have endorsed it because it provides an intellectual framework for short-term plans, long-range strategies, policies, and resource allocations.

## The 2001 Attacks on the American Homeland

> If ... on the morning of September 11, 2001, ... the U.S. Government had a fully integrated intelligence and law enforcement organization ... equipped with state-of-the-art data mining capabilities ... law enforcement officials would have been notified that Mohamed Atta and his roommate (both on terrorist watch lists) had just checked in for flights at Boston Logan Airport. Seconds later they would have detected that four other passengers checking in for other flights had listed the same home address as Atta, that three others checking in for flights had made numerous calls during the past month to a telephone at that same address, and two others checking in for flights had used Atta's frequent flier number just one month earlier.[59]

It is impossible to say if such a system could have prevented the attacks of September 11, 2001. What is clear is that there was little or no chance of preventing the attacks with the system that existed in 2001. Laws, regulations, policies, cultural barriers, and bureaucratic stovepipes were ill-suited for the security challenges of the twenty-first century. Al-Qaeda had studied its enemy well. Like a great quarterback, it knew how to find the seams in our defense.

In his book, *On Guerrilla Warfare,* Mao Zedong wrote, "many people think it impossible for guerrillas to exist for long in the enemy's rear. Such a belief reveals lack of comprehension of the relationship that should exist between the people and the troops. The former may be likened to water and the latter to the fish who inhabit it."[60] Mao was referring to the ability of guerrillas to operate in occupied China during the 1940s, but the 9/11 hijackers followed the same concept in their ability to move freely and unnoticed inside and outside the United States. They wore no beards or Muslim clothing and did nothing to draw attention to themselves. Only in hindsight did the abnormalities become obvious. As FBI Director Robert Mueller likes to say, "They lived among us … they shopped at Wal-Mart, ate at Pizza Hut, and bought their command and control system from our convenience stores."[61] The 19 hijackers primarily used high-tech "cyber cafes" and cell phones to coordinate their plans formulated by their leader, Osama Bin Laden.

Osama Bin Laden's role in the attacks was revealed in a series of videotapes captured in Afghanistan. The videos were made in mid-November 2001. No doubt as Bin Laden and other senior al-Qaeda leaders were watching CNN or other international coverage of the unfolding attacks, they must have been ecstatic to learn that the attacks were more successful than they had anticipated.

> We calculated in advance the number of casualties from the enemy who would be killed based on the position of the tower. … We calculated that the floors it would hit would be three or four floors. I was most optimistic of them all. … [D]ue to my experience in this field, I was thinking that the fire from the gas in the plane would melt the iron structure of the building and collapse the area where the plane hit and all the floors above it only. This is all that we had hoped for.[62]

The tapes also revealed information on al-Qaeda's operations and communications security procedures. Bin Laden commented on those who conducted the operations: "All they knew was that they have a martyrdom operation and we asked each of them to go to America, but they didn't know anything about the operation, not even one letter."[63] These were not amateurs, like Ramzi Yousef's assistant, who tried to get back his deposit on the rental truck after bombing the World Trade Center in 1993. These were seasoned professionals.

Their planning spanned two years and several continents. To ensure the attacks were successful, Mohamed Atta selected airline flights carrying large quantities of fuel. They made test flights on those routes to study the patterns of flight attendants, pilots, and other airline personnel. By September 11, 2001, they were ready.

American Airlines (AA) Flight 11 took off at 7:45 A.M. from Boston Logan International Airport for a long flight to Los Angeles International Airport. On board were Mohamed Atta and the four other men. With box cutters and knives in hand they commandeered the big Boeing 767 and flew toward New York City. One hour later, the aircraft crashed into the North Tower (WTC 1) of the World Trade Center complex between the 80th and 90th floors. The resulting fire burned between 1,500–2,000 degrees Fahrenheit and burned for some 102 minutes. Due to the impact and extreme heat produced by burning aviation fuel, the top 30 floors collapsed onto the 80 floors below, bringing down the entire structure.

United Airlines (UA) Flight 175, a Boeing 767, also took off from Boston Logan International Airport roughly 13 minutes after AA Flight 11 at 7:58 A.M. with a long morning flight to Los Angeles. On board at the planned time, five hijackers took over the flight. As Flight 175 approached New York City, the al-Qaeda pilots could have surely seen the smoke coming from the North Tower. At 9:05 A.M., as the world was watching, UA Flight 175 slammed into the South Tower (WTC 2), above the 90th floor, on one side with a brilliant, almost unbelievable flame coming out of the other. For the millions who watched this scene live on TV, it seemed more like something from Hollywood. The fire burned for 56 minutes before the top 20 floors collapsed on the remaining 90 below in eight seconds.[64] The great buildings that Minoru Yamasaki had designed and that had taken seven years to build, collapsed in seconds.[65]

It is estimated that each jet carried approximately 60,000 pounds of jet fuel and was traveling in excess of 300 miles per hour when they crashed into each building.[66] Both towers were the first supertall buildings designed without any masonry, with a uniquely designed central core and elevator system that allowed for more space on each floor. While originally designed to withstand an impact of a Boeing 707, the much larger 767s provided significantly more kinetic energy and fuel. The initial impact of the planes appeared to have created substantial damage, but not enough to cause the building to collapse; however, the intense fires from the burning aircraft fuel combined with the damage began to weaken the undamaged metal support structures. Once the upper floors began to collapse, the downward momentum could not be stopped.[67]

World Trade Center Towers 1, 2, and 7 collapsed, leaving more than one million tons of debris at what became known as Ground Zero. About 400 structures across a 16-acre area were damaged.[68] Over

13,000 customers lost electrical power.[69] In a matter of minutes, 2,752 people were killed.[70] Before the day was over, 440 first responders were killed (23 New York Police Department, 343 Fire Department of New York, and 74 Port Authority of New York and New Jersey). Over 320 other emergency responders were treated for injuries or illnesses.[71]

On that same morning, United Airlines Flight 93 took off at 8:01 A.M. from Newark for a long flight to San Francisco. As the plane was being commandeered and flown back toward the East Coast, cell phone calls informed passengers onboard of what had happened at the World Trade Center. Taking the initiative into their hands with the words "let's roll," passengers engaged the hijackers, causing the plane to crash in a field near Stony Creek Township, Pennsylvania. All 45 people onboard were killed, leaving the intended target a mystery.

American Airline Flight 77, a Boeing 757, took off at 8:10 A.M. from Washington Dulles International Airport to Los Angeles. Along the route, five hijackers took over the plane and flew it toward the Potomac River. At 9:40 A.M., the plane slammed into the newly renovated and empty section of the Pentagon killing 189 people (125 people on the ground, and 64 on the aircraft). The crash damaged or destroyed three of the five interior concentric "rings" of the Pentagon building.[72] By the time most Americans went to bed that night, they realized the world had forever changed. If there were any doubters left, the first two weeks of October 2001 likely changed their minds.

On October 1, 2001, Robert Stevens, an employee of American Media Inc. (AMI), was admitted to a Boca Raton, Florida, hospital in a near-death condition. Five days later he was dead. Within a few days, anthrax had become a 24/7 news event.

On the day Stevens died, letters claiming to contain anthrax were received at the *New York Times* and *St. Petersburg Times*. Both later turned out to be hoaxes. On the next day, anthrax spores were found on another AMI employee, a mailroom worker, and on Stevens's computer. Later, this second worker was confirmed to have inhalation anthrax. On October 10, 2001, a third AMI mailroom worker tested positive for anthrax and led FBI investigators to suspect that anthrax was being disseminated through letters in the postal system.

On October 12, 2001, one of Tom Brokaw's assistants at NBC reported a case of cutaneous anthrax. Five days later an envelope containing anthrax powder was opened in Senator Tom Daschle's office. Until this point, there was no evidence as to the quality of the pathogen, but tests of the material from Senator Daschle's office proved most disturbing. The fine powder was some of the best quality ever seen by U.S. military personnel. America was under attack with a sophisticated pathogen.

Many now refer to the second attack of 2001 as 5-11—5 deaths due to inhalation anthrax and 11 infected with inhalation anthrax. In many respects, the 5-11 had far more ramifications than did the attacks of 9/11. These five deaths and the botched response by federal, state, and local officials demonstrated that America was woefully unprepared to respond to even a small-scale biological attack. In response, billion dollar programs in research and development and public health would soon receive funding from Congress. The United States was, and still is, playing "catch up" after these attacks exposed its significant vulnerabilities to terrorist threats. Needed was a homeland security strategy, program, and organization to organize our effort.

## The Office of Homeland Security

On September 12, 2001, the former coach of the Georgetown University basketball team, John Thompson, was preparing for his afternoon radio talk show. He knew that his audience would not be interested in hearing about sports, so he asked the Director of the ANSER Institute for Homeland Security to be his guest. His first question was straight to the point, "Is America ready for homeland security?"

Considering the audience, the director responded with a sports analogy, "We don't have a coach, we don't have a game plan, and we aren't practicing. How do you think we will do in a big game?"[73]

On October 8, 2001, President Bush gave the nation a coach, Governor Tom Ridge. Some in Congress were calling for the creation of a new department, but the president chose to create a new office within the White House, the Office of Homeland Security. The critics complained that Governor Ridge had neither operational nor budgetary authority in this position. His staff was only 35 with another 150 detailed from other agencies scheduled to come onboard. How could a leader without authority and with such a tiny staff handle what many were calling the most difficult and complex security challenge America had ever faced?

What the critics failed to realize was that the Office of Homeland Security was just the first step of a much larger plan. Following the attacks of 9/11, the president had to take action to better prepare the nation, but there was great concern that creating a new department overnight would have been a "bridge too far." The Bush administration found wise counsel in the first rule of medicine, "First, do no harm."

The Office of Homeland Security was the first step in a long-term plan. It provided the team that would develop the *National Strategy for Homeland Security* (a game plan) and draft the legislative proposal for the creation of a new department. This proposal was based on commission recommendations, particularly Hart-Rudman, and other bills introduced in the House and Senate, but had several unique elements, such as the inclusion of the Secret Service and elements of the Departments of

Agriculture, Health and Human Services, and the Department of Energy (DOE) National Labs.

# A Homeland Security Strategy

On July 15, 2002, President George W. Bush released the first *National Strategy for Homeland Security*. Despite the name, the document did not provide a strategy, but did provide the first national plan for homeland security. The plan explained how the nation would reduce its vulnerabilities and marshal its resources, but not how they would be applied against any specific enemy.[74]

There were four key themes emphasized in the national strategy document.[75] The first was **federalism,** "the idea that the federal government shares authority, responsibility, the mandate for action and the struggle for resources with states, local governments and private actors."[76] The second theme was **accountability.** "The path to homeland security requires clear organizations, consolidation of authority, and then holding some responsible for performance."[77] The third theme was **fiscal responsibility**. In other words, because of the impossibility of defending every possible target in CONUS, "We have to accept some level of terrorist risk as a permanent condition."[78] The fourth theme, **prioritization,** is closely linked to the last one. During his first month in office as the Director of the Office of Homeland Security, Governor Ridge identified four priorities: (1) first responders, (2) borders, (3) bioterrorism, and (4) improved intelligence and information flow.[79]

These key themes are folded into three overarching strategic objectives: prevent terrorist attacks within the United States, reduce America's vulnerabilities to terrorism, and minimize the damage and recover from attacks that do occur.[80] Under the rubric of these three objectives lie the guts of the "game plan," the so-called six "critical mission areas." Mission areas are divided up to support each of the three strategic objectives.

## Prevent Terrorist Attack

Three mission areas fall under this objective:

- *Intelligence and Warning.* This area would help identify and stop potential terrorist attacks by taking measures to enhance the Federal Bureau of Investigation's analytic capabilities, building new capabilities for information analysis and infrastructure protection, enacting a Homeland Security Advisory System, utilizing dual-use analysis to prevent attacks, and employing so-called "red team" techniques to determine our vulnerabilities.[81]

- *Border and Transportation Security.* Retooling protective measures for our border and transportation infrastructure provides a challenge because it is tied into the global transportation infrastructure. New measures will be taken to ensure accountability in border and transportation security by utilizing new technology to create "smart borders." Other measures include increasing security of international shipping containers; reforming the immigration services, implementing the Aviation and Transportation Security Act of 2001, and changing the structure of the U.S. Coast Guard by placing it into the new Department of Homeland Security.[82]

- *Domestic Counterterrorism.* The key effort to preventing future terror attacks is redefining the mission of federal, state, and local law enforcement agencies to prevent and interdict terrorist activity. To accomplish this requires improved intergovernmental law enforcement coordination, a more effective way to facilitate the apprehension of potential terrorist, a continuing investigation and prosecution, and to track foreign terrorists and bring them to justice. Track and attack terrorist financing. Completely restructure the FBI to emphasize the prevention of terrorist attacks.[83]

## Reduce Vulnerabilities

Two of the six mission areas are designed to reduce vulnerabilities:

- *Protecting Critical Infrastructure and Key Assets.* Our physical and virtual networks are very vulnerable to terrorist attacks. The Department of Homeland Security is given certain powers to ensure these interconnected systems do not fail causing chain reactions in other adjoining systems. Eight initiatives are being pursued to unify the effort toward infrastructure protection. This will include building and maintaining a complete and accurate assessment of America's critical infrastructure, creating effective partnerships between state and local governments and the private sector, building a national infrastructure protection plan, securing cyberspace, utilizing analytic and modeling tools to develop effective protective solutions, guarding from "inside" threats, and partnering with the international community to protect our transnational infrastructure.[84]

- *Defending against Catastrophic Threats.* The threat from chemical, biological, radiological, and nuclear weapons requires new ways to defend against them. The strategy identifies key initiatives to turn this into a reality. First is to prevent any terrorist from using nuclear weapons with better sensors and procedures. Second is to enhance the ability to detect chemical and biological materials and attacks. Third is to improve chemical sensors and decontamination techniques. Fourth is to develop a broad spectrum of vaccines, antimicrobials, and antidotes. Fifth is to bring together the scientific knowledge and tools to combat terrorism. Last is to implement the Select Agent Program, which enables the Department of Homeland Security to track dangerous biological agents and toxins used by the scientific research community.[85]

## Minimize Damage and Recover from Attacks

Being prepared is key to an effective response to terrorist attacks. Under the *Emergency Preparedness and Response* mission area, the strategy proposed 12 major initiatives. Two initiatives with overarching implications are the integration of separate federal response plans into a single all-discipline incident management plan, and the creation of a national incident management system. The other initiatives involve better communications, training, and evaluation systems for the response community; enhanced pharmaceutical and vaccine stockpile, as well as better preparation for health-care providers; planning for military support to civil authorities; and the development of a Citizen Corps. Finally, to enhance victim support systems an active effort will be made to prepare for chemical, biological, radiological, and nuclear decontamination and associated measures.[86] These six "critical mission areas" are fleshed out in the Department of Homeland Security's four major directorates.

## The Department of Homeland Security

On March 1, 2003, the Department of Homeland Security became the federal government's third largest bureaucracy. Secretary Tom Ridge assumed control of a new department consisting of 22 agencies, 170,000 plus employees, and a budget of $37.4 billion. It was the largest reorganization of the federal government since 1947.

Prior to this reorganization, a think tank had produced a chart that attempted to demonstrate the complex organizational structure of homeland security organizations within the federal government. One observer commented that it looked like a combination of a plate of spaghetti and an eye chart. (Of course, a complete diagram would have been far more complex, and confusing, since it would have required federal, state, and local government entities plus many private sector organizations.)

To resolve this, President Bush signed the Homeland Security Act of 2002 on November 25, 2002, in effect creating the Department of Homeland Security. Two months later on January 24, 2003, the new Department became part of the U.S. Government. By March 1, 2003, all the component parts moved to the new Department. The idea was not to create new organizations on top of the existing structure, but to take existing independent agencies and realign them under one chain of command and department, thus streamlining and removing interdepartmental fighting over the sparse monetary "rice bowls" and personnel. Its major goal was to "transform and realign the current confusing patchwork of government activities into a single department."[87] President Bush assigned the new Department three missions:

- prevent terrorist attacks within the United States,
- reduce the vulnerability of the United States to terrorism, and

- minimize the damage, and assist in the recovery, from terrorist attacks that do occur within the United States.[88]

One needs only to look at the new directorates to understand the depth of 9/11's impact on the U.S. Government. The removal of agencies or functions from other departments, once unthinkable, was now fact. DHS organized into five major divisions or "directorates." One directorate is purely for management of the department. However, the other four are the key parts to making DHS a success. The Secret Service and the Coast Guard remain intact and report directly to the DHS secretary.

The **Border and Transportation Security Directorate,** by far the largest, consists of the U.S. Customs Service, Immigration and Naturalization Service, the Federal Protection Service, the Transportation Security Administration, Animal and Plant Health Inspection Service, and other agencies. Many of these have been moved from the Departments of Justice, Agriculture, Treasury, and Transportation.

The **Emergency Preparedness and Response Directorate** prepares the nation for terrorist attacks and natural disasters, and the ability to recover from such events. The directorate oversees domestic preparedness training and coordinates government disaster response. It consists of FEMA, Strategic National Stockpile and the National Disaster Medical System, Nuclear Incident Response Team, Domestic Emergency Support Teams, and the National Domestic Preparedness Office. These agencies moved from the Departments of Justice, Health and Human Services, Energy, and the FBI.

The **Science and Technology Directorate** takes advantage of all emerging technologies and science to secure the homeland. Merged into this high-tech directorate will be DoD's National Biological Warfare (BW) Defense Analysis Center, the Agriculture Department's Plum Island Animal Disease Center, and two programs from the DOE: CBRN Countermeasures Programs and Environmental Laboratory.

The **Information Analysis and Infrastructure Protection Directorate** "analyze[s] intelligence and information from other agencies (including the CIA, FBI, DIA, and NSA) involving threats to homeland security and evaluate vulnerabilities in the nation's infrastructure."[89] Originally, this directorate was considered to be the leading candidate to house a national law enforcement and intelligence fusion center. However, the creation of the Terrorism Threat Intelligence Center (under control of the CIA) was announced in the President's State of the Union address.

Many ask how long it will take for the new Department to become effective. Defining "effective" is a challenge, but when one considers that it took the Department of Defense 40 years to "get it right" (Goldwater-Nichols Act of 1987), one hopes success in the Department of Homeland Security will come much quicker.

# Key Issues

Despite the complaints of political pundits that it took 18 months to create the Department of Homeland Security, this is the most significant reorganization of the federal government since 1947. On the other hand, many critical issues remain to be debated by the Administration, the Congress, the courts, and the American people. Four of the most frequently debated issues are the relationship between the law enforcement and intelligence communities; the role of DoD in homeland security; *Posse Comitatus*; and the integration of federal, state, and local personnel, resources, and planning.

## Intelligence and Law Enforcement Integration

When President Truman created the Central Intelligence Agency in 1947, he made it abundantly clear that it would serve as a foreign intelligence service, not a Gestapo-like organization that would infringe on the civil liberties of American citizens. Ultrasecret government organizations seem almost anathema to many Americans, yet the threat of international communism made it a necessary element in America's Cold War defenses. The excesses of covert actions abroad in the 1950s, and domestic spying here at home in the 1960s, resulted in a two-decade long backlash that prohibited the Intelligence Community from operations inside U.S. borders and even limited capabilities overseas.

The failure to prevent the attacks of September 11, 2001, even though information was available, but not properly collected and analyzed, led many to call for the creation of a domestic intelligence service, similar perhaps to the United Kingdom's MI-5.[90] The firewall that had been constructed between law enforcement and intelligence prevented the collection of certain information and the sharing of considerable critical information. For instance, in August 2001, the FBI began a frantic search for two terrorists believed to be inside the United States and planning a major attack. The FBI readily admits it faced a near impossible challenge of finding them, even though these two individuals used credit cards to purchase their 9/11 airline tickets. These cards had exactly the same names as were on the watch lists, but the FBI was prohibited from accessing this database—a database that corporations and private citizens can access for a small fee.

In response to the September 11, 2001, attacks, Congress passed the USA PATRIOT Act. Some new authorities granted to the Department of Justice and FBI in this act were clearly needed. Many of the procedures for gathering evidence and information were of the pre-Internet and pre-digital era. On the other hand, this 342-page bill, which changed 17 laws, was passed by Congress in just two weeks. One wonders how many of the 535 members actually read this legislation. Clearly, the debate over domestic intelligence has yet to begin. It is one of the most important issues yet to be resolved. It is one of the key issues examined by the National Commission on Terrorist Attacks Upon the United States (9/11 Commission).[91]

## Role of the Department of Defense and U.S. Northern Command

While there will be considerable debate on this subject, one thing is clear. In the vast majority of cases DoD will not be in charge, but will provide support to the lead federal agency, which could be the Department of Homeland Security, the Department of Health and Human Services, or the Department of Agriculture, depending on the nature of the crisis.

DoD has divided homeland security into two general categories: *homeland defense* and *civil support*. Homeland defense includes aerospace and maritime missions plus the protection of key DoD facilities and infrastructures. Civil support includes missions ranging from traditional domestic support roles of disaster relief and counterdrug operations to specialized technical support that would be required following an attack using chemical, biological, radiological, nuclear, and high-yield explosive (CBRNE) weapons. Specialized National Guard units, called Weapons of Mass Destruction-Civil Support Teams (initially called RAID Teams) are currently operational in more than 30 states. Eventually, each state will have at least one of these teams that is organized, trained, and equipped to be DoD's first responders to a CBRNE incident.

Additionally, DoD has identified three types of homeland security missions: *extraordinary, emergency,* and *limited scope and duration*. Extraordinary are those missions when DoD would likely be the lead federal agency: aerospace defense, maritime defense, and when normal measures are insufficient to carry out federal functions (as was mentioned in the Bremer Commission Report). Emergency missions are those carried out in response to natural or man-made disasters. Limited scope and duration missions were conducted in support of the 2002 Olympics and the 2002 Super Bowl. In both emergency and limited scope and duration missions, DoD provides support to the lead federal agency.

### *Posse Comitatus*[92]

This nineteenth century, one-sentence law is one of the most misunderstood issues in homeland security. Many military officers, including some very senior officers do not understand *posse comitatus*. First of all, there is no Constitutional prohibition against military personnel enforcing civil law. *Posse comitatus* is Latin for, "power of the county." This legislation was passed after the American Civil War and during the Reconstruction to prevent southern sheriffs from deputizing federal troops. No one has ever been successfully prosecuted under this law. At one time there was a significant difference in the ability of National Guard troops to conduct law enforcement activities, when operating under U.S. Code Title 32 (under the command of state governors), and federal troops who always operate under U.S. Code Title 10. National Guard troops operating in Title 10 status (federalized) lose their Title 32 status and come under the same restrictions as federal troops—unless a presidentially declared state of emergency exists.

However, Congress has passed considerable legislation in the past 10 years that has significantly blurred this distinction.[93] Because it is often misinterpreted and much of it is without legal precedence, *posse comitatus* is long due for legal reform.

Today, *posse comitatus* is used by DoD officials to avoid missions they do not want to do. Federal troops are not organized, trained, and equipped or funded for law enforcement activities. Furthermore, despite the change in the letter of the law, there remains a significant cultural prohibition against such activities. The requirement and likelihood of federal troops (or National Guard troops operating under Title 10) providing law enforcement is limited and unlikely. There are, of course, exceptions, such as the Rodney King riots in 1992, when President George H. W. Bush invoked the Insurrection Act and deployed troops from the 7th Infantry Division at Fort Ord, California, to quell the riots in Los Angeles.[94]

All military officers and senior noncomissioned officers should receive appropriate education on *posse comitatus* so they are prepared to respond in a domestic crisis if required.[95]

## Integration of Federal, State, and Local Government Efforts

Few challenges of homeland security will pose more difficulty than the integration of efforts of 87,000 different government entities. Nowhere is this better demonstrated than in the public health sector.

One of the greatest threats America will face in the coming decades is a sophisticated attack with biological pathogens. America is not prepared to respond to such an attack today. Unfortunately, this is not a problem that can be solved by just "throwing money at it." America's public health system is in such a state of disrepair that money alone will not lead to better preparedness.

The problem is one of organization. To best understand the problem, imagine if America's military was not a centralized organization. Imagine a military where each county had a tank, a platoon, and an airplane. Imagine a military where promotion was not based on competency, but political connections. Imagine a military where there was little or no standardization. Imagine a military where some funding came from the federal level and some from state and local and few of the funding programs were coordinated. Sound ridiculous? That practically describes America's public health infrastructure today.

Prior to the 1960s, environmental issues were seen primarily as a state and local issue. Eventually, the nation learned that environmental policy would be effective only if coordinated at a national level. The same will be true for public health. At some point in the future, America's public health system will require a national organization, not more than 3,000 independent, uncoordinated departments. For example, the state of New Jersey alone has 116 independent public health departments.[96]

General Eisenhower said, "The right organization will not guarantee success, but the wrong organization will guarantee failure."[97]

Not all elements of the federal, state, and local government teams will require such radical changes. Many improvements can be made with enhanced planning efforts and exercise programs. This will avoid the situation we have seen many times in the past, where the first step in responding to a crisis was "exchanging business cards."

Furthermore, the most cost-effective means of preparing for incident management is to do it on a regional basis. Not every community needs to have every piece of equipment and every specialty. Regional capabilities and integrated federal, state, and local teams will make homeland security affordable. Otherwise, the greatest threat to America will be uncontrolled spending.

## 9/11 Commission Recommendations

When the Commission published its final report it wanted the nation to focus on two major objectives toward protecting itself: (1) what to do and (2) how to do it.

### "What To Do"

The first objective asks the question *"what to do?"*. Its focus is to provide us with a global strategy to deal with the enemy, Islamist terrorism. The Commission wanted us to clearly understand who the enemy really is: "the enemy is not just 'terrorism'." More clearly they stated, "It is the threat posed specifically by Islamist terrorism, by Bin Laden and others who draw on a long tradition of extreme intolerance within a minority strain of Islam that does not distinguish politics from religion, and distorts both. The enemy is not Islam, the great world faith, but a perversion of Islam."[98] So the first phase requires a levelheaded understanding of who the enemy is.

The Commission also attempted to put a realistic face to our enemy.

Al Qaeda and other groups are popularly described as being all over the world, adaptable, resilient, needing little higher-level organization, and capable of anything. It is an image of an omnipotent hydra of destruction … . Our report shows a determined and capable group of plotters. Yet the group was fragile and occasionally left vulnerable by the marginal, unstable people often attracted to such causes. The enemy made mistakes.[99]

Our end goal must be the dismantling of the al-Qaeda network and, eventually, prevailing over the ideology that contributes to Islamist terrorism. Therefore, the Commission proposed a strategy with three thrusts "(1) attack terrorists and their organizations, (2) prevent the continued growth of Islamist terrorism, and (3) protect against and prepare for terrorist attacks."[100] The tricky part would be how to do it.

## *"How To Do It"*

The second objective focuses on a different way to organize the government to prepare and fight terrorism. It is the view of the Commission that "Americans should not settle for incremental, ad hoc adjustments to a system created a generation ago for a world that no longer exists."[101]

Therefore, the recommendations they provide are part of a sum total with one clear purpose, "to build unity of effort across the U.S. Government."[102] The Commission offered up five of them.

1. *A National Counterterrorism Center.* The establishment of this joint unified command would synthesize intelligence and perform joint operational planning. The Commission made it clear that it was not to be a policy-making body.

2. *A National Intelligence Director.* This director would oversee the different national intelligence centers and "combine experts from all the collection disciplines against common targets … and … oversee the agencies that contribute to the national intelligence program."[103]

3. *Sharing Information.* The Commission found that the U.S. Government has vast amounts of information but a weak ability to analyze and use, effectively, what it needs. The members of the Commission want a system that shares information rather than withholds it.[104]

4. *Congressional Oversight.* The Congressional intelligence committees must be made stronger in their responsibility and accountability for intelligence oversight, and they should create a single point for oversight and review for homeland security.[105]

5. *Organizing America's Defense in the United States.* The Commission does not recommend creating a new domestic intelligence agency. It did recommend, however, "the establishment of a specialized and integrated national security workforce at the FBI … to ensure the development of an institutional culture imbued with a deep expertise in intelligence and national security."[106] In the area of national defense, the Commission

clearly wanted to delineate the roles, missions, and authority for both the Department of Defense and the Department of Homeland Security. The Department of Defense should assess Northern Command's strategies and planning to defend against military threats to the homeland, while DHS should assess the types of threats to help the government plan and prepare accordingly.[107]

## Summary

Just prior to his retirement from active military service, General Colin Powell stated that it would take a decade to figure out the international security environment that was replacing the Cold War. Some began to recognize this new environment by the mid-1990s. For most Americans it began on a Tuesday morning in September 2001.

Scholars are still searching for the correct name for this new national security era, but they understand the elements: international terrorism, asymmetric warfare made possible through the technological revolution, and homeland security. This new era will not end with the death of Osama Bin Laden or Saddam Hussein. In fact, a world that is fueled with centuries-old hatred and armed with twenty-first century technology is here to stay. Perhaps historians will say that what followed the Cold War was the War on Terrorism—an era that could last far longer than the Cold War.

Two wide oceans and two friendly neighbors have less meaning in twenty-first century security. Today, a cell phone bought in a convenience store can serve as a global command and control system. A terrorist can sit in an outdoor café in Paris and launch a cyber attack on the Pentagon and Wall Street, and a test tube can hold a weapon that could threaten an entire nation.

The good news is that much has been accomplished since September 11, 2001. Today, America has a coach, a game plan, and we are practicing. Secretary Michael Chertoff is the present coach, and he is implementing the president's game plan, the Homeland Security Strategy. In May of 2003, the second of two national level homeland security exercises (TOPOFF II) was completed. Additionally, hundreds of other exercises at the state and local level have been and will be conducted. A database from these exercises is being developed to identify "best practices" and leverage the investment and success.[108]

We cannot defend against all threats. We cannot deter, prevent, or preempt every truck bomber or sniper. We cannot provide every fire, police, and emergency services department in the country with every piece of emergency equipment on its wish list. We must establish wise priorities to capitalize on limited resources.

This will require continuation of a comprehensive and aggressive counterproliferation program. Washington must focus efforts on deterring, preventing, and preempting the high-consequence events, and U.S. officials must realize that they will not always be successful in these endeavors. Therefore, they must take actions to mitigate the effects of these high-consequence events, determine the identity of the perpetrators, have the capability to respond in a manner that will eliminate the attackers' offensive capability, and send a clear signal to all terrorists and tyrants that will reestablish deterrence.

America's enemies will continue to use America's strengths against us. Americans greatly value privacy, protection of individual liberties and rights of the accused, freedom of movement and access, and open borders. Americans see these values as strengths. The enemy sees them as seams in our defense, just as a National Football League quarterback exploits the seams in a zone defense. Defending the American homeland in the twenty-first century will be the most difficult challenge this nation has ever faced. It will likely cause all Americans to reexamine how they think about the military, the Intelligence Community, privacy, civil liberties, federalism, immigration, international commerce, borders, and the role of corporate America.

CHAPTER **12**

# Seeking a Port in the WMD Storm
## Counterproliferation Progress, Shortfalls, and the Way Ahead

*Barry R. Schneider*

Like a ship running from a hurricane at sea, the U.S. Government is struggling to reach a safe port and shelter from a threatening weapons of mass destruction (WMD) storm. In an era where some adversaries are perhaps on the cusp of achieving the capabilities to destroy forward-deployed American military forces with nuclear weapons (e.g., in a future conflict with North Korea) or to kill thousands of Americans in our cities with aerosolized biological weapons (e.g., if al-Qaeda were to achieve the capability), the United States and its allies are racing to create effective chemical, biological, radiological, and nuclear (CBRN) countermeasures. Serious gaps remain, however, and extreme vulnerabilities persist even 13 years after Secretary Les Aspin announced the beginning of the Department of Defense (DoD) Counterproliferation Initiative (CPI).

Much has been done since the CPI was launched in 1993, but much still must be accomplished before the United States can confidently either deter all adversaries from CBRN attacks or, at least, effectively neutralize any such attacks by a combination of effective counterforce targeting, active defenses, passive defenses, or the ability to recover through superb consequence management actions.

## The Ideal Counterproliferation Posture

Much progress has been made in the 13 years since Secretary Aspin and his deputy, Dr. Ashton Carter, launched the DoD Counterproliferation Initiative. However, progress to date does not equate success. Many additional steps must be taken before the United States and its allies can claim reasonable levels of preparedness in the effort to halt, thin out, manage, rollback, or counter the weapons of mass destruction threats posed by adversary states and groups.

To evaluate the ideal and compare it to the present counterproliferation program and identify the progress and shortfalls of the counterproliferation program, it is useful to look at the various elements where the Department of Defense is the lead agency before offering an overall assessment.

## Deterrence

### Maximum Deterrence Stance

The ideal deterrence posture can be arrived at only if the United States and its partners possess a known retaliatory military and economic capability that can impose costs on an aggressor state that are unacceptably high to its leadership should it elect to attack us. Further, that adversary leadership must believe the United States and its allies will have the will to use such full retaliatory strikes if provoked. Third, this U.S./allied retaliatory force must be able to survive an enemy surprise attack before delivering its response. Fourth, deterrence is most likely to work when the adversary leadership is rational and fully understands the self-defeating nature of starting a conflict and does not believe it can secure a compromise place down the road that would allow it to keep any initial gain made by striking first. Fifth, U.S./allied counterforce, active defense, passive defense, and consequence management capabilities would be so robust in an ideal counterproliferation posture that an adversary chemical, biological, radiological, and nuclear CBRN attack would be neutralized and U.S./allied forces would be better equipped to fight in such a toxic environment than the aggressor forces. Knowing that his CBRN weapons could be neutralized, a rational adversary is likely to be deterred from use of unconventional arms.

Last, but not by any means least, an ideal robust U.S. and allied deterrent would be based on a thorough knowledge of the enemy, both his leadership and order of battle. The full intelligence preparation of the battle space would include political-psychological profiles of enemy leader tendencies and values as well as a full understanding of adversary force characteristics and numbers as well as where their key assets are located. For full deterrent effects, the adversary should be made to understand that U.S. forces can effectively put bombs on key targets of greatest value to the adversary leaders.

Deterrence can be improved if you know the capabilities and mind of your adversary. U.S. intelligence services should seek to learn the CBRN capabilities, locations, and intent of possible adversaries. The recent experience in Iraq indicates a shortfall in U.S. and allied intelligence about Saddam Hussein's nuclear, chemical, and biological weapons potential. The U.S. Government appears to have drastically overestimated the Iraqi weapons of mass destruction threat as a result of depending upon unreliable defector information, relying on inconclusive findings from national technical means, and lacking adequate human intelligence inside Saddam Hussein's regime.

Plausibly, U.S. intelligence concluded from Iraq's inability to document disarmament of its weapons of mass destruction programs, its unwillingness to cooperate with UN inspection teams, and the heavy economic costs of noncompliance that Iraq was hiding a significant weapons of mass destruction arsenal and infrastructure. Saddam Hussein's regime is estimated to have lost $100 billion or more due to sanctions that limited Iraqi oil sales until the UN inspectors could verify that Iraq had truly scrapped its weapons of mass destruction assets. Further, Saddam Hussein, before his defeat in Operation Desert Storm, had invested heavily in his nuclear, chemical, and biological warfare programs, and the tyrant was still in place in early 2003 when Operation Iraqi Freedom was launched into Iraq to disarm his regime.

Many questions remain as to the disposition of Iraqi CBRN weapons:

1. Were these weapons programs discontinued to avoid further UN sanctions?

2. Were they hidden somewhere inside or outside Iraq to be claimed at a later date?

3. Were the Iraqi weapons of mass destruction hardware programs discontinued while "software" analytic efforts to perfect such weapons continued?

4. Was Saddam Hussein too proud to cooperate with the UN inspectors and/ or afraid to look so weak as to admit disarming?

5. Did Saddam Hussein disarm privately but pretend to retain weapons of mass destruction in order to deter enemies such as Iran and the United States from intervention into Iraq?

6. Did Iraqi scientists lie to Saddam Hussein about the extent of their WMD research and production, thereby making it impossible to find weapons never actually produced in quantity after 1991?

We may never know the full story about the Iraqi weapons of mass destruction program. What is clear to the U.S. Select Committee on Intelligence, however, is that U.S. intelligence about the program was far off the mark[1] and largely in the dark, leading analysts to draw speculative conclusions that were wrong because they were grounded in too many uncertainties and because their plausible theory, nevertheless, appears to have turned out to be incorrect.

This has led critics of U.S. intelligence to suggest that analysis of adversary weapons of mass destruction be more careful and rigorous, be increasingly reliant on human intelligence, be dependent on known hard facts, and that interpretations be challenged more by intelligence superiors as well as by decision makers. Furthermore, such analyses should be mated with a more intense scrutiny of the intent of adversary leaders and the factors that shape their decisions.

With regard to the last point, U.S. deterrence capability vs. enemies' war initiation or use of weapons of mass destruction should rest on a clear understanding of the thinking of adversary leaders to enable U.S. leaders to pose retaliatory threats that such adversaries will most fear and best understand.

Profiling of potential adversary leaders, done by intelligence experts dedicated to understanding their goals, decision-making processes, tendencies, personalities, and vulnerabilities can yield useful deterrence results if combined with a very potent U.S. retaliatory capability, an obvious will to respond to attacks, and a clearly crafted communication of both U.S. military muscle and U.S. determination to exact retribution for any losses suffered by U.S. citizens. In the end, adversaries must be taught to fear the American retribution and to conclude that aggression against the United States is a fool's gamble, a path that could lead them only to a terrible end.

Unfortunately, U.S. intelligence services have placed less importance on profiling of enemy leaders in the post-Cold War era than they did when we were threatened by the Soviet Union in the period from 1946 to 1991. These profiling capabilities, if resurrected and heeded, may give us better insights into how to deter, compel, counter, and anticipate the actions ordered by leaders of rogue states and terrorist adversaries.

It is suggested that both the Defense Intelligence Agency and the CIA resurrect such dedicated interdisciplinary profiling groups that can study and help U.S. leaders understand the political/psychological dimensions of adversary leaders, their strategic cultures, military doctrines, and organizational decision processes to determine likely adversary courses of action and tendencies in projected scenarios. A good model to follow would be the Center for the Analysis of Personality and Political Behavior directed by Dr. Jerrold Post at the CIA for a number of years that did profiles of foreign leaders to inform and assist U.S. policy makers who dealt with them.[2] Unfortunately, this center was dissolved and never adequately replaced after the late 1980s.

Such profiling could help U.S. leaders better understand who they are contending with, the things enemies most value and would least like to lose, and the actions that would most likely elicit either more cooperation or more violent responses. Such analysis of adversary leaders might help U.S. leaders better sort out enemy bluffs from real threats and might guide U.S. actions that could help persuade an adversary not to initiate a conflict nor escalate it to weapons of mass destruction use once embroiled.

In addition, it will be important for the U.S. intelligence services to greatly expand their expertise in the Middle East and northeast Asia particularly. More analysts need to be trained in the Korean, Chinese, Arabic, and Farsi languages, and much more emphasis needs to be given to creating human intelligence (HUMINT) on the ground in countries in the conflict zones. HUMINT is in scare supply and it is difficult to "know thy enemy" without it.

# Counterforce

## Maximum Counterforce Capability

The ideal counterforce posture will combine a comprehensive precision-guided munition arsenal of weapons, acquired in such numbers that most known key fixed surface targets in the adversary state can be eliminated. In addition, all airborne attack assets should be on stealthy launch platforms that cannot be readily detected by the radars of enemy surface-to-air missiles and other antiaircraft batteries.

This counterforce capability against fixed surface targets must also be coupled with additional capabilities to locate and destroy both mobile CBRN missile launchers and CBRN assets located in deeply buried facilities, hidden in tunnels bored into hillsides, or concealed in cut-and-cover hardened shelters. The ideal counterforce capability will have the use of robust earth penetrators and have the information and capabilities needed to inflict functional defeats on the hardened underground target sets when absolute destruction is not possible.

The ideal counterforce capability also will be augmented by a comprehensive and accurate intelligence preparation of the battle space. Ideally, all CBRN targets of consequence must be identified, characterized, and located. Then, optimally, after such locations and assets are struck, accurate damage assessments must be capable of being made in order to restrike undamaged CBRN assets, and this process should, within a short time, be able to silence such adversary CBRN weapons.

Ideal counterforce capabilities would be robust enough to tackle the entire range of enemy CBRN assets before a significant number could be employed against U.S. and allied targets. This suggests the need for a persistent overhead shooter and sensor capability, augmented by heavy Special Operations Forces (SOF) incursions on the ground, to slam the door shut on enemy CBRN usage before it could inflict heavy damage. Such an ideal force also will require a 24/7/365 overhead persistent intelligence, surveillance, and reconnaissance (ISR) presence to provide targeting information to shooters until the threat is eliminated.

Finally, the maximum or ideal counterforce capability will require adequate stocks of effective agent defeat weapons to destroy, neutralize, or entomb adversary chemical, biological, radiological, or nuclear weapons assets without significant spillover danger to adjacent civilians or friendly forces.

## Progress and Shortfalls in Counterforce

The advent of precision-guided munitions has greatly improved the accuracy and, therefore, the lethality of U.S. weapons against fixed targets identified on the earth's surface from the time of Operation Desert Storm on. This precision-guided munition revolution has resulted in a dramatic change in the ratio of weapons employed to targets destroyed. Whereas, in pre-1991 wars, air campaign outcomes were described in terms of hundreds or thousands of sorties per target destroyed, in the present era we can now talk of numbers of targets destroyed per sortie.

The introduction of stealthy aircraft also has made the counterforce mission easier and less costly in terms of aviators and aircraft lost on these missions since air defenses have been almost helpless against such hard-to-locate attackers. Stealthy aircraft can not only penetrate to target but can also attack targets at closer range at less risk than if conventional aircraft were used, increasing the chances of successful engagements.

So long as U.S. intelligence can provide exact coordinates for surface targets, U.S. strike aircraft can destroy them with great effectiveness. There, of course, is the rub. Certain high-value, time-sensitive targets, such as ballistic missiles with CBRN warheads about to be launched from hidden or camouflaged mobile launchers or those at fixed sites, may be invisible to U.S. intelligence, surveillance, and reconnaissance assets. It is difficult to destroy targets whose precise whereabouts are uncertain, so counterforce effectiveness against surface targets is dependent on accurate target location information.

Because of the increasing vulnerability of fixed-location assets on the ground, U.S. adversaries have begun placing their command and control centers, missile launchers, and weapons of mass destruction assets either in underground hardened sites, inside tunnels bored into the sides of hills or mountains, or have made them mobile by deploying them on wheeled vehicles or trains. Thus, counterforce attacks may be complicated by an enemy's mole or mobility tactics. North Korea, for example, has hidden most of its missile launchers and artillery in tunnels bored into the sides of mountains north of the demilitarized zone (DZ). Iraq, during the 1990–1991 Gulf War, launched 88 ballistic missiles toward coalition forces and Israel, and the U.S. "Scud hunt" for these mobile assets was deemed almost totally unsuccessful. Despite allocating approximately 1,500 sorties against such targets in the war, there was not a single confirmed kill against Scud transporter erector launchers.

Defeating some of the deeply buried hardened targets through outright physical destruction of the facilities may be outside the capabilities of today's forces. Short of nuclear weapons use, many underground hardened sites cannot be eliminated, and some are so deeply buried that even a nuclear detonation may not suffice. Added to these problems is the fact that nuclear use likely would have so much of a political downside that U.S. decision makers probably would be unwilling to open Pandora's box by employing such precedent-setting weapons and by risking incurring worldwide disfavor, condemnation, and the sanctions that probably would follow.

Perhaps the best and most likely strategy to defeat underground targets is to first locate them and then inflict a functional defeat by denying that facility electrical power, air, heat, connectivity, food, water, ingress or egress, and other essentials. This places an extraordinary burden upon the U.S. intelligence preparation of the battle space in order to locate the wiring, vents, entrances, exits, antennas, and emissions of each such underground facility.

It is difficult to evaluate how much the United States has progressed in its ability to achieve functional defeats on underground targets since it has had little wartime experience since 1991 against such targets. However, clearly there has been a degree of progress in fielding ISR assets needed to do the thorough intelligence assessments necessary to this difficult mission. The addition of Predator and Global Hawk Unmanned Aerial Vehicles (UAVs) gives the military a somewhat more continuous overhead view of such installations, combined with SOF improvements and the still imperfect development of unattended ground sensors.

Still missing is a suite of weapons capable of destroying deeply buried hardened targets, the lack of enough persistent overhead intelligence, surveillance and reconnaissance assets, and the limited numbers of "shooters" that can be kept close to the targets 24/7. Further, only a limited agent defeat weapon capability exists. Therefore, the balance of advantage over the past decade has to be given to adversary defenses over U.S. counterforce offenses. Should the United States field a nuclear earth-penetrating weapon it would bring a number of additional high-value targets within reach that are currently not threatened, although a certain number of such deeply buried facilities would still remain relatively safe from being destroyed. Employing such a nuclear device, however, would likely create diplomatic and political problems that could be seen to outweigh its counterforce advantages.

The U.S. capability to track, target, destroy, and assess damage against mobile missile launches is probably improved a good deal from Operation Desert Storm in 1991 to Operation Iraqi Freedom (OIF) in 2003. Exercises prior to OIF at Nellis Air Force Base, Nevada, led to greater coordination between Special Forces, strike aircraft, and ISR assets and probably would have narrowed the advantages still enjoyed by adversaries in "the Scud hunt." There have been considerable Scud hunting improvements in ISR due to deployment of Global Hawk and Predator UAVs, as well as command and control improvement due to the professionalization, reorganization, and information processing changes in the Combined Air Operations Center.

However, having said all this, U.S. persistent overhead ISR is still lacking over the battle space and many of the information processing, battle management, and automatic target recognition technologies are still in research and development rather than deployed, as many should have been 13 years after the Scud hunt failures of 1991. The continued inability to solve the critical mobile missile problem is an unfortunate failure. Unfortunately, no single organization or agency has been appointed or chosen to step forward to solve this pressing military problem. Hopefully, it will not require a military catastrophe to get proper attention to this problem. It would be very unfortunate if the gravity of this error was realized only after an adversary kills tens of thousands of U.S. or allied personnel when launching a missile carrying a weapon of mass destruction warhead from a transporter erector launcher that otherwise could have been neutralized.

The Scud hunt program needs leadership attention, more persistent overhead intelligence, surveillance, and reconnaissance assets, more shooters and sensors constantly in the target area, and new technology that assists in more rapidly processing battle management information and target tracking to reduce the sensor-to-shooter time to just a few minutes. First, and foremost, someone in the Department of Defense has to own the problem, be responsible for progress, and wield enough influence to bring the multiple research and development solutions now available to the field, where U.S. combatant commanders can wield them in the next war.

Not only should someone be put in charge of coordinating all the cross-functional elements of "Scud hunting," but someone else at the highest levels of the Department of Defense must oversee the progress of the program, ensure proper funding, and hold the commanders and managers accountable for outcomes. Combatant commanders must demand that their forces be properly organized, trained, and equipped to carry out this mission in the future. Additional Congressional oversight and presidential level attention might be needed to direct proper attention to this program.

The issue of preemption has become a controversial topic for policy debate. One component of this debate is the question of when such action is appropriate, legal, and necessary for security. Given the extreme level of damage that could be done by, say, a nuclear or strategic biological weapons attack, it is prudent to destroy those types of threats before they are inflicted upon one's own forces or population, if the attack appears to be imminent and intelligence is such that reasonable certainty of use can be confirmed.

As one recent study by the Center for Counterproliferation Research at the National Defense University with regard to the need for a capability for rapid precision strikes states the following:

> Because the time window for engaging many WMD counterforce targets may be narrow, there will be a premium in these missions on what has come to be called "network-centric operations"—the effective integration of intelligence, surveillance, and reconnaissance (ISR), rapid adaptive planning, collaborative decision-making, strike coordination, and real-time battle damage assessment. The need in some cases for prompt strikes highlights a potential shortfall in current capability. Prompt conventional global strike is a potentially high-value deterrent and combat capability against a range of target types. That is, the ability to deliver decisive effects rapidly may be key to denying adversaries the time to exercise asymmetric strategies, holding strategic assets at risk before effective sanctuary is achieved, and restoring deterrence through rapid, shock-maximizing strikes. In particular, there is advantage for U.S. forces if time-sensitive targets can be held at risk at all times—including when theater-based assets are not available.[3]

## Active Defenses

### Maximum Active Defenses

The ideal active defense force will be robust enough so that it can reduce enemy missile and aircraft attacks to a minimum by intercepting, destroying, or deflecting them before their CBRN warheads and bombs can reach their targets. Such an ideal system will have very high performance SATKA capabilities for surveillance of incoming attackers, acquisition of the targets, tracking of the targets, killing of the attacking missiles or aircraft, and assessing the results to determine whether to go into a reattack mode.

The likely ideal missile defense will probably feature a layered defense with accurate and effective missile interceptors operating in the boost phase, postboost phase, midcourse range, and terminal phases of an adversary missile's flight. A three-layer or four-layer defense, with each phase providing a 90 percent kill probability in its engagements, if deployed in adequate interceptor numbers, should be able to sweep the skies of adversary aircraft or missiles.

This ideal active defense system could also be provided by a multishot speed-of-light system such as the boost-phase airborne laser (ABL) now in development, if it is proven feasible, is procured in adequate numbers, is continuously deployed, and has a high probability of kill (PK) per shot.

The ideal active defense capability will also defend comprehensively against the 360 degree azimuth threat of low flying, relatively inexpensive cruise missiles, possibly launched in swarms. The ideal defense against cruise missiles will probably deploy airborne look-down radars to discern low-flying cruise missiles from the surrounding ground clutter and will be augmented by airborne and ground-based interceptors that can be directed to a full 360 degree layered or multishot defense. An ideal active defense would be robust enough to intercept, simultaneously, even a saturation attack by dozens of cruise missiles.

## The Progress and Shortfalls in Active Defenses

One means of delivering CBRN weapons is by ballistic or cruise missiles and, as of this writing, both present very difficult challenges to U.S. active defenses. The difficulty of the theater ballistic missile (TBM) defensive task is akin to developing a bullet to hit an incoming bullet. Nuclear and biological munitions mounted on missiles will increasingly pose a strategic threat to U.S. and allied forces and citizens in the next two decades. The list of states with such missiles is growing. For example, it has been estimated that 75 states have some form of cruise missiles and that there are roughly 75,000 cruise missiles held by these countries. Compared to nuclear and biological weapons, chemical arms pose no strategic threat unless, for example, many tons of chemical agents are delivered, an unlikely threat. Radiological weapons are strictly tactical, but could be useful to the user in rendering certain limited areas unusable or, at least dangerous, to operate within.

U.S. ballistic missile defense programs have made important improvements since 1993. The Patriot-2 (PAC-2) TBM terminal defense system was introduced in the 1991 Gulf War where it enjoyed some limited success against Iraqi ballistic missile attacks. The PAC-2 has now been superseded by the more accurate Patriot-3 (PAC-3), which introduces new hit-to-kill technology and has a wider range of coverage. Basically, however, U.S. forces will not be very well defended against theater ballistic missiles until the next generation of defense upgrades which will provide a layered defense.

Now in development are no fewer than five other U.S. theater missile defense systems: the Terminal High Altitude Area Defense (THAAD), the Medium Extended Air Defense System (MEADS), the midcourse interceptor Navy Theater-Wide Ballistic Missile Defense system, lower-tier Navy Area Theater Ballistic Missile Defense System, and the ABL. When all or most are fielded, if they work as advertised, and are deployed in sufficient numbers, the United States and its allies will possess for the first time a viable ballistic missile defense against enemies who possess several hundred of such missiles. This will be a breakthrough since no nation-state has had a viable missile defense since World War II when these types of weapons were introduced into combat by the Germans when they barraged Great Britain with their V-1 and V-2 missiles.

The goal in ballistic missile defense is to achieve a multilayered or multishot defense where each layer or shot has, let us say, a 90 percent or higher kill probability against the incoming missiles. Indeed, it may be possible to intercept such enemy systems multiple times when using the Airborne Laser, which is expected to be capable of up to 30 speed-of-light shots or intercepts. One can imagine a three-layer defense made up of the Airborne Laser to intercept missiles in their boost and postboost phases of flight, augmented by the army's THAAD and Navy Area Theater Ballistic Missile Defenses for kinetic kills at midcourse ranges, and PAC-3, MEADS, and Navy lower-tier interceptors to rise to meet whatever enemy missiles got through the first two layers of defense.

Therefore, if a country such as North Korea were to become engaged in combat with U.S. and Republic of Korea forces in the South and fired off a hundred ballistic missiles at Republic of Korea targets, a two-layer (midcourse and terminal interceptor) defense with a 90 percent PK per layer would permit just one leaker to reach its targets. In this case, 90 of the 100 missiles could be eliminated by midcourse interceptors like Terminal High Altitude Area Defense and Aegis Wide Area interceptors. Then, 9 of the remaining 10 missiles might be eliminated by terminal defenses such as the Patriot-3 or the Aegis Navy terminal interceptors. Unfortunately, at present only limited numbers of Patriot-3s are defending these areas where adversary states might possibly one day take action.

Several international partners are also working on theater ballistic missile defensive systems. Lockheed-Martin has collaborated with Israel in its development of the Arrow interceptors now being deployed. In addition, the United States is in the early stages of collaborating with Japan to develop a ballistic missile defense system. And, finally, the NATO allies are collaborating to finance the Medium Extended Air Defense System, a mobile terminal "bubbletop" defense for shielding land forces as they move into or across theater. The Medium Extended Range Air Defense System, for example, could be an excellent terminal defense for an invasion force being landed at ports or being sent across a beach under hostile fire. It is designed to provide the protective bubble over a power projection force being sent into a foreign theater to "kick the doors down" for follow-on reinforcements. Until theater active defenses are augmented with such robust multilayered, multishot interceptors, U.S. forces will be largely at the mercy of enemy ballistic missile attacks.

Adding to this emerging U.S. theater ballistic missile defensive capability will be a new U.S. strategic terminal defensive system to defend the continental United States. Twenty interceptors based in Alaska and California will provide the possibility of a defense against a light enemy missile strike. The beginnings of such a system, no longer restricted by the Anti-Ballistic Missile Treaty, designed initially to be capable of defending against a light ballistic missile attack, was scheduled to be in place and operating by late 2004. Thus, United States territory will be defended against a handful of missiles launched against targets on the West Coast of the United States from potential adversary states such as North Korea or China. It might also be used to intercept stray accidental launches of long-range ballistic missiles that headed toward U.S. territory. Missile defense programs, both theater and strategic, cost $10 billion in fiscal year (FY) 2004 and consume the large majority of Department of Defense funding for counterproliferation capabilities.

Perhaps most disturbing in the area of active defenses is the lack of progress in U.S. cruise missile defenses at a time when foreign cruise missile capabilities have spread to over 75 countries.[4] The leadership of the Missile Defense Agency has focused its work almost exclusively upon defeating the ballistic missile threat, to the neglect of cruise missile defense.

This neglect of cruise missile defense is compounded by the fact that, from an adversary perspective, these are perhaps the ideal adversary weapons to carry biological munitions. Adversary leaders of a relatively poor state might pursue an asymmetrical strategy of coupling the poor nation's best strategic delivery system, cruise missiles, with the poor nation's best weapon of mass destruction, biological weapons, in order to level the playing field against the world's military superpower. Cruise missiles are much cheaper to build or buy than ballistic missiles. They have tiny radar cross sections and fly close to the nap of the earth where they can be lost in the earth's ground clutter, making them difficult to detect, track, and target. Because they are relatively cheap they can be produced and fired in numbers sufficient to saturate even very good air defenses. Further, they can pose a 360 degree threat since they can be programmed to fly predesignated routes and change directions as programmed. Finally, their speed is relatively slow so that they can more easily distribute aerosolized biological warfare (BW) agents on targets below them, as opposed to supersonic ballistic missiles that can be less easily programmed for optimal height of bursts and have problems of heat shielding which, if not perfect, could burn up the biological munitions being delivered.

Thus, a possibly fatal flaw in U.S. active defenses is the neglect of cruise missiles defense during the past decade, and the failure of the U.S. Missile Defense Agency or the Joint Theater Air and Missile Defense Organization to focus on this problem satisfactorily.

Of course, active defenses also need to be conducted on the ground along places like the DMZ separating the two Koreas, along the U.S. and allied borders, and around U.S. military facilities in the continental United States or worldwide. Enemy Special Forces and terrorists could utilize CBRN weapons in various ways without utilizing missile systems: witness the possibilities of using crop duster aircraft to distribute biological agents over targeted areas or saboteurs to detonate explosives where toxic industrial chemicals (TICs) and toxic industrial materials (TIMs) are manufactured and stored. Every American and allied city and port has such targets and guarding against all other types of CBRN attacks is an unenviable active defense job where the odds favor the attackers who can pick the time and place.

## Passive Defense
### Maximum Passive Defenses

The ideal passive defensive system will provide redundant and highly effective biological, chemical, and radiological weapons detectors, lightweight biological warfare masks, and full counterchemical warfare and counterbiological warfare individual protective equipment (IPE) complete with masks, boots, gloves, and overgarments to each U.S. and allied military person, and associated civilian support workers.[5] Indeed, each individual should possess multiple backup protective suits, masks, gloves, and boots so that they can change out of contaminated gear to gain continuous protection over the period of the conflict. The ideal passive defenses will also have administered the full range of biological warfare vaccines and chemical warfare antidotes to the U.S. and allied force and support workers and will have ready access to prepositioned counterbiological warfare and counterchemical warfare medicines, protective equipment, and decontaminants such as are stockpiled in the continental United States in the Strategic National Stockpile (SNS).

Also, the ideal passive defense program will provide effective collective protection shelters for all base personnel and will stockpile adequate medical supplies and equipment to cope with CBRN emergencies. Further, this program will provide plans, training, and adequate resources for dealing with the medical side of a CBRN conflict, including well-thought-out plans for handling evacuations, mass casualties (triage, evacuations, and quarantines), and identification of the physically injured and separation from the "worried well" to prevent the overwhelming of medical staffs and supplies.

The ideal passive defense program will provide both a point detector and a standoff sensor system that detects biological and chemical agents in incoming weapons or in aerosolized clouds approaching U.S. and allied positions. This ideal detect-to-warn sensor alarm will provide enough warning time for friendly forces to don masks and take shelter before the attack arrives, thus substituting for the "detect-to-treat" system now in place.

In addition to the need for excellent point and standoff detectors to sense when a CBRN attack is taking place, and decontamination and medical diagnostic capabilities to sustain the force when it is subject to such enemy weapons, the ideal passive defense system also needs technologies to shield the force, including individual and collective protective equipment and chemical, biological, or radiological prophylaxes. Finally, the ideal passive defense must be designed and run by those who understand the threat environment by providing to the war fighter the optimal battle analysis, battle management tools based on modeling and simulation training. The ideal passive defense will take advantage of an integrated early warning system, an advanced medical surveillance system, and concepts of operation designed to both protect the force and its ability to execute the mission [e.g., the United States Air Force Counter-Chemical Warfare Concept of Operations (USAF C-CW CONOPS)].

## Progress and Shortfalls in Passive Defense

Significant progress has been made in passive defenses in more than a decade since the start of the Defense Counterproliferation Initiative in 1993. Indeed, in no element of U.S. counterproliferation policy has more progress been made than in passive defense, and that is true despite the fact that the active defense investment is 10 times that of passive defense, with far less satisfactory results. This leads some to question the priorities of the overall CP program.

When Secretary Aspin launched the CPI, only a small percentage of the armed forces personnel had been administered anthrax vaccine. Today, most personnel going into harm's way have been inoculated against this primary BW threat, although in late 2004 the anthrax vaccinations were halted by court order, subject to further safety testing of the vaccine. In December 2005, the FDA approved the vaccine as safe, and the DoD has made it available on a voluntary basis to those authorized for the vaccine.

In 1993, those military units that had protective masks, overgarments, gloves, and boots to guard against chemical attacks had only the very bulky, very hot, very restrictive protective gear. Today, much of the active duty U.S. military assigned to forward bases in danger zones such as Iraq,

South Korea, and Afghanistan have ready much lighter, less restrictive, and less oppressive new Joint Service Lightweight Integrated Suit Technology overgarments.

In addition, the force has been given improved protective masks such as the M20 and M42. These replace the M17, M25, and M9 and feature a better face seal, increased useful life, weather and ozone resistance, improved comfort, and ease of cleaning and maintenance. Also, the new M25 mask supports the army and SOF personnel and gives them close-fitting eye lenses, a voice emitter for face-to-face and telephone communication, a drinking tube, and an interphone for aircraft communications. Three other new improved masks are now in research and development (R&D) for deployment in the next several years for helicopter pilots, and selected ground forces and commercial applications.

Further, inspections of U.S. bases abroad in the early to mid-1990s showed that collective protection (COLPRO) shelters had long been neglected and were inadequate to meet the chemical and biological (CB) warfare threats anticipated in the future. Some progress, although not nearly enough, has been made to improve the COLPRO capabilities at key bases such as Osan Air Base in the Republic of Korea and others within close reach of adversaries. Other U.S. bases generally are far less prepared to offer up-to-date, fully equipped and supplied, toxic-free shelters.

In FY 2001, the U.S. military began deploying a 300-square foot Chemical Biological Protective Shelter (CBPS) to replace the older M51 shelters. These CBPS units will help provide relief to personnel who can use such contamination-free zones to rest, get treatment, gain relief from protective overgarments, take care of bodily functions, and get into fresh protective gear.

Other new collective protection shelters used to improve medical service to combatants are the U.S. Army Chemical Protected Deployable Medical System and the U.S. Air Force Chemically Hardened Air Transportable Hospital, which were both introduced to the field in FY 2001 to provide a toxic-free treatment area.

U.S. Navy ships are also being backfitted to accept a Collective Protection System to provide a contamination-free environment in designated locations aboard each vessel. These were designed to protect mission-essential and life-sustaining functions on board while the naval vessel and its crew are subject to chemical and/or biological attacks. This backfitting program began in FY 2001 and will proceed for many years as the United States moves to protect its fleet and personnel.

In addition, the Department of Defense also is working on the Joint Collective Protection Equipment program to provide improved filters to prevent the flow of chemical and biological particulates into collective protection shelters.

Finally, still in research and development is the Joint Transportable Collective Protection System, a modular shelter system that can, when deployed, be used as a stand-alone structure or as a toxic-free shelter within existing structures to protect against chemical and biological agents, toxic industrial materials, and radiological particulate matter.[6]

Medical preparations for CBRN warfare have led to some very useful new passive defense programs in the 13 years since the Counterproliferation Initiative was begun. One such advance is the introduction of the Global Expeditionary Medical System (GEMS), previously known as Desert Cove.[7] The Global Expeditionary Medical System allows for integration of patient evaluation, epidemiological analysis, and command and control linkages of medics at the scene of casualties to commanders in the rear. The Global Expeditionary Medical System uses the Rugged Advanced Pathogen Identification Device (RAPID) to tell medical personnel and commanders in real time what kind of biological warfare agent is being used by the enemy force. This RAPID assessment facilitates command decisions such as what kinds of treatment to administer, whether to isolate casualties, and whether or not to quarantine personnel or sectors. Another GEMS tool is the Patient Encounter Module, a paperless data linked tool for the front-line medic to record and trade individual patient assessments. The Global Expeditionary Medical System also utilizes the Theater Epidemiological Module, an analysis tool designed for far forward use as well as a capable reporting system to aid command and control surveillance of the battle area. Finally, the Global Expeditionary Medical System personnel also use the Theater Occupational Module which assists the user in estimating the level of biological warfare contamination risk in a given area by comparing and contrasting readings with a baseline normal operating environment.

In the past decade, the military medical community has given more attention to the medical risks of different types of biological agents and the intelligence assessments of what different adversary states and groups are thought to possess. For example, they have concluded that for a group of rogue states the medical risks and intelligence assessment of possible possession is greatest for agents such as anthrax, botulinum toxin, plague, and ricin. The possibility of biological warfare agents like smallpox, encephalitis, and Ebola being in the hands of adversaries is not as likely, but should they use such weapons the results could be as or more severe than the first four cited.[8] (See Figure 12.1.)

Medical countermeasures have now been developed to decrease the risk to personnel associated with enemy biological warfare attacks and to continue to carry out U.S. military missions. One such product, new to the inventory in the 1990s, is Pentavalent Botulinium Toxoid (PBT) to treat Botulinium Toxin (BOT). Unfortunately, there is no present manufacturer to produce PBT in the quantities needed. The U.S. military medical

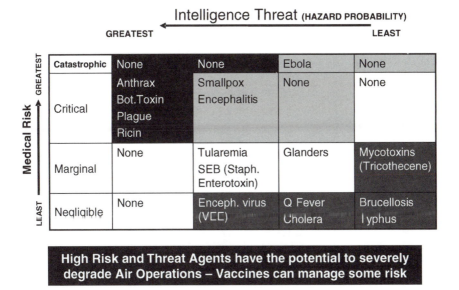

Figure 12.1    Biodefense: Certain Weapons Pose Critical Risk[9]

community works to keep food and water safe, provides a number of relevant vaccines such as the Anthrax Vaccine Adsorbed (AVA), uses systems like the Global Expeditionary Medical System to detect and identify biological agents rapidly, and utilizes protective equipment to protect personnel and field hospitals. If these preexposure measures do not prevent infections, the medical community still utilizes vaccines, antibodies, antivirals, protective equipment, decontamination, disease surveillance techniques, and other treatments to aid casualties and prevent the spreading of contagious diseases.

Still under study is how to treat massive numbers of casualties, what roles the civilian sector can play in such treatment, how to triage a mass casualty event, when to quarantine casualties and exposed personnel, where and when to execute an evacuation of personnel, and how to dovetail the medical response with ongoing combat operations. Also, unresolved is how much forward-deployed stockpiles of medical equipment, vaccines, and medical supplies are required in different Combatant Command areas of responsibility to cope with possible biological warfare attacks.

Recent analysis of what many consider the number one biological warfare threat, anthrax, shows some interesting data on survivability of personnel given the timing and medical countermeasures taken. (See Figure 12.2.)

Note the importance of administering AVA either during the preexposure or presymptomatic phases of an anthrax attack on personnel. A

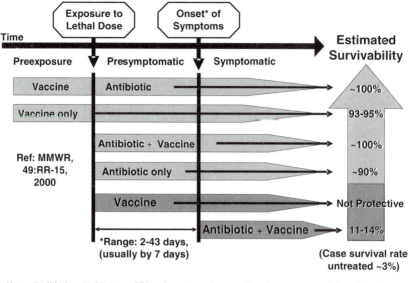

**Figure 12.2** Medical Countermeasures and Survivability Example: Anthrax[10]

combination of both Anthrax Vaccine Adsorbed and the relevant antibiotics (Ciprofloxacin or Doxycycline) should lead to close to 100 percent survival. Failure to treat until after symptoms begin changes the estimated survival rate to only 11 to 14 percent. This shows the need for early warning and good biological warfare early warning sensors. Unfortunately, the United States and its allies are still in the "detect-to-treat" rather than the far more favorable "detect-to-warn" mode of operations, and changes in our alerting capabilities could save tens of thousands of lives in a biological warfare scenario.

The military science and technology (S&T) community has been working very hard to give the war fighter and homeland defender a variety of new tools to help them survive, fight, and win either on the chemical and biological battlefield, or on the home front. Note the array of chemical and biological defense technologies that have been deployed in the field since Secretary Aspin's Counterproliferation Initiative was begun in the areas of individual protection, collective protection, decontamination, medical assistance, contamination avoidance, information systems, modeling and simulation, and CBRN protection and response. (See Figure 12.3.)

However, in some other areas of passive defense, major deficiencies still exist. Out of the 14 biological agents deemed most useful for

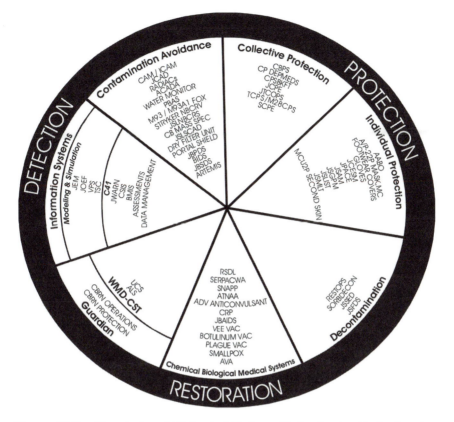

**Figure 12.3** Chemical and Biological Defense Technologies: Reducing the Threat with Enhanced Capabilities[11]

weaponization, the United States has still fielded only four vaccines that have been given the Food and Drug Administration (FDA) stamp of approval. In some cases, even where a FDA-approved vaccine exists, no adequate supply of the vaccine has yet been purchased. In several cases there is no usable vaccine yet in sight despite the passage of over a decade when, with proper funding and dedication to finding workable solutions, vaccines might have been available now to protect U.S. armed forces.

Indeed, had there not been the al-Qaeda attacks of September 11, 2001, followed by the October–November 2001 anthrax-through-the-mail attacks, there would likely have been even less progress in vaccines, antibiotics, antiviral drugs, and the stockpiling of emergency medical supplies.

Because our intelligence is limited about the kinds of chemical and biological agents that rivals such as North Korea or Iran might possess and because such programs are easy to conceal and are inherently difficult to detect using U.S. national technical means, it is wise to adopt a capabilities-based passive defense approach rather than a threat-based one. Thus, even if an adversary CB threat has not definitively been detected, it is wise to prepare for the contingency of adversary CB use if it is within their capability to produce and use such arms.

## DHS Support for Passive Defense

As of FY 2004, nine out of ten federal dollars spent on passive defense against BW are spent by the Department of Homeland Security (DHS). The U.S. Congress has recently passed, and the DHS has pushed, the Bioshield and Biosensor programs that should upgrade the U.S. vaccine development and biological sensor R&D programs. Department of Homeland Security programs already have sparked the acquisition of enough smallpox vaccine to inoculate every American citizen and created a SNS program whereby 50-ton "Push Packages" of all types of vaccines, medicines, decontamination agents, and emergency medical equipment are stored in a dozen locations across the United States in preparation for emergencies in all regions of the country. The Strategic National Stockpile has increased 50 percent from FY 2001 to FY 2004. The Strategic National Stockpile program should be duplicated and/or made available for overseas application as well and likely will be extended and adopted in hot spots abroad in the future where the CBRN threat is greatest.

The al-Qaeda attacks on the World Trade Center and Pentagon on September 11, 2001, have galvanized U.S. biodefense preparedness, even though it still has a long way to go to reach a satisfactory condition. Federal investment in biodefense is up 17 times from $294 million in the Department of Health and Human Services (HHS) in FY 2001 to $5.2 billion in FY 2004.[12] Each of the 50 states of the United States now has bioterrorism response plans in place, including mass vaccination plans, and all have created disease reporting systems that should rapidly detect a bioterrorist event.[13] The U.S. Centers for Disease Control and Prevention (CDC) has drafted model legislation on emergency health powers for states to adopt in order to deal with such crises.

The Laboratory Response Network, connecting labs that can help in a bioattack emergency, has been expanded from 80 labs in FY 2001 to 145 labs by FY 2004.[14] The number of state and local public health labs that are approved for work at the biosecurity level three has expanded to 47, four times the number in 1999.[15] In FY 2003, the CDC provided specialized bioterrorism training to 8,800 key lab technicians. Eleven new high-level biocontainment research laboratories are currently being funded by the National Institutes of Health (NIH). These could be made available also for assistance in a public health response to a bioterrorist event.[16]

Moreover, the Department of Health and Human Services has expanded the U.S. Centers for Disease Control Public Health Information Network to reach 1 million public health professionals, including those in 90 percent of all county public health agencies. Further, almost 174,000 health professionals have been trained in FY 2003 and FY 2004 through Health Resources and Services Administration's Bioterrorism Training and Curriculum Development program.[17]

The Department of Health and Human Services has quadrupled the Readiness Force in the U.S. Public Health Service Commissioned Corps from 600 in FY 2001 to about 2,300 in FY 2004. The Food and Drug Administration has increased its imported food inspections at ports of entry from 40 ports in 2001 to 90 ports in FY 2004 and has conducted eight times more such inspections.[18] Also since the September 11, 2001, al-Qaeda attacks, the Food and Drug Administration created a Food Emergency Network, with 63 laboratories serving 34 states to deal with possible food poisoning events.[19]

The NIH has invested in new and improved vaccines against smallpox and anthrax. The smallpox vaccine supply has increased from 15.4 million to over 300 million doses, enough to vaccinate all U.S. citizens, if required. The NIH has also developed an Ebola virus vaccine that has worked in monkeys and is now being tested on human volunteers.[20]

The National Institutes of Health also established eight Regional Centers of Excellence for Biodefense and Emerging Infectious Diseases Research.[21] Further, in 2002 the U.S. Centers for Disease Control in collaboration with the Department of Justice created a Forensic Epidemiology course to train public safety and law enforcement professionals to aid in investigations. By 2004, 42 of the 50 states had participated and 5,000 professionals were trained.[22]

This progress in biodefense made by HHS and the Department of Homeland Security also arms the United States with greater protection, expertise, and biodefense assets that can be copied or borrowed by the war-fighter community in foreign wars.

## Other Medical Defenses

Clearly, in the realm of vaccine research and distribution to counter infections from biological weapons, there has been some impressive improvement. Most U.S. active duty military personnel assigned to forward areas in conflict zones have been vaccinated against anthrax. Moreover, the United States now has enough smallpox vaccine to inoculate the entire U.S. population, including all U.S. military personnel should the need arise. Unfortunately, as of this writing, the anthrax vaccination program has been at least temporarily halted by court order until more safety tests can be conducted. The DoD is appealing this ruling, arguing that the vaccine is safe.

While it is reassuring that U.S. defenses against these twin scourges, anthrax and smallpox, have been improved, that does not protect U.S. forces and citizens against the consequences of several other biological agents that could be used as weapons of war or terror. The United States currently has only a few FDA-approved vaccines such as those for cholera, plague, smallpox, and anthrax. Even in these, the cholera vaccine is not recommended for routine protection in endemic areas and the plague vaccine, while FDA approved, is no longer available in quantity.[23]

Some counter-BW vaccines are in what is called the "Investigational New Drug (IND)" status, awaiting Food and Drug Administration approval pending further trials. The vaccines for Q fever, tularemia, Venezuelan equine encephalitis, viral hemorrhagic fevers, and botulism are in this IND category and are in very short supply.[24]

No vaccine at all currently exists that is effective against such biological agents as glanders, brucellosis, staphylococcal enterotoxin B, ricin, or T-2 mycotoxins and a myriad of other diseases that could also be weaponized in the future.[25]

It is especially recommended that the Departments of Defense and Homeland Security give top priority to several medical chemical and biological defense S&T programs, namely,[26]

- multiagent biological warfare agent vaccines and medicines,
- programs to provide earlier indications of biological warfare attacks and infections,
- drugs to provide short-term biological warfare agent protection,
- antivirals for pox and hemorrhagic fever virus,
- medicines and vaccines to combat adversary fourth generation chemical warfare agents, and
- plasma technology to neutralize BW agents.

With regard to the nonthermal plasma technology cited above, the Air Force Research Laboratory is presently testing two portable devices to neutralize biological agents, one that uses high powered pulsed microwaves, the other atmospheric pressure plasma to kill the bacteria and viruses. High energy electrons are discharged to preferentially interact with and destroy or neutralize otherwise harmful biological agents. The Non-Thermal Plasma Technology, still in the research and development stage, is designed to suck in air particles, neutralize them, and thereby clean rooms, aircraft, vehicles, and containers without using the foams, solvents, or bleach that could otherwise harm both ordinary and sensitive materials.

## Sensor Upgrades Needed

In addition, new types of biodetectors are needed that can identify the contents of aerosolized clouds being borne by wind currents in the direction of U.S. and allied forces. Biosensors are also needed that can provide rapid and accurate information on biocontamination over a wide area, as opposed to the current point detectors like the Biological Integrated Defense System, a road mobile laboratory developed in the mid-1990s after Operation Desert Storm.

Science and Technology research also needs to provide improved reconnaissance capabilities to detect biological and chemical agents already on the surface and to identify the areas contaminated from those that are clean. Such improved sensors need to be integrated into a centralized battle management command and control system at military bases and ports.

Of course, during the period from 1991 to 2004, the U.S. armed services have shown some improvement in both biological and chemical sensors despite funding problems and a failure to put anyone in charge of the entire effort until the late 1990s. The M-22 Automatic Agent Detector/Alarm was introduced together with the M21 Remote Sensing Chemical Agent Alarm, and the Improved Chemical Monitor. Also, the Combatant Commands began to introduce Dry Filter Units to sample bioagents in the air at their installations. Both the U.S. Army and Marines fielded improved radiacs to help detect radiation and give warning.

A new array of chemical and biological agent detectors were in U.S. hands by 2004[27] including the following:

### *Chemical Sensors*

- Automatic Chemical Agent Detection Alarm, a man-portable vapor alarm that serves as a point detector and identifier of nerve and blister agents;
- Joint Chemical Agent Detector;
- Improved Chemical Agent Monitor;
- Chemical Agent Monitor;
- Improved (Chemical Agent) Point Detection System installed on naval vessels to detect nerve and blister agents;
- Joint Services Lightweight Standoff Chemical Agent Detector;
- Shipboard Automatic Liquid Agent Detector;
- Joint Services Lightweight NBC Reconnaissance Systems (also detects biological, radiological, and nuclear contamination);
- Joint Warning and Reporting System (for CBRN agents); and the
- Artemis, a standoff chemical agent detector still in research and development, which scans threat clouds in all directions out to

20 kilometers or more. It will be used on a variety of land, sea, and air platforms.

## Biological Agent Sensors

- Biological Integrated Detection System (BIDS);
- Interim Biological Agent Detector (IBAD);
- Joint Biological Point Detection System (JBPDS) provides a common sensor that can identify a biological agent in 15 minutes that began to replace IBAD in 2003;
- Joint Biological Remote Early Warning System;
- Joint Biological Universal Detector; and the
- Joint Biological Standoff Detection System is a research and development project that when perfected is expected to use a LIDAR beam to detect aerosol clouds out to a range of 15 kilometers for particulate matter and identify the existence of biological particles out to 3 kilometers.

## Radiation Agent Sensors

- the AN/UDR-13 Radiac Set, a compact handheld, pocket-size tactical radiation meter that measures gamma/neutron doses in the vicinity;
- the AN/VDR-2 Radiac Set, a handheld or vehicle-mounted sensor to detect and measure nuclear radiation from fallout;
- the AN/PDR-75 Radiac Set that measures dose exposure of individuals to gamma and neutron radiation; and
- the AN/PDR-77 Radiac Set that measures doses of alpha, beta, gamma, and x-ray radiation.

The standoff chemical, biological, and radiation sensor systems, in particular, once perfected, will be the beginning of the U.S. military's capability to provide adequate warning to its forces to get into protective gear and shelters prior to the arrival of a chemical or biological attack.

Once the U.S. and allied military forces have turned the corner in transitioning from a detect-to-treat situation to a detect-to-warn capability, all personnel will be significantly safer from chemical and biological attacks. Much research and development work on standoff sensors remains before this becomes a reality.

In addition to these detectors, Portal Shield is also an interim capability for biodetection at high-value fixed overseas sites. It was initially deployed in 1998 and has been introduced to numerous sites as of 2004. Portal Shield uses a network of sensors ringing a base or facility, linked to the command and control of a centralized computer accessible to the site commander. Portal Shield is to be replaced by the more advanced JBPDS, which works faster and is more accurate.

Also, highly desirable will be the invention and deployment of methods and equipment for identifying fourth generation chemical warfare agents and other new technology agents. Moreover, improved decontamination materials are required.

While substantial progress has been made in biodefense, in the area of decontamination of equipment and personnel that have been exposed to chemical agents, only marginal progress has been made. The U.S. military still relies on chemical agent decontaminants such as bleach that are too caustic for cleaning up both contaminated personnel and equipment.

One useful new decontaminant for personnel that has been introduced in the last 10 years is the Skin Exposure Reduction Paste against Chemical Warfare Agents product. Another recent innovation is the XM-100 Sorbent Decontamination System, an aluminum oxide powder to remove chemical contaminants from the surface of facilities and equipment, and it reduces the need for water. Also, it is being examined by the FDA for possible application as a skin or open-wound decontaminant.

There has been limited success in developing new decontaminants that will not ruin the surfaces of equipment or glaze over windshields of aircraft or land vehicles that have been coated with toxic chemicals. Nor has an effective way been found to decontaminate rubber or plastic that has been exposed to chemical warfare agents. Instead, such materials absorb the chemicals and remain toxic for long periods, thwarting all present remedies.

As noted there have been a number of new chemical agent detectors introduced to the field in the past few years. However, laying down M8 detection paper or M9 detection tape is still considered the best way to detect the areas contaminated by chemical warfare agents, to help indicate what places are safe and which are still dangerous. It would be valuable to operations and personnel if chemical "markers" were produced to be sprayed over areas and when in contact with toxic materials, to turn color or otherwise show areas of contamination so that operational workarounds of hot spots could be more safely and rapidly done.

Considerable progress has been made in designing new chemical and biological sensors. The Portal Shield sensor suites are a first step toward ringing military bases and facilities with a detection and warning system vis-à-vis biological warfare attacks, but the system, like most of the other detectors in the field, is far from perfect, causing far too many false alarms.

The Fox Vehicle and the BIDS are mobile, protected laboratories for detecting and identifying chemical and biological agents, respectively, an analysis that can provide point detection and identification within 30 minutes.

Although considerable research and development work on standoff detectors is proceeding, there is nothing yet in the field that can detect aerosolized agents drifting in clouds toward a targeted area. Something like this is needed to provide detection to warn friendly troops to don protective chemical and biological gear before the hazard arrives. At present, our sensors confirm the presence of chemical and biological agents only after they have contaminated an area, and all such detection is point detection, not wide area detection. What is most needed is a detect-to-warn system rather than the present detect-to-treat system where the first sign of an attack may be the physical symptoms of victims reacting to chemical or biological attacks.

## Passive Defense: Is a Quick Fix Possible?

The slow pace of research and development in biodefense sensors and the serious biological warfare threat that exists has led some analysts to search for immediate and commercially available off-the-shelf remedies for protecting personnel living and working at fixed military bases that face potential biological attacks.[28] Much of the danger of biological warfare or biological terrorist attacks could be alleviated if the targeted personnel were to don inexpensive N-95 masks to filter out the biological microbes, since aerosolized BW agents are the main threat.

How would personnel know when to don their masks? This might be required when the threat indicators were highest. For example, it would be wise to wear masks when the intelligence agencies signaled that the threat was higher than usual, for example, Threat Level "Charlie" or "Delta," especially when this warning level coincided with optimal meteorological conditions for a biological warfare attack from the standpoint of those behind it. Thus, masks should be worn when the intelligence warning levels are "Charlie or higher" and, when simultaneously, there were cool cloudy overcast days or cool nights, when a temperature inversion was likely. The N-95 masks are much less cumbersome, restrictive, and uncomfortable than the rubberized gas masks now issued.

The masks normally worn by military personnel are restrictive and expensive, costing anywhere from $170 to $210 or more each. However, a normal $20 painter's filter mask (N-95) can filter out one- to five-micron-diameter biological particles, the kind that is most dangerous and likely to stick when breathed into the lungs.

It would also greatly aid the ability of our Combatant Commands to provide passive defense against CBRN attacks if the science were better understood in several areas where currently some uncertainty exists. One such area for further research is in understanding the evaporation and neutralization rates of toxic chemical and biological agents in different environments. Another area where better understanding could improve passive defense is research in the effects on personnel of lower levels of chemical toxicity than we have previously investigated. A third area where the payoff for passive defense might be very high is research that throws light on the validity for humans of animal testing of chemical and biological agents antidotes and vaccines. A fourth area recommended for closer research investigation is further analysis of the mechanisms by which disease spreads or chemical agents work in the body in order to design appropriate doses of antidotes and other medications.[29] These four S&T research projects, if successful, can help the Departments of Defense and Homeland Security provide more effective passive defense protection to the war fighter, emergency responder communities, and to victims of CBRN attacks.

# Consequence Management

## Maximum Consequence Management

The ideal consequence management capability to cope with CBRN warfare will provide the means of avoiding, decontaminating, and reconstituting operations after such an attack. This ideal reconstitution of a fighting force can be facilitated first by understanding the likely persistence of a toxic CBRN environment. Once the "science" is understood, effective counter-CBRN concepts of operation can be implemented by applying the best and most appropriate tactics, techniques, and procedures (TTPs) to avoid, eliminate, and work around the toxic hazards.

Cleanup of contaminated areas in an ideal system will be conducted by spraying areas with markers that turn color or provide other physical indicators of agent activity when brought in contact with CBRN agent contamination. Then, in the ideal consequence management system, all contaminated personnel, equipment, and areas could be detoxified by applying available, effective, but benign decontamination agents that can completely neutralize the CBRN agents without harming the personnel or equipment being treated.

Further, the ideal consequence management program will have worked out a system for dealing with contaminated aircraft, ships, and other equipment both for decontamination and for isolation and reconstitution. Landing and basing of such assets and procedures for cleaning and recertifying them for renewed use would be worked out in agreements previously articulated to the satisfaction of U.S. and allied governments to facilitate operations in a CBRN theater. Standards would also have to be agreed upon that define minimal standards of how clean the equipment or personnel have to be before they could be admitted on the soil of receiving states or before they could be returned to action. The answer to the "how clean is clean?" question must both protect those dealing with the contaminated persons and equipment and must also not be set so impossibly high that it paralyzes the nation's war-fighting capability.

Moreover, it needs to be addressed well in advance of the conflict so as to facilitate timely and appropriate contingency planning and actions and to avoid nasty show stopping surprises in the middle of a war.

## Progress and Shortfalls in Consequence Management

If, despite our best efforts, an enemy succeeds in inflicting damage through CBRN attacks, it then falls to U.S. (and allied) forces to clean up the target area, resurrect the damaged capability, bind up the wounds of casualties, and bury the dead. Consequences must be managed to limit the damage, reconstitute the force, and keep U.S. and allied operations up and running so as to continue to carry the fight to the enemy.

How much better prepared are we now to manage consequences of CBRN strikes than we were in 1993? What shortfalls remain? Progress in consequence management has been made on several fronts. First, the United States and its allies are somewhat improved in the areas of passive defense, active defense, and counterforce so that against the same level of CBRN attack as could have been launched 13 years ago, there should be fewer consequences to cope with than was the case then. On the other hand, the CBRN threat likely has grown along with U.S. consequence management countermeasures, so that despite U.S. improvements in organization, training, and equipment, we are still falling short of an adequate response capability to CBRN weapons attacks.

Nevertheless, there have been major improvements in our appreciation of the danger of CBRN attacks in the wake of (1) repeated al-Qaeda attacks over the last decade, (2) the October 4 to November 21, 2001, anthrax letter deliveries,[30] and (3) the October 2001 major cyber attack that cost the United States $3 billion in repairs.

This heightened appreciation of CBRN dangers has led both the administrations of President William Clinton and President George W. Bush to issue strong new policy and guidance to the U.S. armed services and to domestic emergency responders to prepare better for consequence management of CBRN attack contingencies both abroad and within the continental United States. Consequence management of CBRN attack effects will be the joint responsibility of the Department of Defense and the Department of Homeland Security, with the origin and location of the attack determining who has primary responsibility for response.

As the Bennett/Love chapter on Consequence Management summarizes, the United States has made progress over the past 13 years in expanding the number of laboratories capable of rapidly identifying chemical and biological agents. Efforts have succeeded in improving the U.S. surveillance and detection of biological outbreaks and in differentiating natural from man-initiated events, and a good deal of thought has gone into how to achieve further early warning and in identifying the sources of outbreaks.[31]

Another area of improvement is in understanding and preparing to combat panic and to provide U.S. forces and private citizens effective public affairs guidance during and after a weapon of mass destruction event to reduce the number of worried well flooding hospitals and to improve constructive responses to a serious crisis either at home or in the battle space.[32]

All this is positive. Nevertheless, much still needs to be done before consequence management preparations can be considered adequate. Since 1993, despite an increased concern about weapons of mass destruction effects, only a small amount of study has gone into what kinds of public information procedures will be needed to limit panic and reduce adverse psychological reactions to a CBRN attack. Medical facilities could easily be overwhelmed both in the military's battle space and at home in terrorist scenarios if the worried well were not rapidly sorted out from the "physically impaired" after a weapon of mass destruction strike.

Only in a preliminary way, through several Defense Threat Reduction Agency conferences and workshops, has this problem of controlling adverse behavior of U.S. and allied personnel during a CBRN crisis or attack been addressed. The USAF Biodefense Task Force and the Strategic Integrated Process Team of the Contamination Avoidance at Sea Ports of Debarkation Advanced Concepts and Technology Demonstration (ACTD) have analyzed, brainstormed, and discussed the means of using public announcements, training, and public affairs bulletins to mitigate panic, provide effective information, and squash rumors before they take on a life of their own.[33]

Modest gains have been made in some areas of consequence management since 1993. The Restoration of Operations ACTD made some progress in policies for handling human remains after a CBRN event at an air base, but considerable further mortuary affairs work remains. Organizing U.S. forces and on-scene responders for weapon of mass destruction events has resulted in the creation of the USMC Chem-Bio Incident Response Force, the U.S. Army Tech Escort Units, and 54 U.S. Army Reserve weapons of mass destruction Civil Support Teams in 50 states by 2006. These second-responder units could help restore services and public confidence and restore order in areas affected at home.

Decontamination agents exist to clean up toxic areas, but much additional work needs to be done to create noncaustic decontamination agents that can be immediately applied. No work appears to have been done to develop CBRN markers to identify the contaminated from uncontaminated areas where chemical and biological attacks had occurred in the proximity. Only M8 paper and M9 tape are currently available to be applied by ground-based personnel. It is to be hoped that markers will be developed that would turn color or otherwise give indication when in contact with toxic chemical or biological agents and that could be delivered over wide areas in a timely manner, perhaps by air, to give commanders and their units a rapid appreciation of where chemical or biological toxicity exists and where safe areas are located.

Within the United States, domestic weapons of mass destruction events will be handled first by the Department of Homeland Security, with Federal Emergency Management Agency taking the lead in consequence management and the FBI in crisis management. The Department of Defense will be a supporting rather than the lead department in domestic consequence management activities.

With regard to overseas weapons of mass destruction events, the U.S. Department of State has the formal lead role in U.S. consequence management activities in aiding a foreign government which takes the overall responsibility for directing such efforts. The Department of Defense will be a key supporter of the State Department in such consequence management abroad, especially in airlifting needed equipment and supplies to the areas affected. Given the paucity of resources directly available to the Department of State, it is certain that the Defense Department will play a key role in support since its resources abroad are far more extensive.

As Bennett and Love point out in their chapter, there are spectrums of new threats that neither U.S. forces abroad nor U.S. responders at home have adequate capabilities with which to cope. These include the ability to neutralize so-called fourth generation nerve agents and genetically altered biological agents. Further, in a target-rich environment, it is likely that defensive and consequence management programs will continue to lag far behind the offensive CBRN possibilities available to rogue states and terrorists.

## Counter-CBRN Operations: Suggestions for Combatant Commander Plans

Counter-CBRN Operations will focus on eliminating enemy weapons of mass destruction as early as possible in a conflict, if possible. We must get them before they can get us. Failing that, effective active defenses become paramount. If you cannot eliminate such massive threats before they are launched, it is imperative to intercept them en route. If there are failures in both counterforce and active defense, then survival of one's forces is reliant on effective passive defenses or dependent upon placing units in positions where they are difficult to eliminate. This means staying out of enemy range or dispersing forces, and removing civilians, if possible, from the combat zones.[34]

Preemption versus enemy weapons of mass destruction assets or preventive war launched with the element of surprise is, in most cases, an unrealistic option against such heavily armed opponents. First, as Operation Iraqi Freedom illustrated all too well, the United States and its allies may have unreliable intelligence about the number, type, and location of adversary CBRN weapons. It is difficult to target assets that you lack such intelligence about.

Furthermore, unless preemption works completely, it is likely that enemy weapons of mass destruction retaliation will take place against the U.S. forces by an enemy leader who figures he had better use, rather than lose, such forces to further U.S. attacks. A wounded enemy with weapons of mass destruction could exact a terrible price for a botched U.S. counterforce strike.

A preemption strategy might work in a very few scenarios such as the Israeli strike on Iraq's Osirak nuclear reactor at a time when there was a single unprotected very high-value target and the Iraqis, embroiled in a fierce war with Iran, were not equipped to retaliate. However, facing an opponent with a weapons of mass destruction retaliatory capability is an altogether more dangerous proposition. A better strategy is to rely on the overwhelming U.S. nuclear and conventional deterrents to such action unless one's intelligence is absolutely complete, the counterforce strike is very likely to be successful, and the WMD threat is deemed imminent.[35]

Should a conflict escalate to the use of chemical, biological, or nuclear weapons, despite the best U.S. effort to deter their use, U.S. counter-CBRN military doctrine and CONOPs will be needed to protect U.S. personnel.

Shortfalls in operational plans still exist in such areas as how to conduct resupply and reinforcement using strategic lift assets in contaminated areas where air and sea transports may become toxically coated. Still to be determined is how to recover such aircraft and ships after VX, sarin, or anthrax contamination. Still to be decided is where to take such aircraft and ships for decontamination, what cleanliness standards to set for reemployment of such aircraft, and what criteria to choose for introducing such valuable assets into a CBRN scenario where contamination might lay waste to a very expensive and hard-to-replace aircraft or ship.

The U.S. Combatant Commands are still evaluating how to fight an opponent who may use an array of biological weapons, a type of war the U.S. military has yet to fight in the modern era. Given the potential strategic nature of biological weapons, this uncertainty is an ominous sign. Indeed, the uncertainties about how to fight a biological war is perhaps the single most serious flaw in U.S. military operational plans at present and needs to be addressed as soon as possible.

In the past decade, the U.S. Air Force has led the way in developing a new Counter-CW (C-CW) concept of operations at air bases to keep aircraft sortie rates high even in the midst of ballistic missile attacks using chemical weapons. The C-CW concept of operations features initial protection of aircraft, crews, and equipment using shelters and coverings, followed by base reconnaissance and split-mission-oriented protective posture operations, where the amount of protection adopted depends on the amount and locations of chemicals. One favorable factor was the discovery that blister and nerve agents are rapidly absorbed by the asphalt and concrete of runways. TTPs for handling potential hazards and risk evaluation decision tools for commanders promise to keep most U.S. attack aircraft in the air despite the base being "slimed."

As previously discussed in great detail, the air force is now working on a counterbiological concept of operations element to augment its C-CW concept of operations. Eventually, this will be augmented by a counterradiological concept of operations element, a counternuclear concept of operations element, and perhaps a counter-high-yield explosive CONOPs element so that an overall Counter-CBRNE concept of operations will provide guidance to commanders if faced with such threats. This goal will be difficult to achieve should an enemy use a combination of, say, both chemical and biological weapons in the same campaign, since the concept of operations for each may differ or even be opposed to each other in some scenarios.

Finally, in the event of another campaign along the lines of Operation Iraqi Freedom, where U.S. forces clash with an adversary armed with chemical, biological, radiological, or nuclear weapons, U.S. forces have to be organized, trained, and equipped for the WMD elimination mission. WMD elimination should not be an ad hoc "pickup game," but must be institutionalized in our deliberate planning.

U.S. forces must be able to systematically and comprehensively remove an adversary state's CBRN programs by eliminating its capacity to do CBRN-related research, production, testing, storage, deployment, or use of such weapons in the foreseeable future. As one recent study summarized,

> Conceptually, WMD elimination may be divided into three main tasks. Exploitation refers to locating, characterizing, and securing and functionally defeating an adversary's WMD sites, documentation, personnel, and materials. Forensic evidence is developed as necessary. Destruction refers to rendering safe, dismantling, destroying, removing, or otherwise safely and verifiably disposing of weapons, materials, equipment, and infrastructure. Monitoring and redirection are intended to prevent the WMD threat from reconstituting, including the "conversion" of WMD activities and personnel. These tasks may be sequential for specific WMD sites but are likely to be simultaneous for larger WMD programs. Planning should reflect this, especially because each of the tasks requires some unique capabilities in terms of skill sets and expertise, equipment, and so forth.[36]

## Counter-CBRN Planning, Education, Training, and Exercises

In the years since Secretary Aspin launched the DoD Counterproliferation Initiative there has been some substantial progress in the way that the Department of Defense and the military services have organized themselves to make decisions on Counter-CBRN issues and programs. Note the reformation in the DoD Chemical and Biological Defense Program that took place from 1996 to 2001 and that serves DoD today. (See Appendix C on page 349.)

In addition, the air force, in 1997, issued a service-wide Counterproliferation Master Plan that set out objectives and called for initiatives to improve USAF counterproliferation capabilities. Among these,

> in the area of passive defense, the Master Plan called for a continuing process of scientific research, operational analysis and capability improvements with the following objectives:
>
> • Improve technical and scientific knowledge of chemical/ biological agent behavior.
>
> • Identify and assess the operational implications of CBRNE attacks with enough precision to understand and quantify their effects on operations.
>
> • Develop and implement USAF policy, doctrine and guidance governing actions to counter the effects of CBRNE attacks.[37]

Other services would be wise to develop their own C-CBRNE master plans and road maps based on this USAF model. In both the USAF Master Plan and the USAF Counter-CBRNE Road Map, the Chief of Staff of the Air Force has required that USAF education, training, and exercises be designed to prepare every airman with the kind of understanding of CBRNE threats and countermeasures that will allow him/her to survive, operate, and win in conflicts where such weapons are available to the adversary. Such Counter-CBRNE education, training, and exercises must be realistic and appropriate to the kinds of career paths each airman takes, at each step during his/her time in the service from when he/she joins to the time he/she separates.

In the professional military education (PME) of U.S. military officers on these Counter-CBRN topics, several PME institutions have taken the lead. The Army Chemical School produces first-rate technical experts in dealing with countering CBRN threats. The Air University, particularly the Air War College in combination with the USAF Counterproliferation Center staff, has provided the most extensive number of elective courses on the subject. Other leading institutions that have specialized courses in this field are National Defense University in combination with their WMD Studies Center and the Naval Post-Graduate School. Several other PME schools have a course or two each on Counter-CBRNE issues, but much work needs to be done to educate, train, and exercise military officers of all ranks on the threats these potent weapons pose and best practices for countering them in future conflicts.

## International CP Cooperation

### Ideal International Counterproliferation Program

In the optimal coalition situation, each unit in the coalition will be equipped fully with the same quality and quantity of IPE, the same collective protective shelters, the same quantity and quality of medicines and vaccines, and have the same high-quality sensors to alert them of contamination and incoming attacks sufficient to warn them in time to don protective equipment and take adequate protective shelter. Each element of the coalition will fall within the protective umbrella of effective and multilayered or multishot missile and aircraft defenses. Further, each element of the coalition will have sufficient counterforce capability and dedicated persistent overhead intelligence, surveillance, and reconnaissance assets to rapidly degrade the launchers and missiles that could threaten CBRN attacks upon them. Finally, each unit in the coalition should possess skilled first and second responders, and other well-equipped and practiced consequence management capabilities against the most likely CBRN threats. The entire coalition should be thoroughly trained in specific counter-CBRN concepts of operations for continuing military operations on land, sea, and air during a conflict, including frequent training in such concept of operations and tactics, techniques, and procedures to sustain operations and accomplish the mission. The entire coalition should also have an integrated command and control structure, should be organized, trained, and equipped for CBRN warfare to a common standard, and employ a common military doctrine and operational war plan for conducting military operations in a CBRN environment.

### Progress and Shortfalls in International Cooperation

Unfortunately, only some grudging progress has been made to get allied states involved and taking steps to counter CBRN threats to their forces and societies but, to date, there has been far more talk than action by most. The NATO states' leaders with one exception (the United Kingdom) either do not appear to believe the weapons of mass destruction threat is imminent or do not want to confront the economic costs of serious preparations against such a threat. They are slowly investing in one missile defense system, the Medium Extended Range Air Defense System, but overall progress in counterproliferation organization, training, and equipping is slow or virtually nonexistent.

The same is true of Japan and Arab states in the Persian Gulf. For example, there have been numerous annual meetings of the Cooperative Defense Initiative group, including the United States and the Arab states of the Gulf, but the physical progress toward either a counterforce, active defense, passive defense, or good consequence management capability is very much more theory than accomplished fact. At least it is a topic for consideration of the military leaders of those allied countries and regularly scheduled meetings on the topic are held, but the political will and budgeting does not currently exist to translate these talks into much concrete action. It is as if each such ally is deciding to let the United States provide the defense, or they are waiting for a weapons of mass destruction disaster before they will be willing to act seriously.

Unfortunately, if Counter-CBRN preparations by the United States over the last decade are still inadequate, they still far exceed the C-CBRN efforts of U.S. allies, with the exception of the United Kingdom and Israel. Among U.S. allies, only Israel has erected its own independent active defenses against ballistic missiles. Israel, the exception to the rule, depends on its terminal-phase Arrow theater ballistic missile defense program, as well as, in some crises, the U.S. Patriot-3 batteries for protection, but even this tandem of missile defenses offers only a partial answer to such threats. Israel also has a serious vaccination program in place and has created programs to give it a practiced passive defense and consequence management capability should enemies attack it with either chemical or biological weapons. Israel also has a serious aircraft-based counterforce capability and has in the past been willing to preempt adversary positions and assets in their ongoing conflict with Palestinian Arabs and adjacent Arab states. For example, Menachem Begin ordered the destruction of the Iraqi Osirak nuclear reactor in June 1981 to prevent Saddam Hussein from developing Iraqi nuclear arms that might have otherwise been used later against Israel.

Japan has just agreed to participate in a bilateral effort to develop theater missile defense systems to offset the North Korean No Dong threat and possible future Chinese missile threats as well. The U.S. allies in Europe have been working with the United States in a joint program to develop the Missile Extended Air Defense System to provide a mobile defensive bubble over allied ground troops moving in wartime within enemy missile range. The Missile Extended Air Defense System is a terminal phase interceptor, as is the Israeli Arrow interceptor. Only the United States is funding R&D work on more extended range (midcourse, post-boost, or boost phase) interceptors such as the Terminal High Altitude Air Defense, the Navy Wide Area Missile Defense, or the Airborne Laser programs.

States such as the Republic of Korea, our Persian Gulf Arab allies, our NATO allies, Japan, and others have very weak passive defense programs lacking in adequate quantities or quality of protective masks, suits, collective protective shelters, decontamination capabilities, vaccines, inoculated personnel, and prepositioned medical supplies and equipment. Only the Israelis and the British forces have adequate vaccine inoculation preparations against possible future biological attacks by adversaries armed with anthrax and smallpox.

U.S. Central Command has worked with U.S. Arab state allies in the Persian Gulf to better prepare them against chemical and biological warfare and chemical and biological terrorist threats. That is the mission of the Cooperative Defense Initiative program, whereby top military leaders from these states have met with top U.S. experts over the past four years on cooperative chemical and biological defense preparations and training.

Similarly, the U.S. Central Command has held a series of Desert Breeze tabletop exercises on how to fight a chemical and biological war in the Gulf, involving the U.S. Central Command Combatant Commander and his planning staff. A similar series of exercises is run by the U.S. Pacific Command Combatant Commander and his staff, titled Coral Breeze, to analyze how to best cope with an adversary such as North Korea that is armed with chemical and biological weapons. These Combatant Commander exercises take into account the state of counter-CBRN readiness of allies in each region, and lessons learned are reviewed and shared with our coalition partners.

One of the serious deficiencies in U.S. and allied defenses against CBRN attacks is the fact that allied military forces are so much more vulnerable to chemical or biological attacks that U.S. forces may find themselves fighting with partners whose military prowess is greatly diminished after such an attack. Allied forces may be very impaired by such chemical and biological warfare scenarios and this, in turn, creates greater danger for U.S. forces.

Further, U.S. forces may become hamstrung if host nation or third-party nationals who work the air bases and ports feel unprotected and refuse to stay and perform their jobs if CBRN weapons are threatened or used by an adversary. This is especially true if such base or port workers have to worry about protecting and/or evacuating families from the danger zones. This problem will be exacerbated if enemy military or terrorist organizations were to target TICs and TIMs in the area of U.S. and allied ports or air bases. The end result might be the same as or worse than if the enemy fired a ballistic missile armed with chemical weapons at the port or air base.

Panic control measures need to be provided to keep host nation and third-party national workers from bolting and abandoning their support roles at these bases and ports in wartime. Precrisis or prewar training and education can solve some of these problems and alleviate unrealistic fears. Excellent command and control procedures coupled with first-rate communications from trusted authorities can cut panic, as can the rapid treatment and removal from sight of dead and wounded. Assignments of specific crisis jobs and protective responses can cut both real and psychological casualties. Also, each key worker needs some basic protection equipment, both individual protective equipment and collective protection shelters. Workers also need to be assured of emergency medical help and should be acquainted with emergency response procedures learned in prewar/precrisis drills. At key foreign ports of entry (seaports of debarkation), the U.S. military and civilian authorities need to have negotiated agreements with host nations for how to administer the port in wartime. They need to agree on the conditions for replacing indigenous or third-party national workers if necessary. Also, sectors of the port should be designated beforehand for use by the combatant forces in unloading equipment, supplies, and personnel. Berths should be assigned for docking military supply ships. Key port and air-base personnel should have dispersed housing, not collocated at the port or air base, and be provided toxic-free shelters near the work area as well as dependable transportation in the event of a CBRN attack or alarm.

Collective coalition plans for protecting all coalition units from CBRN strikes, both by properly equipping and training allied forces that are to fight shoulder to shoulder with U.S. personnel, and by protecting the civilian work forces at key bases and ports, will be essential when facing CBRN-armed opponents. Otherwise, U.S. forces may lack the allied support required for victory against a rogue state military using weapons capable of inflicting mass destruction, disruption, and casualties.

## Summary of the CP Program Progress and Shortfalls
### Areas for Capability Enhancement (ACEs)

Each year for most of the past decade, the U.S. Counterproliferation Program Review Committee produces an Annual Report to Congress and the Executive Branch where it lays out, in priority order, the areas identified by the Department of Energy, the Department of Defense, and the U.S. Intelligence Community that most need improvement in the coming years. These items are called "Areas for Capability Enhancement" or ACEs.

Unfortunately, progress has been slow in important counterproliferation areas and few ACEs have been solved and dropped from the list in the past decade. It is instructive to look at what the Department of

Defense (DoD), Department of Energy (DOE), and the Intelligence Community (IC) all believe are the most important areas for capability enhancement. Note the priorities in Table 12.1 each of the three have assigned to the following U.S. counterproliferation needs.[38]

Obviously each department, agency, or command has a different set of priorities for enhancing U.S. counterproliferation capabilities depending on its own unique missions. Note, for example, the combined ACE priorities of the U.S. Combatant Commanders[39] as shown in Table 12.2.[40]

Despite many progressive steps, much more obviously still needs to be done to provide an adequate U.S. defense against CBRN weapons at home and abroad. Funds are still limited within the U.S. defense budget for passive defenses against CBRN attacks, roughly $1 billion per year as opposed to roughly $10 billion spent in FY 2004 for ballistic missile defenses. Clearly, the U.S. military needs to prioritize better in how it allocates defense funding to U.S. counterproliferation programs.

Some suggest that the relatively slow pace of solving major CBRN threat problems could be partially cured by putting a "czar" over all counterproliferation programs, with an integrated budget and authority, enabling him or her to establish better priorities between the different program elements or pillars. This would create greater coherence among the various units needed to execute, for example, the Scud hunt problem. A single counterproliferation czar would also provide leadership needed to address neglected programs such as cruise missile defense and could be held responsible for successes or failures for a program that, today, either finds no one in charge or too many trying to lead at once with the result that there is not sufficient unity of effort.

Despite key shortfalls in the U.S. counterproliferation effort there is still some consolation in the fact that the sum is greater than its various less-than impressive parts. For the most part, U.S. nonproliferation and counterproliferation policies have, up to now, been sufficient to prevent almost all chemical, biological, radiological, and nuclear attacks on its forces, allies, and population with the exception of the anthrax-mail attacks of October and November 2001 that killed five individuals, caused 22 total casualties, and caused major disruptions on Capitol Hill and elsewhere.

Some consolation can be drawn from the fact that the very great majority of the over 190 countries in the world have neither used nor acquired CBRN weapons. It is only a handful of states that persist in pursuing such mass effects weapons, as well as several terrorist organizations such as al-Qaeda. On the whole, U.S. and international efforts to erect arms control and nonproliferation treaty regimes such as the Non-Proliferation Treaty, Chemical Weapons Convention, and Biological Weapons Convention, augmented by a series of export control regimes like the Missile Technology Control Regime, Australia Group, and two nuclear suppliers control

**Table 12.1**   Areas for Capability Enhancement (ACEs)

| DoD | DOE | IC | ACEs |
|---|---|---|---|
| 1 | | 1 | Timely collection, analysis, and dissemination of strategic, operational, and tactical level actionable intelligence to support CP and CT. |
| 2 | | 2 | Detection, identification, characterization, location, prediction, and warning of traditional and nontraditional CW and BW agents (including medical surveillance). |
| 3 | | 3 | Defense against, and detection, characterization and defeat of paramilitary, covert delivery, and terrorist WMD capabilities (including protection of critical CONUS and OCONUS installations). |
| 4 | 2 | 5 | Detection, location, and tracking of WMD/M and related materials, components, and key personnel. |
| 5 | | 7 | Support for maritime, air, ground WMD/M interdiction, including special operations. |
| 6 | | | Enable sustained operations in a WMD environment through decontamination, and individual and collective protection. |
| 7 | | | Medical protection, training, diagnosis, treatment, and countermeasures against NBC agents, to include surge manufacturing capability and stockpile availability of vaccines, pretreatments, therapeutics, and other medical products. |
| 8 | | 9 | Ballistic and cruise missile active defense. |
| 9 | | | Consequence management in response to use of WMD (including civil support in response to domestic WMD contingencies). |
| 10 | | 6 | Target planning for WMD/M targets. |
| 11 | 3 | 4 | Detection, location, characterization, defeat, and elimination of WMD/M weapons and related facilities while minimizing collateral effects. |
| 12 | | 8 | Detection, location, characterization, and defeat of HDBTs while minimizing collateral effects. |
| 13 | | 10 | Prompt mobile detection and defeat. |
| 14 | 1 | | Protection of WMD/M and WMD/M-related materials and components. |
| 15 | 5 | 11 | Support to export control activities of the U.S. Government. |
| 16 | 4 | 12 | Support to inspection and monitoring activities of arms control agreements and regimes and other nonproliferation initiatives. |

**Table 12.2** Combatant Commander Prioritized Counterproliferation Requirements

| Rank | Counterproliferation Requirement |
|:---:|---|
| 1 | Timely collection, analysis, and dissemination of Strategic, Operational, and Tactical level actionable intelligence to support counterproliferation and counterterrorism. |
| 2 | Detection, identification, characterization, location, prediction, and warning of CW and BW agents. |
| 3 | Enable sustained operation in a WMD environment through decontamination, and individual and collective protection. |
| 4 | Medical protection, training, diagnosis, treatment, surveillance, and countermeasures against NBC agents, to include surge manufacturing capability and stockpile availability of vaccines, pretreatments, therapeutics, and other medical products. |
| 5 | Support for Special Operations including WMD/M interdiction. |
| 6 | Defense against, and detection, characterization, and defeat of paramilitary, covert delivery, and terrorist WMD capabilities (including protection of critical CONUS and OCONUS installations). |
| 7 | Ballistic and cruise missile active defense. |
| 8 | Consequence management in response to use of WMD (including civil support in response to domestic WMD contingencies). |
| 9 | Detection, location, and tracking of WMD/M and related materials, components, and key personnel. |
| 10 | Target planning for WMD/M targets. |
| 11 | Detection, location, characterization, defeat, and elimination of WMD/M, NBC/M, and related facilities while minimizing collateral effects. |
| 12 | Detection, location, characterization, and defeat of HDBT while minimizing collateral effects. |
| 13 | Prompt mobile target detection and defeat. |
| 14 | Protection of WMD/M and WMD/M-related materials and components. |
| 15 | Support to export control activities of the U.S. Government. |
| 16 | Support to inspection and monitoring activities of arms control agreements and regimes and other nonproliferation initiatives. |

groups, have kept the weapons of mass destruction genie in the bottle with just a few important exceptions.

Treaties and export control regimes have been augmented recently by more than 60 states that have joined together in the Proliferation Security Initiative (PSI) to intercept dangerous shipments of missiles, CBRN weapons, CBRN agents, dual-use technologies, equipment, and components to prevent their transfer to other hostile hands. These programs have also been augmented by strong "carrot and stick" diplomacy to facilitate rollbacks in CBRN programs in places such as Libya, South Africa, Ukraine, Belarus, and Kazakhstan.

Further, the U.S.–former Soviet Union Cooperative Threat Reduction Program has achieved considerable success in destroying surplus nuclear, biological, chemical, and associated missile capabilities and in helping to secure fissile material in storage in Russia, Ukraine, and Kazakhstan. Efforts have begun to give alternative employment to scientist weaponeers and to secure existing nuclear, biological, and chemical assets.

This mix of nonproliferation policies, agreements, and programs is one solution to the weapons of mass destruction problem by helping to prevent the spread of these assets to adversaries. However, what treaties, export controls, diplomacy, the Proliferation Security Initiative, and the Cooperative Threat Reduction programs cannot do to dissuade states and groups from CBRN programs and use, U.S. and allied military countermeasures must contain.

Most rogue state leaders, even if they choose to pursue such CBRN capabilities, will likely be deterred from using such mass effects weapons by the U.S. and allied capability and threats to inflict a massive retaliatory attack on any aggressor state. Further, U.S. and allied preparations in counterforce targeting, active and passive defenses, and in consequence management all are likely to persuade any knowledgeable and rational enemy leader that our forces should be able to fight better in a CBRN environment than can their own personnel. This fact, if properly communicated and understood, should make a rational and informed enemy leader hesitate in launching the dogs of a CBRN war.

In conclusion, there are many shortfalls and deficiencies in U.S. and allied counterproliferation readiness and war-fighting capability. Nevertheless, even mediocre capabilities in each area of the counterproliferation program, when combined, can serve as an important safety net against unconventional and asymmetrical attacks. If the cords of such a safety net were made up of a single strand of thread, it is likely to break under pressure. But when many such strands are woven together, the net can provide strength and security. Such, too, is the U.S. and allied counterproliferation safety net. When all elements, "all 8 Ds" of counterproliferation work in tandem (disarmament, diplomacy, defusing, dissuasion, denial, deterrence, defense, and destruction), the whole effort is synergistic and can be greater than the sum of its parts.

This is not to say that the U.S. Government and its key allies can afford to rest and neglect the strands that make up this safety net. It would take only one CBRN war to wreak havoc on us. The United States and its allies can ill afford to be the unready confronting the unthinkable. In this era when even poor countries, small groups, or a few individuals now could possess and use weapons of mass destruction, inflict mass casualties, and cause mass disruption, all efforts must be made to mobilize the best minds and capabilities to meet and defeat the challenge of adversaries with CBRN weapons. To do less is to court a disaster unlike in its dimensions and scope anything we have ever previously suffered. Time and the momentum of events are not on our side. A maximum counterproliferation effort is needed in this second decade of the integrated counterproliferation program and even that might not be enough to protect us from the coming WMD storm.

# "The Counterproliferation Initiative"

## Remarks by Honorable Les Aspin Secretary of Defense[1]

*National Academy of Sciences
Committee on International Security
and Arms Control
December 7, 1993*

Thank you very much, Dr. Alberts, and thank all of you for coming this morning. I'm particularly pleased to be able to talk about this important topic before this audience because I know many of you have thought about this. It's something that's going to take all our best efforts.

The national security requirements of the United States have undergone fundamental change in just a few short years. We won the Cold War. The Soviet threat that dominated our strategy, doctrine, weapons acquisition and force structure for so long is gone. With it has gone the threat of global war. But history did not end with that victory, and neither did threats to the United States, its people and its interests.

As part of the Bottom Up Review we began to think seriously about what threats we really faced in this new era. We came up with four chief threats to the United States. First, a new danger posed by the increased threat of proliferation of nuclear weapons and other weapons of mass destruction. Second, regional dangers posed by the threat of aggression by powers such as Saddam Hussein's Iraq. Third, the danger that democratic and market reforms will fail in the former Soviet Union, Eastern Europe and elsewhere. And finally, we recognize an economic danger to our national security. In the short run our security is protected by a strong military, but in the long run it will be protected by a strong economy.

Of these dangers, the one that most urgently and directly threatens America at home and American interests abroad is the new nuclear danger. The old nuclear danger we faced was thousands of warheads in the Soviet Union. The new nuclear danger we face is perhaps a handful of nuclear devices in the hands of rogue states or even terrorist groups. The engine of this new danger is proliferation.

Let us recall briefly how we dealt with the old nuclear danger— the nuclear danger of the Cold War era. We had three approaches— deterrence, arms control and a nonproliferation policy based on prevention. They worked.

Our policy of deterrence was aimed primarily at the Soviet Union. Our aim was to guarantee by the structure and disposition of our own nuclear forces that a nuclear attack on the United States or its allies would bring no profit, and thus deter it.

We sought to stabilize these arsenals through arms control and eventually to shrink them through arms reduction. Our nonproliferation policy was aimed at preventing the spread of nuclear weapons by persuading most nations not to go nuclear, and denying the materials and know-how to make bombs to those who pursued them. And in fact, these weapons did not spread as quickly as many suggested.

But that was then and this is now. And now we face the potential of a greatly increased proliferation problem. This increase is the product of two new developments. The first arises from the break-up of the former Soviet Union. The second concerns the nature of technology diffusion in this new era. Each of these developments profoundly changes the nature of the proliferation problem.

Let's look at the former Soviet Union. The continued existence of the former Soviet Union's arsenal amidst revolutionary change gives rise to four potential proliferation problems.

First, and most obvious, is that nuclear weapons are now deployed on the territory of four states. Before, there was one. The safe and secure transport and dismantlement of these weapons is one of the U.S. Government's highest priorities.

Second, we have the potential for what I call "loose nukes." In a time of profound transition in the former Soviet Union, it is possible that nuclear weapons, or the material or technology to make them could find their way to a nuclear black market.

Third, nuclear and other weapons expertise for hire could go to would-be proliferators.

Fourth, whatever restraint the former Soviet Union exercised over its client states with nuclear ambitions, such as North Korea, is much diminished. Regional power balances have been disrupted and old ethnic conflicts have re-emerged.

The other new development that exacerbates today's proliferation problem is a by-product of growth in world trade and the rising tide of technology everywhere.

The world economy today is characterized by an ever increasing volume of trade leading to ever greater diffusion of technology. Simply put, this will make it harder and harder to detect illicit diversions of materials and technology useful for weapons development.

Moreover, many potential aggressors no longer have to import all the sophisticated technology they need. They are "growing" it at home. The growth of indigenous technology can completely change the nonproliferation equation.

Potential proliferators are sometimes said to be "several decades behind the West." This is not much comfort. If a would-be nuclear nation is four decades behind in 1993 then it is at the same technological level as the United States was in 1953. By 1953, the United States had fission weapons. We were building intercontinental range bombers and were developing intercontinental missiles.

Realize, too, that most of the thermonuclear weapons in the United States arsenal today were designed in the 1960s using computers that were then known as "super computers." These same "super computers" are no more powerful than today's laptop personal computers that you can pick up at the store or order through the catalog.

These new developments tell us a couple of very important things. The first, of course, is that we face a bigger proliferation danger than we've ever faced before. But second, and most important, is that a policy of prevention through denial won't be enough to cope with the potential of tomorrow's proliferators.

In concrete terms, here is where we stand today. More than a score of countries—many of them hostile to the United States, our friends and our allies—have now or are developing nuclear, biological and/or chemical weapons—and the means to deliver them. More than 12 countries have operational ballistic missiles and others have programs to develop them.

Weapons of mass destruction may directly threaten our forces in the field, and in a more subtle way threaten the effective use of those forces. In some ways, in fact, the role of nuclear weapons in the U.S. scheme of things has completely changed.

During the Cold War, our principal adversary had conventional forces in Europe that were numerically superior. For us, nuclear weapons were the equalizer. The threat to use them was present and was used to compensate for our smaller numbers of conventional forces. Today, nuclear weapons can still be the equalizer against superior conventional forces.

But today it is the United States that has unmatched conventional military power, and it is our potential adversaries who may attain nuclear weapons. We're the ones who could wind up being the equalizee.

And it's not just nuclear weapons. All the potential threat nations are at least capable of producing biological and chemical agents. They might not have usable weapons yet, and they might not use them if they do. But our commanders will have to assume that U.S. forces are threatened. So the threat is real and it is upon us today. President Clinton directed the world's attention to it in his speech to the United Nations General Assembly in September. He said, "One of our most urgent priorities must be attacking the proliferation of weapons of mass destruction, whether they are nuclear, chemical, or biological; and the ballistic missiles that can rain them down on populations hundreds of miles away … If we do not stem the proliferation of the world's deadliest weapons, no democracy can feel secure."

To respond to the President, we have created the Defense Counterproliferation Initiative. With this initiative, we are making the essential change demanded by this increased threat. We are adding the task of protection to the task of prevention.

In past administrations, the emphasis was on prevention. The policy of nonproliferation combined global diplomacy and regional security efforts with the denial of material and know-how to would-be proliferators. Prevention remains our pre-eminent goal. In North Korea, for example, our goals are still a non-nuclear peninsula and a strong nonproliferation regime.

The Defense Counterproliferation Initiative in no way means we will lessen our nonproliferation efforts. In fact, DoD's work will strengthen prevention. What the Defense Counterproliferation Initiative recognizes, however, is that proliferation may still occur. Thus, we are adding protection as a major policy goal.

The chart shows how the two—prevention and protection—combine to make a complete attack on the problem. On the left, we have the policy instruments for prevention. On the right are the steps we take to protect if proliferation occurs. What's new is the emphasis on the right side of the chart where the Defense Department has a special responsibility.

At the heart of the Defense Counterproliferation Initiative, therefore, is a drive to develop new military capabilities to deal with this new threat. It has five elements: One, creation of the new mission by the President; two, changing what we buy to meet the threat; three, planning to fight wars differently; four, changing how we collect intelligence and what intelligence we collect; and finally, five, doing all these things with our allies.

Let's look at each in turn.

First point; new mission. President Clinton not only recognized the danger of the new threat, he gave us this new mission to cope with it. We have issued defense planning guidance to the services to make sure everyone understands what the President wants. I have organized my own staff to reflect the importance of the new mission with the new position of Assistant Secretary of Defense for Nuclear Security and Counterproliferation.

Second point; what we buy. We are reviewing all relevant programs to see what we can do better. For example, we're looking at improved non-nuclear penetrating munitions to deal with underground installations. Saddam Hussein, you'll recall, was building a lot of underground refuges because normal structures were totally vulnerable to our precision air strikes. We cannot let future Saddams escape attack. We're also working hard on better ways to hunt mobile missiles after our difficulties in finding Scuds during the Gulf War. And of course, we have reoriented the Strategic Defense Initiative into the Ballistic Missile Defense Organization so that it concentrates on responding to theater ballistic missile threats that are here today.

We've also proposed a clarification in the ABM Treaty. It would allow us to develop and test a theater missile defense system to meet a real threat without undermining an important agreement. This is an essential element of our counterproliferation strategy.

Third point; how we fight wars. We are developing guidance for dealing with this new threat. We have directed the services to tell us how prepared they are for it. The Chairman of the Joint Chiefs of Staff and our regional commanders in chief—our CINCs—are developing a military planning process for dealing with adversaries who have weapons of mass destruction.

And our concerns are by no means limited to the nuclear threat. We have a new Joint Office to oversee all DoD biological defense programs. This is the first time the department has organized its collective expertise to deal with the tough biological defense problems we face.

Fourth point; intelligence. After the war with Iraq, we discovered that Saddam Hussein had a much more extensive nuclear weapons program going than we knew. Moreover, we learned during the war that we had failed to destroy his biological and chemical warfare efforts. We do not want to be caught like that again, so we are working to improve our counterproliferation intelligence.

As a first step, we are pursuing an arrangement with the director of central intelligence to establish a new deputy director for military support in the Intelligence Community's Nonproliferation Center. And we're tripling the number of Defense Department experts assigned to the center. We're looking for intelligence that is useful militarily, not only diplomatically.

Fifth point; international cooperation. Our allies and security partners around the world have as much to be concerned about as we do. We have tabled an initiative with NATO to increase alliance efforts against proliferation of weapons of mass destruction.

We are also cooperating actively with the Japanese on deployment of theater missile defense systems there, and possibly on developing such systems together.

We are paying special attention to the dangerous potential problem of weapons and nuclear material proliferating from the Soviet Union. Under the Nunn-Lugar program, we are helping Russia, Belarus, Ukraine and Kazakhstan with the safe and secure dismantling of their nuclear weapons. And we're helping them improve the security of fissile material in both weapons and civilian nuclear facilities by helping them set up material control and accounting systems.

We are even including Russia in our attempt to reshape export controls on sensitive technology. The control system used to be aimed at the Eastern Bloc. Now we are incorporating former Eastern Bloc countries in our efforts to impede would-be proliferators. The Defense Department can play a constructive role in balancing economics and security here. In this effort, we have been guided by the excellent work conducted by the National Academy of Sciences.

To sum up, we've undertaken a new mission. For many years we planned to counter the weapons of mass destruction of the former Soviet Union. Now, we've recognized a new problem and we're acting to meet it with counterproliferation. At the same time, our initiative complements nonproliferation in three important ways. It promotes consensus on the gravity of the threat, helping to maintain the international nonproliferation effort. It reduces the military utility of weapons of mass destruction, while nonproliferation keeps up the price, making them less attractive to the proliferator. And it reduces the vulnerability of the neighbors of those holding these weapons, further reducing the motive to acquire them in self-defense.

We are in a new era. We have released our Bottom Up Review that provided a blueprint for our conventional forces for the years ahead. Our Defense Counterproliferation Initiative will allow us to deal with the number one threat identified in the BUR, and it will help provide the real strength America needs to meet the dangers we face. The public expects nothing less from its Department of Defense than the right responses to the new world.

Thank you.

APPENDIX **B**

# National Strategy to Combat Weapons of Mass Destruction[1]
## December 2002

The gravest danger our Nation faces lies at the crossroads of radicalism and technology. Our enemies have openly declared that they are seeking weapons of mass destruction, and evidence indicates that they are doing so with determination. The United States will not allow these efforts to succeed. … History will judge harshly those who saw this coming danger but failed to act. In the new world we have entered, the only path to peace and security is the path of action.

—President Bush
The National Security Strategy of the United States of America
September 17, 2002

## Introduction

Weapons of mass destruction (WMD)—nuclear, biological, and chemical—in the possession of hostile states and terrorists represent one of the greatest security challenges facing the United States. We must pursue a comprehensive strategy to counter this threat in all of its dimensions.

An effective strategy for countering WMD, including their use and further proliferation, is an integral component of the National Security Strategy of the United States of America. As with the war on terrorism, our strategy for homeland security, and our new concept of deterrence, the U.S. approach to combat WMD represents a fundamental change from the past. To succeed, we must take full advantage of today's opportunities, including the application of new technologies, increased emphasis on intelligence collection and analysis, the strengthening of alliance relationships, and the establishment of new partnerships with former adversaries.

Weapons of mass destruction could enable adversaries to inflict massive harm on the United States, our military forces at home and abroad, and our friends and allies. Some states, including several that have supported and continue to support terrorism, already possess WMD and are seeking even greater capabilities, as tools of coercion and intimidation. For them, these are not weapons of last resort, but militarily useful weapons of choice intended to overcome our nation's advantages in conventional forces and to deter us from responding to aggression against our friends and allies in regions of vital interest. In addition, terrorist groups are seeking to acquire WMD with the stated purpose of killing large numbers of our people and those of friends and allies—without compunction and without warning.

We will not permit the world's most dangerous regimes and terrorists to threaten us with the world's most destructive weapons. We must accord the highest priority to the protection of the United States, our forces, and our friends and allies from the existing and growing WMD threat.

## Pillars of Our National Strategy

Our National Strategy to Combat Weapons of Mass Destruction has three principal pillars:

### 1. Counterproliferation to Combat WMD Use

The possession and increased likelihood of use of WMD by hostile states and terrorists are realities of the contemporary security environment. It is therefore critical that the U.S. military and appropriate civilian agencies be prepared to deter and defend against the full range of possible WMD employment scenarios. We will ensure that all needed capabilities to combat WMD are fully integrated into the emerging defense transformation plan and into our homeland security posture. Counterproliferation will also be fully integrated into the basic doctrine, training, and equipping of all forces, in order to ensure that they can sustain operations to decisively defeat WMD-armed adversaries.

### 2. Strengthened Nonproliferation to Combat WMD Proliferation

The United States, our friends and allies, and the broader international community must undertake every effort to prevent states and terrorists from acquiring WMD and missiles. We must enhance traditional measures diplomacy, arms control, multilateral agreements, threat reduction assistance, and export controls—that seek to dissuade or impede proliferant states and terrorist networks, as well as to slow and make more costly their access to sensitive technologies, material, and expertise. We must ensure compliance with relevant international agreements, including the Nuclear Non-proliferation Treaty (NPT), the Chemical Weapons Convention (CWC), and the Biological and Toxin Weapons Convention (BTWC). The United States will continue to work with other states to improve their capability to prevent unauthorized transfers of WMD and missile technology, expertise, and material. We will identify and pursue new methods of prevention, such as national criminalization of proliferation activities and expanded safety and security measures.

## 3. Consequence Management to Respond to WMD Use

Finally, the United States must be prepared to respond to the use of WMD against our citizens, our military forces, and those of friends and allies. We will develop and maintain the capability to reduce to the extent possible the potentially horrific consequences of WMD attacks at home and abroad.

The three pillars of the U.S. national strategy to combat WMD are seamless elements of a comprehensive approach. Serving to integrate the pillars are four cross-cutting enabling functions that need to be pursued on a priority basis: intelligence collection and analysis on WMD, delivery systems, and related technologies; research and development to improve our ability to respond to evolving threats; bilateral and multilateral cooperation; and targeted strategies against hostile states and terrorists.

## Counterproliferation

We know from experience that we cannot always be successful in preventing and containing the proliferation of WMD to hostile states and terrorists. Therefore, U.S. military and appropriate civilian agencies must possess the full range of operational capabilities to counter the threat and use of WMD by states and terrorists against the United States, our military forces, and friends and allies.

## Interdiction

Effective interdiction is a critical part of the U.S. strategy to combat WMD and their delivery means. We must enhance the capabilities of our military, intelligence, technical, and law enforcement communities to prevent the movement of WMD materials, technology, and expertise to hostile states and terrorist organizations.

## Deterrence

Today's threats are far more diverse and less predictable than those of the past. States hostile to the United States and to our friends and allies have demonstrated their willingness to take high risks to achieve their goals, and are aggressively pursuing WMD and their means of delivery as critical tools in this effort. As a consequence, we require new methods of deterrence. A strong declaratory policy and effective military forces are essential elements of our contemporary deterrent posture, along with the full range of political tools to persuade potential adversaries not to seek or use WMD. The United States will continue to make clear that it reserves the right to respond with overwhelming force—including through resort to all of our options—to the use of WMD against the United States, our forces abroad, and friends and allies.

In addition to our conventional and nuclear response and defense capabilities, our overall deterrent posture against WMD threats is reinforced by effective intelligence, surveillance, interdiction, and domestic law enforcement capabilities. Such combined capabilities enhance deterrence both by devaluing an adversary's WMD and missiles, and by posing the prospect of an overwhelming response to any use of such weapons.

## Defense and Mitigation

Because deterrence may not succeed, and because of the potentially devastating consequences of WMD use against our forces and civilian population, U.S. military forces and appropriate civilian agencies must have the capability to defend against WMD-armed adversaries, including in appropriate cases through preemptive measures. This requires capabilities to detect and destroy an adversary's WMD assets before these weapons are used. In addition, robust active and passive defenses and mitigation measures must be in place to enable U.S. military forces and appropriate civilian agencies to accomplish their missions, and to assist friends and allies when WMD are used.

Active defenses disrupt, disable, or destroy WMD en route to their targets. Active defenses include vigorous air defense and effective missile defenses against today's threats. Passive defenses must be tailored to the unique characteristics of the various forms of WMD. The United States must also have the ability rapidly and effectively to mitigate the effects of a WMD attack against our deployed forces.

Our approach to defend against biological threats has long been based on our approach to chemical threats, despite the fundamental differences between these weapons. The United States is developing a new approach to provide us and our friends and allies with an effective defense against biological weapons.

Finally, U.S. military forces and domestic law enforcement agencies as appropriate must stand ready to respond against the source of any WMD attack. The primary objective of a response is to disrupt an imminent attack or an attack in progress, and eliminate the threat of future attacks. As with deterrence and prevention, an effective response requires rapid attribution and robust strike capability. We must accelerate efforts to field new capabilities to defeat WMD-related assets. The United States needs to be prepared to conduct post-conflict operations to destroy or dismantle any residual WMD capabilities of the hostile state or terrorist network. An effective U.S. response not only will eliminate the source of a WMD attack but will also have a powerful deterrent effect upon other adversaries that possess or seek WMD or missiles.

## Nonproliferation

### Active Nonproliferation Diplomacy

The United States will actively employ diplomatic approaches in bilateral and multilateral settings in pursuit of our nonproliferation goals. We must dissuade supplier states from cooperating with proliferant states and induce proliferant states to end their WMD and missile programs. We will hold countries responsible for complying with their commitments. In addition, we will continue to build coalitions to support our efforts, as well as to seek their increased support for nonproliferation and threat reduction cooperation programs. However, should our wide-ranging nonproliferation efforts fail, we must have available the full range of operational capabilities necessary to defend against the possible employment of WMD.

### Multilateral Regimes

Existing nonproliferation and arms control regimes play an important role in our overall strategy. The United States will support those regimes that are currently in force, and work to improve the effectiveness of, and compliance with, those regimes. Consistent with other policy priorities, we will also promote new agreements and arrangements that serve our nonproliferation goals. Overall, we seek to cultivate an international environment that is more conducive to nonproliferation. Our efforts will include:

- **Nuclear**

  – Strengthening of the Nuclear Non-proliferation Treaty and International Atomic Energy Agency (IAEA), including through ratification of an IAEA Additional Protocol by all NPT states parties, assurances that all states put

in place full-scope IAEA safeguards agreements, and appropriate increases in funding for the Agency;
- Negotiating a Fissile Material Cut-Off Treaty that advances U.S. security interests; and
- Strengthening the Nuclear Suppliers Group and Zangger Committee.
- **Chemical and Biological**
    - Effective functioning of the Organization for the Prohibition of Chemical Weapons;
    - Identification and promotion of constructive and realistic measures to strengthen the BWC and thereby to help meet the biological weapons threat; and
    - Strengthening of the Australia Group.
- **Missile**
    - Strengthening the Missile Technology Control Regime (MTCR), including through support for universal adherence to the International Code of Conduct Against Ballistic Missile Proliferation.

## Nonproliferation and Threat Reduction Cooperation

The United States pursues a wide range of programs, including the Nunn-Lugar program, designed to address the proliferation threat stemming from the large quantities of Soviet-legacy WMD and missile-related expertise and materials. Maintaining an extensive and efficient set of nonproliferation and threat reduction assistance programs to Russia and other former Soviet states is a high priority. We will also continue to encourage friends and allies to increase their contributions to these programs, particularly through the G-8 Global Partnership Against the Spread of Weapons and Materials of Mass Destruction. In addition, we will work with other states to improve the security of their WMD-related materials.

## Controls on Nuclear Materials

In addition to programs with former Soviet states to reduce fissile material and improve the security of that which remains, the United States will continue to discourage the worldwide accumulation of separated plutonium and to minimize the use of highly-enriched uranium. As outlined in the National Energy Policy, the United States will work in collaboration with international partners to develop recycle and fuel treatment technologies that are cleaner, more efficient, less waste-intensive, and more proliferation-resistant.

## U.S. Export Controls

We must ensure that the implementation of U.S. export controls furthers our nonproliferation and other national security goals, while recognizing the realities that American businesses face in the increasingly globalized marketplace.

We will work to update and strengthen export controls using existing authorities. We also seek new legislation to improve the ability of our export control system to give full weight to both nonproliferation objectives and commercial interests. Our overall goal is to focus our resources on truly sensitive exports to hostile states or those that engage in onward proliferation, while removing unnecessary barriers in the global marketplace.

## Nonproliferation Sanctions

Sanctions can be a valuable component of our overall strategy against WMD proliferation. At times, however, sanctions have proven inflexible and ineffective. We will develop a comprehensive sanctions policy to better integrate sanctions into our overall strategy and work with Congress to consolidate and modify existing sanctions legislation.

# WMD Consequence Management

Defending the American homeland is the most basic responsibility of our government. As part of our defense, the United States must be fully prepared to respond to the consequences of WMD use on our soil, whether by hostile states or by terrorists. We must also be prepared to respond to the effects of WMD use against our forces deployed abroad, and to assist friends and allies.

The National Strategy for Homeland Security discusses U.S. Government programs to deal with the consequences of the use of a chemical, biological, radiological, or nuclear weapon in the United States. A number of these programs offer training, planning, and assistance to state and local governments. To maximize their effectiveness, these efforts need to be integrated and comprehensive. Our first responders must have the full range of protective, medical, and remediation tools to identify, assess, and respond rapidly to a WMD event on our territory.

The White House Office of Homeland Security will coordinate all federal efforts to prepare for and mitigate the consequences of terrorist attacks within the United States, including those involving WMD. The Office of Homeland Security will also work closely with state and local governments to ensure their planning, training, and equipment requirements are addressed. These issues, including the roles of the Department of

Homeland Security, are addressed in detail in the National Strategy for Homeland Security.

The National Security Council's Office of Combating Terrorism coordinates and helps improve U. S. efforts to respond to and manage the recovery from terrorist attacks outside the United States. In cooperation with the Office of Combating Terrorism, the Department of State coordinates interagency efforts to work with our friends and allies to develop their own emergency preparedness and consequence management capabilities.

## Integrating the Pillars

Several critical enabling functions serve to integrate the three pillars—counterproliferation, nonproliferation, and consequence management—of the U.S. National Strategy to Combat WMD.

## Improved Intelligence Collection and Analysis

A more accurate and complete understanding of the full range of WMD threats is, and will remain, among the highest U. S. intelligence priorities, to enable us to prevent proliferation, and to deter or defend against those who would use those capabilities against us. Improving our ability to obtain timely and accurate knowledge of adversaries' offensive and defensive capabilities, plans, and intentions is key to developing effective counter- and nonproliferation policies and capabilities. Particular emphasis must be accorded to improving: intelligence regarding WMD-related facilities and activities; interaction among U.S. intelligence, law enforcement, and military agencies; and intelligence cooperation with friends and allies.

## Research and Development

The United States has a critical need for cutting-edge technology that can quickly and effectively detect, analyze, facilitate interdiction of, defend against, defeat, and mitigate the consequences of WMD. Numerous U.S. Government departments and agencies are currently engaged in the essential research and development to support our overall strategy against WMD proliferation.

The new Counterproliferation Technology Coordination Committee, consisting of senior representatives from all concerned agencies, will act to improve interagency coordination of U.S. Government counterproliferation research and development efforts. The Committee will assist in identifying priorities, gaps, and overlaps in existing programs and in examining options for future investment strategies.

## Strengthened International Cooperation

WMD represent a threat not just to the United States, but also to our friends and allies and the broader international community. For this reason, it is vital that we work closely with like-minded countries on all elements of our comprehensive proliferation strategy.

## Targeted Strategies Against Proliferants

All elements of the overall U.S. strategy to combat WMD must be brought to bear in targeted strategies against supplier and recipient states of WMD proliferation concern, as well as against terrorist groups which seek to acquire WMD.

A few states are dedicated proliferators, whose leaders are determined to develop, maintain, and improve their WMD and delivery capabilities, which directly threaten the United States, U.S. forces overseas, and/or our friends and allies. Because each of these regimes is different, we will pursue country-specific strategies that best enable us and our friends and allies to prevent, deter, and defend against WMD and missile threats from each of them. These strategies must also take into account the growing cooperation among proliferant states—so-called secondary proliferation—which challenges us to think in new ways about specific country strategies.

One of the most difficult challenges we face is to prevent, deter, and defend against the acquisition and use of WMD by terrorist groups. The current and potential future linkages between terrorist groups and state sponsors of terrorism are particularly dangerous and require priority attention. The full range of counterproliferation, nonproliferation, and consequence management measures must be brought to bear against the WMD terrorist threat, just as they are against states of greatest proliferation concern.

## End Note

Our National Strategy to Combat WMD requires much of all of us—the Executive Branch, the Congress, state and local governments, the American people, and our friends and allies. The requirements to prevent, deter, defend against, and respond to today's WMD threats are complex and challenging. But they are not daunting. We can and will succeed in the tasks laid out in this strategy; we have no other choice.

APPENDIX **C**

# Reforming the Chemical and Biological Defense Program, 1996-2001

*Albert J. Mauroni*

In March 1996, the General Accounting Office (GAO) released a report assessing the military's readiness at that time for chemical and biological (CB) warfare. This report was very critical about the ability of combat units to survive and sustain combat operations in a chemical and biological warfare environment, largely due to shortages of equipment and consumables, insufficient training, and lack of leadership attention. The General Accounting Office report noted the following:

Officials from Army major commands, corps, divisions, and individual units said that chemical and biological defense skills not only tended to be difficult to attain and highly perishable but also were often given a lower priority than other areas for the following reasons:

- too many other higher priority taskings,
- low levels of monitoring or interest by higher headquarters,
- the difficulty of performing tasks in cumbersome and uncomfortable protective gear,
- the time-consuming nature of chemical training,
- heavy reliance on postmobilization training and preparation, and
- the perceived low likelihood of chemical and biological warfare.[1]

In short, despite the noted vulnerabilities U.S. military forces demonstrated during Operation Desert Shield and the immense effort made to develop an adequate chemical and biological defense capability for Operation Desert Storm, not much had visibly changed in the field. On the one hand, there was clear guidance from the 1997 Quadrennial Defense Review that stated "the threat or use of chemical and biological weapons … is a likely condition of future warfare, including the early stages of war to disrupt U.S. operations and logistics."[2]

Despite the rhetoric about the importance of chemical and biological defenses, U.S. efforts to remedy known vulnerabilities lagged far behind the problem. CB defense needed an organizational overhaul and greater funding, and Congress stepped in to assist in that direction.

The National Defense Authorization Act for fiscal year 1994 included language that created an Office of Secretary of Defense program element for all Department of Defense (DoD) CB defense research, development, test, evaluation, and acquisition. The services' acquisition secretaries created a joint CB defense management structure to organize and execute programs under this direction, including committees for joint requirements and for joint research and development.

Until the end of the 1990s, the army, navy, marines, and air force administered the various chemical and biological defense programs as the milestone decision authorities guided by the two joint coordinating committees. The Office of the Secretary of Defense (OSD) retained an oversight role and approved all programming and budgeting issues. Because the final decisions on each program were made by each of the services, duplication of organizations and stovepiping particular projects remained all too common.

The four services defined "ensuring their equities were met" as receiving equal parts of the program rather than assessing the overall Chemical and Biological Defense Program's ability to deliver a balanced capability to the field. While the number of projects was reduced by the nature of being developed as joint efforts, inefficiencies actually grew and new capabilities were not being fielded.

This is not necessarily the fault of various U.S. armed services. The central flaw was the lack of a unified system of control complete with strong Department of Defense oversight and leadership. This problem was finally addressed almost a full decade after these problems were laid bare in Operation Desert Storm at the beginning of 1991.

In August 1999, Deputy Secretary of Defense Rudy DeLeon directed a review of the Chemical and Biological Defense Program structure, considering alternatives that ranged from increasing program oversight to devolving the responsibility for research, development, and procurement of chemical and biological defense equipment back to the services. Some of the reasons why this review was ongoing included increased questions from Congress and numerous audits by the General Accounting Office trying to understand why the overall chemical, biological, radiological, and nuclear (CBRN) defense readiness of the force was not visibly improving despite the management reforms taken five years earlier.[3]

Questions about protective mask readiness and an industry scandal concerning 780,000 defective Battle Dress Overgarments highlighted the point that there was no one person in charge of the program. For example, the Deputy Assistant to the Secretary of Defense for Chemical and Biological Defense programs[4] testified before Congress that there were nine program offices among the four services and the Defense Threat Reduction Agency. These multiple acquisition decision authorities all had specific responsibilities for executing particular joint programs, rather than having a single decision authority for all programs at the Office of the Secretary of Defense.

Furthermore, a new CBRN threat was taking shape at this time. People started talking about CBRN hazards from terrorist attacks aimed at military installations and the general public, but it was unclear who was developing capabilities against this "new" threat. The Defense Advanced Research Projects Agency and the U.S. Army's Soldier and Biological Defense Command had initiatives independent from the DoD program to support the DoD Domestic Preparedness Program, for instance.

In 1996, counterproliferation programs began to increasingly address passive defense issues as well as the traditional (and more influential) missile defense and counterforce capabilities. The combatant commands grew increasingly involved in discussions about desired CBRN defense capabilities, although they had little voice in the service-dominated committees. The Defense Reform Initiative created the Defense Threat Reduction Agency in 1998 and changed the Office of the Secretary of Defense management of the CB defense program.

In 1999, a commission, chaired by the former Deputy Defense Secretary John Deutch and cochaired by Senator Arlen Spector, had spent more than a year assessing federal agencies involved in combating proliferation and found that the U.S. Government was not effectively organized to combat proliferation and lacked a comprehensive approach to combating proliferation of WMDs.[5] Combined with increasing criticisms from the GAO and congressional committees, OSD recognized it was time to review the program for changes.

## DoD Reorganizes CB Defense

Various groups studied the Department of Defense Chemical and Biological Defense Program and offered recommendations, such as the following suggestions:

- the army adopt a single Program Executive Office for Chemical and Biological Defense in 2001,
- the Joint Staff become a voting member on the Joint NBC Defense Board in 2000,[6] and

- the Department of Defense Chemical and Biological Defense Program take oversight of the WMD Civil Support Team acquisition efforts in 2001.

However, there was not much incentive to act, especially with a new administration coming into the White House and several key Department of Defense leadership positions to fill.

That was true until September 11, 2001. The tragic attacks against the World Trade Center and the Pentagon created a concern within the Department of Defense that additional al-Qaeda attacks might include the use of chemical, biological, radiological, or nuclear strikes against military and public targets. Congress and the Office of the Secretary of Defense demanded quick action to address potential vulnerabilities at military installations, equipment shortages within military units, and homeland security overall.

On October 19, 2001, the Under Secretary of Defense for Acquisition, Technology and Logistics directed the formation of a task force led by the Office of the Secretary of Defense to review the need for a Joint Program Executive Office for Chemical and Biological Defense and other reforms necessary to the Department of Defense Chemical and Biological Defense Program.[7]

This was the start of a year-long effort to redesign the overall program into a more flexible, responsive, and streamlined structure. It was decided that the Defense Threat Reduction Agency would retain control of the funds management and would take control of the Chemical and Biological Defense Program science and technology program.

Brigadier General Steve Reeves, the Army Program Executive Officer for Chemical and Biological Defense, had his office transformed into the Joint Program Executive Office for Chemical and Biological Defense and was to assume control over all CBRN defense acquisition efforts.

The Joint Service Materiel Group Executive Office became an "independent" army-staffed program analysis and integration office, responsible for the program's annual research, development, acquisition, and logistics plans. There would be no legislative changes required to the public law that directed the formation of the Department of Defense Chemical and Biological Defense Program.

As the Office of the Secretary of Defense task force was working out the details of a new management structure, the Under Secretary of Defense for Acquisition, Technology and Logistics asked the Joint Staff in late November 2001 to head a joint working group to examine the requirements process. This group delivered its final report to the Joint NBC Defense Board in late February 2002, with that body approving the development of a new requirements office on the Joint Staff to replace the Joint Service Integration Group.

The resistance was not as fierce as what the acquisition task force had faced; many senior service officers recognized that the Joint Service Integration Group was not adequately resourced, staffed, or empowered to make the necessary decisions required to execute the increasing responsibilities of the program.

The Joint Staff working group developed an organizational structure for a Joint Requirements Office for CBRN Defense, which would reside under the J8, Joint Staff, similar to how the Joint Tactical Air and Missile Defense Organization had been organized. As a result, the Joint Requirements Office for CBRN Defense officially assumed its duties on October 1, 2002, with Brigadier General Stephen Goldfein, an air force general officer on the Joint Staff, as its first director.

On September 19, 2002, the Under Secretary of Defense for Acquisition, Technology and Logistics released an acquisition decision memorandum outlining the responsibilities of four primary organizations:

- the Assistant to the Secretary of Defense for Nuclear and Chemical and Biological Defense as the oversight office,
- the Joint Requirements Office as the user requirements office,
- the Joint Program Executive Office as the material developer, and
- the Defense Threat Reduction Agency as the funds manager and head of science and technology efforts.

The Deputy Under Secretary of the Army for Operational Research became the executive agent for Department of Defense chemical and

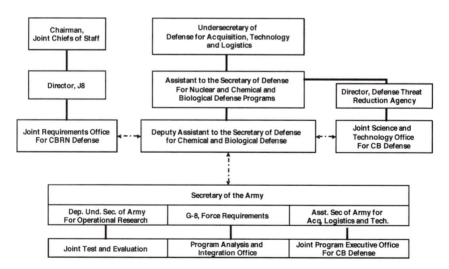

Department of Defense Chemical and Biological Defense Program Management Structure Effective April 2003[8]

biological defense test and evaluation, a change initiated to streamline its joint service approach and give new vitality to the performance of this mission.

On April 22, 2003, the Under Secretary of Defense for Acquisition, Technology and Logistics signed the implementation plan detailing the responsibilities of the new management structure and its efforts to address Defense Department CBRN defense requirements across passive defense, consequence management, force protection, and homeland security.

The Under Secretary of Defense for Acquisition, Technology and Logistics would be the one Milestone Decision Authority for the entire program, delegating the responsibility for individual programs to the Joint Program Executive Office for Chemical and Biological Defense.

The four services would have action officers within the Joint Program Executive Office and Joint Requirements Office, but no longer would joint committees make "least-common denominator" decisions to guide the execution of the Chemical and Biological Defense Program.

Thus, this new reorganization of the Department of Defense Chemical and Biological Defense Program was in place just as the fighting in Operation Iraqi Freedom began.

# Acronyms

**9/11.** September 11, 2001

**AB.** Air Base

**ABC.** American Broadcasting Company

**ABL.** Airborne Laser

**ABM.** Anti-Ballistic Missile

**ACADA.** Automatic Chemical Agent Detection Alarm

**ACDA.** Arms Control and Disarmament Agency

**ACE.** Areas for Capability Enhancements

**ACRS.** Arms Control and Regional Security

**ACTD.** Advanced Concept Technology Demonstration

**ADW.** Agent Defeat Weapon

**AEF.** Air Expeditionary Force

**AFH.** Air Force Handbook

**AFI.** Air Force Instruction

**AFJMAN.** Air Force Joint Manual

**AFMAN.** Air Force Manual

**AFRL.** Air Force Research Laboratory

**AGE.** Aerospace Ground Equipment

**AGE/MHE.** Aerospace Ground Equipment/Materials Handling Equipment

**AKA.** Also Known As

**ALPS.** Accidental Launch Protection System

**AMI.** American Media Inc.

**AMSTE.** Affordable Moving Surface Target Engagement

**AO.** Attack Operations

**APOD.** Aerial Port of Debarkation

**ATO.** Air Tasking Order

**ATP.** Allied Tactical Publication

**ATR.** Automatic Target Recognition

**AVA.** Anthrax Vaccine Adsorbed

**BDA.** Battle Damage Assessment

**BDTF.** Biological Defense Task Force

**BEDAL.** Baseline Equipment Data Assessment List

**BEE.** Bioenvironmental Engineering

**BIDS.** Biological Integrated Detection System

**BLU.** Bomb Live Unit

**BMDO.** Ballistic Missile Defense Organization

**BMDS.** Ballistic Missile Defense System

**BMEWS.** Ballistic Missile Early Warning System

**BMT.** Basic Military Training (Air Force)

**BSL-3.** Biosecurity Level Three

**BTWC.** Biological and Toxins Weapons Convention (Same as BWC)

**BW.** Biological Warfare

**BWC.** Biological Weapons Convention (Same as BTWC)

**C2.** Command and Control

**C4I.** Command, Control, Communication, Computers, and Intelligence

**CALCM.** Conventional Air Launched Cruise Missile

**CAM.** Chemical Agent Monitor

**CANA.** Convulsant Antidote Nerve Agent

**CAOC.** Combined Air Operations Center

**CAPS.** Counterproliferation Analysis Planning System

**CARC.** Chemical Agent Resistant Coating

**CASPOD.** Contamination Avoidance at Seaports of Debarkation

**CB.** Chemical and Biological

**CBPS.** Chemical Biological Protective Shelter

**CBRN.** Chemical, Biological, Radiological, and Nuclear

**CBRNE.** Chemical, Biological, Radiological, Nuclear, and High-Yield Explosive

**CBS.** Columbia Broadcasting System

**CBW.** Chemical and Biological Warfare

**CCA.** Contamination Control Area

**C-CBRNE.** Counter-Chemical, Biological, Radiological, Nuclear, and High-Yield Explosive Warfare

**CC&D.** Camouflage, Concealment, and Deception

**C-CW.** Chemical-Chemical Warfare

**C-CW CONOPS.** Counter-Chemical Warfare Concept of Operations

**CDC.** U.S. Centers for Disease Control and Prevention

**CDI.** Cooperative Defense Initiative

**CENTCOM.** Central Command

**CEP.** Circular Error of Probability

**CEX.** Civil Engineer Readiness (USAF)

**CF.** Counterforce

**CFE.** Conventional Forces in Europe

**CHATH.** Chemically Hardened Air Transportable Hospital

**CIA.** Central Intelligence Agency

**CM.** Consequence Management

**CoCom.** Coordinating Committee for Multilateral Export Controls

**COLPRO.** Collective Protection

**COMPACAF.** Commander of the Pacific Air Forces

**CONOPs.** Concepts of Operations

**CONUS.** Continental United States

**CP.** Counterproliferation

**CP DEPMEDS.** Chemically Protected Deployable Medical System

**CPI.** Counterproliferation Initiative

**CPS.** Collective Protection System

**CPSBKFT.** Collective Protection System Amphibious Backfit

**CrashPAD.** Crash Prompt Agent Defeat

**CSAF.** Chief of Staff, United States Air Force

**CTBT.** Comprehensive Test Ban Treaty

**CTR.** Cooperative Threat Reduction

**CW.** Chemical Warfare

**CWC.** Chemical Weapons Convention

**CWG.** Counterproliferation Working Group (U.S.–Israel)

**DCI.** Director of Central Intelligence

**DGP.** Defence Group on Proliferation (NATO)

**DHS.** Department of Homeland Security

**DIA.** Defense Intelligence Agency

**DMZ.** Demilitarized Zone

**DNA.** Defense Nuclear Agency

**DoD.** Department of Defense

**DOE.** Department of Energy

**DOJ.** Department of Justice

**DOTMLPF.** Doctrine, Organization, Training, Material, Leadership, Personnel, and Facilities

**DPRK.** Democratic People's Republic of Korea

**DSWA.** Defense Special Weapons Agency

**DTRA.** Defense Threat Reduction Agency

**DTRA/TD.** Technology Division of the Defense Threat Reduction Agency

**DU.** Depleted Uranium

**ETA.** Euzkadi Ta Askatasuna or Basque Fatherland and Liberty

**EZLN.** Zapatista Army for National Liberation

**FAA.** Federal Aviation Agency

**FACA.** Federal Advisory Commission Act

**FBI.** Federal Bureau of Investigation

**FDA.** U.S. Food and Drug Administration

**FDNY.** Fire Department of New York

**FEMA.** Federal Emergency Management Agency

**FGA.** Fourth Generation Agents

**FMS.** Foreign Military Sales

**FRP.** Federal Response Plan

**FSTR.** Full Spectrum Threat Response

**FSU.** Former Soviet Union

**GA.** Tabun

**GB.** Sarin Gas (crude form)

**GCC.** Gulf Cooperation Council

**GD.** Soman

**GEMS.** Global Expeditionary Medical System

**GF.** Cyclosarin

**GMD.** Ground-Based Midcourse Missile Defense

**GPALS.** Global Protection Against Limited Strikes

**GPS.** Global Positioning System

**GSDF.** Ground Self-Defense Force

**GWAPS.** Gulf War Air Power Survey

**GWOT.** Global War on Terrorism

**HAZMAT.** Hazardous Materials

**HDBTC.** Hard and Deeply Buried Target Capability

**HE.** High Explosive

**HEU.** Highly Enriched Uranium

**HHS.** Department of Health and Human Services

**HIT.** High Incendiary Temperature

**HPAC.** Hazard Prediction and Assessment Capability

**HQ.** Headquarters

**HQ PACAF.** Headquarters Pacific Air Forces

**HSPD.** Homeland Security Presidential Directive

**HUMINT.** Human Intelligence

**HVAC.** Heating, Ventilation, and Air Conditioning

**IAEA.** International Atomic Energy Agency

**IBAD.** Interim Biological Agent Detector

**IC.** Intelligence Community

**ICAM.** Improved Chemical Agent Monitor

**ICBM.** Intercontinental Ballistic Missile

**IDO.** Initial Defensive Operations

**IG.** Inspector General

**IMEA.** Interactive Multi-Variate Environmental Analysis

**IMEA.** Integrated Munitions Effects Assessment

**IND.** Investigational New Drug

**INS.** Immigration and Naturalization Service

**IOC.** Initial Operational Capability

**IPDS.** Improved (Chemical Agent) Point Detection System

**IPE.** Individual Protective Equipment

**IRBMs.** Intermediate range ballistic missiles

**ISACs.** Infrastructure Sharing and Analysis Centers

**ISR.** Intelligence, Surveillance, and Reconnaissance

**IST.** Information systems terrorism

**JBPDD.** Joint Biological Point Defense Detection System

**JBPDS.** Joint Biological Point Detection System

**JBREWS.** Joint Biological Remote Early Warning System

**JBSDS.** Joint Biological Standoff Detection System

**JBUD.** Joint Biological Universal Detector

**JCAD.** Joint Chemical Agent Detector

**JCPE.** Joint Collective Protection Equipment

**JCS.** Joint Chiefs of Staff

**JDAMs.** Joint Direct Attack Munitions

**JOR.** Joint Operational Requirements

**JPMG.** Joint Political/Military Group

**JPO-BD.** Joint Program Office for Biological Defense

**JRO.** Joint Requirements Office

**JS NBCRS.** Joint Services Lightweight NBC Reconnaissance Systems

**JSIPP.** Joint Service Installation Pilot Program

**JSLSCAD.** Joint Services Lightweight Standoff Chemical Agent Detector

**JSMG.** Joint Service Materiel Group

**JSOW.** Joint Standoff Weapon

**JSTARS.** Joint Surveillance and Target Attack Radar System

**JTAMDO.** Joint Theater Air and Missile Defense Organization

**JTCOPS.** Joint Transportable Collective Protection System

**JVOG.** Joint Venture Oversight Group (U.S.–United Kingdom)

**JWARN.** Joint Warning and Reporting Network

**LADAR.** Laser Detection and Ranging

**LANTIRN.** Low Altitude Navigation and Targeting Infrared for Night

**LIDAR.** Light Detection and Ranging

**LOCAAS.** Low Cost Autonomous Attack System

**LTTE.** Liberation Tigers of Tamil Eelam

**MAD.** Mutual Assured Destruction

**MAJCOM.** Major Command

**MASINT.** Measurement and Signature Intelligence

**MDA.** Missile Defense Agency

**MEA.** Munitions Effects Assessment

**MEADS.** Medium Extended Air Defense System

**MHE.** Materials Handling Equipment

**MOPP.** Mission-Oriented Protective Posture

**MRTA.** Túpac Amaru Revolutionary Movement

**MTCR.** Missile Technology Control Regime

**MTI.** Multispectral Thermal Imager

**MX.** Peacekeeper Missile

**NAAK.** Nerve Agent Antidote Kit

**NATO.** North Atlantic Treaty Organization

**NBC.** Nuclear, Biological, and Chemical

**NBC.** National Broadcasting Company

**NBCC.** Nuclear, Biological, Chemical, and Conventional

**NBC/M.** Nuclear, Biological, Chemical, and Missile

**NDP.** National Defense Panel

**NESA.** Near Eastern and South Asian Affairs

**NEST.** Nuclear Emergency Search Team

**NIE.** National Intelligence Estimate

**NIH.** National Institutes of Health

**NIMS.** National Incident Management System

**NMD.** National Missile Defense

**NORTHCOM.** Northern Command

**NPT.** Treaty of the Non-Proliferation of Nuclear Weapons (also referred to as the Nuclear Non-Proliferation Treaty)

**NRP.** National Response Plan

**NSA.** National Security Agency

**NSC.** National Security Council

**NSS.** National Security Strategy

**NSWC.** Naval Surface Warfare Center

**NTAs.** New Technology Agents

**NYPD.** New York Police Department

**OEA.** Operational Effectiveness Assistance

**OHS.** Office of Homeland Security

**OIF.** Operation Iraqi Freedom

**OPCW.** Organisation for Prohibition of Chemical Weapons

**OPTEMPO.** Operational Tempo

**OSD.** Office of the Secretary of Defense

**PAC.** Patriot Advanced Capability

**PAC-2.** Patriot Advanced Capability 2

**PAC-3.** Patriot Advanced Capability 3

**PACAF.** Pacific Air Forces

**PB.** Pyridostigmine Bromide

**PBT.** Pentavalent Botulinum Toxoid

**PCC.** Prague Capabilities Commitment

**PCCIP.** President's Commission on Critical Infrastructure Protection

**PCR.** Polymerase Chain Reaction

**PDD.** Presidential Decision Directive

**PDD-39.** Presidential Decision Directive 39

**PFLP.** Popular Front for the Liberation of Palestine

**PGMs.** Precision-Guided Munitions

**PIRA.** Provisional Irish Republican Army of Northern Ireland

**PK.** Probability of Kill

**PSI.** Proliferation Security Initiative

**QDR.** Quadrennial Defense Review

**R&D.** Research and Development

**radiac.** radioactivity, detection, indication, and computation

**RAPID.** Rugged Advanced Pathogen Identification Device

**RCC.** Regional Coordination Cell (GCC states)

**RDD.** Radiation Dispersal Devices

**RDT&E.** Research, Development, Test, and Evaluation

**RESTOPS.** Restoration of Operations

**RESTOPS ACTD.** Restoration of Operations Advanced Concept Technology
Development

**ROK.** Republic of Korea

**RPA.** Recombinant Protective Antigen

**S&T.** Science and Technology

**SAIP.** Semi-Automated Imagery Intelligence Processing

**SALAD.** Shipboard Automatic Liquid Agent Detector

**SAM.** Surface-to-Air Missile

**SAR.** Synthetic Aperture Radar

**SARS.** Severe Acute Respiratory Syndrome

**SATKA.** Surveillance of incoming attackers, acquisition of the targets, tracking of the targets, killing of the attacking missiles or aircraft, and assessing the results to determine whether to go into a reattack mode

**SBIRS.** Space-Based Infrared System

**SCPE.** Simplified Collective Protection Equipment

**SDF.** Self-Defense Force

**SDI.** Strategic Defense Initiative

**SDIO.** Strategic Defense Initiative Organization

**SERPACWA.** Skin Exposure Reduction Paste against Chemical Warfare Agents

**SFW.** Sensor-Fuzed Weapon

**SGP.** Senior Political Group on Proliferation (NATO)

**SM.** Standard Missile

**SM-3.** Standard Missile 3

**SNS.** Strategic National Stockpile

**SOF.** Special Operations Forces

**SPODs.** Seaports of Debarkation

**SRBM.** Short-range Ballistic Missile

**SSTS.** Space Surveillance and Tracking System

**START.** Strategic Arms Reduction Treaty

**STRATCOM.** Strategic Command

**TAMD.** Theater Air and Missile Defense

**TB.** Thermobaric

**TBM.** Theater Ballistic Missile

**TCPS.** Transportable Collective Protection Shelter

**TEL.** Transporter Erector Launcher

**TFA.** Toxic-Free Area

**THAAD.** Terminal High-Altitude Area Defense (formerly known as Theater High-Altitude Area Defense)

**TICs.** Toxic Industrial Chemicals

**TIMs.** Toxic Industrial Materials

**TMD.**  Theater Missile Defense

**TOPOFF.**  Congressionally mandated Top Officials Homeland Security Exercise

**TST.**  Time-Sensitive Target

**TTPs.**  Tactics, Techniques, and Procedures

**TUT.**  Targets Under Trees

**UAE.**  United Arab Emirates

**UAV.**  Unmanned Aerial Vehicle

**UGFs.**  Underground Facilities

**UNSCOM.**  United Nations Special Commission on Iraq

**USAF.**  United States Air Force

**USDA.**  United States Department of Agriculture

**USFK.**  United States Forces, Korea

**USSR.**  Union of Soviet Socialist Republics

**USTRANSCOM.**  United States Transportation Command

**VEE.**  Viral Equine Encephalitis

**VLSTRACK.**  Vapor Liquid Solid Tracking

**WDTC.**  West Desert Test Center

**WMD.**  Weapons of Mass Destruction

**WMDI.**  Weapons of Mass Destruction Initiative

**WOT.**  War on Terrorism

**WRM.**  War Reserve Materiel

**WTC.**  World Trade Center

**WWI.**  World War I

**WWII.**  World War II

**ZOG.**  Zionist Occupied Government

# Notes

## Chapter 1

1. Secretary of Defense Les Aspin's full speech given on December 7, 1993, is located in Appendix A of this book.

2. Mark D. Skootsky, "An Annotated Chronology of Post-Soviet Nuclear Disarmament 1991–1994," *The Nonproliferation Review,* Spring/Summer 1995, http://cns.miis.edu/pubs/npr/vol02/23/skoots23.pdf (accessed August 3, 2004).

3. Ken Alibek, with Stephen Handleman, *Biohazard* (New York: Random House, 1999), 43, 293–304.

4. Secretary of Defense Les Aspin's speech to an audience at the National Academy of Sciences, Washington, DC, December 7, 1993.

5. Although the institutionalization of countering proliferation of weapons of mass destruction did not become a top priority within the DoD until the 1990s, it was not a new concept. For example, U.S. counterforce strikes in World War II (WWII) were launched to slow or terminate the Germans' ability to develop nuclear weapons. Air strikes against Nazi heavy water production facilities in Norway persuaded German leaders to move their supplies and equipment back to Germany. A barge carrying this cargo was sunk in a fiord, ending the German A-bomb project for the duration of the war.

6. Stephen Burgess and Helen Purkitt, "The Secret Program: South Africa's Chemical and Biological Weapons," in *The War Next Time: Countering Rogue States and Terrorists Armed with Chemical and Biological Weapons,* ed. Barry R. Schneider and Jim A. Davis (Maxwell AFB, AL: USAF Counterproliferation Center, November 2003), 57–59.

7. James P. McCarthy, "Cooperative Threat Reduction: Building a Concept for National Security," in *Countering the Proliferation and Use of Weapons of Mass Destruction,* ed. Peter L. Hays, Vincent J. Jodoin, and Alan R. Van Tassel (New York: McGraw-Hill, 1998), 122–128.

8. Examples of the increase in international information sharing cross many disciplines. Examples include military, finance, antiterrorism, counterproliferation, and drug trafficking. One such statement of information sharing was by Juan C. Zarate. Juan C. Zarate, Deputy Assistant Secretary, Executive Office Terrorist Financing and Financial Crime, U.S. Department of the Treasury, testimony to the Senate Foreign Relations Committee, March 18, 2003, http://foreign.senate.gov/testimony/2003/ZarateTestimony030318.pdf (accessed May 5, 2004).

9. "HHS Fact Sheet: Biodefense Preparedness," The White House Web site, http://www.whitehouse.gov/news/releases/2004/04/20040428-4.html (accessed May 25, 2004).

10. Robert D. Walpole, National Intelligence Officer for Strategic and Nuclear Programs, "North Korea's Taepo Dong Launch and Some Implications on the Ballistic Missile Threat to the United States," speech, *Center for Strategic and International Studies,* December 8, 1998, http://www.cia.gov/cia/public_affairs/speeches/1998/walpole_speech_120898.html (accessed May 3, 2004); David Wright, "Re: Taepodong 1 Test Flight," *Federation of American Scientists,* September 2, 1998, http://www.fas.org/news/dprk/1998/980831-dprk-dcw.htm (accessed May 3, 2004).

11. "Access to Evil," *BBC News,* January 29, 2004, http://www.news.bbc.co.uk/1/hi/programmes/this_world/3436701.stm (accessed May 4, 2004); Barbara Demick, "North Korea Documents Suggest Political Prisoners Are Gassed," *Los Angeles Times,* February 10, 2004, A3.

12. Conflicting information strategy: while researching the open literature for the status of the countries concerning nuclear, chemical, and biological programs, over a dozen sources were cited. Several sources were found to have conflicting information. Cases where conflicting information was found in various reports were resolved by the author's personal opinion on the most likely accurate data. Sources: Sidney D. Drell, Abraham D. Sofaer, and George D. Wilson, *The New Terror Facing the Threat of Biological and Chemical Weapons* (Stanford, CA: Hoover Institution Press, 1999), 23; Joseph Cirincione, Jon B. Wolfsthal, and Miriam Rajkumar, *Deadly Arsenals Tracking Weapons of Mass Destruction* (Washington, DC: Carnegie Endowment for International Peace, 2002), 8–68; *The Worldwide Biological Warfare Weapons Threat* (Washington, DC: U.S. Government, 2001), 2; Daryl Kimball and Kerry Boyd, *Chemical and Biological Weapons Proliferation at a Glance* (Washington, DC: The Arms Control Association, September 2002); "Chemical and Biological Weapons: Possession and Programs Past and Present," Center for Non-Proliferation Studies, 2002, http://cns.miis.edu (accessed June 15, 2004); "Ethiopia Special Weapons," *Global Security.org,* http://www.globalsecurity.org/wmd/world/ethiopia/ (accessed June 15, 2004); "The Chemical Weapons Convention," Arms Control Association, April 2000, http://www.armscontrol.org/act/2000_04/facap00.asp (accessed June 15, 2004); Anthony H. Cordesman, *National Developments of Biological Weapons in the Middle East: An Analytic Overview* (Washington, DC: Center for Strategic and International Studies, 2001); "Nuclear Facts—Does Canada Contribute to Nuclear Weapons Proliferation?" Canadian Nuclear Association, http://www.cna.ca/english/Nuclear_Facts/07-Nuclear%20Facts-proliferation.pdf (accessed June 15, 2004); "Country Profiles," Nuclear Threat Initiative, http://www.nti.org/e_research/profiles/index.html (accessed June 15, 2004); post-Operation Iraqi Freedom evidence is scant that active programs existed in 2003.

13. Office of the Secretary of Defense, *Proliferation: Threat and Response* (Washington, DC, U.S. Department of Defense, January 2001), 61–64, 109; Brad Roberts, "Conclusion: The Prospects for Mass Casualty Terrorism," in *Hype or Reality? The "New Terrorism" and Mass Casualty Attacks,* ed. Brad Roberts (Alexandria, VA: Chemical and Biological Arms Control Institute, 2000), 279.

14. W. Seth Carus, "The Rajneeshees (1984)," in *Toxic Terror: Assessing Terrorist Use of Chemical and Biological Weapons,* ed. Jonathan B. Tucker (Cambridge, MA: MIT Press, 2000), 115–137.

15. David E. Kaplan and Andrew Marshall, *The Cult at the End of the World* (New York: Crown Publishers, 1996), 92, 251, 294.

16. Nic Robertson, "Tapes Shed New Light on bin Laden's Network," *CNN.com*, August 19, 2002, http://www.cnn.com/2002/US/08/18/terror.tape.main/ (accessed May 4, 2004).

17. "East Texas Man Faces Sentencing for Cyanide Cache," *HoustonChronicle.com*, May 3, 2004, http://www.chron.com/cs/CDA/ssistory.mpl/metropolitan/2546438 (accessed May 5, 2004); Scott Gold, "Hoarder of Arms Gets 11 Years," *Los Angeles Times*, May 5, 2004, http://www.latimes.com/news/nationworld/nation/la-na-krar5may05,1,1737647.story?coll=la-headlines-nation (accessed May 18, 2004).

18. "Fifth Man Charged over Ricin Plot," *BBC News*, January 21, 2003, May 4, 2004, http://news.bbc.co.uk/2/hi/uk_news/2680675.stm (accessed May 4, 2004); also see Joby Warrick, "An Al Qaeda 'Chemist' and The Quest for Ricin," *Washington Post*, May 5, 2003, http://www.washingtonpost.com/wp-dyn/articles/A2159-2004May4.html (accessed May 18, 2004).

19. "Israel Practices for Iraqi Nuke Attack: Holds Large-Scale Exercise to Assess Readiness for Enemy Missiles," *WorldNetDaily*, May 10, 2002, http://www.worldnetdaily.com/news/article.asp?ARTICLE_ID=27571 (accessed May 4, 2004).

20. Margot Dudkevitch and Matthew Guttman, "10 Killed in Ashdod Port Bombings,"*Jerusalem Post*, March 15, 2004; Patrick Goodenough, "Israel to Step Up Strikes Against Terrorists Amid 'Mega Attack' Fears," *CNSNews.com*, March 15, 2004, http://www.cnsnews.com/ViewForeignBureaus.asp?Page=\ForeignBureaus\archive\200403\FOR20040315e.html (accessed May 3, 2004); see also Ohad Gozani, "Suicide Bombs Kill 10 Israelis," *News.telegraph.co.uk*, March 15, 2004, http://www.telegraph.co.uk/news/main.jhtml?xml=news/2004/03/15/wmid15.xml (accessed May 3, 2004).

21. Leonard A. Cole, *The Anthrax Letters: A Medical Detective Story* (Washington, DC: Joseph Henry Press, 2003), 47–55.

22. Carol Morello and Spencer S. Hsu, "Ricin Partially Shuts Senate: 3 Buildings Sealed; Toxin Was Mailed to White House in Nov.," *Washington Post*, February 4, 2004, A01, http://www.Washingtonpost.com/wp-dyn/articles/A10632-2004Feb3.html (accessed May 12, 2004).

23. For example, the author was able to purchase a manual titled *Silent Death* by "Uncle Fester." Uncle Fester is Steve Priesler, who has a degree in chemistry and offers his book for $18 on the Internet through *Amazon.com*. The book tells the reader where to find agents such as *Bacillus anthracis* and *Clostridium botulinum*, how to grow them, how to weaponize them, and how to employ the agents to kill small or large numbers of people depending on your goal. *Amazon.com*, http://www.amazon.com/exec/obidos//ASIN/0970148534/ qid=1012831204/sr=2-3/ref=sr_2_11_3/ (accessed February 4, 2002).

24. See "The Organization for Prohibition of Chemical Weapons," which is the governing body of "The Convention on the Prohibition of the Development, Production, Stockpiling, and Use of Chemical Weapons and on Their Destruction" (also known as the Chemical Weapons Convention or CWC) for the original text of this international treaty, as well as updates and other pertinent information, http:/www.opcw.org/index.html (accessed May 11, 2004).

25. See "The Biological and Toxin Weapons Convention Web site" for the original text of the "The Convention on the Prohibition of the Development, Production, Stockpiling Bacteriological (Biological) and Toxin Weapons and on Their Destruction" (also known as the Biological Weapons Convention or BWC), as well as updates on the Review Conferences and other pertinent information, http://www.opbw.org/ (accessed May 11, 2004).

26. See the United Nations official Web site on "Treaty on the Non-Proliferation of Nuclear Weapons (NPT)," as well as updates on the Review Conferences and other pertinent information, http://disarmament2.un.org/wmd/npt/ (accessed May 11, 2004).

27. Since much of the DoD has varying dollar amounts reported in different reports and accounting practices changed from year to year, these figures must be considered estimates, but should be fairly representative of how DoD dollars were spent. Sources: William J. Perry, Annual Report to the President and the Congress (Washington, DC: U.S. Government Printing Office, February 1995), 273; the estimate is based on totaled CP funding in Figure 1.2 of this chapter; Donald Rumsfeld, "Annual Report to the President and the Congress," Department of Defense, Defense Budget, March 2003, 186, http://www.defenselink.mil/execsec/adr2003/index.html (accessed June 14, 2004); FY03 CP Pillar Breakout was furnished by Mr. R. Stephen Day, USAF Special Assistant for Counterproliferation (AF/XON) on May 11, 2004.

28. Since much of the DoD has varying dollar amounts reported in different reports and accounting practices changed from year to year, these must be considered estimates, but should be fairly representative of how DoD dollars were spent. For example, counterforce is difficult to calculate since many of the systems are dual use. Counterforce does not even appear as a separate item in FY95, and in FY03 includes only a portion of the weapons and other platforms that could or would be used in counterforce. Sources: calculated estimate based on FY96 budget from Steven M. Kosiak, *Nonproliferation & Counterproliferation: Investing for a Safer World?* (Washington, DC: Defense Budget Project, April 1995), 40; estimate from Steven M. Kosiak, ii; William J. Perry, Annual Report to the President and the Congress (Washington, DC: U.S. Government Printing Office, February 1995), 74; The Cooperative Threat Reduction budget was a calculated estimate based on cumulative obligations from FY94 and FY95 in William J. Perry, Annual Report to the President and the Congress (Department of Defense, Chapter 8, Cooperative Threat Reduction, March 1996, http://www.defenselink.mil/execsec/adr96/chapt_8.html (accessed May 17, 2004); William J. Perry, February 1995, Appendix A, Budget Tables, 273; FY03 CP Pillar Breakout was furnished by Mr. R. Stephen Day, USAF Special Assistant for Counterproliferation (AF/XON) on May 11, 2004; CTR breakout was not included with CP Pillar Breakout from Mr. R. Stephen Day but was extracted from Christine Kucia, "CTR Programs Get Boost With Budget Request," *Arms Control Today* 33, no. 2 (March 2003): 27; Donald Rumsfeld, Annual Report to the President and the Congress, Department of Defense, Defense Budget, March 2003, 186, http://www.defenselink.mil/execsec/adr2003/index.html (accessed June 14, 2004).

29. "Growth in United Nations Membership, 1945–2003," United Nations Web site, Department of Public Information, April 23, 2003, http://www.un.org/Overview/growth.htm (accessed May 5, 2004).

30. Frederick R. Sidell, Ernest T. Takafuji, and David R. Franz, eds., *Textbook of Military Medicine: Medical Aspects of Chemical and Biological Warfare*, part 1, *Warfare, Weaponry, and the Casualty* (Washington, DC: Office of the Surgeon General at TMM Publications, 1997), 419; "List of States Parties to the Convention on the Prohibition of the Development, Production and Stockpiling of Bacteriological (Biological) and Toxin Weapons and on their Destruction," The Biological and Toxin Weapons Convention Web site, November 2003, http://www.opbw.org/convention/btwcsps.html (accessed May 10, 2004).

31. "Background on Chemical Disarmament 2000s," *Organization for the Prohibition of Chemical Weapons*, http://www.opcw.org/html/intro/chemdisarm_2k.html (accessed May 10, 2004).

32. U.S. Department of State, Office of the Coordinator for Counterterrrorism, "Overview of State-Sponsored Terrorism," *Patterns of Global Terrorism-2002*, April 30, 2003, http://www.state.gov/s/ct/rls/pgtrpt/2002/html/19988.htm (accessed May 5, 2004).

33. "Fact Sheet, Proliferation Security Initiative, Statement of Interdiction Principles," The White House Web site, September 4, 2003, http://www.whitehouse.gov/news/releases/2003/09/20030904-11.html (accessed April 13, 2004); Colin Robinson, "The Proliferation Security Initiative: Naval Interception Bush-Style," *Defense Monitor, Center for Defense Information*, August 25, 2003, http://www.cdi.org/friendlyversion/printversion.cfm?documentID=1667 (accessed April 13, 2004).

34. Circular error probable: an indicator of the delivery accuracy of a weapon system, used as a factor in determining probable damage to a target. It is the radius of a circle within which half of a missile's projectiles are expected to fall. "Acronyms, Abbreviations, and Glossary," Gulf Link, http://www.gulflink.osd.mil/scud_info_ii/scud_info_taba.htm#TAB%20A%20-%20Acronyms,%20Abbreviations,%20and%20Glossary (accessed May 5, 2004).

35. "The National Strategy For Homeland Security: Office of Homeland Security," The White House Web site, http://www.whitehouse.gov/homeland/book/ (accessed May 5, 2004).

## Chapter 2

1. Consideration of WMD proliferation by nonstate actors is not treated in this chapter although it remains a concern.

2. For further discussion, see Chapter 10 by Lavoy and Meyers, 334. Of the 5,500 that went to hospitals, only 1,000 needed medical attention although 3,800 had some physical symptoms.

3. The White House, *The National Security Strategy of the United States of America* (Washington, DC: U.S. Government Printing Office, September 2002).

4. Given U.S. conventional dominance, states are likely to seek asymmetric ways to deter or confront the United States. At the same time, the United States has every incentive to keep future conflicts conventional so that it can play to its strengths.

5. "The Worldwide Threat in 2003: Evolving Dangers in a Complex World," testimony to the Senate Select Committee on Intelligence of the Director of Central

Intelligence, George Tenet, February 11, 2003, http://www.cia.gov/cia/public_affairs/speeches/2003/dci_speech_02112 003.html (accessed January 14, 2004); "Unclassified Report to Congress on the Acquisition of Technology Related to Weapons of Mass Destruction and Advanced Conventional Munitions, 1 July through 13 December 2001," *Central Intelligence Agency*, http://www.cia.gov/cia/publications/bian/bian_jan_2003.htm (accessed January 5, 2003).

6. South Africa, Belarus, Ukraine, and Kazakstan all gave up nuclear weapons they had manufactured. Other states, such as Romania, South Korea, Taiwan, and Sweden abandoned their programs short of producing nuclear weapons either under pressure or after the regime changed.

7. Fewer than 1,000 of the 5,500 had physical injuries from the sarin attack. The others, more than 4,500, were fearful of having been injured, enough so that they went to the hospital.

8. Office of the Secretary of Defense (OSD), *Proliferation: Threat and Response* (Washington, DC: U.S. Government Printing Office, January 2001), 34.

9. The author was first made aware of this conflict in discussions with George Perkovich.

10. Paul Kerr, "A Sprawling Nuclear Black Market," *Arms Control Today*, March 2004, 23. See also Douglas Frantz and Josh Meyer, "For Sale: Nuclear Expertise," *Los Angeles Times*, February 22, 2004, 1, http://www.latimes.com/la-fg-nuke22feb22,1,6800294.story (accessed July 1, 2004).

11. David Rhode, "Pakistanis Question Official Ignorance of Atom Transfers," *New York Times*, February 3, 2004, 1, http://nytimes.com/2004/02/03/international/asia/03STAN.html?th (accessed July 1, 2004).

12. Marshall Breit, "Iran's Natanz Facility," Carnegie Endowment for International Peace Web site, May 2, 2003, http://www.proliferationnews.org (accessed September 17, 2003).

13. Senate Governmental Affairs Committee, Hearing on Nuclear Proliferation, February 24, 1993. Oehler has now retired from the CIA. He was, at the time, the Director of the CIA's Nonproliferation Center, now part of another division after a reorganization.

14. Russian Federation, Foreign Intelligence Services Report, "A New Challenge after the Cold War: Proliferation of Weapons of Mass Destruction," Joint Publications Research Service (JPRS) report, *Proliferation Issues*, JPRS-TND-93-007, March 5, 1993, 29.

15. U.S. Department of State, *Patterns of Global Terrorism 2002* (Washington, DC: U.S. Government Printing Office, April 2003), 77.

16. "Unclassified Report to Congress on the Acquisition of Technology Related to Weapons of Mass Destruction and Advanced Conventional Munitions, 1 July through 31 December 2001."

17. Glenn Kessler, "N. Korea Nuclear Estimate to Rise: U.S. Report to Say Country Has At Least 8 Bombs," *Washington Post*, April 28, 2004, http://www.washingtonpost.com/wp-dyn/articles/A47833-2004Apr27.html (accessed May 12, 2004).

18. "North Korea Nuke Program Caught By U.S. Intelligence," *Washington Post*, October 18, 2002.

19. A. Q. Khan's clandestine black marketing of expertise and technology has gone to at least North Korea, Libya, and Iran and allegedly provided the DPRK

with centrifuge designs and components. See "A Sprawling Nuclear Black Market," *Arms Control Today* (March 2004): 23.

20. Jon B. Wolfsthal, "Estimates of North Korea's Unchecked Nuclear Weapons Production Potential," *Proliferation News,* http://www.proliferationnews.org (accessed July 25, 2003).

21. Larry Niksch, "North Korea's Nuclear Weapons Program" (Washington, DC: Library of Congress, Congressional Research Service, February 27, 2001), 2.

22. Joseph Cirincione, with Jon B. Wolfsthal and Miriam Rajkumar, *Deadly Arsenals: Tracking Weapons of Mass Destruction* (Washington, DC: Carnegie Endowment for International Peace, 2002), 94.

23. OSD, *Proliferation Threat and Response,* January 2001, 11.

24. Statement of Undersecretary of State John Bolton, Fifth Review Conference of the Biological Weapons Convention, Geneva, Switzerland, November 19, 2001.

25. Cirincione et al., *Deadly Arsenals,* 250.

26. "Pakistan's Nuclear Forces, 2001," NRDC Nuclear Notebook, *Bulletin of the Atomic Scientists* 58, no. 1 (January/February 2002): 20–21, http://www.thebulletin.org/issues/nukenotes/jf02nukenote.html.

27. OSD, *Proliferation: Threat and Response*, January 2001, 43.

28. Ibid., 40.

29. Ibid.

30. Ibid.

31. Ibid.

32. U.S. Department of State, *Patterns of Global Terrorism 2002,* 81.

33. UN Security Council Resolution 687, April 3, 1991.

34. UNSCOM, Seventh Report Under UN Resolution 715, October 4, 1995.

35. E. J. Hogendoorn, "A Chemical Weapons Atlas," *Bulletin of the Atomic Scientists* (September–October 1997): 37.

36. "Iraq's Weapons of Mass Destruction Programs," Director of Central Intelligence, October 2002, 2 (referred to as CIA report on Iraq, October 2002).

37. OSD, *Proliferation: Threat and Response*, January 2001, 40.

38. CIA report on Iraq, 2. See note 5.

39. Ibid.

40. Charles Duelfer, *Comprehensive Report of the Special Adviser to the DCI on Iraq's WMD* (Washington, DC: Central Intelligence Agency, October 2004). This report indicates that, "In Saddam's view, WMD helped save the regime multiple times. He believed that during the Iran-Iraq War chemical weapons had halted Iranian ground offensives and that ballistic missile attacks on Tehran had broken its political will. Similarly, during Desert Storm, Saddam believed WMD had deterred coalition forces from pressing their attack beyond the goal of freeing Kuwait. WMD had even played a role in crushing Shi'a revolts in the south following the 1991 cease fire." (See the section on "Regime Strategic Intent: Key Findings.")

41. Paul Kerr, "IAEA Praises Libya for Disarmament Efforts," *Arms Control Today* (April 2004): 27–28.

42. Ibid., 28.

43. Ibid. For more detail, see also "Libya's Chemical Weapons Program," *Arms Control Today* (March 2004): 8.

44. Paul Kerr, "U.S. Lifts More Sanctions on Libya," *Arms Control Today* (May 2004): 5.

45. Ibid.

46. Paul Kerr, "IAEA Praises Libya for Disarmament Efforts," *Arms Control Today* (April 2004): 27–28.

47. Ibid., 28.

48. Ibid., 24.

49. Paul Kerr, "Libya to Keep Limited Missile Force," *Arms Control Today* (May 2004): 28.

50. Paul Kerr, "IAEA Praises Libya for Disarmament Efforts," *Arms Control Today* (April 2004): 28.

51. Ibid.

52. Chemical arms were used by Egypt in the civil war in Yemen three times: in 1963, 1965, and 1967. See Frederick J. Brown, *Chemical Warfare: A Study in Restraints* (Princeton, NJ: Princeton University Press, 1968); see also Lawrence Scheinman, "NBC and Missile Proliferation Issues in the Middle East," in *Middle East Security Issues: In the Shadow of Weapons of Mass Destruction Proliferation*, ed. Barry R. Schneider (Maxwell AFB, AL: U.S. Air Force Counterproliferation Center, December 1999), 7–8.

53. "Egypt's Special Weapons Guide," *Federation of American Scientists*, http://www.fas.org/nuke/guide/egypt/index.html (accessed July 17, 2003).

54. Russian Federation, Foreign Intelligence Services Report, "A New Challenge after the Cold War: Proliferation of Weapons of Mass Destruction," Joint Publications Research Service (JPRS) report, *Proliferation Issues*, JPRS-TND-93-007, March 5, 1993, 23 (referred to hereafter as the JPRS report).

55. Scheinman, "NBC and Missile Proliferation Issues," 21.

56. Senate Governmental Affairs Committee, Hearing on Nuclear Proliferation (Witness James Woolsey, Director of Central Intelligence), February 24, 1993.

57. Russian Federation, Foreign Intelligence Services Report, "A New Challenge after the Cold War: Proliferation of Weapons of Mass Destruction," Joint Publications Research Service (JPRS) report, *Proliferation Issues*, JPRS-TND-93-007, March 5, 1993.

58. Ibid., 21.

59. "Nuclear Posture Review [Excerpts]," January 8, 2002, http://www.globalsecurity.org/wmd/library/policy/ dod/npr.htm (accessed September 17, 2003).

# Chapter 3

1. This chapter draws on testimony of Dr. Jerrold Post before the National Security Sub-Committee of the Committee on Government Reform hearings on Bioterrorism on October 12, 2001, on testimony before the United Nations International Atomic Energy Agency at a special session on nuclear terrorism in Vienna, Austria, November 2001, and on chapters "Psychological and Motivational Factors in Terrorist Decision Making: Implications for CBW Terrorism," in *Toxic Terror*, ed. Jonathan Tucker (Cambridge, MA: MIT Press, 2000); and "Prospects for

Chemical/Biological Terrorism: Psychological Incentives and Constraints," in *Bioterrorism*, ed. Robert Ursano, Ann Norwood, and Carol Fullerton (Cambridge: Cambridge University Press, 2004).

2. David Rapoport, "Messianic Sanctions for Terror," *Comparative Politics* 20, no. 2 (1988): 195–213.

3. Walter Laqueur, *The New Terrorism* (New York: Oxford University Press, 1999), 11.

4. Jessica Stern, *The Ultimate Terrorists* (Cambridge, MA: Harvard University Press, 1999), 42.

5. Ibid.

6. Jerrold M. Post, *Weapons of Mass Destruction Terrorism: A Systematic Examination of Individual and Group Decision Making* (Washington, DC: Elliott School of International Affairs, George Washington University, 2002), 47.

7. This threshold had already been crossed in 1985 with the bombing of an Air India flight by Sikh terrorists in which 329 were killed.

8. Of the 5,500 that went to hospitals, only 1,000 needed medical attention although 3,800 had some physical symptoms. See Chapter 10, Lavoy and Meyers, 334.

9. "Global Proliferation of Weapons of Mass Destruction: A Case Study of Aum Shinrikyo," *Senate Government Affairs Permanent Subcommittee on Investigations Staff Statement*, October 31, 1995, http://www.fas.org/irp/congress/1995_rpt/aum/ (accessed July 8, 2003).

10. John M. Deutch, "Excerpt from Testimony before the Permanent Subcommittee on Investigations of the Senate Committee on Government Affairs, March 20, 1996," *Super Terrorism: Biological, Chemical, and Nuclear* (Ardsley, NY: Transnational Publishers, 2001), 71.

11. John F. Sopko, "The Cooperative Threat Reduction Program in Transition: From Nukes to Gas, Bugs, and Thugs," *Countering the Proliferation and Use of Weapons of Mass Destruction* (New York: McGraw-Hill, 1998), 43.

12. Gavin Cameron, *Nuclear Terrorism: A Threat Assessment for the 21st Century* (New York: Palgrave McMillan, 1999), 211.

13. Stern, *The Ultimate Terrorists*, 86.

14. Jerrold M. Post, "Killing in the Name of God: Osama bin Laden and Radical Islam," Counterproliferation Papers, Future Warfare Series, No. 18, November 2002, Maxwell Air Force Base, Alabama.

15. Nadine Gurr and Benjamin Cole, *The New Face of Terrorism: Threats from Weapons of Mass Destruction* (London: I. B. Tauris, 2002), x–xi.

16. Bruce Hoffman, *Inside Terrorism* (New York: Columbia University Press, 1998), 149.

17. Stern, *The Ultimate Terrorists*, 2.

18. James Glave, "Have Crackers Found the Military's Achilles' Heel?" *Wired*, April 21, 1998. On-line, Internet, July 8, 2003, http://www.wired.com/news/print/0,1294,11811,00.html (accessed July 8, 2003).

19. B. Meeks and M. Moran, "India's Nuclear Servers Hacked, Compromised," *MSNBC*, June 5, 1998, http://www.msnbc.com/news/170944.asp (accessed July 8, 2003).

20. Jerrold Post, Kevin Ruby, and Eric Shaw, "From Car Bombs to Logic Bombs: The Growing Threat of Information Terrorism," *Terrorism and Political Violence* 12, no. 2 (Summer 2000): 97–122.

21. Alex Schmid, *Political Terrorism* (New York: North-Holland Publishing Co., 1983.)

22. "Patterns of Global Terrorism: 2002," *Office of the Coordinator for Counterterrorism, U.S. Department of State*, April 30, 2003, http://www.state.gov/s/ct/rls/pgtrpt/2002/html/19988.htm (accessed July 8, 2003).

23. Jerrold Post, "Terrorist Psycho-Logic: Terrorist Behavior as a Product of Psychological Forces," in *Origins of Terrorism*, ed. W. Reich (Cambridge: Cambridge University Press, 1990), 25–40.

24. Qur'an (Koran), 2: 190–193.

25. Robert Robins and Jerrold Post, *Political Paranoia: The Psychopolitics of Hatred* (New Haven, CT: Yale University Press, 1997), 153–54.

26. See David E. Kaplan and Andrew Marshall, *The Cult From the End of the World* (New York: Crown Publishers, 1996).

27. For a detailed account of the cult and its use of biological agents, see W. Seth Carus, "The Rajneeshees," in *Toxic Terror: Assessing Terrorist Use of Chemical and Biological Weapons*, ed. Jonathan B. Tucker (Cambridge, MA: MIT Press, 2000), 115–138.

28. Ibid.

29. Christopher C. Harmon, *Terrorism Today* (London: Frank Cass Publishers, 2000), 7.

30. Ibid., 8; see also David Foreman, *Confessions of an Eco-Warrior* (New York: Harmony Books, 1991).

31. An earlier version of this paper can be found in R. W. Mengel, "Terrorism and New Technologies of Destruction: An Overview of the Potential Risk," in *Disorders and Terrorism: Report of the Task Force on Disorders and Terrorism*, U.S. National Advisory Committee on Criminal Justice Standards and Goals (Washington, DC: U.S. Government Printing Office, 1977), 443–73.

32. Jerrold M. Post, Ehud Sprinzak, and Laurita M. Denny, "Terrorists in Their Own Words: Interviews with 35 Incarcerated Middle East Terrorists," *Terrorism and Political Violence* 15, no. 1 (Spring 2003): 171–184.

33. Seth Carus, *Bioterrorism and Biocrimes: The Illicit Use of Biological Agents in the 20th Century*, Working Paper (Washington, DC: Center for Counterproliferation Research, National Defense University, February 2001), 12, http://www.ndu.edu/centercounter/Full_Doc.pdf (accessed July 8, 2003).

34. Richard Falkenrath, who served as special assistant to the President for Homeland Security, has in the past stated that chemical weapons precursor materials are largely dual-use and are commercially available, that there are only moderate requirements to produce the necessary agents, and that weaponization is not difficult. Richard Falkenrath, Robert Newman, and Bradley Thayer, *America's Achilles' Heel: Nuclear, Biological and Chemical Terrorism and Covert Attack* (Cambridge, MA: MIT Press, 1998), 214–15.

35. Ron Purver, *Chemical and Biological Terrorism: The Threat According to the Open Literature: Chemical Terrorism* (Ottawa: Canadian Security Intelligence Service, 1995); and Ron Purver, *Chemical and Biological Terrorism: The Threat According to the Open Literature: CB Terrorism* (Ottawa: Canadian Security Intelligence

Service, 1995), http://www.csis-scrs.gc.ca/eng/miscdocs/tabintr_e.html#toc (accessed June 10, 2004).

36. Ibid.

37. Stern, *The Ultimate Terrorists*, 26–27.

38. Cameron, *Nuclear Terrorism: A Threat Assessment for the 21st Century*, 197–98.

39. R. W. Mengel, *Terrorism and New Technologies of Destruction: An Overview of the Potential Risk* (Disorders and Terrorism: Report of the Task Force on Disorders and Terrorism), U.S. National Advisory Committee on Criminal Justice Standards and Goals (Washington, DC: U.S. Government Printing Office, 1977), 443–73.

40. W. Seth Carus, *Bioterrorism and Biocrimes: The Illicit Use of Biological Agents in the 20th Century* (Washington, DC: Center for Counterproliferation Research, NDU, March 1999), 55–57.

41. After the Tokyo attacks 5,500 Japanese reported to hospitals, but 4,500 were "worried well." Only 1,000 had physical injuries, but more may have suffered post-traumatic stress syndrome.

42. Jonathan B. Tucker, ed., *Toxic Terror: Assessing Terrorist Use of Chemical and Biological Weapons* (Cambridge, MA: MIT Press, 2000).

43. Glassine is a word meaning a thin dense transparent or semitransparent paper highly resistant to the passage of air and grease.

44. Post et al., "Terrorists in their Own Words," 171–184.

# Chapter 4

1. Earlier drafts of this paper have benefited from thoughtful and constructive critiques by Lewis Dunn, Michael Moodie, and Victor Utgoff. The author alone remains responsible for the final arguments presented here.

2. Michael Moodie, "Multilateral Arms Control: Challenges and Opportunities," in *Challenges in Arms Control for the 1990s*, ed. James Brown (Amsterdam: VU University Press, 1992), 71–82. Moodie was, at the time, assistant director for multilateral affairs in the U.S. Arms Control and Disarmament Agency.

3. Richard Hooper, "Strengthening IAEA Safeguards in an Era of Nuclear Cooperation," *Arms Control Today* 25, no. 9 (November 1995): 14–18.

4. UN Security Council Resolution on proliferation: note by the President of the Security Council, UN Document S/235000, January 31, 1992.

5. For a review of the effort to strengthen the BWC, see Jonathan B. Tucker, "In the Shadow of Anthrax: Strengthening the Biological Disarmament Regime," *Nonproliferation Review* 9, no. 1 (Spring 2002): 112–21.

6. For a review of this effort, see Office of the Secretary of Defense, *Proliferation: Threat and Response* (Washington, DC: U.S. Government Printing Office, April 1996).

7. Cited in John Ikenberry, "American Grand Strategy in the Age of Terror," *Survival* 43, no. 4 (Winter 2001–2002): 27.

8. For some analyses of the progress made during the 1990s in working these various problems, see Brad Roberts, "Proliferation and Nonproliferation in the 1990s: Looking for the Right Lessons," *Nonproliferation Review* 6, no. 4 (Fall 1999): 70–82; Jayantha Dhanapala, "Multilateralism and the Future of the Global Nuclear

Nonproliferation Regime," *Nonproliferation Review* 8, no. 3 (Fall–Winter 2001): 99–106; Jonathan B. Tucker, "The Chemical Weapons Convention: Has it Enhanced U.S. Security?" *Arms Control Today* (April 2001): 8–12; and Siegfried S. Hecker, "Thoughts about an Integrated Strategy for Nuclear Cooperation with Russia," *Nonproliferation Review* 8, no. 2 (Summer 2001): 1–24.

9. William Schneider, "Weapons Proliferation and Missile Defense: the Strategic Case," in *Present Dangers: Crisis and Opportunity in American Foreign and Defense Policy,* ed. Robert Kagan and William Kristol (San Francisco: Encounter Books, 2000), 269.

10. Ibid., 269, 271.

11. Phillip C. Saunders, "New Approaches to Nonproliferation: Supplementing or Supplanting the Regime?" *Nonproliferation Review* (Fall–Winter 2001): 123–136.

12. Tucker, "In the Shadow of Anthrax."

13. Statement to the Conference on Disarmament, United Nations, Geneva, Switzerland, January 2002.

14. "Expounding Bush's Approach to U.S. Nuclear Security, an Interview with John R. Bolton," *Arms Control Today* (March 2002): 3–8.

15. In each significant debate over the nuclear era about how to respond to the next nuclear proliferation challenge, there has been a body of opinion reflecting the view that some additional proliferation might serve U.S. interests, whether by strengthening an ally or by providing security to a friendly state for which a security guarantee would not be viable. Such arguments have tended to draw on the thinking of Kenneth Waltz about nuclear proliferation that "more may be better" because it stabilizes competitive relationships. See Scott D. Sagan and Kenneth N. Waltz, *The Spread of Nuclear Weapons: A Debate Renewed* (New York: Norton and Co., 2003). But as a matter of policy, the U.S. Government has opposed each and every new nuclear state, including even Britain.

16. Both are available at the Web site of the White House, White House Web site, www.whitehouse.gov (accessed January 10, 2004).

17. "Countries Draft Guidelines for Intercepting Proliferation," *Arms Control Today* 33, no. 7 (September 2003): 27, 48.

18. Remarks by the President on Weapons of Mass Destruction Proliferation, National Defense University, Washington, DC, February 11, 2004, www.whitehouse.gov (accessed January 10, 2004).

19. "Transcript: David Kay at Senate Hearing," *CNN.com,* January 28, 2004, www.cnn.com/2004/US/01/28/kay.transcript/ (accessed November 22, 2004). David Kay's report also indicated that Iraq still had traces of a BW program but no serious ongoing effort. Also, his team found Iraq was not in full compliance with UN resolution and Desert Storm cease-fire terms with regard to the deployment of ballistic missiles.

20. The Chechen acquisition of a small amount of Cesium-136 and threatened use, with no result, is a possible exception, except that they appeared to have no more than they buried in a Moscow park for police to find. The Aum Shinrikyo cult in Japan manufactured its own biological and chemical weapons. There is also the possibility that the South African chemical and biological weapons programs were exported to Zimbabwe and elsewhere in Africa. See Stephen Burgess and Helen Purkitt, *The Rollback of South Africa's Chemical and Biological Warfare Program* (Maxwell AFB, AL: USAF Counterproliferation Center, April 2001), 17–38; see also

W. Seth Carus, *Bioterrorism and Biocrimes* (Washington, DC: Center for Counterproliferation Research, NDU, March 1999 edition), 47–86.

21. Albert Wohlstetter, "Nuclear Sharing: NATO and the N+1 Country," *Foreign Affairs* 39, no. 3 (April 1961): 355–387.

22. These arguments are elaborated in more detail in Brad Roberts, *Weapons Proliferation and World Order After the Cold War* (Boston, MA: Kluwer Press, 1995).

23. Leonard S. Spector, "Repentant Nuclear Proliferants," *Foreign Policy* no. 88 (Fall 1992): 3–20; Mitchell Reiss, *Bridled Ambition: Why Countries Constrain Their Nuclear Capabilities* (Washington, DC: Woodrow Wilson Center Press, 1995).

24. For more on nuclear recidivism, see Kurt M. Campbell, "Nuclear Proliferation beyond Rogues," *Washington Quarterly* 26, no. 1 (Winter 2002–2003): 7–15; Ariel E. Levite, "Never Say Never Again: Nuclear Reversal Revisited," *International Security* 27, no. 3 (Winter 2002–2003): 59–88.

25. Secretary of Defense Donald H. Rumsfeld, remarks delivered on the 10th anniversary of the George Marshall Center in Garmisch, Germany, June 11, 2003.

26. For the argument that winning is possible by two conservative commentators, see Henry Sokolski, *Best of Intentions: America's Campaign Against Strategic Weapons Proliferation* (Westport, CT: Praeger, 2001); and Baker Spring, *Ten Principles for Combating Nuclear Proliferation*, Heritage Lecture No. 783, Heritage Foundation, Washington, DC, March 27, 2003.

27. *National Strategy to Combat WMD* (Washington, DC: The White House, 2003), 6.

28. Joseph Cirincione, with Jon B. Wolfstahl and Miriam Rajkumar, *Deadly Arsenals: Tracking Weapons of Mass Destruction* (Washington, DC: Carnegie Endowment for International Peace, 2002).

29. See remarks by Richard N. Haass on "hard-headed multilateralism" to the Carnegie Endowment for International Peace and the Center on International Cooperation, November 14, 2001, www.ceip.org (accessed January 10, 2004); see also Richard N. Haass, "What to Do with American Primacy," *Foreign Affairs* 78, no. 5 (September–October 1999).

30. For more on the argument that American primacy is the major foreign policy theme for most of the other actors in the international system, see Brad Roberts, *American Primacy and Major Power Concert: A Critique of the 2002 National Security Strategy* (Alexandria, VA: Institute for Defense Analyses, 2002).

31. Saunders, "New Approaches to Nonproliferation," 133–135.

32. Rumsfeld, remarks delivered on the 10th anniversary.

33. Coral Bell, "Normative Shift," *National Interest* (Winter 2002/2003): 44.

34. William Walker, "Nuclear Order and Disorder," *International Affairs* 76, no. 4 (2000): 703–724.

35. This was an argument made in the context of his case for going to war to expel Saddam in such close succession to the war against the Taliban. See Richard N. Perle, "Next Stop, Iraq," remarks to the Foreign Policy Research Institute, November 14, 2001, www.aei.org (accessed January 10, 2004). More precisely, Perle has argued that a wider war ought not be necessary to achieve desired changes among many countries so long as a good example is made of one or two countries.

## Chapter 5

1. See the remarks of George Ullrich, Director, Weapons Systems, Office of the Secretary of Defense, ODUSD (S&T), "Presentation to the 2003 Munitions Executive Summit," Falls Church, VA, February 12, 2003.

2. *The United States Strategic Bombing Surveys* (European War) (Pacific War) (Maxwell AFB, AL: Air University Press, 1987), 13.

3. David A. Deptula, "Effects-Based Operations: Change in the Nature of Warfare," *Defense and Airpower Series* (Washington, DC: Aerospace Education Foundation, 2001), 5–6, http://www.aef.org/pub/psbook.pdf (accessed July 1, 2004).

4. Ibid., 6. The original source is *The United States Strategic Bombing Surveys*, 13.

5. Ibid., 5.

6. Ibid.

7. Ibid.

8. Lt. Gen. Buster C. Glosson, "Impact of Precision Weapons on Air Combat Operations," *Airpower Journal* (Summer 1993): 5, http://www.airpower.maxwell.af.mil/airchronicles/apj/glosson.html (accessed July 1, 2004).

9. Anthony H. Cordesman, "Instant Lessons of the Iraq War," Washington, Center for Strategic and International Studies, April 14, 2003, 88.

10. Sandra I. Erwin, "Precision-Guided Bombs Labeled 'Transformational,' " *National Defense,* Arlington, VA, October 2001, http://proquest.umi.com/pqdweb?index=0&did=000000082252830&Srch Mode=5&Fmt=3&retrieve Group=0&VInst=PROD&VType=PQD&RQT=309&x=-&VName =PQD&TS= 1061406042&clientId=417 (accessed February 24, 2003).

11. Bill Sweetman, "Scratching the Surface: Next Century Air-to-Ground Weapons," *Jane's International Defense Review,* July 1997, 55.

12. Glosson, "Impact of Precision Weapons on Air Combat Operations," 5.

13. Ibid.

14. Ibid.

15. "Joint Direct Attack Munition (JDAM)," *United States Navy Fact File,* February 18, 2003, http://www.chinfo.navy.mil/navpalib/factfile/weapons/wep-jdam.html (accessed July 1, 2004).

16. Federation of American Scientists (FAS), Military Analysis Network, "Smart Bombs," http://fas.org/man/dod-101/sys/smart/index.html (accessed July 1, 2004). Improved U.S. PGMs include the following: GM-62 Walleye, AGM-65 MAVERICK, AGM-84 HARPOON, SLAM, AGM-86C CALCM, AGM-88 HARM, AGM-130, AGM-142 HAVE NAP, AGM-154 JSOW, AGM-158 JASSM, BGM-109 TOMAHAWK and its variants, LOCASS, FRSW, AARMD, and the HYS-TRIKE/FAST HAWK.

17. Glosson, "Impact of Precision Weapons on Air Combat Operations," 7.

18. FAS, The United States has acquired, for example, 11,000 GBU-10 and 32,000 GBU-12 guided bombs; 13,000 GBU-24s; 3,200 GBU-27s, and 300 bunker-busting GBU-28s. The United States also possesses TV/IR guided bombs such as the GBU-15 munition and other GPS-guided bombs such as the GBU-15, GBU-24 E/B, GBU-29, GBU-32, the GBU-36, GBU-37, and GBU-ADW, and other guided bombs such as the 40,000 WCMDs acquired since 1998.

19. Deptula, "Effects-Based Operations," 7.

20. "Proliferation: Threat and Response," Office of the Secretary of Defense (Washington, DC: U.S. Department of Defense, January 2001), 90.

21. "Nuclear Posture Review [Excerpts]," http://www.globalsecurity.org/wmd/library/policy/dod/npr.htm (accessed July 1, 2004).

22. Barry R. Schneider, "Invitation to a Nuclear Beheading," *Across The Board*, July/August 1983, 13.

23. Nuclear Posture Review [Excerpts]," 90.

24. Ibid., 90–91. The Tunnel Defeat Demonstration Program is jointly sponsored by the Defense Threat Reduction Agency (DTRA) and by the Defense Intelligence Agency (DIA). Currently, the Hard Target Defeat Office is housed in the DTRA Technology Development Division, directed by Dr. Anthony Thomas Hopkins.

25. This is a method of tunnel construction where a trench is excavated, the tunnel structure built, and then it is covered with earth and rock.

26. Michael Giltrud, Briefing, "Emerging Concepts of Counterforce (CF) Weapons," DTRA/TD Slide, presented at Air War College, April 15, 2003.

27. See the *Gulf War Air Power Survey*. See also Rear Admiral Stephen H. Baker, USN (Ret.), "Iraqi Scuds: A Threat We Have To Respect," CDI Terrorism Project, *Center for Defense Information*, December 3, 2002; Baker summarizes, "on 42 occasions, patrolling aircraft spotted a launch plume, leading to eight attacks. Overall, tactical aircraft reportedly failed to destroy any Scud launchers," 2.

28. Baker, "Iraqi Scuds," 2.

29. *Gulf War Air Power Survey;* see also Barry R. Schneider, *Future War and Counterproliferation: U.S. Military Reponses to NBC Proliferation Threats* (Westport, CT.: Praeger Publishers, 1999), 155.

30. Timothy F. Lindemann, "U.S. Nuclear, Biological, Chemical and Missile Counterforce Capabilities," unpublished dissertation, USAF National Security Fellows Program, June 2001 draft, 9.

31. Ibid.

32. Ibid.

33. These thoughts are the personal assessment of Mr. Steven Hancock, an intelligence officer from the DIA's Missile and Space Intelligence Center (MSIC), who was a participant in the Combined Air Operations Center for Operation Iraqi Freedom. MSIC itself has taken no official position on the lessons of OIF.

34. Ullrich, remarks, 11.

35. Lindemann, "U.S. Nuclear, Biological, Chemical and Missile Counterforce Capabilities," 13.

36. Ullrich, remarks, 38-40.

37. Briefing on "JTAMDO 2010 Vision for Attack Operations," by Colonel Rich Harris, USAF, JTAMDO, JCS/J8, to USAF Counterproliferation Center (CPC) Workshop, March 26, 2003. See CPC *Summary Report* submitted to Technology Division, U.S. Defense Threat Reduction Agency, September 30, 2003, 11.

38. Ibid., 10.

39. Ibid., 11.

40. Thomas E. Ricks, "U.S. Military Considers Weapons that Disable Bunkers, Spare People," *Wall Street Journal,* July 1, 1999, 1.

41. Paula R. Kaufman, "Fierce Thermobaric Weapons Readied Against Underground Bunkers," *IEE Spectrum*, November 19, 2002, http://www.spectrum.ieee.org/WEBONLY/wonews/nov02/thermo.html (accessed

September 24, 2003). Thermobaric comes from two Greek words: "therme" for heat and "baros" for pressure. As Dr. Stephen Younger, Director of the Defense Threat Reduction Agency, has stated, "we have several programs ... to look at advanced methods for agent defeat, such as generating a high enough temperature for a long enough period to kill biological organisms. This appears to be a promising route, but lacking that ability the best we may be able to do is immobilize the agent until ground forces have arrived." See "Issues and Events: Younger Speaks From the Frontline of Defense," *Physics Today* (February 2003), http://www.aip.org/pt/vol-56/iss-2/p23.html (accessed July 1, 2004).

42. "The DTRA Thermobaric ACTD," *Global Security*, http://www.globalsecurity.org/military/library/report/2001/010725-thermobaric.htm (accessed July 1, 2004).

43. John Pike, "Agent Defeat Weapon, Agent Defeat Warhead (ADW)," *Global Security*, Washington, DC, December 22, 2002, http://www.globalsecurity.org/military/systems/munitions/adw.htm (accessed July 1, 2004). ADWs are being designed to fit the GBU-15, GBU-24, GBU-27, GBU-28, GB-111B, AGM 130, and GBU-31s.

44. "DoD Readies 'Thermobaric,' Cave-Clearing Bomb For Enduring Freedom," *Inside The Air Force* 13, no. 1 (January 4, 2002), http://www.globalsecurity.org/military/library/news/2002/01/020104-Afws4.htm (accessed July 1, 2004); see also Kaufman, "Fierce Thermobaric Weapons," 1.

45. "U.S. DoD Expedites Anti-Chem-Bio Weapons Development," *Janes Information Group*, September 13, 2002, http://www.janes.com/press/pc020913_1.shtml (accessed July 1, 2004).

46. Mr. Vayl Oxford, Deputy Director, Technology Division, DTRA/TD, Briefing on "DTRA and Counterforce Operations Against Weapons of Mass Destruction," April 2000, USAF Counterproliferation Conference, Maxwell AFB, Alabama.

47. Ibid.

48. Ibid.

49. Ibid., 62.

50. Ibid., 59. The three major aspects of the CAPS program are (1) integration of intelligence and production process analyses to create detailed assessments of suspected proliferating country's WMD assets, (2) identification of critical nodes in each of these country's WMD programs, and (3) consequence management of attack plans.

51. See Counterproliferation Analysis and Targeting System (CAPS) at http://www.llnl.gov/nai/technologies/techinfo2.html. This is the Internet Web site of NISA, a Lawrence Livermore National Laboratory address.

52. "National Strategy to Combat Weapons of Mass Destruction," Washington, DC, The White House, December 2002, 3.

53. Barry R. Schneider quote that has become the motto of the U.S. Air Force Counterproliferation Center, Maxwell AFB, Alabama.

54. In considering the worth of any preemption decision, policy makers will be confronted with a number of important questions. [For an earlier discussion of these points, see Barry R. Schneider, "Offensive Action: A Viable Option?" *Future War and Counterproliferation: U.S. Military Responses to NBC Proliferation Threats* (Westport, CT: Praeger, 1999), 157–182.] For example,

- Should the United States initiate a war to deny a hostile government the use of its weapons of mass destruction? To prevent it from acquiring that capability?
- Or, should the U.S. leadership, in all peacetime cases, abstain from initiating war and take its chances with nonmilitary means of persuasion?
- How immediate is the adversary threat to use WMD? Has the United States exhausted other nonmilitary options first and does it have time to persist in these further?
- How certain is U.S. intelligence about the adversary WMD capabilities and likely timing of future WMD employment? Is the United States and/or its vital interests at immediate risk?
- Are key enemy WMD targets precisely located and vulnerable to U.S. preemptive strikes? Does the United States possess the required counterforce strike capabilities? What levels of damage could the adversary WMD inflict if the U.S. counterforce operation is not completely successful?
- Can the adversary be deterred by U.S. threats and warnings short of war?
- Is surprise achievable? If not, can the counterforce preemptive attack succeed?
- Are the United States and allied states safe from WMD retaliation from the adversary state or its regional allies?
- Is the United States committed to win the conflict once the preemptive strike sparks it? Has it carefully planned the initial campaign, the possible directions such a war might go in, and a reasoned exit strategy and postwar end game?
- Have the U.S. leaders set clear objectives and limits for U.S. military actions and chosen appropriate means?
- Finally, has the U.S. leadership weighed the costs and benefits of preemption as opposed to a nonmilitary set of options backed by the threat of retaliation? Which option holds the greater risk to U.S. national security, counterforce targeting or adopting a wait-and-see diplomatic/deterrence option?

55. Ibid., 162–164. As Daniel Webster, U.S. Secretary of State in 1841, wrote in a note to the British Government in the 1837 Caroline Case, "use of force by one nation against another is permissible as a self-defense action only if force is both necessary and proportionate"; see Zachary S. Davis, with Mitchell Reiss, consultant, "U.S. Counterproliferation Doctrine: Issues for Congress," CRS Report, Library of Congress, September 21, 1999, CRS-19.

56. Elihu Root, "The Real Monroe Doctrine," *American Journal of International Law* 35 (1914): 422. For an unsympathetic view of anticipatory self-defense, see Louis Henkin, *How Nations Behave*, 2nd ed. (New York: Columbia University Press, 1979), 141–145; for a more supportive view, note Myres S. McDougal and Florentino P. Feliciano, *Law and Minimum World Order: The Legal Regulation of International Coercion* (New Haven, CT: Yale University Press, 1961), 217–244; see also Schneider, "Offensive Action: A Viable Option," 169.

57. Brad Roberts, "Military Strikes Against NBC-Armed Rogue States; Is There a Moral Case for Preemption? Unpublished paper, August 3, 1996.

58. Michael Walzer, *Just and Unjust Wars*, 2nd ed. (New York: Basic Books, 1992), 24.

## Chapter 6

1. William Perry, *Annual Report of the Secretary of Defense to the President and the Congress*, February 1993, 73.

2. Counterproliferation Program Review Committee, *Report on Activities and Programs for Countering Proliferation*, May 1995, 27; Counterproliferation Program Review Committee, *Report on Activities and Programs for Countering Proliferation and NBC Terrorism*, May 1997, tables 1.2 and 5.1.

3. See, for example, the arguments made in James Lindsay and Michael O'Hanlon, *Defending America* (Washington, DC: Brookings Institute, 2001).

4. For good short histories, see the following: Donald R. Baucom, "Ballistic Missile Defense: A Short History," Missile Defense Agency, July 2000, www.acq.osd.mil/bmdo/bmdolink/html/briefhis.html (accessed June 11, 2004); Bradley Graham, "Back to the Future," in *Hit to Kill: The New Battle Over Shielding American From Missile Attack* (New York: Public Affairs Publishing, 2001); historical pages on the Web site of the Federation of American Scientists at www.fas.org/spp/starwars/program; John E. Pike, Bruce G. Blair, and Stephen I. Schwartz, "Defending Against the Bomb," in *Atomic Audit* (Washington, DC: Brookings Institution Press, 1998), 269–326; Kerry M. Kartchner, "The Future of the Offense-Defense Relationship," in *Arms Control: Cooperative Defense in a Changing Environment*, ed. Jeffrey A. Larsen (Boulder, CO: Lynne Rienner Press, 2002); Michael Krepon, *Cooperative Threat Reduction, Missile Defense, and the Nuclear Future* (Washington, DC: Henry L. Stimson Center, 2003); Douglas C. Waller, "The Strategic Defense Initiative and Arms Control," in *Encyclopedia of Arms Control and Disarmament*, ed. Richard Dean Burns, vol. 2 (New York: Charles Scribner's Sons, 1993); "Strategic Defensive Arms Control: The ABM Treaty and Star Wars," in *Arms Control and National Security: An Introduction* (Washington, DC: Arms Control Association, 1989), 67–83; and Ivo Daalder, "Deployment Criteria for Strategic Defences," in *Strategic Defences in the 1990s* (New York: St. Martin's Press, 1990), 5–23.

5. The action-reaction dynamic was put forth in a famous speech by Secretary of Defense Robert McNamara in San Francisco, CA, in September 1967, during which he condemned the idea of strategic defenses because of their likely negative influence on international stability, and then with convoluted logic announced the deployment of Sentinel. See Department of State, *Bulletin*, October 9, 1967, 449; and Robert S. McNamara, *The Essence of Security: Reflections in Office* (New York: Harper & Row, 1968), 65.

6. U.S. Arms Control and Disarmament Agency, *Documents in Disarmament 1983* (Washington, DC: U.S. Government Printing Office, February 1986), 199–200.

7. Kerry M. Kartchner, *Negotiating START: Strategic Arms Reduction Talks and the Quest for Stability* (New Brunswick: Transaction Books, 1992), 114–16, 241–43.

8. Highlights of Nitze's 1985 speech to the Philadelphia World Affairs Council found in Krepon, 94.

9. Donald R. Baucom, "Ballistic Missile Defense: A Brief History," Office of the Undersecretary of Defense for Acquisition, Technology and Logistics Web site, http://www.acq.osd.mil/bmdo/bmdolink/html/briefhis.html (accessed April 14, 2004).

10. Most of these are antiship missiles (of 130 varieties, produced by 17 nations); some of these can be modified into land-attack variants. Thirteen nations have or are pursuing land-attack cruise missile capabilities. Barry Schneider, *Future War and Counterproliferation: U.S. Military Responses to NBC Proliferation Threats* (Westport, CT: Praeger, 1999), 119; see also Dennis M. Gormley, "UAVs and Cruise Missiles as Possible Terrorist Weapons," in *New Challenges in Missile Proliferation, Missile Defense, and Space Security,* ed. James Clay Moltz, Occasional Paper 12 (Monterey, CA: Center for Nonproliferation Studies, Monterey Institute of International Studies, July 2003), 3–9.

11. "Foreign Missile Developments and the Ballistic Missile Threat Through 2015, An Unclassified Summary of a National Intelligence Estimate," *National Intelligence Council,* December 2001, www.odci.gov/nic/other _missilethreat2001.html (accessed January 5, 2004).

12. The National Intelligence Council has contained this statement in each annual report on ballistic missile proliferation since 1999.

13. *Ballistic and Cruise Missile Threat* (Wright-Patterson AFB, OH: National Air and Space Intelligence Center, August 2003), 22.

14. For a thorough discussion of the cruise missile threat, with special reference to their application as potential delivery vehicles for biological weapons, see Rex R. Kiziah, "Assessment of the Emerging Biocruise Threat," *Future Warfare Series No. 6* (Maxwell AFB, AL: USAF Counterproliferation Center, Air War College, August 2000); and Michael E. Dickey, "Biocruise: A Contemporary Threat," *Future Warfare Series No. 7* (Maxwell AFB, AL: USAF Counterproliferation Center, Air War College, September 2000).

15. Robert D. Walpole, National Intelligence Officer for Strategic and Nuclear Programs, "Statement for the Record to the Senate Subcommittee on International Security, Proliferation, and Federal Services, on the Ballistic Missile Threat to the United States," February 9, 2000, www.cia.gov/cia/public_affairs/speeches/2000/nio_speech_020900.html (accessed January 5, 2004).

16. "Excerpts from the DCI National Intelligence Estimate: President's Summary," *The Brookings Institution,* www.brook.edu/dybdocroot/press/companion/defendingamerica/appendix_b.htm (accessed February 2, 2004).

17. The unclassified version of the Gates Panel report is available at the Federation of American Scientists Web site, December 23, 1996, www.fas.org/irp/threat/missile/oca961908.htm (accessed January 5, 2004).

18. This conclusion was subsequently misinterpreted to imply that such a threat would materialize within five years of the Commission's report—that is, by 2003—and, when such a threat did not materialize by that date, the Rumsfeld Commission was criticized on this basis. But that is an inaccurate reading of the report's conclusion. The report did not identify any specific date, but simply predicted the amount of time needed to produce a long-range missile should such a country make a decision to do so.

19. The unclassified Executive Summary of the Rumsfeld Commission Report is available at Federation of American Scientists Web site, www.fas.org/irp/threat/bm-threat.htm (accessed January 5, 2004).

20. Ibid.

21. In a speech to the Carnegie Endowment for International Peace, National Intelligence Officer for Strategic and Nuclear Programs, Robert D. Walpole (senior official in charge of producing the missile threat NIEs) said, "Although the launch of the Taepo Dong 1 as a missile was expected for some time, its use as a space launch vehicle with a third stage was not." Central Intelligence Agency Web site, www.cia.gov/cia/public_affairs/speeches/1998/walpole_ speech_091798.html, 6 (accessed January 5, 2004).

22. Robert Walpole, "Statement for the Record to the Senate Subcommittee on International Security, Proliferation, and Federal Services, on the Ballistic Missile Threat to the United States."

23. The official unclassified summary is available at Director of Central Intelligence Web site, www.odci.gov/nic/other_missilethreat2001.html (accessed January 5, 2004)

24. Ibid.

25. "Excerpts from the DCI National Intelligence Estimate: President's Summary," *The Brookings Institution,* www.brook.edu/dybdocroot/press/companion/defendingamerica/appendix_b.htm (accessed February 2, 2004).

26. The specifics regarding individual weapons systems in this section comes from multiple sources, among them the following: Wade Boese, "Missile Defense, Post-ABM Treaty: No System, No Arms Race," and "Factfile: U.S. Missile Defense Programs at a Glance," both in *Arms Control Today* (June 2003): 20–28; Theresa Hitchens, "Technical Hurdles in U.S. Missile Defense Agency Programs," in Moltz, 10–17; the U.S. Missile Defense Agency Web site, www.acq.osd.mil/bmdo/bmdolink/html (accessed January 5, 2004) (see especially their series of short *MDA In-Depth* fact sheets, published in July 2003, including "Ballistic Missile Threat Challenge" and "The Ballistic Missile Defense System"); and the Web site of the Federation of American Scientists, www.fas.org (accessed January 5, 2004).

27. Krepon, *Cooperative Threat Reduction,* 128.

28. A good overview of theater missile defense can be found in Barry Schneider, "Theater Missile Defenses: Key to Future Operations," *Future War and Counterproliferation: US Military Responses to NBC Proliferation Threats* (Westport, CT: Praeger, 1999), 117–145.

29. This debate is best chronicled in Theodore A. Postol, "Lessons of the Gulf War Experience with Patriot," *International Security* 16, no. 3 (Winter 1991/1992): 119–71; and "Correspondence: Patriot Experience in the Gulf War," *International Security* 17, no. 1 (Summer 1992): 199–240; see also Steven A. Hildreth, "Evaluation of U.S. Army Assessment of Patriot Anti-tactical Missile Effectiveness in the War Against Iraq," *Congressional Research Service,* April 7, 1992. Ironically, it was the so-called "arms control community" in the United States, whose members—such as Theodore Postol—were most critical of its failings as an antimissile defense after the Gulf War, that lobbied to have Patriot's antimissile defense characteristics "dumbed down" during its development period in the 1980s for fear of violating the ABM Treaty.

30. Although the acronym remained the same, in 2004 the DoD renamed this program by replacing "Theater" with "Terminal" to Terminal High Altitude Area Defense.

31. David E. Mosher, "The Budget Politics of Missile Defense," in *New Challenges in Missile Proliferation, Missile Defense, and Space Security,* ed. James Clay Moltz, Occasional Paper 12 (Monterey, CA: Center for Nonproliferation Studies, Monterey Institute of International Studies, July 2003), 19.

32. The White House, Office of the Press Secretary, "Remarks by the President on National Missile Defense," Gaston Hall, Georgetown University, Washington, DC, September 1, 2000.

33. "Remarks by the President to Students and Faculty at National Defense University," The White House Web site, May 1, 2001, www.whitehouse.gov/news/releases/2001/05/20010501-10.html (accessed January 5, 2004).

34. For a good discussion of this time line and the associated domestic pressures for an early decision to withdraw from the ABM Treaty, see Graham, *Hit to Kill,* 73–100.

35. "President Discusses National Missile Defense," The White House Web site, December 12, 2001, www.whitehouse.gov/news/releases/2001/12/20011213-4.html (accessed January 5, 2004).

36. "President Announces Progress in Missile Defense Capabilities," The White House Web site, December 17, 2002, www.whitehouse.gov/news/releases/2002/12/20021217.html (accessed January 5, 2004).

37. U.S. Department of Defense, news release, "Missile Defense Operations Announcement," December 17, 2002, http://www.defenselink.mil/releases/2002/b12172002_bt642-02.html (accessed January 5, 2004).

38. Donald Rumsfeld, quoted in Philip Coyle, "Rhetoric or Reality? Missile Defense Under Bush," *Arms Control Today* (May 2002): 3.

39. Bradley Graham, "U.S. Missile Defense Set to Get Early Start," *Washington Post,* February 2, 2004, A10.

40. This issue is addressed, for example, by Lindsay and O'Hanlon, in *Defending America,* 7–16.

41. "National Missile Defense Act of 1999 (H.R. 4 ENR)," reprinted in *Rockets' Red Glare: Missile Defenses and the Future of World Politics,* ed. James J. Wirtz and Jeffrey A. Larsen (Boulder, CO: Westview Press, 2001), 324–325.

42. See Mosher, "The Budget Politics of Missile Defense," 20–21.

43. For one example of this argument, see Philip E. Coyle, "Is Missile Defense on Target?" *Arms Control Today* (October 2003): 7–14.

44. Mosher, "The Budget Politics of Missile Defense," 20.

45. Kiziah, "Assessment of the Emerging Biocruise Threat"; and Dickey, "Biocruise: A Contemporary Threat."

46. For more on TMD requirements, see Schneider, *Future War and Counterproliferation,* 134.

## Chapter 7

1. It would be interesting to know who made the decision to associate NBC defense with the term "passive defense." The Department of Defense CB defense community never liked the idea of being viewed as "passive"; the term had a

negative connotation in the overall operational art of war, especially to the offensive-oriented U.S. military. The Cold War had seen the armed forces develop a nuclear defense strategy consisting of counterforce (bombers and ballistic missiles aimed at Soviet military bases and launch sites), active defense (interceptors and antimissile defenses), and passive defense (civil defense efforts intended to protect noncombatants). The civil defense efforts included radiological detection, individual and collective protection efforts, decontamination, and medical countermeasures. Although it must have seemed natural for counterproliferation experts to label NBC defense as passive defense in the 1990s, it was not a label that the Department of Defense CB defense community would embrace.

2. See Appendix C, Al Mauroni, "Reforming the Chemical and Biological Defense Program, 1996–2001."

3. See Charles Deulfer, *Comprehensive Report of the Special Advisor to the DCI on Iraq's WMD* (Washington, DC: Central Intelligence Agency, September 30, 2004), http://www.cia.gov/cia/reports/iraq_wmd_2004/.

4. Reported by Division and Corps Chemical Officers in various after action reports and at the annual Worldwide Chemical Conferences held at Ft. McClellan, Alabama, in the mid to late 1990s.

5. Nevertheless, forces in a MOPP-4 posture (wearing the full overgarment ensemble, complete with mask, gloves, and boots) in a high temperature environment is very likely to degrade the conventional combat efficiency of the unit. See Barry R. Schneider, "Combat Effectiveness in MOPP-4: Lessons from the U.S. Army CANE Exercises," *The War Next Time* (Maxwell AFB, AL: USAF Counterproliferation Center, 2003), 173–182.

6. Ibid. Depending on the specialty of the wearer, this degradation of effectiveness could range from 25 percent to 50 percent.

7. *Department of Defense Annual Report on Chemical, Biological, Radiological and Nuclear Defense,* Washington, DC, 2004, passim.

8. Anthony Cordesman. *The Iraq War* (Westport, CT: Praeger Publishers, 2003), 65–66.

9. See the unclassified National Intelligence Estimate, October 2002, http://www.gwu.edu/~nsarchiv/NSAEBB/NSAEBB80/wmd15.pdf.

10. Italics as in the report. James Bamford points out in his book *A Pretext for War* (New York: Doubleday, 2004), 329–30, that the UAV program and the potential for their being armed with CB-agent filled drop tanks was a key factor for many Congressmen to vote for the resolution supporting the use of force against Iraq, a vote held two weeks after the delivery of the CIA NIE to Congress.

11. "Remarks by Deputy Secretary of Defense Paul D. Wolfowitz," National Defense University, May 13, 2003, published in *At the Crossroads: Counterproliferation and National Security Strategy* (Washington, DC: Center for Counterproliferation Research, NDU, April 2004), 61–62.

12. Cordesman, *The Iraq War,* 451–55.

13. Ibid., 448.

14. For a discussion of the many handicaps of wearing conventional overgarments vs. those protective against chemical or biological agents, see Barry R. Schneider, "Combat Effectiveness in MOPP4: Lessons from the U.S. Army CANE Exercises," in *The War Next Time: Countering Rogue States and Terrorists Armed with Chemical and Biological Weapons,* ed. Barry R. Schneider and Jim A. Davis (Maxwell

AFB, AL: USAF Counterproliferation Center, 2003), 173–182. An adversary that forces the U.S. military into wearing such protective overgarments, masks, gloves, and boots can significantly degrade U.S. conventional combat effectiveness. The JSLIST improvement over the older battle dress overgarments reduces this disadvantage somewhat.

15. Major General Joseph Kelley, USAF Assistant Surgeon General for Healthcare Operations, Briefing on "Biodefense: The Air Force Medical System Approach," USAF Counterproliferation/DTRA Conference, Alexandria, VA, December 2003.

16. Is the biodefense requirements system broken? Recently, there has been a move to look at detection, individual protection, vaccination, and therapeutics taken together as a more holistic approach to biological defense. However, this move has yet to be reflected when the Department of Defense establishes requirements. If DoD requirements stressed the need for certain specified operational or organizational capabilities, rather than individual safety standards that are set unrealistically high, biodefense products could move much more rapidly from the lab to the field.

Upon identification of promising candidate vaccines by the Technology Base, they are transitioned to Advanced Development. In FY 1996, the Joint Vaccine Acquisition Program (JVAP) was created to serve as the oversight to a prime systems contractor who had the responsibility for the advanced development and procurement of biological defense vaccines. The initial Joint Vaccine Acquisition Program vaccine candidates [vaccinia (e.g., smallpox), tularemia, and Q fever] were selected based on their perceived maturity, not the relative biological warfare threat. While this appeared to be a solid strategy at the time, as of the conclusion of FY 2004, none of these three, or any other new biological defense vaccines, are available for Department of Defense use (see Joint Service Chemical and Biological Defense Program Handbooks for a progression of JVAP vaccine Milestone projections). Most of the initially transitioned candidate vaccines have been moved back into Advanced Development due to the lack of maturity of the products and the need for further preclinical studies.

With the limited funding that is applied to research, development, and procurement of biological defense vaccines as compared to industry, all avenues must be looked at to increase the successful development of these products. In the authors' opinion, problems associated with the lack of progress in moving biological defense vaccines through the process are the following:

- the lack of individuals with commercial vaccine/biopharmaceutical production background in either the Tech Base laboratories or the Joint Vaccine Acquisition Program or Prime Systems Contractor organizations;
- little actual or perceived incentive for the commercial biopharmaceutical manufacturers to participate in Department of Defense programs due to the limited production quantities required for each vaccine;
- the fact that, within the Joint Vaccine Acquisition Program construct, the Department of Defense research Tech Base is not necessarily the primary source of candidates for the Joint Vaccine Acquisition Program;

- the inability of industry to have frank and open discussions with the Prime Systems Contractor; and
- the apparent reluctance of the government to use extramural resources to conduct studies.

Experience with the three vaccines developed in the Joint Vaccine Acquisition Program (tularemia, Q fever, and vaccinia) exemplifies a problem. They were chosen, not based upon their relative importance as threat agents, but upon their perceived maturity at the time the Joint Vaccine Acquisition Program prime systems contract was awarded. In hindsight, none was as "ready" as expected.

17. See Barry R. Schneider, "U.S. Biodefense Readiness: Thoughts After September 11th," in *The Gathering Biological Warfare Storm*, ed. Jim A. Davis and Barry R. Schneider (Westport, CT: Praeger Publishers, 2004), 4; for additional data see USAMRIID, *Medical Management of Biological Casualties Handbook*, 11th ed., February 2001, Ft. Detrick, MD.

18. *Department of Defense Annual Report on Chemical, Biological, Radiological and Nuclear Defense*, Washington, DC, 2004, 3.

19. DoD Acquisition of Vaccine Production—Report to the Deputy Secretary of Defense by the Independent Panel of Experts (aka "the Top Report"), as contained in *Report on Biological Warfare Defense Vaccine Research & Development Programs*, July 2001, DoD response to Section 218 of the Floyd D. Spence National Defense Authorization Act for Fiscal Year 2001, Public Law (PL), 106–398.

# Chapter 8

1. This analysis considers passive defenses and protective concepts of operation only in the context of protecting personnel who are otherwise performing consequence management activities and not the broader applications of these approaches to preventing damage in the first place. It also considers preparation, training, and coordination with allies, only in the context of performing consequence management.

2. This definition is a modification of the definition agreed to by representatives of the United States and the Gulf Cooperation Council (GCC) states (Bahrain, Kuwait, Oman, Qatar, Saudi Arabia, and the UAE) in the Eagle Resolve 2000 conference sponsored by USCENTCOM (U.S. Central Command). That conference focused on consequence management as one of its two key issues. Major Mike Warmack of SOCCENT (Special Operations Command Central) initially proposed this definition. While the original definition also included the use of high explosives and natural/industrial disasters, which the Gulf States considered an integral part of their consequence management efforts, the scope is limited here to weapons of mass destruction uses.

3. "National Strategy to Combat Weapons of Mass Destruction," The White House, December 2002, 5.

4. A redacted version of PDD 39 is widely available. Specifically, PDD 39 directed FEMA to update the Federal Response Plan to ensure that the federal government was prepared to respond to the consequences of terrorist attacks directed at "large" populations in the United States. The Terrorism Annex to the

Federal Response Plan was released on February 7, 1997.

5. National Security Council, Subject: U.S. Policy on Counterterrorism, June 21, 1995. An unclassified version of the document provided to the Pentagon Library on February 24, 1997, was used here. Significant portions of the document were excised.

6. "Fact Sheet: Summary of Presidential Decision Directives 62 and 63," May 22, 1998; and "Fact Sheet: Combating Terrorism: Presidential Decision Directive 62," Office of the Press Secretary, The White House, May 22, 1998, http://www.whitehouse.gov (accessed May 11, 2004).

7 This program is now referred to as the Strategic National Stockpile (formerly the National Pharmaceutical Stockpile), http://www.bt.cdc.gov/stockpile/index.asp (accessed May 11, 2004).

8. "President Requests Additional Funding for Protection against Biological and Chemical Weapons," Office of the Press Secretary, The White House, June 8, 1998, http://www.fas.org/spp/starwars/program/news98/980608-wh3.htm (accessed July 1, 2004); "Press Briefing by Richard Clarke, National Coordinator for Security, Infrastructure Protection, and Counter-Terrorism, and Jeffrey Hunker, Director of the Critical Infrastructure Assurance Office," Office of the Press Secretary, The White House, May 22, 1998, http://www.fas.org/irp/news/1998/05/980522-wh3.htm (accessed July 1, 2004).

9. Kenneth F. McKenzie, Jr., *The Revenge of the Melians: Asymmetric Threats and the Next QDR,* McNair Paper No. 62 (Washington, DC, National Defense University Press, 2000), 1. Although the concept was implicit in some earlier post-Cold War thinking about threats to U.S. security, the QDR represented the first official use of this terminology.

10. Office of the Assistant to the Secretary for Nuclear, Biological, and Chemical Matters, and the U.S. Army Chemical and Biological Defense Command, *Assessment of the Impact of Chemical and Biological Weapons on Joint Operations in 2010: A Summary Report* (McLean, VA: Booz-Allen & Hamilton, November 1997). This so-called *CB 2010* report was funded by the Office of the Secretary of Defense (including the Office of Net Assessment and the Office of the Deputy Assistant to the Secretary of Defense for Counterproliferation and Chemical/Biological Defense), the U.S. Army Chemical and Biological Defense Command, and the Executive Office of the Joint Service Materiel Group. However, the study report explicitly notes that it "is not to be considered an official position of the Department of Defense."

11. Among the attacks postulated was an aerosol release of encapsulated cholera against the U.S. Forces deployed at Diego Garcia, the use of mustard gas against air and sea ports of embarkation used by U.S. Forces deploying to the Persian Gulf, mustard attacks on airports and seaports of debarkation and on prepositioned equipment in the Persian Gulf arena, and a mustard attack on the Pentagon. See *CB 2010,* 12–18. See note 10.

12. *CB 2010,* 23.

13. Ibid., 18.

14. Ibid., 1.

15. President George W. Bush, *The National Security Strategy of the United States of America,* The White House, September 17, 2002, 1.

16. Ibid., 14.

17. Ibid.

18. *National Strategy to Combat Weapons of Mass Destruction*, The White House, December 2002, 5.

19. Ibid., 2.

20. Ibid., 5

21. Ibid.

22. Ibid.

23. Office of Homeland Security, *National Strategy for Homeland Security*, The White House, July 2002, x.

24. Table 8.1 was developed by Bruce Bennett using various sources.

25. Some sources associated enhanced high-yield explosives (like full-air explosives) with WMD; see, for example, the 2001 QDR discussion of CBRNE, p. 4. This chapter does not address enhanced high-yield explosives.

26. Ken Alibek's Testimony to the House Armed Services Committee, Oversight Panel on Terrorism, May 23, 2000.

27. *Proliferation of Weapons of Mass Destruction: Assessing the Risks*, U.S. Congress Office of Technology Assessment, August 1993, 53–54; adapted by Bruce Bennett to a smaller amount of anthrax and corrected for sarin coverage (which is an order of magnitude too low in the original). The numbers for chemical casualties printed by OTA were off by an order of magnitude (a multiplication error?), as confirmed by Steve Fetter, "Ballistic Missiles and Weapons of Mass Destruction: What Is the Threat? What Should Be Done?" *International Security* (Summer 1991): 21–27. The area affected by anthrax and the quantity of anthrax used were both reduced by a factor of 10 to put them more in the range of a quantity that an adversary would likely use. The biological fatalities assume that all of the lethal area is urbanized. Because the biological cloud could be very long and narrow (unless the attacker is very well prepared and very skilled) going well beyond the urbanized area, these fatalities should be considered an upper bound.

28. While in theory each gram of anthrax contains 100 million lethal doses, in practice a much smaller number of people would be affected because of atmospheric dispersal. Thus, the several grams of anthrax contained in the anthrax letters mailed in late 2001 infected only 11 people to the point of showing symptoms before widespread antibiotic prophylaxis was begun.

29. The "worried well" are people who think they have been exposed to WMD effects but have not been, yet they seek medical care.

30. Table 8.3 was developed by Bruce Bennett.

31. Chemical and biological weapons could also be put in food/water and could contaminate a location, though these are not likely means to cause mass casualties.

32. The 1984 incident in Bhopal, India, involved the release of 20 to 30 tons of methylisocyanate. The accident caused 2,500 immediate fatalities and approximately 100,000 casualties requiring some form of medical treatment. There were also several thousand animals injured and roughly 1,000 killed.

33. For example, there has been considerable speculation that the woman in Connecticut who died from the anthrax letters likely received a very low dose of anthrax. At least one expert claims that even a few spores could cause death in some people, even though the dose required for a 50 percent chance of getting anthrax is about 8,000 retained spores. See C. J. Peters and D. M. Hartley,

"Anthrax Inhalation and Lethal Human Infection," *The Lancet,* February 23, 2002, 710–11.

34. One example is a model called NBC Crest.

35. "Almost all inhalational anthrax cases in which treatment was begun after patients were significantly symptomatic have been fatal, regardless of treatment." USAMRIID, *Medical Management of Biological Casualties Handbook,* February 2001, 23. This reference does not clarify what "significantly symptomatic" means. One example of the view which was held prior to the anthrax letters cases is, "Unless there has been prior immunization, once symptoms appear, treatment invariably is ineffective, although there are anecdotal reports of patients surviving after very early confirmation of exposure and extremely aggressive antibiotic and supportive therapy." Lieutenant Commander Pietro Marghella, "The Second, Silent Attack on Pearl," *U.S. Naval Institute Proceedings,* May 1999, 61.

36. All six of the patients who received antibiotics during the first phase of the disease, starting from one to seven days after symptoms began, survived. See John A. Jernigan et al., "Bioterrorism-Related Inhalation Anthrax: The First Ten Cases Reported in the United States," *Emerging Infectious Diseases* 7 (Nov/Dec 2001), http://www.cdc.gov/ncidod/EID/vol7no6/jernigan.htm (accessed May 11, 2004).

37. For anthrax, see Thomas V. Inglesby et al., "Anthrax as a Biological Weapon," *JAMA* (May 12, 1999): 1735–45, http://jama.ama-assn.org/cgi/reprint/281/18/1735.pdf (accessed May 11, 2004); Thomas V. Inglesby et al., "Anthrax as a Biological Weapon, 2002: Updated Recommendations for Management," *JAMA* (May 1, 2002): 2236–52, http://jama.ama-assn.org/cgi/reprint/287/17/2236.pdf (accessed May 11, 2004).

38. A replacement to the NAAK, the Antidote Treatment Nerve Agent Autoinjector, is in the process of being fielded. This new kit combines the atropine and 2-Pralidoxime chloride for delivery from a single needle, delivering antidotes faster from a more compact package.

39. This change in procedures apparently made a significant improvement in the survival of the anthrax letter cases, per Jernigan et al., "Bioterrorism-Related Inhalation Anthrax," 942.

40. The CDC draws the distinctions made here between quarantine and isolation, http://www.cdc.gov/ncidod/sars/isolationquarantine.htm (accessed May 8, 2004).

41. See the World Health Organization Web site, http://www.who.int/csr/disease/en (accessed May 8, 2004).

42. See "Executive Order 13295: Revised List of Quarantinable Communicable Diseases," http://www.cdc.gov/cidod/sars/executiveorder040403.htm (accessed May 8, 2004).

43. See Headquarters, Departments of the Army, the Navy, and the Air Force, "Quarantine Regulations of the Armed Forces," Army Regulation 40-12, January 24, 1992.

44. In February 2003, it was reported that a DoD panel had made recommendations on how to handle human remains contaminated by WMD. See Erin Q. Winograd, "DoD Given Guidelines for Dealing with Soldiers Killed by CBN Agents," *Inside the Army,* February 2003.

45. With chemical agents like VX, which persists for days to weeks on glass surfaces depending upon the temperature, there is a debate on the degree to which they absorb and adsorb into surfaces like concrete, asphalt, and paint, and whether they are then benign. This subject, referred to as "agent fate," is being studied by the DoD to determine the nature and duration of the residual threat, and the need for avoidance or decontamination.

46. In 2002, the defense community fielded a series of new decontaminants (especially several foams), but subsequent testing showed that these agents could fail to decontaminate some CBW agents and still had the corrosive drawbacks of traditional decontaminants like bleach solutions. As of 2004, the community is still seeking a better form of decontaminant.

47. United States Government Interagency Domestic Terrorism Concept of Operations Plan, January 2001, p. B-4. DoD's definitions of recovery and reconstitution are "1. Those actions taken by one nation prior to, during, and following an attack by an enemy nation to minimize the effects of the attack, rehabilitate the national economy, provide for the welfare of the populace, and maximize the combat potential of remaining forces and supporting activities. 2. Those actions taken by a military force during or after operational employment to restore its combat capability to full operational readiness." Joint Publication 1-02: *Department of Defense Dictionary of Military and Associated Terms,* April 12, 2001 (as amended through June 5, 2003), 444.

48. *National Response Plan,* December 2005, 82, http://www.dhs.gov/interweb/assetlibrary/NRPbaseplan.pdf (accessed February 15, 2005).

49. *Homeland Security: Emergencies & Disasters: Planning and Prevention,* http://www.dhs.gov/dhspublic/interapp/editorial/editorial_0566.xml (accessed February 15, 2005).

50. Office of the Secretary of Defense, *Proliferation: Threat and Response,* January 2001, 57.

51. Dr. Kenneth Alibek, "Biological Weapons," briefing presented to the USAF Air War College, November 1, 1999, slide 9.

52. Department of Defense, *Quadrennial Defense Review Report,* September 30, 2001, iv.

53. Ibid., 12.

54. The term "challenge and response cycle" was coined by Sam Gardiner and Dan Fox as part of RAND's early 1990s work on Revolutions in Military Affairs.

55. Department of Defense, *Quadrennial Defense Review Report,* vi.

# Chapter 9

1. Donald H. Rumsfeld, Secretary of Defense, Testimony before the House Armed Services Committee, June 28, 2001.

2. MOPP level 4 is the highest level of MOPP gear and requires the wearing of overgarment, field gear [helmet, web belt, canteen and, if used, body armor (worn over the overgarment)], footwear covers (overboots), mask, hood, and gloves. It is used when the highest degree of CB protection is required, such as Alarm Black notification and also postattack reconnaissance—until the actual hazard has been determined. Only the installation commander can direct the change in MOPP

levels. Notional MOPP levels for forces ashore are presented as follows in Joint Doctrine for Operations in NBC Environments, July 11, 2000:

|  | Level 0 | Level 1 | Level 2 | Level 3 | Level 4 |
|---|---|---|---|---|---|
| **Overgarment** | Readily available | Worn | Worn | Worn | Worn |
| **Overboots** | Readily available | Carried | Worn | Worn | Worn |
| **Mask & Hood** | Carried | Carried | Carried | Worn | Worn |
| **Gloves** | Readily available | Carried | Carried | Carried | Worn |

3. Col. Glenn Burgess, USMC (Ret.), "Counter Chemical Warfare CONOPS Now ... Survive and Operate," *Marine Corps Gazette,* Marine Corps Association, Quantico, VA, December 2002, 47.

4. "Senior Leader's Guide," Update 2002, 5. Headquarters Air Force Civil Engineer Support Agency HQ AFCESA/CEXR Tyndall AFB, FL.

5. USAF Counter-Chemical Warfare Concept of Operations, XONP/ILEX, Washington, DC, January 2, 2002.

6. "Senior Leader's Guide," Update 2002, 8.

7. In the past, MOPP postures were largely binary—which meant the entire base populace was generally in either a MOPP 2 or MOPP 4 posture following an attack. The C-CW CONOPS includes procedures for determining which areas of a base are contaminated and which are clean so that personnel operating in clean areas can reduce MOPP levels according to sectors. It also includes procedures for split-MOPP within a sector. Personnel adopt the appropriate MOPP, as directed by installation leadership, based on their proximity to contaminated areas or surfaces.

8. "Senior Leader's Guide," Update 2002, 7.

9. Some of these include CORAL BREEZE (Summer 1996–Spring 1997), CHEM-WAR 2000 (Fall 1997), and TAEBEK'97 (Fall 1997).

10. Some examples of nerve agents include GA (Tabun), GB (Sarin), GD (Soman), GF (Cyclosarin), and VX. Nerve agents attack the nervous system and affect muscle control, vision, heart, and lung functions. Some examples of blister agents include H (Sulphur Mustard), HD (Distilled Mustard), HN-1 (Nitrogen Mustard), and L (Lewisite). Blister agents attack and destroy cell tissue. They cause skin and eye irritation, inflammation, and severe blisters. This tissue damage increases the chance of infection and may ultimately cause death. In most cases, pain and blisters may not occur until long after exposure.

11. In 1997, the air force and DTRA conducted an operational study of strategic air mobility operations in a chemically contaminated environment (it is referred to commonly as the APOD Study.) Based on the results of the study, other "excursion studies" were conducted, the total of which are referred to as the "APOD family of studies."

12. Live agent testing: testing using actual chemical warfare agents on actual air-base operating surfaces.

13. Results from live agent testing on duration: the first tests were sponsored by the air staff and DTRA between August 1998 and May 1999 and were held at

Dugway, West Desert Test Center in Utah. These tests examined the persistence of VX and two of its isomers as liquid and vapor hazards on concrete and asphalt (samples taken from air bases) at three temperatures. The second test was conducted in two phases from May 1998 through August 1999. This test was sponsored by the Joint Service Materiel Group (JSMG) Decontamination Commodity Area Manager and held in the Czech Republic. This test examined persistence of VX (nerve), GD (nerve), and HD (blister) agents on grass, sand, concrete, and asphalt. A third live agent test was conducted by the Naval Surface Warfare Center in Dahlgren, Virginia, during the spring of 1999, focusing on the liquid and vapor hazard generated over time from VX, HD, and thickened GD agents sorbed into surfaces. Each of these tests concluded that liquid agents rapidly sorb into a wide range of porous surfaces, quickly removing the liquid pickup and transfer hazard. The Dugway results were robust and held true for dry and wet surfaces, surfaces with paint and rubber deposits, as well as surfaces contaminated with petroleum, oil, and lubricants. All shed light on two primary issues affecting airbase operations in the wake of a chemical attack: persistence of the liquid contact hazard and duration of the vapor hazard of agent sorbed into surfaces.

14. PACAF C-CW CONOPS: the risk assessment methodologies, command and control tools, and detailed information on the tactics, techniques, and procedures associated with this C-CW CONOPS can be found in USAF publications, including AFMAN 10-2602, NBCC Defense Operations and Standards, and AFMAN 10-2603, Counter-NBCC Defense Commander's Guide, NBCC Commander's Guide.

15. "Senior Leader's Guide," Update 2002, 7.

16. The CSAF directed that COMPACAF operating procedures become the USAF Counter-Chemical Warfare concept of operations.

17. See note 7.

18. See note 20 on detectors.

19. The term "sorb" is a term of art within the community reflecting the various interactions that occur between liquid agents and surfaces with which they come into contact. This includes the traditional absorption (the wholesale soaking in of a substance) and adsorption (sticking of individual molecules to a surface, such as activated charcoal scavenging poisonous gases in gas masks), as well as the more complicated chemical interactions of physisorption and chemisorption.

20. Some examples of detectors include M8 and M9 paper, M256 A1, and the Chemical Agent Monitor. The M8 paper will detect liquid G and V nerve agents and H blister agents. M8 paper provides the user with a manual liquid detection capability. Technical Order (T.O.) 11H2-14-5-1 is the technical reference. M9 paper, like M8 paper, contains agent sensitive dyes that change color in the presence of liquid chemical agent. M9 paper will turn different colors if liquid agent comes in contact with paper. Color changes to M9 paper identify agent presence, not agent type. T.O. 11H2-2-21 is the technical reference. The M256A1 Chemical Agent Detector Kit manually detects and classifies nerve, blister, and blood agents in vapor or liquid form. The M256A1 sampler detectors are capable of detecting and identifying vapors only. T.O. 11H2-21-1 is the technical reference. The Chemical Agent Monitor (CAM) is a handheld point monitor capable of detecting and identifying nerve and mustard agent vapors. CAMs are intended for use to search out clean areas and to identify contaminated personnel, equipment, aircraft,

vehicles, buildings, and terrain. CAMs can help determine the effectiveness of decontamination and can be used in collective protection shelters. The CAM is a monitor, not a detector, and can become contaminated or overloaded (saturated) if not used properly. The CAM can detect vapors only at the inlet nozzle. It will not give the vapor hazard over an area. The CAM is currently the best fielded device we have to at least approximate the concentrations of chemical agent vapors present at any given time. While it does not provide a digital readout with exact chemical concentrations, the CAM's individual bars do equate to intensity ranges. T.O.11H2-20-1 is the technical reference for inspection and use. Note 31 provides additional detection information.

21. There are many tables based on varying agent-surface-environmental conditions listed in the NBC Detection Guide published by HQ AFCESA, on March 21, 2003. These tables are based on static weather conditions throughout the entire hazard duration listed; uncertainty in actual hazard durations lies with real-time variance in these conditions.

22. Air bases use primarily alkyd- or polymer-based paints, including latex, epoxy, polyurethane, and acrylic. Each paint, including Chemical Agent Resistant Coating (CARC), exhibits unique characteristics in different situations. These include the diffusion and transport of the agents across the surface, the vapor evaporation rates based on the wetted surface area, the rate at which the agent penetrates the surface as a function of time, the transferability of the agent from the painted surface to materials that contact the paint surface (dependent on the two surfaces, the type of agent, and type of contact), and the rate at which agents off-gas after they are sorbed into the paint. The USAF does own some CARC-painted equipment; however, the CARC-painted vehicles (usually operated by Security Forces) have not received the maintenance necessary to maintain CARC's antiabsorbent capability.

23. For additional information, please refer to AFMAN 10-2602, *NBCC Defense Operations and Standards,* Interim Change, May 23, 2003, Attachment 2.

24. See note 11.

25. This is based on compilation of results of eight air bases from the Operational Effectiveness Assessment studies, which include the completed analysis of operations at 15 USAF installations.

26. See note 25.

27. Restoration of Operations (RESTOPS) Advanced Concept Technology Demonstration (ACTD): RESTOPS was a collaborative initiative among United States Pacific Command (PACOM), United States Central Command (CENTCOM), United States Transportation Command (TRANSCOM), Pacific Air Forces (PACAF), United States Forces Korea (USFK), United States Air Force (USAF), Defense Threat Reduction Agency (DTRA), West Desert Test Center (WDTC) at Dugway Proving Ground (DPG), Detachment 1, Air Force Operational Test and Evaluation Center (Det 1, AFOTEC), Joint Service Materiel Group (JSMG) (Joint NBC Defense Program), Joint Service Integration Group (JSIG) (Joint NBC Defense Program), Center for Counterproliferation Research, National Defense University (NDU), Edgewood Chemical Biological Center (ECBC), Soldier Biological and Chemical Command (SBCCOM), Joint Program Office–Biological Defense (JPO-BD), Institute for Defense Analyses (IDA), and the Department of Energy (DOE). The air force was the lead service and DTRA was the executing agent.

As written in the March 2000 Management Plan, the RESTOPS ACTD was designed to demonstrate mitigating actions taken before, during, and after an attack to protect against and immediately react to the consequences of a chemical/biological attack. These actions aim to restore OPTEMPO in mission execution and the movement of individuals and materiel to support combat operations at a fixed site.

28. VLSTRACK training sessions were conducted at each MAJCOM Orientation C-CW CONOPS training (January 2002–December 2002). CW and Biological Warfare (BW) VLSTRACK checklists were provided as handouts to walk the student through the plotting sessions.

29. Three years of analysis and testing, sponsored by AF/XON, the Defense Threat Reduction Agency, the Joint Service Materiel Group, and the Navy Surface Warfare West Desert Center at Dahlgren, provided a greater understanding of chemical effects on air-base operating surfaces.

30. The M17A/A2 Decontamination Apparatus provides the user with a portable decontaminating capability. The system consists of a pump/heater assembly, two spray wands, each with 20 meters of high pressure hose, 12 shower points, 10 meters of suction hose with filter, and an injector for chemical decontaminant. T.O. 11D1-3-9-1, 11D1-3-9-2, and 11D1-3-9-1CL-1 are the technical references.

31. While serious deficiencies still exist, the air force fielded two improved chemical agent detectors over the past 13 years. The additions were the Improved Chemical Agent Monitor (ICAM) and the M22 Automatic Chemical Agent Detector and Alarm (ACADA). The ICAM's primary enhancements over the original Chemical Agent Monitor (CAM) were the ability to automatically switch scales from nerve to blister and the ability to provide an audio alarm when a specified concentration (3 bars) was achieved. The M22's primary enhancement over the M8A1 is the ability to simultaneously detect nerve and blister agents; the M8A1 was a nerve agent only detector.

32. The issue surrounding air force-wide IPE supply requirement shortfall is gaining attention by the USAF, as noted in the 2003 Annual Report to Congress, vol. I, April 2003. This document may be referenced for further information on this topic.

33. The issues listed are the main issues and do not represent the full spectrum of issues requiring further attention. For additional reading on such issues, documents such as AFMAN 10-2602 Paras 1.18; AFJMAN 44-151–NATO Handbook on Medical Aspects of NBC Defense and Operations; AFMAN 44-156(I)–Treatment of Biological Warfare Agent Casualties.

34. AFMAN 32-4005, Personnel Protection and Attack, October 30, 2001, HQ AFCESA/CEXR, Tyndall AFB, FL.

35. "Air Force Plan for Implementing the Anthrax Vaccine Immunization Program under Postemergency Use Authorization Conditions," January 24, 2006, https://kx.afms.mil (accessed February 28, 2006).

36. The M291 Skin Decontaminating Kit provides the user capability to completely decontaminate through physical removal, absorption, and neutralization of chemical agents on the skin. This wallet-sized kit contains six separately packaged laminated pads soaked with the nontoxic decontaminant AMBERGARD XE-555. Ambergard absorbs and neutralizes the chemical agent. M291 pads are to be used to wipe skin, clothing, masks, gloves, personal equipment, and

weapons. The six pads of an M291 kit should be sufficient for three personal decontaminations. The kit operates in ranges from –50°F to 120°F. Technical Order (T.O.) 11D1-1-131 is the technical reference. The M295 Equipment Decontamination Kit allows the individual to decontaminate his or her equipment through physical removal and absorption of chemical agents. Each M295 Kit consists of a carrying pouch containing four individual decon packets. Each packet contains a decon mitt filled with decon powder. The packet is designed to fit comfortably in the pocket of the ground crew ensemble. Each individual mitt is composed of absorbent resin contained within a nonwoven polyester material. The kit operates in ranges from –25°F to 180°F. TM-3-4230-235-10 is the technical reference.

37. Per AFMAN 44-156 (I), Treatment of Biological Warfare Agent Casualties.

38. Contained in Air Force Manual (AFMAN) 32-4005, CE Readiness Technician's Manual for NBC Defense.

39. AF/XOS-FC Web site, https://www.xo.hq.af.mil/xos/xosf/xosfc/.

40. Reference Attachment 2 of AFMAN 10-2602, NBCC Defense Operations and Standards, and Attachment 13 of AFMAN 32-4005, Personnel Protection and Attack Actions.

41. Air force installations are required to include a section on responding to situations where the air base is in the downwind hazard plume of an RDD in Annex C of their Full Spectrum Threat Response (FSTR) Plan 10-2. This requirement is specified in Attachment 3 of AFI 10-2501, FSTR Planning and Operations.

42. Per AFMAN 32-4005, Attachment 1.

43. Per AFMAN 32-4005, 1.12.3; see also Attachment 2.

44. Per AFMAN 32-4005, Attachment 2, A2.2.8.

# Chapter 10

1. Of particular concern was the new information provided by Soviet and Russian defectors of the amazing lethality, enormity, and diversity of the Soviet biological warfare (BW) program, especially when compounded by reports that Russia might have retained some elements of that program and that some of this capability might have leaked into the possession of new military adversaries. For background, see Ken Alibek, with Stephen Handelman, *Biohazard: The Chilling True Story of the Largest Covert Biological Weapons Program in the World—Told from Inside by the Man Who Ran It* (New York: Random House, 1999); and Peter R. Lavoy, Scott D. Sagan, and James J. Wirtz, eds., *Planning the Unthinkable: How New Powers Will Use Nuclear, Biological, and Chemical Weapons* (Ithaca, NY: Cornell University Press, 2000).

2. Secretary of Defense Les Aspin, speech to the National Academy of Sciences, Washington, DC, December 7, 1993. (See Appendix A.)

3. See Leonard S. Spector, "Neo-Nonproliferation," *Survival* 37, no. 1 (Spring 1995): 66–85. Nonproliferation proponents actually had begun voicing this concern even before the CPI was announced. For one prominent example, see Thomas W. Graham, "Winning the Nonproliferation Battle," *Arms Control Today* 21, no. 7 (September 1991): 8–13.

4. Aspin, speech to the National Academy of Sciences.

5. For one prominent example, see "Jane's Interview: Ashton Carter," *Jane's Defence Weekly,* July 30, 1994, 40.

6. Statement of the U.K. Minister of Defence, "UK Defence Strategy: A Continuing Role for Nuclear Weapons?" January 18, 1994; cited in Angus McColl, "Is Counterproliferation Compatible with Nonproliferation? Rethinking the Defense Counterproliferation Initiative," *Aerospace Power Journal* (Spring 1997): 101.

7. French Ministry of Defense, *Livre Blanc sur la Defense* (Paris: Ministere de la defense, Service d'information et de relations publiques des armees, 1994), 77.

8. Virginia S. I. Gamba has argued that Washington's inability to offer a clear-cut definition of what counterproliferation was intended to be "seemed to have worked as a stimulant rather than a hindrance … [and] that months before the U.S. administration had a firm idea of what its own initiative meant and what it entailed, major NATO partners were already busily interpreting Aspin's words on counterproliferation." Virginia S. I. Gamba, "Counterproliferation: Harmony or Contradiction?" in *International Perspectives on Counterproliferation,* ed. Mitchell Reiss and Harald Müller, Working Paper no. 99 (Washington, DC: Woodrow Wilson International Center for Scholars, 1995), 58.

9. This tension was evident inside the U.S. Government as well. The Counterproliferation Initiative sparked a major turf battle between the Defense Department, on one side, and the State Department, the Arms Control and Disarmament Agency (ACDA), and the Department of Energy, on the other side. The interagency debate over what organization had what responsibility in dealing with WMD proliferation caused Daniel Poneman, the Special Assistant to the President for Proliferation Policy at the National Security Council, to intervene. Poneman issued a widely circulated memorandum on February 18, 1994, to Robert Gallucci, Assistant Secretary of State for Political-Military Affairs, and Assistant Secretary of Defense for International Security Policy, Ashton Carter. The memorandum defined counterproliferation as "the activities of the Department of Defense across the full range of U.S. efforts to combat proliferation, including diplomacy, arms control, export controls, and intelligence collection and analysis, with particular responsibility for assuring that U.S. force and interests can be protected should they confront an adversary armed with weapons of mass destruction or missiles." Former Undersecretary of Defense John Deutch's subsequent *Report on Nonproliferation and Counterproliferation Activities and Programs* endorsed this definition and identified two NSC committees with oversight responsibilities for counterproliferation policy. These committees give the NSC the ability to task specific aspects of proliferation policy to the appropriate government agency, thus mitigating interagency turf battles and tensions.

10. See Harald Müller, "Counterproliferation and the Nonproliferation Regime: A View from Germany," in *International Perspectives on Counterproliferation,* ed. Mitchell Reiss and Harald Müller, 29–30, attributed to FRG Foreign Office, "Deutsche 10-Punkte-Erkl rung zur Nichtverbreitungspolitik," Bonn: December 15, 1993, 4; Barry R. Schneider, "Military Responses to Proliferation Threats," in *Pulling Back from the Nuclear Brink: Reducing and Countering Nuclear Threats* (London: Frank Cass, 1998), 295–99; and McColl, "Is Counterproliferation Compatible with Nonproliferation?" 99–110.

11. According to Seongwhun Cheon, "the South Korean government and public have expressed consistent opposition to any measure that might increase

tensions on the Korean peninsula." Cheon also observed that the vast majority of the Korean population opposed a statement made by South Korean Defense Minister Lee Jong-ku in April 1991 that the North's suspicious Yongbyon nuclear complex should be struck by a commando raid. See Seongwhun Cheon "A South Korean View of the U.S. Counterproliferation Initiative," in *International Perspectives on Counterproliferation,* ed. Mitchell Reiss and Harald Müller, 110–12.

12. Israel was not the first country to launch a preventive counterproliferation strike. The Allies launched such strikes against Japan and a German-operated heavy-water facility in Norway to prevent these countries from developing nuclear weapons during the Second World War. Later, Iraq disabled Iran's nuclear reactor during their war in the 1980s. And in 1991 the United States bombed suspected Iraqi WMD facilities.

13. Saudi Arabia was a prime mover in setting up the Gulf Cooperation Council in 1981. Other members are Bahrain, Kuwait, Oman, Qatar, and the United Arab Emirates (UAE). The GCC aims to coordinate resistance to outside intervention in the Gulf and to strengthen cooperation in areas such as agriculture, industry, investment, security, and trade among its members. The presidency of the Gulf Cooperation Council rotates yearly among members. Council headquarters are in Riyadh, Saudi Arabia.

14. Mitchell B. Wallerstein, "The Origins and Evolution of the Defense Counterproliferation Initiative," in *Countering the Proliferation and Use of Weapons of Mass Destruction,* ed. Peter L. Hays, Vincent J. Jodoin, and Alan R. Van Tassel (New York: McGraw-Hill, 1998), 28, emphasis in original.

15. See Iliana P. Bravo, *NATO's Weapons of Mass Destruction Initiative: Achievements and Challenges,* thesis prepared for the Naval Postgraduate School, Monterey, CA, September 2003, v, http://www.nps.navy.mil/Research/ThesisSummer03/ ma_national_security_affairs.pdf (accessed July 10, 2004).

16. "Vershbow Remarks on Euro-Atlantic Security, Defense," *Aerotech News and Review,* May 18, 2001, F8, http://www.aerotechnews.com/starc/2001/051801/ NATO_CPI.html (accessed September 2004).

17. NATO Press Release, Prague Summit Declaration, 21 November 2002, par. 4, sections c-e, g, http://www.nato.int/docu/pr/2002/p02-127e.htm (accessed July 10, 2004).

18. Bravo, *NATO's Weapons of Mass Destruction Initiative.*

19. U.K. Secretary of State for Defence George Robertson, "Written Answers Text for Tuesday 26 Jan 1999," http://www.parliament.the-stationery-office.co.uk/pa/cm199899/cmhansrd/vo990126/text/90126w05.htm (accessed July 10, 2004).

20. *CB Quarterly,* Edgewood Chemical Biological Center, Aberdeen Proving Ground, no. 34 (Fall 2003), http://www.edgewood.army.mil/ip/cb_quarterly/ final_cb_quarterly_fall_2003_issue_34.pdf (accessed July 10, 2004).

21. General Anthony C. Zinni, Commander in Chief, U.S. Central Command, statement before the U.S. Senate Committee on the Armed Services, February 29, 2000.

22. Shawnee McKain, "NSA Bahrain Holds Exercise Desert Sailor 2004, 3/9/ 2004," Commander, U.S. Naval Forces Central Command/Commander, U.S. 5th Fleet Public Affairs.

23. Egypt chose not to participate and generally has been less enthusiastic about CDI than the other seven countries approached by the United States.

24. Center for Strategic Leadership, Army War College, *CSL Quarterly*, 5, no. 4 (July-September 2003), http://www.carlisle.army.mil/usacsl/publications/vol5iss4.pdf (accessed July 10, 2004).

25. Zinni, statement before the U.S. Senate Committee on the Armed Services.

26. Johns Hopkins University Applied Physics Laboratory, "Brainstorming in Bahrain," *In the Spotlight* (2001), http://www.jhuapl.edu/newscenter/aplnews/2001/bahrain.htm (accessed July 10, 2004).

27. "Kuwaiti, US, German Forces Hold Warfare Drill," *Agence France Presse*, October 21, 2002.

28. Table 10.1 was created by Gayle Meyers. Data source: "Reports by the Department of State Pursuant to Section 655 of the Foreign Assistance Act, Direct Commercial Sales Authorizations for Fiscal Years 1999-2003," http://www.pmdtc.org/rpt655intro.htm (accessed July 1, 2004). These reports cover defense articles and defense services licensed for export under Section 38 of the Arms Export Control Act. They show the aggregate dollar value and quantity of defense articles and defense services authorized for sale by American companies to each foreign country. They do not include cover defense articles and services that are provided via the Foreign Military Sales (FMS) program.

29. "Kuwait: Czech-Slovak Battalion Guarding Against NBC Attack," *Radio Free Europe/Radio Liberty,* reproduced in *defense-aerospace.com,* March 13, 2003, http://www.defense-aerospace.com/cgi-bin/client/modele.pl?prod=18896&session=dae.3865913.1085587869.QLTBncOa9dUAAByDRsA&modele=jdc_1.

30. Japan Defense Agency, *Defense of Japan 1996,* http://www.jda.go.jp/e/index_.htm (accessed April 20, 2004).

31. Ibid.

32. David E. Kaplan and Andrew Marshall, *The Cult at the End of the World* (New York: Crown, 1996), 137–46; and Kyle B. Olson, "Aum Shinrikyo: Once and Future Threat?" U.S. Centers for Disease Control and Prevention, *Emerging Infectious Diseases* 5, no. 4 (July–August 1999): 513–16, http://www.cdc.gov/ncidod/EID/vol5no4/olson.htm (accessed July 10, 2004).

33. Olson, "Aum Shinrikyo," 514.

34. Kaplan and Marshall, *The Cult at the End of the World,* 93–98.

35. Ibid.; Sheryl WuDunn, Judith Miller, and William J. Broad, "How Japan Germ Terror Alerted World," *New York Times,* May 26, 1998, A1, A10; and W. Seth Carus, *Bioterrorism and Biocrimes: The Illicit Use of Biological Agents Since 1900* (Washington, DC: Center for Counterproliferation Research, National Defense University, August 1998; February 2001 Revision), 48–50.

36. Japan Defense Agency, *Defense of Japan 2002 White Paper (Summary),* http://www.jda.go.jp/e/index_.htm (accessed April 20, 2004).

37. Ibid.

38. Ibid.

39. Ibid.

40. George W. Bush, "Remarks by the President on Weapons of Mass Destruction Proliferation," speech given to National Defense University, Washington, DC, February 11, 2004, www.whitehouse.gov/news/releases/2004/02/20040211-4.html (accessed July 10, 2004).

41. James Woolsey, unpublished speech given to the Naval Postgraduate School, Monterey, CA, August 21, 2003.

Although North Korea did, ultimately, violate and then terminate the 1994 "Agreed Framework," that does not mean that shutting down the reactors and reactor building programs they had for a decade was a bad idea. Indeed, North Korea might have been much better armed with nuclear arms if they had continued unabated from 1994 to the present.

42. President George W. Bush, *National Strategy to Combat Weapons of Mass Destruction*, December 2002, 1, http://www.whitehouse.gov/nsc/ (accessed July 10, 2004).

43. William S. Cohen, "Message of the Secretary of Defense," in the Department of Defense, *Proliferation: Threat and Response*, January 2001, i, http://www.defenselink.mil (accessed July 10, 2004).

44. Note, for example, that the Bush Administration did not reengage the DPRK and China until 2003, almost three years after it took power.

45. President Bush, *National Strategy to Combat Weapons of Mass Destruction*, 3.

46. George W. Bush, "Remarks by the President to the People of Poland," Krakow, Poland, May 31, 2003, http://www.whitehouse.gov/news/releases/2003/05/20030531-3.html (accessed July 10, 2004).

47. *Comprehensive Report of the Special Advisor to the Director of Central Intelligence on Iraq's Weapons of Mass Destruction*, September 30, 2004, http://www.cia.gov/cia/reports/iraq_wmd_ 2004/index.html (accessed December 6, 2004).

# Chapter 11

1. DARK WINTER was an effort held June 22–23, 2001, led by John Hamre at the Center for Strategic and International Studies. Tara O'Toole and Tom Ingelsby of the Johns Hopkins Center developed the executive simulation for Civilian Biodefense Strategies together with Col. Randy Larsen, USAF (Ret.), and Mark DeMier of the ANSER Institute for Homeland Security. The McCormick-Tribune Foundation and the Oklahoma City Memorial Institute provided funding for the Prevention of Terrorism project. Senior national security leaders, including Senator Sam Nunn, former CIA Director Jim Woolsey, former FBI Director William Session, Governor Frank Keating (R-OK), and David Gergen participated in this two-day event.

2. Comments made to Vice President Cheney by Co. Randall Larsen on September 20, 2001.

3. Abraham Lincoln, "Perpetuation of Our Political Institutions: Address Before the Young Men's Lyceum of Springfield, Illinois," January 27, 1838, http://showcase.netins.net/web/creative/lincoln/speeches/lyceum.htm (accessed November 17, 2003).

4. *National Strategy for Homeland Security*, July 15, 2002, http://www.dhs.gov/interweb/assetlibrary/nat_strat_hls. pdf (accessed November 17, 2003).

5. Albert Einstein, May 1946.

6. However, even al Qaeda has a political agenda as its leaders argue that their actions are aimed at removing U.S. support for Israel, expelling the Israeli Jews, and toppling moderate Arab governments that embrace modernity.

7. John V. Parachini, "The World Trade Center Bombers," (1993) in *Toxic Terror: Assessing Terrorist Use of Chemical and Biological Weapons,* ed. Jonathan B. Tucker (Cambridge, MA, MIT Press, 2000), 91.

8. David Kaplan and Andrew Marshall, *The Cult From The End of the World* (New York: Crown Publishers, 1996), 140–146.

9. For a detailed description of this event and other Aum activities, see David E. Kaplan and Andrew Marshall, *The Cult at the End of the World: The Terrifying Story of the Aum Doomsday Cult* (New York: Crown, 1996).

10. Simon Reeve, *The New Jackals* (Boston: Northeastern University Press, 1999), 109; and Murray Weiss, *The Man Who Warned America: The Life and Death of John O'Neill* (New York: Regan Books, 2003), 89.

11. "Transforming Defense: National Security in the 21st Century," *Report of the National Defense Panel,* December 1997, http://www.dtic.mil/ndp/FullDoc2.pdf (accessed February 16, 2005).

12. Stated in a presentation at the National War College by Executive Director of the PCCIP, Mr. Phil Lacombe, January 7, 1999.

13. Eight ISACs would eventually be created to bring together industry and government. FACA, sometimes referred to as the Sunshine Law, requires that meetings between federal government officials and private industry must be open to the public and press. Both public and private officials have expressed concerns that information regarding industry vulnerabilities could provide targeting information to terrorists. Legislation that created the Department of Homeland Security has allowed for some exceptions to FACA.

14. "Countering the Changing Threat of International Terrorism," *National Commission on Terrorism,* June 7, 2000, 64, http://w3.access.gpo.gov/nct/ (accessed November 17, 2003).

15. All Gilmore Commission reports can be viewed online, http://www.rand.org/nsrd/terrpanel/ (accessed December 15, 2003).

16. Ibid. Report #1, page VIII.

17. Ibid, 47.

18. Amanda Onion, "A Lesson in Biology," *ABC News.com,* http://abcnews.go.com/sections/scitech/DailyNews/wtc_biologylesson011001.html (accessed October 5, 2003).

19. "New World Coming: American Security in the 21st Century: Major Themes and Implications," *The United States Commission on National Security/21st Century* (The Phase I Report on the Emerging Global Security Environment), September 15, 1999, 8, http://www.nssg.gov/Reports/NWC.pdf (accessed November 17, 2003). All the reports are available from http://www.nssg.gov/Reports/reports.htm.

20. The two National Security Strategy documents in the Clinton administration, as well as the 1997 QDR and last couple of national military strategies emphasized asymmetric threats extensively, and from 1998 on there was considerable DoD emphasis on meeting such threats. Thus, some in the Department of Defense were beginning to turn their attention to such asymmetric threats as well. During this time, the DoD created the post of Assistant to the Secretary of Defense for Civil Affairs. Although this was a temporary solution, it was an important step on the path toward creating the position of Assistant Secretary of Defense for Homeland Defense.

21. National Commission on Terrorist Attacks Upon the United States, *The 9/11 Commission Report, Executive Summary*, July 22, 2004, 16, www.gpoaccess.gov/911 (accessed October 27, 2004).

22. "Statement by the President," National Commission on Terrorist Attacks Upon the United States Web site, November 27, 2002, http://www .9-11commission.gov/about/president.htm (accessed October 27, 2004).

23. 107th Congress. *Public Law 107-306, 107th Congress, Short title: "Intelligence Authorization Act for Fiscal Year 2003* (Washington, DC, Congress, November 27, 2002), 116 STAT. 2408-2409, SEC. 603, (a).

24. "The 9-11 Commission Report: About," GPO Access Web site, August 5, 2004, http://www.gpoaccess.gov/911/about.html (accessed October 27, 2004).

25. "Frequently Asked Questions About the 9-11 Commission: What Is the Commission's Budget?" National Commission on Terrorist Attacks Upon the United States Web site, http://www.9-11commission.gov/about/faq.htm#q5 (accessed October 27, 2004).

26. Public Law 107-306, 116 STAT. 2413, Sec. 610(b).

27. "Frequently Asked Questions About the 9-11 Commission: When Was the Commission Created, and When Is It Supposed to Report?" National Commission on Terrorist Attacks Upon the United States Web site, http://www. 9-11commission.gov/about/faq.htm#q2 (accessed October 27, 2004).

28. "About the Commission," National Commission on Terrorist Attacks Upon the United States Web site, http://www.9-11commission.gov/about/index.htm (accessed October 27, 2004).

29. Ibid.

30. "Frequently Asked Questions About the 9-11 Commission: How Many People Have You Interviewed?" National Commission on Terrorist Attacks Upon the United States Web site, http://www.9-11commission.gov/about/faq.htm#q6 (accessed October 27, 2004).

31. "The 9-11 Commission's Web Site Front Page," National Commission on Terrorist Attacks Upon the United States Web site, www.9-11commission.gov (accessed October 27, 2004).

32. *The 9/11 Commission Report, Executive Summary*, xv.

33. Ibid., 3.

34. Ibid., 9.

35. Ibid.

36. Ibid., 10.

37. Ibid., 9.

38. Ibid., 10.

39. Ibid.

40. Ibid., 11.

41. Ibid.

42. Ibid., 12.

43. Ibid.

44. Ibid., 13.

45. Ibid., 13–14.

46. Ibid., 14.

47. Ibid., 15.

48. Ibid.

49. Ibid., 16.

50. Discussion between Col. Randall Larsen and former Representative and Speaker of the House Tom Foley, October 2001.

51. Alan Dershowitz, *Why Terrorism Works* (New Haven, CT: Yale University Press, 2002).

52. "Presidential Decision Directive 39, U.S. Policy on Counterterrorism," U.S. Department of Homeland Security, Office of Domestic Preparedness Web site, http://www.ojp.usdoj.gov/odp/docs/pdd39.htm (accessed April 8, 2004).

53. "Homeland Security Presidential Directive/HSPD-5," The White House Web site, February 28, 2003, http://www.white house.gov/news/releases/2003/02/print/20030228-9.html (accessed April 8, 2004).

54. "Fact Sheet: National Incident Management System (NIMS)," U.S. Department of Homeland Security Web site, March 1, 2004, http://www.dhs.gov/dhspublic/display?content=3258 (accessed March 31, 2004)

55. Ibid.

56. "Initial National Response Plan," *Department of Homeland Security,* Washington, DC; September 30, 2003, 2

57. "Homeland Security Presidential Directive/HSPD-5."

58. President Bush's Address to Congress and the American People; Thursday, September 20, 2001, http://www.newsmax.com/archives/articles/2001/9/21/02114.shtml.

59. Testimony of Randall Larsen, 9/11 Commission, New York City, April 1, 2003.

60. Zedong Mao and Tse-Tung Mao, *On Guerrilla Warfare* (University of Illinois Press: Urbana and Chicago, 1961), First Illinois paperback 2000, 92–93.

61. Robert Mueller, Director of the FBI in a Speech to the National Legal Center, Department of Justice, Washington, DC, November 19, 2002.

62. Jim Garamone, "Tape Proves bin Laden's Complicity in September 11 Attacks," *Defense Link, American Forces Information Service, News Articles,* Washington, DC, December 13, 2001, http://www.defenselink.mil/news/Dec2001/n12132001_200112134.html (accessed July 1, 2004).

63. Ibid.

64. Deputy Chief Vincent Dunn (Ret.), "Why the World Trade Center Buildings Collapsed: A Fire Chief's Assessment," April 19, 2003, http://vincentdunn.com/wtc.html (accessed April 19, 2004).

65. Ibid.

66. Department of State, *2001 Patterns of Global Terrorism* (Washington, DC, April 2002), 3.

67. The University of Sydney, "World Trade Center—Some Engineering Aspects," *Department of Civil Engineering,* http://www.civil.usyd.edu.au/latest/wtc.php#system (accessed November 17, 2003).

68. United States General Accounting Office (GAO), *Potential Terrorist Attacks: Additional Actions Needed to Better Prepare Critical Financial Market Participants, GAO-03-414.* GAO. February 2003, 9.

69. Ibid., 9.

70. Associated Press, "Official WTC Death Toll Is 2,752," *The Salt Lake Tribune,* October 30, 2003, http://www.sltrib.com/2003/Oct/10302003/nation_w/ 106763.asp (accessed November 17, 2003).

71. Brian A. Jackson et al., "Protecting Emergency Responders: Lessons Learned from Terrorist Attacks," *RAND Science and Technology Policy Institute,* Conference Proceedings, 2002, 6.

72. Garamone, "Tape Proves bin Laden's Complicity."

73. Randall Larsen, Director ANSER Institute for Homeland Security in radio interview with John Thompson, September 12, 2001.

74. David McIntyre, "Understanding the New National Security Strategy of the United States," *ANSER Institute for HOMELAND Security* (Institute Analysis 009), September 2002, www.homelandsecurity.org/hlsanalysis/ hlsstrategyanalysis.htm (accessed November 17, 2003).

75. David McIntyre, "The National Strategy for Homeland Security: Finding the Path Among the Trees," *ANSER Institute for HOMELAND Security,* July 23, 2002, 12, http://www.homelandsecurity.org /HLSAnalysis/20020723.htm, 3 (accessed November 17, 2003).

76. Ibid.

77. Ibid., 4.

78. Ibid., 5. Also found in Office of Homeland Security's *National Strategy for Homeland Security,* July 2002, 2.

79. Ibid., 6.

80. *National Strategy for Homeland Security,* July 15, 2002, vii.

81. Ibid., viii.

82. Ibid., viii.

83. Ibid., ix.

84. Ibid., ix.

85. Ibid., vix–x.

86. Ibid., x.

87. "What is the Mission of the New Department of Homeland Security?" Department of Homeland Security Web site, DHS Organization Section, http:// www.dhs.gov/dhspublic/display?theme=10&content=429 (accessed November 17, 2003).

88. "Homeland Security Act of 2002," The White House Web site, http:// www.whitehouse.gov/deptofhomeland/bill/title1.html (accessed November 17, 2003) or http://www.whitehouse.gov/deptofhomeland/bill/hsl-bill.pdf (accessed November 17, 2003).

89. "Who Will Be Part of the New Department?" Department of Homeland Security Web site, DHS Organization Section, http://www.dhs.gov/dhspublic/ display?theme=13 (accessed November 17, 2003).

90. Senator John Edwards, "Senator Edwards Proposes Homeland Intelligence Agency," News from Senator John Edwards North Carolina for Immediate Release-Press Web site, February 13, 2003, http://edwards.senate.gov/press/ 2003/0213-pr.html# (accessed November 17, 2003).

91. From the oral statement by Randall Larsen to The National Commission on Terrorist Attacks Upon the United States (9/11 Commission) in New York City on April 1, 2003.

92. From and after the passage of this act it shall not be lawful to employ any part of the Army of the United States, as a *posse comitatus,* or otherwise, for the purpose of executing the laws, except in such cases and under such circumstances as such employment of said force may be expressly authorized by the Constitution or by act of Congress; and no money appropriated by this act shall be used to pay any of the expenses incurred in the employment of any troops in violation of this section, and any person willfully violating the provisions of this section shall be deemed guilty of a misdemeanor and on conviction thereof shall be punished by fine not exceeding ten thousand dollars or imprisonment not exceeding two years or by both such fine and imprisonment.

93. For more information on *posse comitatus,* go to the following Web sites: http://www.northcom.mil/index.cfm?fuseaction=news.factsheets&factsheet=5, or   http://www.homelandsecurity.org/journal/articles/displayArticle .asp?article=11,  or  http://www.homelandsecurity.org/journal/articles/ displayArticle.asp?article=30 (accessed November 17, 2003).

94. The Insurrection Act (Title 10 USC Sections 331–334). This act allows the president to use U.S. military personnel at the request of the State Legislature or governor to suppress insurrections. It also allows the president to use federal troops to enforce federal laws when rebellion against the authority of the United States makes it impracticable to enforce the laws of the United States.

95. Because if it is required, it means that a serious breach in security has occurred, and DoD must not fail in its mission.

96. Interview with Dr. Elin Gursky, former Deputy Health Commissioner for the State of New Jersey, May 30, 2003.

97. This quote is found in Senator Graham's statement during the proceedings: "I conclude by reading a quote from Dwight David Eisenhower. I think it is very appropriate as we debate the Homeland Security Department and its structure. Ike said: 'the right organization will not guarantee success, but the wrong organization will guarantee failure.'" U.S. Senate Proceedings, "091902 Homeland Security.txt, Homeland Security Act of 2002," *United States Coast Guard Legal Web site* (Homeland Security Act of 2002–Legislative History & Documents–Text Files Listing), September 19, 2002, http://www.uscg.mil/legal/Homeland_legislation/ text/091902%20homeland%20security.txt or http://www.uscg.mil/legal/ Homeland_legislation/Text/, page S8882 (accessed November 18, 2003).

98. National Commission on Terrorist Attacks Upon the United States, *9/11 Commission Report, Executive Summary,* July 22, 2004, 16, www.gpoaccess.gov/911 (accessed October 27, 2004).

99. Ibid., 17.
100. Ibid.
101. Ibid., 20.
102. Ibid.
103. Ibid., 22.
104. Ibid., 25.
105. Ibid.
106. Ibid., 26.
107. Ibid.

108. More information is available at the National Memorial Institute for the Prevention of Terrorism (MIPT) Web site's Library and MIPT Databases, http://www.mipt.org/MIPT-Databases.asp (accessed November 17, 2003).

## Chapter 12

1. William Branigin, "Senate Report Blasts Intelligence Agencies' Flaws," *Washington Post*, July 9, 2004, 1–2.

2. Jerrold M. Post, *Leaders and Their Followers in a Dangerous World* (Ithaca, NY: Cornell University Press, 2004), xv–xvi. The CIA group was composed of an interdisciplinary team made up of area specialists, psychiatrists, social anthropologists, and other specialists.

3. "At the Crossroads: Counterproliferation and National Security Strategy," *A Report of the Center for Counterproliferation Research* (Washington, DC: NDU, April 2004), 34–35.

4. Rex Kiziah, "Assessment of the Emerging Biocruise Threat," *Counterproliferation Papers, Future Warfare Series, No. 6*, August 2000; Michael E. Dickey, "Biocruise: A Contemporary Threat," *Counterproliferation Papers, Future Warfare Series, No. 7*, September 2000. Both were published by the USAF Counterproliferation Center, Maxwell AFB, Alabama.

5. Of course, the ultimate would be to design effective individual protection equipment that is so user-friendly that there is little or no degradation in combat effectiveness when military personnel wear it. In the past and at present, that is far from the case. See Barry R. Schneider, "Combat Effectiveness in MOPP4: Lessons from the U.S. Army CANE Exercises," *The War Next Time: Countering Rogue States and Terrorists Armed with Chemical and Biological Weapons* (Maxwell AFB, AL: USAF Counterproliferation Center, November 2003), 173–182.

6. *Joint Service Chemical and Biological Defense Program FY02-03 Overview* (Washington, DC: Department of Defense, 2003), 28.

7. Major General (Dr.) Joseph Kelley, USAF Assistant Surgeon General for Healthcare Operations, Briefing on "Biodefense: The Air Force Medical System Approach," Washington, DC, December 8, 2003.

8. Ibid.

9. Ibid.

10. Ibid.

11. Ibid.

12. See the "HHS Fact Sheet: Biodefense Preparedness," The White House Web site, April 28, 2004, http://www.whitehouse.gov/news/releases/2004/04/20040428-4.html (accessed July 11, 2004).

13. Ibid.

14. Ibid.

15. Ibid.

16. Ibid.

17. Ibid. CDC's Centers for Public Health Preparedness (CPHP) helps prepare frontline health workers at the local level. There are now 34 such centers in 46 states.

18. Ibid. From 2001 to 2004.

19. Ibid.

20. Ibid.

21. Ibid.

22. Ibid.

23. USAMRIID's Medical Management of Biological Casualties Handbook, 4th ed., February 2001, U.S. Army Medical Research Institute of Infectious Diseases, Fort Detrick, Maryland.

24. Ibid.; see also Barry R. Schneider, "U.S. Bio-Defense Readiness: Thoughts after September 11th," in *The Gathering Biological Warfare Storm*, ed. Jim A. Davis and Barry R. Schneider (Maxwell AFB, AL: USAF Counterproliferation Center, 2002), 1–8.

25. Ibid.

26. These suggestions were made originally by Dr. Charles Gallaway, Director, Chemical-Biological Division, DTRA/TD at a 2004 conference.

27. *Joint Service Chemical and Biological Defense Program FY02-03 Overview*, 8–27.

28. Jim A. Davis and Bruce W. Bennett, "Needed Now: The 85% Solution to the CBW Threat," *The War Next Time* (Maxwell AFB, AL: USAF Counterproliferation Center, 2003), 219–246.

29. These are suggestions of Dr. Charles Gallaway, Director of the Chemical-Biological Division, DTRA.

30. Leonard A. Cole, *The Anthrax Letters, A Medical Detective Story* (Washington DC: Joseph Henry Press, 2003), ix.

31. See Barbara F. Bullock, "Surveillance and Detection: A Public Health Response to Bioterrorism," in *The Gathering Biological Warfare Storm*, ed. Jim A. Davis and Barry R. Schneider (Maxwell AFB, AL: USAF Counterproliferation Center, April 2002), 41–66.

32. See Tanja Korpi and Christopher Hemmer, "Avoiding Panic and Keeping the Ports Open in a Chemical and Biological Threat Environment: A Literature Review," USAF Counterproliferation Center Study, September 15, 2003.

33. Ibid.

34. Barry R. Schneider, *Future War and Counterproliferation: Military Responses to NBC Proliferation Threats* (Westport, CT: Praeger, 1999).

35. See Barry R. Schneider, "Twenty Questions to Ask When Dealing with a NASTI," *Future War and Counterproliferation* (Westport, CT: Praeger, 1999), 157–162, for a discussion of the many questions top U.S. leaders ought to ask before preemptively attacking an opponent's WMD assets.

36. "At the Crossroads: Counterproliferation and National Security Strategy," *A Report of the Center for Counterproliferation Research* (Washington, DC: NDU, April 2004), 38.

37. Major General Roger W. Berg, "U.S. Air Force Goals: Survive, Operate, Sustain," *NBC Report* [Journal of the U.S. Army Chemical and Nuclear Agency], March 2005.

38. "CPRC Areas for Capability Enhancement," Counterproliferation Program Review Committee, *Report on Activities and Programs for Countering Proliferation and NBC Terrorism*, Executive Summary, vol. 1, May 2004, 3–4, http://cms.isn.ch/public/docs/doc_10259_290_en.pdf (accessed February 2, 2005).

39. U.S. Central Command, U.S. Pacific Command, U.S. European Command, U.S. Southern Command, U.S. Northern Command, U.S. Strategic Command, U.S. Special Operations Command, and U.S. Transportation Command.

40. "Department of Defense Chemical, Biological, Radiological and Nuclear Defense Program," *Annual Report to Congress,* May 2004, http://www.acq.osd.mil/cp under the reports section as an Adobe Acrobat (.pdf) file (accessed December 6, 2004).

## Appendix A

1. "Remarks by Honorable Les Aspin, Secretary of Defense, National Academy of Sciences Committee on International Security and Arms Control," *The Navy Public Affairs Library,* December 7, 1993, http://www.chinfo.navy.mil/navpalib/policy/aspi1207.txt (accessed July 13, 2004).

## Appendix B

1. "National Strategy to Combat Weapons of Mass Destruction," The White House Web site, 2002, http://www.whitehouse.gov/news/releases/2002/12/WMDStrategy.pdf (accessed July 13, 2004).

## Appendix C

1. General Accounting Office Report NSIAD-96-103, *Chemical and Biological Defense: Emphasis Remains Insufficient To Resolve Continuing Problems,* March 1996, 15.

2. Online at http://www.defenselink.mil/pubs/qdr/sec3.html (accessed July 6, 2004).

3. See, for example, General Accounting Office (GAO), "Chemical and Biological Defense: Emphasis Remains Insufficient to Resolve Continuing Problems" (GAO/NSIAD 96-103, March 12, 1996); see also GAO, "Report to the Chairman, Committee on Government Affairs, U.S. Senate, Chemical and Biological Defense—U.S. Forces Are Not Adequately Equipped to Detect All Threats," January 1993.

4. Renamed from Deputy Assistant to the Secretary of Defense for Counterproliferation and CB Defense programs [DATSD (CP/CBD)] to Deputy Assistant to the Secretary of Defense for CB defense programs [DATSD (CBD)] in 2000.

5. John M. Deutch et al., "Report of the Commission to Assess the Organization of the Federal Government to Combat the Proliferation of Weapons of Mass Destruction," Washington, DC, July 14, 1999. Hereafter called the Deutch Report.

6. Director, Defense Research and Engineering memorandum to DepSecDef, subject: Chemical and Biological Defense Program (CBDP)—Action Memorandum, dated April 21, 2000, with approval dated May 9, 2000. All four services nonconcurred with the recommendation that the Joint Staff (J5) become a voting member of the Joint NBC Defense Board. The effort was taken to increase the combatant commands' equities in the program, but the services bitterly fought the dilution of their influence.

7. Under Secretary of Defense for Acquisition, Technology and Logistics memorandum, subject: Chemical and Biological Defense Program Management, dated October 19, 2001.

8. DoD CBRN Defense Program Annual Report to Congress, May 2004.

# Index

# About the Contributors

**BRUCE W. BENNETT** is the research leader for strategy, force planning, and counterproliferation within RAND's International Security and Defense Policy Center. He focuses on the future of warfare and military analysis, especially in light of new threats, operational concepts, and technologies required by asymmetric threats. He is examining possible chemical and biological weapon threats in Korea and the Persian Gulf and the character of the U.S. strategy required in response, with a focus on deterrence. He facilitated the Coral Breeze seminars on chemical and biological warfare (CBW) for Commander Combined Forces Command (Korea), the Desert Breeze seminars on CBW for U.S. Central Command (USCENTCOM), and parts of USCENTCOM's Eagle Resolve exercises with the Gulf States. He has worked on defenses against biological weapons in the RESTOPS (Restoration of Operations at airfields after CBW attack) Advanced Concepts Technology Demonstration (ACTD) and the subsequent Biological Weapons Countermeasures Initiative for the Commander of U.S. Pacific Command (USPACOM). He is the Policy Working Group chair for the CASPOD (Contamination Avoidance at Sea Ports of Debarkation) ACTD. He has also worked on the future of warfare and military analysis. Dr. Bennett received his B.S. in Economics from the California Institute of Technology and his Ph.D. in Policy Analysis from the Pardee RAND Graduate School for Public Policy Analysis.

**WALTER L. BUSBEE,** Brigadier General, U.S. Army (Ret.), is the Vice President, CBRNE/WMD Programs, Computer Sciences Corporation, in Arlington, Virginia. He previously served as the Counterproliferation Business Area Executive, Johns Hopkins University Applied Physics Laboratory, and the Deputy Assistant to the Secretary of Defense (Counterproliferation and Chemical-Biological Defense) where he was responsible for oversight and implementation of the congressionally directed joint NBC Defense Program under PL 94-103. He completed 32 years active duty service in the Army Chemical Corps in three consecutive program manager positions —Binary Chemical Modernization, Chemical Weapons Demilitarization, and Biological Defense. He also supported several international arms control initiatives. He is a graduate of the Defense Systems Management College, the U.S. Army War College, the U.S. Army

Command and General Staff College (George C. Marshall awardee), and a graduate of Georgia Tech with an M.S. in Chemical Engineering.

**BERT A. CLINE** is a Senior Analyst at Science Applications International Corporation (SAIC) and has over 26 years of experience in the U.S. Air Force (USAF). Mr. Cline contributed to the development of a methodology for the USAF assessment of Pacific Air Forces (PACAF) Concept of Operations (CONOPS) and authored the PACAF Chemical Warfare (CW) CONOPS that was implemented AF wide. Further, he was a major participant in the successful development and implementation of the Restoration of Operations (RESTOPS) Advanced Concept Technology Demonstration (ACTD) that provided validation of the counter-chemical warfare (C-CW) CONOPS. While in the air force, he held numerous Disaster Preparedness positions, held an Inspector General position, served as a Theater Nuclear, Biological, and Chemical (NBC) Defense Advisor, Superintendent of the Readiness School, and was a Major Command (MAJCOM) Readiness Manager. Additionally, he authored the Desert Shield/Desert Storm NBC Defense portion of the War Plan, the NBC portion of current U.S. Air Forces in Europe (USAFE) and PACAF War Plans, and the USAFE Component Response for Nuclear Weapons Accident Response. Mr. Cline has contributed to numerous SAIC studies and analyses and developed the seven-day Civil Engineering Readiness (CEX) C-CW CONOPS MAJCOM/Wing orientation session, which included lesson plans, tabletop exercises, and progress checks.

**JIM A. DAVIS,** Colonel, USAF (Ret.), is a Senior Program Manager at Battelle Memorial Institute focused on WMD, Homeland Security, Counterterrorism, and Missile Defense. He has a Doctorate of Veterinary Medicine from Texas A&M and a Master and a Doctorate of Public Health from the University of Texas. He is board certified with the American College of Veterinary Preventive Medicine and is a Foreign Animal Disease Diagnostician. He is also a graduate of the Air Command and Staff College and Air War College. Previously to his current position, he spent five years with the USAF Counterproliferation Center where he served as the Deputy Director and also as a Professor at Air War College. Dr. Davis has worked with CENTCOM on Cooperative Defense Initiative, OSD on the Israeli Bilateral Working Group, PACOM on the Biological Weapons Countermeasures Initiative, and many other national and international WMD defense efforts. He has been a sought-after speaker and exercise participant at meetings with city, state, and federal officials. Col. Davis's WMD experiences have also included overseeing stored chemical agents, teaching emergency wartime medicine in surgical labs, and leading decontamination teams. Dr. Davis started his military career with a four-year tour in the Army Veterinary Corps serving in various capacities, some of which dealt with defensive chemical and biological warfare.

During a break in active military service, Col. Davis practiced veterinary medicine for six years but stayed in the Army Reserves. In 1987, Col. Davis joined the USAF as a Public Health Officer and served in that capacity at several bases. He also served as the Deputy Chair for the Department of Future Conflict Studies at Air War College, the USAF Surgeon General's Chair to Air University, and the Commander, 48th Aerospace Medicine Squadron at RAF Lakenheath, U.K. As commander, he was responsible for the largest Aerospace Medicine Squadron in Europe, which directed flight medicine, optometry, preventive medicine, health promotion, public health, industrial hygiene, and bioenvironmental engineering services. He provided daily deployed support to USAFE fighters, European Tanker Task Force, and Military Operations Other Than War (MOOTW) in Europe, Africa, and the Middle East, managed $6 million in resources at eight separate operating locations, and was responsible for the quality of $72 million of subsistence. He also served as U.K. Medical Intelligence Officer and USAFE Consultant for Public Health. His areas of expertise include chemical and biological warfare and terrorism, as well as the Middle East. In addition to the present volume, he has coedited two other books: *The War Next Time: Countering Rogue States and Terrorists Armed with Chemical and Biological Weapons:* Maxwell AFB, AL: USAF Counterproliferation Center, November 2003; and *The Gathering Biological Warfare Storm* (Westport, CT: Praeger Publishers, 2004). Recently one of his articles was published in *Today's Best Military Writing: The Finest Articles on the Past, Present, and Future of the U.S. Military* (New York: Tom Doherty Associates, LLC, September 2004). He has also published several articles on WMD issues.

**LAURITA M. DENNY** is Director of Research at Political Psychology Associates, Ltd. She has specialized in the study of terrorism and terrorist group dynamics, leadership profiling, and the role of religion and ethnicity in conflict, as well as strategic communications. Ms. Denny has most recently conducted research on Palestinian and Radical Islamist terrorism in Israel, Osama Bin Laden and the al-Qaeda network, Radical Islam in Central Asia, Saddam Hussein and the strategic culture of Iraq, Kim Jong Il of North Korea, and the ethnic/religious basis for conflict in the Balkans. Ms. Denny received her Master's degree in International Policy and Practice (with concentrations in terrorism studies and political psychology) from George Washington University and her BA in Political Science from the University of California, Irvine. She was with the U.S. Department of State from 1991 to 1995 during which time she served in the Bureau of Political Military Affairs supporting initial U.S. engagement and humanitarian efforts in Bosnia and Herzegovina and as Executive Assistant to the U.S. Ambassador to Bosnia during the Vance/Owen Peace Process and the initial establishment of the U.S. Embassy in

Sarajevo. Ms. Denny has also worked at the Institute for National Strategic Studies at the National Defense University on Western Hemisphere security issues.

**PATRICK D. ELLIS,** WMD/Homeland Security Analyst to the USAF Counterproliferation Center, specializes in WMD Terrorism, Homeland Security, and Disaster/Emergency Management issues. He has lived, traveled, and worked extensively in the United States, Europe, and Asia. He holds a Bachelor of Arts degree from the University of Maryland in Asian Studies/Government and Politics and a Master of Public Administration degree from the University of Oklahoma. He completed specialized courses at the Defense Nuclear Weapons School, U.S. Army Chemical School, and USAF Special Operations School. His nonmilitary WMD experience includes Department of Justice sponsored training from Louisiana State University, Texas A&M, the Department of Homeland Security's Center for Domestic Preparedness, and Bechtel Nevada's Counter Terrorism Operations Support. Other education and training accomplishments include a University of Maryland Certificate in Korean Studies, courses at the Air University's Academic Instructor School, and the College of Aerospace Doctrine, Research, and Education's *Contingency Wartime Planners* and *Information Warfare Applications* courses. Mr. Ellis participated in WMD exercises such as Consequence Island 2001 (Puerto Rico), Consequence Management 2000, and Launch Relief 2000. In addition, he planned and participated in various field study trips to federal, state, and local counterproliferation and WMD response organizations. Mr. Ellis developed and taught WMD-related lessons for the Air Force Institute of Technology, the Air War College, and the Ira C. Eaker College for Professional Development's USAF On-Scene Commanders course.

**CHARLES R. HEFLEBOWER,** Lieutenant General, USAF (Ret.), currently serves as one of five Air Force Senior Mentors. While on active duty, his assignments included command and staff at every level in the United States, Asia, and Europe. He holds a Bachelor of Science degree from the United States Air Force Academy in Aeronautical Engineering and a Master's degree in International Relations from the University of Arkansas. His other education accomplishments include the National War College, the Program for Senior Executives in National and International Security, Harvard University, the Joint Force Air Component Commander Course, Maxwell Air Force Base, Alabama, and the Joint Flag Officer Warfighting Course, Maxwell Air Force Base. When General Heflebower retired from active duty, he was a command pilot with nearly 4000 hours of flying time, mostly in fighter aircraft. He also has flown over 200 combat missions in Southeast Asia, Bosnia, and Iraq. As an Air Force Senior Mentor, he has participated in numerous war-fighting exercises and mission rehearsals in the Pacific, Europe, and the United States. He also instructs at the Air University. While stationed in the Republic of Korea, he was responsible for the initial implementation of what has become the joint Air Force and Marine Corps Counter-Chemical Concept of Operations.

**KERRY M. KARTCHNER** is Senior Advisor for Missile Defense Policy in the Bureau of Arms Control, U.S. Department of State. He was previously the Senior Representative of the Department of State to the Standing Consultative Commission for the ABM Treaty and, prior to that, the Senior Representative of the U.S. Arms Control and Disarmament Agency to the Joint Compliance and Inspection Commission for the START Treaty. He has also been an Assistant Professor of National Security Affairs at the Naval Postgraduate School and Area Leader for Arms Control Research at Analytic Services, an Arlington, Virginia, think tank. He is the author of *Negotiating START: The Quest for Strategic Stability* (1992), as well as other chapters and edited volumes. He earned his Ph.D. at the University of Southern California.

**JEFFREY A. LARSEN** is a Senior Policy Analyst with the Strategies Business Unit of Science Applications International Corporation in Colorado Springs, Colorado. He is also president of Larsen Consulting Group LLC and an adjunct professor of international studies at the University of Denver. Dr. Larsen is a retired Air Force Lieutenant Colonel who served as a command pilot, associate professor of political science at the Air Force Academy, and first director of the USAF Institute for National Security Studies, where he also designed the Academy's first interdisciplinary course in countering the proliferation of WMD. A native of Wisconsin, Dr. Larsen holds a Ph.D. in politics from Princeton University, an M.A. in international relations from Princeton, an M.A. in national security affairs and European area studies from the Naval Postgraduate School, and a B.S. in international affairs and Soviet area studies from the U.S. Air Force Academy. From 1995 to 1997 he held a Fulbright NATO Research Fellowship, and in 2001 he won SAIC's publication prize in the field of political science, economics, and arms control. Dr. Larsen has served as senior editor of the official Air Force studies of the air campaigns in Kosovo, Afghanistan, and Iraq. He wrote U.S. Space Command's strategy for the region of space, led the team that developed a strategic vision for U.S. Northern Command, and has supported Air Force Headquarters in arms control policy issues, the Nuclear Posture Review, and the development of air force counterproliferation doctrine. He has served as a consultant to the U.S. Navy, the U.S. Air Force, Los Alamos National Laboratory, and the Defense Threat Reduction Agency.

**RANDALL J. LARSEN,** Colonel, USAF (Ret.), is the founder and CEO of Homeland Security Associates, LLC, a private corporation that provides a wide range of homeland security consulting services to industry and government. Previously, he served as the founding Director of the Institute for Homeland Security and as the Chairman of the Department of Military Strategy and Operations at the National War College. Colonel Larsen was one of the first witnesses asked to testify before the 9/11 Commission. He is a frequent expert witness for the U.S. Congress and has recently appeared before the Senate Armed Services, Senate Judiciary, and House Government Reform Committees, plus the House Select Committee on Homeland Security. He is a widely published author who most recently coauthored a book and monograph published by the National Legal Center: *The Executive's Desk Book on Corporate Risks and Response for Homeland Security* (March 2003), and *What Corporate America Needs to Know About Bioterrorism* (July 2003). He is a frequent guest on radio and television, including CBS, NBC, ABC, PBS, CNN, BBC, Fox News Channel, and Larry King Live. Since March 2003, he has been the Homeland Security consultant to CBS News. His analysis and opinions have recently appeared in the *Washington Post, Wall Street Journal, New York Times, Chicago Tribune, USA Today, Newsweek, Time,* and *Business Week.* Colonel Larsen served for 32 years in both the army and the air force. His flying career began as a 19-year-old Cobra pilot in the 101st Airborne Division. He flew 400 combat missions in Vietnam. He also served as military attaché at the U.S. Embassy in Bangkok, the chief of legislative liaison at the U.S. Transportation Command, and the commander of America's fleet of VIP aircraft at Andrews AFB, MD. His decorations include the Legion of Merit, Distinguished Flying Cross, Bronze Star, 17 awards of the Air Medal (three with "V" Device for Valor), and the South Vietnamese Cross of Gallantry.

**PETER R. LAVOY** is Director of the Center for Contemporary Conflict (CCC) at the Naval Postgraduate School (NPS). CCC provides research on contemporary security issues to the makers and executors of U.S. defense policy. At NPS, Dr. Lavoy also is Associate Chair for Research and Assistant Professor in the National Security Affairs Department, where he has been since 1993. He teaches graduate courses and supervises Master's theses on asymmetric conflict, nuclear strategy, weapons proliferation and counterproliferation, South Asian politics and security, and other topics in international relations and defense policy. From June 1998 to June 2000, Dr. Lavoy served as Director for Counterproliferation Policy in the Office of the Secretary of Defense, a position he occupied as an International Affairs Fellow of the Council on Foreign Relations. At the Pentagon, Dr. Lavoy oversaw a staff that was responsible for developing policies to improve U.S. military capabilities to deter, combat, and defend against the use of nuclear, biological, and chemical (NBC) weapons and missiles, and to help allies and coalition partners prepare their armed forces and populations to counter NBC threats. He has published numerous journal articles and book chapters on weapons proliferation and on South Asian security issues. He co-edited *Planning the Unthinkable: How New Powers Will Use Nuclear, Biological and Chemical Weapons* (Cornell University Press, 2000). His newest books are *Learning to Live with the Bomb: India and Nuclear Weapons, 1947–2002* (Palgrave-Macmillan, 2004) and a volume he edited entitled *Asymmetric Warfare in South Asia: The Causes and Consequences of the Kargil Conflict* (2004). Dr. Lavoy received a Ph.D. in Political Science from the University of California, Berkeley, and a B.A. in Government from Oberlin College, where he graduated with High Honors.

**JOHN P. LAWRENCE** is the chief scientist and manager of the Operational Planning and Assessments Department of Science Applications International Corporation. Mr. Lawrence has a history of hands-on, highly responsive technical support involving WMD proliferation issues and CBW proliferation for OSD, DNA, CIA, DOE, ACDA, and the National Laboratories. He pioneered war plans analysis using operational assessment of CW on CONOPS/doctrine and directed CW vulnerability analysis of OCONUS MOBs, APODs, and SPODs. Mr. Lawrence participated in the SHAPE analyses that formed the basis for the SHAPE post-Cold War CP triad, SHAPE TMD MOR, and NATO TMD concepts. Since joining SAIC in 1988, Mr. Lawrence has led the analysis efforts of a series of operational impact analyses conducted for the Air Staff, the Joint Staff, and CINCUNC Korea, which quantifies the impact of CB WMD attacks on operations at key APODs, SPODs, and fighter bases. This work has been central to uncovering "new" science with respect to the difficulties adversaries face with delivering a sustainable hazard environment at these fixed sites. The methodology is broadly recognized as unique, both in the level of operational detail it addresses and the ability to directly measure the interdependencies between passive defense, active defense, and counterforce. It has been the basis for both direct changes to CINC OPLANs, Service CONOPs, and operational procedures. During Mr. Lawrence's July 1999 presentation of analytic results to the Secretary and the Chief-of-Staff of the US Air Force, the Chief-of-Staff directed the Air Staff to begin implementation of the study findings. Additionally, Mr. Lawrence led a series of analyses for SHAPE, which identified the force posture implications of nuclear, biological, chemical, and missile proliferation and led to the development of SHAPE's counterproliferation deterrence triad and the military operational requirement for Theater Missile Defense (TMD). Mr. Lawrence graduated from the United States Military Academy with a Bachelor of Science in Nuclear Engineering. He spent nine years in the United States Army, with four years serving as a Nuclear Weapons Development Staff Officer.

**LAURA J. LeGALLO** has over five years of experience as an Operations Research Analyst focusing on the effects of weapons of mass destruction (WMD), specifically chemical and biological warfare weapons, on operations at key military sites (both homeland/domestic and international sites to include the Pacific, European, and Southwest Asian theaters) and analyzing the implications of those hazards for current and future theater operational planning, acquisition, and force structure. These analyses have been conducted in support of a number of DoD customers including the Air Force Directorate for Nuclear and Counterproliferation HQ USAF/XON [now the Directorate Strategic Security, AF(XOS)], the Defense Threat Reduction Agency (DTRA), U.S. Marine Corps Forces, Pacific (MARFORPAC), U.S. Forces Korea (USFK), and the 7th Air Force. This work has been paramount in revealing the complexities that adversaries face with regard to delivering sustainable chemical or biological hazards to fixed sites and has directly influenced CINC OPLANS, Service CONOPS and Tactics, Techniques, and Procedures (TTPs) and several related ACTDs. She holds a Bachelor's degree from the University of Virginia in Biology and is completing a Master's degree in Systems Engineering from George Washington University. Additionally, Ms. Le Gallo has analyzed passive and active defense postures currently used by the United States and its allies, and the impact of attack operations on strategic sealift and airlift operations, intratheater airlift, and tactical air and port operations. Both the integrated methodology and the associated tools Ms. Le Gallo used to perform the aforementioned analyses are broadly recognized as unique in the level of site-specific operational detail and fidelity that they address and their ability to quantify the interdependencies between passive defense, active defense, and attack operations/counterforce.

**RICHARD A. LOVE** is a Research Professor at the National Defense University in Washington, D.C., where he teaches *Combating the Proliferation of WMD* at the National War College and conducts counterproliferation and consequence management research. Dr. Love lectures on WMD threats and proliferation in the NATO staff officers' course, in the Reserve Components National Security Course, and in the CBRN focus study at the Joint Forces Staff College in Norfolk, Virginia. He is an adjunct professor of law and politics at Catholic University, where he teaches National Security Law, International Law of Armed Conflict, International Organizations and Law, and Security in the Information Age. He serves as counsel for the Financial Crimes and Security Project at the Brookings Institution and as an advisor on homeland security for the Council on Foreign Relations. He holds a Juris Doctor and LL.M. in international law.

**ALBERT J. MAURONI** is a program manager with Innovative Emergency Management, Inc., in Arlington, Virginia, where he currently supports the army chemical demilitarization program and DoD CBRN Defense Program. He has more than 18 years of experience working on joint CBRN defense programs and policy issues. He participated in the city training program and ran the CB Helpline of the DoD Domestic Preparedness Program, supported the CB 2010 study, and facilitated strategic planning for U.S. Army CBDCOM. Mr. Mauroni directly supported the JSMG Executive Office and, while on the Joint Staff, participated as an action officer on the JSIG, the JNBCDB, and OSD CBD Steering Committee. While supporting the Joint Chiefs of Staff between 1999 and 2003, he analyzed the DoD CBD POM for its adequacy in supporting combatant command requirements, ran four annual symposiums for CBRN defense, and developed a biological standoff detection system concept of operation and a joint concept of employment for CBRN defense of military installations and facilities. In 2002, he was a key participant in the formation of the new CBRN defense management structure, and in particular, the Joint Requirements Office for CBRN Defense. Mr. Mauroni coordinated key CBRN defense assessments and issues during Operation Enduring Freedom/Iraqi Freedom while supporting the Joint Staff. Mr. Mauroni is the author of four books and numerous articles on CBRN defense. He has a Bachelor's degree from Carnegie-Mellon University and a Master's degree from Central Michigan University. He lives in Alexandria, Virginia, with his wife Roseann and their three dogs.

**GAYLE D. MEYERS** is the Director of Middle East Regional Security Projects at Search for Common Ground. Based in the organization's Jerusalem office, she manages a dialogue group on strategic security issues composed of retired military and diplomatic personnel, and she is responsible for creating two consortia through which Israeli, Jordanian, Palestinian, and Egyptian officials are working to improve the region's chemical and biological preparedness. Ms. Meyers served for five years in the U.S. Office of the Secretary of Defense, first as a Presidential Management Intern, and then as a foreign affairs specialist in the Office of Counterproliferation Policy. There, she launched and managed the Cooperative Defense Initiative to counter the proliferation of weapons of mass destruction in partnership with U.S. Central Command and the militaries of the Gulf states, Egypt, and Jordan. She staffed WMD-related seminars such as DESERT BREEZE and EAGLE RESOLVE and supported the NATO Senior Defence Group on Proliferation. Ms. Meyers has received several awards, including the Department of Defense Exceptional Civilian Service Award and the Department of State Meritorious Service Award, and is a member of Women in International Security. She is trained in mediation and negotiation and holds an M.A. from the Fletcher School of Law and Diplomacy and a B.A. from the University of Pennsylvania.

**JERROLD M. POST** is a physician serving as Professor of Psychiatry, Political Psychology, and International Affairs, and Director of the Political Psychology Program at The George Washington University. Dr. Post has devoted his entire career to the field of political psychology, coming to George Washington after a 21-year career with the U.S. Government where he founded and directed the Center for the Analysis of Personality and Political Behavior. At George Washington, he cofounded and directs the George Washington University Institute for Crisis and Disaster Management. Dr. Post received his B.A. magna cum laude from Yale College. After receiving his M.S. from Yale, where he was elected to Alpha Omega Alpha, honor medical society, he received postgraduate training in psychiatry at Harvard Medical School and the National Institute of Mental Health, and in international studies from Johns Hopkins. A practicing psychiatrist, he is a Life Fellow of the American Psychiatric Association, a member of the American Academy of Psychiatry and the Law, and the American College of Psychiatrists. Dr. Post has testified before Congress on numerous occasions and is a frequent commentator on national and international radio and television. His books include *When Illness Strikes the Leader: The Dilemma of the Captive King, Political Paranoia: The Psychopolitics of Hatred, Know Thy Enemy: Profiles of Adversary Leaders and Their Strategic Cultures, The Psychological Assessment of Political Leaders, with Profiles of Saddam Hussein and Bill Clinton,* and *Leaders and Their Followers in a Dangerous World: The Psychology of Political Behavior.*

**BRAD ROBERTS** is a member of the research staff of the Institute for Defense Analyses in Alexandria, Virginia, where he contributes to studies for the Office of the Secretary of Defense, DoD support agencies, and the joint military staff. His areas of expertise are NBC weapons counterproliferation, nonproliferation, and counterterrorism. He is also an adjunct professor at George Washington University, a member of DoD's Threat Reduction Advisory Committee, chairman of the research council of the Chemical and Biological Arms Control Institute, chairman of the Threat Reduction Program Review Committee for Los Alamos National Laboratory, and a member of the executive committee of the U.S. Committee of the Council for Security Cooperation in Asia Pacific. He joined IDA in 1995, having served previously at the Center for Strategic and International Studies as a research fellow and as editor of *The Washington Quarterly.* Dr. Roberts has a Bachelor's degree from Stanford University, a Master's degree from the London School of Economics and Political Science, and a doctorate from Erasmus University, Rotterdam, The Netherlands.

**BARRY R. SCHNEIDER** is the director of the USAF Counterproliferation Center at Maxwell AFB, AL, and a Professor of International Relations at the Air War College. Dr. Schneider specializes in NBC counterproliferation and nonproliferation issues. He is the author of *Future War and*

*Counterproliferation: U.S. Military Responses to NBC Proliferation Threats* (Praeger, 1999) and contributor to and coeditor of *The War Next Time: Countering Rogue States and Terrorists Armed with Chemical and Biological Weapons* (USAF Counterproliferation Center, 2003), *The Gathering Biological Warfare Storm.* (Westport, CT: Praeger Publishers, 2004), *Know Thy Enemy: Profiles of Adversary Leaders and Their Strategic Cultures* (USAF Counterproliferation Center, 2002), *Middle East Security Issues: In the Shadow of Weapons of Mass Destruction Proliferation* (USAF Counterproliferation Center, 1999), *Pulling Back from the Nuclear Brink: Reducing and Countering Nuclear Threats* (Frank Cass Ltd., 1998), *Battlefield of the Future: 21st Century Warfare Issues* (Air University Press, 1998), *Missiles for the Nineties: ICBMs and Strategic Policy* (Westview, 1984), and *Current Issues in U.S. Defense Policy* (Praeger, 1976). He has served as a Foreign Affairs Officer and Public Affairs Officer at the U.S. Arms Control and Disarmament Agency, as a Congressional staffer on arms control and defense issues, and was a Senior Defense Analyst at The Harris Group and the National Institute for Public Policy. He has taught at the Air War College since 1993. As a faculty member, he teaches elective courses, which include International Rivals, International Flashpoints, Counterproliferation Issues, and CBW Issues for the USAF. He has taught at six other colleges and universities and has a Ph.D. in Political Science from Columbia University.

**JOHN V. WADE,** a native of Michigan, entered the U.S. Army Veterinary Corps in June 1977 upon receiving Bachelor of Science and Doctor of Veterinary Medicine degrees from Michigan State University. In 1987 he completed graduate education at the University of Kansas Medical Center, earning a Ph.D. in Toxicology. Subsequent assignments focused on medical-chemical and medical-biological defense at the U.S. Army Medical Research Institute of Chemical Defense, the Pentagon, the Medical Research and Materiel Command, and the U.S. Army Medical Research Institute of Infectious Diseases. During Operations Desert Shield and Storm, Colonel Wade was assigned to the U.S. Central Command Surgeon's Office, Riyadh, Saudi Arabia, as special advisor to General Schwarzkopf on the medical effects of chemical weapons. Colonel Wade is a resident graduate of the U.S. Army Command and General Staff College, a Diplomat of the American Board of Toxicology, and served as the Advisor in Toxicology to the U.S. Army Assistant Surgeon General for Veterinary Services. He is the author or coauthor of three book chapters and over 30 scientific articles. Colonel Wade's military career culminated with his appointment as the Acting Deputy Assistant to the Secretary Defense (Chemical and Biological Defense). Dr. Wade retired from the Army in 1999, joining Battelle Memorial Institute as a Senior Marketing Manager. In January 2002, he became Battelle's Vice President for Vaccine Program Development and was instrumental in securing award of the contract to produce and test the "next generation anthrax vaccine." In July 2003, he assumed the position of Vice President and Manager, Biodefense Medical Systems, managing Battelle's medical chemical and biological high-containment laboratories engaged in WMD defense research, development, testing, and evaluation for numerous government and commercial clients.

**JONATHAN B. WOLFSTHAL** is currently the deputy director of the Non-Proliferation Project at the Carnegie Endowment for International Peace and the coauthor of *Deadly Arsenals: Tracking Weapons of Mass Destruction*. He is a frequently cited expert on the proliferation of weapons of mass destruction and has appeared on numerous TV and radio programs. His articles and op-ed pieces have appeared in many domestic and international publications, including *Survival, Current History, Arms Control Today, Bulletin of the Atomic Scientist, the International Herald Tribune, LA Times,* and *The Christian Science Monitor*. His main areas of research include U.S. nuclear weapons and nonproliferation policy, the nuclear weapons program in North Korea, and the risk of proliferation from Russia's nuclear arsenal and facilities. He is the coeditor of the *Russian Nuclear Status Report* (copublished with the Monterey Institute of International Studies) and editor of the English-language version of *Russia's Nuclear and Missile Complex: The Human Factor in Proliferation* by Valentin Tikhonov. Prior to his position at the Carnegie Endowment, Mr. Wolfsthal served as an official at the U.S. Department of Energy where he served in a number of positions. During his five-year tenure at the Department of Energy, he served as the U.S. Government's on-site monitor at North Korea's nuclear complex at Yongbyon, worked to improve security at Russian nuclear facilities, and oversaw several U.S. multimillion dollar programs to eliminate the trade in weapons-usable nuclear materials. He last served as the Special Assistant to the Assistant Secretary for Non-Proliferation and National Security. Mr. Wolfsthal is the founder of New Analysis in International Security and a Term Member of the Council on Foreign Relations. He has conducted graduate-level studies at the George Washington University and holds a Bachelor of Arts from Emory University.

Photo of Fritz Lang © Gretchen Berg, 1967

# Fritz
# LANG

*a guide to references and resources*

*A*
*Reference*
*Publication*
*in*
*Film*

Ronald Gottesman
*Editor*

The Sidney B. Coulter Library
Onondaga Community College
Rte. 173, Onondaga Hill
Syracuse, New York 13215

# *Fritz*
# LANG

## *a guide to references and resources*

E. ANN KAPLAN

## G.K.HALL&CO.

70 LINCOLN STREET, BOSTON, MASS.

Copyright © 1981 by E. Ann Kaplan

*Library of Congress Cataloging in Publication Data*

Kaplan, E. Ann.
   Fritz Lang, a guide to references and resources

   Includes bibliographical references and indexes.
   1. Lang, Fritz, 1890-1976. I. Title.
PN1998.A3L3595   016.79143′0233′0924   81-7164
ISBN 0-8161-8035-0                      AACR2

*This publication is printed on permanent/durable acid-free paper*
MANUFACTURED IN THE UNITED STATES OF AMERICA

*For my mother, Trudie Mercer, without whose help*
*this book could never have been written*

*For my daughter, Brett, and members of the*
*Mercer Family who gave me support*

*For the many friends who gave me invaluable advice along the way*

# Contents

# The Author

E. Ann Kaplan did her undergraduate work in England, where she also taught film and lectured for the British Film Institute. After obtaining her Ph.D. in America, she taught film at Monmouth College and, from 1974 on, at Rutgers University where she is currently an Associate Professor in the English Department.

Her publications include Talking About the Cinema (London: The British Film Institute, 1963); Women in Film Noir, editor (London: The British Film Institute, 1978); and numerous articles on film published in Jump Cut, Quarterly Review of Film Studies, Millenium Film Journal, and Marxist Perspectives.

# Preface

This book is intended not only as a definitive annotated bibliography
of Fritz Lang, but also as a means of providing scholars with detailed
information about Lang's works, including distribution of the films
and resources in film study centers. The introductory chapters consist of, first, a history of Lang criticism, and second, a summary
of the auteur analysis of Lang's works in relation to his life. I
thought it important to put the Critical Survey first, since one result of recent film theories has been the discrediting of the individual importance of the director and of the relevance of his or her
life to the work. It seemed necessary to place the auteur survey of
the evolution of Lang's themes in relation to his life in the context
of available theoretical models as these emerge from a study of film
criticism. Chapter three contains original synopses of the forty
films available for viewing: my aim was to give as concrete a presentation of each film as possible, focusing on the visual as well as
the narrative development. Chapter four is an annotated bibliography
of writings about Lang in English, German, and French (although where
I came across pieces in Italian or, rarely, in other languages, such
as Danish or Finnish, I annotated those also). Chapter five contains
annotations of critical writings by Lang and of his interviews;
scripts Lang wrote and roles he played are also listed here. Chapter
six has information about film institutes and study centers of interest to Lang scholars, and the last chapter lists 16mm distributors of
available Lang films.

Chapter four was the most difficult to write because of decisions
about what to include. I wanted the bibliography to be as complete
as possible, but I had to weigh this against the value of annotating
every review of every Lang film. Reviews have a place in film criticism quite different from that in literary criticism because of the
late development of film scholarship. Particularly in England and
America, journals specially devoted to film did not come into their
own until the 1950s, and relatively few books on film were published
before then; those that appeared rarely dealt with individual directors

or undertook in-depth analysis of specific films, but rather treated film aesthetics or the sociology of film in general terms.

In the 1920s, 1930s, and 1940s, newspaper reviews, and columns in literary and other magazines constituted the main writing about film. For these years in England and America, I have annotated a number of articles from the New York Times, the New York Sun, New World Telegram, the London Times, the Nation, and the Spectator, without attempting to be comprehensive. While the material does not often tell us much of value about Lang's works, it is important from a cultural and sociological point of view. We can learn about attitudes toward film and toward people involved in film; given that Lang worked primarily in popular forms once he came to America, these perspectives are relevant. From the 1950s on, I paid less attention to newspaper materials, since responsible reviews by people seriously involved in film began to appear in The British Film Institute publications (Sight and Sound, the Monthly Film Bulletin), in Le Revue du Cinéma (later Cahiers du Cinéma), in Arts (Paris), and Radio-Cinéma-Télévision. With the rather late reemergence of a film culture in Germany in the mid 1960s, I was able to include reviews from journals like Filmkritik, Film-Dienst, and Filmstudio.

Paradoxically, Germany had developed a film culture as early as the 1920s, well ahead of other European nations, and vied with Russia for the lead in film experimentation. Many film magazines existed in Germany at this time, underscoring the cultural significance granted film. Journals like Der Film, Filmland, Lichtbildbühne, and Der Kinematograph printed articles (many by Lang himself) analyzing the state of film as an art form, and including responsible reviews of Lang's works. This film culture was effectively destroyed by the Nazis, and for twelve years virtually nothing was written about Lang in German or French.

Selections from early German reviews have been gathered by the German film clubs in an impressive collection called Fritz Lang: Documents I and II, available in several of the German Film Institutes, but which I read at the Deutsches Institut für Filmkunde in Wiesbaden. Some of the other early German film reviews I obtained through the kind help of Hans Helmut Prinzler in the Deutschen Film und Fernsehakademie in West Berlin.

I also relied on the collection of Lang materials to be found in Alfred Eibel's Fritz Lang (Paris: Présence du Cinéma, 1964); often texts are only excerpts, however, and they are of course translated into French. Sometimes references are not given for materials Eibel prints, but there is a good general bibliography listing Eibel's sources. Lotte Eisner's recent Fritz Lang also has excerpts from early German reviews of Lang films, and she lists at least the name and year of the journal. Eisner's book was particularly useful for summaries of Lang's earliest films for which no prints remain and about which there is very little information. Many of the later

German newspaper reviews and articles on Lang I found in a large
clippings file gathered together by Herr Eberhard Spiess in the
Wiesbaden archive.

All these sources were invaluable because very little of the
material would have been readily available otherwise.  Many of the
early German film journals are difficult to find, as are the early
and late German newspapers.  Relatively few German newspapers are
available in America, although one can obtain the major ones through
the interlibrary loan system.  I thus was forced to rely on the collections mentioned above, which were often not fully documented.
This accounts for some annotations from newspapers and early journals
lacking page numbers and listing of the cities where they were printed.  Occasionally, a review seemed sufficiently important that I
would annotate it even though the source was unavailable.  In these
cases, I listed the name of the archive where I read the material.
In a few instances, I assigned an entry number to an important piece
of material but was unable to locate it.  I then listed the source
of the reference, and gave the entry number an asterisk to indicate
that I had not seen the article.

As noted earlier, I thought it important to annotate selected
newspaper articles written before film study became a scholarly activity, but I was reluctant to assign a separate entry number for each
review.  Desiring a certain degree of comprehensiveness, however, I
have listed after the credits newspapers and dates of other reviews,
some of which I found in various clippings files in archives (or on
cards, in the case of the British Film Institute).  Unfortunately,
page numbers were often missing from these sources.  Many of these
reviews were from magazines geared to the film industry (such as
Hollywood Reporter, Variety, Today's Cinema and Film Daily), and I
annotated these only where I found them in clippings files and then
mainly to give representative examples of the response Lang's films
received in the industry.  Where a piece of material in a file seemed
interesting, but not sufficiently so to warrant its own entry number,
I added some brief comments in this reviews list.

Again for reasons of comprehensiveness, I have listed, but not
annotated, certain articles that belonged in the same category as
one I was paraphrasing.  For example, beginning in 1960 large numbers
of German newspapers printed articles every time Lang had a birthday,
visited Germany, or produced a new film there.  These articles often
followed a very similar format and thus did not seem to require separate annotation.  But to let scholars know that they were written, I
appended a short bibliography at the end of the entry, and, if the
citation was incomplete, I noted the archive where I had found it.
All the information about location of the film archives I visited,
together with the resources they offer, is to be found in Chapter
five, along with a guide to Lang materials in many other archives
that I did not visit.

I have used standard film bibliographies for references to critical materials on Lang, including Vincent J. Aceto, Jane Graves, and Fred Silva, eds., Film Literature Index, 1973, 1974, 1975, 1976, 1977, and 1978, Albany: Filmdex, 1975, 1976, 1977, 1978, and 1979; Mel Schuster, ed., Motion Picture Directors: A Bibliography of Magazine and Periodical Articles, 1900-1972, Metuchen, N.J.: Scarecrow Press, 1972; Supplement I, 1974; John C. Gerlach and Lana Gerlach, eds., The Critical Index: A Bibliography of Articles on Film in English, 1946-1973. New York and London: Teachers College Press, 1974; Richard Dyer MacCann and Edward S. Perry, The New Film Index, 1930-1970, New York: E. P. Dutton, 1974; Karen Jones, ed., International Index to Film Periodicals, 1972, 1973, New York and London: R. R. Bowker, 1973, 1974; Stephen E. Bowles, Index to Critical Film Reviews in British and American Film Periodicals. Vol. 1, A-M. New York: Burt Franklin, 1974; Linda Batty, Retrospective Index to Film Periodicals, 1930-1971. New York and London: R. R. Bowker, 1975; Workers of the Writers' Program, New York, The Film Index: A Bibliography, New York: H. W. Wilson, Co.: 1941, Reprint: Arno Press, 1966.

I have also used bibliographies from books about Lang to supplement references; most useful here was the extensive bibliography by Hans Helmut Prinzler in the book by Enno Patalas and Frieda Grafe. This was an invaluable aid in locating materials in German, particularly for the 1920s. Other Lang bibliographies, particularly those in the books by Luc Moullet and Paul Jensen, while useful, contained errors. Where possible I located materials myself and corrected the information.

Of all the resources that I used for the book, those which were most unreliable and contradictory were the filmographies. This made determining an accurate list of credits for each film an enormously difficult task. The more sources I used, the more discrepancies I found in spellings and even in names and roles. Particularly unreliable, because so poorly proofread, is the filmography in Lotte Eisner's book, although it does contain some interesting notes on various films. In the end, I had to make my own decision about which sources were most credible. For the German films, I relied mainly on Gerhard Lamprecht, ed., Deutsche Stummfilm 1917-1931, Berlin: Deutsche Kinemathek, 1969 (1919-1929) (which does not however, give roles), and on the filmography in the German book by Enno Patalas and Frieda Grafe. For the American films, I relied mainly on the Studio Releases on fiches in the Museum of Modern Art, and on the filmography in Peter Bogdanovitch's Fritz Lang in America. Eisner's bibliography sometimes had names of actors and actresses (sometimes only the last name) without roles, and, without being able to check these, I simply added them to the Studio list. The German sources sometimes had alternate spellings (e.g., Meinhard/Meinhart; Müthel/Mütel), which I noted in the text. Information on the very early Lang films was scant in all sources, so that many of the categories are omitted. The early films were, of course, produced under extremely different and much simpler circumstances than the later ones, so that producers were not needed. I have tried to be as responsible as possible about getting a correct list of credits.

Several Lang interviews and articles have been translated and published in different countries at different times. Where possible, I have noted the original date and place of publication, even if I had read the material in another language from a later publication.

I wish to thank the many people who have made this book possible. Lotte Eisner and Howard Vernon, whom I interviewed in Paris, gave me invaluable insights into Lang's background and life. Several people at the various film research centers I visited were particularly helpful: Charles Silver, Emily Sieger, and Ron Magliozzi at the Museum of Modern Art; Gillian Hartnoll at the British Film Institute; Hans Helmut Prinzler at the Deutsche Film und Fernsehakademie in West Berlin; Enno Patalas at the Münchner Stadtmuseum; Dorothea Gebauer and Herr Eberhard Spiess at the Deutsches Institut für Filmkunde, Wiesbaden. In addition, I want to thank Monty Arnold and many other staff members at the Lincoln Center Film Research Library, staff members at the Library of Congress, the New York Public Library and Newspaper Annex, the British Museum libraries, the East Berlin Stadtmuseum and the Staatliches Film Archiv, East Berlin, for their patience in tracking down Lang materials and for making useful suggestions. Their support was invaluable in the success of this difficult project.

I want to thank my typists, Lynn Hubers and Laurie Zomermaand who struggled long and loyally with my materials, and Yolanda Rudich, who both typed and did the index, and whose interest, patience, and thoroughness went far beyond what was required. Estelle Berger helped me annotate some of the German materials.

Finally, let me thank the Rutgers Research Council and the Deutscher Akademischer Austauschdienst for the grants that enabled me to do the research necessary for this book.

# Critical Survey

This book goes to press at a point in the history of film criticism when the auteur and thematic approaches, brought from France to America in 1962 by Andrew Sarris, confront the semiological and psychoanalytic theories that also originated in France. In England, these theories combined with Russian formalist and German Marxist ideas (Brecht, Lukacs) to produce a formidable, often fascinating body of work published in Screen and in British Film Institute books. A few American film journals have embraced the new theories (Camera Obscura), undertaken debates about their validity (Jump Cut), or simply printed articles using the new methodologies (Enclitic, the Canadian Ciné-Tracts, Discourse). The mainstream of American film criticism, however, remains suspicious of new developments, sometimes for good reasons (which will be discussed later).

The chronological ordering of materials in this book, together with the coincidence of the emergence of film as an art form and the start of Lang's film career, has resulted in a text that implicitly traces the main shifts in the history of film criticism.

The earliest Lang critics, writing in Germany in the 1920s, were people like Rudolf Arnheim, Herbert Ihering, and Roland Schacht, who saw themselves on the side of high culture, taste, and intellect in a world where such values were being increasingly eroded.[1] They adopted a critical position that evolved out of the Romantic tradition and culminated in Matthew Arnold's Culture and Anarchy. Films were evaluated according to aesthetic and moral standards embodied in certain classic texts and works of high culture. Lang's films were thus often condemned for being sentimental kitsch (literally trash), mere entertainment without redeeming moral value. This was a position later echoed by American critics (their views summarized neatly by Dwight Macdonald in his Masscult article in 1961),[2] who scorned Hollywood films as a group for similar reasons.

Between 1933 and 1945 there was little French or German criticism of Lang; intellectual life throughout Europe, and also in England and America, was completely disoriented during part of this period as a result of World War II.  In America, several newspaper reporters, like Eileen Creelman (New York Sun) followed Lang's progress, but their articles and interviews are mainly of sociological interest.

Understandably enough, in the postwar period film criticism was dominated by political and sociological approaches, most consistently developed in Italian Neo-Realism and Soviet Socialist Realism.  In the wake of the bitter political conflicts that had lead to, and continued during, the war, critics were concerned with the social messages that film propagated.  The new aesthetic discredited films that were studio-made or that attempted to express the inner, psychological life of the individual.  Siegfried Kracauer's From Caligari to Hitler (1947), attempting to combine political and sociological approaches with psychological ones, effectively damaged Lang's critical reputation for at least a decade.  The postwar realist aesthetic made it easy for Kracauer to link the expressionist, antirealist style with the decadence and perversion of fascism.  Trying to come to terms with what had just happened in Germany, Kracauer was distressed that filmmakers in the pre-Nazi period had not made explicitly antifascist, realist films that argued for democracy and might have helped prevent Hitler's rise to power.  Playing with Lang's statement that Dr. Mabuse was a documentary of his period, warning people about what was going on, Kracauer claims that Mabuse is indeed a "document of its time," luxuriating in anarchic fantasies culminating in tyranny, and "not making the slightest allusion to true freedom."  He objects strongly to the "settings of pronounced artificiality," comparing the film to Caligari (the worst word in Kracauer's vocabulary) and branding it as "an emotional vision."[3]

In an unfortunately personal way, Kracauer makes much of the fact that Lang's ex-wife, Thea von Harbou, became a Nazi after Lang left Germany, and of the Nazi interest in some of his films.  Kracauer concludes that Lang's films, along with others of the period, reflect the basic consciousness that later became that of fascism, demonstrating the unhealthy turning away from nature and "reality," an obsession with the perverse and decadent which the Nazis incarnated.

At least partly because he was tainted in this way by fascism, Lang was neglected in the 1940s and early 1950s by serious film critics.  When English-speaking critics did finally turn to him in the mid-1960s, it became commonplace to say that Lang was, at best, not against the tendencies in pre-Nazi Germany--the opinion, for example, of George Huaco and Eric Rhode.  Huaco, an American Marxist, building on Kracauer's analysis, argued that Lang's films, and indeed all the expressionist films, were essentially reactionary.  For Huaco, "the plot of (Lang's) Destiny suggests that it is useless to revolt or protest against death or fate."  He further quotes producer Erich Pommer (Lang's mentor) as saying in an unpublished interview that Dr. Mabuse was about "the fight between the Sparticists [Communists]

and the moderates," with Mabuse representing the Communists. Thus
Lang is accused of identifying the Sparticists "with a nihilistic and
terroristic organization." Huaco says that this is not too surprising in itself "until we realize that this identification of the extreme left with the criminal underworld is the exact reverse of the
actual political situation."[4]

Critics like Eric Rhode in England, while critical of Kracauer,
nevertheless perpetuated his thesis. Rhode modifies Kracauer's analysis to show the development in Lang from a position close to National
Socialism in the Mabuse films to one critical of it in M.[5] More recently, David Thompson revived the tradition of viewing Lang as ide-
ologically suspect in his discussion of Lang's Ministry of Fear, showing the fascination Lang has for secret organizations and plots to
overthrow the world.[6]

As Germany slowly developed its own film culture in the mid-1960s,
people began to discuss Lang again,[7] but the predominately left-wing
critics again adopted Kracauer's position and developed an ideological
approach that placed Lang in a negative light. Eckart Jahnke, writing
from East Berlin about M in 1965, argues that Lang is not a progressive political filmmaker because although he was able to show the
reality of his period he did not provide solutions or interpret what
he saw, thus placing it into its proper historical perspective.[8]
Lang did not understand why what was happening was happening, as
Marxists claimed to do.

But as German film clubs, influenced by the French adulation of
Lang, organized retrospectives of his works, a more complex attitude
began to emerge. Enno Patalas, Ulrich Gregor, and others established
the scholarly German film journal, Filmkritik, which, like the periodical Filmstudio, published balanced reviews and analyses of Lang
films. Wolfram Schütte and Peter W. Jensen initiated the scholarly
Reihe film series and in 1977 published the first German book on Lang,
which contained important introductory essays by Frieda Grafe, comments by Patalas on all of Lang's films, and an excellent bibliography by Hans Prinzler. The approach in this text reflects the newer
developments in Lang film criticism that began to emerge in the late
1950s, but that have only been seriously underway in the past five
years.

Lang scholars everywhere are indebted to the French for two recent
major developments in film criticism that brought Lang out of obscurity, fortunately before he died. The first is the auteur approach
developed in the late 1950s by young French critics (like Truffaut),
who formed a circle around Cahiers du Cinéma and André Bazin. Auteur
criticism, focusing as it does on the themes and stylistic characteristics evident in the entire body of a director's work, was largely
responsible for the reevaluation of Lang's American films, which had
up to this point been neglected as trivial Hollywood genre films.
While some auteur critics took a stance for or against Lang's German

films as superior to his American ones, the majority began to see the works as a whole with a consistent world view and repeated structural patterns.

Two essays by Philippe Demonsablon and Michel Mourlet, published in Cahiers du Cinéma in September 1959, signaled the first break-through. Demonsablon was interested in the way Lang managed to bal-ance opposed tendencies, the one leaning toward extravagance, the other toward barrenness. A dialectic is at work in many films, he argued, so that fear of solitude is balanced by fear of promiscuity, innocence turns to guilt, activity to stasis. Mourlet emphasized Lang's philosophical preoccupations, expressed through mise-en-scène, and showed how he attempts to eliminate chance from his films. In Lang's world, each element is indispensable to the whole and does not exist for itself.

These essays redressed the overemphasis on ideology in the main-stream of English and German analysis and began a new direction in Lang criticism. Occasionally, as in the work of Gérard Legrand, studies became excessively abstract, but they were balanced by other new Cahiers critics (Jean Douchet, Michel Mardore, François Truffaut, Bernard Tavernier), who combined visual analysis with an exploration of Lang's view of society, and who began to undercut Kracauer's over-schematic linking of Lang with fascism. These writers showed that the problem with Lang's point of view is not that he is at heart a fascist, but that he cannot see anything except a choice between chaos or tyranny. While deploring both, they claimed, he lacks a vision of a democratic kind of social interchange that would transcend the undesirable alternatives he portrays so well. Like many expres-sionists in the post World War I period (one thinks of Kafka especi-ally), Lang was haunted by visions of doom and by a sense of the nightmare world that lay behind carefully constructed bourgeois il-lusions. These visions remained with Lang throughout his life and found their most obvious expression in the detective-gangster genre, which Lang used to undercut the comfortable notion of bourgeois "reality." Placing supercriminals at the center of his works (Die Spinnen [The Spiders], Dr. Mabuse, Spione [Spies], Frau im Mond [Woman in the Moon], Das Testament [The Last Will], Lang showed a decadent, chaotic world, peopled by madmen and their followers. Given that expressionism provided the dominant aesthetic at the time, Lang naturally drew on expressionist techniques of visual distortion, achieved in film through subtle use of camera angles and of light and shadow, to reveal the insanity he saw in German society. His world is one where nothing is what it seems--the many "faces" of Dr. Mabuse reflect this perfectly--and where, as Jean Douchet has shown, every-thing always turns into its opposite.[9]

The auteur approach represented in these essays began to place Lang in the existentialist, as against the fascist, camp. From this point of view, Lang's fascination with his supercriminals and tyrants arises more from his scorn for the bourgeoisie and their codes than

anything else.  Like Nietzsche, Lang was impelled toward those who
rose above mediocrity and was himself authoritarian and perfectionist, demanding the highest standards.  His dislike of the currents
that lead to nazism was not thus strictly political, but, like that
of many other artists, aesthetic and cultural instead.  While some
writers, like Brecht, saw themselves as political authors, Lang took
a stance as a creative person.  Contrasting Lang and Brecht, Michel
Mardore shows well where Lang stands from this point of view:  Brecht,
like a true Marxist, saw evil as a result of capitalist society and
did not blame individuals for their plight, while Lang considered
individuals themselves to be guilty.  The corrupt, hostile society,
for Lang, incarnated human fate.

But a second wave of theoretical work, originating in France and
developed in England, took the discussion to another level.  Brecht's
theories of the desirability of alienation and distanciation in art
(i.e., refusing audience identification with characters and punctur-
ing narrative illusion), were combined with ideas from Althusser and
Barthes to produce a completely new reading of apparently realistic
works.  This was to affect profoundly the treatment of Lang's Hollywood films and in turn clarified Lang's expressionist films, making
Kracauer's reading even more indefensible.  Bellour's "Sur Fritz
Lang" (Critique, 1966) marks an important stage between auteur and
later semiotic criticism.[10]  Bellour focuses on Lang's notion of
cinema as ultimate metaphor.  In his last films Lang makes a game of
his hackneyed subjects while actually dealing with the very possibility of cinema.  Bellour outlines elements that need analyzing in order
to understand Lang and deals first, with the constant shifting of
perspective on characters; second, with all the complications of
point of view in relation to objects; and finally, with the perverse
game that Lang plays, erecting a kind of counterscenario that undercuts the surface of the film.

Other critics went on to show how realism, as a film style, reflects not social reality, lived experience, so much as the representations of reality that any society assumes.  These representations carry ideology, now not in the sense of the ideological component in all bourgeois institutions and modes of production, but in
the sense of images, myths, ideas, or concepts.[11]  These images,
myths, and concepts are essentially those of the ruling classes and,
according to this theory they are embedded in the cultural forms of
our society as well as in the predominant realist aesthetic.  Eileen
McGarry, following Barthes, shows that the social world, considered
"natural," actually consists in a series of sign systems that include
"such taken-for-granted things as dress (fashion, class determined
and sex determined dress codes), architecture, interior decoration,
writing, language (especially variations, e.g., slang, accent, etc.),
sexual relations (both emotionally and politically determined by
ideology), body language (and its class and cultural variations),
etc." McGarry goes on to say:

We are accustomed to the existence of these sign systems;
we encounter them and read or interpret them every day,
according to our place within and relation to the super-
structure of the social formation. But when we encounter these sign systems in film, they take on new
contexts in their larger than life reproduction and
thus perpetuation in a cultural object.[12]

These essentially Barthesian and Althusserian ideas are useful in
correcting a simplistic sociological reading of film and in showing
how media representations influence our ways of perceiving in daily
life.

The expressionist revolt against bourgeois forms was premised on
some such understanding, and Kracauer, of course, missed this point
completely. Writing in Germany in the 1920s, Brecht was one of the
first to focus attention on the spectator and to understand the
natural process of identification upon which all great art in the
previous century had relied. If the dominant aesthetic, realism,
encouraged identification with modes of representation that reflected
bourgeois values rather than the "truth" about capitalist society,
then these had to be undercut by art forms that prevented such identification. The expressionists, in revolt against bourgeois values,
tried to replace traditional images with their unique, subjective
ways of seeing, and the only way they could do this was to use new,
nonrealist aesthetic forms. Caligari and Raskolnikov, with their
painted sets, distorted perspectives, dramatic light/dark contrasts,
and subversive themes typify the kind of film art that was being
produced. Noel Burch and Jorge Dana have shown how Caligari breaks
deliberately with all the major film codes of representation and
narrativity that reproduced the codes of linearity and illusionism
governing literature for two centuries. Transparence and the illusion of continuity are destroyed in the film.[13]

Burch is typical of some of the earliest Lang critics influenced
by Metz, Barthes, and semiology in that he sees a distinct break between the German half of Lang's career and the later American half.
In an article written in 1973, Burch argued that the German films
function on a very complex level, while in America Lang simply becomes one of an anonymous herd of directors. The article focuses on
Dr. Mabuse and M, Burch showing how Mabuse terminates one major direction in film form, taken from the nineteenth-century novel, while M
marks a shift to something new, combining forms peripheral to cinema
(like the novel) with those of pure film. In a detailed analysis of
the film, Burch isolates nine parts, showing how each has its own
mode of functioning, its own "laws." In addition, there are two
dominant principles that control the film, the first carrying the
film from the separate parts to coherence, and the second unveiling
its central character--the murderer.[14] The centrality of M for semiotic critics is underscored by Thierry Kuntzel's detailed analysis

of the first sequence of the film, using Barthesian concepts of codes.[15]

While Burch and Jorge (using Secret Beyond the Door as an example) see Lang as perpetuating the illusion of realism in his American films, some recent critics have convincingly shown that even in these works Lang is using cinematic codes to make us question our automatic responses and to reveal a world more complex than we may want to imagine. The best example of this approach is a provocative article on Hangmen Also Die by Comolli and Géré (Cahiers du Cinéma, 1978). The film is often seen as presenting the kind of complex political and moral situation familiar in Brecht's plays; i.e., the resistance workers have to choose between betraying the assassin (an act that would destroy their movement) and permitting hundreds of innocent Czechs, taken hostage by the Nazis, to die needlessly. But Comolli and Géré argue that on a deeper level the film is even more disturbing: not only do we feel forced to choose along with the resistance workers, but we are also made to see links between the Nazis and the Czechs. Comolli and Géré argue that in allowing hostages to be killed, the resistance movement puts itself in the place of the Nazi machine. Through an elaborate series of shots (that Comolli and Géré explain in detail) we are made to identify with the Nazi police inspector Gruber (whom we should, and do, hate), because he has more "life" than all the "good" characters, and because he uses his intelligence in his search for truth. Our simplistic liberal ways of thinking are shaken by Lang's cinematic devices in this film.[16]

Comolli and Géré have shown that just because Lang went to America this did not mean that he drastically changed his basic methods of filmmaking. Since their work provides a model that synthesizes many of the new theories while retaining a clear political perspective, I would like to see the kind of analysis they did of Hangmen Also Die applied to other American films. My own preference is for an eclectic reading that combines new concepts with Brechtian notions of distanciation and with notions of discourse and code as summarized above by Eileen McGarry.[17] Lang did, after all, develop his aesthetic in the period when Brecht was articulating theories and was, evidently, consciously influenced by him.[18] Far from being "perverse," as Kracauer had claimed, or seeming to glorify chaos and tyranny, Lang's Dr. Mabuse, made in Germany in 1922, presents the contradictions and ambivalences of the period. Instead of breaking completely with realist forms like the expressionists, Lang plays with bourgeois representations, doing all he can to distance us from characters and events by forcing identification with figures like Mabuse, whom we abhor; by creating a disjointed narrative through editing techniques so that we are never allowed to stay long enough with one group or action to become fully involved; and by using expressionist visual techniques in specific scenes and with specific characters so as to create a sense of uneasiness, of things being unbalanced, not normal. We are, in Brechtian fashion, encouraged to think about what is going on, to stand apart and evaluate the world

*Fritz Lang*

Lang presents.[19]

$\underline{M}$ once again shows Lang's techniques of distanciation, establishing a cinematic method that looked toward his first American films. Through use of an elaborate system of codes we are made to see the ironic links between two antithetical discourses of the criminal underground, on the one hand, and of law and order, on the other. The authorities in the ascending hierarchical order are revealed as stupid and incompetent, while the criminals ironically embody law and order and run an efficient machine. Besides this moral ambiguity, there is the further ambivalence about the murderer, Beckert. His situation is made so pitiful that we identify with him as the hunted victim, despite the monstrous crime he has committed. He is clearly a victim of his own irrational impulses, rather than of some force outside himself (like the people in Dr. Mabuse), making everything that much more terrifying. Although Lohmann does finally solve the riddle, the criminals have been there before him and he now has to rescue Beckert from their clutches. The ambiguity in the film has produced conflicting critical interpretations ranging from arguments showing Lang on the side of Law and Order to those suggesting that he is supporting anarchy. In fact, Lang is presenting a complex series of discourses that, placed contrapuntally against what we expect, show authorities as fallible, criminals as useful, and murderers as victims as well.

That it has been possible to survey the main shifts in the history of film criticism in relation to work about Lang says something about his significance and stature as a director. His films have attracted some of the leading film scholars because of their complexity and depth, but the actual number of detailed, high quality works on Lang is, to date, minimal. Some forthcoming books and dissertations suggest that we are on the brink of a new wave of Lang criticism stemming from semiology and psychoanalysis. Oudart was one of the first Lang critics to introduce the Lacanian notion of the absent signifier and to talk about Lang in terms of the look of the camera and the spectator (Cahiers du Cinéma, 1969). Two dissertations on Lang (one still in progress) build on some of these concepts: the first, written under the direction of Christian Metz, is on self-reflexive cinema in ten of Lang's American films and takes a semiotic, psychoanalytic approach to the cinematic signifier and the placing of the spectator; the second is on narrative conventions in the American films, including discussion of the relationship between psychoanalysis and melodrama, focusing on woman's place with respect to enunciation (i.e., to the controlling discourse, to who "speaks" the film and to how the female image is constructed). The method combines stylistic, thematic and mise-en-scène analysis. A forthcoming British Film Institute book will locate the auteurist response historically rather than see it as the "key" to the text, translate important French essays, and discuss twelve Lang films, replacing the idea of destiny with that of patriarchy, reading the films as Oedipal drama.[20]

8

# Critical Survey

Future Lang criticism will no doubt develop along the lines prepared for in these new studies, focusing on enunciation, the spectator, psychoanalysis, and semiology, and representing the most recent tendencies in film theory. One hopes that interesting and useful work will also emerge in Germany, but from a perspective that is more political and sociological in analytic terms, as new critics and film-makers begin to integrate the Nazi catastrophe. Lang remained essentially German in his mode of seeing, his depth and complexity continuing to emerge from his contact with expressionism and the lively aesthetic debates of the 1920s; German critics thus may be able to tell us things that foreigners cannot see.

In future years, the material gathered here will seem merely the tip of an iceberg, respectable and solid though it may be. We start the 1980s with film criticism in an important transitional stage, moving toward a seriousness and scholarly rigor previously lacking. One hopes that Lang's works will continue to be analyzed from a variety of critical contexts ensuring renewed insight into his fascinating art. I hope that this book will enable scholars everywhere to extend and deepen our understanding of Lang's formidable body of work.

## NOTES

1  See Donna Baker, "Nazism and the Petit Bourgeois Protagonist: The Novels of Grass, Böll and Mann," New German Critique, no. 5 (spring, 1975), 77-106; also John Tulloch, "Genetic Structuralism and the Cinema: A Look at Fritz Lang's Metropolis," The Australian Journal of Screen Theory, No. 1, 1 (1976), pp. 3-50.

2  Dwight Macdonald, "Masscult and Midcult," Partisan Review, Series No. 4 (New York: Random House, 1961).

3  Siegfried Kracauer, From Caligari to Hitler, rev. ed. (Princeton University Press, 1974), pp. 81-84.

4  George Huaco, The Sociology of Film Art (New York: Basic Books), pp. 45-46.

5  Eric Rhode, Tower of Babel (London: Weindenfeld & Nicolson, 1966), pp. 83-105.

6  David Thompson, "Lang's Ministry," Sight and Sound, 46, No. 2 (Spring 1977), 114-116.

7  This is not to imply that nothing had been written about Lang in the post war years, but the writing was limited to newspaper articles, often on the occasion of his birthdays. A number of articles appeared when Lang returned to Germany in 1956 to arrange the making of a film and then again in 1958

upon the release of the Indian films. There were articles again around the making of Lang's last film, Die Tausend Augen des Dr. Mabuse. But these articles were basically surveys of Lang's life and career, rather than scholarly critical analyses. It is interesting to find the American films being accorded some respect, however.

8    Eckart Jahnke, "Fritz Lang's M," Film (East Berlin), No. 6 (1965), pp. 169-180.

9    Jean Douchet, "L'Etrange Obsession," Cahiers du Cinéma, No. 122 (August 1961), pp. 49-53.

10   The most influential writers in terms of developing a semiotics of the cinema are Roland Barthes and Christian Metz. Barthes first published some articles in 1952-1956 (that later became his Mythologies [1957]), where he began the work of extending the methods of Saussurean linguistics into areas like eating, dressing, going on a vacation, wrestling, etc. He showed the systematic nature of social signification, the existence of highly developed social sign-systems. As he put it in Elements of Semiology (1964):

> Semiology therefore aims to take in any system
> of signs, whatever their substance and limits;
> images, gestures, musical sounds, objects, and
> the complex associations of all these, which
> form the content of ritual, convention or
> public entertainment: these constitute, if
> not language, at least systems of signification.
> [p. 9]

Later on, in S/Z (1970), Barthes distinguished five forms of connotation (codes), which organize the intelligibility of any realist text and which film critics have applied to analyzing realist films. According to Coward and Ellis (in their Language and Materialism), these correspond to the five major critical languages of our time: narrative, thematic, psychological, sociological, and psychoanalytic criticism.

Barthes uses the word discourse in distinguishing language from speech. By language, Barthes means the given social institution and system of values that individuals learn when they learn words and which they cannot by themselves create or modify; speech is the individual's selection made from the given forms. Extended speech becomes discourse, the individual's personal ways of seeing, his or her own thought expressed through the given verbal forms and his or her values and ideas. We can thus talk of a male discourse as against a female one, while agreeing that there is a monolithic, phallocentric language.

11  These essentially Althusserian ideas (see his Pour Marx, Paris, 1965), have been usefully integrated into film criticism by people like Claire Johnston. See particularly "Dorothy Arnzer: Critical Strategies," in Claire Johnston, ed., Dorothy Arnzer, (London:  British Film Institute, 1975); see also Colin MacCabe, "Realism and the Cinema:  Notes on Some Brechtian Themes," Screen, 15, No. 2, (Summer 1974); and J. L. Comolli, "Technique and Ideology," Cahiers du Cinéma, nos. 229-231, 233, 235, and 241.  For a useful summary of these theoretical developments see Douglas Kellner, "Ideology, Marxism, Advanced Capitalism," Socialist Review 42, 8, No. 6 (November–December 1978), pp. 37–66.

12  Eileen McGarry, "Documentary Realism and Women's Cinema," Women and Film 2, No. 7 (Summer 1975):  55–56.

13  Noel Burch and Jorge Dana, "Propositions," Afterimage (U.K.), (Spring 1974), pp. 41–66.

14  Noel Burch, "De Mabuse à M: Le Travail de Fritz Lang," Revue d'Esthétique, 1973 (texts presented by Dominique Noguez), pp.

15  Thierry Kuntzel, "Le Travail du Film," Communications, No. 19. Trans.  Claudia Tysdal, Lawrence Crawford, and Kimball Lockhart, "The Film Work," Enclitic 2, No. 1 (Spring 1978): 39–64.

16  Jean-Louis Commolli and François Géré, "Deux Fictions de la Haine," Cahiers du Cinéma, No. 286 (March 1978), pp. 30–48.

17  The word discourse is now problematic, but when I first used it I was taking the concept from the work of Stephen Heath and Claire Johnston (in her book on Arnzer).  The word then referred to all that pertained to a group of characters (women, for example) or to an individual who belonged to such a group:  thoughts, words, what was defined as permissible for the group culturally--such as sex-roles, established behavior, modes of interaction.

18  In the unpublished interviews I conducted with her, Lotte Eisner talked about Lang's fascination with Brecht, whom Eisner knew and had introduced Lang to.

19  For fuller treatment of this analysis of Dr. Mabuse, see my article "Expressionism and the Flight from Family: A Reading of Fritz Lang's Dr. Mabuse, der Spieler," to be published in a forthcoming anthology of articles, The Legacy of Expressionism.  (See Entry No. 495.)

20  See Reynold Humphries, "Le Cinéma auto-reflexif et la place du spectateur," Ph.D. Diss., Ecole des Haute Etudes en Science

Sociales, 1979; Janet Bergstrom, "Narrative Conventions in the American Films of Fritz Lang," Ph.D. Diss., UCLA, 1980; Stephen Jenkins, Fritz Lang (London: The British Film Institute, 1980). (See Entries Nos. 491, 492, and 494.)

21   E. Ann Kaplan, "Integrating Marxist and Psychoanalytic Concepts in Feminist Film Criticism," Millenium Film Journal, No. 6 (Spring 1980), pp. 8-17.

22   Richard Wollheim, "Dr. Lacan's Cabinet," New York Review of Books, 25, Nos. 21-22 (25 January 1979): 36 ff.

# Biographical Background

One result of some of the new theories discussed in Chapter 1 has
been a discrediting of the individual importance of the director and
of the relevance of his or her life to the work.  This position is,
in part, a reaction to the overemphasis given the director in _auteur_
theory, but it is ironic to find film critics reverting to a position
not unlike that of New Criticism, fashionable from the late 1930s to
the 1960s and now largely discredited.

The position vis-a-vis the director is a function of a larger theoretical point of view that sees art works as the result of external
historical forces (including production) that come together momentarily under a certain director's name.  The perspective is perhaps most
clear in Paul Willemen's introduction to _Ophuls_.  Willemen is at
pains to account for a book's being produced under the title of
_Ophuls_ and proceeds to explain the "Ophuls" of the book as the place
where the disparate sets of discourses created by critics, film historians, family members, and Ophuls himself coincide.  "The information included here," Willemen says, "concentrates on the signposting
of certain sets of discourses in which 'Ophuls' was/is embedded and
which produced him as a specific character in the dramatic narrative
called 'film history.'"[1]

My experiences working on this book to a certain extent corroborate what Willemen says:  I realized early on that Lang's comments,
both about himself and about his work, as well as those of critics
and historians, assumed the guise of a certain "journalistic genre," as
Willemen puts it, of "the melodrama of the life of the great artist."
Lang reiterates the same anecdotes from his youth, the same stories
in relation to aspects of certain films, the same general statements
about young people, about the way society functions, and about his
commitment to making films.  Gradually, these elements take the shape
of a constantly repeated narrative, so that each interview goes over

identical ground, rarely including new material, as in the retelling of traditional fairytales. Toward the end of his life, Lang became bored with interviews and impatient with interviewers, not realizing that his boredom grew out of an unwillingness to explore in a new way; he was clearly tired of his carefully constructed persona.

But I disagree with Willemen when he implies, first, that any truth about the person of the director is unknowable, and second, that such knowledge is irrelevant to a study of the work. For example, one realizes that in young adulthood Lang must have suffered a deep personal loss from which he never recovered and which conditioned his way of seeing ever after. Possibly this was the sudden death of Gerda Maurus, whom Lang loved,[2] shortly after he had made Frau im Mond, together with the rise of nazism, which meant Lang had to leave a nation he loved. We will never know for sure, because Lang consistently refused to discuss his personal life or to reveal anything about his inner self. He was evidently not given to personal introspection, preferring, as he kept saying, that others "psychoanalyze" him and tell him what he is about in his works.

Second, in relation to the significance of a director's life to the work, it is clearly as wrong totally to exclude all material from the life as it is totally to explain works in relation to a life. On the one hand, much in Lang's films can be explained only in terms of the way meaning is produced in a film, and of unconscious societal codes and structures that Lang used automatically.

On the other hand, if the personality of the individual director had no impact on the shape of a film, all Hollywood films would be identical. The events of Lang's inner life, however conditioned by larger, psychological events common to all people, took a specific form for him and account for a unique way of seeing reality. Lang's individual experience intersects with general psychological law and with social codes to produce works at once individual _and_ representative of the society and institutions in which they were made. Lang's Mabuse is an example of a creation that arose naturally out of expressionist Germany and clearly has a personal dimension unique to Lang. His return to Germany and continuing interest in Mabuse can only be explained with reference to Lang, the individual.

Since the familiar Lang persona has been written about extensively (for a recent, fully detailed account, see the introduction to Frederick Ott's book), and since the interviews annotated in this book reiterate all the aspects of the Lang "narrative," I will confine myself here to a cursory repetition of well-known facts, including, however, reference to Lang's writings that occasionally give us ways of assessing some of his publicly stated concerns. The events of Lang's life take their place as part of the overall context in which the films must be viewed. The events do not "explain" the films, but the films may not be completely explicable without reference to what Lang was doing and experiencing.

What follows, then, is an attempt to explain Lang's experiences
and intellectual development as he himself presented it to the world
(through writings, interviews, and statements about his films).
This does not constitute an objective reading of his life and work,
but neither is it correct to say that Lang and others created "a
phantasy figure, a fictional character," as Willemen claimed about
Ophuls.  Instead, we have a reading of Lang's life and work filtered
through his own consciousness.  The history of Lang's work is, as I
proposed in Chapter 1, a history of theoretical models applied to
the films.  The works take on meaning only within certain theoretical
or subjective contexts and have no meaningful existence of their own.
In this chapter, the context for discussion of Lang and his works is
biographical, that is, a survey of Lang's artistic life as put together by critics, film historians, and Lang himself, to the degree
that he was willing to tell us about himself.  Much, of course, remained unsaid while he lived, and now will never be known.

Although Austrian-born (in 1890), Lang spent his formative years
in Germany and had German citizenship.  Refusing to follow his
father's wishes and become an architect, Lang left Austria to study
painting in Munich, after which, influenced like others by the new
travel literature (e.g., Karl May's books about America) he travelled
throughout the world collecting art pieces from exotic places like
the Far East.  Back in Europe in 1911, Lang lived the typical bohemian
life of the period, finally settling in Paris, where he made a living
selling his own postcards, paintings, and occasional cartoons.  During this period, Lang was influenced by the expressionist revolt,
already well underway, and he adopted its dislike of the bourgeoisie
and an identification with the outsider that were never to leave him.

World War I wrenched Lang from his artistic life in Paris.  Back
in Vienna, he was called up, but after being wounded was declared
unfit for service.  He had already become interested in film in Paris
and now began to write film scripts and to do some acting.  In 1918,
Lang signed a contract with Eric Pommer at Decla in Berlin, where he
first acted and wrote scripts, but soon became a director in his own
right.  He married the writer, Thea von Harbou, who later worked with
him on many films.

By the time Die Nibelungen and Metropolis were released in the
mid-1920s, Lang had become a director of note and one of the big men
at the Universum Film A. G.  Granted a status as high as that of producers in the German industry, directors viewed themselves (and were
viewed) as artists equal to those in other fields.  Lang lived the
life of Berlin's cultural elite.[3]

Like many others who went into film in Germany, Lang already had
training in both architecture and painting.  He was thus concerned
with aesthetic and philosophical matters in a way that early American
directors rarely were.  While in America film was quickly linked to
making money, in Germany people were interested in experimenting with

the form and in making "art" rather than purely commercial films. German film magazines of the 1920s reflect this seriousness toward the new art of film, in contrast to its low status in America from the start. Lang's own pieces, annotated in chapter 3, contributed to the ongoing debates about the future of film as an art form, and about the tension between its aesthetic and commercial aspects.

A sampling of the German reviews of Lang's early films shows critics' appreciation for his imagination, his creativity, and his formal experiments. Der müde Tod [Destiny] (1921) was valued for its serious theme and for the creative use of the film medium; the Mabuse films (1922) were honored as incisive comments on the decadence of Germany, while with Die Nibelungen (1924), according to most critics, Lang had reached the apex of his career.[4] While Lang's critical reputation wavered with Metropolis (1927) and Die Frau im Mond [Woman in the Moon] (1929), M (1931) was received enthusiastically as marking a new direction. But it was precisely this new direction that Lang was unable to pursue in Germany due to the rise of the Nazis: his second Mabuse film, Das Testament des Dr. Mabuse [The Last Will of Dr. Mabuse], made in 1932, was never released in Germany because the Nazis objected to its social criticism. They did not, ironically, see Mabuse and the psychologist as parodying Nazi slogans, but complained that no Fuhrer came in at the end to restore order.[5] Alarmed by Goebbels's invitation to head the new German film industry under the Nazis (Hitler reputedly enjoyed Die Nibelungen and Metropolis, and Goebbels saw them as films to emulate), Lang hastily left for France, forfeiting status, career, wealth, and art collection, as well as abandoning the nation he had loved and that had shaped him.

The degree to which Lang's attitude toward art and society had been developed in expressionist, pre-Nazi Germany has not been sufficiently recognized. Lang emerged from the first phase of his career imbued with German intellectual traditions. On the side of high culture, taste, and intellect, Lang and others like him had begun to feel isolated in a world where the ruling classes no longer had the power and vitality to stand up for the values they had originally embodied, and where middle classes lacking taste and culture were gaining power.

America, from this vantage point, seemed in the 1920s to embody much that the German intellectuals feared in terms of commercialism, greed, and materialism. Writing in 1925 about his first visit to America, Lang wrily noted the importance Americans assign to technology. Beginning with a literal wasteland, the Americans, Lang said, have developed a technological haven they consider a paradise; they contrast this positively to the wasteland that has evolved in Europe as nations fell from their original state of Eden. As businessmen and profiteers, Lang saw Americans neglecting higher values, including art, focusing instead on increasing material wealth and exploiting people's needs. But Lang could not help being impressed with American film studios, with the new techniques that had been developed, and with the energetic way in which Americans approached things. Ultimately, however, America seemed to promise much to unwary Europeans that it could not deliver.[6]

How ironic then that in 1935, after a year in France (during which he made Liliom), Lang found himself on the way to the very nation he had depicted so ambivalently! He had been driven out of Germany by the accession to power of the very class he had so feared. Nazism upset Lang's previous conceptions of Germany and America and meant that he had to reconsider his earlier values. In his first American films (Fury, You Only Live Once, You and Me), Lang presents American authorities as being as corrupt as the German ones he had recently left; but when fascism became an articulated political position and when America joined the war, Lang began to see America as a land of freedom and possibility. His anti-Nazi films of the 1940s and his early Westerns show Lang at his most positive about human nature and the possibility of overcoming evil.

But the hopeful note was confined to the war years, and faded as soon as the war was over. Insecure as a German immigrant (with an apparently incorrigible accent), Lang emphasized his appreciation of America and his hatred of nazism while the war was on. Already forty-three when he left Germany, and living among a group of emigrés in Hollywood, Lang never lost his nostalgia for prewar Germany.[7] Despite his efforts to appreciate America (e.g., his traveling throughout the West, getting to know the land and the Indians), Lang remained essentially German and never became integrated into American life. There was always a split between Lang's personal sense of alienation in America and his longing for what he had lost in Germany on the one hand, and his public stance of love for America and what it stood for, on the other. He remained outside the dominant Hollywood groups, and his increasing disillusionment was naturally colored by his difficulties in starting a new career in America. No major studio ever signed Lang on (as, for instance, happened to Hitchcock). Lang thus missed the security of the sort that enables a director to pursue his interests. Things were so difficult for Lang during the years when the House Un-American Activities Committee (HUAC) prevailed, that he set up his own production company in order to be able to work at all. It may be true that Lang was personally hard to get along with and that his perfectionism caused problems for both actors and producers; but it is also true that he faced a basic American prejudice against foreigners that belied the superficial melting pot notions of America.

While Lang's public statements about America are generally positive,[8] they often conflict with the hopeless vision that underlies his films, a vision that goes back to his expressionist period in Germany. The social and public Lang wanted to be positive, but the parts of him that fed his art reflect an unyielding disillusionment, which gradually became despair.

17

The changes in Lang's American films from decade to decade reflect this increasing disillusionment. While they must be seen in the context of Hollywood's response to social and political events, they also show Lang's personal stamp. His films varied according to the genres that predominated, the political and intellectual situation, the sort of institution in which he worked, and the people assigned to work with him. But he inserted his personal assessment of the state of the world and his idiosyncratic, recurring interests. He moved from a position of relief at living in a nation free from tyranny, one in which democracy prevailed, to bitter disillusionment about American values.

Ministry of Fear (1944) marks the transition between Lang's anti-Nazi films and his films noir, which, in different forms, constitute the majority of his last films in America. His movement away from films with a social message had two main causes. First, as the war came to an end, and the focus turned from defeating fascism to upholding the democratic America for which people had died, Lang saw that things were not as simple as they had seemed during the war. He thus became disillusioned about the possibilities for progressive social change. Second, the paranoia about communism that began to develop as early as 1947 (when HUAC was established), prevented one from making explicitly critical films and necessitated a focus on purely entertaining genre films. But, as critics have shown, the criticism continued beneath the surface of certain genres, films noir in particular. The world of the film noir becomes a correlative for American society, reflecting the political and metaphysical unease. For Lang this is especially significant; his films once again show a world where appearances mislead. As in the films made in expressionist Germany, Lang's films noir reveal an illusory "reality" beneath which lurk monstrous desires and evil deeds which, once known, throw the apparently ordered world into chaos.

In the first series of films noir, from 1945 to 1950, the themes are treated in an explicitly Freudian manner. Guilty sexuality lurks beneath the surface of the ordered bourgeois world of the large Victorian households in Secret Beyond the Door and House by the River and of the smart apartments the women inhabit in Scarlet Street and Woman in the Window. Illicit sexuality threatens to tear apart the thin veil of politeness and propriety the characters maintain, exposing the violence behind it. Images of entrapment had always fascinated Lang, but in his films noir, the form has changed from one of literal incarceration to a psychological entrapment. Developing the direction first started in M, and then modified while in America, Lang now shows criminals who internalize what had earlier been external restraints, becoming victims of their own impulses and desires.

These works are saved from total despair by Freudian psychology, which here provides "explanations" for evil and allows for "cure" through reenactment of the original trauma and by the presence of some decent characters who are sincerely trying to get to the bottom

18

of the mystery. None of these elements is present in Lang's second series of films noir (1953-1956), which become increasingly nihilistic and cynical. By the time he made While the City Sleeps and Beyond a Reasonable Doubt (1956), Lang had lost all faith in human nature and in human institutions. He had, moreover, lost faith in the process of making films, which had sustained him through earlier periods of disillusionment. The belief that he was doing some good in showing people the truth about their society had given purpose and direction to his life and work even when what he had to say was despairing. But by 1956, he had lost the hope of influencing people, partly because the world continued in what he considered a disastrous direction, and partly because his films received poor reviews and were not particularly well-attended. He began to doubt the effectiveness of film as a medium for expressing ideas about life and to see little point in making films at all. The questions raised in While the City Sleeps about the possibility for responsible journalism reflect Lang's thoughts about film. Just as Kyne Junior plays cynically with his reporters, who in turn manipulate others, so, Lang seems to be saying, producers manipulate directors, who in turn deceive their audiences. While the theme of the deceptive camera is not new with Lang (going back at least to You Only Live Once),[9] it became an obsession with him in his films of the 1950s, finding its most extreme expression in Beyond a Reasonable Doubt. Here the still camera captures false images of the hero, proving his guilt in a murder we think he did not commit. He is falsely accused, it seems, but Lang's camera has itself deceived us: we discover that Tom Garrett was, all along in fact, the murderer.

In Lang's last American films, we are never sure whether we can trust what the camera is showing us, and we always learn that we were not shown events that would have cleared up the ambiguity. In addition, people in authority broadcast false offers of help through the media (the newspaper in The Blue Gardenia, television in While the City Sleeps) to victims being pursued by the police. The film director likewise offers false solutions, deceiving the audience as much as the victims in the films are deceived.

Lang's disillusionment with cinema itself, together with his bitterness about his treatment in Hollywood, resulted in his decision not to make any more films in America. His last three films were all made in Germany, unfortunately under equally difficult circumstances. Lang made a nostalgic visit to Berlin in 1956, somehow hoping to recover what he had lost long ago.[10] Approached by German producers, he agreed to make the films he had already scripted in 1920 and never directed--Der Tiger von Eschnapur [The Tiger of Bengal] and Das indische Grabmal [The Indian Tomb]. His last film, also made in Germany, again reflected a return to his early filmmaking. With a contemporary setting, Die tausend Augen des Dr. Mabuse [The Thousand Eyes of Dr. Mabuse] (1961) neatly summarized themes that had preoccupied Lang throughout his life and that had their roots in pre-Nazi Germany.

Partly because this period haunted Lang, he sensed and presented
the sort of horror that haunts people in our period living in major
urban centers where community networks have collapsed. Beginning
with M, Lang expressed fears we dare not articulate; the horror is
sometimes heightened by making the victims children or childlike
women (see, besides M, Manhunt, where Jenny's hat pin is used in much
the same manner as Elsie's balloon, The Big Heat, and Moonfleet, where
John Mohune is enmeshed in the evil doings of Jeremy Fox's gang.
While not victims, the presence of babies in You Only Live Once and
Clash by Night increases the horror that the adults are suffering).
As Lang becomes more bitter and disillusioned, innocence is rare and
the films reflect an unmitigated vision of paranoia, deception, and
ambiguity, a world deprived of hope and possibility.

Yet if Lang's vision is despairing toward the end, this had as
much to do with the prevailing political climate in America as with
Lang's inherent metaphysical angst. Although never a member of the
Communist Party, Lang had worked with Brecht and left-wing scriptwriters like Albert Maltz and Ring Lardner. He was known to have
liberal ideas, had deplored censorship in a 1945 article,[11] and
joined a group called Filmmakers for Democracy, which protested what
was happening at the time of HUAC.

Wolfram Schütte is wrong to see Lang's films as essentially conservative.[12] Instead they reflect the bitterness and cynicism of a
disillusioned idealist who, in hoping for too much, ends up believing
in very little. Yet as the 1960s began, Lang became more optimistic.
He began to think that young people might bring about the changes
that he had hoped for, and he planned to make a film dealing with
youth, which might have shown a return to positive ways of seeing
human nature. Failing eyesight and ill health prevented Lang from
undertaking the project, but he was able to enjoy the new recognition
of his greatness in the 1960s. Frequently interviewed and invited to
speak to film students and at film gatherings, Lang must have felt
that he was having an impact, although, according to Howard Vernon,
he still regretted that he had not accomplished enough along these
lines.[13] He had always wanted to make popular films in order to
reach the majority of the people and he never experienced the kind
of popularity that he wanted. Yet his films were shown more than
ever before in the 1970s, and since his death in 1976 there has been
a great deal of interest in his work.

This new critical interest does not, of course, equal the popular
acclaim Lang always wished for, but it does (perhaps ironically) reflect Lang's own interest in what cinema is, and in how audiences
relate to screen images. It is to Lang's credit that scholars keep
turning to his works and that now some of his deepest concerns are
at the forefront of theoretical developments.

NOTES

1   Paul Willemen, ed., Ophuls (London:  British Film Institute, 1978), p. 1.

2   Personal interview with Lotte Eisner, 1977.

3   Ibid.

4   See the German reviews annotated in Chapter 4.

5   See David Hull, Film in the Third Reich (New York:  Simon and Schuster, 1969), pp. 39-40.

6   Fritz Lang, "Zwischen Bohrturmen und Palmen.  Ein kalifornischer Reisebericht," Filmland (Berlin) (3 January 1925).

7   See particularly Howard Vernon's comments in "Unpublished Interviews" (Paris 1977).  Vernon talks about Lang's isolation in Hollywood and the comfort he found with other expatriates.

8   See, for example, Fritz Lang, "Happily Ever After," Penguin Film Review, No. 5 (January 1948), pp. 22-29.

9   See George Wilson, "You Only Live Once:  The Double Feature," Sight and Sound, 46, No. 4 (Autumn 1977), 221-226.

10  Lotte Eisner talks about Lang's nostalgia in Kaplan, "Interviews."

11  See Fritz Lang, "The Freedom of the Screen," Theatre Arts (September 1947), pp. 52-55.

12  Wolfram Schütte, "Kolportage, Stilisierung, Realismus: Anmerkungen zum Werk Fritz Langs von den Spinnen bis zu dem Testament des Dr. Mabuse," Filmstudio, No. 44 (September 1964).

13  See Vernon's comments in Kaplan, "Interviews" for evidence of Lang's regrets late in life.

# The Films: Synopses, Credits, Notes, Reviews

1  HALBBLUT [The Half-Caste] (1919)
   The first of four lost, and five unknown, films by Lang,
Halbblut is the story of a love-triangle comprised of two men
and a half-caste who was originally a prostitute in Mexico.
The young husband is warned by a friend about the danger of
marrying a woman who is a cross between two races, and, over-
hearing this, the half-caste seeks revenge.  After ruining the
two men (one of them dies in a prison, the other in a lunatic
asylum), she befriends another half-caste and together they
make a dubious living by playing cards.  About to flee to
Mexico to live on ill-gotten gains, the woman is killed by a
cheated lover.  (For more details about the film and quotes
from the original reviews, see entry nos.: 461, 478, 493.)

Credits:
Director:              Fritz Lang
Screenplay:            Fritz Lang
Photography:           Carl Hoffmann
Cast:                  Ressel Orla, Carl de Vogt, Gilda
                       Langer, Carl Gebhard-Schröder, Paul
                       Morgan
Filmed at:             Decla-Bioscop, Berlin, 1919
Original Length:       1,608 meters
Released:              3 April 1919 (Marmorhaus, Berlin)

Reviews:
Der Kinematograph, April 1919 (quoted in Eisner's Fritz Lang,
p. 23);
Der Film, No. 141 (1919) (See Eisner, p. 24, for quotation
giving plot summary);
Lichtbildbühne, No. 14 (1919) (See Eisner, p. 24).

2   DER HERR DER LIEBE [Master of Love] (1919)
    The second of Lang's films with no surviving print, Der
Herr der Liebe is another story of unhappy love in the mode
of a society drama. (For more details, see books mentioned
in entry nos.:  461, 478, 493.)

Credits:
Producer:                Fritz Lang
Director:                Fritz Lang
Screenplay:              Oscar Koffler
Photography:             Emil Schünemann
Art Direction:           Carl Ludwig Kirmse
Cast:                    Carl de Vogt (Disescu), Gilda Langer,
                         (Yvette), Erika Unruh, Fritz Lang
Filmed at:               Helios Film Studios, Berlin, 1919
Original Length:         1,436 meters (according to Grafe/Patalas)
                         (Deutsche Stummfilm has 1,316m)
Released:                Mid-September 1919 (Richard Oswald
                         Lichtspiele, Berlin)

Reviews:
Der Kinematograph (Dusseldorf edition), No. 664 (1919) (Parts
of this are quoted in Eisner's Fritz Lang, p. 24.)

3   DIE SPINNEN [The Spiders] Part I:  DER GOLDENE SEE [The Golden
    Lake] (1919)
    As the film opens, an old man (whom we later discover is a
Harvard professor doing research on the Incas and their gold),
is weeping for a dead friend and frightened for his own life.
Indians creep up on him, and he just has time to stuff a rag
with information about Inca gold on it into a bottle and throw
it out to sea before he is killed.
    We cut to the Sail Club of America, where we find Kai Hoog,
an elegant upper-class man, being taken upstairs to join Lio
Sha and other guests.  Hoog tells everyone how he found a bottle containing a message about Inca gold (as he talks there
are flashbacks of what he is describing) and that after doing
some research, he thinks he has found the place on the map.
He plans to leave for the site the next day.  Lio Sha looks
sinister as Hoog is describing his adventure, but Hoog is careful to put the information written on a rag into his pocket.
All drink a toast to Hoog's success; Lio Sha and Hoog clink
glasses so firmly that one breaks.
    Cut to Hoog sitting alone in his lounge at night.  Three
masked men in black creep up on him and knock him out.  Waking
in a daze the next day, Hoog finds all his papers and letters
relating to the Inca gold gone and a spider in their place.
    We next see Dr. Telephas receiving a message from Lio Sha,
telling him he is needed by the Spiders and that the golden
treasure must be theirs.  Telephas goes to an underground
place where bankers and financiers are gathered, and Lio Sha

spies on the meeting from another room through a mirror device. Telephas informs the group that they must put up the money for the trip, since they have to be there before Hoog.

We cut to Cuitan, Mexico, the best starting point for archeological expeditions. Hoog, on his way there by train, persuades Harry, a balloon expert, to fly him over the Cordillera crater into Chile.

In Cuitan Station, Hoog sees Lio Sha gathering men for her trip; Telephas has decided not to go. Hoog arranges to meet Harry at a specific time, but meanwhile runs into Lio Sha's group plotting over the stolen piece of rag. Hoog grabs it and runs off, with the Spiders in hot pursuit. He just manages to reach the balloon and get away before being shot.

Hoog explains that the document he stole is about a secret cache of gold. We cut to the Spiders on their journey, Lio Sha saying that Kai Hoog has the key to the treasure. She has heard of the golden sea in the west where no mortals have been and where each morning a golden woman bathes.

Hoog and Harry meanwhile have sighted the ruins of an old Inca town through their telescope, and Hoog prepares to parachute in. We see him in a swamp and then in the town. The sun priestess is just beginning her bathing ritual as the sun rises. While Hoog watches, a snake creeps down the steps, and he is able to save the priestess and kill the snake. The girl tells Hoog to get out if he can (since no white man has ever left the place alive before), but he finally discovers a cave with a passage that leads into a temple.

The Incas have captured Lio Sha and she is brought to the chief. In three days, they tell her, her heart will be given as a sacrifice to the sun god. When the chief tells the sun priestess that she will sacrifice Lio Sha to the god, she is horrified, but the chief tells her she will thereby help to restore the Incas to their earlier greatness.

The priestess finds Hoog in the temple and tells him again to leave. She takes him to the gold mine under the golden sea where no white people have trodden before. She warns him not to burn the holy candles and begs him to take her away with him.

The day of the sacrifice has come, and Lio Sha, bound, is brought to the Priestess to be slain; the Priestess begs the Chief not to make her do it. Meanwhile, we see the Spiders outside trying to get into the city. They finally burst in with their guns, and a bitter fight ensues. Hoog and the Priestess find each other and run away, but the Spiders discover the treasure and rush to grab it. Hoog lights a bough and it burns by itself. There is intercutting between the men crazed with gold, Lio Sha, and Hoog and the Priestess escaping. The bough becomes a stream of water that pushes the men out of the cave, pulling them into its current. Hoog and the Priestess stay afloat on the bough and are finally rescued by a boat.

A week later in San Francisco, Lio Sha comes to Hoog's

house, where he is now living with the Priestess. Lio Sha asks for the document about the treasure and tells Hoog that she had loved him but that he has now ruined her life. Hoog rejects Lio Sha, telling her that he loves someone else, but she warns him that she will get her revenge. After Lio Sha leaves, Hoog reassures the Priestess that the other woman now means nothing. Forced to leave on business, Hoog takes a fond farewell of the Priestess. When Hoog returns, the Priestess is gone. After a search, he finds her body in the garden with a spider next to it.

Credits:

| | |
|---|---|
| Director: | Fritz Lang |
| Screenplay: | Fritz Lang |
| Photography: | Emil Schünemann |
| Art Direction: | Otto Hunte, Carl Ludwig Kirmse, Herman Warm, Heinrich Umlauff |
| Cast: | Carl de Vogt (Kai Hoog), Ressel Orla (Lio Sha), Lil Dagover (Sun priestess), Paul Morgan (expert), Georg John (Dr. Telephas), Rudolf [Bruno] Lettinger (Terry Landon), Edgar Pauly (Four-Finger John), Paul Biensfeldt, Friedrich Kühne, Harry Frank |
| Filmed in: | Decla-Bioscop Studios, Berlin, 1919. |
| Original Length: | 1,951 meters |
| Released: | books in entry nos. 461, 478, 493.) |
| Note: | Eisner comments that "Lang later made a novel from the material of Der goldene See, which was first serialized in the Berlin Film-Kurier and then published in book form." |

Reviews:
Der Kinematograph (8 October 1919) (reprinted in Eisner, p. 32); Der Film, no. 41 (1919) (Eisner, p. 33); Der Kinematograph (Dusseldorf edition) (1 October 1919) (Eisner, pp. 33-34).

4    HARAKIRI [Madame Butterfly] (1919)
A fragile print of this film survives in The Amsterdam Film Archive, but it was not in any condition to be seen. Filmed between Parts I and II of Die Spinnen, Harakiri is an adaptation of the play Madame Butterfly by David Belasco and John Luther Long. It tells the story of O-Take-San's tragic love affair with a naval officer who deserts her soon after their marriage. Unable to live with the dishonor brought on his family, O-Take-San's father commits harakiri, and this is soon followed by his daughter's suicide. (For more details, see books in entry nos." 461, 478, 493.)

## The Films: Synopses, Credits, Notes, Reviews

Credits:
| | |
|---|---|
| Director: | Fritz Lang |
| Screenplay: | Max Jungk, based on the play <u>Madame Butterfly</u> by John Luther Long and David Belasco |
| Photography: | Max Fassbender |
| Art Direction: | Heinrich Umlauff (with the assistance of the I. F. G. Umlauff Museum of Hamburg) |
| Cast: | Paul Biensfeldt (Daimyo Tokujawa), Lil Dagover (O-Take-San, his daughter), Georg John (Buddhist monk), Meinhart Maur (Prince Matahari), Rudolf Lettinger (Karan), Erner Hübsch (Kin-Be-Araki), Käte Küster [Jüster] (Hanake, O-Take-San's servant), Niels [Nils] Prien (Olaf J. Anderson), Herta Hedén (Eva), Harry Frank, Josef Roemer, Loni Nest (child) |
| Filmed at: | Decla-Bioscop, Berlin, 1919 |
| Original Length: | 2,525 meters |
| Released: | 18 December 1919 (Marmorhaus, Berlin) |
| Note: | Eisner says that "After <u>Hara-Kiri</u>, Hermann Warm, Walter Reimann and Walter Roehrig submitted a story to Lang and Erich Pommer: <u>Das Cabinet des Dr. Caligari</u>. The popularity of the first part of <u>Die Spinnen</u> was so great, however, that Lang had to begin the second part at once. Lang's idea that the expressionistic story be framed by a normal prologue and epilogue was retained by the writers of the script (Carl Mayer and Hans Janowitz), and <u>Caligari</u> was then directed by Robert Wiene and released by Decla in February, 1920." |

Reviews:
<u>Der Kinematograph</u> (31 December 1919) (quoted in Eisner, pp. 25-26); <u>Der Film</u>, 4, No. 51 (1919) (gives plot summary, quoted in Eisner, p. 26); <u>Berliner Börsenzeitung</u>, (21 December 1919) (praises realistic picture of life, quoted in Eisner, p. 28); <u>Erste Internationale Film-Zeitung</u> (Berlin) No. 50, (20 December 1919).

5   DIE SPINNEN [The Spiders].  Part II:  DAS BRILLANTENSCHIFF [The Diamond Ship] (1920)
    This second part of the film begins with the Spiders

robbing a bank under the very noses of the police. Shot from above, the bank looks like a labyrinth, and the robbery is perfectly executed.

At her house, Lio Sha tells a Chinese man that their organization is brilliant and that it's not their fault if they didn't find the jewel shaped like a Buddha's head that they are seeking. We cut to yet one more robbery being carried out and then to Lio Sha and the Chinese man going through the jewels. Lio Sha says she is no longer afraid of Hoog.

We cut to Hoog, planning an invasion of Lio Sha's house. He flies in by plane, entering through the roof. Down below the criminals escape through secret doors while the police try to follow. The Chinese man presses buttons, and the police and Hoog are trapped. They finally kill the Chinese man and find the right button to open the door. Hoog takes a document and a piece of ivory from the dead man and then goes to help other people to escape. One carload of Spiders gets away.

The next day, unable to figure out the document, Hoog takes it to an old professor, who looks up the words in his dusty books. The document says that there is an underground town beneath the Chinese Quarter, and that the ivory permits entrance. He warns Hoog not to let the police know if he visits there.

Meanwhile, we see Lio Sha in the underground town, asking about the famous stone they are looking for. Hoog is permitted to go underground when he shows the ivory, walking down long passages guarded by tigers in cages. He is horrified to see Lio Sha there, but is taken to a room and given an opium pipe. He pretends to be asleep, but overhears Lio Sha saying that the Buddha Stone is not there—it was found on an island long ago. They plan to go there shortly. She needs a captain, however, to guide the boat. Hoog's presence becomes known but he is able to escape by grabbing Lio Sha as hostage. Shortly after, a captain is hired. Hoog, meanwhile, has made plans to get aboard by hiding in a crate marked "secret documents." We see it being loaded.

In Asia, the Spiders are consulting a Yogi to learn where the precious stone is; finding it will mean Asia's freedom from foreign domination. The Yogi just has time to say that John Terry, the great diamond king in London, possesses the stone before he has a heart attack and dies.

We cut back to the ship and see Hoog, in disguise, taking down a message from the shortwave radio, after knocking out the real operator. Hoog is discovered, and, pursued by the captain and sailors, jumps into the water.

Meanwhile, John Terry finds a note saying the Spiders have kidnapped his daughter, Ellen, in exchange for the Buddha Stone. The Spiders question Ellen, but she denies knowing anything about the stone.

Hoog now comes to Terry, who insists that he knows nothing of the stone. They agree that the secret to its whereabouts must lie with Terry, however. His family originated with a sea captain, who left a box with a sea log in it. Hoog and Terry read about a fight over some treasure in a rock cave in the Falklands, but pages are missing. Hearing a movement at the door, Hoog discovers Terry's servant listening; he turns out to be Four-finger John of the Spiders. They lock him up for forty-eight hours to prevent his spoiling their plans, but John sends a pigeon with a note about the Falkland Islands to Lio Sha.

We see Lio Sha receiving the message on the boat and the Spiders set out for the Islands. There before them, Hoog has already discovered the jewel and Lio Sha, having over-whelmed him with her gang, demands that he give it to her. He refuses, so they tie him up and settle down to sleep. During the night, fumes fill the cave and there is an explosion. Hoog just manages to free himself and escape, but most of the Spiders are killed, all but one young man.

Hoog comes back to Terry, whose daughter is still missing. They receive a report that an old man has checked into a hotel with a young girl (who apparently had been hypnotized). The couple is being followed by Indians who, suspecting the Spiders of tyranny, listen at their door. They hear him plotting to make a copy of the jewel and trick the Asians into believing it's the real one. He and Ellen would then be in power. The Indians, learning of the double cross, break in, intending to kill both the leader and Ellen. Just in time, Terry and Hoog arrive and save Ellen, who, having been hypnotized, recalls nothing of what happened.

Credits:

| | |
|---|---|
| Director: | Fritz Lang |
| Screenplay: | Fritz Lang |
| Photography: | Karl Freund |
| Art Direction: | Otto Hunte, Carl Ludwig Kirmse, Hermann Warm, Heinrich Umlauff |
| Cast: | Carl de Vogt (Kay Hoog), Ressel Orla (Lio Sha), Georg John (the Master), Rudolf Lettinger (Terry Landon, dia-mond king), Thea Zander (Ellen, his daughter), Reiner-Steiner (Captain of the Diamond Ship), Friedrich Kühne (All-Hab-Mah, the Yogi), Edgar Pauly (Four-Finger John), Meinhard [Meinhart; Meinhardt] Maur (the Chinese man), Paul Morgan (the Jew), K. A. Römer, Gilda Langer, Paul Biensfeldt, Lil Dagover (Priestess of the Sun God) |
| Filmed by: | Decla-Bioscop, Berlin, toward the end of 1919 |
| Original Length: | 2,219 meters |

Released:                February 1920 (at Theater am
                         Moritzplatz, Berlin)

Notes:                   Eisner says that "this section of
                         Die Spinnen was originally called
                         Das Sklavenschiff [The Slave Ship]
                         in Lang's original four-part cycle;
                         Parts Three, Das Geheimnis der Sphinx
                         [The Secret of the Sphinx] and Four,
                         Um Asiens Kaiserskrone [For Asia's
                         Imperial Crown] were written by Lang
                         but never filmed.'

Reviews:
Der Film, No. 7 (1919) (quoted in Eisner, p. 34); John Gillett,
Program Notes (BFI:  Gillett links the film to Feuillade, noting that Lang has the same flair for exotic adventure and
fantasy.  It's an example of Lang's favorite theme of an
international organization bent on world domination.  He
praises the decor and sets.)

6   DAS WANDERNDE BILD [The Wandering Image] (1920)
    Another lost film, Das Wandernde Bild was the first made
in collaboration with Thea Von Harbou.  Like Halbblut, it involves two men in love with the same woman; this time, however,
she is pure and saintly.  The men live in a remote snow-bound
Alpine village visited by the woman who cures a sick child.
She departs as mysteriously as she came, leaving the villagers
believing that she was the Virgin Mary.  (For more details
about this film, see books mentioned in entry nos.: 461, 478,
493.)

Credits:
Director:                Fritz Lang
Screenplay:              Fritz Lang, Thea von Harbou
Photography:             Guido Seeber
Art Direction:           Otto Hunte, Erich Kettelhut (building
                         of the model)
Cast:                    Mia May (Irmgard Vanderheit), Hans
                         Marr (Georg Vanderheit/John, her
                         brother), Rudolf Klein-Rohden (Wil
                         Brand), Harry Frank, Loni Nest
Filmed by:               May-Film GMBH, Berlin, 1919
Original Length:         2,032 meters; working title Madonna
                         im Schnee
Released:                25 December 1920 (Tauentzienpalast,
                         Berlin)

Reviews:
Lichtbildbühne (1 January 1921) (plot summary and critical
comments, quoted in Eisner, p. 28); Film-Kurier (January 1921).

7    KÄMPFENDE HERZEN (Die Vier um die Frau) [Fighting Hearts or
     Four Around a Woman] (1920)
        The last of the lost early films, Kämpfende Herzen is a
     complicated melodrama.  It involves a dealer, Yquem, whose
     jealousy is aroused when buying his wife some jewelry with
     forged money in a thieves' den.  He sees a man who resembles
     a portrait his wife owns and invites him to his house, with
     disastrous consequences.  After a night full of violence and
     deception, the wife's innocence is established and Yquem ar-
     rested for his crimes.  (For more details about this film, see
     books mentioned in entry nos.:  461, 478, 493.)

     Credits:
     Director:                  Fritz Lang
     Screenplay:                Thea von Harbou, Fritz Lang, from a
                                piece by R. E. Vanloo
     Photography:               Otto Kanturek
     Art Direction:             Ernst Meiwers, Hans Jacoby
     Cast:                      Carola Toelle (Florence Yquem),
                                Hermann Boettcher (Her father),
                                Ludwig Hartau (Harry Yquem), Anton
                                Edthofer (Werner Krafft/William, his
                                brother), Rudolf Klein-Rogge (Upton),
                                Robert Forster-Larrinaga (Meunier),
                                Lilli Lohrer (first maid), Harry
                                Frank (Bobby), Leonhard Haskel/Paul
                                Rehkopf (swindlers), Gottfried
                                Huppertz (head waiter), Hans
                                Lüpschütz (hoodlum), Lisa von Marton
                                (Margot), Erika Unruh (prostitute),
                                Paul Morgan (hustler), Edgar Pauly
                                (man), Gerhard Ritterband (newspaper
                                boy)
     Filmed at:                 Decla-Bioscop, Berlin, 1920
     Original Length:           1,707 meters
     Released:                  February 1921 (Marmorhaus, Berlin)

     Reviews:
     Film und Presse, No. 516 (1921); Lichtbildbühne (13 February
     1921) (both quoted in Eisner, p. 31).

8    DER MÜDE TOD:  EIN DEUTSCHES VOLKSLIED IN 6 VERSEN [Destiny]
     (1921)
        The film opens with a shot of a grave, followed by another
     of some trees from which the stranger, Death, emerges.  A
     horse and carriage come along the road, and we cut to a shot
     of lovers inside who are sitting by an old woman with a goose.
     Death, now standing beneath a cross on the road, stops the
     carriage and enters slowly.  The woman with the goose is agi-
     tated by the stranger, who, after she leaves, looks hard at
     the lovers.

They come to a small town, where everyone gets out at the
inn. We are introduced to the main townspeople--the mayor,
doctor, a priest, notary, and schoolmaster--all of whom are
ridiculed. Discussing the stranger's arrival, the authorities
recall that the gravedigger first saw him, and we flashback
to the graveyard and the stranger buying land next to it. He
surrounds the land with a high wall that has no doors or windows. There is a long shot of Death standing by his enormous
wall.

We cut to the present and the stranger following the lovers
into the inn. While the town authorities look on, the stranger
sits by the young couple, who laughingly drink out of a loving
cup. The man's glass suddenly turns into an eggtimer, and
while the woman goes into the kitchen to play with some kit-
tens, the man and Death leave. The woman, frantic, goes in
search of him, and is seen later wandering in the moonlit
countryside. She arrives again at the village square as the
authorities stumble drunkenly into the night, while an herbalist gathers his plants. Arriving at Death's huge wall, the
girl has a vision of a procession of cripples in white all
moving silently through the wall. Weak with fear and hunger,
the woman faints, but the herbalist finds her and takes her
to his home.

They enter the dark hovel, and the old man mixes her a
soothing potion. But she sees his book and the statement that
"Love is as strong as Death." She decides to take poison, and
raises a vial to her lips. Suddenly she is at the wall again,
only this time she goes through and up the stairs, where Death
waits for her. The woman pleads with him for her lover's life,
and we cut to a cathedral with Death and the woman surrounded
by huge candles. When Death takes one candle, it becomes a
baby, and we see the mother weeping for her dead child. Death
claims that he is weary of seeing human suffering, hates his
duty, and would gladly be overcome, had anyone the strength
to defeat him. Turning to three flickering candles, Death
says that each represents a life about to end. If the woman
can save any of them, Death will give her her lover back.

The stories of the three lives follow. The first takes
place in ninth-century Bagdad. It is the feast of Ramadan,
and the people are worshipping in a mosque. We see the priest
leading the prayers, the dancers moving wildly, and the crowd
swaying in rhythm. Zobeide, the Caliph's sister, is in love
with a Frank, an infidel, who now enters the temple in disguise.
He approaches Zobeide and tells her he wants to see her again.
One of the dancers sees them, however, and when he leaves,
rushes out after him, ripping off his disguise. A wild fight
follows; the Frank single-handedly holds off the crowd of
worshippers and then manages to escape in the chase that
follows.

We cut to Zobeide grieving with her loyal maid and then to
the Caliph being informed about the event. The Caliph comes

to Zobeide, looking evil with a huge knife in his belt, and is unconvinced by her protests of innocence.  Shortly after he leaves, Ayesha, the maid, brings the Frank to Zobeide, but someone outside has seen him come.  The palace is surrounded; Zobeide, frantic, tries to hide her lover, but after another chase, he is caught and bound, to the Caliph's evil delight.

We cut to El Mot, the gardener who is really Death, digging the grave where the Frank will be buried alive.  The Caliph arrives, sits down and takes out his pipe.  He orders Zobeide to come to him, and tells her that El Mot is preparing a surprise for her.  She rushes down to the grave.  El Mot looks sympathetic; we realize he is Death, and we cut back to the Cathedral.

The second story is set in fourteenth-century Venice, and recalls Romeo and Juliet.  A carnival is going on.  We cut to Fiametta, a young girl in love with Giovanfrancesco but betrothed to Girolamo, an old man.  She is standing on a balcony, caressing a flower given to her by her lover hiding down below.  Girolamo, wearing an ugly mask, comes to Fiametta, and guessing who gave her the rose, predicts Giovanfrancesco's death.  Girolamo tells Fiametta that he knows she hates him, but hopes that she'll love him after they are married and Giovanfrancesco is dead.

We next see Fiametta planning to get rid of Girolamo.  She writes two letters and sends them to Girolamo and Giovanfrancesco respectively.  We cut to a cock fight and a Moor's being called away from it by Fiametta.  Meanwhile, Girolamo is reading the letter brought by Fiametta's messenger; he asks the boy if he is delivering another letter, but he denies it.  Girolamo sends his men after the boy, anyway.

We cut to Fiametta and the Moor; she is poisoning a sword and telling the Moor what to do with it.  Meanwhile, the boy is beaten by Girolamo's men, who seize the letter to Giovanfrancesco telling of Fiametta's plan to kill Girolamo.  Girolamo now sends the letter originally meant for him (asking him to visit Fiametta at a certain time and disguised in a certain way), to Giovanfrancesco.  Giovanfrancesco is met by Fiametta, who is disguised as a swordswoman and challenges him (apparently in fun) to a duel.  She guides him to the arras, behind which the Moor is standing with the poisoned sword, and Giovanfrancesco is murdered.  Too late, Fiametta realizes her error, and embraces Giovanfrancesco as he dies.

The third story is set in China.  It opens with an old magician, A Hi, reading a long script from the emperor.  There are some comic moments when the old man makes the paper disappear and reappear, to the delight of his daughter and the assistant she is in love with.  The emperor wants to be entertained, so A Hi goes to the court on his flying carpet, taking his daughter and assistant with him.  He creates a miniature army and a flying horse, but the emperor is much more interested in the magician's daughter than in his tricks.  The magician promises to give him everything except his daughter, but the emperor declares that A Hi will be beheaded unless he gives in. The daughter pleads with the emperor to no avail, and we next see her imprisoned. The emperor comes in and tries to seduce her, but he is fat and ugly and she resists.

A Hi is called in and told to make his daughter obey or he will be killed. A Hi tries to comfort his daughter, but she snatches his wand and breaks it in two in anger. She discovers that the wand works, even if broken, and touches the guards, who turn into pigs. She writes some words, an elephant appears, and she and her lover run away. The path being too narrow, they soon have to get off the elephant and walk. They wander through the woods, but the wand is now small since it shrinks with use; the lovers become desperate when they are pursued by the emperor's men. The emperor tells his servant to take the magic horse, given by A Hi, and bring the lovers back dead or alive. When they see the horse coming, the daughter uses the wand to change herself into a statue and her lover into a tiger. The archer kills the tiger and he dies, tears of blood running down the statue's face as this happens. The archer and his men leave.

We return to the figures of Death and the girl in the cathedral. He tells her that she has one last chance if she can save a life as yet unspent. We cut to the girl still taking the poison; the entire intervening action took place between the moment that she put the poison to her lips and the moment that the herbalist took it from her. She pleads with him for his life in return for her lover's, since he is old and near death anyway, but he refuses. The girl rushes out into the street, and asks several old people for their lives, but none will give it up. In an old people's home, no one will help the girl, but as they run away from her a lamp overturns and the place catches fire. The girl rushes to snatch a baby left in the home, but Death wants to take it in return for her lover. The girl cannot bear to do this and hands the baby to its mother outside. In the crypt, the lovers are united; when Death appears, their spirits rise from their biers and they walk tranquilly away over a grassy hill.

Credits:

| | |
|---|---|
| Director: | Fritz Lang |
| Screenplay: | Fritz Lang, Thea von Harbou |
| Photography: | Erich Nitzschmann [Nilschmann] Hermann Saalfrank (old German episode), Fritz Arno Wagner (Venetian, Oriental, and Chinese episodes). |
| Art Direction: | Robert Herlth (Chinese section, with the exception of the emperor's palace); Walter Röhrig (German section, with the exception of the hillock), Hermann Warm (Venetian and Oriental |

34

|  |  |
|---|---|
|  | sections, emperor's palace, hillock). |
| Costumes: | Chinese and Oriental costumes from the Umlauff Museum, Hamburg. |
| Lighting: | Robert Hegerwald |
| Music: | Peter Schirman |
| Cast: | Lil Dagover (young woman), Bernhard Goetzke (Death), Walter Janssen (lover), Hans Sternberg (Mayor), Carl Rückert (vicar), Max Adalbert (lawyer), Erich Pabst (teacher), Paul Rehkopf (sexton), Hermann Picha (tailer), Edgar Klitzsch (doctor), Georg John (beggar), Marie Wismar (old woman), Aloisha Lehnert (mother); Oriental Section: Lil Dagover (Zobeide), Walter Janssen (Frank), Bernhard Goetzke (El Mot), Rudolf Klein-Rogge (dervish), Eduard von Winterstein (Calip), Erika Unruh (Aisha); Venetian Episode: Lil Dagover (Fiametta), Rudolf Klein-Rogge (Girolamo), Lewis Brody (Moor), Lothar Müthel [Mütel] (confidant), Lina Paulsen (nurse), Walter Janssen (Giovanfrancesco); Chinese Episode: Lil Dagover (Tiaotsien), Walter Janssen (Liang), Bernhard Goetzke (archer), Paul Biensfeldt (A Hi, magician), Karl Huszar (emperor), Max Adalbert (treasurer), Paul Neumann (hangman). |
| Filmed at: | Decla-Bioscop Studios, Neubabelsberg, 1921 |
| Completed: | October 1921 |
| Original Length: | 2,311 meters (2,306m [DS]) |
| Released: | 7 October 1921 (Mozartsaal and U. T. Kurfürstendamm, Berlin). The film was released briefly in America, July 1923, under the title Between Two Worlds, by Artclass. |

Reviews:
H. W. [Hans Wollenberg], Lichtbildbühne (8 October 1921); Der Film, No. 46 (1921) (quoted in Eisner, pp. 45-46); Freiheit (11 October 1921) (quoted in Eisner, p. 43); Brauner, Ludwig, Der Kinematograph (16 October 1921); Balthasar (Roland Schacht) Das Blaue Heft (22 October 1921); Pinthus, Kurt, Das Tage-Buch (22 October 1921) (see entry no. 44); K.H., Der Welt-Film, Nos. 10-11, (5 November 1921) (praises film for marking a re-birth of the form); Acht-Uhr Abendblatt (7 October 1921) (praises the art of this film and the way it uses the old

folksong that it is based on); Film-Kurier (7 October 1921)
(comments on way Lang has caught here something essentially
German, the flickering light of the German fairy tales);
Ihering, Herbert, Berliner Börsen-Courier (30 September 1923)
(quoted in Eisner, p. 43 and reprinted in Ihering, Von
Reinhardt bis Brecht, vol. 1, Berlin: Aufbau, 1958); Lang,
Fritz, "On Benevolent Death," Berliner Tage-blatt (1 January
1927) (reprinted in Eisner, pp. 55-56. See also other comments
by Lang on Der mude Tod in Eisner, particularly in relation to
the Titles, originally verses and now lost, pp. 52-54); Gilles,
Jacob, Cinéma 65, No. 100 (1965); Raynes, Tony, Monthly Film
Bulletin, No. 481 (February 1974) (see entry no. 437).

9    DR. MABUSE, DER SPIELER [Dr. Mabuse, The Gambler] (1922)
     Part I:  DER GROSSE SPIELER--EIN BILD DER ZEIT [The Great
     Gambler--A Picture of the Time]
         The film opens with a close-up of cards being arranged by
     someone into a fan shape; they show a man in different dis-
     guises. The next shot shows Mabuse shuffling these cards,
     picking one out, and handing it to his valet. Mabuse takes
     out his watch, which we see in close-up, and the following
     sequence of Mabuse's being made up is intercut with that of
     Mabuse's man murdering a courier on a train and stealing his
     attache case containing an important treaty which will influence
     the stock market. An aide waits to help the murderer escape,
     while another, disguised as a telephone repairman, phones
     Mabuse that all is well.
         Mabuse, now carefully disguised as an aristocratic elderly
     man, receives one of his workers, Pesche, who brings news
     about the arrival of some loads of medicine and platinum. He
     is blamed for being late by Mabuse, who writes on some bank
     notes Pesche hands him. Mabuse goes out, and, after being
     approached by a one-legged man, gets into a car that shortly
     crashes into another one; Mabuse continues in the other car,
     where we see him open up the contrats commercial stolen on the
     train.
         Cut to the headline of a special edition of the newspaper,
     proclaiming the loss of the documents relating to a signifi-
     cant Swiss treaty, on which the stability of the stock market
     evidently depends. Shots of the Stock Exchange show business-
     men in their tall black hats bustling about in distress at the
     falling prices. Mabuse, now disguised as a businessman, stands
     above the others buying stocks that immediately regain their
     values once the lost treaty is discovered deposited intact at
     the Swiss Embassy. The sequence closes with Mabuse's face,
     in close-up, superimposed on shots of the now empty Stock
     Exchange.
         Cut to the "Folies-Bergère" with the curtain going up. A
     dancer, Cara Carozza, is announced, and Mabuse arrives while
     she is doing her seductive act. He finds a note from Cara in
     his program giving him details about his next victim, Hull,

the only son of a rich industrialist. Cut to Hull, whom Mabuse peers at through his glasses. Cara finishes her dance to loud applause and bouquets of flowers. Mabuse's eyes, in extreme close-up, precede shots of Hull suddenly feeling intense pain in his head and neck. When Hull leaves his friends, Mabuse greets him in the corridor and tells Hull to take him to his secret club. When they arrive, Mabuse is introduced as Hugo Balling, and they sit down to cards. Cara, meanwhile, receives a note that Room 111 is reserved for her in the Hotel Excelsior and that she will receive further instructions.

A series of short shots shows Hull losing badly at cards (hypnotized as he is by Mabuse), his friends looking on anxiously, the management wondering what to do, the time passing. Unable to pay his total debt, Hull asks for Balling's card and Mabuse leaves. Hull begins to come out of his trance.

The next day, when Hull goes to the address on the card, Room 112, Hotel Excelsior, he only finds one of Mabuse's men there; Cara is next door listening, however, and when Hull leaves she pursues and seduces him.

Ten days have passed and Hull, now madly in love with Cara, as intended by Mabuse, is expecting Cara at his rooms. While bustling about making everything perfect, the bell rings, but it is the detective, von Wenk. Wenk tells Hull that he has been the victim of a clever crook using psychic influence to make his opponents lose at cards. Wenk, noting that the crook has many disguises and gives out false cards, wonders why he has not collected his money from Hull. Hull, with his mind on Cara, is hardly interested in his own case, but Wenk looks puzzled. Cara, meanwhile, has delayed going to Hull, waiting in the hotel corridor for Mabuse, whom she finally sees, appealing to him to love her as she loves him. Wenk, now taking his leave of Hull, gives him a card and asks to be called when Balling gets in touch for the money. Hull rips up the card and places it in a bowl of candy.

Cara, arriving as Wenk leaves, is greeted effusively by Hull, who does all he can to pamper her. She finds Wenk's card and warns Hull against being intimate with the police.

We cut to the next evening and the Schwank Grill. A series of shots of the club is apparently designed to show the shady activities that go on behind the restaurant and to make a general comment about the kind of criminal who owns a place like this. We next get shots of the inside of the club, showing expressionist designs and distorted shapes. Countess Told, a beautiful woman, enters, and Detective Wenk, there to watch out for the crook, is immediately taken with her. Countess Told sits down to watch a card game, and we see shots of Hull, Cara, and Mabuse, in yet another disguise, cheating another player. When Hull receives a note from Balling to pay up the money, Wenk sees his chance to capture the crook.

Countess Told invites Wenk to her house, where he views her expressionist paintings and exotic art works. While she talks of her extreme boredom, Wenk says he is involved in a great adventure, tracking down the great unknown.

We cut to Mabuse's house, with Cara's arriving to warn him about Wenk. Mabuse laughs her fears away, apparently believing that he is omnipotent. Countess Told, meanwhile, agrees to help Wenk.

In disguise, Wenk visits the Palais Andalusia, a private club. He sits at Mabuse's table and Mabuse hypnotizes him. Wenk struggles against the influence and Mabuse, realizing who Wenk is, rushes off. Wenk recovers and follows him, tracking him to his hotel, but Mabuse has already fled.

Hull phones Wenk to tell him that Cara is in league with the master criminal. Wenk, meanwhile, raids the club and Cara is arrested.

Cut to Mabuse and his gang, trying to decide what to do about Cara's arrest. Some of the men want to get Cara back at once, but Mabuse decides to let things be.

Meanwhile, Countess Told is approached by Wenk to help in soliciting information from Cara. He suggests that he pretend to arrest the countess and put her in jail with Cara, hoping that Cara will confide in her. We see the countess enter the jail cell and talk to Cara, but Cara merely weeps and talks of her love for her master. Shortly after this, Countess Told is released from the cell.

We cut next to a party at the Told house. Count Told asks Mabuse what he thinks of expressionism (Told's magnificent collection of expressionist paintings is evident in the rear while the men are talking). Mabuse says expressionism is a gamble--that everything in life is a gamble. Told asks Mabuse to play cards, but he refuses. Countess Told says that her husband never plays, but Mabuse fixes his eyes on Told and he sits down at the card table. Countess Told confesses to Mabuse that she recently had an experience that she did not know existed, namely love. Mabuse scornfully replies that there is no such thing as love--only desire and the wish to possess what you desire. As if to prove his words, Mabuse proceeds to hypnotize and capture Countess Told while her husband, already under hypnosis, plays cards. The first part of the film ends with Mabuse bringing Countess Told to his house and placing her on the bed, saying "She is MINE!"

Part II: INFERNO: EIN SPIEL VON MENSCHEN UNSERER ZEIT
[Inferno: A Play about People of Our Times]

The second part of the film opens with the title "Nights without Sleep," and the following sequence intercuts between several sleepless people: Cara, in her cell, her restless image swaying back and forth over the dark walls; Count Told, in his house; and detective Wenk, in his office.

We cut to Mabuse, also having a sleepless night, due to a rowdy drinking party. Countess Told rests in another room.

Cut back to Count Told standing forlornly by his open door, apparently uncertain of what to do. Cut to Wenk's office. Closing his window against the rain, Wenk sees Count Told standing drenched before his door and rushes out. The camera focuses on the room, showing the white curtains blowing in the wind. Wenk brings Told in.

Meanwhile, Mabuse's party is getting wilder, and Mabuse proclaims himself a giant, bigger than all the rest. We see his gang in various stages of intoxication.

Back in Wenk's office, Told, distressed, confesses to having cheated at cards against his will. A flashback to the game (at the end of Part I of the film) shows Told touching his aching head, as we have seen all Mabuse's victims do. Told tells Wenk that he doesn't ordinarily play cards and yet found himself taking all kinds of risk. When he cheated, his friends left in disgust. Under questioning from Wenk, Told says that Mabuse was the only guest he didn't know. Told believes that his wife has left him because she did not want to live with a cheat.

We cut to Countess Told on the couch in Mabuse's house, awakening suddenly but too dizzy to walk. We see more shots of Mabuse and his group, the party now past its height, empty bottles and other debris about the room, while Mabuse gesticulates wildly.

Wenk advises Told to consult a qualified psychoanalyst. Told thinks of Mabuse and decides to phone him at once. At Mabuse's house, we see him, stumbling drunkenly into Countess Told's room, reaching for her; he is interrupted by Told's call and arranges to go to Told's house the next day.

Following the caption "The Consultation," we see Mabuse with Told, telling him he will take his case only on condition that Told agree to isolate himself completely, not talking to anyone who reminds him of his former self.

We cut to Wenk trying to reach Told and being advised by Told's manservant that Told and his wife have just left on a trip, the countess going to her mother's house.

In Mabuse's house, we see Countess Told trying to escape. Mabuse comes in, and she demands her release, saying that Wenk and her husband will track her down. Mabuse laughs and says that her husband is under his medical care; if she wants him to live, she must not think or speak of him.

Wenk, meanwhile, has come to Cara's jail cell and is trying to persuade her to cooperate with the police. If she will help them, they can help her, since they know she loves Mabuse. Wenk cannot understand why she refuses to give them her boss's name. He insinuates that another woman may have taken her place, hoping jealousy will provoke Cara to confess. She asks for two days to think it over.

Mabuse at his house tells Countess Told that they are about

to leave on a long trip. She begs to be allowed to return to her husband, but Mabuse says he is dead. She tries to escape, but all the doors are locked; she says she would also like to die.

Back at his office, Wenk finds Mabuse waiting for him; he tells Wenk that Told must have been under the influence of a strange criminal will. He asks Wenk if he has heard of the Weltman experiments in mass hypnosis and invites him to the next show. Wenk agrees to go. While Mabuse orders his men to follow Wenk, we see Wenk giving orders to his own men, presumably in preparation for the Weltman performance.

Cut to the next evening and the hall with Weltman performing hypnosis. After a series of experiments designed by Mabuse to disarm Wenk, Weltman asks for volunteers to go up on stage, and Wenk responds and is hypnotized. Weltman writes two sets of instructions on sheets of paper. The one he gives secretly to Wenk involves getting into the car outside and driving over the Melior Cliffs. The instructions that are read aloud simply tell him to leave the hall.

Wenk's men, meanwhile, planted in the hall, are worried about how Wenk looked when he left the hall and follow his car, preventing him just in time from crashing to his death. Wenk now realizes that Mabuse is the great unknown, whom he has been searching for all this time. They go to the nearest police station to get reinforcements.

Cut to Mabuse's house and people preparing for a departure. One man rushes in to tell Mabuse that the house is surrounded. There is a fast-paced sequence, intercutting between the police and Wenk outside, who are shooting at the house, and the men and Mabuse inside shooting from the windows. After most of Mabuse's people are killed, Wenk makes a telephone call to Mabuse asking him to give himself up. Mabuse replies: "I don't recognize your justice; if you want me, come and get me." Wenk tells him that they will get him, even if it means blowing up the house, at which Mabuse laughs maliciously, declaring that they will then also kill Countess Told, who is inside. Wenk is furious on hearing this, and they rush into the house. Mabuse goes to get the countess, but she resists him, and one of Mabuse's men persuades him to forget her and save himself. He just manages to get down the secret passageway before Wenk's men come in.

Cut to Mabuse wading through the secret tunnel to the hideout. Wenk meanwhile comes into the house and finds the countess nearly fainting. Mabuse nears the end of his walk in the tunnel and climbs a ladder. He seals the trap door behind him, only to find that he is locked in his own money factory.

Mabuse now goes mad, being haunted by hallucinations of all the people whom he deceived--Cara, Count Told, Hull. They sit down to play cards, and Told calls Mabuse a cheat. By the time Wenk and his men come in, Mabuse is reduced to babbling incoherently on the floor. They pick him up and take him away.

# The Films: Synopses, Credits, Notes, Reviews

Credits:

| | |
|---|---|
| Director: | Fritz Lang |
| Screenplay: | Fritz Lang, Thea von Harbou, from a novel by Norbert Jacques, published in Berliner Illustrirte Zeitung |
| Photography: | Carl Hoffmann |
| Art Direction: | Carl Stahl Urach (died during the filming of Part I), Otto Hunte, Erich Kettelhut, Karl Vollbrecht |
| Costumes: | Vally Reinecke |
| Cast: | Rudolf Klein-Rogge (Dr. Mabuse), Aud Egede Nissen (Cara Carozza, the dancer), Gertrude Welcker (Countess Told), Alfred Abel (Count Told), Bernhard Goetzke (Detective von Wenk), Paul Richter (Edgar Hull), Robert Forster-Larrinaga (Dr. Mabuse's servant), Hans Adalbert Schlettow (Georg, the chauffeur), Georg John (Pesche), Karl Huszar (Hawasch, manager of the counterfeiting factory), Grete Berger (Fine, Mabuse's servant), Julius Falkenstein (Karsten, Wenk's friend), Lydia Potechina (the Russian woman), Julius E. Herrmann (Schramm, the proprietor), Karl Platen (Told's servant), Anita Berber (dancer), Paul Biensfeldt (man with the pistol), Edgar Pauly (fat man), Lil Dagover, Julie Brandt, Auguste Prasch-Grevenberg, Adele Sandrock, Max Adalbert, Gustav Botz, Heinrich Gotho, Leonhard Haskel, Erner Hubsch, Gottfried Huppertz, Hans Junkermann, Adolf Klein, Erich Pabst, Hans Sternberg, Olaf Storm, Erich Walter, Willi Schmidt-Gentner. |
| Filmed in: | Uco-Film Studios, Berlin, 1921-1922; Part I in 8 weeks, Part II in 9 weeks. |
| Completed: | April 1922 |
| Running Time: | Part I, 120 mins.; Part II, 93 mins. These lengths reflect cut versions; original lengths: Part I, 3496 meters; Part II, 2560 meters. |
| Released: | Part I, 27 April 1922; Part II, 26 May 1922 (both at Ufa Palast am Zoo, Berlin) |

Reviews: (Several reviews are annotated in chapter 4)
New York Times (9 August 1928); F. G. [Fritz Goetz].

41

Vossische Zeitung (Berlin) (28 April and 27 May 1922); Herbert
Ihering, Berliner Börsen-Courier (30 April and 11 June 1922)
(reprinted in his Von Reinhardt bis Brecht, vol. 1.  East
Berlin:  Aufbau, 1958); Berliner Tageblatt (30 April 1922);
Vorwarts (30 April 1922); Kurt Pinthus, Das Tage-Buch (6 May
and 3 June 1922); Fritz Olimsky, Der Kinematograph (7 May and
4 June 1922); Oskar Geller, Der Kinematograph (29 May 1922);
p. s. Vorwärts (28 May 1922); Balthasar [Roland Schacht].
Das Blaue Heft (10 June 1922); Margit Freud, Das Blaue Heft
(24 June 1922); Hans Siemsen, Die Weltbühne (Berlin) (17
August 1922); Die Welt am Montag, 1 May 1922 (quoted in Eisner,
p. 57); Roland Von Berlin (4 May 1922) (quoted in Eisner, p.
58); B. Z. am Mittag (28 April 1922) (praises film for reflecting times while also generalizing, for being art as well as
cinema); Verleihkatalog der Decla-Bioscop, Berlin, p. 13 (says
film is more than a detective film giving picture of the time
and combining all coherently); BFI has National Film Archive
Notes by L. O. Laochaire (comments on links between film and
novel and on influence on Hitchcock's The Man Who Knew Too
Much); BFI also has German notes on the film and Lang himself;
MMA has notes on Dr. Mabuse; E. K. Everson, Theodore Huff
Memorial Film Society Notes, March 16 1965 (MMA:  Everson argues that Lang does not care about content but is happy playing with lights and camera and with bizarre scenes of suspense
and thrill); German Vorwort to Mabuse (MMA:  critic argues
that film is not merely sensational but is about the Zeitgeist
with epic and dramatic dimensions of Mabuse as a fascist dictator type, linking him to the Nazis; also discusses expressionism); Wayne Cozart, Notes, The Thousand Eyes (Carnegie
Hall Cinema); Herbert Birett, Filmstudio (Frankfurt), No. 32
(1961); EV [Franz Everschor], Film-Dienst (5 April 1961);
Ulrich Gregor, Spandauer Volksblatt (13 and 20 December 1964);
Tom Milne, Monthly Film Bulletin, Vol 41, No. 484 (May 1974);
112-113.

10    DIE NIBELUNGEN [The Niebelungen] (1924)
      Part I:  SIEGFRIED
      The original version of the film opens with shots of King
Gunther's court, where a minstrel is singing of Siegfried's
adventures.  (In the 1933 reissue version, titled Siegfried's
Tod [Siegfried's Death], there is music accompanying the credits and opening shots.  A narrator recites the first few
stanzas of the Nibelungen Saga in modern German.)  We then cut
to Siegfried fashioning swords in a cave where his master,
Mime, the smith, tells him that he has taught him all he
knows.  Siegfried is now ready to leave for Gunther's court,
where he can make his fortune.
      The men bring a beautiful white horse for Siegfried, set
him on it, and lead him through the tall woods.  We see shots
of him riding proudly, full of strength and confidence, but
his way is soon blocked by a fierce dragon.  A bloody fight

follows, but Siegfried finally manages to kill the dragon. A bird tells Siegfried that if he bathes in the dragon's blood, he will be immortal. Siegfried does this gleefully, but a leaf falls on his back, leaving a vulnerable spot.

He next comes to the realm of the Nibelungs, ruled by Alberich, who can make himself invisible through the use of the magic helmet. He shows Siegfried his incredible treasure trove, meaning to kill him there, but Siegfried tricks him and kills him instead. As he dies, he curses the treasure and then he turns into stone; Siegfried steals the magic helmet.

We cut back to Gunther's court. Siegfried's arrival, with his twelve vassals, all kings, is announced. Hagen Tronje advises against letting Siegfried enter, but Gunther sees no reason to turn him away, and he is welcomed. At the ceremonies, Kriemhild (Gunther's sister) and Siegfried fall in love at first sight. In her room later, Kriemhild tells her mother, Queen Ute, of her love for Siegfried and also of a dark dream she had in which two black eagles fought over a white dove.

Shortly after this, Siegfried comes to ask Gunther for Kriemhild's hand. Gunther agrees on condition that Siegfried help him win the hand of the warriorlike Queen of Iceland, Brunhild, who will marry only the man who can vanquish her. When the Burgundians enter her Hall, Brunhild is attracted to Siegfried, whom she assumes is her wooer. Through his magic powers, Siegfried manages to conquer Brunhild after a long series of contests. When Brunhild realizes she is to marry Gunther, she is disappointed and says that she will return only as his prisoner, not his wife.

Back in Gunther's kingdom, the two couples are married amid splendor, and Siegfried and Gunther swear to be bloodbrothers. Gunther asks for Siegfried's help once more to win Brunhild as wife for him. Siegfried enters Brunhild's room, disguised as Gunther, and by his strength manages to wrest from her the bracelet that signifies her virginity. Gunther then appears and Brunhild submits to him. Siegfried meanwhile goes to Kriemhild and they embrace passionately.

Soon after this, Kriemhild finds the bracelet in Siegfried's room and Siegfried tells her the story of how he came to have it. He also tells Kriemhild the story of the battle with the dragon, of how the leaf fell on one spot, making him vulnerable only there.

Brunhild, jealous of Siegfried's love for Kriemhild, attempts to undercut Gunther's relationship to him. On the cathedral steps, Siegfried is placed above her, and Brunhild asks why a vassel should go higher. She calls Kriemhild "wife of a vassel," and, enraged, Kriemhild blurts out the story of how Siegfried in fact won her for Gunther. Enraged in turn, Brunhild pretends that Siegfried slept with her when he won the bracelet.

Hagen, jealous all along of Gunther's closeness with Siegfried and of the people's attraction to him, plots to have

Siegfried murdered. Gunther, believing what Brunhild says, weakly goes along, despite the bloodbrother pact. Hagen then goes to Kriemhild and, pretending that there is going to be war and that he wants to protect Siegfried, asks her where Siegfried's vulnerable spot is. Kriemhild tells him and agrees to sew a cross on Siegfried's coat marking the spot.

The next day, a big hunting expedition is planned. We see Siegfried joyfully getting ready, full of youthful energy. Kriemhild tells him not to go on the hunt because a dream has left her full of foreboding. But Siegfried brushes all her fears away and they kiss. She last sees him standing beneath a tree in full blossom.

Hagen is planning to murder Siegfried during the hunt. Gunther, although clearly upset and unwilling, does nothing to stop Hagen, and Siegfried is hit by an arrow in his vulnerable spot as he bends to drink from a fresh fountain bursting with spring flowers.

The hunting party returns carrying Siegfried's body, which is placed in state in the castle. When Hagen enters the room, Kriemhild sees blood coming from the wound, a sign that the murderer is present. She realizes that this is Hagen's work and demands revenge, but since Gunther agreed to the murder he will not do anything, and the other members of the family must stick by their King.

Brunhild, at first delighted to hear that Siegfried is dead, now tells Gunther that she lied, and that he killed his blood-brother for nothing. But, unable to endure what she has brought about, Brunhild goes to Siegfried's bier and kills herself. The last shot of this part of the film shows Kriemhild entering the chapel where Siegfried is lying next to Brunhild and kneeling down to mourn for her lover.

Part II:  KRIEMHILDS RACHE [Kriemhild's Revenge]

The second part of Die Nibelungen begins with a brief review of the main events of the first part. The action starts with Kriemhild's accusing Hagen of murdering Siegfried, while Gunther and the members of the court are standing around Siegfried's bier. She demands justice. Gerenot, Gunther's younger brother, however, says that they must remain loyal to one another as Burgundians. Gunther passively assents to do nothing, since he was partially involved in the murder and benefitted politically from it. Kriemhild, now dressed in black, vows vengeance on Hagen.

Some months afterwards, Rüdiger von Bechlarn arrives from King Etzel, leader of the Huns, to ask for Kriemhild's hand in marriage. Gunther, weak and broken, agrees. Kriemhild, full of hate, leaves the court without looking back and rides off through the snowladen forests. When she comes to the place where Siegfried was murdered, she gets off her horse and, crying bitterly, gathers some of the earth into a handkerchief to carry with her to the land of the Huns.

Although Kriemhild despises the Huns for their barbaric way
of life, which contrasts strongly with the elegant, sophisticated Burgundian world, she agrees to marry Etzel, who vows to
defend her against any wrongs. Kriemhild gives birth to a son,
whom Etzel dotes on. Shortly afterwards, Kriemhild invites
her brother to Etzel's court. When they arrive, Etzel receives
them with due honor, preparing a table for them in the main
hall. The men drink together while Kriemhild looks on, revengeful and angry. When Etzel refuses to kill Hagen, since
the Burgundians are his guests, Kriemhild gets one of the Huns
to start a wild party in their underground caves. Etzel meanwhile, against Kriemhild's wishes, asks that his son be brought
into the hall for Gunther and Hagen to see. Hagen plays with
the child, but notes that he does not look as though he will
live long.

The scene in the hall is intercut with the scene of
Burgundians and Huns engaging in a wild party. A fight breaks
out between the two groups when one of the Huns insults a
Burgundian. The Huns go wild and break into the hall, killing
as they go. Chaos breaks out and the Burgundians begin to
fight for their lives. In the uproar, Hagen kills Kriemhild's
child; utterly broken by this, Etzel now also vows revenge and
war is declared. The Burgundians finally manage to secure the
hall for themselves and lock themselves in. Kriemhild offers
to spare the rest of the Burgundians in exchange for Hagen,
but is refused. She sets the hall on fire, and one by one her
brothers inside die. Hagen, however, manages to survive, but
when he staggers out into the open from the ruined hall,
Kriemhild kills him herself. She is then killed by Hildebrand,
one of the Huns who hated her for the devastation she had
wrought.

Credits:
| | |
|---|---|
| Director: | Fritz Lang |
| Screenplay: | Thea von Harbou and Fritz Lang, based on Das Nibelungenlied and Norse sagas. |
| Photography: | Carl Hoffman, Günther Rittau, and Walter Ruttmann for the animated "Dream of the Falcon" sequence |
| Art Direction: | Otto Hunte, Erich Kettelhut, Karl Vollbrecht |
| Music: | Gottfried Huppertz |
| Costumes: | Paul Gerd Guderian (who died during the production), Anne Willkomm; armor, costumes, and weapons of the Huns were manufactured by Heinrich Umlauff in the workshop of his Volksmuseum in Hamburg. |
| Make-Up: | Otto Genath |

Cast:

Paul Richter (Siegfried), Margarethe Schön (Kriemhild), Theodor Loos (King Gunther), Hanna Ralph (Brunhild), Georg John (Mime, the Smith, and Alberich in I, Blaodel in II), Gertrud Arnold (Queen Ute), Hans Carl Müller (Gerenot), Erwin Biswanger (Giselher), Bernhard Goetzke (Volker von Alzey), Hans Adalbert Schlettow (Hagen Tronje), Rudolf Rittner (Markgraf Rüdiger von Bechlarn), Hardy von Francois (Dankwart), Fritz Alberti (Dietrich von Bern), Georg August Koch (Hildebrand), Rudolph Klein-Rogge (King Etzel), Hubert Heinrich (Werbel), Grete Berger (a Hun), Frida Richard (lecturer), Georg Jurowski (priest), Iris Roberts (page), Rose Lichtenstein

Filmed at:

Decla-Bioscop-Ufa Studios, Berlin (Decla-Bioscop and Ufa merged during the production), 1922-1924

Completed:

January 1924

Running Time:

Shortened versions most often distributed: I, 92 mins.; II, 97 mins. Original Length I, 3216 meters; II, 3576 meters.

Released:

Siegfried, 14 February 1924; Kriemhilds Rache, 26 April 1924 (both at Ufa Palast am Zoo, Berlin)

Notes:

Eisner comments that the shortened version of Siegfried (2743 meters) was released by Ufa in 1925 with music from Wagner's Der Ring des Nibelungen and as arranged by Hugo Reisenfeld, while in 1928 a shortened version of Kriemhild's Rache appeared, also 2743 meters. In 1933 Ufa released an even shorter version (688 meters) of Siegfried, which Prinzler notes had a new title, Siegfrieds Tod with voiceover by Theodore Loos and the Wagner music again, arranged by Franz Biermann. Eisner notes: "Needless to say, these shorter versions, particularly with Wagner's music, which Lang dislikes, were not authorized by the director." Enno Patalas in the Munich Stadtmuseum is attempting to restore as much of the original footage as possible and is preparing new titles.

Reviews:  (Several reviews are annotated in Chapter 4)
Herbert Ihering, Berliner Börsen-Courier (15 February and 1 May
1924); Erich Vogeler, Berliner Tageblatt, (15 February 1924);
M. J. [Monty Jacobs], Vossische Zeitung (Berlin) (15 February
1924); H. Fr. [Heinrich Fraenkel] Lichtbildbühne (16 February)
1924); Ernst Ulitzsch, Der Kinematograph (17 February 1924);
Frank Aschau, Die Weltbühne (Berlin) (28 February 1924);
o. V., Der Kinematograph (4 May 1924); Balthasar [Roland
Schacht], Das Blaue Heft (1 March 1924); C. K. [Friedrich
Schnack], Vossische Zeitung (Berlin) (30 April 1924); E. H.,
Berliner Tageblatt (2 May 1924); Kurt Pinthus, Das Tage-Buch
(3 May 1924); Remy M. Hardt, Der Kritiker (Berlin) (May-June
1924); H. U. [Hans Ungureit], Frankfurter Rundschau (13 April
1962); H. P., Der Bildwart, No. 3 (15 April 1924); Mordaunt
Hall, New York Times (24 August 1925); review from a British
newspaper, Berlin Correspondent, written on opening night of
the film in Berlin (BFI: Reviewer describes the opening as a
big national event as brilliant as any opera premiere; this
shows the support being given good films.  For Lang, the
reviewer says, nature spoils art if a certain atmosphere is
desired); another British newspaper review (BFI:  Reviewer
notes the differences between Wagner's Ring cycle and Lang's
version; he praises the sets and fairyland atmosphere while
regretting lack of dramatic effect).  The BFI has a whole
series of notes on the film from different archives and theaters:  Staatliches Film Archiv (of East Germany) Notes;
Italian Film Notes; National Film Theatre Notes; Irish Film
Society Notes; Deutscher Filmkunsttheater Notes, discussing
background to the film, the actors, Lang's career, the sets,
production; (Film Society Program Notes, London, (28 November
1926); excerpts from English and American reviews, Literary
Digest (September 1925); Edward Shanks, Outlook (London)
(28 June 1924); Stark Young, New Republic (13 August 1930);
Joseph R. Fliesler, ed., Siegfried (compilation of reviews and
original articles by Fritz Lang and others, dealing with various aspects of the film's conception and production; copy
available at the New York Public Library, Music Division);
Joseph Wood Krutch, Nation (16 September 1925); Exceptional
Photoplays (October 1925); New York Times (Kriemhild's Revenge),
(16 October 1928).  Discussion and documentation of Die
Nibelungen in Cinémathèque de Belgique (18 October 1955) (MMA:
the treatment includes discussion of the myth and early epic
of Die Nibelungen, the script, comparisons with Eisenstein's
Nevsky and Ivan, the visual style of the film, including discussion of its expressionism; there are quotations from critics
and film historians); Jacques Rivette (short review on occasion
of Cinémathèque [France] showing of Kriemhilds Rache; Rivette
complains about the inadequate print and does not like von
Harbou's script, but he admires the film, noting that with it
Lang became a director of genius).  Klaus Eder, Film (Velber
bei Hannover), No. 2 (1967); P. Jouvert, "Les Images de

Kriemhild." <u>Cinématographe</u>, No. 23 (5-8 January 1977).

11   METROPOLIS (1927)
     The film opens with a series of dissolves of skyscrapers
and elevated highways.  Superimposed on these are shots of
machines turning and factory whistles blowing.  A montage sequence of workers changing shifts follows, and we see a new
shift of workers walking down tunnels to the lifts and the
tired ones clumping home, heads bowed.  Cut to the world of
the leisure class above, and Freder, son of the master of
Metropolis, running races in a stadium.  He plays with his
friends in an elaborate pleasure garden, apparently free from
all cares, until they are interrupted by the sudden appearance
of Marie, a fragile girl in poor clothes, standing in the huge
doorway with a cluster of thin, white-faced children around
her.  Freder and Marie stare at each other, and, after she is
hustled away, Freder desperately tries to find out who she is.
On being told that she comes from the workers' world below,
Freder determines to follow her there.
     Freder is down in the machine area, watching the tired
workers endlessly manipulate the levers that run the machines.
One worker, unable to continue, allows his machine to go out
of control and there is an explosion.  Freder has a vision of
Moloch, whose enormous mouth is devouring people alive.  This
merges into a vision of an ancient tyrannical God and men in
chains climbing up endless steps.  As the smoke clears, Freder's
vision ends, and he sees the new workers taking the place of
the others, while the dead men are carried off on stretchers.
     Above ground, the city life continues, with planes flying
and railways moving along the elevated tracks.  In the heart
of the city, Joh Fredersen, master of Metropolis, is figuring
out problems, while his staff take down moving numbers from a
series of screens.  Freder enters the room, distraught, anxious
to speak with his father, who finally turns to him.  Freder
attacks his father for allowing the workers to continue under
such wretched conditions, but Joh says that nothing is important except the brain that has brought them wealth.  The hands
belong in the depths.  We cut to workers going down in their
lifts and then back to Joh's office and a foreman bringing some
plans found in the pockets of men killed in the explosion
Freder witnessed.  Josephat, Joh's right-hand man, looks nervous and is then fired for failing to stop the plotting.
Shocked at this also, Freder runs after Josephat and asks for
his help in getting back underground.
     Once below again, Freder, seeing a worker about to faint,
changes clothes with him and takes his place at the machines.
Joh, meanwhile, perturbed about the workers' plot, has also
come below ground to speak with Rotwang, an inventor; the only
person Joh respects and fears, Rotwang is also the only one to
remain outside of the entire system that is Metropolis.  He
lives alone in his own medieval-looking house.  Rotwang shows

Joh his progress on the robot he is making to replace human workers. Joh watches in fascination as the female robot gets up and walks; he is pleased with the fact that the machine lacks a soul.

Joh next asks Rotwang about the plans they have found and Rotwang agrees to show Joh the meeting place in the catacombs. In the machine room, meanwhile, the whistles have blown and the new shift has taken over. Exhausted, Freder nevertheless joins a large group of workers who, following the plans, are evidently going to some sort of meeting. We intercut between Rotwang and Joh making their way down the passages and the workers congregating in a large space with an altar-like structure at one end where Marie is standing holding a cross and a sword. The men kneel, and Marie relates the story of Babel, while images of her tale appear on the screen. Streams of laboring men are carrying huge slabs of stone for the construction of an enormous tower, while a richly clad man commands and whips them. Marie talks of the need for a mediator to link head and hands and calls upon the men there to find such a person.

Greatly moved by Marie's tale, and already in love with her, Freder vows to be the mediator himself. He stays behind to talk to her and declare his love. They plan to meet in the cathedral the next day. Through a hole in the brick, Joh and Rotwang have seen everything, and once Joh has left, Rotwang sets about capturing Marie. He chases her through the passages, pinning her down with his torch beam, and finally traps her in his house, whose electronic doors lack handles.

Not finding Marie the next day Freder searches everywhere for her, above and below ground. Hearing her screaming from Rotwang's house, he goes in and is trapped by the automatic doors.

Rotwang begins his work of transforming the robot into Marie's likeness. Marie is strapped down in a scientific laboratory, among the bottles and dials (in a scene that was to be imitated in many Frankenstein movies), and slowly the robot takes on her likeness. Freder, meanwhile, is suddenly able to open a door; he goes upstairs into Rotwang's library, only to find his father and the robot (whom he takes for Marie) apparently making love. He faints, and we next see him asleep in his own room at home, being taken care of by nurses. Joh comes in, on his way to a party, and tenderly kisses his son. At the party, the robot is to be tested for its authenticity in an elaborately staged striptease scene. It succeeds magnificently, and Joh and Rotwang are now ready to let the creature stir up trouble among the workers. Freder, meanwhile, troubled by visions of his father and Marie, cannot rest, and decides to go below ground to find out what is happening.

We cut to the robot beginning to incite the workers to violence. Führer-like, she has no difficulty persuading the people to wreck the machines and go on a rampage. Freder arrives

to persuade them that the robot is not the real Marie, but
they do not believe him and continue with the destruction.
Men and women have all deserted their homes to join the revolt,
and now the children begin to creep down the stairs, since
their homes are being flooded. At this point, the real Marie
finally manages to escape from Rotwang's house and arrives in
time to begin taking the children to safety on a central platform in the housing courtyard. Freder and Josephat now appear
and together they manage to bring the children out of danger.

Joh, meanwhile, has remained cool and calm in his vast
office, looking over his creation and unaware of the extent of
destruction initiated by himself. When he realizes that
Metropolis is being destroyed, he panics and rushes out to
look for his son. In the courtyard, meanwhile, the workers
have made a huge bonfire for the robot Marie, and Freder is
desperate, thinking it to be his beloved. Rotwang, furious
at the destruction of his machine, suddenly glimpes the real
Marie in the cathedral. He runs in after her and chases her
on the cathedral roof. Freder rushes up to help; Rotwang now
chases him, and they have a fight on the parapets. Joh Fredersen
anxiously watches and prays below for the safety of his son.
When Rotwang falls to his death, Marie brings Freder to act as
mediator between Joh Fredersen and the foreman, representing
the workers. She finally achieves her goal of linking head
and hands through the heart.

Credits:
Director:                    Fritz Lang
Screenplay:                  Fritz Lang, Thea von Harbou
Photography:                 Karl Freund, Günther Rittau
Special Effects:             Eugene Schüfftan
Art Direction:               Otto Hunte, Erich Kettelhut, Karl
                             Vollbrecht
Sculptures:                  Walter Schultze-Mittendorff
Costumes:                    Anne Willkomm
Music:                       Gottfried Huppertz
Cast:                        Brigitte Helm (Maria/the mechanical
                             Maria), Alfred Abel (Joh Fredersen),
                             Gustav Fröhlich (Freder), Rudolf
                             Klein-Rogge (Rotwang), Fritz Rasp
                             (Slim), Theodor Loos (Josaphat/
                             Joseph), Heinrich George (Grot, the
                             foreman), Olaf Storm (Jan), Hanns
                             Leo Reich (Marinus), Heinrich Gotho
                             (master of ceremonies), Margarete
                             Lanner (woman in the car), Max Dietze/
                             Georg John/Walter Kühle/Arthur
                             Reinhard/Erwin Vater (workers), Grete
                             Berger/Olly Böheim/Ellen Frey/Lisa
                             Gray/Rose Lichtenstein/Helene Weigel
                             (female workers); Beatrice Garga/
                             Anny Hintze/Margarete Lanner/ Helen
                             von Münchhofen/Hilde Woitscheff

|   |   |
|---|---|
| | (women in the eternal garden), Fritz Alberti (Robot), 750 secondary actors and over 30,000 extras |
| Filmed at: | Ufa Studios, Berlin, 1925-26, in 310 days and 60 nights |
| Running Time: | Original length was 4189 meters; when originally shown, the film ran for two hours, but after its release it was cut to 3170 meters both abroad and in Germany. No complete master copy now exists, but the Staatliches Archiv (East Berlin) has made a new copy compiling all remaining footage. |
| Released: | 10 January 1927 (Ufa Palast am Zoo, Berlin) |
| Notes: | According to Lotte Eisner, the novel Metropolis seems to have been written (as it was published) after the film rather than the film's having been based on the novel by Harbou. |

Reviews: (Several of these are annotated in Chapter 4)
Fred Hildebrandt, Berliner Tageblatt (11 January 1927); E. S. P., Lichtbildbühne (11 January 1927); Herbert Ihering, Berliner Börsen-Courier (11 January 1927); R. A., Die Rote Fahne (12 January 1927); M. J. [Monty Jacobs], Vossische Zeitung (Berlin) (12 January 1927); Kurt Pinthus, Das Tage-Buch (15 January 1927); o. V., Der Kinematograph (16 January 1927); g., Vorwärts (16 January 1927); Axel Eggebrecht, Die Weltbühne (19 January 1927); W. H. [Willy Haas], Die Literarische Welt (Berlin) (21 January 1927); Rudolf Arnheim, Das Stachelschwein (1 February 1927); Balthasar [Roland Schacht], Das Blaue Heft (1 February 1927); Ev. [Franz Everschor], Film-Dienst (19 March 1959); H. G. Wells, New York Times (17 April 1927), trans. in Frankfurter Zeitung (3 May 1927); Hans Siemsen, Die Weltbühne (14 June 1927); Mordaunt Hall, New York Times (7 March 1927); RUR, Variety (MMA clipping: finds film weird and fantastic, but interesting); Frank Vreeland, New York Telegram (7 March 1927) (MMA clipping: positive review, praising the film's serious subject, the acting, photography. The film shows that movies can be art); Review in New York Evening Journal (18 January 1927); Review in New York World Telegram (24 April 1937) (MMA: unfavorable review on occasion of film's revival; cinema has moved so far ahead that the film is disappointing now. Lang has gone on to become a brilliant director, however); Review from Cinémathèque de Belgigue (MMA); Thea von Harbou, "Eine Szene wird geprobt," Uhu (Berlin), No. 11 (26 August 1927); MMA has a press release with stills and an attempt to convey the mood of the film; German notices, some reviews and more comments by Lang and Harbou about the film (MMA); British Film Institute Program Notes (film is praised for its visual

effects, but said to be absurd politically; economic issues
are ludicrously falsified); W. R. Nelson, Program Notes,
1950-1951 (MMA: links Metropolis to the trick films of Méliès,
fantasy films, and science fiction films that emerged in the
sound era, but finds the film lacking in the harsh realism the
Russians are good at); The BFI has several interesting, but
undated and unreferenced, clippings: a French review sees the
film as an odd mixture of realism and romanticism, while the
social message is praised and the stylization said to bring
out the themes more clearly; a British reviewer complains about
the censorship and the producer's concern about time; he fears
for film as an art form in such a situation; Richard Coombs,
Monthly Film Bulletin (April 1976); J. Romains, L'Avant-Scène,
No. 197 (1 December 1977), pp. 29-30.

12   SPIONE [Spies] (1928)
The film opens with the murder of a diplomat. A newspaper
headline tells of his death and of stolen secret documents.
Irate, harassed police are shown yelling into telephones, and
an informer is murdered while on the brink of giving vital information to a high official. Tremaine enters a post-office
with another man, and writes a message in code. He gives this
to the official, and leaves; the first man returns, picks up
the blotting paper on which Tremaine had written, and reads
the message. It's to the Jason Secret Service, saying Tremaine
is being trailed by spies but will report the next day.
We cut to Burton Jason, head of Secret Service, apparently
rather old and inefficient, reading a note from the Minister
of the Interior to the effect that his service must do better
or heads will roll. An aide announces that Tremaine has been
picked up, but, as Tremaine enters, he knocks the aide out,
saying he is a traitor. The aide refuses to say whom he works
for, declaring that he'd rather die.
Jason tells Tremaine that the spy leader is the most dangerous man in Europe and that he must be caught. Although Jason
has lost many men already on this case, Tremaine is not afraid.
We cut to Haighi, the crippled leader, at his secret receiving station in a bank. He receives a card, and Sonja, one
of his top agents, comes in. He asks her to cover Tremaine,
who is staying at the Hotel Olympia.
We cut to Tremaine, entering his hotel room after a night's
work. He hears a gunshot, and suddenly Sonja bursts into the
room, claiming that she has shot someone. While people gather
outside, Tremaine, taken with Sonja's beauty, hides her in an
adjoining room. The police begin to search his room. When
Tremaine indicates it's a discreet matter, the police leave.
Tremaine delays going to Sonja until he has gotten out of his
tramp outfit and is handsomely clothed; they fall in love
immediately, and Tremaine wants to help her. But when he departs for a moment, she escapes, leaving a note saying that it
would be better for them not to see each other again.

Cut to Sonja's telling Haighi what happened and begging to
be taken off the case, but he insists she stay on it until she
has obtained every detail of the secret treaty. He reminds
her of the fate of her brother and father, sent to their deaths
by Tremaine's government, and notes that Tremaine knows where
the treaty is to be signed. Forced by Haighi, Sonja writes a
letter to Tremaine resuming their relationship, and we see him
arrive at her house with flowers. They are more in love than
ever.

Cut to the Café Danielle where Tremaine and Sonja are dancing. After a man hands her a note, Sonja looks concerned and
leaves the floor; we see Haighi and his nurse at a table. Letting her necklace fall, Sonja sends Tremaine to look for it,
and disappears. Tremaine, puzzled, follows her to her house,
only to find that it is empty.

Haighi berates Sonja for her love for Tremaine, while
Tremaine gets drunk in a bar. Matsumoto, Japanese diplomat
and secret agent, tells Tremaine that Sonja is a spy. Sonja
is replaced on the case by Kitty, whom we see sitting provoca-
tively on Haighi's desk. Kitty is to seduce Matsumoto, who
has copies of the treaty, and steal them for Haighi.

We cut to the diplomat, who is going home in a terrible
storm. He finds Kitty dressed in rags, huddled in a doorway,
and takes her with him. There Kitty pretends to be innocent
and naively seductive, and Matsumoto is clearly tempted. She
begs to stay and work for him, and he agrees to keep her.

Haighi is seen having breakfast; Sonja is called to him and
Haighi announces that he will have every copy of the treaty in
his hands that night. We cut to Matsumoto's handing out copies
of the treaty to men to deliver by hand. Haighi, meanwhile,
is drinking champagne in a gay mood; he hands Sonja a glass
with pearls around the base, but Sonja says she cannot be
bought that way. Haighi declares his insane desire to control
the world and proclaims his omnipotence. The stolen copies of
the treaty begin to arrive, but each one turns out to be a fake.
Furious, Haighi throws a fit, but still seems to think he can
win.

At the Japanese diplomat's house, Kitty watches while
Matsumoto packs his suitcase and places the real copy of the
treaty in a special compartment. She then pretends to be
heartbroken at his leaving and finally succeeds in seducing
him. When the diplomat wakes up, Kitty is gone and so is the
treaty. Heartbroken by the deception and his failure to safeguard the treaty, he kneels in front of a statue of Buddha and
commits hara-kiri. Kitty, meanwhile, is enjoying her success
with Haighi, who gives her the pearls originally meant for
Sonja.

Haighi persuades Sonja to do one last thing for him--namely,
take some secret information out of the country. She agrees,
on condition that no harm come to Tremaine.

Jason, meanwhile, is still under pressure from his boss to

succeed in keeping the treaty safe.  He and Tremaine visit
another agent, Nemo, who does a nightly clown act and is, in
fact, Haighi in yet another disguise.  Nemo assures Jason that
he has found a way to get the treaty safely deposited.

Setting out on her journey, Sonja sees Tremaine in the next
train; she happens to notice the number of his carriage, 33-133;
she later recalls Haighi receiving a note about that carriage.
Tremaine, meanwhile, makes himself comfortable, but looks nos-
talgically at the necklace Sonja had lost that night at the
Café Danielle when he last saw her.  Haighi's people, who are
waiting for Tremaine, agree to do their work once the train
enters the tunnel.  Tremaine is woken by Sonja's necklace falling on him as he sleeps; he realizes the train has stopped.
We have seen the men release Tremaine's carriage, so that we
know he is stuck alone in the tunnel.  When he comes out, he
sees another train rushing toward him at a fierce rate.

We cut to Sonja, whose train has come into a station.  She
hears of the crash, recalls Haighi's face and the number, and
rushes to the scene.  She rescues Tremaine just as Haighi's
agent is about to ensure his death.  The lovers are joyfully
reunited; they chase after the agent, whose car crashes.
Tremaine and Jason next go to Haighi's bank, having figured
that he is behind everything.  Haighi, meanwhile, has captured
Sonja and threatens to blow up the bank if the police are not
called off.  Tremaine takes the gamble of finding Haighi's
hideout in the twelve minutes Haighi allotted.  They break
through to Sonja just in time to save her, but Haighi has fled.
Tremaine and Jason realize that Nemo the clown and Haighi
must be one, and come to arrest him at his nightly performance;
when Haighi realizes the police have him cornered, he substitutes a real gun in his act, and kills himself on stage.

Credits:

| | |
|---|---|
| Producer: | Fritz Lang |
| Director: | Fritz Lang |
| Screenplay: | Fritz Lang, Thea von Harbou, based on Harbou's novel |
| Photography: | Fritz Arno Wagner |
| Art Direction: | Otto Hunte, Karl Vollbrecht |
| Music: | Werner R. Heymann |
| Cast: | Rudolph Klein-Rogge (Haighi), Gerda Maurus (Sonja), Lien Deyers (Kitty), Louis Ralph (Morrier), Craighall Sherry (Police Chief Jason), Willy Fritsch (No. 326, detective), Paul Hörbiger (Franz, the chauffeur), Lupu Pick (Dr. Masimoto), Fritz Rasp (Colonel Jellusic), Hertha von Walther (Lady Leslane), Julius Falkenstein (Hotel manager), Georg John (train conductor), Paul Rehkopf |

|  | (hoodlum), Hermann Vallentin, Grete Berger. |
|---|---|
| Filmed by: | Universum Film, AG, in the Neubabelsberg Studios, Berlin, December 1927 to March 1928 in 15 weeks |
| Original Length: | 4364 meters |
| Released: | By Ufa, 22 March 1928 (Ufa Palast am Zoo, Berlin) |

Reviews:
Roland Schacht, B. Z. am Mittag (23 March 1928); Hi. [Fred Hildebrandt], Berliner Tageblatt (23 March 1928); Herbert Ihering, Berliner Börsen-Courier (23 March 1928); Betz (Hans-Walther), Der Film (Berlin) (24 March 1928); o. V., Der Kinematograph (25 March 1928); Kurt Pinthus, Das Tage-Buch (31 March 1928); Paul Ickes, Die Filmwoche (4 April 1928); Balthasar [Roland Schacht], Das Blaue Heft (15 April 1928); Rudolf Arnheim, Das Stachelschwein (May 1928); New York Times (10 August 1928 and 5 March 1929); Erich Hellmund-Waldow, Close-Up (London) (8 June 1928); New York Post (4 March 1929) (MMA: rather facetious review, but ends by noting that the film is perhaps not so fantastic, given real Berlin agents); Variety (25 April 1933) (MMA: the film is having a good run although made before Nazis came to power, because it fits in with trends in public opinion); Review from Münchner Merkur (22 October 1957); William K. Everson, Notes for New Yorker Film Society (18 September 1961) (MMA); Notes from a showing at the Metropolitan Museum, New York, including one from Cinémathèque Française (MMA); Mark Langer, Notes (20 January 1977) (MMA: Langer comments on links with earlier Dr. Mabuse, but sees a development in directing style; the sets are bare, and the earlier tendency toward mysticism is avoided. Haighi is a more realistic criminal and anticipates Lang's later treatment of crime in M. The film is a transitional link between Lang's neoromantic epics and his later extrapolation from current events); Jonathan Rosenbaum, Monthly Film Bulletin, (May 1976).

13   DIE FRAU IM MOND [Woman in the Moon] (1929)
After the caption "Thirty years ago, Professor Manfeldt, a famous expert," we see a shot of Manfeldt lecturing to fellow scientists. He suggests that there are gold deposits on the moon and predicts that the day will come when space ships will fly there. The other scientists ridicule him. The second title, "Today, Professor Manfeldt, an old man," precedes a shot of him disheveled and crazy, still trying to test his theories. Wolf Helius is trying to finance the construction of a space ship and has come to tell Manfeldt that he will have to bring in some businessmen. He mentions that Hans Windegger, an engineer, and Frieda Velten, an astronomy student,

who have just become engaged, are interested in Helius's undertaking. We cut to some financiers very interested in the project, headed by Turner, who has obtained all the information for the group. He shows them charts and designs and a film taken by an unmanned rocket, complete with photos of the far side of the moon. The businessmen agree that if they are to remain in control of the gold on earth they should have the gold on the moon as well.

We return to Helius, telling Manfeldt rather reluctantly that they will have to involve these men, but saying that at least Manfeldt will have his dream fulfilled. Manfeldt gives Helius the worn copy of his study of the moon, and Helius angrily tears up a notice of Frieda and Hans's engagement. The financiers and Hans do not get along, but eventually Helius makes an agreement that permits Turner's presence on the trip.

On the night of the spaceship's take off, crowds come to watch, and newsmen inspect the ship inside and out. Finally all is ready and the space ship is launched. The take off is dramatic; all those on board are buffeted about and become unconscious; Helius gradually wakes up and goes to see if Frieda is all right. Seeing them together, Hans becomes jealous, while Helius, ashamed of his feelings for Frieda (which he can barely hide), slinks away.

In the storeroom, Frieda discovers a small boy, Gustav, who had sneaked on board. There are several shots of Turner, looking very sinister as he gets up and combs his hair and plays with the boy's rucksack. Frieda and Gustav look at some science fiction magazines he has with him and then they see the earth far behind them. Manfeldt, meanwhile, keeps his eyes glued to the telescope, looking at the stars. When the moon's craters come into view, they all strap themselves in again.

Hans begins to get nervous and suggests they don't land at all. He blames Helius for getting them into this and for his ambition. Helius calms him down, and then we see shots of the landing, with the moon's surface rushing toward the craft. There is an explosion as the ship crashes deep into the moon's surface. Pointing to all the damaged equipment, Hans notes that "the only thing we will find on the moon is death."

Since some water casks were ruptured on landing, Manfeldt goes off to look for water with his divining rod. The others all come out of the ship, and Turner offers to find both water and Manfeldt. As Hans and Gustav dig out the craft, Frieda bandages Helius' hand, hurt in the landing, and the love between the two is evident.

Uneasy about Manfeldt, Helius also goes out after him, taking Gustav along. We cut to Manfeldt going over hot springs, with Turner following behind. As Manfeldt enters a huge cave, the word "Gold" is superimposed on the screen in big letters; he discovers gold rocks and begins to hug them until, turning round, he sees Turner following. He loses his footing and falls over the cliff to his death. Turner can hardly believe his eyes and greedily reaches for the gold. Helius and Gustav now come into the cave calling for Manfeldt. Uninterested in the gold, they are shocked to see the old man's body at the bottom of the cliff.

Turner, meanwhile, returns to the rocket and knocks out Hans, tying his hands. Frieda is inside developing film when Turner begins to creep up into the ship; she tries to escape from him, understanding what he is about. While Helius and Gustav slowly make their way home, suspecting nothing, Hans, having freed himself, struggles with Turner, overcoming him. The dying Turner shoots at the oxygen tanks, thinking to get his revenge on the others by preventing their return to earth. Hans and Helius inspect the damage and realize that only one person need stay behind. The men draw lots to see which one it will be. Panicking when he loses, Hans weeps in terror and grief.

Helius decides to drug both Frieda and Hans and stay behind himself, showing Gustav first how to lift the rocket into the air. He says goodbye to the boy and goes outside. We see Gustav at the controls inside while Helius watches the ship lifting off from the moon into outer space. Standing there alone, he begins to weep, and then starts as Freida emerges from behind the supplies; they embrace tenderly as the last caption notes that there is no greater proof of love than this.

Credits:

| | |
|---|---|
| Producer: | Fritz Lang |
| Director: | Fritz Lang |
| Screenplay: | Thea von Harbou, from her novel |
| Photography: | Curt Courant, Oskar Fischinger, Otto Kanturek |
| Special Effects: | Konstantin Tschetwerikoff |
| Art Direction: | Otto Hunte, Emil Hasler, Karl Vollbrecht |
| Backdrop Photographs: | Horst von Harbou |
| Music: | Willi Schmidt-Gentner |
| Technical Advisors: | Dr. Gustav Wolff, Joseph Danilowatz, Prof. Herman Oberth, Willy Ley |
| Cast: | Klaus Pohl (Prof. Georg Manfeldt), Willy Fritsch (Wolf Helius), Gustav von Wangenheim (Engineer Hans Windegger), Gerda Maurus (Frieda Velten), Gustl Stark-Gstettenbaur (Gustav), Fritz Rasp (Walt Turner), Tilla Durieux/Hermann Vallentin/Max Zilzer/Mahmud Terja Bey/Borwin Walth (Financiers), Margarete Kupfer (Mrs. Hippolt), Max Maximilian (Grotjan, Helius's chauffeur), Alexa von Porembsky (Flower vendor), Gerhard |

|  |  |
|---|---|
|  | Dammann (Foreman), Heinrich Gotho, Karl Platen, Alfred Loretto, Edgar Pauly, Josephine (the Mouse). |
| Filmed at: | Universum Film, Berlin in 1929, in 13 weeks |
| Original Length: | 4356 meters |
| Released: | 15 October 1929 (Ufa Palast am Zoo, Berlin). |
| Note: | Eisner remarks that Frau im Mond has also been known in the United States and England under the titles By Rocket to the Moon and Girl in the Moon. |

Reviews: (Several of these are annotated in Chapter 4)
Blass, Ernst, Berliner Tageblatt (16 October 1929); Ihering, Herbert, Berliner Börsen-Courier (16 October 1929); Pol, Heinz, Vossische Zeitung (Berlin) (16 October 1929); Wollenberg, Hans, Lichtbildbühne (16 October 1929); Betz (Hans-Walther), Der Film (19 October 1929) (The same issue has an article by Kurt London on the music to Frau im Mond); Pinthus, Kurt, Das Tage-Buch (19 October 1929); Arnheim, Rudolf, Die Weltbühne (22 October 1929); Kochba, Bar, Der Angriff (24 October 1929); A. A., Film und Volk, No. 9-10 (November 1929) (collected in Film und revolutionare Arbeiterbewegung in Deutschland 1918-1932, East Berlin: Henschel 1975); Drefus, "La Femme sur la Lune", La Revue du Cinéma (May 1939); Review in New York Times, under title By Rocket to the Moon (7 February 1931) (MMA: Basically a positive review discussing the space-rocket aspects of the film); Waly, Variety (11 February 1931); Ackerman, Forest J., "The Girl in the Moon," Parts I and II, Spacemen (April and July 1962); Wetzel, Kraft, Kino, No. 15 (15 July 1974); Carroll, Noel, Soho Weekly (28 September 1978).

14  M, MÖRDER UNTER UNS [M, Murderer(s) among Us] (1931)
The film opens with a high-angle shot of children playing in a courtyard and singing a song about a man and his "chopper," who comes after little girls. The camera pans up to a balcony where a woman, carrying laundry, yells at the kids for singing such an awful song. Cut to Mrs. Beckmann opening the door to the lady with the laundry and the clock showing 12:00 P.M., her child Elsie's lunchtime.
We cut to the school, where a knot of parents is waiting for children. Elsie is seen carrying her books and bouncing her ball on the way home. We see Elsie's ball bouncing on a poster, then Beckert's large shadow over it, his kindly voice admiring the ball and asking if she'd like a balloon. Cut to the mother watching out for Elsie and seeing two other children come upstairs. Cut to Elsie and Beckert, backs to camera, buying a balloon from a blind beggar, while Beckert whistles a theme from Grieg's Peer Gynt suite. At home, Mrs. Beckmann

panicks and calls out Elsie's name while we see a series of
shots of the deserted stairwell and empty basements, followed
by shots of Elsie's ball rolling in the grass and her balloon
caught on a telephone pole.  Cut to a high-angle shot of a
newspaper boy selling the sensational story about the murder.

We next see Beckert, his back to the camera, frantically
writing the editor of the newspaper that he has not reached
the end.

We next follow the response of the police to the crime.
The chief of police reports by telephone to a government minister on what actions have been taken.  When the chief talks
about the various raids on places haunted by the underworld,
we cut to the police, headed by Commissioner Lohmann, setting
out in their trucks on the rainswept streets at night to arrest
criminals at The Crocodile.

After this disruption, the leaders of the underworld, headed
by Schränker, sit down to figure out what they can do about the
murderer who is interfering with their activities.  In a fashion that Welles was to use later, we cut from one of Schränker's
statements to its completion in the parallel meeting being held
by the police to discuss what to do next.  Both rooms are full
of smoke as the men search in vain for solutions.  Lohmann
finally thinks of looking through files of mental institutions
for leads, while Schränker declares that the beggar's organization can protect the children and help catch the murderer.

The police meanwhile are hot on Beckert's trail from the
records they are searching.  We see Beckert leave a house and
then a detective go in to search Beckert's room.  He finds
various clues, including a cigarette package that will identify
the murderer.

Out on the street, Beckert is buying fruit.  A young girl
enters the frame, her reflection alongside Beckert's.  The
murderer gets excited and follows when the girl moves on.
They are next seen reflected in a toy shop window, Beckert
whistling the Grieg theme, but the child's mother comes up in
time and the two walk away.  Barely able to control his emotions, Beckert goes to an outside bar.

We cut to Lohmann's office and the detective reporting to
him.  Lohmann links the cigarette brand with another murder.
On the street, Beckert is identified by the beggars, who recognize his tune, and they follow him while he befriends yet
another girl.  A beggar, Henry, follows them as they buy fruit
and candy, and while Beckert peels an orange with a knife Henry
puts the "M" sign on his back in white chalk.

Back in Beckert's room, Lohmann finds all the evidence he
needs to link Beckert with Elsie's murder, while on the street,
the murderer and the girl are seen through another toy window
display.  When he sees the "M" in the reflection, he panicks
and rushes off, pursued by the beggars, who trap him in an
office building.

The beggars have told Schränker that Beckert eluded them,

but Schränker does not want the police called. He decides
that they will pretend to be police and break into the building
to get Beckert themselves. The beggars track down Beckert in
the attic and capture him. Lohmann learns that the beggars
have captured Beckert and taken him to a factory for a trial.

Cut to this trial just beginning. The room is packed with
underworld people, all hostile and determined to get their revenge on Beckert. The prosecution lawyer presents his case,
and the beggar who sold the balloon to Beckert and Elsie gives
evidence. As he listens to the case against him, Beckert looks
terrified and acts like a trapped animal. The crowd begins to
demand his death, but he protests that he did no wrong and wants
to be handed over to the police. Schränker does not want this,
because he is afraid Beckert will plead insanity and soon return to his crimes. Beckert gives a moving confession about
what it feels like to be the sort of person he is, saying that
he can't help himself, and that he feels pursued by himself.

Neither the crowd nor Schränker is moved. A lawyer argues
in Beckert's defense, but the crowd will not tolerate it and
is ready to lynch Beckert on the spot. As they surge forward,
a whistle is heard and the police break in just in time. The
crowd, stopped in its forward movement, pulls back and all
raise their hands above their heads, Schränker last of all.
The murderer gets up stunned but relieved as the police take
him away "in the name of the law." The last words are those
of Mrs. Beckmann saying that we should all take care of our
children, as the Peer Gynt tune sounds on the track.

Credits:
| | |
|---|---|
| Producer: | Seymour Nebenzal |
| Director: | Fritz Lang |
| Screenplay: | Thea von Harbou, Fritz Lang |
| Photography: | Fritz Arno Wagner, Gustav Rathje |
| Camera Operator: | Karl Vass |
| Art Direction: | Karl Vollbrecht, Emil Hasler |
| Backdrop Photographs: | Horst von Harbou |
| Music: | Excerpts from Peer Gynt by Grieg (murder's tune whistled by Fritz Lang) |
| Sound: | Adolf Jansen |
| Editor: | Paul Falkenberg |
| Cast: | Peter Lorre (Hans Beckert, the murderer), Ellen Windmann (Frau Beckmann, the mother), Inge Landgut (Elsie, the child), Gustaf Gründgens (Schränker), Fritz Odemar (Cheater), Paul Kemp (pickpocket), Theo Lingen (confidence-man), Ernst Stahl-Nachbaur (police chief), Franz Stein (minister), Otto Wernicke (Commissioner Lohmann), Theodor Loos (Commissioner Groeber), |

Georg John (blind peddler), Rudolf Blümner (Attorney), Karl Platen (watchman), Gerhard Bienert (police secretary), Rosa Valetti (servant), Hertha von Walther (prostitute), Fritz Gnass (burglar), Josef Almas, Carl Balhaus, Hans Behal, Joseph Dahmen, Hugo Döblin, J. A. Eckhoff, Else Ehser, Karl Elzer, Erwin Faber, Ilse Fürstenberg, Heinrich Gotho, Heinrich Gretler, Günther Hadank, Robert Hartberg, Ernst Paul Hempel, Oskar Höcker, Albert Hörrmann, Albert Karchow, Werner Kepich, Hermann Krehan, Rose Lichtenstein, Lotte Löbinger, Sigurd Lohde, Alfred Loretto, Paul Mederow, Margarete Melzer, Trude Moos, Hadrian M. Netto, Maja Norden, Edgar Paul, Klaus Pohl, Franz Polland, Paul Rehkopf, Hans Ritter, Max Sablotzki, Alexander Sascha, Leonard Steckel, Karl Heinz Stroux, Wolf Trutz, Otto Waldis, Borwin Walth, Rolf Wanka, Ernst Wulf, Bruno Ziener, Swinborne, Gelin Wannemann, Rhaden, Agnes Schultz-Lichterfeld (extras).

Filmed at: Nero-Film A. G. Verlag Star Film-G.m.b.H. Berlin, in 1931, in 6 weeks.

Running Time: 117 mins.

Released: 11 May 1931 (at Ufa Palast am Zoo, Berlin)

Notes: Eisner comments that "upon its original release, M ran for two hours. Since then the film has often been shortened; it is now most commonly shown in a version of 89 minutes, although rare, complete prints do exist. A 1933 dubbed version was released in the United States with only Lorre speaking his own lines." Eisner mentions the 1951 remake of M directed by Joseph Losey; "although obviously based on the original screenplay and film," Eisner says, "neither Lang nor Harbou are credited, which, given the dubious quality of the film, may be just as well."

Reviews:
D. [K. H. Döscher], Vorwärts (12 May 1931); Ihering, Herbert, Berliner Börsen-Courier (12 May 1931); o. V. Der Kinematograph

(12 May 1931); Wollenberg, Hans, Lichtbildbühne (12 May 1931);
Hirsch, Leo, Berliner Tageblatt (12 May 1931); Pohl, Heinz,
Vossische Zeitung (Berlin) (13 May 1931); Betz, (Hans-Walther),
Der Film (16 May 1931); Arnheim, Rudolf, Die Weltbühne (19
May 1931); Tölle, (Karl), Arbeiterbühne und Film (June 1931);
Magnus, Variety (June 1931); Tergit, Gabriele, Die Weltbühne
(9 June 1931, with a comment by Arnheim in the same issue);
D., Review in Deutsche Filmzeitung (Munich) (14 August 1931)
(Reviewer praises Lang's use of sound, although finding the
children's song coarse; he notes how sound becomes part of the
action); Hamilton, James Shelley, National Board of Review
Magazine (8-11 March 1933); Watts, Richard, Jr., New York
Herald Tribune (April 1933); Crewe, Regina, New York American
(3 April 1933); Hall, Mordaunt, New York Times (3 April 1933);
Bliven, Bruce, The New Republic, No. 74 (10 April 1933); Brown,
John Mason, New York Evening Post (11 April 1933); Watts,
Richard, Jr., New York Herald Tribune (16 April 1933); Troy,
William, The Nation, No. 126 (19 April 1933); Barry, Iris,
Museum of Modern Art Bulletin, 1. No. 1 (June 1933); Philadelphia
Evening Bulletin (29 September 1933) (Reviewer notes that this
is one of the very best commercial films not marked by sensa-
tionalism, heroics and flamboyance of most Hollywood films.
An English dubbed version, but with Teutonic thoroughness show-
ing the steady tracking down of the murderer) (MMA); Notes
from Austen Riggs Cinema Study Group (19 March 1952) (Surveys
Lang's life and career, talks of source for film in Peter
Kurten case, Lang given access to secret publications of the
Berlin Police Department, basing film on real police proce-
dures); Notes from the Brattle Film Foundation Series (Fall
1953) (MMA); Hoff, Edward, Notes for Roosevelt University Film
Society (1956-57) (MMA); Dyer, Peter John, Sunday Observer
(London) (19 May 1957) (The reviews from the British newspapers
are available on fiches in the BFI); BFI Notes, placing the
film in its historical context; Toronto Film Society Notes on
Lang and Crime (BFI): Brisben, Quinn, Wisconsin Film Society
Notes (1957-68); Filmkritik (Munich) No. 3 (1960); Sarris,
Andrew, The Village Voice (9 January 1960); Ramseger, George,
Die Welt (Hamburg) (16 January 1960); H. D. R. [Hans-Dieter
Roos], Süddeutsche Zeitung (10 June 1960) (Roos praises the film
for its originality, still unequalled today; it is a film of
the highest quality and an amazing document from the early
days of film, not to be missed); Seuren, Gunter, Deutsche
Zeitung (22 June 1960); H-nn [Hilde Herrmann]. Film-Dienst
(13 July 1960); Domarchi, Jean, Arts (Paris) (24 April 1961);
Gilson, René, Cinéma 61, No. 59 (August-September 1961); K. H.
[Karl Horn], Frankfurter Allgemeine Zeitung (11 December 1961)
(Collected in Jahrbuch III der Filmkritik (Emsdetter 1962);
Billington, Michael, London Times (26 October 1967); Milne,
Tom, Financial Times (London) (19 October 1967); Gibbs,
Patricia, Daily Telegraph (London) (27 October 1967); Mortimer,
Penelope, Sunday Observer (London) (29 October 1967); Schober,

Siegfried, <u>Süddeutsche Zeitung</u> (7 December 1970); Lang, Fritz,
Notes on <u>M</u> for the Princeton Group Arts Film Workshop, n. d.
(Available in MMA files).

15    DAS TESTAMENT DES DR. MABUSE [The Last Will of Dr. Mabuse]
    (1933)
       Like the films preceeding it, including <u>M</u>, <u>Das Testament</u> has
a confused narrative development relying on techniques evolved
for the silent film.
      At police headquarters, Inspector Lohmann is leaving for
the opera. The phone rings: it is Hofmeister, a dismissed
detective, desperate to talk to Lohmann. He tells Lohmann
that he is on the track of a great crime organization, a gang
of bank forgers, and that he's been in hiding in order to discover the leader. At this point the screen goes black,
Hofmeister screams, and we hear a shot; Lohmann, still holding
the phone, hears strange singing, and we realize that Hofmeister
has gone mad.
      Cut to a hospital where a doctor is lecturing to medical
students about the effects that great shocks can have on people.
He illustrates with a case study of Dr. Mabuse, known for his
psychological gifts and genius for great crimes. Baum tells
how Mabuse first would not stop scribbling and then began to
make proper words; he now writes down the most fantastic
crimes worked out to the nth degree. We cut quickly to Mabuse's
men and then to Lohmann, in the room Hofmeister phoned from,
trying to piece together what happened to him. He reconstructs
the situation, realizing that Hofmeister must have been backed
up against the window by the intruder who caused him to go mad.
Examining the window, Lohmann finds some scratch marks on the
pane, and, figuring that Hofmeister was trying to tell him
something, he has his men cut out the pane and take it to headquarters for analysis.
      We cut to Mabuse in his hospital bed, writing furiously.
As the papers float to the floor they are collected by an assistant, who gives them to Baum. Baum sees a vision and rubs
his eyes.
      Cut to Lilli and Kent having tea in a restaurant. We real-
ize they are in love, and Kent recalls how Lilli helped him a
year ago when he was out of work. We recognize Kent as one of
Mabuse's men.
      Back at the hospital, Dr. Kramm comes in to see Dr. Baum,
and finds Mabuse's writings on Baum's desk. He reads some
pages and then realizes that he is reading an account of a
jewelry store robbery that was just described in the newspaper.
Kramm confronts Baum with this when he comes in, but Baum pretends not to understand. Kramm realizes that Mabuse could
have hypnotized someone who would then carry out his evil
deeds and suggests they go to the police. As he leaves, one
of Mabuse's men, who had been listening outside, makes a call,
and we next see Kramm's car being pursued. Kramm stops for a

traffic light; in a long high-angle shot we see the cars draw
up, side by side. A crook takes out a gun, and, covered by
the noise of honking horns, he shoots Kramm. From a high angle
we now see all the cars move off except Kramm's; he is dead at
the wheel.

We cut to Kent's room, and a half-written letter on his
desk, telling Lilli that he dare not go on with her because
he's afraid she'll find out who he really is. Back at the
hospital, Baum's assistant is looking for Baum, because Mabuse
has stopped writing and is only staring. But Baum says he is
not to be disturbed.

Cut to a close-up of hands opening a secret lock; it is
Mabuse's men gathering in a room with a closed curtain at the
end. They are taking their orders from a voice coming from
behind the curtain. They must get rid of people who are in
the way; Kent is warned that he is pledged to the organization
and must carry out orders.

In the police headquarters, meanwhile, a man has figured
out that the words on the window pane read "Mabuse." Soon
after, a librarian is handing Lohmann a dusty packet marked
"Mabuse." While Lohmann is still trying to figure things out,
a call comes announcing that Mabuse is dead. At the same time,
Kent receives a note saying "Tonight at midnight--Dr. Mabuse."
A close-up of Mabuse's corpse pulls back to reveal both Baum
and Lohmann in the room; Baum is upset by Mabuse's death,
praising his brain, his destructive energy, and his resistance
to police interference. Baum tells Lohmann that Mabuse left a
will that was unusual, of a type to interest a doctor.

We cut to Baum's looking at the pile of Mabuse's writings,
including paintings of strange faces. The title of the papers
is "Mastery of Crime," and we are given excerpts from the pages,
including the statement that when a person becomes haunted by
terror, then it is time for the mastery of crime. Three
ghosts of Mabuse surround Baum, one finally taking its place
right in Baum's body.

In the room with the curtain, Mabuse's men again receive
orders, some about blowing up a chemical works. Kent's group
is called in and told to rob a bank, kill the watchman, and
replace the money with forged notes.

When he gets home, Kent finds Lilli waiting for him. He
warns her that she will not love him when he tells her all,
but she clings to her love through everything he says.

The gang meanwhile has assembled and replaced the bank notes;
Kent has not come. We cut to Kent and Lilli, still in his room;
Lilli says that Lohmann will help them. On their way to him,
however, they are kidnapped by the gang and driven to the room
with the curtain. There the voice tells them that they have
three hours to live. Kent bursts through the curtain shooting,
but finds only a loudspeaker and a cardboard shape of a man.

Meanwhile the rest of Mabuse's men are eating well in a
beautiful room. The bell rings, and the woman answers it; it

is the police. A violent shoot-out follows between Lohmann's men and the gang. The gang is finally beaten and Lohmann interrogates one man, who finally breaks down and blurts out a few pieces of information.

Kent and Lilli decide to flood their room in the hope that they can escape in this way. They finally succeed in getting out. Lohmann, meanwhile, has been on the track of Baum, suspecting him of being the boss the gang have told him about. But when he brings Baum to the police station, none of the gang recognizes him. But Kent and Lilli arrive just when Baum is leaving, and Baum calls out Kent's name in surprise at his escape. Lohmann is suspicious, although Kent now denies ever having seen Baum before. As Lohmann listens to Kent's story, he begins to suspect that the crimes are being committed by someone else in Mabuse's name. In Baum's room, Lohmann finds a map with a circle round a chemical factory and that day's date on it. They all rush to the factory, just in time to see it exploding. Suspecting Baum will be nearby, they hunt the woods around the plant, Kent finally catching sight of the now-crazed Baum. A fantastic car chase follows, with Baum driving at a crazy speed, haunted by Mabuse's ghost. The ghost takes him to the hospital and leads him to Mabuse's own room, where Hofmeister is now lying. Hofmeister gasps when Baum comes in, but Lohmann is close behind, and as Hofmeister is being brought out, he finally tells Lohmann what he had wanted to say at the film's start--that the leader of the gang is Dr. Mabuse. Baum has finally been silenced and sits on the bed pathetically shredding pieces of paper. Lohmann says in closing that this is no longer a case for the police.

Credits:

| | |
|---|---|
| Director: | Fritz Lang |
| Producer: | Seymour Nebenzal |
| Screenplay: | Thea von Harbou, Fritz Lang, based on characters from a novel by Norbert Jacques |
| Photography: | Fritz Arno Wagner, Karl Vass |
| Art Direction: | Karl Vollbrecht, Emil Hasler |
| Music: | Hans Erdmann |
| Cast: | Rudolf Klein-Rogge (Dr. Mabuse), Oskar Beregi (Dr. Baum), Karl Meixner (landlord), Theodor Loos (Dr. Kramm, assistant to Baum), Otto Wernicke (Detective Lohmann), Klaus Pohl (Lohmann's assistant, Müller), Wera Liessem (Lilli), Gustav Diessl (Thomas Kent), Camilla Spira (Jewel-Anna), Rudolf Schündler (Hardy), Theo Lingen (Hardy's friend), Paul Oskar Höcker (Bredow), Paul Henckels (lithographer), Georg John (Baum's |

|  | servant), Ludwig Stössel (worker), Hardrian M. Netto (Nicolai Grigoriew), Paul Bernd (blackmailer), Henry Pless (Dunce), A. E. Licho (Dr. Hauser); Sanitarium Assistants: Karl Platen, Anna Goltz, Heinrich Gretler; Detectives: Gerhard Bienert, Paul Bernd, Ernst Ludwig, Klaus Pohl, Paul Rehkopf, Franz Stein, Ludwig Stossel, Eduard Wesener, Bruno Ziener, Michael von Newlinski, Heinrich Gotho, Josef Dahmen |
|---|---|
| Filmed in: | the Nero-Film A. G. Studios, Berlin, 1932, in 10 weeks |
| Completed: | March 1933 |
| Running Time: | 122 mins. Length: 3334 meters |
| Released: | The Nazis censored the film on 29 March 1933; it was shown in Vienna, 5 December 1933; Eisner tells us that unassembled footage from the French version was smuggled out of Germany when the film was banned and edited in France by Lothar Wolff into a less complete version. This was the print that was released in America in 1943 and for which Lang wrote a special forward. It was not released in Germany until 24 August 1951. |

A French version of the film was shot simultaneously with the same technical crew, the screenplay adapted into French by A. Rene-Sti:

Le Testament du Dr. Mabuse, 1932.

| Cast: | Rudolf Klein-Rogge, Oskar Beregi, Karl Meixner, Jim Gérald, Thomy Bourdelle, Maurice Maillot, Monique Rolland, René Ferté, Daniel Mendaille, Raymond Cordy, Ginette Gaubert, Silvio de Pedrelli, Marcel Merminod, Georges Tourreil, Georges Paulais, Jacques Ehrem, Lily Rezillot. |
|---|---|
| Running Time: | 95 mins. |
| Released: | April 1933, Paris |

Reviews:
Variety (9 May 1933) (MMA: Reviewer sees influence of Dr. Jekyll and the Frankenstein movies); New York World Telegram (11 June 1941); Crowther, Bosley, New York Times (20 March 1943) (C. notes that it is the French version that's being shown; does not credit Lang's statements re film showing up Nazism but it does show the paranoia that Germans suffered at

the time; beautifully directed and acted); MR [Martin Ruppert] Frankfurter Allgemeine Zeitung (13 September 1951); Grit [Max Gritschneder], Film-Dienst (Düsseldorf; later Berlin) (24 August 1951): (A negative review--the film is hardly worthy of the director of Metropolis and M); J.G., Monthly Film Bulletin, No. 240 (January 1954) (The power of the original shows through the ravaged American version; admires firm control of narrative, naturalistic photography, ingenious use of sound and Lang's excellent condemnation of the superman); Sayre, Nora, New York Times (6 December 1960); Note by Gideon Bachman on the film (Summer, 1960) (MMA: Bachman focuses on the two-fold conflict in Lang's work between his formal and contextual approach. The films reflect a "baffling inconsistency"; the main types are spectacles of epic proportion, science fiction design, and crime films); William, Paul, The Village Voice (12 September 1974); Everson, W. K., Notes for the Theodore Huff Memorial Film Society (MMA: Everson compares and contrasts the three Mabuse films, pointing out similarities and differences); Notes from the Staatliches Filmarchiv, DDR (MMA).

16   LILIOM (1934)
     The film opens with shots of a carousel on a fairground in the evening. With his merry song and cheerful manner, Liliom, running the carousel, easily attracts the crowds away from the Strong Man. As Liliom harmlessly flirts with the girls on the carousel, Madame Muscat, the owner, in love with Liliom, looks on benignly, sure that these girls offer no threat to her. But the attention Liliom gives to one girl, Julie, does upset Madame Muscat; after an ugly fight with his boss, Liliom leaves the carousel with Julie and her friend.
     Seriously interested in Julie, Liliom sends her friend home and the two spend a romantic night in the park, despite the attempts of a policeman to warn Julie that Liliom is up to no good. Touchingly innocent, Julie declares "If I loved someone, I'd have no fear of anything, even of dying."
     A shot of the bench in the park engraved with many lovers' names covering those of Liliom and Julie indicates the passing of time and prepares us for Julie and Liliom's new situation. They are living together with her aunt, a photographer, for whom Julie is working. The old lady berates Liliom for not working, but he considers himself an artist. Bored and longing for the fairground, Liliom fights with Julie and is then summoned to the police station. A comic scene ensues, with nearly everything declared to be forbidden, and people kept waiting for no reason. A rich man, however, is given direct access to the inspector. Liliom meets his old friend Albert there, and when they leave the police station, Albert outlines an idea for a robbery. We cut meanwhile to Julie going home mournfully, to find Madame Muscat there looking for Liliom.
     But Liliom, having turned down the robbery job for now, is

enjoying himself at a bar, flirting, and playing cards. Julie's aunt, meanwhile, tries to persuade Julie to marry one of their clients who is interested in her.

Shortly afterward, Madame Muscat arrives at the aunt's house, and finding Liliom home, tries to persuade him to return to her and the fairground. Julie listens passively, but is terrified that she will lose Liliom, who is pulled between the two women and two sides of himself. Julie tells Liliom she is pregnant, but does not wait to see how overjoyed he is, and he also cannot share his delight with her. He meets Albert instead and while they are fishing, Albert outlines the robbery job again. Afraid, but needing the money now more than ever, Liliom agrees. He is bothered about committing a crime, but is aware that society is unjust to him and his class.

As Albert and Liliom wait for the mailman they will rob, a blind sharpener of knives comes along, establishing a sinister tone. They mismanage the robbery, and Liliom, about to be arrested, chooses instead to stab himself. At that moment Julie, at work, grabs her heart as if knowing that Liliom is hurt. Liliom is brought home dying, and Julie, beautiful and statuesque in her pain, bends over him declaring her love. Madame Muscat meanwhile stands nearby watching. Back at the fairground, she asks for some minutes of silence in honor of Liliom.

Soon figures in black come to take Liliom away. Rising from his deathbed, he is carried into the clouds. There he undergoes tribulations similar to those endured in the police station on earth, as he waits to be given information and is shunted from one official to another. Liliom behaves the same here as on earth, flirting and protesting, swearing he is innocent, even when shown films of his wicked deeds, particularly of his brutality to the long-suffering Julie. Beginning to feel ashamed, he nevertheless denies it, viewing shame as weakness. He asks about his child, but is told he will only be allowed to return for one day when the child is sixteen years old. He is packed off to purgatory on a train, the commissioner yelling at the last moment that he has a daughter.

Sixteen years pass, and Liliom returns grey-haired and changed. He is allowed to go down to earth, where he sees his daughter and the enduring Julie. He has stolen a star to give his child, but his good feelings evaporate when the girl tells him her father was no good. He slaps her while the star crumbles, and he is then taken back to heaven. His fate is being decided, and the scales, that had tipped heavily toward evil, level out when the tears of both Julie and her daughter are heard. Their love saves him from going to hell.

Credits:

| | |
|---|---|
| Producer: | Erich Pommer |
| Director: | Fritz Lang |
| Screenplay: | Fritz Lang, Robert Liebmann, based |

| | |
|---|---|
| | on the play by Ferenc Molnar. Dialogue, Bernard Zimmer. |
| Photography: | Rudolph Maté, Louis Neé |
| Art Direction: | Paul Colin, René Renoux |
| Music: | Jean Lenoir, Franz Wachsmann |
| Assistant Director: | Jean-Pierre Feydeau |
| Cast: | Charles Boyer (Liliom), Madeleine Ozeray (Julie), Florelle (Madame Muscat), Robert Arnoux (strong man), Roland Toutain (sailor), Alexandre Rignault (Hollinger), Henri Richard (Commissioner), Richard Barencey (Purgatory policeman), Antonin Artaud (Knife grinder), Raoul Marco (detective), Pierre Alcover (Alfred), Léon Arvel (clerk), René Stern (cashier), Maximilienne (Madame Menoux), Mimi Funès (Marie), Viviane Romance (cigarette girl), Mila Parély (secretary in heaven), Rosa Valetti, Lily Latté. |
| Filmed at: | St. Maurice Studios, Paris, beginning December 1933, in 57 days |
| Completed: | February 1934 |
| Running Time: | 120 mins. |
| Released: | 15 May 1934, Paris |

Reviews:
New York Times (18 March 1935); James Powers, Hollywood Reporter (6 October 1969); Richard Whitehall, Los Angeles Free Press (3 October 1969); Gérard Lenne, Télérama (14 October 1972); André Moreau, Télérama (19 October 1972) (Both Télérama articles are in the British Film Institute. Moreau says that the revival of Liliom reveals a film peripheral to Lang's career. It reflects a mixture of melodrama, populist cinema and the poetical imagination of a great auteur); David Robinson, National Film Theatre Notes (BFI); Ecran, No. 10 (December 1972); Positif, No. 188 (December 1976) (See Entry No. 466).

17    FURY (1936)
     As the film opens, Katherine Grant and Joe Wilson are engaged to be married. Katherine is leaving town to take a job somewhere else until the two have saved enough money to marry. On their way to the train, Joe rips his coat. Katherine is a sensitive, well-educated woman, who jokingly corrects Joe's "mementum" for "memento," obviously loving him for who he is. Katherine then quickly stitches the rip with blue cotton. After the parting, Joe stands glumly on the station steps, eating the peanuts he always has in his pockets. After picking up a stray dog, Joe returns to the dingy apartment that he shares with his brothers, one of whom is well on his way to

becoming a criminal.  Determined to make a better life for
both himself and his brothers, Joe decides to invest in a garage on the off chance that they can make a go of it.  Katherine
meanwhile works hard and longs to be reunited with him.

The day finally comes when Joe has established himself sufficiently to support Katherine, and he sets out happily in his
car to bring her home.  Near the place where he was to meet
Katherine, Joe is stopped in a routine search for kidnappers
who have obtained ransom money.  The mean-looking sheriff and
his men arrest Joe on purely circumstantial evidence:  the
peanuts in his pocket are linked to the crumbs in the kidnap
note; the stray dog is also connected to the affair and they
discover a ransom bill in his wallet.  The sheriff decides to
keep Joe locked up until his innocence is established.

Meanwhile, the arrest is having its affect in the town.
After hearing about it in his shop, the barber calls his wife
who, in turn, begins to gossip to her neighbors.  As word
passes from mouth to mouth, people forget that Joe is only a
suspect, not the convicted criminal, and the sentiment for revenge builds.  The hysteria increases as individuals incite
things for their own interests:  the journalist because he
wants a big story; the stranger because he loves to meddle;
the people who latch onto anything evil that is afoot.  Indig-
nant citizens march to the town hall to insist that the sheriff
convict and punish Joe.  As the crowd gets more and more excited, the sheriff becomes nervous and contacts the governor
for help.  But the governor is concerned about votes and decides that sending in the National Guard will alienate the
people.  Back at the town hall, the sheriff and his men try to
keep order and prevent the large, angry crowd from breaking
into the jail.  We see Wilson becoming more and more frightened
as the noise outside mounts.  Finally, the mob goes out of control, and, carried along by wild emotions, these "honest citizens" become maniacal and charge into the town hall, knocking
out the sheriff and his men, and finally setting fire to the
jail.  In a kind of mad ectasy, the people watch silently as
everything burns.

Katherine meanwhile has been waiting for Joe to join her
and, becoming concerned, finds her way into town just in time
to see Joe's horrified face at the jailbars as he awaits death.
Unable to stand the sight, Katherine faints.  Shortly afterwards, the real kidnappers are caught and people understand
that an innocent man was killed by the mob.  Back at the garage, Joe's brothers bitterly vow revenge.  Suddenly Joe comes
in, having escaped the fire by going down a drainpipe, a
changed, embittered man who is now only interested in getting
back at the mob.

The last part of the film consists of the trial of the
twenty-two citizens involved in the apparent killing.  It
begins with the crowd jaunty and confident of being allowed
to go free, but Joe's brothers are able to build up a strong

case with his secret help. Finally Katherine, who, after
Joe's supposed death has become withdrawn and ill, recognizing
no one, becomes well enough to come to court. She gradually
understands from the stitched raincoat and the error "mementum"
in a note that Joe is alive. But Joe is so corrupted by his
search for revenge that he has no use for Katherine or her
love, and she watches with horror as he turns into a hate-
filled man. Even the brothers begin to sicken at the thought
of twenty-two people being hung for a murder that did not, in
the end, take place, but Joe remains adamant until the last
moment. As the sentence is being pronounced, he suddenly
realizes his utter loneliness and his need of Katherine and
her love. This realization redeems him and, to Katherine's
delight, Joe rushes to the court to reveal that he is alive.
The film ends with their joyful reunion.

Credits:

| | |
|---|---|
| Producer: | Joseph L. Mankiewicz |
| Director: | Fritz Lang |
| Screenplay: | Fritz Lang, Bartlett Cormack, based on the story "Mob Rule" by Norman Krasna |
| Photography: | Joseph Ruttenberg |
| Art Direction: | Cedric Gibbons, William A. Horning, Edwin B. Willis |
| Costumes: | Dolly Tree |
| Music: | Franz Waxman |
| Editor: | Frank Sullivan |
| Assistant Director: | Horace Hough |
| Cast: | Spencer Tracy (Joe Wilson), Sylvia Sidney (Katherine Grant), Walter Abel (District attorney), Bruce Cabot (Kirby Dawson), Edward Ellis (Sheriff), Walter Brennan (Bugs Meyers), Frank Albertson (Charlie), George Walcott (Tom), Arthur Stone (Durkin), Morgan Wallace (Fred Garrett), George Chandler (Milton Jackson), Roger Gray (Stranger), Edwin Maxwell (Vickery), Howard Hickman (Governor), Jonathan Hale (Defense attorney), Leila Bennett (Edna Hopper), Esther Dale (Mrs. Whipple), Helene Flint (Franchette), Frank Sully (dynamiter). |
| Filmed in: | Metro-Goldwyn-Mayer Studios, Hollywood, 1936 |
| Completed: | May 1936 |
| Running Time: | 94 mins. [90 mins. in some sources] |
| Released: | 5 June 1936 |

Reviews:  (Some of these are annotated in Chapter 4)
Monthly Film Bulletin, Vol. 3, No. 30 (1936); Hollywood
Spectator, Vol. 2, No. 5 (6 June 1936).  Nugent, Frank S., New
York Times (6 June 1936) (A very positive review, Nugent prais-
ing the courage of the film, unusual in Hollywood:  direct,
vehement, Fury is brilliantly filmed, cast, and directed);
Listener (22 June 1936); The Cinema (London) (24 June 1936);
Kine Weekly (25 June 1936 and 15 January 1942); Sunday Observer
(26 June 1936); Film Weekly (27 June 1936); London Times (29
June 1936); Sight and Sound (Summer and Autumn 1936); Cinémonde
(20 October 1936); Pour Vous (22 October 1936); Picturegoer
(14 November 1936); Lambert, Gavin., National Film Theatre
Notes (1962); The Manchester Guardian (24 March 1962) (on oc-
casion of a National Film Theatre Retrospective); L'Avant-
Scène, No. 78 (February 1963); Positif, No. 58 (February 1964);
Gregor, Ulrich, Filmkritik (Munich), No. 3 (1965); Thousand
Eyes Magazine, Vol. 2, No. 5 (January 1977), p. 21.  Fiche
Filmographique (Put out by the Hautes Etudes Cinématographiques:
BFI has copy.  The analysis follows the regular format of these
studies with quotes from well known critics on Fury, information on the film--script, narrative, actors, etc.; a critical
summary of the film's style and its importance on artistic and
social levels.  The authors conclude that Fury does not renew
the style of M but uses it in a different mode.  The film was
socially important due to its theme, not often treated in
America).  Murat, P., "Fury." Téléciné, no. 2 (14-15 January
1977).

18    YOU ONLY LIVE ONCE (1936)
    Joan (Jo) Graham, who works for Stephen Whitney, the public
defender, is excitedly awaiting the release from jail of her
fiancé, Eddie Taylor.  Whitney, Jo, and the prison priest,
Father Dolan, all believe in Eddie, but Jo's sister, Bonnie,
and others are more skeptical about Eddie's prospects.  Eddie
himself seems cynical about being allowed to "go straight,"
but things begin well with his wedding to Jo and their honeymoon in an idyllic spot.
    Here, however, there are ominous signs of future trouble as
the couple is suddenly asked to leave in the middle of the
night because the tavern proprietor has discovered that Eddie
is an ex-convict.  Things improve, however, as Eddie starts a
trucking job, and they put down money on a ramshackle house
that will be their family haven.  However, Eddie's lateness
one day is enough to outrage the boss and make him regret hir-
ing an ex-convict.  Eddie is fired, but daren't tell Jo because
of the downpayment on the house.
    Meanwhile, Monk, Eddie's old gang mate who swore to get re-
venge on Eddie when he left the prison, has moved into Eddie's
hotel room.  Monk is seen stealing Eddie's hat.  This same hat
is discovered at the scene of a bank robbery in which a policeman is killed.  Eddie wants to flee but Jo persuades him to

give himself up and trust to justice.

At the trial, circumstantial evidence is used to convict Eddie and he is condemned to death. Bitter and resentful, Eddie rejects Jo, who, along with Whitney, nevertheless proceeds to do all she can to exonerate Eddie. Eddie's mates in the prison, meanwhile, help him to escape, but at the very moment of the daring getaway, news come through of evidence that proves Eddie's innocence. But Eddie is too embittered to believe what he is told, even refusing to honor Father Dolan's word. He kills Dolan and escapes.

Jo had been on the verge of committing suicide to coincide with Eddie's death (in accordance with the myth about frogs [namely that if one dies, the other follows] the two had discussed on their honeymoon), but she hears of the escape just in time. Eddie contacts her and they meet in a deserted railway carriage. Jo vows her love and dedication to Eddie, now blaming herself for his situation, since she was the one who originally persuaded him to give himself up. They take off on the run, Bonnie and Clyde style, stealing to live and hiding out as best they can. In the midst of all this Jo bears their child, whom they keep with them as long as they can. Finally, Jo arranges for Whitney and Bonnie, her sister, to adopt the child. Jo, to their dismay, has decided to stick by Eddie and to attempt to reach the Mexican border and freedom.

Unfortunately, a chance stop for cigarettes alerts a store manager who, mindful of the reward, calls the police. Jo and Eddie are mercilessly gunned down as they reach the Mexican border. As he dies, Eddie hears Father Dolan's voice calling to him that he is finally free to enter the Kingdom of Heaven.

Credits:
Producer: Walter Wanger
Director: Fritz Lang
Screenplay: Gene Towne, Graham Baker, based on a story by Gene Towne
Photography: Leon Shamroy
Art Direction: Alexander Toluboff
Music: Alfred Newman. Song "A Thousand Dreams of You" by Louis Alter, Paul Francis Webster.
Editor: Daniel Mandell
Assistant Director: Robert Lee
Cast: Sylvia Sidney (Joan Graham), Henry Fonda (Eddie Taylor), Barton MacLane (Stephen Whitney), Jean Dixon (Bonnie Graham), William Gargan (Father Dolan), Warren Hymer (Muggsy), Charles "Chic" Sale (Ethan), Margaret Hamilton (Hester), Guinn Williams (Rogers), Jerome Cowan (Dr. Hill), John Wray (warden), Jonathan Hale (district

attorney), Ward Bond (guard), Wade
Boteler (policeman), Henry Taylor
(Kozderonas), Jean Stoddard (stenogra-
pher), Ben Hall (messenger), Walter
De Palma.

Filmed in:             Wanger-United Artists Studios,
                       Hollywood, 1936, in 46 days
Completed:             December 1936
Running Time:          86 mins.
Released:              29 January, 1937

Reviews:
Monthly Film Bulletin, Vol. 4, No. 4 (1937); W. F., Monthly
Film Bulletin, No. 39 (1937) (Positive review, but finds the
film less compelling than Fury; real injustice is not as fundamental as the mass hysteria in Fury); Motion Picture Herald
(30 January 1937); Nugent, Frank, New York Times (1 February
1937) (While less than Fury, in other hands film would have
been mere melodrama; he praises Lang's sense of camera, use of
angles, pace, and mood, even though the film is not the moving
social documentary it could have been); Kine Weekly (25 March
1937); Film Weekly (19 May 1937); Sight and Sound (Summer 1937);
New Statesman (5 June 1937); Spectator (11 June 1937);
Picturegoer (10 July 1937); Today's Cinema (12 April 1946);
Reissue: Sunday Times (14 April 1946) (Surveys Lang's career
and finds You Only better than more recent films); K. B., Film-
Dienst (9 February 1951) (This film, by the German director
whose early works are more famous, shows only traces of Lang's
former greatness in the first part of the film); Film User
(October 1965); Positif, No. 165 (January 1975).

19    YOU AND ME (1938)
       The main narrative of the film is preceded by a musical
montage by Kurt Weill, with Brechtian overtones, showing the
tempting range of consumer goods that people desire.  This is
followed by a series of short scenes in a large department
store where the clerks know a few tricks: Helen Roberts (the
heroine of the film), catches a shoplifter; a salesman coerces
a precocious and snobbish child into buying a toy; another convinces a customer that he knows all about tennis rackets; and
the last one, clearly accustomed to cracking safes, demonstrates
a can opener to the boss's wife.  The boss, Mr. Morris, is a
liberal man, whose policy it is to employ ex-convicts in his
store as proof of his theory that people are essentially good,
if given enough to live on.
       The narrative proper begins as Joe has decided to leave
town, since his parole is over and he is being pressed by members of his old gang to return to them.  Helen Roberts meets
Joe Dennis after work.  The two go out for a drink on the way
to meet Joe's bus, and their love for each other is obvious.
At the last moment, Joe decides to stay with Helen.  They plan

to marry, but it's clear that Helen has a guilty secret she's hiding from Joe. We soon learn that she too is an ex-convict, still on parole, but that she can't tell Joe since part of the reason he's attracted to her is that she's not part of his criminal world. The two get married, although Helen is on dangerous ground here since this is against the rules for parolees.

At first things are idyllic, although Helen is nervous and imagines she's being followed. But everything changes when Joe finds Helen's parole cards. He turns away from her and is soon drawn back into the world of his old criminal gang. Helen, completely unaware of what has upset Joe, is heartbroken and imagines that Joe has a lover.

The climax occurs on Christmas night, when Joe is told by the gang that he's expected at their Christmas party. Estranged from Helen, he finally arrives at the party. We see here the strong ties among the men as a result of their criminal activities and jail experiences. Joe agrees to participate in the next gang crime--robbing the store where he and a number of other gang members work. Hearing about the plan, Helen tells Mr. Morris about it. They decide to allow the robbery to take place, but to make it a lesson for the gang.

On the night of the robbery, the gang members break in, as arranged, and begin collecting goods. But just before they are ready to leave, Helen and Mr. Morris surprise them. Morris convinces them to hear what Helen has to say, and finally they all sit down to listen. Using a blackboard, Helen sets out to demonstrate in economic terms that crime does not pay. She shows the men that, after all the expenses were paid, each man only stood to gain $133.25.

Joe is still angry with Helen and disappears before the lesson is over. Helen is terribly hurt by this, and soon she is nowhere to be found. The gang spreads out over the town searching for her, finally tracking her down in the maternity hospital having her and Joe's baby. The gang and Joe wait anxiously in the hospital, and the film ends on a comic note as they all rush forward when the father is called.

Credits:
Producer:              Fritz Lang
Director:              Fritz Lang
Screenplay:            Virginia van Upp, based on a story
                       by Norman Krasna.

Photography:           Charles Lang, Jr.
Art Direction:         Hans Dreier, Ernst Fegté
Set Decoration:        A. E. Freudeman
Music:                 Kurt Weill, Boris Morros. Songs:
                       "The Right Guy for Me" by Weill, Sam
                       Coslow; "You and Me" by Ralph Freed,
                       Frederick Hollander
Musical Advisor:       Phil Boutelie

75

| | |
|---|---|
| Editor: | Paul Weatherwax |
| Cast: | Sylvia Sidney (Helen Roberts), George Raft (Joe Dennis), Robert Cummings (Jim), Barton MacLane (Mickey), Roscoe Karns (Cuffy), Harry Carey (Mr. Morris), Warren Hymer (Gimpy), George E. Stone (Patsy), Guinn Williams (cab driver), Vera Gordon (Mrs. Levine), Carol Paige (torch singer), Bernadene Hayes (Nellie), Egon Brecher (Mr. Levine), Joyce Compton (curly blonde), Cecil Cunningham (Mrs. Morris), Willard Robertson (Dayton), Roger Grey (attendant), Adrian Morris (Knucks), Joe Gray, Harlan Briggs (McTavish), Paula de Cardo/Harriette Haddon (cigarette girls), Matt McHugh (Newcomer), Paul Newlan, Margaret Randall (clothes thief), Jack Pennick, Kit Guard, Fern Emmet, Max Barwyn, James McNamara, Blanca Vischer, Hetra Lynd, Jimmie Dundee, Terry Raye, Sheila Darcy, Jack Mullhall [Mulhall], Sam Ash, Ruth Rogers, Julia Faye, Arthur Hoyt. |
| Filmed in: | Paramount Studios 1938 in 45 days |
| Completed: | May 1938 |
| Released: | 3 June 1938 |
| Running Time: | 90 mins (according to Lotte Eisner, 94 mins.). |

Reviews:
Frank Nugent, New York Times (2 June 1938) (Lang is courageous in trying to break with Hollywood formulae, but the net effect is poor); E. P., Monthly Film Bulletin, No. 54 (30 June 1938) (treatment uneven and disappointing, but underlying idea is good); Kine Weekly (23 June 1938); Film Weekly (2 July 1938); Publicity release (BFI); G. Greene, The Spectator (1 July 1938) (BFI); Peter Galway, The New Statesman (25 June 1938) (BFI).

20 THE RETURN OF FRANK JAMES (1940)
The film, designed as a sequel to Henry King's Jesse James (1939), begins where that film ended--with the murder of Jesse in his home, shot in the back by the Ford brothers as he was taking down a wall hanging. Hearing about the murder, Frank James (Jesse's brother), who lives on a ranch under a new name, resolves at first to let the law take care of the Ford brothers. But when he learns of their acquittal, he determines to go after them himself. He orders young Clem, son of a dead gang member, who lives with him, to stay with Pinky (their servant)

at the ranch.

Tipped off by Rufus Tod, his friend and editor of the local newspaper, Frank sets out for Denver on the heels of the Fords. He views as poetic justice his robbing the offices of McCoy, the railroad magnate who originally stole the people's land. Unfortunately, as a result of Clem's intervention the watchman is killed by the sheriff's men. Clem and Frank manage to escape, and, much to the former's delight, the two set off for Denver.

There they give a false account of Frank's death to mislead the Ford brothers, Clem pretending to have seen Frank killed in Mexico. A new reporter, Eleanor Stone, is taken in by the performance and writes up the story for the Denver Star, owned by her father. Frank and Clem meanwhile set out, again following the Fords. They catch up with them in a small town where they are starring in a drama enacting the death of Jesse James. Frank watches the performance, but the Fords catch sight of him and try to escape. Frank and Clem follow in hot pursuit, and a shoot-out with Charlie Ford in the mountains ends with his death as he falls into the stream below.

Meanwhile, in Denver, McCoy's railroad detective, Runyan, gets Eleanor to establish that the man who told her of Frank's supposed death was, indeed, Frank himself. Runyan plans to accost Frank and Clem on their return to Denver. He breaks into their hotel room and, when they arrive, captures them. Clem, however, manages to trip Runyan and they hook him inside a closet and escape.

Eleanor meets Frank secretly and tells him that McCoy has engineered Pinky's arrest. They are planning to hang him unless Frank gives himself up. Frank, obsessed with revenge, is unable to relinquish his pursuit of Bob Ford, and he and Clem set out again. Eleanor, disappointed in Frank, whom she loves, decides to go to the trial herself to see what she can do.

At the last moment, Frank is unable to allow Pinky to hang, and he and Clem return posthaste to the town, where Frank gives himself up. A lengthy trial ensues, with Frank brilliantly defended by Rufus Todd. Todd manages to insinuate that the St. Louis railroad has infiltrated the community and he casts doubt on the validity of the prosecution's case. Bob Ford appears just as Frank is acquitted and Frank rushes out after him. Clem, however, has already tried to kill Ford by the time Frank gets outside, and has, in turn, been fatally wounded. After a touching farewell scene with Clem, Frank goes off to get Ford, who has taken refuge in an old, dark barn. Frank narrowly escapes being killed by the mortally wounded Bob Ford, who is dead when Frank finally gets to him.

On his way out of town, Frank, now satisfied that justice has been done, says goodbye to Eleanor Stone, whom he plans to see again.

Credits:
| | |
|---|---|
| Producer: | Darryl F. Zanuck, Kenneth Macgowan |
| Director: | Fritz Lang |
| Screenplay: | Sam Hellman |
| Photography (technicolor): | George Barnes, William V. Skall |
| Art Direction: | Richard Day, Wiard B. Ihnen |
| Set Decoration: | Thomas Little |
| Costumes: | Travis Banton |
| Sound: | W. D. Flick, Roger Heman |
| Music: | David Buttolph |
| Technical Director: | Natalie Kalmus |
| Editor: | Walter Thompson |
| Associate: | Morgan Padelford |
| Cast: | Henry Fonda (Frank James), Gene Tierney (Eleanor Stone), Jackie Cooper (Clem), Henry Hull (Major Rufus Todd), J. Edward Bromberg (George Runyan), Donald Meek (McCoy), Eddie Collins (Station agent), John Carradine (Bob Ford), George Barbier (Judge), Ernest Whitman (Pinky), Charles Tannen (Charlie Ford), Lloyd Corrigan (Randolph Stone), Russell Hicks (Prosecutor), Victor Kilian (Preacher), Edward McWade (Colonel Jackson), George Chandler (Roy), Irving Bacon (Bystander), Frank Shannon (Sheriff), Barbara Pepper (Nellie Blane), Stymie Beard (Mose), William Pawley/Frank Sully (Actors), Louis Mason (Watchman), Davidson Clark (Officer). |
| Filmed at: | Twentieth-Century Fox Studios, Hollywood, in 1940 in 46 days |
| Completed: | June 1940 |
| Running Time: | 92 mins. |
| Released: | 12 August 1940 |

Reviews:
New York Times (10 August and 8 October 1940); Variety (15 August 1940) (MMA); Today's Cinema (22 October 1940); Kine Weekly (24 October 1940); Monthly Film Bulletin, No. 83 (November 1940); Picturegoer (18 January 1941); Film-Dienst (7 April 1952); J. L. Godard in Image et Son, No. 95 (October 1956) (BFI); Radio-Cinéma-Télévision, No. 536 (24 April 1960); E. P. in Filmkritik, No. 3 (1965) (see no. 345).

21  WESTERN UNION (1941)
Western Union begins as Vance Shaw, a bandit, rescues Edward Creighton, a member of a posse sent out after buffalo thieves.

After taking the seriously wounded man to safety, Shaw rides away abruptly.

Creighton, who heads the Western Union outfit in Omaha and is responsible for bringing the telegraph lines to Salt Lake City, realizes soon after that the man who saved him was part of a gang that held up the local bank. He nevertheless decides to hire Vance Shaw to guard his men from Indian attack when they go out on the plains to put up telegraph poles. When Shaw realizes that Creighton knows who he is, he plans to leave, but Creighton persuades him to stay, understanding that he will do an honest job.

Shaw has already met Creighton's daughter Sue, who works in the Western Union office and who is being wooed by Richard Blake, a rich, naive easterner, who has been sent by his father to Omaha in the hopes of toughening him up. Shaw and Blake become rivals for Sue's love and also for the approval of Creighton, who takes very seriously his mission of bringing communication from Washington, D.C. to the West.

After a comic selection process to choose men to join the group going out into the plains, we see them putting up the first poles. When the men have gone a certain distance from the town, Creighton joins them, and Sue is sent back to look after the Western Union office. In another semicomic scene, Shaw and Blake both sneak back into town to see her.

Back at the camp, the first mishap has taken place: one man has been killed and another wounded by some Indians. Shaw discovers that the so-called Indians are none other than his old gang, headed by Jack Slade in disguise. They have been hired by Southern Confederates to stop the telegraph line, since it is viewed as only strengthening Yankee rule. Shaw agrees not to divulge their identities if they leave the line alone.

On a brief visit to the camp, Sue indicates her love for Shaw. He, however, hints at his evil past, believing that it stands between the two of them.

Soon after this, as they are making a first telegraph connection, the Western Union workers are attacked by drunken Indians. They just manage to get the connection through and warn the camp before the Indians arrive. Shaw tells the men to be calm and says that he will deal with the attackers, but Blake gets nervous and kills one of them. In revenge, the Indians raid the main camp before the others return.

Creighton, deeply upset, appeals to Shaw, who realizes that he has to explain the truth about his gang. They drive into town to make a deal with the gang, who agree to set up a meeting with the Indians in return for a large amount of money. Blake, Creighton, and Shaw go out together into the plains to persuade the Indians that the wire is not dangerous and will not interfere with them.

But Jack Slade, whom we later discover is Shaw's brother, cannot forgive him for leaving the gang and reneges on the deal. The gang captures Shaw and then sets fire to the camp, hoping that Shaw will be blamed. He manages to return, but it is too late to save much. The tattered survivors of the camp finally reassemble, but Creighton, unable to get Shaw to tell him about his difficulties, sends him away.

Shaw rides into town, determined now to kill his brother and the gang, who have acted so treacherously. Slade shoots him from behind before Shaw can kill him, but Blake, having followed Shaw, revenges his death, and, at the same time, enters into manhood himself.

Credits:

| | |
|---|---|
| Producer: | Harry Joe Brown |
| Director: | Fritz Lang |
| Screenplay: | Robert Carson, based on a novel of Zane Grey. |
| Photography (technicolor): | Edward Cronjager, Allen M. Davey |
| Art Direction: | Richard Day, Albert Hugsett |
| Set Decoration: | Thomas Little |
| Costumes: | Travis Banton |
| Music: | David Buttolph |
| Technical Director: | Natalie Kalmus |
| Associate: | Morgan Padelford |
| Sound: | Bernard Fredericks, Roger Heman |
| Editor: | Robert Bischoff |
| Cast: | Robert Young (Richard Blake), Randolph Scott (Vance Shaw), Dean Jagger (Edward Creighton), Virginia Gilmore (Sue Creighton), John Carradine (Doc Murdoch), Slim Summerville (Herman), Chill Wills (Homer), Barton MacLane (Jack Slade), Russell Hicks (Governor), Victor Kilian (Charlie), Minor Watson (Pat Grogan), George Chandler (Herb), Chief Big Tree, Chief Spotted Horse, Chief Thundercloud (Indian leaders), Dick Rich (Porky), Harry Strang (henchman), Charles Middleton (stage-coach rider), Addison Richards (Captain Harlow), J. Edward Bromberg, Irving Bacon (barber) |
| Filmed at: | Twentieth-Century-Fox in 56 days |
| Running Time: | 93-95 mins. (assessments vary). |
| Released: | 7 February 1941 (21 February 1941) |

Reviews:
Walt, Variety (New York) (5 February 1941); New York Times (7 February 1941); Thirer, Irene, New York Post (7 February

1941); <u>Motion Picture Herald</u> (New York) (8 February 1941);
<u>New Yorker</u> (15 February 1941); <u>Today's Cinema</u> (28 May 1941);
<u>Kine Weekly</u> (19 May 1941); <u>New Statesman</u> (London) (12 April
1941) (BFI); <u>Monthly Film Bulletin</u> (London), No. 90, p. 74 (30
June 1941); <u>Motion Picture Herald</u> (New York) (14 June 1947);
Feigl, Walter, <u>Film-Dienst</u> (27 December 1949); Hellwig, Klaus,
<u>Filmkritik</u>, No. 4 (1965); Silver, Charles, Program Notes (New
York) (MMA); Publicity Release (BFI, MMA).

22   MANHUNT (1941)
     After a long tracking shot over a forest, the camera picks
up Captain Thorndike poised over the edge of a cliff, peering
intently down a rifle, within range of Nazi guards.  A shot
through the rifle lens shows us that the target is Hitler.
Thorndike pulls the trigger, but no bullet is inside.  He
loads the gun, lines it up again, but this time delays.  A
leaf falls on the gun, and the sun catching it at that moment
alerts the guards.  Thorndike is arrested and taken for inter-
rogation to Quive-Smith, a high-ranking Nazi officer.  Quive-
Smith wants Thorndike to sign a paper admitting that he was
trying to kill Hitler on behalf of the British government.
Thorndike, however, is a famous big game hunter and says he
was doing it merely to see if he could get within shooting
range of Hitler--as a sporting stalk.
     Thorndike's arrest causes the British Government aggrava-
tion, since he is the brother of Lord Risborough, a high-
ranking official.  He also causes the Nazis problems, since he
refuses to sign the paper even after days of torture.  The
Nazis finally decide that they will have to make his death look
like an accident:  they push him over a cliff and leave him for
dead.
     Thorndike, however, is not dead, as the Nazis realize the
next day when they come to pick up the corpse.  A chase ensues,
with Thorndike managing to evade the Nazis because of his hunting expertise.  He makes his way to the sea and is able to
climb secretly on board a Dutch ship with the aid of a young
boy.  Just as the ship is leaving, the Nazis bring on board a
German agent, dressed to look like Thorndike, and bearing his
passport, which they had seized earlier.  After many tense
moments when it looks as though Thorndike will be discovered,
he arrives safely in London.
     Here, however, Thorndike is still not free of the Nazis,
who have a wide network of spies out to catch and murder him.
He narrowly escapes by entering a house where Jenny, a tough
but kindly prostitute, lives.
     Jenny puts him up and lends him enough money to go to visit
Lord and Lady Risborough; he takes Jenny along with him to as-
sure her that he will repay her.  There are some comic scenes
of the Risboroughs' reactions to Jenny.  A touching relationship begins to develop between Thorndike and Jenny, and
Thorndike buys her an arrow-shaped pin for her beret in

gratitude for what she's done for him. Thorndike is now ready to attempt to leave England and goes to his solicitor, Farnsworth, to get money and to make arrangements for Jenny. Outside the window, he sees the agent who is impersonating him feeding pigeons and releasing one (presumably to the central spy office).

Thorndike wants to leave Jenny then and there, but she insists on accompanying him to the subway. They are followed by the agent, Mr. Jones. A dramatic chase follows in the dark subway tunnel: Jones falls on the lines and is electrocuted. A newspaper headline proclaims Captain Thorndike's death. Jenny is heartbroken until, on returning home, she finds Thorndike waiting for her. They say goodbye to each other on London Bridge after Thorndike has given her instructions about sending a letter to Lyme Regis.

Jenny returns home to find Quive-Smith and the Nazi agents waiting for her. They close in on her, demanding to know where Thorndike is. Thorndike, meanwhile, is seen asking for his letters at the post office near the place where he has made a hiding place in the rock. The postmistress looks alarmed, so Thorndike presumes that the agents have found out about his hiding place. He returns and shuts himself in, only to be accosted from outside by Quive-Smith, who has now placed a solid rock in front of the entrance. A tense battle of wits follows, as Quive-Smith tries again to intimidate Thorndike into signing the confession. When Quive-Smith hands Jenny's hat pin in to Thorndike, he knows that she has been killed. But the pin fittingly proves to be his salvation, in revenge for Jenny's death. Thorndike constructs an arrow with the pin, while agreeing to sign the paper and pretending to give himself up. Outside, Quive-Smith prepares to murder Thorndike despite promises to the contrary. When Quive-Smith comes to get the confession, Thorndike shoots the sharp pin at him and kills him. But Quive-Smith has just enough strength to wound Thorndike seriously as he crawls out of his hole.

The film ends with a montage of shots of the war breaking out, Thorndike being operated on, and Thorndike's recovery and enlistment as a secret agent in Europe. The last shot shows him parachuting back into Germany. Thorndike has now discovered that indeed he does wish to murder Hitler rather than playing hunting games.

Credits:
| | |
|---|---|
| Producer: | Kenneth MacGowan |
| Director: | Fritz Lang |
| Screenplay: | Dudley Nichols, based on the novel Rogue Mâle by Geoffrey Household |
| Photography: | Arthur Miller |
| Art Direction: | Richard Day, Wiard B. Ihnen |
| Set Decoration: | Thomas Little |
| Costumes: | Travis Banton |

| | |
|---|---|
| Music: | Alfred Newman |
| Sound: | Eugene Grossman, Roger Heman |
| Editor: | Allen McNeil |
| Cast: | Walter Pidgeon (Captain Thorndike), Joan Bennett (Jenny), George Sanders (Quive-Smith), John Carradine (Mr. Jones), Roddy McDowall (Vaner), Ludwig Stössel (Doctor), Heather Thatcher (Lady Risborough), Frederick Worlock (Lord Risborough), Roger Imhof (Captain Jensen), Egon Brecher (Whiskers), Lester Matthews (Major), Holmes Herbert (Farnsworth), Eily Malyon (Postmistress), Arno Frey (Police lieutenant), Fredrik Vogeding (Ambassador), Lucien Prival (Man with umbrella), Herbert Evans (Reeves), Keith Hitchcock (Bobby). |
| Filmed at: | Twentieth-Century Fox, Hollywood, 1941 |
| Running Time: | 102 mins. (original length 105 mins.) |
| Released: | 20 June 1941 |

Reviews:
New York Times (14 June 1941); New York Herald Tribune (14-15 June 1941) (MMA); Variety (14 June 1941) (MMA); Pacific Coast Musician (21 June 1941) (MMA); New York Daily News (14 June 1941) (MMA); Motion Picture Herald (New York) (14 June 1941); Today's Cinema (3 September 1941); Kine Weekly (4 September 1941); Monthly Film Bulletin No. 93 (30 September 1941) p. 118; Sight and Sound (Summer 1941), p. 25 and (Autumn 1941), p. 46; Hollywood Picture (25 May 1943), p. 22 (MMA); Ferguson, Otis New Republic (23 June 1941) (See Entry No. 155a); Publicity release (MMA).

23    HANGMEN ALSO DIE (1943)
    The film takes place in Czechoslovakia during the Nazi oc-
cupation.  Dissatisfied with the production at the Skoda works,
Richard Heydrich, nicknamed "the Hangman," announces that he
will take fifty lives as punishment, and leaves immediately to
carry out the executions.  Out on the street we see a variety
of different actions that we only later reconstruct as taking
place during the assassination of Heydrich by Franz Svoboda, a
Czech resistance worker.  A cab driver is seen waiting with
the engine running, and a few moments later he is arrested by
some Nazis; an elderly man tells a driver of a horse-drawn
carriage that Vanya has been arrested and to get going; we see
a young girl, Mascha Novotny, buying vegetables from an old
lady, Miss Dvorak; and then Franz Svoboda enters an alley and
changes his hat before stealthily moving on.  Suddenly, some
Nazis come running in haste, blowing whistles.  They question

83

The Sidney B. Coulter Library
Onondaga Community College
Rte. 173, Onondaga Hill
Syracuse, New York 13215

Mascha and she gives them false information.  Svoboda then
steals out, sees where Mascha lives, and goes into a movie.
Whispers soon start regarding Heydrich's murder, and the audience bursts out with applause.  Svoboda leaves, and tries to
rent a room.  After the murder the Nazis are everywhere making
threats and setting curfews, and the people are afraid.

At the Novotny household, preparations for Mascha's wedding
are underway; Jan Horak, Mascha's fiancé, has just left to
beat the curfew when the bell rings.  Svoboda, having just escaped a German dragnet and pretending to be an admirer, enters
with flowers for Mascha.  Novotny, obviously a resistance sym-
pathizer, guesses who Svoboda is, but will listen to nothing
either from his daughter, Mascha, or Svoboda himself, whom she
has just helped save.  The family invites Svoboda to dinner,
the curfew hour having passed.  The family learns from the
radio that Heydrich has been murdered and that citizens should
be on the alert for the assassin.  Boda, Mascha's brother, accidentally cuts his finger on the bread knife and Svoboda bandages it expertly.  The Gestapo meanwhile have begun their in-
terrogations with Miss Dvorak and the cab driver.  The old
vegetable seller refuses to say anything, and the cab driver
jumped out of the window rather than risk giving information.

Alois Gruber, a Nazi detective scornful of the heavy-handed
approach to Czech resistance, prefers more subtle ways of playing with the people.  He and Emil Czaka, a Nazi spy who has
infiltrated the underground, are responsible for the lists of
people to be gathered as hostages and held until the murderer
of Heydrich is found.  They decide that poets and intellectuals
are most dangerous in preventing the Germanization of the
Czechs.

At the Novotny home the next morning, as Mascha and Svoboda
are learning about the feared reprisals for Heydrich's death,
the Nazis come and arrest Professor Novotny.  Because of her
close relationship to her father, Mascha is particularly upset.
Jan tries later on to console her, while her aunt declares that
the assassin ought to give himself up rather than risk the
lives of so many eminent Czechs.  Mascha, fingering Svoboda's
roses, is in conflict because she knows who the assassin is.
Mascha guesses that Svoboda is a doctor and is able to trace
the hospital because of Svoboda's earlier reference to the
chimes he hears every day.

At the hospital, we see Svoboda receiving the leader of the
underground, disguised as a patient, and pleading to be allowed
to give himself up.  The leader, Debège, persuades him that the
cause is greater than individuals and that Svoboda will be
needed when the Nazis are finally driven out.  Mascha then
comes in and hysterically denounces Svoboda as selfish.  She
determines to go to the Gestapo and tell them what she knows.
The underground tries to prevent her from doing this, and the
Czech people seem united behind it, scorning Mascha for collaborating in any way.  But Mascha cannot bear the thought of

her father's being killed and goes to make her statement.

Once at the Gestapo, she begins to think better of her deed, but it is too late. She makes the Nazis suspicious by trying to leave without seeing the chief. They hold her while they ransack the Novotny home. Finding nothing, they arrest the whole family, but they all have the same story, and the Nazis reluctantly let them go. Svoboda, one step ahead of the Nazis, sends Mascha more flowers and then goes to visit her. Knowing the Nazis have bugged the room, he signals Mascha to keep up the pretense of a romance. Nazi detective Gruber remains unconvinced, but has no evidence for his hunch. However, we see him checking out Svoboda's alibi (he revealed his true identity during the conversation with Mascha) and learning that at the time of the murder Svoboda was performing an operation at the hospital.

At a meeting of an underground cell, we find (Nazi spy) Emil Czaka pleading for the assassin to be given up to save the lives of the hostages. Debège, who was in a back room listening, later demands that Czaka be tested. Czaka meanwhile, enjoying a rich dinner with Gruber, is nervous as a result of the group's reaction to his plea. He bribes Gruber into giving him a bodyguard.

Gruber meanwhile continues his game of playing with Mascha in the hope of finding her out. He phones in the middle of the night to say that her father is going to be executed. There is a farewell scene between Mascha and her father. Later on, Mascha learns that her father was not executed, after all.

Gruber remains suspicious and goes on checking Svoboda's records, learning that he is not generally known as the romantic type this affair with Mascha would suggest.

The underground plans a dinner with Czaka to test his background and trick him into revealing his familiarity with German. But the Nazis are waiting outside; Debège is badly wounded but escapes, while several of the cell are captured. Gruber interrogates the driver who took Debège away and guesses that he is at Svoboda's house. Gruber goes there, but is again fooled into thinking Mascha and Svoboda were in bed. Debège is, in fact, in the house nearly bleeding to death. Gruber sends for Jan to see if Mascha will give herself away when faced with her fiancé, but again, Mascha is able to carry it off.

Gruber decides to stick with Jan for the evening, to make sure he is not part of the plot, and they go to a nightclub to drink and pick up prostitutes, whose job it is to test Jan's story.

Just before he dies, Debège helps Svoboda and Mascha think up a way to save both the hostages and Svoboda. It involves an elaborate frame-up of Czaka as Heydrich's assassin.

Circumstantial evidence mounts against Czaka, as he stands appalled that his cover has been blown. The one witness who could have saved him and exposed the false testimony of all

these people is Detective Gruber, but he has been murdered by
Svoboda. The assassination of Heydrich and the murder of
Gruber are pinned on Czaka, who is then brutally gunned down
by Nazis.

The film ends in a reception room with the new governor of
Czechoslovakia sitting under Hitler's portrait and receiving
a report of the whole Czaka affair. We learn that the Nazis
realized that Czaka could not have been the assassin, but that
to save face in the light of Czech resistance, they will accept
him as the murderer. The last ironic note is the caption "NOT
THE END."

Credits:

| | |
|---|---|
| Producer: | Arnold Pressburger, Fritz Lang, T. W. Baumfield [Baumfeld] |
| Director: | Fritz Lang |
| Screenplay: | Fritz Lang, Bertolt Brecht, John Wexley, based on a story by Lang and Brecht |
| Photography: | James Wong Howe |
| Art Direction: | William Darling |
| Costumes: | Julie Heron |
| Music: | Hanns Eisler; Song: "No Surrender" by Eisler, Sam Coslow |
| Sound: | Fred Law |
| Editor: | Gene Fowler, Jr. |
| Assistant Production Manager | Carl Curley Harriman |
| Assistant Directors: | Walter Mayo, Fred Pressburger |
| Cast: | Brian Donlevy (Dr. Franz Svoboda), Walter Brennan (Prof. Novotny), Anna Lee (Mascha Novotny), Gene Lockhart (Emil Czaka), Dennis O'Keefe (Jan Horek), Alexander Granach (Alois Gruber), Margaret Wycherly (Ludmilla Novotny), Nana Bryant (Mrs. Novotny), Billy Roy (Beda Novotny), Hans von Twardowksi (Richard Heydrich), Tonio Selwart (Haas, Gestapo chief), Jonathan Hale (Dedič), Lionel Stander (Cabby), Byron Foulger (Bartos), Virginia Farmer (Landlady), Louis Donath (Schirmer), Sarah Padden (Miss Dvorak), Edmund MacDonald (Dr. Pilar), George Irving (Necval), James Bush (Worker), Arno Frey (Itnut), Lester Sharpe (Rudy), Arthur Loft (General Vortruba), William Farnum (Viktorin), Reinhold Schünzel (Inspector Ritter), Philip Merivale. |
| Filmed at: | Arnold Productions, United Artists, |

Running Time:

Hollywood in 1942 in 52 days
Original length 140 mins. Some versions in distribution lack the last 10 mins.

Released:   26 March 1943

Reviews:
Motion Picture Herald (27 March 1943); Cameron, Kate, New York Daily News (16 April 1943) (see Entry No. 159); T. S. [Theodore Strauss], New York Times (16 April 1943), p. 20; D. P., New York World Telegram (25 April 1943); Davidson, Joe, New Masses (New York) (4 May 1943); D. E. B., Monthly Film Bulletin, No. 114 (June 1943), p. 64; Today's Cinema (2 June 1943); Kine Weekly (London) (3 June 1943); Manchester Guardian (3 June 1943); Evening Standard (London) (5 June 1943); Sunday Times (London) (6 June 1943); Reissue: Today's Cinema (13 September 1950); Philippe, Claude Jean, Télérama (26 November 1961) (BFI); Cahiers du Cinéma, No. 127 (1962), p. 57 (see Entry No. 299); Présence du Cinéma, No. 10 (196–); Cinema 62 (January 1962), p. 116 (see Entry No. 300); Filmkritik, No. 7 (1975); Gersh, Wolfgang,"Der Fall Hangmen Also Die," in his Film Bei Brecht, Berlin DDR: Henschel (1975), pp. 200-217 (see Engty No. 445a.); Deutsche Film Theatre Notes (BFI); Film Daily, Variety, Cue, Harrison's Report, reviews in MMA; National Film Theatre Notes (BFI); Pohodna, Joseph, New York Herald Tribune (MMA); Platt, David, Daily Worker (London) (MMA); Trade Synopsis (MMA); Winsten, Archer, New York Post (MMA) (precise dates not available, but reviews written at time of release).

24   MINISTRY OF FEAR (1944)
   As the film opens, Stephen Neale is seen leaving a dark, prisonlike building that turns out to be a mental institution. While waiting for a train to London, Stephen wanders into a local fair, where, with the help of a fortune-teller, he guesses the correct weight of a cake. As he is leaving with the cake, a man in black, Costa, rushes into the grounds and tries unsuccessfully to take the cake away from him. On the train Stephen finds himself opposite a supposedly blind man who, in fact, has his eye on the cake and makes off with it when the train is stopped during an air raid. Neale follows in chase and is shot at by the "blind" man from a ruin, before a bomb blasts the man and the whole area. Stephen picks up the gun before resuming his journey.
   We next see Stephen in London, going to a private detective, Mr. Rennit. He pretends at first to be above such cases, but in fact seems desperate for business. They go to the headquarters of Mothers of the Free Nations, the group running the fair in the country, to track down the fortune-teller, Mrs. Bellane, in the hope of solving the mystery of the cake. Austrian refugees Carla and Willi Hilfe (brother and sister) receive them and make light of the whole thing, while agreeing

to take Stephen, with Rennit in tow, to Mrs. Bellane's house. There Stephen joins in a séance, and sees Costa, the man from the fair, come in at the last moment. During the séance, Stephen's wife is heard blaming Stephen for her death. Suddenly we hear a shot and Costa is found dead. Hilfe recalls seeing the gun Stephen took from the "blind" man after he died, and Stephen is blamed for the murder.

That night, Stephen returns to Rennit's office, only to find the place ransacked and Rennit murdered. Outside the eerily quiet building Stephen sees a sinister man leaning against the wall. Afraid that he is part of the mysterious group against him, Stephen calls Carla Hilfe, whom he trusts. They meet, but an air raid forces them to spend a night in the subway system. Stephen begins to fall in love with Carla and reveals to her that two years ago he was imprisoned for the murder of his wife, who, terminally ill and in great pain, begged Stephen to buy poison and give it to her. Carla is sympathetic, but it is not at all clear which side she is really on. The men trailing Stephen are seen coming into the subway, but they do not approach the pair.

The next day, after the all clear signal, Carla takes Stephen to an old bookshop where she says he will be safe. In the store, Stephen sees books by a Dr. Forrester, a high Ministry official who was at the séance. In the little room upstairs, Stephen begins to tell Carla of his suspicions that the Mothers of the Free Nations is a front for a Nazi spy organization, but Carla looks very shocked.

Stephen then visits Mrs. Bellane to try to get to the bottom of things. He is now suspicious of her, and pulls a gun out of her bag when she tries to seduce him. Back at the Mothers' headquarters, Carla tells Willi of Stephen's fears, admits she's falling in love with him, and says she will go to the Ministry with Stephen if necessary.

At the bookstore, Carla and Stephen are asked to deliver some books for the owner to Dr. Forrester's apartment. When they get there, they are shown a room under the name "Travers," and discover it is completely empty. When they open the box of books, Stephen hears a noise, and they get out of the way just before the box explodes.

Stephen wakes up in a strange room, to find the man who had been trailing him sitting by the bedside. He turns out not to be a Nazi but from Scotland Yard. Stephen, relieved, tries to convince the detective about the cake and the Nazi organization. Skeptical, the detective nevertheless agrees to give Stephen his chance, and they go out into the country where the bomb exploded on the blind man who had stolen the cake. The police find all kinds of evidence that corroborates Stephen's story, including, at the last moment, a piece of film stolen from the Foreign Ministry. It looks as though Forrester from the Ministry must be a spy.

Trailing Forrester, the police come to his tailor, Travers,

who turns out to be Costa, the man who was supposed to have
been murdered at the séance. Costa makes a call about a suit,
saying the shoulders should be carefully checked before the
customer puts it on. Costa then goes into a room, carrying
his long tailor's scissors, and kills himself. Stephen dials
the number Costa had called and Carla answers the phone.
Neale now begins to suspect her, as the audience has all along.
Rushing out, he gets the address from the delivery boy and goes
there. As he arrives, we see Forrester waiting in his car,
ominously.

Willi tries to keep up pretenses, but it is clear that Carla
is innocent. Willi suddenly pulls his gun, admitting his role
in the whole thing, and his determination now to get away with
the film that is in the suit shoulders. Stephen tries to grab
Willi's gun, but Carla gets it instead. She holds it on her
brother, but Willi, confident that she won't shoot, rushes
out. Carla shoots through the door, and they find Willi dead
outside. Stephen takes the film from the shoulders of Willi's
suit, but then Forrester and his men meet them on the landing.
Carla and Stephen rush up the stairs to the roof, closely followed by Forrester, but the inspector and his men arrive just
in time to save the couple. The last shot of the film shows
the two happily on their honeymoon, recalling ironically that
they had no cake at their wedding.

Credits:

| | |
|---|---|
| Producer: | Seton I. Miller |
| Director: | Fritz Lang |
| Screenplay: | Seton I. Miller, based on the novel by Graham Greene |
| Photography: | Henry Sharp |
| Art Direction: | Hans T. Dreier, Hal Pereira |
| Music: | Victor Young |
| Set Decoration: | Bert Granger |
| Editor: | Archie Marshek |
| Assistant Director: | George Templeton |
| Cast: | Ray Milland (Stephen Neale), Marjorie Reynolds (Carla Hilfe), Carl Esmond (Willi Hilfe), Dan Duryea (Travers), Hillary Brooke (Mrs. Bellane), Percy Waram (Inspector Prentice), Erskine Sanford (Mr. Rennit), Thomas Louden (Mr. Newland), Alan Napier (Dr. Forrester), Helene Grant (Mrs. Merrick), Aminta Dyne (the first Mrs. Bellaire), Rita Johnson (the second Mrs. Bellaire), Mary Field (Miss Penteel), Byron Foulger (Newby), Lester Matthews (Dr. Morton), Eustace Wyatt (Blind man). |
| Filmed at: | Paramount Studios, Hollywood, in 1944, |

| | |
|---|---|
| | in 7 weeks |
| Running Time: | 84 mins. (Reihe Film 7 lists 105 mins. as the original length) |
| Released: | Although produced earlier, the film was released on 16 October 1944, after Woman in the Window on 10 October. |

Reviews: (Some of these are annotated in Chapter 4)
Manchester Guardian (1944); Daily Telegraph (22 April 1944);
Monthly Film Bulletin No. 125 (May 1944); Today's Cinema (12
May 1944); Kine Weekly (18 May 1944); Winnington, R., New
Chronicle (20 May 1944); London Times (22 May 1944); New
Statesman (27 May 1944); LeJeune, C. A., Sunday Observer
(London) (18 June 1944); Motion Picture Herald (21 October 1944);
Harrison's Reports (23 October 1944); Time (6 November 1944);
New York Times (8 February 1945); Bony, Jean-Louis, Le Nouvel
Observateur (29 March 1967) (BFI); Télérama (9 April 1967)
(BFI); Schütte, Wolfram, Frankfurter Rundshau (29 March 1973)
(see Entry No. 430); Jansen, Peter W., Die Zeit (30 March 1973);
Schmidt, Eckhardt, Süddeutsche Zeitung (31 March 1973);
Literature Film Quarterly, Vol. 2, No. 4 (Fall 1974), pp.
310-323; Creelman, Eileen, New York Sun (MMA); Publicity re-
lease (BFI); Reviews from Hollywood Reporter, Film Daily,
Variety, New York Herald Tribune, all in MMA; Trade Release
(MMA).

25  WOMAN IN THE WINDOW (1944)
     Richard Wanley, a professor of criminology and psychology,
is seen lecturing to a class in New York and then sending his
family off on a trip. Alone for the evening, he meets his
friends, the district attorney and Dr. Barkstone, at their
club. Outside, all three admire a portrait of a beautiful
woman, and inside they discuss the degree to which they are
capable of responding to such beauty now that they are firmly
middle-aged. The professor is adamant in claiming that he is
beyond any kind of adventure with women; after saying goodbye
to his friends, he takes down Solomon's Song of Songs and
drinks a bit more. Stumbling out into the street later on,
Wanley pauses once more by the portrait, only this time a real
woman, Alice (the model for the painting), joins him.
     Already in love with her beauty, the professor is easily
tempted first to drink with her and then to return to her
apartment to look at some sketches. They are suddenly interrupted by a man (who turns out to be Howard, a rich man and
Alice's former lover), who immediately becomes violent on finding Wanley there. As Howard is about to strangle Wanley, Alice
hands Wanley a pair of scissors, and he stabs Howard to death.
After some hesitation, Wanley and Alice decide to try to cover
up the deed rather than go to the police. Wanley's career and
reputation are at stake. Leaving his waistcoat for surety,

Wanley goes off to fetch his car. They wrap the body in a
blanket and Wanley drives off to dump the body a little further
away from the city center. After some tense moments, first at
a toll booth and then with traffic police, Wanley gets rid of
the body, but he tears his sleeve on some barbed wire and leaves
tire tracks in soft mud by the roadside.

Back at the club the next night, Dr. Barkstone, Wanley's
friend, notices how pale and edgy he is and gives him a pre-
scription for sleeping pills. His friend the district attorney
is bustling with his new case, the disappearance of a financier,
and Wanley begins to look uncomfortable when the district attorney assumes it's a case of murder.

From this point on, Wanley has difficulty not revealing
himself. Taken on a visit to the murder site by his friend,
he automatically walks in the right direction; he has to account for a nasty cut on his hand and for the ivy poisoning
evident around the cut. His explanations get more and more
complicated, and his state of mind declines.

Finally Alice phones him up. She had retained Wanley's pen
with his initials on it, taken out of the waistcoat he left
temporarily with her, and then saw Wanley's photo in the paper
in connection with an award he received. She herself, however,
presents no threat. But Howard's mysterious bodyguard, who
disappeared after the murder, suddenly arrives at Alice's
apartment and begins to blackmail her. Alice and Wanley, fearing that he will ruin them, decide to get rid of the bodyguard.
They plan to give him an overdose of sleeping pills in a drink,
but the bodyguard is too smart for this. Taking all of Alice's
money and Howard's watch (which Alice had hidden away), he
rushes out, but promises to be back. After talking to Alice
and realizing their dilemma, Wanley takes an overdose of pills.

Meanwhile, there are shots outside Alice's apartment, and
she runs out to find the bodyguard's crumpled body. The police, guarding her apartment, had seen the man run out, but he
had shot first. Since he has the incriminating watch and the
money on him, the police assume that he murdered Howard.

Alice tries to phone Wanley at this point, but gets no answer. We see a close-up of the sleeping professor and the
phone ringing. This gradually changes to an image of the professor asleep in his club, being awakened by the waiter. We
realize that the whole drama has, in fact, been a nightmare
dreamt by Wanley after drinking and reading the Song of Songs.
He goes out into the street, and, pondering the dream, walks
home.

Credits:
Producer:         Nunnally Johnson
Director:         Fritz Lang
Screenplay:       Nunnally Johnson, based on the novel
                  Once Off Guard by J. H. Wallis
Photography:      Milton Krasner

| | |
|---|---|
| Special Effects: | Vernon Walker |
| Art Direction: | Duncan Cramer |
| Set Decoration: | Julia Heron |
| Costumes: | Muriel King |
| Music: | Arthur Lang |
| Editor: | Marjorie Johnson |
| Assistant Director: | Richard Harlan |
| Cast: | Edward G. Robinson (Professor Wanley), Joan Bennett (Alice Reed), Raymond Massey (Frank Lalor, district attorney), Dan Duryea (Heidt, blackmailer), Edmond Breon (Dr. Barkstone), Thomas E. Jackson (Inspector Jackson), Arthur Loft (Mazard), Dorothy Peterson (Mrs. Wanley), Carol Cameron (Elsie), Bobby Blake (Dickie), Frank Dawson. |
| Filmed at: | the studios of International Pictures/ Christie Corporation, Hollywood, 1944. |
| Running Time: | 99 mins. |
| Released: | 10 October 1944 |

Reviews:
London Times (28 July 1944); Motion Picture Herald (14 October 1944); Monthly Film Bulletin No. 133 (January 1945), p. 7; Kine Weekly (1 January 1945); Today's Cinema (3 January 1945); New York Times (16 January 1945); News Chronicle (3 February 1945); Powell, Dilys, Sunday Observer (4 February 1945); Daily Telegraph (5 February 1945); The Spectator (10 February 1945); E. P. M. [Erika Pullner], Film-Dienst (6 May 1950); Reissue: Today's Cinema (6 September 1954); Kine Weekly (9 September 1954); Th. K. [Theodor Kotulla], Filmkritik, No. 7 (1959), p. 196; Trölle, Borge, Danish Film Museum Notes (November 1964) (BFI); Review from Radio-Télévision-Cinéma (no date-BFI); Publicity Release, International Pictures Corp. (BFI).

26   SCARLET STREET (1945)

The film opens on a wet night in New York. Inside a smart club, a business firm is honoring Chris Cross, their cashier of twenty-five years. J. B., the boss, has to hurry off to a date with his glamorous mistress, while Chris and his friend, both lonely men, wander out into the empty streets. After sending his friend off, Chris hears a woman scream and sees a man run away. He helps the woman, Kitty Marsh, and they have a drink together near her apartment. A Sunday painter in fact, Chris misleads Kitty into thinking that he is a rich, established artist.

Kitty and her crooked boyfriend, Johnny, decide to exploit Chris, who, unhappily married, is infatuated with Kitty. Kitty begins to make demands on Chris for money to buy clothes and to set herself up in an apartment where Chris can also come to paint. Not having much money, Chris first takes some of his wife's bonds and is then driven to stealing from his own firm.

Johnny decides to find out just how good a painter Chris is and takes some of the paintings to a street show. There they are seen by some art dealers, who trace the artist to Kitty's apartment. Kitty pretends to be the painter and, helped by Johnny, who acts as her agent, they make profitable deals with the art people. Believing that Kitty loves him, and not knowing about Johnny (who pretends to be the boyfriend of Kitty's old roommate, Millie) Chris is not even angry when he finds out that Kitty has been selling his paintings under her own name. He feels it merely brings them closer.

Meanwhile, Homer, the first husband of Chris's wife, Adèle, supposed dead in action, suddenly returns. He is hoping to blackmail Chris, who, he presumes, wishes to stay with Adèle. Chris, of course, now sees his chance to be free to marry Kitty. He deceives Homer into revealing his existence to Adèle and leaves him to his fate. Having already packed his bags, Chris now goes to Kitty's place in the belief that he can finally have his wish and marry her.

On entering the apartment, Chris hears romantic music and finds Kitty in Johnny's arms, declaring her love. Hurt beyond belief, Chris returns downstairs and hides when Johnny comes down. He creeps out to a bar wondering what to do now. He decides that Kitty must love him anyway and returns to ask her to marry him. We have meanwhile seen Kitty on the phone with her friend, Millie. Millie tells Kitty that Johnny got very drunk and is on his way back to give Kitty hell for allowing Chris to find them together. Kitty smirks confidently, sure that they will, as usual, make up.

Kitty thus thinks it is Johnny when she hears the door open. But Chris comes in and pleads with her to go away with him. Kitty, however, finally fed up with the whole game, turns on Chris and reveals her true feelings about him. She says that she scorns him and that he is ridiculous in his love for her. She has never loved anyone but Johnny. Unable to tolerate the truth about their relationship, Crise grabs an ice pick that Johnny had earlier brought into the apartment and stabs Kitty to death. He then creeps out, not having been seen by anyone.

Johnny soon arrives in a drunken stupor and finds Kitty dead. All the circumstantial evidence points to him as the murderer, and he is arrested. Chris, of course, denies having seen Kitty that evening, and he allows Johnny to be executed for a murder he didn't commit. However, after the execution, Chris is haunted by the voices of both Kitty and Johnny. Fired from his job for embezzlement Chris roams the streets, telling everyone he should be hung for murder, but is disregarded as being out of his mind. He becomes a bum, wandering tormented around the New York streets, not even hearing a rich gallery owner telling his wife proudly that the painting of Kitty that was just sold went for ten thousand dollars.

*Fritz Lang*

Credits:

| | |
|---|---|
| Producer: | Walter Wanger |
| Director: | Fritz Lang |
| Screenplay: | Dudley Nichols, based on the novel and play La Chienne by Georges de la Fouchardière (with Mouëzy-Eon) |
| Photography: | Milton Krasner |
| Special Photographic Effects: | John P. Fulton |
| Art Direction: | Alexander Golitzen |
| Set Decoration: | Russell A. Gausman, Carl Lawrence |
| Costumes: | Travis Banton |
| Paintings: | John Decker |
| Music: | Hans J. Salter |
| Editor: | Arthur Hilton |
| Assistant Director: | Melville Shyer |
| Cast: | Edward G. Robinson (Christopher Cross), Joan Bennett (Kitty), Dan Duryea (Johnny), Margaret Lindsay (Millie), Rosalind Ivan (Adèle), Samuel S. Hinds (Charles Pringle), Jess Barker (Janeway), Arthur Loft (Dellarowe), Vladimir Sokoloff (Pop Lejon), Charles Kemper (Patcheye), Russell Hicks (Hogarth), Anita Bolster (Mrs. Michaels), Cyrus W. Kendell (Nick), Fred Essler (Marchetti), Edgar Dearing/Tom Dillon (Police officers), Chuck Hamilton (Chauffeur), Gus Glassmire, Howard Mitchell, Ralph Littlefield, Sherry Hall, Jack Stratham (Workers), Rodney Bell (Barney), Byron Foulger (Landlord), Will Wright (Cashier). |
| Filmed at: | Diana Productions Studios, Los Angeles, 1945 in 56 days |
| Running Time: | 102 mins. |
| Released: | by Universal, 28 December 1945 |

Reviews:
Motion Picture Herald (29 December 1945); Grant, Jack D., Hollywood Reporter (1946) (MMA); PM (7 January 1946); Time Magazine (21 January 1946); Today's Cinema (25 January 1946); Kine Weekly (31 January 1946); K. F. B., Monthly Film Bulletin, (February 1946); Parade (10 February 1946) (MMA); New York Times (15 February 1946); Daily Mirror (21 February 1946); Evening Standard (22 February 1946); Manchester Guardian (22 February 1946); Daily Express (23 February 1946); Daily Herald (29 February 1946); The Spectator (1 March 1946); New Statesman (2 March 1946); Philadelphia Motion Picture Forum (25 March 1946); Harrison's Reports (4 April 1946); New York Times

(23 September 1956) (MMA); Z., <u>Film-Dienst</u> (23 March 1950);
Everson, William, Lecture on Lang's <u>Scarlet Street</u> in
Pittsburgh (18 June 1976) (MMA); Anon., "Fritz Lang Shows Them
How" (on <u>Scarlet Street</u> and its making); Kreck, Joachim,
<u>Deutsche Film Theatre</u> (film notes-BFI); <u>Showman's Trade Review</u>
(MMA); <u>Trade Synopsis</u> (Universal Studio) (MMA); <u>Variety</u> (MMA);
Wilk, Ralph, <u>Film Daily</u> (MMA).

27    CLOAK AND DAGGER (1946)

We see Alvah Jasper at work in his physics lab in a big
Midwestern university. An old classmate is sent by the Office
of Strategic Services, "the cloak and dagger boys," to enlist
Jasper's help first, in interpreting a message from France and
second, in finding out how far the Germans have gotten toward
making a nuclear bomb. Jasper is to visit a leading German
atomic scientist, Dr. Katerin Loder, who has escaped to
Switzerland. Jasper is against using science to create destructive weapons, but is persuaded to go, especially since he
admires Dr. Loder greatly and is anxious to meet her.

Arriving in Switzerland, Jasper gives himself away at the
airport and German agents trail him to his hotel and to the
meeting with Dr. Loder the next day. Too weak to talk that
day, she promises to give Jasper all the information later on.
Back at the hotel, however, Jasper learns that Dr. Loder has
been kidnapped from the hospital. He is told by his contact
in Switzerland to obtain information regarding Loder's whereabouts from a spy named Dawson.

Jasper finally gets the information out of Dawson, but when
they arrive at the country house where Loder is hidden, they
discover that she has been murdered. Jasper is now told that
the one last hope for obtaining the information about the state
of German science is nuclear physicist Dr. Polda. But Polda
is in Italy, heavily guarded by the fascists.

Jasper is met on the Italian shore by a group of resistance
people, among them Gina, who looks after him. After a few
tense moments in the back of a truck, Jasper arrives safely
at Polda's residence suitably disguised as a German scientist.
Dr. Polda, terrified by the fascists who are holding his daughter, Maria, nearly betrays Jasper, but he finally agrees to an
escape plan providing that his daughter will also be freed.
Two resistance men leave to rescue Maria. Gina and Jasper are
to wait for a message and then take Polda to a place where they
will all be picked up by a plane.

Left alone for several days, Jasper and Gina begin to fall
in love. Gina's tough exterior hides the pain and suffering
she has endured as a resistance worker and her feeling that "if
you fight scum, you become scum." Jasper comforts and encourages her, but they have little time for romance. They
pass several tense days on the run before they receive their
message to meet Polda and other underground members in town.
Jasper has to kill Luigi, Polda's fascist guard, before they

get Polda safely away to a country hut.

There they meet other workers and all anxiously await Maria's arrival, which is to coincide with that of the rescue plane. But when the woman is finally brought in, Polda discovers that it is not his daughter. The fascists have outwitted the resistance and allowed an agent to be captured in order to be led back to Polda. The group now tries to hold off the fascists with gunfire while Gina leads Jasper and Polda out through an underground passage to the woods and so to the rescue plane. They arrive just before the plane leaves, and there is a touching farewell with Gina, who refuses to go along despite her love for Jasper. He promises to come and fetch her when the war is over, and the plane takes off safely as the first glimmer of dawn appears in the sky.

Credits:

| | |
|---|---|
| Producer: | Milton Sperling |
| Director: | Fritz Lang |
| Screenplay: | Albert Maltz, Ring Lardner, Jr., based on a story by Boris Ingster and John Larkin, suggested by a book by Corey Ford and Alastair MacBain |
| Photography: | Sol Polita |
| Art Direction: | Max Parker |
| Set Decoration: | Walter Hilford |
| Special Effects: | Harry Barndollar, Edwin DuPar |
| Music: | Max Steiner |
| Editor: | Christian Nyby |
| Assistant Director: | Russ Saunders |
| Technical Advisor: | Michael Burke |
| Cast: | Gary Cooper (Prof. Alvah Jasper), Lilli Palmer (Gina), Robert Alda (Pinkie), Vladmimir Sokoloff (Dr. Polda), J. Edward Brombert (Trenk), Marjorie Hoshelle (Ann Dawson), Ludwig Stössel (the German), Helene Thimig (Katherine Loder), Dan Seymour (Marsoli), Marc Lawrence (Luigi), James Flavin (Col. Walsh), Pat O'Moore (the Englishman), Charles Marsh (Lingg), Larry Olson (Tommy), Don Turner (Erich), Rosalind Lyons, Connie Gilchrist. |
| Filmed at: | United State Pictures, Inc., Hollywood, in 1946 |
| Running Time: | Original release length, 106 mins; current prints, 102 mins. |
| Release: | by Warner Bros 28 September 1946 |

Reviews:
*Variety* (8 September 1946); *Film Daily* (11 September 1946);

Motion Picture Herald (14 September 1946); Harrison's Reports (16 September 1946); New York Times (5 October 1946); Time (21 October 1946); Monthly Film Bulletin, No. 157 (January 1947); Today's Cinema (3 January 1947); Kine Weekly (9 January 1947); Spectator (31 January 1947); Ruppert, Martin, Frankfurter Allgemeine Zeitung (27 July 1953); Ro. [Frank Rowas], Film-Dienst (11 September 1953); Filmcritica (Rome) (October 1963); Canham, Kingsley, Films and Filming, 15, No. 5 (February 1969); Trade Reviews (MMA); Warner Pressbook (MMA) (very revealing about advertising strategies).

28    SECRET BEYOND THE DOOR (1948)

The tone of the film is set by a surrealist image of a door, followed by a close-up of circles in a pond. Celia Lamphere, who narrates the story, says that it is her wedding day. There is then a flashback to the events preceding the wedding. We learn that Celia, a rich heiress, had rejected many suitors and was again postponing a marriage. The sudden death of her brother and guardian, Rick, upsets Celia, and her lawyer, Bob, advises a vacation in Mexico. There, in a rather ominous manner, Celia meets Mark Lamphere. During a lovers' quarrel, Celia is fascinated by a special quality she sees in Mark's eyes and is sure that he is what she has been waiting for. They fall in love and arrange a hasty marriage. Just before the wedding, Celia seems almost hypnotized by Mark, and on the day itself she senses something is wrong and almost runs away.

On their honeymoon Mark tells Celia of his hobby of collecting rooms, and in a sinister way suggests that the way a place is built determines what will happen in it, certain rooms causing violence, even murder.

Once at Mark's mansion, Lavender Falls, Celia meets Mark's rather cool sister, Caroline, Mark's son, David, and Miss Robey, Mark's secretary (none of whom Mark had mentioned earlier). There are mysterious hints about the death of Mark's first wife.

When Celia sees Mark the next day on his arrival from the city he acts strangely at the sight of the sprig of lilac that Celia had picked to brighten up her suit. Mark continues to be withdrawn, and Celia, tired of the moods and the odd houseful of people, determines to return to her old life in New York. After meeting Mark, however, that life seems empty, and at the station she turns around, deciding to see it through with Mark.

At their housewarming party a few days later, a sudden storm interrupts the gaiety in the garden, and Mark decides to take his guests on a tour of his collection of rooms. As he opens up each room with a special key, he reveals a reconstruction of a famous murder of a woman: a Huguenot countess stabbed by her husband, a mother tied to a chair and drowned by her son, a series of murders by Don Ignazio, who strangled his wives with a scarf. As he enters the third room, Mark notes that murder, as well as love, is a fine art, a comment that horrifies Celia. In relation to one of the murders, Mark mentions a certain fragrance driving the man to kill. A bright psychology major in the crowd suggests an analysis of the murderer as one driven by unnatural love for his victims. Mark refuses to open the seventh door, however, and when pressed by Celia, becomes irritated.

After the guests have left, Celia questions Mark about the rooms he called "felicitous" on their honeymoon. Mark becomes almost ecstatic as he notes that the architecture fits the emotions, and that the desire to murder is as strong an emotion as love. When Celia tries to understand Mark further, he turns on her saying that he has always been hemmed in by women trying to live his life for him.

The next day, talking to Caroline in the garden, Celia learns that Mark's mother loved lilacs, but that Mark had them all pulled up when she died. Caroline notes that she picked Eleanor (Mark's first wife) for Mark and regretted it afterwards; she also mentions a childhood episode when she locked Mark in his room once as a joke, but he became hysterical thinking it had been his mother. Soon after this, David tells Celia that his father killed his mother.

Having been given all this information, Celia now tries to piece together what had been going on in the house and to figure out what Mark's problems are. She decides that the clue to everything must lie in the locked seventh room and has a copy of the key made. Late one night, she creeps down to open it, and is horrified to find that it is a copy of her own room, although there is, as yet, nothing in it. She guesses that Mark is waiting for her murder to complete it. Frightened by the imminence of her death, she panics and rushes out. Miss Robey helps her to escape and she finds a long scarf strewn on the stairs. In the mist-laden garden she searches frantically for her car as a dark figure looms ominously.

Next morning, we see Mark shaving and, apparently guilt-ridden, hallucinating. He imagines a trial where he is judge, jury, prosecutor, defender, and criminal simultaneously. At the breakfast table, Celia appears, evidently not having escaped, and we learn that Miss Robey, Caroline, and David are leaving that day. Mark and Celia will be alone. A storm begins as evening comes, and Mark becomes terrified of his impulses if left alone with Celia. Celia, meanwhile, has decided that if Mark is to be cured, he must meet with her in the seventh room, which she has filled with lilacs. She waits to see what will happen. Mark finally appears, in a sinister manner, twisting a scarf in his hand. Celia tells him that it was Caroline, not his mother, who locked him in, and Mark is suddenly released from his sickness. The last shot of the film shows Celia and Mark on a second honeymoon, Mark aware that he is on the way to being cured, but that it still will take some time.

Credits:
Producer:                    Fritz Lang, Walter Wanger
Director:                    Fritz Lang
Screenplay:                  Silvia Richards, from the story
                             "Museum Piece No. 13" by Rufus King
Photography:                 Stanley Cortez
Set Decoration:              Russell A. Gausman, John Austin
Production Designer:         Max Parker
Music:                       Miklos Rosza
Editor:                      Arthur Hilton
Assistant Director:          William Holland
Cast:                        Joan Bennett (Celia Lamphere),
                             Barbara O'Neil (Miss Robey), Michael
                             Redgrave (Mark Lamphere), Anne Revere
                             (Caroline Lamphere), Natalie Schaefer
                             (Edith Potter), Paul Cavanagh (Rick
                             Barrett), Anabel Shaw (Society guest),
                             Rosa Rey (Paquita), James Seay (Bob
                             Dwight), Mark Dennis (David), Donna
                             Di Mario (Gypsy), David Cota (Her
                             lover), Celia Moore.
Filmed at:                   Diana Productions Studies, in 1947,
                             in 61 days.
Running Time:                99 mins.
Released:                    By Universal International, 13
                             January 1948

Reviews:
Universal Plot Synopsis (6 March 1947) (MMA); Variety (29
December 1947); Hollywood Reporter (31 December 1947);
Crowther, Bosley, New York Times (16 January 1948); Cook, Alton,
New York World Telegram (February 1948) (MMA); Guernsey, Otis
L., New York Herald Tribune (February 1948) (MMA); Newsweek
(2 February 1948); Time (23 February 1948); Today's Cinema
(20 October 1948); Monthly Film Bulletin, No. 179 (November
1948); Evening News (4 November 1948); Evening Standard (4
November 1948); Daily Mirror (5 November 1948); Sunday Observer
(London) (5 November 1948); Daily Worker (6 November 1948);
Manchester Guardian (6 November 1948); Graphic (7 November
1948); Daily Herald (7 November 1948); Times (London) (7
November 1948).

29  HOUSE BY THE RIVER (1950)
    Most of the action takes place in a large Victorian house
situated on a river.  The opening shots show the river and
house on a sunny summer afternoon, when everything is apparently normal.  Stephen Byrne, a not-too-successful writer is plod-
ding away in his garden-study, while his neighbor, Mrs. Ambrose,
gardens next door.  Lang establishes a sinister, foreboding
mood, which intensifies as the film progresses.  Mrs. Ambrose
notices a large, unsightly object floating in the water and

complains about how uneasy the river makes her feel.

Stephen is obviously interested in his maid, Emily, who
rather seductively hands him a parcel (yet one more returned
manuscript) before asking if she can shower in his bathroom
since the plumber did not come to repair her bathroom.  With
his wife not there, and in an ugly mood over his writing,
Stephen stares up at the light in the bathroom where Emily is
showering.  We cut to Emily inside making herself attractive
(it is not clear whether for Stephen or someone else) and putting on Marjorie Byrne's perfume.  At about the same moment,
Stephen enters the now dark house, helping himself to a drink
in the hall, and Emily walks slowly down the stairs.  The sight
of her legs emerging from the negligée borrowed from his wife,
arouses Stephen and he goes to kiss Emily.  She struggles, and
in an effort to prevent Mrs. Ambrose from hearing, Stephen puts
his hand over her mouth.  After the neighbor has gone, Stephen
finds that Emily is dead.

Stephen's crippled brother, John, a lawyer and a frequent
visitor to the house, arrives, and Stephen persuades him to
help in disposing of Emily's body.  When John resists, Stephen
pretends that Marjorie, whom John loves, is pregnant and could
not stand the shock.  They tie Emily up in a sack that Stephen
had borrowed from John and are almost discovered by Mrs. Ambrose.

Stephen and John take the body to the river, their faces lit
only by the moon.  After dropping John off, Stephen once again
enters the dark house, takes his drink, and again hears a woman
stepping slowly down the stairs.  Afraid that it is Emily's
ghost, he jumps, only to find that Marjorie, his wife, had returned and is now looking for Emily.

At a party later that evening, Stephen is lively and entertaining, while John stands gloomily in a corner, critical and
condemning.  The next day, the police begin to investigate
Emily's disappearance.  Stephen lies to Emily's parents, his
wife, and the detectives.  The tension begins to eat at John,
however, who cannot bear to see what Stephen is doing; he is
shorttempered with his maid after seeing a newspaper article
with sketches of Stephen and Emily in it.  Stephen phones to
remind John that his name was on the sack in which they put
Emily, hoping that this will prevent him from going to the
police.

Stephen is cashing in on the publicity, meanwhile, and using
it to increase the sales of his books.  He is now engrossed in
a new novel that he will not let anyone see.  He tells Marjorie
that this novel is about things he really knows, and we learn
that it is, in fact, a thinly disguised account of his murder
of Emily.

Estranged, Marjorie and Stephen spend their evenings separately, Stephen near the river with his novel and Marjorie looking at a photo album.  She is upset to discover that Stephen
has cut out a certain photo, which she remembers was the basis
of the newspaper sketch.  John drops by and the two begin to

share their feelings about Stephen's strange behavior. Their mutual loneliness and need for each other is now clear.

Mrs. Ambrose, meanwhile, has seen what she thinks is the old large object floating by again, but which we and Stephen immediately recognize as Emily's body, which has surfaced. Stephen tries to lodge the body securely, but cannot do it and is constantly haunted by a vision of Emily coming out of the sack alive.

John, meanwhile, is cracking under the strain. He can no longer eat, and this offends his maid. He takes to drinking and loses clients daily. After his maid leaves, he degenerates even more, Marjorie now being his only solace. One night, after trying unsuccessfully to sink the sack, Stephen arrives hysterical at John's house. They both realize that the sack will now be discovered, but Stephen is relieved that it will be traced to John.

At the official trial that follows, Stephen manipulates people and events to ensure his innocence and place the guilt on his brother. Despite the weight of the testimoney against him and the circumstantial evidence, John is exonerated and let go. But the public scandal has ruined his career.

After the trial, Stephen behaves cruelly to Marjorie, from whom he is increasingly estranged. Afraid of Stephen, Marjorie goes to visit John, who is at his lowest point and about to go away. She persuades him to stay, but is concerned that he will take his life. These fears give Stephen the idea of trying to push John to suicide by piling up evidence of his supposed relationship with Emily.

Marjorie sends Stephen out after John one night when John appears especially distraught. Stephen hits John over the head, and leaves him for dead, returning to the house now to kill Marjorie. Marjorie has meanwhile found Stephen's manuscript and understands everything. As he is about to murder Marjorie, Stephen hears foot steps clanking up the stairs. Terrified of what he thinks is John's ghost, he drops Marjorie and rushes into the hall. The white, blowing curtains appear to him in the shape of Emily, and in terror he dashes toward them, becomes entangled, and falls to his death over the bannister. The last shots are of John and Emily standing together, while the pages of Stephen's manuscript flutter around the floor.

Credits:

| | |
|---|---|
| Producer: | Howard Welsch |
| Associate Producer: | Robert Peters |
| Director: | Fritz Lang |
| Screenplay: | Mel Dinelli, based on a novel by A. P. Herbert |
| Photography: | Edward Cronjager |
| Art Direction: | Bert Leven |
| Set Decoration: | Charles Thompson, John McCarthy, Jr. |

| | |
|---|---|
| Special Effects: | Howard and Theodore Lydecker |
| Costumes: | Adele Palmer |
| Music: | George Antheil |
| Editor: | Arthur D. Hilton |
| Production Manager: | Joseph Dillpe |
| Assistant Director: | John Grubbs |
| Cast: | Louis Hayward (Stephen Byrne), Lee Bowman (John Byrne), Jane Wyatt (Marjorie Byrne), Dorothy Patrick (Emily Gaunt), Ann Shoemaker (Mrs. Ambrose), Jody Gilbert (Flora Bantam), Peter Brocco (Attorney general), Howland Chamberlain (District attorney), Margaret Seddon (Mrs. Whittaker), Sarah Padden (Mrs. Beach), Kathleen Freeman (Effie Ferguson), Will Wright (Inspector Sarten), Leslie Kimmell (Mr. Gaunt), Effie Laird (Mrs. Gaunt). |
| Filmed at: | Fidelity Pictures Studios, Hollywood, 1949, in 32 days. |
| Running Time: | 88 mins. |
| Released: | By Republic 25 March 1950 |

Reviews:
New York Times (2 May 1950); G. L. [Gavin Lambert], Monthly Film Bulletin (London), No. 197 (June 1950); Motion Picture Herald (New York) (1 April 1950); Today's Cinema (16 May 1950), p. 6; Kine Weekly (18 May 1950), p. 25; Daily Film Renter (17 May 1950), p. 6; Everson, William K., Film Notes (MMA); Guernsey, Otis L., New York Herald Tribune (2 May 1950) (MMA: mixed review, asserting that the style not suited to plot).

30  AMERICAN GUERILLA IN THE PHILIPPINES (1950)
The opening sequence of the film shows Motor Torpedo 43 being blown up just outside the Philippine Islands. It is 1943. Shots of the burning boat are intercut with those of men swimming to shore, the wounded being carried on boards; we see men running for cover under trees, and Filipinos coming to aid the Americans. The group on shore just escapes being shot.

The voice of Anson Palmer, who functions periodically as narrator during the movie, informs us that he and a few other men were all that remained of Motor Torpedo 43 after helping MacArthur in his historic escape from Corregidor. After hiding out in a deserted hut, the men finally get the news that Bataan, the last post in the Philippines, has fallen to the Japanese. The men, now on their own, decide to try to reach Australia rather than surrender. Palmer and Jim Mitchell set out together, and we follow them alongside hundreds of Filipinos, all seeking to escape. They finally arrive at Daclobe on Leyte, where Colonel Bensen had been in command. Crowds of people are trying to see the Colonel, among them Jeanne Martinez, whom Palmer intercedes to help.

Palmer and his men buy and stock a boat. They last on the sea only seventy-two hours, and we then see the overturned boat. Palmer and Jim are rescued by friendly Filipinos active in the resistance. While resting there, Palmer witnesses the bravery of Miguel and other resistance workers in the face of Japanese aggression.

Palmer then tells how throughout the summer of 1943 he and his group wandered in the jungle, never thinking of fighting back, but trying only to avoid the increasing Japanese patrols. We then see his group battle with such a patrol and have the satisfaction of destroying it.

Palmer and his group arrive in a crowded village square, where an American is urging the people to contribute to his organization, which is trying to free the Philippines. Palmer, suspicious, approaches one man collecting from the people and offers the support of his men; the man is flustered, revealing the fraud, and the group quickly leave. Palmer is then approached by Martinez, who had watched the whole scene. He offers Palmer his assistance and invites him and his men to his house.

We cut to Jim and Palmer entering a serene villa surrounded by flowers. They are greeted by Jeanne Martinez, whom Palmer is delighted to see but disappointed to find married. They exchange news and are then taken to a Filipino Colonel, Demolando, who agrees to give Palmer a boat in return for his contacting a Colonel Phillips, who is coordinating all guerilla activities on the Philippines. Palmer and his men capture a Japanese boat when the officers leave it poorly guarded.

Later, they journey for days through the jungle, footsore and weary, fed by friendly islanders, until finally stumbling on Phillips. Phillips tells Palmer that MacArthur does not want the focus to be on killing Japanese but on creating a people's army ready to go into action when MacArthur is ready. A string of radio stations is badly needed, and Phillips puts Palmer in charge of radio operations on Leyte.

Palmer then narrates how the provisional government of Leyte was set up under the very noses of the Japanese, and an army of men was trained in preparation for MacArthur's return. At a fundraising garden party Palmer meets Jeanne Martinez again. They are delighted to see each other and begin to exchange accounts of their backgrounds as they fall in love. But Mr. Martinez arrives with a message for Palmer from Phillips: he is somehow to set up a radio station.

The next section of the film gives Palmer's account of how he managed this and of the first contact with San Francisco. But we see the Japanese intercept the call, and shortly afterwards they invade the station. The Americans just have time to gather their materials and escape. There is a tense sequence as the Japanese search the jungle.

Things now look bad for the Americans; the Japanese murder

villagers until they get information about the guerilla movement. They then break into the Martinez house, and brutally torture and murder Martinez in front of Jeanne, whom they interrogate about Palmer and abuse generally.

Palmer narrates how he and his men were constantly on the run with their radio, but, despite grave dangers, manage to keep informing the Americans about enemy movements. Jeanne is also a fugitive and they often meet briefly, finally declaring their love.

Palmer tells how though dreary weeks and months still lay ahead, the decisive change had taken place as the American submarines bring supplies and the guerillas make attacks everywhere. We see Palmer give Jeanne his ring before going on a dangerous mission. Palmer and his men give the movements of a Japanese destroyer to the Americans, who blow up the ship before it can escape. Palmer and his men get out just in time. Jeanne comes to them, as they hide out by a roadside, saying that the coast in the village is clear; but they barely enter the village before the Japanese return suddenly. The group takes refuge in a church and would have gone unnoticed had a boy not wandered out eating American chocolate. The Japanese invade the church and a bloody battle follows. Just in time, MacArthur's planes are heard droning overhead, and the enemy beats a hasty retreat. The film ends with MacArthur's triumphal march through the village as Palmer is given a precious bottle of Coke to toast their success.

Credits:

| | |
|---|---|
| Producer: | Lamar Trotti |
| Director: | Fritz Lang |
| Screenplay: | Lamar Trotti, based on the novel of the same title by Ira Wolfert |
| Photography (Technicolor): | Harry Jackson |
| Special Photographic Effects: | Fred Sersen |
| Art Direction: | Lyle Wheeler, J. Russell Spencer |
| Set Decoration: | Thomas Little, Stuart Reiss |
| Costumes: | Travilla |
| Music: | Cyril Mockridge |
| Musical Director: | Lionel Newman |
| Editor: | Robert Simpson |
| Production Manager: | F. E. Johnson |
| Second-Unit Director: | Robert D. Webb |
| Assistant Director: | Horace Hough |
| Cast: | Tyrone Power (Chuck Palmer), Micheline Presle [Prelle] (Jeanne Martinez), Jack Elam (Spencer), Bob Patten (Lovejoy), Tom Edwell (Jim Mitchell), Tommy Cook (Miguel), Robert Barrat (Gen. Douglas MacArthur), Juan Torena |

|  |  |
|---|---|
|  | (Juan Martinez), Miguel Azures (Philippine traitor), Eddie Infante (Col. Dimalanta), Orlando Martin (Col. Benson), Carleton Young (Col. Phillips), Chris de Vera, Erlinda Cortez, Rosa del Rosario, Katy Ruby. |
| Filmed by: | Twentieth-Century Fox on location in the Philippines (Luzon Island) (including interiors), in 1950, in 48 days |
| Running Time: | 105 mins. |
| Released: | 11 November 1950 |

Reviews:
Crowther, Bosley, New York Times (8 November 1950); Cue (16 November 1950) (negative review); Brog, Variety (15 August 1950) (positive review, noting differences from the novel); Motion Picture Herald (11 November 1950), p. 25 and (18 November 1959), p. 571; Ro. [Franz Rowas], Film-Dienst (7 June 1952); Färber, Helmut, Süddeutsche Zeitung (23 January 1969); Anon., "Hollywood Took a Task Force to Luzon" (n.d.) (MMA: interesting description of logistics of the filming); Guernsey, Otis L., New York Herald Tribune (MMA: mixed review--film unprofessional); Time (MMA: negative review--film counterfeit and hackneyed); Today's Cinema, No. 204, p. 200; Trade Synopsis (MMA).

31   RANCHO NOTORIOUS (1952)
    Beth Forbes, left alone to guard her father's store, is visited by Vern Haskell, her fiancé, who gives her a beautiful brooch. They discuss their forthcoming marriage, and then Vern leaves. Two men, Kinch and Whitey, ride into town; Kinch enters the store, evidently with the intent of seducing Beth and then robbing the store. Although the camera remains outside, we understand later that she has been raped and murdered. Vern arrives to find her dead; the brooch has been stolen along with the money.
    Vern vows revenge and sets out on the trail of the criminals. After a while he comes upon Whitey, left to die by Kinch after wanting to take his cut and leave. Whitey mutters something about "Chuck-a-Luck" before he dies, giving Vern the only clue he will have to Kinch's whereabouts.
    The theme song of the film now comes on the track:

    Now where and what is Chuck-a-Luck
    Nobody knows and the dead won't tell
    So on and on relentlessly this man pursues his quest . . .
    And deep within him grows the beast of HATE
    MURDER
    And REVENGE

The song continues and we see Vern interviewing various
people, none of whom knows anything about Chuck-a-Luck.  He
finally learns from an encounter in a barber shop that it is
connected with Altar Keene.

When Vern is chatting with a group of men one afternoon, one
of them suddenly perks up at the mention of Altar Keene and recalls an entertaining evening when the women rode their men
like horses.  We cut to a flashback of Altar's triumphantly
egging on her "horse," the old deputy, Baldy, who is telling
the tale.  Vern next meets with Dolly, Altar's friend, who recalls how Altar was fired from a saloon in Tascosa by Baldy,
because she kicked a man for fondling her.  Before she left,
however, Altar decided to have a turn on the roulette wheel,
and, helped by the man in charge, won all the takings.  Frenchie
Fairmont, a noted gunman and outlaw, happened to be in town,
and he protected Altar until she left the next day.

The flashbacks end with Baldy's delightedly telling Vern
that Altar's relationship with Frenchie is all over now since
Frenchie is in jail in Gunsight.  Vern is next seen entering
the town where Frenchie is imprisoned, and where an election
is going on.  The men advocating law and order have locked up
all the opposition for the duration, so that they cannot oversee the voting.  Vern gets himself arrested and is thrown into
Frenchie's cell.  The two men then engineer a jail-break and
ride out of town.

Frenchie leads Vern to Rancho Notorious, where he says they
will be protected by Altar Keene.  Altar welcomes them in riding gear; she and Vern are obviously attracted to each other.
No questions are asked at the ranch, but the men who come
there have to abide by certain rules, one of which is that no
one must ask any questions about the others.  Vern thus has to
figure out for himself which of the outlaws at the ranch killed
his fiancée.

He decides that getting close to Altar would be the best
strategy, since she surely knows; but this means alienating
Frenchie.  As he woos her quietly Vern realizes that he is
falling in love.  Frenchie becomes jealous and hints that Vern
should leave Altar alone; but Vern is driven on by his need to
find his fiancée's murderer.  On the night of Altar's birthday
party, Vern sees the brooch on her gown and is now more determined than ever to know the killer.

Vern manages to find himself alone at the ranch with Altar
one day.  They ride out to a lonely promontory where they all
but declare their love openly.  Vern's overriding motivation,
however, is to find out who gave Altar the brooch.  When he
discovers that it is Kinch, he plans to murder him when the
opportunity arises.

Frenchie, meanwhile, takes Vern along on their next robbery.
Kinch, suspecting who Vern is from the way he rides his horse,
tries to kill him and sets off a gun battle.  The outlaws manage to escape, and Vern returns to the ranch with Altar's share

of the loot. Frenchie, however, is missing. Once there, Vern berates Altar for harboring men like Kinch and tells her the history of the brooch.

Back in town, Vern meets Kinch in a saloon and tells him that he knows he killed his fiancée. Since Kinch will not fight, Vern hands him over to the sheriff, and Kinch is taken off to jail. On the way there, however, Kinch's friends free him and they all escape.

Frenchie returns wounded to the ranch to find Altar leaving. She has decided to give up her life harboring criminals and return to being a dancer. Frenchie thinks she is leaving with Vern, but Altar bitterly tells him that Vern would not have her. At that moment, Kinch and his friends return to kill Altar, whom they suspect of having betrayed them. Vern arrives in time to help, but Altar stops a bullet meant for Frenchie and dies there between the two men, who both declare their love for her as she dies.

Frenchie and Vern then ride off together, with nothing left to live for. The film concludes with this song:

> Now revenge is a bitter and evil fruit
> And death hangs beside it on the bough
> These men that lived by the code of hate
> Have nothing to live for now . . .
> And the legends tell that when Custer fell
> They died with him in the fight.

Credits:

| | |
|---|---|
| Producer: | Howard Welsch |
| Director: | Fritz Lang |
| Screenplay: | Dan Taradash, based on the story "Gunsight Whitman," by Sylvia Richards |
| Photography (Technicolor): | Hal Mohr |
| Art Direction: | Robert Priestly |
| Music: | Emil Newman. Songs: "The Legend of Chuck-A-Luck" (sung by William Lee), "Gypsy Davey," "Get Away, Young Man" (sung by Marlene Dietrich) by Ken Darby. |
| Editor: | Otto Ludwig |
| Assistant Director: | Emmett Emerson |
| Cast: | Marlene Dietrich (Altar Keene), Arthur Kennedy (Vern Haskell), Mel Ferrer (Frenchie Fairmont), Gloria Henry (Beth), William Frawley (Baldy Gunder), Lisa Ferraday (Maxine), John Raven (Dealer), Jack Elam (Geary), Dan Seymour (Paul), George Reeves (Wilson), Rodric |

Redwing (Rio), Frank Ferguson
(Preacher), Clarles Gonzales (Hevia),
Francis MacDonald (Harbin), John
Kellogg (Salesman), Stan Jolley
(Warren), Jose Dominguez (Gonzales),
John Doucette (Whitey), Stuart
Randall (Starr), Frank Graham (Ace
Maguire), Fuzzy Knight (Barber),
Roger Anderson (Red), Felipe Turich
(Sanchez), Lloyd Gough (Kinch),
Russell Johnson (Dealer)

Filmed at:             Fidelity Pictures, Hollywood, in 1951
Running Time:          89 mins.
Released:              By RKO, February 1952

Reviews:

Crowther, Bosley, New York Times (15 May 1952) (negative review,
See Entry No. 194); Houston, Penelope, Monthly Film Bulletin,
No. 220 (May 1952) (negative review--Lang's style is mechani-
cal, Dietrich worn); Variety (6 February 1952); Motion Picture
Herald (9 February 1952), p. 1229; Today's Cinema (2 April
1952), p. 14; Kine Weekly (3 April 1952), p. 16; Saturday
Review (March 1952); Cameron, Kate, New York Daily News (15
May 1952); Guernsey, Otis L., New York Herald Tribune (15 May
1952) (negative review, "an erratic western"); Winsten, Archer,
New York Post (15 May 1952) (MMA: negative review); ft.
[Friedrich Luft], Die Neue Zeitung (Berlin) (7 January 1953);
F. [Walter Feigl], Film-Dienst (9 January 1953); Farber, Helmut,
Süddeutsche Zeitung (Munich) (4 October 1965); H. G. P. [Hans
Günther Pflaum], Süddeutsche Zeitung (Munich) (October 1973);
Aaronson, Dominique, IDHEC-Fiche Filmographique, No. 182; Anon,
Review in pamphlet Spielfilme im Deutschen Fernsehen, 1971.
(Available in Deutschen Film und Fernsehakademie, West Berlin.)

32   CLASH BY NIGHT (1952)
     The film, set in a fishing town, opens with on-location
shots of the sea crashing against the shore, intercut with
shots of birds and seals and of fishermen hauling in a catch.
We cut to the village and the women in the canning factory
cleaning the fish.
     As a train is leaving the station, a woman, Mae Doyle, walks
into town after a ten-year absence.  In a bar she runs into
Jerry D'Amato.
     Mae arrives to an empty house, but we see her brother Joe
and his girlfriend Peggy on their way there for lunch.  Joe is
cool to Mae, who displeased the family by leaving and who now
returns, having failed to find a husband and wealth in the
city.  Peggy is friendly, and Joe finally agrees to let Mae
stay.
     Jerry, Joe, and the men are mending nets by the sea.  Jerry
admits his attraction to Mae, whom he finally asks out.  He

arrives, looking awkward in a suit, to find Mae still dressing. Before they go to a movie, Jerry talks about his family in Italy. Jerry wants Mae to meet his friend, Earl, the projectionist. Attracted to each other at once, Earl and Mae nevertheless spar later on in a bar.

The next day, Peggy and Mae confide in each other: Mae admits she needs a man to take care of her, while Peggy tells her that Jerry needs a woman to look after him. Soon afterwards, one dark night on a boat, Jerry tells Mae he wants to marry her. She's afraid she will hurt him, but agrees to think about it. The next day at a beach party, Earl gets drunk and starts flirting with Mae. Angry at first, Mae nevertheless confides in Earl, who then wants to know where he stands with her. Attracted to but disturbed by Earl, Mae now decides to marry Jerry. At the wedding that soon follows, Earl is disgruntled and Mae hostile.

Time passes, and Mae and Jerry settle into their home and soon have a baby. It is now a hot summer. We see Mae and Jerry in their home, Jerry taking care of his baby, showing her the moon and rocking her, while Mae seems preoccupied. Earl drops by now in the evenings, and one night tells Mae that he has gotten divorced. Another night he comes by very drunk and tells Jerry to take care of his lovely wife and baby. They let him stay with them after he passes out. While Jerry rocks the baby, Mae stands silent at the window watching the waves crash against the shore. We cut to dawn and the birds flying, and then Jerry is called out.

After he has gone, Mae looks despairingly at the empty apartment, clearly frustrated and bored. Earl comes out. Unable to hold back any longer, they kiss passionately, beginning their affair.

Jerry, rescuing his uncle as usual from a bar, hears the men talking about Earl and Mae. He comes home to an empty house--now the routine--very upset and disturbed. When Mae returns after a long day with Earl, she shouts angrily at Jerry about how bored she is, and how miserable their little life seems to her. Furious, Jerry barely knows how to contain his anger and jealousy, but Mae is determined to honor her love for Earl and leave Jerry. For Earl, also, it is his hope for happiness. Together on the beach, Earl and Mae declare their love, but Mae is grief-stricken at the idea of giving up her baby.

Back in the house, Jerry paces up and down, furious and not knowing what to do. Earl and Mae come in together to say that they have decided to get married. After an ugly scene where they fight about who should keep the baby, Mae leaves. At Joe and Peggy's place, she gets comfort from Peggy but blame from Joe. She joins Earl at his projection booth, but Jerry comes in ready to kill Earl. After a tense scene, Jerry comes to his senses and rushes out.

Earl and Mae decide that they must leave town. Mae goes

home to get her things and the baby, only to find Jerry and the baby gone.  She and Earl have a bitter fight about leaving without the baby; Mae suddenly understands the kind of people she and Earl are--always on the run, afraid of belonging to anyone, afraid of responsibility, wanting things always their way.  She decides to find Jerry and the baby, guessing that he has taken her to his boat.  Begging Jerry's forgiveness, she swears that this time she will stay and find happiness in him and her child.

Credits:

| | |
|---|---|
| Producer: | Harriet Parsons |
| Executive Producer: | Jerry Wald |
| Director: | Fritz Lang |
| Screenplay: | Alfred Hayes, based on the play of the same name by Clifford Odets. |
| Photographer: | Nicholas Musuraca |
| Special Photographic Effects: | Harold Wellman |
| Art Direction: | Albert S. D'Agostino, Carroll Clark |
| Set Decoration: | Darrell Silvera, Jack Mills |
| Music Director: | C. Bakaleinikoff |
| Music: | Roy Webb.  Song: "I Hear a Rhapsody" by Dick Gasparre, Jack Baker, George Fragos (sung by Tony Martin) |
| Editor: | George J. Amy |
| Cast: | Barbara Stanwyck (Mae Doyle), Paul Douglas (Jerry D'Amato), Robert Ryan (Earl Pfeiffer), Marilyn Monroe (Peggy), J. Carroll Naish (Uncle Vince), Keith Andes (Joe Doyle), Silvio Minciotti (Papa D'Amato) |
| Filmed at: | Wald-Krasna Productions/RKO Pictures, Hollywood in 1951.  Shooting took 32 days, including locations at Monterey, California |
| Running Time: | 105 mins. |
| Released: | 16 May 1952 |

Reviews:
Variety (14 May 1952); Motion Picture Herald (17 May 1952); Time (9 June 1952) (MMA: condescending review; Lang's direction is turgid, the movie pretentious); Saturday Review (14 June 1952); Cook, Alton, New York World-Telegraph and Sun (19 June 1952) (MMA: focus is on Monroe; Lang's direction praised); New York Herald Tribune (19 June 1952) (MMA: negative review; Lang blamed for plot's improbability); A. W. [A. H. Weiler], New York Times (19 June 1952); Today's Cinema (23 July 1952), p. 8; Daily Film Renter (23 July 1952), p. 7; Kine Weekly (31 July 1952), p. 13; Daily Herald (1 August 1952); News of the World (3 August 1952); Daily Telegraph (4 August 1952); K. R., Monthly Film Bulletin, No. 224 (September 1952); Morgan, James,

Sight and Sound, 22, No. 2 (October–December 1952); E. (Walter
Feigl), Film-Dienst (1 December 1952); S.F. (Hans Schwab-
Felisch), Die Neue Zeitung (West Berlin) (20 August 1953);
Schwerbrock, Wolfgang, Frankfurter Allgemeine Zeitung (2
October 1956); Daily Express (1 August 1957); Sunday Chronicle
(3 August 1957); Review in pamphlet Spielfilme im Deutschen
Fernsehen 1969/70; Publicity Book (MMA); Studio Press release
and synopsis (MMA).

33  THE BLUE GARDENIA (1953)

In the telephone company of a California town Harry Prebble,
a well-known fashion designer, is seductively sketching Crystal
Carpenter, one of the telephone operators. He is called away
to the phone, and is seen trying to calm an obviously hysterical woman, Rose, on the other end of the line.

At the end of the day Crystal leaves with her friends, Norah
and Sally, who live with her. Left alone at home that evening,
Norah makes an elaborate birthday dinner to share symbolically
with her fiancé, who is in the army in Korea. She toasts her
lover and then opens a letter from him, only to learn that he
is calling off their engagement and marrying the nurse who
helped him recover from a wound.

At this point Harry Prebble phones, hoping to have a date
with Crystal, but finding her out invites Norah instead. Heartbroken, Norah goes off with Prebble to a fancy Hawaiian restaurant, "The Blue Gardenia."

At the restaurant, Prebble begins his usual seduction routine, plying Norah with strong drinks, while Nat Cole plays
the title song, and a blind lady sells them a blue gardenia.

On the pretense of giving a party, Prebble persuades Norah,
now drunk, to go home with him. He shows her some of his incomplete sketches while rain batters the skylight window.
Opening a bottle, Prebble cuts his finger, and Norah gives him
her handkerchief to bandage it with. Prebble plays the "Blue
Gardenia" record while Norah, suddenly sleepy, lies down.

She wakes to find Prebble making love to her and responds
momentarily, since she's confused and thinks it's her lover.
She then tries to push him away, but he is adamant and nasty.
Terrified, Norah picks up a poker and prepares to hit Prebble
on the head. She smashes the mirror instead. Then, drunk and
dizzy, she faints. Awaking to find shards of glass around her
and still frightened, she rushes out into the rainy night, for-
getting her shoes.

The next morning, when Sally gets up to wake the others, she
finds Norah's clothes strewn everywhere and Norah herself sound
asleep on the bed. Her friends finally manage to wake her and
try to find out what happened, but Norah's mind is a complete
blank.

Meanwhile, a police investigation is proceeding in Prebble's
apartment. He had been found murdered that morning. Casey
Mayo, a well-known reporter, notices the record player still

on and sardonically remarks that the artist was murdered to
music. At the telephone company, Norah jumps when some glass
falls out of her friend's bag; she has a quick flash of herself
smashing Prebble's mirror. The girls whom Prebble sketched are
being questioned about their activities the night before, and
Norah becomes anxious. She goes down to get a newspaper, and
is frightened when she sees the police car outside.

Evidently uncertain of her guilt since she cannot recall
anything about the evening, Norah does not go to the police or
tell her friends where she had gone the night before. But
every little event terrifies her and she is in constant fear
of being discovered. She listens to her radio secretly under
the bedclothes, following all the latest developments.

Casey Mayo meanwhile is trying to crack the case of the mysterious woman himself and is heard on the radio speaking directly to the woman, calling her "The Blue Gardenia" and pleading
with her to make herself known to him. He promises to help
her if she can tell him the correct size of the shoes left in
Prebble's apartment. There are comic interludes where we see
the hysterical women who phone in pretending to be The Blue
Gardenia, but finally Norah is moved to phone Casey, feeling
terribly alone and frightened. She meets him at his office
later that night, but pretends that she's come for her "friend."
They have coffee in a diner, while a sinister waiter listens
to all they say and then phones the police. Casey and Norah,
meanwhile, are obviously falling in love.

The police meet them outside and arrest Norah. As Casey
leaves he suddenly recalls that the record on Prebble's machine
was not "The Blue Gardenia" that Norah said was playing as she
blacked out. He rushes to the record store where Prebble shopped and talks to the woman behind the counter. As the woman
goes off to check on Prebble's last purchase, Casey waits im-
patiently. When the woman doesn't return he goes after her
and finds that she's slashed her wrists. She is Rose, the woman
Prebble talked to at the start of the film, who, desperate to
get together with Harry, went to his apartment that night.
When she wouldn't go away, Prebble put on a new record for her,
but she picked up the poker and murdered him.

Norah is seen in a final shot being let out of jail and met
by her friends. Casey is also there, and although Norah shuns
him superficially, he's so sure they will be together that he
hands his little black date book to his friend.

Credits:
Producer:              Alex Gottlieb
Director:              Fritz Lang
Screenplay:           Charles Hoffmann, based on story by
                      Vera Caspary
Photographer:         Nicholas Musuraca
Music:                Raoul Kraushaar. Song "Blue Gardenia"
                      by Bob Russell and Lester Lee,

|  | arranged by Nelson Riddle (sung by Nat "King" Cole) |
|---|---|
| Art Direction: | Daniel Hall |
| Special Effects: | Willis Cook |
| Editor: | Edward Mann |
| Cast: | Anne Baxter (Norah Larkin), Richard Conte (Casey Mayo), Ann Sothern (Crystal Carpenter), Raymond Burr (Harry Prebble), Jeff Donnell (Sally Ellis), Richard Erdman (Al), George Reeves (Haynes, Police captain), Ruth Storey (Rose), Ray Walker (Homer), Celia Lovsky (Blind woman), Frank Ferguson (Drunk), Alex Gottlieb, Nat "King" Cole (himself) |
| Filmed by: | Blue Gardenia Productions–Gloria Films, December 1952, in 21 days |
| Running Time: | 90 mins. |
| Released: | By Warner Brothers, 28 March 1953 |

Reviews:
Motion Picture Herald (6 December 1952); Today's Cinema (6 December 1952 and 3 November 1953); Motion Picture Herald (14 March 1953), p. 1758; Variety (18 March 1953); Film Daily (23 March 1953), p. 14; London Times (23 March 1953) (actors praised, content commonplace); Crowther, Bosley, New York Times (28 April 1953) (good cast but hackneyed script); Kine Weekly (5 November 1953), p. 21; Monthly Film Bulletin No. 239 (December 1953); Jungeblodt, Werner, Film-Dienst (23 April 1954); Publicity notices and Trade synopsis (BFI). (The MMA has several reviews, lacking references, that are basically unfavorable, criticizing the "tired formulas" and cliche-ridden characterizations. All reviews praise the quality of acting performances, which cannot, however, save the film.)

34    THE BIG HEAT (1953)

The film opens with a close-up of a gun on a table. A hand reaches out, fires the gun, and a man falls onto the table. We pan to an envelope addressed to the district attorney, a police badge alongside it. Tom Duncan, police commissioner, has committed suicide, presumably in despair at being controlled by Mike Lagana, a local racketeer. Bertha Duncan, the dead man's wife, coolly picks up an envelope and puts it in the safe before phoning Lagana to tell him the news. Bertha is obviously going to use her husband's letter to the district attorney to blackmail Lagana.

Lagana phones Vincent Stone, one of the gang, and we see Stone playing cards while Debbie, his bored mistress, lounges on the sofa. Their conversation reveals that they have little respect for each other.

We cut to Bertha Duncan's house where the police are

investigating the suicide. Dave Bannion, police sergeant and hero of the film, interviews Bertha, who puts on a convincing act for him.

Bannion goes to a bar where Lagana's gang hangs out and learns from Lucy Chapman, a bar girl, that Tom Duncan lived very well, was in love with her, and was about to get a divorce when he died. Suspicious, Bannion returns to Bertha, who denies any wrongdoing, while admitting that her husband had been unfaithful. Later, at the office, Bannion learns that Lucy Chapman has been murdered. He is more than ever convinced that something is being covered up when his boss tells him to leave Bertha Duncan alone.

Anxious and preoccupied, Bannion arrives at his home. He gets a threatening phone call, and, understanding that Mike Lagana must be at the bottom of this, goes to visit him in his luxurious house. When he mentions Lucy Chapman's death, Bannion is thrown out.

Next day at work, Bannion is told by his boss not to go any further into the Chapman murder or the Duncan case. Bannion is angry and uncooperative and the two part on uneasy terms. That night, Bannion and his wife are planning to go out. Bannion tucks his child into bed while his wife goes to fetch the babysitter. When she starts the car, it explodes. Bannion arrives in time to drag his wife's lifeless body from the wreck.

The next day, Bannion charges Higgins, his boss, with being on Lagana's payroll. Furious and disgusted, Bannion turns in his police badge, vowing to catch Lagana on his own. We cut to Lagana in his lush office talking with Vince Stone and telling him to calm down. Vince's violent actions will give the show away; they cannot attack Bannion directly now that their first plan to kill him has misfired.

Bannion has meanwhile been following leads to get information. A sinister-looking, crippled lady in a used car-lot turns out to be on his side, and she gives him a tip as to where he might find Vince Stone. At the bar used by the gang Bannion gains Debbie's confidence. A member of the gang sees them and tells Stone, who, furious with Debbie, throws scalding coffee in her face. She rushes out, and, not knowing where to turn, goes to Bannion, who takes her in. He sees that her face is attended to and then lets her hide in his room. Debbie tells him that Larry Gordon is the one who killed his wife. After threatening Gordon, Bannion leaves him to be killed by his own gang, and goes to visit Bertha Duncan, intending to kill her. After she is dead, Duncan's letter will be released and Lagana exposed. Bertha phones the police, however, who force Bannion to leave.

Back in his room, Bannion tells Debbie about his wife and mentions that Bertha Duncan stands in the way of everything's being revealed. Bannion then hears that Higgins has called off the police protection for his little girl who is staying with his brother-in-law. He rushes out, leaving Debbie a gun.

At his brother-in-law's house, strange men grab him, and we think Lagana has already taken over. It turns out to be the brother-in-law's friends, and Bannion visits his child safely.

Debbie goes to visit Bertha Duncan and, to get back at Stone and also to help Bannion, kills her. She goes to Vince's apartment to tell him it is the end for him and to get further revenge by throwing hot coffee at him. Vince shoots her just as Bannion arrives. Bannion and Vince try to shoot each other, while Debbie lies dying. The police arrive, and Bannion has time before she dies to tell Debbie that she would have liked his wife.

The film ends with Bannion once more on the job in the police department, going off on a call.

Credits:

| | |
|---|---|
| Producer: | Robert Arthur |
| Director: | Fritz Lang |
| Screenplay: | Sidney Boehm, based on the novel by William McGivern |
| Photography: | Charles Lang, Jr. |
| Art Direction: | Robert Peterson |
| Set Decoration: | William Kiernan |
| Music: | Daniele Amfitheatrof |
| Editor: | Charles Nelson |
| Assistant Director: | Milton Feldman |
| Cast: | Glenn Ford (Dave Bannion), Gloria Grahame (Debbie Marsh), Jocelyn Brando (Katie Bannion), Alexander Scourby (Mike Lagana), Lee Marvin (Vince Stone), Jeanette Nolan (Bertha Duncan), Peter Whitney (Tierney), Willis Bouchey (Lt. Wilkes), Robert Burton (Gus Burke), Adam Williams (Larry Gordon), Howard Wendell (Commissioner Higgins), Cris Alcaide (George Rose), Michael Granger (Hugo), Dorothy Green (Lucy Chapman), Carolyn Jones (Doris), Ric Roman (Baldy), Dan Seymour (Atkins), Edith Evanson (Selma Parker), Linda Bennett, Kathryn Eames, Rex Reason. |
| Filmed by: | Columbia Pictures, Hollywood, in 1953 in 29 days |
| Running Time: | 90 mins. |
| Released: | 6 October 1953 |

Reviews:
Today's Cinema (4 March 1953), p. 32; Motion Picture Herald (28 March 1953), p. 28, and (26 September 1953), p. 2006; Hollywood Reporter (23 September 1953), p. 3; Variety (23 September 1953); Film Daily (6 October 1953), p. 8; Crowther,

Bosley, New York Times (15 October 1953) (positive review, praising especially Lang's direction and the script); Time (2 November 1953) (negative review); Today's Cinema (2 February 1954), p. 6; Kine Weekly (4 February 1954), p. 22; K. Nf. [Karen Niehoff], Der Tagesspiegel (13 March 1954); CK [Christopher Kühn], Film-Dienst (19 March 1954); Monthly Film Bulletin No. 243 (April 1954); Anderson, Lindsay, Sight and Sound, 23 No. 1 (July–September 1954); Thome, Rudolf, Süddeutsche Zeitung (4 February 1964); Almendarez, Valentin, Cinema Texas Program Notes, Vol 8, No. 40 (20 March 1975); MMA has undated reviews from Newsweek, praising Lang's flair for suspense and violent action, and New York Herald Tribune, lauding the film's script, direction and acting; also a publicity magazine on The Big Heat, emphasizing the rough treatment of women and the revenge theme; Beylie, Claude, Ecran (Paris), No. 32 (January 1975), p. 13.

35  HUMAN DESIRE (1954)

As the film opens, Jeff Warren, newly returned from Korea, is driving a train back to the yard with his mate Alec Simmons, with whose family Jeff rooms. The various shots of the train, the tracks, and the rocky scenery establish Jeff's pleasure in being back as well as giving a clear impression of the work and lives of the railway men. John Thurston, the yard master, is cool to Jeff. Carl Buckley, an old friend, indicates how he has come up in the world since Jeff left and mentions that he is now married. We cut to Alec's home, a warm, friendly place, where Jeff is received with fondness by both Mrs. Simmons and her daughter Kathleen, now grown into a woman and obviously in love with him.

At Buckley's home, meanwhile, Vicki Buckley is idling away her time eating chocolates and watching television. Carl comes in sadly, having been fired that day. He asks Vicki to help him by looking up John Owens, for whom Vicki used to work and who has pull with Thurston. Vicki seems reluctant but finally agrees.

The next day Vicki goes to meet Owens, who receives her like a lover, while back at the hotel Carl is getting nervous because Vicki is late. When Vicki comes in, Carl suspects that she has slept with Owens and becomes jealous. He vows revenge. Realizing that Owens will be on their train that night, he makes Vicki write a note to Owens saying that Carl is staying in town and that she'll meet him in his compartment on the train. At the station, Carl has Owens paged and the note handed him. Meanwhile, we see Jeff also getting on the train as a passenger.

The train is seen hurtling through the night, while inside Carl ominously sharpens a piece of wood with his knife and Vicki sits by, terrified. He sends Vicki into Owens's compartment, pushes in after her and murders Owens, taking his wallet and gold watch chain. As they are about to leave they see Jeff Warren smoking in the corridor. Carl sends Vicki to get him out of the way. She flirts with Jeff, who takes her into an empty compartment, hastily kisses her, and goes out. The train is again seen hurtling through the black night.

When they arrive back in town, Vicki and Carl begin to fight about the murder. Carl burns his clothes, but when Vicki tries to take the wallet Carl refuses to let her have it, since it contains her incriminating note to Owens. At the inquest that follows, Jeff, catching Vicki's eye in the audience, does not reveal that he met her in the corridor.

Carl and Vicki's relationship is deteriorating as Carl, guilt-ridden, takes to drink. Jeff helps Vicki home with Carl one night, and Vicki tells Jeff part of the truth, leaving him confused but obviously half in love with her. Vicki and Carl fight bitterly the next evening, Vicki declaring that she cannot love a murderer. She is determined to get the incriminating letter from Carl, but it is not hidden with the wallet and watch. She phones Jeff and they meet secretly at the terminal, where Vicki complains bitterly about her life with Carl. She refers to Jeff's war experience and begins to hint that Jeff should kill Carl so that they could be free together. The two begin to meet secretly at a girlfriend's apartment in town, but Vicki continues to lie to Jeff about Owens, although she has told him about the murder. Jeff, however, begins to suspect that Vicki had been having an affair with Owens, since he knows that Carl must have had cause to be so jealous. Jeff's relationship with his mate Alec meanwhile is becoming very strained, since Alec and his wife disapprove of what's going on, although Jeff continues to room with the family. Kathleen also is despondent about losing Jeff to Vicki Buckley and comes into his room recalling how he had talked when he first returned from Korea about wanting a home and family. But Jeff gets angry and walks out to visit Vicki.

Vicki again complains about her life and encourages Jeff to murder Carl, noting how easy it would be for Carl to have an "accident" since he is regularly drunk and often staggers home. But Jeff is unable to kill a man whom he basically respects and who is so vulnerable. He does, however, steal the note for Vicki. They fight, and as Vicki reveals her true nature, Jeff becomes disgusted and walks out on her for good.

The next day, Carl and Vicki are seen leaving town and getting on the train with all their luggage. Jeff, meanwhile, has obviously made up with Kathleen and things are cheery once again with Alec. In the carriage, Carl begins to appeal to Vicki to love him because he desperately needs her, but Vicki now turns on him. She tells him that she had wanted Owens, wanted his house, and wanted him to divorce his wife and marry her. Infuriated, Carl lunges at her and strangles her. The film ends with the camera on the exhausted Carl, who has finally gotten rid of the rottenness in his life.

Credits:
Producer:               Lewis J. Rachmil, Jerry Wald
Director:               Fritz Lang
Screenplay:             Alfred Hayes, based on La Bête
                        Humaine by Emil Zola
Photography:            Burnett Guffey
Art Direction:          Robert Peterson
Set Decoration:         William Kiernan
Music:                  Daniele Amfitheatrof
Editor:                 Aaron Stell
Assistant Director:     Milton Feldman
Cast:                   Glenn Ford (Jeff Warren), Gloria
                        Grahame (Vicki Buckley), Broderick
                        Crawford (Carl Buckley), Edgar
                        Buchanan (Alec Simmons), Kathleen
                        Case (Ellen Simmons), Peggy Maley
                        (Jean), Diane DeLaire (Vera Simmons),
                        Grandon Rhodes (John Owens), Dan
                        Seymour (Kellner), John Pickard (Matt
                        Henley), Paul Brinegar (Brakeman),
                        Dan Riss (Prosecutor), Victor Hugo
                        Greene (Davidson), John Zaremba
                        (Russell), Carl Lee (John Thurston),
                        Olan Soule (Lewis).
Filmed at:              Columbia Studios, Hollywood, 1954,
                        in 35 days
Running Time:           90 mins.
Released:               6 August 1954

Reviews:
London Times (24 September 1953) (BFI:  note saying that Rita
Hayworth is to have lead in the film); The Star (30 September
1953) (BFI:  another note, saying that Rita Hayworth will be
replaced by Olivia de Havilland in lead role); Hollywood
Reporter (3 August 1954); Gene, Variety (11 August 1954);
Crowther, Bosley, New York Times (7 August 1954); Motion
Picture Herald (6 August 1954); Today's Cinema (22 November
1954), p. 7; Kine Weekly (25 November 1954), p. 16; Monthly
Film Bulletin No. 252 (January 1955); Anderson, Lindsay, Sight
and Sound, 24, No. 4 (Spring 1955); F.T. [François Truffaut],
Cahiers du Cinéma, No. 47 (May 1955); Truffaut, François, Arts
(Paris) (13-19 July 1955); Columbia Picture Corp. Trade synop-
sis (MMA); New York Herald Tribune (MMA:  J. P. praises the
railroad background and the photography, but dislikes the story
and the "cloudy plot").

36   MOONFLEET (1955)
     Set in England in 1757, the film opens with shots of waves
crashing over rocks.  We cut to a small boy, John Mohune, walking alone along deserted paths.  As evening comes, he is seen
on a heath looking at a sign for "Moonfleet."  Sitting down by

a wall to rest his feet, he hears groans coming from the graveyard. There he finds a sinister-looking statue of an angel
among the gravestones, and, terrified by moving shadows, falls
into a hole.

He awakes to find a circle of faces around him. These turn
out to be smugglers, part of the gang headed by Jeremy Fox, the
man Mohune was sent by his dying mother to find. Jeremy Fox
had been in love with John's mother, Olivia, but her family
rejected him. Embittered, he turned to crime. Fox is not
pleased to see young John Mohune and plans to send him away to
school the next morning.

We cut to Fox's men trying to push the reluctant boy into
a carriage. Although they finally get him in and start off,
John jumps out and is shown the way to Fox's mansion by a little girl, Grace. He creeps up to the house and, peeking through
the window, sees Fox and his friends sitting drunkenly around
a table watching Fox's lover dance on the table. Angered at
first to find John there, Fox warms to him because of his courage and his obvious trust in him. He agrees to let John stay,
and the boy meets Fox's jealous lover Mrs. Minton.

After a stormy night, we see John in the garden where he is
joined by Grace. She takes him to the church, where John later
learns about past events from the friendly priest who had known
John's mother. The priest has taken as a topic for the sermon
"Thou Shalt Not Have Strange Gods." He talks about the people's
susceptibility to superstition, and their belief in the power
of "Redbeard" Mohune, whose tomb in the graveyard was feared.
The priest tells John about the search that has been going on
for years for Redbeard's diamond.

Walking back through the graveyard one eery night, with the
noise of waves crashing in the background, John passes the
sinister statue and falls down a hole again. Exploring the
tunnels below, John discovers Redbeard's tomb and takes a locket from the skeleton. Hearing voices, he comes upon the smugglers having a meeting; he learns of Fox's role in the organization and the plans to find the diamond.

Back at Fox's house, a ball is going on. Fox's sophisticated and heartless friends, Lord and Lady Ashwood, suggest
that Fox join them in some shady deal. Fox is uncertain of
what to do.

John, meanwhile, trying to leave the tomb, discovers that
the smugglers have covered the entrance. He calls for help,
only to be found by Fox's men. Realizing he knows their secrets, they take him to their hideout and plan to kill him.
Fox arrives just in time, but a dangerous fight with the men
follows. Mrs. Minton is then seen writing a letter denouncing
Fox to the military. She understands now that his love for
Olivia Mohune stands between them. As Fox and John are escaping, the military descends on them, and after a hectic fight,
Fox gets away, John following him out over the cliffs and heath.
He shows Fox some verses about the diamond that he found in the

locket in the grave, and they manage to break the code.  Finding the diamond involves a dangerous mission to the place where
the soldiers are gathered.  Fox steals a uniform, and he and
John go to the well mentioned in the verses, where John is
lowered in a bucket.  He finds the diamond, but just as they
are about to leave, Fox's disguise is revealed.  He risks his
life to save John, and they finally get away safely.

We cut to John sleeping in a hut by the sea.  That night
the two are to leave to make a new life in the colonies.  Fox
wakes up and leaves without John, taking the diamond with him.
He meets Lord and Lady Ashwood on the road, and the three are
happily on their way when they are stopped by the military,
who are searching all carriages, looking for Fox.  Lady Ashwood
saves him by embracing him when the soldiers look in, and Lord
Ashwood tells them that he is with his daughter and her husband.

Fox is glad to be saved but uncomfortable with what he has
done and with his pact with Lord and Lady Ashwood.  They assume
that he has killed John Mohune, and at this point Fox becomes
so sickened by the situation that he demands that they turn
back.  Lord and Lady Ashwood think he is mad, and they fight.
Fox kills Ashwood, but is mortally wounded himself.  He manages
to make his way painfully back to the hut and to John, where he
tears off the part of the note he had left, saying that John
had been wrong to trust in him, and he puts the diamond in
John's pocket.  The boy wakes just as Fox is leaving, and Fox
tells him he has decided that it would be best for them to go
to his mother's house.  Then Fox goes down to the sea and gets
into the boat, the last shot showing him lying down, holding
the red sail, as the boat floats out to sea.

Credits:
Producer:                            John Houseman, Jud Kinberg
Director:                            Fritz Lang
Screenplay:                          Jan Lustig, Margaret Fitts, based on
                                     the novel of the same title by John
                                     Meade Falkner
Photography (Eastman
  color and Cinemascope):  Robert Planck
Art Direction:                       Cedric Gibbons, Hans Peters
Set Decoration:                      Edwin B. Willis, Richard Pfefferle
Costumes:                            Walter Plunkett
Music:                               Miklos Rozsa.  Flamenco Music:
                                     Vincente Gomez
Editor:                              Albert Akst
Assistant Director:                  Sid Sidman
Cast:                                Stewart Granger (Jeremy Fox), George
                                     Sanders (Lord Ashwood), Joan Greenwood
                                     (Lady Ashwood), Viveca Lindfors (Anna
                                     Minton), Jon Whiteley (John Mohune),
                                     Liliane Montevecchi (Gypsy dancer),
                                     Sean McClory (Elzevir Block), Melville

|            |                                         |
|------------|-----------------------------------------|
|            | Cooper (Felix Ratsey), Alan Napier (Parson Glennie), John Hoyt (Magistrate Maskew), Donna Corcoran (Grace), Jack Elam (Damen), Dan Seymour (Hull), Ian Wolfe (Tewkesbury), Lester Matthews (Major Hennishaw), Skelton Knaggs (Jacob), Richard Hale (Starkill), John Alderson (Greening), Ashley Cowan (Tomson), Frank Ferguson (Coachman), Booth Colman (Captain Stanhope), Peggy Maley (Tenant) |
| Filmed by: | Metro-Goldwyn-Mayer, Hollywood, September to October 1954, in 45 days on location at Oceanside, California |
| Running Time: | 87 mins. (some sources have 89 mins.) |
| Released: | 12 June 1955 |

Reviews:
Hollywood Reporter (9 May 1955), p. 3; Variety (11 May 1955); Motion Picture Herald (14 May 1955), p. 433; Today's Cinema (3 June 1955), p. 8; Kine Weekly (9 June 1955), p. 23; Crowther, Bosley, New York Times (25 June 1955); Monthly Film Bulletin, no. 258 (July 1955); Barnes, Peter, Films and Filming, 1, no. 11 (August 1955), p. 17; Images, 1, No. 2 (December 1955), p. 25; J-t [Werner Jungeboldt], Film-Dienst (12 April 1956); lpk, Frankfurter Allgemeine Zeitung (6 June 1956); L'Écran, no. 1 (January 1958), p. 58; MMA has the following undated reviews: Newsweek (short, negative review); Zunser, Jesse, Cue (short, positive review); Time (reviewer makes comparisons to R. L. Stevenson, and to Dickens' Great Expectations, and says the film is "a string of lively, unrelated escapades.").

37   WHILE THE CITY SLEEPS (1956)
     The opening shots set an ominous tone with dark, rainswept New York City streets. A man in black is seen knocking at an apartment door, but before it is opened, an older man comes up the stairs and enters the apartment. He talks to the girl inside, who is evidently bathing, and then leaves. The man in black meanwhile has been hiding on the stairs. He now comes down and, after giving the girl some drugs she ordered, fixes the door so that it will open. We hear the water running, see the man rush in, and as a scream is heard, the credits come on the screen. A close-up of her robe pans up to a newsman reporting at the scene of the crime and on to letters scrawled on the wall "Ask Mother."
     We cut to Kyne, Inc. and the New York Sentinel office. Walter Kyne, an old man now, is sick and dying. Upset about the way his paper is handling the new murder case, he reflects bitterly on the mistakes he has made in his life. He had

wanted to leave the paper in Ed Mobley's hands, trusting him
more than his own son.  He talks about the responsibility of
the press to the people, stressing how important it is to have
correct information.  Then suddenly he has a heart attack and
dies.

We cut to an empty room and Walter Kyne, Jr., standing awk-
wardly in bow tie and formal dress.  He calls the three main
men on the paper—Ed Mobley, Mark Loving, John Griffith—into
his office and begins his plan to turn them against one another.
Kyne, hurt that his father had excluded him from the firm, intends now to get his revenge.  We learn shortly that his wife
Dorothy is having an affair with Harry Kritzer, who also works
on the paper, and who hopes to gain power through Dorothy's
influence.

We next see Ed Mobley returning with his girlfriend, Nancy
Liggett, to her modern apartment.  A little drunk, Mobley forces
his way in, then pretends to leave, but first fixes the door in
the manner that the murderer had done earlier.  He thus is soon
back and gives Nancy a lecture on making sure she closes her
door properly.  As he is making love to Nancy and asking her
to marry him, the phone rings; it is Griffith asking him to
come to the police station where the janitor of the apartment
house is being interviewed.

Mobley finds the evidence against the janitor too pat and
begins to think about the possibility of someone's fixing the
door between the janitor's visits.  His police officer friend
talks about the suggestive comic books sold to kids of all ages
in drug stores, but Mobley concludes that it was a premeditated
murder by a psychopath.  In a line that recalls M, Mobley notes
that the murderer seems to be asking for help, saying in effect, "Catch me, I can't help myself."

After the next murder, Mobley decides (in a fashion similar
to that of Casey Mayo in The Blue Gardenia) to appeal to the
killer through television announcements.  He hopes the murderer
will be listening and then proceeds to psychoanalyze him, suggesting that he is a mama's boy who hates his mother, and,
through her, all women.  We cut to the killer's room and see
the truth of Mobley's analysis:  the boy Manners is adopted
and overprotected; worse still, his mother wanted him to be a
girl.

Mobley guesses correctly that his analysis will have angered
the killer, who will now most likely try to hurt Mobley.  He
decides to use Nancy as bait to catch Manners, deliberately
letting the killer know who his girlfriend is.  Nancy, hurt at
the notion of being used to catch the murderer, nevertheless
goes along because of her love.  She is to have a bodyguard at
all times.

Mark Loving, meanwhile, anxious to win Mobley's support for
a job, sends his girlfriend Mildred, once a columnist on the
paper, to seduce him.  Not at all unwilling, Mildred finds
Mobley disconsolate in the bar—it is Nancy's night at the Red

Cross--and when they are drunk, they leave for her place in a cab.

At home, Kyne is pleased with the latest issue of the paper and even more with the way his power over the men at the office is working. Dorothy phones from Kritzer's apartment (which is opposite to that where Nancy lives), pretending to be at her mother's and unable to get away. Kritzer calls for more liquor from the drugstore, and Manners delivers it; seeing Dorothy fixing her stockings in the back room, he gets excited but is prevented from fixing the door by Kritzer's bringing the money. On his way out, Manners sees Nancy's name on the opposite door.

The next day at the office, everyone knows that Mobley went out with Mildred. Nancy is hurt and cold to him, refusing to see him. Kyne is at home with Dorothy when Kritzer phones, saying he needs to see Dorothy at once. Dorothy leaves to meet him, pretending it's a friend who wants her to go shopping.

Mobley and Nancy, meanwhile, meeting in a bar, are still at odds over Mobley's night with Mildred. Nancy leaves upset, while her guard follows. The killer, however, is also waiting outside for her. At the bar Mobley continues to talk about the killer's getting more and more daring, saying that he may even try to kill a woman when she is protected. At this point, he becomes frightened and rushes out to Nancy's apartment. We meanwhile see Nancy taken to her apartment by the guard, who then says he's going to get something to eat, and leaves the building. The killer comes up the stairs and pretends to be Ed. Nancy nearly opens her door, but says she is still angry. He bangs at the door, but at that moment Dorothy comes out of the opposite apartment. The killer rushes into her room but Dorothy just manages to escape. The killer runs off, but Mobley is hot on his trail and pursues him into the subway. He is caught by the police as he rushes out of an escape exit.

Mildred, coming to talk to Kritzer, sees him leaving his room with Dorothy. We soon hear that Kyne has awarded the new post to Kritzer and that Mildred has been given a syndicated column on the paper. Obviously, the whole thing was a deal to protect Kyne's marriage.

Mobley and Nancy have made up and are married. We see them on their honeymoon in Florida. The phone rings, and we learn that, after all, Kyne did not give the position to Kritzer. Evidently he finally stood up for himself, threw Kritzer out, and put Griffith in the new job, with Mobley as managing editor.

Credits:
Producer:        Bert E. Friedlob
Director:        Fritz Lang
Screenplay:      Casey Robinson, based on the novel
                 The Bloody Spur by Charles Einstein

Photography
 (Superscope):   Ernest Laszlo
Art Direction:   Carroll Clark

| | |
|---|---|
| Set Decoration: | Jack Mills |
| Costumes: | Norma |
| Music: | Herschel Burke Gilbert |
| Editor: | Gene Fowler, Jr. |
| Sound Editor: | Verna Fields |
| Assistant Director: | Ronnie Rondell |
| Cast: | Dana Andrews (Edward Mobley), Rhonda Fleming (Dorothy Kyne), Sally Forrest (Nancy Liggett), Thomas Mitchell (Griffith), Vincent Price (Walter Kyne), Howard Duff (Lt. Kaufman), Ida Lupino (Mildred), George Sanders (Mark Loving), James Craig (Harry Kritzer), John Barrymore, Jr. (Robert Manners), Vladimir Sokoloff (George Pilski), Robert Warwick (Amos Kyne), Ralph Peters (Meade), Larry Blake (Police sergeant), Edward Hinton (O'Leary), Mae Marsh (Mrs. Manners), Sandy White (Judith Fenton), Celia Lovsky (Miss Dodd), Pit Herbert (Bartender), Andrew Lupino. |
| Filmed at: | Thor Productions-RKO Teleradio Pictures, New York, July-August 1955, in five weeks |
| Running Time: | 100 mins. |
| Released: | By RKO Radio, May 1956 |

Reviews:
A. W., New York Times (17 May 1956) (Film is a qualified success. A. W. praises the script, the fast pace of the film, and the professional acting); P. V. B., New York Herald Tribune (17 May 1956) (unfavorable review, condescending toward the film); Kove, Variety (2 May 1956) (praises Fritz Lang for deft plot, authenticity, and pace of the film); Today's Cinema (6 April 1956), p. 8; Daily Film Renter (9 April 1956), p. 6; Kine Weekly (12 April 1956), p. 20; Monthly Film Bulletin 23, No. 268 (May 1956); Motion Picture Herald (5 May 1956), p. 882; Hollywood Reporter (2 May 1956), p. 3; Film Daily (14 May 1956), p. 8; Carroll, John, Films and Filming, 2, No. 8 (May 1956); Mg [William Mogge], Film-Dienst (28 February 1957); Delling, Manfred, Die Welt (Hamburg) (11 May 1957); Anon: Review in pamphlet Spielfilme im Deutschen Fernsehen, 1969/70.

38  BEYOND A REASONABLE DOUBT (1956)
    As the film opens, Tom Garrett, a novelist, and Austin Spencer, owner of a newspaper, are watching an execution in a prison presented in all its grim reality. Garrett then listens while Spencer, his prospective father-in-law, debates the validity of capital punishment with District Attorney Thompson. Spencer is against capital punishment and would like to show

Thompson the danger of relying on circumstantial evidence (as in the case of the man just executed) when the death penalty is involved.

Spencer takes Garrett home, where Susan, Spencer's daughter, is waiting for them. Garrett and Susan were to be married soon, but for some reason (ostensibly to finish a novel he has begun), Garrett wants a delay. Garrett and Spencer then discuss the problem of possibly innocent men's being executed, and Spencer comes up with the idea of using Garrett to make a test case when the next murder happens.

Shortly afterwards, a dancer, Patty Gray, is found strangled, but there are no clues. We see the police interviewing the girls who roomed with Patty. Garrett and Spencer decide to create enough purely circumstantial evidence to convict Garrett. Spencer will take photos of everything they are doing as they go along so that there will be evidence of the fake if, and when, Garrett is convicted. As a start, Garrett goes to meet Patty's friends at the burlesque hall and begins to date Sally. He takes her in his car to the place where Patty's body was found, Spencer secretly taking photos of everything.

Garrett and Spencer work on the car in the garage, creating all the clues necessary to prove that Garrett had been in it with Patty and had murdered her afterwards. Spencer takes photos of everything with a Polaroid camera, so that we constantly see the still shots of their actions. Once the car is ready, Garrett takes Sally out in it. Her friend, suspicious of Sally's male companion, and thinking he looks rather like the one who called for Patty on the fatal night, has alerted the police, who now follow the couple and arrest Garrett.

Thompson is delighted to see Garrett brought in because he now sees a way to get back at Spencer for his criticism. A colleague warns Thompson that he could be in serious trouble if anyone ever thinks he convicted Garrett for personal reasons. But for Thompson, this is the case that will make his name and get him promoted.

The trial starts, and as Spencer expected, Thompson uses all the circumstantial evidence they have provided to convict Garrett. Realizing that the moment has come to reveal the truth and expose Thompson, Spencer returns for all the photos. In a hurry, concerned now for the fate of his future son-in-law, Spencer does not look as he backs out of his driveway. He is killed by an oncoming truck, and all the evidence is burned.

Thompson, of course, will not believe Garrett that this was all a put-on job to test Thompson, and Garrett is sent to death row. We see Garrett in jail, the camera slowly panning the prisoners on death row as it had in the first scene, now stopping at his cell. Susan, meanwhile, is seen at her father's desk, writing letters to prove that Thompson is doing all this for personal reasons. Furious, Thompson denies it all, but he will not give in.

Susan is determined to prove Garrett's innocence, and, helped by a journalist, finds out that Patty's real name was Emma Bloker. At this point, Spencer's partner returns from Europe and finds a letter from Spencer in which he outlined the whole plan to falsify evidence so as to prove the inadequacy of circumstantial evidence.

Susan joyfully meets Garrett in the prison, but, as the reprieve is about to go through, Garrett makes a slip and refers to "Emma." Susan suddenly understands that he really did commit the murder and is totally confused by his confession. He tells how he had been forced to marry Emma and how she had been blackmailing him since the engagement. Susan leaves in turmoil, wondering what to do. The journalist convinces her that it is her duty to give Garrett up, despite their love, and he phones the governor just as he is signing the reprieve. Garrett is returned to death row, ironically to be executed on false evidence for a crime he did commit.

Credits:

| | |
|---|---|
| Producer: | Bert E. Friedlob |
| Director: | Fritz Lang |
| Screenplay: | Douglas Morrow |
| Photography (RKO-Scope): | William Snyder |
| Art Direction: | Carroll Clark |
| Set Decoration: | Darrell Silvera |
| Music: | Herschel Burke Gilbert. Song: "Beyond A Reasonable Doubt" (sung by The Hi-Los) by H. B. Gilbert, Alfred Perry. |
| Assistant Director: | Maxwell Henry |
| Editor: | Gene Fowler, Jr. |
| Cast: | Dana Andrews (Tom Garrett), Joan Fontaine (Susan Spencer), Sidney Blackmer (Austin Spencer), Philip Bourneuf (Thompson), Barbara Nichols (Sally), Shepperd Strudwick (Wilson), Arthur Franz (Hale), Robin Raymond (Terry), Edward Binns (Lt. Kennedy), William Leicester (Charlie Miller), Dan Seymour (Greco), Rusty Lane (Judge), Joyce Taylor (Joan), Carleton Young (Kirk), Trudy Wroe (Hat check girl), Joe Kirk (Clerk), Charles Evans (Governor), Wendell Niles (Announcer). |
| Filmed in: | the studios of Thor Productions-RKO Teleradio, New York, July-August 1955, in five weeks |
| Completed: | August 1955 |
| Running Time: | 80 mins. |
| Released: | May 9 1956 |

Reviews:
Crowther, Bosley, New York Times (14 September 1956); P. H.
[Penelope Houston], Monthly Film Bulletin, No. 275 (December
1956); Variety (11 September 1956); Today's Cinema (4 January
1956), p. 9; Hollywood Reporter (12 September 1956), p. 3;
Motion Picture Herald (15 September 1956), p. 65; Today's
Cinema (22 October 1956), p. 7; Film Renter (22 October 1956),
p. 6; Kine Weekly (25 October 1956), p. 18; Film Daily (1
October 1956), p. 7; Zinsser, William, New York Herald Tribune
(14 September 1956) (reviewer notes tight security designed to
conceal ending and praises the script, although finding it below Hitchcock's thrillers); Sanders, Rino, Die Welt (Hamburg)
(10 August 1957); Bazin, André, Radio-Cinéma-Télévision (20
October 1957) (see Entry No. 231); Rohmer, Eric, Arts (Paris)
(15 September 1957).

39   DER TIGER VON ESCHNAPUR [The Tiger of Bengal] and DAS INDISCHE
     GRABMAL [The Indian Tomb] (1959)
        The two-part film opens with the journey of architect Harald
     Berger to the palace of Chandra, Maharajah of Eschnapur.  In the
     jungle along the way, Berger rescues a beautiful young woman,
     Seetha, a dancer in Chandra's palace, from a tiger.  He sug-
     gests that they travel together and the two begin to fall in
     love.
        From there we cut to Chandra in his palace.  We see his
     brother, Ramigani, plotting to overthrow Chandra because of
     his modern ideas.  In particular, Ramigani objects to Chandra's
     plan to marry Seetha and to bringing a European architect to
     the palace.
        On his arrival, Berger is warmly received by Chandra, who
     takes to him at once.  Knowing nothing of Chandra's interest
     in Seetha, Berger seeks her out and manages to meet with her
     in her rooms, thanks to the help of her maid-servant.
        Setting out to explore the palace and temple, Berger acci-
     dently sees Seetha doing a religious dance that is forbidden
     to men's eyes.  He also finds a network of tunnels underneath
     the palace, some of which lead to horrible dungeons where
     hordes of lepers are kept.
        The conspiracy against Chandra grows, and we see Ramigani
     plotting with neighboring warlords to depose his brother.
     Chandra meanwhile is seen feeding the tigers he uses to punish
     those who oppose him.  Chandra begins to suspect that Berger
     and Seetha are in love and meeting secretly with the help of
     Seetha's maid.  At a large banquet, he insists that the maid
     partake in an entertainment that involves a disappearing act.
     She is put into a box that is then sliced through with knives,
     murdering her.  Chandra next traps Berger in the underground
     vaults and forces him to fight for his life against a tiger.
     Berger manages to win, but Chandra orders him to leave the
     palace at once.  Berger leaves, but takes Seetha with him.
        On discovering the flight of the lovers, Chandra is furious

and vows to kill his men unless they bring the couple back
alive. He now plans to hold as hostages Berger's sister and
brother-in-law, who had come to visit him at Eschnapur and who
know nothing about what has happened.

We cut to the lovers fleeing in the desert, pursued by
Chandra's forces. They finally escape them, but having run
out of food and water, are near death. This part of the film
ends with both Berger and Seetha lying on the sand as if dead,
while vultures hover above.

Chandra, back at the palace, is seen asking Berger's brother-
in-law to build a tomb for Seetha when she is brought back.

Das indische Grabmal begins with a short reiteration of the
main events in the first part of the film. As the narrative
resumes, we see a friendly caravan discovering Seetha and
Berger. The people rescue them and nurse them back to health
in a village. Chandra's soldiers, meanwhile, order the villagers not to harbor the lovers on pain of death. The lovers are
almost betrayed but flee just in time. They hide out in a
cave, but even with nature on their side, they are finally
captured.

In the palace, we learn that the war lords in league with
Ramigani are getting restless and threatening to attack the
palace at once. Chandra is now very worried about his situation, but is unable to find out exactly what is going on.

When the lovers return, Seetha is forced to undergo a dangerous ritual dance with a snake in order to discover whether or
not she is innocent. Chandra, watching, interrupts at the last
moment, unable to see his beloved die. He comes to Seetha,
hoping that she still loves him, but it is clear that she loves
Berger. Seetha does agree to marry Chandra, however, in order
to save her lover.

Berger languishes in a gruesome cell, his neck bound with
heavy chains. Escape seems impossible until a servant comes
to murder him. Berger is able to trap the man under his
chains, kill him, and seize the key.

Berger's sister and brother-in-law are meanwhile trying to
find out what is going on. Suspecting that Berger is imprisoned, they obtain maps of the underground tunnels and go to look
for him. They find him wandering around dragging his chains.
At this point, Ramigani's group stages the rebellion, the palace is blown up, and Chandra is defeated. Seetha and Berger
together with his sister and brother-in-law depart.

Credits:

| | |
|---|---|
| Executive Producer: | Artur Brauner |
| Producers: | Eberhard Meischner, Louise de Masure |
| Director: | Fritz Lang |
| Screenplay: | Fritz Lang, Werner Jörg Lüddecke, based on a novel by Thea von Harbou and a script by Thea von Harbou and |

Fritz Lang

| | |
|---|---|
| Photography (color and Colorscope): | Richard Angst |
| Art Direction: | Helmut Nentwig, Willy Schatz |
| Costumes: | Claudia Herberg, Günther Brosda |
| Music: | Michel Michelet (Tiger); Gerhard Becker (Grabmal) |
| Set Decoration: | Willi Schatz, Helmuth Nentwig |
| Choreographer: | Robby Gay, Billy Daniel |
| Editor: | Walter Wischniewsky |
| Assistant Director: | Frank Winterstein |
| Cast: | Debra Paget (Seetha), Paul Hubschmid, Henri Mercier in French version (Harald Berger), Walter Reyer (Chandra, the Maharajah of Eschnapur), Claus Holm (Dr. Walter Rhode), Sabine Bethmann (Irene, his wife), Valery Inkijinoff (Yama, high priest), René Deltgen (Prince Ramigani), Jochen Brockmann (Padhu), Jochen Blume (Asagara), Luciana Paoluzzi (Bahrani), Guido Celano (General Dagh), Angela Portulari (Peasant--Grabmal only), Richard Lauffen (Bhowana), Helmut Hildebrand (Ramigani's servant), Panos Papadopoulos (Messenger), Victor Francen. |
| Filmed by: | West German-French-Italian Co-Production: CCC Films/Regina Films/Criterion Films/Rizzoli Films/Imperia Films. Filmed in West Berlin in 89 days, and 27 on location in India in 1958 |
| Running Time: | Tiger, 97 mins.; Grabmal, 101 mins. |
| Released: | Tiger, 22 January 1959 (Hanover), Grabmal, 5 March 1959 (Stuttgart). |
| Note: | According to Lotte Eisner, "the films were released with the original German and French titles in July and August of 1959. American International released, in October 1960, a badly-dubbed version of the two films edited into one feature of 95 minutes titled Journey to the Lost City (U.S.) or Tiger of Bengal (U.K.). Paul Hubschmid was billed as Paul Christian in the English-language version." |

Reviews:
Filmblätter, No. 35 (1958), p. 1091, and No. 11 (1959), p. 224;

E.P. [Enno Patalas], Filmkritik (Munich) No. 3 (1959); Film-
Dienst (29 January 1959) (Tiger); EV. [Franz Everschor], Film-
Dienst (19 March 1959) (Grabmal); Filmwoche (13 June 1959),
p. 5; Variety (1 July 1959); Moullet, Luc, Arts (Paris) (22
July 1959); Demonsablon, Philippe, Cahiers du Cinéma, No. 98
(August 1959) (see Entry No. ·243); Hoveyda, Fereydoun, Cahiers
du Cinéma, No. 99 (September 1959) (see Entry No. 247); Le Film
Français (11 September 1959); Cinémathèque Française (24
October 1959), p. 19; Archer, Eugene, New York Times (8
December 1960); P.J.D. [Peter John Dyer], Monthly Film Bulletin,
No. 340 (May 1962); Durgnat, Raymond, Films and Filming (London)
8, No. 9 (June 1962); Gillet, John, Sight and Sound, 31, No.3
(Summer 1962); Vialle, Gabriel, La Revue du Cinéma-Image et
Son, No. 244 (1970); Patalas, Enno, Die Zeit (25 December 1970).

40 DIE TAUSEND AUGEN DES DR. MABUSE [The Thousand Eyes of Dr.
Mabuse] (1960)

The titles appear over a dark cityscape, followed by shots
of eyes floating, surrealist-fashion, over city shapes. Dissolve to a close-up of a man, whom we later realize is reporter
Peter Barter, in a car stuck in traffic. Another car comes
alongside, and we see the driver nod his head. The camera
pans to a man in dark glasses in the back seat tapping a case
on his lap. Cut to a police department, with officials who
recall those in M, and then to a blind seer phoning the police
and predicting a murder about to happen. We cut back to the
man in the car getting out his gun and shooting Barter. A
high-angle shot down on the road shows the second car pulling
off, while the first remains. With a sensational story, a
newscaster reports the death of Barter on his way to the studios while the killer phones in the results of the murder to
his boss. We cut to hands manipulating a machine recording
the man's words and then the camera pans down to a huge club
foot.

In the police station, Cornelius, the seer, discusses the
dead reporter, whom he knew was a skeptic. A call comes
through that the reporter had not died of a heart attack, as
supposed, but from fine needles evidently shot into him. Cut
to the reporter's room completely ransacked except for the
photo of a woman.

We next hear a report of the weapon, evidently a top secret
one, suggesting that the murderers have infiltrated the military. One official begins to talk of a certain Dr. Mabuse,
who once tried to dominate the world and who, as rumor has it,
never died. Someone suggests digging up the old case; a di-
lapidated folder is taken out. Cut to the machine and the
man's hands working it and then some members of the gang in a
truck full of recording devices. The men talk about keeping
track of a man called Travers, and we cut to Travers at the
Hotel Luxor, making a deal about buying an atomic weapons
plant.

Back in the police department, the officials, circled in smoke in the fashion of those in <u>M</u>, listen to a record of all the unsolved cases that have taken place at the Luxor over the past ten years. We cut to the hotel and a high-angle shot of a crowd standing outside. We realize we are seeing the crowd from the point of view of a young woman standing on the ledge and about to jump. We cut to the police taking out a net and then to people in windows, to reporters downstairs, and to the hotel manager and detective trying to coax the woman, Marion, inside. Instead, she reaches out to Travers, whose room happens to be next to hers. He brings her in, reassuring her until a doctor comes to take her to her room.

Downstairs, the bartender talks to Commissioner Kraus about Barter's having met Marion there. We cut to Marion's room and the police rather pointedly asking her what happened. Down in the bar, an insurance salesman (who is really Mistelzweig, a spy) discusses astrology and complains that because the hotel was designed by the Nazis it has had a curse on it from the start.

Dissolve to Travers driving. Cornelius runs across his path, but Travers is courteous. Kraus watches the incident and we follow Cornelius now in the car with Travers. He helps him avoid a crash. Then confessing that he can see into the future, he predicts an explosion at the atomic plant Travers was going to buy. Kraus is waiting for Cornelius when he comes in, each apparently trying to get information from the other.

Marion and Travers are seen dancing together, watched by Mistelzweig. The camera pulls back, however, as we realize that they are also being watched by someone monitoring a huge panel of television screens. The observer can see what people are doing in all the rooms in the hotel.

Beginning to fall in love, Marion and Travers plan to marry and return to the United States, but Marion gets a message from her husband, who is coming to meet her. Meanwhile, a hotel official has shown Travers a two-way mirror through which he can see into the next room. Learning that this is Marion's room, Travers goes down to watch her receive some flowers he has sent. Marion's husband, a huge ugly man with a club foot, arrives to take her away. He is about to kill Marion when Travers breaks through the mirror, seizes the gun, and shoots the husband. Professor Jordan arrives promptly, and, to save Travers from trouble, agrees to take the body away and pretend that the husband died of a heart attack.

Once in the ambulance, the husband's foot begins to move, and we understand that the entire scene was staged, a further part of the plot to confuse Travers. As Travers and Marion are planning their departure, Marion, now really in love, tells Travers of the plot to trick him into marrying her, after which he would be killed, the whole of Travers's wealth then falling to Mabuse. She tells him about the television screens and says they must hurry to escape. But it is too late. Once

they are in the elevator, it continues to descend. When the
lovers get out, they are trapped in the television center,
built originally by the Nazis, from which Mabuse has controlled
all the events in the hotel. Jordan is there and is revealed
as the heir of Mabuse; he locks Travers and Marion into the
center, leaving a gun in case they prefer to commit suicide.

Mistelzweig, the secret agent, has meanwhile been piecing
things together. He had earlier noted that Cornelius's dog was
hostile to him but friendly to Marion; he had also tricked
Cornelius into revealing that he could see. In the lobby, when
he sees the elevator continue to descend, he decides to investigate. Jordan meanwhile, walking through the lobby undisguised,
is given away by Cornelius's dog. Jordan, Cornelius, and Mabuse
are revealed to have been one person. Mabuse tries to escape,
but his car crashes during the chase and drops into the river.

Mistelzweig has found the television center, the lovers are
rescued just before shooting themselves, and they are reunited
in the hospital, where Marion is recovering from wounds.

Credits:

| | |
|---|---|
| Producer: | Artur Brauner |
| Director: | Fritz Lang |
| Screenplay: | Fritz Lang, Heinz Oskar Wuttig, based on an idea of Jan Fethke's and the character created by Norbert Jacques |
| Photography: | Karl Loeb |
| Art Direction: | Erich Kettelhut, Johannes Ott |
| Costumes: | Ina Stein |
| Music: | Bert Grund |
| Editors: | Walter and Waltraute Wischniewsky |
| Cast: | Dawn Addams (Marion Menil), Peter von Eyck (Travers), Wolfgang Preiss (Jordan), Gert Fröbe (Commissioner Kraus), Lupo Prezzo (Cornelius), Werner Peters (Hieronymous P. Mistelzweig), Andrea Checchi (Hotel detective Berg), Reinhard Koldehoff (Clubfoot), Howard Vernon (No. 12), Nico Pepe (Hotel manager), David Camerone (Parker), Jean-Jacques Delbo (Servant), Marieluise Nagel (Blonde woman), Werner Buttler (No. 11), Linda Sini (Corinna), Rolf Moebius (Police officer), Bruno W. Pantel (Reporter), Albert Bessler (Hotel engineer) |
| Filmed by: | West-German-French-Italian Co-Production: CCC Filmkunst, Berlin; Criterion Films, Cei-Incom, Rome; Omnia Distribution. Filmed in Berlin, 1960, in 42 days. |
| Running Time: | 103 mins. |

Released:                    14 May 1960, Gloria-Palast (Stuttgart)

Reviews:
Th. [Theodor Kotulla], Filmkritik, No. 11 (1960); M., Film-
Dienst (3 October 1960); MR [Martin Ruppert], Frankfurter
Allgemeine Zeitung (29 November 1960); J.G. [John Gillett],
Monthly Film Bulletin, No. 345 (October 1962); Durgnat, Raymond,
Films and Filming, 9, No. 2 (November 1962); Linder, Herbert,
Süddeutsche Zeitung (Munich) (5 May 1970); Lowry, Edward,
Cinema Texas Program Notes, 12, No. 1 (24 February 1977) (MMA).


### Films Lang Worked on but Did Not Complete

41   THE CABINET OF DR. CALIGARI (1920)
    Producer:              Eric Pommer
    Director:              Robert Wiene
    Screenplay:            Carl Mayer, Hans Janowitz
    Photography:           Willy Hameister
    Art Directors:         Hermann Warm, Walter Reiman, Walter
                           Röhrig
    Cast:                  Werner Krauss, Conrad Veidt, Lil
                           Dagover, Friedrich Feher, Hans
                           Heinrich von Twardowski
    Filmed at:             Decla-Bioscop, Berlin, in 1919
    Length:                1,703 meters
    Released:              1920

Pommer first assigned Fritz Lang to direct Caligari, and,
according to Lang, it was his idea to add the framing sections
to the original tale, which now becomes the invention of an in-
mate of an asylum. Lang was quickly replaced by Wiene, because
the popularity of the first part of Die Spinnen [The Spiders]
necessitated making a sequel.

42   CONFIRM OR DENY (1941)
    Director:              Archie Mayo [and (uncredited) Lang]
    Producer:              Len Hammond
    Screenplay:            Joe Swerling, based on a story by
                           Samuel Fuller and Henry Wales
    Photography:           Leon Shamroy
    Editor:                Robert Bischoff
    Cast:                  Don Ameche, Joan Bennett, Roddy
                           McDowall, John Loder
    Filmed at:             Twentieth-Century Fox, Hollywood,
                           1941
    Running Time:          73 mins.
    Released:              12 December 1941

According to Eisner, "Mayo took over when Lang suffered a
not unfortunate illness (he never liked the work and was merely
fulfilling his contract)."

43   MOONTIDE (1942)
          Producer:                    Mark Hellinger
          Director:                    Archie Mayo [and (uncredited) Fritz
                                       Lang]
          Screenplay:                  John O'Hara, based on the novel by
                                       Willard Robertson
          Photography:                 Charles Clark
          Art Directors:               Richard Day, James Basevi
          Music:                       Cyril J. Mockridge, David Buttolph
          Editor:                      William Reynolds
          Cast:                        Jean Gabin, Ida Lupino, Claude Rains,
                                       Jerome Cowan, Thomas Mitchell
          Filmed at:                   Twentieth-Century Fox studios,
                                       Hollywood, 1942

    According to Eisner, "Mayo replaced Lang after only four
days of shooting."

# Writings About Fritz Lang

1921

44    Pinthus, Kurt. "Sehenswerter Film--Der müde Tod." [Review of
          Destiny] Das Tage-Buch (Berlin) (22 October).
              Pinthus notes that Lang wanted to rely on an old folk-
          song in order to bring out the spiritual and metaphysical
          side to the film. But while one can express magic and
          wonder in film, it is hard to deal with problems of relig-
          ion and the occult. The best and most inspired parts of
          the film are the three intermezzi set in the land of
          Mohammed, in China, and in Venice. Lang was able to draw
          on a generation of cultivated film directors in making the
          film worthwhile. Soon, Pinthus fears, there will only be
          uncultivated directors, interested in profit and that will
          signal the end of the art of film.

45    H. W.  "Der müde Tod: Ein deutsches Volkslied in 6 Versen."
          Lichtbildbühne (Berlin) (8 October).
              H. W. first praises Destiny for being a real film, as
          contrasted with a literary work that merely illustrates
          themes. This film is made by a man totally immersed in
          film creation per se. The reviewer notes how the film
          achieves unity through a central idea--the oldest one in
          Western culture, namely the riddle of death. While the
          actors help Lang to express his vision, it is Lang's tech-
          nical effects, above all his use of light and shadow, and
          his rhythmic organization of the whole, that are responsible
          for the film's beauty. Whoever believes in the future of
          the cinema should see this film, H. W. concludes.

### 1922

*46   Balthasar [Roland Schacht]. Review of Dr. Mabuse, der Spieler.
      Das Blaue Heft (Berlin) (10 June).
          Source: Grafe, Frieda, and Enno Patalas. Fritz Lang.
      Munich: Hanser, 1976, p. 168.

47   Ihering, Herbert. "Filmfragen (Dr. Mabuse)". Berliner
     Börsen-Courier (11 June). Reprinted in his Von Reinhardt
     bis Brecht, vol. 1. East Berlin: Aufbau, 1958. Pp.
     426-428.
         Ihering begins by contrasting Klein-Rogge in Dr. Mabuse
     with Werner Krauss in Zirkus des Lebens. In relying on
     masks, beards, wigs, etc. to portray the transformations
     of Dr. Mabuse, Klein-Rogge remains within the stage tradi-
     tion, while Krauss becomes someone else merely through
     facial expressions. The artist who needs masks to assume
     another likeness is a mere observer of life as contrasted
     with the artist who can intuitively assume another person-
     ality. Ihering argues that in film one needs only the free
     use of face, limbs, and body.
         Ihering next shows how Dr. Mabuse is a masterpiece visu-
     ally, using the devices of film direction and theater to
     their fullest. He praises the film's theme--the depiction
     of the chaos of a modern city. But he criticizes the film's
     tempo, finding it too rushed and unbalanced. The narrative
     does not live up to the beauty of the image.
         Ihering concludes by contrasting the respective abilities
     of theater and film to conceptualize. While ideas are quite
     easily expressed in theater through its main symbolic mode,
     the word, they are difficult to convey in film, which must
     work with the image. Films try to express through images
     what can, in fact, only be communicated in words.

48   Olimsky, Fritz. Review of Dr. Mabuse, der Spieler [Dr. Mabuse,
     the Gambler]. Der Kinematograph (Düsseldorf), No. 794
     (7 May).
         Olimsky argues that Lang makes art out of a story that
     is essentially Kitsch. Lang was fortunate in the people he
     had working for him--his architect, Stahl-Urach, and camera
     man, Carl Hoffmann.

*49   Pinthus, Kurt. "Dr. Mabuses Welt." Das Tage-Buch (Berlin),
      No. 18 (6 May).
          Source: Grafe, Frieda, and Enno Patalas. Fritz Lang.
      Munich: Hanser, 1976, p. 168.

50   Pinthus, Kurt. "Nochmals: Dr. Mabuses Welt." Das Tage-Buch
     (Berlin) (3 June).
         Pinthus defends his support for Lang's first Mabuse
     film, praising the way in which Lang and Hoffmann took care

not to photograph reality but instead to present elements of it in brilliant compositions, which render film "art." He finds similar visual aspects to praise in the second part of Dr. Mabuse, der Spieler [Dr. Mabuse, the Gambler], noting the play of shadow and light, the use of space, and the decor. Lang and Hoffman realized that film is not theater, but is composed of images combined in space.

Pinthus finds the treatment of part II less satisfactory than part I because the main elements of the Jacques novel had been used in the first half. Mabuse is here more of an ordinary criminal, but Pinthus mentions as excellent the scene where, following the word "melior" von Wenk rushes out of the hall and drives toward the cliffs. This is something that has not been done by the Americans.

## 1923

51 Harbou, Thea von. Das Nibelungenbuch. Berlin: Decla-Bioscop; Munich: Drei Masken Verlag.
Apparently written after the movie, this book contains many stills from the film.

52 Ihering, Herbert. "Das Brennende Geheimnis/ Leute aus Wermland/ Der müde Tod." Berliner Börsen-Courier (30 September). Reprinted in his Von Reinhardt bis Brecht, vol. 1, East Berlin: Aufbau, 1958.
Der müde Tod (Destiny) represents the start of a specifically German film genre--that of the song- and ballad-film. But the variation in quality is very noticeable today: two of the three tales, the Oriental and the Italian, inevitably deviate from the tone of the framing plot since they belong to a group of conventional hunt and chase films. The tales are costumed detective stories inserted into a lyrical ballad. Lang deserves credit for discovering this film genre, despite the fact that he is not yet successful in realizing it. Although he has a good sense of the image, he knows little about acting.
A fantastic film is dependent on its pictorial treatment: this is still elementary in Der müde Tod, and may be explained by its early date. The film also lacks subtlety.

## 1923/24

53 Sch. "Kriemhilds Rache im Film." Kunstwart und Kulturwart (No. 10).
Sch. condemns Die Nibelungen as the mere product of technology, capital, and ambition. Having followed Lang for some years, the reviewer predicts that Lang will soon burst from boring pomposity. In spite of all its grandiosity, Sch. considers Die Nibelungen a trashy film.

*54   W. B.   "Ein Nibelungenfilm."  Der Kunstwart und Kulturwart,
      No. 8.
         Source:  Verband des Deutschen Film Klubs:  Dokumentation
      Bad Ems, 1964.  (Available in Deutsches Institut für
      Filmkunde, Wiesbaden.)


                              1924


55    Anon.  "Der Aussenminister über den deutschen Film."  Der
      Kinematograph (Berlin), No. 887 (17 February), p. 15.
         The article summarizes a speech by Norman Wright about
      the German film.  Wright praises it highly, singling out
      Lang's recent Die Nibelungen for special mention as a work
      that brings film-form to a new height both culturally and
      aesthetically.  He is optimistic about the future of German
      films, believing that they will become some of the very best
      in the world.


56    Anon.  Review of Between Two Worlds [American version of Der
      müde Tod].  New York Times (7 July).  [The New York Times
      also has a notice on 3 February 1927 of an edited version
      of Between Two Worlds called Beyond the Wall.]
         The reviewer finds the film a depressing German produc-
      tion that is full of weird symbolism.  He also notes that
      the film reminds him of Thief of Bagdad [evidently not know-
      ing that Fairbanks stole from Lang, ed.].  The film, says
      the reviewer, was made at a time when lighting, photography,
      and construction of settings had not reached their present
      high standards.  He does not like the acting, but finds the
      Venetian sequences impressive, although at times too dark.
      The reviewer finds the Chinese sections less impressive
      than those in Fairbanks's film.  He or she concludes by
      gently mocking Lang's allegorical strivings as shown by the
      huge walls and unending stairs.


57    Anon.  "German Director, Fritz Lang, Here."  Telegraph (New
      York) (14 October).
         The writer notes that Lang, "reputed to be the greatest
      film director on the continent," is visiting America with
      Eric Pommer of Ufa.  They came to study American methods in
      New York and Los Angeles, but Lang evidently does not intend
      to direct here.  Lang tells the writer that he could not
      work well in America without knowing all about the society
      and the film industry; he is here to see the new cameras
      and to study the big cities for his next feature, Metropolis.
      He is interested in American methods of printing and devel-
      oping and in the "steady cameras that are used to make your
      trick pictures."  Pommer notes that Lang's films are made
      for the future and that Siegfried should be interesting to
      future generations.  He says that Ufa does not want to


                              138

undersell the Americans or flood the country with German
films, but they do want to make worthwhile pictures with
international casts. They are negotiating with Lillian
Gish for a new Faust film in which Emil Jannings will play
Mephistopheles. He notes further that "society dramas are
the vogue in Germany now, and the demand for Westerns has
fallen off. Only the greatest American stars are known in
Germany, and the people won't go to see even their pictures
if the production is not good." The article ends with a
note to the effect that Ufa Berlin was recently incorporated
in America as UFA-USA.

58   Anon. "German Director Tells of Visit to Hollywood." New
     York Times (30 November).
     The article describes Lang's American visit, which had
just ended. At the Hollywood studios, he met with prominent
producers and screen celebrities. The German Ufa officials
with Lang were impressed with what they saw, especially the
laboratories (which were superior to German ones) and the
sets. They were allowed to see all the technical details
of the movie version of Conan Doyle's The Lost World. Talking with Mary Pickford, Lang learned of her admiration for
foreign directors who were willing to risk a lot for originality, while American directors were afraid to deal with
anything different or controversial. Douglas Fairbanks
noted that in America producers relied on stars, while in
Germany, according to Lang, "it was usually the idea to
make the picture the attraction for the star."
     Lang admired Fairbanks's technical setups in his studios,
and they saw The Thief of Bagdad with pleasure. They ended
their trip to America by visiting D. W. Griffith in
Montclair, N. J., where he was making Isn't Life Wonderful?
which the German group also thought highly of because of
"the human touches."

59   Barry, Iris. "The Nibelungs." Spectator (London) (14 June),
     p. 955.
     Barry begins by noting that most important cinematic ex-
periments continue to come from the continent. Fritz Lang
is famous in England for Destiny and Sumurum [Iris mistakenly credited Lang for this Lubitsch film, ed.]. Once a
painter, Lang insists that the visual beauty of a film is
as important as its dramatic effectiveness.
     In The Nibelungs, Lang has subordinated the dramatic to
the visual element. The characters are legendary and the
architecture, trees, and dragons become protagonists. Shot
in the Ufa studios, the film astounds with its visual feats
rather than its emotions. Barry particularly admires the
visual symbolism in Kriemhild's dream.
     Barry objects to the lumpish acting, but even more to
the atrocious translations in the subtitles.

139

In conclusion, Barry notes the importance of The
Nibelungs in showing how much can be done in film visually,
whereas before emphasis had mainly been on how to tell a
story well.

60  Dey, Martin. Nibelungenbuch und Nibelungenfilm. Betrachtungen
eines Laien. Dortmund: Ruhfus.
    The basic position Dey takes in this booklet is that
while each generation has a right to its own view of the
Nibelungen legend, the Lang-Harbou film cheapens, sensation-
alizes, and popularizes the original. The depiction of the
Huns goes against historical evidence, and the heroes are
made sentimental in order to fit the expectations of modern
film audiences. Dey concludes that film had better have
nothing to do with great literature if this is all that it
can offer. But he hopes that at some point a more authentic
Nibelungen film will be made.

61  H. Fr. "Der Nibelungen-Film." Lichtbildbühne (Berlin)
(16 February).
    A very positive review of the film, which H. Fr. denies
is either a costume film or a monumental film. He praises
all aspects of the film, talking of the excellence of von
Harbou's rendering of the original epic, of the brilliant
set decoration by Otto Hunte, of the acting, and the photography. He mentions the contribution of Lang's ability
as a painter to the success of the film.

62  Hardt, Remy M. "Ufa Palast: Kriemhilds Rache." Der Kritiker
(May-June).
    Hardt considers it ridiculous to have attempted a film
of the Nibelungen epic. The film is "monumental" in its
boredom, and interesting only for its images and technical
aspects. It is like a succession of pictures in a museum,
lacking all vitality and movement, and ending up as Kitsch,
not art. While Lang directed earlier films like Der müde
Tod [Destiny] well, here nothing works cinematically.
    The film has some good qualities: Hoffmann's photography,
Lang's painterly eye, Hunte's designs; the contrast between
the Burgundians and Huns, chaos and culture, is well done.
Had Lang only made the film work as cinema, it would have
been beautiful.

63  Higgins, Bertram. "Destiny at the Polytechnic Hall."
Spectator (London) (23 February), pp. 284-285.
    Higgins begins by surveying the state of film as an art
and notes that three new German films -- Destiny and two
others coming shortly, Caligari and The Street -- lift film
to a new level. The conventions of spectacular realism,
begun by Griffith, are exhausted, but the German films offer
a new form of psychological fantasy that should be encouraged.

After briefly outlining the plot of Destiny, Higgins concludes that a summary of the narrative cannot convey the
beauty of the film directed so well by Lang. He praises
the screen play, the producer, and the acting of Goetzke
and Lil Dagover. Even allowing for the new conceptions of
time, however, the story is metaphysically confusing and
the subtitles poor. But taken as a whole, the film is original and impressive.

64    Ihering, Herbert. "Der erste Nibelungen-Film." Berliner
      Börsen-Courier (15 February). Reprinted in his Von
      Reinhardt bis Brecht, vol. 2. East Berlin: Aufbau, 1959,
      pp. 474-475.
          Ihering notes that Lang tried [in The Nibelungen Part I:
      The Death of Siegfried] to find a style that would unite
      painterly and architechtural elements fitting for this fam-
      ous legend. But the result is that the film is uncinematic;
      the inflexibility and static quality of Siegfried come from
      its one-sided conception. Ihering finds the film lacking
      in dramatic intensity, being too academic and decorative.
      The theatrical quality in all Lang's films is a weakness;
      he depends on technical surprises too much and does not know
      how to achieve cinematic effects in other ways. He would
      have done better to create a more living, human film.

65    t. "Leute, die man im Film nicht sieht: Fritz Lang." Die
      Filmwoche (Berlin), No. 24.
          This is a rather mocking account of an interview with
      Lang, in which the critic exposes Lang's pretentiousness,
      pomposity, and overearnestness. The piece is interesting
      in that it shows how early Lang adopted certain styles of
      behavior and ways of relating to people that later got him
      into trouble in Hollywood.
          The critic begins by complaining that it was very diffi-
      cult to get answers from Lang, who also avoided any ques-
      tions he did not like. The author comments on the fact that
      Lang speaks kindly only of people like Eric Pommer and Thea
      von Harbou whom he was very close to. All his famous films
      were made with Pommer at Decla, Lang's situation there being
      very privileged. Lang refuses to answer any questions about
      his future plans.

66    Ulitzsch, Ernst. "Die Nibelungen: Uraufführung des ersten
      Teiles Siegfried am Ufa-Palast am Zoo." Der Kinematograph
      (Dusseldorf) (17 February).
          In a very positive review, Ulitzsch begins by praising
      the use Lang makes of light and shade and the way he has
      managed, like Goethe, to build an entire world that reflects
      the Middle Ages. Lang is the Wagner of film, creating some-
      thing grand and Germanic. Turning to Thea von Harbou, Lang's
      coworker on the film, Ulitzsch notes how she has made more

of the Nibelungen myth than did Hebbel or Wagner. While
the film is not so dramatic as the epic, being more lyrical
and episodic, it is beautifully done. He praises the style
for being Nordic rather than Gothic, admiring the purity of
line and of the silhouettes. Most of the technical tricks
work and the choice of actors was good.

67  Vogeler, Erich. "Der Nibelungenfilm: 1. Teil: <u>Siegfried</u>."
    <u>Berliner Tageblatt</u>, No. 79 (15 February).
        According to Vogeler, the <u>Nibelungenlied</u> [Niebelungen
    saga] is a great legend that resists being pressed into a
    form. Thea von Harbou has produced a clean work without
    <u>Kitsch</u>. Lang's direction has similar qualities and often
    includes wonderful pictures. But the whole is a bit cold,
    more a historical drama than a legend or a song.

68  Ybarra, T. R.  "<u>Die Nibelungen</u> Meets Disaster in Berlin."  <u>New
    York Times</u> (29 April).
        The subtitle of the article reads: "First showing of
    Nationalist Propaganda Film Interrupted on account of
    Protests." Ybarra goes on to describe the offensive adver-
    tising that had preceded the film's release, which evidently
    had favored the German Siegfried over the Niebelungen.
    Kriemhild, the heroine of the piece, is seen committing mur-
    der in response to treacherous dealings. Ybarra concludes
    that the film was intended as propaganda for the German
    nationalist spirit, and he criticises the management for
    having created such intense feelings with its tactless
    advertising.


<u>1925</u>

69  Anon.  "Dr. Lang Finds Us Inartistic."  <u>New York Sun</u> (11
    February).
        This article reports on a lecture Lang gave in Berlin
    following his visit to America. Noting that American direc-
    tors were too commercial and less devoted to art than were
    German filmmakers, Lang found only Griffith to be concerned
    with ideas. While Germany has better actors, there is more
    variety in America and one can find actors able to play
    themselves. Unlike German actors, American ones keep in
    top shape. Lang admires the pervasive sense of vitality in
    America: while Germans complain all the time, Americans in-
    variably claim to be fine.

70  Anon.  "How Siegfried was Produced."  <u>New York Times</u>
    (6 September).
        The reviewer obtained information about details of the
    making of <u>Siegfried</u> from Gwynne Jones, managing director
    for Ufa in America. The enormous feat of creating and

filming the dragon is discussed, along with the way in
which the brilliant lighting effects were achieved, how the
fog was made, how models were created according to painstak-
ing study of the laws of perspective, and what special
lenses produced certain special effects. The reviewer concludes by noting the great care with which the film was
made, especially in terms of obtaining the proper rhythm of
action.

71    Hall, Mordaunt.  Review of Siegfried.  New York Times
      (24 August).
            Hall notes that the film invades the sacred realm of the
      opera, taking a different view of the familiar heroic fig-
      ures.  Nevertheless, it should be taken seriously.  Although
      the film was made inside a studio, the narrative is fascin-
      ating, particularly since it is put together using techniques
      that belong to old legends.  Scenes unfold with a grace
      helped by "the wizardry of the camera."  The huge sets and
      the fight with the dragon are especially impressive.
            Hall praises Brunhild's dignity, magnificent at times,
      although at other times she seems too normal and modern.
      In concluding, Hall singles out for mention the acting per-
      formances of Richter, Schoen, and Schlettow, along with the
      Wagnerian score.

72    Spitzer, Ludwig.  "Fritz Lang über den Film der Zukunft."  Die
      Filmtechnik (Halle) (15 July), pp. 34-36.  (A translation
      of this article may be found in Albert Eibel's Fritz Lang)
      (See Entry No. 478).
            Spitzer prefaces the interview by noting how friendly
      Lang was and how willingly he answered questions, except
      those relating to his forthcoming film, Metropolis.  Recent-
      ly famous for Die Nibelungen, Lang would only say that
      Metropolis picks up from Dr. Mabuse.
            Spitzer next discusses the possibility inherent in film
      to show the spiritual and psychological dimensions of human
      beings -- the area that psychoanalysis reveals.  In view of
      this ability, mastery of technique alone is insufficient --
      directors must also understand the intricacies of the human
      soul.  Questioned about this, Lang agrees that filmmakers
      must have a firm grasp on human life and experience if inner
      events are not to be falsified.
            Continuing to speculate about the possibilities for film,
      Spitzer suggests that combining the language that literature
      has always used with the visual expressiveness of the screen
      will produce the highest form to date, the deepest explora-
      tion of the human soul.  We will soon be able to talk about
      a film art rather than an art of the film.  Spitzer asks
      Lang how this combination could be brought about in film,
      and Lang discusses the importance of mastering the camera
      and all the tricks involved in film art.  He regrets that

these "secrets" are so freely given away to the public.

The interview concludes with speculation about the coming generation and the future of film. Lang already seems to doubt that youth will be able to continue along the same lines as his generation. The students that flock to him do not know what they really want to do. He hopes he is wrong in seeing them this way.

73    Ulsen, Hans. 8 Uhr Abendblatt (Berlin), No. 249 (23 October), Sec. 3.

Ulsen begins with a discussion of the relatively new art of film and of the tensions between technical achievements --the artistry of film--and what the public expect. But the director is most important, since it is he who must combine artistry with technique, working tirelessly to get everything right. Lang is an example of a director who uses his imagination to make works of art; he builds each image on an idea and makes harmonious links between one image and the next. Lang's new film, Metropolis, deals with the city of the future, showing the conflicts between the individual and the mass, and between those who work with their heads and those who work with their hands. Lang lives with his themes, thus providing enthusiasm for those who work with him.

Ulsen goes into Lang's background and history, noting his original interest in architecture and painting and his work as a scriptwriter for Joe May. Halbblut [Half-Caste], Lang's first film, was succeeded by Der müde Tod [Destiny], where Lang went more deeply into his themes. His last film, Siegfried, brought him close to his goal of making art films, and Ulsen hopes that Metropolis will represent that level of achievement. Aiming higher than mere commercial success, Lang works tirelessly to produce the best, trying to solve the problems of filmmaking generally and of the art film specifically.

## 1926

74    Fraenkel, Heinrich. "The Story of Fritz Lang, Maker of Siegfried." Motion Picture Classic, 23 (March), 38.

This early article was written while Lang was making Metropolis and still working in Germany. At that time, he was known mainly as the director of Siegfried, his most impressive work to date. The reviewer briefly surveys Lang's background--his bohemianism, his antibourgeois life-style, and the many careers he had, from trying to carry out his father's wish that he be an engineer, attempting architecture, working in a cabaret, trying to become a painter, and finally getting into film through scriptwriting.

His new film, Metropolis, does not resemble the earlier

Wagnerian effort in <u>Siegfried</u>, but is instead a modernist film.

75    Kurtz, Rudolf.  <u>Expressionismus und Film</u>.  Berlin:  Verlag der
      Lichtbildbühne.
           Although there is very little explicit mention of Lang's
      films in Kurtz's book, it is important in providing an early
      analysis of the expressionist aesthetic, which clearly in-
      fluenced Lang.  As the first discussion of expressionism
      and film, the book outlines the origins of the movement in
      painting and then its literary manifestations before turn-
      ing to such early expressionist films as <u>Caligari</u> and
      <u>Rasknolnikov</u>.  Many of Kurtz's insights are now standard in
      any discussion of expressionism, and Lotte Eisner develops
      his work in <u>The Haunted Screen</u> (<u>See</u> Entry No. 375).


                              1927


76    Anon.  "Metropolis Film Seen.  Berlin Witnesses a Grim Portrayal
      of Industrial Future."  <u>New York Times</u> (10 January), p. 36.
           The film had its premiere in Berlin before a large audi-
      ence including Chancellor Marx, cabinet officers, members
      of the diplomatic corps and leading figures from the Berlin
      art world.  According to this reviewer, what success the
      film has will be due to its mechanical, rather than its
      human, aspects.  He notes that "the grandiose artistry of
      the machines is gripping" and praises Lang's imaginative
      conception of the futurist tower of Babel.  The reviewer
      notes in passing the likeness of John [sic] Fredersen to
      John Ford, suggesting that this is deliberate, and goes on
      to marvel at the creation of the robot.
           Brigitte Helm alone among the actors is praised for a
      performance that stands out from the general staginess.
      The audience only really became enthusiastic when viewing
      the scenes in the underground machine room.

77    Anon.  "Metropolis Film Cost $2,000,000.  Germany's Latest
      Thriller a Thing of Awe and Beauty."  <u>New York Sun</u>
      (11 January), p. 25.
           The reviewer talks about the film's high cost and extreme
      length.  It was shown to a full house in Berlin, but did
      not impress the reviewer.  "The social struggle," he says,
      "is left unresolved, and the director has mingled in a lot
      of fantastic nonsense."  Considered as a whole, "the film
      serves only to indicate the possibilities of the movies,
      should technique, skill and unlimited money ever be joined
      with the genius of a great creative artist."

78    Anon.  "Kritik der Leinwand:  <u>Metropolis</u>."  <u>Die Filmwoche</u>
      (Berlin) (19 January) (Available through the Deutschen Film

und Fernsehakademie, West Berlin.)

The author begins by criticizing Lang's emphasis on the hard work that went into making Metropolis; all great works, he notes, require as much, and the only difference is that this one cost a lot.

The writer then objects to von Harbou's unrealistic portrayal of the future. He believes that current social values are the opposite of those portrayed in the film: religiosity has in fact declined, and democratic thought seems guaranteed by a republican constitution. People believe that the development of technology will result in improved social conditions. Even fantasy should have a certain degree of probability, according to the reviewer, and he goes on to ridicule the image of workers cooped up underground after a historical period in which strong workers' organizations arose.

The reviewer condemns von Harbou for playing with logic; if workers could sink to the level of idiots, then nothing would call them back to humanity so suddenly. She irresponsibly throws fantastic and biogenetic elements together, and does not even indicate the purpose of the machines.

Furthermore, the writer points out that von Harbou's novel (on which the film is based) does not even present a credible future world; automobiles, matches, streets, furniture are all the same as in the present; and the seven deadly sins are revived, a young man reads Revelations, a magician draws a pentagram over his electric chair, and the Leipziger Illustrierte is displayed on a newsstand.

The critic concludes that it is the most disenchanting film that he has seen in a long time. The poor actors only further dehumanized an already lifeless novel. The writer admonishes Lang for focussing on beautiful images at the expense of intellectually responsible ideas. This dangerous tendency was already evident in Der müde Tod [Destiny], but an idea was still present in that film; images dominated in Die Nibelungen, but the force of the legend was there; in Metropolis things have got irretrievably out of hand.

79   Anon.   Review of Metropolis.   New York Times (7 March).
The reviewer notes that Metropolis stands alone as a remarkable film achievement and then goes on to praise the visual style and the crowds of men and women. The setting is astounding. The film combines something of a treatise on capital and labor, the R.U.R. idea, and Mary Shelley's Frankenstein.

After praising the acting and the up-to-date appliances in Masterman's office, the critic discusses the enormous work that went into the production of the film, listing the huge numbers of extras and mentioning in particular the scene where the robot is made.

80    Anon.  "Metropolis."  National Board of Review Magazine, No. 2
      (April), p. 12.
           This is a very short notice, stating simply that
      Metropolis is a fantasy about our future industrial civili-
      zation, showing people entirely subordinated to the machine.
      "The futility of antagonism between capital and labour, and
      the need of [sic] brotherly love is brought out allegorical-
      ly."  The review ends with reference to the novel by Thea
      von Harbou from which the film was made.

81    Anon.  "The Crooked Hypnotist."  (Review of Dr. Mabuse, the
      Gambler).  New York Times (9 August).
           The reviewer complains about the poor acting and the ver-
      bose titles.  A few scenes are interesting, such as those
      in the gambling clubs when the people talk about the strange
      Dr. Mabuse at one end of the room, while the doctor hypno-
      tizes them from the other.  But the reviewer thinks that
      Wenk waits too long to use his wits and that the film is
      lengthy and old-fashioned.  "It is something like a serial
      posing as a mystery play."  Since this early film, Lang has
      earned a reputation as director of Siegfried and Metropolis.

82    Arnheim, Rudolf.  "Metropolis."  Das Stachelschwein (1 February).
           Arnheim discusses the elaborate publicity that Metropolis
      was given and how arid this film, built on the desert of
      von Harbou's manuscript, proved in the end.  The value of
      the film lies in its visual style rather than in the con-
      tent, which Arnheim scorns.  The film symbolizes, he says,
      the fusion of American and German film; on the one hand,
      there are the boyish fantasies of the technical future; on
      the other, all the traditions of European literature from
      the idealized maiden to the great Gothic cathedral.  There
      is not a trace here of the "new realism" [Neue Sachlichkeit].
           There are some good scenes, like the flood-scene, and
      some excellent performances.  Coming from a hard day's work,
      one could find the film entertaining.

83    Barry, Iris.  "Metropolis."  Spectator (London) (26 March),
      p. 540.
           If Metropolis fails, it is not due to the brilliant pro-
      ducers, the subject matter, or the treatment, but to the
      state of film, an art form as yet inadequate to deal with
      large themes.
           Barry admires the concrete picture of oppressive future
      city life and praises Lang's imagination.  The conception
      of television and the making of the robot are convincing
      and we sympathize with the downtrodden workers.  But the
      depiction of the rich upper class is false and their cos-
      tumes hideous.  Some of the film is expressionist, some
      naturalist, but some also "is mere picture-post card."
           The story--pure melodrama recalling Griffith--is the

main weakness of the film; cinema, having a mental age of seventeen, is more concerned with the medium itself than with what the medium can express. But Metropolis is the most nearly-adult film yet seen. The architecture is grand, the handling of crowds good, and there are several great moments in the film. Although the subtitles are awful, the photography is brilliant and the acting, especially when stylized, is fine.

Barry concludes by wondering how the Welsh coal miners would respond to the film and if the Coal Owners' Association had been asked to see it.

84    Bartlett, Randolph. "German Film Revision Upheld as Needed Here." New York Times (13 March).

Bartlett begins by praising the editing of German films as the basis of their success. The Germans are good at presenting powerful forces, as in Metropolis, and are also good with light, as in the scene of the robot's creation in the same film.

Where the Germans are weak, however, is in telling a story, which is surprising, given their technical abilities. Bartlett saw all seventeen reels of Metropolis before it was cut, and the British editors simply tried to bring out the real thoughts that were lost in the German version. Unavoidable cuts included the character of Hel, who would have been impossible in a British version.

Bartlett ends by suggesting that German films are overrated for their artiness: the snob appeal in liking the films is similar to that of owning a Parisian hat.

85    Buñuel, Luis. "Metropolis." Gazeta Literaria de Madrid, 1927. Reprinted in Cahiers du Cinéma, No. 223 (August–September, 1971), pp. 20-21. An English translation of the article may be found in both Arnanda, Francis. Luis Buñuel: A Critical Biography. Translated and edited by David Robinson. New York: DaCapo Press, 1976, and Braudy, Leo and Dickstein, Morris, eds. Great Film Directors. New York: Oxford University Press, 1978, pp. 590-592. (Annotation taken from Cahiers du Cinéma.)

Buñuel argues that Metropolis is really a film with two separate levels that clash with each other. There is first the narrative level, on which the film fails, for the story is "trivial, bombastic, pedantic, of an antiquated romanticism." But on the second level, which Buñuel calls the "plastic photogenic basis of the film," Metropolis fulfills all that one could wish for. We are overwhelmed with "the most marvellous picture book imaginable." Thus, while the one level, "the pure-lyrical" is excellent, the other, "the anecdotal, or human, is ultimately irritating."

Buñuel notes that this is not the first time that one finds such a disconcerting dualism in Lang's films (he

refers particularly to Destiny here). He blames Thea von
Harbou for the dangerous sentimentality of the story, with
the simplistic ending, where head and hands are united by
the heart, but he praises Otto Hunte and Walter Ruttmann for
the magnificent visual effects, particularly the images of
machines. Buñuel admires Hunte's vision of the city of the
future (the year 2,000), which he says has been surpassed
but is, nevertheless, beautiful and technically perfect.

Buñuel notes that the main fault of the film is its departure from Eisenstein's idea in Battleship Potemkin that
the mass of people can be made the hero. In Metropolis,
people are used instead as decorative elements, and the central characters are people with large, indecent passions.

Buñuel ends with the sobering thought that the enormous
cost of the film (40,000 people were used and two million
feet of film were shot--the final version originally had
five thousand feet) was not enough to make it great.

86   E. S. P. "Metropolis." Filmbesprechung (no issue given; found
in file in Deutschen Film-und Fernsehakademie, W. Berlin).

E. S. P. comments first on the direction in the film and
on the script and actors, praising the treatment of the
mass, the creation of the robot, etc. He then discusses
the politics of making a film like this, saying it was
wrong to take such a financial risk. The cost was permitted
on the assumption that the film would be a success in
America; but even if this were the case, how long must the
German industry wait to get the actual boxoffice money? He
concludes that films like Metropolis should be made only
out of profits and not out of working capital or on credit.

87   Axel Eggebrecht, "Metropolis." Die Weltbühne (Berlin), No. 3
(18 January).

[In this review, the author maintains the conceit of a
film history written in 2003, ed.]

Lang was one of those who made the peculiar attempt to
revive the old, once holy, art of representation in the new,
still primitive medium of film. The rich gave him money so
that he could play prophet for an age that knew less than
any other where it was headed.

Metropolis was a gigantic labyrinth of half-truths and
misunderstandings, a true mirror of its time. Lang wanted
to depict all the tendencies and possibilities of the spirit
and reconcile them in a "Super-Chicago" of the future. He
took a little bit of class consciousness, some more of industrial Caesarism, a lot from the powers of the advancing
church, and mixed them up with hundreds of other notions.
However, the author of the novel, von Harbou, forgot to
provide the film with a connecting idea, an overall concept.
The gigantic piecework fell apart miserably. This fanatic
organizer of details was moved by the forebodings of his

dying age, but was not stirred by hope, much less certainty.

Lang lacked even the most basic understanding of his age's industrial technology, so that he constructed problems that had long been overcome. His work is typical evidence of the reactionary influence of a supposedly progressive intellectual class in a transitional phase of history. He errs greatly in his portrayal of proletarian and even capitalist psychology.

In order to give life to a future that he cannot imagine, he reviews symbols of the past. The inventor of the artificial human being bears the characteristics, dress, and pentagram of Dr. Faustus, the whore Babel dances among the gentlemen of leisure, the masses disappear in the gorge of the idol Moloch. But when the head and the hands of the city are reconciled through the heart of the rich son in the weakest part of the film, one feels the desparate longing of the age to find a fairytale-like happy ending to its troubles.

The relentless unrest of his times torments Lang. As an artist, he desires reconciling peace; he is a painter, not an actor. He has arranged beautiful mass scenes and hundreds of sketches into a filmstrip. That is what at the time was called film. His machines had decorative value, but the people in this marvelous city were exactly the same uncertain, theatrical, phony, unwise, and impractically dressed people of his own time. The film is trivial work of incredible size; the true genius of the two cameramen was lost without effect.

This great effort brought forth the proof that the soul, the power of hope and fantasy, and the heart of this age were long dead--a late and costly funeral.

88    Freund, Karl. "Meine Arbeit an Metropolis." B.Z. am Mittag (Berlin) (7 January).

Freund talks about his role as cameraman on Metropolis, seeing it as that of aiding Lang to bring out his vision of the city of the future. He tried to make Lang's ideas visually truthful and probable. Metropolis is unusual, Freund says, in its reliance on the camera to express its themes.

Freund goes on to discuss specific difficulties in filming certain scenes, mentioning that he had to work fourteen to sixteen hours a day in the boiler room of the underground city, where it was hot and damp.

89    Gerstein, Evelyn. "Metropolis." The Nation (New York) (23 March), pp. 323-324.

Gerstein begins by contrasting the parasitical nature of Hollywood, which "lives for money and sex" and "borrows or buys its art," with the German directors, who have experimented with the medium, giving us camera movement, imagination, and new lighting techniques.

Having more in common with <u>Siegfried</u> than with Murnau's
<u>The Last Laugh</u>, <u>Metropolis</u> reflects Lang's interest in sheer
beauty, composition, and rhythm. The influence of Reinhardt's
theater is evident in the use of groups and masses. But the
film lacks subtlety and is immobile and static, apart from
the excellent shots of the machinery and of the rebellious
workers in motion.

The film does convey well the chill of the future mechanized world where only the machines seem real, where people
are inanimate, and where there is no loveliness, except in
the gardens of the rich. Yet this is stylized fantasy rather
than realism, there being nothing of the reality of revolution as staged by the Russians. Lang's artistic imagination
sets the film above another on a similar theme, <u>R. U. R.</u>

The film's lack of cohesion may stem from the original
version, a novel by Thea von Harbou. Like the novel, the
film is intellectual, has no humor or individual development,
but is full of sentimental symbolism.

Gerstein concludes that it is the city itself that makes
the film magnificent.

90   Herring, Robert. "Metropolis." <u>London Mercury</u>, 16 (May),
     92-93.
     Herring begins by doubting that <u>Metropolis</u> would have
been any better if uncut; the story was so awful that one
did not want more of it. He considers the view of the future
superficial and disappointing, not even redeemed by the images of machines.

The image of the city was a letdown, Masterman in particular looking ridiculous in his effete clothes. The point
of the film--the contrast between the boss and the workers
--did not come across effectively. The effort as a whole
was unimaginative and the plot silly.

Visually, there were some good scenes, such as the making
of the robot and the explosions. While the photography was
good, satisfying the eyes, there was nothing for the mind
or the imagination here.

91   Hildebrandt, Fred. "Metropolis." <u>Berliner Tageblatt</u>, No. 17
     (11 January).
     The author watches <u>Metropolis</u> being filmed, is favorably
impressed by it, and then goes after the film's premiere to
the Schwannecke, a bar in Berlin frequented by artists and
intellectuals, to hear the clientele's reactions to the
movie.

They maintain it was an artificial, contrived fabrication
with wonderful photography, a phony ethos, an unparalleled
technique, sentimental, pretentious <u>Kitsch</u>, old and new
tricks, hollow symbolism and empty chatter, lopsided realism
and lopsided romanticism at the same time, unrealistic content, and with a dependence on well-known literature.

The author summarizes the plot. He wonders if the tremendous effort and the large amount of time and money spent
on the film has been wasted. He attributes the public's
disappointment to the huge amount of publicity the film received while it was in the making. The film could not match
the expectations raised by the widespread publicity of each
phase in the film's production and by the great advertising
campaign.

92  Ihering, Herbert. "Der Metropolis-Film." Berliner Börsen-
    Courier (11 January). Reprinted in H. Ihering, Von
    Reinhardt bis Brecht, vol. 2. East Berlin: Aufbau, 1959,
    pp. 523-524.
        Ihering gives a review similar to that he gave Die
    Nibelungen, arguing again that Lang ruins everything by
    overstylization and reliance on technical effects. He real-
    izes that it is hard to call such a film a failure, but sees
    Metropolis inevitably failing because of the conflict between
    Thea von Harbou's romantic fantasies and the theme dealing
    with the world of the future. The two aspects work against
    each other.

93  Omicron [pseud.]. Review of Metropolis. Nation (London), 40,
    No. 26 (2 April), 925.
        Mainly positive, the review praises the photography,
    lighting, and acting in Metropolis. "Above all, in its
    amazingly ingenuous and effective decor, it is quite one of
    the most exciting and entertaining films that have ever been
    made."

94  Schacht, Roland. "Der Metropolisfilm der UFA." Der Kunstwart
    (No. 5). (Available in the Deutschen Film und
    Fernsehakademie, West Berlin.)
        Schacht begins by objecting to the sentimental solution
    that Thea von Harbou [responsible for the script of the
    film, ed.] provides for social problems in Metropolis.
    That the heart should mediate between head and hands is
    clearly inadequate as a remedy for social ills.
        According to Schacht, Metropolis is colorful and romantic,
    beautiful as well as abstruse, original as well as tasteless,
    fantastic as well as perverse. While it begins flawlessly,
    it later becomes pompous, and the plot gets lost in the
    overwhelming mass scenes.
        Schacht concludes that Metropolis is technically perfect,
    and amazing for its formal innovations. Even in America,
    there is no director who could make anything like it.

95  Scheffauer, Herman G. "An Impression of the German Film
    Metropolis." New York Times (6 March), p. 7.
        Scheffauer begins by describing the feat of producing
    Metropolis; Lang worked for two years on it, with thousands

of hands, and millions of dollars were spent.  It was a combination of American capital and German knowhow.
    The final effect is disappointing and perhaps had to be,
since the advance publicity was so tremendous.  The film is
ultimately not that new, relying on earlier ideas of the
future.  The characters are torn by emotions similar to
those of people today; this perhaps was necessitated by
commercial considerations.
    Lang's film doesn't quite fit anywhere, being not fully
of the past, nor of the present, nor yet really about the
future.  It shows the influence of Jules Verne, H. G. Wells,
and Mary Shelley.  Yet Scheffauer is impressed by the film:
a certain new wonder does seize us; we see that new forces,
unleashed on earth, could make people their slaves.  The
sinister nature of machines is shown, and Scheffauer admires
the depiction of the future city; it has something of
America in it and seems real.  The film represents the
European perspective on America, showing the danger of certain current tendencies if they are allowed to continue.
    The article ends with an account of the facts and figures
relating to the film's production.

96   Siemsen, Hans von.  "Eine Filmkritik, Wie sie sein soll."
     (Review of Metropolis).  Die Weltbühne (Berlin), No. 24
     (14 June).
        Siemsen uses this discussion of Metropolis to berate
     German critics for falling for such a stupid film.  He cites
     H. G. Wells's negative review of the film as the type of
     criticism that Germans should aspire to, but despairs of the
     German public's ever desiring this kind of analysis.  He is
     glad to see, however, that despite the ravings of German
     critics, the people have not flocked to the film.  The pub-
     lic, he concludes, is not as hopeless as the film itself.

96a  von Harbou, Thea.  "Bis eine Szene so weit ist. . . ."  Ufa
     Magazine (Berlin), No. 3 (14-20 January) (Available in the
     Museum of Modern Art Library).
        This essay is interesting as giving a clear sense of
     Lang's way of working on the set, which established his
     pattern for the rest of his career.  Von Harbou clearly ad-
     mires Lang's perfectionism and the kind of masterly control
     that is evident.  The scene in-the-making is one from
     Metropolis.

97   W.H.  "Zwei grosse Filmpremieren: Metropolis."  Die
     Literarische Welt (Berlin), (21 January), p. 7.
        W.H. begins by noting that Metropolis surpasses even the
     high expectations that it had, leaving all American achieve-
     ments far behind, technically and artistically.  Lang is in
     perfect control of the composition of the images, creating
     fantastic effects, as in the scene where Maria is chased

through the catacombs, pursued by the light from Rotwang's
torch. W.H. also admires the amazing shots of the city,
with airplanes skimming above gliding cars.

But W.H. goes on to criticize Lang and von Harbou for
failing to provide a theme commensurate with the time, effort,
and expense the film required. Taking a tiny portion of
world history, they mix in everything--a bit of Christianity,
a bit of socialism, of Nietzsche--in an allegorical manner
so carefully arranged that no one is offended. W.H. deplores precisely this result found often in the so-called
"monumental" films, that causes them to be empty.
Metropolis, says W.H., offers a romantic view of the past
and the future that avoids real life and the actualities of
the present. None of the burning questions of people's
daily existence is to be found here.

W.H. concludes that the only deeper idea in the film is
the Doppelgänger motif--namely, the physical identity of the
delicate, virtuous virgin and of the hellish, sensual, unfaithful Maria. But this was certainly not intended by the
authors.

98    Wells, H. G. "Mr. Wells Reviews a Current Film." New York
      Times (17 April), pp. 4, 22. Reprinted in Frankfurter
      Zeitung (3 May). Commentary on the piece by Hans Siemsen
      in Die Weltbühne (Berlin) (19 June).
      Wells begins by saying that he has seen a silly film by
a big German studio. The film apparently plagiarized
Capell's Robots and lacks originality and independent
thought. The image of the city, all right for 1897, is now
out of date, let alone able to be the city of the future.
      Wells next attacks the main premise of the film regard-
ing the enslaved masses. A mechanical civilization has no
need for human drudges as shown here.
      Wells goes on to describe the film's plot in an ironic
tone so as to bring out its "silliness." He mocks the fact
that the film seems to come out against machines, which can
do much to ease the human lot. It is "all on the side of
soul and love and such like."
      He now discusses what he calls "the crowning imbecility
of the film," namely the conversion of the robot into Maria,
linking this to German romanticism, and the German love of
magic and fantasy. The ending is particularly awful, Wells
says, and the whole very dull. "It has nothing to do with
any social or moral issues before the world, or with any
that can conceivably arise."
      Wells ends by blaming the filmmakers for not getting
ideas about the future from the modern technical schools
and for giving merely Victorian notions. The issue of the
relation of industrial control to politics is important,
but Ufa was too dense to see how to make these questions
live. The waste of money is deplorable and even more so is

the way that people flock to see such films.  Lang has furthermore ruined the chance for someone else to do a similar
project.


<u>1928</u>


99    Anon.  Review of <u>Kriemhild's Revenge</u>.  <u>New York Times</u>
          (16 October), p. 7.
             The reviewer is surprised that the film was disregarded
          for three years, especially since people had already had a
          chance to see <u>Siegfried</u>.  He praises the realism of the
          whole and the comedy.  Compared to the efforts of a novice,
          the film is like a Tintoretto painting.  While there are
          some improbabilities, the film is generally impressive.


100   Anon.  "Claims <u>Metropolis</u> Play.  Plagiarism charge".  <u>New York</u>
          <u>Times</u> (23 December), Sec. 5, p. 8.
             According to <u>Acht Uhr Abendblatt</u>, Thea von Harbou and
          Fritz Lang have been accused by Frau Diebeke of plagiarism
          in the making of <u>Metropolis</u>.  She says that she sent an
          exposé that contained in condensed form the entire script
          that Harbou and Lang later made into a film.  She sent it
          to a number of directors, including Eric Pommer, who re-
          turned it saying he could not use it.
             Ufa asked Frau Diebeke what terms would satisfy her, but
          after a while she let the matter drop.


101   Arnheim, Rudolf.  "<u>Spione</u>" [Spies].  <u>Das Stachelschwein</u> (May).
          (Available in the Deutschen Film und Fernsehakademie, West
          Berlin).
             Arnheim begins by complaining about the careless way in
          which Thea von Harbou has put together the film's plot,
          apparently with no concern for logic or consistency.  He
          goes on to note that the characters in the film seem em-
          ployed less for the purpose of espionage than for serving
          the technical apparatus.  All kinds of passions are kindled
          --love, hate, ambition, betrayal--but the characters remain
          dead and unreal, as is nearly always the case in Lang's
          films.
             Arnheim concludes that while Lang filmed all this adeptly
          and neatly, one would not call <u>Spies</u> cinematic art.  It is
          rather analagous to a luxury edition of a trashy detective
          novel.


102   Balthasar [Roland Schacht].  "<u>Spione</u> und Amerikaner."  <u>Das</u>
          <u>Blaue Heft</u> (Berlin), No. 8 (15 April).
             Schacht spends some time comparing the von Harbou novel
          and the film, finding the novel more focused on the world
          of spies and the police.  We get more suggestion from the
          novel, Schacht says, and notes that the better the novel,

the worse it is for a film made from it. The film remains
on the superficial, sensational level, merely showing the
facts of the world of spies rather than the purpose and
meaning of espionage. The plot in the film is confused,
leaving spectators puzzled. The problem is the bad influence of American cinema. Americans, he says, make film
the way one cooks dinner from a cookbook. Everything is
too realistic, too true to life, and you cannot make good
films this way. If this is the only way to reach the masses,
we should at least make films out of our own cookbooks.

102a  De Beauplan, Robert. Review of Metropolis. La Petite Illustration
(Paris), No. 372 (Cinéma, No. 11) (3 March), pp. 3-12.
This entire issue is devoted to Metropolis, but it consists mainly of a plot outline. However, De Beauplan's introductory essay is interesting for its survey of German
cinema, and the excerpts from various French newspaper reviews.
De Beauplan sees Metropolis as representing something
unusual; it is in the "colossal" genre, he says, and he
goes on to list all the figures involved in the film's production. Referring to H. G. Wells's criticism of Metropolis
(see entry no. 98) for its invalid picture of the future,
De Beauplan notes that the film is important for its moral
message even if the conflict does not pertain to our times.
De Beauplan next gives brief summaries of some press reviews: the Le Temps reviewer admires the technical virtuosity, the hectic rhythm and the grandeur of the presentation. The rhythm, he notes, has little to do with real
life, being unique to Lang and attaining the status of ideology. The La Presse and L'Homme Libre reviews comment on
the halluncinatory scene of the transformation of the robot
and on the romantic spirit of the film, with its similarity
to Wagner. De Beauplan ends by praising the actors and giving Lang special praise for this and other films that have
justifiably made him famous.

103  H. P. Review of Spione. Der Bildewart, No. 5 (May).
In a rather mocking review of Spies, H. P. complains of
the childish nature of the plot, with its world made up entirely of spies and counterspies. As always, Lang's direction and technical handling are professional, but von Harbou
cannot produce material suitable to a worthy film. Gerda
Maurus and Lien Deyers, two good new actresses, should be
in better films. H. P. ends by deploring the money spent
on a film like this, although luckily Spione did not cost
what Metropolis did. Unfortunately, it is the poor American
films that are being imitated instead of the few good ones.

104  Hall, Mordaunt. "An Artistic Production" (Section of a longer
article on new films). New York Times (21 October), Sec. 10,

p. 7.
Hall thinks it a shame that <u>Kriemhild's Revenge</u> is only
now being shown, four years after it was made.  It is a
pity that commericalism means that shoddy films are shown
while the brilliant ones are not.  The film looks fresher
than von Stroheim's new feature, for despite its legendary
theme, it is finely acted.  Lang's direction shows more
imagination than did his mechanical project, <u>Metropolis</u>.
One gets the sense that a great deal of study went into
<u>Kriemhild's Revenge</u>, enabling Lang to give a sense of realism.

105   Hooper, Trask C.  "Some New German Films."  <u>New York Times</u>
        (20 May), p. 8.
        The context for the article is a new batch of German
films that Hooper says reflect the "good, honest workman-
ship in the continental manner, but are not sensational
enough to lift them over the hurdle of the European outlook."
        Discussing <u>Spione</u> [Spies], Hooper recalls <u>Dr. Mabuse</u>,
noting how breathtaking that film was.  <u>Spione</u>, however, is
merely an imitation of <u>Mabuse</u>, using the same theme of a
mystery criminal whose identity is never fully disclosed.
The plot now seems ridiculous and the direction commonplace.
There are no personal moments in the film, and Hooper thinks
that Hollywood is now putting out better films of this type.

106   Leprohon, Pierre.  "Le Cinéma allemand."  <u>Cinéma</u>:  Cahier
        Spécial de la revue <u>Le Rouge et Le Noir</u> (Paris) (July).
        (Available in BFI Library).
        Leprohon defines the unique German sensibility as arising
from the vacillation of the German soul between passion for
the divine and a terrible human pride, with the tension resulting in anguish.  One can find this psychology in Fritz
Lang's <u>Die Nibelungen</u> and in Goethe's entire work--Goethe
himself drawing on Kantian ideas--but particularly in Faust's
seeking a pact with the devil.  The German cinema has resumed the tradition, although individual films vary greatly
in style.
        Leprohon outlines the different types of German film and
then discusses the work of the two greatest artists, Wiene
and Lang, who typify the German sensibility.  They both reflect the pessimism and pride of the German tradition.  In
Lang's works there is always an impasse, with the human
spirit finding no way out.
        Leprohon goes on to differentiate this German focus,
with its emphasis on artificial sets, from the French love
of nature.  The two aesthetics are quite opposed.  <u>Metropolis</u>
represents a synthesis of German tendencies to date, linked
as it is to Schopenhauer's voluntarism.  After admiring the
opening montage sequence, Leprohon says that the narrative
is poorly conceived, the psychology false, and the film full
of stupidities.

Leprohon concludes, however, that between <u>Caligari</u> and <u>Metropolis</u> the German cinema reached new heights, discovering new forms and ideas. He praises the visual style, but says that the distortions of the external world entailed a distortion of human beings. Despite their greatness, the new techniques lead to a dead end.

107   o.V. "<u>Spione</u>. Der neue Ufa-Film von Fritz Lang." <u>Berliner Tageblatt</u> (28 March). (Available in Deutschen Film und Fernsehakademie, West Berlin).
      o.V. begins by noting that Lang has made a film having similar motifs and following the same format as <u>Dr. Mabuse, der Spieler</u>. While <u>Spione</u> shows great virtuosity and is a conscientious and careful work, o.V. finds it ultimately tedious and confused. He finally characterizes the film as a superbly thrown-together piece of detective trash.

108   Pinthus, Kurt. "Fritz Lang und Spione." <u>Das Tage-buch</u> (Berlin) (31 March).
      Pinthus uses the opportunity of this review [of <u>Spies</u>] to complain about the crisis in German film brought about by the popularity of American films. He notes that one has respect for Lang because he at least tries to do new things, even if often using false, monumental methods. Pinthus points out some good scenes in <u>Spione</u> among the empty ones and notes that we should not present our own directors as worse than they are, just because of the American golden age in film. Things are not so bad that the German film industry cannot be improved.

109   Schacht, Roland. "<u>Spione</u>." <u>B. Z. am Mittag</u> (Berlin) (23 March).
      According to Schacht, the movie's sensationalism is hampered by the fact that its underlying concept is novelistic, not cinematic. The film is confusing. Trying to include important secondary plots, the movie as a whole falls apart. The characters are denied all possibility of developing into human beings and remain chess pieces. Nevertheless, Schacht says it is a film by Fritz Lang, which means that there is always something to note in the imagery, photography, and technical finesse.

### 1929

110   Anon. "<u>Spione</u>." (Review of <u>The Spies</u>) <u>Filmkritische Rundschau</u> (October). (Available through the Deutschen Film und Fernsehakademie, West Berlin.)
      The reviewer begins by placing <u>Spione</u> in the context of Lang's recent films (<u>Die Nibelungen</u>, <u>Metropolis</u>) which dealt with past legends and future prospects. The fear was that he would rely on images in <u>Dr. Mabuse, der Spieler</u> [Dr.

Mabuse, the Gambler], made five years earlier.

According to the reviewer, Lang avoided this danger; instead of trying to make Spione fit contemporary events, he made a broader film about life, combining this with the necessary tension and suspense suitable for improbable events.

Commenting on the film's structure, the writer notes that because events are not presented in sequential order, the film relies on the audience's ability to piece things together; scenes need to be shortened and gaps filled in with explanatory subtitles if the spectator is to follow Lang's intense emotional flow.

The reviewer concludes that while any Lang film is technically amazing, in Spione he has outdone himself in certain scenes; he has in addition elicited excellent performances from the two leads, Willi Fritsch and Hertha von Walter, for whom the film starts a new era.

111 A. A. "Deutsche Spitzenproduktion. Die Frau im Mond." Film und Volk (Berlin), Nos. 9-10 (November), p. 13ff.
In this very negative review of Frau im Mond [Woman in the Moon], A. A. sees the film as pure Kitsch, useful neither from a cultural nor a technical point of view. It is yet one more example of the spiritual bankruptcy of the German film industry.

112 Arnheim, Rudolf. "Die Frau im Mond." Die Weltbühne (Berlin), (22 October).
Arnheim regrets that Ufa, producing this kind of film [Woman in the Moon], has come to represent the German film industry abroad. While praising the technical accuracy of the rocket ship, Arnheim deplores the sensational nature of the narrative.

113 Creighton, Peet. "Spies." New York Post (4 March).
In a lighthearted review, Creighton begins by noting how impossible everything is--the intrigues, fake identities, etc. But he notes that under Lang's direction things take on a pictorial quality that makes the film entertaining. After outlining the plot briefly, Creighton remarks that, after all, if we recall recent arrests in Berlin of agents who had manufactured false state documents, Spies may be closer to life than we think.

114 Ihering, Herbert. "Frau im Mond." [Review of Woman in the Moon] Berliner Börsen-Courier (16 October). Reprinted in his Von Reinhardt bis Brecht, vol. 2. East Berlin: Aufbau, 1959, pp. 577-579.
Ihering begins by bemoaning the fact that Lang, who has the authority to command huge sums of money, wastes his talents on manuscripts from Miss von Harbou. One cannot

tell, he says, where the artist in Lang ends and the businessman begins. The problem in Frau im Mond is that although Harbou's people belong to an earlier era, they are made to deal with machines we do not yet have. There is a marvellous precision about machines in the film, but a wondrous lack of human insight.

Ihering complains about the impossibility of the plot and concludes that the technical aspects of the film are worth nothing, since they are used to express false things.

115   No Entry.

116   Pinthus, Kurt. "Frau im Mond." Das Tage-Buch (Berlin) (19 October).

Pinthus suggests that Frau im Mond [Woman in the Moon] would be better if taken as a parody, for Lang has exaggerated all the elements of the adventure film. The theme--the flight of a rocket to the moon--is a magnificent one, but Gerda Maurus--a fresh new actress--is made to look like a wax figure in a hairdresser's window, ridiculous in knickerbockers. The plot is as sentimental as a middle-class sob story, resulting in emptiness behind the colossal mechanical operations.

Lang's adventure films all lack real substance. Frau im Mond is cavalier and does not represent the progress Lang has been making over the last ten years. Yet it is technically excellent, particularly the montage and trick effects. Lang could, however, use the talents of an acting director.

## 1930

117   Arroy, Jean. "La Femme sur la Lune." Cinémagazine (Paris), No. 6 (June), pp. 16-21.

Arroy surveys briefly the films preceding Frau im Mond [Woman in the Moon], regretting only the ideological confusion in Metropolis and the inept cutting of Spione [Spies] by the censors.

The most recent film exalts the liberating effect of the machine, which is capable of freeing people from all constraints of time, space, and gravity. One can now reach hitherto inaccessible parts of the universe. In fact, Arroy notes, this is not such a fantastic notion, since people soon will in reality have the scientific expertise to travel throughout the universe and will then have to deal with the serious material and spiritual consequences of such flight.

The astronaut is no figment of the imagination but rather the projection of a reality soon to come. Lang aimed at authenticity in this film, and hired H. Oberth, a well-known expert in interplanetary travel, as his technical advisor.

To prevent people from taking the film as pure fantasy, Arroy goes into some detail about the technology of interstellar aviation. He discusses the speed needed to pull people out of the earth's gravitation and the weight individual human bodies can support, as well as dealing with Oberth's modification of the combustion engine to make it capable of sending a rocket into space.

Arroy is most impressed with Lang's combination of scientific and cinematic genius. Excited by the concept of freedom from servitude to the earth, he admires Lang's moon landscapes, which no one else could have imagined without diminishing them. Lang tells it all: the construction of the rocket, the agonizing preparation, the awesome departure, the physical effects of the journey, the first sight of the moonscape, the mountains of gold, the rivalry between the lovers, with the tragic struggle ending in the destruction of the oxygen equipment, and the return to earth, leaving the delirious couple behind on the dead planet. This first interstellar epic opens up unsuspected vistas to all other artists.

118   Greenidge, Terence. "Present-day Tendencies in the Cinema." Socialist Review (London), No. 1 (March), pp. 261-267.
     Although the reference to Lang at the end of the article is rather brief, the comments are significant in giving us an idea of how Lang was received in England as early as 1930. Greenidge considers him a great filmmaker, praising him highly for the films he has made so far. He discusses Lang's forthcoming Woman in the Moon, a supposedly "shocking" film, as one might expect now that Thea von Harbou "has been let loose on the set." Greenidge notes that the blast-off is supposedly terrific and the moonscapes stunning, but word is that the film is not up to Lang's usual standard.

119   H. P. Review of Frau im Mond. Der Bildwart, No. 1 (January).
     H. P. notes that Lang has made both good and bad films with Harbou--the bad including Metropolis and, to some extent, Spione [Spies]. Frau im Mond [Woman in the Moon] is important for the photography and technical feat of the use of the rocket: the take-off section is the best edited in the whole film, which is worth seeing just for this sequence. The plot of the film, however, is poor; H. P. does not like the mixing of the theme of space exploration with the love triangle.
     H. P. points out some confusing elements in the plot and praises some of the acting. While most of the technical details are good, he or she finds some discrepancies.

120   Rotha, Paul. The Film Till Now. London: Jonathan Cape. Annotation based on New York: Funk and Wagnalls, 1949 edition, pp. 272-276. For annotation of American films, see

entry no. 177a.)

Rotha praises Destiny and Siegfried as excellent examples
of the German film, stressing their studio-made aspects,
decorative elements, and architecture. Siegfried's restrained pageantry is far from the naturalism of the Soviets
or the individualism of Pabst. Rotha admires the trick photography and illusionary setting in Destiny and singles out
Lil Dagover and Bernhard Goetzke for their acting skills.

Moving on to Lang's thrillers, Rotha notes that Mabuse
was the first to reach the United States and was acclaimed
for its technique. The action is rapid and is full of startling incidents. It is interesting in its linking of the
prewar long-shot with the tentative methods of the newer
school. Spione [Spies] is great, fast-moving entertainment,
brilliantly and efficiently produced.

Rotha discusses the adverse criticism Metropolis received,
seeing it as in part due to changes in the cut version. It
is, in fact, a remarkable work, based on a specifically cinematic concept, and it is the kind of thing the British are
very poor at.

He concludes that Lang is an intelligent director of
broad views and rare imagination. Though he lacks constructive editing of the Soviet kind, he has initiative.

121  Arnheim, Rudolf. Review of M. Die Weltbühne (Berlin), No. 20
     (19 May).
         Arnheim says that Lang and Harbou have finally made a
     better film, giving up sensational topics for politics and
     a study of society's problems. The only remnant of the old
     Fritz Lang style is a penchant for round table conferences.
     We get an excellent picture of the jovial hostility between
     police and criminals, who are homey, bourgeois types. Hav-
     ing a murderer with a boyish face is good. Arnheim praises
     the editing and subtle use of sound and finds the indirect
     treatment of the murder especially powerful.

122  Hirsch, Leo. "Fritz Lang: M." Berliner Tageblatt, (12 May).
         In this negative review, Hirsch calls M "a mixture . . .
     of grandeur and banality," which, while technically great
     and wonderfully acted, is humanly merely repugnant.

123  Ihering, Herbert. Review of M. Berliner Börsen-Courier (12 May).
     Reprinted in his Von Reinhardt bis Brecht, vol. 3. East
     Berlin: Aufbau, 1960, pp. 342-344.
         Ihering says that as long as Lang remains on the level
     of realistic analysis of the police investigation, the film
     is excellent, both cinematically and from the acting point
     of view. But when he uses literary devices, giving psycho-
     logical commentary, then things get shaky.
         Ihering praises the search for clues at the start of the
     film, but thinks that ultimately the narrative fails because

it lacks proper connection to social reality, particularly
the real issue of capital punishment. The murderer is given
a literary rather than a realistic treatment. Paradoxically,
Brecht's stage version of The Threepenny Opera conveyed more
realism about beggars and criminals than Lang, who was working in a medium where greater realism is possible.

Ihering concludes by praising the actors who do bring
the characters alive. Lorre's physiognomy is perfect.

124   L. L.   "Im Seminar von Professor D. Hinderer Sprechen berliner
      studenten mit Fritz Lang über Kulturwert und Wesen des
      Films." Film-Kurier (Berlin), No. 119 (23 May).
         Lang is invited by Professor Hinderer to talk to his stu-
      dents about his film M and other matters related to film.
         Lang notes that the special value of film lies in its
      ability to make abstract statements emerge from realistic
      situations. Hinderer notes that Lang's M is a good example
      of the presentation of an everyday problem in artistic form.
      There is a debate about why Lang did not express an opinion
      on capital punishment and about whether film, given its
      realism, can be ahead of culture. Asked about the fact
      that not enough worthwhile films are shown, Lang notes that
      the public must be roused out of its lethargy to demand bet-
      ter films.

125   St.; D.; and S., "M." Deutsche Filmzeitung (Munich), No. 33
      (14 August).
         The authors begin by noting that Lang is, technically, a
      great director; but they go on to wonder why he doesn't make
      detective and sensationalist movies that are thrilling as
      entertainment. The problematic concept of "the murderer
      among us," established in M, goes beyond Lang's ability.
         Although Thea von Harbou's script is well-constructed,
      the authors believe that the idea of the film belongs rather
      to the study of pathology and to the psychiatric hospital
      than to film. A pathological murderer simply cannot be the
      subject of a work of art. Debates over difficult cases of
      criminality and sexual pathology are for scientific discus-
      sion rather than for the general public.

126   Steinmetz, Hans. "Die Moral von der Geschichte M." Deutsche
      Filmzeitung (Munich), No. 35 (28 August).
         Steinmetz maintains that "despite all the talk of good
      moral intentions, the film panders to the sensation-
      seeking of the masses by portraying the case of a psychotic
      sex-murderer." He questions the moral necessity of depict-
      ing abnormal murder cases (which deserve only disgust and
      hate) in "crass realism" for the public, when the everyday
      person is struggling to survive and is also working on the
      development of a new state.

127  Tölle. "M: Tonfilm von Fritz Lang." Arbeiterbühne und Film,
     No. 6, (June).
         The bankruptcy of the bourgeoisie, says Tölle, is evident
     with each attempt to deal with any of the problems bringing
     about the collapse of capitalism.  One should therefore mis-
     trust the attempt to deal with child-murder and capital
     punishment; Fritz Lang was the most unsuitable person for
     such a task, given his earlier films.
         Tölle complains that Lang did not use the details of the
     Kurten case as he could have done, but chose instead to make
     a horror film, playing on people's anxieties and avoiding
     all moral and ideological analysis.  All the sympathy goes
     to the police and the criminals; it is no wonder that the
     censor passed the film, since the ending consists in a warn-
     ing to parents to take care of their children.  Yet we know
     that it is the state's responsibility to guard citizens from
     such events; the state creates the conditions for murder and
     then its censor punishes those who wish to expose this
     truthfully.


                              1932


128  Hunter, William.  "Metropolis," in his Scrutiny of Cinema.
     London:  Wishart, pp. 24-25.
         The general theme of Hunter's book is the dangerous in-
     fluence of film.  The form has a powerful effect on people's
     beliefs and behavior, although the process is a complex one,
     reflecting the level on which a culture works in any given
     period.  Hunter discusses the best film examples to date
     and finds that most are noted for technical achievement
     rather than creative power.  The discussion of Metropolis
     begins with a quotation from Paul Rotha praising the film,
     but Hunter proceeds to show that, in fact, there is no
     "great vision" here at all.  The content is banal and, in
     the end, the brilliance lies mainly in the visual style.
     He concludes that "excellence of production does not trans-
     mute a fundamentally worthless theme into a work of art,
     nor ever will."

129  Wright, Basil.  "Let's Be Perverts."  Cinema Quarterly
     (Edinburgh), 1, No. 1 (Autumn), pp. 23-25.
         Wright begins by talking generally about films with
     pathological subjects; he notes how few there are, but also
     how these tend to be both good and box office successes.
     There are few Hollywood films on the list.  Turning to M,
     Wright says that the main interest, apart from the spectacu-
     lar visuals, which are as good as usual in a Lang film, is
     the way Lang has gotten inside his hero.  According to
     Wright, "Lang has succeeded in showing us the subtle dif-
     ference between this man normal and this man homicidal."

Wright notes the effectiveness of the whistling and how Lang works with suggestion.

Wright contrasts this excellence with the rather cheap Hollywood version, Mervyn Le Roy's Two Seconds, which was ruined by "hysterical over-emphasis on the part of the director and appalling over-acting on the part of Robinson . . ." One day, he concludes, "Hollywood will acquire the great gift of reticence. Till then, it must leave pathological and other soul-searching matters to its less affluent European rivals."

### 1933

130 Anon. "Siegfrieds Tod: Wieder im UFA-Palast am Zoo." Lichtbildbühne (Berlin) (30 May).
  The author begins by noting how short a life a film has and how rarely films are revived. When this does happen, although the film is known and valued by a few film buffs, the majority consider it old-fashioned, and it is taken off.
  Siegfrieds Tod [Death of Siegfried] has been revived, however, with the addition of music and the opening words of the Nibelungen Saga, so that it stands as a sound film. Ten years after its production, the film still has a lot to tell us, although technically it is dated. A 1933 film would give a more realistic sense of the film's characters, and the change in film frame-size since 1923 means that the symmetry is lost. But the themes and images remain powerful. The film belongs with the greatest artistic and folk works that Germany has produced, and the ten years that have passed have not been able to destroy the response in the audience. Thus the film should still find sympathy throughout Germany, especially since the new Germany is willing to pay tribute to the past and traditions.

131 Rotha, Paul. Celluloid: the Film Today. London: Longman, Green, pp. 227-238.
  Rotha deals with Lang as one of the few directors who attempt to use cinema for fantastic effects. He always selected the most skilled cameramen, most creative architects, and most attractive actors, and thus enhanced the quality of his films.
  According to Rotha, Lang's work can be divided into two main types: on the one hand, there are the romantic, semi-historical and mystical films, with their slow, pageant-like processions; on the other hand, the quick-moving melodramas, thrilling in action.
  Lang always tried to convey the modern state of mind, and his work reflected modern styles in art and architecture; he was influenced by trends in modern painting like cubism, expressionism, and surrealism.

165

Rotha sees <u>Spies</u> as combining the best of Lang's two
tendencies, but he goes on to discuss <u>The Woman in the Moon</u>
as the most typical Lang film: while it is made out of excellent material, it is ultimately uncinematic. Rotha faults
Lang for the way he assembles shots on the screen.

<u>1934</u>

132   Daumal, René. "Avant la Présentation de <u>Liliom</u>." <u>Aujourd'hui</u>
      (13 March). Reprinted in René Daumal and Fritz Lang. "A
      Propos de Liliom." <u>Positif</u> (Paris), No. 188 (December
      1976), pp. 6-7.
         Daumal begins by saying that while the theme of <u>Liliom</u>
      is not new and the film develops in a familiar way, the par-
      ticular genius of the director of <u>Metropolis</u> has revitalized
      these elements. He makes use of the possibilities for ex-
      pressing himself and lifts the psychological drama into the
      metaphysical realm. The film is full of moving images and
      is touchingly humorous.
         Daumal outlines the plot briefly, showing how in the
      second part of the film Lang follows the moral dilemma of
      the hero beyond death. Usually this fails utterly, as in
      the American films showing black heavenly fantasies, but
      the stars, Madeleine Ozeray and Charles Boyer, help to make
      this a success. The film finally manages to pose the ter-
      rible question of the fatality of human actions and to il-
      lustrate the idea that among people, as in nature, the same
      causes produce the same effects. Would a criminal placed
      in the same situation again perform the same deeds? Where
      does responsibility lie? What is the nature of freedom?

133   Forrest, David. "Exiled German Here to Direct Film Marvels."
      New York <u>World Telegram</u> (14 June).
         Forrest met with Lang in New York on his arrival from
      France. Lang's first reaction is amazement at the similarity
      between New York and his futurist film, <u>Metropolis</u>. Asked
      about current films, Lang deplores the Nazi pictures and
      notes that the Russians have not fulfilled their early prom-
      ise in directors like Eisenstein.
         Forrest quotes Lang in his 1926 and 1927 interviews as
      having scorned Hollywood for debasing artists and taking
      away their creativity; left to themselves, Lang had said,
      the Americans "could kill the greatest art in the world."
      Asked about those comments now, Lang repudiates them and
      says how pleased he is to be in America. He notes that he
      particularly admires American women.

134   Rotha, Paul. "Last Will of Dr. Mabuse." <u>Cinema Quarterly</u>
      (Edinburgh), No. 3 (Autumn), pp. 49-50.
         Rotha sees this film as following the same formula as

the earlier Mabuse works, e.g., the incredible robberies,
the unseen master criminal, houses that are flooded.  The
literary use of sound helps build tension and Lang has borrowed from one or two American gangster films, but for Rotha
the story is "atrocious drivel, lacking in human psychology
and reasoning."  The film is ingenious and well staged in
the old German style.  Rotha regrets that Lang is so superficial, since his knowledge of melodrama might have been
useful in cinema.

## 1935

135   Kalbus, Oskar.  Vom Werden deutscher Filmkunst.  Part I:  Der
      Stummfilm.  Altona-Bahrenfeld:  Cigaretten-Bilderdienst,
      pp. 49, 67, 96-101.
          This first volume of Kalbus's history is interesting in
      its focus on films as presenting certain types of characters.
      Lang's Metropolis is discussed in terms of Brigitte Helm's
      representing a certain kind of vamp that was special to
      Lang, while Frau im Mond [Woman in the Moon] belongs with
      the monumental films.  Spione [Spies] is described as show-
      ing Lang's taste for nastiness.  Stills from the films and
      their production accompany discussions of how films were
      made.

## 1936

136   Anon.  "Fury is Fritz Lang's First American Film."  New York
      Post (29 May).
          Lang's genius in directing has made each of his foreign
      films a worldwide cinematic event.  People were hoping for
      another Metropolis or M with his first American film.  The
      reviewer surveys Lang's background, schooling, and entry
      into film, noting that his first hits were Metropolis and M.
      Lang travelled extensively and has a collection of primitive
      art from the South seas, China, Africa, and Japan.  He has
      a library of 5,000 volumes reflecting his interest in poli-
      tical science, modern art, religion, and politics.

137   Anon.  "New Films in London:  An Indictment of Lynching."
      [Review of Fury]  London Times (29 June), p. 126.
          The reviewer of Fury begins by noting that Hollywood is
      often at its best when exposing crime or satirizing politi-
      cal pretension.  Lynching, he notes, is a serious thing in
      America--it has taken 6,000 lives in the last fifty years
      --and Lang's honest statement may shock the public into as-
      suming responsibility for this.  Lang is known for his path-
      ological study of the Dusseldorf murderer and, after his
      long apprenticeship in the European school, was allowed by

Hollywood to make this harsh indictment of lynching.

Lang works hard to create the prelynching atmosphere; and Spencer Tracy's acting, as Joe Wilson, a man lost in a world where he cannot establish his innocence, is excellently done.

The writer admires the scenes showing that the mob must have its way, their march to the jail and their burning of it. He also praises the court scenes.

138    Cooke, Alistair. "Fritz Lang: $8,000,000: Fury." The Listener (22 July).

Cooke discusses the ambivalence over the film due to its theme of lynching. The producers thought that it would never make money, but Cooke thinks it admirable that Hollywood would make a film that, if not critical of an American institution, at least analyzes the emotion that "unites nice middle-class people in obscene hysteria." It also manages to be a film about a man "who loses his girl and who, in the end, won her back again, as Hollywood allows that he should."

139    D. W. C. "Fritz Lang Bows to Mammon." New York Times (14 June), Sec. 10, p. 2.

This article is a thoughtful discussion of the conflict Lang found himself in at Metro Goldwyn Mayer (MGM): while the producers demanded successes that brought in money, Lang wanted Fury to be a social message film. MGM saw the content of Fury as B fare, only to be used in a film that would definitely make money. D. W. C. points out however that other social message films have made money by sheer word of mouth and the support of the critics.

D. W. C. goes into Lang's background as a new director from Germany, but notes how much Lang likes America. Although Lang is viewed with suspicion because of his German accent and his monocle, he in fact has been travelling around America and talking to people. Lang does not see lynching as a peculiarly American problem, but rather as part of a worldwide tendency: people turn too easily to hate. He thinks producers can make routine films for money, but that they should also do other things.

140    Fearing, Kenneth. "Fury." The New Masses, 19 (16 June).

Fearing first links the film to I Am a Fugitive from a Chain Gang and then goes on to praise the first half for its opposition to lynching. But Fearing asserts that the second half is full of improbable surprises, revelations, and sudden reversals and that this dilutes the impact of the whole.

141    Stebbins, Robert. "Fritz Lang and Fury." New Theatre (New York) (July), pp. 11-12.

Stebbins admires <u>Fury</u> for its integrity of purpose, which, he says, must have caused difficulties for the Hollywood producers. Lang's work, Stebbins notes, continually unfolds and grows.

While Vanzetti would have approved of Lang's film because it avoids the debilitating effect of romances and false stories, he would have objected to the compromises the film makes. The guilt is transferred from the lynchers to Joe Wilson himself, and Lang neglects the economic and racist aspects of lynching as an institution.

Stebbins then discusses the film's strengths: there is a forceful indictment of lynching and a powerful evocation of Joe's sordid life before he works hard to win Katherine. Vivid visual details enforce the emotional bleakness and loneliness, and there is the marvellous device of having the film played back to the pathetic victims in the courtroom.

Stebbins praises the people who worked on the film, but says that the MGM part in the film was not noble. The company did not want to make the film and still regrets having done so.

## 1937

142    Anon. "Lang: New Dynamo of Films." New York <u>World Telegram</u> (27 January), p. 18.

The reviewer starts out discussing how fashions in directors change: a short while ago, the director was in jodhpurs behind a megaphone; now he is a mystery man, unapproachable and unpredictable. He is businesslike and follows regular hours. Lang typifies this new type and, having just finished <u>You Only Live Once</u>, is already the focus of contrasting opinions: some call him an ogre, others a genius; he is mad or colorful, didactic or ruthless. Actually, the reviewer says, Lang is mild-mannered and a very hard worker. No detail was too much for him, and it was necessary for him to keep going at a fast pace so as to be able to have breathing space as needed.

143    Barnes, Howard. "<u>You Only Live Once</u>." New York <u>Herald Tribune</u> (1 February), p. 10.

In this film, Barnes says, Lang shows his talent for achieving suspense and terror on the screen. The production is powerful and there is a strong social message; while the film shocks and moves one, it may offend in the end. Lang's handling of the camera is excellent, but the ending is sentimental. While the acting is also good, it is Lang's direction that makes the film succeed, and that puts it alongside <u>M</u> and <u>Fury</u>.

144  Creelman, Eileen. "Fritz Lang, Director of Fury, Discusses
     His Film 'You Only Live Once.'" New York <u>Sun</u> (28 January).
        Creelman begins by noting how Lang continues to fight for
     his independence in directing.  Viennese by birth, he direct-
     ed films in Germany before coming to the United States.
     Lang notes that he took out German citizenship simply be-
     cause it was fashionable at the time.  He loves America
     partly because people have room to solve their problems
     here and he has no intention of going back to Germany.  He
     explains how at first he was kept writing scripts that came
     to nothing, but finally <u>Fury</u> was approved.  However, there
     were problems over the ending, since, according to Lang,
     producers are always afraid of offending somebody.  He had
     wanted to end with a list of lynchings in America, but the
     producer demanded the happy ending and the courtroom kiss,
     which Lang felt was totally wrong.  The film was originally
     intended to be about the woman, but somehow ended up the
     man's story.  He is glad to be directing Sylvia Sydney again.
     After discussing briefly how he got into film, Lang says he
     regrets that Hollywood makes it so hard for a director to
     put an unknown person into an important role as he had been
     able to do in Germany, discovering Peter Lorre and Brigitte
     Helm in this way.

145  Tazelaar, Marguerite.  "Fritz Lang Likes Hollywood, America,
     and Social Themes."  New York <u>Herald Tribune</u> (7 February),
     Sec. 7, p. 3.
        This article is based on a discussion Tazelaar had with
     Lang.  She notes that Lang believes the screen is an impor-
     tant means of conveying social messages and then refers to
     his impressive background as a German expatriate director.
     He made <u>M</u>, <u>Metropolis</u>, and <u>Dr. Mabuse</u> before he left Germany,
     and his films are now banned there.  After a brief descrip-
     tion of Lang, Tazelaar gives a history of his career, of
     how he got into films through writing scripts, and of his
     meeting with Erich Pommer.  She notes that Lang likes both
     to write scripts and to direct and thus making a film takes
     a long time.  He likes doing films with social themes, and
     has always been interested in contemporary affairs.  He
     wants to show people both what interests them and what im-
     prisons them.
        There are many themes he would like to make films about,
     such as kidnapping, dictators, and people who live in
     trailers, but the censors will not allow it.  Emigration
     also fascinates him--the effect on Europe of so many people
     leaving--and he prefers his films to be controversial rather
     than forgotten.  He sees no connection between the stage
     and the film--the stage can deal more with ideas, but the
     screen far outdistances theater when the ideas can be visu-
     ally treated.

146   Thirer, Irene. "Director Fritz Lang No Propagandist, He Says"
      [on the opening in New York of You Only Live Once]. Screen
      Views and News (28 January).
          Lang denies that he is committed only to making films
      with a social message, but says that it is possible to get
      a point of view across with the camera. "He believes,"
      Thirer says, "that the real dramatic impact on the screen
      is achieved by what he calls 'camera mobility' and 'judici-
      ous cutting.'"


                              1938


147   Bagai, Ram. "Fritz Lang, Master of Mood." Cinema Progress
      (Los Angeles) (May-June), pp. 10-11.
          This is an interesting short piece about Lang's forth-
      coming You and Me, showing how he builds tension and sus-
      pense through his use of lighting, music, and the linking
      of sound-rhythms with the visuals. Bagai gives examples of
      Lang's control of rhythm and tempo from You Only Live Once,
      his latest picture, and of "indirect suggestion" from M.
      He concludes that "every Lang picture brings with it some
      new departure in the subtle use of light and shadow, in
      sound and angle shots, in human touches. Some may call
      Lang's distinctive style 'arty,' but most find it interest-
      ing and gripping. Certainly, it has contributed to the en-
      richment of cinematic expression."


                              1939


148   Jacobs, Lewis. "Contemporary Directors" in his Rise of the
      American Film. New York: Harcourt and Brace, pp. 462-463.
          Jacobs writes about Lang shortly after Lang's arrival in
      America. He talks of Lang's awareness of society and of
      his genius for original film expression. With only three
      American films behind him, he has become one of our most
      significant filmmakers. Perhaps because he is an immigrant,
      he is able to deal with American national characteristics
      better than a native-born American could. Jacobs sees a
      virtue in Lang's being an "older craftsman," steeped in the
      traditions of the medium, and one who had already contributed
      to these traditions before coming to the United States. He
      compares Lang to Hitchcock in intensity. It is easy, Jacobs
      says, to miss Lang's brilliant imagery and cutting on a
      first viewing.
          Jacobs goes briefly into the first three American films,
      giving plot summaries. He praises the frightening tension
      in Fury and its inspired commentary on bigotry; You Only
      Live Once could have been melodramatic, but in Lang's hands
      is a tense tragic social document; You and Me, Lang's least

important film, has an unconvincing story but a few good moments. Jacobs concludes that Lang combines visual skills with a deep understanding of character and society. All his material is from daily life.

149    Snyder, W. L. "Cinema and Stage." Cinema Progress (Los Angeles) (June–July), pp. 11–29.
        Apparently based on an interview with Lang, this article consists in Snyder's paraphrases of Lang's thoughts about various topics. He or she begins by quoting Lang as saying that film is the art form of the century, since it is made for the masses. Going on to contrast the stage and film, Snyder shows how film can present many different moods. While viewing the stage, the audience must create situations with their imagination; the camera puts the spectator in the place of the character. The use of close-ups and the subjective camera, as in Murnau's The Last Laugh, enable this to happen.
        Lang advocates the use of symbolism as a means of cinematic expression, giving Destiny as an example. He notes how important rhythm is, especially that obtained by effective cutting and intelligent planning at the time of the film's making. Cutting should be pleasing and logical and should help express a strong narrative, without which visual effects will dominate.
        Complaining that American audiences do not like symbolism, Lang goes on to emphasize that people have real problems and he would like to make films about them. But censorship in the film industry prevents this (in the theater more is permitted). One cannot make films about war, marital problems, kidnapping, politics, etc.
        The main problem facing directors, according to Lang, is whether to give people a pipe dream or something real to think about. Films have, to date, been mainly escapist, but Lang is hopeful of change. Producers would dare to take the risk if only audiences would demand realism.

### 1940

150    Dana, Robert W. "The Return of Frank James." New York Herald Tribune (10 August), p. 6.
        In a very favorable review, Dana notes the excellence of Lang's methodical direction. While the film moves a bit slowly, it is because Lang is giving attention to detail. The color is superb, as is the action, and there is an attention to character unusual in a Western. "We can recall no previous Western," Dana concludes, "that has combined so expertly the beauty of nature with the actions and laughter of men."

151  Dana, Robert W. "Fritz Lang Changes His Mind: Concedes Color
       Films May Do." New York Herald Tribune (11 August), p. 3.
          In 1937 Lang had said that color in cinema was nothing
       but decoration, but he now agrees that color can add a lot,
       although the use of color is expensive and still at an ex-
       perimental stage. In the Return of Frank James, one scene
       was hard to do because it had to be dark enough for the
       train's headlight to be visible, but light enough for the
       crew to film. They ended up with five minutes to do it.
       Lang recalls that he had made a Western before in Germany,
       The Golden Sea [part one of The Spiders], and that there he
       had used 200 gypsies for Indians.

152  Strauss, Theodore. "Footnote on a Patriotic Occasion." New
       York Times, (11 August).
          The article was written on the occasion of Lang's becom-
       ing an American citizen. Although now an assimilated
       American, Lang has an accent, and is making a Western (The
       Return of Frank James) to prove how much of an American he
       has become. Strauss mentions some of the difficulties Lang
       had with the film--the heavy equipment for the on-location
       scenes, the problem of having to shoot so much at night, of
       actor John Carradine's starring in another film at the same
       time, etc. This is not filming as it was for Die Nibelungen,
       Strauss notes, and is an unorthodox assignment for a man who
       was one of the giants of the golden age of German cinema.
       But Strauss concludes that there may be some thread linking
       his new film with the earlier works, for it is about one of
       the west's desperadoes. Zanuck thought that a European di-
       rector might have fresh insights into American history.

153  T. S. [Theodore Strauss]. Review of The Return of Frank James.
       New York Times (10 August), p. 16.
          Strauss blames the Hayes Code for not allowing Frank, as
       hero, to kill any of the people who ought to die, a fact
       that makes things very improbable. But Strauss praises the
       gorgeous technicolor shots and the flavor of the small town
       that Lang creates.

## 1941

154  Anon. "Fritz Lang Puts on Film the Nazi Mind He Fled From."
       New York World Telegram (11 June).
          Fritz Lang talks of how Germany has changed since the
       Nazis came to power; even the language has broken down, as
       a friend who translated a Nazi diary emphasized. The diary
       wavered between a soft, sugary sweetness and a bark. While
       reading German newspapers in preparation for Manhunt Lang
       also found the language sentimental and unrealistic--"noth-
       ing normal, nothing human." Having just finished Manhunt,

Lang claims that the film is not propaganda, but adventure
with a Nazi background, where the Gestapo plays the hunters.
Lang repeats the history of his German film, M, and the
story of Goebbels's asking him to head the Nazi film industry. Lang concludes by saying how much he likes Manhunt,
feeling that it is one of the best things he has done. It
is an honest film, showing the Nazis as humans but with
warped minds. Lang does not like pure propaganda--the public has the right to see something intelligent.

155    Barnes, Howard. Review of Manhunt. New York Herald Tribune
       (14 and 15 June).
           Barnes takes a very positive stance toward Manhunt, prais-
       ing the way it combines melodrama with social and political
       content. The film is a defense of the democratic way of
       life, with excellent script, acting, and directing.
           In the second review, Barnes calls Manhunt "the most wel-
       come offering since Citizen Kane." Nichols and Lang, he
       says, "have missed no inflection of this terrible chase--
       they have created passages of magnificent pictorial imagery."
       He praises Twentieth-Century Fox not only for producing an
       excellent melodrama, but in addition for keying the film to
       present day events, giving it "enormous emotional and ideo-
       logical compulsion."

155a   Ferguson, Otis. "Behind the Camera." New Republic, No. 103
       (June 23), No. 104 (June 30), p. 887, and No. 105 (July 7),
       p. 21. Reprinted in Robert Wilson, ed. The Film Criticism
       of Otis Ferguson. Philadelphia: Temple University, 1971,
       pp. 374-378.
       1.  "Fritz Lang and Company"
           This review of Manhunt starts with Ferguson's contrast-
       ing the novel on which it was based (Rogue Mâle by Geoffrey
       Household) and the film and noting that Lang and (script-
       writer Dudley) Nichols had to rework, in terms of action,
       material having originally to do with mental states. After
       outlining the plot of the film, Ferguson notes that, as in
       the book, the hero gradually understands that what he is
       doing represents his disgust for the Nazis. Ferguson re-
       grets that the film contains too much dialogue and that the
       climax is insufficiently prepared for and over too quickly.
       But he praises Lang's direction for its depth, careful de-
       tail, and concern for the correctness of each fragment.
       That Lang is an artist is evident in the way that "camera,
       lighting and background give shape to action and meaning to
       a situation." The film is limited in that it is uneven and
       lacking in balance, but its strength lies in the care with
       which it is made.
       2.  "Behind the Camera: Lang" (In two parts)
           Noting that Hollywood directors need to be smart about
       the image they create, Ferguson shows that Lang has failed

in this:  instead of maintaining a certain prestige, he
allowed an image of himself as irascible and difficult.
According to Ferguson, he was not justified in such arrogant
behavior, since he could not rest on M forever and, while
Fury was good, it was followed by two weak films.

156  Mishkin, Leo.  "What's Wrong with Films?  Here's Fritz Lang's
     Version."  New York Morning Telegraph (8 June), pp. 1-2.
        What is wrong today, Lang says, is that it is no longer
     possible to experiment as one could in the old days when
     Lang had his own company and was using his own money.  If
     he had an idea, he simply tried it.  The one concern of pro-
     ducers now is getting people into the cinema.  One is not
     allowed to do things purely for aesthetic reasons, unless
     the innovations would bring people in.  Today people have
     their minds elsewhere--on the war, the radio, the state of
     the nation.
        Lang does not think that we have exhausted experiments
     --for instance, sound has not been fully explored, but there
     is little interest in experimentation.  He is awaiting the
     response to his new film, Manhunt, where he was trying to
     do something like M or Fury--something that has a message
     but is also a thrilling experience and a romance all in one.

157  Skolsky, Sidney.  "Watching Them Make Movies."  New York Post
     (19 April), p. 16.
        This article is interesting in that it deals with Lang's
     filmmaking process.  Watching Lang directing Manhunt,
     Skolsky notes how seriously he takes his work, functioning
     like a general in command, while the performers try to in-
     ject some humor.  He gives a few anecdotes, including one
     about Lang's wading in mud, and another, where, complimented
     by Zanuck on the excellent noises in the rushes, Lang admits
     that he did the barking himself.


                              1942


158  Anon.  "Fritz Lang Creates a Mood Movie Audiences Applaud."
     Eagle (20 December).
        The article is a semicomic description of Lang's filming
     Hangmen Also Die, then still under the title Unconquered.


                              1943


159  Cameron, Kate.  Review of Hangmen Also Die.  New York Daily
     News (16 April).
        Cameron argues that Hangmen Also Die deals truthfully
     with the war, despite the fact that it was made during its
     course.  It was based on an actual occurrence in


                               175

Czechoslovakia--the killing of a hated Gestapo chief, Heydrich. Cameron says that "Lang gives a good look into the workings of the Czech underground army . . . The film is an important part of the record that is piling up against the Nazis and so should be seen by everyone with a stake in the war."

## Circa 1944

160    Anon. "German Films." Clipping from an unnamed Hollywood newspaper at the Museum for Modern Art.
       This article is worth annotating, despite the lack of precise information, because the author reprints Lang's comments about the German film industry after the war. Lang suggests that it would be best for the Allied cause if the Russians were to dominate the Film Industry in Germany after the war. The Russians, Lang says, are realists and will understand how to deal with the Germans and how to handle any attempt at subtle propaganda that a German audience would grasp, while it may pass by Americans. Lang comments on how seriously films deteriorated after Hitler took over.

## 1946

161    Anon. "Film Censors Ban Scarlet Street." New York Times (5 January), p. 16.
       The reviewer simply notes what a dramatic action the banning of Scarlet Street was. The film had been passed by Maryland, Ohio, and Pennsylvania, and had been approved by the Industry's Production Code, and yet was still being censored in New York State.

162    Borel, Jacques. "Lettre de Londres: Hollywood n'a pas standardisé Fritz Lang." L'Écran Française, No. 49, (5 June), pp. 12-13.
       Borel comments first on the sombre films, basically films noir, showing in London at the time, which are in marked contrast to the musicals and patriotic films that prevailed after Pearl Harbor. The latest Fritz Lang and Renoir films (Scarlet Street and Diary of a Chambermaid, respectively) fit in with the film noir mood. Each had trouble with local censors, showing the dangers in departing from conventional morality.
       Since his arrival in America, Lang has taken serious themes. Working now without Thea von Harbou, Lang came into his own, giving us Fury, in which he combined the Anglo-Saxon taste for realism with his romantic vision and understanding of irrationality. Lang gained most from Hollywood

because he did not lose his old qualities and remained
fundamentally German. Despite the large number of people
working for him, Lang managed to make each film his own and
to retain what was best in the German cinema.

Borel next turns to Lang's most recent films, Woman in
the Window and Scarlet Street. He finds the dream device
in Woman in the Window unsatisfactory and suggests that Lang
chose to make Scarlet Street because he had a chance to deal
with the same themes again without making the same mistakes.
This time, however, Edward G. Robinson (who played the lead
in both films) is not trapped in a police labyrinth; his
fall is purely sentimental and sensual. Comparing the film
briefly to Renoir's La Chienne, Borel finds Lang's images
much less enduring. The actors overdo their parts, whereas
in the Renoir film everything is fitting. Lang's film is
less convincing and powerful.

Borel concludes by commenting on the perfect technical
and material surface of Lang's films. If the whole is
schematic and unconvincing, it has to do with the actors
not filling their parts adequately. Borel also agrees that
his position on Lang's Scarlet Street may have been biased
by his memories of the original (novel and play by La
Foucharchière), and he looks forward to Lang's next film.

163    Bourgeois, Jacques. "La Tragédie Policière: La Femme au
       Portrait." La Revue du Cinéma, No. 2 (November), pp. 70-72.
         Bourgeois begins by noting the common theme that runs
through all of Lang's works--that of people overcome by
their destiny after a struggle that forms the climax of the
work.

He then compares the form of Lang's tragedy to that of
ancient Greece before Sophocles, where the hero is neither
good nor evil but victim of a particular destiny: the punishment has no moral dimension. This kind of tragedy may
be seen in modern French authors like Giroudoux, Anouilh,
and Cocteau, who take ancient themes, but destroy the tragic
essence. Bourgeois blames this on modern rationalism, showing the human fear of the inexplicable despite scientific
developments.

Lang shows us what fate is in his Woman in the Window.
As powerfully as in M, Lang makes the tragic emerge from
elements of daily life, all of which suddenly become a trap,
proof of guilt, and the arm of a pitiless destiny.

Discounting the ending of the film, which shows that
everything had been a dream, he notes what a terrifying experience the film is. The horror is linked to Lang's formation in preNazi Germany, where artists thought that brutal-
izing viewers was a way of touching them more deeply.

164    Hirsch, Helen. "Political Censorship: A Mental Atomic Bomb."
       The Jewish Forum (March). (Available in MMA.)

As a former concentration camp internee, Hirsch deplores any attempts to limit freedom of speech or thought. She argues that Scarlet Street does not, even ultimately, violate the Hays Code. In fact, it teaches a great moral lesson, although in a rather unusual way. But even the Cain and Abel story, taken from the very Bible the code makers relied on, shows a murderer free to live, but tormented inwardly with guilt.

Hirsch ends by noting that we fought the war to eliminate restrictive legislation used by the Nazis and fascists.

165   McManus, John T. "Scarlet Street and Censorship." PM (January 7).

McManus is concerned here with the banning of Scarlet Street by the Motion Picture Division of the State Board of Education. He deplores the power of the Educational Department "to rule on mass entertainment in the State in the guise of protecting school children."

166   Weinberg, Herman G. An Index to the Creative Work of Fritz Lang. Index Series, No. 5 (February). Special Supplement to Sight and Sound.

This is a reliable bibliography of Lang's films to date.


### 1947

167   Anon. "Beyond the Door: Gripping and Suspenseful Drama." Hollywood Reporter (December 31), p. 3.

The reviewer begins by noting the high professional quality of Joan Bennett's and Michael Redgrave's acting and also the successful collaboration again of (coproducer) W. Wanger and Fritz Lang. "Their production," he says, "is an artful blend of several patterns which derives dramatic impact from such elements as the flashback technique and a dream sequence . . . " Lang's direction is praised for enabling the "expressive exposition of the jumbled plot threads." Cortez is commended for his photography, Hilton for his editing, Parker for his designs, and Rozsa for the excellent musical score.

168   Eisner, Lotte H. "Notes sur le Style de Fritz Lang." Le Revue du Cinéma, No. 5 (1 February), pp. 22-24.

Eisner places Lang's German films in the context of post-World War I Germany and the expressionist movement. She argues that Lang never totally succumbed to expressionism, but always used elements of the style as they suited his individual purposes. She contrasts Lang's use of light to reveal the contours of the set with the expressionist method of working with light and shadow. Eisner goes on to discuss Lang's use of architectural form; his classic designs and

solid planes reflect the influence of Max Reinhardt's
theater and the Russian experiments with form.  Finally,
Eisner shows how in the American films to date Lang has relaxed his earlier, more rigid visual style, replacing it
with emphasis on psychological relationships.  Elements of
his earlier German style nevertheless remain in the use of
light and in his visual design.

169   Kracauer, Siegfried.  From Caligari to Hitler:  A Psychological
      History of the German Film.  Princeton:  Princeton University
      Press, 1947.  (Page numbers from the fifth Princeton Paper-
      back printing, 1974.)
      (1)   Chapter 6:  "Procession of Tyrants," pp. 81-84 (On Dr.
            Mabuse, der Spieler [Dr. Mabuse, the Gambler])
      Kracauer notes that Lang and Thea von Harbou intended
Mabuse as a document of contemporary life.  Its hero was a
contemporary tyrant, who, like Caligari, was unscrupulous
and wanted unlimited power.  Like Caligari, Mabuse hypnotizes his victims and impersonates different people.
      Kracauer asserts that the film is far from the documen-
tary Lang claimed it to be.  He objects to its length, the
artificiality of the settings, and its expressionist elements.  Using strongly perjorative language, Kracauer calls
the film "trash" and scorns its depiction of a depraved
world, subject to anarchy.  The attack on Mabuse's house
recalls the street fights between the Spartacus and Noske
troops.
      (2)   Chapter 7:  "Destiny," pp. 88-95 (On Der müde Tod
            [Destiny] and Die Nibelungen)
      (a)   Kracauer discusses Der müde Tod in relation to the no-
tion that to the Germans of this period there seemed no alternatives to tyranny and chaos, both of which spelled doom.
Spengler's Decline of the West was partly responsible for
the preoccupation with doom.  Lang's two films discussed
here emphasize the role of fate, which Kracauer links to
Spengler's idea that the laws of history make decline
inevitable.
      After a detailed outline of the plot of Der müde Tod,
Kracauer shows that the main point of the film is to demonstrate that "the actions of tyrants are realizations of
fate."  The agent of fate supports tyranny both in the individual stories and in the framing story; subject to fate
himself, Death cannot help the girl.
      (b)   Kracauer interprets Lang's statement that he wanted
not merely to make a costume film but a film about "the
German mind" as anticipating Goebbels's propaganda.  Fate
manifests itself here not, as in Destiny, "through the actions of tyrants," but "through the anarchical outbursts of
ungovernable instincts and passions."  Hagan, according to
Kracauer, foreshadows a well-known type of Nazi leader, and
Lang's use of architectural sets and rigid compositions

gives the sense of Fate's irresistible power. Kracauer
discusses the use of people for ornamental designs and links
this to the way that Hitler's regime "manifested strong
ornamental inclination in organizing masses." Leni
Riefenstahl's Triumph of the Will proves, says Kracauer,
that the Nazis drew their inspiration from Die Nibelungen
in shaping their mass ornaments.

(3)    Chapter 12:  "Frozen Ground," pp. 149-151 (On
       Metropolis, Spione [Spies], Die Frau im Mond [Woman in
       the Moon])

(a) While admitting that Metropolis is a cinematic achievement, Kracauer again objects to the film on the grounds of
formalism; he takes exception to Lang's placing of the masses in aesthetically pleasing arrangements.

(b) Kracauer links Spione to the Mabuse films, only now,
he says, the master spy is engaged in meaningless activities.
There is again no distinction between criminals and the
representatives of law, and the situation is one of constantly changing identities.  The film suffers from the same
pompousness as Metropolis: "Virtuosity alienated from content posed as art."

(c) Frau im Mond is condemned also for "showy virtuosity"
and its pathetic plot.

(4)    Chapter 13:  "The Prostitute and the Adolescent,"
       pp. 162-164 (On Metropolis)

Returning briefly to Metropolis, Kracauer now points
out the dangers in positing the heart as mediator between
head and hands.  This proposition could have been formulated
by Goebbels, since Fredersen acknowledged the heart only for
the purpose of manipulating it.  Freder's rebellion has
ironically resulted "in the establishment of totalitarian
authority."

(5)    Chapter 18:  "Murderer among Us," pp. 218-222 (On M,
       Mörder unter uns)

M (1931) looks back to the achievements of Lang's
earlier films after the "pretentious duds" of the intervening period.  The murderer is seen as the victim of uncontrollable impulses, which are now within himself, and he
sums up the main tendencies in German cinema from The
Student of Prague (1913) and Caligari (1920) to the phil-
istine in The Street (1923).  Kracauer praises the use of
sound in the film, the visual images that express the murderer's dilemma, and the documentary portrayal of police
activities.

(6)    Chapter 20:  "For a Better World," pp. 248-250 (On
       Das Testament des Dr. Mabuse [The Crimes of Dr.
       Mabuse])

Made as a last stand against nazism, this film was
banned by Goebbels, who came into power before it was released.  Lang later said that the film was made as an
"allegory to show Hitler's processes of terrorism."  As a

sequel to the earlier Mabuse film, Das Testament shows
Mabuse first as living in an insane asylum and second as
controlling a noted psychiatrist from the grave.  Not as
good as M, the film merely accumulates sensations; Kracauer
further believes that even if Goebbels had not banned the
film, audiences would hardly have seen the likeness between Hitler and Mabuse-Baum or been encouraged to stand
up against the Nazis.  Lang's antagonist to Mabuse is the
unattractive Lohmann, no match for the fascination of the
criminals.

170    Wilson, Harry.  "The Genius of Fritz Lang."  Film Quarterly
       (London), No. 5 (Summer), pp. 11-20.
            Wilson surveys Lang's career up to the date of writing
       [the last film was Cloak and Dagger, ed.], noting that
       Hollywood has not destroyed Lang as it did other German ex-
       partriate directors.  After a brief biographical account,
       Wilson proceeds to comment on the works.  He notes the bril-
       liance of Destiny and its historical importance in initiat-
       ing the German school of mysticism and death.  Douglas
       Fairbanks copied elements in the film for his Thief of
       Bagdad, which appeared before Destiny was released in
       America.
            The Dr. Mabuse films, made in collaboration with Thea
       von Harbou, continue the master-criminal motif used earlier
       in Spiders, but it was Die Nibelungen that made Lang's repu-
       tation.  Woman in the Moon was technically ambitious, and
       his German career culminated in M.  After that, Lang made
       one more anti-Nazi film, The Crimes of Dr. Mabuse before
       leaving Germany.
            Wilson continues with a survey of Lang's career in
       America, noting the success of Fury and the next two films
       with their sociological content, commenting on the Westerns
       and Lang's anti-Nazi trilogy.  Wilson likes the anti-Nazi
       films, while taking exception to the falseness of the English
       scenes.  So far, Lang has been a social commentator, contin-
       uing the stance he took in Germany.
            Scarlet Street and Cloak and Dagger seem a departure from
       this, Wilson says.  In Cloak and Dagger, Lang is no longer
       interested in the details of the atom bomb but rather in
       the adventure aspects of the script, which does not measure
       up to 13 Rue Madeleine or other more documentary spy films
       of the period.


## 1948


171    Gesek, Ludwig.  "Fritz Lang: Suggestion und Stimmung."  In
       his Gestalter der Filmkunst, von Asta Nielsen bis Walt
       Disney.  Vienna: Amandus.  Pp. 79-94.
            Gesek begins by outlining Lang's life and then focuses

on his first major films.  According to Gesek, Lang was
never a realist in Eisenstein's sense, but worked with
ideas, space, atmosphere, and suggestion.

The early films reveal the elements basic to Lang's
style:  Der müde Tod [Destiny] reflects Lang's links with
expressionism and romanticism, Dr. Mabuse his enduring interest in the gangster genre, Die Nibelungen his feeling
for architecture and form, Frau Im Mond [Woman in the Moon]
his fascination with technology, while Metropolis combines
all these elements.

Gesek tries to show how these early films foreshadow
Lang's mature style, laying the ground for all his later
themes and preoccupations.  M is Lang's first mature work,
the culmination of all the previous films.  One finds here
a perfect balancing of concepts of space and character, the
building of a complete atmosphere, and Lang's characteristic
tone.  Each shot is carefully composed and full of precise
visual details.  Lang is above all the master of atmosphere,
and locale, conveying the feeling of a place rather than being interested in its precise photographic "reality."

M prepares for the early American films, which continue
the same style.  Fury (1936) is a brilliant handling of the
theme of lynching, while You Only Live Once (1937) is fast-
paced and laden with fatality.  The two Westerns in 1940
and 1942 (The Return of Frank James and Western Union) belong to a different world, but Lang returns to familiar
ground with Manhunt (1941) and Hangmen Also Die (1942).
Gesek basically believes that the American works show a
deepening of themes present in the early films.  Lang was
always individualistic and did not start any particular
school of filmmaking.

172   Jaeger, Ernst.  "Ich spreche mit Fritz Lang (in Hollywood)."
      Film Review (Baden-Baden), Nos. 5-6, p. 133.
      Jaeger interviews Lang at the time he had his own film
company (Diana Productions) and had just completed Secret
Beyond the Door.  Noting how hard he has had to work since
becoming independent, Lang nevertheless plans to make what
he wants in the two years that he thinks he yet has to make
films.

While somewhat skeptical about Lang's decision to remain
in Hollywood, Jaeger says that Lang has solved his dilemma
in his own way, namely, by working within Hollywood conventions, knowing their limitations, but producing quality
work from an ironic distance.

Lang wants to have it as good as any Hollywood manager,
but Jaeger cannot understand why he has allowed Hollywood
to beat him--successful, renowned European director that he
was before he came.  It is possible, Jaeger says, that this
very success made it hard for Hollywood to accept him.

173    Robillot, Henri. "De la Réalité à la Légende." In L'Écran
       Français, No. 143 (23 March).
           The article was prompted by a showing of Lang's The
       Return of Frank James, but Robillot talks mainly about the
       differences between historical legends and their screen
       treatment. Lang's film, in particular, departs from true
       accounts, since Frank James did not in reality attempt to
       avenge his brother. He gave himself up twice, was acquitted
       twice, and lived out his life peacefully. Robillot is in-
       terested in the mythic dimensions Westerns have for American
       audiences.

174    Romano, Sergio. The Testament of Doctor Mabuse. Cinema (Rome),
       n.s., No. 2 (10 November). [In Italian]
           Testament [The Last Will] is a key to Lang's work because
       it marks the transition from one style to another. It con-
       tains elements of the old period--the sense of horror en-
       veloping the characters--and of the period to come, with the
       characters reduced to more human proportions. In this film,
       the early Lang manifests itself in certain romantic and hal-
       lucinatory images, the more modern Lang in the tighter images
       of a middle-class suspense film. Testament is Lang's last
       German film. The author notes that one scene is picked up
       years later by Billy Wilder in La fiamma del peccato [Double
       Indemnity], a film with Fred MacMurray.

175    Wollenberg, H. H. Fifty Years of German Film. London:  Falcon
       Press.
           This short book is useful as background to Lang's work,
       since Wollenberg places the films in their larger context.
       An early survey of the history of German film from the 1890s
       to 1948, the book studies commercial and industrial tenden-
       cies, artistic and spiritual trends, and the political in-
       fluences of the period. Lang's works are given their due
       place as having started new developments.


                              1949


176    Anon. "One Facet of Lang's Art Prophetic of Hitlerism." New
       York Herald Tribune (21 March).
           The article notes that there are three Fritz Langs:
       first, the "ingenious creator of cinema miracles," as rep-
       resented by Siegfried, Metropolis, Spies, and Woman in the
       Moon; second, the Lang "who made excursions into the macabre,
       ferreting out aberrations of the mind," as represented by M
       and The Last Will of Dr. Mabuse; finally, there is the
       American Lang, director of Fury, You Only Live Once, Manhunt,
       and the recently finished Hangmen Also Die.
           The reviewer notes that a fourth Lang may yet emerge--the
       poet and dreamer who made Destiny and Liliom, and who would

like to make a film about Villon or the legend of the Golem.
The lawless in Lang's films are psychopaths and his most
recent film, Hangmen, again deals with this type.  Goebbels
banned The Last Will of Dr. Mabuse because it prophesied
Hitler as the type that emerged from the Mabuses of this
world.

177    F. [Walter Feigl].  "Überfall der Ogalalla."  [Review of
       Western Union] Film-Dienst (Düsseldorf; later Cologne),
       27 December.
          Recalling Lang's fame as an early German filmmaker, Feigl
       notes how disappointing this Western is.  He wonders why
       Lang's Hollywood films lack the quality that made his German
       films famous.  Lang is unable to convey the endlessness of
       the American continent, the political and financial power
       struggles, or the intrigue behind the scenes.
          Furthermore, Feigl says, Lang mishandles the dramatic
       conflict between the hero and his brother, who is evil.  The
       hero's death seems his own fault rather than the result of
       some higher power.

177a   Rotha, Paul.  The Film Till Now.  New York:  Funk and Wagnalls.
       Revised and enlarged edition, pp. 480–482.  (For annotation
       of German films, see Rotha, entry no. 120.)
          In this 1949 edition, Rotha adds a section on Lang's
       American films, praising Fury as a social document.  Lang
       is not so much interested in the incident that provoked the
       lynching as in the small-town prejudices that led to it.
       The ending spoils the film, but otherwise it almost equals
       M.  It did not, unfortunately, influence other social mes-
       sage films of the period.
          Rotha likes Lang's next American films less, finding
       them melodramatic.  You Only Live Once, however, was effec-
       tive as entertainment, but You and Me was disjointed and
       wandering.
          Rotha surveys briefly the films made in the 1940s,
       praising Manhunt (which restored Lang's prestige), but find-
       ing Hangmen Also Die stagey and false.  Woman in the Window
       and Scarlet Street showed only occasional signs of Lang's
       inventiveness.  Lang failed to find interesting stories,
       and while his "attempt to express the dislocation of this
       age of anxiety in terms of melodrama is an interesting and
       thoughtful idea," it needs a deeper approach than Lang has
       given.  Rotha concludes that Lang has a "commercial rather
       than a philosophic" interest in topicality.

## 1950

178    Crowther, Bosley.  "American Guerilla in the Philippines:  A
       Review."  New York Times (8 November).

This review is worth annotating partly because so little has been written about American Guerilla and partly because the position Crowther takes evidently set a trend that has yet to be reversed. Most critics disregard the film as showing no marks of Lang's preoccupations and style and therefore as worth very little. While this attitude was often corrected in the case of other films Lang made in Hollywood, this has not yet happened with American Guerilla.

Crowther does respond to the war scenes, which he finds timely, given America's involvement in a war in the Far East. But he goes on to object to the stiffness of the script and the artificiality of the acting.

179 Granich, Tom. "Fritz Lang." Ferrania (Milan) (August), pp. 27-28 [In Italian] [This review typifies the accepted critical stance on Lang throughout the 1950s--a stance only reversed in the late 1950s by the French Cahiers du Cinéma critics.]

Granich begins by noting that Lang is essentially a European director, with links to René Clair and Pabst. Lang made interesting films in the silent era, creating his greatest work at the very start of the sound period, but then, instead of deepening the aesthetic, formalist, and intellectual tendencies that had emerged in working with Thea von Harbou, he directed films in America according to formulas, compromising his talent. The result was that his career went into a decline.

Granich proceeds to analyze the development of Lang's film art from Destiny onwards. Destiny first showed the benefit of collaboration with Thea von Harbou, but Lang's social and moral concerns also emerged in embryo here as in the Mabuse films.

Die Nibelungen and Metropolis, the next two films, are usually seen as rich examples of art films and are often placed within expressionism. Granich argues that there is ultimately little evidence for this, the films instead anticipating cubist and modern mise-en-scène. The expressionism is certainly contaminated by constructivism and realism. After two interesting but mediocre films, Spione [Spies] and Woman in the Moon, Lang went on to make his first sound film, M, which represents the height of his career. Here expressionism cedes to a sociological and psychological realism shot through with poetic lyricism, especially in terms of the film's rhythm.

M introduces a new turning toward realism and care for the concrete detail of everyday life, which Lang continued in his first three American films. The films confront a major modern social problem--that of the criminal and the judicial system--in a progressive way. Granich warns, however, that the America of these films is not the authentic one, but an America seen through a consciousness formed in

185

Europe and pervaded with a philosphical point of view that
diminishes the force of the social criticism.

With 1940 and The Return of Frank James, Lang's first
Western and first color film, the director finds himself
using a genre that will not admit of his social and psychological interests. The film thereby initiates the decline
of this Austrian filmmaker, there being only two exceptions
to the lesser quality of the rest of his films--Hangmen Also
Die (which was made in collaboration with Brecht) and Woman
in the Window. The last three films--Scarlet Street, Cloak
and Dagger, and Secret Beyond the Door--are neither good
films nor typical of Lang at all. It is disappointing to
see an originally excellent director adapting to the commercial Hollywood situation.

180    J-t. "Jenseits allen Zweifels." [Review of Beyond a Reasonable
       Doubt]. Film-Dienst (Düsseldorf: later Cologne) (6 May).
       After a short plot summary, the reviewer says that while
it all sounds very ingenious, the film is quite primitively
contrived. It is not really a criticism of circumstantial
evidence in the administration of justice, and Lang does
not even attain his formerly easily achieved suspense. The
criminal milieu has a particularly vulgar appearance, in
addition, and this makes the film even more inappropriate
for youth.

181    Jungk, Robert. "Der Star, von dem man spricht." Stuttgarter
       Nachrichten (8 December). [This article is a shortened
       version of the one entitled "Guerrilla in Hollywood," which
       appeared in Die Tat, (Zurich) (17 December 1950)].
       No ten out of Hollywood's 365 directors are as "non-
Hollywoodish" as Fritz Lang. This is the result of a tough,
patient guerilla war against the tyranny of taste.
       He has made the necessary connection with the financiers
and producers. But that meant extensive compliance with
Hollywood's working methods.
       "Please don't misunderstand me," Lang says. "I don't
use Hollywood's particular rules as an excuse for bad reviews. Two 'invisible directors' come more into play here
than elsewhere: the necessity of being a financial success
and the increasingly petty censors. Do you think I still
could have made a film like Fury, an indictment of mass
hysteria, today?"
       Lang is not the person to be hindered by the censors in
expressing his opinions. He left Germany when offered a
post by Goebbels. He has not had it easy in Hollywood, for
Lang wants to say something in his films.
       Lang has up until now made twelve films in Hollywood,
including masterpieces such as Fury and You Only Live Once,
in which he portrays American life with keener eyes than an
American could have. In Manhunt and Hangmen Also Die he

portrayed dictatorship in its full horror and erected a
memorial to the resistance movements without heroic Kitsch
figures.  In Woman in the Window and Scarlet Street he once
again treated the problem of crime and the criminal with so
much understanding for the offender that it did not please
the censors.  But curiously, he has had the greatest success
with films about the Wild West and is currently finishing
Rancho Notorious.

Lang concludes with the hope that some European director
will offer him a project so that, far from Hollywood, he can
create a true Lang film once again.

182   Land, Hans.  "Gefährliche Begegnung:  Zu neuen Fritz Lang
Filmen" [Review of Woman in the Window].  Generalanzeiger
für Bonn (5 August).

Land gives a brief overview of Lang's background and
early works, noting how visual power was always dominant in
Lang's films.  Now in his sixtieth year, Lang remains a master of visual style.  Since he emigrated to America, what
he has lost in artistic breadth he has gained in intensity
of depiction.  While he can no longer make works on the
level of Die Nibelungen, he is instead speaking to the broad
public, as did Shakespeare, in ways it can understand.  And
he is still managing to insert his own vision and style.

183   M. E. P. [Erika Pöllner].  "Gefährliche Begegnung."  [Review
of The Woman in the Window] Film-Dienst (Düsseldorf; later
Cologne) (6 May).

Pöllner gives a brief outline of the plot of Woman in
the Window.  She then notes that Lang depicts the way in
which the professor and the woman scheme to hide the body
in a careful, concentrated manner.  The situations shown
burst with irony.  But when the film becomes most tragic
and the professor's suicide seems inevitable, everything returns neatly to reality:  the professor had only dreamed the
nasty adventure.  The charming conclusion provokes gentle
laughter.  The fascinating portrayal of the increasing
criminal involvement is not, of course, healthy entertainment for children.

184   Manvell, Roger.  "Siegfried 1922-1924."  Sight and Sound, vol.
19, no. 2 (April), 83-85.

Manvell first places the film in the political context
of the post-World War I revival of legendary heroes.  After
summarizing past criticism by Kracauer, Sadoul, and Eisner,
Manvell gives his own impressions of the film, agreeing that
for a modern audience all moves too slowly and clumsily.
Few of the actors are convincing:  he likes Gunther and
Hagan, however, and Siegfried to a degree.

Manvell concludes by saying that human characterization
was not Lang's aim.  He wanted to give a pictorial feeling

and atmosphere was everything. If you like grandeur and symmetry of design, Manvell notes, this film will please. He praises particularly the beauty of the forest scenes when Siegfried first leaves Mime. But the film will pall if projected at the correct speed and he recommends running it at sound speed.

184a    Porges, Friedrich. "Filmkunst für die Praxis: Zu den neuen Fritz Lang Filmen." Rundschau (Cologne) (27 May).

In a tribute to Lang on the occasion of his sixtieth birthday, Porges surveys his background and career, noting his place in film history. Lang's interest in visual style derives in part from his early preoccupation with painting; in the recent works, Lang's images are more adept than his sound. Porges sees the use of the voices of the dead at the end of Scarlet Street as a mistake.

Lang never made films of the quality of Die Nibelungen after going to Hollywood, but he still kept his personal vision. Like Shakespeare, Lang works with popular material that the public wants, but raises it to the level of art through his treatment, as, for example, in The Woman in the Window. Porges considers Lang's gangster films as studies of the human soul.

In conclusion, Porges notes that Lang is neither a realist nor a surrealist, but makes psychological films. Within the Hollywood conventions, one can still see the master hand at work.

Other sixtieth birthday tributes:
H. R., "Fritz Lang wird sechzig: Als Pionier der Filmkunst in Deutschland unvergessen." Illustrierte Filmwoche (Karlsruhe) (2 December 1950).

185    Wortig, Kurt. "Aus Constantins Presse-Büro: Fritz Lang wird 60 Jahre alt." (Clipping without reference in Wiesbaden file.) (5 December).

Wortig looks back on Lang and his career on the occasion of the re-release of You Only Live Once (1936) in Germany. He notes that Lang was one of the film personalities who made the German film internationally known and raised the quality of film to art.

Once Lang had left Germany, his work declined because he could not adjust to American culture. Wortig concludes with the hope that the reshowing of You Only Live Once will stimulate interest in Lang and provide him with the chance to make a thriller in Germany, which would be an honor to the German industry.

186    Z. "Strasse der Versuchung." (Review of Scarlet Street). Film-Dienst (Düsseldorf; later Cologne) (23 March). Available in Deutschen Film und Fernsehakademie, West Berlin.

Z. notes that the theme of Scarlet Street was old, and had already been made into a great film by Jean Renoir in 1932. Lang reshaped the material into another excellent movie.

According to Z., while Renoir's La Chienne is made in a naturalist style without concern for moral strictures, the realism of Lang's Scarlet Street is hampered by the Hays Production Code, so that the film never goes beyond the limits of propriety. But Z. says that, like every other Lang film, this movie leaves one with a feeling of emptiness and inner dissatisfaction. However, the film is typical of Lang in that both large and small details in some scenes and the psychological development are unsurpassed.

## 1951

187 A. T. "Fritz Lang." Le Soir (Brussels) (26 January).

A. T. says that among the disparate films of this German-American director we find powerful moments that come close to defining a personal, tragic view of life. Lang's best works reveal an inevitable machinery, which traps his characters and brings about their downfall. But Lang narrowly avoids a truly pessimistic philosophy of life, standing instead on the brink of familiar romantic attitudes.

With the exception of You Only Live Once (being revived in Brussels at the time of writing), A. T. says that we find only a feeble echo of ancient tragedy in Lang's films. The fatal situations in his works emerge finally from the theatrical rather than the "true," despite the surface realism.

But, according to A. T., it is wrong to try to find the moralist in Lang; he is a master of the thriller and of a powerful visual style evident as early as Die Nibelungen in 1923.

Lang's work falls clearly into two periods: there is his German career, which A. T. finds the more creative, and which was characterized by the fantastic and sensational, and his American career, where Lang took on Hollywood realism, making dramatic films with social and psychological import. While A. T. likes the early American works, he sees a decline in the forties, Scarlet Street and Woman in the Window being the only films to recall Lang's brilliant past.

188 Gérard, Olivier. "Rétrospective: La Femme au Portrait, Ondine ou Femme à L'Encan." Raccords, No. 8 (Summer), pp. 19-20.

Gérard begins with a quotation from Mitry that he thinks illuminates Lang's aesthetic. According to Mitry, cinema is the only art that creates symbols out of real life. In Lang's work, visual style and mise-en-scène have to render the richness of N. Johnson's screenplay.

189

For Lang, Gérard argues, the moment has more meaning
than events stretched through time, so that the image must
always hold the spectator's attention.  The drama is expressed through a series of symbols, which function as profound
correlatives for the screenplay.  The heroine in Woman in
the Window is not so much a real woman as the incarnation
of a portrait.  The image never ceases to be a sign.  The
exotic mise-en-scène perhaps comes from Lang's experience
of German expressionism.

Gérard goes on to discuss how the importance given to
the composition of perfect images governs the rhythm of the
montage; the still shots therefore have a jarring effect.
For the most part, the figure of Professor Wanley (played
by Edward G. Robinson) becomes a dramatic counterpoint to
the other images in the film.

The mystery in the film emerges from the perfect union
of image and montage, and the world of the film takes on a
surreal quality.  Women are as fascinating as statues, while
every police officer bears the look of death.  The two guilty
characters are haunted by the fear of punishment that they
see in the eyes of the most innocent passerby.  According
to Gérard, Lang moves us from mystery to horror, showing
that horror lies in that which is immobile.

The ending of the film has been criticized, even though
this is the happy ending producers demanded.  But the last
sequence may be justified in other terms.  It is a carica-
ture of narrative in general, rendering this particular
narrative more subtle and mysterious.

189    KB. [Klaus Brüne].  "Gehetzt" [Review of You Only Live Once].
       Film-Dienst (Düsseldorf; later Cologne), (9 February).
       Brüne says that while Fritz Lang's name calls up many
       memories in Germany, this film is a polished disappointment.
       There are traces of Lang's famous works in the first part
       of the film, but the second half foregoes all probability
       and lapses into sentimentality, especially in the very last
       scenes.  The promising beginning deteriorates into a stan-
       dard Hollywood product.

190    MR [Martin Ruppert].  "Die Herrschaft des Verbrechens: Das
       Testament des Dr. Mabuse."  Frankfurter Allgemeine Zeitung
       (13 September).
       Ruppert reviews The Last Will of Dr. Mabuse on its first
       release in Germany since being banned by the Nazis.  He be-
       gins by looking briefly at film history between 1921 and
       1933, seeing the period as bounded on the one side by
       Caligari and on the other by The Last Will of Dr. Mabuse.
       The connection between the films is the flight from the pain
       of war and traditional, bourgeois life.  Films of the period
       revealed the power of emotional life over the physical realm
       and had a "utopian" aspect:  people are under the hypnotic

power of a tyrant who begins with merely criminal acts, but ends in full-blown tyranny of the kind that Orwell described in 1984.

The film, according to Ruppert, shows the abnormality of the period in the madhouse setting, but it also looks toward the future chaos. The theme of suppression of personal freedom through terror still has meaning for us today.

Ruppert concludes that the power of the film lies not in its dialogue but in the force of the images. He goes on to discuss visual aspects of the film, praising the use of light and shadow, the creation of an atmosphere of terror, and of world of madness. Lang has depicted well the domination of one person by the will of another.

191 Seelmann-Eggebrecht, Ulrich. "Dämonie des Untergangs: Das Abgründige in Herrn Fritz Lang." Der Mittag (Düsseldorf) (22 March).

Seelmann-Eggebrecht begins by outling in detail the plot of Fury and then sketching those of Der müde Tod [Destiny], M, and Scarlet Street. He concludes that Lang's films always show people lost in a labyrinth of woe. Briefly surveying Lang's early aspirations as a painter, Seelmann-Eggebrecht notes that this interest led Lang at first into the monumental film, but he thinks Kracauer went too far in finding the forerunner of Nuremberg in this style. Lang went on to expose the totalitarian state in his Mabuse films.

Beginning to work in the period of Caligari and Paul Wegener's films, Lang never rid himself of his interest in the demonic and in terror. But he learned from Eisenstein the concept of montage and the importance of objects and space. Once in America in the 1930s, he picked up the realist style of King Vidor and Henry Hathaway. Having taken an outsider for hero in M, he took a similar hero in You Only Live Once.

Seelmann-Eggebrecht concludes that Lang combined the suspense of the gangster film and the demonic Dostoevskian world. Even in his conventional dramas, Lang revealed the underlying human suffering and delusion and his tendency for violence and destruction.

## 1952

192 Anon. "Filmgespräche mit Fritz Lang." Frankfurter Neue Presse (Frankfurt a. M.) (28 June).

The author visits Lang in his Beverly Hills home and reports the gist of their conversation. Lang has just completed Clash by Night, but the film has not been released. Since the theme of the film is the eternal triangle, Lang talks about the problem of marriage. He next discusses eroticism in American films and the unrealistic happy

endings, which are not really any solution. He concludes
by criticizing the recent remake of M, noting that he would
like to make a film in Europe and that he has some ideas
for it.

193    Anon. "Fritz Lang: 'Director of Directors': Filmregisseur
in Zwei Erdteilen und drei Ländern." Mannheimer Morgen
(29 November).
    The author begins by noting Lang's pioneering work in
the early days of the German film. The Nibelungen,
Metropolis, and Dr. Mabuse, der Spieler [Dr. Mabuse, the
Gambler], took the art of film forward, and Lang's Der müde
Tod [Destiny] made the German film internationally known.
While not belonging to any one group, Lang learned from
others, especially Reinhardt, who taught him about handling
large crowds. Lang combined naturalism and expressionism
and pioneered in all the film techniques we now take for
granted. Lang's training in engineering, architecture, and
painting all came in useful.
    After briefly discussing Frau im Mond [Woman in the Moon]
and Das Testament des Dr. Mabuse [The Last Will of Dr.
Mabuse], the author describes Lang's departure from Germany.
In America, he says, Lang was not so autonomous, but still
managed to put his stamp on his work. Scarlet Street and
Clash by Night show Lang as interpreter and investigator of
the deepest reaches of the soul.

194    Crowther, Bosley. Review of Rancho Notorious. New York Times
(15 May), p. 39.
    Crowther writes a negative review, finding Marlene
Dietrich here listless, lacking the power of her earlier
Destry Rides Again. Crowther blames Taradash, the scriptwriter, for using Dietrich merely as a pawn. While praising certain excitingly staged gunfights, Crowther concludes
that this Western does not match the character of its female
star.

194a   Eisner, Lotte. L'Écran Demoniaque. Paris: André Bonne.
Annotation and page numbers from English language version,
translated from the French by Roger Greaves and published
as The Haunted Screen: Expressionism in the German Cinema
and the Influence of Max Reinhardt. Rev. enl. ed. Berkeley
and Los Angeles: The University of California Press, 1969.
    (1)  Chapter 13: "Handling of Crowds--Metropolis (1926):
the influence of the Expressionist Choruses and
Piscator," pp. 223-236.
    Eisner is critical of Metropolis, seeing it as "old-
fashioned and vaguely ridiculous . . . overloaded with
sentiment." But she proceeds to show how Lang had been influenced by both Max Reinhardt and expressionist choruses,
especially those of Piscator, who was himself influenced by

Russian stage production. The influence of Otto Rippert, who directed <u>Homunculus</u> (1916), is clear in the way the crowds are directed. Eisner sees Rippert's film as setting the trend for expressionist films even before <u>Caligari</u>. Lang uses expressionist stylization to great effect in the underground town in <u>Metropolis</u>. The masses employ the echelon movement found in expressionist choruses, and the procession of Moloch's victims moves with the same mechanical motion in their rhomboidal divisions. The crowds, the human element in the film, are stylized into a mechanical element. While this geometrical stylization is the last vestige of expressionist aesthetic, it never becomes trite. There is borrowing from <u>Caligari</u> in the way that Rotwang, like Cesare, goes mad and bears Maria off over the rooftops.

Eisner does not like the scenes in Joh Fredersen's office as much as those in the underground and generally attributes a lot of the film's mawkishness to Thea von Harbou: "Her sentimentalism and deplorable taste for false grandeur made her lapse rapidly into the darkness of Nazi ideology."

The use of lighting, Eisner notes, is brilliant in <u>Metropolis</u>, particularly in the creation of the robot, where light is used to give the impression of sound.

(2) Chapter 14: "The Fritz Lang Thriller," pp. 237-249.

　　(a) <u>Die Spinnen</u> [The Spiders]

Eisner praises Lang's innovations here, particularly the scenes filmed on the train without back projection. There are still ridiculous aspects to the film--the comedy is too emphatic, and there are borrowings from Feuillade's <u>Vampires</u> in the hooded figures. Many elements are drawn from the common stock of the suspense film, and at one point the film turns into a Western.

But there is already foreshadowing of future films; hypnotism plays a major role as it will in <u>Dr. Mabuse, der Spieler</u>; the televising of scenes with the vamp prefigures the "television" screen in <u>Metropolis</u> and <u>Die tausend Augen</u> [The Thousand Eyes]; the scene where the hero is imprisoned in a cellar looks toward <u>Dr. Mabuse</u> and the many scenes in other films that reflect Lang's fascination with fantastic caves deep in the bowels of the earth (e.g., Joe May's 1920s version of <u>Das indische Grabmal</u> [The Indian Tomb]; the lunar caverns in <u>Frau im Mond</u> [Woman in the Moon]; the caves in <u>Die Nibelungen</u>, and finally Lang's 1958 <u>Das indische Grabmal</u> [The Indian Tomb]).

　　(b) <u>Dr. Mabuse der Spieler</u>

This film marks a change in that there is some attempt to convey the individual psychology of the master criminal, but most of the critics of the time saw the film as reflecting the decadence of the period. It is significant that Lang uses a contemporary setting (as contrasted with that in <u>Die Spinnen</u> [The Spiders]), but there is more influence from art nouveau than from expressionism. Lang has now

learned how to create chimeric states--as when the count is
under hypnosis--but, as Eisner notes, "In Lang, the real
world is never far removed from fantasy." Eisner ends this
section by noting some influences from Caligari, The Golem,
and Homunculus.

(c) Spione [Spies]

Eisner finds this film disappointing, attributing the
failure of the film again to Thea von Harbou's taste for
pompous melodrama. Harbou dwells excessively on the feelings and the reactions of her characters. Seeing only a
few scenes of pure Lang, Eisner points to his influence on
the visual aspects of the film.

(d) Die Frau im Mond [Woman in the Moon]

Again Eisner finds this film heavily influenced by
Harbou, discerning the genius of Lang only in the rocket
launching episodes that predict the future.

195 -e- [Walter Feigl]. "Vor dem neuen Tag" [Review of Clash by
Night]. Film-Dienst (Düsseldorf; later Cologne), (1
December).

Feigl summarizes the plot briefly and then complains
that the Odets play on which it was based has not been
translated into film but instead remains as it was in the
theater: the pauses between acts are taken up with shots
of the sea and fishing boats. Everything remains external,
the director not having succeeded in penetrating to the
roots of things. Ultimately, everything is superficial.

196 G. H. "Rache für Jesse James." [Review of The Return of
Frank James]. Film-Dienst (Dusseldorf; later Cologne),
(7 April).

G. H. notes that this film is a follow-up to King's
Jesse James, but although made by the famous director Lang,
it is not at all original. The actors struggle valiantly
with their material, and the cameraman tries hard, but on
the whole this is just another genre film in the usual,
wild West manner.

197 Jeanne, René and Charles Ford. Histoire encyclopédique du
cinéma, vol. 2: Le Cinéma Muet. Paris: S. E. D. E.
(La Société D'Édition de Dictionnaires et Encylopédies)
pp. 149-185, but esp. pp. 174-180.

Jeanne and Ford say that Lang stands as the incarnation
of German cinema of the golden age with Destiny, The
Nibelungen, and Metropolis. After a brief outline of Lang's
background and career, the authors discuss these three films.

Destiny is seen as representing symbolic expressionism;
the spectacular sets reflect a purification of what Wiene
was trying to do in Caligari and of what other expressionists had done. The excellent choice of actors added to the
film's success. Jeanne and Ford see a decline in the Mabuse

films that followed. Although they are superior police
films, they are, nevertheless, only that.

The Nibelungen is more in accord with Lang's natural
tastes and aspirations. The response to the first part
[Death of Siegfried] was unprecedented, but the second part
was less enthusiastically received, due in part to Wagner's
popularization of the characters. The artifical sets, similar to those in Caligari, make the first part of the film
expressionist. While the film may appeal to those who enjoy careful composition and modelling, film is not a static
art.

Lang tried to build more dramatic intensity into
Kriemhild's Revenge. After praising the group of actors
Lang had working for him, the authors conclude that Lang
was the most poetic, romantic, and German of all German
cineastes. The Nibelungen significes the end of expressionism proper.

198   Morgan, James.  Review of Clash by Night.  Sight and Sound,
      22, No. 2 (October-September), 80.
      Morgan finds Clash by Night unsatisfactory because pre-
      tentious.  It has a dated 1930s charm, but not even its
      highly assured acting can infuse the film with life.

199   Ro. [Franz Rowas].  Review of American Guerilla in the
      Philippines.  Film-Dienst (Düsseldorf; later Cologne)
      (7 June).
      Rowas outlines the plot and then wryly notes that one
      cannot expect a nation that won the war to give up making
      profit from the episodes.  One could only have hoped that
      the theme would not be treated in the manner of a wild West
      adventure film--improbably patriotic and sentimental--as in
      this case.  Rowas deplores the acting of Micheline Presle,
      who is here far from the great actress she was in other
      films.

200   Werner, Gösta.  "Metropolis och Fritz Lang."  Biografbladet
      (Stockholm), final issue, pp. 28-32.
      Werner begins by stating that the chaos in cultural life
      in Germany after World War I led to expressionism, well
      illustrated in the work of Reinhardt and Piscator, and in
      the homunculus motif taken from romanticism.  But perhaps
      the phenomeon of the times can best be seen in the abstract
      film Metropolis, with the magnificent creation of the robot,
      the brilliant handling of the masses, and the spontaneous,
      wild destruction of the workers' town.
      Werner goes briefly into Lang's background and career
      before he made Metropolis and then discusses the enormous
      cost and scale of the film, comparing the project to
      Griffith's Intolerance.  He discusses the various artists,
      technicians, and actors who worked on the film, describing

the film's reception as at first enthusiastic and later critical.

Werner sees the film as a mixture of pseudoidealism, Marxism, and Christianity. The vision of Babel is a combination of Cecil B. De Mille and Max Reinhardt. Werner proceeds to isolate the various motifs taken from earlier German films like Caligari, Nosferatu, and The Golem. An essentially romantic work like Metropolis, which placed all on the heart, also interested Hitler, who asked Goebbels to appoint Lang head of the German film industry.

Werner ends by discussing the claustrophobic element in Metropolis and tracing the recurrence of this motif in many later Lang works such as M, The Last Will of Dr. Mabuse, Fury, and Secret beyond the Door.


## 1953

201   Dorsday, Michel. "Symphonie Nuptiale." Review of Clash by Night [along with Cukor's The Marrying Kind.] Cahiers du Cinéma, No. 19 (January), p. 41.

Dorsday notes how paradoxical it is that Americans, who are misogynist (with reason) [sic], are also happier and freer than people of other nations. They hate what the industrial machine has done to their lives, but also know that they have to live with it.

Dorsday briefly outlines the situation of Mae (played by Barbara Stanwyck) as she appears at the start of the film. According to Dorsday, the two themes of the film are the responsibility and indestructability of marriage. This is revolutionary in a period when divorce has become a hypocritical game. Stanwyck refuses to be good and just, yet she also does not want to abandon her husband and child. In the end, she attains a certain peace, but it is a strange kind, analogous to that of the character played by Bette Davis in Little Foxes: watching the one being she's ever loved, her daughter, leave with the lover whom Davis has liberated.

202   F. [W. Feigl]. "Engel der Gejagten" [Review of Rancho Notorious]. Film-Dienst (Düsseldorf; later Cologne) (9 January).

Feigl begins by giving a summary of the film's plot and then says that when the "hunter" whose bride was murdered by one of the bandits reaches the farm, gold and money are no longer the issue. Different kinds of conflicts arise, growing out of loyalty, love, betrayal, and jealousy among the bandits. People exonerate themselves through the unshakable intention of the pursuer to turn the murderer over to justice. Altar Keene, played by Marlene Dietrich, the star, has to die at the end. That is the standard solution.

This is one of Lang's best American films: a Western, but an uncommon one even in its form. Ballad-like, the Moritat [ballad] is sung at the opening and closing and, when necessary, during the action. Of course there is much riding and shooting, but this is not much more than decoration for the mental and spiritual processes of the characters' personalities.

203 F. T. [Friedrich Luft]. "Marlene auf Wild West: Engel der Gejagten." Die Neue Zeitung (West Berlin) (7 January).
     Luft finds the value of Lang's Rancho Notorious to lie mainly in Marlene Dietrich's performance and role. Luft at first thought Lang was parodying the traditional Western, but the film turns out to take itself seriously. It does at times evoke a kind of ironic laughter at the German slant given the cowboy songs.

204 Porges, Fr. "Eine Kamera, die alles sieht: Fritz Lang erfand das 'Opernglas' System." Berliner Morgenpost (27 February).
     Porges writes this article after having visited Lang on the set of The Blue Gardenia. He is impressed with Lang's skillful use of the camera, which he now has mounted on a newly developed trolley. Lang talks about how the new camera enables much more movement. The old camera is no longer suitable, since now the camera must be free to move throughout the space, like a curious person looking at everything taking place before him or her. Lang believes that the new methods bring out more dramatic meaning and intensity. The camera now functions as a living entity within the film. Lang will use the new method, developed with Nick Musuraca, in all his future films.

205 Ro [Franz Rowas]. "Im Geheimdienst." [Review of Cloak and Dagger]. Film-Dienst (Düsseldorf; later Cologne) (11 September).
     Rowas says that this long-awaited film (completed in 1946), billed as an atom spy story, makes one think of the contemporary American-Russian tensions rather than of the German-American adversity in the last world war. After a brief outline of the plot, Rowas concludes that while the successful outcome of the love story provides a touching ending to the film, it has few other outstanding features.

206 S.F. "Vor dem neuen Tag." (Review of Clash by Night). Die Neue Zeitung (West Berlin) (20 August).
     According to S.F., the film's origin in the theatre is unmistakable, but Lang has made it work as a careful, impressive film. The actors are good, and S.F. finds the film enlivened with convincing emotional scenes.
     S.F. says that the story is about existential anxiety, reflecting disgust and heartlessness combined in a love-

triangle. Its conclusion seems to be a Hollywood compromise. In conclusion, S.F. notes that Clash by Night is not a film for sentimentalists. Convincing in details, especially in the dialogue, it lacks the sweeping movement that could have made it great as a whole.

207 Sadoul, Georges. "Fritz Lang." In his Histoire générale du cinéma, vol. 3: "Le Cinéma devient un art: La première Guerre Mondiale." Paris: Denoel. Pp. 385-402.
Although quite brief, the discussion of Lang here is useful in setting his work in the historical context of World War I, the revolution in Berlin, and the general social upheavals of the time. Sadoul emphasizes Lang's early taste for social metaphors, which were to become a distinctive mark of his talent.

## 1954

208 Anderson, Lindsay. "The Big Heat." Sight and Sound, 24, No. 1 (July-September), 36.
Anderson begins by commenting on the length of time since Lang has made a good film. His recent work has manifested a sense of strain and pretentiousness when "it has not been mere commercial hokum." But he goes on to praise The Big Heat as a good thriller, noting its intelligence, speed, tautness, "modesty of intention," and "craftsman-like writing." Without using the term, Anderson essentially places the film in the film noir tradition and praises Charles Nelson, the photographer, for the lighting.
Anderson concludes that The Big Heat is like many Hitchcock films, balanced in style and vision. It is more satisfying than more ambitious works and shows that Lang is still a master.

209 Autera, Leonardo. "Il Parabola di Fritz Lang." Cinema (Rome), n.s., no. 9 (15 January). [In Italian]
Light was the most important element in Der müde Tod [Destiny] and would continue to be the key stylistic element in Lang's subsequent work. While there are similarities between Murnau's and Lang's use of light it is important to note where the two diverge: Murnau concentrates on characters described minutely; Lang indulges in scenographic monumentality that is purely decorative (as in Die Nibelungen and Metropolis). In Die Nibelungen Lang's taste for geometric composition is apparent: shots are always dominated by the scenographic element, under which everything else is subsumed. His composition is always geometrically static.
Stylized, grandiose architecture dominates Metropolis and clashes with the banal humanitarianism of the story. The story reflects the negative influence of Lang's wife,

Thea von Harbou, who wrote the script. Her bad scripting is evident in all Lang's German films. Autera agrees with Kracauer that Dr. Mabuse, der Spieler [Dr. Mabuse, the Gambler] reflects the political paralysis of Germany.

The theme of the victim, the individual persecuted without reason by a tyrant who sometimes is identified with society itself, will remain the most sincere element in Lang's sound films. In M Lang combines masterful technique with expression of a psychological state.

In Das Testament des Dr. Mabuse [The Last Will of Dr. Mabuse], the theme of terror interests Lang more than the theme of freedom. The sound track is used innovatively to communicate a constant sense of fear.

Autera disagrees with those who say that Lang's Hollywood films are better because more humanitarian. Lang was, in fact, always more interested in style. Hangmen Also Die is his best Hollywood film, the only one as good as the German films. His American films are cold and distant, because he was never able to adjust to the American environment and mentality.

210    J-t [Werner Jungeblodt]. "Gardenia, eine Frau will vergessen." [Review of The Blue Gardenia]. Film-Dienst (Düsseldorf; later Cologne) (23 April).
       After saying how unappetizing he finds the plight of the three telephone operators in their apartment, J-t goes on to give a rather mocking summary of the film's plot. He concludes that a few scenes reveal Lang's mastery of visual tension, but on the whole finds the film routine, complete with its music by Richard Wagner. One might expect some real analysis of the problem of guilt or of a troubled conscience, but the film is all psychological froth, lacking in any real ethical viewpoint.

211    Rohmer, Eric (Maurice Schérer). "Un realisme méchant." Cahiers du Cinéma, No. 36 (June), pp. 58-59.
       Rohmer begins by stating that this film will be as big a disappointment as Scarlet Street to those who won't allow the director of Metropolis to renew his themes and style. Rohmer finds two main leitmotifs in Lang's films: first, the notion of the will triumphant or broken, perverse or revengeful; second, the way Lang maintains distance from his characters. While this distance contributes a certain realism, there is an evil element to it, for if Lang does not love or exalt his characters, he feels a need to punish them.
       This evil element is familiar from German expressionism and provides the key to understanding The Blue Gardenia, which might otherwise be viewed as banal. After giving a brief plot outline, Rohmer defends the forced happy ending, noting that an awful ending is not necessary for the drama's

violence to be evident. It is there as the film proceeds
in the tension between opposing forces. Lang's skill lies
in bringing events to a shocking level and then managing
to get out of it all gracefully, with clean hands. The
seduction scene in Prebble's apartment vies in its suspense
with the famous one in Queen Kelly.

Rohmer ends by commenting that Lang may have used the
script more to move characters around than to justify events,
but he praises the detailed observation and the presentation
of the lives of the three young women. In addition, the
editing technique is new, with one frame flowing into the
next. This is not Lang as we usually know him. The film
recalls Backer or De Sica and shows Lang battling with neo-
realism on its own grounds.

212   Tasiemka, Hans. "Wiedersehen mit Fritz Lang." Berliner
      Morgenpost (14 September).
          Tasiemka describes his meeting with Lang in the Dorchester
      Hotel, London, during preparations for the Indian films. He
      notes that young people flock around Lang, while leaving
      Wilder, Preminger, and Litvak alone. Lang says he wants to
      work in Germany, but only on the condition that he can have
      a say in the script, as in the old days, and in the cutting
      of the film.

213   Truffaut, François. "Aimer Fritz Lang." Cahiers du Cinéma
      (Paris), No. 31 (January), pp. 52-54.
          Truffaut begins by noting that Lang's main theme is that
      of people struggling alone against a hostile universe. Many
      films follow the same pattern: a man gets involved in a
      fight through duty or desire, becomes weary of the fight,
      and is on the point of abandoning it all when something
      makes him take it up again--often the death of a wife, as
      in The Big Heat. The conflict now becomes strictly personal,
      with the individual's own reasons for revenge taking the
      place of the social or political ones that may have been
      important before.
          Everything in a Lang film is set against a very moral
      backdrop, although the morality is not of a conventional
      kind. The representatives of the law are cowards and his
      heroes always fight for themselves and only revenge the one
      victim who meant a lot to them.
          The Big Heat, Truffaut says, is a beautiful film, reveal-
      ing Lang's skill with actors. He notes how critics typically
      find the American films lacking in symbolism and how they
      clearly prefer the German works because they are "art."
      But Truffaut is struck by how much of Hollywood there is in
      the German films and how much of the German work is retained
      in the American ones, such as the lighting, decor, taste for
      perspective, and sharp angles. The best Hollywood works, in
      fact, come from European directors. A good director "saves"

the works he's given, redeeming the horrible subjects.

Lang's films, although signed by different scriptwriters, all have a common style. His themes and his vision merely borrow the banal appearance of the thriller, for Lang, in fact, is a true author of films. One must love Fritz Lang and welcome each of his films as it arrives.

## 1955

214   Anderson, Lindsay. Review of Human Desire. Sight and Sound (London), 24, No. 4 (Spring), 198.

In this positive review, Anderson finds Human Desire more successful than Lang's earlier attempt at a Zola-Renoir story in Scarlet Street. Lang's alterations of the novel are an improvement: the hero now is an honest driver brought to ruin by the seduction of a femme fatale.

One can sense the appeal that this old narrative has for Lang's harsh German temperament and he infuses it with new life. The relationships have an interesting European quality and the harshness makes them real. But Anderson says that the film inevitably collapses. Glenn Ford [Jeff Warren] cannot kill the jealous husband. The good parts of the film make one regret the disintegration.

215   Chabrol, Claude. "Évolution du Film Policier." Cahiers du Cinéma (Paris), No. 54 (Winter).

Although this article does not deal directly with Lang's work, it is relevant to the genres that he worked with mainly in America. The entire issue of Cahiers du Cinéma is devoted to Hollywood cinema. Lang is included in the "Dictionary of Contemporary American Directors."

216   Demonsablon, Philippe. "La Difficulté d'Être." [Review of Human Desire]. Cahiers du Cinéma (Paris), No. 50 (August-September), pp. 44-46.

Demonsablon begins by saying that he is not going to compare Lang's film with either Zola's novel or Renoir's earlier adaptation of it. His main reasons are that he dislikes Zola and that the fifteen years separating Renoir's and Lang's films make comparisons hard, since cinematic language has changed so much during this time. In addition, it is hard to compare works made by men at such different stages in their lives.

This last difference perhaps accounts for the contrasting points of view that Lang and Renoir take. Lang's film centers not on the characters played by Glenn Ford or Gloria Graham, but on that of Broderick Crawford. We see again Lang's recurring interest in the relationship of an older man with a younger woman.

The people in Human Desire, according to Demonsablon,

see age only in terms of decline of the flesh. They do not
know how to use aging to liberate the spirit and thus
Crawford wants to destroy his wife because life is eluding
him. He hopes to reconquer his loved one by linking her
with the guilt of murder. But this turns out to be impossible, and Crawford can offer his wife freedom only in
death. Behind all this, Demonsablon says, is a fear of
loneliness, a need for attachment.

We are here on familiar Langian ground, and Demonsablon
goes on to show how Lang uses mise-en-scène to explore the
complex links people have to their past, which always half
absorbs them. He concludes that Human Desire is a bitter
film, full of empty images, and deprived of all action,
where time is cruelly emptied of the future. This complex
work reveals the difficulty of existence.

217    H. M. S. "Deuter der Menschenseele: Am 5.12 wird Filmregisseur
       Fritz Lang 65 Jahre alt." Westdeutsche Rundshau (Wuppertal-
       Barmen) (3 December).
           H. M. S. surveys Lang's background and career, his de-
       parture from Germany and arrival in America. He concludes
       that Lang's thrillers went beyond the formulas to deal with
       metaphysical matters. Lang had most success with Westerns.

218    Lambert, Gavin. "Fritz Lang's America." Sight and Sound
       (London), 25, No. 1 Summer 1955, 15-21; No. 2 Autumn 1955,
       92-97.
           Lambert describes the status of the German film industry
       before Lang left Germany in 1934. He discusses a few of the
       German films briefly, but then analyzes several of the
       American films in depth--Fury, You Only Live Once, You and
       Me, and The Big Heat. He concludes that Lang's work often
       lacks the "twin advances of a broadening assimilation of
       human experience and enrichment of technique." If this is
       working properly, Lambert says, "the business of creation
       becomes a constant search for the forms by which to express
       new experiences, new visions."
           The first American films reflected the stimulus of Lang's
       new experiences (especially in Fury and You Only Live Once).
       In The Big Heat, again, one finds Lang's imagination trans-
       forming the run-of-the-mill American thriller. But between
       You Only Live Once and The Big Heat, Lang's imaginative
       vision was often undernourished. Scarlet Street and Woman
       in the Window are variations on his usual themes rather than
       enlargements of experience. "In Lang's best films," Lambert
       notes, "society is always composed of victims and aggressors.
       For his characters to really live, he needs to place them
       on one side or the other. The same struggles are fought
       over and over again. Nor are they necessarily ennobling,
       for the director's impassivity excludes a tragic feeling.
       The violence as such is untouched by pity or anger; it

admits only of an intellectual terror."
Lambert finds Lang's world deviod of beauty and notes
that his America is really not that different from his
Germany. Both are actually another country, a haunted place
in which the same dramas occur. Lang's films deal with the
mechanized, artificial world and hardly ever with the natural one. His work shows the relentless advance of a destiny
that is neither beautiful nor pleasant but "the breakout of
the Caligari within." The persistent projection of anxiety
neurosis gives Lang's films their unique power, but as works
of art they are limited by passivity. "In the shadows of
the premonition human relationships break down. Guilt and
violence are at large."

219  Truffaut, François. Review of Human Desire. Cahiers du Cinéma
     (Paris), No. 47 (May), pp. 31-32.
     Truffaut notes that Human Desire is a remake of Renoir's
     La Bête Humaine, but, as in the case of Woman in the Window
     and La Chienne, comparisons are meaningless. Lang is search-
     ing for something different than was Renoir. While Renoir
     is interested in the relationship between the heroine and
     her lover, Lang is fascinated by the old man in love with
     the young woman, as in Scarlet Street and Woman in the
     Window. Gloria Grahame's low-life appearance challenges
     bourgeois morality. Truffaut sees a harmonious connection
     between Lang's Spione and Human Desire.

220  Truffaut, François. "Desirs humains de Fritz Lang." Arts
     (Paris) No. 524 (July 13-19), p. 5.
     Lang's Human Desire is a remake of Renoir's film rather
     than a new adaptation of the Zola novel. Alfred Hays, the
     scriptwriter, may never have opened the novel, but the in-
     fluence of Renoir's film is evident throughout. Lang and
     Renoir apparently share the taste for a similar theme--that
     of an old husband, a young wife, and her lover; they also
     have in common a predilection for the feline type of heroine.
     But that is as far as the comparison goes, for the authors
     have quite different ends in mind.
     Renoir introduced spiritual themes not in the original
     novel, stressing his hero's atavism. Lang's film is more
     austere, but is not worth less for pleasing less. Human
     Desire is a bitter, cynical film in which Lang creates a
     mood of constant oppressiveness. Many scenes are shot with-
     out background, for this might mitigate the effect or dis-
     tract the eye. There are many long scenes in close-up,
     with grey walls behind the actors. The two main themes here
     are the Corneille-like notion of revenge and unhappy marri-
     age. Despite its gloom, it is a strong, solid film.
     The juxtaposition of the two films is enriching; one
     sees how differently these two great auteurs treated the
     same subject in terms of content and point of view. But
     each made one of the best films of his career.

## 1956

221  Domarchi, Jean.  "Lang Le Constructeur" [Review of While the
     City Sleeps].  Cahiers du Cinéma (Paris), No. 63 (October),
     pp. 40–41.
          Domarchi comments first on Lang's icy detachment from
     his characters.  After pointing out his unwillingness to
     believe that even in America the director of a newspaper
     would use such methods to control his staff as shown in
     While the City Sleeps, Domarchi notes that documentary ex-
     actitude is beside the point.  Lang is merely demonstrating
     the modern social pathology of corruption through money,
     protecting us from the full force of his insight by
     distanciation [distancing].  All is as neat and proper as
     an operating room.
          Lang destroys the myth of journalist as savior, refusing
     (unlike Wilder) to bring in anything to relieve the bitter-
     ness.  Mobley, who has access to justice, uses it only to
     manipulate, and the women represent all that is basest in
     human nature.  Such humanity deserves neither pardon, nor
     even vengeance.
          Domarchi ends by protesting the unjust treatment accorded
     Lang's American films.  He claims that in American technique
     Lang found his real talent, abandoning all the expressionist
     trappings for an inimitable rigor.  Lang increasingly moved
     toward linear construction, retaining only what was essen-
     tial, and thus founded a neoclassical school of filmmaking.
     Although having become an American metteur-en-scène, Lang
     remained German.

222  Fraenkel, Heinrich.  Unsterblicher Film:  Von der Laterna
     Magica bis zum Tonfilm.  Munich:  Kindler, pp. 140–143.
          Fraenkel usefully surveys Lang's evolution as a film
     director, commenting briefly on the early scripts Lang wrote
     for Otto Rippert and Joe May, and showing how they prepared
     for his first films and especially for Der müde Tod (Destiny).
     The early work reveals Lang's interest in two main themes
     that would dominate his career--that of the femme fatale
     and of the supercriminal.
          Fraenkel notes the international success that Lang and
     Harbou gained with Der müde Tod, especially in France and
     England where critics talked of the ghosts of Dürer and
     Grünewald hovering over the film's images.
          Commenting on the Hollywood appropriation of Der müde Tod
     in Douglas Fairbanks' Thief of Bagdad, Fraenkel goes on to
     discuss the disastrous financial impact of the Hollywood
     industry on German films.  Metropolis lost money partly be-
     cause the huge anticipated American distribution failed to
     materialize, while American films became increasingly popu-
     lar in Germany.  But he concludes that the artistic impulse
     of the German films was a victory, since it introduced

variety in a boring diet of repeated plots and forms, and
pushed film ahead both aesthetically and technically.

223  Godard, Jean-Luc. "Le Retour de Frank James." Image et Son
     (Paris), No. 95 (October-November), pp. 41.
         As part of the Fiche culturelle U.F.O.L.E.I.S. series,
     this study of The Return of Frank James follows the usual
     format, starting with a discussion of Lang as director and
     of the Western genre. Godard next considers the dramatic
     value of the film. Its main theme, that of revenge, is
     common to many of Lang's films. As for the cinematic value
     of the film, Godard points out that mise-en-scène is always
     central in Lang and that a single image can define his
     aesthetic. Godard discusses the film's happy ending, noting
     that while Lang is fascinated with the man who sins, he is
     even more interested in regeneration. This can happen only
     after a man has paid his moral dues, as happens with Frank
     James. Finally, there is a section on documentation, where
     Godard provides excerpts from various books and articles on
     Lang.

224  Moullet, Luc. "Faulkner Contre Faulkner." Cahiers du Cinéma
     (Paris), No. 63 (October), p. 35.
         Moonfleet is a genial, admirable film that needs defend-
     ing, Moullet says, since on the surface everything would
     seem to be against it (it is similar in this way to Rancho
     Notorious). Moullet notes that as a child he read the novel
     Moonfleet, by Faulkner, and liked it, but that it has been
     totally changed in the film. While the book is merely a
     series of adventures, the film is a severe criticism of
     decadence and of moral failure. One needs to have seen the
     insane dance on the table or the scene where Joan Greenwood
     (Lady Ashwood) embraces first Stewart Granger (Jeremy Fox),
     then her dog, and finally her husband, to understand this
     fully. Lang does not like any of the people, not even the
     young boy, John Mohune, who, tempted by a terrifying vision
     of evil, falls into a cave and is all but interred.
         Moullet concludes by referring to Beyond a Reasonable
     Doubt (Lang's next film). Having just read the script,
     Moullet comments on its severity as well. This film con-
     cludes a series--The Blue Gardenia, Moonfleet, While the
     City Sleeps--all of which have similar bitter themes. Lang,
     as one of the greatest auteurs, is behind them all.

225  Niehoff, Karena. "Europa ist immer noch unbequem." Der Tages-
     spiegel (21 October), p. 30. Collected in Niehoff, Karena.
     Stimmt es Stimmt es nicht? Munich: Herrenalb-Erdmann,
     1962.
         Niehoff introduces a discussion of how Lang "sees" by
     analyzing the symbolism of his monocle. Having just arrived
     from America, Lang carries the monocle with a democratic air.

Lang sees more evil with his one eye than others with both, but he seems tired of giving us images of our time.

Continuing the theme of "seeing," Niehoff shows how Lang established a new direction for film with his painterly use of light, and she gives specific examples from Die Nibelungen, Metropolis, and Der müde Tod [Destiny]. With M Lang had the courage to risk more realistic kinds of filming in a period when surrealism was dominant. It was at this time, with Hitler coming to power, that Lang allowed his uncanny Dr. Mabuse to die. But Goebbels wanted to rescue the madman and make him healthy again through the passion of the people. The irony of this could not be understood at the time. It was difficult for Lang when Goebbels asked him to head Hitler's film industry, and he left Germany.

Now, after twenty-two years, he has returned to visit friends. He would like to direct in Germany and seems to enjoy talking openly with the press. He is surprised to hear the reporters discuss a recent play, noting that that kind of talk rarely goes on in Hollywood. The food in Germany is good, Lang says, but apart from that Europe is still uncomfortable.

226 PEM. "Der deutsche Film hat ihnen viel zu danken." Der Kurier (Berlin) (18 August).

Meeting Lang in London after twenty-four years (PEM last saw him on the set of Das Testament [The Last Will]), PEM recalls Lang's hasty departure from Germany after a successful series of films. Finding Lang little altered, PEM notes how Lang himself was the star in Germany and, instead of relying on famous actors, brought those he chose to prominence.

Lang always remained European in Hollywood, and his works bear his personal stamp. Some of the American films are among his very best.

PEM believes that Lang is on his way to Berlin in order to meet with German film companies in the hope of making a film in his own language on a theme that really interests him.

Other articles on the occasion of Lang's European trip:
Mautner, Michael. "Wanderer zwischen zwei Welten: Fritz Lang--Kassenmagnet ersten Ranges." Braunschweiger Nachrichten (24 October 1956).
                            close up
P. A. "Gestalter des Hintergründigen: Filmpionier Fritz Lang besucht Deutschland." Hannoversche Allgemeine (1 September 1956).

227 PEM. "Heimkehr in die Fremde." Allgemeine (Düsseldorf) (26 October).

Writing on the occasion of Lang's return to Germany after 23 years, PEM describes Lang's shock at the changes he found and also notes that Lang clearly wants to work again in Germany. As yet he has not been offered any project that interests him. Lang is anxious to meet young people and they greet him warmly, asking him to set a new standard in film. Lang replies that they should look for new talents, for people who will find a new form for the new content.

PEM concludes with the hope that Lang will find a suitable project now that new contact has been established with him.

228    Ross, Don. "Lang, Director of M, Seeks to Escape Net." New York Herald Tribune (20 May).
    In an interview with Ross, Lang surveys his own career, calls M his greatest film, but he also likes Scarlet Street, Clash by Night, Fury, and Woman in the Window. He is pleased with his latest film, While the City Sleeps. He talks of a future project--a film called Dark Spring, from a novel by Michael Ladde [never made, ed.].

229    Schnog, Karl. "Die Nibelungen." Filmspiegel (East Berlin), No. 7. (Available in Deutschen Film und Fernsehakademie, W. Berlin.)
    Schnog wrote this review on the occasion of a retrospective of the film. He recalls the context in which it was first produced--that of inflation-ridden Germany--and how the film, begun by Decla, was finished by Ufa.
    Despite the shortage of material, everything is on a huge scale. Fritz Lang, originally Austrian, and with a monocle even then, built his huge sets at Babelsberg. The film consists of beautiful images in black and white. Use of space, time, and lighting is brilliant. But the film community financed a grandiose, sentimental work.
    After discussing the main actors and actresses briefly, Schnog talks of how rich some of them became, while the hundreds of extras ate and slept on the set, glad to be earning some bread. The whole style of the film is inflated, consisting of masks and decoration rather than character. The whole thing cost five million marks, and then this monumental saga was sent, with great success, around the world.

230    Truffaut, François. "La Cinquième Victime." Arts (Paris), no. 581 (22-24 August), 1956, p. 3.
    Truffaut first comments on the way that Lang has been underestimated to date. Film historians recognize the value of some German works and of a few American ones, but as soon as Lang makes war films, Westerns, spy films, and thrillers they deny him all genius. But in fact, to one who loves Fritz Lang, none of his films is unworthy of Die Nibelungen or Fury, despite having the surface appearance of the B film.
    Lang never had the freedom in Hollywood that one or two

financial successes won for luckier directors, or that
directors had who were more in accord with the public mood.
He had to express himself through scripts that were often
badly constructed, improbable, or hastily rewritten by Lang
himself a couple of days before shooting.  His reputation
as difficult and stubborn meant that he had to change producers often.

As he grew older, Lang became more austere and grew
further from the public.  Although he was never sentimental,
in his early works he allowed himself cinematic effects--
visually or in the script.  He was lyrical, humorous, and
inventive in the early days, and it was this side of him
that influenced Hitchcock.  Bitterness took the place of
lyricism as Lang evolved and purified his style.  Truffaut
argues that Lang is now even more profound and great, despite the fact that he pleases less.  He is now sure of his
technique and has mastered his skills.  Lang manages to
include his favorite obsessions in the scripts he is given
and expresses himself freely.

It seems to Truffaut that after seeing While the City
Sleeps, he knows who Lang is and what he thinks.  He proceeds to outline the plot of the film as it relates to a
group of people around a newspaper.  Lang never liked
police mysteries, so he shows us the criminal at work as
the film opens.  Lang's total scorn for his characters is
what is most remarkable in the film:  they are all damned.
There is nothing less sentimental and more cruel than a
love scene directed by the mature Lang.  Even the better
guy in the film, played by Dana Andrews, behaves badly to
his girlfriend.  Lang multiplies his vicious comments on
people out of disgust and pessimism, his cruelty coming out
of his bitterness.  He never resettled in America in the
manner of other Germans fleeing nazism, and he never really
liked America.  No films are more bitter about American
civilization than those of Fritz Lang.  He never recovered
from nazism and in Hollywood never wanted to join leftist
groups.  But it is significant that when the Hollywood Ten
were arrested, it was he who took the initiative in raising
money so that they could hire a lawyer, all the while char-
acteristically convinced that they would be electrocuted
and he along with them.

1957

231   Bazin, André.  "Un incroyable film."  Radio-Cinéma-Télévision
(Paris), No. 405 (October 20), P. 46.
Bazin begins by noting that if Fritz Lang's name hadn't
been on Beyond A Reasonable Doubt, it would not have been
shown on the Champs Elysées (he doubts it will make the suburbs).  We already know, he says, that Lang has been reduced

to making B movies, which could have been given to a lesser director. But B films, because less supervised and low-budget, give filmmakers greater freedom. The films reflect Lang's genius, albeit only peripherally and in paradoxical forms.

But Bazin thinks that Lang scorned the script for Beyond and was unable to retain his sense of himself as a great director. Bazin leaves it to the auteur critics to see the culmination of Lang's career in the film, since to him the script is that of a routine police film and is not at all convincing. Lang's intelligence mixes badly with the total emptiness of the plot.

232   Kyrou, Ado. "L'Amour Revolte: You Only Live Once and Gun Crazy." In Amour-erotisme et cinéma. Paris: Eric Losfeld, pp. 424-429.
      Kyrou believes that Lang made his two best films when he arrived in America. The ending of You Only Live Once is, according to Kyrou, a sublime affirmation. At the mercy of the murderers of love, the characters played by Henry Fonda and Sylvia Sidney have to strive hard to love freely, to find here on earth even one moment of love. Their love has a very touching quality in a world that gives the right to love to those who do not know how to love. Each time they look at one another, they reveal an infinite joy. The film represents a plea for love, hurled at a society that must learn again how to love.

233   Mg [Wilhelm Mögge]. Review of While the City Sleeps. Film-Dienst (Düsseldorf; later Cologne) (28 February).
      In a short review, Mogge notes that while there are some sharp insights into relations between people in While the City Sleeps, the moral is old and the murder story worn. Neither the script nor the direction manages to illuminate the murderer's motives sufficiently, and the two stories—that of the murder and that of the newspaper contest—are not integrated. The murder story is particularly weak, and neither the good actors nor the director can redeem the lack of mastery of the material.

234   Rivette, Jacques. "La Main." Cahiers du Cinéma (Paris), No. 76 (November), pp. 48-51.
      Rivette notes that one is first struck by the apparent "nakedness" and "purity" of the images in Beyond a Reasonable Doubt. One suspects a trick just because all seems so totally objective. This impression is reinforced by the total disregard for probability or reality, as well as for narrative illusion. We enter a world of necessity established next to the arbitrariness of the hypotheses. Lang always searches for the truth beyond the probable, and here the search reaches to the improbable. Refusing all other

pleasurable diversions, Lang plunges us into a morgue-like
world that suggests his scorn for his subject and for his
audience. He is trying to create a totally closed universe
like that in Frau im Mond.
Five minutes before the end of the film, however, Lang
reverses all the givens in the situation in a manner that
Rivette calls "poetic." Lang manages to destroy the notion
of "character." The people exist instead as human abstractions. If the film is negative, it is so in the pure
Hegelian sense of abstract intelligence.
Lang is, first and foremost, the director of the concept,
which means that one cannot discuss him without recourse to
abstraction and necessity. The film is nevertheless a
simple description of existence on two levels. There is
first the discovery of the vanity of human justice, but
second the realization that there is no such thing as a
falsely accused, innocent person. For Lang we are all, a
priori, guilty. People who were, by grace, erroneously
called "innocent," immediately condemn themselves. We are
in a pitiless world in which the only possible attitude is
absolute scorn. While in You Only Live Once and Fury innocence had the appearance of guilt, in Beyond a Reasonable
Doubt guilt has all the appearance of innocence.


1958

235   Anon. "Soviel Pracht." Der Spiegel (8 October).
The reviewer's tone in this article is arch and condescending, toward both Lang and film itself. He begins by
feigning surprise that Fritz Lang, the director of monumental UFA silent films, is actually doing re-makes of Der Tiger
Von Eschnapur [The Tiger of Bengal] and Das Indische Grabmal
[The Indian Tomb]. The project is one of the most expensive
of the German post war film industry.
The reviewer considers the risky investment in a trite
adventure-spectacle film a misguided attempt by film producers to wean people away from television. Hollywood has
demonstrated that television viewers could be lured back
into the film theatres if they were offered spectaculars
that could not be projected on the small television screen.
Turning to Lang, the author notes that when Richard
Eichberg was making Das Indische Grabmal and Der Tiger Von
Eschnapur in Germany in 1938 (this is the first re-make of
the films, which were originally scripted by Lang in the
1920's and directed by Joe May, ed.), Lang was already in
Hollywood. According to the reviewer, Lang was unable to
establish himself as an artistically renowned Hollywood
director and so had to content himself with detective and
adventure films. Making the Indian films in Germany provides Lang with his first chance in many years to command

hosts of actors through gigantic sets.  It has been said
(the reviewer concludes) that Lang is using these films "to
unload himself of every idea that he has carried around with
him for a lifetime."

236    Anon.  "Ein Magier des deutschen Films."  (Newspaper not given.
       From file in Deutsches Institut für Filmkunde, Wiesbaden.)
           The author sets the context for his article by noting
       that Lang is in Germany to film Das Indische Grabmal [The
       Indian Tomb] and Der Tiger von Eschnapur [The Tiger of
       Bengal].  While many younger film goers may not know Lang,
       the author says that his name will be familiar to older
       generations.  Director of Dr. Mabuse, der Spieler, Frau Im
       Mond, Metropolis, and many other films that made film his-
       tory, Lang is an unforgettable magician of the screen.
           Lang's desire to direct the Indian films is understand-
       able, since he drafted the first versions, which were filmed
       by Joe May in 1922.  His passion is to remake them in his
       own style.
           The author concludes by hoping that Lang, now sixty-seven
       years old, will once again be successful with the German
       film; if he arouses shock and enthusiasm, his return home
       will be meaningful.

237    Andersson, Leo.  "Fritz Lang's Nya Fas" [Fritz Lang's New
       Phase].  In Aito Makinen, ed. Studio 4:  Elokuvan Vuosikirja
       1958 [Fourth Film Year Book] pp. 81-90, published by the
       Finnish Archives.  [Available at The British Film Institute].
       [In Swedish].
           The article on Lang appears in the part of the yearbook
       devoted to German directors who went to America.  Andersson
       is declared the only critic in the yearbook who follows the
       Cahiers du Cinéma line, and his position on Lang reflects
       this.  Andersson does not accept Gavin Lambert's opinion of
       the decline in Lang's work after he went to America; instead,
       like the French, Andersson sees Lang reaching a high point
       in the works after Scarlet Street.  His career culminates
       in While the City Sleeps and Beyond a Reasonable Doubt.

238    Douchet, Jean.  "You Only Live Once."  Cahiers du Cinéma
       (Paris), No. 81 (March), pp. 53-55.
           Douchet argues that You Only Live Once is a pure tragedy
       in which Lang shows the necessity of every event.  The film
       is structured around the Greek idea of fate and reflects a
       terrifying world of strict necessity, which excludes all
       chance.  Douchet denies the validity of all psychological
       or sociological interpretations.  He concludes by saying
       that Beyond A Reasonable Doubt carries the ideas of You
       Only Live Once to an even higher level.

239    Hecht, Hans.  "Mit Monokel und Kamera-Auge:  Matter Abglanz

oder neue Brillianz?" <u>Der Tag</u> (Berlin) (16 February).
  This is one of a series of articles written on the occasion of Lang's return to Germany to make his Indian films. Hecht notes Lang's charm and passion when he meets him in his Berlin studio and then surveys Lang's career briefly, discussing the differences between the German and American periods. He mentions the most important films and the actors Lang used in Germany, and then characterizes Lang's film style as a mixture of realism and abstraction, detail and vastness. Hecht traces the influences on Lang of Reinhardt and expressionism, talks about his work with Thea von Harbou, and then recounts his departure from Germany, his brief stay in France, and his arrival in America.
  Hecht outlines Lang's American career briefly, noting the change from social message films to gangster films and thrillers, and comments that Lang never renounced his expressionist tendencies or psychological subtlety. Hecht sees it as a good sign that Lang has returned to Germany to remake the Indian films, and hopes for great results.

Other similar articles:
  Anon. "Fritz Lang bleibt in Deutschland." <u>Frankfurter Neue Presse</u> (28 February 1958).
  Hecht, Hans. "Fritz Lang wieder in Berlin: Er will den Tiger von Eschnapur und <u>Das indische Grabmal</u> wiederverfilmen." <u>Hannoversche Allgemeine</u> (15 February 1958).
  H. H. "Das indische Kolossalgemälde: Fritz Lang verfilmt zwei Monsterwerke von einst." <u>Bielefeld</u> (4 October 1958).
  H. H. "Wegbereiter des Films: Fritz Lang." <u>Badisches Tageblatt</u> (Baden-Baden) (22 November 1958).
  pth. "Bibel und Dostojewski allein schaffen es nicht. Altmeister Fritz Lang filmt nach 25 Jahren wieder an der Spree." <u>Hamburger Echo</u> (11 October 1958).
  Schmieding, Walter. "Die Rückkehr des Tigers." <u>Westfalenpost</u> (Hagen), No. 26 (31 January 1959).

240   Moullet, Luc. "Le Film Policier: Peut-il avoir un sens Moral?" <u>Radio-Cinéma-Télévision</u> (Paris), No. 419 (26 January).
  After discussing the detective genre and its moral possibilities, Moullet goes on to discuss two films that used the form in an original way--Clouzot's <u>Les Espions</u> and Lang's <u>Beyond a Reasonable Doubt</u>. Both deal with individuals who are out of control. But while Clouzot gives the impression of a Kafka-like nihilistic universe that does not want to exist, Lang's film deals with the ambiguity of guilt and innocence. Based on a novel by Agatha Christie (<u>Murder in the Vicarage</u>), <u>Beyond</u> shows a hero who begins as innocent, makes himself appear guilty, turns out to be innocent, and

is finally found guilty just as the film ends. The only
sure thing is that we never know who is really guilty.
Lang thus converts the genre to a negative one that conforms
to his vision of life.

241  Patalas, Enno. "Fritz Lang--Endstation 'Indisches Grabmal'?"
     Kirche und Film, No. 10 (October 11).
        Lang has returned to Germany. He has surprised those
     interested in film with his announcement that he wants to
     film Das indische Grabmal [The Indian Tomb]. No other re-
     turned Hollywood expatriates have until now tried to make
     a contribution to the contemporary German scene. Is it
     Lang who can give new impulses to the benumbed West German
     film?
        Der müde Tod [Destiny] was Lang's breakthrough. Never
     before had sets and lighting been so rigorously put in the
     service of the director. All the means of expression avail-
     able to silent film worked together, creating a fatalistic
     atmosphere. Hereafter, the fascination with an unaviodable
     fate was a leitmotif not only in Lang's films, but also in
     other representative German works.
        While in Der müde Tod, fate, the real main character in all
     of Lang's German films, appeared as a fairy-tale messenger
     of death in black robes, in Dr. Mabuse, der Spieler [Dr.
     Mabuse, the Gambler], fate appeared in the contemporary
     figure of a brilliant criminal. Although not personified
     in Die Nibelungen, fate pulled all the strings here too.
     Its agents were the heroes' overpowering passions.
        The powerful and effective stylization of Metropolis
     makes it a formal masterpiece despite its naive-sentimental
     resolution of class conflict on the level of utopian pulp
     novels. Again Lang devised optic formulas for fate, whose
     expressive power leaves the subject matter of the film far
     behind. The child murderer in M is, like Mabuse, an insane
     criminal, but he is more a subordinate agent of fate--like
     all the heroes in Lang's German films.
        Hitler never allowed Das Testament des Dr. Mabuse [The
     Last Will of Dr. Mabuse] to be shown, although he openly
     admired Die Nibelungen and Metropolis. The reason for
     Hitler's divided reaction must be sought in Lang's works.
     They demonstrate a strong fascination with the aura of
     power as an expression of fate, but Lang also communicated
     a sense of its destructive capacity.
        Lang's first three American films belong to the genre of
     social criticism. Fury, You Only Live Once, and You and Me
     deal with lynch justice, discrimination against exconvicts,
     mistaken verdicts, and other flaws of society. Neverthe-
     less all these films see social ills as agents of unescap-
     able fate.
        With The Return of Frank James a new Fritz Lang was re-
     vealed: the skilled director who learned the lessons of

American films and adapted himself to changed circumstances
The best film of his American period, Hangmen Also Die, is
as much the work of the scriptwriter, Bertolt Brecht, and
of the composer, Hanns Eisler, as it is Lang's.

Lang expressly turned away from his earlier pessimistic
attitude after the war. He does not require the unquali-
fied happy ending, but instead seeks positive solutions.
In Lang's postwar films, which are routine, undemanding
melodramas, this was scarcely expressed. Was it his failing or that of a commercial production? Will he take greater freedom in Germany? The choice of the dusty Indische
Grabmal [Indian Tomb] for his German comeback seems to answer these questions in the negative.


### 1959

242   Borde, R.; Buache, F.; and Courtade, F.  "M--Le Maudit."  In
      Le Cinéma Realiste Allemand.  Lausanne:  Cinémathèque
      Suisse, pp. 59-68.
         This article consists of a summary of the plot, a list-
      ing of the main shots in the film, and a study of themes.
      The authors argue that M reflects the concerns of the per-
      iod in which it was made rather than being an individual
      case study.  The film reflects Lang's concern over the in-
      crease in fascism, both as a Jew and as a leftist.  He ex-
      poses the decadence of his society--the scorn for the po-
      lice, the effective criminal organization, the sense that
      anything is possible.  The murderer stands for everyone.
         The article concludes with an analysis of Lang's cine-
      matic techniques, camera movements, montage, shots, and
      sound.  The techniques serve the narrative rather than be-
      ing mere expressionist decoration.

243   Demonsablon, Phillipe.  "Le Tigre d'Argol."  Cahiers du Cinéma
      (Paris), No. 98 (August), pp. 58-59.
         Demonsablon notes how many echoes of Lang's earlier films
      are contained in the remake of Der Tiger von Eschnapur [The
      Tiger of Bengal], but says that this is what one would ex-
      pect of a project originally conceived at the start of a
      long career.  Lang seized the opportunity to affirm the
      continuity of his work, not wishing to deny anything.  There
      are echoes of Metropolis, Destiny, You Only Live Once,
      Ministry of Fear, and Woman in the Window.  Characteristic
      of Lang is the achievement of unity within diversity.
      Demonsablon notes the careful symmetry of the film--torn
      apart for commercial reasons--with events from the first
      half repeated in the second.  But there is also a balancing
      between opposed tendencies--the one toward profusion and
      extravagance and the other toward barrenness.  Far from be-
      ing mutually exclusive, Demonsablon asserts, these depend

on each other.

The order in many Lang films rests on the paradox that intelligence is used in a rigorous way to control chaos. Lang works hard to create a world that has little to do with the one we know. He chooses India for these films because of its exotic, fabulous palaces, its fasts, and charlatans. The "real" does not interest Lang, who deals in appearances, presenting a beautiful disorder of images.

Lang here confirms his aim of reconstructing the real. Das indische Grabmal [The Indian Tomb] is an example of a cinema freed from verisimilitude, with no other object than pure spectacle. Made for simple contemplation, the film continues Lang's trend toward abstraction.

244    Demonsablon, Phillipe. "La Hautaine Dialectique de Fritz Lang." Cahiers du Cinéma (Paris), No. 99 (September), pp. 10-18.

Demonsablon outlines Lang's major abstract themes:  revenge, innocence and defiance, fear of solitude, and fear of promiscuity.  But within the constancy of themes there is a certain diversity.  Contradictions and reversals are typical of Lang's films, for once he has assembled enough in one direction, the film turns in the opposite one.  Giving examples from four key films (M, You Only Live Once, Woman in the Window, and The Big Heat), Demonsablon shows that a dialectical movement is at work.

You Only Live Once, for example, again introduces notions of guilt and innocence.  The dialectic here is between the hero and society, with which he is always out of harmony. Eddie is found guilty at the very moment when innocence is established or innocent at the moment that guilt is established.  Unlike Hawks, who wanted to unite the individual and society, Lang insists on the inevitability of opposition.

Fascinated with Woman in the Window, which he sees as an earlier version of Beyond A Reasonable Doubt, Demonsablon argues that the film presents a world not so much imaginary as rigorously possible.  It attributes to reality that which belongs in a world of fiction and shows that people are the only anomaly in a world governed by fixed laws.  Everything in a Lang film is premeditated and inevitable, so that the more active heroes are, the more they in fact stay still.

Lang often prepares for disaster by allowing characters a moment of repose, as, for example, in The Blue Gardenia, where the character played by Anne Baxter sits down for a meal before she opens her fiancé's letter.  He also arranges things so that we have to confront horror, e.g., the corpse in Woman in the Window, the accused in Fury watching the film of their lynching, the character played by Marlene Dietrich in Rancho Notorious being shot in the exact spot where the brooch was.  But Lang gives us occasional glimpses of softness, particularly in Sylvia Sidney's roles when she

is allowed certain sensuous moments. It is as if Lang is
permitting us a moment of respite while he gathers his
thoughts for the horror to come.

245    Douchet, Jean. "L'Oeuvre de Fritz Lang à la Cinémathèque.
       Le Piège Considéré Comme l'un des Beaux-Arts." Arts (Paris),
       No. 729 (1-7 July), p. 6.
          Douchet surveys Lang's achievement as a director on the
       occasion of a retrospective at the Cinémathèque Française,
       when Lang was acclaimed by young people. Commenting on the
       influence Lang has had on directors from Hitchcock to Max
       Ophuls and from Eisenstein to Welles, Douchet notes that
       Lang's persistent expressionism can be annoying today. The
       films of his youthful period are particularly tiresome be-
       cause of his taste for the colossal, the geometrical con-
       struction of the sets, his love of sharp angles, and his
       oppressive contrasts of shadow and light. Yet these sys-
       tematic elements make it easier to see the great idea under-
       lying Lang's work.
          Unlike Murnau or Hitchcock, Lang refuses to see the
       dramatic struggle in life. While he is a tragic director,
       he presents a closed universe, surrounded by shadow that is
       never penetrated by light. People, for Lang, are eternally
       trapped in a silent, immobile world deprived even of the
       possibility of drama. The only movement Lang can introduce
       is that of time; obsessed with the notion of fate, Lang
       establishes circumstances that always lead necessarily in
       a certain direction.
          But the rigorous logic of Lang's narrative sits uneasily
       with his romanticism, which denounces the vices of society
       --lynching, police corruption, the corrupt press. Thus he
       is sometimes sentimental or naive. The Langian hero is
       always a noble man caught in a solid web of events that
       work against him. Revolted by injustice, the hero seeks
       revenge and becomes a victim of absolute justice.
          The moral of Lang's work is resignation, acceptance of
       one's lot. Only by practicing the most noble virtues may
       one live safely. His films do not expand outwards in some
       kind of progressive development, but instead with each new
       film Lang becomes more abstract, more oriented toward genre
       and mise-en-scène. His world is a haunted, passionate one,
       but Douchet questions whether it is sufficient.

246    Franju, Georges. "Le Style de Fritz Lang." Cahiers du Cinéma
       (Paris), No. 100 (November), pp. 16-22. [First printed in
       another form in Cinématographe, March 1939 and reprinted in
       Vialle, G., Franju (Paris, 1968). A complete translation
       by Sally Iannotti may be found in Braudy, L., and Dickstein,
       Morris, eds., Great Film Directors. New York: Oxford
       University Press, 1978. Pp. 583-589.
          A series of notes rather than a developed argument, this

piece focuses on important aspects of Lang's themes and style. Although Lang's approach is not sociological, he always dreams of justice. His outlook is definitely philosophical to begin with, but with Metropolis he introduces the sociological dimension and in M places absolute justice in opposition to the laws that are manifest in specific institutions.

Giving examples from M, Dr. Mabuse, der Spieler, and Liliom, Franju shows how Lang always sympathizes with people who are down, no matter what their sins or the ways in which they might have fought against the dogmas of a corrupt society.

Franju next turns to Lang's editing techniques, claiming that he discovered "intuitive" editing early, as contrasted with editing to follow the narrative at one extreme or seeking to be artistic by using an impressionistic camera at the other. (Examples here from Destiny, M, Liliom, and Das Testament.) Denying that Lang relies on theatrical elements in his mise-en-scène, Franju argues that Lang's decor instead manifests a primordial concern for a spiritual energy. One can see this in Lang's love of the spectacular, as in the explosions in Metropolis and Woman in the Moon or in the flood scenes in Metropolis and Dr. Mabuse, der Spieler. In line with this are the intense, dramatic facial expressions of key Lang actors--Brigitte Helm, Bernard Goetzke, Klein-Rogge, Peter Lorre.

Franju concludes that Lang's concern with truth is marked by a personal sense of injustice and an identification with the lowly, which is reflected in his visual style. An energy both spiritual and physical dominates his work, sometimes touching the heart and always the nerves.

247  Hoveyda, Fereydoun. "Les Indes Fabulées." [Review of The Tiger of Bengal and The Indian Tomb]. Cahiers du Cinéma (Paris), No. 99 (September), pp. 56-58.

Hoveyda begins by anticipating complaints that future Lang critics will make of these films and agreeing that, looking from the outside, one could take a scornful attitude. Hoveyda believes, however, that these films show us more about Lang than do earlier works and are important.

Hoveyda discusses briefly how the films evoke childhood pleasures in the serials with their chain of escapades, quasi-metaphysical element, and one-dimensional characters in the grip of inexorable destiny. The films look back to Die Spinnen [The Spiders], but also continue the abstract trend and linear construction of the last American films.

Discussing in some detail the visual style of these works, especially the beautiful decors, Hoveyda shows how scenes of great simplicity alternate with bravura shots and complicated camera movements. Lang uses the glance to create suspense, the eyes replacing the parallel montage found in a director like Hitchcock. The decor of the films recalls that in Die Nibelungen and Metropolis, while the use of color is at times hallucinatory. Lang's use of rhythm and composition attain their height, and it is here that we find the films' importance rather than in the story line. We realize from the start that this is not realism.

Although Hoveyda does not scorn the story line, he thinks it worth asking why Lang chose it; possibly Lang had in mind a homage to Thea von Harbou, who had written the script for the Joe May Indian films with Lang. Here for once love triumphs. Although good and evil are simplistically opposed in the films, the real meaning for Lang lies in the beauty of renunciation. Apparently in the Joe May films, the German engineer and the Indian dancer are the heroes, but the Maharaj is most important for Lang. The theme, in any event, is not so slight, since it deals with the problem of solitude and the ability of East and West to understand each other.

The films are finally interesting in showing that Lang is more moralist than psychologist. A recent Lang retrospective makes this clear. The Indian films are important for their hallucinatory visual style, their perfect mise-en-scène and their ultimate moral.

248  Luft, Herbert G. "Eric Pommer: Part Two." Films in Review (New York), (November), pp. 518-33

Luft begins by noting that Pommer was put in charge of Ufa's production in 1923. The German government then no longer had a say in what films would or would not be produced. It was Pommer who insisted on the happy ending in The Last Laugh and on the framing story for Caligari.

The major Ufa production in 1926 was Lang's Metropolis. Luft notes in passing that neither Lang nor Thea von Harbou had had any contact with workers. He then goes into detail about the film's production, e.g., the fact that the sets were models built by architect Kettlebut who had worked with Lang on Die Nibelungen and the fact that some of the actors were ones already used by Lang (Klein-Rogge and Abel), but that the young lovers (Gustav Fröhlich and Brigitte Helm) were totally new.

When Hitler became Chancellor of the Third Reich in January 1933, Pommer resigned from Ufa and left Germany for Paris, where he was put in charge of Fox's European production. It was through this contact that Lang made Liliom in 1934 and then, when Fox could no longer afford to make films in Europe, Pommer and Lang went to the United States.

249  Moullet, Luc. "Excercise de Style." Arts (Paris), No. 733 (July 22), p. 7.

Moullet notes that Lang, finally disillusioned with the American experience, returned to Germany where he made Der

Tiger von Eschnapur [The Tiger of Bengal] (1958). While it
is the best film to come out of Germany in twenty-six years,
this is due rather to the meager talent in the German cinema
than to the film's excellence. In the context of Lang's
whole work, Der Tiger is a minor film; we catch only glimpses
of Lang's genius in a film that he had wanted to make for
forty years. The script is nothing, the characters are unreal (which is rare for a Lang film), and Lang did not try
to humanize this schematic work.

Paradoxically, Moullet says, the degree to which the film
is empty is also the degree to which it is rich. It is a
cold, icy world, a world of absences, and this creates a
sense of mystery and anxiety not unlike that in recent
Hitchcock films. This iciness gives the film its beauty
more than the scenes where Lang uses pastiches of his earlier films or posits an easy opposition between people and
the universe.

250   Mourlet, Michel. "Trajectoire de Fritz Lang." Cahiers du
      Cinéma (Paris), No. 99 (September), pp. 19-35.
      Mourlet begins with philosophical speculations about the
ultimate nature of cinema and then discusses Lang's attempt
to eliminate chance in his films. Lang's frames are composed so compellingly that the spectators, fascinated, are
unable to detach themselves.

Since Lang began making films in the silent era, it is
not surprising that his work reflects the progression of
cinematic form. He began when it was legitimate for cinema
to be a geometry of space, as contrasted with what it would
become in the sound era, a geometry of the soul. Expressionism was a perfect movement for the silent cinema, since
it encouraged abstraction. Gestures became decorative and
subject to the laws of symmetry.

For Mourlet, therefore, Lang's sound period represents
a falling-away from the pure state of the silent film, its
rigorousness sacrificed to ideas and the impurity of moral
postulates that falsify the play of existence. M and You
Only Live Once fail because Lang has not yet mastered ideas
and words, or found ways to integrate them into the mise-
en-scène. Only with the films made after the war does Lang
again manage to integrate image and concept (See Ministry
of Fear, Rancho Notorious, Human Desire, The Big Heat, and
Moonfleet), and Mourlet finds the culmination of Lang's
mature work in Beyond A Reasonable Doubt and Das indische
Grabmal [The Indian Tomb].

Lang's work does not, of course, progress in a direct
line. There were false starts and reversals (Fury, for example, was the best of the prewar films), but in general
the films follow the pattern outlined. By 1948, Lang no
longer makes the image the mere support of sound, a superficial decoration, but rather mise-en-scène is innate to

meaning. The change, according to Mourlet, comes about because Lang detached himself from those who thought of mise-
en-scène merely as a way of presenting a story on the screen.
 Mourlet illustrates this point by showing the development
from Clash by Night, where the mise-en-scène is too literal
and relies on psychological clichés, through Human Desire,
which is closer to integration, on to The Tiger of Bengal
which Mourlet considers a brilliant representation of love
and hate in their pure state; there are no more themes,
ideas of mise-en-scène, or characters here, but rather naked
passions themselves constituting the filmic world.
 Lang's art, Mourlet goes on to argue, is formalized:
he creates a world where each element is indispensable to
the whole and does not exist for itself. He objectified
his passions and placed them in an absolute, silent, and
lucid world close to that of the mathematician. He is like
Mallarmé in his interest in pure art and in form.
 Mourlet ends by discussing the typical Langian universe:
the individual is plunged into a hostile milieu, brilliantly
expressed by Lang's use of decor, which evokes feelings of
terror, of suffocation, and of the awful. It is a terrifying unalterable universe full of hate, premeditated murder,
and a sad eroticism, offering only the alternatives of killing or being killed. In a kind of Hegelian dialectic, every
conscience wishes the death of the other, using as pretexts
personal vengeance, legal punishment, or collective persecution. Cold relationships, worn faces, and frigid women
dominate a universe in which the individual waits for the
lash to fall.

251 Mourlet, Michel. "Billet Londonien." Cahiers du Cinéma
 (Paris), No. 102 (December), pp. 38-41.
 Mourlet notes that House by the River appeared three
years later than Secret Beyond the Door, but nevertheless
he sees the two films as forming a unit thematically and in
terms of mise-en-scène. House by the River is a terrifying
film, where desire leads to strangulation. More clearly
than in any other film, Lang here explores erotic obsession.
 The unit that these films form is part of a general movement in Lang's later career that culminated in Der Tiger von
Eschnapur [The Tiger of Bengal]. The mise-en-scène, however, is partially abandoned as Lang learned to be more
disciplined and sparse. House by the River lacks the bleak
sense of eternity that spreads over Beyond a Reasonable
Doubt.

252 P. S. "Un Super-navet signé de Fritz Lang." Radio-Cinéma-
 Télévision (Paris), Nos. 500-501 (16 and 23 August).
 Writing from a moral and political position, the reviewer
takes a dislike to the Indian films. He finds the first
part extremely boring and pretentious and mocks the heavy-

handed themes ("subject cornelienne comme vous voyez--
conflit entre deux civilizations") ("It's theme, you see,
is one found often in Corneille--the conflict between two
civilizations."). He notes sardonically that the film cost
one million dollars, while in India a bowl of rice could
save a life.

The reviewer is equally ironic about the second part of
the film. He says that the boredom here is as fatal as in
the first half and that the whole is insipid, despite a few
scenes where Lang parodies his own earlier works.

253   Th. K.  "Gefährliche Begegnung."  [Review of Woman in the
      Window].  Filmkritik, (No. 7).

Th. K. begins by discussing the way Lang incorporates
important elements of the type of criminal melodrama he
developed in Germany, in his Hollywood films. The New York
setting of Woman in the Window is as abstract as the
Dusseldorf of M; the surface "reality" of its streets and
interiors is transformed by the sinister story to create the
twilight atmosphere of a nightmare world. Lang achieves
this effect by building sets with cold, anonymous buildings
and then creating a painterly look through the semidarkness
of the lighting. In addition, the film takes place mainly
at night and indoors, and its rhythm is deliberately slow-
moving.

According to Th. K., the super-human aspect of this
world exercises a power like that of fate itself, causing
people to move about like puppets. We share the anxieties
of the people, but we learn almost nothing about them, so
that their actions have a relentless, somnambulant logic.

Th. K. points out the similarity between the scene in M
where the little girl sees the reflection of the murderer
in the shop window and that in Woman in the Window where the
professor watches as the portrait of the model merges with
her reflection. The events move deliberately to their catastrophic end, at which point we find out that the horror,
enacted so powerfully, was only a dream. Th. K. can only
conclude that Lang was trying to combine art and light entertainment here, since he denies that the "happy end" was
added for commercial reasons.

254   W. F.  "Ausgerechnet der Tiger von Eschnapur."  Rhein-Neckar-
      Zeitung (Heidelberg) (22 November).

The critic notes how the post-World War II German film
industry tried hard to become engaged again in the international film market, and how it needed a good director to
get things going. Lang's name often came up as the person
able to give German film the lift it needed. The German
film clubs attempted to bring Lang's work to people's notice with retrospectives of his films. Lang finally came
and made the Indian films, choosing an adventure film set

in an exotic land with which to enliven cinema. He presents
an old tale in modern style.
The critic concludes by stressing his belief in Lang's
ability to do good work.


## 1960

255   Anon. "Der Vater des Dr. Mabuse: Fritz Lang wird 70 Jahre
      alt." Stuttgarter Zeitung (2 December).
      The author briefly outlines Lang's contributions to the
      early German film, noting how he sent the expressionist
      film on its way with Der müde Tod [Destiny]. In his Mabuse
      films, Lang achieved a remarkable mixture of the mystery
      film, the grotesque, and daily realities. He predicted the
      terror of the dictator in his last Mabuse film and intro-
      duced politics in M. He made Fury, a film about lynching,
      in America and then returned to Germany to make the Indian
      films and yet another film about Mabuse.

256   Arbois, Janick. "Moonfleet." Radio-Cinéma-Télévision (Paris),
      No. 533, (3 April), p. 52.
      Arbois relates the film to the novels of Stevenson and
      Dickens. But he says it's not at all an ordinary film. It
      does not evoke other films so much as adventure stories from
      childhood. Yet while the film is attractive and pleasant,
      it does not reflect Lang's genius. It was a film Lang had
      to make and not one where he was in charge of the material.

257   Bernard, Marc. Brief Notes on Die tausend Augen des Dr. Mabuse
      and Moonfleet. Cahiers du Cinéma (Paris), No. 109 (July),
      p. 42.
      Bernard begins by noting Lang's complaint that Moonfleet
      was not edited in the way he wanted. Although he has not
      made a film for two years, Lang was under contract with a
      German company for three films--the two Indian ones already
      done and another Mabuse film (with an original script by
      Lang), which is about to be released. All those who liked
      the Indian films are waiting excitedly for the Mabuse.
      The film had its origin in a newspaper article about a new
      American weapon that does not produce a visible wound.
      Lang says the film has no political or aesthetic preoccupa-
      tion, but "will be a brutal, realistic film. The first to
      be killed will be a T.V. reporter."

258   Clarens, Carlos. "Journey to the Lost City." Films in Review
      (New York), 8, No. 11 (December), 617.
      Clarens discusses the history of the film, noting that
      it is a remake of the Joe May movie from the 1920s and that
      the American version is a truncated one combining the two
      parts of the original. He still considers it fun, concluding

that "the result, if not taken seriously, is a fun-show all
the way. The cliché climaxes are intact."

259    Davidson, Bernard.  Review of <u>Moonfleet</u>.  <u>Cinéma 60</u> (Paris),
       No. 46 (May), pp. 124-125.
          Davidson makes a few general comments about Lang and then
       argues that in <u>Moonfleet</u> Lang was unable to capture the
       beautiful theme in the novel of the same name (by John Meade
       Falkner) of the strange relationship between a young boy and
       the leader of an outlaw gang.  The rich language of the
       English text is not translated into film terms.  While he
       praises Lang's sense of the fantastic, Davidson regrets
       that this is not integrated into the film as a whole.

259a   De Laura, David.  "Notes on Lang's <u>Metropolis</u>."  In Lennig, A.,
       ed., <u>Film Notes of the Wisconsin Film Society</u>.  Madison:
       Film Society Press, pp. 36-37.
          According to De Laura, <u>Metropolis</u> marks the high point
       of the expressionist film, although he thinks that it suf-
       fers from being made without sound.  Its magnificent use of
       lighting and spatial effects and the symbolic involvement
       of people and machines in the modern world are especially
       noteworthy.

260    Douchet, Jean.  "<u>Moonfleet</u>."  <u>Cahiers du Cinéma</u> (Paris), No.
       107 (May), pp. 44-47.
          Noting the introduction to the film-the shots of surging
       waves-Douchet says we need to recognize the poetry that lies
       at the base of all Lang's films, without denying Lang's
       ability to handle concepts dialectically.  Divorced from all
       social context, <u>Moonfleet</u> is freed to be a drunken explora-
       tion of adventure.  While the film has been compared to
       works by Dickens, Stevenson, and Poe, Lang has made the
       subject his own.
          The film is about the descent of innocence into the
       guilt of passions and human turmoil.  Everything seeks in-
       evitably to destroy the child and innocence, but, true to
       the genre, innocence triumphs.
          Douchet links the sensation of descent to the reverie of
       a poet; in the very midst of the dark passages and corridors,
       the places where terror lurks-like the lepers in <u>Der Tiger
       von Eschnapur</u> [The Tiger of Bengal]-and even when the child
       is faced with horror directly, Lang explores the intimate
       corners of his soul.  All exorcism involves freeing monsters
       -the dragon reemerges in each Lang film and presents a chal-
       lenge to the hero, who has only high moral values with which
       to fight.  In <u>Moonfleet</u>, Lang takes a terrifying look at
       himself, uncovering his most secret impulses.  Monstrous
       degradation is pitted against what is most beautiful in the
       human being.
          Four people reflect the different sides of Lang:  the

boy, innocence; Fox, ambition and greed (although he is able
to respond to innocence); Lord Ashwood, cynicism; and the
old procurer, pure evil. Fox is the Langian hero who is
torn between two movements--the one towards greed, the self;
the other, a higher one, towards the pure kind of love he
manifests for the boy. The way Fox breaks the circle he is
in is presented visually each time he saves the boy; his
own conscience, his superior self breaks his criminal course.

Douchet concludes with a short discussion of the function
of women in the film. Olivia, John Mohune's mother, is the
ideal woman, who haunts Jeremy Fox and represents his better
self. But there are three degraded images of her, representing the reverse of the ideal: the sensual dancer; the
passionate, jealous lover; and the cruel, greedy Lady
Ashwood.

261   The Editors. "Le Retour de Frank James," in the section
      "Chacque Semaine L'Analyse d'un Grand Film." Radio-Cinéma-
      Télévision (Paris), No. 536 (April 24), pp. 47-48.
      Following the format for these analyses, there is first
      a Lang filmography. The editors next explain the relation-
      ship of Lang's film to the real history of the James brothers,
      quoting largely from J. L. Rieupeyrout, Le Western, and con-
      cluding that the film does not stick very closely to history.
      The following discussion of Henry King's Jesse James shows
      that King also took liberties with the truth.
      The next section deals with the main theme of the film,
      vengeance, with quotations from Godard's essay on The
      Return of Frank James in Image et Son, No. 95 (See Entry
      No. 223).
      The section on Lang's style deals mainly with the mise-
      en-scène in the film. The authors show that Lang's main
      aim is not to evoke passion or pity for his hero but to
      present him as confronting a destiny larger than himself.
      The abstractness of Lang's vision arises from his refusal
      to isolate his heroes from the spatial context through which
      their destiny is revealed. Far from wanting to show pity
      for a suffering man, which is after all quite easy, Lang at
      his best shows instead the inextricable link between indi-
      vidual human destiny and the universe.
      Beyond a Reasonable Doubt is an example of the mathema-
      tical rigor of Lang's mise-en-scène, while Der Tiger von
      Eschnapur [The Tiger of Bengal] demonstrates a brilliant
      geometric design. The script only has validity once it has
      been transcended by the mise-en-scène and given its function
      as spatial sign. "The mise-en-scène consists in transcrib-
      ing the signs of a story in space with the greatest effi-
      ciency and economy."

262   Krusche, Dieter. "Der Architekt auf dem Regiestuhl."
      Frankfurter Rundschau (5 December).

Krusche accounts for the ornamental style of many Lang
films by the fact that he first studied architecture. Both
the interest in architecture and in fate can be seen in his
first work, Der müde Tod [Destiny], which Lang made after
being wounded in the war. The forms and themes of the early
works prepared for Lang's future films. People interest him
less as individuals than as objects of fate or, as in Die
Nibelungen, for their mythic dimension. These themes are
reflected in the use of the camera to create magnificent
compositions, including huge lines and decoration, which
surround people, leaving them as faceless entities in the
mass.

The Mabuse films, reflecting the insanity of the period
following the First World War, take on meaning in the light
of the above themes; one can also understand Lang's interest
in the child murderer, caught between the force of evil, on
the one hand, and that of the police and the underground on
the other.

The American films that parallel the monumental ones of
the German period reflect the same theme of the unwilling
criminal. Once in the United States, Lang specialized in
thrillers in the style of Mabuse and M, but he also made
films about the war and Westerns.

His return to Germany to do two remakes was a mistake,
although Der Tiger von Eschnapur [The Tiger of Bengal] has
good visual effects and Die tausend Augen des Dr. Mabuse
[The Thousand Eyes of Dr. Mabuse] reflects the hard-nosed
reality of the present.

Lang is seventy years old. Krusche hopes that he will
discover his own links with the past, and that he will
emerge from the political disfavor that had been his. He
also hopes that Lang's films will be known not only as an
important part of film history, but as crucial for understanding the present.

263 Lennig, A., ed. "Notes on Lang's Nibelungen Saga" in his Film
Notes of the Wisconsin Film Society Madison: Film Society
Press, pp. 13-20.

Lennig spends most of the article justifying Lang's crea-
tion of a nationalist epic in the light of Siegfried
Kracauer's criticism in From Caligari to Hitler:  A
Psychological History of the German Film (1947). He derides
Kracauer's method as simplistic, a mere arbitrary assigning
of blame for the emergence of Hitler.

He then discusses the decorative aspects of Siegfried--
the impressive studio sets, and the larger-than-life quality
of the mythic tale that recalls Eisenstein's Nevsky or Ivan
the Terrible. The pace of the film is carefully varied to
suit the action. Kriemhild's Revenge contains none of the
supernatural, mythic elements of the first part, the atmosphere instead being one of somber revenge suited to the new

situation. Kriemhild's Medea-like behavior is perhaps too sympathetically viewed, from the Christian standpoint anyway. The moral rightness of seeking this kind of revenge is not raised. Kriemhild is too inhuman and abstractly treated for us to feel her dilemma as tragic.

264   Luft, Friedrich. "Ein Expressionist an der Kamera." Die Welt (Hamburg) (3 December).
      Writing on the occasion of Lang's seventieth birthday, Luft notes that Lang was one of the great visual artists of the silent film, coming, as he did, out of painting and architecture and never abandoning those arts. He dealt with more than just the narrative and the actors, since realism was never his style.
      When his films were good, which was not always, they represented expressionism at its best. We remember them for their stark power. One recalls Siegfried's ride through the forest, the Dance of Death in Der müde Tod [Destiny], or the flood-scene in Metropolis, a film now often considered silly. Lang's penchant was for the uncanny, the terror of the unknown, the game with danger; beauty was not his interest. Using his camera expressionistically, Lang created an image of madness on the screen. His best work, M, came between the silent and the sound film, and influenced Hitchcock greatly.
      He went to Hollywood after this, where he made Fury and then the Germans called him back in the late 1950s and he made sentimental Indian films. However, the long-awaited return of the Great Director was a flop.
      Luft ends by hoping that Lang will once again make an outstanding film.

265   Moullet, Luc. "L'Enfer des films de Fritz Lang, est-il l'antichambre de la sagesse?" Radio-Cinéma-Télévision (Paris), No. 551 (7 August), pp. 42-43.
      Moullet argues that Moonfleet is imperfect but nevertheless reveals the typical Langian world, despite the fact that many scenes are missing due to conflict with the producers. The boy, representing innocence, moves through a cruel and evil world to which he remains as indifferent as Lang himself. If Lang tries to expose the most repugnant aspects of vice, greed, and violence, this is a deliberate attempt to reach a public that is impervious to Christian appeals. While Lang condemns vice, he does, like many Germans, also recognize its aesthetic attraction. Moullet notes that all his life Lang was fascinated by adventure, horror, and the fantastic. He concludes that Moonfleet would be less beautiful if the people were less ugly, both physically and morally. Fox himself, nevertheless, is vulnerable to the boy's innocence and offers him friendship.

266    Pem [Paul Marcus]. "Der umstrittene Klassiker des Zelluloids."
       Film-Telegram (1 December) [written on the occasion of
       Lang's seventieth birthday]. Available in Deutschen Film
       und Fernsehakademie, W. Berlin.
            Marcus begins by emphasizing how controversial Lang was
       in the early German period. Berlin critics were split at
       each Lang premier because of the tension between form and
       content in the films: some critics hated the Wagnerian
       subject matter, others the monumental sumptuousness of
       Lang's visual style. But the controversy did not hinder
       Lang's career or prevent his films from being shown all over
       the world.
            Marcus next goes briefly over Lang's background and ca-
       reer, listing the early films and the actors and actresses
       that he used. According to Marcus, Lang was particularly
       lucky to have Erich Pommer as a friend and both Pommer and
       Seymour Nebenzal as producers. After a worldwide success
       with M, Lang's Fury (made in America) also did well and
       showed that Lang had not lost his mastery. While he aban-
       doned his German style, Land did not forget his European
       origins, working with Kurt Weill on You and Me. Woman in
       the Window was noteworthy, and Lang later won a prize with
       Moonfleet.
            Lang was a pioneer in a new art form, carving out a place
       for himself here. While his films sometimes disappointed
       his followers, he always hoped for box office successes.
       Marcus ends by noting that behind Lang's monocle, which gave
       him a snobbish air, there was a man who had dedicated his
       life to film, living it twenty-four hours a day. This has
       been both his strength and weakness as a pioneer in film
       for fifty years.

267    Pepe, Nico. "Fritz Lang In Patria Con Un Nuovo Mabuse" [Fritz
       Lang in His Country with a New Mabuse]. Corriere Lombardo
       (1 June).
            Nico Pepe, an Italian actor, reports from Berlin that
       Lang, the famous German director, back from Hollywood, is
       making a new film with his old terrifying character. Pepe
       notes that while at an art cinema M is being shown, Lang
       is directing Die tausend Augen des Dr. Mabuse [The Thousand
       Eyes of Dr. Mabuse], the continuation of a film made thirty
       years ago.

268    Porges, Friedrich. "Filmschöpfer in zwei Erdteilen: Fritz
       Lang." Aufbau ("Die Westküste"), (2 December).
            This article was written just after Lang had returned
       from making his last Mabuse film in Germany. Porges notes
       how Lang has always been able to work in any country in the
       world, and is now planning a new project, although he will
       not say where it will be filmed.
            Now seventy years old, Lang has behind him a whole series

of interesting and artistic films. Porges proceeds to survey the main films, noting that both his silent and early
sound films are classics, M in particular being shown in
cinemas all over the world.

Porges concludes that Lang has influenced the standards
of film as an art form and improved the American film with
his dynamic, realist style. An intense, serious artist,
Lang views film as a vocation, not a job.

269   Ramseger, Georg. "30 Jahre alt und alterlos: In der Urania
      ist Fritz Langs M jetzt wieder greifbar." Die Welt
      (Hamburg) (16 January).

      According to Ramseger, the restoration of the movie M
has been so successful that the technical limitations of a
thirty-year-old film are hardly noticeable. Beyond that,
the quality of the film remains wonderfully preserved.

      Ramseger notes that the pictorial language is still that
of expressionism. This is balanced by the constant, reso-
lute forward motion of the plot. This film is steeped in
the cynicism of Berlin in the twenties. Today, when the
detective film indulges in brutality, it has the crude division between good and evil as an alibi. With Lang, this
division is anything but crude.

270   Reimar, Richard. "Ein Wegbereiter unseres goldenen
      Filmzeitalters: Am 5. Dezember vollendet Filmregisseur
      Fritz Lang das 70. Lebensjahr." Recklinghauser-Zeitung
      (3 December).

      Reimar notes ironically how differently Lang is viewed
in America (where he's seen as a commercial director), in
France (where he is considered the greatest director in the
world), and in Germany (where until recently he was known
only for his early German masterpieces). When he returned
to Germany in 1958 he fullfilled his wish of making the
Indian films that he had planned as early as 1920.

      Reimar reviews Lang's career briefly, concluding that
his visual style marks him as a great filmmaker. His compositions always have a dynamic element that, combined with
symbolism, produces a refined psychological analysis of
human experience. For Lang, people are always held fast in
the grip of fate.

      Other reviews on the occasion of Lang's seventieth birthday:
        Baer, Volker. "M brachte Ruhm und Feindschaft." Der
          Tagesspiegel (Berlin) (4 December 1960).
        Anon. "Wegbereiter des goldenen Filmzeitalters." West-
          deutsche Rundschau (Wuppertal-Barmen) (2 December 1960).
        Hdr [Hans-Dieter Roos]. "Ein Meister des expressionisti-
          chen Films." Süddeutsche Zeitung (Munich) (5 December).

271   MR [Ruppert, Martin]. "Der Filmpionier. Fritz Lang zum

siebzigsten." <u>Frankfurter Allegemeine Zeitung</u> (6 December).
After reviewing Lang's career and personal history,
Ruppert describes his influence on the art of film in the
early days of the film industry in Germany, when the Ufa
had Murnau, Weine, and many other great directors working
for it. He discusses briefly Lang's departure for Europe
and then America, his founding of Diana Productions in the
1940s, and his return to Germany in 1958 to make some films
that gave new life to the German film industry.

272    Sarris, Andrew. "El and <u>M</u>." The <u>Village Voice</u> (New York) (1
       September), pp. 6, 8.
       The review appears in connection with the showing of <u>El</u>
(by Buñuel) and <u>M</u> at the Bleecker Cinema. According to
Sarris, neither film is completely successful judged by
traditional standards. "Much of <u>M</u> bogs down somewhat in an
amicable underworld sub-plot." The acting is uneven, although Lorre's performance was ahead of its time.
       Each film provides a rare visual excitement that makes
up for deficiencies. Sarris refers to the shot of Elsie's
ball rolling on the grass as she is being murdered and to
the slow, symbolic evocation of violence. As in all his
films, Lang here evokes a sense of the danger endemic to
modern life.
       While both Lang and Buñuel are masters in their medium,
neither is Sarris's favorite. Sarris objects to Lang's
contempt for realism and detail in "his relentless quest
for violent climaxes . . . ." Yet both are inspired image-
makers, and this is interesting in an age when realism is
at a dead end.

273    Seuren, Gunther. "Der Alptraum ist gelieben: Fritz Lang's
       <u>M</u>." <u>Deutsche Zeitung</u> (Stuttgart-Köln) (22 June).
       Seuren begins by noting that for decades <u>M</u> has represent-
ed a standard for the quality film. He is writing on the
occasion of the showing of a restored print of the film,
which had been lost for years.
       According to Seuren, the film remains a Berlin nightmare
of beggars, unemployment and the social dissonances that
spawn the seeds of mass hysteria. The actual growth in
strength of the masses since the film's making gives <u>M</u>, a
film which raises doubts about modern life, an uncanny
relevance.
       <u>M</u> documents the days of organized crime in Berlin; Seuren
notes that the film's climax, with the victim's breakdown
in the face of lynch justice, represents the triumph of the
masses. Ultimately, however, Seuren argues that <u>M</u> reveals
the fact that being preyed upon is an irrevocable aspect of
life.

274    Vernon, Howard. "Lang." <u>Cahiers du Cinéma</u> (Paris), No. 111

(September), pp. 50-51.

Howard Vernon discusses his experiences as an actor in Fritz Lang's Die tausend Augen des Dr. Mabuse [The Thousand Eyes of Dr. Mabuse]. Noting the awe in which he held Lang, Vernon says he wanted to serve as material for Lang, using as his analogy the painter's assembling dots of paint on a canvas. Keeping up this comparison, Vernon recalls how Lang referred to himself as a "worker" rather than an "artist". In order to work successfully with Lang, Vernon says, one must value the film as much as oneself. All objects have importance in the mise-en-scène of a film, and the actor's face becomes simply one of the beautiful details in the whole.

Agreeing that Lang was often difficult, Vernon notes that Lang had as much right to demand perfection as did Michaelangelo. He concludes by saying how glad he is to have met Lang, whom he considers a great man.

275 Willmer, Herbert. "Lebt Dr. Mabuse noch?" [Newspaper not given. From file in the Deutsches Institut für Filmkunde, Wiesbaden].

The author begins with a plot summary of the film. Lang wants to repeat his Mabuse-successes of the twenties and thirties with Die tausend Augen des Dr. Mabuse [The Thousand Eyes of Dr. Mabuse]. To be sure, Dr. Mabuse died in an insane asylum at the beginning of the Hitler era, but his files have been stolen. One suspects that the methods and legacy of this awful monster are behind these crimes.

Lang does not give away all the connections. So far he has been able to keep the solution of this new movie a secret, which will only be revealed at the premiere of the film.

## 1961

276 Anon. "Fritz Lang und Bert Brecht." Neue Zürcher Zeitung (16 December).

The reviewer is writing on the occasion of a retrospective showing of Lang's Hangmen Also Die in Paris. He notes that while the extent of Brecht's participation in this film (never shown in Germany) is unclear, according to Joseph Losey, the idea for the plot came from Brecht while J. Wexley rewrote the final script. The main idea of the film, the reviewer comments, is original in a way reminiscent of Brecht; but Brecht's contribution was obviously reduced to a minimum, covered up with typical Hollywood dialogue attributable to Wexley.

This movie, according to the writer, brings us no closer to solving the puzzle of Fritz Lang, who made technically grandiose movies in the 1920s, realistic detective films in the 1930s, and thrillers afterwards, all evidencing a fascination with fate.

Returning to Hangmen Also Die, the reviewer notes that Lang thought it his best film since M; the writer agrees that Lang produced some brilliant moments from obstinate material. He concludes that while the film is an odd mixture of Lang's masterfully constructed detective world, Brecht's concept of a people united against a traiter, and intrusive Hollywood-style dramatic episodes, the film marks an important stage in Lang's work.

277    Bellour, Raymond. "M, Le Maudit." Cinéma 61 (Paris), No. 58, pp. 114-115.

Bellour describes the two main tendencies in the German cinema and in the German soul during the period when the film was made as the drives toward realism and toward expressionism. Lang creates a brilliant balance between these tendencies in M, synthesizing them primarily through creative use of sound.

278    Brunel, Philippe. "Fritz Lang Aujourd'hui." L'Express, No. 516 (4 May), pp. 48-49.

Brunel notes that although Lang's name does not mean much today, this was not always the case. From 1920 to 1940, a Lang film was a cinematic event, Lang was internationally famous, and his films were well attended. It is amazing that since 1940 he has worked in near obscurity; except for Woman in the Window, French critics have not received his films well; condescending to Lang, they constantly asked what had happened to the once great director.

Making a comparison to painting, Brunel argues that Lang moved from a kind of realism that was based on strong scripts (analogous to portrait painters) to focussing more and more on mise-en-scène. This is analogous to the impressionist painters, who showed that the theme of a painting was less important than how it was done. Many of the New Wave directors prefer Lang to all other filmmakers.

Brunel next goes into an extended account of Lang's personal background and outlines the main stages in his career. The last section of the article deals with Lang's cynicism regarding people. He increasingly came to believe that people strive only for material gain—for money, status, and power—ignoring the inner life, morality, and spirituality. The bleak mise-en-scène of the later films was intended to show the poverty of people's lives: characters are trapped by the frames, confined by their own attempts to control the world and to suppress everything that does not lead to material gain. Ironically, as Lang shows, all external conquest is vain; his heroes fail in their goals because people can conquer only themselves and for this must turn to their inner life.

279   D. K. [Dietrich Kuhlbrodt].  "M:  Wieder in Deutschland."
      Filmkritik (Munich), No. 3.
           Kuhlbrodt begins by noting the paradox that the Nazis
      allowed M to be shown once they realised that the sub-title,
      Mörder unter uns [Murderer(s) among us] did not refer to
      them.  But in fact the film does mirror the period and
      fascism.
           Kuhlbrodt next describes the surface level of the film,
      with the police and the underworld both hunting down the
      murderer.  But while the police win theoretically, Kuhlbrodt
      believes that the real power lies with the underworld.  He
      notes that the film shows the truth of things in the last
      year of the Weimar Republic, with the hierarchical govern-
      ment arrangement and the rebellious underworld.  But the
      government and the people take second place to the murderer,
      who is depicted as victim both of authority and of his inner
      impulses.

280   Domarchi, Jean.  "Avec M, Le Maudit, Fritz Lang en 1932
      Annonçait la Destinée de L'Allemagne."  Arts (Paris), No.
      819 (26 April-2 May), p. 7.
           The revival of M on the eve of the new Mabuse film,
      Domarchi says, allows us to reconsider the work of Lang as
      a great cinéaste.  Partly expressionist--for example, in
      its use of camera, decor, and mode of interpretation--and
      made on the eve of Hitler's rise to power, M shows a deep
      disturbance in the German sensibility.  First looking back
      to 1919, Domarchi suggests some of the economic and cultural
      causes for the disturbance.  He then looks even further
      back, to the Reformation, noting how the Germans inherited
      from the Greeks the idea of fate.  Habituated to the notion
      of the Apocalypse since the Thirty Years War, Germans have
      lived in simultaneous fear of, and wish for, the end of
      time.  Feeling guilty about omnipotent fantasies, the
      Germans gladly suffer punishment for them.
           The German antagonism to the Jews, Domarchi suggests,
      results from their sharing this German way of seeing.  The
      Germans want to annihilate Jews for a way of being that is
      too close to their own.
           Lang's films express this wrenching of conscience, etern-
      ally divided between delight in destruction and nostalgia
      for a calm life.  The murderer in M represents the German
      people, always driven to attack the good and innocent--
      hence Lang's sympathy for him.  The only safety is for the
      Germans to surrender to a higher international authority.
      M illustrates the theme that Metropolis and Frau im Mond
      [Woman in the Moon] had earlier expressed--that of what
      Hitler's world would be like.  The evil Maria in Metropolis
      is Hitler, dazzling everyone and leading them on, as the
      greedy capitalists in Frau im Mond [Woman in the Moon] lead
      everyone to destruction.

Lang remained interested in the underworld in his
American films, and his latest German films deal with the
theme again. One sees Lang's cinematic genius here, except
that the new films lack the excesses of the earlier ones.
Losey's remake of M suffers by comparison, not because Losey
is not a great filmmaker, but because he lacked Lang's feeling for horror.

281   Douchet, Jean. "Fritz Lang, un vieux seigneur." Arts (Paris),
      No. 827 (21-28 June), p. 13.
      This is essentially a profile of Fritz Lang on the occa-
sion of his visit to the Cinémathèque in Paris. Douchet
starts out with a filmography and then summarizes Lang's
view of the world and his kind of creativity. Lang has essentially one main theme--that of the individual's struggle
against events--a kind of modern version of the Promethean
combat. Fritz Lang's tragic universe, founded on the necessity for struggle, would not be great without the magnificence of his visual style, which deepens the major theme.
      Lang has always lived for cinema, and in the practical
realm he has no equal. He views himself as a simple craftsman, who makes the object demanded with love and care, and
his greatness lies in his creative use of form. He goes
for what is essential and thus tends to be abstract, so
that his films are peopled by characters obsessed with love,
hate, vengeance, money, and power. Death is the inevitable
result of the degradation of what is most noble in human
beings, namely the will to conquer. Innocence alone author-
izes a return to human greatness.
      Douchet ends by claiming that Fritz Lang's thought is
essentially that of a great classic writer.

282   Douchet, Jean. "L'Étrange Obsession." Cahiers du Cinéma
      (Paris), No. 122 (August), pp. 49-53.
      Douchet begins by discussing the purpose of criticism,
objecting to the new school of French critics who rave about
the visual beauty of Lang's and other directors' films.
Worthwhile criticism is that which tries to get to the heart
of the film. Douchet will neither declare Lang's Die tausend
Augen des Dr. Mabuse [The Thousand Eyes of Dr. Mabuse] beautiful nor defend its rigorous structure.
      For Douchet, art is a personal attempt to recover lost
equilibrium; Lang's fascination with the Mabuse theme since
1922 must reflect a fundamental and personal obsession. We
have to ask: Who is Mabuse? Why Mabuse?
      Mabuse's madness, Douchet says, concerns not only the
destruction of humanity but also the return to cosmic chaos.
Mabuse wants to annihilate the world, having decided that
to possess is to destroy. He suffers, through pride, due
to the idea of being only a neglible movement in a universe
full of movements and here is linked to the original

*Fritz Lang*

Promethean revolt.

This theme--that to possess is to destroy--is a typical Langian one. Everything in Lang's films turns to its opposite: personal love turns to murderous hate, justice to injustice, innocence to guilt, truth to lies. Mabuse tries to conquer the secrets of an indifferent universe, to make it recognize him as master.

Douchet goes on to show how this interpretation of Lang's characters can be seen in the mise-en-scène itself. In the scene where one car remains while the others move, each shot is the result of the preceding one and the cause for the next one. We are plunged into the realm of ideas, where each object attains the status of an archetype. The succession of shots illustrates Lang's theme: each shot, caught in its own trap, destroys itself by the very movement that brings the next one into being. This movement reproduces that of the universe and reveals the inexorable situation of humanity.

Mabuse, however, refuses to accept this tragic movement and tries to organize the world according to his convenience. In his attempt to penetrate the secret of souls, he takes on two identities, that of the blind Cornelius, a poet, and of the psychoanalyst, Jordan. But it is all an immense bluff: Mabuse is simply a craftsman using tools and machines, not to explore and know the world, but to dominate and destroy it.

Douchet sees all this as analogous to the process of making films and elaborates on this idea in the last section of the article. The scene where Mabuse looks at the television screens is the most obvious reference to the process of making films. Douchet shows the connections between the images, noting that at the very moment when Mabuse seemed totally in control of everything, there is a movement that he cannot control; namely Marion's falling in love with Travers, whom she was supposed to trap.

The aim of mise-en-scène is to eliminate chance, and one can sense the temptation that this has for Lang. His films always seem to be a series of fixed shots, because all movements of the camera annhilate those of the people.

Lang's work, Douchet concludes, is a series of introspections, of which Mabuse is the most monstrous. It is logical that at the end of his life Lang would criticize the artistic activity that emerges from his obsession. Central in Der Tiger von Eschnapur [The Tiger of Bengal] is movement, and in Mabuse Lang took mise-en-scène for his subject.

283    Douchet, Jean. "Le Cinéma est un art autonome." Les Lettres Françaises, No. 897 (18-24 October), p. 6.
Douchet complains about the prevailing critical assumption that subjects for films are either good or bad and that a good director cannot do anything with a poor script.

He asserts that all depends on how artists put their material together. It is their shaping vision, their use of mise-en-scène that counts, not what the film is ostensibly about. Several directors, including Lang, have suffered from the old critical approach, and Douchet notes that had Moonfleet not happened to win a prize, all of Lang's subsequent films would have been disregarded, including Beyond a Reasonable Doubt.

Douchet goes on to use Lang's Die tausend Augen des Dr. Mabuse [The Thousand Eyes of Dr. Mabuse] as an example of his remark about the importance of mise-en-scène. If one studies the mise-en-scène, one finds that Lang's film is about the process of filmmaking itself. The evil doctor has television channels in every room, so that he can see "reality" and then intervene to control and change people's lives. We are kept confused about identities and about people's functions and know only that there is some unknown person controlling everything. According to Douchet, this is fascism in action. One sees here the difference between a mise-en-scène that seeks total control and one that respects life. The artists' view of the world is contained in their mise-en-scène.

The article concludes with a detailed look at Godard's Une Femme Est Une Femme from the same point of view, i.e., that of demonstrating how meaning lies not in narrative but in mise-en-scène.

284  Everschor, Franz. "Über Dr. Mabuse, der Spieler." Film-Dienst (Düsseldorf; later Cologne) (5 April).

Everschor is writing on the occasion of the long, three-and-one-half-hour version of Dr. Mabuse, the Gambler being shown at the University of Bonn. He notes that what is most remarkable in hindsight is the way in which one can find in the film all the characteristics of later criminal and horror films. Expressionist use of light and shadow and the atmosphere of decadence are linked to a powerful narrative.

Mabuse continued a long line of tyrants already depicted in German films. None of these earlier versions, however, provided such a critical look at the contemporary period as Dr. Mabuse. Lang deals with sexual perversion, criminality, and political manipulation, creating a new realism within the detective genre. While the allusion to Hitler is explicit in the second Mabuse film [The Last Will of Dr. Mabuse], the whole pattern is already there in Dr. Mabuse, der Spieler. The likeness to Hitler stands out clearly for the modern viewer.

Everschor concludes by noting that the film is important both in terms of film history and also of Lang's personal development. All the tendencies in Lang's later films emerge from the silent works.

285 Gilson, Rene. "M, Le Maudit." Cinéma 61 (Paris), No. 59
(August-September), pp. 112-113.
Gilson first notes the possibility that old films by
great cinéastes may be commercially successful. He mentions
that the recent success of M has less to do with its links
to the police and suspense genres (many such films from the
same period do not hold up) than with the fact that M is a
perfect film--in its rhythm, structure, and movement and in
the achievement of each scene. M shows the importance of
mise-en-scène, of a successful écriture, which Lang saw no
need to change thereafter. The style has become the man.
Gilson goes on to discuss some of the many brilliant
scenes in M, most of which are now well known. We do not
appreciate these so much for aesthetic reasons, i.e., as
carefully planned compositions, as for their moral, as
compared with purely dramatic or psychological, values.
With M, Lang freed himself from the theatrical and architectural influences that dominate Die Nibelungen. His camera does not move about in the manner of Murnau, but we get
slow, deliberate movements that reveal reality.
In this film, Lang shows his ability to deal with actors.
Each of the gangsters who pass before Lohmann is an individual and alive. M finally reveals a solid sense of humor--
the opposite of the tragic--and as a whole embodies the birth
of Lang's mature style.

286 K.K. "Kein Mörderspiel: Fritz Lang's M von 1931."
Frankfurter Allgemeine Zeitung (11 December).
K.K. begins by noting that M, one of the greats of film
history, reflects pre-fascism in a unique way. Analysis of
the film helps to understand the past and the dangers of a
possible future.
According to K.K., the film's main theme is the disturbance to the order in a modern city caused by a psychopathic
murderer who cannot be found. Collective hate and loathing
descend on him, while the police are nervous as a result of
the hysteria, paranoia, and hatred among the citizens that
the case ignites.
K.K. moves next to public reaction to the film, which
showed people's familiarity with the hysteria it revealed.
At the time, viewers believed that the film advocated the
elimination of capital punishment and tried to arouse sympathy for perversion. Today, M still forces people to take
a stand, and many continue to react incorrectly and dangerously. Behaving like the frightened people in the film,
they are angry that the police do not apprehend the murderer
immediately. The film shows that instead of trusting the
social order, people begin to undermine it; it is an alarming portrayal of the outbreak of hostility in society.
K.K. concludes by pointing out that M carries the irony
of this inversion so far as to endow the underworld with a

form of order. In addition, the film will please spectators through its visual power, particularly the expressionist settings of barren ruins, decayed factories, and cellars. Far from being a tasteless murder game, as some aver, M anticipated, already in 1931, much of what was to happen in the following years.

287   Lebesque, Morvan. "Diabolique de Pacotille." L'Express
      (6 July), p. 34.
      Lebesque gives a negative review of Die tausend Augen
des Dr. Mabuse [The Thousand Eyes of Dr. Mabuse], which he
sees as an inferior remake of the much better, earlier
Mabuse films. Lang imitates poorly elements in the previous
works, made when he still had a tremendous imagination. The
creativity that went into Metropolis is not evident here.
All that remains is the German theme of obsession with evil
and power. While this theme reached its height in the great
films like Spione [Spies], Mabuse and M, here it becomes
mediocre.

288   *Leprohon, Pierre. Histoire du Cinéma. I:Vie et Mort du
      Cinématographie (1895-1930). Paris: Cerf. (Coll. 7e art).
      Source: Fritz Lang. Reihe 7. Munich: Carl Hanser
Verlag, 1976, p. 167.

289   Mardore, Michel. "Le Diabolique Docteur Mabuse." Cinéma 61
      (Paris), No. 59 (August-September), pp. 110-111.
      Mardore begins by noting that anyone who does not love
Lang's last film [The Thousand Eyes of Dr. Mabuse] reveals
an ignorance of cinema, while those who do love it risk doing so for the wrong reasons. The apparent return to the
style of Die Spinnen [The Spiders] and Das Testament des
Dr. Mabuse [The Last Will of Dr. Mabuse] may captivate the
film buff who adores the old modes of cinema, which recent
technological developments have eliminated from the screen.
Yet the modernist, interested in the new, alienated cinema,
which lacks drama and is full of philosophical speculations,
only finds Die tausend Augen [The Thousand Eyes] puerile.
While there may be some truth to this if one still expects
from cinema the depth of ideas easily expressed in literature, the film can really be appreciated only by the lovers
of "pure" cinema, who believe that mise-en-scène is what
film is all about.
      Mardore next examines the style in Die tausend Augen,
noting how the elliptical form--both within and between
scenes--is, in fact, a form of simplicity. Lang here shows
his mastery of mise-en-scène and of the art of narration.
      Switching for a moment to the two films made prior to
this one--Das indische Grabmal [The Indian Tomb] and Der
Tiger von Eschnapur [The Tiger of Bengal]--Mardore notes
that these bring together the height of the supple American

classical style and the synthesizing Germanic inspiration.
The apparently rigid Langian frames are, in fact, dynamic
and thus become the opposite of the aesthetic of expressionism, which is that of the prison.

It is thus easy to show how wrong the people are who
naively believed that Lang had regressed to an earlier cinema. Even if both Mabuse films are ultimately linked to
the same Faustian myth that is at the heart of Lang's work,
Lang's pure style transcends the baroque themes. The film
is close to the pure poetry of Rancho Notorious. Die
tausend Augen represents the mise-en-scène of a bunch of
liars and in doing so transforms the cliché-ridden plot into a powerful dreamlike vision.

290  Martin, Marcel. "Les Bourreaux Meurent Aussi: Fritz Lang et
     Brecht Vingt Ans Après." Les Lettres Françaises, No. 904
     (7 December), p. 8.
        Martin begins by noting that when Hangmen Also Die first
     appeared, World War II was still on, and the film seemed
     like a documentary in the manner of Open City. Seen today,
     the film looks very different, yet it is still relevant be-
     cause of the questions about democracy that it raises. It
     is ironic that the film reappeared at the same time as a
     film about Nazi Germany, called Mein Kampf.
        Based on a real historical event, Hangmen is less violent
     than was the reality. Like Lubitsch's To Be or Not to Be,
     it is done in a satirical tone and conveys the Nazi reality
     brilliantly. Although it is hard to tell what in the film
     derives from Brecht and what from Lang, we must attribute
     the creative imagination in the film to Lang. The collabor-
     ation was far from easy, and Brecht must have found the last
     third of the film naive and laborious. While the plot mach-
     inations are improbable, this is great cinema, and we get a
     sense of the involvement of all the people in the revolt
     against the Nazis. The film is a remarkable work of atmos-
     phere and passion, Lang's plastic expression of the narra-
     tive being of the first order. Perhaps Brecht's corrosive,
     penetrating message, however, is reflected through too
     classical a narrative structure, and there may be too much
     attempt to capture and retain audience attention. The au-
     thor of M and Fury was obviously sincere, and the film shows
     both his cinematic genius and his faith in defending free-
     dom and dignity.

291  Mauriac, Claude. "Les Bourreaux Meurent Aussi de Fritz Lang
     et Bertolt Brecht." [Review of Hangmen Also Die].
        Mauriac plays with Brecht's notion of distanciation
     ["Verfremdung," "distancing"] in this article. He talks
     briefly about the history of the making of Hangmen Also Die,
     noting Brecht's statement to the House Un-American Activities
     Committee that he had provided only the idea for the film

and that he had withdrawn early from the project. Mauriac outlines the film's main themes and comments on some historical inaccuracies which are due to the American distance from the European scene.

Mauriac then suggests that Brecht must have been displeased by how the film was made, because Lang does not use distanciation techniques here. Mauriac launches into a fairly detailed account of Brecht's theories and then describes what kind of distanciation does take place as we watch Hangmen Also Die today. The main kind relates to time: we now know the events of the film--they are part of our history and no longer appear in the same light. But there is also a personal distanciation for Mauriac, resulting from the fact that he had been in Prague in 1938 and had friends who resemble the heroes in the film. Earlier, in 1933, he had watched Lang making Liliom in Paris.

These kinds of distanciation are poetic rather than political, and they are not ones that Brecht would have liked, as they are of little interest to Marxists. Mauriac concludes by noting how each individual "creates" his or her own art work in the act of appreciation.

292    Taylor, John Russell. "The Nine Lives of Dr. Mabuse." Sight and Sound (London) 31, No. 1 (Winter), 43-46.
Taylor begins by contesting the notion that Lang has continually revised and remade works from his past. Taylor lists the remakes Lang has actually done and mentions several chances to do others that were offered Lang in the 1960s, particularly in Germany. Taylor does, however, agree that "certain themes run inescapably through his career . . . and of them all that represented by Dr. Mabuse, which reaches its apotheosis and logical conclusion in the latest episode, is the most persistent and pervasive."

Although Die Spinnen [The Spiders] (1919) is merely on the level of popular adventure, the fantasy of criminals conquering the world provided the germ for the later Dr. Mabuse films in 1922. The master criminal now begins to look like a Caligari with supernatural powers. In Spione [Spies] (1928), Haighi has lost ordinary criminal aims and wants a general disruption of society. Das Testament des Dr. Mabuse [The Last Will of Dr. Mabuse] in 1933 clearly shows the antisocial aims of the leader who has made lack of normal motivation into a principle of life. According to Lang, the film is a reflection on the Nazi party, but it is interesting that Goebbels liked it, saying that it only lacked a Führer to come and save the world from those who would destroy it by perverting true ideas.

Although Lang did nothing directly connected with Mabuse for the next ten years, Taylor sees Hangmen Also Die in 1943 as picking up where Das Testament left off, for the Heydrichs, Himmlers, and Hitlers are the heirs of Mabuse. Ministry of

Fear (1944) contains the idea of madness in the hero (seen leaving a mental home at the start), but as the tide turned against Hitler, Lang moved from the supermale to the super-female, and we have the femmes fatales of Woman in the Window and Scarlet Street.

Taylor points out that the superman is a substitute for fate in the lives of ordinary people, who are often present-ed as dull and colorless beside the master criminal. In the American films, of course, the ordinary person becomes the hero and the "madmen" are authorities or women. Die tausend Augen des Dr. Mabuse [The Thousand Eyes of Dr. Mabuse] (1961) represents the culmination of Lang's thinking about criminals, taking elements from both of the earlier Mabuse films.

Taylor concludes by noting that Lang is not a philosophi-cal director, because he makes films with ideas rather than about ideas. His power to embody ideas visually is his strength, so that the main conflict is not good versus evil, but light versus darkness. Mabuse represents the archetypal power of darkness.

## 1962

293    Bernard, Marc C. "Les Bourreaux Meurent Aussi." In Présence du Cinéma (Paris), No. 10 (January), pp. 40-41. [Review of Hangmen Also Die].
Bernard begins by noting how central James Wong Howe's photography is to the success of Hangmen Also Die. Howe's work shows the importance of lighting to powerful mise-en-scène. The brutality of Howe's images adds to their force and proves the necessity of brutality to great art.

While Fritz Lang's intentions were not identical with Brecht's, they were also not that different. Lang always tries to expose the social, economic, sexual, and domestic implications of things. Lang's mise-en-scène was in harmony with Brecht's dialogue in working for clarity and action.

Bernard concludes by saying that brutality is a necessary and honest approach to reality.

294    Durgnat, Raymond. "Der Tiger von Eschnapur." Films and Filming (London), 8, No. 9 (June), 38-39. [Review of The Tiger of Bengal].
Writing on the occasion of a Lang Festival at the National Film Theatre (London), Durgnat comments on how predictable the results of the festival were, the "classics" remaining fresh, while other films (like Human Desire) were obviously lesser works. He notes that the American version of Der Tiger was half the length of the original two-part film. While the story is childish and full of Saturday matinée clichés, the film is visually stunning--full of

colors, exciting use of forms, movements, texture, and
architectural space, all "orchestrated with Lang's slow,
eerie, muscularity." The tense fights have the quality of
choreography. Halfway between the dramatic and the decorative, the film encourages one to meditate rather than participate. Its sinister poetry is akin to that in Metropolis.

295    Durgnat, Raymond. "The Thousand Eyes of Dr. Mabuse." Films
       and Filming (London), 9, No. 2 (November), 40.
          Durgnat begins by noting how hard Lang found it to rid
       himself of Mabuse and compares the situation to Conan Doyle
       and Moriarty. Lang tries to recreate his villain in the
       latest film to reflect the sources of chaos in the modern
       world. Mabuse here throws the stock market into turmoil by
       spying on guests in his hotel, and he plans to gain control
       of a vast atomic plant, holding the world as hostage.
          But the film, for Durgnat, lacks the conviction of earl-
       ier versions. While certain scenes work and are exciting,
       the film as a whole does not succeed; it falls far short of
       the superb Der Tiger von Eschnapur [The Tiger of Bengal].

296    Gregor, Ulrich, and Patalas, Enno. "Deutschland: Expression-
       ismus und Neue Sachlichkeit." In Geschichte des Films.
       Gütersloh: Sigbert Mohn. Pp. 55-75 [on Lang specifically,
       pp. 65-68], reprinted in 1974.
          The authors begin with a brief description of the politi-
       cal and social situation in Germany after the First World
       War, noting that it was during a period of inflation, pover-
       ty, and crisis that Germany produced its richest films. Af-
       ter a short discussion of Lubitsch and the historical film,
       they turn to expressionism, outlining briefly the main char-
       acteristics of the movement. Gregor and Patalas see Wegener
       and Reinhardt as preparing the ground for expressionism with
       their focus on the crisis of identity, particularly through
       their use of devices like the mirror and the shadow.
          But Gregor and Patalas see Mayer and Janowitz's Caligari
       as initiating the classic period of German film and as play-
       ing a role analogous to that of works by Zavattini in ini-
       tiating Italian neo-realism. The themes of Caligari were
       to set a trend and to be copied in many films, even in those
       with a more realistic style. Most important were the idea
       of fate looming over humanity and the view of the world as
       objectification of spirit, feeling, and emotion. All became
       symbolic, and nature and the real world were excluded from
       the screen.
          Gregor and Patalas give a brief analysis of the
       Kammerspielfilm [The chamber-play film], which they see as
       continuing, rather than breaking with, the tendencies of
       Caligari. It is true that the heroes are not ruined by a
       supernatural power, but rather by their own pathetic in-
       stincts. But this amounts essentially to the same thing

[that is, an internalization of outside evil, ed.], and the world of the film is still filled with the dreamlike atmosphere of expressionism.

The discussion of Fritz Lang that follows continues the tendency, evident in the whole chapter, of describing expressionism in terms similar to Kracauer's, i.e., as unhealthy. The authors see Lang as very much influenced by the expressionist aesthetic and themes, although they point out that Der müde Tod [Destiny] is dominated by architectural forms in contrast to the painted decor of Caligari or the moving camera and montage of Murnau. Above all, Lang uses light to model space and create his atmosphere of fate and transiency.

According to the authors, Mabuse belongs very much with Caligari in its theme of the superman leading others to murder through hypnotising them and ending up insane himself; but on the other hand, this film, more than any others of Lang, looks toward the thirties.

Gregor and Patalas criticise both Metropolis and Die Nibelungen for their abstractions and lack of spontaneity. Both show affinities with tendencies in National Socialism: Die Nibelungen in the cult of the Nordic, the defamation of the "un-German," the submission to the will of the leader, and the glorification of the death of the hero; Metropolis in the camouflaging of social contrasts, the redemption of the proletariat by superiors, and in its ending. The authors conclude that the division between the early fascist Lang and the later antifascist Lang is too neat; Lang's work always retained fascist elements in his fascination with chaos and in his inability to see alternatives other than having a dictator. Order comes only from a powerful central authority and never emerges as a result of choice.

With the failure of Metropolis, Lang returned to earlier themes, but these no longer reflected the times, and his films became mere thrillers.

297    Lefèvre, Raymond. "M, Le Maudit." Image et Son (Paris), No. 152 (June), pp. 17-23.
       The article follows the format of the Image et Son film treatments, beginning with a brief discussion of Lang's background, followed by excerpts from articles where Lang talks about his art. A short introduction to the subject of M is followed by a list of the main sequences, themes, and characters. M is placed in the context of both realism and expressionism: on the one hand, the film had documentary value in its presentation of a pathological case in realist settings and in its clear social message; but on the other hand, it is a visionary and prophetic film.

298    Leutrat, Paul. "Actualité de l'Expressionnisme." In two parts: Cinéma 62, No. 69, pp. 80-96 and Cinéma 62, No. 71,

pp. 91-126.

While dealing only briefly with individual Lang films,
this article is important for its discussion of the connection between German expressionism and film noir, which Lang
is at least partly responsible for.  Leutrat builds on the
pioneering work by Borde and Chaumeton on film noir.

In Part I, Leutrat surveys the origins of expressionism
in Germany and lists films made between 1913 and 1924 that
reflect expressionist tendencies.  A detailed account of
Caligari is followed by a long discussion of Lang's Der müde
Tod [Destiny], which Leutrat sees as having broken new
ground for expressionism.  The use of stairways and the
sculptural placing of the actors look toward The Nibelungen.

Part II begins with a discussion of the social crisis in
1924, which Leutrat sees as having affected interest in expressionism.  On the one hand, the movement reflected the
revolt of the individual against the social situation, and,
on the other, allowed for indulgence in dangerous passions
that could be exploited politically.

Unfortunately, the repetition of the same formulas resulted in the deterioration of the expressionist style.

Leutrat next deals with the links between expressionism
and the horror and science fiction film.  He traces a tradition from Frankenstein and King Kong, both of which draw on
expressionism, through Dreyer and the vampire movies of the
1930s to the "fantôme" films of the 1940s, which include
Dr. Jekyll and Mr. Hyde and The Invisible Man, to the works
of H. G. Wells and Conan Doyle.

Film noir emerges directly out of these films, which in
turn look back to expressionism.  Victor Fleming in Dr.
Jekyll revived all the expressionist themes developed by
Lang, Paul Leni, Murnau, and Siodmak, most of whom, fleeing
nazism, ended up in Hollywood.

Drawing next on Borde and Chaumeton's work, Leutrat lists
films now called noir and suggests that these films rejoin
the expressionist film in the unravelling of an action that
is illogical and absurd, although it is now treated in a
realistic manner.  The films create a nightmare world where
people are caught up in complicated intrigues whose thread
gets lost.  The type begins in 1941 with The Maltese Falcon
and Shanghai, which are expressionist in their use of fog and
and in their unexpected decor.  He mentions Lang as continuing film noir with Manhunt, Scarlet Street, and Woman in the
Window.  According to Leutrat, however, Lang increasingly
detached himself from expressionism.  Leutrat concludes by
considering the tradition of expressionism among various
American and European directors from Eisenstein to Bergman.
He suggests that Lang's Die Nibelungen influenced Eisenstein's
Alexander Nevsky.

299   Marcorelles, Louis.  "Gehalt und Gestalt." Cahiers du Cinéma

No. 127 (January), p. 57.

This article deals mainly with the collaboration between Brecht and Lang on Hangmen Also Die. Marcorelles notes that Brecht's ideas are essentially not transferable to the screen, primarily because in the theater we are in the realm of the "real," where economic situations apply, while in film we are transported elsewhere.

Marcorelles summarizes briefly Lang's attitude to the world--that of believing in original sin, in the evil inherent in people. From this point of view, the three social message films made with Sylvia Sidney in America are an anomaly. Brecht, meanwhile, in the 1930s was inaugurating his epic theater and had given up the nihilism of the 1920s. Lang brought him to America to work on a project about the assassination of Heydrich in Czechoslovakia.

Marcorelles discusses briefly the confusion about the screenplay for Hangmen Also Die. He notes how much of Brecht's ideas remain in the completed version. He finds that the originally Brechtian idea of a trick played on brute force becomes through Lang's vision something more Faustian--that of the struggle against evil.

Marcorelles concludes by noting that Lang returned after an interval of ten years to the realistic style of his German sound films, but he put this realism to very different uses than did Brecht. While with Brecht spectators are made to collaborate actively, to judge the events they see, Lang's realism is situated in the moment, at the level of appearances. Both deal with ideas, but while with Brecht the idea resides in a content with social dimensions, with Lang it exists only in space, in the illusion of the screen. Brecht perhaps never took cinema seriously precisely because of its power to transpose everything into another realm.

300   Mardore, Michel. "Les Bourreaux Meurent Aussi." Cinéma 62, No. 62 (January), pp. 116-118.

Mardore addresses himself to an audience apparently hostile to Lang, which either misunderstands his works or considers them childish and improbable. While these people never consider Lang a serious filmmaker, Mardore notes that Lang actually loves serious ideas and has often expressed them openly rather than through exotic adventures. Hangmen Also Die is one such film that deals with real events--the oppression of the Czech people during World War II and the actions of the resistance group. Showing the superiority of the revolutionary ethos over the bourgeois one, Lang's film could have been made in the 1960s.

Mardore refuses to be defensive about the film. But he notes that the fact that it was acted by emigrés, who had lived the experience, accounts somewhat for the exaggerated view of the Nazis, and that a more rigorous documentary approach would have hindered Lang's style. For Lang's aim is

always utimately to create a sense of fate, and this involves
abstraction: his work, therefore, is never limited to the
actual event described. Paradoxically again, Lang's most
timeless films have a social message, so that Das indische
Grabmal [The Indian Tomb] is, in fact, a realistic description of nazism. But the compositions in Lang's films are
so stylized that the most burning problems never provoke
excessive emotion. The simplicity of the surface narrative
masks the severity of the abstraction.

Looked at from afar, Hangmen Also Die appears banal.
Mardore summarizes the main aspects of the plot and notes
that Brecht's participation is evident in the ending, which
is worthy of a Brechtian fable, and in certain other scenes.
But there is a basic contradiction between the thought of
the two men: for Brecht, the individual is not guilty, but
problems are instead due to an evil capitalist society;
while for Lang individuals are guilty and the cruelty of
society simply reflects their fate.

Mardore concludes that while the theme of the film in
some ways contradicts Lang's vision (e.g., Svoboda, although
guilty of murder, does not suffer the vengeance of the people), the film's mise-en-scène and overall style remain
typically Langian. The structure of the film is that of
laying a trap, and there is the familiar Langian preoccupation with objects. In Hangmen Also Die, one finds the seeds
of the great American films and it is, in fact, thirty years
ahead of its time.

301  PEM. "London feiert Fritz Lang: Eine Chance für die Werbung
     mit deutschen Filmen is verpasst worden." Film-Telegramm,
     No. 11 (13 March). (Available in Deutschen Film und
     Fernsehakademie, W. Berlin.)
         PEM is writing on the occasion of Lang's visit to London
     for a retrospective of his works at the National Film
     Theatre. He is interested to see that London has welcomed
     Lang enthusiastically, not as a Hollywood director, but as
     representing the golden age of the German film and because
     of his recent German works. The British Film Institute had
     wanted to show Die tausend Augen des Dr. Mabuse [The
     Thousand Eyes of Dr. Mabuse], but the German production
     company was reluctant to give it to them for fear of nega-
     tive reviews, which might hinder the film's sale in England.
     PEM finds this attitude hard to understand, since Paris
     loved the film and since the British are so interested in
     the German Lang. If there is still a prejudice against
     German films (as the German industry fears), then Lang would
     be the very director helpful in overcoming it.

302  *Patalas, Enno. "Das Phänomen Mabuse." Neue Zürcher Zeitung
     (24 March).
         Source: Grafe, F. and Enno Patalas. Fritz Lang.
     Munich: Hanser, p. 164.

302a "Unusual Opportunity to Study the Work of Fritz Lang." Times
(London) (2 January).
Writing on the occasion of a retrospective of Lang's
work at the National Film Institute, London, the author
notes how, out of all the directors of silent films, Lang
is the only one still successful. His return to Europe has
not meant the loss of his old skills or his sensitivity to
public taste. The reviewer notes also the success of Lang's
recent film, Die tausend Augen [The Thousand Eyes], in
Europe. He ends with describing the retrospective as divided between Lang's early German works and a selection of his
American films.

303 Shivas, Mark. "The Thousand Eyes of Dr. Mabuse." Movie
(London), No. 4, (November), p. 6.
Shivas argues for the film as "a simple fable." The
stark black and white contrasts, the clear stereotypes, and
the obvious connections made through editing all reveal a
complex world; but Lang also shows how simply this criminal
world can be overcome by the love of a good woman for the
good man. This is as it should be in a fable.

304 Tavernier, Bernard. "Lang." Cahiers du Cinéma (Paris), No.
132 (June), pp. 18-19. [Review of House by the River].
Tavernier argues that like Rancho Notorious and Moonfleet,
House by the River represents one of those pauses in Lang's
career where he "gives free rein to a profound romanticism."
While in Rancho Notorious Lang attacked the myth of the
hero and in Moonfleet that of the outsider or lawbreaker,
so in House by the River Lang deals with the notion of guilt,
one of his major obsessions.
Tavernier sees a similarity between the hero in House by
the River and that in Beyond a Reasonable Doubt (where the
hero takes photos of his own acts), particularly in the way
each central character refuses to accept guilt for his deed.
This, of course, is reminiscent of the hero in the various
Mabuse films. Here Lang is interested in dissecting the
relationship between guilt and society, showing how the
murderer misleads the representatives of justice (the police,
detectives), and how he undertakes elaborate schemes to ac-
cuse an innocent person.
House by the River differs from Beyond a Reasonable Doubt
largely in terms of atmosphere. The film's opening moments
are beautiful--it is a lovely summer evening on the river--
and throughout the film we wish to return to this beauty.
In this film, the anguish arises from tenderness rather than
from cruelty, as in the later film.
Tavernier concludes by recalling the haunting visual moments in the film, such as the scenes of the woman suddenly
murdered, of the fish leaping out of the water, of the river
that carries the body, or the last images of the pieces of
paper, the only proof of a perhaps imaginary crime.

305  Tyler, Parker. "<u>M</u>."  In his <u>Classics of the Foreign Film</u>.
New York: Citadel Press.  Pp. 70-73.
Tyler begins by contrasting the German treatment of
guilt with that of Russian writers like Dostoevsky, Gorky,
and Gogol.  While the Russians express their guilt in "a
clamour of human confusion," the Germans take an intellectual, examining attitude, making guilt into a psychological
issue.
Tyler sees <u>Caligari</u> as starting the trend in expressionist films of dealing with the psychological realities of
crime and guilt.  Lang, however, was ultimately more interested in making <u>M</u> into a gripping movie.
Tyler ends with a brief analysis of the film's high
points, praising Lorre's acting and Lang's "reporting" and
noting how the force of the film depends on the murderer's
being hunted down by the underworld.

306  Werth, German.  "Fritz Langs <u>Metropolis</u>:  Zum Marmorhaus-
Jubiläum."  <u>Der Tagesspiegel</u> (West Berlin), (31 March).
Werth discusses Lang's <u>Metropolis</u> as one of the films
being shown in a retrospective of the German silent film.
He begins by discussing the occasion in general terms, objecting to a certain arrogance that accompanies the show-
ings.  While the films are in many ways anachronistic, even
laughable, we are supposed to feel that we have seen something worthwhile.
Werth then talks of <u>Metropolis</u>, saying that its vision
of the present mitigates the social pathos and the naive,
romantic aspects derived from expressionism, including the
renewal of the moral nature of humankind.  Lang has set
this warning about the machine age in a monumental structure,
mixing in fairy-tale and ghostly elements, but showing a
world divided into two distinct parts, two separate classes.
Lang could not resist sweetening his vision with a love story
and making of love the heavenly power that unites head and
hands.


1963


307  Aprà, Adrian.  "<u>Cloak and Dagger</u>:  esempi dello stile di Fritz
Lang."  [An Example of Lang's Film Style].  <u>Filmcritica</u>
(Rome), No. 138 (October), pp. 614-624.
Aprà's concern is to establish the validity of the
American Lang, dealing with visual style in detail in order
to prove the aesthetic worth of the films.  He discusses
the typically Langian structure of <u>Cloak and Dagger</u> and the
themes dealing with will and the irrational.  The film is
analyzed in detail, particularly in relation to <u>mise-en-
scène</u>, and there are many references to other works by Lang.

308  Courtade, Francis. <u>Fritz Lang</u>. Paris:  Le Terrain Vague.
     Courtade's book, appearing in the same year as that by
Moullet (<u>See</u> Entry No. 315), takes a much more conventional
position on Lang.  He values the earlier German films and
the first American ones for their social content; while he
praises the German ones for their visual style, he assumes
that the American films are generally less worthy than the
German works.  The name of Lang alone gives the American
films validity and caused them to be noticed.  He criticizes
<u>American Guerilla in the Philippines</u> particularly, although
he does do some justice to the <u>films noir</u>.  He overpraises
the anti-Nazi films, on the other hand, because of their
political content.
     Courtade's book is divided into sections on Lang in
Europe, Lang in Hollywood, and Lang's return to Europe,
followed by a conclusion.  After outlining Lang's beginnings,
Courtade discusses the expressionist movement briefly, which
Lang became aware of during World War I, and his involvement
with a theatrical group.  Lang became even more involved
with expressionism after the war, when he made <u>Harakiri</u> and
worked on <u>Caligari</u>.  Courtade goes on to show how <u>Der müde
Tod</u> [Destiny] is an expressionist film and then analyzes
the films in chronological order, focusing particularly on
<u>Dr. Mabuse, der Spieler</u> as an interesting mixture of realism
and expressionism.  It is fantastic or subjective realism.
Courtade goes on to discuss the expressionist elements in
both <u>Die Nibelungen</u> and <u>Metropolis</u>.  There are some interesting comments on <u>Das Testament</u> [The Last Will] by Lang himself, from his introduction to the film at the World Theater
in New York in March 1943.
     Courtade argues against the current Lang cult among the
<u>Cahiers du Cinéma</u> group.  He believes, in fact, that the
new interest shows that Lang is not so great a director and
that he has always bent with the wind.
     There is a filmography, followed by a bibliography of
French reviews on the films and a short general bibliography.

309  Legrand, Gérard.  "Notes pour un éloge de Fritz Lang."
     <u>Positif</u> (Paris), No. 50-52 (March), pp. 130-136.
     This piece consists of rather enigmatic reflections on
Lang and his films, intended to reveal the complex, ambiguous, and dialectical nature of his work.  Legrand first
talks about Lang's brave way of opening his films with the
climax (e.g., <u>The Big Heat</u>) and of the way one can begin
anywhere in his films, since they are in fact circular.
Lang refuses to take sides, to belong in any camp.  Legrand
points out the two main schools of Lang critics:  those who
see a natural evolution in his work, and those who view the
American works as a betrayal of earlier work.  He goes on
to talk about Lang's main themes and of his obsession with
architecture, his taste for secret heights, his cerebral

curiosity about evil, and his frigid women characters. Not interested in agreement between the content and the form, Lang paradoxically uses a medium of communication (that is, film) in such a manner that it does not serve as communication.

Legrand notes that there is something tragic about Lang's choosing themes that only very great artists can really handle; he has often been seen as being at the mercy of inferiority feelings in relation to his father. In the Langian world, only children are accorded respect (e.g., John Mohune in Moonfleet and the child in Secret Beyond the Door).

Lang uses decor and objects as the means by which necessity makes itself felt. While there is no reason to suspect the sincerity of Lang's statements, his fascination with evil is suspect. Lang has no progressive vision; his idea of history comes dangerously close to being a history of crimes. The reoccurrence of the Mabuse figure suggests that Lang, in fact, identifies with Mabuse and with the all-powerful nature of technology. The Hitlerian overtones to Mabuse are confirmed by Goebbels's calling on Lang to head the Nazi film industry after the second Mabuse film.

Legrand sees a kind of dialectic at work in Lang between two sides of himself--the one that identifies with Mabuse and the other that criticizes him. The ultimate metaphor for what Lang is doing occurs in Die tausend Augen des Dr. Mabuse [The Thousand Eyes of Dr. Mabuse], where the Mabuse figure directs everything from behind a secret mirror. For Lang, making films was a way of controlling the different parts of himself. In America, the increasingly complex dialectic expressed itself in ever simpler form.

Legrand ends with a quotation from de Sade and suggests that Lang's heroes are ephemeral but act as if they were eternal. Lang's work itself reflects his own intense drive to achieve closure; giving us in fact a sense of always becoming, the films are intended to discover how to be.

310    Luft, Herbert G. "Karl Freund." Films in Review (New York) (February), pp. 93-108.

Luft surveys the career of this photographer who is significant here for his work on Lang's Die Spinnen [The Spiders] and then again on Metropolis. Luft shows the general influence of Freund in the early days of film, noting how many of the great classic films of the period were photographed by him--The Last Laugh, Variety, Wiene's Eva, The Golem, and other films by Murnau and Wegener.

Freund evidently admired Lang, especially for the compositions and mise-en-scène, but did not get on with him personally and avoided working with him between 1921 and 1926. Luft describes the many special effects and trick shots that Freund helped with in Metropolis.

311   Moullet, Luc.  <u>Fritz Lang</u>.  Paris:  Seghers.  [Includes a
      biofilmography and bibliography].

One of the first books on Lang (Courtade's book came out
in the same year), this study was important for its solid,
responsible <u>auteur</u> approach, which included a sophisticated
understanding of visual style.  The first half of the book
consists of a long essay by Moullet, where he surveys Lang's
entire career, dividing the films into clear periods.  In
an introductory section, Moullet generalizes about Lang's
themes, noting that his films combine a personal series of
concerns with an external interest in social morality.
Moullet describes briefly the atmosphere in post-World War
I Germany, showing how Lang's early scripts demonstrated an
interest in dream and forgetfulness, although the other side
of Lang, his skepticism and pessimism, soon began to appear.
<u>Der müde Tod</u> [Destiny] was a breakthrough and revealed Lang's
expressionist style.

For Moullet, the German works fall into two categories--
those showing people dominated by the world and those showing people who hope to dominate the world.  These culminate
in <u>M</u>, where Lang initiates the theme of conflict between
official and individual justice.  With <u>M</u>, the abstract
superman is replaced by the Nazi revolutionary, although
still disguised, while in <u>Das Testament</u> [The Last Will],
Mabuse is clearly Hitler.

Moullet concludes that while the German works do not form
a separate thematic unit and are not defined by expressionism (only four films, he says, are expressionist), they are
linked by themes central to Germany of the time and by the
group of actors and technicians that Lang worked with.

After a brief discussion of <u>Liliom</u>, which Moullet appre-
ciates for its whimsical, poetic, and comic qualities,
Moullet takes up Lang's American career.  While hesitant
about the ultimate value of the films, Moullet admires their
ambitious aims; he sees Lang's ideas as diluted by the required realism--they get lost in the banal, daily gestures.
He analyzes the first three American films as a trilogy,
defending <u>You and Me</u> for its poetry and for what it shows
about Lang's metaphysics.

Moullet sees a change in the films between 1940 and 1949:
this period is devoted to the question "Must people either
revolt or conform?"  Lang the metaphysician is now replaced
by Lang the moralist; while in the first films, Lang refused
to judge his heroes or to show the way forward, now he begins to reflect on what he has produced in three genres--
the Western, the thriller and the psycholgical melodrama.
Moullet discusses each group of films, noting that as the
war started Lang continued his personal fight against fascism, which had begun with the <u>Mabuse</u> films.  The spy films
have been unjustly derided, Moullet says, and while agreeing that the films show no respect for realism or local

color, this was deliberate. There are separate discussions
of Manhunt, Ministry of Fear, Cloak and Dagger, and Hangmen
Also Die.

Moullet discusses the police melodramas made between 1944
and 1949 as a unit, calling them more personal films. After
the fight against nazism comes the struggle against one's
self. He has some interesting comments on the repetition
in this group of films—Woman in the Window, Scarlet Street,
Secret Beyond the Door, House by the River—where Lang uses
the same actors and actresses and the same photographer.
Noting Lang's penchant for the remake, Moullet sees this as
the first form of repetition. Lang offers different forms
of the same theme and uses similar forms for different
themes; often he has conceived of two different endings for
his films, this habit of thinking reflecting his metaphysical position, in which people always oscillate between two
poles—those of revolt and of submission to the law or to
their own reason. The choice depends on chance, and it is
this aspect of chance that Lang honors in the two possible
endings. Moullet sees a personal aspect to Lang's preoccupation with the theme of the older man seduced by the young
woman—Lang was himself at this point 55 years old.

Moullet dislikes Secret Beyond the Door (it fails, he
thinks), views Guerillas as showing no mark of Lang and has
not seen House by the River.

Part II of the book is titled "Maturity" and traces the
films from 1951 to 1960. Moullet groups the films between
1951 and 1955 under the heading "The Critic," seeing the
mature Lang as now turning a scornful, sarcastic glance at
the world around him. With Lang bitter and isolated, his
work reflects his violent reaction to the social order imposed by the American way of life. Lang now critiques eras
he had earlier idealized—like the old West (Rancho
Notorious) or the eighteenth century (Moonfleet). He shows
myths of the old West as moribund and gentlemen as corrupt.
There is a severe critique of contemporary manners in Clash
by Night, The Blue Gardenia, The Big Heat, and While the
City Sleeps.

The final group of films between 1954 and 1960 Moullet
groups under "Contemplation," and here he sees Lang replacing the bitter critic with the lofty, godlike stance of one
who knows the indifference of the universe in relation to
human beings. He shows the difficulty of communication between people locked into the social order. This stance is
evident in Human Desire and Beyond a Reasonable Doubt, the
latter representing an extreme abstraction. The last three
German films fit into this category. Moullet claims that
the Indian films are neither as brilliant nor as awful as
other critics have asserted, but do show a lack of creativity, a falling off in imagination, which is also evident in
Lang's last Mabuse film.

In the final section of the essay, Moullet describes
Lang's place among the German and American directors,
stressing the unity of his entire career. None of his
films makes sense outside of the others, and the work takes
on meaning in terms of the evolution of the whole. Finally,
Moullet stresses the importance of Lang's experience in
Germany in the 1920s as shaping his world view.

The second half of the book consists of selections from
Lang's interviews and own writings, as well as excerpts
from articles and books by critics (most of which are annotated in my own study). It is a useful and well-chosen collection of texts.

312    Sarris, Andrew. "Fritz Lang." Film Culture (New York)
       (Spring), pp. 9-52.
       This article presents Sarris's initial division of
American directors into groups, beginning with the best,
"The Pantheon," and moving on down through "The Second Line"
and "The Third Line" to "Esoterica," "Beyond the Fringe,"
and "Fallen Idols." The whole piece was later expanded and
developed into the book American Cinema.

Sarris places Lang in "The Second Line," noting that
Lang's cinema is that of nightmare, the fable, and philosophical dissertation. The plots are inadequate, going silly or sour at the end, and Lang's characters lack psychological depth. While the world of the films lacks details
and verisimilitude, the visual forms carry Lang's meanings.
To make his point about Lang, Sarris compares Renoir's version of Zola's novel La Bête Humaine, with that of Lang's
(Human Desire).

Lang's cinema has not declined over the years, according
to Sarris; Metropolis and Moonfleet share the same bleak
vision of people struggling against their fate. There is
something of the voyeur in Lang (e.g., the flashlight sequence in Metropolis and the false mirror in Die tausand
Augen [The Thousand Eyes]). Sarris concludes that Lang's
films "are cold and unpleasant, but their formal brilliance
and intellectual conception are incontestable. Lang is the
cerebral tragedian of the cinema, and his lapses into absurdity are the evidence of a remote sagacity and intellect
without intelligence."

1964

313    Anon. "Begegnung mit Fritz Lang." Kultur Filmprämie des
       Bundesinnenministeriums. (Available in Deutschen Film und
       Fernsehakademie, West Berlin.)
       In a discussion of Lang's role in Godard's Le Mépris,
the author notes the documentary aspect of Lang's playing
himself. There are scenes that recall Lang's films,

especially <u>Die Nibelungen</u>, <u>Der müde Tod</u> [Destiny], <u>M</u>—this
is reporting as art.  The author praises <u>Le Mépris</u> for its
mixture of New Wave style, musical motifs and for bringing
together themes from various earlier films by Lang.

314    Eibel, Alfred, ed.  <u>Fritz Lang</u>.  Paris:  Présence du Cinéma.
       Eibel's book is extremely useful in that it gathers to-
gether a wide range of materials on Lang written in German
and English as well as French and covers Lang's career from
1890 to 1964.  There are excerpts from newspaper reviews of
Lang's films, from his interviews and his own writings, and
statements about Lang by people who worked with him in various capacities.  Especially useful are selections from inaccessible German and French reviews of the early films
(the German materials are translated into French).  While
Eibel unfortunately does not (for the most part) document
the materials as they occur in the text, there is an excellent bibliography at the end of the book citing references
for the materials he quoted from.
       The first part of the book deals with the first German
period, from 1890 to 1933.  An account by Lang himself gives
an overview of the period, interspersed with statements by
Eibel, filling in the sequence of events.  Interesting here
is Eibel's discussion of the relative merits of the Norbert
Jacques novel on which <u>Dr. Mabuse, the Gambler</u> was based
and of the film.  Important also is the detailed analysis
of the reception of, and controversies over, <u>M</u>, with quotations from newspapers published in many countries.  The section ends with Lang's departure from Germany after being
interviewed by Goebbels.
       This is followed by Thea von Harbou's discussion of <u>Die
Nibelungen</u>, Lang's account of his visit to California (<u>See</u>
Entry No. 520), his response to a questionnaire about
American films (<u>See</u> Entry No. 521), his article on <u>M</u> (<u>See</u>
Entry No. 527), and excerpts from an article on <u>Dr. Mabuse,
der Spieler</u> printed in <u>Cinema Nuovo</u> in 1952.  Parts of his
interview with Ludwig Spitzer are also reprinted (<u>See</u> Entry
No. 72).
       The next section contains statements on Lang by actors
and technicians who worked with him, including Siodmak,
Carl de Vogt, Lil Dagover, Joseph Losey.
       Part one ends with selections from newspaper reviews of
early films scripted by Lang (<u>Pest in Florenz</u> [Plague in
Florence], <u>Das indische Grabmal</u> [The Indian Tomb]) and directed by him (<u>Harakiri</u>, <u>Der müde Tod</u> [Destiny], <u>Dr. Mabuse,
der Spieler</u>, <u>Metropolis</u>, <u>Die Frau im Mond</u> [Woman in the
Moon]).
       Part II covers Lang's American period, from 1934 to 1957.
Eibel follows the same procedure, beginning with excerpts
from texts by Lang himself.  The selection here is particularly good, including an interesting piece called "The

Person from Porlock," another that comments on the making of You Only Live Once ("The Frog and I"), and an essay entitled "Why Am I Interested in Murder?" (1947). Eibel reprints Mary Morris's 1945 interview with Lang, and there is again a series of statements by people involved with Lang in various capacities during these years. There are extracts from newspaper reviews of Fury, You and Me, Manhunt, and Hangmen Also Die.

Part three deals with Lang's second German period, from 1958 to 1964. Extracts from statements by Lang are followed by excerpts from two Lang screenplays and statements by various coworkers. An article by Pommer about discovering Lang is followed by press reviews of the Indian films. The filmography and bibliography complete the book.

315    Eisner, Lotte H.  "Le Style de M, Le Maudit."  L'Avant-Scène
       39 (15 July-16 August), pp. 5-46.
            This thorough look at M follows the usual format of the
       L'Avant-Scène analyses. The introduction describes the
       main stylistic and thematic elements of the film, the use
       of sound, and the use of light and composition. A selec-
       tion from the script of M in French is followed by a section
       entitled "M et le Presse," which has excerpts from critical
       analyses and reviews. Included are the following: Cinema
       61, No. 59 (1961); Objectif 63, No. 25 (December-January
       1964); Arts, No. 819 (24 April 1961); and Cinémonde (14
       April 1932). A section on Peter Lorre includes a filmogra-
       phy and a tribute to him. The book ends with a Lang film-
       ography, put together by Claude Beylie, covering Lang's
       German works from 1919 to 1932.

316    Everschor, Franz.  "Ein Mythos wurde begraben."  Film-Dienst
       (Düsseldorf; later Cologne) (13 May).
            Writing on the occasion of the Bad Ems retrospective,
       Everschor notes the tone of reverence used now for Lang,
       but also the fact that the American films are still barely
       known in Germany. Twenty-one films are being shown at the
       retrospective, enabling consideration of Lang's whole career
       for the first time. Good documentation from the film clubs
       enriches the experience.
            Everschor thinks that Lang has a good feeling both for
       social reality and for human fantasies. His themes remained
       the same for twenty years, e.g., the war of the individual
       against organized power, and the struggle of the good man
       against corruption. In whatever genre Lang worked, he had
       a similar male hero, trying to fight established power.
            But Lang never thinks his conflicts through rationally to
       the end; Fate really controls everything, and the happy end-
       ing is simply added on. Everschor concludes that while
       Lang's material is banal, his treatment of it is original.
       Lang's significance in film history lies in his genius for

bringing together all the various elements in an harmonious form.

317    Fouquet, Alexander. "Ich glaube, ich mag Fritz Lang: Stenogramm zu einigen amerikanischen Filmen." Filmstudio (Frankfurt), No. 45 (1 November), pp. 23-31.

Fouquet discusses each of Lang's films from Fury onward, trying to account for some of Lang's themes--his antifascism, his eroticism, and his predilection for a noir world. Linking some of the American films with Lang's early German works, Fouquet sees the anti-Nazi films in America as a reflection on the Mabuse-cycle; Lang returns to his fascination with the erotic and the idea of fate in Scarlet Street and Woman in the Window.

Admitting to gaps in his knowledge of Lang's American films and talking in a frankly subjective way much of the time, Fouquet concludes that there are few high points in Lang's work in the past thirty years. His was the kind of talent that would not appeal to large numbers of people and yet he became ever more entrenched in the director's ghetto that is Hollywood. His vision became increasingly narrow, and he is to be pitied, like Chaplin, for the shoddy treatment that he received in Hollywood. With Le Mépris by Godard, however, Lang has finally become a great man of the cinema, a living myth.

318    Gregor, Ulrich. "Ein Prototyp der Zeit: Allegro: Dr. Mabuse, der Spieler." Spandauer Volksblatt (13 December) and "Dr. Mabuse; Inferno des Verbrechens," (20 December).

Both reviews were written on the occasion of a retrospective of German silent films. Gregor says the program is well planned, has good interpretations of the films shown, and the addition of modern music gives the works a new appearance.

Discussing Lang's Dr. Mabuse, the Gambler, Gregor notes that this two-part film is virtually unknown in Germany; Lang here used a theme that he was to return to in 1932 and 1961 and that fascinated the French New Wave. Half criminal, half Nietzschean underground man, Mabuse is representative of his period, using all kinds of methods to perpetuate his criminal acts.

Gregor discusses some of the techniques used to create the magical aspects of Mabuse; he then praises the music of the film for underscoring the expressionist, unrealistic dimensions and causing the sentimental, cliché-ridden aspects to be less obvious.

In reviewing the second part of the film, Gregor talks of the atmosphere of terror that Lang was to create in all later films. It here sometimes borders on the grotesque, but one must note how artistically Lang has treated his theme, creating a surreal, urban landscape.

One theme that was repeated in later films like M̲ is the panic of someone locked in a small space. Nearly all the characters in Mabuse̲ are confined in one way or another, and some of Mabuse's people commit suicide in prison. Gregor discusses again the visual techniques that emphasize the film's theme, especially the use of light and shadow and expressionist forms.

Gregor notes that the film's rhythm is distorted, if not totally destroyed, by being projected at the wrong speed.

319   Hartmann, Rainer. "Wirklichkeit statt Menschheitsfragen." Frankfurter Neue Presse̲ (26 May).
      Hartmann begins by noting that M̲ marked the end of the first phase of Lang's career, during which he tried to solve the problems of humanity and made films full of false pathos and pseudophilosophy. Lang returned to Germany in 1960 to make a vulgar Mabuse̲ film full of clichés. Die tausend̲ Augen̲ [The Thousand Eyes], according to Hartmann, had nothing in common with Lang's American films, which Hartmann admires. He picks out Fury̲, Ministry of Fear̲, and Manhunt̲ for special mention and praises Lang's deftness with the conventions of the Western. Hangmen Also Die̲, Hartmann says, is much more than a political thriller, standing instead as a testimonial to community action.
      In America, Lang was known mainly as a director of gangster films, but The Big Heat̲ and While the City Sleeps̲ show Lang's ability to use the genre for social criticism. The new German film, which also specializes in thrillers, has nothing to set beside Lang's films.
      Hartmann is less satisfied with Human Desire̲ and Beyond̲ a Reasonable Doubt̲, which raise the issue of circumstantial evidence, mainly because of the improbabilities in the works. Human Desire̲ shows people at the mercy of uncontrollable forces. Hartmann notes that Lang never succeeded in making convincing love scenes, but he praises the mise-en-̲ scène̲ in Lang's films, demonstrating that the "realist" Lang still "thinks in pictures." He praises the Westerns for the use of color and for their rhythm.
      Hartmann ends by saying how he values the Bad Ems Retrospective for what it showed about Lang's development and he hopes the film clubs will do more.

320   Hull, David Stewart. "About Fritz Lang." The Playgoer̲ (January 23), pp. 9-13.
      In these notes for a viewing of Fury̲, Hull surveys Lang's career, briefly commenting on the main films up to Fury̲ and noting critical disagreements regarding his subsequent American works, films that the French have recently applauded.

321   Jacob, Gilles. "L'Erreur Judiciaire: Fritz Lang." In Le̲

Cinéma Moderne. Lyons: Serdoc, pp. 75-82.

This article begins by linking You Only Live Once to Lang's preoccupation with fate and with society as the cause of people's turning to crime. Jacob focuses on the way Lang uses images to express his themes: the heavy court buildings symbolize the inflexibility of the law and the haunting honeymoon scene is full of foreboding. Lang's films have always used decor expressively, and he has also always refused to show the violent deed itself. Horror and sex are presented indirectly.

Jacob links Lang's obsession with the haunted man to his Jewishness and his knowledge of a haunted people. He is also haunted by the notion of judicial error, so that while Antonioni shows the fragility of love, Lang shows the fragility of testimony. His major theme is that of a man wrongly suspected of crime, imprisoned, and only too late found to be innocent.

Jacob compares Hitchcock's The Wrong Man to You Only Live Once. Both star Henry Fonda, but while Hitchcock's film is good, it is not the film of a serious, committed filmmaker.

Jacob attributes the claustrophobia of Lang's film to the fact that the camera barely leaves Fonda. We are tricked into judging wrongly, according to false testimony, so as to give us the experience of belonging in a false, blind society. Lang's dishonesty, Jacob feels, is forgivable. We are tricked in a different way in Woman in the Window, where the whole murder turns out to have been a dream.

The unimpeachable style, the unity, and the heavy atmosphere, which Lang recreates so well in his films, are witness to a basic tragic sensibility. There are few sympathetic people in Lang's films: Lang stands outside his filmic world, looking at it through his famous monocle, disdaining these people, while masking his tenderness for them. He remains an indispensable objective presence behind his films.

322 Lefèvre, Raymond. "Fritz Lang Dossier." Image et Son (Paris), No. 169 (January), pp. 61-70.

Lefèvre has compiled this "dossier" by gathering together excerpts from various previously published books and articles on Lang (most of which have been annotated in this bibliography). He groups the selections under the following headings: (a) a biography of Lang; (b) the man himself; (c) Lang's cinematic style; (d) expressionism; (e) Lang's main themes; (f) the evolution of the art and the perfecting of his mise-en-scène; and (g) a bibliography (often without full citations, unfortunately).

There is no original material by Lefèvre here.

323 Leiser, Erwin. "Notizen über Fritz Lang." Atlas Filmheft 38.

(Available in Deutschen Film und Fernsehakademie, W. Berlin.)

Leiser notes that in Godard's Le Mépris Lang incarnates the Lang legend of a demonic film director, who cites Hölderlin, Dante, and Brecht out of weariness and despair. The real Lang, Leiser says, is different: generous, humorous, and charming, he is interested in young people and in all kinds of experiments. Lang believes that his generation had things much easier than the present one, in that they were in a situation when film form was new, leaving lots of room for experimentation.

Lang's main theme, according to Leiser, is the struggle of people against their destiny. Yet Lang now sees his early film, Der müde Tod [Destiny], as presenting a utopian idea of human nature; M, his first sound film, provided the opportunity for new technical experiments; Das Testament des Dr. Mabuse [The Last Will of Dr. Mabuse] was banned by the Nazis because it revealed the mechanisms of social terror before National Socialists practiced them.

Lang's films combine personal themes with those relating to political events of his period.

324    Napolitano, Antonio. "Fritz Lang." Il Mattino (28 August).
Napolitano surveys Lang's career, but focuses on the problem of von Harbou and on defining her role. How much was she responsible for? What was Lang's contribution? He goes on to discuss how Harbou stayed in Germany after the Nazis came to power and wrote scripts for Nazi films aimed at the deformation of humanity.

325    Patalas, Enno. "Fritz Lang, der Unbekannte: Jahrestreffen der deutschen Filmclubs." Frankfurter Allgemeine Zeitung (7 May).
Patalas begins by noting the new seriousness with which film is being viewed in Germany as evidenced by the emergence of film clubs. While the bias has so far been toward New Wave films, it is now time to look at German films produced both before and after the war.

The occasion for the article is the Bad Ems Lang retrospective. Patalas notes that it is now time to reconsider Lang's work and to ask key questions. What, for example, is the truth about Lang in relation to fascism? Was he a proto-fascist or an antifascist? What made him the darling of Goebbels and Hitler? How did Lang adapt German cultural tradition to the New World? Was there a basic difference in the way Lang reflected social reality before and after leaving Germany? Does Lang belong in the first order of auteurs or not? What can we say about his style from Die Nibelungen to M and from The Big Heat to Die tausend Augen [The Thousand Eyes]? Is there a progression or a falling-off in style?

Patalas concludes by saying that the American films, too little known in Germany, now need reexamining in the way that has been done in France. Surveying the few books on Lang, largely from France, Patalas complains about there being no German Lang text and urges that this lack be remedied. The retrospective provides a good opportunity for new work on Lang.

See also:
> Schröder, Peter H. "M und Die tausend Augen des Dr. Mabuse." Die Welt (Hamburg) (12 May).
> N. [Nettelbeck] U. [Uwe] "Die Zerstörung einer Legende." Die Zeit (Hamburg) (15 April).

326   Ponzi, Maurizio. "Rapporti fra Uomo e Societa: Fritz Lang" ["Links Between Man and Society: Fritz Lang"]. Filmcritica (Rome), (September), pp. 462-467.

Writing on the occasion of a retrospective of You Only Live Once, Ponzi says that it is ridiculous to admire the Lang of M and The Last Will while ignoring the importance "of Lang's other films. The focus on love-relationships, for example, unites Lang's films from M to Das Indische Grabmal." Lang's interest throughout his work was in the struggle rather than in winning.

Ponzi next discusses the way the narrative of You Only Live Once reveals Lang's criticism of a society where justice is impossible. The individual is oppressed by an egotistical world; Lang's heroes are always alone.

Ponzi discusses the links between You Only Live Once and the later Human Desire. He praises the geometrical design of the film--the music, the sounds, the images of trains throughout. He notes the film's pessimism, but sees it as leaving open the possibility for change, since the conditions are seen to arise from capitalism.

Ponzi concludes that the Indian films represent the culmination of Lang's career, despite the poor reviews in Italy, where Lang means M and little else. To deny an evolution in Lang's work is a severe error: Lang's constant theme is the stifling of people in a capitalist society; social laws are seen to limit human capacities. But the power of Lang's work lies in the hope he leaves for salvation.

327   Porter, Miguel. "La Estructura Profética en M" [The Prophetic Structure of M."]. In Spanish edition of the script, M: El Vampiro de Dusseldorf. Barcelona.

Porter begins by noting that, while film generally represents a vision of human experience, classical works create a special difficulty of understanding because of their location in a past reality. In addition, there is the author's personal presence and the projection of indi-

vidual issues. The medium of film itself presents
further problems in that there is a special language and a
collective spectator. Recently there have been attempts to
circulate classical film more commerically and to provide
written materials giving background and interpretation.

Porter proceeds to an examination of M, which he finds
constructed according to the principles of classical theatre
--having a prologue, three parts, and an epilogue. He examines each section in turn:

(1) the prologue:  Intended to create tension and introduce
the protagonists, this section consists of the children's
choir, the scenes with the mother (juxtaposition of
normality and intuitive discomfort), and the blindman,
who represents the force of destiny that plays a role
in the tragedy;

(2) part I:  Here we see reactions to the murder--the collective excitement and panic, the police reactions, and
reactions of the underground, whose livelihood is
threatened;

(3) part II:  Here we see the parallels between the police
and the beggar association and the mixing of emotive
and rational elements. The basic elements of the story
are interwoven, changing the course of the story;

(4) part III (conclusion):  Here the paths of the argument
converge and characters suffer individually and collectively; the murderer becomes a victim and destiny, in
the shape of the blind beggar, tips the balance toward
tragedy. Justice and injustice are united in a dangerous game, and anonymous collaborators--the psychiatrist
and the police--give the film the semblance of truth.

(5) the epilogue:  This section questions the whole concept
of justice. The judgement of the legal tribunal is most
likely the same as would have been given by the impro-
vised, beggar/thief tribunal. Mothers are warned to
take care of their children.

The interpretation of M should be based on an understanding of Lang's particular ways of thinking; the film should
be placed in the context of his nation's historical situation and of the form of production.

Lang's work is not revolutionary, since there is no
break with his world, but it does reflect his ethical viewpoint. In contrast to eighteenth- and nineteenth-century
storytellers, Lang offers no final solutions, but merely
projects a view of the future. The structure of M is drawn
from Brecht's Threepenny Opera, but ends up being quite different: while Brecht is dialectical, Lang is demonstrative.
He responds to Germany's socioeconomic situation and concludes that Germany must take care of its children. With
its mixture of realistic and expressionistic styles, its
combination of a dramatic-classical context and documentary
style photography, M attains an unexpected maturity. The

main idea is the Rousseauistic one of the individual versus
destiny.

327a    R. H.  "Verführung durch Dämon und Bild:  Ein Querschnitt
durch das Werk von Fritz Lang."  <u>Stuttgarter Zeitung</u> (8 May).
        R. H. gives an account of the retrospective of Lang's
films at Bad Ems, where representative works from <u>Die
Spinnen</u> [Spiders] to <u>Die tausend Augen</u> [The Thousand Eyes]
are being shown.  R. H. does not like the early works, finding them visually splendid but empty, cold, and politically
dangerous.  <u>M</u> marks the turning point toward realism before
Lang had to <u>l</u>eave Germany.  R. H. regrets that so few
American films were available for viewing, but praises the
ones he saw for their realism and accuracy about corruption
in America.  He hopes the film clubs will do more retrospectives.

328     Sandras, Michel.  "M, Le Maudit et L'Expressionisme."  <u>Image
et Son</u> (Paris), No. 169 (January), pp. 71-84.
        This article consists of detailed information useful for
audiences to have before a viewing of the film and of suggestions for discussion topics afterwards.  There is first
an analysis of the historical background of the term "expressionism," necessary for a full understanding of its
meaning; next, the more general historical, political, and
aesthetic context of the film is surveyed, i.e., the 1930s
as a period, surrealism, and the expressionist aesthetic.
Sandras argues that the themes and styles of <u>M</u> emerge from
its historical moment.
        The following topics are briefly discussed as suitable
for consideration:
(1) the film as a police film, its realistic aspects;
(2) the expressionist aesthetic as it emerges from the film:
        (a) the lighting (expressionist in its effort to trans-
            late a mental state into visual terms);
        (b) the importance of decor, <u>mise-en-scène</u>, and camera
            movement;
        (c) the use of sound counterpoint;
        (d) the total structural conception of the film.
(3) the significance of <u>M</u> and of expressionism needs to be
    discussed in relation to metaphysical, social, and moral
    issues.
Sandras concludes his analysis with general remarks and
ends with a biography of Lang and a brief bibliography.
        The same <u>Image et Son</u> issue contains a Lang "dossier,"
compiled by Raymond Lefèvre and consisting of a Lang biography, discussion of his visual style, his relation to expressionism, his main themes, the evolution of his art, and a
bibliography.  (<u>See</u> Entry No. 322.)

329     Schröder, Peter.  "Ornament und Ideologie:  Zu einer Fritz Lang

Retrospective." Film (Munich), No. 8 (June-July).

Schröder announces his intention as that of analyzing
the specific reasons for Lang's recent acclaim in both
France and England. The Bad Ems Retrospective, he says, in
many ways destroyed the Lang legend. He will look at aspects
of Lang's style, personal aesthetics, and philosophy in order to give concrete form to the myth built up by Luc Moullet
and Courtade.

In his first section, titled "Sensationalism and Bourgeois
Needs," Schröder traces Lang's career back to writing scripts
for May and Rippert, where he became used to fulfilling bourgeois fantasies. He was to continue to do this, never denying that sensationalism was an important part of his depiction of his times. Schröder stresses that Lang's fantasy
world does rest on reality and sees a common line from the
Kay Hoog figure on through Lohmann, Frank James, Vance Shaw,
Captain Thorndike, Svoboda, and the architect in the later
Indian films. Primarily a bourgeois figure, this type takes
on different colorings according to the period when each
film is made, giving a sociological survey of these eras.

Lang discovered, according to Schröder, what the French
now call mise-en-scène, and his films satisfy through their
use of light and their architecture. The French love his B
films because he presents reality through melodrama.

In the second section, "The Past and the German Soul,"
Schröder analyzes the German elements in Der müde Tod
[Destiny] and the feeling for the tragic that this film
shares with Die Nibelungen. The elements Spengler isolated
as typically German are evident, especially the yearning to
break all bounds found in Faustian man. Schröder then analyzes Lang's mise-en-scène in these films in detail, likening
it to that found in Caligari, particularly the use of light
and dark and the sets that create a sculptured world. Nature is reduced to decor, but there is not as much expressionism in these films as Moullet and Courtade think.

Schröder next discusses the politics of the ornamental
style, finding prefascist tendencies.

In a third section, "Decor and Man," Schröder contrasts
the use of mise-en-scène vis-à-vis characters in Die
Nibelungen (an extreme) and in the later American films.
Schröder praises Die Nibelungen for its visual magnificence,
but notes that here decor triumphs over people, who are
merely statutes placed in a totally conditioned world. With
M and the sound film, more montage possibilities became
available to Lang, and in the American films one finds only
traces of the original use of decor in details in the interiors. American cinema eschewed the colossal sets, huge ex-
teriors, and ornamental designs.

In a final section, "Vision and Antifaschism," Schröder
argues that Fury is Lang's most antifascist film because it
deals with the arousal of fascist feelings among the mass

of the people. But he criticises the banal characters and
the homespun feeling that remains from the German films.
Schröder concludes that Lang did not indulge his liking for
adventure and melodrama only twice--in M and Fury--but that
it is wrong to see value only in films with social ideas.
These are not the films that the French admire; German filmmakers can learn from Lang what is equally important for
cinema and what they lack, namely brilliance in visual style.
Lang has yet to be properly discovered by the German public.

330   Schütte, Wolfram. "Kolportage, Stilisierung, Realismus.
      Anmerkungen zum Werk Fritz Langs von den 'Spinnen' bis zu
      dem 'Testament des Dr. Mabuse.'"  Filmstudio (Frankfurt),
      No. 44 (September).  Reprinted from Neue Zürcher Zeitung
      (28 July and 4 August).
         Schütte begins by saying that although Lang is not a
      naive director, his works are naive in their simplistic
      world view (i.e., the social/political elements) and their
      handling of emotions (i.e., the focus on broad feelings--
      love, hate, and violence--and on the basic struggle between
      good and evil).  There is a contradiction between this rather
      naive material and the sophisticated artistic treatment.
      The most problematic aspect of Lang's work is the tension
      between form and content, which was never transcended.  The
      films become sensational when Lang cannot fuse form and
      content.
         Schütte goes on to account in part for the sensationalism
      of Lang's films by noting that Lang began working at a time
      when all films were naive and sensational.  The earliest
      forms were the melodrama and the burlesque; film was merely
      intended as an escape from the trials of life.  Die Spinnen
      [The Spiders] already contains many of the naive elements
      that were to recur in later Lang films--such as the woman
      in the power of some crime organization--and that were much
      influenced by Karl May's travel novels with their compli-
      cated adventures.  There is the division of the world into
      good and evil, the concept of the underworld (repeated in
      the Huns in Kriemhilds Rache [Kriemhild's Revenge], the
      workers' world in Metropolis, the beggars in M, the lepers
      in Der Tiger von Eschnapur [The Tiger of Bengal]), and the
      mixture of realism, stylization, and ornamental grandeur.
      As with all sensationalism, it is hard to find one's way
      through Lang's junglelike texture, but the films up to 1933
      and Das Testament des Dr. Mabuse [The Last Will of Dr.
      Mabuse] reflect in their form the historical angst, with
      people not what they projected and no one believing in what
      they were.  The pessimism and death-leaning madness that
      fascinated Thomas Mann in Wagner also dominated Lang's
      world through M.  Der müde Tod [Destiny] shows well Lang's
      latent romanticism and his leaning toward death, the mys-
      terious, and the exotic.  Lang talks of a film's creating

myths like fairy tales, and his early work is a synthesis
of myths having to do with hell and Grimm's fairy tales.
The films lack psychological depth and function on a simple
level.

Schütte next turns to Lang's visual style and comments
on the effects of Lang's interest in architecture and painting. Lang is influenced by the expressionist movement,
especially in his use of lighting, as Lotte Eisner has
shown, but thematically he differs. While the expressionists tried to show the essence of one's being when freed
from all restraints, Lang's people are always confined within mythical or social-utopian limits, a fate that conditions
their existence. Echoing this theme, Lang's camera fixes
the characters as the painter fixes objects on the canvas;
they are reduced to ornamental faces, passively placed as
the director desires for compositional reasons.

Schütte agrees with Kracauer's view of Metropolis, for
example, that Lang treats the workers in a formalist way,
making the masses into a picturesque entity rather than a
political one. The high degree of formal stylization prepared for the fascist works of Leni Riefenstahl. Schütte
is not saying that Lang's works are fascist or prefascist,
but he notes that they do not reflect the "democratic
spirit." Lang is too fascinated with the hierarchical,
archaic, and mythic order of honor, love, revenge, and hate.
His works are essentially aristocratic in their treatment
of the material, that is, in their formalism and the abstract ethical system they present. They reflect a kind of
nihilism rather than belonging to either fascist or democratic ideology.

M freed Lang from the shadows of Die Nibelungen that so
unfortunately influenced his later work. Sound freed Lang
from the passive, static nature of the silent works, and M
represents the high point of his work. For the most part,
Lang does not present a perspective on the world through
the ironic distancing of the author (as, for example, in
Thomas Mann). His works are instead founded in nineteenth-
century bourgeois culture and are informed by a sentimental
romanticism. What was only dimly present in Lang's early
works became dominant and central during the Nazi period.

331    Ungureit, Heinz. "Fritz Lang, der Unbekannte und Verkannte."
       Frankfurter Rundshau (16 May), p. 5.
       Ungureit finds Lang an unrewarding director, who, never-
theless, has been accorded much praise in France and England.
The Germans soon dropped interest in him once they found
fascist elements in the works, and although some older people began to make a place for Lang in film history, redeeming the early films, they knew as little as the younger
people about his American works. Because of all the contradictory criticism, Lang remains an enigma. The retrospective

organized by the film clubs in Bad Ems was interesting, but did not help much.

Ungureit launches into a discussion of the politics of Lang's films, evidently relying on Kracauer's analysis in From Caligari to Hitler. The early films reflect the tendencies that were to result in nazism--the playing with death, the presence of uncontrollable evil, the idea of revenge, the use of people as an enslaved mass, etc.

But Ungureit notes that Lang did leave Germany and quotes Gavin Lambert to the effect that the tendencies in German films of the 1920s have as much to do with elements of Romanticism in the culture generally as with fascism per se. The world view was nevertheless a perverted one, according to Ungureit, showing that justice could come only from the underworld and that chaos prevailed.

Yet somehow in America Lang, a protofascist, developed into a solid antifascist. Patalas points out that the American films negate the prefascist concerns that had interested Lang earlier, but that he continues to see no alternative between chaos on the one hand and a repressive, mechanical authority on the other. There is no possibility for a vital and democratic social exchange.

Once in Hollywood, Lang was limited by the film industry itself and by the Hays Code. Yet the early films did reflect a criticism of both lynching and justice in the United States. Hangmen Also Die was a political film, but Lang did not understand as well as Brecht the resistance of the group to a repressive authority.

332    Verband des Deutschen Filmklubs. Retrospektive Fritz Lang: Dokumentation. Bad Ems.

The book consists of two volumes and is an extremely useful collection of reviews on Lang (many of which have been annotated here) reprinted from newspapers and film journals internationally. Volume 1 deals with the German films. There is a general introduction, consisting of a discussion of the 1920s generally and then of the German situation specifically, comments on whether or not film is an art and on film in relation to literature. Second, there is a large number of excerpts from reviews of the early films from film journals and newspapers and third, materials on Lang's contribution to the development of the German film, giving an overview of his early films. Volume 2 has similar material on Lang's American films.

333    Waldekranz, Rune. "Fritz Lang und die deutsche Malerschule." Atlas Filmheft 38. [Excerpt from a lecture given in Kiel, 1960].

Waldekranz begins by noting that Lang's importance for film history lies in the early German works preceding Hitler's coming to power. Lang stands out as the expressionist filmmaker who used film both as a sculptural, decorative medium and as a means of commenting on his times.

While Lang was not really original--he drew upon the various movements of the period, which was, after all, one of artistic revolutions--he is the most vital and famous of the artists. In an attempt to reconstruct some possible influences on Lang, Waldekranz lists all the new German films that Lang might have seen in Paris from 1913 on, speculating particularly on the influence of Paul Wegener's films and of some of the early Italian epic films like Quo Vadis? and Anthony and Cleopatra or the Italian Die Nibelungen.

Waldekranz surveys Lang's background and history, noting that he was the son of an architect who wanted Lang to take up that career. Film seemed to combine Lang's own interest in painting with his training in architecture. His youthful style is best seen in the paintings and book illustrations that Lang did in Paris, and that combine the decorative style with literary fantasy.

Lang was a born creator of thrillers, as can be seen in the first scripts that he wrote for Joe May after the First World War. One already finds here Lang's preoccupation with the brutal and the macabre, which he raised to the level of art. The war meant that death became a reality for Lang, and fate and death dominated his films from then on. While Der müde Tod [Destiny] reflects Lang's own experience, it also symbolized that of his generation in its depiction of the struggle between love and death.

Lang began to develop the notion of women as potentially destructive in the first films. Der müde Tod combines inspiration from Renaissance painters, like Dürer and Grünewald, with Lang's own style as developed in his illustrations for fairy tales. In this way Der müde Tod prepares for Die Nibelungen and Metropolis.

Waldekranz concludes by noting how expressionism as a style had permeated all the arts up until the 1920s. The new art of film gave a subjective and soulful vision of reality. Paradoxically, the late romantic belief in the artist as the purveyor of 'truth,' as the prophet, won, in film, a new attention to "reality." Yet the influence of the Reinhardt theater, with its emphasis on symbolism, was also there.

1965

334   Alexandre, Alexander. "Die Kopien reichen nicht aus:  Paris feiert Fritz Lang und die grosse deutsche Stummfilmzeit." Neue Rhein-Ruhr-Zeitung (Köln-Essen) (3 November).
      The article was written on the occasion of a program, "The Haunted Screen," being shown in Paris that included several Lang films. Alexandre talks with Lang briefly in

his hotel, noting that when not in public Lang does not wear his monocle. When asked about the state of the German film, Lang contrasts the excitement between the two world wars, which Hitler's coming to power destroyed, with the dirth of films in contemporary Germany, despite the twenty years that have passed since the end of the war. Alexandre comments that a new wave seems about to break as young film-makers begin to get organized financially.

Lang gives high praise to Godard and Truffaut in France and predicts that Nicolas Gessner has a great future.

See also:
> PEM. [Paul Marcus]. "Klassiker mit Monokel und Millimeter Papier." Film-Telegramm (30 November).

335   Färber, Helmut. "Die Gejagten wiederaufgeführt." Süddeutsche Zeitung (Munich) (4 October). [Review of Rancho Norotious].

According to Färber, the world of the Western with a story of revenge, love, and death must have well suited Lang's predilection for the fateful melodramatic elements in human life. Nevertheless, his relation to that world has something brittle and crumbling about it. A Western is always a story of something long past. Yet whereas John Ford calmly depicts epic scenarios and portrays even a brawl as a loving memory, a ballad that is only in part elaborated further is sung throughout Lang's entire film. Situations fall apart without having properly solidified, and the colors and decor have a curious coolness and artificiality. In fact, sometimes one almost doesn't want to believe that these heroes really shoot so well. One sees the world of the Western and yet doesn't see it: one sees it dissolving.

For Färber, this mood of resignation, emptiness, and transitoriness is made concrete in the two main characters. Both fit the archetype of legendary characters of the Western and both are these no longer, for they have grown old. Marlene Dietrich appears as an aged beauty--portrayed not in a psychologically believable manner, but instead in a fascinating, playful way; therein lies more "human truth" than where one tries to make everything meaningful.

336   Freund, Rudolf. "Zwischen Kunst und Kolportage." Filmspiegel (East Berlin), No. 24 (1 December).

According to Freund, Lang is one of the few great old men of film who are still alive--one of those who had already made a name for themselves in silent film and (even rarer) who did not lose their artistic potency with the advent of sound.

The artist's gloomy works, in which crime, violence, and death rule, began to take shape in Dr. Mabuse, der Spieler [Dr. Mabuse, the Gambler]. The film is still true sensationalism, but the beginnings of a dark realism emerge:

the crisis-ridden Wiemar Republic is mirrored in the game
halls and streetfights. Yet Lang wanted to be an artist
and pursued this goal on an entirely different path, namely,
the molding of a particular form while the content remained
relatively unimportant. During this time he married von
Harbou, later a Nazi follower, who wrote the scripts, which
were a mostly uneven, somewhat "folkisch" literary hodge-
podge.

Freund notes that one of von Harbou's first, and artistically still interesting, films was Der müde Tod [Destiny],
a "German ballad" based on an old fairy-tale motif. The
famous Nibelungen became a favorite of the right-wingers.
Lang certainly did not intend the racial implications of
the film; rather, he took naive pleasure in his slow-moving
collossal images.

Lang later noted that, as an artist, he was still "politically naive." The best evidence of this is Metropolis.
Today Lang comments that "I personally . . . don't like
Metropolis because I believe that the way in which the film
tries to solve a social problem is childish."

Lang, in his first sound film, M, reached surprising
artistic heights. Up until now conventional antinomies
flowed through his film: good and evil, hate and love,
crime and punishment. Lang frees himself from this contrived world in M. Freund says that in 1933 Lang was one of the
most important directors of the sound film. With M he was
one of the first who did not use sound naturalistically,
but rather set it "against" the picture: sound-montages
supplement and connect the changing sequences of the film.
Sound is used as a dramaturgical leitmotif.

According to Freund, Lang's first Hollywood films confirmed that he could maintain these heights in a foreign
land. In Fury, the director, whose political conscience
was strengthened by his emigration, treats a burning wound
of American society: the problem of lynch justice. The
conclusion of the film is obviously a compromise for the
public taste after this gloomy picture of violence and
cruelty.

Freund notes that Hangmen also Die was one of a series
of antifascist films Lang made during World War II, its message superficially attached to a spy story. The film lacks
Lang's old fatalism, probably due to Brecht's influence.
His heroes are not loners, but rather prove themselves collectively. The film is somewhat uneven.

In 1958 Lang went back to West Germany, but he was only
offered remakes of themes he had already dealt with. He
died artistically at this point. Two years later Lang played himself in Godard's Le Mépris--a tired, old, bored film
director. Freund concludes that, instead of leaving Lang
on this note, we should instead lay claim to his best films
and to the artist who had the courage to say "No."

337  Gregor, Ulrich.  "Fury."  Filmkritik (Munich), No. 3, pp.
     149-151.
        The article was written on the occasion of the first
     showing in Germany of Fury, Gregor noting how little is
     known of Lang's early American works.  The film is usually
     seen in the tradition of social message films and if not
     the best that Lang has done, is at least vivid and real.
     Often critics note that the film's themes also fit in with
     those common to Lang's work as a whole.
        Gregor, however, sees the film as sentimental and full
     of clichés, particularly in connection with Americans' sup-
     posed hatred of foreigners.  (Gregor does admit that, newly
     arrived as he was from Germany, Lang may have actually ex-
     perienced this prejudice.)  He deplores the rhetorical, po-
     lemical elements in the film, especially the sentimental
     use of the dog and the artificial happy ending with Joe's
     sudden conversion to humanitarianism.
        In both good and bad ways, Fury represents Lang's special
     interests:  it recalls Mabuse in Joe's pretending to be dead
     and directing things from a secret place and M in the lynch-
     ing, although in that film the lynching was a very private
     thing and here it is public.  The film is better viewed in
     terms of Lang's major themes--claustrophobia, terror, and
     anxiety--than as documenting real social situations.  But
     the combination of Lang's personal themes with the social
     analysis of America makes Fury a high point, not only in
     his career but also in that of the American film generally.

338  Hollman, Reimar.  "Fritz Lang, Regisseur ohne Engagement."
     Film (East Berlin), 3, No. 12 (December), 27-32.
        Hollman argues that Lang is a cold, antihuman, possibly
     even misogynist, director, maintaining distance from both
     his characters and his work.  Interested more in form than
     in content, Lang compromises, working within established
     fashions or conventions.  His training in painting and arch-
     itecture accounts for his use of mass in his compositions.
     Lang complies rather than invents, and he shows no interest
     in people per se.  Siegfried shows Lang at his most abstract,
     concerned here as he is with composition, lines, and mass,
     while in Metropolis and M the characters are mere objects
     for the camera.
        Lang leans toward a romanticism of a bleak kind related
     to Brentano, E. T. A. Hoffmann, and Poe.  When under the
     influence of Brecht, Lang overcame this, but from the time
     of the Caligari project, Lang had been interested in mad-
     ness, as the Mabuse films show.
        In terms of technique, Lang replaces Eisenstein's montage
     with overlapping, preceding Welles in having a sentence that
     starts in one scene being completed in the next.
        In general, Lang sees the faults of institutions but does
     not think in terms of changing the world.  Godard's Le

Mépris [Contempt] summarizes as well as anything Lang's
prevailing attitudes to his work.

339    Huaco, George A.  "Introduction" and "German Expressionism."
       In his The Sociology of Film Art.  New York:  Basic Books.
       Pp. 3-7, 25-92.
            George Huaco's book is interesting primarily as an ex-
       ample of a kind of sociological/political methodology now
       largely discredited because too schematic.  The part of the
       book relevant to Lang is that dealing with German Expression-
       ism, which has plot outlines of Der müde Tod, Dr. Mabuse,
       Die Nibelungen, Metropolis and M.  Huaco accounts for the
       rise of expressionism in film on the basis of four "struc-
       tural factors":  (1) the trained cadre of technicians, cam-
       eramen, directors, and actors; (2) an industrial film plant
       consisting of studios, laboratories, and equipment; (3) a
       mode of organization of the film industry favorable to the
       ideology of the future film wave; and (4) a climate of po-
       litical norms favorable to this ideology.  After outlining
       twenty-one plots, including those of five of Lang's films,
       Huaco concludes that they reveal "a consistent and self-
       reinforcing pattern of conservative and frequently reaction-
       ary themes and interpretations."  He accounts for this by
       the fact that the film industry had a semimonopolistic mode
       of organization, which ensured that the ideology of expres-
       sionist films would be conservative and devoid of social
       criticism.
            The problem with Huaco's book is his reliance on Kracauer,
       whom he quotes extensively, and the reductive nature of his
       treatment of film.  He draws conclusions about the ideology
       in films simply from a particular interpretation of the
       plots.  He applies, in addition, certain external factors,
       like a director's social background or political develop-
       ments of the period, whose exact bearing on the shape of a
       film is highly questionable.
            Most useful perhaps is the brief history of the sources
       of the expressionist style in painting, drama, and litera-
       ture with which the chapter on expressionism concludes.

340    Jahnke, Eckart.  "Fritz Lang's M."  Film (East Berlin), No. 6,
       pp. 169-180.
            Jahnke places M in the context of the emergence of sound
       and of Eisenstein's montage experiments.  Lang's use of mon-
       tage conveys hectic city life well.
            The city sequences also show Berlin in a time of crisis:
       many were questioning the political system and were attract-
       ed to either the Communist or the Nazi party.  Those, like
       Lang, who could not see the historical necessity of what
       was taking place, fell into despair, and came under the in-
       fluence of pessimistic philosophers like Spengler and
       Schopenhauer.  People looked to metaphysics to account for

the state of affairs, and thus fate and guilt took on mystical dimensions.

The notion of the human being confronting destiny had
early on been a central Langian theme. This took on psychological form under the influence of Freud, who showed that
people are governed by driving forces beyond their control.
Mabuse is driven by a lust for power, and the murderer in
M by a pathological sexual drive.

Jahnke criticizes Lang for offering no solutions in M;
he does not agree with some critics who say that the underworld represents sound popular instinct as an alternative
to authority. On the contrary, Lang tends to favor the
established law of bourgeois society and to see this as the
answer. Yet, as Kracauer notes, Lang is also attracted in
some way to lawlessness. It is hard ultimately to find
social criticism in Lang; it is all "served up with sensual
enjoyment." Although Lang himself in interviews claims that
he was engaged in social criticism, Jahnke believes that in
the end it all ends up as metaphysics. Lang cannot, like
Brecht, get to the essence of things, because he does not
understand economic relations. He remains superficial, because he believes in predetermined destiny. While he is
able to grasp tendencies of his period and reflect them in
his films, he cannot present a scientific analysis of social
problems.

Lang is often praised for his presentiment in foreshadowing the Nazi regime in the parallel montage sequence in M,
where police and gangsters are equated. But Jahnke understands this sequence instead as reflecting two contradictory
tendencies within Lang himself--that toward the law and that
toward anarchy. He was inspired by outcasts and anarchic
situations, but all he ever did was to transpose these to
film. Following Brecht's Threepenny Opera, Lang chose
Verfremdung [distancing] for his style, but presents only a
shallow treatment of problems.

Jahnke concludes with a detailed look at some of Lang's
technical achievements, particularly in relation to sound.
He gives many examples of contrapuntal uses and then praises
Lang's grasp of atmosphere and dramatic use of details. But
ultimately Lang fails for Jahnke because he offers no solutions to the issues he introduces. Jahnke quotes Lang as
saying rather hesitantly that film is, or should be, a form
of social criticism and even declaring that he is a leftist.
Jahnke leaves no doubt that he cannot accept this--it all
depends, he says, on one's point of view.

341   Jansen, Peter W. "Appell zu einem Happy-End. Fritz Lang wird
am 5. Dezember 75 Jahre alt." Frankfurter Allgemeine Zeitung
(4 December), p. 2.
      Praising Lang's first great film, Der müde Tod [Destiny]
for its architectural style and the use of light and shadow,

Jansen also notes that in this film nothing was left to
chance. So a new director was born, one who never deviated
from the aesthetic approach that he started with, and who,
furthermore, established a new direction for German film
with his insistence that people be shown as "responsible."
For at this time the idea of fate was dominant, reflecting
the fear of some dark horror underlying society. This notion was initiated by the catastrophe of World War I, which
also sowed the seeds for fascism.

Jansen notes that Lang could not help it if Hitler liked
his Die Nibelungen and Metropolis; Hitler did not understand
the warning signs that Lang had inserted in Metropolis,
where the workers are swallowed by a gigantic mouth. M
linked the establishment to criminals, while Das Testament
des Dr. Mabuse [The Last Will of Dr. Mabuse] figured Hitler
himself.

Once in America, Jansen says Lang made social message
films, later becoming a routine Hollywood filmmaker (Hangmen
Also Die, which was made with Brecht, is an exception in
this period). His remake of Das indische Grabmal [The
Indian Tomb] and Der Tiger von Eschnapur [The Tiger of
Bengal] are, according to Jansen, not typical Lang films,
but they did spark a revival in the German film industry.

Lang's American films remain unknown in Germany, although
a few were recently shown in a retrospective program. In
France, Lang has been made a grand old man of the cinema,
honored in Godard's Mépris and given an award by André
Malraux. Lang does not, however, want to become a living
monument and is currently developing plans for new films.

Jansen's birthday wish for Lang is not so much that he
will make new films but that Germany will grant him a place
of honor analogous to that he has rightly won in France.
In the words of Lang's friend, Theodor Adorno, "the happy
end is the discovery of passionate artists."

342   Jensen, Peter. "M," in Lennig, Arthur, ed. Classics of the
      Film. Madison, Wisconsin: Film Society Press, pp. 110-120.
      Jensen begins by noting how often Lang's heroes are in-
dividuals who are isolated in society. For Lang, society
is composed of two warring groups--organized justice on the
one hand and criminals on the other--and the individual is
caught between them. Jensen shows how the conflict is presented in Lang's films. The revenge theme is most evident
in Siegfried and Fury, while The Big Heat reveals the idea
of delayed justice. M focuses on the notion of impulsive
criminality, but Beckert is caught between the worlds of
Lohmann and the police, on the one hand, and on the other,
Schränker and the criminals. Lohmann and Schränker differ
in their approaches to finding the criminal, in personal
style, and in ultimate integrity.

Jensen next discusses the way in which M represents a

change in Lang's directing style. The overall style is
more naturalist and straightforward than in the earlier
films, although there are some remaining expressionist elements. Jensen comments on the excellent construction of
the film and ends by analyzing the subtle use of sound that
gives M a central place in the history of film.

343  K. H. Western Union. Filmkritik (Munich), No. 4 (April),
     p. 196.
     K. H. sees Western Union as a weary film, in which Lang
     took his lead from Ford's Iron Horse and tried to introduce
     an epic dimension through the conflict between two brothers,
     a device usually found in B films. While in Ford's film
     the theme is presented in a coherent manner, Lang only pre-
     sents picturesque details. Lang had wanted to make a film
     on a subject from American history, but he attains only
     the spectacular level here, with the semirehabilitation of
     the bad guy in the final showdown.

344  Michelson, Ole. "Fritz Lang." Kosmorama (Copenhagen), 12,
     No. 72 (December), 70-74.
     Michelson deals mainly with the early German works. The
     focus is primarily on showing the degree to which Lang does,
     or does not, belong to expressionism.

345  Patalas, Enno. "Rache von Frank James: Kurzkritik in
     'Kommentierte Westernografie II.'" Filmkritik (Munich),
     No. 3, p. 133.
     The film belongs to a series of Westerns that adhered to
     myths and attempted to present their heroes in the best
     light. In reality, Frank James did not revenge his brother's
     death, but in the legend Lang found the theme that had been
     evident in his earlier works: a man must follow his fate
     so that he can say, "Now I can look at myself in the mirror
     again."
     In its details and particularly in the court scene,
     Return of Frank James looks back to Lang's earlier films.
     While it has none of the epic atmosphere of Westerns, but
     instead a synthetic feeling, nevertheless the moral common
     to the genre shines through. The main interest in the film
     is the brilliant use of technicolor, as Gavin Lambert has
     shown.

346  Schmidt, Eckart. "Fritz Lang 75 Jahre alt." Süddeutsche
     Zeitung (Munich) (December 4), p. 35.
     Schmidt begins by wishing he could honor Lang less am-
     biguously than he has to, given Lang's controversial status.
     Lang has been both disdained and highly praised, and his
     forty-five films are often judged as a unit. Some consider
     Lang's pre-Hitler works as his greatest, while others find
     films like Metropolis and Die Nibelungen naive and

sentimental. Some people say that in America Lang remained under the sway of his bosses, while others assert that he never made a film he did not want to make; they place the American films next to, if not above, the German work. All agree that his return to Germany was unfortunate.

One can quickly find agreement on the greatness of certain films, such as M, Das Testament des Dr. Mabuse [The Last Will of Dr. Mabuse], Fury, Hangmen Also Die, and The Big Heat. But it is hard to accept the fact that Lang was continuously creative over a forty-year period. Critics often see an abrupt break between the German and the American periods; yet while M clearly emerged out of the earlier work, it also prepares for the realism that Lang was to develop in America. The more ordinary the content of his American films became, the more visually and stylistically artistic the films were. Lang's main theme remained the human struggle against an overriding fate, and his obsession with this reflected something deep in Lang's personality.

Next to Pabst and Murnau, Lang is considered the greatest of German directors. Now seventy-five years old, he is seen at all international film festivals, and he is known from Godard's Le Mépris and from numerous interviews. He is apparently planning a new film, Death of a Career Girl.

347  Schröder, Peter H. "Orientalischer Irrgarten und Grossberlin." Filmkritik (Munich), No. 12, pp. 670-682.
This long article contains an overview of Lang's career and works, as well as quotations from his own early writings and his French interviews. Schröder finds in the early German works a preoccupation with the exotic and the Romantic, which reflect Lang's travels in the East. Schröder basically finds the American films shockingly naive, picking out only Hangmen Also Die and Moonfleet for commendation. He finds some links with the themes and interests of the early German period, but while arguing for a certain unity in Lang's works, sees a decline in the American period.
There is a biofilmography at the end of the articles, following the quotations.

348  Schröder, Peter H. "Der Bürger zweier Welten". Filmreport, No. 16. [On the occasion of Lang's seventy-fifth birthday]. (Available in Deutschen Film und Fernschakademie, W. Berlin.)
Schröder points out how Lang's life is typical of that of many others of the period, in that he grew up in Germany, but is now an American citizen. He briefly surveys Lang's career, both in Germany and in America.

349  Schröder, Peter H. "Dekor, Licht und Schatten." Die Welt (Hamburg) (4 December).
Written on the occasion of Lang's seventy-fifth birthday,

this article surveys his life and career. Schröder notes
that while Lang worked with ordinary genres in his American
films, he retained his own vision of the world--his preoccupation with fate, misogyny, the play of light and shadow,
decor. While Lang's early films are revered as great works,
ironically they cannot be seen outside of their dim life
circulating around the film clubs.

Lang's modernity and talent have been honored in France,
where young filmmakers (for example, Godard, Rivette,
Truffaut, Rohmer) look at his films often. Germany should
have a Lang retrospective analogous to that held in Paris.

Lang will no longer make films in Germany, but Schröder
wishes him well with a new project, Death of a Career Girl,
to be made in Paris. This work should be a fitting conclusion to Lang's long career, consisting of forty-three films
in forty-five years.

See also on the occasion of Lang's seventy-fifth birthday:
   Patalas, Enno. "Altmeister der Regie." Abendzeitung
      (Munich) (4 December).

350  W. I. "Brigitte Bardot in Contempt: Fritz Lang als
     Schauspieler," Aufbau (New York) (29 January).
        W. I. gives a short description of the film, focusing on
     Bardot's role and her change from a soft, submissive wife
     to a hostile woman. W. I. discusses the collapse of strong
     feeling between people that the film shows. He or she goes
     on to mention Lang's acting himself in the film--the director
     with the confidence of a veteran and the worldly philosopher
     with charm and wit. With her soft voice, Bardot is convinc-
     ing in her tragic role. W. I. ends with praise for Godard's
     version of the Moravia original, and for the stunning color
     that pervades the film, giving it an electric texture.


### 1966

351  Bellour, Raymond. "Sur Fritz Lang." Critique, No. 226
     (March). Reprinted in Raymond Bellour. Le Livre des Autres.
     Editions de L'Herne: Paris, 1971. Translated in Sub-Stance,
     No. 9, 1974 (BFI).
        Bellour begins by noting what a strange destiny Fritz
     Lang has had: he is one of the first great film directors
     and yet embodies the very notion of mise-en-scène. Once in
     America, Lang became known as a great Hollywood director
     but nothing more, since "greatness" in Hollywood usually
     connotes absence of critical distance.
        In 1958, however, when Lang left Hollywood, the so-called
     New Wave group in France (including Astruc, Rivette, Rohmer,
     and Douchet) saw that Lang's works revealed the possibili-
     ties of cinema itself (this is not to say that Lang was

necessarily greater than other American directors). For
instance, in Fury, Lang inserts the vision itself, the
image, into the text of the film. This is evident in the
courtroom scene when a film of the lynching is shown and in
the presence of the investigator in so many of his works.
For Lang, the notion of seeing, the vision, is the ultimate
metaphor. Lang often said that a director should know life;
Bellour believes Lang here meant "life" as the place where
one perceives.

Bellour is especially impressed with Lang's last films
in Germany, Das indische Grabmal [The Indian Tomb] and Die
tausend Augen des Dr. Mabuse [The Thousand Eyes of Dr.
Mabuse], because they reveal Lang's interest in the cinema
as metaphor. A good example of this is Godard's Le Mépris,
where Lang is a director trying to make a film of The
Odyssey. During the forty years of his career, he tried to
formulate his ideas in visual terms. He plays a clever,
refined game with his themes and is personally authoritarian
and secretive. For this reason, his own words, in interviews, do not help much, for he played with the questions
and amused himself by giving contradictory responses, eluding the investigator much as the truth eludes people in his
films.

Bellour outlines the elements that need analyzing if one
is to understand Lang:

(1) Lang's use of point of view in relation to people; his
    perspective is ambiguous, shifting constantly;
(2) His use of point of view in relation to objects; he
    frequently uses close shots allowing his camera to ex-
    plore an environment gradually and coming in to focus
    on the significant object;
(3) His use of movement within the frame;
(4) His frequent use of photographs, plans, maps, letters,
    etc.
(5) His use of space--the dialectical movement between sub-
    ject and object, such as that between Jeff Warren and
    his train (Human Desire), the woman and the rocket (Die
    Frau im Mond [Woman in the Moon]), or Thorndike and his
    gun (Manhunt);
(6) The repetition of certain configurations; Lang will re-
    peat a specific scene, complete with mise-en-scène and
    actors, but the actors will be arranged differently
    within the frame, or different actors will be present
    to reflect how things have changed since the first time
    we saw the scene, or to remind us of what went on before;
(7) Finally, the perverse game that Lang plays needs analyz-
    ing, for he errects a kind of counterscenario, an under-
    cutting of the surface of the film.

Bellour concludes that a Lang film is always in the process of being made. By emphasizing the precariousness of
the "real," Lang shows how false the notion of a harmonious

universe really is. He breaks the illusion by inserting
elements antithetical to the presentation.

352  De Mandiarques, André-Peyre. "L'Écran Démoniaque." Cinéma 66,
     No. 100, pp. 64-107.
        The article consists of discussions by different authors
     of three early Lang films:
        1. Gilles Jacob, Der müde Tod [Destiny]
           Jacob considers the second section of the film as by
     far the most successful. What touches us today is the pro-
     fusion of forms that emanates from all the parts and the
     visual style that is not, as in Siegfried and Metropolis,
     pushed to a pure extreme but that instead shows a strong
     plastic sense carefully controlled. Jacob notes all the
     forms, shapes, spirals, and arabesques that hem the pro-
     tagonists in, inside the rigid frame.
        2. Marcel Martin, Metropolis
           Martin deplores the sentimental plot of the film,
     which he blames on Thea von Harbou, and again stresses the
     brilliant use of form and mise-en-scène.
        3. Marcel Martin, Dr. Mabuse, der Spieler [Dr. Mabuse,
           the Gambler]
           Martin places the film within the thriller genre
     generally and more specifically in the context of Lang's
     spy films. The film still has a strong impact today, and,
     together with other Lang films, has influenced key directors
     like Welles or Chris Marker. Martin ends by placing Dr.
     Mabuse in relation to expressionsim.

353  Rhode, Eric. "Fritz Lang (The German Period, 1919-1933)." In
     his Tower of Babel. London: Weidenfeld and Nicholson.
     Pp. 83-105.
        Rhode begins by discussing Lang's politics. His first
     films trace the confusion and anxieties of the Weimar
     Republic, but, while Lang did play briefly with easy solu-
     tions to these problems, he merely flirted with National
     Socialism. By the time of M and Das Testament des Dr.
     Mabuse [The Last Will of Dr. Mabuse], he had explicitly re-
     jected any form of Nazi solution. This, according to Rhode,
     was a better political contribution than that of the young
     Eisenstein.
        Rhode denies that Lang's films are myth in the sense of
     Nazi lies (as generally claimed in England), but says that
     they are instead mythopoetic, since they at once work on
     the level of common experience and convey a sense of moral
     discovery; in addition, they manifest the formal qualities
     of harmony and complexity. Lang evolved a telling image of
     the modern city and presented the difficulties of the post-
     war era honestly.
        Rhode notes the destructive role of Kracauer's book on
     Lang's reputation, suggesting a personal reason for the

attack. Kracauer's thesis crumbles under questioning, and
Lang does not fit into his categories anyway. A personal
blend of fantasy and realism dominated Lang's work from the
start and his architectural training prohibited typically
expressionist distortions.

Lang's view of the world is close to that of Spengler
(whose Decline of the West was published in 1918), particularly in terms of the destructive effect of the modern city
on people. According to Spengler, when disconnected from
nature, people attach themselves to alien things--money,
power, and intellectuality. Lang's early films show people
doomed in the city, endlessly hatching plots, but with M he
moves on to show that the city could be the site of sanity
and order.

Rhode supports this thesis by detailed analysis of how
Die Spinnen [The Spiders] and the Mabuse films reflect
Spengler's idea of a society enervated by pleasure. Although disjointed, the films are gripping visually and thematically. Playing on the primitive in all of us, Lang
treats science and technology as a form of magic. Politics
has degenerated to private interest and police authority is
precarious. Lang presents a mad world well, but does not
have perspective on it. By means of a compelling visual
style, Lang permits us to believe, by identification with
Mabuse, that through magic and infantile power we can overcome the chaos of the city and impotence.

Lang appreciated hypnotism as a form of control, because
of its invisibility. Rhode notes that Lang was apparently
moving toward an intuitive understanding of Hannah Arendt's
arguments (in Totalitarianism) in relation to uncontrollable
forces. Without fully grasping what they entailed, Lang
nevertheless uses their filmic possibilities. Insofar as
order exists, it is maintained by the police, but their
authority is precarious; von Wenk is as much a victim as
anyone else.

According to Rhode, Mabuse is close to Lang himself in
that he carries out mass hypnotism much as film is supposed
to do. Rhode fancies that Lang is replaying the rebellious
child in his parents' Gothic home. The films let us believe
that we too can surpass the fear of chaos aroused in us; but
there is no distance here--Lang is so involved in the game-
playing that he cannot stand back to judge it.

Metropolis, Spengler's city of the future, also simpli-
fies urgent problems having to do with technology and political repression and presents social issues in mythological
terms. The religious allegory further plays with our emotions, especially since it is linked to Oedipal myths.

M, Lang's most mature film, finally speaks to the adult
in us, since the infant-adult conflict is central to the
film. The world of the film is one of chaos, where good
and evil cannot be distinguished, where evidence is

ambiguous and perceptions doubtful. But in contrast to
Kracauer's thesis about Lang, Rhode says that the appeal
to the irrational is moderated by the figure of Lohmann,
who stands up for what is right and returns order to the
city. There is no pleasure in the chaos as in Mabuse.

Lohmann's role is continued in Das Testament [The Last
Will], where he again solves the riddles. The many references to the Nibelung Saga and Wagner's Ring of the
Niebelungen here reveal the moral implications of the film
rather than merely confusing us as does the religious allegory in Metropolis. The shaky power of Mabuse and Baum,
although intimidating when exercised, is defeated partly by
Lilli's love for Kent, but mainly by Lohmann's intelligence.

Rhode concludes by emphasizing Lang's influence on other
filmmakers, an influence not merely to do with lighting and
frame composition, but with the force of his visual ideas.


### 1967

354    Agel, Henri. "Fritz Lang." In Les Grands Cinéastes que je
       Propose. Paris: Cerf, pp. 67-74.
       Agel argues for the amazing continuity of themes and
inspiration in Lang's films. He early on submitted to a
tragic view of the world, being the victim of a guilt complex that creating his art exorcised.

Lang structured the lines of this despair in terms of a
legendary mythology (as in Destiny, Die Nibelungen) or in
terms of the future (Metropolis). After his arrival in the
United States, he conveyed it through ordinary life, the
urban landscape, criminal acts, conventions of the Western,
and the whole Hollywood repertoire.

From the start, Lang worked with mass, volume, and architectural compositions, to express his vulnerability to implacable forces, which he experienced as the supreme reality. Lang always remained faithful to the structuring of
space, which was the major ambition of German expressionism.
The heritage of Max Reinhardt can be seen in the large surface, where shadow struggles with light, in the geometry of
stairs, and the distortions imposed on forms. The tension
between light, decor, and human beings is presented with
exceptional force in Lang's films. All his work is dominated by a high degree of stylization, obtained by using
studio sets almost exclusively. He eliminates all contingency and the result is very austere.

Hollywood softened Lang's rigidity, but it can still be
found in the editing and rhythm of his films. His last
film is especially disorienting because of the increased
dehumanization and nihilism. Metropolis and You Only Live
Once present society as blind and arbitrary; Lang's experience of America only deepened his feelings about society,

and his films became increasingly cold. He began to dissect human nature in films like The Blue Gardenia.

Lang presents things in an implacable way--whether this be Greek or Jansenist is hard to say. His films are claustrophobic but moral, as Rivette noted when talking about Beyond a Reasonable Doubt. Lang shows that we are all a priori guilty and that we live in a pitiless world, devoid of mercy. People seem to be crushed by forces beyond their control. Human Desire typifies this--it's a film cruelly lacking in any future at all and not made to please. Lang's genius for cinematic "writing" expresses itself in the elaboration of an algebra of the inner world.

355   Bogdanovich, Peter. Fritz Lang in America. London: Studio Vista. Later edition: New York: Praeger, 1969.

Bogdanovitch's book emerged at a time when little was known of the French criticism of Lang and when, despite auteur theory, Lang's American films were still largely viewed as works of mere entertainment and of far less value than his artistic German films. Bogdanovitch's introduction attempts to correct this view: he gives a brief survey of Lang's American films, tracing the various changes in emphasis and grouping the films according to type. Bogdanovitch takes the auteur approach, seeing Lang's films as forming an homogenous whole, united by visual style and thematic continuity despite the changing emphases. He sees the fight of the individual against fate as evident from Metropolis to Moonfleet and concludes that

> as a creator of nightmares, Lang has few peers;
> his world--whether it's the 18th century England
> of Moonfleet or the middle-class railroad community
> of Human Desire (1954)--is one of shadows and
> night--ominous, haunted--filled with foreboding
> and violence, anxiety and death. The tears he
> elicits for the damned figures who inhabit it
> . . . are born from the depth of his personality;
> in his words, they have all my heart [p. 14]

This statement neatly summarizes the auteur position on Lang, particularly the assumption that Lang's life and work are intimately connected. The rest of the book consists of a series of edited transcriptions of six days of interviews with Lang in 1965. Lang begins with his arrival in America and the making of Fury, and he and Bogdanovitch move through his entire American career, film by film. Lang recalls various incidents that happened with producers or actors while making a film, discusses some special difficulties with filming a scene, or talks about what his films meant and his intentions in doing certain things. There is information here that is, at times, illuminating, but much had appeared already in published interviews or would appear later on. Lang is, however, unusually relaxed and open with

Bogdanovitch, so that one gets a very good impression of
the man, often as much through what is not said as through
what is articulated.  Many of the discussions are expanded
and developed in Lotte Eisner's book (See Entry No. 478).

356   Durgnat, Raymond.  "Caligari is Dead--Long Live Caligari," in
         his Films and Feelings.  London:  Faber and Faber, pp. 87-98.
         Durgnat's chapter is important in its demonstration that
      expressionism is a style as much as an artistic or socio-
      logical movement (the positions of Eisner and Kracauer
      respectively).  He discusses Metropolis as an example of
      Lang's emphasis on visual aspects of film and has interest-
      ing comments also on Human Desire (the restless movements of
      the trains), Woman in the Window, and Der Tiger von Eschnapur
      [The Tiger of Bengal].  Durgnat is interested in the color
      symbolism in this latter film, showing how Lang uses it to
      present "good" as dull and "evil" as a mosaic of rich,
      glinting patterns.

357   Eder, Klaus.  "Nibelungen Nötigung."  Film (Velber), No. 2,
         pp. 28-29.
         Eder compares Lang's version of Siegfried with Harold
      Reinl's 1966 version.  He discusses the decorative style of
      both versions, but Reinl's, filmed in color, is much less
      tasteful than Lang's.  Lang's conception of his hero sprang
      from the needs of the period when types like Siegfried were
      called for to lay the corner stone of the twentieth century;
      but in the 1966 version, Siegfried is silly, since he is not
      grounded in his historical moment.

358   Sarris, Andrew.  "Retrospective of Lang's Work at the Museum
         of Modern Art."  Village Voice (New York) (7 December), p.
         39.
         The article was written on the occasion of Lang's visit
      to the Museum of Modern Art at the age of seventy-seven.
      Sarris notes that Lang has not made a film since Die tausend
      Augen [The Thousand Eyes] in 1961 and comments on the re-
      spectful reception he received as he introduced the retro-
      spective.  Sarris summarizes the main elements of Lang's
      style, repeating much of what he said in 1963 in Film
      Culture.  He mentions again that Lang's cinema is that "of
      nightmare, the fable and the philosophical dissertation,"
      adding that his style "is most conspicuous in its over-
      expressive expressionism."  He emphasizes the degree to
      which Lang communicates through visual forms rather than
      through the verisimilitude so dear to realist critics and
      goes on to compare Renoir's and Lang's versions of Zola's
      novel, La Bête Humaine.  While Renoir's film shows "a doomed
      man, caught up in the flow of life," Lang reveals the "night-
      mare of an innocent man enmeshed in tangled strands of fate."
      Recalling Lang's use of the geometrical lines of the trains

and their tracks and the fateful camera angles, Sarris concludes that "as Renoir is humanism, Lang is determinism.
Renoir is concerned with the plight of his characters, Lang
is obsessed with the structure of the trap."

### 1968

359   Beylie, Claude. "Fritz Lang's Fury." L'Avant-Scène, No. 78
      (February). [Entire issue devoted to the film].
          The issue contains the following material:
      (1) An article on the film by Claude Beylie, outlining the
      film's main theme. Beylie points to a contradiction in the
      film, which seems at first bitter and pessimistic, perhaps
      because Lang had just come from fascist Germany. But Beylie
      goes on to argue that the film is not so pessimistic after
      all and instead betrays Lang's confidence in people. There
      are two conflicting notions in the film. On the one hand,
      we find two major premises that reflect Lang's bitterness:
      there is nothing except injustice on earth; each act of
      justice, if done merely for oneself, becomes an "assassina-
      tion" (or a revenge type of justice). But, on the other
      hand, superseding these premises, is the idea that we are
      all guilty, and in the act of accepting our guilt we also
      reveal the innocence of everyone.
      (2) A complete scenario of the film--cutting dialogue, list
      of scenes.
      (3) There are quotations from reviews and history texts as
      follows:
            (a) excerpt from review by Odile Cambier, Cinémonde,
                No. 419 (29 October 1936)
            (b) excerpt from Lotte Eisner, Revue du Cinéma, No. 5
                (February 1947)
            (c) excerpt from Maurice Bessy, Histoire en 1000 Images
                du Cinéma (Paris: Edition Pont Royal, n.d.)
            (d) excerpt from Jean Mitry, Dictionnaire du Cinéma
                (Paris: Ed. Larousse, 1963)
            (e) excerpt from Georges Sadoul, Histoire du Cinéma
                Mondial (Paris: Editions Flammarion, 1949)

360   Beylie, Claude. "Le Secret Derrière La Porte: Le Tournois
      d'âmes Dechirés." Cinéma 68, No. 126 (May), pp. 99-102.
          Beylie mentions the way that Lang's American works have
      previously been disregarded, but notes that now they are
      seen as even more pure than the German films, since unen-
      cumbered by the romantic, expressionist elements. When it
      first appeared, critics saw Secret Beyond the Door as not
      representing the "great" Lang.
          Beylie notes that it is wrong to see Secret as belonging
      in the Freudian film tradition of Spellbound or Rebecca.
      Psychoanalytic study had been a regular component in Lang's

works long before Freud's influence reached Hollywood; while evident in Scarlet Street and Woman in the Window, it goes all the way back to M. The hero in Secret has the typical Langian preoccupation with, and linking of, love and death, Eros and Thanatos.

Secret is about the evil deep in the human mind, which emerges to invade the real world. Death invades all of Mark's actions. Beylie concludes by commenting on the mise-en-scène in the film, which is ultimately the best part.

361    Chapier, Angel. "Le Secret Derrière La Porte:  Un Onirisme Fascinant."  Combat (Paris) (20 February), p. 13.
          Chapier begins by noting that while psychoanalytic inter- pretations are often given indiscriminantly for American films, that approach is totally appropriate for Secret Beyond the Door, since psychoanalysis is the very basis for the film.
          More than anyone else, Lang knows how to bring out the poetry in dream.  The film opens with a waking dream of a haunted woman who little by little discovers that her hus- band has an obsession with murder and death.
          The film does not reveal any part of the mind we are un- familiar with today--analysts now interpret the most deeply hidden motivations--so that the explanation in the film is itself commonplace.  But what is superb is Lang's direction, his mise-en-scène, the beauty of his sets, and his venture into the world of the imagination.  The reconstruction of the rooms that had been scenes of famous murders is shock- ing, but Lang inserts the cold note into the Sternberg-like baroque profusion.
          As in many other films, Lang here shows a man who gra- dually puts himself outside the law and creates a monstrous, deformed version of reality.  The strange people, the de- formed woman and the ghosts all help in the creation of a disturbed perception.  We think we know the world but dis- cover we do not.
          The fire in the house and the flight in the garden are scenes worthy of a film anthology and should convince those who still need it of the value of conserving art works like these, which represent their period as much as did Renaissance paintings.  While all of Lang's works require in-depth study, the resurrection of this film, which slipped by unnoticed in 1947, is the least that we can do.

362    Del Ministro, Maurizio.  "Introduzione A Lang Espresionista." Sections reprinted in Il Ponte (Florence) (July 1969), pp. 965-967.
          Before studying Lang in the context of the rigid, though interesting, tradition from Caligari to Hitler, we must an- alyze him in the context of his own work between 1921 and

1924.

According to Del Ministro, Der müde Tod [Destiny] reveals Lang's main themes and characteristics: the world is a tragic stage, dominated by fate, where good struggles against evil; evil, the stronger, is inevitable and multifaceted. Evil is the leitmotif of all his films, making them much more than thrillers. In a mythic representation, where cynicism, vice, gambling, and criminal wealth dominate, Lang represents the chaos of an age.

Del Ministro believes that expressionism was the appropriate stylistic vehicle for Lang's world view. The antinaturalistic tendencies of expressionism lead to a style that Del Ministro finds merely ornamental; Lang sets a fantastic stage on which an epic battle takes place, as in Siegfrieds Tod [Death of Siegfried].

363  Godard, Jean-Luc.  Jean-Luc Godard.  Paris:  Pierre Belfoud. Republished as Milne, Tom and Narboni, Jean, eds.  Godard on Godard.  Translated by Tom Milne.  New York:  Secker and Warburg, 1972.

Although there is no prolonged discussion of Lang here, the book is important for anyone studying Lang's influence on the French New Wave and Godard in particular.  Godard often refers to Lang as representing a tradition and type of cinema that he obviously admires greatly.  At one point, for example, he places Franju's La Tête contre les Murs in the tradition "of rational frenzy, of controlled madness, of Fritz Langian dislocation such as Baudelaire loved in Poe, the orbit where reigns the atmosphere of Ministry of Fear rather than of M, and even more than Ministry of Fear, of Dr. Mabuse."  In other places, Godard links Lang with Hitchcock (e.g., p. 25, English edition) noting that Foreign Correspondent and Manhunt are each director's best film.

364  H. F.  Reviews of Der Tiger von Eschnapur and Das indische Grabmal.  Süddeutsche Zeitung (Munich) (13 November). [Reviews of The Tiger of Bengal and The Indian Tomb].

These films, H. F. notes, made ten years ago in Germany, won praise in France from Godard, Rivette, and Jean-Marie Straub.  The films are very modern in their style, construction, use of space, and abstraction.  H. F. concludes that the works are new and exciting.

365  Image et Son (Paris), No. 216 (April).  [Entire issue devoted to Lang].

The issue contains the following:

(1) Lefèvre, Raymond.  "Fritz Lang," pp. 9-62

Lefèvre surveys Lang's entire career, giving plot summaries of all the films and quoting from critical analyses, such as those by Lotte Eisner, Godard, and Eibel; although there is little new analysis or interpretation, he instead

gathers together usefully what has been done to date.
(2) Tabès, René. "Lang et le Western," pp. 63-66
    In the form of notes rather than an article, Tabès
tries to show that Lang's Westerns are an integral part of
his total work. They reflect his interest in broad, simple
themes--the "classic" side of him--and follow a familiar
plan. A Langian hero finds himself accidentally embroiled
in a tragedy, alone against the power of certain individuals.
The Westerns are touched by a pessimism that comes directly
from German romanticism. Tabès isolates three main themes:
vengeance, the concept of honor, and time. He sees the
Langian hero as always controlled by time, whether he is
marked by the past or sees the present as the beginning of
his end.
    Tabès concludes by looking at the heroines in Lang's
Westerns. The first two have traditional heroines, but
Rancho Notorious departs from this with Dietrich as a femme
fatale. Talking to Bogdanovitch, Lang insisted that one
needed new Westerns each year because each year there is a
new generation to appeal to.
(3) Ganne, Claude. "Filmographie de Fritz Lang," pp. 67-77

366    Jensen, Paul. "Metropolis." Film Heritage (Dayton, Ohio), 3,
    No. 2 (Winter), 22-28.
    Jensen begins by outlining the plot of Metropolis, point-
ing out its narrative weaknesses, which he finds due, in
part, to the reediting that took place in Britain, but in
part to ideological inconsistencies (e.g., why would Joh
Fredersen create a robot to incite the workers to revolt?).
Jensen then links some of the themes of the film to Lang's
general concerns (e.g., the outsider-hero, the contrast between a good and an evil woman, the conflict between the
intellect and emotions, the master-criminal). Finally,
Jensen praises the film's visual style, which provides pleasure despite the "silly" content. Lang was wrong to treat
Metropolis as if it were a romantic legend.

367    Legrand, Gérard. "Le Génie des Lieux." Positif (Paris), No.
    94 (April), pp. 62-64.
    By giving a brief plot outline of Secret Beyond the Door,
Legrand shows how the film can seem to belong with Rebecca
or Jane Eyre--typical women's films. But Lang, in fact,
has transformed the basic material into something quite
different, which perhaps accounts for the commercial failure
of the film.
    Elements that might seem like symbols, Legrand argues,
are not really so. The lilacs really are lilacs, the storm
is linked to the theme of nature, and the character played
by Redgrave refuses the sinister secretary because the latter is a liar. Lang parodies Freud when an earnest psychology student, accompanying the group on the tour of rooms,

by chance happens upon the truth about Mark. Believing
that in fact everyone has the potential to be a criminal,
Lang thinks that the filmmaker is freer than others to explore that self.

Legrand next discusses Lang's use of interior monologue
in the film, showing that his aim is not so much to give
the subjective view--as in Dark Passage or Marienbad--but
instead to remain in control. Although Lang might well
have succumbed to expressionism in the film, as he did in
Woman in the Window, he has not done so; the film, in fact,
paradoxically moves toward harmony. According to Legrand,
Lang here sacrifices psychological truth in the interests
of resolution. He ends by noting the formal beauty of the
film and the warmth of Joan Bennett's performance.

368   Legrand, Gérard. "Nouvelles Notes pour un éloge de Fritz
      Lang." Positif (Paris), No. 94 (April), pp. 1-7.
      In this second section of a three-part article (See
Entries Nos. 309 and 466), Legrand begins by setting out
the elements that make up a great work of art. The art of
film, he says, consists in the presentation of an emotion
so rich that others can find it briefly in themselves.

Noting that Lang did not "use" expressionism as one uses
the subway--instead it informed his work in a basic way--
Legrand goes on to discuss the way Lang effortlessly establishes a dialectic in his work, creating a constant sense
of anxiety. Not giving us a puzzle to solve in the Hitchcock
manner, Lang instead creates tension through a series of
contrapuntal elements. He also uses space rather than time
(as is usually done) to create fear and terror. (Legrand
gives an example here from While the City Sleeps.)

Legrand next discusses Lang's interest in the process of
cinema itself, often showing a film within a film (e.g., in
Fury, the projection booth in Clash by Night, television in
While the City Sleeps and in Beyond a Reasonable Doubt).
He uses architecture similarly, giving us images of buildings within buildings (e.g., the window shots in M). His
editing works to prevent a subjective point of view through
building in a series of contradictions. Here we have the
paradox of continuity in a world that is always on the brink
of ruin.

Giving examples from Mabuse, Moonfleet, and Beyond a
Reasonable Doubt, Legrand shows how Lang plays upon two contradictory wishes in the spectator, making us first identify
with the evil figure and then deny this identification.
Lang's world is essentially a magical one, Lang giving us
a sense of space constricted within time.

The article ends with a discussion of Lang's ideas about
his own works, Legrand showing that we cannot rely on what
he tells us. It is not surprising that Lang settled so
easily into America since, first, Pommer's productions had

already accustomed him to a mixture of modern subjects and
fantasy/myth; second, because Lang saw cinema increasingly
as a criticism of cinema; and finally, because Lang's work
was the kind that nourished itself. His work is more onto-
logical than metaphysical--note the role played by objects
in his work--and we can believe in the sincerity of his rejection of expressionism in which he saw an exaggerated
subjectivity alien to him.

369   Roulet, Sebastien. "La Septième Porte." Cahiers du Cinéma
      (Paris), No. 204 (September), pp. 60-62. [Review of Secret
      Beyond the Door].
         The theme of the film, according to Roulet, is the process
      of filmmaking itself. The opening of the film establishes
      the film as the evocation of a narrative through the devices
      of the voice-over, the images of drowning, and the surreal-
      ism. Lang manages to create a feeling of suspense beneath
      the surfaces of the actual objects filmed. The movie ends
      up being an analysis of its own reason for being; it becomes
      the revelation of its means of expression, deciphering it-
      self.
         The characters create themselves as they go along. Mark
      in particular flees from himself in the face of his progres-
      sive definition. According to Roulet, "the only indications
      of Mark's existence are those parts of himself that he is
      hiding--the flowers, the rooms."
         The key to it all is the seventh door where, having com-
      mitted sacrilege in stealing the key, Celia finds her own
      room. Cinema here confronts itself just as Celia finds
      herself, her intended fate, behind the door. As soon as
      the character faces the reality that cinema has suddenly
      revealed, the fiction ends, and the internal coherence of
      the film's structure is revealed.

370   Sarris, Andrew. The American Cinema: Directors and Direction,
      1929-1968. New York: Dutton. Pp. 63-65. Originally
      printed as "A Second Line: Fritz Lang," in Film Culture
      (Spring 1963). [See Entry No. 312].
         Sarris places Lang in his top category of "Pantheon
      Directors," and this was important in the regeneration of
      interest in Lang. In a succinct evaluation of the director,
      Sarris emphasizes the centrality of Lang's visual style to
      an understanding of his cinema, contrasting Renoir's Human
      Beast with Lang's Human Desire to make his point. While
      faces are what we recall in Renoir, Human Desire leaves us
      with images of the trains, tracks, and fateful camera angles.
         Sarris notes the constancy of Lang's themes, from
      Metropolis to Moonfleet, films that share the same bleak
      view of the universe; he comments on the closed world of a
      Lang film, on Lang's tendency to be a voyeur, and on the
      pattern of paranoia evident from the first Mabuse film to

the last, and running through Lang's best American films.
The prevailing Lang image is that of "a world ravaged and
in flames," although there are occasional sentimental exceptions in the existence of the pure love of beautiful
women.

371    Tabès, René. "La Cinquième Victime et L'Invraisemblable
       Vérité." Image et Son (Paris), No. 214, pp. 71-75.
       [Documentation on While the City Sleeps and Beyond a
       Reasonable Doubt].
            This documentation consists of the following items:
       (1) Plot summaries of both films; (2) Background information
       on Lang; (3) Discussion of the use of the theme of the press
       in Hollywood cinema, with reference to Citizen Kane and a
       Richard Brooks film. Hollywood is fascinated by the milieu
       of the press, but Lang reveals the corruption of the press
       in a capitalist society; and (4) a series of quotations
       from critical books and articles on both films.

372    Vialle, Gabriel. "L'Ange des Maudits." [Part of a special
       section, "L'Ecran Demoniaque," which includes notes on
       Destiny, Dr. Mabuse, and Metropolis, as well as quotations
       from renowned critics on Lang and some notes by Lang him-
       self]. Image et Son (Paris), No. 214 (February). Section
       on Rancho Notorious, pp. 17-21; other material, pp. 97-103.
            This study of Rancho Notorious follows the usual French
       documentation format: it begins with a plot summary, fol-
       lowed by a filmography; there are then notes on the most
       important actors in the film and on those working on the
       film. The "Analyse Dramatique" follows: here Vialle ar-
       gues for the film as tightly structured with two key epi-
       sodes in each of the two parts, the division being the ar-
       rival at the ranch. The film contains the same themes as
       Lang's other films--death, vengeance, the tracking down of
       a man, and the implacable mechanisms by which people are
       trapped. Vialle relates these themes to the early German
       and American works and then discusses each in more detail.
       He notes that Lang's fascination with tracking down a man
       may have to do with his own exile; he links Lang to Brecht
       in their interest in mechanisms by which people are trapped,
       commenting that both use distanciation [distancing]. There
       is a final section on the women in Rancho Notorious, Dietrich
       being analyzed as a type of femme fatale.
            Vialle discusses the despair of the film, noting that in
       Germany Lang had been one of the few expressionists to in-
       ject a gleam of hope and of humanism into his work. His
       films became bitter once he went to America.
            A final section covers the cinematic interest of the
       film, particularly in relation to Dietrich. The film re-
       tains only the exterior elements of the Western, with Lang
       using the genre instead to present a tragedy about the force

of destiny.

The material in the "L'Écran Démoniaque" general section
has a collection of quotations by various critics on Destiny,
Mabuse, and Metropolis. This is followed by a discussion,
relevant to Lang, of all the films covered in relation to
expressionism. Vialle deals with recurring images, thematic
tendencies, and cinematic techniques such as lighting, types
of shot, and composition.

## 1969

373   Burch, Noel. Praxis du Cinéma. Paris: Editions Gallimard,
      pp. 27-28. Reprinted as Theory of Film Practice. Translated
      by Helen R. Lang. New York: Secker and Warburg. Pp. 14-15.
      Although the reference to Lang is short, it is signifi-
cant in terms of establishing a new approach to him that,
along with the work of Oudart and Bellour, was to be developed further in the 1970s. Burch talks of Lang's M as an
example of a certain kind of editing. Lang begins with
shots that are spatially and temporally autonomous. Elipsis
and decor play a large role. The film proceeds with a use
of shot change, increasingly approximating real time. This
culminates in the trial sequence, where time and space are
fixed for a period of fifteen minutes of real time. The
most significant use of time elipsis in editing is that
where a member of the underground is seen working his way
through floors in the abandoned factory while the search
for Beckert is taking place. We cut from the discovery of
Lorre to this man's working his way through a floor. We
have not seen the others take Lorre away and expect the
workman to come up to be greeted by his friends. Instead,
the police are awaiting him.

374   Dorr, John H. "Abstractions in Silence." UCLA Daily Bruin
      (15 October).
      Dorr begins by contrasting public response to Lang's
silent and to his sound films. The silent work is revered
for its stunning visual power, the films being appreciated
on an abstract level. But audiences cannot tolerate the
same abstraction in sound films, where realism is more in
demand. It is harder to see beyond the surface narrative
in the sound era.
      But for Dorr, appreciation of the abstract level of
Lang's films is essential; he makes a distinction between
passively watching a film and actively seeing it. He briefly comments on the films being shown in the retrospective
at the Los Angeles County Museum and on the expressionist
background that shaped them. He contrasts expressionism
with the Griffith tradition that Americans are used to.
While Lang's American films adhere superficially to this

tradition, his grounding principle is the concept of the frame and he does not follow the action or the actors. Dorr gives examples from specific films to show how Lang's interest in fate, in people as victims in a heartless world, is evident in the frame compositions.

Dorr concludes that Lang's is not a cinema of plots, characters, or actors, but rather that of a mathematical universe where everything is conditioned and nothing happens by chance. Like Eisenstein, Lang is "one of the great formalists of the cinema," more concerned with "the mechanisms that restrain men from living rather than with the process of living."

375   No Entry

376   Fritz, Walter. "Lilith and Ly: A Forgotten Film of Fritz
      Lang." Action (Austria), No. 4 (April), pp. 26-28. (Available in BFI Library).
        Fritz discusses Lang's script for a little-known Austrian
      film, Lilith and Ly, directed by Erich Kober in 1919. Fritz
      surveys briefly Lang's background and career and notes that
      1919 was his most productive year ever. The idea for the
      film came from Lang's Asian travels, and, after outlining
      the plot, Fritz concludes with some interesting comments
      about the women's roles, noting that they are either completely holy or evil.

377   Hull, David Stewart. Film in the Third Reich. Berkeley:
      University of California Press. Reprinted by Simon and
      Schuster, New York, 1973.
        Although most of Hull's book deals with the years after
      Lang left Germany, the prologue and the first chapter are
      of interest in that they deal with pre-Nazi Germany and the
      first years of the Nazi regime, when Lang's last German
      film, Das Testament des Dr. Mabuse [The Last Will of Dr.
      Mabuse], would have been released. The book is interesting
      to the degree that it contributes to the debate about the
      latent prefascist content or style of Lang's early films
      and for what is shows about Nazi reactions to Lang's films.
        Hull mentions Goebbels's speech to the film organizations,
      SPIO and DACHO, which were resisting Nazification. SPIO had
      sent Goebbels a list of names of Jews they wanted to retain
      because of heroic service in the First World War or for
      their contribution to the film industry. Trying to bring
      the groups into line, Goebbels mentions four films that he
      wanted emulated, one of them being Lang's Die Nibelungen,
      which Goebbels admired for showing modern themes set in
      early times.
        A little later on, Hull discusses the banning of Lang's
      Das Testament, which was first shown in Vienna on 12 May
      1933. Goebbels disliked the film because of his general

aversion to crime films, Hull says.  In an article printed in Film-Kurier (29 September 1933), Goebbels refers to "a criminality tainted with Metropolis fantasies, gigantic destructiveness, and decay," arguing that the real German film will consist "in the great service done for the people by the tireless exponents of speed, intelligence, and justice . . . ."

In a later chapter, Hull mentions Frank Wysbar's Fährmann Maria, made in 1936, as "one of the highpoints of the German sound cinema" and the film that "to all intents and purposes . . . closes the series of films which began with Der Student von Prag in 1914." One scene in the film he thinks is directly descended from Lang's Der müde Tod [Destiny], since the figure of the stranger recalls Lang's character, Death; he is, Hull says "destroyed at the end of the film by pure faith . . . much as Wegener's Golem is at last put out of action by a small child . . . ."

A final mention of Lang is made in the context of the list Goebbels issued in 1938 of banned German directors.

Recently, Julian Petley has cast doubt on Hull's thesis regarding the resistance of the German film industry to Nazification in his Capital and Culture:  German Cinema 1933-45 (London:  British Film Institute, 1979).  According to Petley, the industry was much more willing to cooperate than Hull allows.  Important also on the Nazi cinema are a short book by Erwin Leiser, Deutschland erwache! (Hamburg:  Rowohlt, 1968) and a longer, more recent book by Francis Courtade and Pierre Cadars, Geschichte des Films im Dritten Reich (Munich and Vienna:  Hanser, 1975).  The latter is well documented, has a bibliography of materials about film in the Third Reich, a filmography listing the most important Nazi films, a chronology of important historical events, and a large number of stills.  All of these books have brief discussions in the early chapters of Lang's being invited to head the Nazi propaganda film unit, of the Nazi interest in certain of his films, and about his emigration to America.

378   Hymson, Joseph.  "Fritz Lang's M."  UCLA Daily Bruin (7
      November).
      Hymson notes how universal the themes of M are and anal-
yses the film's style in detail.  He comments on the lack of
a clear viewpoint and on the deliberate creation of a pseudo-
documentary approach.  It is up to the audience to decide on
the "correct" position vis-à-vis events in the film.
      Hymson shows how Lang deliberately creates moods in every
scene, giving examples to support his point that Lang brings
out "the terror existing in the common place." Lang employs
textures and patterns to control moods.
      Turning to Lang's brilliant use of both editing and sound
in M, Hymson shows how Lang tells the story in images rather
than in words.  While M dispelled doubts as to Lang's ability

to handle actors, Hymson notes that Peter Lorre never lived
up to the promise he showed as the murderer in M.

379   Jensen, Paul M.  The Cinema of Fritz Lang.  New York:  A. S.
      Barnes; London:  A. Zwemmer.
          At the time it was written, Jensen's book was significant
      as the first book on Lang in English.  Its structure and
      methodology are now limited, since Jensen was working within
      traditions of film criticism that have recently been called
      in question.  In his introductory chapter, Jensen finds
      corollaries between Lang's life and his films, his thesis
      being that the combination of romanticism and pessimistic
      fatality has to do with Lang's rejection of his career as an
      architect and his exotic travels, followed by the severe
      discipline of the army.  Lang continued throughout his career,
      according to Jensen, to be concerned with "the earthly forces
      which affect the actions of individuals; society, psychology,
      and environment are depicted with the objective, and scien-
      tific eye of a naturalist."  But he also, like the expres-
      sionists, injected the feeling of vague evil into ordinary
      reality.
          Having established these main Langian themes, Jensen
      proceeds, in the traditional manner, to go through Lang's
      works, film by film, giving in each case a summary of the
      plot, discussing themes and narrative structure, and noting
      any links with previous films or those to come.  In what
      had been the accepted position vis-à-vis Lang until the
      French criticism of the late 1950s, Jensen clearly favors
      the early German works over the American ones.  More than
      half the book focuses on the nine main German films, and
      many of the Hollywood films are dismissed in the then stan-
      dard manner as improbable, cliché-ridden genre films.
      Jensen's bibliography betrays his lack of detailed knowledge
      of French criticism (only Mourlet and Demonsablon are there,
      as well as a couple of French interviews), and most material
      comes from American newspapers and standard American film
      journals.  (Jensen's bibliography, by the way, has several
      errors in citation.)
          Nevertheless, Jensen did provide a breakthrough in terms
      of the English-speaking response to Lang and in pursuing a
      standard auteur, thematic approach he was squarely in the
      mainstream of what was going on in American criticism at
      the time.  However, were I to need material from this point
      of view, I would rely instead on Lotte Eisner's recent text,
      which has the virtue of Lang's personal corroboration of
      information.

380   Johnston, Claire.  Fritz Lang.  British Film Institute Pamphlet
      (available only in the BFI Library, London).
          Johnston begins by outlining some possible approaches to
      Lang, for example, Lang as German director with a style

derived from expressionism or Lang as a director working
mainly in thriller and crime genres.  But she believes that
the auteur approach is most valid.

Johnston does, however, realize the importance of the
expressionist movement in the development of Lang's unique
style and vision, and in the section "An Introduction to
German Expressionism" she outlines the main themes of the
movement, the predominant style, and the political/social
orientation of expressionist artists.  Johnston traces the
origins of expressionism back to romanticism and the idealist, nineteenth-century tradition; the main world view is
one in which life is oppressive and meaningless, and people
are doomed.  Only by moving from life back to nature can
the artist find hope.  He or she searches for an absolute,
objective truth, for what lies behind reality as we experience it.  Artists attack the major power structures, which
are seen as a threat to the individual's integrity, turning
him or her into a tool of abstract forces.

Expressionist artists reflect two possible responses to
the dilemma.  Some artists internalize the terror of social
oppression and show individuals who embody irrational evil.
Others replace objective reality with that of the artist-
hero who tries to control everything, aiming for a totality
of all possible experiences (e.g., such superhuman heros as
Dr. Mabuse and Haighi).

Johnston traces the origin of these world views to
Scandinavia and Strindberg.  Stellan Rye made the first
Student from Prague film with Paul Wegener, which was to
influence the German expressionist film.  The importance of
expressionism, according to Johnston, lies in its revolutionary negation of bourgeois society; but its weakness is
that it leads to despair and desolation.  Because expressionists rejected society outright, they never criticised
it.  Lang is important because he moulds the expressionist
world view into a criticism of society.

Johnston ends this section by noting how key elements of
expressionism have entered the mainstream of cinema in the
thriller, gangster, and horror genres, particularly in relation to lighting techniques.

The second part of the pamphlet consists of a bibliography on expressionism, followed by a list of extracts and
films available for rent.  The next section is about Lang
himself--his main themes, his main types of heroes, and his
links with expressionism, which Johnston argues conditioned
his central concerns.  Johnston notes the frequency of the
femme fatale type in Lang's films and Lang's understanding
that, given partriarchal society, male-female relationships
will be negative.

Concluding sections are:  a Lang bibliography and filmography; an extract from the Lang interview with Jean
Domarchi and Jacques Rivette (Cahiers du Cinéma, No. 99,

1959), and finally, credits, plot summaries, and comments on some key films--Metropolis, Die Nibelungen, M, Secret Beyond the Door, and The Big Heat.

This is an extremely useful, concise introduction to Lang and it is regrettable that the pamphlet is not more generally available.

381    Mamber, Stephen. "The American Films of Fritz Lang." UCLA Daily Bruin (15 October).

Mamber's article was written to persuade people to attend a retrospective of Lang's films at the Los Angeles County Museum.  Aware of the special sort of commitment that a retrospective involves, Mamber nevertheless deplores the short notices accorded old films by reviewers and their bias toward works of high culture.  Lang's films, disturbing as they are, remain beyond the confines of safe art.

Lang's films are difficult to discuss because they lack the humanism of Renoir or the humor of Hitchcock and instead reveal a bleak, terrifying view of people and their world. Lang emphasizes the ungovernable conflicts that lead to crime and the susceptibility of the innocent to evil.  The rise of the Nazis in part accounts for Lang's awareness of the extremes of human evil.

Lang's American anti-Nazi films are superior to other war films in their focus on individual conflicts rather than on patriotism per se.  Using Manhunt as an example, Mamber shows how the hero only gradually realizes that he had been capable of murdering Hitler because the Nazis used force to advance their ideas.  The film has continuing relevance in that fascists today still try to use force to impose their views on others.

Turning to Hangmen Also Die, Mamber sees Brecht's influence in the overemphasis on the political implications of the situation, but some lively moments compensate for this. Ministry of Fear shows that Lang was able to make routine Hollywood assignments his own.

Discussing the "reverse cultural bias in so-called intelligent film audiences," Mamber shows how it works against taking Lang's films seriously.  People prefer his foreign films, like Liliom, to the American ones, not seeing how Lang has found a way to express his world view within the context of conventional melodrama.

According to Mamber, Lang is a product of the twentieth-century world of mass murder and technology rather than being a transplanted German director.  His American films make sense both as a whole and as individual works of art.  Mamber denies that Lang went into a decline in the late 1950s, believing instead that his last two Hollywood films reflect his criticism of America's economic system and values.

382    Mitry, Jean.  Histoire du Cinéma:  Art et Industrie.  Vol. 2:

1915-1925. Paris: Edition Universitaires, pp. 458-459 and 467-468, plus other references throughout.

Mitry has quite a long discussion of Die Nibelungen in the context of demonstrating the love expressionists had for recreating nature in the studio. He notes how suitable the abstract, artificial forest is for the Nibelungen legend: it takes on archetypal qualities suitable for myth. With its slow dramatic movement, the film joins with liturgical ceremony. Quoting Eisner, Mitry praises the second half of the film, which is often overlooked; the film builds to a crescendo in which all the people responsible for Siegfried's death are brought down.

Der müde Tod [Destiny] is discussed for its use of light and the architectural forms. The three stories parody expressionism, according to Mitry. Using architecture symbolically, Lang is able to achieve a foreboding of death and of the search to escape destiny.

383   Oudart, Jean Pierre. "La Suture." Cahiers du Cinéma, No. 211 (April), pp. 36-39; No. 212 (May), pp. 53-55.

While this article does not deal at length with Lang, it is important in presenting an approach to him that was developed further in the 1970s, particularly by Bellour and Noel Burch. Oudart's first article is about how the image given evokes its absent corollary. All great cinéastes, he says, use effects of retroactive signification; they set up an exchange between two images, only one of which is, in fact, shown. The other is located on the imaginary plane. Oudart mentions Lang's Kriemhilds Rache [Kriemhild's Revenge] as one of the few real examples of what he calls the "champ-contre-champ" method of filming, where the protagonists take on an aura of unreality because of Lang's total refusal to link the camera movements with the glance of the characters (that is, the camera never shows us what anyone is looking at).

In the second part of the article, Oudart mentions Lang, along with Hitchcock, as one of the directors who has experimented--at first innocently and then more consciously--with cinematic form. Lang understood cinema as a language that functions according to its own laws rather than in order to present a certain "content."

Oudart concludes that cinematic language is essentially erotic--a discovery which, he says, goes back to Lang. All the consequences of this may not yet be known, but Oudart believes the erotic movement governs all cinema. Through erotic means, cinema leads beyond eroticism to a figurative, symbolic reality found in films like Lang's Der Tiger von Eschnapur [The Tiger of Bengal], Jeanne d'Arc, and Une Histoire Immortelle.

384   Canham, Nicholas. "Surface Signs." Films and Filming (London),

15, No. 5 (February), pp. 74-75.

Canham discusses briefly Cloak and Dagger and Secret Beyond the Door in an article surveying the development of cinema since the start of the industry in 1897 and noting the new films released in London. He talks about the advances made by German expressionist directors like Lang, who abandoned realism for fantasy, and used symbolic acting to capture the truth through the artist's subjective intuition. He argues that the emphasis on science fiction and fantasy amounted to the first instance of genre filmmaking.

Discussing new releases, Canham notes the tense atmosphere of Cloak and Dagger and the uniformly good performances; he complains of the lack of suspense in Secret Beyond the Door, but says that the good performances partially redeem the film, while the photography and Rozsa's score do the rest.

385   Thomas, Kevin. "Fritz Lang Tribute: Liliom First Film in Series." Los Angeles Times (3 October), Sec. IV, p. 8.

Writing at the start of a long overdue tribute to Lang at the Los Angeles County Museum of Art, Thomas notes that if at last the director is coming into his own, it is because the quality of Lang's work deserves acclaim. Made in Paris in 1934, Liliom has been a "lost" film, rarely shown. The first half resembles the films that Clair and Renoir made during that period. With the entry into heaven, however, the film takes a Mèlies-like fantasy direction to make its point about the "eternity of injustice." The film is unusual for Lang in its number of comic touches, but Liliom does have the typical Lang theme of the struggle against fate.

386   Thomas, Kevin. "Die Nibelungen On Screen Tonight." Los Angeles Times (10 October), Sec. IV, p. 16.

The occasion for the review is the presentation of Die Nibelungen as part of the County Museum's Lang retrospective. According to Thomas, the films represent "movie-making at its most monumental. Larger-than-life figures of legend enact Thea von Harbou's theme of memorable fate . . . The films possess Greek tragedy's quality of inevitability," but their main appeal is that they become "the embodiment of a stirring saga of profoundly mythical appeal." Thomas goes on to compare the films to Japanese spectacles with their Samurai heroes and then outlines the main plot of Die Nibelungen. He concludes by commenting appreciatively on the operatic style, the stately pace, and the tableauxlike series of episodes in the works. They remain a high point in Fritz Lang's career and a landmark in the so-called golden age of German cinema.

Early 1970s

387   Aaronson, Dominique.   "Rancho Notorious."   Fiche Filmographique,
      No. 182.   Produced by the Institut des Hautes Études
      Cinématographiques (I. D. H. E. C.), Paris.
          As usual in this series of analyses, there are four main
      sections.  A short introduction, giving the history of the
      film's release and reception in France and England, is fol-
      lowed by a brief account of Lang's background and career,
      including a filmography.
          The second section consists of a summary of the plot of
      Rancho Notorious, followed by a brief account of the main
      sequences.  Aaronson then analyses three major themes:
      (1) the typical Langian theme of a man forced outside the
      law because of the death of his loved one, whom he must
      avenge (Vern's story); (2) the passing of time, with Frenchy
      and Altar struggling against aging.  Altar tests her power
      over men, while Frenchy still needs to be the fastest draw;
      and (3) a social theme--that of the necessity of struggling
      against society if one is to remain a man (e.g., Vern's
      conflict with the men of his village who refuse to pursue
      the murderer).
          This section also provides analyses of the main characters
      --Vern, Frenchy, and Altar.  Aaronson admires the way Lang
      has drawn his characters and the deep understanding of human
      nature that this reveals.  The narrative follows the psycho-
      logical development of Vern from a simple cowboy into a
      gangster.  The inevitability of the deaths of the main char-
      acters makes the film tragic.  Lang has used the genre of
      the Western and its legendary appeal to create an allegory;
      here an ordinary man, in becoming a hero by accident, kills
      the legendary hero, Frenchy.
          The third section deals with the film's visual style.
      Aaronson shows how the style is governed throughout by the
      needs of the action.  He goes into a detailed account, im-
      possible to summarize here, of the following aspects of the
      film:  editing; the use of frame and camera angles; the
      camera movements; the length of the shots; the use of color,
      lighting, decor, and sound (the music, the ballad, sound
      effects, and dialogue); the acting.
          In the concluding section, Aaronson notes that Rancho
      Notorious proves that even in America Lang remained true to
      himself.  He moved without difficulty from expressionism to
      realism, from the silent film to cinemascope, but did not,
      in all this, alter his basic vision, which is that of the
      struggle of the individual against circumstances.  For Lang,
      the struggle itself is what counts, and he does not try to
      offer solutions.  Aaronson praises Lang for not trying to
      make "art" films, but accepting himself as a craftsman.
      After analyzing briefly the place of the Western both in
      Lang's work and in the cinema in general, Aaronson concludes

that the genre is suitable for Lang in that it essentially
concerns the search for liberty by individuals who must, in
the end, create their own justice.  Love motivates people
in Lang's films, and thus, for Lang woman becomes the cata-
lyst for men's actions, providing in this way the tragic
basis for events.

### 1970

388  Barsaq, Leon.  "Toward a Film Aesthetic:  Sweden and Germany
     1917-1922."  In Le Décor de Film.  Preface by René Clair.
     Paris:  Editions Seghers.  Pp. 31-39.  Reprinted in English
     as Caligari's Cabinet and Other Grand Illusions, rev. ed.
     prepared by Elliott Stein.  Boston:  New York Graphic
     Society, 1976.
         Barsaq begins by showing the influence on Lang's Die
     Nibelungen of the Swedish filmmaker, Stiller, particularly
     his Sir Arne's Treasure (1919), with remarkable sets by
     Dahlstrom and Bako.
         Turning to the German expressionist film, Barsaq discusses
     Lang's Der müde Tod [Destiny]; he notes the strong influence
     of Reinhardt on Lang but stresses that Lang went on to de-
     velop a very personal vision.  He is preoccupied with death
     in this film, creating, for example, a satanic atmosphere
     in the apothecary's laboratory.  His use of lighting is es-
     pecially effective, the lighting coming from below so as to
     emphasize the architecture and bring out the relief surfaces.
         Barsaq goes on to discuss the powerful landscapes re-
     created in the studio for Die Nibelungen.  The three set
     designers worked together as a team, Hunte making the pre-
     liminary sketches, Kettelhut elaborating on them, while
     Vollbrecht was responsible for the construction.  As a
     painter, Lang tried to bring to life the famous canvases of
     Arnold Böcklin.  Everything was calculated--the balanced
     volumes, linear arabesques, lighting effects, and the pre-
     cise degree of black/white contrast.
         Barsaq finds Metropolis the most interesting from the
     point of view of design; even though the plot is puerile
     and the acting outdated, the sets are contemporary and there
     is much that is prophetic in the film.  Lighting is especial-
     ly brilliant.
         Barsaq's main point is that design was given an unprece-
     dented place during the expressionist period in Germany.
     "Expressionism proved the value, often disputed, of systema-
     tic set design . . . ."  The sets became elements as active
     and important as the characters.

389  Blum, Heiko R.  "Hollywoodregisseur mit deutscher
     Filmvergangenheit."  Filmreport (W. Berlin) (2 December).
     (Available in the Deutschen Film und Fersehakademie, West

Berlin.)

Blum notes that Lang doesn't count for much in Germany. His fame ended with M and when he returned to Germany in 1956, one resented the fact that he did not come as the savior of the German film. But Blum wonders what there was to save in a country which, at least in the realm of film, has not overcome the spirit of the past?

Lang undoubtedly has entered the annals of film history with his silent films like Nibelungen, Metropolis, and Dr. Mabuse, der Spieler. For the German public he remains the classicist of the early German film, of which H. Ihering said as early as 1924, "There is no development on this path. The poverty and perplexity of the stylized film has finally been demonstrated--despite the technical perfection, despite the marvelous photography. And Lang himself must realize that he must take another path in order to go further."

His new path led to failure: in 1932 he made a new Mabuse-film, with explicit references to Hitler. Hitler wrote Mein Kampf while incarcerated in Landsberg; Mabuse writes his textbook of crime in a cell--the parallel and dedication were unmistakable. The film was banned after the Nazi takeover--it could have given rise to undesirable comparisons.

While in America, Lang remained true to his basic theme of the relentless fight against a merciless fate. He is exemplary in his success in harmonizing his unique style with the demands of American cinema. Lang does not surrender to Hollywood methods without criticism and uses them for his own purposes. If his hero in the 1920s was a cliché-figure of German film mythology, the protagonist of the American films is an average citizen, with whom the public can identify. Yet the first three films were not successful commercially. This was due to the themes and their sociopolitical relevance. He restored himself with two Westerns and won prestige with the political thrillers Man Hunt, Hangmen Also Die, and Ministry of Fear. The best of these films are paragons of American cinema and thanks to a few typical bits of inspiration, quite personal pieces of work, as, for example, The Big Heat.

It is regrettable that few of Lang's films are shown in Germany.

390     Blum, Heiko R.  "Ein Mörder und sein Schicksal."  (Newspaper not given.  From file in Deutsches Institut für Filmkunde, Wiesbaden.)

Writing on the occasion of Lang's eightieth birthday, Blum notes that while Lang is justly being honored as one of the most important German-speaking film directors, the cinemas in Germany have neglected him.

Blum goes on to discuss M (1931), the film based on the

case of Peter Kurten and originally intended to be a warning
against child murderers. The film alternates between realism and symbolism, and becomes more than the story of a manhunt. The sick criminal hero, like those in Lang's other
films, cannot control his own destiny; he is hunted by the
relentless forces of the state, which has fascist characteristics. According to Blum, it is not surprising that the
Nazis banned the film.

Blum does not, however, see Lang as primarily a political
director. One should not fault him for failing to see the
latent fascism in his Metropolis, nor claim that he prophesied the persecution and terror of the Nazi regime in movies
like M and Das Testament des Dr. Mabuse [The Last Will of
Dr. Mabuse]. Like every sensitive artist, he captured the
mood of his times.

Blum notes that Lang has been criticized by the left for
his apolitical stance. Herbert Ihering, one of the leading
critics of the time who recognized Lang as an important
filmmaker, criticized him for romanticizing the criminal
underworld and for his indecision about capital punishment.
Blum concludes that M is nevertheless an important document
in film history.

391   Grafe, Frieda. "Er erfand den Countdown: Zum 80 Geburtstag
      Von Fritz Lang am 5 December." Süddeutsche Zeitung (Munich),
      Nr. p. 291 (5-6 December).
         Grafe uses Die Frau im Mond [Woman in the Moon] to demon-
      strate the mixture of realism and fantasy characteristic of
      Lang's work; in that film, he "discovered" the countdown
      while in the process of creating artistic tension. Similar-
      ly, in 1924, it was the real city of New York that inspired
      his futuristic vision in Metropolis. Once in Hollywood,
      however, Lang made no more fantasy films but settled into
      Hollywood realism. Realizing that the superman was not
      appropriate in America, he now dealt rather with the "man
      of the street."
         Grafe then discusses the enormous difference between
      notions of high culture in Germany and the predominance of
      popular culture in America. She says that the German cinema
      was the poorer for never becoming popular; links to popular
      culture make for vitality and richness, as in the many li-
      terary traditions, like surrealism in France, that have
      drawn on it.
         After noting the difference between the German and
      American works, and listing the groups of actors that under-
      score the changes, Grafe deplores the fact that Lang took on
      the American style and refused, in interviews, to take his
      American work seriously.
         The concluding comments deal with the violence in Lang's
      American films and with the sad fact that in America a di-
      rector cannot work through symbols, but must show violence
      to reach people.

392   *Guilleminault, Gilbert and Bernet, Philippe. "Fritz Lang, le
      magnifique Prince de la nuit germanique." In Les princes
      des années folles. Paris: Plon, pp. 255-382.
            Source: F. Grafe and Enno Patalas. Fritz Lang. Munich:
      Carl Hanser Verlag, 1976, p. 167.

393   Haas, Willy. "Fritz Lang wird 80 Jahre alt." Die Welt
      (Hamburg) (5 December).
            Writing on the occasion of Lang's eightieth birthday,
      Haas notes that when Lang went into filmmaking, the high
      point of the monumental, monster film had passed, and the
      genre was degenerating into Kitsch. Murnau, Lupu Pick, and
      Carl Mayer were beginning to make the Kammerspiel [Chamber
      play] film. Always a compromiser, Lang took the mass scenes
      and adventure from Lubitsch and good taste from more re-
      fined films. He tried something expressionist and symbolic
      in Der müde Tod [Destiny], but his works always ended up
      being imitative in a negative way, perhaps because of the
      influence of Thea von Harbou.
            Haas rejects Die Nibelungen as imitative and Metropolis
      as prefiguring Nazi ideology. But he goes on to praise
      Fury as presenting a true picture of its time, as well as
      looking toward the future; seen today, the film holds up.
            Dr. Mabuse, der Spieler and M are thrillers in a good
      sense of the word, and other films made in Europe were only
      moderately successful. Haas feels that recent German and
      French critics have perhaps overemphasized Lang's merits as
      an artist.

394   Harmssen, Henning. "Von Siegfried bis Mabuse. Filmklassiker
      Fritz Lang zum 80. Geburtstag." Stuttgarter Zeitung (4
      December). Note: This article is reprinted almost word
      for word in the same newspaper on 5 December 1975, and in
      Lübecker Nachrichten (6 December 1970). An abbreviated ver-
      sion appeared in Saarbrücken Zeitung (4 December 1970).
            Harmssen notes that Lang visited the South seas,
      Indonesia, China, Japan, and Russia, where he gathered ex-
      otic impressions, which play a dominant role in some of his
      early films (Halbblut, Die Spinnen [The Spiders], Harakiri,
      Spione [Spies]). "I simply had the desire to make adventure
      movies," said Lang in 1964. "I was young then and loved
      everything exotic. Besides, I wanted to use my travel
      souveniers."
            The film Der müde Tod [Destiny], which is characteristic
      of Lang's directing style (shadows, reflected light, and
      emphasis on architectural structures) is considered to be
      an early masterpiece.
            Whereas Lang's Mabuse films were anxious political
      "premonitions" (Kracauer), the other world-famous Lang films
      are extremely contradictory creations with a disconcerting
      affinity with nazism, especially Die Nibelungen and Metropolis.

Commenting on Die Nibelungen, which contained presentiments of and supported National Socialist ideology (the cult of the Nordic, the Führer-principle, and the worship of heroic death), Goebbels explained: "Here is a film-fate not taken from contemporary times, but so modern, so relevant, that it deeply moved the warriors of the NS-movement." That a film like Metropolis, which according to Kracauer is "a cross between Krupp and Richard Wagner," with its masking of social conflict and its deceptive picture of class harmony, was hailed by the Nazis is not surprising.

The strange affinity with the Nazi ideology in Die Nibelungen and Metropolis has to this day not been plausibly explained. Was the subject matter simply value-free, just an opportunity to utilize his directorial talent and technical tricks? Or did Lang lie under the influence of an unconscious fascination with oppositions due to his predilection for romanticism? In both cases, "Lang's directorial conception was objectively not so free of fascist ideology as his subjective convictions would have it" (Gregor/Patalas).

According to Lang, he became politically mature after the Nazis forced him to drop the subtitle of the film M, Mörder unter uns [Murderer(s) among Us].

In 1936, Lang made his most important American film, Fury, a passionate study of mass hysteria, which was directed against lynch justice.

It is characteristic of Lang's rather pessimistic outlook that most of his film heroes are not strong enough to fight successfully against a dark fate.

Of his American films, Lang values Fury, Woman in the Window, Scarlet Street, and While the City Sleeps the most.

Lang is highly regarded in France, but almost unknown in Germany.

Other newspaper articles honoring Lang on his eightieth birthday:

Freund, Rudolf. "Schon zu Lebzeiten legendär," Leipziger Volkszeitung (6 December 1970).

sth. "In Hollywood nur schlechte Laune: Filmregisseur Fritz Lang wird 80 Jahre alt. Der unübertroffene Meister des 'Thrillers'." Rheinische Post (5 December 1970).

Ebeling, Rago T. "Fritz Lang." Westfalen-Blatt (19 December 1970).

Dvorak, P. "Ein Wiener Preusse mit Monokel: Fritz Lang wird heute 80 Jahre alt." (6 December) Newspaper not given.

Tölke, Susanna, and Maibohm, Ludwig. "Immer das Monokel vorm linken Auge: Fritz Lang, der Meisterregisseur der deutschen Stummfilmzeit, feiert heute seinen 80. Geburtstag." Abend-Zeitung (Munich) (6 December 1970).

Anon. "Legende seiner selbst: Fritz Lang 80 Jahre alt.
Bedeutender Filmpionier." Thüringer Neueste Nachrichten
(27 November 1970).

Reichow, Joachim. "Fritz Lang--Macht des Schicksals?"
Der Morgen (Berlin) (6 December 1970).

PEM [Paul Marcus]. "Fritz Lang ohne Monokel." Film-
Telegramm (1 December 1970).

See also Entries Nos. 398, 399, and 402.

395    Joannides, Paul. "Aspects of Fritz Lang." Cinema (London),
Nos. 6/7 (August), pp. 5-9.

Joannides attributes much of the negative critical response to Lang to the emphasis on the literary rather than
the visual aspects of his films. He goes on to show how
complex Lang's view of the world actually is: while Lang
may condemn the mob (as in Metropolis and Fury), he sympathizes with individuals and places the responsibility on
society. Lang is able "to see different values as the necessary product of different conditions." Apparently similar
situations in Rancho Notorious and The Big Heat are evaluated differently; for example, Ford becomes virtuous in his
revenge, while Kennedy deteriorates because of his. Yet,
paradoxically, Lang distances us from Ford (the objective
situation makes his case justifiable) and encourages us to
identify with Kennedy, whom we might otherwise simply reject.
But Joannides notes that overriding all of this moral
sensitivity is Lang's fatalistic world view. A pursuing
force hunts down its victims, so that hate and revenge take
on "a creative intensity." There is a sense of everything's
hanging over a precipice: death, madness, danger, and pain
are ever present, enhanced by the objective camera. Objects
take on meanings that suggest the metaphysical. Lang's
images reflect psychological states and abstract ideas, and
Joannides gives examples from The Big Heat and Rancho
Notorious as proof.
Quoting Lang himself, Joannides suggests that the source
of Lang's abstractions is the occult, rather than expressionism. He refers to Metropolis and Der müde Tod [Destiny]
here, but notes that while with sound the framework of
Lang's films became realistic, the same effects are to be
found. Objects in M, Manhunt, Rancho Notorious, and Scarlet
Street continue to have a life of their own.
Joannides concludes by showing how narrative takes on
the quality of dream in Lang's films; the plots interest
Lang little, since he thinks instead in cinematic terms of
image in relation to image. He handles movement expressively to highlight emotional states. The two "Indian" films
(made in Germany) offer an extreme example of film as dream:
"Narrative becomes symbolism, reality dissolves, the film
is moulded entirely by subconscious measures."

396    Lyons, B. "Fritz Lang and the film noir." Mise-En-Scène
       (Great Britain) (January 11), n.d. (BFI library has a copy.)
           This is a rather general, rambling survey of Lang's life
       and work, covering the major films. Lyons presents the
       broad outlines of the film noir visual style and goes on to
       apply what he says in an unfocused way to Lang's work. Ac-
       cording to Lyons, the very length of Lang's career and all
       the political and technical changes he witnessed make him
       interesting.
           The best part of the article is Lyons's discussion of the
       visual texture of certain specific scenes in Manhunt and
       You Only Live Once.
           Lyons sees no break between Lang's early German and his
       American films, pointing out a consistency in theme and
       style. Lang constantly uses buildings "as though they were
       a microcosm of the universe," and his overriding theme is
       the struggle to master the environment.

397    Patalas, Enno. "Prophet im Ausland." Die Zeit (Hamburg)
       (25 November).
           Patalas notes that Lang was driven out of Germany three
       times: by the Nazis in 1933, by the German film industry
       in 1957, and by the supervisors of film culture (including
       critics), who stubbornly ignore him even today.
           Having made three films for Arthur Brauner (CCC) in 1956
       and 1957, Lang was disillusioned with the German film indus-
       try and gave up the idea of doing more films. "The leaders
       of the film industry," he said, "want to make a profit be-
       fore the film is begun. They are not interested in making
       good films." Lang had undertaken the remake of the two
       Indian films halfheartedly. Despite the anachronistic sub-
       ject, the catastrophic working conditions, and a rare col-
       lection of talentless actors, Patalas says that one can
       still see Lang's skill in the design and flow of the images,
       in the colors, and in such scenes as the conclusion of Der
       Tiger von Eschnapur [The Tiger of Bengal], where the lovers
       are covered by the sandstorm.
           The prestige of Lang's German silent films diverts atten-
       tion from the American films, making them almost invisible.
       Patalas objects to the current critical distinction between
       a "German" Lang, who made expressionist, monumental films,
       and an "American" Lang, who made conventional, well-crafted
       melodramas. While still in Germany, Lang sought the
       American soul and made thrillers, serials, and science fic-
       tion films; Metropolis was a German dream of America.
       Hollywood Westerns like Rancho Notorious, on the other hand,
       continue the direction of Die Nibelungen. The Indian films
       are an amalgam of the German longing for distant places and
       the Ziegfield Follies. Fairy tales and legends were never
       far from reality and the present for Lang, and he linked
       film to folk tales.

Patalas concludes that Germany has suppressed an important part of film history in suppressing Lang. New Wave directors in France benefit from watching Lang films frequently at the Cinemathèque Française. Comparing a new German film with one by Chabrol, Godard, Truffaut, or Straub reveals how much Germans lack through not knowing Lang.

398     Schirmer, Arnd F. "Der Metaphysiker auf dem Regiestuhl: Zum 80. Geburtstag von Fritz Lang." (5 December) (Clipping available in Deutschen Film- und Fernsehakademie, W. Berlin--newspaper not given.)

Schirmer begins by quoting Lang on the cinema, saying that it is a vice that he worships. "I have often said," Lang continues, "that it is the art form of our century . . . I love this art, which unfortunately has become an industry in most countries . . . ." This, according to Schirmer, is spoken by a man who has been unable to make the leap from the nineteenth to the twentieth century, and who wants to create art in a medium that can no longer be brought into harmony with the artistic ideas of the past.

Lang goes on to discuss the main theme of his films, concluding that it is the struggle of the individual against events, the Greek problem of the struggle against fate. Asserting that we fight against rules today that we do not consider good or just, Lang notes that the struggle is more important than the outcome.

For Schirmer, Lang is one of the great originals of film history, who has made many conflicting films. Schirmer finds the irrationalism in many of the films embarrassing: the frenzied stylization, the fatalism, and the dark whispering that pervade his films fascinated the originators of the French New Wave in the 1950s. Regarded more highly in France than here in Germany, Lang belongs among the great directors such as Hawks, Ford, and Sternberg, because his unique mark is evident even in his weakest films.

Claude Chabrol claims that Lang remained true to himself even in his commercial films. His themes--the inevitability of decay, the occult power of secret societies, and spy networks--are as important to him, Chabrol says, as his aesthetics. His characters are confined to a frame from which they escape only through everyday activities.

399     Schütte, Wolfram (WoS). "Ein Meister: Fritz Lang wird am 5. Dezember 80 Jahre alt." Frankfurter Rundshau (5 December), p. 6.

Schütte considers Lang to be the last of the great German film directors who have not outlived their glory. Honored in France, the Austrian filmmaker is viewed as reflecting the essence of German cinema, his life work an example of a great cinéaste.

His name is mainly associated with Die Niebelungen and

Metropolis, which the Nazis so enjoyed.  Lang made the two
best films of his career before he left Germany after
Goebbels' overtures:  M represents the high point of the
realist film, while Das Testament [The Last Will] foreshadowed the madness to come.

Lang's American films look back to the realist, social-
issue films of the German period, but, because of the connection between his personal development and historical
events, his work is stamped with fatalism.  The mature Lang
worked in Hollywood genres--the films often made ultimately
by several people--and these little-known films are generally
not highly regarded.  A recent retrospective by the film
clubs brought both Lang and his work to notice.  But his
last monumental films made in Germany were a mistake, Lang
suffering the kind of treatment that the industry usually
affords to young directors.

400    Vialle, Gabriel.  Review of Der Tiger von Eschnapur.  Image et
       Son, No. 244, pp. 189-195.
       Vialle briefly summarizes the plot of The Tiger of Bengal
and its history, mentioning Lang's early involvement with
the script for the Karl May film.  He next lists the major
people involved in the project, followed by a general overview of the narrative techniques used in the film, which is
a series of episodes.  Vialle notes that while Lang tried
to make his people real, he also tried to give a sense of
their destiny.  The film contains typical Langian themes,
such as the struggle between love and faith.  Vialle lists
the main sequences in each part of the film and then goes
on to say that Lang ultimately gives more attention to
decor and objects than to characters.

Vialle sees the film as Lang's personal realization of an
old project, shaped by his experiences in pre-Nazi Germany
and his involvement with expressionism.  The film is an exciting, classical adventure story reflecting Lang's hatred
of all that oppresses and suppresses the individual, as well
as his search for a transcendent kind of love.  Vialle
enumerates the cinematic devices through which Lang expresses these themes, citing movements of the camera, mise-en-
scène, color, and lighting.  Vialle concludes that the film
is deliberately artificial and ends up being surreal, simply
the means for Lang's expression of his abstract themes:
love, hate, jealousy, and betrayal.

Vialle complains about the way in which the actors were
directed and about the musical track.  He regrets Lang's
loss of restraint since having gone to America, but admires
the sumptuousness of the costumes and accessories.

401    Weinberg, Herman G.  "Welcome, Fritz Lang."  Originally written
       for the Souvenir Program of the Montreal Film Festival, 1967,
       where Lang was guest of honor.  Reprinted in Saint Cinema:

Selected Writings, 1920-1970. New York: Drama Book
Specialists publications, pp. 9-11.
 Weinberg surveys Lang's cinematic career from the pre-
history of film to his comments on our own period in Die
tausend Augen des Dr. Mabuse [The Thousand Eyes of Dr.
Mabuse] and his acting in Godard's film. He considers Lang
one of the great directors, whose classic films are now
taken for granted. Weinberg finds the high points of Lang's
career in the early German period and glosses over the
American films. He concludes by mentioning Lang's new project for a film about American youth.

402 Wiegand, Wilfried. "Der Regisseur von 'M.'" Frankfurter
 Allgemeine Zeitung (5 December), p. 282.
 Wiegand begins by reciting some of the negative British
opinions about Lang (that he is a mere showman, that
Metropolis is childish and M melodramatic) that the Germans
adopted. The British deliberately rejected expressionism,
but in Germany critics have also condemned Lang's films,
honoring only Die Nibelungen, Dr. Mabuse, and M, as they
have value for film history rather than in themselves. In
France, on the contrary, Lang is honored as a great director;
he received a high award from Malraux and is recognized as
a genius by New Wave filmmakers, being given the status of
a living myth in Godard's Le Mépris (1963).
 German appreciation of Lang has been hindered by the
fact that the American films have barely been shown in
Germany. The recent German films have likewise been condemned out of hand. Secondly, there is a lot of ignorance
about Lang's work.
 M has been considered an inhuman film because of the
censored version that is always shown. Kracauer's book
also did a great deal of harm. Its methodology is questionable, and it comes down to whether or not in Das Testament
[The Last Will] Lang was providing a model for National
Socialism, since Hitler wanted him as film director for the
Third Reich.
 Wiegand responds to these charges by saying that the
general influence was from Max Reinhardt and expressionism
--elements that also touched socialist writers and directors
like Brecht and Piscator. Furthermore, Lang himself considers
some of his endings weak. Focusing particularly on the greatness of M, Wiegand goes on to praise the way Lang, like Pabst,
moved from expressionism to realism.
 A final reason for the low opinion of Lang has been that
one has looked at his works as isolated units rather than as
a whole (with the later works commenting on earlier ones).
Thus Fury can be seen as a reflection on Metropolis, with
Lang now showing that we must watch out for the fascism
that can come out of inciting a mob.
 Wiegand concludes with a summary of all the elements

standing in the way of proper appreciation of Lang in
Germany in the hope that these can now be overcome.


1971

403    Anon.  "Engel der Gejagten."  (Review of Rancho Notorious.)
       Spielfilme im deutschen Fernsehen.  (Available in Deutschen
       Film und Fernsehakademie, West Berlin.)
          The author begins by discussing how well Lang understands
       creating a satiric drama out of an idyll and a legend out of
       the hero's downfall.  The use of the old Western ballad gives
       the film its legendary air, which naturally extends to the
       ending.  The female leader of the gangsters repents of her
       evil ways but, as is inevitable, dies in the final battle.
          According to the reviewer, Marlene Dietrich acts one of
       her most sinister roles as a woman who plays with other
       people's lives.  She participates in the unrelenting game
       of her rival lovers.  Taking their fate into their own hands,
       the three main characters assume legendary status for the
       other men.
          The author concludes that Rancho Notorious has an aura of
       unreality from the start; Lang is perhaps so good at making
       Westerns because he never pretends to reproduce reality but
       remains instead on the legendary plane, as he did also in
       The Return of Frank James.

404    Anon.  "Präfaschistischer Horror?"  [On the showing of the
       three Mabuse films on German television].  Fernsehen und
       Film, No. 3 (March).  (Available in the Deutschen Film und
       Fernsehakademie, West Berlin.)
          The critic says that the second of the silent films ends
       with Mabuse's succumbing to a childlike madness and being
       taken away by a von Wenk filled with pity.  We all pity
       King Kong's fall from the Empire State Building to Fifth
       Avenue, but the same arguments were made for Hitler--namely,
       that he had fallen into a genial, feeblemindedness.  Lang
       has said that his Mabuse films are ciphers for the twentieth
       century, but they also anticipate the coming totalitarian
       society.  The reviewer thinks the films are both anticipa-
       tions of, and preparations for, totalitarianism.  He con-
       cludes by noting that the Mabuse retrospective will be
       followed by a talk by Klaus Kreimeier on Lang's German films
       and their relation to the Weimar period.

405    Brochier, Jean-Jacques.  "Fritz Lang."  In Jean-Français Bory
       and C. Cluny, Dossiers du Cinéma, Cinéastes I, Tournai
       Casterman, pp. 145-148.
          Brochier notes the originality of Lang's first German
       period.  While linked to expressionism, Lang made modern
       adventure stories, while expressionists turned to traditional

literary themes, often from the romantic period or popular
literature.  Brochier denies that Dr. Mabuse represented
Hitler, arguing that while Hitler stood for metaphysical
evil, Mabuse signified the evil of industrial capitalism.
A few films do seem expressionist, but then a critique of
the style is present along with the perfecting of it, e.g.,
in Die Nibelungen.  The continuity between the German and
American films would have been impossible for a director in
the Caligari tradition.

M represents the model for Lang's political films, with
themes expressed through mise-en-scène rather than dialogue.
The montage in the trial scene is repeated in Fury in the
scene where Tracy is nearly lynched.

In both Germany and America, whether Lang was making
popular adventure films or psychological dramas, the truth
of his work resides in the mise-en-scène.  For Lang (in contrast to Hitchcock) the image is at once enigma and solution;
Brochier gives examples of Lang's use of mirrors and of his
repetition of images in a dialectical relationship.  Beyond
a Reasonable Doubt shows best the literalness with which
Lang's image must be taken.

Brochier concludes that Lang's is a realist (but not
naturalist) cinema; because truth rests in the image itself,
Lang's films cannot be put in any of the usual categories
True realism, Brochier says, consists in refusing the illusion of realism, and in this way Lang is striving for the
same result as Brecht, although their means are different.

406   *Hanisch, Michael.  "Der Vater des Dr. Mabuse."  Neue Zeit
(East Berlin) (3 January).
Source:  F. Grafe and Enno Patalas, Fritz Lang.  Munich:
Carl Hanser Verlag, 1976, p. 165.

407   Henry, Michael.  Le Cinéma Expressioniste Allemand.  Paris:
Editions du signe, pp. 32-35.
The whole first chapter is important as background for
Lang, but Henry also discusses the three Mabuse films in
the course of more general observations.  Lang is compared
to his creation, Mabuse, in that while Mabuse hypnotizes
his followers, Lang fascinates his spectators.  Dialectical
man par excellence, Mabuse hides behind his disguises; a
totalitarian leader, he synthesises the positions of all
his opponents.  Typically expressionist, Henry says, is the
doubling that results from Mabuse's hypnotism of others and
also the way that the hero damns himself; Mabuse, like Mark
in Secret Beyond the Door, is at once criminal and his own
accuser.

Henry proceeds to make some distinctions between the three
Mabuse films in terms of their world view, concluding that
expressionists tried to substitute for an indifferent universe a world ruled by the idea.

408   Maltin, Leonard.  Behind the Camera.  New York:  New American
      Library, pp. 81-83, 129-130.
          Maltin interviews two cameramen who worked with Lang and
      who have interestingly diverse views on their experiences.
      Both agree that Lang is a great director whom they admire,
      but Arthur Miller also seemed to find a way to get along
      with Lang, while Hal Mohr objected to the way that Lang
      "abused" people.  Miller discusses working with Lang on
      Manhunt; he found Lang anxious to learn from him and easy
      to please.  Miller thought his bad reputation unjust.  Miller,
      it seems, was inventive in his camera work and thus earned
      Lang's admiration.
          Mohr on the other hand, working with Lang on Rancho
      Notorious, resented Lang's insistence on looking through the
      camera viewfinder himself.  According to Mohr, the director
      should leave the filming to the cameraman.

409   Manvell, Roger and Heinrich Fraenkel.  The German Cinema.  New
      York and London:  Praeger Publishers, pp. 12-31.
          Manvell and Fraenkel discuss Lang in the context of a
      survey of the major film directors of the 1920s in Germany.
      They survey Lang's silent films in a conventional manner,
      placing them in the context of expressionism.  They use
      Lotte Eisner's analysis of expressionism (See Entry No. 375)
      and Lang's reflections on the period (See Entry No. 532) to
      support their views.


                              1972

410   Beylie, Claude.  Review of Liliom.  Écran 72, No. 10 (December),
      pp. 55-56.
          Beylie notes that many archive versions of Liliom lack
      the last few minutes, so that critics think Liliom was damned
      eternally instead of ultimately being pardoned.  Lang con-
      tinually undercuts the realism of the film by nonrealism,
      so that a theatrical treatment of the section on earth is
      followed by close attention to detail in the celestial part.
      There is, Beylie notes, a strange section in which Liliom
      is shown scenes from his past life, while on the soundtrack
      we hear his thoughts about what he sees.  (Lang created a
      similar sequence in Fury and again in the last Mabuse film.)
          Noting the often contradictory and puzzled critical re-
      ception of the film, Beylie emphasizes three points as ex-
      planation:
      (1) although Lang is uneasy in Molnar's universe, he brings
          a certain rhythm to it;
      (2) the actors, except for Antonin Artaud, are mediocre,
          this being perhaps due to Lang's unfamiliarity with
          French and to his recent escape from Nazi Germany; and
      (3) there is perhaps a parallel between Boyer's brief return


                              310

to earth from purgatory and Lang's escape from Nazi
barbarism.

411    Hempel, Rolf. "Fritz Lang-Mythos--für wen?", in Knietzsch,
       Horst, ed., Prisma. East Berlin: Henschel, pp. 236-251.
           Hempel begins by discussing Lang's works in relation to
       the social events of his time. In a manner typical of East
       German critics, Hempel focusses on the contradictions in
       the political positions in Lang's films, and criticizes him
       for not objecting more to the whole social system.
           At the beginning of his career, Hempel says, Lang faught
       ardently for the cause of the German-Austrian monarchy as a
       high-ranking officer. But he did not deal with the war in
       his works or, like other artists, take a pacifist position.
       According to Hempel, those of Lang's works made between
       World War I and the Nazi seizure of power always supported
       bourgeois ideology. When at all present--mainly in his
       first American period--Lang's social criticism was divided,
       contradictory, and never against the social organization as
       a whole.
           Even in exile, then, Hempel says, Lang never became a
       politically aware or committed artist, but rather served
       Hollywood. Hangmen Also Die--about the anti-fascist resist-
       ance in Czechoslovakia--is an exception. Nor did Lang
       demonstrate any new attitude after World War II. When he
       returned to West Germany to make films, he produced two
       pieces of grand trash: Hempel concludes that these works
       reveal the decline of a director who, for most of his career,
       was a propagandist for the bourgeoisie.

412    Kauffmann, Stanley, and Henstall, Bruce. American Film
       Criticism. New York: Liveright Press.
           This is a useful collection of reprints of the best cri-
       ticism of early Lang films, many of which are annotated in
       this bibliography. The following articles are included:
       (1) Krutch, Joseph Wood. Review of Siegfried. The Nation
           (16 September 1925), pp. 165-167.
           A basically positive review, praising the artistic in-
       telligence that went into the film; Krutch notes the stylis-
       tic unity, often lacking in films, and sees the structure
       of the narrative as an advance on what had been done before.
       (2) A series of reviews of Metropolis, pp. 184-190:
           (a) Vreeland, F. New York Telegram (7 March 1927).
           (b) Gerstein, E. The Nation (23 March 1927).
           (c) Beaton, Welford. The Film Spectator (3 September
               1927).
           Metropolis is fascinating as a film, but contains
       an unsatisfactory picture of the future. The human
       element is reduced in the American version.
       (3) A series of reviews of M, pp. 282-288:
           (a) Watts, Richard, Jr. New York Herald Tribune

(3 April 1933).
(b) Troy, William. The Nation (19 April 1933).
(c) Lorentz, Pare. Vanity Fair (May 1933).
(4) Reviews of Fury, pp. 337-340.
(a) Nugent, Frank S. New York Times (6 June 1936).
(b) Fearing, K. The New Masses (16 June 1936).

413   Kinder, Marsha and Houston, Beverle. "M". In their Close-Up:
A Critical Perspective on Film. New York: Harcourt, Brace
Jovanovich, pp. 58-66.
      Primarily intended for students, the discussion of M is
still generally useful, since there is detailed reference
to the use of sound, camera angles, and imagery. The authors
analyze "the pattern of entrapment that particularly threatens Beckert and the children, thereby linking them as victims
of the orderly society." The extensive use of the overhead
angle, Houston and Kinder argue, expressed "the omniscient
view of the film as it examines the nature of society,
stressing the similarities between the police and underworld." They conclude by suggesting that Lang invites us
to share the power that the omniscient view provides and
"use it to fight against capital punishment and to improve
society."

414   Kuntzel, Thierry. "Le Travail du Film." [On M].
Communications, No. 19. Reprinted as "The Film Work."
Translated by Lawrence Crawford, Kimball Lockhart, and
Claudia Tysdal. Enclitic (University of Minnesota), 2, No.
1 (Spring 1978), 39-64.
      This article is a detailed semiotic reading of the first
sequence of M, divided into fourteen sections, and relying
on Barthesian concepts of codes, lexia, seme, etc. Kuntzel
spends the first few sections establishing his methodology
and his reasons for focusing on the first sequence of M.
He intends not so much to deal with certain codes evident
in the first sequence "with a view toward reconstruction of
a system which would give the film's overall functioning in
brief," but instead to choose specific codes that stand out
in some way.
      Kuntzel discusses the significance of the letter "M" as
it crosses the screen in the titles, justifying Lang's traditional practice of not beginning analysis with the first
diegetic image. The "M" refers to "Mabuse" in Lang's works,
to the subtitles of the film containing the word "murderer",
to Freud's "wolf man," to the symbolics of lettering in certain alphabets, etc. Kuntzel next discusses the various
visual codes, showing how the motif of circularity is established and how conventional polarities ("small/large,"
"overwhelmed/overwhelming," "dominated/dominating") are set
up, only later to be played with humorously by Lang. He
goes on to show the function of the rhyme in the several

sound codes in the sequence and then discusses the code of
decor evident when the camera begins to move up the building
and the code of actions, which contrast play (the children)
and work (the woman with the washing).  The words spoken
reinforce the fear already established and the impotence of
speech.  The children don't respond, and when the woman goes
off, the camera remains.  But, says Kuntzel, the void and
silence are far from the Bergman metaphysical heaviness;
instead "waiting and absence are inscribed in the text and
not in an interpretation of the world."

Kuntzel provides a shot-by-shot analysis of the sequence
at this point--26 shots listed in all, complete with stills.
He shows the alternation between places (interior and exterior), related characters (Mrs. Beckmann and Elsie), and
actions (working and playing).  This alternation figures a
dissymmetry, since there are only six exterior and twenty
interior shots.  The drama thus rests on the fact of "waiting" rather than on the actual murder.  He proceeds to analyze the series of shots in detail, showing how "the presence
of objects gauges the absence of the subject," and similarly,
"the presence of a voice . . . lets another person's absence
(Elsie's) be read."  Kuntzel ends by discussing the last two
shots of the sequence revealing Elsie's death:  here the
ball "designates not only the child, but the murderer's desire as well."

Kuntzel declares that his reading of M has "attempted to
stage two modes of work:  generation by demonstrating what
any object having a meaning obliterates . . .; and structura-
tion of the phenotext itself--the dynamics of motifs in the
shot and of shots in the syntagem, the contrapuntal inter-
play of sound and visuals."

415   McArthur, Colin.  "Fritz Lang."  In his Underworld U.S.A.
      London:  Secker and Warburg.  Pp. 71-81.
         McArthur deals mainly with the themes in Lang's thrillers,
      focusing on M, The Big Heat, and Beyond a Reasonable Doubt.
      Setting his discussion in the context of Lang's early German
      experiences (the First World War, the Nazis, the mood of
      early German cinema), McArthur shows how extremely bleak and
      despairing Lang's vision always was.  He points out the in-
      teresting pattern of detection and conviction and the re-
      currence of court scenes in Lang's films, where justice is
      an illusion.  Chance comes into play as yet another cruel
      aspect of human life.
         McArthur discusses the role of violence in Lang's films,
      noting its sexual dimension, and the femmes fatales who pro-
      voke violence through their cold seductiveness.
         Respectability and criminality are barely distinguishable
      in Lang's films noir, with McArthur giving examples from
      several.  After noting the artificiality of Lang's style,
      with its focus on lighting, its baroque fondness for mirrors

and deliberate creation of unease, McArthur gives a detailed analysis of the motifs in The Big Heat, which he considers Lang's most restrained and beautiful film.

416    Ostroff, Roberta. Interview with Henry Fonda. Take One, No. 10 (March-April), pp. 14-17.
       Fonda makes some interesting, if negative, comments about Lang in the course of an interview on what it was like working with different directors in Hollywood. Fonda is explicit about his dislike for Lang and seems particularly irritated by Lang's perfectionism. He describes spending an entire day on the set-up for a scene in You Only Live Once, where Lang could not get some dessert dishes and the spoon exactly as he wanted them. Fonda seems to think that Lang was the wrong person to make The Return of Frank James; he had not wanted to work with Lang again but was under contract and had no choice. Fonda describes one scene in Return where he was required simply to enter and leave. After rehearsing for a while, Lang decided he wanted some cobwebs, and it took twenty minutes for someone to come back with them. But Lang was still not satisfied, wanting an "old" cobweb, and ended up pulling the whole thing apart.
       Fonda seems to believe that Lang was essentially a director of silent films: "I think he greatly resented the fact that sound came in and he was not able to talk to an actor during the performance." He notes how involved Lang was with the camera, standing always close to it and making excited gestures.

417    *Toeplitz, Jerzy. Geschichte des Films, 1, 1895-1928 Translated from the Polish. East Berlin: Henschel; Munich: Rogner and Bernhardt, 1973.
       I could locate only the Polish edition (published 1955-1969), available in the Lincoln Center Library.


## 1973

418    Anon. "Ministerium der Angst." [Review of Ministry of Fear]. Spielfilm im deutschen Fernsehen. (Available in Deutschen Film und Fernsehakademie, West Berlin.)
       According to the reviewer, Ministry of Fear belongs to a group of four films criticizing the Nazis, which Lang made between 1941 and 1945. Ministry recalls Spione [Spies] in the mysterious organization manipulating everything behind the scenes. While the story has many clichés, Lang imbues his work with his "fantastical realism." After a summary of the plot, the reviewer concludes that one can see Lang's handiwork in the film: he has created a suspenseful atmosphere and succeeded in introducing symbolism and an artistic dimension. One should not miss a film that has been unknown for so long in Germany.

419   Burch, Noel.  "De Mabuse à M:  Le Travail de Fritz Lang."
      Revue d'Esthétique, special issue.  (Texts collected and
      edited by Dominique Noguez.)
         Burch begins by arguing against the prevailing view of
      Lang's work as a thematic and stylistic whole.  He sees a
      distinct break between the first German period and the
      American period.  The German films are far superior and on
      quite a different plane.  Once in America, Lang simply be-
      came one of the anonymous herd of Hollywood directors.
         Dr. Mabuse terminates one main direction in film form,
      representing the culmination of aspects taken from the
      nineteenth-century novel.  The kind of discourse in this
      cinematic form is literary--that is, reducible to another
      narration, a dimension of the film separate from the film
      itself.  Silent films in the tradition of Caligari, however,
      represent another kind of cinema, which Metz refers to as
      "le langage sans langue."
         Burch shows how the nineteenth-century novel relies on
      the illusion of the characters' human resemblance.  We are
      invited to think of characters in terms similar to the way
      we think about people in our daily lives.  Literally, of
      course, these "characters" are merely a set of grammatical
      functions.  Dr. Mabuse works in exactly the same way; we be-
      lieve in the characters and they are as real and vivid today
      as in 1922.  Lang creates the illusion of "reality" better
      than Griffith, Ince, or Feuillade.
         The main section of the article is a detailed analysis
      of M from the structural point of view.  Burch places M
      after Potemkin and Vampyre as a leading example of composite
      forms.  We find a coherent combination of forms peripheral
      to cinema and those of pure film.  The film is divided into
      nine parts, each of which has its own mode of functioning
      and obeys its own "laws."  But there are also a few large
      controlling principles in the film, and it is the complex
      interaction among the principles that determines the film's
      form.  The nine parts that Burch isolates are as follows:
      (1) the murder of Elsie; (2) the psychosis of the killer;
      (3) the diligence/powerlessness of the police; (4) the in-
      vestigations by the underground and the police; (5) the
      meeting of the two investigators; (6) the end of the investi-
      gation; (7) the murderer on the run--he is caught; (8) the
      police on the trail of the murderer; (9) the two trials.
         Burch shows how two large movements run across these nine
      parts, creating a complex structure.  These are, first, the
      movement that carries the film from the separate parts to
      coherence; and second, the movement consisting of the un-
      veiling of the central person in the film--the murderer--in
      seven scenes.
         Burch then analyzes each of the nine parts outlined above,
      showing how it works, and how the elaborate structure estab-
      lishes Lang's meanings.

420    Casty, Alan.  "Fritz Lang:  Expressionist Epic and Expressive
        Realism."  In his Development of the Film:  An Interpretive
        History.  New York:  Harcourt, Brace, Jovanovich, pp. 52-56.
        [For an additional discussion of Lang, see pp. 151-154 and
        for Lang and film noir, pp. 255-257].
            In discussing Lang's early films, Casty notes that Lang
        employed expressionist techniques while extending the orna-
        mental manner of Caligari to topics with mythic scope and
        grandeur.  Lang focuses on the theme of the split in the
        individual between emotions and intellect, body and spirit,
        aggression and love.  These reflected conflicts in the ex-
        ternal society.
            Casty discusses Destiny and Die Nibelungen briefly, not-
        ing the odd mixture of artificial scenery, magical camera
        tricks, grandiose posturing, and inventive visual symbolism.
        When the mixture works, great images result, but in general
        Casty finds these films self-indulgent.  He likes Metropolis
        better, viewing it in terms of the theme of individual versus
        technology.  But Casty again criticizes the overindulgence
        and sentimentality, which result merely in plot conflicts
        rather than expressionist protest.  Praising the visual as-
        pects of the films, Casty provides examples of the powerful
        images produced by the symbolic use of ornamental architec-
        ture.
            He finally turns to Dr. Mabuse, der Spieler and M as
        representing a more literal, realistic rendering of Lang's
        social and psychological themes.  Dr. Mabuse is a thriller
        with a basis in contemporary life and its visual design is
        a fascinating blend of the literal and the expressionist;
        Mabuse represents the disorder and evil of a rapacious
        society.  Casty concludes with some comments on M:  although
        a sound film, it represents the culmination of expressive
        devices used to reveal extreme inner states within a real-
        istic treatment.  Casty discusses Lang's use of editing and
        of the way he makes objects assume symbolic dimensions.
            Casty considers Lang's first three American films in
        terms of their social themes.  He sees Fury as continuing
        the direction toward realism begun in M, while integrating
        the American style at the same time.  Lang's three films
        help to change the attitude toward the criminal from one
        which glorified the gangland heroes while condemning them
        to one which viewed criminals largely as victims of forces
        beyond their control.
            Casty concludes by discussing Lang's Woman in the Window
        and Scarlet Street as exemplifying the characteristics of
        film noir that he describes in his chapter on "Modifying
        Realism and Expressiveness."

421    *Clancy, L.  "Fritz Lang:  The Ambiguity of Innocence."
        Lumière (24 June), pp. 23-27.
            An analysis of the films of Fritz Lang.  (I was unable to
        locate the journal).

421a    Elsaesser, Thomas. "Why Hollywood?" <u>Monogram</u> (London), No. 3,
       pp. 4-10.

          In this article, Elsaesser attempts to place Hollywood
directors in terms of their adherence to a classic tradition. Lang is discussed as one of a group who fall outside
the mainstream; while these directors' films are comprehensible within the framework of traditional American cinema,
their work is exceptional because of the directors' personalities and their vision of the cinema. In Elsaesser's
words, "One might say that the great directors within the
tradition have created and formulated the standards for
their fields and genres . . . ," while the others share "a
far more explicitly intellectual, analytic approach to the
medium, in which the tradition is reflected only obliquely
or reformulated altogether."

          Elsaesser discusses Lang's careful use of <u>mise-en-scene</u>,
and shows how Lang is a director whose works constitute a
philosophy of life. His themes progress as his career goes
forward. Elsaesser goes on to talk of the way Lang's films
are structured through focus on a single person--a focus
that ensures the predominantly unilinear yet essentially
"closed" development of the typical American movie. However,
Lang's best films--<u>Fury</u>, <u>You Only Live Once</u> and <u>The Big Heat</u>
--use this stock dramatic device critically. According to
Elsaesser, Lang is thus able "to dismantle the ideology of
personal initiative and private morality in a mass-society,
while still giving his heroes the tragic dignity of a unique
existence."

422    Garnham, Nicolas. "Reply to Thierry Kuntzel's 'The Treatment
       of Ideology in the Textual Analysis of Film.'" <u>Screen</u>
       (London), 14, No. 3 (Autumn), pp. 55-58.

          As one of the critics accused by Kuntzel of reducing
film texts to ideological messages (<u>see</u> Entry No. 424a),
Garnham defends himself and denies that Kuntzel is ultimately doing anything different. He claims first, that Kuntzel
merely reworks Garnham's own introduction to <u>M</u> (in his edition of the script) that he tried to refute methodologically;
second, Garnham denies that his own method is symbolic in
the sense of "showing a deep belief in one meaning--the true
meaning--of the text"; third, Garnham claims that Kuntzel
in the end refuses to describe a method of critical analysis
for the treatment of ideology; fourth, Garnham says that
while Kuntzel criticizes the "decoding" method Kracauer
uses, he in fact employs that same method himself; finally,
Garnham denies that one can study a non-arbitrary sign system as a "system which knows only its own order." He says
that "we can never derive meaning from the study of a filmic
fact in isolation."

422a    Greenspun, Roger. "Film Favorites: The Thousand Eyes of Dr.

Mabuse." Film Comment (New York) (March-April), pp. 54-55.
Greenspun deplores the poor reception the film received
in New York. Although it was a premiere, the dubbing was
bad and it was not even listed in Cue Magazine. While unable to compare the film to the earlier Mabuse films,
Greenspun finds The Thousand Eyes superb--"dense, complex,
exuberant, mysterious." It recalls Feuillade's Vampires in
the extraordinary beauty of the images and the respect given
to the potential for evil inherent in the objects and impulses of the world of the film.

The title is a misnomer, since Mabuse actually died in
1932 [in The Last Will of Dr. Mabuse, ed.], but Lang presents a Mabuse carrying on the doctor's tradition for his
own ends. The Hotel Luxor is important since it was built
by the Nazis, who planned to establish a microphone system
to use to spy on diplomats after the war. Lang changes the
mikes to cameras, which are "the thousand eyes."

According to Greenspun, Mabuse has two selves--Cornelius
and Jordan--played by two different actors. [Lotte Eisner
notes that, in fact, the same actor did the two parts, but
Lang gave two names in the titles so as not to give away the
plot, ed.]. The mechanisms Mabuse uses are interesting in
and of themselves, but as with all Mabuse schemes, things
get out of hand. Fritz Lang's precisely controlled camera
discloses a causal world; Mabuse's sin "amounts to a sin
against the nature of things as they are and are seen to
be."

Greenspun focuses the rest of his discussion on the way
the Cornelius/Jordan split works. The function of Cornelius
is to render Jordan vulnerable. The entire world of Mabuse
is a cursed one, partly as a result of the Nazi legacy and
partly because of a universal resignation. Mabuse is willing only to look at all the scenes of disorder; he is unable
to perceive any meaning behind the message.

Greenspun concludes that Lang's statement in the film
has to do with its being possible only to know uncertainty,
but there is neither comfort nor truth in this assurance.
Mabuse, the master of illusion, "becomes the dupe of his
own techniques as soon as he stops producing the show."
The pathos of Mabuse's position is that of "every mad, impotent movie genius who cannot hope to possess the girl
anesthetized on his diabolical operating table, or embrace
the world whose future bubbles ominously in his laboratory
retorts."

423   Günther, Winfried. "Ministerium der Angst." [Review of
      Ministry of Fear] Medium (March). (Available through the
      Deutschen Film und Fersehakademie, West Berlin.)
      Günther notes that Lang made this film in 1943, between
      his two masterpieces, Hangmen Also Die and Woman in the
      Window. Its plot is an old one; a man with a shady past,

through seemingly harmless circumstances, falls into a
dangerous net of intrigue and becomes involved in espionage
and murder.
  Lang himself claims not to like the film too much, but
this may simply result from his not having had control over
the script. According to Günther, Lang had originally been
sufficiently interested in the Graham Greene novel [on which
the film was based, ed.] to want to buy the rights to it,
but Paramount outbid him.
  Günther concludes that despite Lang's disclaimers, he
has made an ordinary genre story into something personal,
which retains the standard of his earlier detective films.

424  Jansen, Peter. "Ein Loch in der Tür." [Review of Ministry of
     Fear]. Die Zeit (Hamburg) (30 March).
       Jansen discusses Lang's own negative attitude to Ministry
     of Fear as reflected in his interview with Bogdanovitch,
     but shows that despite Lang's complaints about having to use
     someone else's script, the film does indeed belong to Lang
     in its theme of a man trapped by an espionage group and in
     its visual style. Picking up Lang's statement that "I saw
     it on T.V. . . . and fell asleep," Jansen notes that al-
     though Lang resented the coming of television, it was often
     the only means for showing his films not seen before or re-
     showing ones rarely seen. It is unfortunate that the tele-
     vision setting resulted in an altered response to the film.

424a Kuntzel, Thierry. "The Treatment of Ideology in the Textual
     Analysis of Film." Screen (London), 14, No. 3 (Autumn),
     pp. 44-54.
       Kuntzel's main aim in this essay is to delegitimize es-
     tablished modes of reading films, using Lang's M as an ex-
     ample. In his first section, "Semiotic Preliminaries,"
     Kuntzel distinguishes between cinematic fact and filmic
     fact, and states that he will use M to illustrate how key
     terms (text, code, system) distinguished by Metz function
     within the question of ideology.
       The second section of the article, "Ideology: Non-
     Specific Codes," begins by showing how M critics have tra-
     ditionally used two methods which Kuntzel calls "Symbolic"
     and "Decoding." He gives examples to show how M is reduced
     to ideological messages of various types through these ap-
     proaches. Kuntzel then argues for reading the film with
     the murderer as Other; he also shows the ambiguity of the
     Police, who are both with and against the Gang.
       Kuntzel concludes by discussing first, the filmic system
     and the role of specific codes in the ideological process,
     and second, textual overdetermination and systematic over-
     interpretation.

425  Manvell, Roger. "Introduction" in his Masterpieces of the

German Cinema [scripts for The Golem, Nosferatu, M, The Threepenny Opera]. New York: Harper & Row, pp. 7-18; script for M, pp. 97-177.

Manvell discusses the political situation in Germany in the 1920s--the unrest, disturbances, inflation, and general instability. However, the cinema between 1920 and 1924 was at its height, involving great artists of various types. Nearly all of the Ufa productions of this period became classics.

Referring to Eisner's The Haunted Screen, Manvell discusses the influence of Max Reinhardt and his theater on the cinematic conventions and techniques that led to expressionism. But expressionism merged with earlier theatrical concepts of the supernatural and the horrific; forces of darkness, magicians, hypnotists, and a whole host of gothic fancies dominate the films. To these were opposed loyalty, love, and self-sacrifice.

Manvell notes, in an aside, the simplicity of Kracauer's thesis about the expressionist film, saying that the rise of Hitler was due to far less "metaphysical" causes.

Manvell sees M as moving in the direction of social and psychological realism while retaining "the expressionist imagery and shadowed pictorialism" of the silent films. The realism behind the melodrama points toward the American films, and Lorre's acting raises the film to a high level. Lang's last German film, Das Testament des Dr. Mabuse [The Last Will of Dr. Mabuse], showed a crazed criminal, representing Hitler, trying to overpower the sane world. Goebbels banned the film and Lang left Germany, like so many others, to make a new career elsewhere.

426    Mitry, Jean.  Histoire du Cinéma:  Art et Industrie, vol. 3, 1923-1930.  Paris:  Edition Universitaires, pp. 202-207 and passim.

Mitry focuses on Metropolis--a film that he is critical of, at least partly because he, like some other critics, sees Thea von Harbou as Lang's evil genius. The problem with the film is the attempt to apply expressionism to a social theme showing how the conflicts of capitalism could be solved. But the characters are mere abstractions projected onto a symbolic future world that is itself only extrapolated from the present one. This, says Mitry, dooms the film to anachronism; Lang has given us a false present projected onto an improbable future. While the film may be seen as a criticism of National Socialism before the fact-- there is the single, supreme authority, directing millions of others--many aspects of National Socialism are not dealt with. Mitry complains that the social problem is mixed with the moral one, and that Lang has a poor grasp of economics.

Mitry discusses the anacronisms in the film, but shows how Lang, as usual, expresses ideas through form. But if

the ideas are poor, the forms are magnificent. Mitry refers
to Paul Ramain's article that shows the musical construction
of Metropolis in order to emphasize the limits of pure formal beauty in a film that has a narrative and characters.
One may construct a film like a symphony, but a film is not
a symphony. People cannot be reduced to mere rhythmic patterns. Metropolis is like a magnificent house built on
sand.

Mitry ends this section with a brief discussion of Lang's
return with Spione to the thriller genre where fantastic
improbabilities have more place. He praises Frau im Mond
as a solid achievement in relation to the rocket, but deplores the mixture of such a serious theme with a thriller
narrative.

427   Petley, Julian. "The Films of Fritz Lang: The Cinema of
      Destiny." Master's thesis, University of Exeter.
          Petley's thesis usefully integrates the work of Cahiers
      du Cinéma critics in the late 1950s and early 1960s, prior
      to semiology. Although his thesis follows the film-by-film
      format, the films are intelligently grouped, and interesting
      statements precede the analyses. The approach is essentially
      auteur, with a lot of emphasis on mise-en-scène and world
      view as reflected through visual style.
          Discussing Lang's Mabuse films and Spione [Spies], Petley
      notes the blurring of good and evil, which results in empha-
      sis on characters' moral ambivalence. He talks of Lang's
      paranoid universe and of the presentation of a labyrinthine,
      unfathomable world, with expressionist techniques communi-
      cating mental states. Petley notes that as Lang's romanti-
      cism waned, his view of women became more pessimist and
      negative, until they come to embody the destructive forces
      of the hero's environment.
          Petley discusses the change in Lang's style after he
      went to America and, following Brunel and Tavernier, notes
      the lessening of expressionist techniques, the increasing
      pessimism, and the reduction of mise-en-scène to the abso-
      lutely essential. An implacable logic now governs every-
      thing, the fatality-ridden world view being expressed through
      the austere style. Small, insignificant objects take on a
      life of their own and serve ultimately to trap the hero.
      In contrast, the feeling of fate in the German films was
      conveyed through huge settings and enormous space, with
      people reduced to a tiny element. It is significant, Petley
      says, that when film is shown in Lang's films, it is danger-
      ous and misleading.
          In an interesting comment on Lang's Westerns, Petley
      notes that their subject matter is a lucid analysis of the
      mythology of Westerns and the process whereby an outlaw came
      to be seen as a hero.
          Taking the concept from the French, Petley discusses

Lang's dialectical thinking (See Entries Nos. 244 and 250);
Lang's films, he notes, often have two parts, and he often
remade his own films as well as those of others. The two
parts or versions often have a dialectical relationship,
the one commenting on, or adding to, the first. This dialectical way of proceeding is seen in the ambivalence and
ambiguities built into his filmic world.

Analysing Lang's use of distanciation [distancing],
Petley notes that Lang's mise-en-scène is even more crucial
in the later films, a fact that Anglo-Saxon critics have to
date overlooked. Remnants of Lang's expressionism may be
seen in the handling of space, in the placing of actors,
and in the geometrical patterns. The characters in Clash
by Night are almost as abstract and dehumanized, Petley says,
as those in Die Nibelungen. The increasing abstraction only
heightens Lang's actual preoccupations. In the late films,
Lang's universe is more hostile and claustrophobic than ever
--the mise-en-scène is bleak and austere, conveying doom
and a sense of entrapment.

Unfortunately, Petley did not get to see many of the
films himself, presumably because they were at the time unavailable in England. There are some errors in plot outlines (e.g., in Woman in the Moon) and some confusing of
critics (e.g., Gilles for Levèbre).

428   Sayre, Nora. Review of Das Testament des Dr. Mabuse. New
      York Times (6 December).
         Sayre begins by referring to the statement Lang made in
      his forward to The Last Will of Dr. Mabuse in 1943. He
      said then that he had designed the film in order to show
      the processes of Hitler's terror. He "hoped to expose the
      masked Nazi theory of the necessity to deliberately destroy
      everything which is precious to people. Then, when every-
      thing collapsed and they were thrown into utter despair,
      they would try to find 'help' in the new order." Sayre
      next comments on Lang's skill in creating a sense of being
      trapped. Lang specializes in people who are desperate to
      escape from intolerable situations or from places where
      they might be killed. Sayre concludes that Lang's Mabuse
      films remind us of what Lang himself escaped from.

429   Sayre, Nora. "Dr. Mabuse." [Review of new long version].
      New York Times (15 October).
         Dr. Mabuse, der Spieler is reviewed on the occasion of
      the film's being shown at the Lincoln Center Film Festival.
      Sayre outlines the plot, marvelling at how Lang, before the
      rise of Hitler, looked back to the military power of the
      emperor and exposes the impact of Nietzsche on German cul-
      ture. She comments on the mixture of expressionism and sur-
      realism and the very real documentary touches. Lang shows
      the vulnerability of the rich as well as of the poor.

430   Schütte, Wolfram. "Mehr als ein Thriller: Fritz Langs
      <u>Ministerium der Angst</u>--deutsche Premiere." <u>Frankfurter
      Rundschau</u> (29 March).
         Schütte begins by linking Lang's <u>Ministry of Fear</u> to
      Hitchcock's spy films, noting that the genre came into its
      heyday in the post-World War II period. The films were anti-
      fascist propaganda.
         Schütte then places Lang as the director of films (e.g.,
      <u>Metropolis</u> and <u>Die Nibelungen</u>) that had unmistakeable links
      with fascism. Yet when he came to America, Lang made four
      antifascist films. Schütte shows how in <u>Ministry of Fear</u>
      Lang creates a dense world that casts doubt on people's
      motives and functions.
         The film recalls not only Hitchcock's early period but
      also later films like <u>Frenzy</u>; like Hitchcock, Lang plays
      with his audience. But Schütte sees Lang's greatness as
      ultimately different from Hitchcock's. Lang's power lies
      in creating a feeling of threat and horror merely through
      the sight of an empty room or the gleam of light in darkness.


                              1974


431   Anon. "Höllischer Kampf." <u>Der Spiegel</u> (30 September).
         According to the reviewer, foreign critics have always
      honored Lang as a great director and a brilliant creator of
      nightmares. German critics, on the other hand, have con-
      sidered him overpraised and, at best, thought him interest-
      ing in terms of film history.
         When Lang emigrated in 1933 and filmed commercial Westerns,
      detective stories, and propaganda movies for Hollywood, all
      critics agreed that "a myth had been buried." (Cf. F.
      Everschor)
         Yet in the meantime, the reviewer says, the intellectuals
      have reconciled themselves with Hollywood, and Lang's long-
      unrecognized American work now receives more judicious cri-
      ticism.
         According to the writer, the highlights of the Lang-
      cycle being shown on television are the Western <u>Engel der
      Gejagten</u> [Rancho Notorious], the criminal stories <u>Die Frau
      im Fenster</u> [Woman in the Window] and <u>Heisses Eisen</u> [The Big
      Heat], and the anti-Nazi films <u>Menschenjagd</u> [Manhunt] and
      <u>Auch Henker Sterben</u> [Hangmen Also Die].
         These are realistic stories, true to their milieu, of
      outlaws and justice-fanatics, of individual battles against
      the power of fate, of hate, murder, and revenge. Lang con-
      tinually varied the <u>leitmotifs</u> of his silent films and did
      so also while in exile. Only the ingenious lighting effects
      in his Hollywood films are reminiscent of his symbol-laden
      expressionism. A producer told him early on: "The Americans
      don't like symbols."

The reviewer notes that Lang quickly understood what the
Yankees wanted. Nevertheless, he remained obstinate and
contrary. He fought with the bosses and the censors, who
did not let any of his films go uncut. Lang fought with
authors and stars who feared the "Goddamn foreigner" as the
studio-despot and precision-fetishist.

His quarrel with Brecht was of more consequence. In the
script for Hangmen Also Die, Brecht "had of course emphasized the scenes of the people." But Lang was not interested
in the collective. He raged, "I want to make a Hollywood
picture and to hell with scenes of the people."

As much as Brecht complained about the "dictator," he was
also impressed by his opponent's directorial talent. He
said: "When Lang directs a brawl, the result is almost artistic, the work has dignity."

The writer concludes by noting Lang's vain hope for better
working conditions in Germany. He is now retired in Beverly
Hills. He looks back skeptically at his cinematic work:
"In none of my films have I achieved what I had envisioned."

432 Appel, Alfred, Jr. "Film Noir: The Director. Fritz Lang's
American Nightmare." Film Comment, 10, No. 6 (November-
December), 12-17.

Appel begins by noting that many of Lang's films are
still neglected; while he thinks many should remain so,
Woman in the Window deserves discussion. Appel states that
it belongs with other films noir as a reflection of the
"nightmare" many people were experiencing in the postwar
period.

Through a close reading of the film's style and structure,
Appel attempts to prove that "the telling, rather than the
outline of the tale, is everything."

Appel spends a good deal of time on the dream-device,
noting the similarity with the framing device in Caligari
(suggested by Lang originally). He shows how carefully the
dream is prepared for in the brief classroom scene and in
the scene with Wanley and his friends in the club, both of
which show the trap of Wanley's middle-class life. The
dream mechanism is equally well managed at the end of the
film.

Having shown the dreamlike quality of Wanley's labyrin-
thine nightmare world, Appel discusses devices like the
straw hat, intended to heighten anxiety, and Lang's clever-
ness in making us share Wanley's point of view. The pur-
ported "faults" in the film, such as low-budget sets and
unexplained characters, in fact point to the illogic of
dream. Appel shows how the use of mirrors and glassy surfaces deepens the idea of the nightmare trap.

The popular Freudian underpinnings of the film reveal
Wanley's dream as a wish fulfillment, but, sadly, the film
shows that all is too late for Wanley and his friends.

Appel ends with comments on Lang's style as a <u>film noir</u> director; he praises Lang's economy and precision and his subtle evocation of violence without directly showing it. Lang's gentle parody of American middle-aged men reflects a European perspective: as a "survivor of the nightmare of history," Lang shows Americans as "wondrously innocent ex-scouts."

433  Burch, Noel, and Dana, Jorge. "Propositions." <u>Afterimage</u> (United Kingdom) (Spring), pp. 41-66. Reprinted in <u>Kino</u>, No. 20 (15 November) and No. 21 (15 December).

Burch and Dana's article contains a brief discussion of <u>M</u> and a longer one on <u>Secret Beyond the Door</u> in the context of developing a theoretical position based on the work of Umberto Eco and Christian Metz. They begin by noting the confusion of perspectives in film criticism in contrast to other arts; in film, critics use the same tools and the same methods for films differing widely in quality and type. Cinema is too young to have roots in exemplary "textual practices," but Burch and Dana think elementary classifications are essential and set out to describe one.

They discuss the problem of the aesthetic message, using work done by Shklovsky, Jakobson, and Eco. The best films (i.e., the "masterpieces" singled out by critics and historians) reflect the deconstruction and subversion of dominant codes, through a redistribution of signifiers.

The authors proceed to show the development of film-forms through a brief study of the early film period. Between 1895 and 1919 the main film codes of representation and narrativity were constituted, in effect reproducing the codes of linearity and illusionism that had governed literature for two centuries.

<u>M</u> is introduced not so much as an example of deconstructing narrative codes, as of their reorganization into a "diversified superstructure." While Lang adhered to all the principles of cinematic illusionism and had even developed these with his <u>Dr. Mabuse</u>, his work nevertheless provides a comment on narrative codes comparable to that of Flaubert or Proust in literature. <u>M</u> has "that self-reflexive quality which Umberto Eco defines as destined to 'draw the attention of the addressee (of the artistic message) primarily to its specific form.'"

The authors next divide films into four categories:
(1)  "Films totally accounted for and informed at all levels by the dominant codes."
(2)  "Films totally accounted for by the codes, but in which this fact is masked by a stylistic (which the dominant terminology describes as 'form')."
(3)  "Films which intermittently escape the ideological determination of the codes."
(4)  "Films which are informed by a constant designation/

deconstruction of the codes which, however ideo-
logically determined at the strictly diegetic level,
implicity question this determination by the way
they situate the codes and play upon them."

I will deal only with group (1), as Secret Beyond the
Door is included there.

The authors chose a Lang film mainly in order to attack
the latest "universalist theories of cinema--whose ultimate
aim is to validate linear discourse in film." They complain
that films of great authors like Lang are held up as models
of filmic "writing," and that a difference is set up between
their formal contribution and "the anonymous machinery of
'ordinary' cinema." The authors believe that films need to
be placed in their historical context; their function as a
vehicle for representation of the dominant class needs to
be revealed. Secret Beyond the Door is a perfect illustration of linearity.

The authors describe briefly the historical background
of the development of these codes of linearity, showing how
once film became a commercial industry, the businessmen en-
sured that the representational systems associated with their
own class, ones that had dominated the nineteenth-century
theater and novel, would be continued in film. The codes
of linearity include: (1) the reproduction of the spectator/
stage relationship from the theater; (2) the fourteenth-
century concept of deep space; and (3) the transparent narrative time associated with the nineteenth-century bourgeois
novel.

Lang's film is a good example of the codes the authors
have listed, particularly in relation to the basic element
of linearity, namely, the cause-effect relationship. According to Burch and Dana, the "whole film is organized to facilitate the development of a diegesis whose economy consists
in loading the slightest detail with signification, of flat-
tening every signifier under the tyrannical weight of the
signified." They proceed to give examples of this from the
film, referring first to the scene in the Mexican inn where
Mark suddenly leaves Celia, where the "saturation" of devices makes us share the character's anxiety; and second to
an apparent exception to the system, where Celia first enters
the house, a movement that turns out to be serving the same
ends of "naturalising" the signified. Finally, Burch and
Dana show how the two honeymoon sequences complement one
another in the end, completing the camouflage process in
emphasizing "the rebirth of all things"--a basically linear
concept.

434    Flinn, Tom. "The Big Heat and The Big Combo: Rogue Cops and
       Mink-Coated Girls." The Velvet Light Trap (Madison, Wisc.),
       No. 11, pp. 23-38.
          Flinn discusses the two films in the context of Hollywood

films that began in the 1950s (in the wake of the Kefauver hearings) to deal with organized crime. A new figure, on the right side of the law, now emerges, the "rogue cop," who opposes the political and departmental bureaucracy. Dave Bannion, according to Flinn, is the model for this type; he gives examples of Bannion's impatience with due process and legal procedure, especially after his wife's death. Flinn shows that Lang makes us identify with Bannion through stressing his ordinariness and his domestic life. Lang idealizes middle-class marriage in order to intensify Bannion's loss and make his thirst for revenge (analogous to Kriemhild's) more acceptable.

Flinn finds The Big Heat more than a personal revenge story, also being an "examination of the politics and procedures of a gangland controlled police department." Flinn gives examples of this from the film and then briefly contrasts Lagana and Vince Stone as representing the old style and more modern types of gangster.

Turning next to Gloria Graham, Flinn shows how the character she plays (Debby Marsh) humanizes Bannion; her seemingly spontaneous acting is effective. Flinn finds that the visual style of the film has little in common with postwar film noir, since there are few shadowy scenes. The Big Heat proves that film noir does not have to be dark in order to depict a corrosive mood, the links being in the content and the characters.

After discussing The Big Combo, Flinn concludes that both films say a lot about social conditions in post-World War II America. The Big Heat shows the corruption of the police force and the emotional dynamics of revenge in the modern world. He regrets that neither film had anything to say about combating crime organizations and, in fact, distort reality in showing that a determined individual can defeat corruption. There is the further problem that a rogue cop's violence is associated with that of the gangsters--his violence is justified because it mimics theirs.

435   Milne, Tom.  Review of Dr. Mabuse, der Spieler.  Monthly Film
      Bulletin, 41, No. 484 (May), 112-113.
      Milne says that there is nothing in Dr. Mabuse, der
      Spieler to equal the 1933 Das Testament des Dr. Mabuse [The
      Last Will of Dr. Mabuse]. Lang cannot duplicate the shattering opening of that film or the chilling resonance of the
      madmen. The earlier films are further away from nazism and
      are closer to the world of Feuillade. Yet the films are engaging and full of surprises.

436   Phillips, Gene D.  Discussion of Fritz Lang's Ministry of Fear
      in Graham Greene: The Films of His Fiction.  New York:
      Teachers College Press, Columbia University.  Pp. 27-32.
      Phillips notes that the Graham Greene novel on which the

film was based works on a deeper level than melodrama. The
"Ministry of Nazis" is also "a ministry as large as life itself to which all who loved belonged; if one loved, one
feared." Lang's film remains largely on the level of melodrama, and it omits the whole third part of the novel where
Rowe goes to an asylum to work things out. This was not
Lang's fault, but the studio's. The script obviously appealed to him, and he was able to convert it into a typical
Langian one, where the hero finds himself amidst hidden
forces, unable to find out who is following him.

437    Rayns, Tony. "Destiny." Monthly Film Bulletin (BFI, London),
       No. 481 (February), pp. 36-37.
            Rayns praises the film's range and Lang's ability to
       combine the diverse parts into a coherent whole. Rayns
       sees the film as exemplifying expressionism and its idea of
       fate and of dark forces destroying bourgeois stability as
       reminiscent of romanticism. The exoticism of the tales
       comes from the pulp adventure cycle that Lang himself had
       been instrumental in developing (cf. Die Spinnen [The
       Spiders]). Rayns sees in Destiny the first tentative work-
       ing toward the later Lang/Harbou Catholic mysticism and
       German fatalism, which was to bloom in Metropolis, and cites
       the church/death scenes as evidence of this.

438    Welsh, James M. and Barrett, Gerald R. "Graham Green's
       Ministry of Fear: The Transformation of an Entertainment."
       Literature/Film Quarterly, 2, No. 4 (Fall), 310-323.
            Welsh and Barrett argue that Lang's film is a disappoint-
       ing adaptation of Greene's book. While the novel is called
       "an entertainment," signalling a light work, the authors
       find a philosophical level to the text. Lang's changes
       serve to increase the purely thriller aspect, "popularizing
       and cheapening the original, depriving it of too much sub-
       stance."
            The authors attempt first, to discover the degree to
       which Lang is to blame for the "transformational failure,"
       and second, to see what satisfactions a viewer might gain
       from the film.
            Concluding that Lang's world view is not that far from
       Greene's, Welsh and Barrett decide to look elsewhere for
       the problems. The fact that Seton L. Miller wrote the
       script while Lang was away and refused to let Lang change
       it radically, might account for a lot.
            The authors go on to discuss the positive aspects of the
       film, praising the creation of the paranoid mood and the de-
       piction of a world of illusory appearances. They then dis-
       cuss Lang's effective use of light/dark imagery to convey
       ambiguousness and his clever use of scene transitions and
       of camera movement to create the sense of a world in flux.
            The authors conclude that Lang does more than show a

world where things are not what they seem. Lang charts
Neale's spiritual progress, showing that there was something
wrong with his way of perceiving. Once this is corrected,
even though the world remains ambiguous, it is not so
frightening. The real value of the film lies in the handling
of formal materials, however.

439   Wetzel, Kraft. "Fritz Lang: Frau im Mond." Kino, No. 15
      (15 July).
         Wetzel argues that, on the one hand, Frau im Mond [Woman
      in the Moon] is a trivial melodrama with reactionary over-
      tones, for which he blames von Harbou. Lang's realistic
      adaptation of Harbou's novel is so turgid that the film re-
      mains sentimental. Yet, on the other hand, Lang's careful,
      persevering approach, together with his strong feeling for
      detail, renders the first half of the film (before the ar-
      rival on the moon) beautiful.

440   William, Paul. Review of Das Testament des Dr. Mabuse. The
      Village Voice (New York) (12 September).
         In a sensitive and intelligent review, William begins by
      discussing the inaccuracies of much writing on film. He
      comments on Lang's moral vision in The Last Will of Dr.
      Mabuse, noting that although Lang does keep good and evil
      separate, they seem after all not that dissimilar. Lang is
      perhaps anticipating his later films where good and evil are
      found in the same person. William sees underlying the whole
      film "a despairing vision that finds a wellspring of good
      and evil in the depths of the human psyche."

441   Williams, Alan. "Structures of Narrativity in Fritz Lang's
      Metropolis," Film Quarterly (Berkeley, Ca.) 27, No. 4
      (Summer), 17-24.
         Williams uses the concepts developed by A. G. Greimas in
      his Elements d'une grammaire narrative for analysis of
      Metropolis. Greimas outlines three distinct levels in a
      text: the structural (mythic), the anthropomorphic, and
      "the level of inscription in which narrative is presented"
      (here, according to Williams, "the filmic text as read").
         Beginning with the anthropomorphic level, Williams notes
      that Metropolis, like all narratives, begins with a lack,
      here the alienated condition of the workers, who are the
      collective hero of the film. The different spaces that
      "will make possible various transfers or disjunctions" are
      also introduced in the first section, where the workers
      descend from the machines to their houses, presenting the
      main machine/human opposition central to the film's themes.
         In the second segment, Maria fails to take the children
      from the world of the workers to the pleasure garden, but
      this will be achieved by the end of the film. Freder is
      now seen as an individual hero through his discovery of his

own lack of knowledge about the workers, while his father
is a kind of antihero--he lacks knowledge about the workers'
plot. Both father and son try to gain the knowledge that
each lacks, but their goals are opposed: while Freder seeks
the liberation of the workers, Joh Fredersen seeks to control or eliminate them. Maria becomes an object of desire
for each in attaining his goals. Fredersen tries to deceive
Freder and the workers by making a robot in Maria's likeness, which incites the workers to violence, including the
potential destruction of their children. But Freder's power
is restored once he realizes that the robot is not Maria.
The heroes--Maria and Freder--then undo the deception of
the workers and the robot is destroyed. Freder saves Maria
from Rotwang and saves the children at the same time. In
doing this, he transforms his father from traitor to hero.
By the end of the film, "the lacks of the subjects are removed, the traitors destroyed, and the imbalance which set
the narrative in motion is eliminated."

Williams notes that some problems with the film arise
from the fact that portions of the original movie are missing. However, the basic problem is the division of the
functions of hero and traitor among six different characters.
Making things even more complicated is the treatment of
Maria as an object and the presence of the Maria-robot.
Williams goes into some detail about the effect of this
technique on the overall narrative structure, using narrative concepts first from Propp and then from Greimas.

Williams concludes with a discussion of the film's meaning. The apparent restoration of the children from the
alienated, deprived world of the workers to the plentitude
of the pleasure garden contains a paradox, for nothing has
really changed through the accord between the master of
Metropolis (the head) and the workers (hands). In Williams's
words: "What appears to be socially radical in the film's
overt content is negated by the deeper structure set up by
its circulation of values." The most important oppositions
in the film are, on the one hand, the mechanical/human, and
on the other, the Christian-mystical/alchemical. The
mechanical/human opposition is clear at the start with the
shots of the machines contrasted with those of the pleasure
garden. Two of the traitors are mechanical (the robot;
Rotwang has a mechanical hand), while Joh, although human,
functions as a machine. He becomes fully human at the end,
when transformed into a hero.

The workers' modes of transportation also reflect this
opposition: when they act as heroes, they go on foot; when
as traitors, serving someone else's interests, they use
machines (the elevators). This almost-Marxist discourse,
however, is "belied by the contexts into which the production of this meaning is inserted."

The Christian-mystical/alchemical opposition is contained

in the Rotwang/Maria contrast. Rotwang is a medieval sorcerer, with an overtly Semitic appearance, in contrast to the typically Aryan Maria and Freder. Freder is a Christ figure, crucified on the machine, who "saves" humanity, while Maria is the Virgin Mary.

Finally, there is the psychoanalytical context, with Joh Freder as the father (Jehovah), Freder the son (Christ) and Maria, the mother. Freder needs access to the mother to negate the power of the father. The film "portrays an individual and collective, Oedipal and primal, revolt against the Father, for Maria is also Mother to the masses." Freudian also is the analysis in terms of the life and death instinct; the machines and the traitors stand for death, while the heroes represent life and preserve the culture.

## 1975

442    Buchka, Peter. "Aber ich bin Lang." Süddeutsche Zeitung
       (Munich) (5 December).
          According to Buchka, the lack of attention paid to Lang
       seemed justified after the production of his India films.
       Since then, fortunately, the situation has changed drasti-
       cally, for the simple reason that Lang's earlier films are
       being shown again.
          Buchka says that his films are, in a curious, mysterious
       way, deeply German, perhaps especially where, on the surface,
       Hollywood is reproduced at its flashiest. Romanticism, ex-
       pressionism, and New Objectivity [Neue Sachlichkeit] merge
       in a fascinating and disturbing alliance, so that the most
       contradictory interpretations are possible. He filmed the
       stories of good and evil superheroes, set in the dim past
       as well as in the modern asphalt jungle.
          The contradictions seemed to grow stronger in Hollywood.
       He who had refused to make films in Germany that would
       "please Lehmann's Anna," (i.e., that were geared simply to
       a mass audience) all of a sudden made films about John Doe,
       the average American. But is this really a contradiction?
       Lang had already said in 1924 that "the essence of film is
       convincing only when it is congruent with the essence of
       the times from which it was born." The results seem to
       support him; even today his films are marked with a dense,
       contemporary atmosphere.
          Buchka concludes that the contradictions of this director
       are those of his time. One should view Lang's films with
       this in mind.

443    DeNitto, Dennis and Herman, William. "M, directed by Fritz
       Lang." In their Film and the Critical Eye. New York:
       Macmillan. Pp. 104-136.
          This detailed study of M, primarily intended for students,

is nevertheless generally valuable because of the almost
shot-by-shot description of the film.  The authors begin by
placing the film in the context of the development of sound,
exploring Lang's use of devices of synchronization and asyn-
chronization; they next give a general overview of the story
and the characters, followed by a discussion of the main
themes.  DeNitto and Herman deny that Lang's own statement
about the film--that it was meant "to warn mothers about
neglecting their children" (see also Marguerite Tazelar,
"Fritz Lang Likes Hollywood, America and Social Themes,"
New York Herald Tribune, 7 February 1937)--covers its essential meaning.  They assert that its social message is that
one shouldn't judge the mentally-ill criminal by the same
standards as the "rational" criminal.  The film also "involves the relationship of the individual to the community,"
Lang asserting the need for "the law to control dangerous
individuals."  This theme is, however, mitigated by the
sympathetic treatment of the murderer.

Under "Style and Approach," the authors discuss Lang's
use of camera angles, editing techniques, and visual symbols,
such as the circle, the mirror, and the knife.  Finally,
DeNitto and Herman place the film in the context of expressionism, agreeing that while there are echoes of the movement in the film's style, the approach is, on the whole,
not expressionist.  (See also pp. 10-15 and 207-209 for
more on expressionism.)

444   Dürrenmatt, Dieter.  "Fritz Lang--Der missverstandene Regisseur"
      (12 December).  Article from the Internationales Archiv für
      Filmgeschichte, Switzerland [to be found in the Deutsches
      Institut für Filmkunde, Wiesbaden].

Dürrenmatt begins by raising the question of whether or
not Lang created fascist films.  Francis Courtade called
the world-famous film Metropolis "une oeuvre fasciste pré-
nazie" in his study of Lang.  Many others have taken up this
opinion.  Dürrenmatt considers this a bad misunderstanding!
Lang has a robot appear in Metropolis, which stirs up the
already dissatisfied workers with simplistic statements
against the industrialists.  The film demonstrates, therefore, how much the masses respond to brutality and simplifi-
cations--conclusions to which Hitler also comes in Mein
Kampf.

Yet Lang then demonstrates--and here he powerfully separates himself from fascist ideologues--what senseless acts
the masses allow themselves to be driven to by the Führer
figure.  This is absolutely not "fascistically" intended,
since salvation for the fascists comes from the infallible
Führer, who only wants to help and not--like the robot in
Metropolis--harm the masses.  Also contrary to fascist ideology, the workers destroy their Führer after becoming aware
of their betrayal by the robot.

According to Dürrenmatt Metropolis is an extremely intelligent film about manipulation of the masses. It anticipates in a visionary manner the catastrophic developments in Germany after 1933. The thesis that Lang's Nibelungen films are tinged with National Socialism simply because of their theme is as absurd as the assertion that Wagner was a Nazi because he composed the Ring of the Nibelungen. Lang perceived in 1919 the crushing and humiliating demands that the victorious powers imposed on Germany. Germany was supposed to regain its self-understanding by pointing to its historic roots.

Dürrenmatt next questions whether or not Lang's American films are decadent. The Swiss Radio-und-Fernsehzeitung wrote in 1970 that Lang grew increasingly "commercial" after making his masterpiece M. One speaks of the "decadence" of the "American" Lang. The fact is that Lang made five films of high artistic value in Hollywood: Fury, You Only Live Once, Hangmen Also Die, The Woman in the Window, and Scarlet Street. The seventeen other films are solid, well-crafted pieces. That Lang made more works with a spark of imagination in the Weimar Republic than in Hollywood is due to the fact that he was working under different conditions; for example, his wife, von Harbou, provided him with outstanding scripts for ten years, whereas he often had to be content with only mediocre scripts in the United States.

Dürrenmatt concludes that Lang viewed himself more as a craftsman than as an artist and finds himself in good company--John Ford, for example, also regarded himself as a craftsman. Of the over 125 films Ford made, a dozen are artistic creations; the others are good pieces of craftsmanship. Yet no one speaks of a "decadent" John Ford.

445  Gersch, Wolfgang, Bitomsky, Harmut, and others. "Hangmen Also
       Die. Fritz Lang--Bertolt Brecht." Filmkritik (Munich), 19,
       No. 7 (July), 290-323.
       This issue of Filmkritik is devoted almost entirely to
an analysis of the Lang-Brecht collaboration on Hangmen Also
Die. It contains the following articles:
(1) Bitomsky, Harmut. "Die Erklärung des Krieges" [Declara-
       of War]
       This is less an article than a collection of documents
relevant to the Lang-Brecht project: an announcement of the
collaboration in Brecht's Journal (the film was then called
Never Surrender); an outline of the film's plot; quotations
about the film from Theodor Adorno and Hans Eisler's book,
Komposition für den Film [Music Composition for Film] (one
excerpt deals with Eisler's score for the film and the fact
that in the final scene the music represents illegality);
quotations from Bogdanovich's interviews with Lang. Bitomsky
criticizes the film because it does not explain to the bourgeoisie the reasons for America's entry into the war.

(2) There is an account by Lang himself of the whole Hangmen project. He recalls how he and Lilli Latte (a friend of Helene Weigel, Brecht's wife) helped Brecht come to America, how he got the idea for the project, and how the misunderstandings with Brecht came about.
(3) In parallel columns with Lang's account are entries from Brecht's Journal, giving his view of the collaboration. (14 November 1941-26 June 1943). Much of this section is summarized by Gersch in his article that follows (and in his book, See Entry No. 445a).
(4) Harun Farocki's "Geschichte" follows, presenting the actual history of Heydrich's assassination.
(5) Wolfgang Gersch's article on Hangmen Also Die summarizes and surveys the misunderstandings between Lang and Brecht, accounting for them in terms of each man's personality, experiences, and expectations. For a more detailed version, See Entry No. 445a.
(6) Bitomsky concludes with selections from "Brecht und der Film [Brecht and The Film], where the differences (in Brecht 73 [East Berlin, 1973], pp. 259-263) between Lang's film and Brecht's "ideal" script are discussed.

Note:  For more information on the Lang-Brecht collaboration:
Special issue of Screen devoted to Brecht (Vol. 16, No. 4, 1976) (See Entry No. 456);
Screen, Vol. 15, No. 2 (Summer 1974) analysis of the episode in Lotte Eisner's Fritz Lang (See Entry No. 478), pp. 221-238;
Winge, Hans. "Brecht and Cinema." Sight and Sound, 26, No. 3 (1956-57), pp. 144-147;
Losey, Joseph. "Über Brecht." Cahiers du Cinéma, No. 114 (December, 1960), pp. 21-32.

445a   Gersch, Wolfgang. "Der Fall 'Hangmen Also Die,'" in his Film bei Brecht. East Berlin: Henschel, pp. 200-217; (West German Edition, Munich: Hanser, 1976).
Gersch says that the case of Hangmen Also Die is particularly interesting for what it shows us about Brecht's situation in America and for the light it casts on Hollywood itself. Brecht's political and aesthetic orientation are evident from his experience with Hangmen, itself an example of an antifascist film that could not have been produced without his intervention.
The murder of Heydrich interested Hollywood because it included violence, persecution, and flight. Brecht was interested in it from a communist point of view, as an example of the oppression of a people.
Brecht's links with Lang came not from common ideology or politics, but from being part of the emigrant colony in Hollywood; people here were linked by their common hatred

of Hitler, but adhered to different political positions.

Gersch traces the gradual development of the plot of Hangmen Also Die as Brecht and Lang first worked on it in June and July of 1942. He notes the differences that soon arose over the plot, Lang wanting to include narrative devices (what Brecht called "surprises") from the thriller genre, while Brecht scorned these as a dilution of the main theme. Brecht wanted meaning to be focused on the oppression of the people and a severe conflict emerged.

At this point, Wexley was brought in, and Gersch presents Wexley's interpretation of events. Wexley saw Brecht as in need of learning Hollywood's methods; Lang, he says, although not conservative was not nearly so far to the left as Brecht, and he was very cautious. Brecht's ideas were often just not feasible. For Wexley, Brecht's way of working was too static and abstract, since Wexley was trying to make a dramatic story that did not fit Brecht's way of working. Brecht deplored the use of a series of situations geared to create excitement; this suggested that the actors could not act and that the audience could not think. Brecht tried to influence the script at this point and got Wexley to collaborate on some new scenes, "The Ideal Script," largely dealing with the mass of the people.

But these scenes were rejected by Lang in the final version, and the film ended up being closer to a spy film than a political analysis of oppression. What Brecht had wanted, Gersch concludes, was just not possible in Hollywood.

Gersch ends by discussing the script of Hangmen, trying to figure out exactly what Brecht's contribution was. He concludes that Lang did not want to follow Brecht's intentions. Thus the film should not be placed in the context of Brecht's own work but instead seen as part of Lang's filmography and in the context of the standard Hollywood antifascist film. From this point of view, Hangmen stands out as one of the few really antifascist films that came out of Hollywood.

446  Harmssen, Henning. "Des Teufels Traumfabrik: Aus den Sitzungsprotokollen der Ufa 1932 bis 1941 (1)." Saarbrücken Zeitung (8 May).

This article is part of a series documenting works produced by Ufa. Harmssen begins by quoting a passage from Ufa documents barring Lang from being given work and suggesting he be treated coolly.

Harmssen then analyses Metropolis in terms of its cost and box office return. In this light, it was a fiasco. Because of it, the industry was in such financial straits that it had to borrow heavily to make the change over to sound. Lang's last German films were made through Nero, not Ufa.

447  Knapp, Gottfried. "Man stellt Denkmäler nicht auf den flachen
     Asphalt." Süddeutsche Zeitung (Munich) (19-20 January).
     Knapp notes that the fascination with architectual illu-
sions in cinema is as old as celluloid illusion itself.
Film architecture was never more ambitious, more thematically
contemporary than in the German expressionist silent films,
and seldom did film reproduce more closely the stylistic
sense of its own time than in the movies Die Nibelungen
and Metropolis, which Lang created in close conjunction with
the architects Otto Hunte, Erich Kettelhut, and Karl
Vollbrecht.
     Knapp says that in the city and factory scenes, Metropolis
portrays futuristic architecture in its purest, most fantastic form.  One could say today that the only larger,
completed project of futuristic architecture was that model
of the city in the Berlin Ufa Studio.  It has noticeable
parallels to Antonio Sant'Elia's futuristic Città Nuova
(1914).
     Knapp notes that Lang broadened the language of film
greatly in movies like Metropolis.  When Goebbels banned
Das Testament des Dr. Mabuse [The Last Will of Dr. Mabuse]
in 1933, while at the same time offering Lang a central
position in the Nazi film industry, Lang fled that same
night to Paris.  He did not want to aid the new regime's
irrational despotism, which he had prophetically portrayed
out of the reigning mood of fear and decline in 1922 (Dr.
Mabuse, der Spieler [Dr. Mabuse, the Gambler]).
     Kriemhild's prescient nightmare in Siegfrieds Tod [Death
of Siegfried] (1924) conjures up the unformed powers of the
1920s in the free dynamic of graphic abstraction.  This
scene not only characterizes the times, but is also a good
example of Lang's visual relation to his environment, of
his ability to express the "essence of the times" through
the "substance of film."
     Lang's interest in architectural and graphic stylization
is obvious in his films--basic cinematic instincts that were
seldom valued in Germany.  Lang exhibited an unliterary
pleasure in exotica, fairy tales, and sensationalism, which
were increasingly counterpointed through highly artistic
imagery.  Thus a unique split in Lang's films arose:  on
the one hand, high artistic demands, modern motifs, and
bold models for a new cinematic art-form; on the other hand,
anachronistic, almost medieval thrillers, mysticism, and
naive plots.
     According to Knapp, in Metropolis, the most contradictory
film of this time, the monumental science fiction world is
confronted with the antiquated aura of the inventor-figure
of the German, demonic alchemist from the theater.  The
plot stumbles from its great beginning down through the centuries.  One symbolic setting follows another, one proto-
typical figure is attached to another.  Only a suspect

compromise brings the film to a happy ending.

Knapp regrets that the great design with which the film began seems to have been forgotten. The film slides back from the "brave new world" into the good old days, from a monumental hell of organized exploitation through a hand-shake into a melodramatic, Christian feudalistic Middle Ages. Lang himself made fun of this false conclusion while in America. It is indicative of his artistic demands at that time that this conclusion did not disturb him while the work was in progress.

One already finds in <u>Die Spinnen</u> [The Spiders] (1919) this typical mixture of mystical fairy tale and practical engineering. Trapdoors and all sorts of occult hocus-pocus appear next to telephones and airplanes. The art deco film <u>Die Frau im Mond</u> [Woman in the Moon] (1929), produced at the end of the silent film era, achieves a charming cinematic form in its Jules Verne mixture of space exploration, espionage, a love triange, and finally a melodramatic treasure hunt on the moon. Film did not yet have precise genres. Lang did not put much emphasis on dramatic concentration of the plot. He preferred to shape his material in epic proportions.

Knapp notes that <u>Die Nibelungen</u> (1924) gave Lang the opportunity to exercise his unique abilities on material particularly well suited to the epic form. Quietly and steadily the individual "songs" take shape in the middle of a static image. Max Reinhardt's theatre and the images of C. D. Friedrich, Schwind, Böcklin, and art nouveau influenced Lang. The figures move through buildings and landscapes of materialized light to the places of fate. Guilt or innocence--the central questions of Lang's American films --and also love, jealousy, revenge, and hatred--which in earlier films were overdone and trivialized--receive their due through the silent ritual of optical oppositions. Carefully developed, myth and fairy-tale motifs retrieve their psychological symbolic value.

Knapp concludes that Lang found the best connection to the public with this stylized staging. He wrote that the film could become a "document of its time" for the "man of 1924" only through the <u>Nibelungen</u>-like "enlargement." Undoubtedly <u>Die Nibelungen</u> is one of the most successful cinematic monuments of these years.

448    Lebens, Brigitte. "Morgen begeht Filmregisseur Fritz Lang in Hollywood seinen 85. Geburtstag: America's Jugend liebt ihn." <u>Abend-Zeitung</u> (4 December).

On the occasion of Lang's eighty-fifth birthday, the author interviewed Lilli Latte, Lang's longtime friend and secretary in Beverly Hills. Latte notes how ill Lang has been. Nearly blind, he can make no more films, but for nearly two years has been honored by students all over

America, who flock to see his films.

This piece is accompanied by one by "Ponkie," who compares Lang with John Ford; what Ford did for the Western, Land did for the expressionist film. Ponkie corrects the notion that because Lang's early German films reflect the fatalism of their period and the flight into the irrational, they are therefore sympathetic to nazism. He or she notes that Lang merely reflected his period and emigrated as soon as the Nazis came into power [sic].

On Lang's 85th Birthday, see also:
    sth. "Wachsender Ruhm: Fritz Langs 85 Jahre."
    Rheinische Post (Düsseldorf) (5 December).

449    Legrand, Gérard. "Le Regard Froid." [Review of You Only Live Once]. Positif, No. 165 (January), pp. 68-70.
    Legrand begins by pointing out a certain duality of intention between Helen's [should be Jo, ed.] story (that could have been a domestic comedy) and Eddie's story (the thriller genre). The general tone is despairing, and there is nothing even in the lovers' relationship to introduce joy.

    The main dramatic action hinges on Lang's principle of contradiction, namely that the consequence of an act will be the opposite of that intended. The film is a deepening of ideas in Fury, Legrand says, and he goes on to show the way objects are given symbolic value. Helen [Jo], for example, betrays Eddie through buying him cigarettes; when Helen gives up her baby, we see shots of a long, empty road.

    It is easy to see that Lang was very taken with Sylvia Sidney's charm in making the film. While the character she plays [Jo] is innocent, her sister, representing morality, is harsh. Eddie obviously appealed to Lang because he reflects Lang's interest in the man who is up against all odds.

    Legrand ends with noting how You Only Live Once looks toward certain later films like Secret Beyond the Door and Beyond a Reasonable Doubt. While an attractive naiveté was lost, Lang's films gained in rigor. You Only Live Once reveals ultimately the same powerful style that Lang first showed in M.

450    Overby, David. "Fritz Lang's Career Girl." Sight and Sound (London), 44, No. 4 (Autumn), 240-244.
    Overby refers to Lang's many uncompleted projects (some mythic but several quite real), mentioning how delightful it is to work with the scripts for Lang's completed films because they are covered with Lang's own comments. One can get closer to the heart of the creative process in this way. But scripts like the Death of a Career Girl, which were never made into films, can tell even more.

    Lang nearly came out of retirement to make this film,

encouraged by Jeanne Moreau's desire to work with him and
her suitability for the lead. He first thought of the idea
in Mannheim in 1964 and it was finally complete by 1975.
Cancellation of the project was due mainly to the difficulty
of getting all the necessary people involved at the same
time.

The scenario was written in three languages, but Overby
is working with the English one, which has speeches the
others lack. Overby outlines the basic plot. There are
eight sequences tracing the life of a woman from 1943 to
1966, with two framing scenes in 1966. The film opens in
1966 in a luxurious apartment. The woman is about to commit
suicide. She meditates upon her life, and we go back to
1943 and her work with the marquis. Several disillusioning
experiences alienate her and after the war she goes to Rome.
Pregnant but unable to pay for an abortion, she has the
child and then leaves him, placing a special chain around
his neck. She begins to use men to get money and has an
affair with Richard Feling (anagram for Friedrich (Fritz)
Lang), an art dealer, who falls in love with her. Experiencing love, the woman becomes afraid and leaves him for an
even wealthier man. She becomes more cynical and hard, ambitious now only for power and wealth. At the height of
her power in Paris, she entertains highly successful people.
Having equipped her apartment with concealed recording devices, she monitors private conversations to consolidate
her power. Deciding to produce an heir, she gets pregnant
by Feling, but then has an abortion, because there is a
chance to grab one more company for her cartel. Feling
dies. Guilt-ridden, she goes to Italy to drink and lose
herself. Unwittingly, she sleeps with her son. It is on
her return that she plans to commit suicide, but back in
the present, her servant announces that officers of her
company have arrived, and she opens the meeting.

Overby makes a few comments on this material:

(1) He notes that while this material is very melodramatic,
    Lang often managed to transform such plots through
    "working visually against the melodramatic grain."

(2) He talks about Lang's fascination with women and about
    the fact that women in his films, whether good or bad,
    are always stronger than the men. Femme fatales have
    been a constant type from Die Spinnen [The Spiders] on;
    Kriemhild is an early version of the Career Girl, pur-
    suing a goal to its logical, destructive conclusion
    and rejecting love and maternal feelings. Marion Menil
    in Die tausend Augen [The Thousand Eyes] was a more
    recent version, but she succumbs to her feelings in the
    end.

(3) Overby notes the similarities between the Career Girl
    and Dr. Mabuse himself. She too uses electronic record-
    ing devices. In the animated dream in Die Nibelungen

and the film footage in <u>Fury</u> (representing truth), Lang
shows the progressive perversion of the image in modern
life.  The corruption in <u>Career Girl</u> is even more hor-
rifying than before, since now it is entirely for personal ends, without even the mad ambition for world
power that Mabuse had.

(4) Overby talks of the religious underpinnings of the Girl's
damnation in the film, noting that Lang never gave up
his Catholic beliefs entirely.  He never allowed a suicide in any film, claiming that death was no solution;
how could one say definitely that the Career Girl is
beyond redemption?  There are several religious overtones in the film.

(5) Overby notes that one could tell a lot about how the
film would have looked from the script, for Lang, while
claiming that it was dangerous to read symbols into objects, also paid careful attention to such things as
decor and costume.

(6) Finally, Overby sees the <u>Career Girl</u> project as coming
full circle back to <u>Der müde Tod</u> [Destiny].  There Death
was weary, but love triumphed over it.  Now everything
is reversed; it is love that is weary.  Happy endings
were possible when the protagonists died, as in <u>You
Only Live Once</u>, but this ending, with the protagonist
still alive, is ironically the saddest that Lang ever
made.

451   Tessitore, John A.  "The German Film I:  Expressionism in <u>M</u>."
<u>Bright Lights</u> (United Kingdom), 1, No. 3 (Summer), 27-28.
Tessitore argues that while Lang is basically a realist
director, his style reflects links to expressionism.
Tessitore discusses the expressionist elements in <u>M</u> that
remain despite the introduction of sound, which humanized
the German cinema and led to realist conventions.  He lists
the following expressionist aspects:

(1) the emotional impact of the opening credits where the
real world is seen as distorted;

(2) the use of high- and low-angle shots in many sequences;

(3) the variety of angles used for the murderer and the way
many shots actually veil him;

(4) the use of light/dark contrast, despite the fact that,
in general, expressionist decor is at a minimum;

(5) the use of reflections and mirrors;

(6) the manipulation of crowds for expressionist effect, as
in the underworld café and the beggar's trial;

(7) Lorre's acting, which is seen as a blend of realism
and expressionism.

Tessitore ends with a discussion of Lang's use of sound
in the film, which shows him at his most expressionist.

452   Thomas, Kevin.  "Director Fritz Lang Turns 85."  <u>Los Angeles</u>

Times (5 December).

Thomas notes that Lang is the last of the three great
early German directors, having outlived Murnau and Pabst.
In Hollywood, despite the lack of backing analogous to that
Erich Pommer gave him in Germany, Lang managed to retain
his style and integrity.

Thomas lists the honors Lang has received in recent
years, including a retrospective of forty films at the
Munich Stadt Museum and one of twenty films at the Moscow
Film Institute. Two new books on Lang--one by Enno Patalas
in Germany and another by Lotte Eisner (England and America)
--are due to be published shortly.

Thomas concludes with a quotation from Lang about a film
he would now want to make: given the state of the world,
it would be critical of many things, including the way in
which television has robbed youth of its imagination.

453 Truffaut, François. "Fritz Lang en Amérique." In Les Films
de Ma Vie. Paris: Flammarion. Pp. 89-93. Translated by
Leonard Mayhew. The Films of My Life. New York: Simon &
Schuster, 1978.

After noting the large number of German-sounding names
among Hollywood directors, Truffaut goes on to discuss You
Only Live Once and the idea of fatality that it rests on.
There is the paradox of society's first pushing the character that Henry Fonda plays into crime and then his escape
at the moment that his innocence is declared. Lang contrasts the baseness of the authorities with the beauty of
the outcast couple. Despite the romanticism in the film,
it holds up well today.

Lang always shows people who are outside the law. He is
obsessed with the problems of justice and conscience; his
pessimism grows with each film, his last ones being among
the most bitter in the cinema. The victim-hero gives way
to a revengeful hero, who in turn, is replaced by the man
stained with sin. According to Truffaut all the people in
the later films are depraved. He thinks this development
is perhaps an inevitable result of Lang's experiences under
nazism, of his deportation [sic], the war, and McCarthyism.

Truffaut dwells a moment on While the City Sleeps, admiring Lang's rough attitude toward the characters, who are all
damned. Even the character played by Dana Andrews is willing to use his girlfriend for his own ends and to flirt
with the character played by Ida Lupino. Convinced that
people are born evil, Lang allowed pessimism to overwhelm
him. His vision recalls that of Night and Fog or of Genet
in its attitude that the whole world is guilty and that all
people are victims.

Truffaut says that Lang's style reflects his world view:
everything is planned for a specific effect, as in the scene
in You Only Live Once where the character played by Fonda

asks his wife to get him a gun.

Truffaut concludes by noting that Lang is a great but isolated artist, who is the least understood of contemporary directors.


## 1976

454    Baer, Volker. "Er machte Filmgeschichte." Der Tagesspiegel (West Berlin) (4 August).

In this obituary, Baer notes that in the past few years Lang had become a living legend. Although he had not produced any new films since 1961, his work constantly received new interpretations; he found new admirers along with new critics, and no German director won as much international respect as Lang.

Turning to a survey of his works, Baer comments on the contradictions the films contain, being at once genre films and films about ideas. Many works combine entertainment with social criticism, Lang taking issue with capital punishment, lynch law, corruption, and the sensational press. All his films are suspenseful, although it is hard to see Die Nibelungen or Metropolis other than as products of their time.

Baer concludes that Lang was a brilliant director, endowed with psychological insight. He was interested in the battle of the individual against fate and an artist who, for all his involvement, still saw the world in broad, simple terms.

455    Blumenberg, Hans C. "Kino der Angst." Die Zeit (Hamburg) (13 September).

Blumenberg begins by discussing the critical reception of Lang's films, particularly the lack of recognition awarded those made in America. He goes on to question the myth that Lang, the brilliant filmmaker from Germany, was defeated by Hollywood. Lang did after all tell Bogdanovitch in 1967 that he found the technical aspects of American films indescribably superior to German ones.

Blumenberg turns next to Lang's work as a whole, objecting to the attempt often made to polarize the German Lang of Die Spinnen [The Spiders], Die Nibelungen, and Dr. Mabuse, der Spieler, and the American Lang of the 1940's and 1950's. Blumenberg rather sees a development similar to that between Hitchcock's British and American films. Lang moved on from the ornamental pomp of Der müde Tod [Destiny] and Metropolis to develop his cinema of fear, which he continued to perfect. What had originally been a self-conscious attempt to make "art" became in Hollywood an icy functionalism devoid of superfluous frames or merely ornamental camera movements. Hollywood was in this sense an excellent training ground

for directors, Blumenberg notes, since it forced extreme
concentration on filmmakers.

Blumenberg ends by observing that despite all the retrospectives, Lang still awaits discovery in Germany because
of prejudices against his German films. But the German Lang
represents only half of what he has produced; the more mature half of his work deserves recognition.

456   Brewster, Ben. "Brecht and the Film Industry. (On The
      Threepenny Opera film and Hangmen Also Die)." Screen
      (London), 16, No. 4 (Winter), 16-33.

Brewster begins with a brief outline of the context for
Brecht's involvement in both The Threepenny Opera and Hangmen
Also Die. Brecht's dilemma is usually seen as that of the
poet attempting, in both Germany and America, to function
within the industry and finding his work distorted beyond
recognition. In both cases Brecht sued and lost. In fact,
Brewster says, things were actually more complex; drawing
on Brecht's own account of the making of Hangmen Also Die
as revealed in his Arbeitsjournal [Work Journal], Brewster
reveals the contradictions in Brecht's position. On the
one hand, he views traditional intellectuals as his enemies,
because they "defend the freedom of the creative individual
against the encroachments of the market economy (from which
they derived their incomes)." Yet, as Brewster goes on to
show, in America these were the very people who were his
neighbors and friends. He shared their status and their
hostility to America. In his relations with Lang, he saw
himself as the writer, versus Lang as representative of the
film industry, although Brecht would never have consciously
allowed himself that status.

Because he saw himself in this way, Brecht blamed Lang
for what happened with Hangmen Also Die (to Lang's indigna-
tion) rather than Pressburger or Wexley.

Nevertheless, the Hangmen project was never the collaborative one Brecht desired. According to Brewster, Hangmen was,
for Brecht, ultimately "an unfortunate reactionary by-
product," the positive results being the money he made and
the record in the Archive. Brecht did not understand Lang's
insistence that only certain things were possible in Hollywood
and that a Hollywood film had to have intrigue. Brecht evidently had hoped to make certain scenes with the hostages
that could later have been separated as a quasidocumentary
film to demonstrate the nature of the Nazi regime to Germans
after the war. And Lang had originally agreed to this. In
the final version, however, according to Brewster, "the
Brechtianism of some of the scenes is completely subordinated to a dramaturgy of empathy whenever it is the heroes,
the representative of the people or the people themselves
who appear." Brewster concludes that what is left of
Brecht's part in the film is too little for us to assess

what Brecht's influence really was or how successful his
intentions might have been.

This article is a transcription of the Brecht Event II
(held at the Edinburgh International Film Festival in Summer
1975) and interesting comments by participants follow
Brewster's paper.  In replying to a question about whether
or not Brecht could have made an antifascist film in
Hollywood, Brewster notes that Brecht simply did not understand Hollywood's aesthetic or what could be done within its
terms.  He "overestimated his capacity for imposing a certain amount of Brecht onto Lang," Brewster says, and goes
on to compare him to Sirk, who did manage to build critiques
of American capitalism into his works.  A final interesting
point is made by Colin McCabe about the political issue in
the film that divided Brecht and Lang.  While Lang found
the bourgeois characters central, including the terrorists
(the people being ambiguous), for Brecht the common people
are all-important, especially as critics of their resistance
leaders.  McCabe sees this tension revealed in various sequences.

457   Dadoun, Roger.  "Le Pouvoir et 'sa' folie."  *Positif* (Paris),
      No. 188 (December), pp. 13-20.
      This is a compact, dense, and difficult article about M
that is hard to paraphrase.  The main idea is that Lang
catches in M the place where primitive emotion and history
intersect, giving us an insight thereby into prefascist
Germany on both the emotional and social planes.  The originality and importance of the article lies in Dadoun's
analysis of how the film's structure and themes lay bare
essential aspects of fascism.

Dadoun's first section deals with the way in which
Beckert causes the polarization between the law and the
criminal world, and exposes another polarity, that between
the law and maternity.  The maternal rage at the murder of
children takes its place alongside the hate toward the murderer that the criminal underground generates.  But Dadoun
shows how, ultimately, both the law and the underworld want
to eliminate Beckert and are identical in their modes of
operation.  Moreover, the law also cannot remain pure and
innocent and above the terror generated by the mothers in
the town.  It is here that Dadoun finds the first similarity
with fascism:  namely, that those in power are on the side
of extermination and terror.

Dadoun next turns to the figure of the murderer himself,
showing how he takes the shape of a madness that the rigidly
defined and determined society represses.  Beckert takes
onto himself all the characteristics that the ordered, civi-
lized world cannot permit; and he evokes in those in power
all the terror and destruction that he embodies.

Thirdly, Dadoun shows how Beckert represents the massive

sexual repression leading to death, which was one of the
foundations of the fascist conscience. The fascists hoped
to transform sexual energy into destructive power, murder.
In addition, in his isolation from people and the external world, Beckert represents the individual that modern society has made, ready to form part of the interchangeable
mass of beings who need a dictator. Beckert is treated as
an undesirable, who can easily be exterminated because declared such. Beckert's crimes come out of his attempt to
get out of the trap of himself and to make contact with the
exterior world. All the elements of his character as Dadoun
has outlined them were, he claims, present in preNazi German
society.

458    Daumal, René, and Lang, Fritz. "A Propos de Liliom." Positif
       (Paris), No. 188 (December), pp. 6-7.
           This article consists of reprints originally published
       in 1934. Lang's piece is "Mes Amis, Le Ouvriers," from
       Excelsior (27 April 1934). (See Entry No. 529). René
       Daumal's piece is "Avant la Presentation de Liliom," from
       Aujourd'hui (13 March 1934). (See Entry No. 132).

459    Doneux, Marcel. "Hommage à Fritz Lang: Le Borgne Visionnaire."
       Revue Belge du Cinéma (Brussels), No. 2 (November), pp.
       59-66.
           Doneux notes the varied nature of Lang's work and the
       fact that it touched both expressionist and realist extremes.
       Lang's expressionism only enhanced his realism, although he
       never got rid of a certain German romantic essence.
           Doneux next discusses Lang's genius as a stylist, men-
       tioning his brilliant composition of every shot, each perfect
       in isolation. Lang's main themes are those of fate, destiny,
       death, and power. His universe has a Kafkaesque quality.
       While Lang's works vary in quality, his style is unique, and
       his films all have an incontestable originality.
           Doneux ends his hommage with a brief biofilmography, sur-
       veying Lang's life, career, and background and writing short
       comments on each of the major films. He comments finally on
       the directors Lang has influenced, especially Hitchcock and
       Carné, and Lang's role as father of the New Wave.

460    Goelz, Else. "Der Mann mit dem Einglas." Stuttgarter Zeitung
       (4 August).
           Writing on the occasion of Lang's death, Goelz notes
       that, due to the new importance being accorded film directors
       by the younger generation, his passing does not simply evoke
       the sentimental memories of an older group.
           Goelz proceeds to survey Lang's background and career
       briefly, commenting on the fact that Lang was a Viennese
       shaped by late-nineteenth century values, but that, in keep-
       ing with the times, he was more interested in psychological

problems than in social issues.

Technical and artistic perfection distinguishes Der müde Tod [Destiny], the film that gave Lang his breakthrough. Like Murnau, Lang's social criticism has personal overtones; Dr. Mabuse, in Dr. Mabuse, der Spieler [Dr. Mabuse, the Gambler] simply incarnates evil, and while Metropolis does deal with the conflict between rich and poor, the main theme is how love can overcome class difference.

According to Goelz, Lang, one of the most successful emigres in America, made a number of artistic and entertaining films. His last German films were unsuccessful because looking back to a time long past.

Goelz concludes that while Lang continued to deal with fated, hopeless people in Hollywood, he became more realistic and less concerned with destiny in later years.

461    Grafe, Frieda, Enno Patalas, Hans Helmut Prinzler. Fritz Lang. Reihe Film 7 (Peter W. Jansen and Wolfram Schütte, eds.). Munich: Hanser. Stills (by Peter Syr).

This book is especially important in being the first full-length work on Lang to come out of Germany. It reflects the culmination of the revival of interest in Lang in Germany since the mid-1960s, influenced by the French. There are three main sections to the book:

(1) A long and important essay by Frieda Grafe (82 pages) covers various aspects of Lang. Grafe begins by noting the coincidence of Lang's personal development, artistically, with that of film-form itself; she points out that Lang was essentially a silent film director and that he perfected film as mass art, annhilating the old conflict between high art and popular forms. Far from fearing sensationalism, stereotyping, and genres, Lang instead built his idea of cinema out of these elements. He realized early on that cinema, unlike theater, which worked through physical presence, obtained its effects with images, signs for things.

Grafe stresses the variety of film forms Lang experimented with and surveys briefly the dominant critical approaches to him. While some critics have always scorned the American films, Godard and the New Wave admired the Hollywood films for their brilliant use of mise-en-scène and the way they broke with Hollywood meanings while retaining the required overall format. For this very reason, Lang was never popular in Hollywood and often went without work. In addition, he was said to be cold and inhuman in his dealings with people. Reality and probability are excluded from Lang's filmic world, and only the rules of that universe remain.

Grafe ends this section by noting that Lang's films span fifty years, thus representing a large slice of film history. The Germans have been slow in accepting and exploring his work, but they now have the advantage of distance for assessing its worth.

The second section is titled "Lang and Brecht." Grafe notes the two men's very different personal and political styles, but sees a common abhorence for nature, or pseudo-nature, which they nevertheless employed in their works. Both were experts in alienation, but it was easier for Brecht in that it is easier to eliminate the appearance of reality from the theater than from film. Grafe notes the irony of Brecht's and other Germans' coming to Hollywood expecting great things. Brecht hoped to rebuild cinema in the image of his theater, and when it did not happen, he blamed Lang. Lang understood and accepted the Hollywood system in ways Brecht never could, and he knew how to make it serve his ends. Brecht saw only that Lang was using a form, melodrama, that he despised. Lang's films, in fact, have little to do with realism, taking discontinuity as their basis, and despite the surface realistic details, reality is reduced to a skeleton.

In a section on "Fritz and Thea," Grafe tries to correct the idea that von Harbou is responsible for all that is wrong with certain films, especially Metropolis. The faults come from other sources, for example, the conflict between the science fiction form and treatment of a real social problem. Lang was at first happy to make films from popular fiction and only later went to newspapers and facts for his themes. Grafe sees a change after Frau im Mond [Woman in the Moon], in that Lang now became interested mainly in the power of visual forms and began to treat diverse themes in similar forms. In all the films, Lang plays with the situation of the spectator in the cinema. Coming from painting and architecture, Lang found the sketch of a building more interesting than the building itself. While the Russians were fascinated with the camera, Lang was interested in its laws.

When reduced to formulations, Lang has few themes—good and evil, guilt and innocence, love and death, hate and revenge. But art cannot be so reduced, and his themes are mere structuring entities for his abstract meanings.

In the next section, Grafe deals with Lang's politics and his departure from Germany. She notes that Lang was not a communist and was put on the black list simply by siding with the communists against fascism. Dr. Mabuse is closer to Lang's American outlaws than he is to Hitler, and Lang's films have more to do with ancient tragedy than with social criticism. The German films certainly are melodrama, while the American works are more socially oriented. If anxiety has more place in the German films, fear of the terrible unknown is more evident in the American works. Psychoanalysis and the new film techniques resulted in Lang's no longer placing the individual at the center of his films; the individual is now seen as part of the social community.

A section titled "X Marks the Spot" deals with the

symbolism in Lang's work. Despite Lang's statement that
Americans did not want symbols, Grafe says that symbols
continued to be present, but masked by the accurate mirror-
ing of surface realism. That objects are filmic signs is
hard to see here. But Grafe notes the change in the way
symbols are used in the early German films and in the
American ones. Lang now tries to show the irrational that
underlies the organized, surface world.

Grafe moves from here to a discussion of how the atmosphere of fatality in Lang's films arises from his use of
obsessional objects, such as the arrow-pin in Manhunt or
the cigar-snipper in Woman in the Window. Lang insists on
details in his films, and in this way he is like Balzac,
who uses description to tell us about his characters. De-
spising psychological analysis, Lang uses mise-en-scène to
express what we need to know about his people; he puts his
films together as if constructing circumstantial evidence
about an event. The characters in his films have as much
likeness to real people as does the sketch of a murderer,
compiled from several descriptions, to the real criminal.

Using Liliom (a film that Lang, a harsh critic of his
own work, still admires), to make the point, Grafe notes
that Lang's world consists in the space between the real and
the unreal. He takes fictional characters and gives them
bodies, but changes real people into spirits.

Grafe sees Die Nibelungen as demonstrating how ahistorical
Lang's films really are. They exist outside of time and
yet, paradoxically, Die Nibelungen, in its very emphasis on
decor, shows how conditioned the people are by their environ-
ment--their dwellings, their armour, clothes, and citadels.

Grafe next focuses on the centrality of architecture to
Lang's films (son of an architect and student in the field
that Lang was). She points out the frequent alternation of
people situated either on the top of buildings or underneath
the ground floor, these placings occurring within structures
signifying might and force versus powerlessness and vulnerability. Secret Beyond the Door is especially interesting as
a demonstration of Lang's method of filmmaking, that is, a
demonstration about buildings. In addition, Grafe notes
that Lang's houses are rarely homes; they have imposing
fronts, but are usually official places like law courts,
hotels, or stores, symbolizing authority.

In the section that follows, Grafe notes how the imposing
facades are ironic commentaries on the absence of what they
ideally stand for, such as justice or truth.

Grafe then discusses the social impulses in Lang's work,
concluding that it is present less for itself than as the
starting point for different perspectives, and as part, ultimately, of mise-en-scène.

Grafe goes on to show that all architecture in Lang in
the end must be blown up, since all representations are

actually images of emptiness. The buildings are only hollow forms, mere surfaces that conceal another, dangerous world, where chaos reigns. Hence the emphasis on holes and underground tunnels where criminals hide and that signify the irruption of chaos onto the surface, the ordered world.

Grafe's last section, called "The Thousand Eyes," deals with the emphasis throughout Lang's work on the notion of "seeing." Those who know are "blind," like the beggar in M--a very old concept; the best workers are those who don't see what they are doing. Grafe also shows how central the glance is in Lang's films--glances are often dazzling and misleading, bringing people to grief. Lang plays with the concept of sight in many ways, but the most remarkable blind man is that played by Artaud in Liliom, who represents fate.

Blind in one eye himself, Lang saw more than many with two eyes; yet Grafe's last image of Lang, that of his glistening monocle, suggests that Lang wanted to present surfaces that merely reflected, that ultimately concealed the depth they contained.

(2) The second section of the book consists of short notes on all of Lang's films by Enno Patalas. Although very brief, the comments are illuminating, often picking up elements dealt with by Grafe in her long essay. Patalas tries to single out one dominant aspect of each film that in some sense places and defines it, rather than telling the plot.

(3) The last section of the book by Hans Helmut Prinzler contains a short biography of Lang, a reliable and detailed filmography, and an excellent bibliography, divided into critical works in German, English, and French, followed by a list of reviews and other materials on each film. (See Entry No. 475 for a German review of this book).

462    *Grisolia, Michel. "Un Oeil Irremplacable." Le Nouvel
       Observateur (Paris) (9 August).
            Obituary for Lang.

463    H. H.  "Kühle Reserve Empfohlen: Wie sich der Vorstand der
       Ufa von Fritz Lang distanzierte." Stuttgarter Zeitung
       (6 August).
            H. H. begins with a quotation from a Ufa document saying
       that as of 1932 Lang was out of favor with the organization.
       H. H. then goes on to describe Lang's first films, the cata-
       strophe of Metropolis, and the meeting with Goebbels.

464    Hartman, Rainer. "Der Mann, der den Dr. Mabuse erfand."
       Frankfurter Neue Presse (4 August).
            Hartmann begins by praising Lang's greatness, and his
       contribution to both the technical and artistic development
       of film, which, as a result of his efforts, moved away from
       being a sentimental imitation of the theater.

Despite the sentimental nature of Lang's plots, Hartmann notes that the director created new effects with his new techniques. He showed visually how humans come up against anonymous powers; the demonism of fate is embodied in Lang's use of shadows and of closed rooms that become dungeons from which escape is no longer possible.

According to Hartmann, the expressionist Lang, with his perfect, deliberate and carefully controlled mise-en-scène, can be contrasted with the Russian Eisenstein, whose montage celebrates dynamic movement.

Hartmann next explores the contrast between Lang's mastery of the art of film, and his lack of intellectual and political rigor. The Mabuse films betray blind surrender to the demonic, while Die Nibelungen glorifies Germanic heroes; Metropolis is misguided in its irrational solution to class conflict through the heart.

Hartmann notes that critics have begun to explore this split in Lang's work and the presence of some pre-fascist platitudes. But by 1931, according to Hartmann, Lang had already distanced himself from "Blüt und Boden" (blood and earth) in M. Furthermore, he emigrated after Goebbels asked him to head the German film industry, and Lang later called Metropolis a "terrible movie."

Hartmann concludes by drawing attention to the decisive turning point in Lang's work once he got to America. The architect of the expressive and fantastic in Germany, once in America Lang favored Hollywood's view of reality, adapting himself to genres like the detective film and the Western. Hartmann points out that Lang's importance for film history is evident in the active discussion of his work and by the fact that in France he is revered as one of the models for the New Wave. For Hartmann, one of the great masters of the early film died with Lang.

464a    Jameson, Richard T. "Götterdammerung in Technicolor: Fritz Lang's Rancho Notorious". Movietone News (Seattle, Washington), No. 52 (11 October), pp. 16-23.

Jameson begins by noting what a peculiar Western Rancho Notorious is. The film makes more sense in the context of Lang's previous work than in that of the Western genre, since it quickly becomes a manhunt by a revengeful hero.

Jameson next focuses on the highly formal structure of the film, commenting particularly on the use of the concepts of the Chuck-a-Luck roulette game and of the frame. The frequency of the framing in doorways and windows symbolizes "an intensely restricted awareness within an intensely restrictive environment. . . . Frames trap Lang's characters as his films' plots trap them." Lang uses lighting, camera angles, and gestures to create a sense of people impinged upon.

In order to establish the desolation and barrenness, Lang

abandons both conventional realism and conventional narrative. The film is structured in a symmetrical manner, and
each event is joined to the next by some direct sound or
image. The beautiful balladic movement of the film has a
poetic effect.

Giving concrete examples from the film, Jameson shows how
the concept of the circle has a temporal as well as a structural dimension. Time repeats itself, but will not, however,
reverse. Aging preoccupies both Altar and Frenchie.

Relationships are difficult throughout the film, and
Vern deteriorates until he is like the very men he seeks
revenge on. The film ultimately belongs in Lang's Mabuse
series--Altar is herself a kind of Mabuse figure, controlling
her world and the men at the Ranch--and deals with greed,
lust, betrayal. For most of the film, Jameson concludes,
"Lang honors only personal, stylistic imperatives."

465   Krebs, Albin. "Fritz Lang, Film Director Noted for 'M', Dead
      at 85." New York Times (3 August).
      Krebs notes Lang's fame as director of M and his influ-
      ence on many younger film directors. He "put an indelible
      stamp on the art of cinema." Krebs quotes Lang's saying
      that he is profoundly fascinated by "cruelty, fear, horror,
      death," the pathology of violence.
      After naming Lang's most famous American films, Krebs
      mentions how famous Lang was for his "crisp, inventive,
      pictorial style," and for his experiments with sound. But
      on the set Lang was known as tyrannical and difficult.
      Reviewing briefly the main German films, Krebs recalls
      how in Frau im Mond [Woman in the Moon] Lang invented the
      countdown. He repeats Lang's hesitations regarding the
      ending of Metropolis, quoting from the interview with
      Bogdanovitch. Krebs gives concrete examples of Lang's
      power to create horror and tension in M. Lang made a bold
      film once in America, Fury, but he got into trouble on the
      set, because used to the Germanic system, where the director
      had complete power.
      Krebs goes briefly through the American films, noting
      how Lang managed to dwell on his favorite themes. Lang
      liked his next-to-last film best (While the City Sleeps)
      and left Hollywood after Beyond a Reasonable Doubt, because
      of all the trouble with producers. Krebs does not see much
      in the late German films and ends with recalling Lang's
      last thin years in Beverly Hills, when he was still tyranni-
      cal and opinionated, sure that he would yet make the greatest
      film ever.

466   Legrand, Gérard. "Homage à Fritz Lang: 1890-1976." Positif
      (Paris), No. 188 (December), pp. 8-12.
      The last in a series of notes on Lang, those offered
      here, Legrand says, are more than ever inconclusive. Lang's

work represents too large and formidable an amount of material to master. He reiterates his error in an earlier discussion of Beyond a Reasonable Doubt, where he noted that the scene of the lorry's crashing into the editor's car was so important because at that moment the editor was going to remake the past; yet instead he is literally and visually displaced. Legrand moves from there to mention the conflict in Lang between the symbolic artist and the man simply doing his job.

Legrand shows how Lang at once fascinates the viewer and criticizes this fascination. Yet, according to Legrand, critics have insisted too much on Lang's use of distanciation [distancing]. Despite his efforts in You and Me, Lang is essentially unaware of the problems of identification and distanciation. He can only create heroes through the mythological dimension.

Lang is economical in the strict sense of the term, refusing camera movements and relying on the use of emptiness to create a sense of menace, which weighs upon the community. This menace is by no means entirely external, much of it coming from within the individual, and here Legrand sees a similarity between Lang's preoccupations and those of Freud in Civilization and Its Discontents (1930). Neither of these pessimists, however, totally despairs of human perfectability, at least in the enlightenment sense.

Time and space in Lang, freely divided up in the silent films before M, are arranged in symmetrical planes in the great films. They become Kantian—or better—Hegelian time and space, so that space is the screen itself, that is, the film covering the screen; the division of space is thus totally symmetrical. But the humanist and democratic content of Lang films prevents him from being a formalist.

In conclusion, Legrand says that Lang was the director who made him think most about his true relationship to cinema. Legrand regrets that so much commentary is descriptive rather than working from within the work. That is why he, Legrand, should also stop here.

467   Overby, David. "Fritz Lang, 1890-1976." Sight and Sound (London) 54, No. 4 (Autumn), 226-27.

This sensitive obituary begins with reference to Lang's ironic humor regarding the recent auteur criticism of his works and the earnest obsessions of film students. Overby remembers Lang as a complete man, who loved his work but who did not confine himself to it. He loved to talk of world affairs, believing that there was a political trend favoring the forces of reaction; he mused frequently about capital punishment, a topic dealt with so much in his films.

468   Sarris, Andrew. "Fritz Lang (1890-1976) Was the Prophet of Our Paranoia." Village Voice (Films in Focus) (16 August),

p. 99.

Sarris surveys Lang's career and notes how his films foreshadowed the film noir genre. Never sufficiently appreciated or understood, Lang, like Hitchcock, was "afflicted by the genre prejudices of his critics throughout his career." He was denounced by Fonda for "caring more about the placement of the props in a scene than about the motivations of the actors and the meanings of the characters." Sarris concludes that while in terms of narrative Lang was a fatalist, all his creative energies went into the visual design of fate. "His is the cinema of the nightmare, the fable and the morality tale . . . If Renoir is humanism, Lang is determinism; if Renoir is concerned with the plight of his characters, Lang is obsessed with the structure of the trap."

Sarris sees little change in Lang's vision from the German to the American films: both show people struggling with their personal destiny and inevitably losing. Lang's films take place in a closed world, but their formal brilliance is incontestable. He is "the cerebral fatalist of the cinema, and his lapses into absurdity are the evidence of a remote sagacity and intellect that transforms images into ideas." Sarris comments on the paranoia in Lang's films, but says that he could never ask Lang about this any more than about the sentimental exceptions in the love of a pure woman for the hero.

Sarris concludes that Lang believed that the world had to be destroyed before it could be purified. He consistently undercut audience expectations of "a moral balance regained." Cultists and auteurists are now spending their time revising Lang's own estimation of his efforts, demonstrating how Lang's personality is actually stamped on all that he did.

469   Thackeray, Ted, Jr., and Tuchman, Michelle. "Fritz Lang Perfectionist Film Director, Dies at 85." Los Angeles Times (3 August), pp. 1, 5.

The authors begin by noting how dedicated to perfectionism Lang was, and they refer to a few of his important films. They survey his background and early life, mentioning his period of wandering, his being wounded in the war, his meeting with Pommer, and his directing his first film.

While Lang belongs in expressionism, German critics in the 1920s did not like his work, which they considered "superficial." Only the French treated Lang kindly, comparing him to Dürer and Grünewald. Dr. Mabuse, der Spieler set the tone for much of Lang's later work.

Once in Hollywood, Lang was seen as an oddity, with his accent and monocle, and because he shot lots of film, he was considered expensive. Lang never enjoyed the financial and moral support in Hollywood that he had had in Europe.

Lang directed all the top stars and in his last years was honored in many nations at film festivals and won lots of awards. If he were to make a film of the 1970s, Lang said that he would show that television had robbed children of their imagination.

470    Tulloch, John. "Genetic Structuralism and the Cinema: A Look at Fritz Lang's Metropolis." Australian Journal of Screen Theory, No. 1, pp. 3-50.
       Functioning as the editorial statement in the first issue of the journal, this article covers a wide range of topics. Tulloch's main aim is to demonstrate the kind of theoretical approach the journal will favor, and he has chosen to make a case study out of German expressionism (and within that, Lang's Metropolis), since that movement has tempted critics to find links between film and society. Tulloch attempts to develop a methodology which, while incorporating sociological approaches, intends to move beyond them by using structure as the main tool of analysis. His method requires, first of all, extensive criticism, along with recognition of the importance of Kracauer and Huaco, and, later on, explanation of the mandarin theories of sociologists F. K. Ringer and Friedrich Schürr (and others quoted by Ringer).
       Tulloch grants Kracauer his place in the development of sociological film criticism, but then goes on to show how content analysis of this kind creates problems. An image has no meaning apart from its context, since a film is a structural whole; the relationship of elements to one another is more important than the frequency with which an image occurs. Huaco, Tulloch shows, errs in a manner similar to that of Kracauer; his method for arriving at the variable he has isolated is too arbitrary, and Tulloch reveals the contradiction between the supposed right-wing ideology of the filmmaker in Huaco's system and the negative way capitalists are shown in expressionist films.
       A detailed contrast of Eisenstein's October and Lang's Metropolis reveals the way pure content analysis can lead to false conclusions. According to Tulloch, an examination of the structural relations between items of content in these films would lead to different results.
       Tulloch discusses Metropolis at length, showing how the structure of the film is dialectical rather than binary, for "the whole direction of the film is to resolve the major antithesis of worker and capitalist in the culminating act of synthesis on the Cathedral steps." The early sequences, Tulloch shows, set up a pattern of thesis, antithesis, and synthesis.
       Focusing next on how helpless the people are shown to be, whether worker or capitalist, Tulloch sees the two groups as ultimately making up the one inhuman world of Metropolis.

Having dealt with the Christian symbolism in the film at some length, Tulloch shows how the film contains a series of "shifting antinomies"--Christian/diabolic, spiritual/ materialist, and human/mechanical--but goes on to assert the need to explain "the genesis of this vision which fused capitalist and worker within a concept of materialism." To do this, he has to move beyond structuralism to sociology. He intends to use Mannheim and F. K. Ringer for this, citing again as failures the methodologies of Kracauer and Huaco. He praises Ringer's analysis of German intellectuals and professionals and goes on to show that Lang was part of the mandarins, or cultural elite, these groups represent. The mandarins' alienation and isolation in the face of the new practical, industrial classes is reflected in Metropolis, where the soulless city creates soulless people, governed by hard, capitalist men of science. Maria and Freder embody the values of the alienated mandarins--love, passion, and the longing for a return to an earlier, preindustrial or- ganization of society. Anarchy was attractive to the manda- rin mind in this situation, but while the people may smash the machines, the danger is that they will forget the spiri- tual revolution that Maria finally does bring about in the film.

Tulloch concludes this section with discussion of the paradoxical function of Rotwang as at once symbolic of the Jews--false materialist religion--and of the false "Weberian 'materialist-Marxist' intellectual, against whom is erected . . . the hero-synthesis representative of the youthful renewal." Rotwang demonstrates the mandarin belief that "divisive weltanshauung, Marxist or otherwise, were created by the development of industrialism and capitalism."

Tulloch next outlines certain basic areas of sociological research necessary if his thesis is not to remain tentative: (1) Other expressionist films must be analyzed in the same manner as Metropolis here to see if the same relationships can be found and thus the "film wave" be made general. Possibly different social classes needed the films in dif- ferent ways. Tulloch finds that at the level of structure similar relationships do appear in other Lang films--especi- ally Dr. Mabuse and Destiny--and in Murnau's Faust. The triumph of love through death seems to run through Lang's Hollywood films, only now the opposition between intellect and emotion is played out on the psychological rather than the social/political plane. The mandarin position, Tulloch suggests, continued right up to the last project Lang en- visioned, namely his Death of A Career Girl. (2) The re- lationship of the expressionist film to other forms of German expressionism also needs proper examination, particu- larly in connection with influence that artists from the group Der Sturm were able to exert to counteract the manda- rin values of the films.

In the final section of the editorial, Tulloch summarizes the main aspects of his approach to German expressionism and Metropolis. First, the approach is sociological rather than based in New Criticism (where film criticism is focused on analysis of the few masterpieces as models to be learned from); second, the approach assumes that artists are deeply involved in their social period. He next distinguishes his kind of structuralism--genetic--from that derived from linguistics; following Lucien Goldmann, Tulloch says that elements in a work of art can be understood only in the context of the system as a whole, and that analysis must go beyond mere surface content to uncover the underlying structure. While linguistic structuralism focuses only on the internal organization of a work, Tulloch's method operates on several levels at once, moving from the work to the social group and the wider socio-historical context. Tulloch spends some time attacking, and also explaining, the development of linguistic structuralism, which "'considers the structure as a cause in itself' thus 'liberating it from the determinations of the subject and of history.'"

In explaining how Goldmann avoids reducing the work to the social group, Tulloch outlines briefly two forms that a political stance can take; he calls "ideology" that stance where a privileged group seeks to maintain the social structure as it is; and a "world view" that stance in which a group's interests are directed toward transforming the social structure. After mentioning some problems with Goldmann's theory, Tulloch ends by describing the four levels appropriate for film analysis that Christian Metz has outlined. He finds a special place for the genetic structuralist in Metz's assertion that films contain "signifieds of extra-cinematic origin." While these signifieds need not enter into a purely cinematic analysis, they are essential for understanding the "total signification of a particular film." He warns, however, that the signified elements must not be reduced to the socio-cultural and uses here Kenneth Burke's notion of art forms as "critical and imaginative answers to a social problematic" to explain his position.

471   Ulrich, Jörg. "Der Mann mit den 1000 Augen." Münchner Merkur (4 August).

Ulrich begins by discussing criticism of Lang's last films, made in Germany. All of them were full of involuntary parodies of his first works, and Ulrich accounts for this by noting that Lang, in his seventies when he attempted a new start in Europe, was probably too preoccupied with his past fame. His American films, especially those of the 1950s, destroyed all his earlier artistic and commercial credit; unfortunately, his European efforts also failed.

However, Ulrich says that when early films became

fashionable again, Lang's films of the 1920s began to attract interest. Lang was not only reclaimed for the Golden Age of the German film, but underwent a thorough reevaluation by a young generation that placed social relevance above other categories. Adopting an approach similar to Kracauer, they argued that the Indian films represent the wishful dreams of a prisoner longing for exotic, far away places, the prison in this case being the blockaded and mutilated Fatherland.

According to Ulrich, films like Die Nibelungen and Metropolis, arguably full of pre-fascist forebodings, made Lang famous beyond his purely artistic abilities as a director; his use of light and shadow, his architectural sense, together with his thematic fascination for the masses and grandiose, fate-driven heroes, appealed to a generation that knew little of Lang's times.

Ulrich ends by evaluating Lang's ultimate aesthetic worth; he agrees that Lang had a penchant for kitsch, but notes that both he and his wife, von Harbou, were sensitive to the dangerous political tendencies of the period. This is clear in a film like M, which goes beyond a mere crime film to providing a lesson in organized persecution. This timeless film, Ulrich says, with its successful blend of realism and expressionism, brought Lang international fame, and he remained basically known for his work in Berlin preceding the Nazi disaster.

472    Veszelits, Thomas. "Herr Maulwurf spielte gerne Skat: Zum Tode von Fritz Lang: Zeitgenossen erinnern sich an den Meisterregisseur." Abend-Zeitung (Munich) (4 August).
Some of Lang's contemporaries, including Fritz Rasp, and others who worked with him, like Artur Brauner and Paul Hubschmied, talk about what Lang was really like, how he worked and lived.

473    Wenders, Wim. "Sein Tod is keine Lösung" [His Death is No Solution] Der Spiegel (4 August). Reprinted and expanded in Pflaum, Hans Gunther, ed. Jahrbuch Film 77/78. Munich: Hanser, 1977.
Writing at the time of Lang's death (called upon by Der Spiegel, he suspects, because of his film Kings of the Road, where he mentions Lang's Die Nibelungen and inserts a couple of photos of him), Wenders begins by picking up the sentence Lang originally spoke in Godard's film Le Mépris (and later quoted in a French interview) to the effect that "Death is no solution."

Perplexed by this sentence, Wenders tried to read everything by and about Lang, but was unable to solve the enigma the phrase contains. The retrospectives in the newspapers and film clubs did not dispel Wenders's uneasiness about the sentence. While Lang will now, he thinks, be made into

a myth, the truth is that Lang has been poorly treated in
Germany. He recalls Lang's statement that he was glad to
leave Germany after Goebbels approached him, glad to become
an American; but Lang, in fact, never got over the pain of
what happened in Germany, which he had loved dearly as the
place where all his roots were.

Wenders then notes that Lang made not only his first,
but also his last, films in Germany and goes on to describe
the unfortunate experiences Lang had doing the last German
films. He arrived in Germany under an illusion about what
his situation would be, lived in hotels, friendless, and
without public recognition, and found the people he had to
work with intolerable. They were interested only in making
money.

Wenders suggests that perhaps there is a basic antagonism
between the artistic and commercial aspects of film, but he
quotes Lang as hoping, in 1924, that the fact that film appealed to the masses did not mean that it could not also be
art.

Wenders next quotes a rather negative statement by Frieda
Grafe to the effect that Lang was a cold, impenetrable man.
He notes that he has seen few Lang films (the first ones
being those shown in Paris) and says how strange they seemed
to him. His mind was full of other images, other kinds of
cinema--the American, the French, and the Russian. The
images did not appeal to him; he found himself struggling
against them, yet there was something familiar within the
strangeness.

Wenders ends by commenting that he in fact knows very
little about Fritz Lang; he recalls asking Samuel Fuller
some idiotic question about Lang, who had lived near him.
Fuller told him laconically that he had liked Lang and that
Gene Fowler, who had been with Lang during the last days,
had arranged a kind of wake for Lang, so that his friends
could drink and tell stories about the dead man. This somehow finally releases Wenders from his puzzlement about Lang's
sentence: "Death is no solution."

474    Wiegand, Wilfried. "Der Mensch im Ornament. Zum Tod des
       Filmregisseurs Fritz Lang." <u>Frankfurter Allgemeine Zeitung</u>
       (4 August).
       Wiegand begins by noting that much of Germany's political
history and practically the entire history of German film
is mirrored in Lang's life.
       According to Lang, his first decisive encounter with film
was in 1909 in Brugge (Belgium): "In the loneliness of this
city, a picture of film is fixed in me that never lets me
go. I sense new possibilities. Again in Paris, I am already
under the spell of film." An unusual acknowledgment since
at that time film was far from being a recognized art form.
       Wiegand says that Berlin became the center for film in

the 1920s. Practically every new idea brought forth by the
artists was tested in film. As a result, cubist painting
and the staccato speech of expressionism left their marks
on German film. Most decisive, however, was the borrowing
from theater, particularly Max Reinhardt's stage, whose
stylized mass-scenes insert people into a large supra-
personal ornament: the individual becomes a part of a moving picture.

Lang and Lubitsch were the most radical in carrying this
style over into film. The architecture in Die Nibelungen
films, as well as Metropolis, consists in gigantically en-
larged stage sets, in front of which the people shrink almost to the size of decorations. To be sure, Lang is often
successful in bringing these ornamental masses into motion,
binding them dramatically with the architecture.

Wiegand notes that much has been written about the affinity
of Lang's expressionist style to the aesthetics of Nazi
mass marches. The scripts of the most important Lang films
were written by his former wife, Thea von Harbou. Her books
exhibit no lack of the superman cult à la Nietzsche, and the
temptation is to ascribe all those traits which now seem
antiquated solely to her.

But Wiegand notes that this argument, while it exonerates
Lang, does not say much for him, since no artist is forced
to rely on his wife's books. It is better to find grounds
within Lang's works themselves to free him from the fashionable charge of pre-fascism. Wiegand claims that this is
not difficult in that his style is one that distances him
from his heroes, making them ultimately unbelievable. His
plots are always laden with symbols. According to Wiegand,
Lang's expressionism is related to that of his predecessors
in the manner that Heine's lyric is to romanticism, or
Mendelsohn's music to Beethoven. His use of irony, mis-
perceived as lack of intellectual rigor, cost him due recognition.

Wiegand concludes by noting that Lang's American films,
far from being inferior as is usually claimed, reflect his
great talent. He comes close to Hitchcock's demonization
of the everyday in the psychological criminal films like
Woman in the Window. Lang was indeed able to make good use
of the demands of Hollywood because his own film, M, anticipated as early as 1931 many of the techniques that later
re-entered film language via Hollywood.

475   Wiegand, Wilfried. "Der Film als Schattenbeschwörung."
      Frankfurter Allgemeine Zeitung (25 August). (Review of the
      first German book on Lang by Enno Patalas and Frieda Grafe.
      Munich: Hanser, 1976.)
          Wiegand begins by noting that when Lang died [a few weeks
      before Wiegand's review, ed.], his work had long been fin-
      ished. His last film appeared in 1960 (Die Tausend Augen

des Dr. Mabuse [The Thousand Eyes of Dr. Mabuse]), and when
Lang portrayed himself in Godard's Le Mépris in 1963, he
was already, at seventy-three, a living legend.

Proceeding with his review, Wiegand deplores the fact
that the slim book by Patalas and Grafe is the first written
in German about the greatest film director Germany has produced.

Wiegand continues with a critique of the book for a certain heavy, esoteric quality--a quality that is ironically
the opposite of that which Lang himself possessed when discussing his own works. Wiegand complains about the lack
of plot summaries and about Grafe's affected use of foreign
words; but he does concede that her introductory essay is
one of the best in recent film criticism. Her methodology
is far superior to the simplistic ideological one initiated
by Kracauer. Wiegand praises Grafe's acceptance of film as
a popular art, and her notion that Lang was perfectly fitted
for the entertainment world. Given this, one need no longer
attribute all the flaws in the early works to Thea von
Harbou; her material was exactly what suited Lang's talents.

According to Wiegand, film succeeds as a mass art because
it relies on images, and because it has no need to concern
itself with "reality." Lang was a master of this kind of
art: his films transform the reality that is their raw
material into a metaphysical universe.

Wiegand concludes by commending Grafe's critical methodology that is informed by psychoanalysis, sociology, and,
most unusual for a German film critic, semiology and structuralism. Grafe has begun the necessary dialogue with foreign theorists that will counterbalance the dominant bias
toward sociology in German film criticism.

476   Witte, Karsten. "Der müde Tod: Zum Tode Fritz Langs." [The
      Tired Death (film by Lang): On the Death of Fritz Lang]
      Frankfurter Rundschau (4 August).
         Witte begins by noting the impressive way in which Lang,
      working within the industry, always dared to experiment
      with new things. He made history with each of his films,
      which varied from the magical and fairytalelike to the ad-
      venture and trick film and on to monumental stylization and
      finally realism. But Lang always tried to create a second
      nature in the studio, and in doing this he advanced cinema.
         Witte then goes on to discuss how Lang was one of the
      first to understand that film was a mass medium, reflecting
      in his work the collective anxiety and terror, rather than
      the wishes and hopes, of humankind. But he reflected the
      truth about the end of the Weimar period, finding forms
      that fit the reality.
         Referring to the first German book on Lang, Witte notes
      that it is no longer simply a matter of whether or not Lang's
      Mabuse prefigured fascism: Lang's works are complex and

ambivalent, designed to overcome the enemy.

Other obituaries:
> Niemeyer, Kai. "Die Hand am Puls der Zeit: Der Filmregisseur Fritz Lang ist im Hollywood gestorben." Abend-Zeitung (Munich) (4 August 1976).
>
> Harmssen, Hennig. "Seltsame Affinitäten: Zum Tode des Filmregisseurs Fritz Lang." Rheinische Merkur (n.d.: See Deutsches Institut für Filmkunde file).
>
> Feldman, Sebastian. "Angst und Verhängnis: Zum Tod des Filmregisseurs Fritz Lang." Rheinische Post (Dusseldorf) (4 August).
>
> WR. "Nestor des deutschen Films: Zum Tode des Regisseurs Fritz Lang." Wiesbaden Zeitung (4 August 1976).
>
> "In Memoriam Fritz Lang." Ekran (Ljubljana, Czechoslovakia) No. 6 (1976), p. 747.
>
> G. H. "Fritz Lang." Film-Echo, No. 42 (1976), p. 7.
>
> Anon: "Fritz Lang." Le Film Français, No. 1638 (1976), p. 6.
>
> "Fritz Lang disait à L'Express. . . ." L'Express (5 August 1976).
>
> PMT. "Fritz Lang, architecte faustian du 7e art." Le Figaro (4 August 1976).
>
> F. M. "Fritz Lang, l'un des maîtres de l'expressionnisme, n'est plus." L'Humanité (4 August 1976).
>
> Rainer, S. "Die Emigrationen des Fritz Lang." Badische Zeitung (4 August 1976).
>
> Th. L. "Fritz Lang, cinéaste maudit." La Libre Belgique (4 August 1976).
>
> Grandjean, P. "Le cinéaste Fritz Lang est mort." Journal de Genève (4 August 1976).
>
> Ulrich, J. "Der Mann mit den 1000 Augen." Münchner Merkur (4 August 1976).
>
> f. h. w., "Er machte Filmgeschichte." Volksstumme (7 August 1976).
>
> Anon. "Fritz Lang, 85, An Early Great: Film Fest Fave." Variety (4 August 1976).
>
> Trölle, B. "Fritz Lang 1890-1976." Spotlight, No. 15, (1976), p. 68.
>
> "Mr. Fritz Lang, A Pioneer of Silent Films." The Times (4 August 1976).
>
> Savioli, A. "Fritz Lang fra arte et industria." L'Unità (4 August 1976).
>
> M. T. "Maestro de Maestros." La Vanguardia (4 August 1976).

## 1977

476a    Basset, V. and D. Sotiaux. "Deux textes pour servir une problématique, L'Ouvrier dans le cinéma allemand des années

20." Revue Belge du Cinéma (Brussels) (5-6 June), pp. 6-13.
A study of the representation of workers in three German films, Lang's Metropolis, Brecht's Kuhle Wampe, and Lang's M.

477  Del Ministro, Maurizio. "Una ipotesi psicoanalitica per la lettura di 'M.'" Cinema Nuovo (Turin), No. 250 (November-December), pp. 451-454.
Del Ministro argues that the source of M is to be found in Lang's early childhood guilt about innocent pleasure. Beckert symbolizes an externalization of Lang's internal "monster," who needed to destroy the child in him.

478  Eisner, Lotte H. Fritz Lang. Translated by Gertrud Mander and edited by David Robinson. London: Secker and Warburg, 1976; New York: Oxford University Press, 1977. 416 pp. Filmography.
Lotte Eisner's new book on Fritz Lang, in the same attractive (and expensive) format as her other books, is a fitting testimonial to Lang, who died shortly after its publication. Written largely in collaboration with Lang, it is a dedicated survey of his entire work by a loyal, lifelong friend. Aging and ill, Lang wanted to make sure that posterity would be left with correct information about his life and work, and Lotte Eisner was the obvious choice for the task of setting the record straight. As Eisner notes, Lang was "conscious how often his remarks have been misunderstood and misinterpreted" (p. 397), for he did not even consider the tape recorder inviolable and often complained of critics' distortions. A second purpose of the book was to bring to public attention films still insufficiently known and appreciated.
The logical structure to accomodate both aims was the usual film-by-film analysis, moving chronologically from the German works into Lang's long career in America. Lang wanted detailed descriptions that would convey a vivid impression of the thematic and visual aspects of each film; this is, of course, the kind of writing about film that Eisner is good at (partly as a result of her art history background and her interest in visual style), and the accounts are never merely monotonous retellings of plots. Eisner's energy and enthusiasm bring each film alive and our attention is drawn to hitherto neglected aspects.
The discussion of Lang's German films is better than the discussion of the American ones, partly because the early German film has been Eisner's special area of study over the years and partly because an underlying theme gives the descriptions some coherence. At Lang's request, Eisner is at pains to dissociate him from expressionism--a link that Eisner herself had established originally in The Haunted Screen (1952). Lang evidently disliked the assertion that

362

he had been influenced by expressionism, since this seemed
to detract from his individuality and creativity as an artist.  Eisner agrees that critics have overdone the association and now attempts to distinguish aspects of Lang that
emerge from romanticism from those that arise from expressionism.  For example, when discussing Destiny, she says,
"The mode of calling the characters The Young Man, The Girl,
The Wanderer and so on is characteristic of Expressionist
drama.  The little town in the middle of nowhere, smacks
more of romanticism than Expressionism" (p. 52).  Eisner
objects to the easy way in which critics refer to expressionist elements in Lang's films, thus betraying their ignorance of the true meaning of the term.  Discussing a review of Dr. Mabuse, Eisner comments:  "The review also mentions 'the expressionist rooms at the Tolds', and 'the expressionist nightclub'; but it is possible that more Expressionism has been read into the film than was intended
. . . The only genuinely Expressionist feature is the
restaurant with its flame walls . . . Nor are Told's rooms
Expressionist, though some of the art works in them are"
(pp. 61-62).  Eisner is also amazed that in Die Nibelungen
"for some curious reason, many people still regard the well-
balanced, symmetrical, spacious sets as Expressionist.  Yet
there are none of the ecstatic distortions, the oblique
angles of Caligari or Raskolnikov" (p. 69).
    The discussion of Metropolis reveals well the kind of
criticism Eisner excels at, since she is able to show that
the film contains several different aesthetic styles.  There
are first some purely expressionist moments, such as the
accident, when Freder, "all elegant in white," is "frozen
into an Expressionist diagonal as the dark figures bearing
the casualties file past, shot against the light" (p. 84).
At other times Eisner notes that the expressionism is pitted
against surrealism, as in the visions of the skyscrapers,
or in Freder's fevered dreams when "he seems to be falling
through circulating shapes into an abyss" (p. 86).  Finally,
Metropolis also looks toward the "New Objectivity" [Neue
Sachlichkeit] in the use of geometrical structuring of bodies and in the "documentary" techniques used in the flood
scenes (p. 89).
    In this first section, Eisner is also concerned with set-
ting the record straight and with revealing interesting
practical details about the production of certain films,
but not to the degree that she is in the second part.  For
example, in the chapter on Die Nibelungen, Eisner devotes
some time to rebutting Kracauer's allegations of anti-
Semitism in the film and also denies the charges of racism
in Lang's portrait of the Huns.  In discussing Destiny,
Eisner gives a good deal of space to Lang's account of how
they did the lighting first in his Der Herr der Liebe
[Master of Love] and second in Destiny itself.  Eisner

learned from Lang that when he did the film, certain of
the episodes were arranged in a different order, and that
"the film originally had three decisive verses, though today even the German copies have only prose titles" (pp.
52-54). But for the most part, the focus is on placing the
films in relation to the art movements of the period, and
this links the separate discussions.

This sort of coherence is missing once Eisner gets to
the American films. One senses her difficulty in fully ap-
preciating the American films, but she makes good use of
the Cahiers du Cinéma critics, who for the last twenty years
have been revealing the complexity and importance of the
American films. The most valuable aspect of her accounts
is the way in which she brings out the brilliance of Lang's
visual patterns and compositions, his use of lighting to
evoke atmosphere, and his creation of a nightmare world in
the gangster, thriller, and war films.

Apart from this, the value of each account lies in the
somewhat arbitrary pieces of information that Eisner obviously obtained from Lang. There are three main types of comments. First, Eisner includes quite practical information
regarding a film's making. In discussing Manhunt, for example, Eisner relates how the scene of the parting between
Jenny and Thorndike on the bridge was almost lost. Zanuck
did not want Jenny, "a decent girl," to have to play the
prostitute before the man she loved. But Lang went ahead
with the scene anyway, and since there was no budget for it,
they used existing set materials from earlier street scenes
and Lang paid for the rest himself. As they could not get
studio workers, "Lang and his cameraman shot the scene
themselves at 4 a.m. in the deserted studio" (p. 218). At
the very end of the chapter on Ministry of Fear, Eisner includes details of the scene where Willy is killed--a scene
that was particularly hard to do. "Lang had to make the
hole cut by the bullet visible at exactly the right angle.
It took 1 ½ hours to set up. Then, because of union rules,
Lang was not allowed to drill the hole himself or let any
of the crew do it . . . " (p. 247). These are details that
suddenly bring the making of the film close and add interest.

A second group of interesting comments has to do with
differences between Lang's original intention in a film and
the version we now have. Often a production company would
not allow Lang's point of view to prevail. A striking example is Cloak and Dagger, which Lang had intended as "a
kind of concluding commentary on the terror of the Reich,"
as well as "a warning against the new-born terror of the
spread of the destructive capabilities of atomic power"
(p. 267). The pacifist-oriented ending was filmed, but "it
was removed with the entire last reel of the film by the
production company, and was destroyed with the film's release" (p. 267).

A third group of comments arises out of Eisner's privileged access, as Lang's friend, to many film scripts unavailable generally. By referring to underlining by Lang, she is able to see what effects he tried to bring out. For example, the script of Manhunt shows Lang's deletion of his scriptwriter's detailed description of Thorndike after his torture by the Nazis. Lang notes in the margin "Shadow—don't show Thorndike throughout the whole scene," and, later on, "Close shot of dragging feet . . . blood drops could be all". The deletion demonstrates Lang's genius for understatement, his awareness that the human imagination can conjure up horror more effectively than any literal presentation of it.

The chapter on Hangmen Also Die is almost completely concerned with unravelling the tangle of bitterness and recriminations surrounding the film, particularly in connection with Brecht's role in writing the script and in the conception of the whole film. Eisner quotes extensively from Brecht's diaries and obtained the final word on the affair from Lang.

The close involvement of Lang in the text naturally imposed some limitations on Eisner and affected the total conception of the book. Eisner sent each chapter as it was finished to Lang for changes and additions, and at his bequest she would delete sections. For instance, Eisner wanted to be critical of Thea von Harbou, but Lang decided that he preferred to let bygones be bygones. The lack of critical analysis in general is apparently also motivated by the desire to accomodate Lang. But Eisner had even more difficulties to contend with in bringing out the English edition. The number of people working on the text turned into a "too many cooks" situation, resulting in various errors that were pointed out later by some reviewers. (The filmography is particularly unreliable because of the many spelling errors.)

On balance, however, Fritz Lang is a well-researched and faithful book, which fulfills its intention of bringing attention to hitherto neglected aspects of Lang's work. The excellently reproduced stills corroborate Eisner's points about Lang's visual style, and this constant focus confirms Lang as a master of the visual dimension of film form. The book is a welcome commemoration of Lang, in the year of his death.

[For annotation of a review of Eisner's book, See Entry No. 482].

479   Eyman, Scott. "Fritz Lang Remembered." Take One, 5, No. 8 (March), 15-16.

Eyman writes about Lang as a personal friend, giving touching tribute to him as a human being and an artist. He was with Lang during the last months of his life, when he was clearly in much pain and detesting the process of aging. His world-weariness and disillusionment with America emerge from the comments Eyman recalls. Lang notes, first, how competition has ruined the Americans whom he had at first trusted; he is, second, upset by the violence he sees now in America, particularly since it reminds him of the violence that preceded Hitler's rise to power in Germany; third, he deplores the fact that directors are now making immoral films, which show a lack of respect for the human condition, and, in addition, don't allow the audience to think anymore. Lang considers that only he and von Stroheim in Hollywood made films without regard to box office success.

Eyman ends by recalling some touching personal moments with Lang and with a tribute to Lang's personal and professional greatness: "As an artist, Fritz Lang was a Titan wrestling with the Gods; as a man, he had the rare ability to both give and receive love."

480 Lowry, Ed. "Die tausend Augen des Dr. Mabuse." [Review of The Thousand Eyes of Dr. Mabuse] Cinema Texas Program Notes, 12, No. 1 (24 February). (In MMA).

After noting the similarities to the other Mabuse films, Lowry focuses on the differences in relation first, to the way Mabuse becomes reliant on modern technology, and second, to the voyeurism which comments on cinema-going experiences. We are aware, in this version, of Lang as omniscient director and of our voyeurism as audience. Like Mabuse, Lang manipulates events he watches and knows the master scheme that links everything. Excluded, the audience is forced to submit to whatever Lang chooses to show.

The mirror scenes, Lowry says, show first, how perversely fetishistic our relationship with the film image is, and second, how we as audience can be manipulated through our passivity.

The Mabuse in Die tausend is no longer responding to a decadent society, but is evil personified, desiring destruction for its own sake. It is significant that the disguises he chooses are those of a psychiatrist and seer, both of whom deal with the unconscious and with the irrational aspects of human beings.

Lowry ends by referring to the political moment of the film's making: it was the period of the cold war and the building of the Berlin Wall. The concept of nuclear brinksmanship is evident in the central paradox of Dr. Mabuse--we find the most irrational human impulses ordered by the most cold-blooded logic.

481 Prawer, S. S. "The Cost-Effective Visionary." Review of Lotte Eisner, Fritz Lang. Translated by Gertrud Mander, edited by David Robinson. London: Secker and Warburg. Times Literary Supplement (January 21), pp. 60-62.

Prawer begins by recalling the strong impression that Lang's Das Testament des Dr. Mabuse [The Last Will of Dr. Mabuse] had on him, with its evocation of madness, the roots of crime, and power and its misuse. He proceeds to list the large number of films that drew on Lang's techniques, from Eisenstein's Nevsky to Franju's Les Yeux Sans Visages. Noting that Lang has, in turn, been influenced by other directors, Prawer concludes that Lang gave more than he took.

Turning to Eisner's book, Prawer sees her functioning as Lang's Boswell or Eckermann [biographer of Goethe], but complains of her too uncritical acceptance of all that Lang says. Prawer is, however, grateful for a positive look at Lang, given the many negative evaluations, like those of Kracauer and Peter Gay. The book is timely in relation to the battering that the auteur theory was receiving at the time of Prawer's review: Eisner shows how a director could "pursue themes and develop a theme-related style" even under the adverse Hollywood conditions.

Prawer then lists the many reasons why Lang was able to do this, including his energy, his technical mastery, his managing to insert his own ideas in the scripts, and his creation of a "repertory company" whenever possible, continuing the practice he had started in Germany. Lang got a string of excellent performances out of German and American actors and actresses, but Prawer notes that Eisner omitted mention of the many figures who played an important role outside the cinema and whom Lang asked to act for him (e.g., Rosa Valetti--the German cabaret singer, Antonin Artaud, Nat King Cole).

Lang kept control of his work in America by shrewdly abandoning his monumental style and working with low budgets. He hired gifted cameramen and technicians, like Karl Freund, Fritz Arno Wagner, and James Wong Howe. As Eisner noted, "economy proved a stimulus to Lang's invention."

Finally, Lang remained an auteur by always trying to do more than make box office successes, dealing also with social morality. By founding the Screen Directors' Guild, he helped others to free themselves from the Hollywood machine. But as Eisner shows, Lang could not prevent the mutilation of some of his works by editors and producers.

Prawer concludes by briefly reviewing the many aspects of Lang's work that Eisner touches upon. He praises the book for its "combination of structural and thematic analysis with close technical descriptions of Lang's procedures and effects." He mentions a few mistakes in the text (such as a wrongly described shot in M) and complains of the typing errors and sloppy writing, but essentially values the book for its contribution to our understanding of Lang.

482    Reiss, Curt. Das gab's nur einmal: Die grosse Zeit des deutschen Films, vol. 11 Vienna-Munich: Molden Taschenbuch.

Reiss's discussion focuses on Spione [Spies], Frau im
Mond [Woman in the Moon], M, and Das Testament des Dr.
Mabuse [The Last Will of Dr. Mabuse]. Reiss's is a rather
lighthearted, anecdotal approach, in which he draws on accounts of what actually went on as Lang was making his
films; Reiss focuses on personalities, particularly those
of Lang himself and the actors and actresses he used. The
accounts are interesting in that they give a lively sense
of the period and of Lang's ways of working, although everything is naturally colored by Reiss's subjectivity. There
is a quite amusing discussion of Lang's discovery of Gerda
Maurus and of the painful time she had working with him on
Spione. But he did make her into a famous star--so much so
that Max Reinhardt wanted her to act in a classic play for
him--but Lang, of course, would not let her go, and he went
on to use her in Frau im Mond.
  There is a similarly anecdotal and interesting account
of how M came to be made, and how Lang managed to get Peter
Lorre for the part of the murderer, weaning him away from
a project with Brecht that interested Lorre much more, but
that ultimately failed. M, Reiss points out, is still
played today. The discussion about Lang ends with comments
on Das Testament and Lang's disillusionment with power in
the face of Hitler. Thea von Harbou, Reiss notes wryly,
was a good scriptwriter, but had no head for politics and
was taken in entirely by Hitler's propaganda.

483   Thomson, David. "Lang's Ministry." Sight and Sound (London),
      46, No. 2 (Spring), 114-116.
      Thomson begins by showing how false he finds Lang's image
as created by Godard in Le Mépris. Nothing is spontaneous
in a Lang film, and Thomson thinks the final slogan that
"one has to finish what one has started," while apparently
solemn, is, in fact, hollow. Lang deserves more skeptical
examination than Godard and conventional views of Lang have
provided. If he was a great director, Lang was also an un-
encouraging man who created an atmosphere of insecurity and
unreliability. Critics need to take more seriously the
fact of Goebbels's interest in Lang and ask what the implications of this are.
      Thomson next discusses the Graham Greene novel from which
Lang's film Ministry of Fear was taken. While Lang retains
the major incidents, he alters their resonance in a way
that exposes his own coldness. Greene's novel "shivers
with pathos and pain," exploring as it does inner torment,
while for Lang "fear is a reaction to bombs, conspiracy and
fate." Quoting from Lang's interview with Bogdanovitch,
Thomson notes how many directors mouth commonplace thoughts
and how Lang "never appeared other than a shrewd, ingenious
entertainer." Rejecting Ministry because the script was altered, thus eliminating what Thomson considered to be its

deeper aspects, Thomson asserts that all Lang's best films
work on a similar level. "Lang's quality is a narrow but
intense visualization of action conveying fear, claustrophobia and malign fate." The conception of fear is the
best part of Ministry, but Thomson sets out to argue that
"the film is itself like a product of the Ministry it ostensibly hates."

A detailed analysis of the film's opening follows, showing how the power of these scenes lies not in depiction of
character but in the composition and editing. Character
is not important in Lang films, and there are thus few
outstanding acting performances. Even Lorre in M, according
to Thomson, arouses curiosity rather than compassion. For
similar reasons, there are few homes in Lang's work, the
interiors rather being atmospheric geometry.

The creator of a self-conscious cinema, Lang rarely
trusts nature or reality. The artificial studio set-ups
sap vitality, as in the opening scenes of Ministry, where
Neale leaves the asylum and wanders into the garden fête,
with its fake lawn and painted sky. Thomson goes on to
describe in detail the opening sequence with its gloomy,
leaden atmosphere. While Greene's novel gets close to the
reality of London during the Blitz, Lang suggests that wars,
and the ministries that conduct them, are eternal.

Noting that Lang's films are restless, and full of action,
Thomson next shows how in Ministry objects are focused on
until they almost acquire the force of characters; he demonstrates this through analyzing the use of doorways in the
film. After a long description of the last sequence in the
film where the character played by Dan Duryea (Willi Hilfe)
is shot through a door by his sister, Thomson concludes that
for Lang "spatial relationships are as profound as human
beings. Doors last, but human beings pass in and out."

Thomson deplores the false happy ending to Ministry, but
notes how common this is in Lang. Discussing Metropolis,
Thomson shows how forlorn the ending is and links Lang's
confidence to that of the fascists, who used it to "overlay
their brutal cleansing solutions." According to Thomson,
there is a contradiction in Lang's work between his conscious
rejection of nazism and his presentation of a world fit only
for tyrants. Overwhelmingly pessimistic, Lang shows humans
as inevitable victims of fate. Despite his claims to be
moving toward "character" when he came to America, Thomson
believes that Lang adhered to the style of his German works.
While Lang may have been an authentic liberal, he made authoritarian films.

484   Wilson, George. "You Only Live Once: The Doubled Feature,"
      Sight and Sound, 46, No. 4 (Autumn), pp. 221-226.
      Wilson argues that we need to go beyond the standard
      remarks on You Only Live Once to reconsider the nature of

Lang's thematic materials and the strategies through which
they are expressed in his work. The film is full of references to various aspects of perception and blindness.
"Through the visuals and the dialogue we are repeatedly
introduced to questions concerning sight and the failure
to see, pictures and picturing and the various senses of
the word 'vision.'" In addition, Lang comments on the potential unreliability of film itself in the way he manipulates the audience's perceptions.

Wilson first discusses the way in which Lang has built
into his film ambiguity about Eddie's guilt or innocence.
On the evidence we are given, we do not actually know who
Eddie is or what he has done. We may want to believe in
Eddie's innocence, but we are actually in no position to
judge. His innocence cannot be proved by logic; the robbery
and getaway sequences are filled with references to the
difficulty of seeing, so that we cannot perceive the event
clearly for ourselves; finally, Lang manipulates the viewer's
perceptions in two key sequences that might establish definite innocence--the one with Monk and Eddie in their room
together, and that of the robbery itself, where we are not
sure whose eyes we see in the back of the car.

Wilson goes on to discuss the connection Lang makes between the way people are seen and the way they are "pictured"
in various scenes. "It is," he says, "a simple transition
from questions about the pictures in the film to the same
questions about the pictures that constitute the film we
are watching." This question is dealt with directly in the
sequence where Eddie is taken off to prison, and again in
the prison scene when Joan visits Eddie. Wilson argues
that Lang is warning the audience that the film image may
reveal much less than it appears to do.

Proceeding from the central ambiguities in the film
around seeing and perceiving, Wilson moves on to consider
the ambiguities inherent in the presentation of each of the
three main characters. Eddie may be the innocent victim
of injustice that he seems to be, but he may also be a
desperate criminal who uses Joan for his own ends when cornered, and who lies to her. Joan is usually considered a loving, loyal, devoted wife, but there may be something blind,
and a little insane, about her extreme devotion to Eddie.
Her determination to see goodness in him represents a blind
faith not substantially based. Joan, Wilson concludes, "can
be read as a character whose perception of the world is
clouded by a larger vision which she will cling to at all
costs."

Father Dolan, who also sees redeeming virtue in Eddie
has similar ambivalent aspects. Lang questions the validity
of his Christian philosophy of life and death as he had
Joan's romanticism by showing how Dolan gets things wrong,
or only partly right. The last scenes of the film, where

Eddie sees Father Dolan calling him up to heaven, are intended as the final misperception that culminates a whole chain of misperceptions.

Wilson ends his article by suggesting that further work needs doing on You Only Live Once, particularly in the area of the hierarchy of human relationships that is established. Relationships in the film are always threatened by the failure of the people involved to understand each other. It is, Wilson notes, a despairing vision that Lang presents.

## 1978

485   Armour, Robert A.  Fritz Lang.  Boston:  G. K. Hall, Twayne,
      199 pp.  Filmography, short bibliography.

Yet one more book written from an unreflective, auteur point of view, Armour's text does at least break with the traditional film-by-film format.  Taking Bartlett's notion of "the dark struggle" between "the tendencies toward good and evil in man's nature" (See Entry No. 564) that fascinated Lang as the basis for his study of the works, Armour traces the theme as it emerged from the German period onwards.

Two introductory chapters present an overview of Lang's life and career; Armour shows how Lang's involvement with the notion of struggle arose from his experiences in the world wars and from the rise of nazism.  Looking at plots of Lang films throughout his career, Armour points out the focus on the exterior struggle between human beings and their fate.  Lang uses several devices to underscore the notion of struggle:  violence, hallucination, mistaken identity, and Christian symbolism.

Chapter three deals with some of Lang's visual techniques for presenting the dark struggle, such as lighting, color, sound, editing, and camera angles; Armour gives concrete examples from various films to support points.

The next two chapters argue first, for The Nibelungen as a prime example of the dark struggle, and second, for Lang's Mabuse films as reflecting his career-long fascination with the theme of the struggle between society and the criminal forces that try to rule it.

Chapter six traces the idea of social protest in Lang's films from M, Fury, and You Only Live Once to Beyond a Reasonable Doubt.  Chapter seven deals with the Westerns as representing the struggle in the West, while chapter eight explores the war and spy films from the point of view of the international struggle.  The final chapter deals with Lang's "criminal struggle," discussing briefly Scarlet Street, Woman in the Window, The Blue Gardenia, The Big Heat, Human Desire and While the City Sleeps.

The problem with the text is its lack of methodological

sophistication together with the choice of a theme that is too broad to be really useful. Given the format of the book, Armour had to find a way to include all the films somehow, and often one senses the tension in stretching the concept of the "dark struggle" to fit the works. Little that is new is illuminated through this approach.

486    Carroll, Noel. "Two Evil Geniuses. Review of <u>Spione</u> [Spies]." <u>Soho Weekly</u> (New York) (28 September).
    This article was written on the occasion of the screening of Lang's original version of the film at the Lincoln Film Festival in New York. The complete version was a reconstruction done by the Munich Stadtmuseum and took twice the time of the prints now available. After a brief outline of the plot, Carroll notes that Haighi is more than an individual, symbolizing rather the "disruption and chaos that is associated with a monomaniacal drive for power." The world of the film is one where most people are not what they originally seemed to be and where people spy on each other. Yet despite the paranoia in the film, true love manages to overcome evil.
    According to Carroll, the film is more like a serial than a narrative that moves toward an inevitable denouement. Yet this fits in with Lang's reflection of "the paranoid belief in virtual omnipotence and the indestructability of wickedness."
    Carroll ends by commenting on the richness of Lang's visual style and his brilliant use of symbolism. Haighi's disguise as a cripple suggests that a life devoted to the pursuit of power is a maimed one. The ending, with the crosscutting and the lack of establishing shots, conveys the atmosphere of paranoid fantasy splendidly. While the composition is sparse, for the most part, Lang introduces profusion reflecting the rush of feeling when fitting, as in the scene where Tremaine and the agent fall in love.

487    Carroll, Noel. "Lang, Pabst and Sound." <u>Cine-tracts</u>, 2, No. 1 (Fall), 15-23.
    Carroll discusses Lang's <u>M</u> in the context of analysing various responses by directors to the coming of sound in 1930. He divides directors into those like Eisenstein, who recommended montage as the paradigm for dealing with sound, resulting in the "silent sound" film; and those like Renoir, who (in Bazin's theory) "opposed the silent film predisposition towards stylization and manipulation" and believed in film as recording.
    The first part of Carroll's article deals with <u>M</u> as an example of the first type of sound film (with Pabst's <u>Kamaradshaft</u> as the second type). Carroll shows the importance of montage in <u>M</u> and analyses the parallel development of the gangster and police strategies for capturing

the murderer. Lang's commitment to montage shapes his attitude to the sound track, so that he makes sound imitate
editing in a montage parallel to the visual one.
    Carroll next shows the links between this approach to
sound and Lang's themes, Eisenstein being the model for what
Lang is doing. <u>M</u> is, above all, about the process of investigation, and Lang's visual and sound techniques force the
viewer to become an investigator in relation to the film,
as the detective within the film is in relation to his clues.
The viewing experience of the spectator thus simulates that
of the fictional characters within the film.
    Carroll concludes, after the discussion of the Pabst
film, that sound caused a major theoretical crisis in the
film world. It could function as an element of manipulation
in the silent paradigm (as in <u>M</u>) or could enhance film's
capacity for recording. Carroll makes it clear that he is
not valuing one use over the other, but showing that both
exist.

487a*  Clancy, L. "Director and Screenwriter: a Reading of Lang's
       <u>While the City Sleeps</u>." <u>Australian Journal of Screen Theory</u>
       (Sydney), No. 4, pp. 33-38.
           This article discusses the problematical relationship
       between the roles of director and scriptwriter, with special
       reference to Lang's <u>While the City Sleeps</u>.

488    Comolli, Jean et Géré, François. "Deux Fictions de la Haine."
       <u>Cahiers du Cinéma</u> (Paris), No. 286 (March), pp. 30-48.
           The authors begin by wondering what function Hollywood
       films can serve today--can they be more than a collection
       of souvenirs or fetishes?
           In their first section, Comolli and Géré discuss the
       odd conjunction of two films, <u>Hangmen Also Die</u> by Lang and
       Lubitsch's <u>To Be or Not to Be</u>. Both made in 1942, neither
       film has been revered by cinéastes, Lang's because of the
       Brechtian games, Lubitsch's because it was too bitter.
       Poland and Czechoslovakia, the referents of the film, are
       alike in recalling old Europe before the Nazis; they symbol-
       ize the origins of many American values like democracy and
       humanism, according to the myth that America is made up of
       bits of old Europe.
           In the second section on Hollywood propaganda, the
       authors place the films in the context of the need to coun-
       teract pacifist, isolationist tendencies. Many Americans
       hesitated to go against nazism because of a certain attrac-
       tion to it, so films were made showing nazism as <u>mise-en-
       scène</u>--the manipulation of appearances, a false show. Each
       film contains two kinds of representation: one showing
       nazism as evil, the other showing its opposite--forces of
       truth, liberty, and generosity. Like all propaganda,
       Hollywood sets up an enemy that is not only detestable but

which can also be resisted and overcome.

The third section of the article begins the detailed examination of <u>Hangmen Also Die</u>. The authors note the contrasting images of the two opposed groups, the rigidity of the Nazis being set off by the relaxed, derisive attitude of the workers. Heydrich demands that the machines roll, but the next time we see him, he is dead. Comolli and Géré discuss the image of his body as having a sexual, erotic element, which is linked to the castration the Nazis imposed on others; Heydrich alone, as the all-powerful one, was allowed sexuality. One can see here the pattern of Lang's symbolism, which attaches the look to death, desire to loss, and joy to castration. This fits in with Lang's metaphysic of loss and punishment, a system of negation, of lack, which can be seen in a pattern of flight and pursuit through which the fiction advances. Even before we learn of Heydrich's death, we see Svoboda in flight; he is seen by Miss Novotny, who, perceiving what she was not supposed to, is caught in a web of lies. The audience, by virtue of knowing that she has seen Svoboda, is made to participate in the trap to which the fiction predestines them. In Lang's system, truth leads to death--even if it is only the symbolic death of the forced happy endings--and lies, no matter how justified, are bad.

The resistance group in the film is in an impossible trap, caught between the two sides of death: if they tell the truth, and declare the assassin, they kill the popular resistance movement completely; if they conceal it, hundreds of hostages die. Lang's slyness lies in his placing of the old debate between life and ideas, individual sacrifice versus collective responsibility, in a context familiar to the liberal, humanist, democratic American spectator. This point of view is clear in the debates within the Novotny household and among the people of Prague. It also results in an identification with the oppressed Czechs: if they give up Svoboda, they reinforce the power of the Nazis; but if they refuse, they lose the hostages and make themselves part of the Nazi death machine by putting the machine above individual lives. Those who have the secret cannot declare it (the resistance workers for the above reasons; Svoboda because his life is no longer his own--he's a symbol of revolt; Novotny because he represents the Law, a transcendental value). Miss Novotny, however, represents the doubting conscience of the ordinary person and is most caught up in all the ambiguities.

The Nazis, on the other side, are nearly all put in one group: they are suffused with Nazi negativity--uniforms, arrogance, brutality, stupidity; they lack truth, not so much because they are evil as that they lack anything human. Unthinking machines, they represent pure hate.

But on the Nazi side is also police inspector Gruber--

without rituals and uniform, not professing nazism. A
classic Lang detective, Gruber's search for truth is for
its own sake, for the challenge that it offers, but also
because of the relief of finding someone on the Nazi side
who is human and uses his intelligence. Gruber is moreover
given a solid presence accorded few characters; the good
characters are particularly invisible--Prof. Novotny, Miss
Novotny, Svoboda, the fiancé. Svoboda is especially phan-
tomelike, since he had to be "invisible" to do the murder,
and he has a double who covered for him at the hospital.

Only a few secondary characters have bodies: Heydrich,
Czaka, Gruber. But Gruber, as we have seen, is so placed
in the narrative as to prevent identification with him; yet,
because of his bodily actions, he has vitality and energy,
and presents a strong contrast always to the others, highlighting their unreality. The authors make their point by
using the scene where Miss Novotny and Svoboda fake a love-
scene to provide a cover for the wounded resistance leader
they are hiding. Gruber is not taken in by any of the surface arrangements and appears to us as the most real person
in the situation, highlighting the bloodlessness of the
others and their links with death. Significant is the fact
that Gruber, being a working-class man, only drinks beer,
but the wine of these bourgeois resistance workers ironically
saves them from detection: the wine covers the blood from
the wounded leader. Gruber leaves, but still tries to test
the scene that he has witnessed. He provides the audience
with a lesson in reading, making us aware of the difficulties
of knowing, of detecting truth. A little later on, the
authors show how we are attracted to Gruber, despite the
side he is on, because he uses his intelligence, his powers
of logic and deduction, while the rest of the Nazis are
emptied of all proper substance. And finally Gruber does
arrive at the truth. The authors analyze this moment in
some detail.

Knowing that something is not right, Gruber takes Miss
Novotny's fiancé out for a night on the town hoping to prize
some information out of him. In the morning as the prostitutes leave, Gruber, with the help of the fiancé, finally
stumbles on the truth that he lacked. The fiancé sees a
smudge of lipstick on Gruber's cheek, and at once realizes,
through comparing the natural look of this smudge with the
now clearly artificial one on Svoboda's cheek, that the
other scene had been fake. Gruber, catching the fiancé's
look in the mirror, suddenly understands it all himself.
Comolli and Géré explore in a fascinating way all the implications of the exchanges between the two men, including
their effect on the audience, who sees Gruber seeing. We
are put in a state of conflict through the forced identification with Gruber and have to examine what being on the
side of the hostages really means. Is it really a different

375

side from that of the executioners?

In the final section, "The Hate of the Spectator," the authors show how Gruber, knowing truth, now necessarily runs to his death. Going to the hospital, he at once sees through Svoboda's alibi, since he meets him coming from an operation, the surgical mask making him indistinguishable from his assistant. Comolli and Géré analyze in the same fashion the scene where Gruber is killed as that where Gruber detected truth, showing how we see the resistance men as Gruber sees them--two implacable machines converging on him, two forces of hate occupying the place of the executioners. The previously heroic resistance workers are now reduced to the level of the Nazis; the Nazi machine is opposed by an equally implacable, pitiless, and unyielding machine. The death of Czaka, which follows, reinforces the machine aspect of the resistance workers, for although Czaka did much wrong, he is killed for what he did not do. The spectator is condemned also: we have to pay for being spectators and are made to lose all our ideological support for good causes, our desire for truth, and our illusions of justice. We have to submit to the law of deceit and have no more choice than the characters but to come to the point of absolute hate.

489    Hennelly, Mark M., Jr. "American Nightmare: The Underworld in Film." Journal of Popular Film (Bowling Green, Ohio), 6, No. 3, 240-261.

Hennelly uses Lang's You Only Live Once and The Big Heat as examples in an article on the American gangster film. The scene in You Only Live Once where the hotel keeper and his wife quarrel over Eddie Taylor (played by Henry Fonda) suggests both domestic tranquillity, in the reference to Whistler, and the attraction of the criminal world for a nation of frustrated and repressed shopkeepers (e.g., the way the husband is determined to track down Eddie's image in his piles of magazines about convicts). Hennelly later discusses the film in connection with the helplessness of both orthodox religion and of established justice in the underworld.

The Big Heat is referred to in connection with the iconography of the gangster film, and (linked now to You Only Live Once) in a discussion of underworld "estrangement." Both Bannion and Eddie are forced into vengeful lawlessness.

Hennelly finally returns to You Only Live Once as representing the ambivalent attitudes of the American middle class to the underworld and criminals. The audience is lead by Lang to consider Eddie guilty, only to find out that he's in fact innocent. When Eddie turns to the lynch mob and cries, "It's fun to see a man die, isn't it?", he is really hurling the insult at the voyeuristic mob in the theater.

490    Kaplan, E. Ann.  "The Place of Women in The Blue Gardenia."
       In Women in Film Noir.  Edited by E. Ann Kaplan.  London:
       British Film Institute, pp. 83-90.
           Kaplan begins by noting that in the typical film noir
       the world is presented from the point of view of a reassur-
       ing, male investigator, who seeks to unravel a mystery that
       he has been presented with.  The female characters, on the
       other hand, symbolize all that is evil and mysterious, and
       they stand outside the male order as a challenge to it.
       They use their sexuality to entrap the investigator, so
       that he must guard against their desireability if he is to
       succeed in his quest.
           Kaplan goes on to argue that in The Blue Gardenia, Lang
       turns film noir conventions upside down by presenting two
       separate discourses, two modes of articulating a vision of
       reality.  Lang has inserted the discourse of Norah, a young
       telephone operator, alongside that of Mayo, a journalist
       here functioning as the investigator.
           Through a close analysis of The Blue Gardenia, Kaplan
       shows how Lang's treatment of Norah exposes male assumptions
       about women in films noir.  By juxtaposing the male dis-
       course, within the mode of film noir conventions, to that
       of Norah, Lang reveals elements of the discourse that usually
       go unquestioned.
           Moving through the film sequence by sequence, Kaplan
       shows the gradual invasion of the comfortable women's world
       of work and home by the increasingly threatening presence
       of men, first in the form of a letter of rejection from
       Norah's fiancé, then in the form of the determined seducer,
       Harry Prebble, and finally that of the police and Mayo,
       relentlessly tracking down the murderer.
           The alternation between the discourses, particularly
       those of Mayo and of Norah, "places" what Mayo is doing,
       allowing us to see it for what it is.  In the usual film
       noir, the investigator's entrapment of the murderer is a
       sign of his triumph over sexuality and evil, but here Mayo
       is seen as engineering a despicable betrayal of Norah, whose
       dilemma he exploits for a publicity stunt.
           As often in Lang films, the ending undercuts the move-
       ment of the film proper, but despite the fact that all the
       structures defining men and women are safely back in place
       in the last shots, Lang has exposed the place women occupy
       in films noir.  The view men have of women is seen to be
       false, in that the set of implications about Norah generated
       by the male world turn out to be invalid.  The Blue Gardenia
       reveals the essential contradiction between the dominant
       male discourse and the subordinate (repressed) discourse
       of women in patriarchy.

490a   Roth, Lane.  "Metropolis: The Lights Fantastic:  Semiotic
       Analysis of Lighting Codes in Relation to Character and

Theme." Literature/Film Quarterly (Salisbury, Maryland), 6, No. 4 (Fall), 342-346.

Roth begins by noting the importance of the main theme of Metropolis--that of the negative impact of technology on man's social and spiritual progress. This theme is express- ed through the lighting codes used in connection with three main characters--Rotwang, Maria, and the robotrix.

The contrast between the real and false Maria is develop- ed, according to Roth, through the use of light. The real Maria is lit either by a halo of sunlight or by the "natural" light of candles, while the false Maria is created in the artificial electric light of the laboratory.

Furthermore, Roth shows how the real Maria is linked to spirit and to God, while the false Maria is soulless, en- tirely manmade. Like the city that she represents, the false Maria lacks warmth, a heart.

Roth goes on to contrast Rotwang and the real Maria; she signifies community, while he represents cold isolation; she represents innocence, purity and Christianity, while he stands for a mixture of the evil use of science and sorcery. Their roles are designated by their contrasting white and black dress; furthermore, she is encircled by light, he by darkness. Rotwang stifles Maria's candlelight with his electric torch, with which he then entraps her.

Roth notes the symbolism of Rotwang's truncated arm; the loss of his hand reflects the destructiveness of technology and underscores the main theme that mechanical marvels will not alone improve man's condition.

In conclusion, Roth notes the symbolic descent of Rotwang from the Cathedral roof to his death (Hell). Meanwhile the false Maria's artificial light is extinguished in natural fire and the whole city is reborn in the dawning day.

## 1979

490b* Audibert, L. "L'ombre du son." Cinématographe (Paris), No. 48 (June), pp. 5-10.
The article studies the reactions of three directors to the coming of sound, looking at Murnau's Tabu, Lang's M, and Von Sternberg's Der Blaue Engel [The Blue Angel].

491 Bergstrom, Janet. "Narrative Conventions in the Films of Fritz Lang." Ph.D. Dissertation, University of California at Los Angeles.
Bergstrom's dissertation is a study of conventions of the American cinema as they emerge from close analysis of selected Lang films, including Die Nibelungen, Fury, You Only Live Once, Scarlet Street, Secret Beyond the Door, Human Desire, Beyond a Reasonable Doubt, Der Tiger Von Eschnapur [The Tiger of Bengal], and Das Indische Grabmal

[The Indian Tomb].

Bergstrom begins by contrasting the pre- and post-American Lang; she continues with a chapter contrasting Lang's Scarlet Street and Human Desire with the La Fouchardière and Zola novels on which they were based, and with Renoir's La Chienne and La Bête Humaine, made from the same originals.

The chapter on Secret Beyond the Door deals with the relationship between psychoanalysis (in the American cinema of the 1940s), and melodrama, examining in particular the woman's place with respect to enunciation, for example, the voice-over and the organization of the flash-backs.

A further chapter explores the films that deal with circumstantial evidence and "truth," the law and inferential judgement--Fury, You Only Live Once, and Beyond a Reasonable Doubt.

Another chapter compares Die Nibelungen and the Indian films, while the one on Le Mépris includes discussion of Godard's fascination with the conventions of the American cinema and particularly with Lang's films.

Bergstrom's method combines stylistic, thematic, and psychoanalytic approaches.

491a   Haller, Robert. Review of Eisner, Lotte. Fritz Lang. New York, 1977; Ott, Frederick. The Films of Fritz Lang. Secaucus, N. J.: Citadel Press, 1979; Focus on Fritz Lang: An Audio-Text Cassette (Center for Cassette Studies Los Angeles, 1973); and Die Spinnen [The Spiders]. Field of Vision (West Coast), No. 7, pp. 29-30.

Haller notes the increase in the quality and quantity of works on Lang available since his death in 1976. There is a growing awareness that Lang's films represent a unique and vital body of work, involving much more than some peripheral connection to a film movement like expressionism.

While recognizing the new information about Lang contained in Eisner's book, Haller regrets the errors in dealing with the American films and the evident bias against many of these works. Eisner apparently was relying on Lang's scripts rather than the films themselves. Her treatment of the Lang-Harbou relationship is also inadequate.

Ott's book is useful, according to Haller, for the translations of reviews and reports of interviews with Lang. There are also many pictures and posters, but Ott again gives less space and value to the American films.

The cassette tape does not provide new information on Lang, but is valuable simply for giving us his strong, confident voice.

Haller concludes with a brief discussion of the new print of Die Spinnen toned in several colors and comments on what an excellent print does for these old films. The film, while slow-moving in the second half, nevertheless prepares for Lang's later German projects.

492  Humphries, Reynold. <u>Le Cinéma auto-reflexif et la place du spectateur</u>. Ph.D. Dissertation, École des Hautes Études en Sciences Sociales. (Director of Studies: Christian Metz).

The thesis is on self-reflexive cinema with reference to ten of Lang's American films. (The choice of films was determined partly by availability, but also by their interest and significance for the project.) The dissertation includes a chapter on Welles's <u>Lady from Shanghai</u> as a way for Humphries to show the ambiguity inherent in any attempt, within the dominant cinema, to draw attention to the cinematic signifier.

Humphries takes a semiotic, psychoanalytic approach to the cinematic signifier and the placing of the spectator. He deals with the problems of representation--the articulation of the spectatorial look, the look of the camera, and the diegetic look. This problematic is discussed in relation to the means of representation within the diegesis: newsreel (<u>Fury</u>); photography (<u>Beyond a Reasonable Doubt</u>); newspapers (<u>The Blue Gardenia</u> and <u>You Only Live Once</u>); the problem of identification and role-playing (<u>Hangmen Also Die</u>, <u>Ministry of Fear</u>, <u>Cloak and Dagger</u>, <u>Rancho Notorious</u>). Reynolds focuses particularly on <u>Woman in the Window</u> and <u>Scarlet Street</u>, the first because of the conflict between the supposed meaning of the dream and the extreme naturalism of the enunciation; the second because of the subversion of the film's literal project (only the husband is mad) by a variety of specific cinematic codes, such as voice-off and lighting, which show that the wife is also neurotic. There is a final chapter on elements of suture in Lang, such as fade-out, and ways of linking scenes (the imaginary reference).

492a  Nau, Peter. "Die Kunst des Filmsehens." <u>Filmkritik</u> (Munich), No. 270 (June), pp. 250-252. (Reviews of <u>Hangmen Also Die</u> and <u>While the City Sleeps</u>.)

In a very brief review, Nau compares <u>Hangmen Also Die</u> to Lubitsch's <u>To Be or Not To Be</u> in that the heroes in both cases scheme to outwit the Nazis in a nerve-wracking situation. <u>Hangmen</u>, according to Nau, is constructed so that actions belie the reality; this is particularly true in relation to the comical love-affair, which contradicts the actual entanglement of the lovers that is grounded in the struggle against the Nazis.

Nau begins his review of <u>While the City Sleeps</u> with discussing the myth of the City that the film revolves around. The film conjures up the myth of the city as a living creature that gradually lays down to sleep, but in whose womb, as morning dawns, there lies a pretty girl who will wake no more. But in the end the film works to destroy the Hollywood myth of journalists that is unjustified by actual careers.

Nau next goes into some detail about the complicated plot

of the film, and concludes that Lang overloads his films with actions. He is here contrasted with Straub, whose Nicht versöhnt also contains a complicated plot. But all is carefully constructed in Straub, while Lang's film, in depending on coincidences (such as Dorothy and Harry meeting in an apartment next to Nancy's) runs the danger of falling from a veritable thriller into a domestic comedy.

493    Ott, Frederick W. The Films of Fritz Lang. Secaucus, N. J.:
       Citadel Press.
            This is an attractively produced text, full of stills
       and photographs of materials related to the films (such as
       the German posters advertising works being shown). Ott in-
       troduces his filmography with a lengthy biography of Lang,
       gathering together information by Lang and critics about
       his work and life. Ott interviewed Lang himself, and he
       has done research on Lang and his films in German film in-
       stitutes. Each film is introduced by quotations from re-
       views, which are particularly interesting in relation to
       the early German works. There is a short synopsis of and
       comment on each film. While not adding anything really
       new, this text is responsibly put together. It is, however,
       somewhat redundant in the light of Lotte Eisner's recent
       book, which contains much more information. (See Entry No.
       478.)

493a   Petley, Julian. "Review of Hangmen Also Die." Focus on Film
       (London), No. 32 (April), pp. 34-38.
            Petley begins by surveying briefly the problems Brecht
       encountered when working on Hangmen Also Die and that un-
       fortunately paralleled those he had already experienced
       twelve years earlier in Germany with The Threepenny Opera.
       According to Petley, the generally accepted view is that
       Lang and Wexley betrayed Brecht.
            However this may be, Petley says that Hangmen differs in
       many ways from the usual Hollywood war films and also de-
       parts from traditional Hollywood narrative form in ways
       that can be related to Brecht's theatrical practice and to
       certain Brechtian strategies in Lang's own work.
            Petley proceeds to compare Hangmen to a Brechtian
       lehrstück (didactic play), aimed at teaching people in
       America about a war that was little understood.
            Giving concrete examples from the film, Petley shows how
       Hangmen departs from the fiercely individualistic ethos of
       most Hollywood cinema of the time by having brute force and
       cunning overwhelmed by mass action and the bravery of ordi-
       nary people. The schematism of the characters is, accord-
       ing to Petley, quite deliberate, and shows Lang's applica-
       tion of Brecht's theories of acting as the externalization
       of feelings and the display of attitudes.
            Petley concludes by noting the indirect violence that

lies beneath the film's surface. He also comments on the
way the film grows out of Lang's earlier concerns with
supercriminals like Dr. Mabuse. Heydrich is a direct des-
cendent in that he is at once fascinating and horrendous.
He reflects the modern tendency of eroticizing fascism.

<u>1980</u>

493b    Fischer, Lucy. "Dr. Mabuse and Mr. Lang." <u>Wideangle</u>, 3, No.
3 (Winter).
Fischer begins by outlining a theoretical framework concerning the relationship between authorial style and moral
position, which she will use in her analysis of Lang's <u>Das
Testament des Dr. Mabuse</u> [The Last Will of Dr. Mabuse].
Robert Weimann's <u>Structure and Society in Literary History</u>
provides the context for a political reading of the film,
which Fischer justifies by noting the historical moment of
the film's making and the way the narrative style itself
raises questions about the author's narrative method and
social point of view. The film was produced at the moment
of Nazi accession to power and was followed shortly by
Lang's departure from Germany.
Fischer summarizes the complicated reaction to the film,
both on the part of Goebbels, as Culture Minister, and Lang
himself, who subsequently claimed that the film was directed
against the Nazis (a claim that critics have often questioned).
Fischer proceeds to demonstrate the superficiality of
analogies between the mad Dr. Mabuse and Hitler and between
events in the film and the period of Hitler's rise to power.
But Fischer agrees that on the narrative level the film is
antiauthoritarian: the plot establishes Mabuse's illegiti-
macy as a leader and it proceeds to have him defeated. But
Fischer goes on to show that the narrative <u>style</u> reveals a
message counter to that of Lang's professed intentions.
Beginning with an analysis of offscreen sound, Fischer
shows that it connotes a menacing power. Baum controls the
band of criminals through his offscreen voice (the recording
machine), while Mabuse controls Baum in turn through offscreen voices (the spirit of Mabuse working through him).
But the most powerful offscreen narrator is the film director, presenting the tale to us.
According to Fischer, the normal, Hollywood spatio-
temporal or causal relationship of events to one another is
replaced in Lang's film by sequences linked by associational
leaps. She distinguishes three kinds of leaps: those linking events by a related concept (e.g., madness); those linked through repetition of the subject of the shot; and sequences linked purely through sound. This, Fischer says,
reveals the offscreen presence of the director as a powerful

mind, and she finds this significant in a film about the
hypnotic powers of a Mabuse.

Next, Fischer turns to iconography to develop further
her analysis of the links between the offscreen narrator
and Mabuse. The "sound" illusion that Baum creates for his
men is a metaphor for the sound medium in film; there is an
analogy between the tools of the dictators--Baum, Mabuse--
and of Lang. "His narrative style," Fischer notes, "strongly posits the sense of an overriding mental force which controls the presentation of the cinematic story . . . ."
Lang seems both to assert and to relish his power as offscreen narrator and is here very like Mabuse, who is a menacing political force. She concludes that "Lang does not so
much defeat the authoritarian powers of Baum/Mabuse as substitute for them the authorial powers of Lang."

494    Jenkins, Stephen, ed. Fritz Lang. London: British Film
       Institute.
           Part of the BFI's Occasional Publications series, Jenkins's
       book consists, first, of an introduction describing English
       and French critical responses to the Lang text and locating
       the auteur position historically rather than seeing it as
       the 'key' to works. Jenkins here argues that there is no
       possible 'key,' since the text is unstable, created anew
       with every reading of it. Similar to Willemen in his Ophuls
       book (BFI, 1978) (cf. chapter 2 of this text, ed.), Jenkins
       sees Lang as "the space where a multiplicity of discourses
       intersect and interact." He shows the interaction of a
       specific group of films (Lang's filmography) with particular
       (and historically locatable) ways of reading and viewing
       those films.
           There follows a series of translations of central French
       texts:
       (1) Philippe Demonsablon's "La Hautaine Dialectique de
               Fritz Lang." Cahiers du Cinéma (September 1959);
               (See Entry No. 244).
       (2) Michel Mourlet's "Trajectoire de Fritz Lang." Cahiers
               du Cinéma (September 1959); (See Entry No. 250).
       (3) Jean-Louis Comolli and François Géré's "Deux Fictions
               de la Haine." Cahiers du Cinéma (March 1978); (See
               Entry No. 488).
       (4) Raymond Bellour's "Sur Fritz Lang." Translated in
               Sub-Stance, No. 9 (1974); (See Entry No. 351).
           Jenkins concludes by providing notes for twelve Lang
       films, replacing the idea of destiny with that of patriarchy,
       and thus reading the films as workings through of the oedi-
       pal drama, with woman as "problem" for the text to deal with.
       Focus is on the foregrounding of forms of representation/
       specularity across the text.

494a   Kaplan, E. Ann, and Don Willis. "Lang and his Critics." Film

Quarterly (Berkeley, Calif.), 33, No. 4 (Summer), 62-63.
This consists first in a letter by Kaplan replying to
Willis's article "Fritz Lang: Only Melodrama" (see Entry
No. 495b), followed by Willis' response. The argument
hinges essentially on the degree to which Lang has been
overpraised as an artist; Willis and Kaplan disagree about
the critical context suitable for evaluating Lang's achievements, and about his ultimate importance. Willis remains
convinced that Lang reduces "complex social issues to melodrama (and low-level melodrama at that, in some cases),"
while Kaplan argues that Lang at times uses the melodrama
form to make important political, moral, and human statements using the cinematic apparatus in a sophisticated
manner.

495  Kaplan, E. Ann. "Expressionism and the Flight from Family:
     A Reading of Lang's Dr. Mabuse, der Spieler." Socialist
     Review, No. 57 (May-June), pp. 115-127.
     Kaplan begins by tracing briefly the damage done to Lang's
critical reputation by Siegfried Kracauer's From Caligari to
Hitler (1947). She then outlines some of the recent theoretical developments that have resulted in renewed interest
in Lang and that show the influence of Brecht, Gramsci, the
Frankfurt School, and of semiology and structuralism in
France. These theories of ideology and culture are useful
in correcting simplistic sociological readings of film and
in showing how media representations affect our ways of
perceiving in daily life.
     Kaplan turns from here to the expressionist revolt and
its underlying aesthetic, which tried to replace traditional
bourgeois images with the individual artist's unique way of
seeing. This entailed a rejection of realist forms for nonrealist ones, for example in Caligari and Raskolnikov, which
break with the conventional codes of representation and
narrativity in film.
     Recent work by Comolli and Géré on Lang's Hangmen Also
Die showed that even when working with surface realism,
Lang plays with realist representations in order to expose
their falseness and simplicity.
     Kaplan then turns to a detailed analysis of Lang's Dr.
Mabuse, the Gambler, showing how Lang produces a powerful
sense of abnormality by the deliberate repression of the
idea of the family. She argues that the flight from family
was one of the elements that shaped expressionism and that
involved a basic contradiction between the rejection of
family as an oppressive institution and the simultaneous
longing for the comfort and safety that the family symbolizes.
     Analyzing the main worlds of Dr. Mabuse, Kaplan shows
that the absence of the family in both the worlds of the

ruling class and of the disaffected petty bourgeoisie en-
tails emptiness and alienation. The absence of the family
in addition means the disturbance of traditional sex-roles,
particularly in relation to men. The decline of old-style
governmental authority in the state is reflected in the decline of the traditional, patriarchal family; ruling class
men have now become weak, passive, and effeminate. The
women represent an extreme negation of the mother image and
are even more passive than the men.

After detailing the mise-en-scène that reflects Lang's
attitude to the world of the rich, Kaplan turns to the petty
bourgeois world ruled by Mabuse. Here it is the absence
of the family that enables Mabuse to take control; he becomes the patriarch, offering a surrogate family. There
is a degree of energy here due to the dedication to a cause,
even if a perverse one, and Kaplan demonstrates the contrast
between listlessness and activity by contrasting Countess
Told and Cara, the dancer. Kaplan also contrasts von Wenk,
nominally the investigator, who is weak, passive, and inadequate to his role, with Mabuse, whose drive, energy, and
masculinity reflect the qualities that the representative
of order ought to have (and in fact does have in the normal
detective genre).

In the concluding section of the article, Kaplan shows
how Lang deliberately manipulates the spectator's identifi-
cations so as to produce the ambivalences and contradictions
that give Dr. Mabuse its complexity and status as art.
Most disturbing of all is the forced identification with
Mabuse himself. Like other expressionist works, this film
functions by negating bourgeois codes in order to reveal
their inadequacy and vulnerability to subversion from tyrannical forces. Paradoxically, Dr. Mabuse evokes by negation
images of the repressed idealized family that the expressionists were in flight from. Lang's vision is limited in
that, not seeing alternatives between chaos and tyranny, he
allows for nostalgic images of a mythic, idealized past pre-
dating the machine.

Lang's limitations are, Kaplan concludes, those of expressionism itself. While trying to delegitimize bourgeois
codes, the movement was never able to transcend them; expressionist attacks on bourgeois rationalism are evident in
the rejection of logic, scientific causality, and instrumental reason. But by tying themselves to a rejection of
bourgeois codes, the expressionists were unable to move beyond them. The delegitimation of rationalism was progressive and the assertion of love, passion, and concern for
the human person defied materialistic, bourgeois codes, but
Lang's films do not provide adequate solutions to the problems depicted.

495a   Kaplan, E. Ann. "Patterns of Violence Toward Women in Fritz

Lang's <u>While the City Sleeps</u>." <u>Wideangle</u>, 3, No. 4
(Spring), 55-59.

Kaplan begins by noting that, as feminist historians have
shown, violence against women changes according to changes
in the traditional bourgeois family. The extension of violence upward through the classes after the two world wars
is reflected in films from Griffith, through <u>films noir</u> and
on up to the films of the 1950s, where representations become more complex due to a shift away from the tough, viril
hero to images of weak, feminized men. Lang's images of
such men are particularly interesting because he links them
to the public sphere, showing the implications for social
institutions.

Kaplan includes a brief discussion of Lang's <u>M</u>, because
of its close links to <u>While the City Sleeps</u>. <u>M</u> exposes the
psychosis that modern civilization has increasingly spawned;
Beckert, the murderer, is a prototype of the sick, alienated,
and "feminized" male (evident in his stance and appearance),
who became more frequent in the post-World War II period.
Trapped by impulses deep in his unconscious, Beckert's violence against little girls is his attempt to assert his
masculinity. Elsie is especially vulnerable since her
father is absent and her mother bowed down by hard work.
The level of the unconscious is repressed in <u>M</u> since Lang
was at the time more interested in criticizing an inadequate
leadership and bankrupt social institutions.

Kaplan goes on to show that in <u>While the City Sleeps</u>
Lang returns to the themes of <u>M</u>, only now he links the theme
of the decline of male authority to that of violence against
women. This linking is clear first in the figure of the
young murderer, Manners, who is presented as suffering from
overidentification with his mother, the father being weak
and absent. But it is repeated in the character of Walter
Kyne, also presented as a weak, effeminate son, this time
because of an overindulgent father. Unlike Manners, who
projects his violence outward onto innocent women, crippling
his personal relations, Kyne projects his violence onto the
people he deals with as new director of the Kyne firm.

After contrasting the old-style leadership of Amos Kyne,
Walter's father, with Walter's cynical, new-style leadership, Kaplan explores the degeneration of the virile, <u>noir</u>
investigator represented by Ed Mobley. No longer an aggressive, heroic figure, Mobley is morally, ambiguous both in the
methods he uses to trap Manners and in relation to his girlfriend, Nancy. Ed, like Kyne, stands in close relation to
the murderer, Manners, who simply represents a more extreme
version of tendencies in the men who have power.

Lang's conservative longing for the patriarchal male
figure who (the work of the film suggests) could prevent
such expressions of violence and such cyncicism, is evident
in his treatment of the three main women in the film,

Dorothy Kyne, Mildred, and Nancy Leggett. Walter's effeminacy is seen as resulting in his wife's promiscuity and her rather distasteful lustfulness, while Mildred is an example of the single woman who inevitably becomes seductive and scheming because her sexuality is not safely tied to a man. But while we expect negative images in these variations of the noir femme fatale, more surprising is the negative treatment of the one "good" presence in the film, Mobley's girlfriend, Nancy. Again, the suggestion is that Nancy's prudishness is a result of Mobley's lack of reliability and moral strength.

The "revolutionary" aspects of the film thus lie in the exposure of the bankruptcy of established male values in capitalism; but while Lang exposes the abuse of women once they are no longer protected by the bourgeois family, he does not allow women to speak for themselves or to assert a discourse in the face of the corrupt male one. Rather than seeking alternatives to the decline of the family, Lang instead suggests that modern society's ills stem from the erosion of old-style patriarchal authority.

495b   Willis, Don. "Fritz Lang: Only Melodrama." Film Quarterly, 33, No. 2 (Winter 1979-80), 2-11.

Don Willis notes that the context for his article is the publication of a series of English-language books on Lang over the past few years. Willis states that Lang's reputation looks less formidable now than at the time of the Los Angeles County Museum retrospective of his films ten years ago.

Willis discusses briefly the books of Eisner and Armour, finding both unenlightening and unsatisfactory. He suggests that there may be a correlation between the quality of an artist's work and the quality of the criticism it inspires. Willis notes that several critics defending Lang sound as though they are apologizing for him; in the end, Willis says, we find that Lang was indeed no more than a director of "thrillers."

Moving chronologically through Lang's German films, Willis points out their stiffness and awkwardness, their dramatic inadequacy, and clichés.

Turning to the American films, Willis objects first to the terminology used to describe Lang's work and universe; while people talk grandiosely of the world of fate or chance, what they all seem to be talking about in the end is simply plot. It amounts, says Willis, to the difference between trying to hide the mess one has made (Metropolis) or calling attention to it (You Only Live Once). Discussing each American film in turn, Willis points to the plot contrivances that critics claim reflect a concept of fate. He contrasts the hollowness of Lang's work to the richness and depth in von Sternberg's films, and he finds only Scarlet Street really well constructed. The films reflecting the "darker" Lang--<u>M</u>, <u>Das Testament</u> [The Last Will], <u>Fury</u>, <u>The Big Heat</u>, and <u>While the City Sleeps</u> are more worthwhile, but Willis concludes that <u>Liliom</u>, the film least shown or known, reflects Lang at his finest (except for <u>Kriemhild's Revenge</u>).

# Writings, Performances, and Other Film Related Activity

(This list of scripts is from Frieda Grafe and Enno Patalas, Fritz Lang. Munich: Hanser, 1976.)

496    Die Hochzeit im Exzentrik Klub
       1917
       Director:            Joe May
       Screenplay:          Fritz Lang
       Photography:         Carl Hoffmann
       Cast:                Harry Liedtke [Joe Debbs], Magda
                            Magdaleine, Bruno Kastner, Paul
                            Westermeier, Käthe Haack
       Produced by:         May-Film

497    Hilde Warren und der Tod
       1917
       Director:            Joe May
       Screenplay:          Fritz Lang
       Photography:         Curt Courant
       Cast:                Mia May, Fritz Lang, Hans Mierendorff,
                            Bruno Kastner, Georg John
       Produced by:         May-Film

498    Die Rache ist mein
       1918/19
       Director:            Alwin Neub
       Screenplay:          Fritz Lang
       Cast:                Otto Paul, Alwin Neub, Arnold Czempin,
                            Helga Molander, Marta Daghofer (= Lil
                            Dagover), Hanni Rheinwald
       Produced by:         Decla

389

499 Bettler GmbH
    1918/19
    Director:                    unknown
    Screenplay:                  Fritz Lang
    Cast:                        Alwin Neub, Fred Selva-Goebel, Fritz
                                 Achterberg, Otto Paul, Marta
                                 Daghofer (= Lil Dagover)
    Produced by:                 Decla

500 Wolkenbau und Flimmerstern
    1919
    Director:                    unknown
    Screenplay:                  Wolfgang Geiger, Fritz Lang
    Cast:                        Margarete Frey, Karl Gebhard-Schröder,
                                 Albert Paul, Ressel Orla
    Produced by:                 Decla

501 Totentanz
    1919
    Director:                    Otto Rippert
    Screenplay:                  Fritz Lang
    Photography:                 Willy Hameister
    Art Direction:               Hermann Warm
    Cast:                        Sascha Gura, Werner Kraub, Joseph
                                 Roemer
    Produced by:                 Helios-Film
    Released:                    19 June 1919

502 Die Pest in Florenz
    1919
    Director:                    Otto Rippert
    Screenplay:                  Fritz Lang
    Photography:                 Willy Hameister
    Cast:                        Theodor Becker, Marga Kierska, Erich
                                 Bartels, Juliette Brandt, Erner
                                 Hubsch, Otto Mannstaedt
    Produced by:                 Decla
    Released:                    23 October 1919

503 Die Frau mit den Orchideen
    1919
    Director:                    Otto Rippert
    Screenplay:                  Fritz Lang
    Photography:                 Carl Hoffmann
    Cast:                        Werner Kraub, Carl de Vogt, Gilda
                                 Langer
    Produced by:                 Decla

504 Das indische Grabmal (Part 1:  Die Sendung des Yoghi; Part 2:
    Das indische Grabmal)
    1921

| | |
|---|---|
| Director: | Joe May |
| Screenplay: | Fritz Lang, Thea von Harbou |
| Photography: | Werner Brandes |
| Cast: | Mia May, Conrad Veidt, Lya de Putti, Olaf Fonss, Erna Morena, Bernhard Goetzke, Paul Richter |
| Produced by: | Joe May |
| Released: | 22 October and 19 November 1921 |

Performances
_____

1917
____

504a    Hilde Warren und der Tod (for details, see entry no. 497).
        Lang evidently played four roles in this film directed by
        Joe May but scripted by Lang. He recalled playing Death,
        an old priest and a young messenger, but was unable to re-
        member the fourth role.

1963
____

504b    Le Mépris [Contempt]

| | |
|---|---|
| Director: | Jean Luc Godard |
| Producers: | Joseph E. Levine, Georges de Beauregard, Carlo Ponti |
| Screenplay: | Jean Luc Godard, from the novel Il Disprezzo by Alberto Moravia |
| Photography: | Raoul Coutard (in color and Franscope) |
| Music: | Georges Delerue |
| Editors: | Agnès Guillemot, Lila Lakshmanan |
| Cast: | Brigitte Bardot (Camille Javal), Jack Palance (Jeremy Prokosck), Michel Piccoli (Paul Javal), Fritz Lang (Fritz Lang), Giorgia Moll (Francesca Vanini), Jean-Luc Godard (Lang's assistant director), Linda Veras (a siren) |

Filmed on location in Rome and Capri by Films Concocordia-
Compagnia, Cinematografica Champion-Marceau-Cocinor
Distributors, April-June, 1963.

| | |
|---|---|
| Running Time: | 100 mins. |
| Released: | December 27, Paris premiere |

Godard asked Lang to play a director named Fritz Lang in
his picture about a group of people filming an adaptation
of The Odyssey. As many of the interviews show, Lang
clearly admired Godard and his work, while recognizing

391

their different approaches to the cinema. Judging by the comments in Peter Bogdanovitch's book, Fritz Lang in America (p. 142) (see Entry No. 355), Lang thoroughly enjoyed working on the film.

## The Unrealised Projects

Reprinted from Lotte H. Eisner, Fritz Lang. Translated by Gertrud Mander, and edited by David Robinson. New York: Oxford University Press, 1977. Entries marked with an asterisk are reprinted from P. Bogdanovitch, Fritz Lang in America. London: Studio Vista, 1967.

In the filmographies, books, and articles devoted to Lang and his work, a good many unfilmed projects are attributed to the director. Most of them are apocryphal, dreamed up by press agents, hopeful producers, and even critics. Lang insists he has never heard of the majority of them. Nonetheless, there are a small number of such projects, authenticated by Lang himself, which he had had the intention of making as films, and which had reached various stages of completion before being abandoned for equally various reasons.

505   Die Legende vom letzten wiener Fiaker (The Legend of the Last Viennese Fiacre). In 1933, after Das Testament des Dr. Mabuse, during the dark time of Hitler's rise to power, Lang wrote (without the aid of Thea von Harbou) the outline for a scenario full of humour and gaiety, reminiscent of his Viennese origins and prefiguring to a degree the fairy tale, picture book heaven of Liliom.
      Lang's story has all the drollery of Raimund, the once famous and popular comedy writer of early 19th century Vienna.
      The 'Fiaker' (he shares the appellation with his coach) is a proud proprietor-driver. With haughty graciousness, he gives his lowly 'Waterer' (the man who looks after the horses and gives them water) a lottery ticket which he had been forced to buy, but which he believes is beneath his dignity to keep. Contrary to all expectations, the 'Waterer' wins a huge sum, which he immediately invests in a factory which manufactures the new automobiles which the 'Fiaker' strongly detests. With his new found wealth, the social barriers between the 'Waterer' and the 'Fiaker' dissolve, and the 'Waterer's' son is able to marry his beloved, the 'Fiaker's' daughter.
      Only one consolation rests for the 'Fiaker' who is so proud of his horses: those 'damned poor, horseless cars' are not allowed to drive on the principal allée of the Prater. Yet, while the two new fathers-in-law are drinking

a toast with new wine ('Heurigen') to the young couple, an
'extra' headline in a newspaper announces that Emperor Franz
Josef has given a special dispensation:  the automobiles are
now allowed on the allée.  The news shatters all the 'Fiaker's'
illusions; he suffers a stroke.

At the Heavenly Gates, Saint Peter receives the dead
'Fiaker', but when the coachman wants to drive in with his
horses and coach, Saint Peter furiously bangs the gates
shut, and rushes off to arrange a special concert for Saint
Cecile.  Although all of the great composers have been invited, Saint Peter can't find them in their bungalows when
the concert is about to begin.  He finally discovers them
all sitting on comfortable clouds, listening in bliss to
the 'Fiaker' singing his Viennese lieder.  Saint Cecile is
waiting; there is only one thing to do:  report the entire
matter to the Lord.

Our Lord arrives at the gates and speaks to the coachman.
As the 'Fiaker' refuses to budge without his horses, the
Lord appoints him His special coachman, gets into the fiacre,
and proudly the 'Fiaker' drives into Heaven.  As the wheels
turn, a new constellation is born:  The Big Wagon.  The
story is worth repeating in some detail if only to remind
those critics who tend to forget Lang's Viennese background
that he is not the total pessimist they sometimes describe
him as being.

506   Hell Afloat.  In 1934, Lang wrote, with Oliver H. P. Garrett,
a story based on the S.S. Morro Castle fire in which over a
hundred people died.  David O. Selznick rejected the story
for M.G.M.

507   The Man behind You.  In 1935, Lang wrote this modern Jekyll
and Hyde story concerning a doctor who identifies more and
more with the evil nature of man.  It is a pity that the
director was unable to make the film; it seems a natural
subject for the director of M.

508   Men without a Country.  After You and Me, in 1939, Lang planned
this film for Paramount in collaboration with Jonathan
Latimer.  It was to have been a story dealing with a secret
weapon which destroys eyesight.

*508a   Americana (1939, unrealized project).  Lang did considerable
research for a Western that would tell one hundred years
of the country's history through the story of a lost mine.
It was this interest in the West that led Darryl Zanuck to
offer him his next film.

*508b   Billy the Kid (1942, unrealized project).  Lang:  'I would have
loved to make a picture about Billy the Kid.  You know the
original man?  In the photos, he looked like a moron, which

he probably was. And if I could have had the chance to
make the first picture, I would have made a moron out of
him, not Bob Taylor [star of the 1941 film, Billy the Kid].
But motion pictures have spread the legend, and because an
audience is educated, they know from the films that Billy
the Kid was a handsome, dashing outlaw, and if somebody
would make him today as he really was, it would probably be
so much against the grain of an audience that it couldn't
be a success.'

*508c  The Golem (1943, unrealized project). Lang planned a modern
version of the old Jewish legend, to be set in France during
the Nazi occupation, and based on an adaptation by Paul
Falkenberg and Henrik Galeen-who had made two German films
of Der Golem (in 1915, co-directed by Paul Wegener, and in
1920). Julien Duvivier did a French adaptation, Le Golem,
in 1936.

509   Winchester 73. In 1948, Lang worked with Silvia Richards (who
had done the script for Secret Beyond the Door) on a script
of Stuart N. Lake's novel. The film was planned for Lang's
own company, Diana Productions, for release by Universal.
The film directed by Anthony Mann in 1950 has no relationship to the Lang project. There was never more than the
first page of the outline at any rate.

*509a  All the King's Men (1948, unrealized project). Very briefly,
Lang worked at adapting the Robert Penn Warren novel, but
had nothing to do with Robert Rossen's version, produced
the following year.

*509b  Rocket Story (1948-49,unrealized project). Lang tried unsuc-
cessfully to interest several studios in making a contemporary story of rocketship development and attempts to reach
the moon. Less than two years later, the first picture in
this vein, Destination Moon, came out and was a great success.

*509c  The Running Man (1953, unrealized project). A Lang story-
inspired by a New Yorker article entitled 'Lost' about a
man who uses amnesia as a subconscious excuse to avoid his
responsibilities. (No relation to Carol Reed's 1963 film
of the same name.)

510   Dark Spring. In about 1954, Lang planned to shoot a script by
Michael Latté, and only gave up his plans to film it when the
problem of casting the child's role became insurmountable.
The story concerns a girl of eleven or twelve who is to in-
herit an enormous fortune from her dead father when she
comes of age. Her mother marries again. Her second husband
is a seemingly successful lawyer, who is being forced to pay

a huge sum to a group of gangsters he once cheated. The
lawyer attempts to kill the girl three times in order to
gain control of the inheritance. Only a friend of the
girl, a boy of fifteen, understands what is actually happening. The mother believes her husband when he tells her that
Bettina, the girl, is paranoid and is only imagining things.
Before he can carry out his fourth attempt at murder, the
lawyer is himself killed by a gangster. One is inclined to
wonder if it were only casting problems which decided Lang
against making the film. While at first glance the subject
seems appropriate to Lang, on closer examination certain
elements become apparent which might well have made Lang
more uncomfortable as the project progressed. Cold-blooded
murder for profit has never been central to his work. In M
and Secret Beyond the Door, for example, Lang deals with
psychopaths who cannot help themselves; the victim in Beyond
a Reasonable Doubt is not an innocent girl, but a hardened
blackmailer.

511   Taj Mahal. In 1956, the Indian government invited Lang to
      India to make a film. The project was about the 17th cen-
      tury maharajah who built the Taj Mahal in memory of his
      love. Lang dropped the project when it became clear that
      the Indian ideal of beauty was completely different from
      that in Europe, so that casting became a great problem.
      This stay of several weeks, however, was of great help later
      for his German films set in India.

*511a  Störtebecker (1958, unrealized project). Lang registered this
       name as the title for a film he had planned about the pirate
       'who lived during the times of the Hanseatic League and
       whose story is very well known in Germany.'

*511b  Faust (1959, unrealized project). After the Indian pictures,
       the producers asked Lang to remake any one of several classic
       German films, among them his own Der Müde Tod, Die Nibelungen
       or Metropolis, Joe May's Herrin der Welt, Murnau's Nosferatu,
       or even Caligari. Lang vehemently turned down all of these
       and proposed instead a new adaptation of Faust (which Murnau
       had also made, in 1926). After due consideration, the pro-
       ducers rejected this and suggested another remake--of Das
       Testament des Dr. Mabuse. Lang again refused but then came
       up with an idea for a new film inspired by the Mabuse series
       (see below).

512   Unter Ausschuss der Offentlichkeit (Behind Closed Doors).
      Although this title appears regularly in filmographies and
      has been treated in detail by Alfred Eibel (see bibliogra-
      phy), Lang insists it is a pure invention on the part of
      Arthur Brauner (Lang's producer on the last three German
      films) as a publicity stunt for Peter van Eyck in 1960.

It was never a Lang project, and the film which was produced
in 1961 with the same title has, of course, no connection
with Lang.

513   Kali Yung and Moon of Dassemra.   In about 1960, Lang was offer-
      ed the chance to make two further films set in India.   The
      projects were finally dropped, however, when the Italian
      producer insisted on certain script alterations, in spite
      of his contract with Lang giving the director full artistic
      control.   The Kali Yung film would have concerned the great-
      est criminal conspiracy in Indian history, the Brotherhood
      of Thugs.   More than ten million innocent travellers were
      strangled with the 'rumal', a kerchief curiously knotted
      at the corners, presumably in honour of the bloody goddess
      Kali, in order to rob them of their valuables.   The fact
      that even Mahradschahs and other high level personalities
      belonged to the secret organisation made it even more diffi-
      cult for the British authorities to exterminate the evil
      cult.
           Set in 1875, the film centres about a young doctor who
      runs a cholera clinic.   When his Sikhs disappear while
      bringing him supplies, he requests the resident, a sick old
      man who wants to avoid trouble, to investigate; the request
      is refused.   The matter is further complicated when the
      doctor discovers that the girl he had loved in England was
      already then the resident's wife.   A Thug murder is commit-
      ted and the doctor falls under suspicion.   In order to clear
      himself, he and an Indian companion undertake their own in-
      vestigation (a dancing girl leads them to the Thugs) and
      become involved in various adventures.   His love and under-
      standing of India prevail, the Thugs are exterminated, and
      his name is cleared.

514   ...Undmorgen: Mord!   (...and Tomorrow:  Murder!)  Planned in
      1962 (written in Beverley Hills in 1961 and in Munich in
      1962), the story deals with a seemingly respectable bour-
      geois, a severe defender of moral traditions, president of
      many social associations who in his youth had suffered vari-
      ous repressions which caused him to commit obsessive, sexual
      crimes.   When he is discovered, he commits suicide.   Only
      the police commissioner, with some few others, know the
      reality behind the lauditory-obituary of the dead man.

515   Death of a Career Girl.   In 1964, Lang was president of the
      Jury at the Cannes Film Festival; Jeanne Moreau was a member
      of the Jury and suggested that they make a film together.
      With the actress in mind, Lang wrote a detailed outline of
      a script.   A mature and still beautiful woman, the head of
      an international economic network contemplates committing
      suicide because her life and ambitions seem to her to be
      empty.   Her whole life is then seen in flashbacks.

Beginning as a young girl working with the French resistance
during the Nazi 'occupation', and, like Gina in Cloak and
Dagger, by 'touching scum becomes scum' in having affairs
with Nazi officers.  Poor and ambitious she uses men un-
scrupulously to further her career.  As the only man who
lovers her and treats her with respect sadly explains to
her, in the struggle upwards she has lost her soul.  At the
end of the film, she decides against suicide:  as one of
the living dead she opens yet another business conference
with cold triumph.  The agents of Lang and Moreau were unable to settle the conditions of production to their mutual
satisfaction and the project was cancelled.

After this, Lang seriously considered making one last
film in spite of his failing eyesight.  Claude Chabrol,
long an admirer of Lang's work, brought him together in
Paris with his own producer, André Génoves, who offered him
both complete artistic liberty and an adequate budget.  Lang
planned a story about contemporary youth, their conflicts
and desires, their striving to free themselves from the traditions of the establishment, and their use of drugs.  He
described to me one beautiful sequence:  coloured balls leap
from a roof terrace and glide easily down stairs and through
the air.  A young girl intensely involved in a LSD dream
glides down with them.  Lang finally decided that his failing sight would not allow him to make the film.

## Articles by Fritz Lang

### 1922

516   "Äusserungen zum Thema Kontingents-Verfahren und Qualitätsfilme."
      Der Film (Berlin), No. 30.
      Lang has a short paragraph in a series of statements by
eminent film people on the future of film.  He begins by
noting how important it is for there to be a proper exchange
of worthwhile films among nations.  For the time being, each
nation is working alone, but exchange is essential to create
a climate in which the very best can be produced.
      As it is, the wealthy nations cheat the poor ones in
terms of flooding markets with their films.  Such a procedure will end up corrupting the film industry at the moment
when it has just begun to live.  Businessmen should apply
all their experience--of a kind that artists lack--to preventing this from occurring.

### 1924

517   "Arbeitsgemeinschaft im Film."  Der Kinematograph (Dusseldorf
      and Berlin), No. 887 (2 February), pp. 7-9.

# Fritz Lang

[This article is important in revealing a certain kind of sentimentality and idealism that one rarely associates with Lang. Possibly written by Harbou, the article is full of emotional language of a disturbing kind, but it does give one a clear sense of Lang's ardent involvement in these early film projects. It also emphasizes the difficulties of working in film in the days when technology was primitive and conveys the exciting sense of experiment and discovery that was possible then.]

After noting that nothing is impossible in film, Lang goes on to say that film is a communal activity--everyone works together on a problem. The newness of film as an art form, as well as its fragility (it's very easy to make mistakes), means that one must concentrate hard.

Moving on to discuss content, Lang says that what counts is not so much the power of the legends one is filming but instead human power. In making Die Nibelungen, Thea von Harbou and Lang wanted to do something good and beautiful. They were fortunate in having an excellent working relationship, and their common aims helped make the project successful. Both were committed to making art rather than something in the American style, which involved profit and commercialism. For them, it was the project itself that mattered, and they worked on it for the most part joyfully. The spirit that hangs over the Die Nibelungen sets has more to do with the breadth of the universe than with the soil of Los Angeles. The film was made with a devotion analogous to that of the great works of the Middle Ages.

Turning next to the people who collaborated with them on the film, Lang has praise for Otto Hunte, who built the sets [Hunte had worked previously with Lang on Dr. Mabuse], for the painter Paul Gerd Guderian and his plain, stark style, and for Carl Hoffmann and his camera work. Hoffmann managed to achieve, through subtle use of light and shadow, all that Lang had dreamed of, revealing the inner, spiritual meanings of the scenes. The dragon had been a difficult problem and it took everyone's ingenuity to solve it satisfactorily.

In conclusion, Lang reiterates how the love of their work united everyone involved on the film. Quarrels there certainly were, but what mattered was that everyone believed in the project. Given how very difficult making a film is and how long it takes to make only a very small piece of a film, it is essential for all involved to feel a sense of unity and a commitment to the aims of the task.

See also by Lang in 1924:
"Was ich in Amerika sah." Film-Kurier (11, 13, and 17 December).
"Der künstlerische Aufbau des Filmdramas" (Referat). Filmbote (Vienna), No. 20; also in Volksbildung

(Vienna), Nos. 4-5 and in Film-Kurier (20 and 21 May).
"Stilwille im Film" (Aufsatz). Jugend (Berlin), No. 3.
"Mein ideales Film-Manuscript." Film-Kurier (Berlin)
(24 April).

518   "Kitsch--Sensation--Kultur und Film." In Beyfuss, E. and
Kossowsky, P. eds. Das Kulturfilmbuch. Berlin: Chryselius,
pp. 28-31. Part of this article is reprinted in Manz, H. P.
ed. UFA und der frühe deutsche Film. Zurich: Sanssouci,
1963.
   Lang begins by asserting the need for the new art of
film to stand on its own, refusing to be measured by old
aesthetic ideas. For Lang, film is the art of the twentieth
century and thus becomes an index of modern culture.
   While we struggle to recreate past eras through documents,
remaining buildings, etc., later generations will have only
to open a can of film to bring alive a piece of past history.
   Film has, according to Lang, the special property of reflecting the essence of its time, and it is this that at-
tracts people. More than live theater, film mirrors the
loves and obsessions of the masses. But if people then
complain that film merely appeals to the sensational, Lang
replies that then it is only doing what folk tales in all
nations have always done. He goes on to show that fairy
tales, made for children, are full of as much violence and
horror as any film. Examining the fascination that fairy
tales have for children and adults, he concludes that it
has to do with the depiction of the eternal struggle between
good and evil, in which good triumphs and order is restored
to the world.
   Lang shows that film provides a similar satisfaction,
only in the context of the modern world. He gives a few
examples of successful films to show that it is not only
the sensational film that wins public approval. He argues
that even a sensational film like his Dr. Mabuse was successful mainly because it documented the Germany of the period.
   The primitive sensational film, like the American
Western, shows contemporary people in the guise of the
fairy tale, while the film showing comtemporary reality
still speaks to universal aspects of human experience.
Film thus has a double aspect, dealing with eternal truths
but also reflecting modern culture worldwide. For film has
become, Lang concludes, the Esperanto of the day, a common
language. To understand this language, one has only to
open one's eyes.

519   Lang, Fritz, and Harbou, Thea von. Programmbroschüre fur Die
Nibelungen. (With articles by Lang and Harbou.) (Xerox in
Museum of Modern Art).
   (1) Lang. "Worauf es beim Nibelungen-Film ankam."
   Lang discusses how he and Thea von Harbou decided to

make <u>Die Nibelungen</u>. They were fascinated by the appeal of the old legend as something quintessentially German.
(2) Lang. "Die Darsteller des Nibelungen-Films."
    Discusses the actors in <u>Die Nibelungen</u>.
(3) von Harbou. "Wie der Nibelungen-Film geschaffen wurde."
    Discusses the actual production of the film and the problems encountered.

### 1925

520  "Zwischen Bohrturmen und Palmen. Ein kalifornischer Reisebericht." <u>Filmland</u> (Berlin) (3 January).
     This is an interesting early piece on Lang's first impressions of America, showing the typically European concept of America that he held before he came here. He begins by describing how the landscape developed, derricks being followed by asphalt roads and finally by the palm trees. While the old world conceives of itself as having first been a paradise and as developing into a wasteland, American mythology conceives of the land as having first been a wasteland and subsequently becoming a paradise.
     Lang turns next to what happens to German artists when they come to America, reciting the story of a German actor, well on the way to a good career, being attracted by America but unable to find work or recognition here. He goes on to stress America's skill at selling itself and mentions the techniques used to get people to buy land; the offer of unlimited wealth spurs people on, appealing to their greed.
     Lang concludes with a discussion of Hollywood, which impressed him. He describes Carl Laemmle's Universal City, noting how he built a model to scale of the Paris Opera house to film <u>Phantom of the Opera</u> and an oriental city to film <u>The Thief of Bagdad</u>. Mentioning many of the well-known artists and personalities of the period, Lang comments on the fairy-tale quality of their lives, lived in luxurious surroundings with unlimited wealth. There is good reason for America's being called the land of opportunity.
     Not wishing to appear ungrateful, Lang ends by noting the warm reception he personally received in America.

521  "Was lieben und hassen wir am amerikanischen Film." (Antwort auf eine Rundfrage.) <u>Deutsche Filmwoche</u> (Berlin) (2 October), p. 13.
     Lang has a short answer in this series of interesting responses by different people to the question of what one loves and hates about the American film. He says that the second half of the question is worthless, and that he loves what is essentially American in films made in the United States--namely, the sense of joy, the excellent comic sensibility, the fast tempo of the Westerns, the energy of the

adventure film. He does not like the sentimentality of
American films, the hypocrisy in regard to morality, or the
monotony of the conventions.


### 1926

522 "Ausblick auf Morgen: Zum Pariser Kongress." Lichtbildbühne
(Berlin), No. 229 (25 October).
In the beginning, Lang says, there was neither deed nor
work but movement. Film, that is, movement, is proceeding
from a primitive to a viable art form, but it is hard to
keep the movement forward toward art because of the public
interest in film. The most subtle artist, according to
Lang, "wanders helpless in the morass of sentimentality,"
and few see film in terms other than those of profit. The
majority of directors do not see the potential film has for
raising the spiritual level of people.
Both technique and imagination are necessary for creativity in film: technique because it can bring greatness out
of the most banal content; the imagination because it gives
poetry to narrative. But the rebirth of film will ultimately take place only through the genius of the director.
But if film is the twentieth-century form of poetry, it
is also the means of speaking to the masses. By giving
people an image of how they really are, film can bring them
out of their chaos. While we have no idea what film will
become in the future, it is clear that it can present people
to themselves--what they are, what they can be--in a useful
way. We have been presented with the human face--the external image--but now we need to be shown the soul. Film
should follow the flow of life. The ultimate goal of film
should be to combine technique with artistic vision in the
service of showing people to themselves ever more clearly,
presenting at the same time the right way, the good in the
world.

See also by Lang in 1926:
"Wohin treiben wir? Kritische Prognosen zur neuen
Saison." (Includes comments also by F. Th. Csokar,
Herbert Ihering, and Richard Weichert.) Die
Literarische Welt (1 October).


### 1927

523 "Was ich noch zu sagen habe." In Porges, Friedrick, ed.
Mein Film (Vienna), No. 59, p. 3.
The piece is introduced by Porges, talking about
Metropolis as a landmark in film creation and technical
development. He admires the way Harbou reduced her original

book without losing anything.

Lang then has a short comment on the experience of making the film. Obviously worn out by the effort and pleased that it is over, Lang praises those who worked with him, hoping that the project had as much meaning for them as it did for him. While the film was the goal during its making, it now seems merely one goal on the way to further goals. Since film is a wonderland without limits, Lang concludes, it is hard ever fully to finish anything.

524    "Moderne Filmregie" (Aufsatz). <u>Die Filmbühne</u> (Berlin), No. 1 (April), pp. 4-5.

[The following article is important in showing that, as early as 1927, Fritz Lang had a clear notion of <u>mis-en-scène</u>; he was self-consciously creating backgrounds and decor that fitted in with his themes. It is also fascinating to see how aware he was of elements like line, rhythm, tempo, and image, and also of the necessity for a governing idea that united all the parts of a film harmoniously. Although Lang ironically notes that the director is a mediator rather than the one who creates everything, in fact he means that the director works with his crew and designers, so that they understand his governing idea in making the film and can produce his vision. So while he does not do it all himself, as the novelist does, nevertheless he is the author of it all in having the ruling vision that governs the work, ed.]

Lang begins by noting that film differs from the other arts in requiring familiarity with all art forms: from the painter, the filmmaker needs the knowledge of building an image; from the sculptor, the knowledge of line; from the musician, rhythm; and from the poet, the concentration of an idea. The filmmaker must be a universal artist. But above all, Lang says, the director has to understand tempo, in the sense of the harmony produced by the different strings on an instrument. A pursuit scene is quite different from a love scene, and each has its own specific tempo.

Filmmakers, Lang notes, differ enormously in temperament and each has an individual way of seeing. While this is good, the best director is the one who understands all the different elements of film form, can work with them, and still keep the whole in mind at one time. He considers it fortunate that Germany does not have the star system and that production of a film is considered a joint project, with people doing their own task as best they can. The director, however, has to see that all the parts work for the good of the whole.

Other skills required of the director are an understanding of the psyche of performing artists and an ability to work closely with technicians and architects. A director must know how to give the set builders an idea of the style

wanted so that they make what is right for the film.  The
film director thus functions as a mediator for the task
rather than as the sole author.

Film is only in its infancy as an art form, and Lang
wonders what its future will be.  Right now, the essential
is that all people involved in the making of a film have a
sense of their role in relation to the whole.


## 1928

525    "Über sich selbst."  In Treuner, Hermann, ed., Filmkünstler:
       Wir über uns selbst.  Berlin: Sibyllen Verlag.
       This short autobiography provided the basis for later
descriptions of Lang's background and career, and the facts
in it are often repeated by Lang himself in interviews.
Lang describes his bourgeois upbringing in Vienna and how
early on he wanted to be an artist and put all his energies
into this against his father's will.  Because his father
wanted him to undertake academic studies, Lang enrolled in
engineering school, but realized this was not for him and
left to wander all over the world, earning his living as
he could by painting and sculpture.  He first encountered
film in Brugge [Bruges, Belgium] in 1909 and from then on
was under its spell.  War interrupted his travels, and soon
after that he got his chance to make films.
       For the future, he hopes to pursue all the possibilities
of film as an art form and to make a new synthesis.  He
hopes to show the problems of humankind in his work.  He
ends with a tribute to Thea von Harbou, his coworker and
friend, who has helped him discover his themes.


## 1929

526    "Die mimische Kunst des Lichtspiels."  Der Film (Berlin), No.
       1, p. 2.
       A statement by Lang is included in a series of comments
by different people on the general topic of "Metaphysik der
filmischen Kunst [The Metaphysics of Film-Art]."  He begins
by noting that in such a short space he will not be able
to conclude whether or not film, as it develops, will deal
with deeper matters as well as with character.  Lang notes
that he has elsewhere argued that film has presented people
with a new outlook on things in a way that no previous art
form could do.
       Theater works through the word that has to be carried
through space to the audience, while film brings the human
face right up to the spectator.  When people have learned
how to read the human visage in the silent film, the image,
perhaps because of its silence, can move people as nothing

before.  Lang goes on to cite instances of the way film can
evoke deep reactions simply through the batting of an eyelid,
the wince on a face, a door's opening or closing, an empty
stool, or a room that someone has just left.  Film, in its
play of light and shadow, functions as the rhapsody of our
period; in addition, film tells stories of human fate--be
they tragic or comic, of innocence or guilt--for all time.
A final advantage of film is that because it is silent, it
can be understood throughout the world.

<u>See also</u> by Lang in 1929:
>"Das Ausland erwartet alles von uns" (Antwort auf eine
>    Umfrage:  "Hat der deutsche Film 1929 künstlersiche
>    Chancen?").  <u>Vossische Zeitung</u> (Berlin) (1 January).
>"Mein Steckenpferd."  <u>Die Filmbühne</u> (Berlin), No. 5
>    (May).
>"Film-Reportage."  (Aufsatz).  <u>Vossische Zeitung</u>
>    (Berlin), No. 484 (13 October).

### 1931

527   "Mein Film <u>M</u>:  Ein Tatsachenbericht."  <u>Die Filmwoche</u> (Berlin),
No. 21 (May), pp. 655-658.
Lang begins by noting that modern people no longer need
the thousand and one tales of Scheherazade to arouse their
imagination because modern life has itself become so fantastic.  We read daily in the newspapers about the tragedies
and comedies that occur, and Lang believes that film should
reflect this daily reality.  Various famous murder cases
have been publicized in recent years, and Lang comments on
the demonstrations they evoked, on the searches of derelicts
by the police, sometimes for good reasons, often for evil
ones.

Lang wanted to introduce these daily realities in <u>M</u> and
to use his film to warn people, especially youngsters, of
the dangers awaiting them.  The problem was that the "truth"
would seem banal, but his aim was to function as a torch-
light does and expose the heights and depths of these events.
He was particularly concerned to show that any child outside
the bosom of his or her family can be lured into danger.
Basing his work on an actual event that he read about in the
newspapers, Lang hoped that <u>M</u>, in alerting us to dangers,
would help us elude them.

### 1932

528*  "Der Wille des Publikums."  <u>Reichsfilmblatt</u> (Berlin) (2
January).
Source:  F. Grafe and E. Patalas, <u>Fritz Lang</u>.  Munich:

Hanser, 1976, p. 163.

<u>See also</u>:
"Existenzkampf des Films." <u>Reichsfilmblatt</u> (20 February).

### 1934

529   "Mes Amis, les Ouvriers." <u>Excelsior</u> (Paris) (27 April). Re-
      printed in Daumal, René and Lang, Fritz, "A Propos de
      Liliom." <u>Positif</u>, No. 188 (December 1976), pp. 6-7.
          As part of an issue devoted to honoring Lang, recently
      dead, Daumal reprints two pieces, including this one by
      Lang, written around the time of making <u>Liliom</u> in Paris.
      It is a poetic and sensitive piece in which Lang describes
      the process of making a film and the role the crew plays.
      He notes how one can immediately tell whether a film is
      good or bad by the attitude of a crew on the set. If the
      film is bad, they complain about the director and their
      tasks, but if it is good, they are alive, involved, and
      friendly toward the filmmaker. Lang is happy that, for the
      most part, his crews have been his friends and describes
      how uncomplainingly they tolerate making many retakes and
      working late into the night, only to be up and on the set
      bright and early as usual.

### 1946

530   "Director Presents His Case Against Censorship of Film."
      <u>Los Angeles Daily News</u> (15 August). Reprinted, in French,
      in Eibel, Alfred ed. <u>Fritz Lang</u>. (<u>See</u> Entry No. 314).
          Lang begins by declaring that he is against censorship
      and that freedom of speech is the hallmark of democracy.
      Where censorship exists, it signifies a refusal to face the
      real problems a nation is having.
          Lang notes that procensorship arguments always assert
      the need to protect adolescents from things, but in fact,
      he says, a real education is one that introduces children
      to the realities of life.
          Lang recognizes the grave responsibility of film direc-
      tors, given the powerful influence of this medium. He
      thinks the industry's own code is sufficient protection,
      however, and that local censorship is unnecessary and dan-
      gerous in that it ends up being political, enforced as it
      is by town mayors and the police.
          Lang concludes that the best censorship of all is that
      of the box office.

530a  "Préface." In Bulleid, H. A. V. <u>Famous Films</u> (Delivered as
      a speech at the occasion of showing <u>M</u> in 1946, and reprinted

in Eibel, Alfred, ed. <u>Fritz Lang</u>). (<u>See</u> Entry No. 314).

Lang begins by noting that film is the art of the people, and that this close relationship between the masses and a contemporary art is a result of the development of a modern, industrial democracy. Democracy, he explains, is merely the word for the goal we are striving for rather than a state already achieved, since we, in fact, live in a class-stratified society.

Lang surveys briefly the history of art, noting how first it was the privilege of the ruling class and that only recently has the working class won enough rights and wealth to have the leisure for entertainment. Classic works naturally will not suffice for workers, since they have too long been the property of the rich and are therefore esoteric and inaccessible. Film filled the need for a popular art form.

Social and economic causes underlie the development of this supple, open art form, capable of unifying a fragmented civilization. Lang goes on to show how film developed out of people's desires and dreams and that film today still rests in hands that may be coarse but that are alive.

Turning to the subtle collaboration going on between a director and the people, Lang says that to succeed a director must work with the realities of life as the masses know them and in a form comprehensible to the people.

Lang goes on to discuss the way in which film is a collective art, drawing on the different arts and on the various talents of people. The visual aspects of film-form render it available to a broad range of people, along with the fact that film has developed its own, new language.

He ends with noting the recent dangerous tendency toward increasingly expensive films and the growth of huge corporations that cut the links with the people. This results in a decline in the quality of films, since people's real needs are neglected for trivial, superficial pleasure. Lang argues for a return to the roots of cultural life which are to be found in the past. The cinema of today is, in fact, dependent on what cinema has been before, and only a solid understanding of past achievements can lead the future director to do the task properly. Lang urges his readers to study Bulleid's study of famous films from earlier eras.


1947

531    "Director Tells of Bloodletting and Violence." <u>Los Angeles</u>
       <u>Herald Express</u> (12 August). (Reprinted in Eibel, Alfred,
       ed. <u>Fritz Lang</u>). (<u>See</u> Entry No. 314.)
           Lang begins by raising the question as to why murder has
       such power over people's imaginations, and why it occupies
       the central place in newspaper headlines. Why was

Shakespeare, who writes constantly of murder, considered
the greatest dramatist ever? All this is partly explicable,
according to Lang, if one assumes that murder and violence
are innate in people--a fact that is confirmed if we look
at the basic Bible story, which involves Cain's murder of
Abel.

According to Lang, we are all most probably potential
murderers and, given a momentary mental lapse, would commit
crimes. All his own films containing murders represent
potential murders by Lang himself, safely and fortunately
contained within the world of entertainment. Often murder
is necessary merely to solve script problems. In his next
film, Secret Beyond the Door, Lang says that he intends to
show how an irresistible desire to kill may be overcome.

Lang believes that the urge to kill is planted in the
human brain very early, but the stupidity and incomprehensi-
bility of so many crimes leads one to despair of ever understanding the human brain. Lang deplores the low level of
science in this area. He thinks that the dramatist can
perhaps help those who have suffered psychic damage and who
are unaware of the danger of what happened to them. Many
now harboring murderous desires could be helped by psychoanalysis or a friend to talk to.

532   "The Freedom of the Screen." Theatre Arts, No. 31 (December),
pp. 52-55. Reprinted in Koszarski, Richard. Hollywood
Directors 1941-1976. New York: Oxford University Press,
1977, pp. 134-142.

Lang argues strongly against censorship in film as "an
unwarranted intrusion on the civil liberties of a great
nation." He begins by talking of the way the Nazis withdrew
his Frau im Mond [Woman in the Moon], and goes on to say
that free discussion is the lifeblood of democracy, that
civilization can only move forward through the presentation
of new ideas. Censors view new ideas as subversive, however;
Lang notes that the ideas persist anyway and to prevent their
expression is to treat people like children. "Censorship,"
he says, "never cured a social problem." Although crime is
forbidden, it continues to exist; we need to explore the
sources of crime and eliminate them.

Lang complains of the way sex has to be treated on the
screen and argues that sex is an essential element in the
healthy life of a nation. Films must draw from life, for
only in this way can they interest people; films can drama-
tize society's problems and suggest solutions.

Censorship implies that people are not mature enough to
decide for themselves, and Lang deplores this. Why should
one suppose that the mass of the people is less mature than
those who govern them? Lang is willing to have separate
rules for children and adolescents but believes that parents
should mainly do the deciding for their own children. It

is dangerous to bring up children guarded from the realities of the world.

Lang recounts briefly the history of the Hays Code, noting that outcries against Hollywood are often the work of a small, narrow-minded minority. His own film, Scarlet Street, was banned in New York State, Milwaukee, and Memphis and allowed to play only after a prolonged legal case. There is no justification for permitting individual states to impose their views on everyone; for example, the politicians of the South have imposed a limited and narrow view of blacks on the entire United States.

Lang ends by noting the irony that people left Europe to avoid religious or political persecution and found that in America too they are told what to think. The only viable "censorship" is that of the public box office, Lang concludes.

## 1948

533 "Happily Ever After." Penguin Film Review, No. 5, pp. 22-29. Collected in Geduld, Harry M. Film Makers on Film Making. Bloomington: Indiana University Press, 1969, pp. 224-231; in French, Echo (August 1948); in German, Der Monat (Berlin), No. 7 (April 1949), and Filmstudio (Frankfurt), No. 44 (September 1964).

Lang talks first about there being no surefire formulas for successful picture making. It all depends on the context and the creativity of the individual director.

He turns next to the question of film endings and the assumption that audiences demand the "happily ever after" conclusions. This kind of ending is culturally a late development and resulted from increased living standards in the West. Asians and Indians still prefer tragic endings. World War I changed Western intellectuals drastically, moving them from the naive nineteenth-century notion of "sweetness and light" to the opposite extreme of despair for its own sake. Including himself in this group, Lang notes that intellectuals rebelled against the old answers and outworn forms. He fought for the "unhappy ending," but reluctantly gave it up. At the end of World War II, intellectuals again resorted to despair, and audiences again rejected their views.

Lang next explores audiences' apparent need for optimistic endings. Classical tragedy showed people as victims of fate, of forces beyond their control. This was necessary at a time when people could not solve most of their problems; it enabled them to retain a sense of dignity. But the twentieth century has shown people that they can solve a great deal through scientific and technological developments. We can no longer say that people are trapped by fate when we see that they can overcome pain and suffering.

Thus endings showing people mastering their problems and getting what they want fit the time we live in.

This does not, however, mean that we should be unfaithful to reality; he cites Open City and his own Hangmen Also Die as examples of films that show a truth (i.e., that fascism cannot easily be overcome), but give people a sense of dignity through the power of the struggle against evil.

Lang concludes that how a film ends will be based on the cultural and political situation of the nation the film is made in. Fascist states return to the mystical concept of fate as it existed in Greek tragedy, but after two world wars people can no longer accept the fairy-tale success of good over evil; they instead want to see virtue triumph through struggle. Lang defends his ending to Woman in the Window as necessary to avoid a totally fatalistic view of things; he sees Scarlet Street as showing that evil in its many forms must result in physical or mental punishment; the characters themselves bring about their punishment. "The highest responsibility of the film creator," Lang says, "is to reflect his times.

## 1953

534* "Il dottore Mabuse non era nazista." [Dr. Mabuse Was Not a Nazi]. Cinema Nuovo (Turin) (15 January).
[I could not find this issue of the journal.]

## 1964

535 "Bilder der Zeit." Frankfurter Rundshau, No. 170 (25 July).
Lang discusses the consciousness of the period in which his early films--Dr. Mabuse, der Spieler [Dr. Mabuse, the Gambler] and Dr. Mabuse, Inferno des Verbrechens [Dr. Mabuse, Inferno of Crime]--were made, on the occasion of the films' being reshown in Frankfurt.

## 1965

536 Berg, Gretchen, ed. "La Nuit Viennoise: Une Confession de Fritz Lang." Part 1. Cahiers du Cinéma, No. 169 (August), pp. 42-61. (See Entry No. 538 for Part 2.)
This long, rambling monologue published in two parts consists of notes edited by Gretchen Berg, from an informal session with Lang, reminiscing with friends (including Herman Weinberg) and Cahiers editors. This first monologue is less coherent and focused than the second one, but both reveal a good deal about Lang. Lang begins by discussing the sad state of the postwar German film industry, which is

way behind the American one, and talks of how shocked he
was to be asked to do yet one more Mabuse film.  Although
he had really wanted to make a film about modern youth,
Lang is pleased with Die Tausend Augen [The Thousand Eyes]--
it is at least better than the Indian films.  He describes
how he came to do these, seizing on the second chance to do
what he had planned originally in 1920.

He next discusses all kinds of unrealized projects he
has had at various times, including a film, Behind Closed
Doors, about a man imprisoned by the world of money and
lacking love; The Running Man, about a person suffering
from amnesia, but really running away from himself; The
Devil's General, about the German pilot who refused to fly
for the Nazis, and so on.

Lang returns to the filming of Mabuse and then recalls
the censoring of Das Testament [The Last Will] and the
problems he had getting M made and shown.  In 1948, he recalls, he tried to persuade film companies to make a rocket
film, without success.  By the time someone did do one,
people had forgotten Lang's Frau im Mond [Woman in the Moon].

Lang mentions his liking for Westerns because they have
necessity built into them.  Talking of how he gets an idea
for a film, Lang describes seeing first a vague silhouette,
then people already living, then imagining their movements
and environments, faces, etc.

Lang denies that he uses objects as symbols and believes
that he moved away from expressionism when he went to
America.  He does not believe in theories, but thinks that
the cinéaste must be a psychoanalyst; Lang agrees that he
utilized expressionism, but he tried to dominate it.

Returning to Frau im Mond, Lang notes how impossible
individualism is in the rocket era and how correct he was,
after all, in Metropolis, in showing people as attached to,
and increasingly like, the machine.

Going from here to the topic of heroism, Lang talks about
Godard's Le Mépris and then says more about unfinished projects.  He says that he never made a film that was not a
compromise; when he was broke in the early 1950s, he made
The Big Heat and Human Desire.  He concludes by noting that
he no longer wants to make films, but he does mention being
phoned by Jeanne Moreau, who was interested in working with
him, and whom he considered for Death of a Career Girl.

537   "Zum Selbstverständnis des Films IV."  Filmkritik (Munich),
No. 12, pp. 675-680.
      This piece consists of a series of quotations from vari-
ous articles by Lang ranging from the 1920s to the 1960s.
Since these pieces are annotated here, I will simply list
the sources of quotations:
(1) "Moderne Filmregie."  Die Filmbühne, No. 1 (April 1967),
    p. 4.

(2) "Mein Film M." Filmwoche, No. 21 (May 1931), p. 658.
(3) Moullet, Luc. Fritz Lang. (Paris, 1963), p. 20.
(4) "Kitsch-Sensation-Kultur und Film." In Beyfuss, E.
    Das Kulturfilmbuch (Berlin, 1924), pp. 28-31.
(5) "Und wenn sie nicht gestorben sind." Originally in
    Penguin Film Review, No. 5 (1948), pp. 22-29; reprinted
    in German Filmstudio (Frankfurt), No. 44 (September
    1964).
(6) "Fritz Lang Vous Parle," Cinéma 62, No. 70 (November
    1962), p. 71.
(7) "Interview with Jean Domarchi and Jacques Rivette."
    Cahiers du Cinéma, No. 99 (September, 1959), pp. 103-118.

## 1966

538    Berg, Gretchen, ed. "La Nuit Viennoise: Une Confession de
       Fritz Lang." Part 2. Cahiers du Cinéma, No. 179 (June),
       p. 50-63. (See Entry No. 536 for Part 1.)
           Lang talks about how he began in film as an actor, play-
       ing four parts in the film he scripted, Hilde Warren und
       der Tod (directed by Joe May) and about his recent part in
       Godard's Le Mépris. Noting that actors were not important
       in the early days, he goes on to say how casually films were
       made then. The director was king, while the producer either
       had a small role or did not exist. Lang himself prefers
       working with unknown actors, because stars always want the
       film to revolve around them, and they always play themselves.
       It is a mistake to make a film for anyone--star, producer,
       or director--for film is a mass art, speaking to the masses,
       and that must always be born in mind. Lang believes that
       he adjusts his reactions, albeit unconsciously, to the mass-
       es. Having lived through two world wars, Lang is very aware
       of how the masses change and of the constant flux of things.
           Lang views film as his vice--he is addicted to making
       films--but he goes on to discuss the tension between the
       commerical and aesthetic aspects, noting that what began as
       an art had ended as an industry. He claims that he is most
       interested in the content, as against the form, of his films
       [despite the fact that critics are always saying that the
       reverse is true, ed.]. While he likes to have everything
       very precisely planned before he gets on the set, Lang says
       that he nevertheless tries to leave room for his actors to
       make changes, as far as this is possible. He takes pains
       to explain their roles to actors, but not to tell them ex-
       actly what to do, and he does not insist on something if
       actors have not seen it for themselves. Only bad directors
       simply tell actors to go ahead and do their scenes without
       any thought or discussion beforehand.
           At this point, Herman Weinberg (present at the interview)
       produces some stills from Metropolis and Lang recalls the

inspiration for the film during his visit to New York one
hot summer. He recalls his and Thea von Harbou's original
notions of a rich class's living in luxury on the sweat of
workers laboring below, but says that he later came to dislike his simplistic solution of heart as mediator between
head and hands. He now sees the problem as a social rather
than a moral one. He also disliked his too easy linking of
people and machine in order to express the evils of mechani-
zation; but he has recently begun to think there was truth
to it, especially in connection with astronauts.

Lang next looks at a photo of the flood and the children
escaping and proceeds to explain how this part of the film
was achieved, technically, through the ingenuity of Eugene
Shuftan. The shots of the futuristic-looking city, which
last one or two minutes on the screen, took six days to
film. But most difficulties occurred with the laboratory
work. The film was wrongly developed the first time and
Lang and his crew had to do the whole thing over again.
Lang says he learned gratefully that one does not make films
alone and compliments the crew he worked with. Lang goes
on to discuss the technicalities of a few more scenes, including that where the machine explodes. He recalls that
Eisenstein happened to be in the studio that day, and that
they had a long discussion about the relative virtues of
the fixed, and the mobile, camera. Lang was using a subjective camera here to make the audience feel the shock of
the explosion. Eisenstein left Berlin before Lang could
see him again, but Lang was told that he was studying his
method of working, and that he had edited the Mabuse films
in Russia.

Lang notes that opinions about Metropolis varied widely,
Wells believing the film was stupid, while Conan Doyle
loved it. Turning to Die Nibelungen, Lang recalls how they
actually planted the flowers on the set that surround
Siegfried when he is cut down by Hagen. He discusses techniques used in filming Das Testament des Dr. Mabuse [The
Last Will of Dr. Mabuse] remembering the excitement of experimenting and the closeness of those working together.

Turning to M, Lang recalls that, after the large, fresco-
like films Die Nibelungen, Metropolis, and Frau im Mond
[Woman in the Moon], he became interested in human beings,
their motives, and acts. The idea for the film came from
a newspaper clipping rather than the Dusseldorf murderer,
and some real criminals, whom Lang knew through his work in
the Berlin equivalent of Scotland Yard, acted in the film.

Moving on to Rancho Notorious, Lang discusses the structural advantages of the ballad, the first time such a device
had been used in a Western; he mentions the change in title
forced by the producer, which leads to a discussion of his
resentment at the producer's power generally--a power only
mitigated by previews. He talks about his subtle uses of

sound in <u>M</u> and notes that this film would not have been
made had he had a producer to contend with then.
   Recalling <u>Hangmen Also Die</u>, Lang notes that at the time
it was made people did not want to be reminded of the war,
but nineteen years later it was well received in Paris.
Thinking about <u>Fury</u>, he says he would have liked to make a
film that would stop lynching, but realizes that a film
director can only hope to raise, not solve, social problems.
Lang reflects on working with Marilyn Monroe in <u>Clash by
Night</u>, noting how pretty she was, but how misguided; Stanwyck
was the powerful one in that film.
   Lang comments on how a director has to be a kind of
psychoanalyst in order to make his characters live on the
screen.  The uniqueness of a director comes, he believes,
from the unconscious, and a good critic could perhaps explain to Lang what he is doing.  But believing that the
source of creativity lies in frustration and anxiety, Lang
would not want to be psychoanalyzed.  A film is, for Lang,
like a child he has put into the world, and although he
can't choose among his many offspring, he singles out as
favorites <u>M</u>, <u>Woman in the Window</u>, <u>Scarlet Street</u>, and <u>While
the City Sleeps</u>.  He thinks that his basic theme is the
Greek problem of the struggle of the individual against
events--the happy ending does not exist in art any more
than in life.


                          1969


539   "Autobiography."  In Higham, Charles, and Greenberg, Joel.
      <u>The Celluloid Muse:  Hollywood Directors Speak</u>.  London:
      Angus & Robertson, pp. 104-127.
         Lang picks up the history of his life at the moment of
      his arrival in America, noting how hurt he was by his
      country's turning to nazism--he never spoke German again.
      Most of the article deals with his career in America, and
      is full of interesting details about the making of various
      films.  Talking about his early experiences with MGM, Lang
      says that working in America was strikingly different from
      working in Germany.  He was surprised at the exclusion of
      blacks from real parts (e.g., in <u>Fury</u>, <u>House by the River</u>)
      and from cigarette ads (e.g., in <u>You Only Live Once</u>).  He
      discusses making his Westerns and then his anti-Nazi films
      and then turns to a film he never completed, <u>Confirm and
      Deny</u>, saying how glad he was to be taken off the project,
      since he could not do what he wanted with it.  He wanted to
      do a musical with Rita Hayworth, but was instead given one
      with Jean Gabin--<u>Moontide</u>--that everyone was unhappy about
      and that was not completed due to the war.
         After saying a few words about most of his American
      films, Lang discusses the film he did with Godard, <u>Le Mépris</u>.


                          413

While admiring Godard very much, Lang notes that he disagrees with putting in realistic sound--all that is happening at the time of filming. He thinks art is based instead
on selection.

While noting that little of value is yet being made in
postwar Germany, he says he has heard of one or two new
young people coming up, although they did not grow up in
Germany. Young people are most likely creating their own
new forms.

540  "Ob Brecht mich beeinflusst hat?" [Lang talks about M].
     Thüringer Tageblatt (30 June).
         Excerpts from Lang's interview with Gero Gandert (See
     Entry No. 568.)

541  "What Directors are Saying." Action (Los Angeles), 4, No. 6
     (November-December), 28.
         This is simply a very short quotation from Bernard
     Rosenberg's The Real Tinsel [See Entry No. 542], where Lang
     talks about the Hollywood system.


## 1970

542  "Autobiography." In Rosenberg, Bernard, and Silverstein,
     Harry. The Real Tinsel. London: Macmillan, pp. 333-348.
         Lang talks about his early life in Vienna and then tells
     how when he left home, he roamed the world getting the ex-
     perience that a director needs. It is, he believes, im-
     portant for filmmakers to have real, specific knowledge.
     After discussing briefly the making of Clash by Night and
     Western Union, particularly in relation to producers Jerry
     Wald and Daryl Zanuck, Lang notes that Western Union gave
     the spirit of the West even if it did not show "truth." He
     sees You and Me as his only flop, and then it was because
     he was trying to copy Brecht. He notes that he often made
     pictures just for the money and then talks of how much he
     appreciates audiences: a film like M functions on many
     levels and can appeal to many different people at once.
     Ultimately, Lang says, you have to make the picture for
     yourself.
         He moves on to discuss Hollywood and the alienation he
     experienced there; people use each other, and you are only
     interesting as long as you are in the limelight. Lang com-
     plains of the star system, which he sees as good for busi-
     ness but bad for art. He also deplores the lack of status
     given the writer, who now is a mere mechanic. In addition,
     things go awry when the director can no longer be in charge,
     when producers try to control directors by making hard and
     fast rules. He left Hollywood ten years ago and will never
     make a film there again; the place lacks a spirit of commun-
     ity and comraderie.

543    "Preface." In Weinberg, Herman G. Saint Cinema:  Selected
          Writings 1929-1970. New York: Drama Book Specialists.
          Rev. ed., n.d.; New York: Dover, 1973, pp. 9-11.
               This essay is written in a personal, literary style;
          Lang describes himself sitting down after dinner to coffee,
          brandy, and cigars, recalling Weinberg's column in Film
          Culture called "Coffee, Brandy, and Cigars." He goes on to
          note how insightful and witty Weinberg's essays on film al-
          ways were.

544    "What Directors are Saying." Action (Los Angeles), 5, No. 6
          (November-December), p. 22.
               This is a quotation from Bogdanovich's book of interviews
          with Lang [See Entry No. 355], where Lang talks about the
          Hollywood system and about films being seen only in terms
          of money rather than in terms of how good they are.

545    "Ein Brief von Fritz Lang (über Kracauers 'Caligari'
          Interpretation)." In Deutsche Kinemathek (ed.). Caligari
          und Caligarismus. Berlin. (Available in Deutschen Film
          und Fernsehakademie, West Berlin.)
               The letter is prefaced by a note from the editors saying
          that since Lang's role in the making of Caligari is often
          mentioned, they asked him to clarify exactly what he did.
               Lang begins by saying that the only correct statement in
          Kracauer's discussion of this film is that Wiene took over
          the direction. All the rest is wrong. Lang denies that it
          was his idea to insert the framing story and says that the
          main idea for the film came from the two painters, Reimann
          and Röhrig, before Pommer had a proper scriptwriter. Their
          idea was to show the world of the madman in an expressionist
          manner.
               His own contribution to the film, Lang says, was the
          shooting of one of the "normal" (realist) scenes, the one
          where the two men sit down and tell each other their stories.
          The reason for this introduction was not to abandon the
          original idea for the film but to cushion the public from
          the new techniques that they were using. It would have been
          too startling to begin the film with them. But the expres-
          sionist style certainly did represent the crazy, mad world.
          Lang denies hearing anything about Mayer and Janowitz's be-
          ing against the opening scene, and he could not get Kracauer's
          assertion confirmed by Carl Mayer. As far as Lang can recall,
          Janowitz began alone as scriptwriter, but was taken off later
          on (after Mayer had joined) because of a falling out.
               Lang does not agree with Kracauer's conclusions about
          the film (nor with much else in the book). The framing
          story does not take away from the revolutionary implications
          of the story, which is essentially a plea against authority.
          For Lang, the opening scene only strengthens the original
          intentions.

## 1972

546   "What Directors are Saying." Action (Los Angeles), 7, No. 3
(May-June), 28.
     This is simply a short quotation from Charles Champlin's
Film Odyssey (BBC Program), where Lang talks about violence
and M and his dislike of explicit scenes.


Interviews with Fritz Lang

## 1929

547*   Anon. "Interview with Fritz Lang." Mon Cine (Paris) (9
September).
     I was unable to find this issue of the journal.


## 1941

548   Creelman, Eileen. "Fritz Lang Discusses the Directing of
Manhunt Now at the Roxy." New York Sun, 17 June.
     Lang describes Manhunt as a modern adventure story. Al-
though it might also be called a propaganda film, it was
made for entertainment rather than for preaching against
the Nazis. Lang was pleased that the film was financially
successful--46,522 people went to see it. The success of
the two Westerns [The Return of Frank James and Western
Union] had made it possible for him to do a more serious
drama.
     In Manhunt, Lang made every effort not to show Nazi cru-
elty directly; Lang notes that the Nazis are, after all,
human beings, not monsters.
     Lang understands that he is still celebrated for M, al-
though he is always surprised to hear it called a melodrama
--for him, it was a psychological study. He would not do
a remake of M because movies are so much a function of the
particular social moment. They are aimed at the contemporary audience, and one cannot rely on their appeal to later
generations.
     Lang ends by discussing his next modern adventure story--
Confirm or Deny--now being written. It is about a war correspondent in London, but he says he will not show any bombing in the picture.


## 1943

549   Creelman, Eileen. "Fritz Lang Discusses Two of His Films:
Hangmen Also Die and a Very Old One." New York Sun, 20
March.

Lang says that <u>Hangmen Also Die</u> was the hardest film he
has ever made.  He is pleased with the fact that it shows
no atrocities, leaving it up to the audience to do its own
imagining.  The film was difficult to produce because it is
set in Europe and yet made in Hollywood, and also because it
is an independent production; now Lang is having to do himself what he had many people do in the studio situation.
The sets were a headache, since he couldn't find anything
that looked like Prague.  <u>Das Testament</u> [The Last Will],
opening at the same time, displeases Lang because it is a
French version, which he has never seen.  The film was made
just before Hitler came to power, and Lang puts Nazi slogans
in the mouths of criminals.


## 1944

550   Creelman, Eileen.  "Fritz Lang Discusses His Latest Film,
      <u>Woman in the Window</u>."  New York <u>Sun</u>, 6 October.
         Lang feels a need to discuss his latest film, since it
      is the first one without any specific social significance.
      The story is universal, one that could happen to anyone,
      and perhaps it does have social significance.  To Creelman,
      it sounds like a top-notch thriller.  Years ago, Lang made
      <u>M</u> (a study of a psychiatric murderer), which is often still
      played today.
         Lang tried not to whitewash the girl in <u>Woman in the
      Window</u>, as is often done in this type of film, and praises
      Joan Bennett for her acting--all Hollywood actors want to
      play the good guys these days.
         In Germany, Lang was given individual credit for his
      films, but here he says that directing is team work and
      collaboration, so that he should not be seen as totally
      responsible for the result.


## 1945

551   Creelman, Eileen.  "Fritz Lang Talks of Forming His Own Company
      and of His Next Drama, <u>Scarlet Street</u>."  New York <u>Sun</u>, 17
      April.
         Lang begins by talking about <u>Woman in the Window</u> and how
      he shot photographs first to get ideas so as to make the
      sets look more authentic.  He liked the book on which it
      was based [<u>Once off Guard</u> by J. H. Wallis] better than the
      film, since there the man is an English, and not a psycholo-
      gy, professor; he had wanted the woman to be lower class,
      but the Hays office prevented this.  The trick ending was
      the producer's idea, not his.
         Lang does not want to compromise with <u>Scarlet Street</u>;
      since he did not know Greenwich Village in 1932, he is

concerned about making the film authentic. He ends by noting that in America he is never allowed to forget M.

552    Morris, Mary. "Fritz Lang: Monster of Hollywood." [No name for newspaper; MMA Files].
       This is a pleasant conversation between Mary Morris and Lang, where we get a good sense of the kind of person Lang is as much from how he and Morris interact as from anything said. They talk about Lang's interest in murder and violence. Lang says that he is innately curious about why people murder and about the inevitable guilt that follows. "Criminals," he says, "are just the ones getting caught. I only try to have an understanding of them--I am not condemning. I want to see the causes--why they are giving in." He sees crime as linked to the social structure and hopes his films will encourage people to look more deeply into the causes of crime.
       Morris and Lang next talk about Lang's having moved from Germany to America, about the problem of changing status from that of a famous director to simply one of many in Hollywood, and about the additional language problem. Lang states that he has been trying to say what he believes in his films, especially in relation to the Nazis; he does not think his is a period for simply "telling stories," and he goes on to mention his interest in politics and the large amount of reading that he does. Morris, surveying his shelves, notes the wide range of books from the Bible to history to thrillers.
       Lang says that films should be information disguised as entertainment. It makes no sense, he says, to make films that depress people: "We should be making films that make people think about Allied unity, and about how closely our American history is paralleling that in Europe today. The problem is how to arrange to tell these things, and make them tasty to the masses. Movies are the art of our century, the art of the people. I am on the side of the people." In reply to a question as to why, then, he is not doing such films, Lang notes that one is not free to do what one wants in Hollywood, but he does what he can.
       They conclude by talking briefly about love and romance; Lang notes how hard it is to find one's match in life and sets up the ideal relationship as that where one shares everything with the loved one.


1956


553    Hart, H. "Fritz Lang Today." Films in Review, 7, No. 6 (June-July), 261-263.
       Lang begins by repudiating the subject matter of Siegfried and Metropolis, although valuing what he did with

sets and decor. He no longer likes the idea in Metropolis
of the heart as mediator between brain and hands, because
it suggests that the emotions will be the form of mediation
between the proletariat and the future managerial oligarchy.
Looking back over his career, Lang notes that the films that
he thought were good when he made them have stood the test
of time, but that time has also exposed the faults of films
he was unsure about. He likes M the best, partly because
it made money, which Lang admits is important to him. While
Lang agrees that the existence of crime must partly be
blamed on criminals themselves and partly on the larger society, he also feels keenly that "the individual's valor is
as nothing in the midst of the madnesses of men in the mass."
Lang believes that violence is necessary in films today, because people have lost their belief in hellfire and brim-
stone. Their fear of physical pain, thus, is all that can
keep them doing right.

554    Kipfmuller, Erwin. "Gespräch Mit Fritz Lang." Süddeutsche
       Zeitung (Munich) (9 October). Reprinted in Film (Munich)
       (December 1956).
           Kipfmuller introduces the interview by noting that Lang
       has returned to Germany after twenty-three years; he has
       aged gracefully, but is otherwise the same, still interested
       in a thousand things, passionate and enthusiastic, loving
       film and living for it.
           The first section of the interview is taken up with Lang's
       going over his background, early education, flight to Munich,
       world travels, sojurn in Paris, and war experiences. He
       first became interested in film in Paris where he was fas-
       cinated by the way it could show lifelike movement. He
       began writing scripts in the hospital and was taken on by
       Erich Pommer, for whom he both wrote scripts and acted.
       Here he received the experience necessary for later becom-
       ing a director.
           Lang explains his role in shaping Caligari before Pommer
       asked him to leave the project to make Die Spinnen [The
       Spiders], which he wrote with Thea von Harbou. Lang notes
       that the theme of Caligari fascinated him and reappears in
       his Mabuse films.
           Lang discusses Der müde Tod [Destiny], a film close to
       his heart, and Douglas Fairbanks's imitation of certain
       tricks in Thief of Bagdad. Der müde Tod was the first of
       a series of films focusing on the German people, the others
       being Dr. Mabuse (the war period), Die Nibelungen (German
       history), Frau im Mond [Woman in the Moon] (the future tech-
       nicians). With prompting from Kipfmuller, Lang comments
       briefly on each of these films, noting the similarity in
       theme between Mabuse and Woman in the Window, the influence
       of Böcklin on Die Nibelungen, his dissatisfaction with
       Metropolis, the Nazi interest in Frau im Mond because of

the authentic space-age technology. The Nazis confiscated all his films except <u>Die Nibelungen</u>, which they ran with a new sound track.

Turning to <u>M</u>, Lang recalls the controversies over the film, both with Ufa, which Lang then left, and the Nazis. His last <u>Mabuse</u> film was censored by the Nazis, and soon after, Lang left Germany for Paris, where he made <u>Liliom</u>; in 1935, Lang went to Hollywood.

With <u>Fury</u>, Lang sees himself continuing a direction that he started in <u>M</u> and that he picked up in his next two American films. <u>You and Me</u>, Lang notes, was influenced by Brecht, although Brecht was not yet in America. Lang comments briefly on his American films.

Kipfmuller's final question is about the German cinema. Lang says that he has seen few of the films, but admires <u>Des Teufels General</u>, starring Oskar Werner, whom Lang thinks is a great actor. He has many plans, as usual, but nothing definite as yet.

## 1957

555    Bachmann, G. "The Impact of Television on Motion Pictures." <u>Film Culture</u> (New York), 3, No. 2 (December), 5.
       Lang's comments here are part of a series of interviews by Bachmann with various film directors. Gilbert Seldes explains in an introduction that the intention was to find out what directors thought could be done about the declining movie business and the competition with television.

       Lang notes that Hollywood does not experiment enough; while he can understand why independent companies would not risk anything new, he fails to see why the major studios are so conservative. Lang views film both as an art and as an industry; for him it was never "mere entertainment," but an art that became an industry through its wide appeal. "What I try to do," he says, "is make pictures about modern people and modern problems. I think we have to try to make pictures about the problems of our own days. That is the first step."

## 1959

556    Delahaye, Michel and Wagner, Jean. Interview with Fritz Lang. <u>Présence du Cinéma</u>, Nos. 2-3 (July-Sept.), pp. 48-50.
       The interview is included in an issue of <u>Présence du Cinéma</u> devoted to Lang's Westerns, and thus the interviewers begin by asking how Lang, as a European, could make a Western. Lang replies that when he went to America he wanted to plunge into the life there and had lived among Indians. The advantage in being a foreigner was that he could see

things that people born in America wouldn't see. <u>Western Union</u>, he says, showed that he could make a film about another culture and about an ordinary man as against the Nietzschean superman. His factual material was all correct. Asked what attracted him to Frank James, Lang says that it was the idea of the outlaw, the individual alone against society. <u>Rancho Notorious</u> is one of his favorite films, but Lang notes that he rewrote the script to make it reflect his own interests, although the film's title was not his. Among contemporary Westerns, Lang likes <u>Shane</u>.

557  Domarchi, Jean and Rivette, Jacques. "Entretien avec Fritz Lang." <u>Cahiers du Cinéma</u>, No. 99 (September), pp. 1-10. Collected in <u>La Politique des Auteurs</u>. Paris: Editions Champ Libre, 1972, pp. 103-118.

The interviewers begin by asking Lang which period of his work he prefers; Lang replies that he can't really say, but that one is always trying to make a great film. He sees <u>M</u> as a new development, showing movement from the mere entertainment of the <u>Mabuse</u> films and <u>Spione</u> [Spies] toward the social criticism evident in <u>Fury</u>, <u>Scarlet Street</u>, <u>Woman in the Window</u>, and <u>While the City Sleeps</u>. He deepened the level on which his films work, now criticizing people's social environment, laws, and conventions. Lang feels that too many people function on a merely materialistic level, oblivious any longer to the inner, spiritual world. In making a film, Lang says he tries to translate an emotion.

Pressed by the interviewers to say what exactly he is attacking, Lang says he is intrigued not so much by a certain kind of alienation as by the ancient Greek problem of the struggle of the individual against circumstances, laws, and imperatives. He goes on to criticize <u>Metropolis</u> for its simplistic vision of the heart mediating between head and hand; he now thinks that one has to look to economics to define the problem. Noting that one cannot give instructions to others as to how to live life, Lang says that he prefers the individual ending of <u>Fury</u> to that in <u>Metropolis</u>. One has to struggle against the trap of circumstances, but all have to find their own way. Murder is not the answer.

Denying that <u>While the City Sleeps</u> has a pessimistic ending, Lang explains that the four men struggle for the new position for different reasons, and that the one with the ideal wins. Lang values self-respect—if one can face oneself in the mirror in the morning, one will have what one desires. Pressed on this some more, Lang pleads that artists have to make money and cannot choose their scripts. If <u>While the City Sleeps</u> did not ring true, he hopes the films he now wants to make will, with their criticism of modern life, where people no longer have a personal existence.

Turning to his Westerns, Lang says that what attracted him to times past was that the word of honor was still

central.  He was interested in the idea of an older man's
being surpassed by a younger one on the draw.

Asked about Human Desire, Lang notes that he is not fond
of the film, finding Renoir's version (La Bête Humaine) much
the better, and he did not understand the positive Cahiers
du Cinéma review of the film.  Questioned about his interest
in melodrama, Lang says that he is most interested in the
response of the public and not so much in what critics have
to say.  He was moved by the positive response of young
people at the Cinemathèque.

The interviewers turn next to expressionism and its influence on Lang.  Unable to say precisely what he took from
expressionism, Lang notes that he had little time to think
about theories in the manner of Eisenstein.  He believes
that one has to create emotions, and that one cannot make
films according to rules.  If he took anything from expressionism it was interest in certain emotions:  Kracauer's
book is wrong because too intellectual.

Lang mentions that he likes Murnau--particularly Nosferatu
and Tabu--and that he admires Renoir.  He knows that Ray took
a lot from him in They Live by Night, but admits that he also
learns from other directors.


## 1961


558    Anon.  "Fritz Lang:  43 ans de métier."  L'Express (6 July),
       pp. 36-37.

The editors begin by noting the contradictory views of
Lang that have appeared, from those like Lebesque (in the
same issue of L'Express) talking of Lang's decline, to the
MacMahon group who brought Lang to Paris and are showing
his films.  They intended to ask Lang himself who he is and
perhaps solve the mystery that way.

Lang says first that he never goes to see his films once
they are made.  Knowing every detail, he is tired of them.
But he did once see M because of doing an interview that
was to precede a television showing of the film in Germany.
He then insisted on seeing a particular version, knowing
that Goebbels had taken portions of one copy to illustrate
his film Entartete Kunst [Depraved Art].  Lang did the show
only on the condition that he be allowed to interrupt the
film at the censored spots and explain why there were gaps.

Asked how he chooses his subjects, Lang replied that
sometimes he gets them from the newspapers, but goes on to
say that one can only do what one wants if one has money.
He explains that he did a remake of the Indian films because
it meant finally having a chance to do what he had planned
so many years ago--as if fate had brought him full circle.
He loves India, wanted to go back there, and knew the locations he wanted to use.  Mabuse was different:  that was

not a remake but a new scheme.

Replying to a question about why Mabuse continues to
interest him, Lang notes that in the 1920s he had been passionately interested in mental illness. He spent eight days
in an asylum and madness fascinated him.

He next discusses exactly how he goes about making films.
While one creates the narrative in writing down the script,
directing is like rediscovery; it's making the words on the
page come alive. The process of the making often takes over,
the film having its own life after a while. Cinema is his
life. He plans everything out in detail beforehand, so that
he knows exactly what he is doing on the set. He tries to
bring out the best in actors and explains what he wants
clearly.

Lang states that he does not care how much a film makes
in terms of money, but he does want a lot of people to see
his films. For him, film is a mass art, so that one is
failing if many people do not see the works. Lang believes
that we no longer live in a society where art is the province
of the elite few, and thus one must adapt works to a mass
audience. This does not mean making simpleminded films:
the producers and directors have a mental age of nine, but
not the public. He only once went to see audience response
to a film of his: it was positive, but what has always upset Lang has been the mostly negative reviews his films have
gotten.

559    Baby, Yvonne. "Recontre avec Fritz Lang: Ce que vous ne
       saississez pas, jamais vous ne le comprenez." Le Monde
       (3 July).

The interview took place on the occasion of the preview
of Die tausend Augen des Dr. Mabuse [The Thousand Eyes of
Dr. Mabuse] in Paris, which drew huge crowds of young people. At the start of the interview, Lang warns Baby that
although he loves the cinema he does not want to talk about
how he makes films. Young people always want recipes, but
Lang insists that there aren't any: making a film means
living with one's characters. He himself lives day and
night with his films, and he uses everything that he sees
daily. For example, he got the idea for the scene in While
the City Sleeps where Mildred (played by Ida Lupino) leads
viewers to believe she's looking at dirty pictures, from a
New York restaurant.

Turning to the new Mabuse film, Lang says he knows it too
well to like it. But he asserts that the film was intended
as a warning to people and was not meant merely as a thriller. He wanted to show how corrupt American gangsters were
engaging in destruction simply for profit. But he leaves it
to the audience to draw their own conclusions. Mabuse represents both the evil and the genius of crime.

Baby cites an anecdote regarding Lang's notorious

independence from producers in Hollywood. Lang comments
that recently he was offered a contract for a film with
Brando and Elizabeth Taylor and turned it down because he
could not work with those actors and would have wanted to
choose his own. He mentions a new project involving India
and Rome and how it fell through because the producer would
not let him decide on the actors.

The article ends with a comparison of Das Testament [The
Last Will] and Die tausend Augen [The Thousand Eyes]. Lang
sees the second film as a good follow-up to the first, carrying the ideas even further and placing reality at even yet
one more remove.

560   Baby, Yvonne. "Mon film le plus important depuis M: C'est un
      film anti-Nazi avec des 'signes' policiers." Le Monde
      (9 December).
          Lang begins by noting that the assassination of Heydrich
      gave him the idea for Hangmen Also Die. He asked Brecht,
      an old friend, to collaborate with him on the film, since
      Brecht knew a lot about the resistance. John Wexley came in
      to translate the script into good English. Lang saw the
      film as rendering a kind of service to Americans in letting
      them know what was going on in Europe. This made the film
      the most important one since M, where Lang was also trying
      to do a service to people, in that case warning mothers to
      look carefully after their children. There are technical
      links between the two films in that the murder of the child
      is shown by a shot of a balloon and that of Heydrich by a
      shot of his hat.
          Lang concludes by saying that although Hangmen has some
      elements of the crime film, it is mainly an anti-Nazi film.
      The resistance theme is most important, but there are traces
      of the police film, admittedly. He thinks the film will be
      better understood today than in its own time.

561   Mardore, Michel. "Fritz Lang dit: L'Amérique ne m'a pas
      devoré; j'y ai beaucoup appris.'" Interview in Les Lettres
      Françaises, No. 904 (7 December), pp. 1, 8.
          In his introduction to the interview, Mardore notes that
      Lang has just had his seventy-first birthday and that he is
      in Paris for a showing of Hangmen Also Die. They were able
      to interview him briefly, but Mardore comments on the diffi-
      culty of getting Lang to explain his work. He hides behind
      his monocle or glasses, eludes questions with a laugh or a
      joke, or alters their meaning. He wants to run his own in-
      terview and have total control, something that reflects his
      way of directing films.
          Mardore begins by asking if Lang would remake Hangmen the
      same if doing it today, given that his style and his thought
      have undergone modification over the years. Lang avoids the
      question by replying that whatever he answered, he would look

bad. Mardore next asks Lang to comment on the fact that in
Hangmen action takes precedence over psychological studies.
Lang notes that the psychological dimension of a character
always exists for the necessity of the action. He says he
has only a sketch for the person involved, working very much
on the empirical level; he does not know what is in his subconscious and suggests that it is the task of the critic to
find out.

Mardore wonders about Lang's use of objects--like flowers
and jewels--and asks if that has to do with expressionism.
Lang replies that Mardore will go wrong if he reads too much
into symbols. Symbols have only concrete significance in
his work. Expressionism and its use of symbols is now out-
moded, and Lang does not like to see directors going back
to that way of working. While everyone tries to place him
in expressionism, he thinks he belongs more in realism. He
wants to link objects to themes through association rather
than having an object stand rigidly for something in particular. He denies that he is rejecting expressionism, but
says that he is far from it now. He explains that he abandoned symbolism when he went to America, since people there
told him that they were intelligent enough to understand
things directly. Far from being devoured by America as
people say, in fact his experience in America has enriched
him and taught him a lot.

Mardore notes the apparent evolution in Lang's work
toward an increasing bleakness occasioned by his preoccupation with the theme of original guilt. Lang accepts this
view of his main theme only if one is talking from the point
of view of Nietzschean notions dominant in Germany. This
didn't hold up in America. Fury was about the common man.
Lang asserts that, once in America, he adopted a more practical, everyday approach to the world than had been possible
in Germany, where the focus was on the unconscious.

562   Mazars, Pierre. "Fritz Lang S'Explique: 'Je ne recherche pas
      le crime pour lui-même.'" Interview in Le Figaro Littéraire
      (9 December).
      The interview took place when Lang was in Paris for the
      showing of his Hangmen Also Die. Mazars begins by asking
      Lang what he thinks of his film, and Lang replies that it
      was an anti-Nazi film designed to show how people unite
      against the dictator. Mazars recalls Lang's last film in
      Germany, Das Testament des Dr. Mabuse [The Last Will of Dr.
      Mabuse], and how it too was against the Nazis. Lang notes
      that in his new Mabuse film (The Thousand Eyes of Dr. Mabuse),
      the character is neither a doctor nor a Nazi but instead
      involved in the crime syndicates that now interest Lang.
      Mazars asks how Lang first became interested in crime, and
      Lang reflects that there is something of the criminal in
      all of us. He goes on to discuss how he likes to suggest

horror rather than show it directly. Noting that people
talk too much in the contemporary cinema, Lang says that he
liked working in the silent film because then people could
supply their own words. But he lists some films that could
not be made without sound (e.g., La Dolce Vita, Bridge on
the River Kwai), and how certain silent films, like Murnau's
Nosferatu, could well be remade with sound, to show that he
does not have a bias against sound in itself. His own Die
Nibelungen, however, could not be made with sound. It would
be impossible to find suitable words for the actors to speak,
and, worse still, it would be impossible to discover actors
capable of playing the roles. When asked by Mazars about
which New Wave films he admires, Lang mentions Truffaut's
400 Blows, Clouzot's La Balaire, and Franju's Eyes Without
a Face. He refuses to answer a question on the contemporary
German cinema, noting that he should not be the one to explain why the German cinema is not now what it once was.

563    Philippe, Claude-Jean. "Une entretien avec Fritz Lang."
       Télérama, No. 599 (9 July), pp. 29-30.
          Philippe introduces the interview by commenting on Lang's
       presence and appearance, noting his experience, politeness,
       and refusal to be led astray by any theory, as well as his
       general youthfulness and intelligence.
          Philippe notes the solid reality of some of Lang's old
       films, and Lang replies that the films where he was abso-
       lutely himself retain their truth, while others die with
       the years. Lang refuses to choose among the three main
       periods of his career, saying only that film was always his
       life. He sees an unbroken line of films representing what
       he has seen, learned, and sensed over his lifetime. The
       variation in his American films comes from his hatred of
       contracts, fear of being trapped, and his need for freedom.
       Lang thinks his most important theme is the need to combat
       evil in all forms and that as a result M and Hangmen Also
       Die are most significant. Mabuse incarnates evil in the
       form of a desire for power that ends destroying itself.
          In his Westerns, Lang says, he showed the West as the
       Westerners wanted to remember it. Appreciating the simple
       morality of the Western, Lang nevertheless refuses to say
       whether he thinks people are ultimately good or bad. In
       his detective films, Lang says he aimed at social criticism;
       in The Big Heat he exposed the corrupt police, in While the
       City Sleeps the power struggle at a big city newspaper. Al-
       though Philippe thinks the view of people in this latter
       film too severe, Lang insists that he simply described what
       he saw. Made under contract, Beyond a Reasonable Doubt is
       less satisfactory, and Lang feared that the public would
       not accept the sudden change in perception of the hero at
       the end.
          Lang denies making any special effort over mise-en-scène

or that there have been changes over the years. He simply
does what seems right, imagining it all beforehand.
Metteurs-en-scène that he admires are Wilder, Cuckor, Wyler,
and Ford.

The last section of the interview deals with the recent
German films, especially Der Tiger von Eschnapur [The Tiger
of Bengal] and Das indische Grabmal [The Indian Tomb].
Tired of being asked if the films are great, Lang simply
notes that when a film is a commercial project done under
contract, he always gets involved in what he is doing.
Evasive about future projects, Lang only hints that he has
a film in mind that will be made either in India or Italy.
He concludes by hoping that the revival of Hangmen Also Die
will be a success.


## 1962

564    Bartlett, Nicholas. "The Dark Struggle." Film (London), No.
32 (Summer), pp. 11-13.

The article consists of quotations from an interview
with Lang about his work, followed by Bartlett's comments.

Lang notes that his main theme has been fate and the
fight of the individual against an implacable power. M
gave him most satisfaction because people liked it, it made
money, and many films were derived from it. He says that
he never uses violence for its own sake but instead to draw
a moral conclusion, which he would rather have people see
for themselves than be shown directly. In discussing Mabuse,
Lang notes how both critic and director function as a certain
kind of psycholanalyst. Lang recalls next that the Hays
Office objected to Hangmen Also Die, saying it encouraged
lying. Lang concludes with the comment that one tries to
do things that are close to one's heart, but that one also
has to make a living.

Bartlett summarizes Lang's main characteristics as a
director: he is first a social message filmmaker who is
interested in the picturesque and who avoids explicit violence. Lang was not political until the Nazis came to power
and the democratic instincts then aroused were developed
in America. Lang's style is one where nothing is wasted;
he achieves his effects within static frameworks, through
composition and exact editing. Lang believed in the necessity of protest and of the fight against corruption.

565    Lang, Fritz. "On the Problems of Today." Films and Filming
(London), 8, No. 9 (June), 20-21.

The statements Lang makes here repeat those he has already made since he began to be interviewed in the late
1950s (and which he will continue to make in the numerous
interviews to come).

He begins by commenting on how both directors and critics
need to be a certain kind of psychoanalyst to do their jobs
properly. He next mentions that although he liked Metropolis
while he was making it, he later found fault with the symbolism. He now thinks that the film represented "an unconscious
'inside' of something."

He talks about his new project for a film about the problems of youth today. A main theme will be the lack of possibility for individualism for contemporary youth. Astronauts are typical in carrying to conclusion only something
that a whole team of people has prepared for. In showing
the links between humans and machines, Metropolis anticipated
astronauts Glenn and Gagarin.

Fate today, Lang says, no longer has its original Greek
meanings; it implies either a dictatorship or some social
force that represses the individual. You Only Live Once and
The Big Heat represent the struggle of the individual against
society. The important thing for Lang is to go on fighting,
even if one does not believe that things can be changed.
Hangmen Also Die now looks prophetic, since similar oppression is presently occurring, only from the other side.

Lang is delighted that in Paris and Rome there now seems
a desire to do something new in cinema, something close to
art in contrast to the big American pictures, which are mere
commodities. He hopes that his own new film will be a serious exploration of why youth today are bad; what happened
to them? We can assume that it has to do with television,
but one cannot expect things to stay the same. Lang would
like to work in Europe, where it is possible to make films
about real emotions and ideas in contrast to the large
American productions, which are merely animated posters.
Many people are now working in television because that is
where the jobs are, but the demand to fill seven channels
for so many hours daily makes it impossible to provide good
creative work.

M, Lang says, became a classic and was copied by other
directors, yet he is not sure that it is "art." Who is to
say? It will take time to decide this. He has always
wanted to reach the masses and was pleased that an old film
of his recently played for eighteen weeks in Paris. He made
some films, like Western Union, that were escapist fantasies,
but he wanted to produce films (like Fury and his crime
films) that would make people think about social wrongs.
Democracy, for Lang, is not so much a particular form of
government as a balancing of things.

Making a film, Lang notes, requires teamwork, and this
can be a problem particularly if the producer is powerful.
But the director does not always have to lose out, as he
shows by referring to Fury.

566 Lang, Fritz. "Fritz Lang Vous Parle." Cinéma 62 (Paris),

No. 70, pp. 70-75.

Lang surveys topics he has discussed elsewhere, particularly in the Films and Filming interview that follows this one closely, beginning with the notion of the director as psychoanalyst and of the critic's being able to see in works what the director's unconscious is all about. Turning to Hangmen Also Die, Lang notes that the struggle against fascism is not over.

Lang thinks that there is a new desire to experiment in cinema. He regrets the invention of television, but realizes that many film directors can get work only there. He notes that M is now being considered art, but the problem is in defining what is and what is not art. Lang talks about films appealing to escapist needs in people and agrees that his Westerns in particular did this.

Lang states that he wanted always to reach a vast public, desiring to give a social message. He has always been against capital punishment, and that has been one of his main messages. In Fury, he wanted at least to show the evils of lynching, even if the film would not bring it to an end.

Lang ends by noting that democracy is a balance of forces. He says that the power of the director has been overstressed; filmmaking is a collective art.

567    Shivas, Mark. "Fritz Lang Talks About Dr. Mabuse." Movie (London), No. 4 (November), pp. 4-5. Reprinted in Sarris, Andrew. Interviews with Film Directors. Kansas City and New York: Bobbs-Merrill, 1969. Pp. 257-261.

Lang reviews how he got into the first, second, and final Mabuse films, each time thinking that he had finished with Mabuse, only to find someone trying to get him to make another version. He talks about his closeness with Norbert Jacques, the author of the novel on which the first film was based, of the way Thea von Harbou helped with the script for the second Mabuse film, and of being coerced into making the third Mabuse film and then liking the idea.

## 1963

568    Gandert, Gero. "Fritz Lang über M: Ein Interview." In Gandert, Gero and Gregor, Ulrich, eds. M. [Script of the film]. Hamburg: Marion von Schroder.

Gandert first asks how Lang arrived at the theme of M, and if the film was really modelled on child murderers. Lang replies that it is hard to say how a theme emerges--he has always been interested in finding out about people, something that requires a lot of personal and general life experience. Once he has a theme, Lang does a lot of research on it. While there were many child murderers around at the

time of the film's making, Beckert was not modelled on any
specific person. M investigates the process of murder, but
is mainly intended as a warning to mothers to look after
their children better. Commissioner Lohmann was not modelled
on a specific person either, but reflected a type dominant at
the time. Lang consulted with the police about their methods
of working and discussed the psychology of the murderer with
psychoanalysts.

Asked about romantic scenes in the film, especially those
with the underground, Lang says he views these scenes as
picturesque instead--only Der müde Tod [Destiny] and Moonfleet
have romantic elements. Lang agrees that he was influenced
in M by Brecht's The Threepenny Opera, as were many people
at the time.

Discussing his use of sound in the film, Lang mentions
his method of using sentences that overlap scenes as a way
of speeding up the film's rhythm, as well as making an association between the scenes. The conversations among the
police and among the beggars are handled contrapuntally, so
that there is really only one discussion.

After some discussion of the change in title from
Murderer(s) among Us to M, the interview ends with comments
on Lang's fascination with guilt and innocence.

569   Lang, Fritz. "Was bin ich, was sind wir? (Aus französischen
      Interviews mit Fritz Lang)." Filmkritik (Munich), No. 7,
      p. 308.
            The editors have translated large sections from three
      French interviews. The first, from L'Express, No. 624, is
      about Lang's work with Godard on Le Mépris. Lang is tired
      and resigned, but clearly admires Godard enormously. In
      the second, from Cahiers du Cinéma, No. 99 (See Entry No.
      557), Lang is asked about which of his own films he likes
      best and questioned about his themes. The final extract,
      from L'Express, No. 525 (See Entry No. 558), deals with how
      Lang goes about making a film. He is questioned about his
      interest in the Mabuse figure and in madness generally.


1964


570   Manceaux, Michèle. "Avec Fritz Lang." L'Express, No. 673
      (7 May), p. 27.
            The occasion for the interview is the Cannes Film
      Festival, over which Lang is presiding. Lang seems to value
      the festival as providing a forum for films that otherwise
      would not have an audience. He says that he tries to be as
      objective as possible when judging. He is bored by imper-
      sonal films, but quickly gets involved if there are charac-
      ters.
            Asked about the most important quality in directors, Lang

answers that they must know life, have experience, read the
papers, and be cultivated. The main change in film in his
lifetime was the introduction of sound; before that, one
had to have action, but now one must try to do everything.
He refers to M as an example of a film that pleased people
with different needs: for some it was an adventure film,
for others a psychological one, yet others saw it as a defense of the criminal.

Asked if film offers as many possibilities as literature,
Lang says the interviewer ought to have asked about film in
relation to the fine arts. He notes that cinema is the art
of the century, the art of the people.

571   Moser, Wolfgang. "Interview Mit Fritz Lang unter Zeugenaufsicht."
      Mannheimer Morgen (17 October).
      Moser prefaces the interview by noting how difficult it
was first, to get to see Lang, and second, how reserved he
was. They had wanted to ask him about the current state of
German films, but when he refused, they turned to questions
about his position as president of the jury evaluating films
being shown at the Mannheim Documentary Film Festival.
Brief though the answers were, Moser thought the interview
worth publishing for the light it threw on Lang's personality.

Asked about presiding at the film festival, Lang notes
that although he is a fiction filmmaker, he believes that
all films should have a documentary aspect. Thus, he is
glad to be evaluating documentary films. Moser tries to
get Lang to talk about a split he has heard of between those
on the jury who favor New Wave techniques and those defending more conservative tendencies. Lang refuses to discuss
the goings-on, but says that people have the right to express their convictions and that an exchange of ideas, far
from being detrimental, may indeed be beneficial. Lang
notes that only in the case of a tie would his vote have
special power.

Asked about his future plans, Lang says that he is not
sure where he is going after the festival. He is too super-
stitious to discuss new projects, but says that he is planning a film about modern youth. He is interested in any
theme that has to do with the modern period and that helps
people understand more about what is going on.

572   Noames, Jean-Louis. "Nouvel Entretien avec Fritz Lang."
      Cahiers du Cinéma (Paris), 26, No. 156 (June), 1-8.
      The interview took place in Hollywood at Lang's home in
the presence of Gene Fowler.
      Noames begins by asking Lang about his statement that
cinema is like a vice for him. Lang explains that he means
that for him making films is like taking a drug--it's an
addiction. All artists have a need to create because of
something within themselves; recounting an interaction with

a critic over the interpretation of M, Lang remarks that
he used to think he knew what he was doing in making a film,
but he now realizes it may all go much deeper.

He notes that he does not want actors just to do what he
says: he instead tries to help them create the part they
are acting, behaving here rather like a psychoanalyst.
Noames can perhaps answer his own question better than Lang
and tell him why he made such a film or why he needs film
in order to live. Qualifying this, however, Lang says he
is afraid of finding out too much, since this might take
away his creative urges.

Noames asks if Lang believes that a director's personal
problems are indeed expressed through his style, his mise-
en-scène. Answering a more general question, Lang notes
that often directors can communicate more through dialogue
than through visual means. In Antonioni's films, a woman
walking restlessly through the streets expresses something,
but it's too vague and imprecise. Lang suggests that films
can have a great influence on people's lives--so that, for
example, Antonioni's films could make one give up on life.
Noames comments that Lang's films also show people hopeless-
ly tracked by destiny, but Lang asserts that he has always
tried to show that an attitude of struggle was vital. Happiness is the search for happiness: Lang is happiest when
in the midst of a film project rather than when it's done.

Noames and Lang next get into a discussion of the tension
in film between stillness and movement. Lang does not see
inaction as necessarily stillness, since a character may be
absorbing the force of some shock. Working in the silent
film perhaps gave directors the notion that movement is
essential.

Lang notes that Godard, for example, is interested not
so much in action as in the result of action. He goes on
to discuss working on Le Mépris and ways in which his and
Godard's approaches to making films are similar and different. [See Take One Interview, 1968, Entry No. 576]. Godard
is doing something new in cinema unlike those trying only to
make millions.

Noames wonders if people trained in the silent cinema
don't have a better idea of conveying character through
mise-en-scène since they had to work without dialogue, but
Lang denies this, again using Godard as the example. According to Lang, Godard is a very inventive filmmaker, and
he uses words in a fascinating way. Lang recalls the use
Godard made of Lang's statement that "Death is no solution,"
having Bardot read it out of a book on Fritz Lang. Godard
does not create his film in the cutting room but makes it
as he is going along, giving it a personal form.

Lang reiterates comments he often makes about producers
and how they influence films and about how film has now become an industry rather than an art. The French, he says,
seem to be reviving its artistic possibilities, however.

573   "Qui-êtes-vous, Fritz Lang?" <u>Le Film Français</u> (4 April).  In
      German, in <u>Film</u> (Munich), No. 8 (June-July).
          This short interview is one of those where Lang clearly
      does not want to say much and makes things difficult for
      the interviewer.  The occasion is the Cannes Film Festival,
      at which Lang was presiding.  Asked how he feels being fam-
      ous enough for such a role, Lang merely plays with the ques-
      tion.  He refuses to discuss <u>Le Mépris</u> or what he thinks
      about the French view of him, but refers his interviewer to
      the <u>Cahiers</u> critics when asked who his friends are.  Avoid-
      ing most questions about actors who worked with him, Lang
      nevertheless notes that he would love to see Peter Lorre
      again.  He agrees that film is his greatest love and that
      he would not have it otherwise.  Refusing to comment on the
      state of film as an art, Lang merely notes that one always
      hopes for a rosy future.  Asked what he thinks about his
      own work and about what he has contributed to the art of the
      film, Lang notes only how much daily life has always in-
      fluenced him.  He wryly comments that he is working hard on
      his next "mistake."  Asked if he can provide a happy recipe
      for life out of his long experience, Lang says that he hopes
      the festival will treat young film directors as generously
      as he was treated as a young man.

## 1967

574   Madsen, Axel.  "Fritz Lang:  An Interview." <u>Sight and Sound</u>
      (London), 36, No. 3 (Summer), 109-112.
          Madsen recapitulates an interview with Lang, writing
      from a subjective point of view.  Madsen first reflects on
      Lang's age and on the fact that "his vision has its origin
      in a fallen Germany."  For Lang, Madsen says, the twentieth-
      century means Dachau and Hiroshima more than Einstein, the
      development of knowledge, or the new abundance.  He out-
      lines the paradox of Lang, Goethean man, living isolated in
      the most American of cities, Los Angeles, which reflects
      values Lang deplores.
          He next analyzes the characteristic poses Lang assumes--
      the difficulty of interviewing him, his contrariness, his
      constant taking of an oppositional position.  Taboo topics
      include the collaboration with Brecht and money.
          Lang's relations with contemporary Germany are uneasy,
      although he did return in the 1950s and again in 1961 to
      make films.  Lang likes the new young German filmmakers and
      is supportive of them, but finds them misguided and spoiled.
      Noting that "no nation has a monopoly on cruelty," Lang
      criticized American studies of Germany and the obsession
      with things German as seen in <u>Hogan's Heroes</u>.  What America
      needed was an atomic war in order to be human.
          Turning to critics of his work, Lang comments on his

disappointment:  he attacks Sadoul for emphasizing his fascination with guilt and he considers Luc Moullet's text full
of inaccuracies.

The article ends with a series of comments by Lang on
the Mabuse films, on the film industry, and on his own work.
He condemns the American cinema for being too dependent on
dialogue and says that his own most creative period was in
the 1920s, in Germany.  Directing is applied psychology,
Lang believes, and he ends by contrasting his generation's
film techniques with those of men like Godard whom he admires.  Lang supports contemporary youth but fears for their
future.

575   Walker, Alexander.  Interview with Fritz Lang:  BBC, London,
      25 August.  Transcription in British Film Institute Library.
          In responding to Walker's questions, Lang discusses vari-
      ous issues that have come up in earlier interviews, but here
      he is relaxed, mellow, and less defensive.  He first talks
      about the changed role of the film director, from the one
      controlling things to one who is now at the mercy of produc-
      ers.  He refers to his conflict over Fury to demonstrate the
      point.  He then mentions something that will recur through-
      out the interview--namely that he would like a psychoanalyst
      to tell him why he makes certain films.  Turning to M, Lang
      describes how he and Thea von Harbou arrived at their theme,
      noting that the film was not based directly on the Dusseldorf
      murderer.  He comments on choosing and then directing Peter
      Lorre in M, stressing their close working relationship; for
      Lang, getting the best out of one's actors is the mark of a
      good director.
          Asked about his departure from Germany, Lang repeats
      the story of Das Testament des Dr. Mabuse [The Last Will of
      Dr. Mabuse], of the interview with Goebbels, and his sudden
      trip to Paris.
          Walker notes that Lang essentially started the spy genre
      and asks what Lang thinks of James Bond.  Lang is unimpressed,
      finding Bond full of clichés and improbabilities; he stresses
      that he got all his own ideas from the newspapers.  When
      Walker asks about Woman in the Moon, Lang notes his interest
      in technical things and the future at the time.  He had
      rocket experts working with him on the film, and later on,
      Werner von Braun put into practice what Lang had shown.
      Discussing Die Nibelungen, Lang notes his attempt to relate
      architecture to culture, providing contrasting settings for
      the sophisticated Burgundians and savage Huns.
          Walker turns to the theme of fate and destiny in Lang's
      work, and Lang again notes that he wishes a psychiatrist
      would explain his fascination with this.  While Lang admits
      to belief in some eternal law or mathematical concept in
      the universe, he says it is hard to make films showing this
      in post-World War II America.  He sees a decline in belief

in all institutions--the family, country, religion.  Physical pain alone makes people afraid, and this in some way
explains the violence in his films.  Violence is never there
for its own sake, however.

Lang notes that many of his films are deliberately critical of America--he names Scarlet Street, Woman in the Window,
and The Big Heat.  He believes that it is the duty of the
filmmaker to show people what is wrong in their society.

Discussing the relative virtues of working on location
and in a studio, Lang says that one can control a film's
rhythm much better in a studio.  He is unable to list his
particular directorial touches, noting again that that is for
the psychiatrist to reveal, but Walker points out the preva-
lence of mirrors and shadows.  Lang agrees that these symbolize the terror of the unknown.

Walker then asks Lang to discuss the experience of working with Godard on Le Mépris, and Lang ennumerates the differences between his and Godard's ways of working, while
noting his enormous respect for Godard and also his awareness of his influence on Godard and other New Wave directors.
Lang agrees that he stands by everything he says in the picture, since, in the end, Godard told him simply to play himself.

The topic of collaboration leads to discussion of Lang's
work with Brecht on Hangmen Also Die and also with his wife,
Thea von Harbou, in Germany earlier on.  Lang describes
their gradual alienation as von Harbou got closer to nazism,
the break finally coming over Das Testament.

The interview ends with a brief discussion of Lang's new
project about contemporary youth.  He is doing his research
for it now, talking to lots of young people, but he admits
that it is difficult to find out what he wants to know.  He
hopes the project will finally come off.  Young people, he
says, want to save themselves from the world Lang's generation created and are searching to create something new.

## 1968

576   Berg, Gretchen.  "Fritz Lang."  Take One (Montreal), 2, No. 2
      (November-December), 12-13.
         Lang begins by talking about making Contempt [Le Mépris],
      which becomes the central point of the interview.  He offers
      the following contrasts between his and Godard's ways of
      working, which he noticed while doing the film:
      (1) While Lang always comes to the set knowing exactly what
          he wants and will do, Godard improvises as he goes along;
      (2) Lang shoots a lot of close-ups, while Godard works main-
          ly in long-shots, partly because he cannot afford many
          takes or a lot of editing.  He thus does not have much
          material at his disposal;

(3) Godard strives hard to achieve a very personal form for his films, while Lang says he is more interested in the content than in the form;

(4) Lang notes that Godard is trying to follow in the footsteps of the old silent film masters, but Lang can see that since Godard never worked himself in that period he is really doing something entirely different. While the silent directors focused their shooting around action, Godard seems more interested in the results of action.

(5) Finally, Lang notes that he had always liked to shoot in the studio before he worked on Contempt, but that working with Godard he came to see the advantages of on-location shooting.

577    Ciment, Michel, Goffredo Fofi, Louis Seguin, Roger Tailleur. "Fritz Lang à Venise." [Discussion of expressionism, led by Lotte Eisner]. Positif (Paris), No. 94 (April), 9-15.
         Lang begins by saying that he is not an expressionist and does not know what expressionism means. He does not think that it is the job of a director to define expressionism, but he mentions Wegener as typical, perhaps, and disassociates himself from the kinds of film often called expressionist. Asked if Wiene was an expressionist, Lang comments that his films were "Caligarism." A critic outlines a few expressionist techniques--the painted decor, the use of shadows, exaggeration of gestures, the presentation of inner vision--but Lang says the deformation is not necessarily expressionism; if a man is drunk and one shows the world as he sees it, that is realism instead.
         In an attempt to explore some expressionist influences on Lang, a critic talks of the Austrian painter, Schiele, but Lang says that he had little contact with Viennese culture after 1908. He notes that the Americans were impatient with symbols and he tried not to use them. Mabuse did not contain symbolism, but was instead a history of its period.
         Lang agrees that his mise-en-scène became increasingly simple in America, but denies that he deliberately chose actors for their blank neutral look. He mentions that he would rather work with little-known actors than with stars, and while he usually works well with scriptwriters, he complains about what was done to Ministry of Fear. Mabuse could not have been made in America, because while the super-criminal expressed well the German obsession with obedience, the Americans wanted a man of the people for their hero.
         Asked about House by the River, Lang says that he undertook that film only because he was out of work due to the House Un-American Activities Committee witch-hunts. His leftist sympathies resulted in his being branded a communist. He was, however, interested in the atmosphere of doom, the water, the drowned woman. A little later on in the interview,

Lang complains about being rejected by MGM, about the effect
of McCarthyism on his career, about the way that directors
generally have to prostitute themselves in Hollywood, about
the despicable Hollywood ethic of making only safe films.
It is for all these reasons that he hasn't worked there for
so long.

Lang denies that he is obsessed with guilt in his films,
preferring to see his theme as a struggle against destiny,
and notes that it is more effective to suggest, rather than
show, violence. He uses as much violence as he does because
after the war people were disillusioned and no longer believed in traditions and the family. He says that he tried
to give a feel of the American West in his Westerns, but
that he had to depart from documentary truth if he was to
stick to the demands of the genre for idealization.

He made the Indian films, he says, in order to fulfill a
lifelong ambition, denied forty years ago, and when asked
about his future projects mentions his wish to make a film
about contemporary youth. He finds significant the recent
phenomenon of unmotivated violence, which eludes even the
psychiatrists. Films, he concludes, reflect their period
and thus remakes rarely work. Although frequently asked to
remake M, he refused for that reason.


1969


578    Blume, Mary. "Fritz Lang Visits His Children." International
       Herald Tribune (4 April), p. 14.
       Lang is in Paris for a showing of his Woman in the Window
       at the Cinémathèque. Madame Ozeray, who acted in Lang's
       Liliom, is with him at the interview. When she's asked how
       it was to work with Lang, she declares it was marvellous,
       but Lang characteristically berates her for lying. Blume
       notes what an imposing man Lang is, although seventy-eight
       years old, and, sadly, that he will not make any more films.
       Until the late 1950s in France, little attention had been
       given to the American films, but people are now interested
       in them.

       Lang begins by complaining that interviews are boring
       but that this is not because the questions are all the same
       but rather that the answers are. He defends the ending of
       Woman in the Window by commenting that it would be too much
       for people to take if a man was punished so cruelly for one
       moment's inattention. Asked about resemblances between You
       Only Live Once and Bonnie and Clyde suggested by Pauline
       Kael and Arthur Schlesinger, Lang denies there is anything
       to it. He goes on to say that he is against violence him-
       self, but that since people today are violent, filmmakers
       must insert violent scenes to satisfy them.

       Lang likes to visit campuses and talk to students, but

is confused as to what he can teach the young. He agrees
that they have inherited a rotten world. He then recalls
how very much he learned from coming to America, giving up
talking and reading German immediately so that he could
really get to know the people. He lived with Indians, read
comic books, and had affairs only with Americans. Cinema
has always been his life, his main love, he says, and concludes that a man like him cannot anyway really consider
one place his home, since he has always had to travel around
and does not now belong anywhere.

579   Langlois, Gérard. "Fritz Lang: Une main tendue vers la
        jeunesse." Les Lettres Françaises (16 April), p. 16.
        In his introduction, Langlois notes how Lang is now known
as one of the greatest directors, both in terms of his visual style and his themes. More has been written about Lang
than almost any other director, crowds flock to his films,
he has established contact between the generations and overcome the split between form and content. He most understood
both Freud and Brecht and gave us moral values. Because of
him, we understand America better, and he ennobled traditional genres like the gangster and Western. The interview took
place on the occasion of the showing of Lang's Woman in the
Window in Paris. Although he has not made a film in the
last ten years, Lang has kept his watchful eye on the world.
        Langlois asks Lang to situate his film in its political
and social context, but instead of doing this, Lang discusses
the debate surrounding the ending of the film, when all is
found to have been a dream. He didn't think that people
would have stood for a man's being so severely punished for
one moment's inattention.
        The next question has to do with the symbolism of Lang's
camera movements in the film. Lang asks for an example of
symbolic camera movement and then notes that he is not interested in symbolism--he tried to give his films a documentary feeling.
        Asked about whether shooting in a studio or on location
is better, Lang replies that since in Hollywood studios are
built like reality, why not use them? He complains that one
cannot hear the actors in New Wave films on location. The
last question is about his not liking his own films; using
Ministry of Fear and Moonfleet as examples, Lang complains
of the interference in the projects by scriptwriters or production managers. That way of working does not please him,
because he does not have full control. Hence, films rarely
turned out as he wanted.

1970

580   Jensen, P. M. "Fritz Lang and Reflections of Present Day

Moods." Filmograph (Orlean, Virginia), 1, No. 3, 21.

Jensen begins by talking negatively about Lang, suggesting that few of his works are great and seeing the repetition of similar themes over forty films as a limitation.
He mentions how difficult Lang is in personal relations--
with actors, producers, and interviewers.

After this, Jensen turns to Lang's world view, denying
that it is pessimistic in the sense of an implacable fate.
God does not rule humanity, for people can gain freedom if
they want to.  Three types of control emerge in Lang's films:
that of the mastermind criminal, that of the mob, and finally that of inner compulsions, where the heroes themselves
contribute to their downfall.

Lang offers no solutions, however; while he presents
things subjectively, he does not enter into his characters'
lives, remaining coldly dispassionate about the people he
creates.  This distance, according to Jensen, makes Lang's
films "modern."  Like many other contemporary filmmakers,
Lang emphasizes technique over content, but his style differs
from the new, jazzy, brightly colored, fast-paced modes; instead, Lang takes a slow, steady look, which brings out the
eeriness in things.  Lang is contemporary also in his use
of familiar genres for more than straight narrative, concen-
trating on setting and mood.

Finally, Lang is modern in the kind of irrational violence that takes place in his work, and in the sense of terror at large in the world, echoing the reality of people's
lives in the big cities today.


### 1971

581  "Selbstdarstellung: Fritz Lang."  Frankfurter Rundschau
     (15 May).

The eighty-year-old Lang in an interview:

"I am blind . . . my eyes were never very good.  In my
left eye I wore a monocle.  With this eye I directed.  With
the other I edited. . . ."

"It is often asserted that there was always something of
Hitler in my German films.  They called my films fascist.
That is nonsense.  I wanted to portray the German person.
Der müde Tod [Destiny] was the romantic German.  Mabuse was
the postwar German.  It is said today that Mabuse was the
first gangster film.  That may be.  Unlike the American
gangster, Mabuse does not commit crime for money.  Mabuse is
a child of Nietzsche.  He wants power.  Die Nibelungen was
the German legend.  Metropolis was the man of a future that
had already begun.  With Metropolis I began to think politically for the first time.  Metropolis actually turned out to
be something different from what I intended.  That's why I
don't like the film much."

582    Wendevogel, N. [Heinz Ohff].  "Scharf und Schnell:  Fritz Lang."
       Der Tagesspiegel (1 July), p. 4.
            The interview takes place at the Berlin Film Festival,
       Wendevogel prefacing the discussion by referring to the
       patch Lang is now wearing over one eye, like an old pirate,
       together with thick spectacles--both a dramatic contrast to
       the aristocratic monocle Lang was famous for in the 1920s.
       Lang says he is as blind as a bat, but like a bat he is ac-
       tive, although eighty years old; he sits there, the incarna-
       tion of film history, and as sharp and alert as if he had
       not just flown for two days without sleep.  But he is not
       a promising interviewee, says Wendevogel, for the smallest
       interchange may end in a row.  He will complain about being
       blamed for what goes on in his films, claiming that he al-
       ways worked collectively.  Asked about expressionism, Lang
       claims not to know what the word means, admitting only that
       he liked Kokoshka and some of the expressionist painters.
            Questioned about having laid the groundwork for the Nazi
       propaganda film with his Die Nibelungen, Lang shrugs his
       shoulders and denies having even seen the films.  But he is
       now revising his opinion of Metropolis, since Hollywood has
       become so materialistic, with directors and producers work-
       ing like computers.  He is now not sure that he was wrong
       to see the lack of "heart" as crucial.  He does not believe
       that money alone can produce good movies.
            Wendevogel mentions the way in which Lang has been re-
       ceived in France, with Der Tiger von Eschnapur [The Tiger
       of Bengal] being viewed as the best film of the century.
       He is now rumored to be considering a film about modern
       youth but when asked about it, Lang notes that this was
       also the theme of his last film, which was butchered by the
       editor.  Lang has become bitter because he fell between
       things in Hollywood, wanting neither to be an art director
       nor to be simply commercial.  He was essentially a humanist
       director with aristocratic tendencies.
            Lang brushed aside any notion of regret as is his manner,
       Wendevogel says.  Having had a long life, Lang does not want
       to complain.  He is a wise man, who understands a lot about
       the world, Wendevogel concludes.


                                1972


583    Bagh, Peter von.  "En diktares solnedgång."  Chaplin 112
       (Stockholm), No. 1, 22-25.
            [Lang becomes increasingly belligerent and uncooperative
       with interviewers during the 1970s, and this discussion with
       Bagh is a good example of the way he can make things diffi-
       cult for them, ed.]
            The interveiw takes place at the 1971 Berlin Film
       Festival.  Bagh begins by discussing how difficult it was


                                440

to get to see Lang, relating this to the hatred for critics that Lang had developed by this time. Lang gets into a fight with Bagh over whether or not Lang produced his own films, whether or not his films contain violence, and about the degree of realism in the films. Lang denies here that he dealt with fantasy, claiming instead that his films were always documentaries, about real people.

## 1973

584    Kirk, Cynthia. "Pioneer '73: Four Evenings with Directors Fritz Lang, Henry King, Norman Tauroe and Robert Lee." Action (Los Angeles), 8, No. 6 (November-December), 27-28.
       The discussion takes place on the occasion of a retrospective showing of Manhunt in Hollywood. With Lang in the question-and-answer session are Kevin Thomas, Ernst Lazlo, R. McDowell, Dan Taradash, and Julia Heron. Most of them remain quiet in order to allow Lang the center stage.
       Lang notes that he no longer believes in the concept of fate, thinking now that each of us creates our own destiny. After Ford had turned down Manhunt, Lang says he gladly took up the project, since he wanted to help Americans understand nazism. Discussing the scene in the film with Jenny (played by Joan Bennett) on the boardwalk, Lang says that Zanuck objected to the implications that she was a prostitute. Zanuck also did not want Lang to insert a lot of swastika imagery in the film. Questioned about his use of violence, Lang states that he is opposed to it in films and on television, arguing that it is much more effective not to show either explicit sex or violence. Asked what he thinks about Westerns, Lang says that he sees them as legends rather than history, notwithstanding a letter from an old Westerner asserting that Western Union represented the truth. Discussing the problems of film crews, Lang notes that he no longer had the privilege of a handpicked crew that moved with him from film to film (as he had had in Germany), but that he found a way to get along with crews, which was to turn up at 7:00 A.M. each day.

## 1974

585    Lang, Fritz. "Interviews." Dialogue on Film (The American Film Institute), 3, No. 5 (April), 2-13.
       In this interview, Lang discusses many aspects of his life, his career as a film director, and his thought. After a brief comment about his having learned more from bad films than from good ones, Lang surveys his background, youth, and the process by which he got into film. He mentions his experiences living a bohemian life in Paris, and then notes

how important it is for directors to love and know all kinds
of people.  Asked about contemporary films, Lang says he
finds them mainly amoral and aimless.  He particularly disliked Deep Throat, because it invaded what Lang considers a
private area, showing people what they should discover for
themselves through passion and love.  He stopped making
films at the end of the 1950s because he foresaw the decline
of the motion picture industry; there were also too many
people ready to go to producers with information that directors would rather have kept secret, thus causing working
problems.  Lang had great difficulty, for example, with the
sequence showing the execution in Sing Sing (at the start of
Beyond a Reasonable Doubt), which his producer wanted cut.

     Asked about his Westerns, Lang notes that he simply
wanted "to build legends with human beings."  He goes on to
say that he had always thought Westerns were a kind of religion for the American people.

     There is a brief discussion at this point of two anti-Nazi
films--Manhunt and Hangmen Also Die.  Lang got Manhunt after
it was turned down by Ford, and he was concerned to show how
awful the Nazis were.  He discusses the use of actors in
Hangmen here but toward the end of the interview returns to
the film to talk about the collaboration with Brecht and the
misunderstandings around introducing Wexley.  [Note:  the
best summary of this controversy can be found in Eisner's
Fritz Lang, ed.  See Entry No. 478.]

     Lang talks about the good relations he has always had
with crews and the long working hours, which he enjoys.
About actors, Lang notes how one must listen to what an
actor has to say.  He suggests that certain actors [he most
likely has Henry Fonda in mind, ed.] are saying false things
about him, but agrees that he does know exactly what he
wants and that must make him difficult to work with.

     Finally, Lang discusses his interest in violence and
murder, talking about gruesome cases he came across when at
the Berlin equivalent of Scotland Yard.  He notes that he has
wanted to be direct with his audience, respecting them and
not assuming a sixteen-year-old mentality.  He has always
tried to please people.


### 1975

586   Phillips, Gene D.  "Fritz Lang:  An Interview."  Focus on Film
      (London), No. 20 (Spring), pp. 43-51.  A section of this is
      reprinted in Atkins, Thomas R., ed.  Science Fiction Films.
      New York:  Simon & Schuster, 1976.
         Introducing his interview, Phillips compares the dominance
      of Lang's splendid Los Angeles house to his place in film
      history; his career culminated in winning an award from new
      young German filmmakers in 1973.

Phillips next asks about Lang's early life and Lang relates the way he ran away from home, saw his first film in
Brugge [Bruges, Belgium], traveled through Europe and the
Orient, how he felt at the outbreak of war, was inducted
into the army and wounded in battle, and fell into acting.
He got the lead in Peter Ostermeyer's play on account of
his Austrian accent; but he soon left the stage to write
scripts and finally to direct films.

Lang recounts again the work he did for Erich Pommer,
how he nearly directed Caligari, and that it was he who suggested the framing story; he tells of leaving Decla for Joe
May's company, where he wrote scripts and met Thea von
Harbou.  He recounts the story about the Indian films and
then how Harbou promised to write a script especially for
him to direct, which turned out to be Der müde Tod [Destiny].
This film failed at first in Germany, but was later taken up
enthusiastically after succeeding in Paris.  He tells how
Douglas Fairbanks bought the American rights, not to release
the film but to copy the tricks for his Thief of Bagdad.

Lang notes that his work always preoccupied him to the
expense of his social life; he never made an effort to meet
great directors.

Discussing Kracauer's comments on Die Nibelungen, Lang
rejects the interpretation; he was not looking toward a
leader like Hitler there, but simply hoping that Germans
could draw on the inspiration from the past in a period when
people were cynical and leaning toward death.

Lang speaks highly of Pommer as a producer who always
brought Lang in on decisions.  Recalling Metropolis, Lang
reiterates his later dislike for the film but is interested
in young people's taking it seriously; in a computer age,
the notion of the heart as mediator takes on new meaning.
Lang notes that he did not want to add sound for Die Frau
im Mond [Woman in the Moon], and Ufa was so angry that it
wanted to withdraw its contract with Lang.  Lang received
an offer to do a film with an independent company--and
agreed on condition that he have full control.  The film
made was M.  He tells the story of how he came to do the
whistling himself.

Talking about his early negative experiences with MGM
and Fury, Lang notes how he always insisted on having a
part in the script, the essential aspect of any film.  Asked
about his working routine, Lang tells how he always prepared the scenes in detail on paper the night before, thus
saving a lot of studio time.  He was never popular with producers anyway, mainly because he had founded the Screen
Directors' Guild; he got little support for Fury, if obstacles weren't deliberately placed in his way, and was unable
to be gracious to Louis B. Mayer when it was a success.  He
has recently tried to take negative comments more lightly.

His Westerns were popular, he thinks, because of the

realistic touches that the old cowboys appreciated.  In fact, the Westerns are analogous to legends like Die Nibelungen.

Phillips recalls how Lang was blacklisted by the House Un-American Activities Committee, and Lang admits he was on the list although he never had been a member of the Communist Party.  About his later films, he notes that he was drawn to While the City Sleeps through a newspaper article describing a murderer who said, "Catch me before I kill more."  About Secret Beyond the Door, Lang notes that the real criminal was the character played by Joan Fontaine, who refused to bail out her lover because she was in love with another man. He feels a personal link with the film, but refuses to talk about his personal life.  The films speak for themselves, he concludes.

## 1976

587   Phillips, Gene D.  "Fritz Lang Gives His Last Interview." Village Voice (Films in Focus) (16 August), p. 99.  Reprinted in Séquences, No. 86 (October 1976), pp. 19-24.

This interview adds nothing new to ones that went before. Phillips notes Lang's high place in film history and the recent award he won for best German film director.  Lang makes a comment about Dr. Mabuse and his intention of showing the despair and vice that followed the First World War; he negates Kracauer's reading of Die Nibelungen, saying that he merely wanted to provide a way out of pessimism for Germans, through identification with their epic past.

Phillips discusses the neglect of Lang's Das Testament des Dr. Mabuse [The Last Will of Dr. Mabuse], and regrets that Scarlet Street is not in distribution.  [The film is now available, ed.  See list at end of book.]

# Archival Sources

In this section, I have followed the format established by Robert Carringer and Barry Sabath in their Ernst Lubitsch: A Guide to References and Resources (G. K. Hall, 1977), and have copied their descriptions of libraries where appropriate. Elaine Burrows, NFI Viewings Supervisor at the British Film Institute, helped in compiling the information presented here.

## (1) American Libraries and Archives

588 Margaret Herrick Library, Academy of Motion Picture Arts and Sciences and Academy Foundation, 8949 Wilshire Boulevard, Beverly Hills, California, 90211; Susan Oka, Temporary Librarian, (213) 278-4313.
  9:00 A.M.-5:00 P.M. Monday, Tuesday, Thursday, Friday. Open to the public. Photograph duplication services available.

Scripts: Paramount Collection
You and Me--script material (first revised final script); pressbook; loose stills
Ministry of Fear--script material (censorship dialogue script, release dialogue, loose stills, script); pressbook

Stills: RKO Collection (Stills)
The Woman in the Window
Rancho Notorious
Clash by Night

While the City Sleeps
Beyond a Reasonable Doubt

Production Files (Clippings and Stills):
Der müde Tod (under Destiny)
Die Nibelungen (Siegfried)
                (Kriemhilds Rache)
Metropolis
Spione (under Spies)
Frau im Mond (under By Rocket to the Moon)
M
Das Testament des Dr. Mabuse (under The Will of Dr. Mabuse)
Liliom
Fury
You Only Live Once
You and Me
The Return of Frank James
Western Union
Manhunt
Hangmen Also Die
Ministry of Fear
The Woman in the Window
Scarlet Street
Cloak and Dagger
Secret Beyond the Door
House by the River
American Guerilla in the Philippines - clippings only
Rancho Notorious
Clash by Night
The Blue Gardenia
The Big Heat
Human Desire
Moonfleet
While the City Sleeps
Beyond a Reasonable Doubt
Das indische Grabmal (under The Indian Tomb) - clippings only

589    The Charles K. Feldman Library, American Film Institute Center
       for Advanced Film Studies, 501 Doheny Road, Beverly Hills,
       California, 90210; Anne G. Schlosser, Librarian, (213) 278-8777.
       9:00 A.M.-5:30 P.M.  Monday through Friday.  Open to
       scholars, historians, writers, educators, and advanced
       graduate students, as well as members of the entertainment
       industry.

Scripts:
Fury
The Big Heat

589a    George Eastman House, 900 East Avenue, Rochester, New York,
        14607; Dr. J. B. Kuiper, Department of Film, (716) 271-3361.

        Prints:
        Dr. Mabuse (35mm); abbreviated version for circulation in
        English-speaking countries; titled The Fatal Passions, inter-
        titles in English.
        Die Nibelungen:  Kriemhilds Rache (35 mm); version originally
        circulated in America; intertitles in German and English.
        Die Nibelungen:  Siegfrieds Tod (16 mm); 1933 reissue with
        music track and intertitles in French.
        Fury (35 mm)
        You Only Live Once (16 mm)
        Die Tausend Augen des Dr. Mabuse (16 mm); dubbed into English.


590     Lincoln Center Library for the Performing Arts, Theater
        Collection, New York Public Library, 111 Amsterdam Avenue/
        Lincoln Center, New York, New York, 10023; Paul Myers, Curator,
        (212) 799-2200 ext. 213 or 214.
            12:00 M.-8:00 P.M., Monday and Thursday; 12:00 M.-6:00 P.M.,
            Tuesday, Wednesday, Friday, and Saturday
            Photographic Service is available Monday through Saturday,
            12:15-6:00 P.M.

        Scripts:
        Fury
        Manhunt
        Hangmen Also Die
        The Big Heat
        You Only Live Once

        Published Scripts (in the Lincoln Center Circulating Library):
        Manvell, Roger, ed. Masterworks of German Cinema.  New York
            and London:  Harper & Row, Icon Editions, 1973; contains a
            script of M and a general introduction by Manvell.
        Garnham, Nicholas, ed. and trans.  M.  Classic Film Scripts.
            New York:  Simon & Schuster; London:  Lorrimer, 1968.
        Jensen, Paul, and Kracauer, Siegfried, eds.  Metropolis.  New
            York:  Simon & Schuster, 1973.  Introduction by Jensen and
            Kracauer.
        Gessner, John, and Nichols, Dudley, eds.  Twenty Best Film
            Plays.  New York:  Crown, 1943; contains script of Fury.

        Other:
        The Theater Collection at Lincoln Center contains an immense
        treasure of specialized materials for research on films by Lang.
        The cataloguing system is complex, and materials on Lang and
        his associates are to be found under several different classi-
        fications.  There is a file for virtually every Lang film re-
        leased in the United States.  For the silent era, the files

typically contain a few photographs, clippings (largely New York area newspaper reviews), a program, and a press sheet or pressbook. For the sound films there are clippings, a pressbook, and usually a larger number of photographs. (The clippings at Lincoln Center usually indicate source and date but not page number.)

591   Library of Congress, Motion Picture Section, Prints and Photographs Division, 1046 Thomas Jefferson Building, Washington, D.C., 20540; Barbara Humphrys, Emily Sigel, Reference Librarians, (202) 426-5000.
      8:30 A.M.-4:30 P.M., Monday through Friday
      The Motion Picture Section maintains the Library's film collections for scholarly study and research. Public projection, preview, and loan services are not available. The Section staff answers written and telephone inquires about the holdings and makes appointments for the use of the reference facilities by individual scholars. The viewing facilities may be used free of charge by serious researchers only; viewing times must be scheduled in advance. The facilities may not be used by high school students; undergraduate college students must provide a letter from their professor endorsing their project. The Section maintains a reading room with extensive card files describing the Library's motion picture holdings. The files include a shelflist, a dictionary catalog, a nitrate film file, a directors file, and chronological and production company files for silent films. Copies of film footage not restricted by copyright, by provisions of gift or transfer, or by physical condition may be ordered through the Section. The requester is responsible for a search, either in person or by mail, of Copyright Office records to determine the copyright status of specific works.

Prints:
While the City Sleeps, 1956.  (RKO)
Human Desire, 1954.  (Col)
The Blue Gardenia, 1953.  (WB)
Clash by Night, 1952.  (RKO)
Rancho Notorious, 1952.  (RKO)
American Guerilla in the Philippines, 1950.  (20th Century-Fox)
Scarlet Street, 1945.  (U)
Cloak and Dagger, 1946.  (WB)
Woman in the Window, 1944.  (RKO)
Ministry of Fear, 1944.  (Paramount Pictures)
You and Me, 1938.  (Paramount Pictures)
Dr. Mabuse, der Spieler, 1922.  (Germany)
Siegfrieds Tod, 1924.  (Germany)
Kriemhild's Revenge, 1924.  (Germany)
Metropolis, 1927.  (Germany)

592    Museum of Modern Art, Film Study Center, 11 West 53rd Street,
New York, New York, 10019; Charles Silver, Supervisor, (212)
956-4212.
Materials in the Film Study Center are made available
only to qualified scholars working on specific research
projects.  Students who wish to view films must present a
letter from their instructor requesting permission, stating
the nature and validity of the project, and listing the
films required.  Writers who present a similar letter from
their editor or publisher may also obtain permission to view
films.  The Department of Film retains the right of approving all requests.  Due to the limited facilities available,
no projects requiring extensively detailed analysis (i.e.,
shot analysis) of individual films can be permitted.  An
appointment is necessary.  The hours are from 1:00 P.M.-
5:00 P.M., Monday through Friday.  Appointments for viewing
films must be made at least one week in advance.  Film books
and older bound periodicals are located in the Museum Library.
Those who anticipate using these materials should make a
separate appointment with the library (212) 956-7236.  Film
stills are available through appointment with the stills
archivist only, (212) 956-4209.

Prints:
Die Spinnen, I & II (tinted)--English titles
Der müde Tod--English titles
Dr. Mabuse (abridged)--English titles
Die Nibelungen, I & II (some prints of Siegfried have English
titles; Eng. and German titles for Kriemhild)
Metropolis--English titles
Spione--English titles
Die Frau im Mond--English titles
M--English titles
Liliom--No titles
You Only Live Once
The Return of Frank James (B & W)
Western Union
Man Hunt
Hangmen Also Die (incomplete)
Scarlet Street
American Guerilla in the Philippines
Rancho Notorious
Beyond a Reasonable Doubt

Stills:
There is a sizeable collection of Lang stills in the MMA.

Scripts:
Hangmen Also Die (original MSs)
Rancho Notorious (original MSs, with Rancho Notorious pencilled
over first title The Legend of Chuck-A-Luck)

Woman in the Window (original MSs, title still Once off Guard)
You Only Live Once:  A series of scripts:
1. An early version, called Three-Time Loser, with Lang's notes, comments, and crossings out;
2. Fritz Lang's sequence notes and annotated sequence breakdown;
3. Two second drafts, with notes, comments, and deletions by Lang;
4. Two third drafts incorporating changes made in earlier versions with few notes by Lang;
5. A final draft with no notations.

There are copies of English titles to Metropolis, Siegfried, and Destiny

593   Theater Arts Library, University of California at Los Angeles, 405 Hilgard Avenue, Los Angeles, California, 90024; Audrae Malkin, Librarian, (213) 825-4880.
       9:00 A.M.-6:00 P.M., Monday through Friday, 12:00 M.-4:00 P.M., Saturday

Prints:
Die Spinnen I & II--35mm
Die Nibelungen--16mm
Spione--16mm (short version)
M--16mm
Ministry of Fear--35mm
The Woman in the Window--35mm

Scripts:
Metropolis (published screenplay)
M (published screenplay)
Fury (original MSs)
You Only Live Once (original MSs)
The Return of Frank James (original MSs)
Western Union (original MSs)
Hangmen Also Die (original MSs)
The Woman in the Window (original MSs)
Scarlet Street (original MSs)
Cloak and Dagger (original MSs)
Secret Beyond the Door (original MSs)

594   UCLA Film Archive, University of California at Los Angeles, 1438 Melnitz Hall, Los Angeles, California, 90024; Robert Rosen, Director, (213) 825-4142.
       Arrangements should be made in advance.

Prints:
Die Nibelungen--16 mm
Spione--16mm

M--35mm
You and Me--Paramount nitrate print, 35mm
Woman in the Window--35mm, nitrate
Ministry of Fear--35mm, nitrate

595   University Library, Communications Department, University of
      Illinois, Urbana, Illinois, 61801; Maynard Brichford, Nancy
      Allen, Archivists, (217) 333-2216.
          8:00 A.M.-12:00 M., 1:00 P.M.-5:00 P.M., Monday through
          Friday

      Scripts:
      American Guerrilla in the Philipines.  Revised final script
      dated 16 August 1945.  It includes notes from a script confer-
      ence involving Zanuck, Trotti, Lang, and Hakim.  It indicates
      script changes by Lang, and contains extensive notes.
      Return of Frank James.  Continuity and dialogue taken from the
      screen, dated 8 August 1940.
      Western Union.  Revised final screenplay dated 10 September
      1940.

596   Wisconsin Center for Film and Theater Research, 816 State
      Street, Madison, Wisconsin, 53706; Maxine Fleckner, Film
      Archivist, Steve Masar, Manuscripts Archivist, (608) 262-0585,
      262-8975.
          8:30 A.M.-4:30 P.M., Monday through Friday

      Prints (16mm):
      Der müde Tod
      Die Nibelungen (Parts 1 & 2)
      Spione
      M
      The Woman in the Window

      Scripts:
      You Only Live Once--(also negatives and pressbook)
      Hangmen Also Die--(also negatives)
      The Woman in the Window
      Secret Beyond the Door

      Stills:
      Metropolis
      M
      Das Testament des Dr. Mabuse--(also negatives)
      Liliom
      Fury
      You Only Live Once
      Return of Frank James
      Western Union

Hangmen Also Die
The Woman in the Window
Scarlet Street
Cloak and Dagger
Secret Beyond the Door
American Guerilla in the Philippines
Rancho Notorious
Clash by Night
The Blue Gardenia
The Big Heat
Human Desire
Moonfleet
While the City Sleeps
Beyond a Reasonable Doubt


(2)   Foreign Libraries and Archives

597   AUSTRALIA
National Film Archive, National Library of Australia, Parkes
Place, Canberra, ACT, 2600, Australia.

Prints:
M--16mm (3457 ft)
Metropolis--16mm (3286 ft)


598   BRAZIL
Museu de Arte Moderna do Rio De Janeiro, Cinemateca, Avenida
Beira-Mar Caixa Postal 44, End. Tel. Museuarmo, Rio De Janeiro
Rj Brasil, Telephone:   231 18 71.

Prints:
Der müde Tod--16mm (English intertitles)
Siegfrieds Tod--16mm (sound version, French intertitles)
Kriemhilds Rache--16mm (English intertitles)
Metropolis--16mm (English intertitles)
Spione--9.5mm (Portuguese intertitles)
Spione--16mm (English intertitles)
Die Frau im Mond--16mm (German intertitles)
M--35mm (Portuguese subtitles)
Western Union--16mm (English version)
The Secret Beyond the Door--35mm (Portuguese subtitles)
The Secret Beyond the Door--16mm (Portuguese subtitles)


599   CZECHOSLOVAKIA
Czechoslovak Film Archives, Czechoslovak Film Institute,
Národní, 40, 110 00 Praha 1; Slavoj Ondroušek, Director,
Telephone:   2600 87.
     The curator sent a list of written materials, which included

books, clippings, press materials, and articles from foreign
magazines. The list is long and contains, besides the
French, English, and German documents (annotated here),
materials in Eastern European languages not researched.
There was no mention of either prints or stills.

600    DENMARK
       Det Danske Filmmuseum, St. Søndervoldstraede, 1419 København K;
       Ib Monty, Director, Telephone:  Asta 6500.

Prints:
The Danish Film Museum has prints of the following films:
Das Brillantenschiff
Der Goldene See
Der müde Tod
Die Nibelungen (Siegfrieds Tod and Kriemhilds Rache)
Metropolis
M
Das Testament des Dr. Mabuse
Fury
You Only Live Once
Clash by Night
Moonfleet
The Woman in the Window
Die tausend Augen des Dr. Mabuse

Script Materials:
Rancho Notorious (Cutting continuity)
The Big Heat (picture continuity + dialogue continuity + title
instruction list)
Human Desire (picture continuity + dialogue continuity +
spotting list)
Beyond a Reasonable Doubt (cutting continuity)
While the City Sleeps (cutting continuity)
Die tausend Augen des Dr. Mabuse (German dialogue list)

Stills:
Die Spinnen (1 still)
Harakiri (1 still)
Der müde Tod (6 stills)
Die Nibelungen (16 stills)
Metropolis (65 stills, most of them production stills)
Frau im Mond (52 stills)
M (45 stills)
Das Testament des Dr. Mabuse (25 stills from French version)
Liliom (2 stills)
Fury (45 stills)
You Only Live Once (33 stills)
You and Me (6 stills)
The Return of Frank James (18 stills)

Western Union (14 stills)
Manhunt (81 stills)
Hangmen Also Die (30 stills)
Ministry of Fear (21 stills)
The Woman in the Window (34 stills)
Scarlet Street (44 stills)
Cloak and Dagger (39 stills)
Secret Beyond the Door (6 stills)
House by the River (20 stills)
American Guerilla in the Philippines (11 stills)
Rancho Notorious (33 stills)
Clash by Night (12 stills)
The Blue Gardenia (8 stills)
The Big Heat (1 still)
Human Desire (49 stills)
Moonfleet (41 stills)
While the City Sleeps (9 stills)
Der Tiger von Eschnapur (9 stills)
Die tausend Augen des Dr. Mabuse (41 stills) + 40 personality
stills of Lang.

Clippings:
Files of newspaper clippings (mainly Danish material) and Danish
souvenir programs of the following films:
Die Spinnen
Harakiri
Der müde Tod
Die Nibelungen
Metropolis
Spione
Frau im Mond
M
Das Testament des Dr. Mabuse
Liliom
Fury
You Only Live Once
You and Me
The Return of Frank James
Western Union
Manhunt
Hangmen Also Die
Ministry of Fear
The Woman in the Window
Scarlet Street
Cloak and Dagger
Secret Beyond the Door
House by the River
American Guerilla in the Philippines
Rancho Notorious
Clash by Night
The Blue Gardenia

The Big Heat
Human Desire
Moonfleet
While the City Sleeps
Der Tiger von Eschnapur
Die tausend Augen des Dr. Mabuse

Other:
The Danish Museum has an extensive library containing most of
the standard materials on Lang in English, some in French, and
a few in German.  There are some additional Danish materials.


601   FRANCE
      Service des Archives du Film, 78390--Bois D'Arcy, France;
      Nicole Schmitt, Librarian, Telephone:  460-20-50.

      Prints:
      La Mort de Siegfried, 1922 (silent)
      La Vengeance de Kriemhild, 1924 (silent), (incomplete)
      Metropolis, 1927
      La Femme au Portrait, 1944, negatifs
      Le Tigre du Bengale, 1958, 16mm
      Le Tombeau Hindou, 1959, 16mm


602   La Cinémathèque Française, 82 Rue de Courcelles, Paris 8e;
      Madame Meerson, Director.
           It is extremely hard to obtain information about holdings
      in the Cinémathèque and difficult to set up appointments
      for viewings.  I understood from Lotte Eisner that there are
      a large number of Lang films in the collection, including
      Die Spinnen and a color version of Western Union.  Eisner
      also told me that the Cinémathèque was trying to organize
      some kind of documentation section, and that she had given
      her own collection of Lang scripts, left with her by Lang
      himself.  These contained, she said, notes by Lang.  There
      is a collection of set design materials for Metropolis.


603   GERMANY (EAST)
      Staatliches Filmarchiv der DDR, Hausvogteiplatz 3-4, 108 Berlin
      (East); Wolfgang Klaue, Director, Eckhardt Jahnke, Archives,
      Telephone:  21-243-24.
           I did not receive a complete list of prints in this archive,
      but I know they have many of the early works, including
      those by Otto Rippert and Joe May for which Lang wrote
      scripts.

604   GERMANY (WEST)
Deutschen Film und Fernsehakademie, Pommernallee 1, 1000 Berlin
19 (West); Heinz Rathsack, Director, Telephone:   3036-212 and
234.

Prints:
Der müde Tod
Dr. Mabuse, der Spieler
Die Nibelungen, Part 1
Spione
Die Frau im Mond
M
Das Testament des Dr. Mabuse
Die tausend Augen des Dr. Mabuse

Stills:
about 600

Other:
Architectural drawings for the following films:
Die Nibelungen
Metropolis
M
Das Testament des Dr. Mabuse

Sketches for costumes for Metropolis
Masks of the seven deadly sins from Metropolis
A number of posters, among them Dr. Mabuse, der Spieler by
Theo Matejko (collection Gero Gandert)
Fragment of the scenario Das Testament des Dr. Mabuse
Comprehensive parts of handwritten orchestra scores for Die
Nibelungen
Two letters by Fritz Lang
Press clippings concerning the personality and work of Fritz
Lang up to 1933
Three novels, deluxe special editions signed by Thea von Harbou
    and Fritz Lang on the occasion of the first showing of
    Metropolis, Spione and Die Frau im Mond (Collection Gero
    Gandert)
2 volumes "Decla-Abenteuerromane" (adventure novels) to Die
    Spinnen (Collection Gero Gandert).

Scripts:  (Published)
Gero Gandert and Ulrich Gregor, eds., M.  Hamburg:  Marion von
Schroder, 1963.


605   Deutsches Institut für Filmkunde, Schloss, 6202 Wiesbaden-
Biebrich; Eberhard Spiess, Library Director, Dorothea Gebauer,
Archives, Telephone:  69074-75.
      This is a well-organized and well-run library, containing

all the standard materials on Lang.  In addition, there is
an impressive collection of newspaper clippings in various
languages, although the focus is naturally on German papers.
Also important is the nearly complete run of rare German
trade periodicals like Der Film (late 1918 to 1926) and
Der Kinematograph (1908 to 1935).  Herr Spiess is particularly helpful in tracking down materials.

Prints:
I was unfortunately unable to obtain a full list of Lang films
in the archive, but they have a number of early works, including Die Spinnen.  Scholars should write to Dorothea Gebauer for
more information.


606   Münchner Stadtmuseum, St. Jakobs Platz 1, D 8 München 2; Enno
Patalas, Curator.


Prints:
Die Spinnen (Der goldene See, Das Brillantenschiff)
Der müde Tod (with original titles)
Dr. Mabuse, der Spieler (Der grosse Spieler; Inferno)
Die Nibelungen (Siegfried:  complete, with original titles;
Kriemhilds Rache (nearly complete)
Metropolis (American version)
Spione (complete, with original titles)
Die Frau im Mond
M (complete)
Das Testament des Dr. Mabuse


Scripts:  (Published)
Gero Gandert and Ulrich Gregor, eds., M.  Hamburg:  Marion von
Schroder, 1963.


607   GREAT BRITAIN
The British Film Institute, Information and Documentation, 127
Charing Cross Road, London WCH2 OEA; Gillian Hartnoll, Susan
Huxley, Research Librarians.  National Film Archive, 81 Dean
Street, London W1V 6AA; Contact:  Elaine Burroughs.
    9:00 A.M.-6:00 P.M., Monday to Friday; open late two even-
ings a week.
Scholars must be members of the British Film Institute or
make special arrangements to use the collection.  The BFI
is an unusually convenient film library.  There are open
stacks containing a wide range of film books in various
languages.  These books may be borrowed by Institute members.  More books are available on reference shelves, but
these must be read in the library.  There are individual
cards for each film director, listing all the main reviews
and articles, but there are also cards for each film, listing

articles and reviews. There are, in addition, fiches for each film, containing newspaper reviews and other materials from film clubs and theaters, such as program notes. The librarians are particularly helpful in locating materials. The BFI has a good collection of early film journals and of the lesser known, often unavailable, journals in various languages.

Prints:
The following are definitely available for viewing:
Die Nibelungen
Metropolis
Das Testament des Dr. Mabuse
M
Liliom
Fury
You and Me
Hangmen Also Die
Ministry of Fear
Cloak and Dagger
Human Desire
The following are sometimes available:
Dr. Mabuse, der Spieler (both parts)
Die Frau im Mond
You Only Live Once
Manhunt
Scarlet Street
Secret Beyond the Door
The Blue Gardenia
The Big Heat
Moonfleet
Das indische Grabmal
Der Tiger von Eschnapur

Stills:
The BFI has a fairly large and varied collection of stills.

608   HUNGARY
Magyar Filmtudomanyi Intézet És Filmarchivum (Hungarian Cinémathèque and Film Research Institute), Nepstadion ut 97, Budapest XlV, Hungary; Dr. Istvan Molnar, Head of Archive.

Prints:
Doktor Mabuse, der Spieler
Die Nibelungen, I & II
Metropolis
Frau im Mond

609   ITALY
Museo Nazionale del Cinema, 10122 Torino - Palazzo Chiablese,
Plazza S. Giovanni 2; Roberto Radicati, Librarian, Telephone:
510-370.

Prints:
You Only Live Once:  Italian version Sono innocente, 16mm
copy
Siegfrieds Tod

Other Material:
Die Niebelungen:   4 pages of presentation of the film (in
                      German) 1923
                   8 pages of presentation of the film (in
                      Kriemhilds Rache (in German) 1923
                   Booklet with presentation of the film
                      Siegfrieds Tod in 4 pages of photos and
                      1 page with F. Lang and Thea von Harbou
                      portraits (in German).
Die Frau im Mond:  La femme sur la Lune - La Petite Illustration
No. 47
Metropolis
Issue of La Petite Illustration, No. 372--Cinéma No. 11
(3 March 1928) (in French) 12 pages
The posters of the Italian version of:
The Return of Frank James (1940
Western Union (1941)
Hangmen Also Die (1942)
Scarlet Street (1943)
Cloak and Dagger (1947)
The Secret Beyond the Door (1948)
House by the River (1950)
American Guerrilla in the Philippines (1950)
Clash by Night (1952)
Rancho Notorious (1952)
The Blue Gardenia (1953)
The Big Heat (1953)
Beyond a Reasonable Doubt (1956)
While the City Sleeps (1956)
Also article in Cinéma No. 15 - 22 March 1930--pp. 15-18.


610   NORWAY
Norsk Filminstitutt, Aslakveien 14 B, Postboks 5 Røa--Oslo 7,
Norway; Jon Stenklev, Librarian, Telegram:  Filminstitutt,
Telephone:  (02) 24 29 94.

Prints:
Das Testament des Dr. Mabuse
M (Mörder unter uns)
Rancho Notorious
Clash by Night

611   SPAIN
Filmoteca Nacional de españa, Carretera de la Dehesa de la
Villa s/n, Madrid 35; Catherine Gautier, Librarian, Telephone:
243 47 95.

Prints:
Siegfried--Incomplete; 1200m (Spanish titles)
Kriemhilds Rache--2200m (Spanish titles)
M--2714m (dubbed into Spanish)
Le Testament du Dr. Mabuse--(French version, Spanish subtitles)

# Film Distributors

Below is a list of 16mm Lang films currently available for nontheatrical rental in the United States, arranged alphabetically, with an abbreviation opposite indicating the rental source. Following the list of films is an alphabetical list identifying rental sources and giving addresses and phone numbers of the agencies. A few titles are also listed as available for purchase and are so indicated here.

| Film | Distributor |
|---|---|
| American Guerrilla in the Philippines (1950) | FNC |
| Beyond a Reasonable Doubt (1956) | BUD, CHA, KPF, UF, WCF, WHO, IVY, VCI |
| The Big Heat (1953) | BUD, CON, MAC, SEL, WCF, WHO, WIL |
| Clash by Night (1952) | AIM, BUD, KPF, MAC, UF, WCF |
| The Crimes of Dr. Mabuse (1933) (Das Testament des Dr. Mabuse) | CFM, IMA, NCS (Sale), BUD, JAN, IMA; longer version of the film, titled Last Will of Dr. Mabuse is available from JAN (120 min.) |
| Die Spinnen (1919/1920) | KPF |

Destiny (1921)

NCS, IMA (sale), KPF, BUD, CFM,
EMG, IMA, JAN, MMA, TMC, UF, SKY,
CLA

Dr. Mabuse, King of Crime
(1921/22), Pt. II

JAN

Dr. Mabuse, der Spieler, Pt. I

THU (sale), BUD, CFM, CSV, EMG,
IMA, JAN, KPF, MMA

Fury (1936)

FNC

Hangmen Also Die (1943)

CTH, BUD

Human Desire (1954)

BUD

Journey to the Lost City (1960)
(American edited version of Der
Tiger von Eschnapur and Das
indische Grabmal) (1959)

NAT

Kriemhild's Revenge (1924)

BAU, BUD, CAL, CFM, EMG, IMA,
KPF, MAC, MMA, RAD; sale: BLA,
RAD, SEL; sound version: KPF

M (1931)

BAU, BUD, CAL, CFM, IMA, JAN,
KPF, MAC, NIL, SEL, TWY, VCI, WHO,
WIL; sale: CIE, GME, IMA, NCS

Manhunt (1941)

FNC

Metropolis (1927)

AIM, BUD, CAL, CFM, CFS, CWF,
EMG, FNC, IMA, JAN, KER, KPF,
MAC, MMA, NIL, RAD, ROA, SEL,
TMC, UNI, VCI, WCF, WHO, WIL;
sale: CIE, FIN, GME, IMA, MAN,
NCS, RAD, SEL, THU; sound version:
VCI, WHO

Ministry of Fear (1944)

UNI

Moonfleet (1955)

FNC

Rancho Notorious (1952)

AB, BUD, KPF, UF, MAC, MOD, ROA,
VCI; lease: VCI

Return of Frank James (1940)

SEL, VCI, WIL, BUD, UF, WC

Scarlet Street (1945)

AIM, BAU, BUD, EMG, IMA, KPF,
MAC, TMC; sale: CIE, GPS, KPF

Siegfried (1924)    BAU, BUD, CAL, EMG, JAN, KPF, MAC, MMA, RAD; sale: EMG, GPS, RAD

Spies (1928)    BAU, BUD, EMG, CLA, IVY, JAN, KPF, MAC, MMA, RAD, UF, VCI; sale: BLA (sound version), BLA, RAD (silent version)

Thousand Eyes of Dr. Mabuse (1961)    EMG, BUD, KPF, MAC

Western Union (1941)    FNC (color and B & W)

While the City Sleeps (1956)    MAC, BUD, KPF, UF

Woman in the Moon (1929)    MAC, CLA, KPF

Woman in the Window (1944)    UAS

You and Me (1938)    UNI

You Only Live Once (1937)    KPF, LCA, MAC, WCF; sale: LCA

## Directory of Addresses and Telephone Numbers

AIM    Association Instructional Materials (Association Films), 866 Third Ave., New York, NY 10022    (212) 736-9693

BAU    Bauer International, 119 N. Bridge St., Somerville, NY 08876 (201) 526-5656

BLA    Blackhawk Films, Eastin-Phelan Corp., Davenport, IA 52808 (319) 323-9736 and (800) 553-1163

BUD    Budget Films, 4590 Santa Monica Blvd., Los Angeles, CA 90029 (213) 660-0187

CAL    University of California, Extension Media Center, 2223 Fulton St., Berkeley, CA 94720    (415) 845-6000

CFM    Classic Film Museum, 4 Union Square, Dover-Foxcroft, ME 04426 (207) 564-8371

CFS    Creative Film Society, 7237 Canby Ave., Reseda, CA 91335 (213) 881-3887

CHA    Charard Motion Pictures, 2110 E. 24th St., Brooklyn, NY 11229 (212) 891-4339

CHU    Churchill Films, 622 N. Robertson Blvd., Los Angeles, CA 90069

CIE    Cinema Concepts/Cinema Eight, 91 Main St., Chester, CT 06412
       (203) 526-9513

CNF    Cine Information, PO Box 315, Franklin Lakes, NJ 07417
       (201) 891-8240

CTH    Corinth Films, 410 E. 62nd St., New York, NY 10021
       (212) 421-4770

CWF    Clem Williams Films, 2240 Noblestown Rd., Pittsburgh, PA 15205
       (412) 921-5810

EMC    Educational Media Corp., 2036 Le Moyne Ave., Los Angeles, CA
       90026    (213) 660-4076

EMG    Em Gee Film Library, 16024 Ventura Blvd., Suite 211, Encino,
       CA 91436    (213) 981-5506

FIN    Edward Finney, 1578 Queens Rd., Hollywood, CA 90069
       (213) 656-0200

FMC    Film-Makers' Cooperative, 175 Lexington Ave., New York, NY
       10016    (212) 889-3820

FNC    Films Incorporated, 1144 Wilmette Ave., Wilmette, IL 60091
       (312) 256-4730    (rental)

GME    Griggs-Moviedrome, 263 Harrison St., Nutley, NJ 07110

GRA    Graphic Curriculum, 600 Madison Ave., New York, NY 10021
       (212) 688-0033

IMA    Images Motion Picture Rental Library, 2 Purdy Ave., Rye, NY
       10580    (914) 967-1102

IMP    Impact Films, 144 Bleecker St., New York, NY 10012
       (212) 674-3375

IVY    Ivy Films/16, 165 W. 46th St., New York, NY 10036
       (212) 765-3940

JAN    Janus Films, 745 Fifth Ave., New York, NY 10022
       (212) 753-7100

KPF    Kit Parker Films, PO Box 227, Carmel Valley, CA 93924
       (408) 659-4131 or 650-3474

LCA    Learning Corp. of America, 1350 Ave. of the Americas, New York,
       NY 10019    (212) 397-9330

MAC    Macmillan Films/Audio Brandon Films, 34 MacQuesten Pkwy. S., Mount Vernon, NY 10550    (800) 431-1994 or (800) 742-1889

MAN    Manbeck Pictures, 3621 Wakonda Dr., Des Moines, IA 50321

MMA    Museum of Modern Art, Department of Film, 11 W. 53rd St., New York, NY 10019    (212) 956-4204 or 956, 4205

MOD    Modern Sound Pictures, 1402 Howard St., Omaha, NE 68102 (402) 341-8476

NAT    National Film Serv., 14 Glenwood Ave., Raleigh, NC 27602 (919) 932-3901

NCE    New Cinema Enterprises, 35 Britain St., Toronto, Ontario, Canada M5A 1R7

NCS    National Cinema Service, 333 W. 57th St., New York, NY 10019 (212) 247-4343

NIL    Niles Inc., 1019 S. Michigan St., South Bend, IN 46618 (800) 348-2462

RAD    Film Images/Radim Films, 17 W. 60th St., New York, NY 10023 (212) 279-6653

ROA    ROA's Films, 1696 N. Astor St., Milwaukee, WI 53202 (414) 271-0861 or (800) 558-9015

SEL    Select Film Library, 115 W. 31st St., New York, NY 10001 (212) 594-4500

THU    Thunderbird Films, 3501 Eagle Rock Blvd., Los Angeles, CA 90054 (213) 256-1034

TMC    The Movie Center, 57 Baldwin St., Charlestown, MA 02129 (617) 242-3456

TWF    Trans-World Films, 3222 S. Michigan Ave., Chicago, IL 60604 (312) 922-1530

TWY    Twyman Films, 4700 Wadsworth Rd., Dayton, OH 45414 (513) 222-4014 or (800) 543-9594

UAS    United Artists 16, 729 Seventh Ave., New York, NY 10019 (212) 575-4715

UF    United Films, 1425 South Main, Tulsa, OK 74119    (918) 584-6491

UNI    Universal 16, 445 Park Ave., New York, NY 10022    (212) 759-7500

VCI    Video Communications Inc., 6555 E. Skelly Dr., Tulsa, OK 74145
      (918) 583-2681

WCF    Westcoast Films, 25 Lusk St., San Francisco, CA 94107
      (415) 362-4700

WEL    Welling Motion Pictures, 454 Meacham Ave., Elmont, NY 11003
      (516) 354-1066/7/8

WES    Weston Woods Studios, Weston, CT 06880    (203) 226-0600

WHO    Wholesome Film Center, 20 Melrose St., Boston, MA   02116
      (617) 426-0155

WIL    Willoughby-Peerless, 110 W. 32nd St., New York, NY 10001
      (212) 564-1600 and 415 Lexington Ave., New York, NY 10017
      (212) 687-1000

# Appendix A:

## Novels, Stories, and Plays from which Films were made

| FILM TITLE | AUTHOR--NOVEL/SHORT STORY/PLAY |
|------------|-------------------------------|
| Die Spinnen (The Spiders) | Fritz Lang--Der goldene See (novel-written after the film) |
| Harakiri | John Luther Long and David Belasco--Madame Butterfly (play) |
| Dr. Mabuse, der Spieler | Norbert Jacques--Dr. Mabuse, der Spieler (novel) |
| Metropolis | Thea von Harbou--Metropolis (novel-written after the film) |
| Spione | Thea von Harbou--Spione |
| Das Testament des Dr. Mabuse | Based on characters from a novel by Norbert Jacques |
| Liliom | Ferenc Molnár--Liliom (play) |
| Fury | Norman Krasna--"Mob Rule" (short story) |
| You Only Live Once | Based on a story by Gene Towne |
| Western Union | Zane Grey--Western Union (novel) |
| Manhunt | Geoffrey Household--Rogue Mâle (novel) |
| Hangmen Also Die | Based on a story by Lang and Brecht |

| | |
|---|---|
| Ministry of Fear | Graham Green--Ministry of Fear (novel) |
| The Woman in the Window | J. H. Wallis--Once off Guard (novel) |
| Scarlet Street | Georges de la Fouchardière (with Mouëzy-Eon)--La Chienne (novel and play |
| Cloak and Dagger | Based on a story by Boris Ingster and John Larkin, suggested by a book by Corey Fork and Alastair MacBain. |
| Secret Beyond the Door | Rufus King--"Museum Piece No. 13" (short story) |
| House by the River | Based on a novel by A. P. Herbert. |
| American Guerrilla in the Philippines | Ira Wolfert--American Guerrilla in the Philippines (novel) |
| Rancho Notorious | Silvia Richards--"Gunsight Whitman" (short story) |
| Clash by Night | Clifford Odets--Clash by Night (play) |
| The Blue Gardenia | Based on a story by Vera Caspary |
| The Big Heat | William P. McGiven--The Big Heat (novel) |
| Human Desire | Emil Zola--La Bête Humaine (novel) |
| Moonfleet | John Meade Falkner--Moonfleet (novel) |
| While the City Sleeps | Charles Einstein--The Bloody Spur (novel) |
| Der Tiger von Eschnapur | Based on a novel by Thea von Harbou and a scenario by Fritz Lang and Thea von Harbou |
| Die tausend Augen des Dr. Mabuse | Based on an idea of Jan Fethke's and the character created by Norbert Jacques |

# Appendix B:

## Translations of Film Titles

| German | English | French |
|---|---|---|
| Halbblut | The Halfcaste | Le Rastaquouère |
| Der Herr der Liebe | Master of Love | Der Herr der Liebe |
| Der goldene See: (first part of Die Spinnen) | The Golden Lake (first part of The Spiders) | Le Lac d'Or (first part of Les Araignées) |
| Harakiri | Madame Butterfly | Madame Butterfly |
| Das Brillantenschiff (second part of Die Spinnen) | The Diamond Ship (second part of The Spiders) | Le Cargo d'Esclaves (second part of Les Araignées) |
| Das wandernde Bild | The Wandering Image | Das wandernde Bild |
| Der müde Tod | Destiny | Les Trois Lumières |
| Dr. Mabuse, der Spieler: Ein Bild der Zeit (I) Inferno: Menschen der Zeit (II) | Dr. Mabuse, the Gambler: A Picture of the Time (I) Inferno: Men of the Time (II) | Le Docteur Mabuse |
| Die Nibelungen: Siegfrieds Tod (I); Kriemhilds Rache (II) | The Niebelungen: Death of Siegfried (I) Kriemhild's Revenge (II) | La Mort de Siegfried (I) La Vengeance de Kriemhilde (II) |
| Metropolis | Metropolis | Métropole |

469

| | | |
|---|---|---|
| Spione | Spies | Les Espions |
| Frau im Mond | Woman in the Moon | La Femme sur la Lune |
| M, Mörder unter uns | M, Murderer Among Us | M, Le Maudit |
| Das Testament des Dr. Mabuse | The Crimes of Dr. Mabuse or The Last Will of Dr. Mabuse | La Testament du Dr. Mabuse |
| Liliom | Liliom | Liliom |
| Fury | Fury | Furie |
| Gehetzt | You Only Live Once | J'ai le Droit de Vivre |
| You and Me | You and Me | Casier Judicaire |
| Rache für Jesse James | The Return of Frank James | Le Retour de Frank James |
| Überfall der Ogalalla | Western Union | Les Pionniers de la Western-Union |
| Menschenjagd | Manhunt | Chasse à L'Homme |
| Auch Henker sterben | Hangmen Also Die | Les Bourreaux Meurent Aussi |
| Gefährliche Begegnung | The Woman in the Window | La Femme au Portrait |
| Strasse der Versuchung | Scarlet Street | La Rue Rouge |
| Im Geheimdienst | Cloak and Dagger | Cape et Poignard |
| Geheimnis hinter der Tür | Secret Beyond the Door | Le Secret derrière la Porte |
| House by the River | House by the River | House by the River |
| Der Held von Mindanao | American Guerrilla in The Philippines | Guérillas |
| Engel der Gejagten/ Die Gejagten | Rancho Notorious | L'Ange des Maudits |
| Vor dem neuen Tag | Clash by Night | Le Démon s'éveille la Nuit |

| | | |
|---|---|---|
| Gardenia--Eine Frau will Vergessen | The Blue Gardenia | La Femme au Gardenia |
| Heisses Eisen | The Big Heat | Reglement de Comptes |
| Lebensgier | Human Desire | Désirs Humains |
| Das Schloss im Schatten | Moonfleet | Les Contrabandiers de Moonfleet |
| Die Bestie | While the City Sleeps | La Cinquième Victime |
| Jenseits allen Zweifels | Beyond a Reasonable Doubt | Invraisemblable Vérité |
| Der Tiger von Eschnapur (I) Das indische Grabmal (II) | The Tiger of Bengal (I) The Indian Tomb (II) Edited USA version: Journey from the Lost City | Le Tigre du Bengale (I) Le Tombeau Hindou (II) |
| Die tausend Augen des Dr. Mabuse | The Thousand Eyes of Dr. Mabuse | Le Diabolique Docteur Mabuse |

# Appendix C:

## German Films about Fritz Lang

1959    Künstlerporträt: Fritz Lang [Portrait of an Artist: Fritz Lang]. By Friedrich Luft and Guido Schütte.
Produced by NWRV Television, Hamburg.
Length: 30 mins.
Released: 23 June, 1959 (NDR)

1963    Begegnung mit Fritz Lang [Meeting with Fritz Lang]. By Peter Fleischmann.
Producers: Jacques Rozier and Klaus Borkmann
Photography: Maurice Perrimond
Length: 14 mins.
Released: February 1964, Westdeutsche Kurzfilmtage, Oberhausen

1964    Das War Die Ufa [That was the Ufa]. Lang Interviewed by Erwin Leiser.
Produced by Atlas-Retro
According to Bogdanovitch (Fritz Lang in America, p. 142), this was "one in a series of West German television programmes concerning the history of Ufa. Sequences from Dr. Mabuse der Spieler (Parts I and II) were shown, along with scenes from Caligari and Murnau's Der Letzte Mann (1924)."

1968    Zum Beispiel Fritz Lang [For Example, Fritz Lang]. By Erwin Leiser.
Part I: Der Ästhet und die Wirklichkeit [The Aesthete and Reality]
Part II: Der Idealist und die Zivilisation [The Idealist and Civilization]
Part III: Der Bürger und die politische Macht [The Citizen and Political Power]
Produced by WDR Television
Length: 45 mins., each part
Released: Part I 17 March, 1971; Part II 24 March 1971;

Part III, 31 March 1971 (WDR III)

1973    Cassette Tape.    Interview with Lang available on tape from
University of Southern California Film Archive.    Produced in
Los Angeles.

1974    Die schweren Träume des Fritz Lang [The Bitter Dreams of Fritz
Lang].    By Werner Dütsch.
Produced by WDR Television
Length:    45 mins
Released: 3 December 1974 (WDR III)

# Index of Proper Names

# Film Title Index

481

# Subject Index

The following topics are of particular relevance to Lang's work and career and to Lang criticism: